Banking Law

Anu Arora

PEARSON

Harlow, England • London • New York • Boston • San Francisco • Toronto • Sydney
Auckland • Singapore • Hong Kong • Tokyo • Seoul • Taipei • New Delhi
Cape Town • São Paulo • Mexico City • Madrid • Amsterdam • Munich • Paris • Milan

PEARSON EDUCATION LIMITED
Edinburgh Gate
Harlow CM20 2JE
United Kingdom
Tel: +44 (0)1279 623623
Web: www.pearson.com/uk

First published 2014 (print and electronic)

ISBN: 978-1-4082-9784-1 (print)
       978-1-4082-9786-5 (PDF)
       978-1-292-01498-2 (eText)

British Library Cataloguing-in-Publication Data
A catalogue record for the print edition is available from the British Library

Library of Congress Cataloging-in-Publication Data
Arora, Anu author.
   Banking law / Anu Arora.
      pages cm
   ISBN 978-1-4082-9784-1
   1. Banking law—Great Britain.   2. Banks and banking, International—Law and legislation.   I. Title.
   KD1715.A97 2014
   346.41'082—dc23

                                                                      2014006485

10 9 8 7 6 5 4 3 2 1
18 17 16 15 14

Print edition typeset in 9/12.5pt ITC Giovanni by 35
Printed in Malaysia, CTP-PJB

NOTE THAT ANY PAGE CROSS-REFERENCES REFER TO THE PRINT EDITION

Brief contents

Contents

Companion Website

For open-access **student resources** specifically written to complement this textbook and support your learning, please visit **www.pearsoned.co.uk/arora**

ON THE WEBSITE

Preface

The UK banking sector performs a crucial role in support of the real economy and enjoys international pre-eminence. Both have, however, been severely eroded by the profound loss of trust resulting from the 2007–09 banking crisis which has shown that the effects of mis-management, lapse in banking standards and poor corporate governance were significant factors in the financial crisis. The Turner Report highlighted that the interconnectedness of the global economies meant that the financial crisis resulted in severe financial problems in many different countries simultaneously. It was this interconnectedness that made it impossible for regulators and governments to manage the crisis nationally within the confines of national boundaries and national banking systems. It also highlighted the lack of preparedness of the tripartite authorities to deal with a financial crisis. This was followed by the Walker Report, which examined the failings in corporate governance that led to risky banking products and practices, which senior management and non-executive did not fully understand, or challenge. Remuneration and the bonus culture rife in the banking sector came under scrutiny and disrepute as million pound bonuses were paid whilst the banks paying them crumbled and governments were forced to bail out failing banks. Whilst the Labour Government's response was to fine-tune the existing regulatory sector the Conservative Party proposed reform of the tripartite authorities and adopting a banking regulatory structure with the Bank of England at the centre of banking regulation.

This book explores some of the causes and effects of the banking crisis and examines the legal and regulatory responses. In the aftermath to the banking crisis the UK banking sector has seen a new regulatory structure with separate bodies responsible for macro and micro regulation and with the Bank of England, once again, at the centre of that regulatory structure. Governmental response, including the special resolution regime, is intended to preserve financial stability and confidence in the financial sector. New legislation has been enacted to ensure a managed response for resolving arrangements for distressed bank and a special insolvency regime for financial institutions. At the same time the government intends to ring fence the retail-banking sector to safeguard the depositor base of the banks. Standards within the banking sector have come under scrutiny and the Parliamentary Commission on Banking Standards has proposed that senior management be made to accept individual responsibility in banking; reforming governance within banks and other financial institutions to reinforce responsibility for each bank's safety and soundness and for the maintenance of standards; creating better functioning and diverse banking markets to empower consumers and provide greater discipline on banks to raise standards; reinforcing the responsibilities of regulators; and specifying the responsibilities of the current, and future, governments. Reform across all these areas is essential and no single change will address the problems of banking standards. There is recognition that more legislation is not necessarily the answer: what is required is a raising of standards in the banking sector and an acceptance of ethical and moral responsibility.

At the same time banking products, consumer protection and banking services have all come under scrutiny. The book, therefore, examines the law relating to the banker and customer relationship and explores the debates around the fairness of the banking contract. The effect of standard form contracts and exclusion or limitation of liability contracts in banking law, and the scope and nature of work of the Financial Services Authority and the Office of Fair Trading in the area of unfair contract terms in banking contracts are examined. With the increased use of electronic fund transfers and plastic cards, i.e. debit and credit cards, the developments in the law in these areas are examined. At the same time the relative ease with which a bank account can be opened and the ease with which money can be transferred abroad means that bank accounts can be used to misappropriate funds quickly and with ease. The book, therefore, examines the law on mistaken payments, tracing of funds through a bank account and money laundering as an exception to bank confidentiality. The book also examines the more common forms of bank lending and concludes with a chapter on the forms of security frequently taken by a bank.

This book is intended to give a thorough understanding of banking law to those studying the subject at the undergraduate and postgraduate degree levels. Each chapter sets out its aims and concludes with a section of further reading for those who wish to consult primary sources or undertake a more in-depth study.

Anu Arora

Guided tour

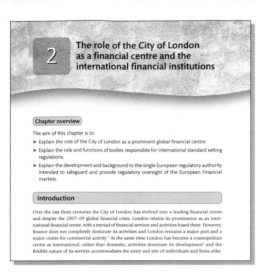

Chapter overviews at the beginning of each chapter outline the main topics you will be covering. You can go back to these as a checklist of what concepts you should be familiar with during the course of your reading.

End of chapter conclusions draw together the key points you need to be aware of following your reading of each chapter.

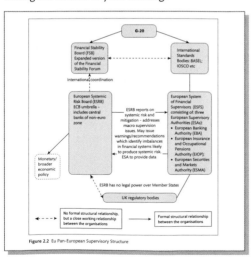

Figures and diagrams are used to strengthen your understanding of complex legal processes in banking law.

Banking Law in Practice boxes throughout the text provide you with relevant examples of the law in action so that you can identify legal issues, analysis and application in context.

competence and the fiduciary concepts of honesty and loyalty.[64] The initial expressions of the duty to exercise reasonable skill and care have stood the test of time and even the more modern formulation of the duty of care is based on the statement by Romer J in *Re City Equitable Fire Insurance Co Ltd*[65] where it was held that 'a director need not exhibit in the performance of his duties a greater degree of skill than may reasonably be expected from a person of his knowledge and experience'. The modern view of the duty to exercise skill and care is, however, a reflection of the fact that directors are expected to be more professional and experienced in the discharge of their responsibilities to stakeholders and the public, and the courts demand a more objective standard of care. Holding a directorship is no longer a hobby for the gentleman seeking a not too demanding distraction. In *Commonwealth Bank of Australia v Friedrich*,[66] Tadgell J expressed the view that:

> In particular, the stage has been reached when a director is expected to be capable of understanding his company's affairs to the extent of actually reaching a reasonably informed opinion of its financial capacity . . . I think it follows that he is required by law to be capable of keeping abreast of the company's affairs, and sufficiently abreast of them to act appropriately if there are reasonable grounds to expect that the company will not be able to pay all its debts in due course and he has reasonable cause to expect it.

Similar views have been expressed by the UK courts in *Norman v Theodore Goddard*[67] and in *Re D'Jan of London Ltd*,[68] in the context of an examination of s.214 of the Insolvency Act 1986, which introduced a more objective standard of care through consideration of the general knowledge that may be reasonably attributed to a director in the same position. More recently, examining the duty to exercise reasonable skill and care in *Lexi Holdings (in administration) v Luqman and Other*[69] the court described s.214 of the Insolvency Act 1986 as the model from which s.174 of the Companies Act 2006 is derived. All directors must, therefore, attend to their duties including taking reasonable steps to supervise and control the conduct of their company's business.

An action for misfeasance under s.212 of the Companies Act 2006 may be available, as an alternative, against the directors. Such action provides a remedy where the directors have misapplied or retained, or become accountable, for money or assets of the company, or where they commit a breach of fiduciary duty owed to the company. Following *Re D'Jan of London Ltd*, misfeasance can include a breach of duty of care, as the court held signing a form without reading it amounted to negligence, thus giving rise to misfeasance.[70]

A number of failings in corporate governance could amount to a breach of duty of care. The FSA, the previous financial services regulator, raised concerns, in 2004, that key parts of the Halifax Bank of Scotland (HBOS) group were posing 'medium or high' risks to maintain-

---

Further reading

➤ Hudson, A. (1999) Money as property in financial transactions, 14(6), *Journal of International Banking Law*, 170–176.
This article considers the implications of how courts deal with financial products for English law's understanding of the nature of money in the context of sophisticated cross-border transactions and tracing, and the benefits of treating money as value rather than as property.

➤ Vroegop, J. (1990) The time of payment in paper-based and electronic funds transfer systems, *LMCLQ*, 64.
This article examines the issue of when payment is made, not only when the mandate to make the payment is given in paper form, for example a payment by cheque, but also when the payment instruction is given electronically. The issue of when payment is made using the different systems and also when there are more than two banks involved in executing the payment mandate, for example where there are intermediary banks involved is also discussed.

➤ Sir John Vickers, Independent Commission on Banking: The Vickers Report and the Parliamentary Commission on Banking Standards, http://www.parliament.uk/briefing-papers/SN06171, September 2011.
The Vickers Commission proposed fundamental changes in the framework in which banks operate in the UK financial sector. The fundamental changes include the concept of ring fencing which would separate retail banking deposits from the riskier activities such as investment banking and proprietary trading. The Vickers Commission further proposes enhanced capital and loss absorbency mechanisms than under the Basel III rules.

➤ Sir James Sassoon, The Tripartite Review, A Review of the UK's Tripartite System of Financial Regulation in Relation to Financial Regulation, March 2009.
The Sassoon Report was commissioned by the opposition Conservative Party in October 2008 to form the Conservative Party's position on the regime of financial regulation in the UK. The report recommended an overhaul of the tripartite regime which shared responsibilities between the Financial Services Authority (FSA), HM Treasury and the Bank of England, due to a lack of communication and awareness of who bore overall responsibility.

➤ FSA Internal Audit Division, The Supervision of Northern Rock: a lessons learnt review, March 2008, http://www.fsa.gov.uk/pubs/other/nr_report.pdf.
This report concluded that the FSA's prevailing framework for assessing risk was not appropriately applied in relation to Northern Rock, so that the supervisory strategy was in line with the firm's risk profile. The report recommended that the FSA's senior management should have increased engagement with high impact firms, while the FSA should increase its focus upon prudential supervision, including liquidity and stress testing.

➤ Financial Services Authority (FSA) Board Report, The failure of the Royal Bank of Scotland,

---

Extracts from key legislation, legal judgements and official sources highlight the important primary materials you need to be aware of in your study of banking law.

Annotated **further reading** at the end of each chapter directs you to further resources available, allowing you to delve deeper into the subject.

Acknowledgements

Author's acknowledgements

I would like to thank my family, friends and colleagues during the writing of this book: a task made that much more challenging by the 2007–09 financial crisis and the ensuing changes and developments in banking law and practice. I would particularly like to thank Michael Pinder, my former student and research assistant, for all his help and assistance during the summer of 2013. The book would not have been concluded without your invaluable input. I would also like to thank Dr Rob Stokes for his comments on the chapter on money laundering. And to both my beautiful daughters: thank you for your patience. To my family I thank you all.

I would like to thank the publishers for keeping me on track with the book. The law in this area is changing as we publish this book. There will be twice yearly updates on the Pearson legal updates site at www.pearsoned.co.uk/legalupdates.

Publisher's acknowledgements

We are grateful to the following for permission to reproduce copyright material:

Figures

Figure 14.3 from CHAPS Technical Requirements, http://www.chapsco.co.uk/files/chaps/technical_requirement_document.pdf, CHAPS Clearing Company Limited.

Text

Extracts on page 35, 36, 277 and 482 from *Libyan Arab Foreign Bank v Bankers Trust* [1989] QB 728; Extract on page 51 from *Trenax Steamship Co Ltd v Reinate Transoceanica Navegacion SA, The Brimnes* [1973] 1 WLR 386 at 400B–C; Extract on page 51 from *A/S Awilco of Solo v Fulvia SpA di Navigazione of Calgiari, The Chikuma* [1981] 1 WLR 314 at 319H; Extracts on page 52 and 521 from *Momm v Barclays Bank International Ltd* [1977] QB 790; Extract on page 104 from Institute of Internal Auditing – UK and Ireland (2004, 1 January), *Code of Ethics and International Standards for the Professional Practice of Internal Auditing*, http://www.theiia.org/?doc_id=1499, Copyright © by The Institute of Internal Auditors, Inc. All Rights Reserved; Extracts on page 107 and 453 from *Space Investments Ltd v Canadian Imperial Bank of Commerce Trust Co (Bahamas)* [1986] 1 WLR 1072; Extract on page 113 from *Re Patrick and Lyon Ltd* [1933] Ch 786; Extract on page 232 from *George Mitchell (Chesterhall) Ltd v Finney Lock Seeds Ltd* [1983] AC 803; Extract on page 232 from *Smith v Eric S. Bush* [1990] AC 831; Extracts on page 233 and 584 from *Director General of Fair Trading v First National Bank Plc* [2002] 1 AC 481; Extracts on page 241, 324, 591, 595, 600, 607 and 616 from *Barclays Bank Ltd v*

W.J. Simms & Cooke (Southern) Ltd [1980] 1 QB 677; Extract on page 251 from *Crantrave Ltd v Lloyds Bank Plc* [2000] QB 917; Extract on page 252 from *Rolls Razor Ltd v Cox* [1967] 1 QB 552 at 574; Extracts on pages 255, 255, 296–7 and 258 from *Tai Hing Cotton Mill Ltd v Liu Chong Hing Bank Ltd* [1986] AC 80; Extracts on page 259 and 263 from *Parry-Jones v Law Society* [1969] 1 Ch 1 at 9; Extract on page 259 from *Attorney-General v Guardian Newspapers Ltd (No 2)* [1990] 1 AC 109 at 281–282; Extract on page 261 from *Lipkin Gorman v Karpnale Ltd* [1989] 1 WLR 1340; Extract on page 261 from *Barclays Bank Plc v Taylor* [1989] 1 WLR 1066 at 1070; Extract on page 267 from *Williams v Summerfield* [1972] 2 QB 512; Extract on page 270 from *Bankers Trust Co v Shapira* [1980] 1 WLR 1274; Extract on page 275 from *MacKinnon v Donaldson, Lufkin and Janrette Securities Corporation* [1986] Ch 482; Extract on page 280 from *Cunliffe-Owen v Teather and Greenwood* [1967] 1 WLR 385 at 391; Extract on page 293 from *Phelps v Hillingdon LBC* [2001] 2 AC 619 at 654; Extract on page 297 from *London Joint Stock Bank v Macmillan* [1918] AC 777; Extract on page 299 from *Greenwood v Martins Bank Ltd* [1933] AC 51; Extract on page 302 from *National Westminster Bank Plc v Morgan* [1985] AC 686 (HL); Extracts on page 303, 305 and 451 from *Bristol and West Building Society v Mothew* [1998] Ch 1; Extract on page 304 from *Re Goldcorp Exchange Ltd* [1995] 1 AC 74; Extract on page 306 from *Lloyds Bank Ltd v Bundy* [1975] QB 326; Extracts on page 311, 314 and 315 from *Royal Bank of Scotland v Etridge (No 2)* [2002] 2 AC 773; Extract on page 314 from *Barclays Bank Plc v O'Brien* [1994] 1 AC 180; Extracts on page 328 and 584 from *Bank of Baroda v Panessar* [1987] Ch 335; Extract on page 330 from *Yourell v Hibernian Bank Ltd* [1918] AC 372; Extract on page 330 from *National Bank of Greece SA v Pinios Shipping Co (No 1)* [1990] 1 AC 637; Extract on page 342 and 347 from *National Westminster Bank Ltd v Halesowen Presswork and Assemblies Ltd* [1972] AC 785; Extract on pages 332–3 from *Deeley v Lloyds Bank Ltd* [1912] AC 756; Extract on page 353 from *Bavins Junior and Sims London and South Western Bank Ltd* [1900] 1 QB 270; Extract on page 365 from *Bank of England v Vagliano Brothers* [1891] AC 107; Extract on page 370 from *Arab Bank Ltd v Ross* [1952] 2 QB 216; Extract on page 384 from *Marfani & Co Ltd v Midland Bank Ltd* [1968] 1 WLR 956 at 971; Extract on page 389 from *Marfani & Co Ltd v Midland Bank Ltd* [1968] 1 WLR 972; Extract on page 389 from *Marfani & Co Ltd v Midland Bank Ltd* [1968] 1 WLR 957; Extract on page 393 from *Lloyds Bank Ltd v E.B. Savory Co* [1933] AC 201; Extracts on pages 419, 440 and 422–3 from *Royal Brunei Airways Sdn Bhd v Tan* [1995] 2 AC 378; Extracts on page 422, 427 and 592 from *Agip (Africa) Ltd v Jackson* [1990] Ch 265; Extract on page 438 from *Macmillan Inc. v Bishopsgate Investment Trust Plc (No 3)* [1995] 1 WLR 978; Extract on page 439 from *Bank of Credit and Commerce International (Overseas) Ltd v Akindele* [2001] Ch 437; Extract on page 442 from *Boscawen v Bajwa* [1996] 1 WLR 328; Extract on page 447 from Trustees of the Property of *F C Jones & Sons (a firm) v Jones* [1997] Ch 159; Extract on page 448 from *Re Diplock* [1948] Ch 465 at 521; Extract on page 449 from *Re Hallett's Estate, Knatchbull v Hallett* (1880) 13 Ch D 696; Extract on page 451 from *Agip (Africa) Ltd v Jackson* [1991] Ch 547; Extract on page 452 from *Chase Manhattan Bank v Israel-British Bank (London) Ltd* [1981] Ch 105; Extract on page 454 from *James Roscoe (Bolton) v Winder* [1915] 1 Ch 62; Extracts on pages 424–5 and 427 from *Twinsectra Ltd v Yardley* [2002] 2 AC 164; Extracts on pages 442–3 and 455 from *Foskett v McKeown* [2001] 1 AC 102; Extract on page 473 from *Squirrell Ltd v National Westminster Bank Plc* [2006] 1 WLR 637; Extracts on page 513 and 524 from *Tenax Steamship Co Ltd v Brimnes (Owners Of), The Brimnes* [1975] 1 QB 929; Extract on page 517 from *R v Preddy* [1996] AC 815; Extract on pages 540–1 from *Re Charge Card Services Ltd* [1987] 1 Ch 150; Extract on page 577 from *UBAF Ltd v European American Banking*

Corporation [1984] 1 QB 713; Extract on page 587 from *Secretary v State for Trade and Industry v Deverell* [2001] Ch 340; Extract on page 589 from *Fibrosa Spolka Akcyjna v Fairbairn Lawson Combe Barbour Ltd* [1943] AC 32 at 61; Extracts on page 593 and 601 from *Lipkin Gorman (a firm) v Karpnale Ltd* [1991] 2 AC 548; Extract on page 599 from *Westdeutsche Landesbank Girozentrale v Islington* [1986] AC 669 at 683; Extract on page 600 from *R.E. Jones Ltd v Waring and Gillow Ltd* [1926] AC 670; Extract on page 601 from *Allcard v Skinner* (1887) 36 Ch D 145; Extract on page 615 from *London and River Plate Bank Ltd v Bank of Liverpool Ltd* [1896] 1 QB 7; Extract on page 616 from *National Westminster Bank Ltd v Barclays Bank International Ltd* [1975] QB 654; Extract on page 631 from *Agnew v Inland Review Commissioners* [2001] 2 AC 710; Extract on page 632 from *Re Spectrum Plus Ltd* [2005] 2 AC 680; Extract on page 633 from Company Security Interests, http://lawcommission.justice.gov.uk/docs/lc296_Company_Security_Interests.pdf.

In some instances we have been unable to trace the owners of copyright material, and we would appreciate any information that would enable us to do so.

Picture Credits

The publisher would like to thank the following for their kind permission to reproduce their photographs:

(Key: b-bottom; c-centre; l-left; r-right; t-top)

Pearson Education Ltd: © Pearson Education, Inc. 485tl, 485tr, 485bl, 485br

All other images © Pearson Education

Every effort has been made to trace the copyright holders and we apologise in advance for any unintentional omissions. We would be pleased to insert the appropriate acknowledgement in any subsequent edition of this publication.

Table of cases

Table of European legislation

Decisions

Guidelines & Frameworks

Tables of equivalences

Treaty on European Union

Old numbering of the Treaty on European Union	New numbering of the Treaty on European Union
TITLE I – COMMON PROVISIONS	TITLE I – COMMON PROVISIONS
Article 1	Article 1
	Article 2
Article 2	Article 3
Article 3 (repealed) [2]	
	Article 4
	Article 5 [3]
Article 4 (repealed) [4]	
Article 5 (repealed) [5]	
Article 6	Article 6
Article 7	Article 7
	Article 8
TITLE II – PROVISIONS AMENDING THE TREATY ESTABLISHING THE EUROPEAN ECONOMIC COMMUNITY WITH A VIEW TO ESTABLISHING THE EUROPEAN COMMUNITY	TITLE II – PROVISIONS ON DEMOCRATIC PRINCIPLES
Article 8 (repealed) [6]	Article 9
	Article 10 [7]
	Article 11
	Article 12

[1] Tables of equivalences as referred to in Article 5 of the Treaty of Lisbon. The original centre column, which set out the intermediate numbering as used in that Treaty, has been omitted.

[2] Replaced, in substance, by Article 7 of the Treaty on the Functioning of the European Union ("TFEU") and by Articles 13(1) and 21, paragraph 3, second subparagraph of the Treaty on European Union ("TEU").

[3] Replaces Article 5 of the Treaty establishing the European Community ("TEC").

[4] Replaced, in substance, by Article 15.

[5] Replaced, in substance, by Article 13, paragraph 2.

[6] Article 8 TEU, which was in force until the entry into force of the Treaty of Lisbon (hereinafter "current"), amended the TEC. Those amendments are incorporated into the latter Treaty and Article 8 is repealed. Its number is used to insert a new provision.

[7] Paragraph 4 replaces, in substance, the first subparagraph of Article 191 TEC.

Old numbering of the Treaty on European Union	New numbering of the Treaty on European Union
TITLE III – PROVISIONS AMENDING THE TREATY ESTABLISHING THE EUROPEAN COAL AND STEEL COMMUNITY	TITLE III – PROVISIONS ON THE INSTITUTIONS
Article 9 (repealed) [8]	Article 13
	Article 14 [9]
	Article 15 [10]
	Article 16 [11]
	Article 17 [12]
	Article 18
	Article 19 [13]
TITLE IV – PROVISIONS AMENDING THE TREATY ESTABLISHING THE EUROPEAN ATOMIC ENERGY COMMUNITY	TITLE IV – PROVISIONS ON ENHANCED COOPERATION
Article 10 (repealed) [14] Articles 27a to 27e (replaced) Articles 40 to 40b (replaced) Articles 43 to 45 (replaced)	Article 20 [15]
TITLE V – PROVISIONS ON A COMMON FOREIGN AND SECURITY POLICY	TITLE V – GENERAL PROVISIONS ON THE UNION'S EXTERNAL ACTION AND SPECIFIC PROVISIONS ON THE COMMON FOREIGN AND SECURITY POLICY
	Chapter 1 – General provisions on the Union's external action
	Article 21
	Article 22
	Chapter 2 – Specific provisions on the common foreign and security policy

[8]   The current Article 9 TEU amended the Treaty establishing the European Coal and Steel Community. This latter expired on 23 July 2002. Article 9 is repealed and the number thereof is used to insert another provision.

[9]

 – Paragraphs 1 and 2 replace, in substance, Article 189 TEC;
 – paragraphs 1 to 3 replace, in substance, paragraphs 1 to 3 of Article 190 TEC;
 – paragraph 1 replaces, in substance, the first subparagraph of Article 192 TEC;
 – paragraph 4 replaces, in substance, the first subparagraph of Article 197 TEC.

[10] Replaces, in substance, Article 4.

[11]

 – Paragraph 1 replaces, in substance, the first and second indents of Article 202 TEC;
 – paragraphs 2 and 9 replace, in substance, Article 203 TEC;
 – paragraphs 4 and 5 replace, in substance, paragraphs 2 and 4 of Article 205 TEC.

[12]

 – Paragraph 1 replaces, in substance, Article 211 TEC;
 – paragraphs 3 and 7 replace, in substance, Article 214 TEC.
 – paragraph 6 replaces, in substance, paragraphs 1, 3 and 4 of Article 217 TEC.

[13]

 – Replaces, in substance, Article 220 TEC.
 – the second subparagraph of paragraph 2 replaces, in substance, the first subparagraph of Article 221 TEC.

[14] The current Article 10 TEU amended the Treaty establishing the European Atomic Energy Community. Those amendments are incorporated into the Treaty of Lisbon. Article 10 is repealed and the number thereof is used to insert another provision.

[15] Also replaces Articles 11 and 11a TEC.

Old numbering of the Treaty on European Union	New numbering of the Treaty on European Union
	Section 1 – Common provisions
	Article 23
Article 11	Article 24
Article 12	Article 25
Article 13	Article 26
	Article 27
Article 14	Article 28
Article 15	Article 29
Article 22 (moved)	Article 30
Article 23 (moved)	Article 31
Article 16	Article 32
Article 17 (moved)	Article 42
Article 18	Article 33
Article 19	Article 34
Article 20	Article 35
Article 21	Article 36
Article 22 (moved)	Article 30
Article 23 (moved)	Article 31
Article 24	Article 37
Article 25	Article 38
	Article 39
Article 47 (moved)	Article 40
Article 26 (repealed)	
Article 27 (repealed)	
Article 27a (replaced) [16]	Article 20
Article 27b (replaced) [16]	Article 20
Article 27c (replaced) [16]	Article 20
Article 27d (replaced) [16]	Article 20
Article 27e (replaced) [16]	Article 20
Article 28	Article 41
	Section 2 – Provisions on the common security and defence policy
Article 17 (moved)	Article 42
	Article 43
	Article 44

Old numbering of the Treaty on European Union	New numbering of the Treaty on European Union
[16] The current Articles 27a to 27e, on enhanced cooperation, are also replaced by Articles 326 to 334 TFEU.	
	Article 45
	Article 46
TITLE VI – PROVISIONS ON POLICE AND JUDICIAL COOPERATION IN CRIMINAL MATTERS (repealed) [17]	
Article 29 (replaced) [18]	
Article 30 (replaced) [19]	
Article 31 (replaced) [20]	
Article 32 (replaced) [21]	
Article 33 (replaced) [22]	
Article 34 (repealed)	
Article 35 (repealed)	
Article 36 (replaced) [23]	
Article 37 (repealed)	
Article 38 (repealed)	
Article 39 (repealed)	
Article 40 (replaced) [24]	Article 20
Article 40 A (replaced) [24]	Article 20
Article 40 B (replaced) [24]	Article 20
Article 41 (repealed)	
Article 42 (repealed)	
TITLE VII – PROVISIONS ON ENHANCED COOPERATION (replaced) [25]	TITLE IV – PROVISIONS ON ENHANCED COOPERATION
Article 43 (replaced) [25]	Article 20
Article 43 A (replaced) [25]	Article 20
Article 43 B (replaced) [25]	Article 20
Article 44 (replaced) [25]	Article 20
Article 44 A (replaced) [25]	Article 20
Article 45 (replaced) [25]	Article 20

[17]   The current provisions of Title VI of the TEU, on police and judicial cooperation in criminal matters, are replaced by the provisions of Chapters 1, 5 and 5 of Title IV of Part Three of the TFEU.
[18]   Replaced by Article 67 TFEU.
[19]   Replaced by Articles 87 and 88 TFEU.
[20]   Replaced by Articles 82, 83 and 85 TFEU.
[21]   Replaced by Article 89 TFEU.
[22]   Replaced by Article 72 TFEU.
[23]   Replaced by Article 71 TFEU.
[24]   The current Articles 40 to 40 B TEU, on enhanced cooperation, are also replaced by Articles 326 to 334 TFEU.
[25]   The current Articles 43 to 45 and Title VII of the TEU, on enhanced cooperation, are also replaced by Articles 326 to 334 TFEU.

Old numbering of the Treaty on European Union	New numbering of the Treaty on European Union
TITRE VIII – FINAL PROVISIONS	TITLE VI – FINAL PROVISIONS
Article 46 (repealed)	
	Article 47
Article 47 (replaced)	Article 40
Article 48	Article 48
Article 49	Article 49
	Article 50
	Article 51
	Article 52
Article 50 (repealed)	
Article 51	Article 53
Article 52	Article 54
Article 53	Article 55

Treaty on the Functioning of the European Union

Old numbering of the Treaty establishing the European Community	New numbering of the Treaty on the Functioning of the European Union
PART ONE – PRINCIPLES	PART ONE – PRINCIPLES
Article 1 (repealed)	
	Article 1
Article 2 (repealed) [26]	
	Title I – Categories and areas of union competence
	Article 2
	Article 3
	Article 4
	Article 5
	Article 6
	Title II – Provisions having general application
	Article 7
Article 3, paragraph 1 (repealed) [27]	
Article 3, paragraph 2	Article 8
Article 4 (moved)	Article 119
Article 5 (replaced) [28]	

[26] Replaced, in substance, by Article 3 TEU.
[27] Replaced, in substance, by Articles 3 to 6 TFEU.
[28] Replaced, in substance, by Article 5 TEU.

Old numbering of the Treaty establishing the European Community	New numbering of the Treaty on the Functioning of the European Union
	Article 9
	Article 10
Article 6	Article 11
Article 153, paragraph 2 (moved)	Article 12
	Article 13 [29]
Article 7 (repealed) [30]	
Article 8 (repealed) [31]	
Article 9 (repealed)	
Article 10 (repealed) [32]	
Article 11 (replaced) [33]	Articles 326 to 334
Article 11a (replaced) [33]	Articles 326 to 334
Article 12 (repealed)	Article 18
Article 13 (moved)	Article 19
Article 14 (moved)	Article 26
Article 15 (moved)	Article 27
Article 16	Article 14
Article 255 (moved)	Article 15
Article 286 (moved)	Article 16
	Article 17
PART TWO – CITIZENSHIP OF THE UNION	PART TWO – NON-DISCRIMINATION AND CITIZENSHIP OF THE UNION
Article 12 (moved)	Article 18
Article 13 (moved)	Article 19
Article 17	Article 20
Article 18	Article 21
Article 19	Article 22
Article 20	Article 23
Article 21	Article 24
Article 22	Article 25

[29] Insertion of the operative part of the protocol on protection and welfare of animals.
[30] Replaced, in substance, by Article 13 TEU.
[31] Replaced, in substance, by Article 13 TEU and Article 282, paragraph 1, TFEU.
[32] Replaced, in substance, by Article 4, paragraph 3, TEU.
[33] Also replaced by Article 20 TEU.

Old numbering of the Treaty establishing the European Community	New numbering of the Treaty on the Functioning of the European Union
PART THREE – COMMUNITY POLICIES	PART THREE – POLICIES AND INTERNAL ACTIONS OF THE UNION
	Title I – The internal market
Article 14 (moved)	Article 26
Article 15 (moved)	Article 27
Title I – Free movement of goods	Title II – Free movement of goods
Article 23	Article 28
Article 24	Article 29
Chapter 1 – The customs union	Chapter 1 – The customs union
Article 25	Article 30
Article 26	Article 31
Article 27	Article 32
Part Three, Title X, Customs cooperation (moved)	Chapter 2 – Customs cooperation
Article 135 (moved)	Article 33
Chapter 2 – Prohibition of quantitative restrictions between Member States	Chapter 3 – Prohibition of quantitative restrictions between Member States
Article 28	Article 34
Article 29	Article 35
Article 30	Article 36
Article 31	Article 37
Title II – Agriculture	Title III – Agriculture and fisheries
Article 32	Article 38
Article 33	Article 39
Article 34	Article 40
Article 35	Article 41
Article 36	Article 42
Article 37	Article 43
Article 38	Article 44
Title III – Free movement of persons, services and capital	Title IV – Free movement of persons, services and capital
Chapter 1 – Workers	Chapter 1 – Workers
Article 39	Article 45
Article 40	Article 46
Article 41	Article 47
Article 42	Article 48

Old numbering of the Treaty establishing the European Community	New numbering of the Treaty on the Functioning of the European Union
Chapter 2 – Right of establishment	Chapter 2 – Right of establishment
Article 43	Article 49
Article 44	Article 50
Article 45	Article 51
Article 46	Article 52
Article 47	Article 53
Article 48	Article 54
Article 294 (moved)	Article 55
Chapter 3 – Services	Chapter 3 – Services
Article 49	Article 56
Article 50	Article 57
Article 51	Article 58
Article 52	Article 59
Article 53	Article 60
Article 54	Article 61
Article 55	Article 62
Chapter 4 – Capital and payments	Chapter 4 – Capital and payments
Article 56	Article 63
Article 57	Article 64
Article 58	Article 65
Article 59	Article 66
Article 60 (moved)	Article 75
Title IV – Visas, asylum, immigration and other policies related to free movement of persons	Title V – Area of freedom, security and justice
	Chapter 1 – General provisions
Article 61	Article 67 [34]
	Article 68
	Article 69
	Article 70
	Article 71 [35]
Article 64, paragraph 1 (replaced)	Article 72 [36]
	Article 73

[34] Also replaces the current Article 29 TEU.
[35] Also replaces the current Article 36 TEU.
[36] Also replaces the current Article 33 TEU.

Old numbering of the Treaty establishing the European Community	New numbering of the Treaty on the Functioning of the European Union
Article 66 (replaced)	Article 74
Article 60 (moved)	Article 75
	Article 76
	Chapter 2 – Policies on border checks, asylum and immigration
Article 62	Article 77
Article 63, points 1 et 2, and Article 64, paragraph 2 [37]	Article 78
Article 63, points 3 and 4	Article 79
	Article 80
Article 64, paragraph 1 (replaced)	Article 72
	Chapter 3 – Judicial cooperation in civil matters
Article 65	Article 81
Article 66 (replaced)	Article 74
Article 67 (repealed)	
Article 68 (repealed)	
Article 69 (repealed)	
	Chapter 4 – Judicial cooperation in criminal matters
	Article 82 [39]
	Article 83 [39]
	Article 84
	Article 85 [39]
	Article 86
	Chapter 5 – Police cooperation
	Article 87 [40]
	Article 88 [40]
	Article 89 [41]
Title V – Transport	Title VI – Transport
Article 70	Article 90
Article 71	Article 91
Article 72	Article 92
Article 73	Article 93

[37] Points 1 and 2 of Article 63 EC are replaced by paragraphs 1 and 2 of Article 78 TFEU, and paragraph 2 of Article 64 is replaced by paragraph 3 of Article 78 TFEU.
[39] Replaces the current Article 31 TEU.
[40] Replaces the current Article 30 TEU.
[41] Replaces the current Article 32 TEU.

Old numbering of the Treaty establishing the European Community	New numbering of the Treaty on the Functioning of the European Union
Article 74	Article 94
Article 75	Article 95
Article 76	Article 96
Article 77	Article 97
Article 78	Article 98
Article 79	Article 99
Article 80	Article 100
Title VI – Common rules on competition, taxation and approximation of laws	Title VII – Common rules on competition, taxation and approximation of laws
Chapter 1 – Rules on competition	Chapter 1 – Rules on competition
Section 1 – Rules applying to undertakings	Section 1 – Rules applying to undertakings
Article 81	Article 101
Article 82	Article 102
Article 83	Article 103
Article 84	Article 104
Article 85	Article 105
Article 86	Article 106
Section 2 – Aids granted by States	Section 2 – Aids granted by States
Article 87	Article 107
Article 88	Article 108
Article 89	Article 109
Chapter 2 – Tax provisions	Chapter 2 – Tax provisions
Article 90	Article 110
Article 91	Article 111
Article 92	Article 112
Article 93	Article 113
Chapter 3 – Approximation of laws	Chapter 3 – Approximation of laws
Article 95 (moved)	Article 114
Article 94 (moved)	Article 115
Article 96	Article 116
Article 97	Article 117
	Article 118
Title VII – Economic and monetary policy	Title VIII – Economic and monetary policy
Article 4 (moved)	Article 119

Old numbering of the Treaty establishing the European Community	New numbering of the Treaty on the Functioning of the European Union
Chapter 1 – Economic policy	Chapter 1 – Economic policy
Article 98	Article 120
Article 99	Article 121
Article 100	Article 122
Article 101	Article 123
Article 102	Article 124
Article 103	Article 125
Article 104	Article 126
Chapter 2 – monetary policy	Chapter 2 – monetary policy
Article 105	Article 127
Article 106	Article 128
Article 107	Article 129
Article 108	Article 130
Article 109	Article 131
Article 110	Article 132
Article 111, paragraphs 1 to 3 and 5 (moved)	Article 219
Article 111, paragraph 4 (moved)	Article 138
	Article 133
Chapter 3 – Institutional provisions	Chapter 3 – Institutional provisions
Article 112 (moved)	Article 283
Article 113 (moved)	Article 284
Article 114	Article 134
Article 115	Article 135
	Chapter 4 – Provisions specific to Member States whose currency is the euro
	Article 136
	Article 137
Article 111, paragraph 4 (moved)	Article 138
Chapter 4 – Transitional provisions	Chapter 5 – Transitional provisions
Article 116 (repealed)	
	Article 139
Article 117, paragraphs 1, 2, sixth indent, and 3 to 9 (repealed)	
Article 117, paragraph 2, first five indents (moved)	Article 141, paragraph 2

Old numbering of the Treaty establishing the European Community	New numbering of the Treaty on the Functioning of the European Union
Article 121, paragraph 1 (moved) Article 122, paragraph 2, second sentence (moved) Article 123, paragraph 5 (moved)	Article 140 [42]
Article 118 (repealed)	
Article 123, paragraph 3 (moved) Article 117, paragraph 2, first five indents (moved)	Article 141 [43]
Article 124, paragraph 1 (moved)	Article 142
Article 119	Article 143
Article 120	Article 144
Article 121, paragraph 1 (moved)	Article 140, paragraph 1
Article 121, paragraphs 2 to 4 (repealed)	
Article 122, paragraphs 1, 2, first sentence, 3, 4, 5 and 6 (repealed)	
Article 122, paragraph 2, second sentence (moved)	Article 140, paragraph 2, first subparagraph
Article 123, paragraphs 1, 2 and 4 (repealed)	
Article 123, paragraph 3 (moved)	Article 141, paragraph 1
Article 123, paragraph 5 (moved)	Article 140, paragraph 3
Article 124, paragraph 1 (moved)	Article 142
Article 124, paragraph 2 (repealed)	
Title VIII – Employment	Title IX – Employment
Article 125	Article 145
Article 126	Article 146
Article 127	Article 147
Article 128	Article 148
Article 129	Article 149
Article 130	Article 150
Title IX – Common commercial policy (moved)	Part Five, Title II, common commercial policy
Article 131 (moved)	Article 206
Article 132 (repealed)	
Article 133 (moved)	Article 207
Article 134 (repealed)	

[42]
- Article 140, paragraph 1 takes over the wording of paragraph 1 of Article 121.
- Article 140, paragraph 2 takes over the second sentence of paragraph 2 of Article 122.
- Article 140, paragraph 3 takes over paragraph 5 of Article 123.

[43]
- Article 141, paragraph 1 takes over paragraph 3 of Article 123.
- Article 141, paragraph 2 takes over the first five indents of paragraph 2 of Article 117.

Old numbering of the Treaty establishing the European Community	New numbering of the Treaty on the Functioning of the European Union
Title X – Customs cooperation (moved)	Part Three, Title II, Chapter 2, Customs cooperation
Article 135 (moved)	Article 33
Title XI – Social policy, education, vocational training and youth	Title X – Social policy
Chapter 1 – social provisions (repealed)	
Article 136	Article 151
	Article 152
Article 137	Article 153
Article 138	Article 154
Article 139	Article 155
Article 140	Article 156
Article 141	Article 157
Article 142	Article 158
Article 143	Article 159
Article 144	Article 160
Article 145	Article 161
Chapter 2 – The European Social Fund	Title XI – The European Social Fund
Article 146	Article 162
Article 147	Article 163
Article 148	Article 164
Chapter 3 – Education, vocational training and youth	Title XII – Education, vocational training, youth and sport
Article 149	Article 165
Article 150	Article 166
Title XII – Culture	Title XIII – Culture
Article 151	Article 167
Title XIII – Public health	Title XIV – Public health
Article 152	Article 168
Title XIV – Consumer protection	Title XV – Consumer protection
Article 153, paragraphs 1, 3, 4 and 5	Article 169
Article 153, paragraph 2 (moved)	Article 12
Title XV – Trans-European networks	Title XVI – Trans-European networks
Article 154	Article 170
Article 155	Article 171
Article 156	Article 172

Old numbering of the Treaty establishing the European Community	New numbering of the Treaty on the Functioning of the European Union
Title XVI – Industry	Title XVII – Industry
Article 157	Article 173
Title XVII – Economic and social cohesion	Title XVIII – Economic, social and territorial cohesion
Article 158	Article 174
Article 159	Article 175
Article 160	Article 176
Article 161	Article 177
Article 162	Article 178
Title XVIII – Research and technological development	Title XIX – Research and technological development and space
Article 163	Article 179
Article 164	Article 180
Article 165	Article 181
Article 166	Article 182
Article 167	Article 183
Article 168	Article 184
Article 169	Article 185
Article 170	Article 186
Article 171	Article 187
Article 172	Article 188
	Article 189
Article 173	Article 190
Title XIX – Environment	Title XX – Environment
Article 174	Article 191
Article 175	Article 192
Article 176	Article 193
	Titre XXI – Energy
	Article 194
	Title XXII – Tourism
	Article 195
	Title XXIII – Civil protection
	Article 196
	Title XXIV – Administrative cooperation
	Article 197

Old numbering of the Treaty establishing the European Community	New numbering of the Treaty on the Functioning of the European Union
Title XX – Development cooperation (moved)	Part Five, Title III, Chapter 1, Development cooperation
Article 177 (moved)	Article 208
Article 178 (repealed) [44]	
Article 179 (moved)	Article 209
Article 180 (moved)	Article 210
Article 181 (moved)	Article 211
Title XXI – Economic, financial and technical cooperation with third countries (moved)	Part Five, Title III, Chapter 2, Economic, financial and technical cooperation with third countries
Article 181a (moved)	Article 212
PART FOUR – ASSOCIATION OF THE OVERSEAS COUNTRIES AND TERRITORIES	PART FOUR – ASSOCIATION OF THE OVERSEAS COUNTRIES AND TERRITORIES
Article 182	Article 198
Article 183	Article 199
Article 184	Article 200
Article 185	Article 201
Article 186	Article 202
Article 187	Article 203
Article 188	Article 204
	PART FIVE – EXTERNAL ACTION BY THE UNION
	Title I – General provisions on the union's external action
	Article 205
Part Three, Title IX, Common commercial policy (moved)	Title II – Common commercial policy
Article 131 (moved)	Article 206
Article 133 (moved)	Article 207
	Title III – Cooperation with third countries and humanitarian aid
Part Three, Title XX, Development cooperation (moved)	Chapter 1 – development cooperation
Article 177 (moved)	Article 208 [45]
Article 179 (moved)	Article 209
Article 180 (moved)	Article 210
Article 181 (moved)	Article 211

[44]   Replaced, in substance, by the second sentence of the second subparagraph of paragraph 1 of Article 208 TFUE.
[45]   The second sentence of the second subparagraph of paragraph 1 replaces, in substance, Article 178 TEC.

Old numbering of the Treaty establishing the European Community	New numbering of the Treaty on the Functioning of the European Union
Part Three, Title XXI, Economic, financial and technical cooperation with third countries (moved)	Chapter 2 – Economic, financial and technical cooperation with third countries
Article 181a (moved)	Article 212
	Article 213
	Chapter 3 – Humanitarian aid
	Article 214
	Title IV – Restrictive measures
Article 301 (replaced)	Article 215
	Title V – International agreements
	Article 216
Article 310 (moved)	Article 217
Article 300 (replaced)	Article 218
Article 111, paragraphs 1 to 3 and 5 (moved)	Article 219
	Title VI – The Union's relations with international organisations and third countries and the Union delegations
Articles 302 to 304 (replaced)	Article 220
	Article 221
	Title VII – Solidarity clause
	Article 222
PART FIVE – INSTITUTIONS OF THE COMMUNITY	PART SIX – INSTITUTIONAL AND FINANCIAL PROVISIONS
Title I – Institutional provisions	Title I – Institutional provisions
Chapter 1 – The institutions	Chapter 1 – The institutions
Section 1 – The European Parliament	Section 1 – The European Parliament
Article 189 (repealed) [46]	
Article 190, paragraphs 1 to 3 (repealed) [47]	
Article 190, paragraphs 4 and 5	Article 223
Article 191, first paragraph (repealed) [48]	
Article 191, second paragraph	Article 224
Article 192, first paragraph (repealed) [49]	
Article 192, second paragraph	Article 225

[46] Replaced, in substance, by Article 14, paragraphs 1 and 2, TEU.
[47] Replaced, in substance, by Article 14, paragraphs 1 to 3, TEU.
[48] Replaced, in substance, by Article 11, paragraph 4, TEU.
[49] Replaced, in substance, by Article 14, paragraph 1, TEU.

Old numbering of the Treaty establishing the European Community	New numbering of the Treaty on the Functioning of the European Union
Article 193	Article 226
Article 194	Article 227
Article 195	Article 228
Article 196	Article 229
Article 197, first paragraph (repealed) [50]	
Article 197, second, third and fourth paragraphs	Article 230
Article 198	Article 231
Article 199	Article 232
Article 200	Article 233
Article 201	Article 234
	Section 2 – The European Council
	Article 235
	Article 236
Section 2 – The Council	Section 3 – The Council
Article 202 (repealed) [51]	
Article 203 (repealed) [52]	
Article 204	Article 237
Article 205, paragraphs 2 and 4 (repealed) [53]	
Article 205, paragraphs 1 and 3	Article 238
Article 206	Article 239
Article 207	Article 240
Article 208	Article 241
Article 209	Article 242
Article 210	Article 243
Section 3 – The Commission	Section 4 – The Commission
Article 211 (repealed) [55]	
	Article 244
Article 212 (moved)	Article 249, paragraph 2
Article 213	Article 245

[50] Replaced, in substance, by Article 14, paragraph 4, TEU.
[51] Replaced, in substance, by Article 16, paragraph 1, TEU and by Articles 290 and 291 TFEU.
[52] Replaced, in substance, by Article 16, paragraphs 2 and 9 TEU.
[53] Replaced, in substance, by Article 16, paragraphs 4 and 5 TEU.
[54] Replaced, in substance, by Article 295 TFEU.
[55] Replaced, in substance, by Article 17, paragraph 1 TEU.
[56] Replaced, in substance, by Article 19, paragraph 2, first subparagraph, of the TEU.

Old numbering of the Treaty establishing the European Community	New numbering of the Treaty on the Functioning of the European Union
Article 214 (repealed) [57]	
Article 215	Article 246
Article 216	Article 247
Article 217, paragraphs 1, 3 and 4 (repealed) [58]	
Article 217, paragraph 2	Article 248
Article 218, paragraph 1 (repealed) [59]	
Article 218, paragraph 2	Article 249
Article 219	Article 250
Section 4 – The Court of Justice	Section 5 – The Court of Justice of the European Union
Article 220 (repealed) [60]	
Article 221, first paragraph (repealed) [61]	
Article 221, second and third paragraphs	Article 251
Article 222	Article 252
Article 223	Article 253
Article 224 [62]	Article 254
	Article 255
Article 225	Article 256
Article 225a	Article 257
Article 226	Article 258
Article 227	Article 259
Article 228	Article 260
Article 229	Article 261
Article 229a	Article 262
Article 230	Article 263
Article 231	Article 264
Article 232	Article 265
Article 233	Article 266
Article 234	Article 267
Article 235	Article 268

[57] Replaced, in substance, by Article 17, paragraphs 3 and 7 TEU.
[58] Replaced, in substance, by Article 17, paragraph 6, TEU.
[59] Replaced, in substance, by Article 295 TFEU.
[60] Replaced, in substance, by Article 19 TEU.
[61] Replaced, in substance, by Article 19, paragraph 2, first subparagraph, of the TEU.
[62] The first sentence of the first subparagraph is replaced, in substance, by Article 19, paragraph 2, second subparagraph of the TEU.

Old numbering of the Treaty establishing the European Community	New numbering of the Treaty on the Functioning of the European Union
	Article 269
Article 236	Article 270
Article 237	Article 271
Article 238	Article 272
Article 239	Article 273
Article 240	Article 274
	Article 275
	Article 276
Article 241	Article 277
Article 242	Article 278
Article 243	Article 279
Article 244	Article 280
Article 245	Article 281
	Section 6 – The European Central Bank
	Article 282
Article 112 (moved)	Article 283
Article 113 (moved)	Article 284
Section 5 – The Court of Auditors	Section 7 – The Court of Auditors
Article 246	Article 285
Article 247	Article 286
Article 248	Article 287
Chapter 2 – Provisions common to several institutions	Chapter 2 – Legal acts of the Union, adoption procedures and other provisions
	Section 1 – The legal acts of the Union
Article 249	Article 288
	Article 289
	Article 290 [63]
	Article 291 [63]
	Article 292
	Section 2 – Procedures for the adoption of acts and other provisions
Article 250	Article 293
Article 251	Article 294
Article 252 (repealed)	

[63]   Replaces, in substance, the third indent of Article 202 TEC.

Old numbering of the Treaty establishing the European Community	New numbering of the Treaty on the Functioning of the European Union
	Article 295
Article 253	Article 296
Article 254	Article 297
	Article 298
Article 255 (moved)	Article 15
Article 256	Article 299
	Chapter 3 – The Union's advisory bodies
	Article 300
Chapter 3 – The Economic and Social Committee	Section 1 – The Economic and Social Committee
Article 257 (repealed) [64]	
Article 258, first, second and fourth paragraphs	Article 301
Article 258, third paragraph (repealed) [65]	
Article 259	Article 302
Article 260	Article 303
Article 261 (repealed)	
Article 262	Article 304
Chapter 4 – The Committee of the Regions	Section 2 – The Committee of the Regions
Article 263, first and fifth paragraphs (repealed) [66]	
Article 263, second to fourth paragraphs	Article 305
Article 264	Article 306
Article 265	Article 307
Chapter 5 – The European Investment Bank	Chapter 4 – The European Investment Bank
Article 266	Article 308
Article 267	Article 309
Title II – Financial provisions	Title II – Financial provisions
Article 268	Article 310
	Chapter 1 – The Union's own resources
Article 269	Article 311
Article 270 (repealed) [67]	
	Chapter 2 – The multiannual financial framework

[64]   Replaced, in substance, by Article 300, paragraph 2 of the TFEU.
[65]   Replaced, in substance, by Article 300, paragraph 4 of the TFEU.
[66]   Replaced, in substance, by Article 300, paragraphs 3 and 4, TFEU.
[67]   Replaced, in substance, by Article 310, paragraph 4, TFEU.

Old numbering of the Treaty establishing the European Community	New numbering of the Treaty on the Functioning of the European Union
	Article 312
	Chapter 3 – The Union's annual budget
Article 272, paragraph 1 (moved)	Article 313
Article 271 (moved)	Article 316
Article 272, paragraph 1 (moved)	Article 313
Article 272, paragraphs 2 to 10	Article 314
Article 273	Article 315
Article 271 (moved)	Article 316
	Chapter 4 – Implementation of the budget and discharge
Article 274	Article 317
Article 275	Article 318
Article 276	Article 319
	Chapter 5 – Common provisions
Article 277	Article 320
Article 278	Article 321
Article 279	Article 322
	Article 323
	Article 324
	Chapter 6 – Combating fraud
Article 280	Article 325
	Title III – Enhanced cooperation
Articles 11 and 11a (replaced)	Article 326 [68]
Articles 11 and 11a (replaced)	Article 327 [68]
Articles 11 and 11a (replaced)	Article 328 [68]
Articles 11 and 11a (replaced)	Article 329 [68]
Articles 11 and 11a (replaced)	Article 330 [68]
Articles 11 and 11a (replaced)	Article 331 [68]
Articles 11 and 11a (replaced)	Article 332 [68]
Articles 11 and 11a (replaced)	Article 333 [68]
Articles 11 and 11a (replaced)	Article 334 [68]
PART SIX – GENERAL AND FINAL PROVISIONS	PART SEVEN – GENERAL AND FINAL PROVISIONS
Article 281 (repealed) [69]	

[68]   Also replaces the current Articles 27a to 27e, 40 to 40b, and 43 to 45 TEU.
[69]   Replaced, in substance, by Article 47 TEU.

Old numbering of the Treaty establishing the European Community	New numbering of the Treaty on the Functioning of the European Union
Article 282	Article 335
Article 283	Article 336
Article 284	Article 337
Article 285	Article 338
Article 286 (replaced)	Article 16
Article 287	Article 339
Article 288	Article 340
Article 289	Article 341
Article 290	Article 342
Article 291	Article 343
Article 292	Article 344
Article 293 (repealed)	
Article 294 (moved)	Article 55
Article 295	Article 345
Article 296	Article 346
Article 297	Article 347
Article 298	Article 348
Article 299, paragraph 1 (repealed) [70]	
Article 299, paragraph 2, second, third and fourth subparagraphs	Article 349
Article 299, paragraph 2, first subparagraph, and paragraphs 3 to 6 (moved)	Article 355
Article 300 (replaced)	Article 218
Article 301 (replaced)	Article 215
Article 302 (replaced)	Article 220
Article 303 (replaced)	Article 220
Article 304 (replaced)	Article 220
Article 305 (repealed)	
Article 306	Article 350
Article 307	Article 351
Article 308	Article 352
	Article 353
Article 309	Article 354

[70]   Replaced, in substance by Article 52 TEU.

Old numbering of the Treaty establishing the European Community	New numbering of the Treaty on the Functioning of the European Union
Article 310 (moved)	Article 217
Article 311 (repealed) [71]	
Article 299, paragraph 2, first subparagraph, and paragraphs 3 to 6 (moved)	Article 355
Article 312	Article 356
Final Provisions	
Article 313	Article 357
	Article 358
Article 314 (repealed) [72]	

[71]   Replaced, in substance by Article 51 TEU.
[72]   Replaced, in substance by Article 55 TEU.

Source: © European Union, 1995–2014

Table of UK legislation

Statutory Instruments

Statement of Principles

White Papers

Working Papers

Table of US legislation

Table of international agreements

1 What is money?

Chapter overview

The aim of this chapter is to:

➤ Explain the role and function of money in society.

➤ Explain the classification of banks and functions of banks.

➤ Explain the nature of services provided by banks.

➤ Explain the legal effect of opening an account – whose money is it?

➤ Explain the payment and clearing system and the issues relating to when payment is made in law.

Introduction

It is because the term 'money' is so prevalent and central to human activity that we rarely pause to ask 'what is money?' Money is a concept that every human being acquires an early acquaintance with: it is the notes and coins each of us carries but any definition of money must recognise and accept the different functions and roles fulfilled by money. The constituents of money have at various times been embodied in gold, silver, copper or paper bills, and even further back in shells, beads, salt, slaves etc. In *Moss v Hancock*[1] the court defined money as:

> that which passes freely from hand to hand throughout the community in final discharge of debts and full payment for commodities, being accepted equally without reference to the character or credit of the person who offers it and without the intention of the person who receives it to consume it or apply it to any other use than in turn tender it to others in discharge of debts or payment for commodities.

In *Reference Re Alberta Statutes*[2] the Supreme Court of Canada adopted an even broader definition of money describing money, as 'any medium which, by practice, fulfils the function of money which everyone will accept in payment of a debt is money', even though it may not be legal tender.

[1] [1899] 2 QB III at 116.
[2] [1938] SCR 100 at 116.

It is because money is used as a means of exchange, as a bargaining tool, as a means of a final discharge of legally enforceable debts and forms the basis of our commercial contracts that we need to understand what is money? Professor Friedman in his work, *Money Mischief*, defined money as:

> whatever is generally accepted in exchange for goods and services – accepted not as an object to be consumed but as an object that represents a temporary abode of purchasing power to be used for buying still other goods and service.[3]

Money, therefore, allows the holder to manage and organise his affairs in the way best suited to him and, will often, enhance his negotiating power. However, money can only be used as an instrument of such power if it is recognised within society as a means of regulating conduct and compelling performance. The use of money thus enables the holder to alter his legal position by exchanging money for goods and services at an agreed, or to be determined, price. For this system of exchange to work effectively society must have confidence that tokens that represent money will be accepted as a means of exchange, both immediately and in the future. While, money as a vehicle for exchange has a fundamental role in society it also has other key functions. Money is therefore:

1 A unit of account: this function is only fulfilled if money, as a unit of account, is given a value that is uniform throughout the monetary area concerned. The law will again have significance since it will underpin the unit of account.

2 A medium of exchange: if a country's system of trade and commerce is to be based on a medium of exchange then the law must support that position and allow for the discharge of monetary debts by payment in that medium. The law will, therefore, require the creditor to accept payment through that medium. In turn, the law must support that position by requiring the creditor to accept payment of debts by those means.

3 A standard of measuring deferred payment: this allows for payment to be expressed with certainty regardless of when payment falls due under the contract.[4]

Economists have frequently expressed the view that money has three features namely: (i) as a medium of exchange, (ii) as a unit of account and (iii) as a store of value.[5] The pound sterling satisfies all these attributes because it is used as a means of acquiring something, whether goods or services, while at the same time serves as a means of measuring value and as a repository of purchasing power. Thus, a pound received today will still be a pound next week or next year and, therefore, an effective store of purchasing power over time, although the value of that purchasing power may depend on inflationary trends, the rate of exchange for the pound against other currencies etc.

The constituent elements of money are irrelevant but what is important is that money in the abstract is given certain legal relevance and thus a piece of paper is treated not merely as paper or metal, as coinage, but as a legal concept embodying certain legally enforceable rights. Money in the abstract is also a fungible concept, and it is this freely exchangeable character that often causes complexities in the understanding of *'What is money?'*

---

[3] Friedman (1992) *Money Mischief*, London: Mariner Books. Professor Friedman was awarded the Nobel Prize in Economics in 1976.

[4] Nussbaum (1937) 'Basic Monetary Conceptions in Law', 35 *Mich. L. Rev.*, 865 at 867.

[5] Mishkin (2012) *The Economics of Money, Banking and Financial Markets*, Harlow: Pearson Publishing, pp. 49–51.

The legal nature of money

Money can only exist as some form of a chattel; that is in a physical form.[6] In the past these chattels could consist of commodities or metals, but in modern society money consists of banksnotes and coins. Banknotes and coins are chattels in possession and those in possession of such notes and coins can exercise certain rights over them.[7] These rights include rights of ownership and transfer.

However, banknotes additionally constitute a chose in action, and may be enforced through action rather than taking possession. In the UK, banknotes express 'a promise to pay the bearer on demand a sum of . . . Pounds'. Banknotes are therefore promissory notes within section 82 of the Bills of Exchange Act 1882, but they are unlike other commercial contracts to pay. Banknotes are the currency of the country[8] and a banknote therefore embodies a promise to pay that which could only be discharged by proffering a replacement note or equivalent value in coins, in exchange. Thus, a Bank of England note only constitutes money because it incorporates a promise to pay. The precise features of banknotes and coins in circulation in a country will be defined by the legislation, which establishes the monetary system of that country.

Within the UK, the Bank of England Act 1694 did not confer any note-issuing powers on it, and neither did it attempt to confer a note-issuing monopoly on the Bank. Nevertheless, the Bank began to issue notes immediately after its incorporation, alongside many other country banks without government control. As the growth of money in circulation was not subject to any effective form of regulation the quality of money could be affected by the solvency of the particular issuer. The function of issuing notes and coins is now confined to the Issue Department of the Bank of England, which operates in much the same way as a commercial bank. The total volume of the banknote issue is determined from time to time by direction of the Treasury and the Bank executing government money policy depending on the demand for currency.

To control inflation, the note issue of the Bank of England was linked to the gold reserve. However, since the gold standard was abandoned in 1931, only part of the note issue is backed by gold coin and bullion held in the Issue Department. By far the greater issue of notes, known as the fiduciary issue, is covered by securities issues to the Bank by the Treasury on behalf of the government, which illustrates that sterling is backed by government securities.[9]

---

[6] This concept is to be distinguished from payment which in the legal sense connotes an act offered and accepted in performance of a monetary obligation although if parties agree that the debtor should discharge a debt by handing over his car, instead of making a cash payment, that should not give the car the characteristics of money. This arrangement merely allows the discharge of a monetary obligation by means other than payment; see *Charter Reinsurance Co Ltd* v *Fagan* [1997] AC 313 at 384.

[7] Property in money generally passes with possession, *Sinclair* v *Brougham* [1914] AC 398 at 418.

[8] *Suffel* v *Bank of England* (1882) 9 QBD 555, 563 and 567; see also *The Guardian of the Poor of the Lichfield Union* v *Greene* (1857) 26 LJ Ex 140.

[9] Currency and Bank Notes Act 1954, s.2.

History of money

Eventually societies around the world accepted gold as a means of exchange and value. This form of money is called '*specie*'. Blackstone explained the desirability of gold and silver as money as follows:

> Money is a universal medium, or common standard, by comparison with which the value of all merchandise may be ascertained: . . . a sign, which represents the respective values of all commodities. Metals are well calculated for this sign because they are durable and capable of many subdivisions: and a precious metal is still better calculated for this purpose, because it is the most portable. A metal is also the most proper for a common measure, because it can easily to be reduced to the same standard in all nations: and every particular nation affixes it own impression on it . . . The coining of money is in all states the act of the sovereign power . . .[10]

By the nineteenth century the use of gold as a monetary commodity led to the adoption of the gold standard. Under the gold standard the currency of the country operating within it was directly linked to the value of gold and convertible into gold. This meant that for countries operating under the gold standard there was a fixed rate of exchange, which was fixed and convertible by and into gold.[11] By the 1870s most of the major currencies in the world were backed by the gold standard and it governed international economic relations and international monetary relations until the end of the First World War. The advantage of the gold standard was that it prevented countries from the uncontrolled issuing of money and governments could only issue money if it was supported by their gold reserves: this meant that the supply of money could not be used as a political tool.

While governments adopted the gold standard as the means by which international monetary relations were governed, the use of gold on an individual basis had its drawbacks. Gold is heavy because of its density and its transportation and delivery presented challenges. An owner of gold would also be concerned with its security because of the value attached to it, and his personal safety when carrying it on his person. In response, the practice developed among businessmen particularly, of depositing their gold, for safekeeping, with goldsmiths who, in turn, issued a receipt, redeemable, for the amount of the gold deposited. In due course, the practice developed of trading these receipts for goods and services and effectively discharging the debt, since the receipts were redeemable for the value of the gold they represented. Thus, began the practice of circulating receipts that represented their value in gold and which could be redeemed for the equivalent in gold. By the time the gold standard was adopted paper money representing the equivalent value in gold had become common practice, as goldsmith bankers began to exchange receipts for gold coins from the sixteenth century onwards. Transactions no longer required gold to be exchanged at the place of contract and the paper money that symbolised the gold deposited with goldsmiths became common currency. However, the link between paper money and the symbol it represented (gold) was broken on the 15 August 1971 when President Richard Nixon terminated the obligation the United States had assumed, at Bretton Woods, to convert dollars held by foreign monetary authorities into gold at the fixed price of $35 an ounce. This reflected the decision of the UK to leave the gold standard in 1931.

---

[10] Blackstone 266 (1765), *Commentaries on the Laws of England*, William S. Hein & Co. Inc. eds 1992.
[11] Mishkin (2012) *The Economics of Money, Banking and Financial Markets*, Harlow: Pearson Publishing, pp. 49–51.

While money is necessary for modern society, gold or another commodity no longer backs it. All money is, therefore, fiat money and, yet, something so necessary and powerful has such fragile foundations. Money is a matter of belief in the legitimacy that the paper notes in circulation will be accepted for the face value they represent and the promise of the Treasury to pay the bearer the equivalent in smaller notes. Section 1(4) of the Currency and Bank Notes Act 1954 provides that the holder of banknotes of any denominations, shall be entitled, on demand made during office hours either at the head office of the Bank of England, or at some other place[12] to receive in exchange for the banknotes, notes of a lower denominations, being legal tender, as he may specify. Thus, the holder of a £20 note can exchange that at a bank for four £5 notes or other equivalent: he can longer claim the equivalent in gold. Public trust in the pound is now maintained by the operation of monetary policy, the objective of which is price stability.[13] It is because money is no longer backed by gold that the concept of fiat money as legal tender has become important.

The concept of fiat money and legal tender

In addition to the pound sterling satisfying the functions of money, other currencies for example the US dollar, the Swiss franc, the euro within the Member States of the eurozone, the Indian rupee etc., all satisfy the functions of money because they are recognised as legal tender by the sovereign state that issues them.[14] However, while a shopkeeper, or the provider of services, may voluntarily accept a foreign currency as discharging a legally enforceable debt under contract, he cannot be compelled by law, to do so. The reason the seller of goods or services, in the UK, will be justified in refusing to accept payment in a currency other than pound sterling is that the foreign currency is not legal tender in the UK.[15] Thus, 'legal tender is money which, if tendered by a debtor in payment of his debt, must not be refused by the creditor'.[16] Therefore, an agreement for the payment of goods or services, unless otherwise agreed, in a currency other than pound sterling may be refused.

Legal tender is locally legally designated tokens that will justify the discharge of legally enforceable payment obligations. Thus, it is unlawful for a creditor to refuse payment in pound sterling unless it is specifically agreed between the parties that payment will be in a foreign currency, or unless the creditor is willing to agree to a variation of the contractual terms and accept payment in the foreign currency. For example, there may be a proper variation of a contract where the debtor agrees to pay in US dollars instead of pound sterling.[17] The ability to discharge debts through payment, therefore, depends on the law's legal designation of pound sterling, as legal tender. The effect of the legal designation is particularly apparent in the context of fiat money. Fiat money is currency that has value because the government[18] has recognised it as legal tender for the purposes of paying taxes and discharging other legally

---

[12] See: Currency and Bank Notes Act 1954, s.1 (3).

[13] Bank of England, Frequently Asked Questions, http://www.bankofengland.co.uk/banknotes/about/faqs.htm#top.

[14] The right to demand payment in legal tender is illustrated in *Libyan Arab Foreign Bank* v *Bankers Trust Co.* [1989] QB 728.

[15] Currency and Bank Notes Act 1954, s.1(2); Coinage Act 1971, s.2 as amended by the Currency Act 1983, s.1(3).

[16] Nussbaum (1937) 'Basic Monetary Conceptions in Law', 35 *Mich. L. Rev.*, 865 at 867.

[17] *Pinnell's Case* (1601) 77 ER 237 which provided that the variation of a contract is not legally enforceable unless supported by fresh consideration and 'the gift of a horse, a hawk or robe' will provide valid consideration.

[18] Mann (1992) *The Legal Aspect of Money*, Oxford: Clarendon Press, p. 14.

enforceable debts, and for monies owed under a contract. Fiat money, therefore, represents a right to claim payment against other forms of valuable commodities, for example gold or silver, and is money solely because government has legislated that it is money and the public has confidence that others will recognise it as having value. The role of the sovereign state and the law becomes key in giving the attributes of money. Thus, a commodity becomes legal tender because the sovereign state so determines.[19] The tender of fiat money therefore discharges debts and other payment obligations; it does not represent a claim on some other commodity to discharge indebtedness. Banks are a key component in the circulation and transfer of money from one person, entity or agency to another and it is important to understand the structure and classification of the banking system and the nature of the business undertaken by them.

Banking system: structure and classification

This section of the chapter will examine some of the activities traditionally associated with the business of banking, then explore classification of banking institutions and go on to examine the structure of the UK banking sector.

Business of banking

Banks are characterised as dealing with money they receive in the form of deposits and using those funds in the course of their business, either by means of lending or investing. Thus, while it is true to say that bankers deal with money, i.e. those chattels which are attributed the character of money by law and by the authority of state,[20] to define the business of banking as dealing with money adopts a narrow approach to the business undertaken by banks. What is significant is that bankers then use the money deposited with them, or those funds they have access to, in the course of their business on the understanding that the bank will return an equivalent amount on demand.[21] In reality the description of the nature of the banking business will, therefore, vary depending on the approach adopted. A broader approach to banking would define the bankers' business as a means of safeguarding and facilitating the exchange of chattels (money) for goods and services, and the accumulation of financial wealth. It is, therefore, not difficult to see why banks receive deposits: bank accounts allow customers to keep their money and savings in a relatively safe environment with the legal right given to the customer to demand repayment of the funds, together with any interest.[22]

From a customer's view, maintaining a bank account is an essential form of social inclusion[23] and the customer will be able to use the current account as a means of safekeeping for any

---

[19] Chung (2009) Money as a Simulacrum: The Legal Nature and Reality of Money, *Hastings Business Law Journal*, 5(109), http://papers.ssrn.com/sol3/papers.cfm?abstract_id=1141383.

[20] Mann (1992) *The Legal Aspect of Money*, Oxford: Clarendon Press, p. 14.

[21] *Foley* v *Hill* (1848) 2 HLC 28.

[22] *Foley* v *Hill* (1848) 2 HLC 28.

[23] The Banking services and poorer households, Financial Inclusion Task Force, December 2010, report found that 52% of the UK unbanked population would like access to bank accounts, p. 6, http://www.hm-treasury.gov.uk/d/fin_inclusion_taskforce_poorerhouseholds_dec2010.pdf.

savings, as a means of receiving his salary directly into the account, facilitating payments to, and from, third parties efficiently and swiftly, either by means of a cheque or by standing orders or credit transfers. Banks offer a wide range of options in respect of the types of accounts available ranging from the current account to the long-term deposit accounts, which may enable the customer to take advantage of better interest rates. Banks also offer customers and third party clients a range of other services, which will be examined below.

Overdrafts

The overdraft[24] is a common way of obtaining short-term funds for personal use, or in business to finance the day-to-day expenditure of the business, or stock in trade. While, the overdraft may be considered a short-term facility, in reality businesses often operate on a continuous overdraft. Thus, the overdraft is a credit line extended to the customer through the use of the current account. An overdraft facility is usually granted by agreement but the bank may allow a customer to overdraw even if an overdraft facility has not been agreed.[25] The customer will pay interest on the overdraft facility with the interest normally calculated on a daily basis, but usually debited against the account periodically.

Term loans

A term loan[26] will invariably state the amount of the loan and the period of the loan. Such loans can be drawn down either by successive regular instalments, or over a number of years. Term loans of up to 5 or 7 years are commonly advanced but banks, sometimes acting as part of a syndicate, may agree to even longer-term loans, for example term loans of up to 20–25 years may be agreed. The loan agreement is legally binding and the insertion of a term specifying the duration of the loan precludes any subsequent claim by the lending banks that the loan can be withdrawn at any time. Normally default provisions will be written into the agreement so that the bank may have the option to accelerate payment in case of such material default. The borrower normally agrees to a commitment fee.

Consumer finance

There has been a tremendous increase in the level of consumer finance consisting of personal loans, revolving credit accounts and budget accounts. All banks provide credit cards[27] to private and business customers alike and banks have also rapidly expanded their lending activities to include house mortgage lending, traditionally a building society activity. The relentless growth of credit and the level of mortgage defaults contributed heavily to the global financial crisis of 2007–08.[28]

Financial services

As the financial markets have been deregulated banks have diversified into the provision of financial services. Consequently, banks represent a substantial proportion of new insurance policies, pensions, long-term savings provision and unit trusts business.

---

[24] See Ch. 9.
[25] See *The Office of Fair Trading* v *Abbey National Plc & Others* [2009] UKSC 6.
[26] See Ch. 15.
[27] See Ch. 14.
[28] The Turner Review: A regulatory response to the global financial crisis, March 2009, p. 87, http://www.fsa.gov.uk/pubs/other/turner_review.pdf.

Export credits and bills of exchange

Banks have undertaken the finance of international trade either through the use of the traditional overdraft or acceptance credits under which they are willing to accept the credit and make payment on the due date, thereby guaranteeing payment. However, the commercial banks moved into the finance of international trade only in the last century and since then the nature of documentary credits and reinsurance activity has become highly technical and sophisticated. Bills of exchange[29] have traditionally been the means of facilitating payment under the letters of credit, although their use has declined. A bill is a promise to pay a specific sum of money, usually provided by the importer, while he waits delivery of the goods. The exporter who receives the draft can either negotiate the bill to the bank or discount house or wait for the bill to mature to receive payment. Banks have also developed the use of guarantees and bonds to safeguard their customers, while at the same time funding the growth of international trade and the growth of the world's economies.

Forfeiting

This is a form of supplier's credit ranging from six months to five years or longer. Banks will purchase bills of exchange or promissory notes where these are evidence of a trade debt. The exporter and importer negotiate a sale contract and the exporter will ascertain the terms of forfeiting. The exporter will quote a contract price to the overseas buyer by loading the discount rate and commitment fee on the sale price of the goods to be exported and enter into a contract with the forfeiter. Export takes place against the documents guaranteed by the importer's bank and discounts the bill with the forfeiter and presents them to the importer for payment on the due date. The bills or notes are arranged to mature at regular intervals.

Factoring and leasing

Traders and exporters may use the services of a factoring agent (usually a subsidiary of a bank) to alleviate cash flow. Factors provide cash based on the quality and liquidity of the business assets, primarily based on the quality of the accounts receivable. Banks, or their leasing subsidiaries, will finance the acquisition of equipment, machinery, vehicles etc. through leasing. The assets in question are hired out to the borrowing company but remain the property of the bank or the leasing company.

Venture capital

Venture capital is start up capital for new or small business; it is in essence risk capital in the form of equity or fixed interest loans, coupled with expertise in management buy-outs or acquisitions. The aim of the financial support is to enable small or new companies to grow rapidly so they can be sold or floated on the stock exchange. The British Venture Capital Association[30] represents enterprises willing to provide venture capital for small and medium-sized companies.

Other facilities will normally be extended by banks, for example mortgage lending, investment advice, will and probate advice etc. and reinforces the nature of business undertaken by

---

[29] See Ch. 11.
[30] http://www.bvca.co.uk/about-bvca/our-mission.

modern banks. Nevertheless, the business of banking may be altered if the recommendation of ring-fencing retail banking assets proposed by Sir John Vickers is introduced.[31]

Classification of financial institutions

Businesses may be classified in a number of different ways including according to the type of commodity produced, the turnover of the business and the number of employees.[32] Any classification of financial institutions under such criteria does not give any indication of the nature of business activities undertaken or the risks involved but it will assist, for example, to determine whether such service providers will need authorisation to accept deposits. In 1959, the Radcliffe Committee on the Working of the Monetary System[33] concluded that although the various markets for credit in an economic sense succeeded in functioning as a single unified market, there were nevertheless a great many differences in the activities of particular financial institutions, for example the clearing banks and the traditional investment banks. Each type of institution had its 'special type of business and by tradition or commercial arrangement a preference for one form of lending rather than another'.

However, since the Radcliffe Report banking business has changed to such an extent that the traditionally recognised demarcation lines within banks themselves, and then between banks and other financial institutions, particularly the building societies, has blurred to such an extent that Gordon Brown, in 1997, the then chancellor of the Exchequer, announced that as one of the main reasons for introducing a single unified regulator for the financial services sector.[34] Not only has the degree of banking specialisation altered since the Radcliffe Report but also the multifunctional banking institution has superseded the traditional bank that offered only limited banking services. For the same reason the classification proposed by Revell[35] that categorised banks as (i) deposit banks; (ii) secondary banks; and (iii) retail secondary bank is no longer adequate. While deposit banks enable an account holder to deposit and withdraw deposited funds, secondary banks provide financing to other banks. Retail secondary banking constitutes loans such as credit cards and mortgages to personal and commercial customers.[36]

The modern structure of the financial institutions prevents any simple single classification, especially as some financial institutions placed within one category may span a variety of financial activities. The discussion in this chapter is, therefore, organised along the lines of the classification in the Wilson Committee Report, which reviewed the *Functioning of Financial Institutions*.[37] The Wilson Committee recognised and distinguished between three types of financial intermediaries:

---

[31] Sir John Vickers, Independent Commission on Banking: The Vickers Report & the Parliamentary Commission on Banking Standards, http://www.parliament.uk/briefing-papers/SN06171, September 2011.

[32] For example the Companies Act 2006, ss.381–384 exempts small companies from certain accounting requirements.

[33] Cmnd 827, London: HMSO, 1959.

[34] Gordon Brown HC Deb, 20 May 1997, c. 510.

[35] Revell (1973) *The British Financial System*, London: Macmillan.

[36] http://www.publications.parliament.uk/pa/cm201011/cmselect/cmtreasy/612/612i.pdf.

[37] Wilson Committee Report on the Functioning of Financial Institutions, Cmnd 7937 HMSO, London, 1980.

Deposit-taking institutions

The common feature ascribed to deposit-taking institutions is that they accept deposits that constitute the liquid and nominal capital of the institution. These institutions then use the deposits as part of their core business to make loans, extend credit and provide other financial facilities, and in turn make a profit for themselves. While these activities reflect the nature of the retail-banking sector the 2007–08 banking crisis has reinforced the extent to which the expansion in banking activities has left any attempted classification inadequate. The extent of dependency within the banking sector was highlighted when, at the height of the financial crisis, banks themselves lost confidence in each other's ability to repay borrowings and the inter-bank lending markets failed, leading to a global banking crisis.[38]

Despite the City of London being a major financial centre for several decades, the law had failed to provide a definition of a bank until 1966, when Lord Denning attempted to characterise the nature of the banking business in *United Dominion Trust* v *Kirkwood*.[39] The Court of Appeal concluded that the distinguishing feature of a clearing bank,[40] apart from the direct or indirect participation in the clearing system, is that it holds itself out as prepared to accept deposits of money from members of the public on current or deposit accounts maintained for them, to collect cheques drawn by its customers on their current accounts, and to collect cheques, and other items, payable to its customer and drawn on or issued by other banks. Nevertheless, by modern standards the court took a narrow approach to the description of activities undertaken by banks. Even the current statutory system of regulation,[41] while more in-line with the nomenclature used by the Wilson Committee, emphasises the traditional range of banking activities, namely accepting deposits from customer's and then re-using these deposits in the ordinary course of the business. Such banks are prepared to accept deposits for small amounts from business and personal customers and must be distinguished from 'wholesale or investment banks',[42] that deal with large commercial or industrial companies, or large or bulk deposits, although these banks are usually either subsidiaries or an extension of the larger clearing banks and therefore the risk of losses in the latter could affect the stability of the clearing sector.[43]

Investing institutions

Investing institutions are those institutions that specialise in collecting funds from individuals, mostly on a longer-term basis and investing the pooled funds in long-term securities, or directly, in property. In the UK, investment savings institutions can be categorised as (a) contractual savings institutions, and (b) portfolio institutions. Contracting savings institutions obtain

---

[38] House of Commons Treasury Committee, The run on the Rock, Fifth Report of Session 2007–08 Volume 1, Ordered by The House of Commons, printed 24 January 2008, HC 56–I, pp. 15–16, http://www.parliament. the-stationery-office.com/pa/cm200708/cmselect/cmtreasy/56/56i.pdf, found that the loss of confidence in Northern Rock was exacerbated when the media reported that the retail banks failed to lend to Northern Rock.

[39] [1966] 1 ALL ER 968.

[40] See page 38 for a description of their business and activities.

[41] Financial Services and Markets Act 2000 (Regulated Activities) Order 2001, SI 2001/544.

[42] Independent Commission on Banking, Final Report, September 2011, ISBN 978-1-845-32-829-0, http:// www.ecgi.org/documents/icb_final_report_12sep2011.pdf, has recommended that the domestic retail banking sector business be separated from the global wholesale business. The report recommended that 'structural separation should make it easier and less costly to resolve banks that get into trouble'.

[43] Independent Commission on Banking, Final Report, September 2011, ISBN 978-1-845-32-829-0, http:// www.ecgi.org/documents/icb_final_report_12sep2011.pdf.

funds from personal savers under long-term contractual arrangements under which savers make regular contributions over a period of years in return for a terminal lump sum in the future, or in return for an annuity in the future. In the UK such savings schemes are usually linked to life assurance policies and pensions funds. These institutions permit individuals to participate in pooled investment funds, which are used to acquire portfolios of marketable securities. Investing in this way can reduce investment risks by portfolio diversification, as marketable securities may be readily bought or sold to raise cash. In the UK, the two major types of institutions undertaking such investments are unit and investment trusts.[44] A unit trust represents the collective investment of a large number of investors. However, an investment trust is quoted on the London Stock Exchange and invests its shareholders fund; it is limited by a fixed number of shares.

Specialist financing agencies

Specialist financing agencies are institutions created to fill gaps in financial markets with respect to the requirements of certain types of borrowers. Such institutions may be public sector agencies financed by the government, or private sector agencies set up with official support, raising funds from banks and other financial agencies or by directly issuing securities. Their common feature is the provision of finance in situations where the risk factor or time period before a return on the investment is unacceptable to other providers of finance. In 1945, in an effort to provide funds for the small and medium-sized businesses, the Bank of England, with the support of the Scottish and London clearing banks, established the Industrial and Commercial Finance Corporation (ICFC). The idea behind ICFC was to provide long-term funds for firms that were too small to raise stock exchange capital. A sister company was also established with the support of the Bank of England and a number of insurance companies and unit trusts in 1945, called Finance Corporation for Industry, which offered financial support for larger companies. The two firms were established to plug the financial gap that the banks were failing to satisfy. In 1973, a single holding company was established, Finance for Industry, which again was reorganised in 1983 and now exists in the form of a venture capital company called 3i. Between 1979 and 1984, a number of bodies were established (the so called Enterprise Boards) to promote regional and local economic growth. Thus, the Greater London Enterprise Board, West Midlands Enterprise Board, West Yorkshire enterprise Board and Greater Manchester Enterprise Fund were started. They provided investments of the venture capital type and between 1982–85 the enterprise boards invested approximately £35 million in 200 businesses. Some of the boards continue to exist, mostly in a privatised form; for example, the Greater London Enterprise Board[45] became an independent company in 1986 and reinvests profits from commercial activities into non-for-profit activities. A regional initiative, established under the Industry Act 1971, was the Scottish Development Agency, which was established in 1975. The Agency, operating under a new name, Scottish Enterprise[46] and as a network organisation, is still active in the area of equity investments. Following the banking crisis in 2007–09, Lord Mandelson, the then Business Secretary, suggested the need for a new ICFC[47] given the banks' refusal to lend and,

[44] Coggan (2009) *The Money Machine: How the City Works*, 6th edn, London: Penguin Books.
[45] http://www.gle.co.uk/who-we-are.php.
[46] http://www.scottish-enterprise.com.
[47] Industrial and Commercial Finance Corporation, 15 January 2009, http://www.thisismoney.co.uk/30-second-guides/article.html?in_article_id=466511&in_page_id=53611.

on the 14 January 2009, he announced the establishment of a £75 million Capital for Enterprise Fund to invest in small firms struggling because of the withdrawal of loan funding by the banks. With the growth of state influence, as the government sought to fill the gaps left by banks too reluctant to lend, there may be further ICFC type initiatives.[48]

A banking sector able to meet the demands of the rest of the financial services sector is fundamental to the success of any advanced economy, and therefore the classification of banks has become complex, as their business and structures have evolved. We will now examine the structure and functions of the UK banking sector.

The UK banking sector

The UK banking structure has developed gradually over the past 300 years; it is neither logical nor symmetrical and is constantly evolving. Although there is some overlap in the nature of banking firms the structure is flexible and until 2007–08 privately owned banks, accountable to shareholders, dominated the banking sector. The financial crisis saw taxpayer ownership of a number of banking institutions as the government intervened to nationalise Northern Rock and the Royal Bank of Scotland.[49] Over the past 20 years two other significant events have occurred which have changed the face of the banking sector:

1 The Bank of England Act 1998 and the Banking Act 2009 made fundamental changes to the structure and functions of the Bank of England.

2 In an effort to restore confidence in the UK banking sector and prevent a systemic collapse during the banking crisis, in 2007–08, several banks and building societies were temporarily nationalised.[50]

The Bank of England

The Bank of England stands at the head of the UK banking system and remains at the centre of the City of London, both physically and functionally. The original Royal Charter, granted in 1694,[51] stated that the bank should 'promote the Public Good and benefit our people'. It was established with a capital of £1,200,000,[52] raised by public subscription, and those contributing to this capital became the subscribers and Governor of the Bank. The Bank was invested with perpetual succession and a common seal,[53] and effectually granted separate

---

[48] Alf Young, Brown looking to the past for ways to revive British industry, 21 April 2009, http://www.herald-scotland.com/brown-looking-to-the-past-for-ways-to-revive-british-industry-1.908085.

[49] Financial Services Authority (FSA) Board Report, The failure of the Royal Bank of Scotland, December 2011, http://www.fsa.gov.uk/static/pubs/other/rbs.pdf.

[50] In the midst of the banking crisis, the government passed the Banking (Special Provisions) Act 2008 in order to enable the nationalisation Northern Rock. The Act lapsed in February 2009 when the Banking Act 2009 came into force.

[51] Bank of England Act 1694, s.19, http://www.bankofengland.co.uk/about/Documents/legislation/1694act.pdf.

[52] Equivalent to approximately £146,677,500 in the value of sterling in 2012 by considering the percentage increase in the Retail Price Index (RPI) between 1694 and 2012. The RPI is used to measure inflation and represents the change in the cost of living through assessing the change in the cost of goods and services which are commonly used. Calculation Resource: http://www.measuringworth.com/ukcompare/relativevalue.php.

[53] Bank of England Act 1694, s.19, http://www.bankofengland.co.uk/about/Documents/legislation/1694act.pdf.

legal personality. The object of the Bank was to raise money required to fund the war with Louis XIV and the early years of the Bank's existence were dominated by the government's pressing demands for finance and the issue of a new coinage. The Bank also embarked upon conventional banking business, accepting deposits and discounting bills.[54] The Bank of England Act 1696[55] granted the bank a monopoly in carrying out a fully-fledged banking business, by a corporation.

Although, the Act does not refer to the Bank's status as a note issuing authority there is evidence to indicate that the Bank was engaged in printing and circulating notes that constituted legal tender from the beginning.[56] Apart from its dealings in bills of exchange and in issuing banknotes, the Bank was also involved in the remittance of money to Flanders for the purposes of the war with France. The dealings in foreign currency, therefore, remained one of its activities and the Bank also started to open accounts for private bankers–goldsmiths. Where two banks maintained accounts with the Bank of England, it was convenient for one bank to pay a balance owed to the other by directing the Bank of England to make a transfer between the accounts. The development of the clearing house in the eighteenth century saw this function rooted into the Bank's activities.[57]

When the charter of the Bank of England was renewed in 1781 the Bank was described as the 'public exchequer'. By then, the Bank of England was also acting as the banker's bank, but theatrically, it could fail if its depositors decided to withdraw money at the same time. However, the Bank was confident that it kept sufficient gold reserves, in its own right, to meet unexpected demand.

The three main functions of the Bank of England namely, (i) issuing notes, (ii) acting as central banker, and (iii) as a settlement bank became firmly established in the nineteenth century. The Bank's role as a supervisory authority developed later although the idea of conferring formal supervisory powers was mooted in the later half of the nineteenth century. However, the Bank was able to exercise informal control over those banks for which it maintained accounts through the interest rates it applied to these accounts. In 1873, Bagehot emphasised the Bank's duties in its role as lender of last resort and asserted that it should be granted supervisory powers, but despite the lack of formal supervisory powers the Bank of England and a consortium of 16 other banks, in 1890, guaranteed the debts of Barings bank.[58] The emergence of private and powerful joint stock banks, in the nineteenth century, limited the *de facto* control the Bank of England had been able to exercise earlier but it continued to attempt to supervise the system by its manipulation of interest rates. The Bank continued to lend at competitive rates to its customers: government departments; joint stock banks, merchant banks, and foreign banks; discount houses; and small number of individual customers, but when the Bank was called upon to act as lender of last resort, usually to one

---

[54] Bank of England Act 1694, s.27, http://www.bankofengland.co.uk/about/Documents/legislation/1694act.pdf.

[55] 8 and 9 Will, 3, c. 20.

[56] The preamble to the 1696 Act refers to the frequent counterfeiting of Bank of England notes. See also *Bank of England v Anderson* (1837) 3 Bing. NC 589, 653.

[57] See: The English Banking System, US Monetary Commission 1910, 269, 280; Holland, The London Bankers' Clearing House.

[58] Sayers (1976) *The Bank of England 1891–1944*, Cambridge, i. 1–3; The Bank collapsed in 1995 following dealings on the futures market of a trader amassing losses of £837 million in Singapore. See: Eisenhammer, Brown, and Willcock, Bank of England offloads blame for Barings collapse, 19 July 1995, *The Independent*, http://www.independent.co.uk/news/bank-of-england-offloads-blame-for-barings-collapse-1592093.html; see also Bair (1995) Lessons from the Baring Collapse, *Fordham Law Review*, Vol. LXIV, 1–10.

of the banks, it granted the extension at an 'official rate' which was considerably higher than the market rate. During the early 1900s the Bank acquired the power to determine the margins to be maintained with it, by the commercial banks. While this acted as a safeguard for banks who might need temporary emergency funds it also enabled the Bank of England to facilitate the settlement of accounts between the banks and allowed it funds to increase its gold reserves. The Bank acquired a new function during the First World War, and as a temporary measure from the beginning of the Second World War, which was the administration and monitoring of exchange control in the UK. The functions ceased in 1980 with the removal of exchange controls.[59]

The structure of the Bank of England

The Bank of England was nationalised in 1946,[60] when the whole of the capital stock of the Bank was transferred to the Treasury against compensation in the form of government stock for the former private stockholders.[61] The Bank has been a public corporation since the compulsory acquisition of its share capital by the Treasury and its current governance and accountability framework was established under the Bank of England Act 1998, which revised the membership of the Court of Directors, established a non-executive committee within the Court, and established a Monetary Policy Committee.[62]

The Court of Directors

The Court of Directors is responsible for managing the affairs of the Bank,[63] other than the work of the monetary policy committee. Under the Banking Act 2009 the Bank of England has a statutory objective to 'contribute to protecting and enhancing the stability of the financial system of the United Kingdom' and the Court will, after consultation with the Treasury, formulate the Bank's strategy in respect of that objective.[64] Under the Bank of England Act 1998, the Court's responsibilities include determining the Bank's objectives and strategy, and ensuring the effective discharge of the Bank's functions and use of resources.[65] The Court consists of the Governor of the Bank of England, the two Deputy Governors[66] (appointed under the Bank of England Act 1998) and nine directors who are all non-executive appointments. The Crown appoints the Governors for a period of five years, and the Directors are appointed for three years. The Banking Act 2009 provides for the Court to be chaired by a Director designated by the Chancellor of the Exchequer, instead of the Governor.[67]

---

[59] Government controls to restrict the transfer of currencies from one country to another.

[60] Bank of England Act 1946, s.1, http://www.bankofengland.co.uk/about/Documents/legislation/1946act.pdf.

[61] See: Radcliffe Report, Committee on the Working of the Monetary System, 1959, Cmnd 827, Ch. 9.

[62] Bank of England Annual Report, 2013, http://www.bankofengland.co.uk/publications/Documents/annualreport/2013/2013report.pdf.

[63] Governance of the Bank Including Matters Reserved to Court, Approved at Court November 2009, Revised version to include changes to Committee Terms of Reference October 2010, http://www.bankofengland.co.uk/about/pdfs/matters_court.pdf.

[64] Banking Act 2009, ss.4 and 11. Section 2 of the Financial Services Bill 2012 was enshrined in s.2 of the Financial Services Act 2012, and amended the Financial Stability Objective embodied in s.2A of the Bank of England Act 1998.

[65] Section 2, amended by ss.239(1) and 239(2) of the Banking Act 2009.

[66] Section 1, amended by ss.239(1) and 239(2) of the Banking Act 2009.

[67] Section 3, amended by ss.239(1) and 239(2) of the Banking Act 2009.

Since 2000, members of the Court have been indemnified by the Bank (approved by the Treasury in accordance with the practice of the government in relation to board members of non-departmental public bodies) against personal civil liability in respect of carrying out their functions provided they act in good faith.[68]

The Monetary Policy Committee

The Bank of England Act 1998[69] established the Monetary Policy Committee (MPC) as a committee of the Bank, although it is subject to oversight by the non-executive directors committee. The Bank of England's objectives in relation to monetary policy are to maintain price stability,[70] and subject to that, support the government's economic policies including the objectives of economic growth and employment.[71] The MPC, therefore, sets the Bank of England base rate and controls interest rates in the UK. The government will state its price stability, growth and employment objectives at least once a year[72] and the MPC will meet at least once a month to implement and monitor these objectives.[73] The membership of the MPC comprises the Governor, the two Deputy Governors, two of the Bank's Executive Directors and four members appointed by the Chancellor.[74] The decisions of the MPC are announced after each meeting and minutes of the meetings are published six weeks later.[75] The quarterly inflation report includes the MPC's projections of inflation and output.[76] In the aftermath of the global financial crisis, the MPC has adopted the unconventional method of quantitative easing to achieve monetary stability. Quantitative easing involves asset purchases of government debt or gilts, which are designed to stimulate the economy, as yields on government gilts fall once nominal demand is increased. In theory, this facilitates the economy through encouraging investors to purchase alternative assets such as corporate bonds and shares. By July 2012, the quantitative easing programme had reached £375 billion.[77]

The Financial Stability Committee

The Bank of England Act 1998[78] created the Financial Stability Committee[79] as a Committee of Court and its functions are to make recommendations to Court concerning the Bank's financial stability strategy,[80] to advise in relation to institutions relevant to the financial

---

[68] Bank of England Act 2009, s.233.
[69] Bank of England Act 1998, s.13.
[70] Bank of England Act 1998, s.13.
[71] Bank of England Act 1998, s.11.
[72] Bank of England Act 1998, s.11.
[73] Bank of England Act 1998, sch. 3, para. 10.
[74] Bank of England Act 1998, s.13(2).
[75] Bank of England Act 1998, s.15.
[76] http://www.bankofengland.co.uk/publications/inflationreport/index.htm.
[77] Bank of England, 'Quantitative Easing Explained', http://www.bankofengland.co.uk/monetarypolicy/pages/qe/default.aspx.
[78] Bank of England Act 1998, s.2B.
[79] Governance of the Bank Including Matters Reserved to Court, Approved at Court November 2009 Revised version to include changes to Committee Terms of Reference October 2010, http://www.bankofengland.co.uk/about/pdfs/matters_court.pdf.
[80] The Memorandum of Understanding between HM Treasury, the Bank of England and the FSA establishes a framework for cooperation between the three in respect of financial stability, http://www.bankofengland.co.uk/financialstability/mou.pdf.

stability objective,[81] to advise on the use of stabilisation powers in specific cases and to monitor the use of such powers. The Committee will also monitor the Bank of England's use of the payment system's oversight powers and to carry out any other functions delegated to it by Court. The membership of the Financial Stability Committee consists of the Governor and Deputy Governors of the Bank of England, four directors appointed by the Chairman of Court and a non-voting member appointed by the Treasury. The Committee may co-opt other non-voting members as necessary.

The non-executive directors committee

The Bank of England Act 1998 provides for a committee of Court consisting of non-executive directors, with the chairman designated by the Chancellor.[82] This committee is responsible for reviewing the Bank's performance[83] in relation to its objectives and strategy, and monitoring the extent to which the Bank's financial management objectives are met.[84] The non-executive directors are also responsible for the procedures of the Monetary Policy Committee, for reviewing the Bank's internal controls, and for determining the pay and terms of employment of the Governors, Executive Directors and the external members of the MPC.

In addition the Remuneration Committee advises the committee of non-executive directors on remuneration[85] of the Bank's senior executives including the Governor, the Executive Directors, the advisers to the Governor and members of the Monetary Policy Committee appointed by the Chancellor of the Exchequer, the Audit Committee[86] which functions to assist the Court in meeting its responsibilities for an effective system of financial reporting, internal control and risk management, and receives reports from, and reviews, the internal and external auditors and the Transactions Committee which is consulted about transactions outside the normal course of the Bank's business support, the internal functioning and management of the Bank.

The functions of the Bank of England

While the Bank of England has reigned supreme as the UK central bank its roles and functions have been subject to scrutiny, debate, modification and criticism particularly since the late 1990s. This section will discuss the main functions of the Bank of England:

Monetary policy

Changes announced by the then Chancellor of the Exchequer, Gordon Brown, in May 1997 had an unprecedented effect on the role of the Bank of England. Since then a core function of the Bank of England has been to pursue monetary policy and maintain financial stability; with a focus on fighting inflation and the key objective of delivering price stability and support

---

[81] Financial Services Bill 2012, s.9C, enacted in the Financial Services Act 2012, s.9C.

[82] Bank of England Act 1998, s.3(4).

[83] Bank of England Act 1998, s.3.

[84] Bank of England Act 1998, s.3.

[85] Bank of England Act 1998, s.3, sch. 1, para. 13.

[86] Governance of the Bank Including Matters Reserved to Court, Approved at Court November 2009 Revised version to include changes to Committee Terms of Reference October 2010, http://www.bankofengland.co.uk/about/pdfs/matters_court.pdf.

for the government's economic policy.[87] The Bank of England's Monetary Policy Committee is, therefore, responsible for setting interest rates, while the government will set its inflation target for each 12-month period. The Bank, acting through the Monetary Policy Committee, will have operational responsibility for achieving this target.[88] A key objective of the Bank of England is, therefore, to safeguard the value of sterling in terms of what it can purchase at home and what it can purchase in term of other currencies. Monetary policy is, therefore, directed at achieving this objective and to providing a framework for non-inflationary economic growth. As with other developed countries, monetary policy operates in the UK through influencing the price of money (i.e. the cost of borrowing), in other words interest rates. The government's price stability objective also has another objective and that is a commitment to an open and accountable policy-making regime with the result that the MPC announces its decisions in respect of interest rates, even if they remain unchanged, and the minutes of its meetings are published.

Financial stability

Financial stability, while a nebulous concept, will safeguard the financial sector and the economy from unplanned movements likely to damage confidence in the sector. Financial stability therefore means maintaining an efficient flow of funds within the economy and confidence in the financial sector through financial intermediaries. The Bank's financial operations as lender of last resort, the decisions of the MPC, PRA's regulation of the financial sector, the Bank's role as a resolution authority, and the Bank's oversight of the key payment, settlement and clearing systems all contribute towards maintaining financial stability.[89] Financial stability, therefore, does not mean that firms will not fail but it will envisage failure threatening the stability of the whole system and it was in order to restore financial stability that the UK acted in the 2007–08 banking crisis. The Bank of England, working with the Treasury, launched a number of initiatives to restore confidence in the UK banking sector, including, as lender of last resort, a special liquidity scheme[90] under which it granted loans to ailing banks including, the Royal Bank of Scotland and the Halifax Banking Group.

Prudential bank supervision

A sound and stable financial system is a major objective of any developed central bank and the Bank of England has, usually, played a key role in bank supervision and ensuring public confidence. However, between 1997–2011, responsibility for prudential bank regulation rested with a quasi-governmental body, the Financial Services Authority (FSA). While, the Bank of England acquired responsibility for the financial stability of the sector,[91] the newly created

---

[87] Section 11 Bank of England Act 1998; Part 2 of the 2006 Memorandum of Understanding provides that the Bank of England is to contribute to the maintenance of the stability of the financial system as a whole as part of its monetary policy function and to oversee the infrastructure of the financial system, Memorandum of Understanding between HM Treasury, the Bank of England and the Financial Services Authority, http://www.fsa.gov.uk/pubs/mou/fsa_hmt_boe.pdf.

[88] Section 13, schedule 3.

[89] Bank of England Annual Report, 2013, http://www.bankofengland.co.uk/publications/Documents/annualreport/2013/2013report.pdf.

[90] Bank of England, News Release, Special Liquidity Release, 21 April 2008, http://www.bankofengland.co.uk/publications/news/2008/029.htm; see also: http://www.bankofengland.co.uk/markets/sls/index.htm and http://www.bankofengland.co.uk/markets/marketnotice090203c.pdf; see also *The Telegraph*, Bank of England's Special Liquidity Scheme 'will not be extended', says Fisher, 30 October 2011.

[91] Bank of England Act 1998, s.13.

FSA was given powers to supervise individual banks and the wider financial services sector, as a unitary regulator.[92] The 1996 Memorandum of Understanding (MoU)[93] formalised, between the Bank of England, the Treasury and the FSA, the allocation of responsibility for regulation of the financial sector and financial stability[94] and the Bank of England Act 1998[95] formally removed the supervisory powers previously vested in the Bank of England. Instead, the 1998 Act made provision for a high-level standing committee to provide a forum within which the FSA, the Bank of England and HM Treasury could develop a common position on sectorial problems. The Standing Committee was expected to maintain a free flow of information and coordinate a response to the management of a financial crisis.

Following the 2007–09 crisis, one of the major failures identified in bank regulation was perceived to be a failure in the tripartite authorities to develop a common understanding of their roles, particularly the failure to develop an effective forum to deal with, and respond to, financial crises.[96] From 1 April 2013, a new system of bank regulation was implemented with the Bank of England restored to a central role in banking supervision. The new system of regulation, sometimes called the 'twin peaks' approach to regulation, makes the Prudential Regulation Authority (PRA) responsible for the prudential regulation and supervision of around 2,000 financial institutions, including banks, building societies and major investments firms.[97] From a micro-prudential perspective, the PRA will promote the safety and soundness of these firms,[98] while at a macro-prudential perspective, the PRA will make forward-looking judgements on the risks posed to the UK financial system as a whole. Alongside PRA the Financial Conduct Authority (FCA),[99] is established to protect consumers, enhance the

---

[92] Section 11 Bank of England Act 1998; Part 2 of the 2006 Memorandum of Understanding provides that the Bank of England is to contribute to the maintenance of the stability of the financial system as a whole as part of its monetary policy function and to oversee the infrastructure of the financial system, Memorandum of Understanding between HM Treasury, the Bank of England and the Financial Services Authority, http://www.fsa.gov.uk/pubs/mou/fsa_hmt_boe.pdf.

[93] Part 2 of the 2006 Memorandum of Understanding provides that the Bank of England is to contribute to the maintenance of the stability of the financial system as a whole as part of its monetary policy function and to oversee the infrastructure of the financial system, Memorandum of Understanding between HM Treasury, the Bank of England and the Financial Services Authority, http://www.fsa.gov.uk/pubs/mou/fsa_hmt_boe.pdf.

[94] http://www.bankofengland.co.uk/financialstability/mou.pdf.

[95] Bank of England Act 1998, s.21.

[96] Sir James Sassoon, The Tripartite Review, A Review of the UK's Tripartite System of Financial Regulation in Relation to Financial Regulation, March 2009.

[97] PRA will be responsible for the prudential supervision of over 2,000 firms, of which around half will be deposit-takers. On current data, it will regulate 157 UK-incorporated banks (of which over 60% form part of overseas banking groups), 48 UK building societies, 652 UK credit unions and 162 branches of overseas banks, split roughly equally between the European Economic Area (EEA) and elsewhere. Through its supervision of UK-authorised deposit-takers PRA will be responsible for the prudential regulation of firms holding £9 trillion of assets in the United Kingdom and globally, equal to around seven times UK GDP. Within this total, UK-owned banks alone hold assets equal to five times UK GDP. Additionally, PRA will be responsible for the prudential supervision of passported branches of EEA banks, which together hold a further £2 trillion of assets in the UK, FSA, The Bank of England, Prudential Regulation Authority Our approach to banking supervision, May 2011, paras 20 and 22, http://www.bankofengland.co.uk/publications/other/financialstability/uk_reg_framework/pra_approach.pdf.

[98] Bank of England and FSA, The Bank of England, Prudential Regulation Authority Our approach to banking supervision, May 2011, http://www.bankofengland.co.uk/publications/other/financialstability/uk_reg_framework/pra_approach.pdf; Financial Services Act 2012, ch. 2 inserts a new s.2B(3) to the Financial Services and Markets Act 2000.

[99] Financial Services Act 2012, ch. 1 inserts a new s.1A to the Financial Services and Markets Act 2000.

integrity of the UK financial system and promote effective competition.[100] The UK's response to the financial crisis will be explored in further detail in Chapter 4.

All other functions of the Bank of England can now be examined in the context of its main two roles, i.e. maintaining price stability and ensuring financial stability:

The Bank of England as a lender of last resort

Henry Thornton[101] and Walter Bagehot[102] both justified the need for the lender of last resort facility for a number of reasons:

> . . . (1) to protect the money stock, (2) to support the whole financial system rather than individual financial institutions, (3) to behave consistently with the longer-run objective of stable money growth, and (4) to preannounce its policy in advance of crises so as to remove uncertainty.

The stability of the banking, and the wider financial services, sector ultimately rests on the confidence reposed in it by the public and that, in part, depends on customers being able to redeem their bank deposits, on demand. In response to a number of banking crises, the Bank of England evolved the role of lender of last resort and since around 1870, the Bank has underpinned the stability of the banking sector through this role. The role of lender of last resort normally falls on the central bank[103] and serves to protect depositors, maintain confidence and prevent widespread panic withdrawals to prevent damage to the wider economy that may be caused by the collapse of a banking institution. While the term 'lender of last resort' may be used in different ways it reflects the provision of discretionary liquidity to a financial institution or to the banking sector as a whole.[104] The 2006 Memorandum of Understanding places specific responsibilities on the Bank of England, in exceptional circumstances and with approval of the Chancellor of the Exchequer, to undertake official financial support to limit the risk of problems affecting particular institutions spreading to other parts of the financial system.[105] The Bank will dictate the rate of interest payable on the borrowed funds and generally makes these terms 'penal'[106] and defines the classes of bills that are acceptable for re-discount and the types of bonds eligible as collateral security for loans.

---

[100] HM Treasury, A new approach to financial regulation: the blueprint for reform, para.1.40, June 2011, Cm 8083, http://www.official-documents.gov.uk/document/cm80/8083/8083.pdf. Financial Services and Markets Act 2000 Part 1A, s.1B, as amended by the Financial Services Act 2012.

[101] Thornton (1802) *An Enquiry into the Nature and Effects of the Paper Credit of Great Britain.*

[102] Bagehot (1873) *Lombard Street: A Description of the Money Market*, London: H S King.

[103] Freixas, Giannini, Hoggarth and Soussa: *Lender of Last Resort: a review of the literature*, Financial Stability Review, November 1999, 151, http://www.bankofengland.co.uk/publications/fsr/1999/fsr07art6.pdf.

[104] Quantitative easing is a term used to describe a form of monetary policy used to stimulate an economy when the use of interest rates, which are at, or close to, zero have failed as a stimulus. When interest cannot be lowered any further the government may authorise the central bank to purchase assets, including government paper and corporate bonds from financial institutions, e.g., banks, using money it has created, http://www.telegraph.co.uk/finance/breakingviewscom/4175704/Quantitative-easing-the-modern-way-to-print-money-or-a-therapy-of-last-resort.html.

[105] Part 2 (iv) of the Memorandum of Understanding 2006 provides the Bank may act in exceptional circumstances to limit the risk to the financial system as a whole.

[106] Northern Rock only requested Bank of England support after private sector funding failed to materialise, House of Commons Treasury Committee, The run on the Rock, Fifth Report of Session 2007–08, HC 56–I, http://www.publications.parliament.uk/pa/cm200708/cmselect/cmtreasy/56/56i.pdf.

The Bank of England may decide to provide support as lender of last resort not only where a solvent institution[107] finds itself temporarily short of liquidity but also where the insolvency of a banking institution may raise the fear of systemic collapse. Because it may often be difficult, in the short period available to the Bank, to determine whether or not an institution is insolvent, temporary support may be granted while a longer-term solution through the private sector is sought. Such borrowing is not usually resorted to by the commercial banks, except in times of severe crisis but a feature of banks is that their assets are largely illiquid term loans, while their liabilities tend predominately to be unsecured short-term deposits which become payable, in full, on demand and on a first come first repaid basis. Consequently, lack of confidence in a banking institution or the banking sector may lead to a run on the bank.

BANKING LAW IN PRACTICE

In the wake of the liquidity crisis the Chancellor, Alistair Darling, authorised the Bank of England, on 14 September 2007, to provide Northern Rock loans against appropriate collateral and at an interest rate premium. The facility was intended to provide Northern Rock with temporary support in order to enable it to secure an orderly resolution to its financial problems. The decision to provide support was made by the Chancellor on the recommendations of the Governor of the Bank of England and the Chairman of the FSA in accordance with the framework set out in the Memorandum of Understanding.[108] The FSA judged Northern Rock as solvent and an institution that exceeded its regulatory capital requirement with a good quality loan book.[109] The decision to provide a liquidity support facility to Northern Rock reflected the difficulties it had in accessing longer-term funding and in the mortgage securitisation market, on which Northern Rock had been particularly reliant.[110] In order to stabilise the banking market and restore customer confidence the Bank of England also announced its readiness to make similar facilities available to other institutions facing short-term liquidity problems and the Bank, indeed did, provide both the ailing Royal Bank of Scotland (RBS) and the Halifax Banking Group (HBOG) with a credit facility of £62 billion without public disclosure, in October and December 2008.[111] In evidence given to the McFall Committee,[112] the Bank of England

---

[107] In September 2007 customer's queued outside branches of Northern Rock when it became public that Northern Rock has failed to gain temporary support from the private banking sector, House of Commons Treasury Committee, The run on the Rock, Fifth Report of Session 2007–08, HC 56–I, http://www.publications.parliament.uk/pa/cm200708/cmselect/cmtreasy/56/56i.pdf.

[108] Part 2 of the 2006 Memorandum of Understanding provides that the Bank of England is to contribute to the maintenance of the stability of the financial system as a whole as part of its monetary policy function and to oversee the infrastructure of the financial system, Memorandum of Understanding between HM Treasury, the Bank of England and the Financial Services Authority, http://www.fsa.gov.uk/pubs/mou/fsa_hmt_boe.pdf.

[109] House of Commons Treasury Committee, The run on the Rock, Fifth Report of Session 2007–08, HC 56–I, http://www.publications.parliament.uk/pa/cm200708/cmselect/cmtreasy/56/56i.pdf.

[110] House of Commons Treasury Committee, The run on the Rock, Fifth Report of Session 2007–08, HC 56–I, http://www.publications.parliament.uk/pa/cm200708/cmselect/cmtreasy/56/56i.pdf.

[111] *The Guardian*, Bank of England reveals secret £62 billion loans used to prop up RBS and HBOS, Hopkins and Treaner, 24 November 2009, http://www.guardian.co.uk/business/2009/nov/24/bank-england-rbs-hbos-loans.

[112] House of Commons Treasury Committee, Banking Crisis: Regulation and Supervision, Fourteenth Report of Session 2008–09, July 2009, http://www.publications.parliament.uk/pa/cm200809/cmselect/cmtreasy/767/767.pdf.

revealed that use of the emergency facilities peaked at £36.6 billion for RBS, on 17 October 2008, and at £25.4 billion for HBOS, on 13 December 2008. RBS repaid the cash by 16 December 2008, and HBOS by 16 January 2009. The collateral provided by the two banks included residential mortgages, personal and commercial loans and UK government debt with a total value in excess of £100 billion.

The Bank of England as banker to the government

The Bank of England has, from its inception, acted as the primary banker to central government. The Exchequer, the central account of the government, is kept with the Bank of England, along with other government accounts. They all appear in the bank's published accounts under the single heading, 'Public Deposits'. The services the Bank of England performs on a daily basis are in essence similar to the services provided by any bank for its customer: the receipt of monies due, the transfers of payments out, advice and assistance to the customer on the conduct of the account, and occasional overnight assistance if the account goes temporally 'in the red'. In order to ensure stability of the financial sector and to comply with the government's monetary policy the Bank also manages the government's borrowing operations on the open market.[113] The Bank receives tenders for each week's issue of Treasury bills and having allotted the bills receives the subscriptions and credits them to the Exchequer.

The Bank also manages new issues of government bonds and stocks, whether for cash or conversion; it advises the government on the terms appropriate for an issue, publishes a prospectus, receives applications and issues and allots the bonds and stocks. It will arrange the 'underwriting' of the issue. At the heart of its work as the central bank, and in the course of management of the money market and operations in government bonds, lie the Bank's open market operations in government debt, including Treasury bills. The Bank of England operates on a daily basis in the money market both buying (thereby putting money into the economy) and selling Treasury bills (thereby taking money out of the economy) to smooth out shortages and surpluses of money in the economy. The purpose of these operations is to maintain an orderly market and to fund government activity by selling Treasury bills. The Bank also maintains a register of stockholders and is responsible for the payment of dividends to stockholders on the due dates.

Following the market turmoil in 2007–08, and as part of its efforts to support the UK economy, the Bank of England was granted permission in April 2008 to announce details of a £50 billion plan to allow banks to swap potentially risky mortgage debts for secure government bonds[114] and, in August 2009, to inject an additional £50 billion to the government support package in the banking sector, with the government also offering up to £200 billion in short-term lending support to improve the availability of credit. The Bank was authorised to buy mainly government bonds but also some corporate debt with newly created money. The Bank continued its asset-purchase programme, or quantitative easing, despite some positive signs from the manufacturing and service sectors because of the lack of credit in the

---

[113] Bank of England, Sterling Monetary Framework Operations, http://www.bankofengland.co.uk/markets/Pages/money/default.aspx.

[114] http://news.bbc.co.uk/1/hi/business/7351506.stm.

economy with banks still reluctant to lend.[115] This process is called open market operations and the creation of the new money is intended to grow the overall supply of money, through deposit multiplication, i.e. by encouraging bank lending and reducing the cost of borrowing; thereby stimulating the economy. Quantitative easing is described as 'printing money' and the central bank creates it by increasing the credit in its own account.

Exchange Equalisation Account

The Bank of England manages the Exchange Equalisation Account (EEA), on behalf of the Treasury. The account was established in 1932 to provide a fund that can be used to check 'undue influences in the exchange value of sterling' and is the official repository of the nation's gold and foreign currency reserves and International Monetary Fund (IMF) Special Drawing Rights (SDRs).[116] The function of the account is to implement any government policy in respect of the exchange rate. Under the Exchange Equalisation Act 1979, the account may also be used to secure the conservation or disposition, in the national interest, of payments abroad; and for certain purposes arising out of the UK's membership of the IMF, including the holding, purchase and sale of SDRs. Under the Finance Act 2000,[117] the Treasury has a statutory obligation to publish a full set of annual financial accounts for the EEA. These accounts are audited by the National Audit Office and laid before both Houses of Parliament.

The Bank of England as the bankers' bank

The role of the Bank of England has several multi-faceted aspects to it. At a basic level, the Bank maintains accounts for the clearing banks and other organisations, including the government and its departments, as well as inter-governmental organisations. As banker to the bankers, and as the institution holding credit balances for these banks, the Bank of England is enabled to provide certain 'banking services' to them. The Bank of England's role of maintaining balances for the clearing banks serves as a convenient method for settling inter-bank indebtedness arising from payment and other inter-bank dealings. At the end of each settlement day the clearing banks will settle this indebtedness[118] by the transfer of balances between accounts held by the respective banks with the Bank of England. This settlement of indebtedness between the banks is in practice an automated exercise and, in some instances, in real-time. The Banking Act 2009, Part V, establishes a new formal regulatory framework for oversight and supervision of the recognised inter-bank payment systems: a role previously undertaken by the Bank of England on a non-statutory basis. This role was given prominence under the MoU between the Treasury, the FSA and the Bank, which provides that it is the

---

[115] Quantitative easing is a term used to describe a form of monetary policy used to stimulate an economy when the use of interest rates, which are at, or close to, zero have failed as a stimulus. When interest cannot be lowered any further the government may authorise the central bank to purchase assets, including government paper and corporate bonds from financial institutions, e.g., banks, using money it has created, http://www.telegraph.co.uk/finance/breakingviewscom/4175704/Quantitative-easing-the-modern-way-to-print-money-or-a-therapy-of-last-resort.html.

[116] http://www.hm-treasury.gov.uk/ukecon_eea_index.htm; SDRs are supplementary foreign exchange reserve assets defined and maintained by the IMF. SDRs represent a claim to currency held by IMF member countries for which they may be exchanged for certain currencies, http://www.imf.org/external/np/exr/facts/sdr.htm.

[117] Finance Act 2000, s.154.

[118] See p. 48 for an explanation of the clearing cycle.

latter that is responsible for providing advice to the Exchequer in relation to payments. In this context, the Bank's function is to safeguard the integrity of the payments systems and safeguard the overall robustness and resilience of the financial system.[119] The Banking Act 2009 gives the Bank power to give directions to settlement houses to maintain the stability of the financial sector.[120]

It is through its role as the bankers' bank that the Bank of England is able to perform its function as the central note-issuing authority, in England and Wales. The Bank of England is the only institution to have a note-issuing authority and therefore enjoys a monopoly in this role.[121] Its notes and coins are legal tender and, while no longer in circulation in England, its £1 notes are still legal tender in Scotland.[122] In normal circumstances an increase in the demand for cash from the general public (through an increase in withdrawals from bank accounts and greater borrowing) is reflected in a decrease in the stocks of notes held in the tills by banks. In order to meet the demand and replenish their stock of notes, the banks will make drawings, in the form of notes, from their deposits with the Bank of England. The stock of notes held as reserves in the issue department of the Bank of England will decline and if the issue department wishes to replenish its own reserves then a change in the fiduciary issue has to be authorised.[123] The banking department will then pay for the additional notes by transferring securities of equivalent value to match the increase in its liabilities. The Treasury determines the total value of the banknote issue and only a part of it is backed by gold reserves, held in the issue department. However, the greater part of the notes and coins in circulation, known as the fiduciary issue, is covered by securities issued to the Bank of England by the Treasury. The issue department is for accounting purposes a part of the central government sector and its resources are separate from the banking department, which operates in much the same way as a commercial bank. This is now an administrative task rather than a policy-making role. In ensuring monetary stability the level of currency in circulation is a core function of the Bank, but that function is discharged in accordance with government policy. The Banking Act 2009[124] introduces a new framework for the issuance of Scottish and Northern Ireland banknotes for which the Bank has an overseeing role. Part VI of the Banking Act 2009 now makes regulations in respect of note issuing in Scotland and Northern Ireland. Section 213 of the Act provides that a bank already authorised to issue notes may continue to do so but if for any reason it stops to issue notes s.219 provides that it cannot later recommence the issue of notes under s.213. If for any reason a Scottish bank stops to issue notes in the course of its business it will lose that power for the future.

---

[119] Memorandum of Understanding between HM Treasury, The Bank of England and The Financial Services Authority, http://www.bankofengland.co.uk/about/legislation/mou.pdf.

[120] Financial Services Act 2012, s.104(3) inserts a s.191 in the Banking Act 2009, which confers powers on the Bank of England to give directions to a recognised payment system. Such directions may, for example, be given for the purposes of securing compliance with a requirement imposed or may be given for the purposes of addressing an immediate threat to financial stability.

[121] Bank of England, A brief history of banknotes, http://www.bankofengland.co.uk/banknotes/pages/about/history.aspx.

[122] Currency and Bank Notes Act 1954, s.1(2).

[123] All Scottish banks have the right to print their own notes and three do so: the Bank of Scotland (founded 1695), the Royal Bank of Scotland (founded 1727) and the Clydesdale Bank (owned by National Australia Bank). Only the Royal Bank of Scotland prints pound notes.

[124] Banking Act 2009, s.207.

The Bank of England's international role

The growth in cross-border financial activity has heightened the importance of UK authorities working effectively and efficiently with their counterparts in other countries. The Bank of England has regular contact with central banks, regulators, and other authorities outside the UK that have an interest in the maintenance of financial stability. It also participates in the activities of key international bodies involved in global financial stability work, such as the Financial Stability forum. The global financial crisis of 2007–09 has shown that management also has an important international dimension and given the international nature of many UK banks and financial firms, and London's role as an international financial centre (which will be examined fully in Chapter 2), it is important that the UK and foreign authorities work collectively to manage a financial crisis affecting cross-border financial firms. The EU MoU[125] on financial stability sets out the principles and processes that guide cooperation between authorities within the EU in such circumstances. The Bank also works alongside foreign authorities in a number of other international groups to manage international financial crisis.

We wil now examine the role of the commercial banks and other institutions that provide banking services in the UK.

Clearing banks

In evidence submitted to the Committee of London Clearing Bankers established to review the 'Functioning of the Financial Institutions',[126] it was submitted that the role of the clearing banks (sometimes known as retail banks or commercial banks because of the services they provide to individual customers) is primarily that of financial intermediation; that is they channel funds from those who have them to those who need them. This is done through the extensive network of branches operated by the main clearing banks (Barclays, HSBC, Lloyds/HBOS, National Westminster, Santander). The Scottish banks also have a considerable branch presence throughout the country. It was also emphasised that what distinguishes these banks from other banks, for example the building societies, or the Post Office, which also provides certain banking services, is the extent to which this role is dependent on the provision of current account facilities and money transmission services. The transmission of payments is facilitated by the participation of these banks in the daily clearing. Non-clearing banks tend to play a lesser part in the money transmission facilities and will use one of the clearing banks as an agent to clear payment instructions.[127] By providing these money transmission services the banks have not only provided much of the infrastructure on which the nation relies for the conduct of its financial transactions, but they have expanded their services to include lending to the consumer and businesses, payment of bills facilities, mortgage facilities, insurance and credit card services, financial investment, advice and management, wills and probate etc.

Since the 1960s the clearing banks have followed a policy of growth and expansion, which has included growth into those areas of activity traditionally considered outside the

---

[125] Memorandum of Understanding on Cooperation between the Financial Supervisory Authorities, Central Banks and Finance Ministries of the European Union on cross-border financial stability, http://www.ecb.int/pub/pdf/other/mou-financialstability2008en.pdf.

[126] Wilson Committee, Committee of London Clearing Bankers established to review the Functioning of the Financial Institutions, November 1977, HMSO.

[127] *Importers Co. Ltd* v *Westminster Bank Ltd* [1927] 1 KB 599.

banking domain (e.g. mortgage lending, growth of investment and advice to businesses) and the development of new products (e.g. automated money transfers, same day money transfers, derivatives etc.). In the 1960s and 1970s, the clearing banks bought up the main hire purchase companies, and then broadened their activities into general finance houses. During the 1980s the big clearing banks extended their business activities abroad and while this has clearly sustained the growth of the UK economy there have also been some major banking disasters with cross-border ramifications.[128] Banks have also extended their market base by extending services to the 'unbanked' section of the population. The Wages Act 1986 made it cheaper to pay wages direct into bank accounts and systems like Bankers Automated Clearing System (BACS) now allows regular payments to be made via the bank account without standard fixed amounts having to be paid manually. There are four major clearings[129] in the UK undertaken by three companies working through the UK Payments Administration Ltd,[130] a company established in 2009 when the Association for Payment Clearing Services ceased to exist, and these supply services to a range of companies that have individual responsibilities for facilitating customer payments.

Banks and the 2008 financial crisis

Over the past 20 years banking has moved away from its dependence on retail deposits as the 'originate and distribute' model[131] has been adopted by the global banking sector.[132] Banks thereby raise money from other institutions in the wholesale markets and lend that to customers, individuals and corporates. Loans made to bank customers are bundled together into pools of assets and sold to outside investors so that the banks can lend the money raised from outside investors on a continuing cycle. Banking regulations require banks to set aside reserves (usually in the form of low yielding investments with little or no risk) for certain loans on their balance sheets and there is, therefore, an incentive for banks to transfer these loans off their balance sheets. From 1990 to 2000, from the investors' point, these asset-backed securities offered higher returns than the yield on government bonds and were attractive to investors seeking a higher return. The asset-backed securities might be pools of mortgages, car loans or credit card debt and, in theory at least, losses should have been predictable. This process of securitisation and selling these loans made it impossible to assess where default may lie when the property market collapsed during the 2008 financial crisis.

---

[128] For example, the growth of BCCI as a global bank without proper cross-border supervision led to branch closures across many countries. The market turmoil in 2007–09 had a global effect as a result of global growth of banking with UK bank exposure to the subprime mortgage market in the USA.

[129] Financial Services Act 2012, s.104(3) inserts a s.191 in the Banking Act 2009, which confers powers on the Bank of England to give directions to a recognised payment system. Such directions may, for example, be given for the purposes of securing compliance with a requirement imposed or may be given for the purposes of addressing an immediate threat to financial stability.

[130] UK Payments Administration – About UK Payments, http://www.ukpayments.org.uk/about_ukpayments/.

[131] An originate-to-distribute (OTD) model of lending, where the originator of a loan sells it to various third parties, was a popular method of mortgage lending before the onset of the subprime mortgage crisis, Puranandam, Originate-to-Distribute Model and the Subprime Mortgage Crisis, http://papers.ssrn.com/sol3/papers.cfm?abstract_id=1167786.

[132] See: Buiter, W.H., Lessons from the North Atlantic financial crisis, revised 28 May 2008, http://www.nber.org/~wbuiter/NAcrisis.pdf.

The crisis was made worse by the fact that mortgage-backed bonds themselves had been bundled up and repackaged.

Additionally, securities, known as collateralised debt obligations or CDOs, made up of bundles of asset-backed bonds, had been created. The CDOs were sliced and diced into different elements, known as tranches. The riskiest slice, known as equity, paid the highest yield but they were the first to suffer losses when the underlying assets defaulted. The higher and top tiers of the pyramid securities theatrically carried less risk but paid a lower return on the investment. However, risks became concentrated when portfolios of securities were pooled together, rather than diversified. The problem was compounded by the use of money borrowed, albeit at low interest rates, which was used to buy the less risky mortgaged backed securities. Nevertheless, when the scale of the subprime crisis became clear, the prices of these securities became apparent. The problem was made worse by the existence of structured investment vehicles (SIVs)[133] which, like the banks, had borrowed money to invest in mortgaged backed securities.[134]

BANKING LAW IN PRACTICE

The Northern Rock collapse

Northern Rock plc was formerly a building society, which demutualised on 1 October 1997. At the end of 1997, Northern Rock had assets on a consolidated basis of £15.8 billion and by the end of 2006 its consolidated balance sheet had grown more than six-fold so that the value of its assets was £101.0 billion, which comprised mainly secured lending on residential properties. Adam Applegarth, the then Chief Executive of Northern Rock, told the House of Commons Select Committee[135] looking into the collapse of Northern Rock that its assets had been 'growing by 20% plus or minus 5%' for the last 17 years. This pace of growth led to Northern Rock entering the FTSE 100 in September 2001. In order to achieve this level of growth in assets, the company changed the structure of its liabilities. In 1999, Northern Rock began to borrow more money from the wholesale markets, adopting the 'originate to distribute' model of funding and began to parcel up mortgages and use them as collateral for further funds, a process known as 'securitisation'.

While wholesale funding to Northern Rock grew, there was no corresponding rapid growth in its retail funding. On a group basis, retail deposits and funds made up £9.9 billion of the liabilities of Northern Rock at the end of 1997, and by the end of 2006, retail deposits and funds had only grown to £22.6 billion, compared with the six-fold increase

---

[133] An SIV was an operating finance company established to earn a profit between its assets and liabilities like a traditional bank. The strategy of SIVs was to borrow money by issuing short-term securities, such as commercial paper and medium-term notes and public bonds at low interest rates, and then lend that money by buying longer-term securities at higher interest rates, with the difference in rates going to investors as profit. Long-term assets could include, among other things, residential mortgage backed securities (RMBS), auto loans, student loans, credit cards securitisations, and bank and corporate bonds. Because of this structure, SIVs were considered to be part of the shadow banking system.

[134] Economic and Monetary Affairs Committee, The International Financial Crisis: its causes and what to do about it, 27 February 2008, http://www.alde.eu/fileadmin/webdocs/key_docs/Finance-book_EN.pdf.Upta nulp

[135] House of Commons Treasury Committee, The run on the Rock, Fifth Report of Session 2007–08, HC 56–I, http://www.publications.parliament.uk/pa/cm200708/cmselect/cmtreasy/56/56i.pdf.

in Northern Rock's assets. This meant that, as a proportion of the total liabilities and equity of Northern Rock, retail deposits and funds had fallen from 62.7 per cent at end-1997 to 22.4 per cent by the end of 2006.[136] Northern Rock's continued expansionary lending policy required the continued success of its funding strategy at a time when there were indications of potential problems on the funding side. In April 2007, the Bank of England 'identified the increasing wholesale funding of banks as a potential risk if markets became less liquid'. In August 2007, Northern Rock's traders noted a 'dislocation in the market' for its funding which was the result of a global shock to the financial system. Two aspects of this worldwide liquidity squeeze appeared to surprise Northern Rock: namely that the funding markets would close to it simultaneously and the mistaken belief that good quality credit would continue to attract funding. Northern Rock had raised money in the markets in January and May and was due raise further funding in September.

In August 2007, it was therefore low in cash and had not thought to have emergency funding in place. So Northern Rock turned to possible private partners for support. The Lloyds TSB was willing to come to a deal but wanted a £30 billion loan from the Bank of England, which the latter refused. On 13 September 2007,[137] the BBC announced that the Bank of England had provided liquidity support for Northern Rock, and the Bank of England[138] made a formal announcement the following day. On 22 February 2008, Northern Rock was nationalised[139] but, worried that other banks seen to be vulnerable would become the targets of short-selling, Alistair Darling, Chancellor of the Exchequer, announced a government guarantee for deposits held not only by Northern Rock customers but those held by any UK banks. The credit crisis claimed another retail bank when the HBOS was forced into a merger with Lloyds TSB but fragility in customer confidence led to a continued fall in share prices of both banks.[140] In addition, the government closed Bradford and Bingley.[141] Confidence in the financial markets continued to plummet and in October 2008, the government was forced to announce a £400 billion rescue package,[142] which involved buying bank shares, guaranteeing their loans and lending them money to stabilise the markets.

---

[136] The figure was low when compared to other banks that were previously building societies: at the end of 2006, Alliance & Leicester's proportion was 43 per cent and Bradford & Bingley's was 49 per cent, House of Commons Treasury Committee, The run on the Rock, Fifth Report of Session 2007–08, HC 56–I, http://www.publications.parliament.uk/pa/cm200708/cmselect/cmtreasy/56/56i.pdf.

[137] BBC News, Northern Rock gets bank bail out, 13 September 2007, http://news.bbc.co.uk/1/hi/business/6994099.stm.

[138] Bank of England, News Release, Liquidity Support Facility for Northern Rock plc, http://www.bankofengland.co.uk/publications/news/2007/090.htm.

[139] BBC News, Northern Rock to be Nationalised, 17 February 2008, http://news.bbc.co.uk/1/hi/business/7249575.stm; BBC News, full text: Alistair Darling's statement, 17 February 2008, http://news.bbc.co.uk/1/hi/business/7249720.stm. On 17 November 2011 it was announced that Virgin Money were going to buy Northern Rock for £747 million, from UK Financial Investments Limited (UKFI). The deal was finalised on 1 January 2012.

[140] BBC News, Bank shares fall despite bail-out, 18 September 2008, http://news.bbc.co.uk/1/hi/7622380.stm.

[141] Cooksey, Sunderland, and Robinson, Government poised to nationalise Bradford & Bingley, The Guardian, 28 September 2008, http://www.guardian.co.uk/business/2008/sep/28/bradfordandbingley.

[142] BBC News, Rescue plan for UK banks unveiled, 8 October 2008, http://news.bbc.co.uk/1/hi/business/7658277.stm.

Investment banks

Most people have some understanding and role of the functions of clearing banks but a lesser understanding of the role and functions of investment banks, more commonly in the UK known as merchant banks, for example Hambros and Augusta & Co. Since the 2008 financial crisis these banks have effectively ceased to exist as independent banks.[143] Thus, Lehman Brothers filed for bankruptcy, in September 2008, and Bears Stearns and Merrill Lynch were both acquired by bank holding companies in September 2008. Investment banking is only a part of the type of business carried on by institutions such as Goldman Sachs, which are also known as broker-dealers. Larger banking groups, such as the HSBC and Santander, also have their own investment banking arms.

BANKING LAW IN PRACTICE

Although investment banks have tended to specialise in their activities the principal business of investment banks has included (i) investment banking focused on raising capital, and mergers and acquisitions transactions for corporate clients and raising capital for governments; (ii) the buying and selling of securities or other financial instruments. Typically an investment bank will perform these tasks on behalf of itself and its clients. In market making, traders will buy and sell financial products primarily to facilitate the investment and trading activities of their clients with the goal of making an incremental amount of money on each trade; and (iii) asset management, also called investment management and money management, which refers to the professional management of investment funds for individuals, families, and institutions. Investments include stocks, bonds, convertibles, alternative assets (such as hedge funds, private equity funds and real estate), commodities, indexes of each of these asset classes and money market investments.

Although investment banks, therefore, act as intermediaries between interested parties, they take an extensive stake in commercial ventures themselves, either by medium- or long-term loans or by subscribing or underwriting issues of securities. It was the latter which changed the nature of the traditional merchant banking business as corporate clients sought advisers who could commit capital to deals. Investment banks therefore moved into new areas of business and sold their business to clients as asset managers. They sold new products, particularly on the derivatives market, on a global basis, thereby placing them at the heart of the global financial system. The free flow of business and capital across national markets made these investment banks powerful players in the global economies and risks were increased by the high level of leverage (borrowed money) employed by them. They used gearing ratios, which meant that their risks were many times their core capital. In this environment traders could make enormous bonuses as part of their remuneration package with million pound pension packages. There was public outrage at the pension package awarded to Sir Red Goodwin, CEO of the Royal Bank of Scotland, when he was ousted from office following the government bailment of RBS. His gold-plated pension package negotiated on his appointment when RBS was a strong

---

[143] See: Sorkin, and Vilas, Shift for Goldman and Morgan Marks the End of an Era, 21 September 2008, *The New York Times*, http://www.nytimes.com/2008/09/22/business/22bank.html.

market force was seen as a reward for failure in 2009.[144] Unsupervised or improperly regulated traders could also do serious damage to the health of their banks. The activities of Nick Leeson, the chief Barings bank trader in Singapore, left the bank bankrupt with losses amounting to £800 million and it was eventually sold to ING, the Dutch banking and insurance group for £1.[145] However, for many years traders and banks alike reaped the benefits of a global financial market, which was supported by a relaxed regulatory and supervisory attitude on an international scale.

At the height of the financial crisis in 2008, the US Federal Reserve was compelled to rescue Bear Stearns, an investment bank which, while it had no consumer customers (unlike Northern Rock in the UK), was felt too big to fail. The Bear Stearns business model was too complex in the dynamics of the rapidly unfolding global financial crisis. Bear Stearns was a participant in a multitude of complex deals in which investors and companies took positions on everything from, for example, exchange-rate movements to the price of commodities and the corporate failure. The ramifications of the failure of Bear Stearns would have taken many years to sort out and with unforeseen consequences because of the complexity of the financial markets and their global dependence. The panic and failure in the money markets was apparent when Lehman Brothers failed and this forced other investment banks into mergers and takeovers.[146] The lack of confidence following the failure of Lehman Brothers led to AIG, an insurance giant, to seek US government protection[147] and the mortgage giant Freddie Mac and Fanny Mae to seek a government bailout.[148] At the same time other investment banks sought private sector rescue, for example Merrill Lynch opted for a takeover by Bank of America.[149] Recognising the economic risks that may stem from government-backed mortgage schemes in encouraging more borrowing than customers can eventually repay, Sir Mervyn King, the former Governor of the Bank of England, warned against the UK government's 'Help to Buy' mortgage guarantee scheme in May 2013.[150]

[144] BBC News, Stand-off over Sir Fred's pension, 17 February 2009, http://news.bbc.co.uk/1/hi/business/7912651.st; see also Treanor, J., Fred Goodwin's pension package under fire from top shareholders, *The Guardian*, 29 March 2009, http://www.guardian.co.uk/business/2009/mar/29/fred-goodwin-pension-rbs.

[145] See BBC News, How Leeson broke the bank, 22 June 1999, http://news.bbc.co.uk/1/hi/business/375259.stm.

[146] *The Economist*, Rethinking Lehman Brothers The price of failure, 2 October 2008, http://www.economist.com/node/12342689; see also: *Case Study: The Collapse of Lehman Brothers*, Investopedia, 2 April 2009, http://www.investopedia.com/articles/economics/09/lehman-brothers-collapse.asp#axzz1cpfF6qdU.

[147] Karnitschnig, Solomon, Pleven, and Hilsenrath, U.S. to Take Over AIG in $85 Billion Bailout; Central Banks Inject Cash as Credit Dries Up, *The Wall Street Journal*, 16 September 2008, http://online.wsj.com/article/SB122156561931242905.html.

[148] Associated Press, Freddie Mac reports $6 billion loss for third quarter; asks for $6 billion in federal aid, *The Washington Post*, 3 November 2008, http://www.washingtonpost.com/business/freddie-mac-reports-6-billion-loss-for-third-quarter-asks-for-6-billion-in-federal-aid/2011/11/03/gIQADBKRiM_story.html.

[149] Gasparino, Bank of America to Buy Merrill Lynch for $50 Billion, CNBC, 14 September 2008, http://www.cnbc.com/id/26708319/Bank_of_America_to_Buy_Merrill_Lynch_for_50_Billion; Stempel, and Comlay, Bank of America takeover to end independent Merrill, Reuters, 15 September 2008, http://www.reuters.com/article/2008/09/15/us-merrill-bankofamerica-idUSN1445019920080915.

[150] BBC News, Sir Mervyn King issues Help to Buy mortgage warning, 19 May 2013, http://www.bbc.co.uk/news/business-22581191; see also, Hughes, D., 19 May 2013, Outgoing governor of the Bank of England Sir Mervyn King issues warning over 'Help to Buy' scheme, *The Independent*, http://www.independent.co.uk/news/uk/home-news/outgoing-governor-of-the-bank-of-england-sir-mervyn-king-issues-warning-over-help-to-buy-scheme-8622531.html.

Overseas and foreign banks

London has been a premier banking and financial centre for a number of decades and most of the world's major banks have a presence in the City of London.[151] A number of organisations represent these banks:

- The Association of Foreign Banks has one of the largest memberships of financial institutions in the City and has around 175 members.[152] The membership consists of foreign banks or securities houses whose ownership rests outside the UK. The association has a number of committees including banking committees that cover corporate and institutional banking, markets, and private banking while the operational committees cover human resources, operations, information technology, finance, legal and regulatory issues. The association has its own board of directors and an advisory committee. Member banks are involved in a range of banking activities although each bank is likely to have strong links with its country of origin. Their business is mainly concerned with wholesale activities rather than retail banking.

- The American and Japanese banks have their own associations concerned wholly with the interests of their members.

- The British Bankers' Association is a trade association made up of around 200 member banks and other financial firms operating in the UK. It has a large non-UK membership (75 per cent of its members are non-UK associations) representing 60 different nations. Membership of the BBA[153] is of two types: namely, those authorised under the Financial Services and Markets Act 2000 to carry out one or more of the following regulated activities – accepting deposits, dealing in investments as a principal, dealing in investments as an agent, managing investments, and arranging deals in investments; and secondly, any institution which is not regulated by the FCA but is regulated by another EU Member State. Membership is also open to any other organisation serving the financial services industry that does not fall within the normal criteria of the BBA. The main objects[154] of the BBA are to promote the interests of the banking sector in the UK and, where necessary, represent and promote the views of its membership within the UK, EU and elsewhere. The BBA allows members to agree on policy and was one of the associations sponsoring the development and adoption of the original voluntary Banking Codes of Practice. Another objective of the BBA is to support the role of London as a major banking and financial centre.

Other institutions providing banking services

Historically, a number of other institutions have provided banking services to the public. The Trustee Savings Bank was established following a number of Acts of Parliament. Initially its objective was to provide banking facilities for the working classes who were unable to open bank accounts. In order to establish depositor trust the Savings Bank (England) Act 1817,

---

[151] See also Ch. 2.
[152] Association of Foreign Banks, http://www.foreignbanks.org.uk/.
[153] http://www.bba.org.uk/about-us.
[154] http://www.bba.org.uk/about-us.

enacted that deposits by the TSB could only be invested in government bonds or deposited with the Bank of England. The bank was restructured under the Trustee Savings Act 1985 which resulted in the Trustee Savings Bank of England and Wales, with similar banks in Scotland and Ireland. It merged with the Lloyds Bank Plc, in 1995, to form the Lloyds TSB Group. The National Girobank was established by the Post Office Act 1969. The Act authorised the Post Office to provide such banking services it thought fit and classed it as banker for all practical purposes. The National Girobank was privatised in the late 1980s and became Girobank Plc, which was acquired by the Alliance & Leicester Building Society. Girobank Plc is now an authorised institution and maintains branches through the Post Office. Initially, it merely provided money transfer services but its activities now extend to the full range of account facilities including offering overdrafts and transmission of money. The building societies currently derive their powers under the Building Societies Act 1986, although the Act has been amended on several occasions, and was substantively revised by the Building Societies Act 1997, and by and under the Financial Services and Markets Act 2000. The effect of the Acts, cumulatively, has been to increase the commercial freedom of building societies and enhance the scope for increased competition and wider choice for consumers. The main provisions of the 2000 Act relevant to building societies include:

- The transfer of most of the functions of the Building Societies Commission to the Financial Services Authority. The Commission's prudential functions were superseded by equivalent functions of the FSA and the registration, and most other functions of the central office of the Registry of Friendly Societies relating to building societies (and other mutual organisations), were transferred to the FSA.

- The replacement of the previous different statutory authorisation criteria for banks, building societies, insurance companies, investment firms etc. by a single statutory process, with broadly harmonised prudential and regulatory requirements.

- The establishment of a single financial services compensation scheme and a single financial ombudsman scheme.

Many provisions of the Building Societies Act 1986 were repealed by or under the Financial Services and Markets Act 2000. However, the provisions of the 1986 Act relating to the constitution, governance and principal purpose of building societies remain in place. A building society may, therefore, be established if its primary purpose is that of raising money, primarily by subscription from members for the purposes of making advances secured on land for residential use.[155] The Building Societies Act 1997 gave building societies the freedom to pursue any activities set out in their memorandum[156] and, in essence, it is the principal purpose, the nature of limits and restrictions, together with the fact that most of a building society's customers are its members, which help to retain a building society's fundamental character, and differentiate it from other financial institutions.

The traditional business of building societies, therefore, was the acceptance of deposits from members and the granting of loans for home purchase secured by a mortgage. The Building Societies Act 1986 represented the first comprehensive review of the legislative framework regulating building societies for over a century. Although, the Act extended the scope of

---

[155] Building Societies Act 1986, s.5(1).
[156] Building Societies Act 1986, schedule 2.

the nature and activities that could be undertaken by building societies, it also ensured they did not stray too far from their primary purpose. A building society also faces significant restrictions in respect of certain types of business, e.g. trading in commodities or currencies and derivatives, and a building society cannot create a floating charge over the whole or part of its undertaking.[157] The Building Societies Act 1997 allowed them to carry out any activity in their objects and that Act, together with the earlier Acts, means that building societies can now undertake the whole range of banking and financial activities for their members. Building societies, like banks, operate through a branch network and over the years the gap in the nature of services offered by them has become blurred. Consequently, it was to be expected that with the introduction of a single financial services regulator building societies should be regulated by the FSMA 2000, and the Financial Services Compensation Scheme established under the Act protects depositors both with the building societies and the banks.

Despite significant deregulation the commercial activities of building societies are restricted. A number of building societies, therefore, converted from being mutual societies to banks over a number of years, for example, Abbey National plc, Alliance and Leicester plc, Halifax plc and Woolwich plc, but many are now part of the banks that have dominated the UK banking sector. Many of the institutions worst hit by the 2007–08 financial crisis were building societies that demutualised and, on reflection, public confidence might have been better maintained and the crisis less intense if they had remained mutual societies conducting business within their original remit.

Competition in the UK banking sector

Clearing banks are at the core of the UK banking system and the provision of banking and financial services to personal and business customers has become increasingly competitive. This competition has come not only from within the traditional banking sector as these banks have expanded their activities, but also from the building society sector as they have grown the scope of their business. A range of supermarkets and other non-banking institutions have also expanded and diversified their businesses into banking and financial services, for example, Tesco, Sainsbury, Marks and Spencer and Virgin. Tesco was initially in partnership with the Royal Bank of Scotland, although Tesco acquired the shares of Royal Bank of Scotland in this joint venture in 2008 and Tesco Personal Finance became a bank in October 2009, while Sainsbury's Bank is the result of a joint venture between Sainsbury's supermarket and the Bank of Scotland (now part of the Lloyds Banking Group). Virgin Money was originally formed as a result of a joint venture between Virgin and Norwich Union, although the Virgin Group has since acquired its entire shareholding. Nevertheless, the government commissioned a review of the level of competition within the UK banking sector in 1988 and the review committee published its final report in March 2000.[158] The Cruickshank Committee focused on the levels of competition in three key areas: money transmission (flow of money

---

[157] Building Societies Act 1986, s.9B. However, a building society may create a floating charge if the Bank of England has provided the society with relevant financial assistance. This provision resulted from an Order made under the emergency legislation passed after Northern Rock's collapse, and was re-enacted and widened under s.251 of the Banking Act 2009. Section 104A allows for registration of such charges.

[158] Cruickshank, Competition in the UK Banking – A Report to the Chancellor of the Exchequer, London, March 2000, available at www.bankreview.org.uk.

through the payment systems),[159] the provision of banking services to personal customers, and the provision of banking services to small and medium-sized businesses. The government concluded there was a competition problem in all three areas and accepted the majority of the 55 recommendations.[160] In the area of banking services the report concluded that there was still a significant section of the population, for example the unemployed and the elderly, who did not have access to banking facilities and the committee recommended it should be made easier for this section of the population to access basic banking services.[161] The government expressed its support for this recommendation and supported the idea of a universal bank through the Post Office. The clearing banks responded by introducing a bank account, which does not provide an overdraft facility; a basic bank account.[162]

The Cruickshank Report noted that OFT research indicated that up to a quarter of applications for a current account might be refused. Nevertheless, the area remains controversial with the British Bankers Association relying on an independent report[163] suggesting that the lack of accounts was the absence of desire or need to use a current account, rather than the banks refusing to make accounts available. Nevertheless, the Committee concluded that it should be made easier to gain access to basic banking facilities and the government responded by developing a universal bank run through the Post Office network. Banks and other retail banking institutions have responded by introducing 'universal banking services' which include the provision of 'basic banks accounts' through branch and ATM networks but which do not provide overdraft facilities. Research undertaken by the British Bankers Association indicates that since April 2003, 3.2 million Post Office accessible accounts have been opened with half for customers having no previous banking facilities. Additionally, since April 2003, a net total of 751,700 basic accounts have been opened by banks and 210,100 upgraded.[164]

The importance of encouraging competition within the banking sector following the merger of Lloyds TSB with the Halifax Plc, which formed the Lloyds Banking Group, has been the subject of public and political debate.[165] Although the European Commission approved the state recapitalisation of £17 billion on 13 October 2008,[166] the Commission ensured

---

[159] The Committee found that money transmission services were run through a series of unregulated networks controlled mainly by the large major clearing banks which dominated the market for services to individuals and small and medium enterprises. The Committee also examined the entry restrictions on membership of these schemes, including membership of APACS (now UKPA) clearings and concluded that the membership criteria distorted competition by restricting full membership to banks and other deposit-taking institutions, Cruickshank, Competition in the UK Banking – A Report to the Chancellor of the Exchequer, London, March 2000, 3.94, available at www.bankreview.org.uk. The Committee recommended a licensing regime for payment systems that would allow non-discriminatory access to the payment system, Cruickshank, Competition in the UK Banking – A Report to the Chancellor of the Exchequer, London, March 2000, 3.186 and 3.197, available at www.bankreview.org.uk.

[160] The government refused to accept the recommendation that all mergers between financial institutions should be referred to the Competition Commission if the institutions have a material share of the relevant market (Recommendation 12).

[161] HM Treasury, Competition in UK Banking: the Cruickshank Report – Government Response, London, August 2000, www.hm-treasury.gov.uk.

[162] See Lending Code, section 5, http://www.lendingstandardsboard.org.uk/docs/lendingcode.pdf.

[163] Kempson and Whyley, Kept Out on Opted Out? Understanding and Combatting Financial Exclusion, www.pfrc.bris.ac.uk/reports/kept_out_opted_out.pdf. University of Bristol.

[164] http://www.bba.org.uk/media/article/7.3-million-basic-bank-accounts-at-the-end-of-the-1st-quarter.

[165] BBC News, How collapsed Lloyds and Co-op deal affects customers, 24 April 2013, http://www.bbc.co.uk/news/business-22277153.

[166] Europa, IP/08/1496, State aid: Commission approves UK support scheme for financial institutions, 13 October 2008, http://europa.eu/rapid/press-release_IP-08-1496_en.htm?locale=en.

effective competition within the UK retail-banking sector would be preserved, and ordered Lloyds to create a divested entity.[167] This entity was required to have a 4.6 per cent market share of the personal current account market and at least 600 branches. While the proposed sale to the Co-operative Group, known as 'Verde', collapsed in April 2013,[168] Lloyds Banking Group has announced it intends to divest the 'TSB Bank' through an Initial Public Offering by the end of 2013.[169] The implications of this were explored by the Treasury Select Committee on 18 June 2013 through its questioning of António Horta-Osório, Group Chief Executive, Lloyds Banking Group and Sir Winfried Bischoff, Chairman, Lloyds Banking Group.[170]

The nature of the banker and customer relationship

While the banker and customer relationship is clearly embedded in contract law the courts have examined the nature of that contract. Historically, banking business is thought to have developed from the early goldsmiths who undertook the function of depositors of gold and plate for their clients. In that capacity goldsmiths acted under a bailor and bailee relationship which demanded the bailee return the exact gold and plate to the bailor at the end of the relationship, or as agreed. The bailee was, therefore, expected to maintain the goods *in specie* and return those exact goods. If he used them contrary to the terms of the bailment the bailee was not only in breach of contract but would be liable to account to the bailor for any profit made. The application of the bailor and bailee relationship, or trustee and beneficiary relationship where the latter could assert proprietary rights over the property, or the agent and principal or other similar relationship, where the bank merely acquired limited rights to the money placed on deposit, in exchange for the payment of a fee, would defeat the traditional foundations of the banker and customer relationship. According to Chorley and Smart[171] the imposition of fiduciary duties in connection with the normal bank account would be too onerous to the relationship and applying the debtor and creditor principles allows the bank complete latitude in the way deposit balances are utilised, in the course of the banking business.

The courts have therefore held that the banker and customer relationship is one of debtor and creditor in respect of monies held to the credit of a customer's bank account.[172] In *Foley* v *Hill* a bank's customer paid money to the credit of his account on the understanding that it would earn interest at the rate of 3 per cent per annum. Interest not having been credited to the account for a period of approximately six years the customer brought an action, in the Court of Chancery, for an account. The customer alleged that he was entitled to the remedy either on the basis of the trustee and beneficiary relationship, or the customer being the bank's principal and the relationship being that of a fiduciary nature meant that the limitation

---

[167] Europa, IP/09/1728, State aid: Commission approves restructuring plan of Lloyds Banking Group, 18 November 2009, http://europa.eu/rapid/press-release_IP-09-1728_en.htm?locale=en.

[168] Lloyds TSB, Update on 24 April 2013, http://www.lloydstsbtransfer.com/update-on-24th-april-2013/.

[169] Lloyds TSB, We've agreed to transfer some of our branches and accounts to a new owner, http://www.lloydstsbtransfer.com/.

[170] Treasury Select Committee, Project Verde, 13 June 2013, http://www.parliament.uk/business/committees/committees-a-z/commons-select/treasury-committee/inquiries1/parliament-2010/project-verde/.

[171] Chorley and Smart (1990) *Leading Cases in the Law of Banking*, London: Sweet & Maxwell Ltd.

[172] *Foley* v *Hill* (1848) 2 HLC 28.

period, then in force, did not prevent a legal action being pursued. The House of Lords having analysed the nature of the banking business as being one in which a bank agrees to return to the customer an amount equivalent to that deposited by him, and not the exact notes and coins deposited, held the relationship between a banker and customer at common law as one of debtor and creditor. Consequently, the customer must pursue an action in debt to recover the value of the deposited funds rather than an action for account, as once deposited the funds belong to the banker without additional equitable obligations imposed through a fiduciary relationship. Lord Cottenham LC[173]explained:

> Money placed in the custody of a banker is, to all intends and purposes, the money of the banker, to do with it as he please; he is guilty of no breach of trust in employing it; he is not answerable to the principal if he puts it into jeopardy, if he engages in a hazardous speculation; he is not bound to keep it or deal with it as the property of his principal; but he is, of course answerable for the amount, to repay to the principal, when demanded, a sum equivalent to that paid into his hands.

A bank, therefore, makes no promises regarding the use of deposits and is not accountable to the customer about the usage of that money. Money placed in a deposit account is an outright transfer of funds to the bank. Thus, in *Hirschhorn v Evans (Barclays Bank Garnishees)*[174] a bank operating an account on behalf of a Lloyds' insurance syndicate was held not to hold that money on trust, without something more in the arrangement to impose those additional obligations. Again in *Space Investments Ltd v Canadian Imperial Bank of Commerce Trust Co (Bahamas) Ltd*[175] the Privy Council expressed the view that the same principle applies where the bank, acting as a trustee, makes an authorised deposit of trust funds with itself as banker.[176] The relationship is that of debtor and creditor when depositing trust funds in an ordinary bank account. While the courts have established that the banker and customer relationship is one of debtor and creditor they have distinguished it from some of the usual features associated with that relationship, for example those which require the creditor to seek out the debtor in order to make repayment. That principle is reversed in the banker and customer relationship and in a situation where the customer places money to the credit of his account it is the customer (creditor) who must seek out the bank (debtor) to demand the repayment relationship.[177] In *Libyan Arab Foreign Bank v Bankers Trust*[178] Staughton J said:

> [s]tudents are taught at an early stage of their studies in the law that it is incorrect to speak of 'all my money in the bank'.

What must be remembered is that once money is placed to the credit of a bank account it is no longer the customer's money and legal and equitable title in those funds rests with the bank. The customer is entitled to the return of the money deposited on demand and so long as the bank is in a position to return an amount equivalent to the demand the bank is not obliged to return the deposited funds *in specie*. The House of Lords in *Foley v Hill*[179] also

---

[173] (1848) 2 HLC 28 at 36.
[174] (1938) 2 KB 801.
[175] [1986] 3 All ER 75.
[176] See Ch. 16.
[177] *Bradford Old Bank Ltd v Sutcliffe* [1918] 2 KB 833 at 848.
[178] [1989] QB 728 at 748.
[179] (1848) 2 HLC 28.

established that the limitation period to bring an action for non-payment would run from the date of the un-met demand and not from the date of the deposit.[180]

The principle established in *Foley* v *Hill*[181] was further illustrated in *Joachimson* v *Swiss Bank Corporation*[182] where a partnership maintained an account with a credit balance of £2,312 with the defendant bank. When the First World War broke out the partnership became an enemy alien because its membership comprised German and English nationals. At the cessation of the war the English partner brought an action in the name of the partnership for the repayment of the credit balance. As the commencement of the action had not been preceded by a demand for repayment the Court of Appeal held that the action could not succeed. Atkin LJ, describing the banker and customer relationship as a single contract made between the bank and its customer, continued:

> The bank undertakes to receive money and to collect bills for its customer's account. The proceeds so received are not held in trust for its customer's account, but the bank borrows the proceeds and undertakes to repay them. The promise to repay is to repay at the branch of the bank where the account is kept, and during banking hours. It includes a promise to repay any part of the amount due against the written order of the customer addressed to the bank at the branch, and as such written orders may be outstanding in the ordinary course of business for two or three days, it is a term of the contract that the bank will not cease to do business with the customer except upon reasonable notice. The customer on his part undertakes to exercise reasonable care in executing his written orders so as not to mislead the bank or to facilitate forgery.

Atkin LJ's judgment in the *Joachimson* case[183] on the incidents of the nature of the banker and customer (while not exhaustive) is certainly comprehensive and in *Tai Hing Cotton Mill Ltd* v *Liu Chong Hing Bank Ltd*[184] Lord Scarman described Atkin LJ's analysis as 'the classic, though not necessarily exhaustive analysis of the incidents of the banker and customer relationship'. This view was further reinforced in *Libyan Arab Foreign Bank* v *Bankers Trust Co*[185] where Staughton J held that while there was a single contract between the bank and its customer, on the facts, that contract was governed 'in part by the law of England and in part by the law of New York'.

The *Foley* v *Hill*[186] and *Joachimson* v *Swiss Banking Corporation*[187] cases have a number of ramifications for the banker and customer relationship, as follows:

● While the analysis of the banker and customer relationship in *Foley* v *Hill*[188] and *Joachimson*,[189] as debtor and creditor, is based on an account being maintained there are many instances when that relationship will be based on the provision of services by the bank and where the right to act for the customer specifically prevents the debtor and

---

[180] *National Bank of Commerce* v *National Westminster Bank* [1990] 2 Lloyd's Rep. 514; *Bank of Baroda* v *A.S.A.A Mahomed* [1999] Lloyd's Rep. Bank, 14.

[181] (1848) 2 HLC 28.

[182] [1921] 3 KB 110.

[183] [1921] 3 KB 110.

[184] [1985] 2 All ER 947 at 956.

[185] [1989] QB 728.

[186] (1848) 2 HLC 28.

[187] [1921] 3 KB 110.

[188] (1848) 2 HLC 28.

[189] [1921] 3 KB 110.

creditor relationship from arising. Thus, the bank may hold valuables for safe custody for its customer and the bank acts as a bailee, or it may manage a portfolio of investments with specific relationships under each investment. Even to reduce the management of the current or deposit account to a simple debtor and creditor relationship is, in many ways, to take a simplistic approach as the management of these accounts also involves the creation of an agent and principal relationship in respect of the duties the relationship imposes. Thus, for example, the bank comes under a contractual obligation to conform to the customer's mandate when making payments against the account; the bank is under a duty of confidentiality in respect of the customer's affairs etc.

- While the relationship is that of debtor and creditor it is the customer (creditor) who must make a demand for the repayment of credit balance and not the bank (debtor) that must seek out the customer. This obligation for the creditor (customer) to seek out the debtor (bank) reverses the general rule that the debtor must seek out the creditor to make repayment. Furthermore, the need for a demand only exists in respect of a credit balance on a current or deposit account where sums can be credited for an indeterminate time. Where the money is deposited for a fixed period, usually because the bank offers a higher interest rate on fixed-term deposits, the bank, in the absence of other instructions, will normally credit such sums to the credit of a current account on the fixed period having expired. If the bank retains the money on a fixed deposit it will be obliged to pay interest.[190]

- The requirement that the demand is made at the branch where the account is maintained, while complying with traditional banking practices, can no longer be strictly observed particularly in respect of the current account where customers can withdraw funds from any automated teller machine (ATM), generally whether or not they have an account with the bank maintaining that ATM, or where the customer makes payment for purchases using a debit card. What is therefore required is that the demand must constitute a 'clear intimation that payment is required'.[191] Indeed, in *Damayanti Kantilal Doshi v Indian Bank*[192] the Singapore Court of Appeal said:

  > [i]n the light of modern technological and business development it is doubtful whether the principle of banking law that a demand for payment must be made at the branch where the account is kept in order to found a cause of action is still good law.

- Atkin LJ in *Joachimson*[193] did not address the issue whether the demand had to be in writing and verified by the customer's signature, but again modern banking practice often allows for alternative means of making a demand with a PIN often substituting for a signature or acting as an digitised signature.

- The debtor and creditor role is reversed where the customer is overdrawn on his account so that with an overdrawn account the customer becomes the debtor with the bank's role being that of creditor. An overdraft may be granted as a result of express or implied agreement and unless expressly agreed the overdraft is repayable on demand.[194] However, a bank cannot bring an action to recover the amount of the overdraft six years after the bank

---

[190] *Bank of America National Trust and Savings Association v Herman Iskandar* [1998] 2 SLR 265.
[191] *Re A Company* [1985] BCLC 37, per Nourse J who accepted the view expressed in *Re Colonial Finance, Mortgage, Investment and Guarantee Co Ltd* (1905) 6 SRNSW 6.
[192] [1999] 4 SLR 1 at 11.
[193] [1921] 3 KB 110.
[194] *Bradford Old Bank Ltd v Sutcliffe* [1918] 2 KB 833.

makes a demand for repayment of the overdraft amount.[195] The limitation period is extended to 12 years where the overdraft is secured by a mortgage or charge.[196]

- Any amounts standing to the credit of the customer's account, including in a current account, become immediately payable and without a demand from the customer if the bank goes into liquidation[197] or if the banker and customer relationship is terminated by closure of the account.

Although the written mandate signed by the customer when opening a current account is still largely based on implied contractual terms it lacks the detail of the legal rules the courts have developed over the years. In their turn, the courts have been reluctant to impose terms that are not sufficiently well known to customers[198] and the Jack Committee[199] stressed the need for transparency and fairness in the banker and customer relationship but recommended that be achieved through a voluntary Code of Good Practice.[200] In 2002, the Cruickshank Report into Competition in UK Banking[201] resulted in the banking sector publishing the Business Banking Code, which set out standards of best practice when dealing with small businesses. Both codes were last revised in 2008 but the need to implement the conduct of business aspects of the Payment Services Directive,[202] in November 2009, promoted a further reconsideration of the codes. The Payment Services Regulations 2009[203] set out detailed conduct of business rules applicable to 'payment services' effected by banks and other payment service providers. To complement these rules the FSA introduced a new Banking Conduct of Business Sourcebook (BCOBS) to regulate deposit taking so as to create a new Banking and Payment Services regime. In 2009 the BCOBS was superseded by the Lending Standards Boards, which issued the *Lending Code* in 2011,[204] a successor to the previous two codes. The *Lending Code* establishes rules of good practice in respect of loans to individual and micro-enterprises, credit cards and other facilities provided by subscriber banks and building societies.[205] However, the customer still has to rely on a number of sources of regulation, including the common law, statute and voluntary codes of practice.

The clearing system and when is payment made?

Payment is the transfer of money from the debtor to the creditor in order to discharge legally enforceable debts. Payment by the physical delivery of money from the payer to the payee

---

[195] Limitation Act 1980, ss.5–6.

[196] Limitation Act 1980, s.20.

[197] *Re Russian Commercial and Industrial Bank* [1955] 1 Ch 148.

[198] See *Turner v Royal Bank of Scotland Plc* [1999] 2 All ER (Comm.) 664; and *Kitchen v HSBC Plc* [2000] (Comm.) 787 at 795, per Sedley LJ.

[199] Banking Services: Law and Practice, Report by the Review Committee, 1989, Cm. 622, paras 4.04, 6.23, 16.10–16.12.

[200] The industry response to the Jack Report came in the form of a voluntary code which sets standards of good banking practice for financial institutions to follow when they are dealing with personal customers in the United Kingdom.

[201] Cruickshank, Competition in UK Banking – A Report to the Chancellor of the Exchequer, London, March 2000, Cm. 5319.

[202] Directive 2007/64/ECC.

[203] SI/2009/209, came into force on 1 November 2009.

[204] Revised in 2012; http://www.lendingstandardsboard.org.uk/docs/lendingcode.pdf.

[205] http://www.lendingstandardsboard.org.uk/docs/lendingcode.pdf.

carries with it risks of loss or theft and can be expensive to transport. This has allowed the development of various methods of money transfer and settlement, and payment is, therefore, often made through the transfer of funds from the bank account of the debtor to that of the creditor by an adjustment of balances between the payer and payee. The payer's account is debited and the payee's account is credited. Thus the debt owed by the payer is extinguished and payee's credit balance is increased. Payment systems therefore allow money to fulfil its function in society as an accepted means of exchange of purchasing power. Individuals and businesses use payment systems to make and receive payments for goods and services, including the payment of bills and salaries. Speed, efficiency, reliability and trust are indispensable to the operation and workings of any payment systems since they will affect the lives of most individuals and the domestic and global economies on a daily basis. Payment systems[206] will include private and corporate customers, financial intermediaries, commercial and central banks each motivated by the need to have access to an efficient, reliable and cost effective system of payment. Geva[207] defined such facilitation systems as:

> Any machinery facilitating the transmission of money which bypasses the transportation of money and its physical delivery from the payor to the payment is a payment mechanism. A payment mechanism facilitating a standard method of payment through a banking system is frequently referred to as a payment system . . .

Goode[208] identified four key components of a national payment system:

1 An inter-bank communications network for the online electronic transmission of large volume payment orders and associated messages.

2 A clearing house for the physical exchange of paper-based payment orders (bills, cheques, bank giro payments) and the netting of matured payment obligations.

3 An automated clearing house for the batch processing of large-volume offline, mainly low-value (retail) payment orders, stored on magnetic tape or computer disk.

4 The involvement of the central bank as the vehicle for the settlement dealings between participants in the clearing (settlement banks) by means of transfers in the books of the central bank, where all settlement banks hold an account.

Each payment system will therefore reflect a compromise between the needs and demands of the users and the system providers within which the level of security and risks will play a significant part. These will therefore determine the most efficient and appropriate operating methods, the legal framework within which the system operates, the level of security, the technologies used and the level of innovation. Competition will therefore play a key part in the continuous development of the payment systems, for example the development of paperless payments.

A payment system will consist of a mechanism for the transfer of funds with either the payment element being completed in cash or by a payment instrument, for example a cheque or other means of effecting a non-cash payment. Thus, the transferor is required to give payment

---

[206] Financial Services Act 2012, s.104(3) inserts a s.191, which confers powers on the Bank of England to give directions to a recognised payment system. Such directions may, for example, be given for the purposes of securing compliance with a requirement imposed or may be given for the purposes of addressing an immediate threat to financial stability. Bank of England, *A brief history of banknotes*.

[207] Geva (1992–2000) *The Law of Electronic Funds Transfers*, loose-leaf, New York: Matthew Bender, s.1.103 [1].

[208] Goode (2009) *Commercial Law*, London: Penguin Press.

instructions to transact a payment through a particular scheme, which allows the payment to be processed and finalised according to certain rules, and practices, which governs the handling of funds on behalf of the payer and payee and the relationship between the service providers and any intermediate parties. The law, which operates within such a framework, will need to provide comprehensive legal rules to determine the finality and irrevocability of the payment. Consequently, these rules will determine issues including: when is payment made so the debtor's obligation is discharged in accordance to any deadlines, where loss lies if there is a failure in the scheme caused either by negligence or breakdown of the system, and where the transaction is affected by fraud or other dishonesty, or the insolvency either of the payer or payee and/or the paying or receiving banks. The role of the settlement agent is normally vested with the central bank, which settles accounts between the banks.

Clearing and settlement

Payments effected through a payment system are initiated by payment instructions given by the payer or by his authorised agent, to the payer's bank.[209] Where the payer's instruction is not an inhouse payment the instruction will involve further payments passing between the payer's bank and the payee's bank, sometimes through intermediate banks. The process of exchanging payment instructions between participant banks is known as clearing and takes place through a series of bilateral exchanges of payment instructions between banks in the UK. However, it is common for clearing to take place multilaterally through a centralised clearinghouse.[210]

Where the payer and payee have accounts at the same bank, the transfer of the funds between the two accounts will normally involve a simple 'inhouse' accounting exercise.[211] The position will be different where the payer and payee's accounts are held with different banks so an inter-bank payment is made and the payment instruction will pass between the banks, sometimes using a correspondent agent bank. The bank sending the instruction will make each inter-bank payment to the bank receiving it and the process by which payment is made between the banks themselves is known as settlement. Settlement therefore occurs either on a bilateral or multilateral basis. Bilateral settlement occurs where the bank sending the payment instruction and the receiving bank are correspondents, meaning that one of them holds an account with the other and settlement is effected through an adjustment of that account. Multilateral settlement involves the settlement of accounts of the sending and receiving bank held with a third bank, either a common bank where they both have accounts or more commonly the central bank.

Settlement may be either net or gross. With gross settlement (real-time gross settlement) each payment obligation is settled when processed so that the balance held by the banks with the central bank will fluctuate as each payment is sent and received. With real-time gross settlement banks will only forward settlement requests to the Bank of England when they have sufficient funds to settle the account which enables the transaction to be processed

---

[209] *Chitty on Contracts*, 30th edn, vol. 1, para. 21–041, London: Sweet & Maxwell; *Treasure & Son Ltd* v *Martin Dawes* [2008] EWHC 2420 (TCC); Cf *Barclay's Bank Ltd* v *WJ Simms, Son & Cooke (Southern) Ltd* [1980] QB 677.

[210] See page 48 for an explanation of the Clearing system.

[211] *Libyan Arab Foreign Bank* v *Bankers Trust Co* [1989] QB 728 at 750–751, per Staughton J. However, see Cranston (2002) *Principles of Banking Law*, Oxford: Clarendon Press, p. 236.

immediately.[212] Consequently, banks need to manage their liquidity carefully during the day to ensure they have funds to settle these payments immediately when the payment is processed. Net settlements may be bilateral or multilateral. In a bilateral net settlement the participant's exposure is determined by reference to its net position in respect of each individual counterparty and not by reference to the system as a whole. Each participant will therefore end up as a net debtor or net creditor in relation to all the participants in the system as a whole.

While there are some advantages to net settlement, for example it reduces the number and value of inter-bank settlement operations and leads to reduced transaction costs, the major risk of a system of net settlements is that the receiving bank may not be placed in funds. Further, acting on a customer's instructions the receiving bank may pass on payment instructions to other banks, which themselves may generate further payment instructions to other banks. The failure of one bank to make payment may mean that other banks in the chain cannot meet their own payment commitments and this causes systemic risk. Although there are various ways in which the risks associated with net settlement can be reduced[213] concern about systemic risk associated with large-value transfer systems led to the establishment of a Working Group on EC Payment Systems[214] which recommended that Member States should develop their own real-time gross settlement system for large-value payments.[215] In 1996, the UK developed the Clearing House Automated Payments System (CHAPS), a real-time gross settlement system for large-value payments. The lack of credit means that participants must have funds available to meet their payment obligations.

There are several European measures that affect the provision of payment services in the UK with the main provisions dealt with below.

Directive on settlement finality in payment and securities settlement systems

On 19 May 1998 the European Parliament adopted the Directive on settlement finality in payments and securities settlement systems[216] which was implemented in the UK through the Financial Market and Insolvency (Settlement Finality) Regulations 1999.[217] The Directive has two main aims: (i) to reduce systemic risk in payment systems which operate on the basis of payment netting, especially multilateral netting, and (ii) to minimise the disruption caused by insolvency proceedings against a participant in a payment or securities settlement system. The Directive is intended to cover domestic and cross-border payment and securities settlement systems, and applies to any settlement system for money and securities governed by the

---

[212] European Monetary Institute, *Payment Systems in the European Union*, April 1996, p. 628, http://www.ecb.int/pub/pdf/othemi/bluebook1996en.pdf.

[213] Dale (1997) *Controlling Risks in Large-Value Interbank Payment systems*, 11, JIBL, 426; Sappideen (2003) *Cross-Border Electronic Funds Transfers Through Large Value Transfer Systems, and the Persistence of Risk*, JBL 584.

[214] Committee of Governors of the Central Banks of the of the Member States of the European Economic Community, Payment Systems in EC Member States, September 1992, prepared by an Ad hoc Working Group on EC Payment Systems.

[215] Committee of Governors of the Central Banks of the of the Member States of the European Economic Community, Payment Systems in EC Member States, September 1992, prepared by an Ad hoc Working Group on EC Payment Systems; see Cranston (2002) *Principles of Banking Law*, Oxford: Clarendon Press.

[216] Directive 98/26/EC [1998] OJ L 166/45.

[217] SI 1999/2979.

law of a Member State and operating in any currency, the euro or in various currencies which the system converts one against another.[218] To constitute a 'system' within the Directive three conditions must be satisfied:[219]

1 The system must consist of a formal arrangement between three or more participants with common rules and standardised arrangements for the execution of the transfer orders between participants (in certain cases Member States may reduce the requirement to two participants). The term transfer order[220] is defined as an instruction to carry out a transfer of money (credit or debit) or of securities.

2 The system must be governed by the law of a Member State chosen by the participants at least one of whom must have its registered head office in that Member State.

3 The system must be designated as such and notified to the European Commission by the Member State whose law is applicable.

The Directive extends to all participants, which can be an institution, a central counterparty, a settlement agent or clearinghouse,[221] in a payment or securities settlement system. The term 'institution' is defined by Art. 2(b) as a credit institution, an investment firm, a public authority or publicly guaranteed undertaking, or an undertaking whose head office is located outside the EC but whose functions correspond to an EC credit institution or investment function and which participates in a system and is responsible for discharging the financial obligations arising from transfer orders within that system. An indirect participant, i.e. a credit institution which is not a member of the payment or securities settlement system but which employs a member to act on its behalf, may be designated a participant if its failure may result in systemic risk. The Directive provides, *inter alia*, that:

1 The transfer orders and netting are to be legally enforceable and binding on third parties, even in the event of insolvency provided the transfer orders were entered into the system before the opening of the insolvency;[222]

2 There is to be no unwinding of a netting because of the operation of the national laws or practice which for the setting aside of contracts and transactions concluded before the insolvency proceedings;[223]

3 A transfer order is not to be revoked by a participant or a third party from the moment defined by the rules of that system;[224] and

---

[218] *Directive on settlement finality in payments and securities settlement systems*, Art. 1(a), Directive 98/26/EC [1998] OJ L 166/45.

[219] *Directive on settlement finality in payments and securities settlement systems*, Art. 2(a), Directive 98/26/EC [1998] OJ L 166/45.

[220] *Directive on settlement finality in payments and securities settlement systems*, Art. 2(i), Directive 98/26/EC [1998] OJ L 166/45.

[221] *Directive on settlement finality in payments and securities settlement systems*, Art. 2(f), Directive 98/26/EC [1998] OJ L 166/45. Each of the terms referring to participants is defined in the Directive (Art. 2(b)–(e)).

[222] *Directive on settlement finality in payments and securities settlement systems*, Art. 3(1), Directive 98/26/EC [1998] OJ L 166/45.

[223] *Directive on settlement finality in payments and securities settlement systems*, Art. 3(2), Directive 98/26/EC [1998] OJ L 166/45.

[224] *Directive on settlement finality in payments and securities settlement systems*, Art. 5, Directive 98/26/EC [1998] OJ L 166/45.

4 Insolvency proceedings are not to have retrospective effect on the rights and obligations of a participant arising from, or in connection with, its participation in a system earlier than the opening of such proceedings.[225] The moment of opening of the insolvency proceedings is the moment when the judicial or administrative authority delivered its decision.[226]

Directive on payment services

The Payment Services Regulations 2009[227] implemented in the UK the Directive on Payment Services.[228] The aim of the Directive was to establish the common legal framework necessary for the creation of an integrated payments market. It applies to domestic payments in sterling within the UK and to certain cross-border payments from and to the UK. Its two main objectives are:

- To generate more competition in payments markets by removing barriers to entering and providing fair market access; and
- To provide a simplified and harmonised set of rules in relation to the information requirements and rights and obligations linked to the provision and use of payment services.

The Directive establishes an authorisation regime for non-bank payment service providers, such as money remitters and non-bank credit card issuers (known as 'payment issuers') and stipulates conduct of business rules for all 'payment service providers' including banks, e-money institutions and payment institutions. The intention is that payment institutions, for example supermarkets or phone companies, will be able to compete with banks in providing cashless payment services,[229] without being subjected to the same level of regulation as banks.

The Electronic Money Directives

In July 2006, a review by the European Commission found that the e-money market was developing at a slower rate than expected, although the number of e-money accounts in Europe grew from 15 million in 2005 to 125 million in 2009[230] and the total value of outstanding e-money has risen from €400 million to €1.7 billion over the same period.[231] The Commission reported, in October 2008, that the legal framework set by the first Electronic Money Directive was holding back the development of the market. The principal causes identified were uncertainty over the application of the legal framework to new business models, excessive prudential requirements, and inconsistent application of the rules by Member States.

---

[225] *Directive on settlement finality in payments and securities settlement systems,* Art. 7, Directive 98/26/EC [1998] OJ L 166/45.

[226] *Directive on settlement finality in payments and securities settlement systems,* Art. 6(1), Directive 98/26/EC [1998] OJ L 166/45.

[227] SI 2009/209.

[228] Directive 2007/64.

[229] See Ch. 14.

[230] Electron Money Association, http://www.e-ma.org.

[231] European Central Bank e-money statistics 2008.

The Second Electronic Money Directive[232] was implemented in the UK on 30 April 2011 through the Electronic Money Regulations 2011.[233] The aims of the Directive are to foster competition among electronic money issuers and payment service providers, to facilitate technological innovation[234] and to share information and experience with other nations who may be considering setting up regimes for the regulation of e-money. Under the revised Electronic Monetary Directive the definition of electronic money has been amended to provide that electronic money is an electronically, including magnetically, stored monetary value as represented by a claim on the issuer which is issued on receipt of funds for the purpose of making payment transactions (as defined by the Payment Services Directive) and which is accepted by a natural or legal person other than the issuer. The definition covers e-money held on payment devices in the holder's possession (e.g. pre-paid cards and electronic purse) or stored remotely at a server.[235]

Euro payment and settlement systems

The European System of Central Bankers (ESCB)[236] comprises the national central banks of all EU Member States whether or not they have adopted the euro. Its objectives include the promotion of the 'smooth operation of the payment systems'.[237] However, because the ESCB includes Member States who have not adopted the euro, the separate eurosystem group was established comprising the ECB and the central banks of those Member States that have adopted the euro.[238] The eurosystem has developed a system for the payment of euros between participant banks in different countries in real time or by the end of the day, with immediate settlement, known as TARGET2.[239] This is the successor to TARGET (Trans-European Automated Real-Time Gross-settlement Express Transfer) which was originally introduced in 1999 to facilitate transfers of euros between participants in different Member States using the new currency. Under the TARGET system, a payment instruction would be directed to, and authorised by, an individual national central bank and transmitted using TARGET to the national central bank of the payee. All countries that are members of the euro participate in TARGET2 but it is possible for the central banks of other countries to choose to participate. The Bank of England does not participate in TARGET2 and for its own transactions accesses TARGET2 through the De Nederlandsche Bank (the Dutch National Bank).

TARGET2 is the dominant method for large value euro payments with 89 per cent of the market in 2009, representing around a total of 88 million payments with a value of 551,174 billion euros.[240] For 2012, the peak in volume turnover was 29 June 2012 with

---

[232] 2009/110/EC [2009] OJ L 267/7. The original Electronic Money Directive was implemented in the UK in April 2002.

[233] http://www.legislation.gov.uk/uksi/2011/99/contents/made.

[234] FSA, The Second Electronic Money Directive, http://www.fsa.gov.uk/pages/about/what/international/pdf/emd.pdf.

[235] HM Treasury, Laying of regulations to implement the new E-Money Directive a consultation document 2010, http://www.hm-treasury.gov.uk/d/emoney_directive_consultation.pdf.

[236] Article 107.1 TEU.

[237] Article 105.2 TEU.

[238] The European Central Bank, The Eurosystem, The European System of Central Banks, ECB and Eurosystem, 2010, http://www.ecb.int/pub/pdf/other/escb_en_weben.pdf.

[239] http://www.ecb.europa.eu/paym/t2/html/index.en.html.

[240] Target Annual Report 2009, 15–16, http://www.ecb.int/pub/pdf/other/targetar2009en.pdf.

536,524 transactions and peak value turnover was on 1 March 2012 with €3,718 billion.[241] TARGET2 applies to credit transfer, direct debit and liquidity transfers with payment orders submitted up to five days before the settlement date.[242] TARGET2 essentially consists of individual payment systems operated by each central bank with each separate system called a 'payment module'. A bank (or permitted institution) participates in TARGET2 by participating in an individual payment module operated by the particular central bank and the Single Shared Platform (SSP).

Single Euro Payments Area

The Single Euro Payments Area (SEPA) project was initiated by the European Payments Council to develop common standards and rules for retail payments and credit and debit payments in euros.[243] The idea is that all euro payments will be treated as domestic payments and the euro area has one retail payments market known as the Single Euro Payments Area. The SEPA encompasses all EU Member States and Iceland, Liechtenstein, Norway, Switzerland and Monaco. The SEPA Credit Transfer Scheme (SCT) was launched on 28 January 2008 to facilitate a credit transfer service in euros throughout the SEPA and, by 2010, SEPA credit transfers accounted for some 8 per cent of the total cross-border euro payments. The SEPA Direct Debit Core Scheme (SDD Core) was launched on 2 November 2009 to enable the transfer of funds between the payer's bank and the biller's bank in euros. In February 2012, the European legislator adopted the Single Euro Payments Area (SEPA)[244] to harmonise national euro credit transfer and direct debit schemes through the uniform adoption of the SCT and SDD schemes.[245]

The UK clearing systems

The clearing banks used to be the only active participants of the clearing house but that position changed in the 1980s when three other banks (the Trustee Savings Bank of England and Wales (now part of the Lloyds Halifax Group), the Co-operative Bank and the National Girobank (now part of the Spanish Santander Banking Group)) became functional members of the clearing house but without seats on the Committee of London Clearing Bankers (CLCB). These three banks were, therefore, permitted direct access to the clearing house through their own clearing departments but could not participate in policy decisions or any periodic reviews. However, the Child Report[246] made several recommendations regarding the three

---

[241] TARGET2 Facts, http://www.ecb.europa.eu/paym/t2/html/index.en.html.

[242] See 2007 Guideline for TARGET2, ECB/2007/2 and the ECB Information Guide for TARGET2 Users.

[243] The European Single Market, Single Euro Payments Area (SEPA), http://ec.europa.eu/internal_market/payments/sepa/.

[244] Regulation (EU) No 260/2012 establishing technical and business requirements for credit transfers and direct debits in euro and amending Regulation (EC) No 924/2009 (the Single Euro Payments (SEPA) Regulation) OJ L 94/22 30/03/2012, http://eur-lex.europa.eu/LexUriServ/LexUriServ.do?uri=OJ:L:2012:094:0022:0037:En:PDF.

[245] Regulation (EU) No 260/2012 establishing technical and business requirements for credit transfers and direct debits in euro and amending Regulation (EC) No 924/2009 (the Single Euro Payments (SEPA) Regulation) OJ L 94/22 30/03/2012, http://eur-lex.europa.eu/LexUriServ/LexUriServ.do?uri=OJ:L:2012:094:0022:0037:En:PDF.

[246] Payment Clearing Systems, Review of Organization, Membership and Control, Report prepared by a Working Party appointed by the ten member banks of the Bankers Clearing House, published by Banking Information Services 1984; reprinted by APACS in 1990.

clearing systems operational in the mid-1980s each of which was under the control of a separate company, including that they should be brought within the framework and under the control of an 'umbrella organisation',[247] The three clearing systems operating at that time were: (i) the 'general clearing' of cheques and paper-generated giro credits issued in England and Wales, and the 'town clearing' used for same day clearing of instruments with a minimum value of £10,000 drawn and payable on a branch within the City of London; (ii) the Bankers Automated Clearing Services (BACS) clearing electronically generated payments, for example direct debits or other periodic payments made in the UK such as salary payments to employees; and (iii) the Clearing House Automated Payment Systems (CHAPS) clearing high-value electronic transfers on the same-day basis in the UK. The report also called for a widening of membership so that all settlement members and individual clearing companies, and other appropriately regulated institutions that previously used agents for clearing purposes, should be offered associate membership. The Child Report, therefore, recommended that membership of the three clearing systems should be liberalised.

These recommendations were given full effect in 1985 and the Association for Payment Clearing Services (APACS) was established as an unincorporated association with 33 members, including the Bank of England, 31 banks and one building society. The effect of the new structure, following the Child Report, was that APACS gained control over the various clearing systems. Another change following the Child Report was that membership of the clearing house was no longer restricted to banks and APACS membership now extends to banks and building societies operating in the UK and any institution based in the EU, EEA or the members of the G10. Membership of APACS was opened to any institution that is a principal member of a payment scheme (i.e. a payment scheme that handles more than 1 per cent of the UK's payment volumes and/or more than 0.1 per cent of the UK's payment values). APACS also has an associate membership scheme that provides payment services for its customers through an agency arrangement[248] with a full member.

From 6 July 2009, APACS ceased to exist and was re-established as the UK Payments Administration Ltd (UKPA), which acts as a portal company for each of the respective sectors of UK payment services such as BACS, CHAPS, the Cheque and Credit clearing company and others who now exist as their own individual businesses. Although UKPA services a significant part of the UK payments industry its remit does not extend to Visa, MasterCard, LINK or SWITCH Maestro but it does operate as an umbrella body for the four payment industry groups (Financial Fraud Action UK, the Payments Council, the UK Cards Association and SWIFT). The Cheque and Credit Clearing Company has control of the general clearing, which consists of the clearing of cheques and paper-based giro credits, in England, Wales and Scotland.[249] The company also manages the clearing of euro cheques and US dollar cheques drawn on UK banks. The company's shareholders are the Bank of England, the clearing banks and one building society.[250] The CHAPS Clearing Co. Ltd manages the UK's real-time gross

---

[247] The ownership of the clearing house was vested in a company, the principal shareholders of which were the clearing banks themselves, while direct control was with CLCB.

[248] 400 banks, building societies other payment service providers operate cheque clearing services for their customers and obtain indirect access to the cheque and credit clearing mechanism by means of agency arrangements with one of the settlement members, http://www.chequeandcredit.co.uk/membership/.

[249] http://www.chequeandcredit.co.uk/about_us/.

[250] http://www.chequeandcredit.co.uk/membership/-/page/list_of_members/.

settlement,[251] same-day value, and electronic sterling credit transfer system frequently used for high value payments.[252] However, in May 2008, CHAPS introduced the 'Faster Payments Service', which was designed to extend the benefits of CHAPS payments to lower value transactions, namely Internet and telephone payments for less than £10,000. The BACS Payment Services Ltd has taken over the activities of BACS Ltd. Members do not have to participate in all three clearing systems but, in practice, they all do with the exception of the Bank of England, which is not a member of the euro cheque clearing system.

While the methods of payment may have changed in the UK, with more emphasis on debit card payments, the volume of payments handled annually continues to show the system facilitating a high turnover. In 2008 those systems processed approximately 82.8 million faster payments; 5.6 billion BACS direct credits and direct debits; 35.8 million CHAPS payments; and a billion cheques and credits, with a combined value of £88.1 trillion. This is nearly four times the value of the whole world economy.[253] The year ending June 2009, showed a slight decline in the volume of payments processed by these systems, but still with very significant amounts being processed and approximately 294.7 million faster payments; 5.6 billion BACS direct credits and direct debits; 39.1 million CHAPS payments; and 949 million cheques and credits, with a combined value of £69.4 trillion being handled. In 2010 there was a further decline in the combined value of payments to £66.6 trillion. The volumes processed were: 425.7 million faster payments; 5.6 billion BACS direct credits and direct debits; 32.1 million CHAPS payments; and 837 million cheques and credits. This signifies a substantial decrease on the preceding years.[254] This is probably a reflection of the 2008 financial crisis and a slowing of the global economies.

Year	Faster Payments	BACS Direct Credits and Direct Debits	CHAPS payments	Cheques and credits	Combined value
2008	82.8 million	5.6 billion	35.8 million	1 billion	£88.1 trillion
2009	294.7 million	5.6 billion	31.9 million	949 million	£69.4 trillion
2010	425.7 million	5.6 billion	32.1 million	837 million	£66.6 trillion

However, the decline in the use of cheques has led to the payments industry publishing guidance reminding customers on how to draw cheques[255] and more recently the Commons Treasury Select Committee[256] wanted to strip the Payments Council of its powers to abolish cheques and other payments instruments.[257]

---

[251] Real Time Gross Systems are funds transfer systems, which enable the transfer of money or securities to take place from one bank to another on a 'real time' and on a 'gross' basis. Settlement in 'real time' means payment transactions are not subjected to any waiting time.

[252] CHAPS also operated the euro-denominated credit transfer system but this was decommissioned on 16 May 2008.

[253] http://www.ukpayments.org.uk/about_ukpayments/.

[254] UK Payments Council, Annual Summary of Payment Clearing Statistics 2010, http://www.ukpayments.org.uk/files/stats/annual_summary__clearing_stats_2010.pdf.

[255] Cheque and Credit Clearing, Advise When Writing and Receiving Cheques, 16 September 2009.

[256] House of Commons Treasury Committee, The Future of Cheques, Eighteenth Report of Session 2010–12, HC1147, http://www.publications.parliament.uk/pa/cm201012/cmselect/cmtreasy/1147/1147.pdf.

[257] Jones, Ministers bounce plans to abolish use of cheques, The Guardian, 12 July 2011, http://www.guardian.co.uk/money/2011/jul/12/cheques-abolition-plan-scrapped.

International funds transfers

An international funds transfer occurs when either or both of the payer's bank or the payee's bank, is located in a country other than that of the currency of the transfer. Most international funds transfers are credit transfers and operate in a similar way to domestic credit transfers, although greater use of correspondent banks may be made. Each payment message, whether between the payer and his bank, or payee and his bank, or between the banks may be communicated in writing, electronically or even orally, although the bank will normally require written confirmation.

The clearing cycle

The Bills of Exchange Act 1882 requires that a cheque must be presented for payment 'at the proper place' which requires the physical presentation of the instrument at the branch where the drawer's account is kept (i.e. the branch of the paying bank on which the instrument is drawn).[258] Originally, the clearing system was divided into the 'town clearing' and the 'general clearing'. 'Town clearing' was used for cheques and bankers' payments for less than £500,000 drawn on, and collected, by bank branches within the City of London. All other instruments, including paper-based giro transfers, were collected through the 'general clearing'. The 'town clearing' was abolished in 1995 so that only the one system remains for the clearing of paper-based money transfers. The general clearing is based on the use of two separate documents handed by the payee (as most cheques in the UK are drawn 'A/C payee only'[259] it is no-longer possible to endorse and transfer title to a third party holder, who might then claim title and thereby payment) of a cheque to the collecting bank, i.e. the cheque which is drawn by the drawer, and the credit slip which is filled by the payee (or more rarely by the holder). In addition to the drawer completing the cheque-form with the name of the payee, the date and the amount payable in words and figures, he will place his signature on the cheque form above his name, which is pre-printed on the form. The foot of the cheque form will also contain a line of information, in magnetic ink, which sets out the bank's clearing number and identifies the branch (through the branch sort code) at which the account is maintained, the drawer's account number and the number of the relevant cheque. This magnetic line is readable by the banks' reader-sorter machines. The credit slip will contain similar information, in magnetic ink, which helps to identify the name and details of the payee so that payment can be made into his account when received from the paying bank. The cheque and credit slip, therefore, serve different functions in the clearing cycle with the credit slip used to facilitate the credit into the payee's account, while the cheque serves as a mandate and facilitates the debiting of the payer's account.

The clearing of cheques drawn on a different bank or branch originally took three days[260] but since 1994 the major clearing banks have opted for a two-day clearing cycle[261] and have given an undertaking to abide by the standardised maximum time limits for the clearing

---

[258] *Barclays Bank Plc v Bank of England* [1985] 1 All ER 385 at 392–394.
[259] Cheques Act 1992, s.1, inserting s.81A into the Bills of Exchange Act 1882.
[260] *Barclays Bank Plc v Bank of England* [1985] 1 All ER 385 at 392–394.
[261] *Emerald Meats (London) Ltd v AIB Group (UK) Plc* [2002] EWCA Civ. 460.

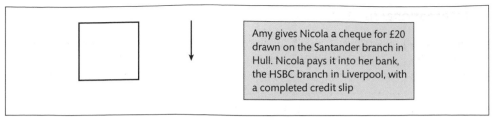

Amy gives Nicola a cheque for £20 drawn on the Santander branch in Hull. Nicola pays it into her bank, the HSBC branch in Liverpool, with a completed credit slip

Figure 1.1

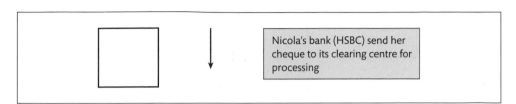

Nicola's bank (HSBC) send her cheque to its clearing centre for processing

Figure 1.2

of cheques.[262] These timescales apply to cheques, bankers' drafts, bankers' cheques and building society cheques paid into a UK sterling current account or basic bank accounts. Under the '2-4-6' commitment the clearing banks undertake to credit the proceeds of cheques into a current account, for the purposes of the payee earning interest, from the second working day following the deposit of the cheque.[263] However, the customer will not be permitted to withdraw funds from the account until the fourth working day. The customer is assured that the cheque will not be dishonoured by the drawee bank from the end of the sixth working day from the day of deposit.[264] Where a cheque is paid into a savings account the time scale is longer and banks give the 2-6-6 commitment so that the customer is allowed to draw against those funds from the sixth day following payment of the deposit.[265] Although the actual procedures adopted vary slightly the mechanics of the clearing cycle are now explained.

Assume that on Monday morning (day 0), Amy gives Nicola a cheque for £20, drawn on the Santander branch in Hull, and Nicola pays it, later the same day, into her bank, the HSBC branch in Liverpool, together with a completed credit slip.

Monday is day 0 in the 2-4-6 timeline for clearing Nicola's cheque. Cheques are generally paid in by the customer to a current or basic bank account, or a savings account at his bank (known as the collecting bank). They can also be paid in at a cash machine at some banks, a post office or sent by post and different methods will affect when the collecting bank receives the cheque for collection and how quickly the processing starts.

The amount of the cheque is encoded in magnetic ink on the cheque form itself, and a computerised credit entry made on the customer's account. A special crossing is added to

[262] Cheque and Credit Card Clearing Company, http://www.chequeandcredit.co.uk/information/-/page/the_cheque_clearing_cycle/.

[263] Cheque and Credit Clearing Company, 2-4-6 Timescales for cheque clearing, http://www.chequeandcredit.co.uk/246/.

[264] 2-4-6 Timescales Explained, http://www.chequeandcredit.co.uk/246/-/page/113/

[265] Cheque and Credit Clearing Company, 2-6-6 Timescales for cheque clearing, http://www.chequeandcredit.co.uk/246/.

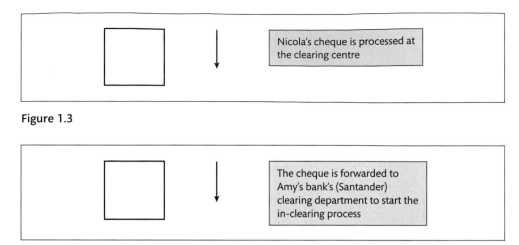

Figure 1.3

Figure 1.4

the cheque so that the branch arranging collection is identified on the cheque, itself. The credit slip remains at the branch and the cheque is bundled with other cheques drawn on the same bank.

Nicola's cheque is fed through reader-sorter machines for three reasons:

1 It places Nicola's cheque, along with all the others drawn on the same branch, in a batch for collection by that bank.

2 The machine will read the information in the magnetic ink line on the cheque with the information passed onto the drawer's (Amy's) (Santander) bank which will calculate the balance in the drawer's account on the subsequent day.

3 The reader-sorter machine will also keep a tally of amounts due from and to each participating clearing bank.

If the balance in the drawer's account is insufficient to meet the cheque the computer will place the cheque in an 'out of order list', comprising items drawn specifically to the attention of the branch manager.

First of all the computer checks the digital signature to ensure that there has been no fraudulent tampering and then it passes the cheques through reader-sorter machines to separate them into branch order. The bank needs to be sure that all the cheques it has brought back from the exchange centre belong to it, as it will have to settle for them the following day (Wednesday, day 2). This happens before banks have had time to examine the individual cheques to make their pay or no pay decision. The Cheque and Credit Clearing Company

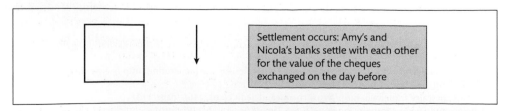

Figure 1.5

calculates how much the banks (in this case Santander and HSBC) owe each other and settlement takes place across accounts held at the Bank of England.

Later on that morning, Amy's bank (Santander) checks to see if she has sufficient money in her account to pay the cheque, also that it has been signed, dated, written correctly and is genuine. Based on this information, the Santander bank decides whether to pay Amy's cheque to Nicola (at her HSBC account), or to return it unpaid to Nicola's bank.

If the cheque is paid (Wednesday afternoon, day 2), Nicola will start to receive interest on the money and the deducted item will appear on Amy's statement. On Friday (day 4) Nicola can draw money against the cheque, if the instrument was paid into her current account. If Nicola had paid in the cheque into a savings account, she would not be able to withdraw the money until the end of day 6.

If Amy's bank (Santander) decides not to pay the cheque to Nicola (HSBC), her bank will send the unpaid cheque back to Nicola's bank by special courier on Wednesday (day 2).

The decision to return a cheque unpaid must be made on the morning of the day after exchange so that the cheque can be returned straightaway to the bank, which collected the cheque for advice to the beneficiary. Cheques may be returned unpaid for a number of reasons: for example, the customer has insufficient funds to pay the cheque, or if it has been improperly drawn, or if it has not been signed, dated or written correctly, or it appears to be fraudulent. The paying bank will write to its customer to tell them that the cheque has been returned unpaid and the customer might be charged for the unpaid cheque.

On Thursday morning (day 3), the unpaid cheque arrives back at Nicola's bank (HSBC) and is reclaimed from her account, so she cannot withdraw the funds on day 4. Depending on the reason for the return of the cheque unpaid, the collecting bank may try to get the cheque paid again, or send the cheque back to its customer and advise them that it has bounced.

Completion of payment

Determining the time of completion of payment as between the drawer (originator) and the payee (beneficiary) may be important in a number of circumstances, for example where the drawer attempts to countermand payment, or where the payee seeks to terminate a contract on the basis that payment was not made strictly on the due date. Thus, for example, in *The Brimnes*,[266] Brandon J had to determine the time of payment of hire under a charterparty, which the owners claimed had been paid late. The charterparty called for 'payment . . . to be made . . . in cash', and Brandon J concluded that in 'modern commercial practice' this included, 'any commercially recognised method of transferring funds the result of which is to give the transferee the unconditional right to the immediate use of the funds transferred'.[267] The word 'unconditional' was interpreted in *The Chikuma*[268] to mean 'unfettered or unrestricted', and not merely 'that the transferee's right to use the funds transferred is neither subject to fulfilment of a condition precedent nor defensible on failure to fulfil a condition subsequent'. A payment is, therefore, complete when the beneficiary is given an unfettered or unrestricted right against his own bank to the immediate use of the funds transferred.

---

[266] *Tenax Steamship Co Ltd* v *Reinate Transoceanica Navegacion SA, The Brimnes* [1973] 1 WLR 386.
[267] [1973] 1 WLR 386 at 400B-C.
[268] *A/S Awilco of Solo* v *Fulvia SpA di Navigazione of Calgiari, The Chikuma* [1981] 1 WLR 314 at 319H, per Lord Bridge.

Intra-branch transfers

Where the drawer (originator) and payee (beneficiary) hold accounts with the same branch of the bank, payment is deemed to take place the moment the bank decides to make the transfer of funds unconditionally, assuming that the bank has the payee's (beneficiary's) actual or ostensible authority to accept the transfer on his behalf. In *Momm* v *Barclays Bank International Ltd*[269] the defendant bank's customer, the Herstatt Bank, as part of a currency exchange transaction with the claimant, ordered the bank to transfer £120,000 from its account to the claimant's account with the same branch, which the claimant had identified for the receipt of the funds in question. Although, Herstatt's account was overdrawn at the time, the bank decided to make a transfer and initiated the computer transfer process to carry out the payment. Later that day, it was announced that the Herstatt bank had ceased trading and gone into liquidation. The defendant bank took no further action and the payment from Herstatt's account to the claimant's account was completed that night. The following morning the defendant bank reversed the transfer and the claimant, on discovering the transfer from the Herstatt account and the reversal of the payment, claimed that the transfer was irrevocable and the defendant bank had wrongly debited its account. Kerr J giving judgment for the claimant held that as between the claimant and Herstatt, the payment was complete the moment the defendant bank decided to credit the claimant's account and initiated the internal payment process. Kerr J also held that, following banking practice, that 'a payment has been made if the payee's account is credited with the payment at the close of business on the value date, at any rate if it was credited intentionally and in good faith and by error or fraud'. Therefore, where it is not possible to identify when the decision to make a payment is made, it is to be assumed that payment is made at the end of the day on which the payment message is processed.[270] Kerr J also made a number of points relating to the completion of payment where both the payer and payee maintain accounts with the same branch of the bank that:

1 The transfer was complete when the bank decided to credit the claimant's account and initiated the computer process for making the transfer. However, initiation of the mechanical process amounts to objective evidence of the decision to credit the beneficiary's account, which also may be available from other sources. Nevertheless, the paying bank's decision to transfer funds to the payee's account must be unconditional so a credit that allows reversal of the transaction would not be absolute payment.[271]

2 Kerr J emphasised that payment was complete even though the beneficiary had not been informed of it. In *Momm* Kerr J distinguishing *Rekstin* v *Severo Sibirsko AO*[272] stressed that in the latter case the bank had no authority to accept a transfer on its behalf, nor could it have anticipated that the payment would be made. By contrast, in the *Momm* case the defendant bank had the claimant's authority to accept the transfer.

3 Payment was held to be complete in the *Momm* case before any credit was made to the beneficiary's account. This approach is consistent with the view taken by Brandon J and affirmed by the Court of Appeal in *The Brimnes*[273] where the charterers' bank in London

---

[269] [1977] QB 790.
[270] Geva, *Payment into a Bank Account* [1990] 3 JIBL 108 at 112–115.
[271] See *Sunderland and Sunderland* v *Royal Bank of Scotland Plc* [1997] 6 Bank LR 132.
[272] [1933] 1 KB 47 at 57 and 62.
[273] *Tenax Steamship Co Ltd* v *Reinate Transoceanica Navegacion SA, The Brimnes* [1973] 1 WLR 386.

(Hambros) had an account with the ship owners' bank in New York (MGT). On receipt of instructions from the charterers to pay hire under the charterparty, Hambros telexed MGT instructing it to transfer the amount of the hire to the ship-owners' account, i.e. to make an intra-branch funds transfer. The Court of Appeal, affirming the decision of Brandon J held that the payment was complete when MGT decided to debit Hambros' account and credit the ship owners' account. The decision seems to emphasise not only that notice to the beneficiary's account is not necessary, but that the decision to transfer the funds need not have been carried out, either in whole or in part, before the payment is deemed complete.

Inter-branch transfers

An inter-~~bank~~ branch transfer involves the transfer of funds between accounts held with different branches of the same bank and, like an intra-bank transfer, does not involve the use of a clearing house or any correspondent bank relationship. By analogy to the *Momm* case, payment is complete when the bank decides to credit the payee's (beneficiary's) account unconditionally, with his apparent or actual authority to accept the transfer. The decision of the payee (beneficiary's) bank branch to credit the payee's account was looked at in *Libyan Arab Foreign Bank* v *Manufacturers Hanover Trust Co (No 2)*[274] where Hirst J had to decide whether a transfer of US $62 million had been made from the claimant's (LAFB's) account at the New York branch of the defendant bank (MHT New York) to LAFB's account at the same bank's London branch (MHT London) before MHT New York purported to revoke the transfer. On 7 January MHT New York notified MHT London by telex that it was crediting the London branch with US $62 million for the account of LAFB. Later the same day, and anticipating the issue of a US presidential order freezing the assets of Libyan nationals held by US nationals and corporations, MHT New York instructed its computer in New York to reverse the transfer. However, on the morning of 8 January MHT London acted on the telex and credited LAFB's account with the US $62 million on its computerised books. MHT London then notified LAFB of the credit. On 10 January MHT New York telexed MHT London to cancel the transfer and this was affected on 13 January. Hirst J held that MHT London had intentionally and bona fide debited its account with MHT New York and credited LAFB's account on 8 January in satisfaction of the telex dated 7 January. It was, therefore, too late to revoke the instructions on 10 January. Hirst J therefore concluded that the actions of MHT London constituted a full completion of the payment of the $62 million and was not affected by the absence of similar and corresponding entries in MHT New York. 'The notification to LAFB confirmed the completion of the payment.'[275]

Inter-bank transfers

In the case of an inter-bank transfer funds are transferred between accounts held at different banks. Payment is complete when the payee's (beneficiary's) bank receives instructions from the drawer's (originator's) bank and decides to make an unconditional credit to the payee's (beneficiary's) account for the specified amount and the payee's (beneficiary's) bank has actual

---

[274] [1989] 1 Lloyd's Rep 608.
[275] [1989] 1 Lloyd's Rep 608 at 631.

or ostensible authority to accept the transfer.[276] It is irrelevant that the payee's (beneficiary's) bank has yet to credit the beneficiary's account or to notify him of the transfer.[277] In *Mardorf Peach & Co Ltd* v *Attica Sea Carriers Corpn of Liberia, The Laconia*[278] the charterers of a ship made a late tender of a hire payment to the owners' bank. The tender was accepted by the owners' bank without objection, but later rejected when the owners became aware of the fact of the purported late payment and attempted to invoke a forfeiture clause in the charterparty, on the grounds of the late payment. The charterers argued that the late payment had been waived by the acceptance of the late tender of payment by the owners' agents, the payee's (beneficiary's) bank. The House of Lords, reversing the Court of Appeal, decided the case in favour of the owners on the grounds that the owners' (beneficiary's) bank had only limited authority to receive the payment and that did not include receiving late payment. Neither did they have authority to waive the owners' right to withdraw the vessel. Although the bank had taken delivery of the payment order and had begun processing the payment, these were merely ministerial acts and therefore reversible and provisional.

In some cases the payee's (beneficiary's) bank will require it be placed with funds before it makes the decision to transfer funds unconditionally, but in other cases that decision may be made before the payee's (beneficiary's) bank is placed with funds, for example where the drawer's (originator's) bank and payee's (beneficiary's) banks are correspondents. However, once the beneficiary's bank has made the decision to credit the beneficiary's account unconditionally the bank accepts the payee (beneficiary) as its creditor for the amount in question and is substituted for the drawer (originator) as the beneficiary's debtor. Payment is thereby complete between the drawer (originator) and the payee (beneficiary).

The decision of the payee's (beneficiary's) bank is critical and the bank may not be able to make that decision for any one of a number of reasons: for example the payment mandate does not adequately identify the payee (beneficiary), or where it is unclear whether it has the payee's (beneficiary's) authority to accept the payment or where crediting the account is a breach of the law (e.g. where regulations prohibit accounts of certain foreign nationals to be credited with certain payments).[279] Until the beneficiary's bank makes the decision to accept the funds for the beneficiary's account, it holds the funds as agent of the drawer (originator) and not the beneficiary. In such cases the funds constitute an unaccepted tender of funds by the drawer (originator) and the underlying payment obligation between the drawer and payee is not discharged.

Conclusion

This chapter gives the reader an understanding of certain key features relating to the structure of the UK banking sector and the nature of the business undertaken by banks, including the effect of legal title passing to the bank when an account is opened. The chapter also deals with the clearing cycle and when payment is made in law.

---

[276] *A/S Awilco of Solo* v *Fulvia SpA di Navigazione of Calgiari, The Chikuma* [1981] 1 WLR 314; *Mardorf Peach & Co Ltd* v *Attica Sea Carriers Corp of Liberia, The Laconia* [1977] AC 850.

[277] *Mardorf Peach & Co Ltd* v *Attica Sea Carriers Corp of Liberia, The Laconia* [1977] AC 850 at 880 and 889, per Lords Salmon and Lord Russell.

[278] [1977] AC 850.

[279] Goode (2009) *Commercial Law*, London: Penguin Press.

Further reading

➤ Hudson, A. (1999) Money as property in financial transactions, 14(6), *Journal of International Banking Law*, 170–176.
This article considers the implications of how courts deal with financial products for English law's understanding of the nature of money in the context of sophisticated cross-border transactions and tracing, and the benefits of treating money as value rather than as property.

➤ Vroegop, J. (1990) The time of payment in paper-based and electronic funds transfer systems, *LMCLQ*, 64.
This article examines the issue of when payment is made, not only when the mandate to make the payment is given in paper form, for example a payment by cheque, but also when the payment instruction is given electronically. The issue of when payment is made using the different systems and also when there are more than two banks involved in executing the payment mandate, for example where there are intermediary banks involved is also discussed.

➤ Sir John Vickers, Independent Commission on Banking: The Vickers Report and the Parliamentary Commission on Banking Standards, http://www.parliament.uk/briefing-papers/SN06171, September 2011.
The Vickers Commission proposed fundamental changes in the framework in which banks operate in the UK financial sector. The fundamental changes include the concept of ring fencing which would separate retail banking deposits from the riskier activities such as investment banking and proprietary trading. The Vickers Commission further proposes enhanced capital and loss absorbency mechanisms than under the Basel III rules.

➤ Sir James Sassoon, The Tripartite Review, A Review of the UK's Tripartite System of Financial Regulation in Relation to Financial Regulation, March 2009.
The Sassoon Report was commissioned by the opposition Conservative Party in October 2008 to form the Conservative Party's position on the regime of financial regulation in the UK. The report recommended an overhaul of the tripartite regime which shared responsibilities between the Financial Services Authority (FSA), HM Treasury and the Bank of England, due to a lack of communication and awareness of who bore overall responsibility.

➤ FSA Internal Audit Division, The Supervision of Northern Rock: a lessons learnt review, March 2008, http://www.fsa.gov.uk/pubs/other/nr_report.pdf.
This report concluded that the FSA's prevailing framework for assessing risk was not appropriately applied in relation to Northern Rock, so that the supervisory strategy was in line with the firm's risk profile. The report recommended that the FSA's senior management should have increased engagement with high impact firms, while the FSA should increase its focus upon prudential supervision, including liquidity and stress testing.

➤ Financial Services Authority (FSA) Board Report, The failure of the Royal Bank of Scotland, December 2011, http://www.fsa.gov.uk/static/pubs/other/rbs.pdf.
This report provides an account of why RBS failed, which resulted in a government bail-out of £45.5 billion in October 2008. This report identifies the multiple factors which combined to produce RBS's failure, while focusing upon errors of judgement. The report further considers deficiencies in the overall global framework for bank regulation which made a systemic crisis more likely, and more general flaws in the FSA's approach to the supervision of banks.

➤ HM Treasury, A new approach to financial regulation: judgement, focus and stability, 26 July 2010.
The Coalition Government, which took office in May 2010, sought to reform the UK's financial regulatory framework. The proposals sought to provide the Bank of England with control and oversight of micro-prudential regulation. These proposals outlined the creation of a Financial Policy Committee within the Bank of England. Furthermore, the Financial Services Authority (FSA) would

be dismantled in favour of a twin peaks approach to regulation. In place of the FSA would be the Financial Conduct Authority (FCA) and the Prudential Regulation Authority (PRA).

➤ HM Treasury, A new approach to financial regulation: the blueprint for reform, June 2011, http://www.official-documents.gov.uk/document/cm80/8083/8083.pdf.
This blueprint encompasses the UK government's response to the previous system of regulation under the tripartite system. The blueprint confirms that the responsibility for financial stability at both the macro-prudential and micro-prudential level rests within the Bank of England.

➤ Parliamentary Commission on Banking Standards, Changing Banking for Good, 19 June 2013, Volume I, http://www.publications.parliament.uk/pa/jt201314/jtselect/jtpcbs/27/27ii02.htm.
Following the LIBOR manipulation scandal which engulfed the financial sector, the Commission was established in July 2012 to conduct an inquiry into the professional standards in the UK banking sector. This report outlines the radical reform required to improve standards across the banking industry. The proposed key recommendations encompass increased responsibility for senior individuals, a new criminal offence of reckless misconduct in the management of a bank, and a new remuneration code to better align risks taken and rewards received in remuneration. Volume I is a summary of the key recommendations.

➤ Parliamentary Commission on Banking Standards, Changing Banking for Good, 19 June 2013, Volume II, http://www.publications.parliament.uk/pa/jt201314/jtselect/jtpcbs/27/2702.htm.
Volume II provides enhanced detail to the key recommendations outlined in Volume I.

2 The role of the City of London as a financial centre and the international financial institutions

Chapter overview

The aim of this chapter is to:

➤ Explain the role of the City of London as a prominent global financial centre.

➤ Explain the role and functions of bodies responsible for international standard setting regulations.

➤ Explain the development and background to the single European regulatory authority intended to safeguard and provide regulatory oversight of the European Financial markets.

Introduction

Over the last three centuries the City of London has evolved into a leading financial centre and despite the 2007–09 global financial crisis, London retains its prominence as an international financial centre, with a myriad of financial services and activities based there. However, finance does not completely dominate its activities and London remains a major port and a major centre for commercial activity.[1] At the same time London has become a cosmopolitan centre as international, rather than domestic, activities dominate its development[2] and the flexible nature of its services accommodates the entry and exit of individuals and firms alike.

The role of the City of London

In the mid-1980s McRae and Cairncross observed that by almost '. . . any measure you can take, the City of London is the world's leading international financial centre . . . if anything

---

[1] Lombard Street Research, Growth prospects of City Industries London, Executive Summary, 2003, http://217.154.230.218/NR/rdonlyres/34B595A0-6322-4166-A91D-ADA502337666/0/BC_RS_growth_0309_ES.pdf.

[2] Michie (2005) A Financial Phoenix: The City of London in the Twentieth Century, in *London and Paris as International Financial Centres in the Twentieth Century*, edited by Cassis and Bussiere, Oxford: Oxford University Press.

57

in the 1960s and 1970s London's dominance increased'.[3] In 2000, the Chancellor of the Exchequer, Gordon Brown, declared that 'as the world's foremost financial centre, London is a vital asset to the British and European economies, attracting investment and boosting competition'.[4] Brown considered the City's contribution so significant to the well-being of the UK and the global financial sector that one of the 'five tests' he set in 1997 for the UK's readiness to join the euro was that such membership should not harm or damage the City.[5] Yet by the beginning of the new millennium not a single investment bank was British.[6]

The wealth and employment opportunities resulting from the dominance of the City of London in the financial services sector has encouraged others to challenge the City's dominance, with Paris and Frankfurt, particularly, attempting to take advantage of the UK's decision not to join the single currency. Within the UK itself, the congestion, high property prices, increased taxation and regulation have at times threatened the City's dominance, but the growth of financial services has encouraged firms to expand their businesses to other UK cities with Birmingham, Leeds and Manchester developing as large commercial and business centres.

Expansion of City activity

While, the City is a geographical area, the mediaeval City of London, in financial terms the City is the 'square mile' housing the major financial institutions, including the Bank of England. Since the 1980s the growth of the financial services sector has resulted in some international and wholesale banks dispersing to other areas, including Canary Wharf. However, the term, the City, continues to be used for the wholesale financial services sector in London, based both in the square mile and beyond. As the City has continued to grow and the global financial services sectors have continued to develop specialised products the numbers of people employed in the 'City-type' wholesale financial services sector has continued to mushroom.

Estimates from the early 1910s indicate that there were approximately 194,000 people employed in the commercial and financial services sector, while estimates for 1964–66 suggest 195,000 people were similarly employed, in financial and commercial services.[7] In 1971 the wholesale financial services sector employed approximately 178,000[8] and despite international recessions and stock market slumps in the mid-1970s and early 1990s, when the City lost 50,000 jobs, the high figures of the 1910s and 1964–66 were surpassed in the early 1980s and by 2000 the financial sector employed 335,000 people. Banks located in the UK provided employment for 435,000 people in 2008 while net exports of UK banks totalled

---

[3] McRae and Cairncross (1985) *Capital City: London as a Financial Centre*, London: Methuen Limited.

[4] Corporation of London, The Global Powerhouse: thecityoflondon (London, 2000), p. 7.

[5] The UK's Five Tests, BBC Home, 21 November 2002, http://news.bbc.co.uk/1/hi/uk_politics/2423783.stm.

[6] Roberts and Kynaston (2002) *City State: A Contemporary History of the City of London and How Money Triumphed*, pp. 102–104, London.

[7] Michie (1992) *The City of London: Continuity and Change, 1850–1990*, London, p. 17; Dunning and Morgan, *An Economic Study of the City of London*, London, pp. 130–131.

[8] Roberts and Kynaston (2002) *City State: A Contemporary History of the City of London and How Money Triumphed*, London, p. 61.

Table 2.1 Number of people working in financial services

Year (approximate)	Number of people
1910	194 000
1964–66	195 000
1971	178 000
1980	
2000	335 000
2008	435 000
2011	1 000 000 (+ 900 000 supporting services)
2012	

a record £31 billion in 2008, up 31 per cent on the previous year.[9] By 2011, the financial services industry accounted for 10 per cent of UK GDP[10] and 11 per cent of UK tax receipts. The sector employed 1 million people of whom 66 per cent worked outside London.[11] A further 900,000 are employed in professional services supporting the financial services sector.[12] (See Table 2.1.)

Underlying the expansion of City employment has been the growth of the international financial sectors and services, backed by long-term economic development and growth across the world, which saw a more prosperous and economically sophisticated consumer and businesses who sought a higher return on savings, investments and financial products. This, together with the expansion of the Asian markets, particularly China and India, saw an era of expansion of financial products and financial services. The financial services sector, therefore, saw unparalleled growth until the recent global financial crisis, which saw some of the major financial players seek help from governments through bail-outs alongside heavy job losses.

Since 1945, world trade has supported the growth of several City activities, for example, foreign trade, foreign exchange, shipping and finance, international insurance etc. As the leading international banking centre and the foremost player in the international capital market (Eurobond), London benefited and was in a prime position to take advantage of these developments. These developments were supported by the collapse of the Bretton Woods system with many countries abandoning exchange controls and freeing up regulation allowing for the free movement of capital. In the aftermath of the Second World War, the Bretton Woods system had established a series of rules to operate as a framework for the international monetary system. Although these rules collapsed in 1971, the continuing relevance of Bretton Woods is demonstrated by the central role of the International Monetary Fund (IMF) and the International Bank for Reconstruction and Development (IBRD).

The 1960s saw an explosion in offshore banking and investment banking, which allowed the contracting parties to choose the regulatory and legal framework that would govern their business contracts. UK membership of the European Community, in 1971, and the free movement

[9] International Financial Services London Research Banking 2010, February 2010, http://www.thecityuk.com/media/2372/IFSL_Banking_2010.pdf.

[10] Bank of England and FSA, The Bank of England, Prudential Regulation, Our approach to banking supervision, May 2011, http://www.bankofengland.co.uk/publications/other/financialstability/uk_reg_framework/pra_approach.pdf.

[11] About TheCityUK, http://www.thecityuk.com/who-we-are/about-thecityuk.aspx.

[12] Statistics and the City Economy, City of London, http://www.cityoflondon.gov.uk/Corporation/LGNL_Services/Business/Business_support_and_advice/Economic_information_and_analysis/statistics.htm.

of trade and capital within Member States saw additional opportunities for the expansion of financial services. At the same time advances in telecommunications and the computer industry allowed for the radical expansion of the quality and quantity of financial information that could be transferred across national boundaries at a fraction of the cost.

The rapid movement of funds allowed the internationalisation of investment and boosted the City of London's banking and investment services. From the 1980s the UK saw the development of a number of factors aimed at growing the dominance of the City of London as a global financial centre:

- The advantages of law, language, learning, culture and politics enhanced the attraction of the City of London as a place for financial business. The English language has always been the official language of international financial business and many US banks established offices in London, in the 1960s, to enable them to undertake Euromarket operations.

- While English is the language of commerce the UK courts and the London-based arbitration and mediation services have a reputation for independence. The availability of specialist training and education centres has also been an attraction for a competitive workforce enjoying living and working in a cosmopolitan city.

- Successive UK governments saw the wealth of the country linked to the growth of the City of London and supported a regulatory framework that encouraged the adoption of a flexible approach, which allowed the City to self-regulate. This encouraged the expansion of the financial services sector and attracted financial firms from across the world.

- The deregulation of the telecom industry since the 1980s and the 'big bang' resulted in London being the first major financial centre to be computerised, which resulted in major communications advantages. The financial infrastructure also saw the banks providing and operating quality payments and settlements systems which encouraged the depositing of both corporate and individual wealth within the UK.

- A favourable corporate taxation environment encouraged corporations and individuals to retain their wealth within the UK.

- Flexible working hours and working practices encouraged international firms to establish places of business in London and the City. Since the 1980s trade unions have been less militant.

- The quality of international transport links from London and other UK cities was a significant attraction for business travel.

Despite the attractions of the City of London as a major financial hub, the City had outstripped its needs by the mid-1980s with congestion of office space and rocketing office rentals. The City of London Corporation relaxed planning restrictions and encouraged planning and development within the square mile with an expansion of modern office accommodation to meet the needs of the financial sector. The physical pressures faced by the City of London were also eased by the development of the Docklands into a linked second international financial centre within London. The development of Canary Wharf began in 1985 with state of the art modern trading floors and telecommunications facilities. The 1990s and the early years of the new millennium saw the City consolidate its position in the domestic market and in the international financial markets. Institutions were also looking to grow activity in the provincial cities and outsource activity within the UK. The growth of offshore banking had three main strands: offshore banking; offshore bond issuance, underwriting and trading; and offshore swaps and derivatives markets.[13] While, in theory, offshore centres could be located anywhere in the world, and some markets were successful in establishing reputable centres able to provide a wider range of innovative financial services at a lower cost, the City of London was a major beneficiary of these developments and remains a competitive financial centre for a number of reasons.[14]

The nature of City activities

A financial centre will undertake both retail and wholesale activities in order to satisfy the needs of both the domestic and business customer. The retail financial services sector mainly accommodates the needs of domestic customers, including small businesses, while wholesale financial activities serve the needs of corporations, governments, public agencies and the financial services industry itself. The City of London specialises in the wholesale markets and operates within a, predominately, international market. By 2000, the financial sector was dominated by massive global banks undertaking the full range of banking and securities activities supported by a range of international legal firms, accountants, insurance companies and fund managers. A plethora of financial services activities can be found in the City but the main activities undertaken in the square mile remain as follows.

Wholesale banking centre

The City of London, like New York is a major wholesale financial services centre and thus attracts business from other financial centres. A number of other centres channel their financial services business through the City of London, for example Singapore, Nassau, Bahrain and Hong Kong. Thus, the London insurance and re-insurance markets are able to accept large risks that other markets cannot facilitate. Countries that have nationalised their own insurance companies often re-insure their domestic risk in London. The need to finance international banking transactions also attracts non-British business to the foreign exchange market[15] while arbitrage business is attracted to London from all over the world. The London commodity markets attract business between commodity producing countries and third countries. The London Metal Exchange handles over 90 per cent of the world's turnover amounting to 112 million metal contracts per annum.[16] Notably the London Metal Exchange was sold in July 2012 to Hong Kong Exchanges and Clearing for approximately £1.4 billion.[17]

---

[13] Lombard Street Research (1998) Growth Prospects of City Industries, London, pp. 14–15.

[14] Lombard Street Research (2003) Growth Prospects of City Industries, London, http://www.cityoflondon.gov.uk/business/economic-research-and-information/research-publications/Documents/2007-2000/Growth%20Prospects%20of%20City%20Industries.pdf.

[15] Data on the level of activity shows that each day the London markets had a $1.9 trillion foreign exchange turnover, accounting for 37 per cent global share, including foreign exchange derivatives, City of London, http://www.thecityuk.com/who-we-are/about-thecityuk.aspx.

[16] Clarke (1999) How the City of London works, London: Sweet & Maxwell; see also City of London, http://www.thecityuk.com/who-we-are/about-thecityuk.aspx.

[17] Chinese buy London Metal Exchange in £1.4 billion takeover, The Independent, 16 June 2012, http://www.independent.co.uk/news/business/news/chinese-buy-london-metal-exchange-in-14bn-takeover-7855200.html.

Eurobond market

The largest securities market is the offshore Eurobond market. A Eurobond is a long-term loan issued in a currency other than the place of issue and such bonds were originally devised in London. Approximately 70 per cent of global Eurobond turnover is traded in London.[18]

Derivatives market

Derivative products such as options, futures and swaps are used for hedging financial risk or for betting on movements in securities and commodities prices, currencies and interest rates. In 2000, the London International Financial Futures and Options Exchange (LIFFE) was Europe's largest derivatives exchange[19] and London, in 2010, accounted for the largest share (43 per cent) of the world over the counter derivative turnover. A futures contract constitutes the obligation to buy or sell an agreed quantity of an asset at a fixed price at a set time. An option constitutes the right but not the obligation to buy or sell a security or alternative financial instrument at an agreed price, which provides more flexibility than purchasing a futures contract. Options enable hedgers to reduce (hedge) the risk of holding an asset, while purchasers (traders) may speculate on the security's price increasing. Furthermore, a swap enables two parties to exchange financial instruments, for example interest rate swaps or currency swaps. A swap may be explained by reference to the following interest rate example discussed through the scenario of party A and B both receiving loans. Party A has a strong credit rating and receives a fixed rate loan below that of party B, who as a result of a weak credit rating can only receive a variable interest rate. A swap of these interest rates benefits party B, as party B gains increased certainty from a fixed interest rate. Due to party A's strong credit rating, party A could benefit from a lower interest rate from the flexible interest rate than it would otherwise under a fixed interest rate.

Fund management

London is the largest fund manager in the world employing over 40,000 people. The range of activity includes managing pension funds and insurance and related activity. Pension funds arise out of efforts to provide security of income on retirement. Some pension schemes are financed out of the Exchequer but the majority of pensions are from schemes which allow regular individual payments to be pooled into a trust fund from which future pensions will be paid. The pooling of resources allows for large funds to be invested on the stock markets. Pensions funds are basically trust funds and trustees are constrained by their trust deeds and the law.

Insurance, marine services, commodities markets

Insurance is one of the oldest activities undertaken in the City of London and is about sharing risk. There are approximately 1,050 insurance companies authorised to undertake business in the UK and about 790 of them carry out general business (e.g. motor, household and

---

[18] City of London, http://www.thecityuk.com/who-we-are/about-thecityuk.aspx.
[19] Clarke (1999) *How the City of London works*, London: Sweet & Maxwell, p. 119.

commercial insurance).[20] Much of the global insurance is transacted through Lloyd's of London. The latter is not an insurance company, like Zurich, Aviva, Legal and General etc. but a market for insurance. It attracts business from around the world and in 2008 had the capacity to write £15.9 billion worth of business. In 2009 London transacted 20 per cent of the global market business in marine insurance.[21]

Professional and specialist services

The City of London's financial services sector is serviced by a range of specialist service providers ranging from lawyers, accountants and insurance brokers with access to appropriate resources, facilities and training. The UK has built up a service industry to support the specialist financial services that are key to the City.[22]

Economies of scale

The larger financial centres are able to provide a more advantageous operating environment ranging from lower operating costs for the services provided, to greater liquidity with finance more easily available. A specialised workforce with key staff located and concentrated in key business locations able to provide face-to-face operations are essential. A larger number of staff and a more competitive and innovative environment may produce new business opportunities and products. Further, competition between firms is likely to lead to quality client care, as firms compete for them. Financial firms operating within the large and established financial centres will enjoy economies of scale in related activities so there is a ready availability of commercial lawyers, accountants, information technology experts, public relations consultants etc. specialising in financial services.

An international dimension to banking

Over the past two decades the internationalisation of the financial system has grown exponentially[23] with the growth of world trade and business, and since the 1970s most countries have removed capital controls and opened their financial centres allowing the free movement of capital. Financial turmoil in one country may, therefore, have an impact across national boundaries[24] and lead to global systemic collapse. The international financial system must have built-in protections and be able to act effectively and efficiently to try and restrain cross-border

---

[20] City of London, http://www.cityoflondon.gov.uk/NR/rdonlyres/D05040A6-D6CC-4FEE-BBE2-F1DEA7210A0E/0/MC_keyfactsDec2010.pdf.

[21] City of London, http://www.cityoflondon.gov.uk/NR/rdonlyres/D05040A6-D6CC-4FEE-BBE2-F1DEA7210A0E/0/MC_keyfactsDec2010.pdf.

[22] Lombard Street Research (2003) Growth prospects of City Industries, London, http://www.cityoflondon.gov.uk/business/economic-research-and-information/research-publications/Documents/2007-2000/Growth%20Prospects%20of%20City%20Industries.pdf.

[23] King (2007) Through the looking glass: reform of the international institutions, *Australian Business Review*, p. 123.

[24] See Chapter 1 and discussion on the 2008 financial crisis which was the result of defaults on loans mainly in the USA.

financial turmoil. Attempts to regulate the international financial markets take place through the development of international policy[25] but this tends to concentrate on the more general standards. There is no global financial regulator responsible for common standards and the regulation of global banks. However, the work of some of the international agencies has had an impact in developing common international standards for financial regulation and the EU has taken some important steps towards establishing a pan-European regulator, as well as legislating for EU-wide common financial standards. While some of the international financial institutions are intergovernmental organisations, others have been created as a result of intergovernmental initiatives; others still are sector-specific groupings of supervisors or regulators.[26] The work of some of these international standards agencies has had a considerable impact on the development of common international standards. These will now be examined.

Intergovernmental organisations

International Monetary Fund

The International Monetary Fund (IMF) monitors and promotes international monetary cooperation and exchange rate stability, helps to facilitate the balanced growth of international trade, and provides resources to help members in balance of payments difficulties or to assist with poverty reduction.[27]

The IMF is a specialised agency of the United Nations but has its own charter, governing structure and finances. Its 186 members are represented through a quota system broadly based on their relative size in the global economy. The IMF works closely with governments and other financial agencies to promote the soundness of financial systems in member countries. The work of the Financial Sector Assessment Programme (FSAP)[28] aims to 'identify the strengths and vulnerabilities of a country's financial system, to determine how key sources of risk are being managed, to ascertain the sector's developmental and technical assistance needs, and to help prioritise policy responses'. The focus of the FSAP assessments is to gauge the stability of the financial sector and to assess its potential contribution to growth and development. In order to assess the stability[29] of the financial sector, FSAP teams examine the soundness of the banking and other financial sectors; conduct stress tests; rate the quality of bank, insurance and financial market supervision against accepted international standards; and evaluate the ability of supervisors, policy-makers, and financial safety nets to respond effectively in case of systemic stress. The FSAP does not evaluate the health of individual financial institutions and cannot predict or prevent financial crises but it can help identify the main vulnerabilities that could trigger a crisis. The FSAP will also examine the quality of the legal framework and of the financial infrastructure, for example, the payments and settlements

---

[25] Ferran and Alexander (2010) Can soft law bodies be effective? The special case of the European Systemic Risk Board, 35(6), *European Law Review*, 751–776; Arora, A. (2010) The global financial crisis: a new global regulatory order?, 8 *Journal of Business Law*, pp. 670–699.

[26] For a full examination of the origins, roles and work of the various international standard settings agencies, see Giovanoli (2000) *International Monetary Law Issues for the New Millennium*, Oxford: OUP, Chapter 1.

[27] http://www.imf.org/external/about/overview.htm.

[28] http://www.imf.org/external/NP/fsap/fssa.aspx.

[29] IMF Factsheet, The Financial Sector Assessment Program (FSAP), 15 March 2013, http://www.imf.org/external/np/exr/facts/fsap.htm.

system; identify obstacles to the competitiveness and efficiency of the sector; and examine its contribution to economic growth and development.

The 2007–08 financial crisis identified both the strengths and some of the weaknesses of the FSAP. The voluntary nature of the programme meant that countries that might have benefited from an in-depth examination of their financial sectors had not undergone an FSAP assessment and where the assessments were relatively recent, they did not always identify the nature of the risks: for example, liquidity risks and cross-border or cross-market linkages were underappreciated.[30] Where risk was identified, the warnings were not always clear. In September 2009, the IMF and World Bank revamped the programme, although key elements remain unchanged. The new features of the FSAP are:

- The introduction of a Risk Assessment Matrix, developed by the IMF, which is designed to make the analysis of stability assessments in the context of the FSAP more systematic, candid and transparent.

- New assessment methodologies developed to better identify linkages between the broader economy and the financial sector; and covering a greater variety of sources of risk.

- More frequent, targeted and focused assessments of either financial stability (IMF) or financial development (World Bank).

- An examination of cross-border capital flows and ownership of financial institutions, global liquidity conditions, and supervisory information-sharing and cooperation arrangements.

- More targeted, risk-based assessments of the standards that apply to the regulation and supervision of banks, securities markets and insurance.

Some of the new features will help with a more integrated approach to the IMF, including by giving greater scope for higher frequency, more focused assessments and by encouraging greater cross-country comparability.

Bank of International Settlements

The Bank for International Settlements (BIS), based in Basel, Switzerland, is an international organisation that fosters international monetary and financial cooperation and serves as a bank for central banks, for example the Bank of England, the US Federal Reserve etc. The BIS fulfils this mandate by acting as a forum to promote discussion and policy analysis among central banks and within the international financial community; a centre for economic and monetary research; a prime counterparty for central banks in their financial transactions; and as an agent or trustee in connection with international financial operations.

As its customers are central banks and international organisations, BIS does not accept deposits from, or provide financial services to, private individuals or corporate entities. One of the key objectives of BIS is to promote monetary and financial stability and BIS hosts a number of standard setting and coordination committees. Thus, the Committee on the Global Financial System (CGFS) monitors developments in global financial markets for central bank Governors.

---

[30] IMF Factsheet, The Financial Sector Assessment Program (FSAP), Lessons from the global Financial Crisis: a revamped FSAP, 15 March 2013, http://www.imf.org/external/np/exr/facts/fsap.htm.

The Committee's mandate is to identify and assess potential sources of stress in global financial markets, to further the understanding of the structural underpinnings of financial markets, and to promote improvements to the functioning and stability of these markets.[31]

Sector specific groupings of bank regulators and supervisors

Many of the sector specific groupings of regulators have been established as a result of inter-governmental initiatives set up through a number of groupings established at the level of finance ministers and central bank governors or their deputies, tasked with acting as fora for developing agreement on national and regulatory policies. However, of the so-called 'G' groupings only the Group of Seven (G-7) meets at the level of heads of government or state. The G-7 has been responsible for a number of international initiatives, including the G-22[32] and the G-20,[33] as well as the Financial Action Task Force established, in 1989, to counter money laundering.

Basel Committee on Banking Supervision

The Basel Committee on Banking Supervision, based in Basel, Switzerland, remains an important international policy-maker. The Basel Committee was established in 1974[34] following the Franklin Bank crisis, in the US, and the Bankhaus Herstatt, in Germany. The Franklin Bank was closed down in 1974 following significant foreign exchange losses, in May 1974. The Federal Reserve with a total of $1.7 billion being made available in support, including $60 million for its London operations, launched a support operation. The bank was eventually closed down in August 1974 after a managed rundown of its operations. Meanwhile Bankhaus Herstatt, in Germany, also suffered significant foreign exchange losses in June 1974 and was closed down, on 25 June 1974. At the time of its closure Bankhaus Herstatt had failed to make Deutschmark payments on outstanding foreign currency contracts and its correspondent bank in New York, Chase Manhattan, consequently refused to complete the $620 million in payment orders and cheques. This led to an immediate crisis in the international financial markets and payments systems. In response to the crisis the Governor of the Group of Ten (G-10) industrialised countries issued a communiqué of support confirming that necessary funds would be made available to settle outstanding obligations as necessary.

The governors of the G-10 also established a new committee on banking regulation and supervisory practices, which became known as the Basel Committee on Banking Supervision. The Basel Committee was originally concerned with attempts to establish a framework for supervisory cooperation between national regulators at the international level. The Committee does not have supranational powers and it formulates supervisory guidelines and standards. The crisis in the mid-1970s had highlighted that there was little ongoing contact,

---

[31] http://www.bis.org/cgfs/index.htm.

[32] The initiative to establish this group was taken by the US Treasury following the Asian Crisis, with a view to broadening the group of countries included in the effort to reinforce the international financial system. See: Giovanoli (2000) *International Monetary Law Issues for the New Millennium*, Oxford: OUP.

[33] The G-20 was established, in 1999, as the successor to the G-22, as a broader forum for informal discussion on monitoring risks in the international financial sector: Giovanoli (2000) *International Monetary Law Issues for the New Millennium*, Oxford: OUP, Chapter 1.

[34] Bank for International Settlements, History of the Basel Committee and its Membership, http://www.bis.org/bcbs/history.htm.

cooperation and coordination of supervisory work between national supervisory authorities. The Basel Committee therefore produced the First Concordat in December 1975, which established an outline cooperation and coordination framework based on principles of joint responsibility:

- Primary responsibility of the host authorities for liquidity.
- Primary responsibility with the parent authorities, i.e. where the institution is registered, for solvency, cooperation and exchange of information.

Following the collapse of Banco Ambrosiano Spa a revised concordat was produced, in May 1983, underlining the earlier principles and the consolidated supervision of banking groups was provided for and a new 'dual key' mutual review mechanism introduced. This mechanism required that home and host authorities should monitor each other's performance and take any corrective measures, if required.

The Committee produced an information Supplement in 1990 following a review of the 1983 Revised Concordat including a number of measures designed to improve the exchange of information between national authorities. In 1991, and following the collapse of BCCI, the Basel Committee produced a set of Minimum Principles in September 1992. The objective was to produce a set of minimum standards that all countries should observe and would replace the earlier principles. The four minimum principles were based on home country consolidated supervision, prior consent to the establishment of cross-border operations, effective information gathering and a revised host country corrective action plan. The latter was intended to support intervention by host authorities such as the Bank of England or the US Federal Reserve Bank of New York in closing down BCCI or other banking groups.

The Basel Committee Offshore Group produced a report in 1992 on minimum standards for the supervision of international banking groups and their cross-border establishments[35] and this was followed in October 1996 by a further report on the supervision of cross-border banking.[36] The 1996 report made further recommendations designed to improve the access of home supervisors to necessary information in order to undertake consolidated supervision. International supervision is generally carried out on the basis of the 1992 report as supplemented by the 1996 recommendations.

Following the Third World Debt Crisis in the 1980s the Basel Committee became concerned that international bank capital levels had dropped dangerously low and could threaten the stability of both domestic and international financial banking systems. The Committee agreed a formal set of recommendations for international capital standards under the 1988 Capital Accord and following the 2008 financial crisis the Committee has introduced Basel III, which is intended to provide a minimum guideline for global capital standards.[37]

Following the Asian financial crisis, in July 1997, the G-7 Heads of Government tasked the Basel Committee to produce a comprehensive and consolidated national and international model for combined bank supervision and regulation. A sub-committee established by Basel subsequently produced a draft set of Core Principles for Effective Banking Supervision in

---

[35] http://www.bis.org/publ/bcbsc314.htm.

[36] http://www.bis.org/publ/bcbs27.htm.

[37] Basel III: A global regulatory framework for more resilient banks and banking systems, December 2010 (revised June 2011), http://www.bis.org/publ/bcbs189.pdf.

1997, which were revised in 2006.[38] These Core Principles form the basic model for bank supervision and control across the world. The Core Basle Principles comprise 25 basic principles that need to be in place for a supervisory system to be effective, including licensing and authorisation rules, adequate risk management processes, internal control systems, maintenance of ethical and professional standards etc. The global financial crisis of 2008 resulted in a further review of the core principles and the Basel Committee has issued a further revision of the principles in 2011.[39] These principles (increased from 25 to 31) set out the strengthened powers of supervisors to ensure they can address issues of soundness and safety of banks. The IMF and the World Bank use the Core Principles as the main banking standards in conducting financial stability examinations.

Financial Stability Forum

Following the Asian financial crisis in the late 1990s it was accepted that closer cooperation and coordination was essential to stave off, or manage effectively, major financial crises. A new Financial Stability Forum was established, in 1999, following a report by the former chairman of the German Bundesbank, Hans Tietmeyer, to promote 'international financial stability through information exchange and international cooperation in financial supervision and surveillance'. The FSF was re-established as the Financial Stability Board, in April 2009,[40] with a remit to coordinate at the international level the work of national financial authorities and international standard setting bodies (SSBs) in order to develop and promote the implementation of effective regulatory, supervisory and other financial sector policies. In collaboration with the international financial institutions, the FSB will address vulnerabilities affecting financial systems in the interest of global financial stability.

The FSF (now the FSB) has made a significant contribution to the production of a Compendium of Standards in the financial area and consists of all the major papers produced by international financial institutions such as the IMF, the World Bank and the OECD as well as the work of specialist committees such as Basel, the International Organisation of Securities Commissions (IOSCO), the International Association of Insurance Supervisors (IAIS), the Committee on Payment and Settlement Systems (CPSS) and the Financial Action Task Force (FAFT). This now forms the basis of a global rulebook for financial oversight and control.

The FSB has been mandated by G-20 governments to investigate the oversight and regulation of shadow banking as part of their wider efforts to ensure the stability of the global financial sector. The FSB has issued a number of consultative documents[41] that set out a range of policy recommendations.[42] It is anticipated that the FSB will issue its final recommendations in September 2013. Shadow banking means lending by entities that are partly, or fully, outside the regulated banking system.[43] So lending by funds, specialist lenders and high net

---

[38] Core Principles for Effective Banking Supervision, October 2006, http://www.bis.org/publ/bcbs129.pdf.

[39] Basel Committee on Banking Supervision: Consultative Document Core Principles for Effective Supervision, (2011), http://www.bis.org/publ/bcbs213.pdf.

[40] Ref no: 14/2009, 2 April 2009, http://www.financialstabilityboard.org/press/pr_090402b.pdf.

[41] Strengthening Oversight and Regulation of Shadow Banking: An Integrated Overview of Policy Recommendations – Consultative Document, 18 November 2012, http://www.financialstabilityboard.org/publications/r_121118.htm.

[42] Shadow Banking: Strengthening Oversight and Regulation, Recommendations of the Financial Stability Board, October 2011, http://www.financialstabilityboard.org/publications/r_111027a.pdf.

[43] Global Shadow Banking Monitoring Report 2012, http://www.financialstabilityboard.org/publications/r_121118c.pdf.

worth individuals falls into this category, as do corporate bonds and securitisation. The FSB estimates that the shadow banking sector amounts to $67 trillion worldwide,[44] or a quarter of all banking activity.

The FSB has been investigating ways to control risks to financial stability that can arise from bank-like activities. As banking regulation is strengthened there are incentives for institutions to transfer their riskier business to the shadow banking sector and the FSB wants to ensure that evasion of tough new banking standards is no longer possible by these means. The main concerns relate to entities that borrow excessively in order to fund their lending and entities that borrow short-term funds, such as customer deposits, in order to lend long term. These risks were highlighted when the debt capital markets closed down in 2007–08.

The FSB has stated that shadow banking can bring benefits to the financial system and the real economy, particularly the provision of alternative financing to the banks and, by creating competition, the possibility of increased innovation, efficient credit allocation and cost reduction.

The FSB's recommendations reflect a series of clear principles: (i) casting the net wide when gathering data about shadow banking so as to ensure that regulators have full information about the areas where risks may arise, and (ii) focusing more narrowly for policy purposes on those shadow bank activities which either increase risks of mismatches of maturity, imperfect credit transfer and/or excessive leverage, and/or indicate a level of regulatory arbitrage which is undermining the benefits of financial regulation.[45] When setting policy, the FSB has put forward a set of overarching principles, which focus on defining the types of entity to be regulated by reference to their economic function rather than their legal form; and on the collection of information from and disclosure by market participants to enable the authorities to assess where the risks lie and when problems may arise.

The International Organisation of Securities Commission (IOSCO)

The International Organisation of Securities Commission (IOSCO) is an international organisation that brings together the regulators of the world's securities and futures markets. It, together with the Basel Committee on Banking Supervision and the International Association of Insurance Supervisors, make up the Joint Forum of International Financial regulators. Currently, IOSCO members regulate more than 90 per cent of the world's securities markets. The IOSCO is recognised as the international standard setter for securities markets. In 1998, the IOSCO adopted a comprehensive set of Objectives and Principles of Securities Regulation (IOSCO Principles)[46] which are today recognised as the international regulatory benchmarks for all securities markets and which establish the responsibilities of regulators and minimum standards for issuers, collective investment schemes, market intermediaries and secondary markets. The Organisation endorsed, in 2003, a comprehensive methodology (IOSCO Principles Assessment Methodology)[47] that enables an objective assessment of the level of implementation of the IOSCO Principles in the jurisdictions of its members and the development of practical action plans to correct identified deficiencies. In 2002, the IOSCO adopted a

---

[44] Global Shadow Banking Monitoring Report 2012, http://www.financialstabilityboard.org/publications/r_121118c.pd.

[45] Global Shadow Banking Monitoring Report 2012, http://www.financialstabilityboard.org/publications/r_121118c.pdf.

[46] http://www.iosco.org/library/pubdocs/pdf/IOSCOPD154.pdf.

[47] https://www.iosco.org/library/pubdocs/pdf/IOSCOPD155.pdf.

multilateral memorandum of understanding (IOSCO MOU) designed to facilitate cross-border enforcement and exchange of information among the international community of securities regulators and in 2005 the IOSCO endorsed the IOSCO MOU as the benchmark for international cooperation among securities regulators and set-out clear strategic objectives to rapidly expand the network of IOSCO MOU signatories by 2010. It approved as an operational priority the effective implementation of the IOSCO Principles and of the IOSCO MOU, which are considered as primary instruments to facilitate cross-border cooperation, reduce global systemic risk, protect investors and ensure fair and efficient securities markets. The IOSCO also adopted a comprehensive consultation policy designed to facilitate its continuous interaction with the international financial community and in particular with the industry.

The Financial Action Task Force (FATF)

The Financial Action Task Force (FATF) was established[48] to examine measures to combat money laundering and in 1990 the FATF issued a report containing a programme of 40 Recommendations[49] intended originally to provide a comprehensive blueprint for action against money laundering and covering, *inter alia*, the financial system and regulation, and international cooperation. The Recommendations have been extended to terrorist financing, which together with the eight special Recommendations on this area provide a comprehensive framework to combat it. The Recommendations were updated on a number of occasions and the current ones incorporate the 2004 revisions. The Recommendations are not a binding convention but FATF member countries[50] have made a commitment to counter money laundering and terrorist financing. A key role for the FATF task force is the need to monitor implementation of the FATF measures.

The work of these organisations, together with the work of regional organisations, for example the EU and national regulators, has resulted in a formidable raft of banking supervision and regulation. The challenge is to be able to predict, forestall and manage financial crises, which wreak damage on the national and global economies. Figure 2.1 attempts to show the range of bodies involved in banking and financial oversight.

An international financial system

The international financial regulatory system has not developed to the same extent or level as the advanced domestic financial systems and hence the former does not have the inbuilt protections found in most national systems. Most national domestic systems have their own systems of criminal law, commercial law, tax laws, bankruptcy laws, a financial regulator and a lender of last resort, as well as their own enforcement systems. Most countries also have rules that govern participation in the financial system, the nature and extent of disclosure that needs to be made to investors, the management and running of firms and an independent dispute

[48] The FATF was established by the G-7 Summit in Paris, in 1989, and has its secretariat at the OECD in Paris.

[49] FATF Standards, 40 FATF Recommendations, 2003 (incorporating the October 2004 revisions), http://www.fatf-gafi.org/dataoecd/7/40/34849567.PDF.

[50] FATF currently has 33 members: 31 countries and governments, 2 international organisations and more than 20 observers, http://www.fatf-gafi.org/document/52/0,3343,en_32250379_32236869_34027188_1_1_1_1,00.html.

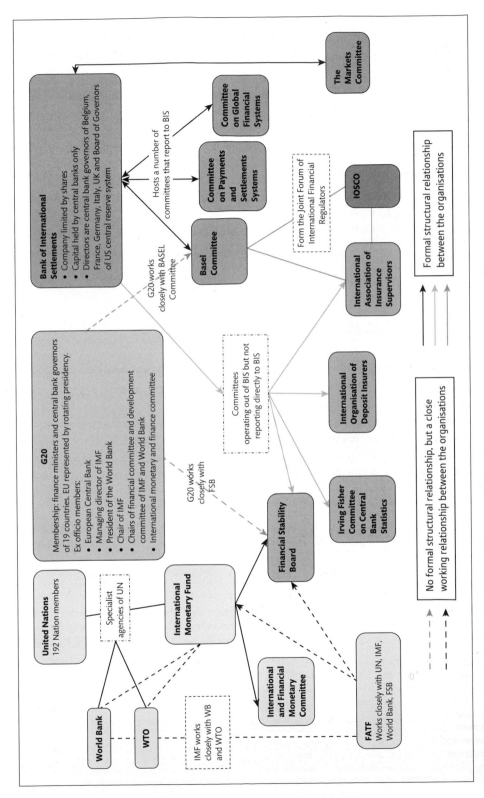

Figure 2.1 The main international standards setting agencies

resolution system.[51] Added to this is the fact that all independent jurisdictions will have their own economic and political policies and ambitions. These and other factors are sometimes impossible to reconcile at the international levels and the result is that international financial transactions and banking activity may take place in a legal vacuum. The rules that, therefore, regulate the international financial markets are largely both domestic and inward looking, and implemented mainly to protect the domestic markets and customers, or established by standard-setting agencies that have no power to legislate for the global market. Further the various international standard-setting agencies neither individually, nor collectively, have the mandate or the budget to fulfil the role or functions of a global financial regulator.[52]

While a number of international standards have been agreed between supranational standard-setting agencies that guide and encourage consistency in approach,[53] some political and economic groupings have attempted to meet the challenges posed by international financial regulation on a regional basis. Thus, the EU has implemented minimum uniform standards of prudential supervision regulating entry and exit of financial institutions to the market, but the monitoring of the financial services sectors and enforcement of the regulations has been left to the domestic regulators.[54] Domestic regulators and governments are left to deal with failing banks, crisis management and the costs of finding a resolution. Since Member States have primary control over fiscal policy[55] EU governance, currently, is confined to policy areas specified now in TFEU,[56] with the result that the European Central Bank, does

---

[51] The Financial Services and Markets Act 2000, amended by the Financial Services Act 2010, deals with the framework for the regulation of the financial services sector in the UK.

[52] At the simplest level international standard-setting bodies are merely national regulators who group together with their foreign counterparts to discuss standards, exchange knowledge and experience, and offer cooperation, but without offending against national sovereignty. Thus, basic rules are agreed and memoranda of understanding govern the level of cooperation, information sharing and levels of joint activity. Standard-setting bodies have been established in a number of fields including telecommunications (International Telecommunications Union; The European Telecommunications Standards Institute), airlines (The International Civil Aviation Organisation), shipping (International Maritime Organisation), international payments (Committee on Payments and Settlements Systems, BIS) and meteorology (The World Meteorology Organisation). However, the level of success achieved by these bodies tends to vary as internationally established standards tend to be vague and even the more specific standards can be evaded although the Basel Accord on capital adequacy is an example of agreed international standards that have been almost universally adopted by national supervisory authorities. The next level of cooperation is the coordination of international financial activity, for example through the work of the Bank of International Settlements (BIS) and the International Organisation of Securities Commission (IOSCO). In the areas of work represented by these bodies domestic governments and regulators have accepted that many transactions are of a truly international nature and regulators must, of necessity, cooperate and coordinate their efforts to achieve domestic stability. Therefore, domestic regulators are increasingly coordinating arrangements to improve cross-border supervision, e.g., colleges of supervisors have been established to monitor and regulate internationally active financial institutions.

[53] The work of the Basle Committee has significantly increased the level of coordination in respect of capital adequacy, while the IOSCO has become the key standard-setter for the securities industry.

[54] Banking Consolidation Directive, Directive 2000/12/EC came into force on 15 June 2000. The BCD was recast in June 2006 (2006/48/EC) OJ L 177, 30.6.2006.

[55] Watson (1997) *Aspects of European Monetary Integration,* Macmillan Press Ltd; McNamara (2006) Managing the Euro: The European Central Bank, Chapter 9 in *The Institutions of the European Union,* eds, Peterson and Shackleton, Oxford: Oxford University Press.

[56] As from 1 December 2009 TFEU replaced the EC Treaty. See: Consolidated versions of the Treaty on European Union and the Treaty on the Functioning of the European Union Charter of Fundamental Rights of the European Union, OJ C 83, 30.3.2010, http://www.consilium.europa.eu/showPage.aspx?id=1296&lang=en. See: Herbert Smith, The Lisbon Treaty – brief overview of the key changes, http://www.herbertsmith.com/NR/rdonlyres/0E23F501-9FA6-4BF1-B793-988FE6DAF533/13364/EUTheLisbonTreaty161109.html.

not have the fiscal resource or the mandate to act as lender of last resort or to bail out ailing banks in Member States.[57]

The effectiveness of this framework was severally challenged by the recent financial crisis. In order to stabilise the financial markets, reinforce consumer confidence, link national supervisors into a strong EU network, and better equip the markets and regulators for the management of future crisis, the EU took steps to establish a pan-European regulator with a formal mandate to coordinate EU action.[58] The focal point, however, for day-to-day supervision will remain at the national level, with national supervisors remaining responsible for the supervision of individual domestic entities.

The European institutions

Part of the EU's response to the 2007–09 financial crisis was to move towards the establishment of a pan-European regulator with a formal mandate to support the work of the national regulatory bodies and ensure stability of the EU financial markets, while the focal point for day-to-day supervision would, largely, remain at the national level, with national supervisors remaining responsible for the supervision of individual domestic entities. The EU response is borne out of a belief that coordinated EU action will stabilise the financial markets, reinforce consumer confidence, link national supervisors into a strong community network and better equip the markets and regulators for the management of crisis.

Background

The European Commission mandated a high-level group chaired by Jacques de Larosière (the de Larosière Group) to make recommendations on how to strengthen European supervisory arrangements with a view to protecting EU citizens and rebuilding trust in the financial system. In February 2009, the de Larosière Group recommended transforming the three existing EU high-level committees in the financial services sector with advisory powers (the Committee of European Banking Supervisors (CEBS), the Committee of European Insurance and Occupational Pensions Committee (CEIOPS) and the Committee of European Securities Regulators (CESR))[59] into European authorities with increased powers to coordinate the work of national supervisory authorities, arbitrate between national supervisors in supervisory colleges in cases of disagreement regarding cross-border financial institutions, take steps to harmonise national regulatory rules and move towards a common European Rulebooks, and supervise certain pan-European institutions regulated at the EU level, for example Credit

[57] European Central Bank, Eurosystem, Fiscal policies, http://www.ecb.int/mopo/eaec/fiscal/html/index.en.html; see also: Sciamarelli, Fiscal Policy in the Member States under EMU, EIPA, http://aei.pitt.edu/816/01/scop98_3_4.pdf.

[58] For a discussion on the power to establish new EU agencies see: Ottow and Van Meerten, The Proposals for the European Supervisory Authorities: The Right (Legal) Way Forward?, 2 December 2009, *Tijdschrift voor Financieel Recht*, Vol. 1, 2010.

[59] Often known as the 'Lamfalussy level 3 committees' because of the role they played in the EU framework for financial services legislation and established by Commission Decision 2009/78/EC (2) OJ L 25, 29.1.2009, p. 23, the Committee of European Insurance and Occupational Pensions Supervisors established by Commission Decision 2009/79/EC(3) OJ L 25, 29.1.2009, p. 28, and the Committee of European Securities Regulators established by Commission Decision 2009/77/EC.

Reference Agencies.[60] In its Communication entitled *Driving European Recovery*[61] the Commission welcomed and supported the recommendations of the de Larosière Group. At its meeting of 19 and 20 March 2009, the European Council agreed to the need to improve the regulation and supervision of EU financial institutions and to use the de Larosière recommendations as the basis for action.

Following these recommendations the European Commission developed a number of proposals to effectively reform the European financial systems so that the financial markets remained, in the future, stable and less risky for consumers and investors. These reforms were aimed at ensuring that 'all relevant actors and all types of financial instruments are subject to appropriate regulation and oversight . . . grounded in the values of responsibility, integrity, transparency and consistency'. At its meeting on 17 June 2010, the Council called on the European Parliament to adopt the legislative proposals to ensure that the ESRB and ESAs can commence operations from the start of 2011.[62]

The European system of financial supervisors

On 27 May 2009, the Commission adopted a Communication[63] describing plans to put into effect the recommendations of the de Larosière Report and introduced legislative proposals in September 2009.[64] On 22 September 2010, the European Parliament, following agreement by all Member States, voted through the new supervisory framework proposed by the Commission.[65] The ECOFIN Council confirmed this on 17 November 2010.[66] Three European Supervisory Authorities (ESAs) and a European Systemic Risk Board (ESRB)[67] were established as from January 2011[68] to replace the three former supervisory committees. The plans included replacing the 'Lamfalussy level 3 Committees'[69] with the European Supervisory Authorities, with the mandate to improve the functioning of the internal market, including ensuring a high, effective and consistent level of regulation and supervision taking account

[60] http://ec.europa.eu/internal_market/finances/committees/index_en.htm#review.

[61] Communication for the Spring European Council: Driving European Recovery, Brussels, 4 March 2009, COM (2009) 114 final, http://eur-lex.europa.eu/LexUriServ/LexUriServ.do?uri=COM:2009:0114:FIN:EN:PDF.

[62] European Council 17 June 2010 Conclusions, CoEur 9 Concl 2, http://www.consilium.europa.eu/uedocs/cms_data/docs/pressdata/en/ec/115346.pdf.

[63] Financial Services: Commission proposes stronger financial supervision in Europe, IP/09/836, Brussels, 27 May 2009.

[64] Proposal of the European Parliament and the Council on Community macro-prudential oversight of the financial system and establishing a European Systemic Risk Board, Brussels, 23 September 2009, COM(2009) 499 final, 2009/0140 (COD), http://ec.europa.eu/internal_market/finances/docs/committees/supervision/20090923/com2009_499_en.pdf.

[65] European Parliament, Parliament gives green light to new financial supervision architecture, http://www.europarl.europa.eu/en/headlines/content/20100910FCS81938/012/html/Parliament-gives-green-light-to-new-financial-supervision-architecture.

[66] Financial supervision: Council adopts legal texts establishing the European Systemic Risk Board and three new supervisory authorities, Brussels, 17 November 2010, 16452/10, Presse 303, http://www.consilium.europa.eu/uedocs/cms_data/docs/pressdata/en/ecofin/117747.pdf.

[67] Regulation (EU) No 1092/2010 of the European Parliament and of the Council of 24 November 2010 on European Union macro-prudential oversight of the financial system and establishing a European Systemic Risk Board, http://www.esma.europa.eu/system/files/Reg_1092_2010_ESRB.pdf.

[68] Financial Supervision Package – Frequently Asked Questions, Memo/10/434, Brussels, 22 September 2010, http://europa.eu/rapid/press-release_MEMO-10-434_en.htm?locale=en.

[69] Ferran and Alexander (2010) Can soft law bodies be effective? The special case of the European Systemic Risk Board, 35(6), *European Law Review*, 751–776.

of the varying interests of Member States: for example the Authorities will promote a consistent approach in the area of deposit guarantees to ensure a level playing field and equitable treatment of depositors.[70]

BANKING LAW IN PRACTICE

The European Supervisory Authorities (ESAs) form part of a European System of Financial Supervisors (ESFS)[71] and include three European Supervisory Authorities created by transforming the three European Supervisory Committees[72] into a European Banking Authority (EBA)[73] (based in London), the European Insurance and Occupational Pensions Authority (EIOPA) (based in Frankfurt), a European Securities and Markets Authority (ESMA) (based in Paris) to function as a network of national and Community supervisors, leaving the supervision of individual institutions to national regulators. The EBA, EIOPA and ESMA can impose temporary bans on very risky financial products and have direct supervisory responsibility for systematically important financial institutions, which means that national supervisors will act as agents of the EU authority. There is a greater role for the ESRB before and during crises that affect financial stability and the EBA is specifically empowered to evaluate the accessibility, availability and the cost of credit to households and small and medium-sized businesses.

The objectives of the European Supervisory Authorities[74] entail:

(i) Improving the functioning of the internal market, including in particular a high, effective and consistent level of regulation and supervision.

(ii) Protecting depositors, investors, policyholders and other beneficiaries.

(iii) Ensuring the integrity, efficiency and orderly functioning of financial markets.

(iv) Safeguarding the stability of the financial system.

(v) Strengthening international supervisory coordination.

(vi) Enhancing consumer protection.

---

[70] Proposal for a Regulation of the European Parliament and of the Council establishing a European Banking Authority (Brussels, 23 September 2009), COM (2009) 501 final, 2009/0142 (COD), Article (9), http://ec.europa.eu/internal_market/finances/docs/committees/supervision/20090923/com2009_499_en.pdf.

[71] Proposal for a Regulation of the European Parliament and of the Council establishing a European Banking Authority (Brussels, 23/09/2009), COM (2009) 501 final, 2009/0142 (COD), http://ec.europa.eu/internal_market/finances/docs/committees/supervision/20090923/com2009_499_en.pdf; see Regulation (EU) No 1092/2010 of the European Parliament and of the Council of 24 November 2010 on European Union macro-prudential oversight of the financial system and establishing a European Systemic Risk Board, http://www.esma.europa.eu/system/files/Reg_1092_2010_ESRB.pdf, Article 2.

[72] The Committee of European Banking Supervisors (CEBS), the Committee of European Insurance and Occupational Pensions Committee (CEIOPS) and the Committee of European Securities Regulators (CESR).

[73] The European Banking Authority was established by Regulation (EC) No. 1093/2010, L331/12, of the European Parliament and of the Council of 24 November 2010, http://eur-lex.europa.eu/LexUriServ/LexUriServ.do?uri=OJ:L:2010:331:0012:0047:EN:PDF.

[74] Regulation (EU) No 1093/2010 of the European Parliament and of the Council of 24 November 2010 establishing a European Supervisory Authority (European Banking Authority), Article 1, amending Decision No 716/2009/EC and repealing Commission Decision 2009/78/EC, http://eur-lex.europa.eu/LexUriServ/LexUriServ.do?uri=OJ:L:2010:331:0012:0047:EN:PDF.

The European Supervisory Authorities (ESAs) are Community bodies with legal personality[75] and play a significant part in the European System of Financial Supervisors (ESFS)[76] with the latter functioning as a network for national supervisors of the Member States. The ESAs are also members of the Joint Committee of European Supervisory Authorities, to cover cross-sectoral issues.[77] The main decision-making body of each ESA is its Board of Supervisors, consisting of the heads of the relevant national supervisors and the Chair of the respective Authority.[78] The ESAs are responsible for establishing a single EU rulebook[79] applicable to all financial institutions in the single market and differences, derogations or ambiguities in the adoption by Member States of EU legislation must be identified and removed, so there is a single set of core common standards applied in the financial services sector within the Member States.[80] The areas where the ESAs may develop such draft standards relate to issues of a highly technical nature where uniform conditions for the application of EU legislation are essential but do not extend to issues of policy. The development of the standards by the ESAs ensures that they benefit in full from the specialised expertise of national supervisors. The regulations establishing the European Supervisory Authorities (ESAs) and the European Systemic Risk Board (ESRB) include provisions for the Commission to review their structure and performance within the ESFS and the ESFS as a whole. This review was launched in April 2013.[81]

However, even the application of a single set of harmonised rules may lead to differences of opinion or interpretation, and without prejudice to the Commission's right to initiate infringement proceedings against a Member State, the ESAs have powers to investigate the non-compliance with EU financial legislation and make recommendations to enforce compliance, or in exceptional circumstances the ESAs may adopt a decision addressed to financial institutions in respect of EU law which is directly applicable to them (i.e. regulations). This is without prejudice to the Commission's powers to enforce its own decision.

[75] Regulation (EU) No 1092/2010 of the European Parliament and of the Council of 24 November 2010 on European Union macro-prudential oversight of the financial system and establishing a European Systemic Risk Board, Article 5, http://www.esma.europa.eu/system/files/Reg_1092_2010_ESRB.pdf.

[76] Regulation (EU) No 1092/2010 of the European Parliament and of the Council of 24 November 2010 on European Union macro-prudential oversight of the financial system and establishing a European Systemic Risk Board, Article 2, http://www.esma.europa.eu/system/files/Reg_1092_2010_ESRB.pdf.

[77] Regulation (EU) No 1092/2010 of the European Parliament and of the Council of 24 November 2010 on European Union macro-prudential oversight of the financial system and establishing a European Systemic Risk Board, Article 2, http://www.esma.europa.eu/system/files/Reg_1092_2010_ESRB.pdf.

[78] Regulation (EU) No 1092/2010 of the European Parliament and of the Council of 24 November 2010 on European Union macro-prudential oversight of the financial system and establishing a European Systemic Risk Board, Article 6, http://www.esma.europa.eu/system/files/Reg_1092_2010_ESRB.pdf.

[79] In order to strengthen the reforms of the European supervisory architecture, a single European rulebook is needed which will provide a common legal basis for supervisory action in the EU to ensure strengthened stability, equal treatment, lower compliance costs for companies as well as removing opportunities for regulatory arbitrage. Such efforts do not require full harmonisation of all aspects of EU legislation, but rather focus on one harmonised core set of key standards, http://europa.eu/rapid/press-release_MEMO-10-434_en.htm?locale=en.

[80] Regulation (EU) No 1092/2010 of the European Parliament and of the Council of 24 November 2010 on European Union macro-prudential oversight of the financial system and establishing a European Systemic Risk Board, Article 2(3), http://www.esma.europa.eu/system/files/Reg_1092_2010_ESRB.pdf.

[81] Financial Supervision, http://ec.europa.eu/internal_market/finances/committees/.

To ensure that the EU is able to respond efficiently and rapidly to possible events that threaten to jeopardise the integrity of the EU financial markets, the ESAs are required to fulfil an active coordination role between national supervisory authorities.[82] Where the financial turmoil is so extensive that national supervisors lack the resources and tools to individually respond to an emerging cross-border crisis the ESAs should, in such exceptional circumstances, have the power to require national supervisors to jointly take specific action. The determination of what constitutes a cross-border emergency situation involves a degree of appreciation of economic, political and financial factors and should therefore be left to the European Commission.[83]

To ensure that the relevant national supervisory authorities take due account of the interests of other Member States, including within colleges of supervisors, where a domestic supervisory authority disagrees on the procedure or content of an action or inaction undertaken or proposed by another domestic supervisory authority where the relevant legislation requires cooperation, coordination or joint decision making, the ESA, at the request of the domestic supervisory authority concerned, may assist in reaching a common approach.[84] This may involve the ESA in undertaking a mediation process[85] to resolve a disagreement between national supervisors, but if conciliation is unsuccessful and domestic supervisors fail to reach an agreement, the ESAs may, through a decision, settle the matter.[86] The dispute settlement mechanism should only address material issues, for example cases where action or inaction by a supervisory authority has a serious detrimental impact on the ability of a supervisory authority to protect the interest of depositors, policyholders, investors, or persons to whom services are provided in one or several other Member States, or on the financial stability of these Member States.

The ESAs are required to play an active role in building a common European supervisory culture and ensuring uniform procedures and consistent supervisory practices throughout the Community. In addition to the power to settle disagreements between national supervisory authorities, the common supervisory culture should help build trust and cooperation, and may increasingly create opportunities for supervisors to delegate certain tasks and responsibilities to one another.[87] The ESAs will facilitate this by identifying tasks that may be delegated or responsibilities which can be jointly exercised, as well as by promoting best practices. In

---

[82] Regulation (EU) No 1092/2010 of the European Parliament and of the Council of 24 November 2010 on European Union macro-prudential oversight of the financial system and establishing a European Systemic Risk Board, Article 18, http://www.esma.europa.eu/system/files/Reg_1092_2010_ESRB.pdf.

[83] Regulation (EU) No 1092/2010 of the European Parliament and of the Council of 24 November 2010 on European Union macro-prudential oversight of the financial system and establishing a European Systemic Risk Board, Article 18 (2), http://www.esma.europa.eu/system/files/Reg_1092_2010_ESRB.pdf.

[84] Regulation (EU) No 1092/2010 of the European Parliament and of the Council of 24 November 2010 on European Union macro-prudential oversight of the financial system and establishing a European Systemic Risk Board, Article 19, http://www.esma.europa.eu/system/files/Reg_1092_2010_ESRB.pdf.

[85] Regulation (EU) No 1092/2010 of the European Parliament and of the Council of 24 November 2010 on European Union macro-prudential oversight of the financial system and establishing a European Systemic Risk Board, Article 19, http://www.esma.europa.eu/system/files/Reg_1092_2010_ESRB.pdf.

[86] Regulation (EU) No 1092/2010 of the European Parliament and of the Council of 24 November 2010 on European Union macro-prudential oversight of the financial system and establishing a European Systemic Risk Board, Article 19(4), http://www.esma.europa.eu/system/files/Reg_1092_2010_ESRB.pdf.

[87] Regulation (EU) No 1092/2010 of the European Parliament and of the Council of 24 November 2010 on European Union macro-prudential oversight of the financial system and establishing a European Systemic Risk Board, Article 11 and 12, http://www.esma.europa.eu/system/files/Reg_1092_2010_ESRB.pdf.

this respect, the ESAs will encourage and facilitate the set-up of joint supervisory teams and the ESAs will periodically conduct peer review analysis of national supervisory authorities.[88] Although the ESRB will be responsible for macro-prudential analysis of the EU financial sector, the ESAs will continue the work of the existing European supervisory committees as the focus of their analysis is different, i.e. micro-prudential analysis provides a bottom-up analysis focusing on individual institutions, rather than macro-prudential analysis which is top-down and concentrates on sectoral wide issues, and their analysis may have a valuable input into the work carried-out by the ESRB. Therefore, the ESAs and ESRB will cooperate in the discharge of their functions.[89]

European Systemic Risk Board

In addition to the establishment of the European Supervisory Authority the de Larosière Group recommended establishing a European Systemic Risk Board (ESRB)[90] responsible for macro-prudential oversight of the financial system within the EU[91] in order to prevent or mitigate systemic risks, to avoid episodes of widespread financial distress, to contribute to a smooth functioning of the Internal Market and ensure a sustainable contribution of the financial sector to economic growth. Only with arrangements in place that properly recognise the interdependence between micro- and macro-prudential risks can all stakeholders, e.g. financial institutions, investors and consumers, have sufficient confidence to engage in cross-border financial activities.

In the past, the focus of prudential supervision[92] has been exclusively at the micro-level, with supervisors assessing the balance sheets of individual financial institutions without due consideration for interactions between institutions and between institutions and the broader financial system. Providing this broader perspective is the responsibility of macro-prudential supervisors who will assess potential financial-stability risks arising from developments that can impact on a sectoral level or at the level of the financial system as a whole. The interconnectedness of the financial institutions and markets implies that the monitoring and assessment of potential systemic risks should be based on a broad set of relevant macro-economic and micro-financial data and indicators. The ESRB will therefore have access to all the information necessary to perform its duties while preserving the confidentiality of the

---

[88] Regulation (EU) No 1092/2010 of the European Parliament and of the Council of 24 November 2010 on European Union macro-prudential oversight of the financial system and establishing a European Systemic Risk Board, Article 30, http://www.esma.europa.eu/system/files/Reg_1092_2010_ESRB.pdf.

[89] Regulation (EU) No 1092/2010 of the European Parliament and of the Council of 24 November 2010 on European Union macro-prudential oversight of the financial system and establishing a European Systemic Risk Board, Article 36, http://www.esma.europa.eu/system/files/Reg_1092_2010_ESRB.pdf.

[90] Proposal for a Regulation of the European Parliament and of the Council on Community macro-prudential oversight of the financial system and establishing a European Systemic Risk Board (Brussels, 23.9.2009), COM (2009) 500 final 2009/0141 (AVC) established under Regulation No 1092/2010 of the European Parliament and of the Council on 24 November 2010 on European Union macro-prudential oversight of the financial system and establishing a European Systemic Risk Board, Article 1, http://www.esma.europa.eu/system/files/ Reg_1092_2010_ESRB.pdf.

[91] Regulation No 1092/2010 of the European Parliament and of the Council on 24 November 2010 on European Union macro-prudential oversight of the financial system and establishing a European Systemic Risk Board, Article 3(1), http://www.esma.europa.eu/system/files/Reg_1092_2010_ESRB.pdf.

[92] Focused on controlling the solvency and liquidity of participating firms.

data.[93] The ESRB is able to rely on the broad set of data already collected through the euro system by the European Central Bank (ECB) on Monetary and Financial Institutions. Given its expertise on macro-prudential issues, the European Central Bank (ECB) is mandated to make a significant contribution by the provision of analytical, statistical, administrative and logistical support to the ESRB.[94]

Additionally, to ensure the necessary consistency between the micro-supervisors and the ESRB, the ESRB can request that ESAs provide information available to them. The ESRB may also request data directly from national supervisory authorities, national central banks (NCBs) or other authorities of Member States, as required.[95] The ESRB will monitor and assess potential threats to financial stability that arise from macroeconomic developments and from developments within the financial system as a whole. The ESRB will provide early warning of systemic risks and issue recommendations to deal with the risks.

Thus, the ESRB is an essential building block for an integrated EU supervisory structure necessary to promote timely and consistent policy responses among the Member States thus preventing diverging approaches and so improve the functioning of the Internal Market. The ESRB[96] is an entirely new European body with no precedent and will be responsible for macro-prudential oversight with the following objectives. It will:

- develop a European macro-prudential perspective to address the problem of fragmented individual risk analysis at national level;
- enhance the effectiveness of early warning mechanisms by improving the interaction between micro-and macro-prudential analyses. The soundness of individual firms was too often supervised in isolation with little focus on the degree of interdependence within the financial system;
- allow for risk assessments to be translated, into action.[97]

The ESRB does not have binding powers to impose measures on Member States or on national authorities. It has been conceived as a 'reputational' body and should influence the actions of policy-makers and supervisors by means of its moral authority. To this end, it will not only provide high-quality assessment of the macro-prudential situation but it may also issue risk warnings and recommendations which identify the potential unbalances in the financial system which are likely to increase systemic risks and the appropriate remedial actions. Warnings and recommendations of the ESRB may address any aspect of the financial

---

[93] Regulation No 1092/2010 of the European Parliament and of the Council on 24 November 2010 on European Union macro-prudential oversight of the financial system and establishing a European Systemic Risk Board, Article 8, http://www.esma.europa.eu/system/files/Reg_1092_2010_ESRB.pdf.

[94] Council Regulation No 1096/2010 of 17 November 2010 Conferring Specific Tasks on the European Central Bank Concerning the functioning of the European Systemic Risk Board, Article 2, http://www.esrb.europa.eu/shared/pdf/ESRB-ECB-en.pdf?3e7579eb5feaf569bb09508a56634ea3.

[95] Council Regulation No 1096/2010 of 17 November 2010 Conferring Specific Tasks on the European Central Bank Concerning the functioning of the European Systemic Risk Board, Article 5, http://www.esrb.europa.eu/shared/pdf/ESRB-ECB-en.pdf?3e7579eb5feaf569bb09508a56634ea3.

[96] Regulation No 1092/2010 of the European Parliament and of the Council on 24 November 2010 on European Union macro-prudential oversight of the financial system and establishing a European Systemic Risk Board, Article 3, http://www.esma.europa.eu/system/files/Reg_1092_2010_ESRB.pdf.

[97] Regulation No 1092/2010 of the European Parliament and of the Council on 24 November 2010 on European Union macro-prudential oversight of the financial system and establishing a European Systemic Risk Board, Article 3, http://www.esma.europa.eu/system/files/Reg_1092_2010_ESRB.pdf.

system that may generate a systemic risk and these warnings will act as an early warning system to avoid the build-up of wider problems and, possibly, eventually a future crisis. If necessary, the ESRB may also recommend specific actions to address any identified risks. It will also be expected to cooperate with the relevant international financial institutions, for example the IMF, FSB and third countries bodies, on issues related to macro-prudential oversight.

The ESRB will decide, on an individual basis, whether the warnings and recommendations should be made public. While the publication of a recommendation may increase the pressure for prompt corrective actions, such publication could also trigger panic in the financial markets and therefore there is no blanket rule relating to the publication of such warnings and recommendations. The recipient of the warnings and recommendations may be the Community as a whole, one or more Member States, one or more European Supervisory Authorities, and one or more national supervisory authorities. All warnings and recommendations must be transmitted to the Council, while those related to supervisory issues should also be transmitted to the relevant ESA. The transmission to the Council and to the ESAs of warnings and recommendations is not intended as a way to water down their content, but is intended to increase the moral pressure on the addressee to act or explain themselves, and offer the Council to comment on the issue.

The Secretariat of the ESRB is supported by the European Central Bank (ECB) and, to this effect, the ECB should provide the ESRB with sufficient human and financial resources. The ECB will provide analytical, statistical, administrative and logistical support to the ESRB. A task of the ESRB is to cover all aspects and areas of financial stability and the ECB should involve national central banks and supervisors to draw on their specific expertise.[98]

Effective regulation of cross-border banking institutions

A long-standing problem has been the effective regulation of cross-border banking institutions. Among, the many failures in the regulation of BCCI was the failure to regulate the bank's global structure and activities, with a failure on the part of national supervisors to coordinate the regulation and business activities of BCCI, and to share information.[99] While the post-BCCI Directive[100] and the Minimum Principles of Banking Supervision produced by the Basel Committee in 1992 and supplemented by the 1996 Supervision of Cross-Border Banking recommendations[101] were intended to redress the failure in cross-border supervision, the 2007–09 banking crisis has further highlighted the significant shortfalls in the systems of cross-border regulation. The de Larosière Group recommended that by the end of 2009, the EU should expand the restricted use of supervisory colleges to all major cross-border firms in the EU.

---

[98] Regulation No 1092/2010 of the European Parliament and of the Council on 24 November 2010 on European Union macro-prudential oversight of the financial system and establishing a European Systemic Risk Board, Article 15, http://www.esma.europa.eu/system/files/Reg_1092_2010_ESRB.pdf.

[99] See the report of the Bingham Inquiry into the supervision of the Bank of Credit and Commerce International, HC Paper (1992–3), No 198.

[100] Prudential Supervision Directive, Council Directive 95/26/EC of 29 June 1995.

[101] The 1992 principles were based on home country consolidated supervision, prior consent to the establishment of any cross-border operations, effective information gathering and a revised host country corrective action clause. The 1996 revisions were intended to improve access of information to home regulators and to ensure that all banking operations were the subject of effective home and host supervision.

The European Commission proposal establishing a European Banking Authority recognised that colleges of supervisors were central to the EU supervisory system and play an important role in ensuring a balanced flow of information between home and host authorities.[102] As such the ESAs contribute to promoting the efficient and consistent functioning of colleges of supervisors and monitor the coherence of the implementation of Community legislation across colleges. Against this background, the ESAs may participate as observers in colleges of supervisors and receive all relevant information shared between the members of the college. Disputes between home and host supervisors will be subject to the authority of the EU institutions and the latter authorities will be tasked with ensuring consistency of prudential supervision among institutions registered in different EU states. The proposed revisions to the Capital Adequacy Requirements make colleges obligatory and the set of ten common principles proposed by the Committee of European Banking Supervisors are in line with that Directive.[103] The common principles include that within the banking sector there may be 'General Colleges'[104] consisting of all supervisors participating in general multilateral meetings for sharing information on group wide issues, as well as 'Core Colleges'[105] which consist of a limited number of relevant authorities participating in restricted multilateral meetings ensuring close cooperation in supervisory activities.

The College of Supervisors provides an effective and flexible permanent forum for cooperation and coordination among authorities responsible for and involved in the supervision of the group where appropriate colleges of supervisors may cooperate with other relevant authorities.[106] Those involved as supervisors will contribute their information and assessments of supervised firms to the overall assessment of risks[107] and financial soundness of the banking group. The exchange of information is bound by the rules of confidentiality. Moreover, the ESA, in collaboration with the supervisors operating in colleges of supervisors, define and collect as appropriate relevant information from supervisory authorities, to facilitate the work of colleges of supervisors. It will establish and manage a central system to make such information accessible to the supervisory authorities in colleges of supervisors. Further, the ESRB is empowered to develop a common set of indicators to permit uniform ratings of the risk of cross-border financial institutions, making risk levels more easily understandable.

There is a binding mediation mechanism in the event of conflicts between national supervisors. If regulatory supervision does ultimately move from existing national regulators to the EBA, ESMA and EIOPA, as proposed, there is likely to be a great deal of uncertainty surrounding the attitudes of the new 'super-regulators'. As a result, financial institutions will be concerned that the 'know-how' existing regulators have built up about various different aspects of the financial services industry they regulate may be lost.

---

[102] Regulation (EC) No. 1093/2010, L331/12, of the European Parliament and of the Council of 24 November 2010 establishing a European Supervisory Authority (European Banking Authority), amending Decision No 716/2009/EC and repealing Commission Decision 2009/78/EC, Article 21, http://eur-lex.europa.eu/LexUriServ/LexUriServ.do?uri=OJ:L:2010:331:0012:0047:EN:PDF.

[103] Colleges of Supervisors – 10 Common Principles, CEIOPS-SEC-54/08 CEBS 2008 124 IWCFC 08 32, 27 January 2009.

[104] Principle 1.

[105] Principle 1.

[106] Principle 2.

[107] Principle 4.

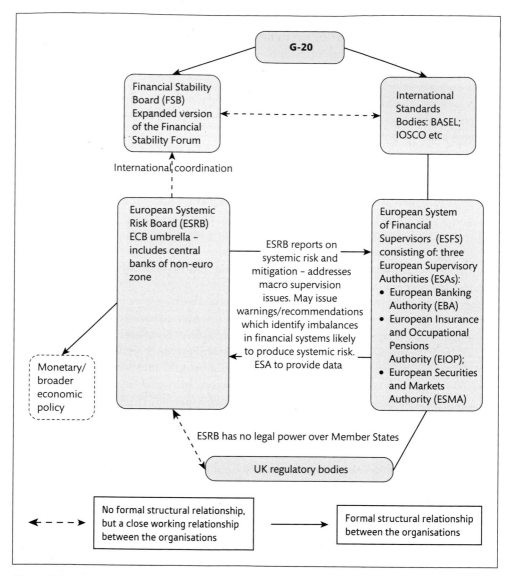

Figure 2.2 Eu Pan-European Supervisory Structure

Weaknesses of the proposed pan-European regulator

The massive failures in the regulation of global financial services has led to calls for more and better oversight of financial services, but in the heat of the debate more should not be mistaken for better. While there has clearly been a lack of regulation in certain areas of financial services activity, the failures and the crisis has been exacerbated by lax supervision and failings in enforcement. Within the EU the failures in the national financial services sectors has seen a fundamental tenet of EU banking regulation, based on the 'single passport' regime, with the home regulatory authority carrying supervisory responsibility come under severe strain. Striking the right balance between home and host country responsibility for supervision has always been both challenging and crucial, and the EU has responded to calls for reinforced international banking regulation by unveiling plans for a pan-European regulator. However, the proposed new European regulatory system has certain inbuilt challenges,[108] which may also be its downfall:

(i) The de Larosière Group's proposals appear to adopt a narrow interpretation of macro-prudential supervision and the Commission proposals appear to give the ESRB rather general and limited high-level powers. The main responsibility of the ESRB is to assess the stability of the EU financial system and monitor trends in the financial services sectors of Member States. The Commission has also limited the powers of the ESRB to giving warnings and issuing recommendations for remedial action, with the ESRB having no legally binding powers. The Commission specifically states that warnings and recommendations issued by the ESRB could be of a general nature or could concern individual Member States. These warnings and/or recommendations will be channelled through the Ecofin Council and/or the new European Supervisory Authorities, rather than to national regulatory bodies.[109] This, itself, may result in delays and inconsistency in implementation. It is, therefore, unlikely that warnings and recommendations are likely to be an ineffective tool to ensure compliance. Indeed, with regard to the effectiveness of warnings, Mervyn King, the then Governor of the Bank of England expressed the view that:

> The Bank finds itself in a position rather like that of a church whose congregation attends weddings and burials but ignores the sermons in between . . . Warnings are unlikely to be effective when people are being asked to change behaviour which seems to them highly profitable. So it is not entirely clear how the Bank will be able to discharge its new statutory responsibility if we can do no more than issue sermons or organise burials.[110]

The role of the ESRB therefore appears to be that of analysing macroeconomic conditions and their implications for systemic risk and issuing warnings. Instead, a more effective role for the ESRB would be for it to be given responsibility for ensuring that EU financial institutions build counter-cyclical capital buffers so that in stable conditions they establish reserves of capital to support them in a crisis or recession.[111] The European Parliament has called for stronger supervisory powers be conferred on the supervisory institutions with the ESRB being given stress testing powers.[112]

---

[108] House of Lords, European Union Committee, 14th Report of Session 2008–09, The future of EU financial regulation and supervision, 2009 Vol. I, analysed the proposals for a new EU structure with several proposals on the European Commission proposals. The European Parliament – Economic and monetary Affairs Committee, 2010, has also proposed several amendments to the Commission proposals.

[109] In its press release on 7 July 2010 the European Parliament recommended that the ESRB should have the power to issue decisions directly to a financial institution where a national supervisor has been unable to change practices considered unsound. They should also have powers to settle disputes between national supervisors. MEPs back root-and-branch reform of financial supervision, Economic and Monetary Affairs, 7 July 2010, http://www.europarl.europa.eu/news/expert/infopress_page/042-77910-186-07-28-907-20100706IPR77909-05-07-2010-2010-false/default_en.htm.

[110] King, Speech at Lord Mayors Banquet, The Guardian, 18 June 2009, http://www.guardian.co.uk/business/2009/jun/18/bank-of-england-mervyn-king.

[111] Whelan, Directorate General for Internal Policies Policy Department A: Economic and Scientific Policies Economic and Monetary Affairs, The ECB Role in Financial Supervision, 2009, http://www.europarl.europa.eu/document/activities/cont/200909/20090922ATT61027/20090922ATT61027EN.pdf.

[112] More powerful EU financial supervisory bodies and less national interest, demand MEPs, http://www.europarl.europa.eu/sides/getDoc.do?pubRef=-//EP//NONSGML+IM-PRESS+20100223IPR69355+0+DOC+PDF+V0//EN&language=ENhttp.

(ii) The ECB should play a key role in macro-prudential supervision whereas under the current proposals its role is closely tied to the work of the ESRB.[113] The ECB should be given an independent function so it can resolve differences of opinion between Member States and regulatory organisations. Thus, the ECB should have powers to enforce compliance if national regulators fail to conform to warnings and regulations. The ECB should be an independent body, with its own budget, in-charge of micro-prudential supervision. Instead, the European Commission proposes a simple advisory technical committee to support the ESRB, including preparing detailed technical analysis of financial stability issues. Its independence is also at risk with a Commission representative having a seat on the ESRB Council with voting powers. No doubt the role of the ECB will change[114] but its independence should be reinforced so it can work efficiently with European central banks.

(iii) The de Larosière Report fails to identify problems that are systemic by nature and the Commission therefore assigns some of these areas for micro-level supervision. There are clear areas of the operational aspects of payments systems for which responsibility for orderly oversight could be transferred to a pan-European agency, for example the clearing and processing of payments could be the responsibility of the ECB, rather than the central banks of Member States.[115] This may potentially enable the ECB to develop the role of lender of last resort.

(iv) The de Larosière Report does not comment on the nature of the existing powers of the national regulators or the lines of responsibility. The Turner Report[116] highlighted what might be considered a weakness of the current UK system of regulation, with the Bank of England focused on monetary policy analysis and the Financial Services Authority focused too much on the supervision of individual institutions. Vital activity of macro-prudential analysis and supervision 'fell between two stools'. In cases of systemic failure the Treasury is also closely involved and this led to added confusion regarding the lines of responsibility in a financial crisis.[117] Within the UK the lines of responsibility therefore

---

[113] Proposal for a Council Decision entrusting the European Central Bank with specific tasks concerning the functioning of the European Systemic Risk Board (Brussels, 23/09/2009) COM (2009) 500 final, 2009/0141 (AVC), Article 2. In its press release on 7 July 2010 the European Parliament recommended that ESRB credibility would be enhanced if it were chaired by the President of the ECB and board membership extended to include academics. MEPs back root-and-branch reform of financial supervision, Economic and Monetary Affairs, 7 July 2010, http://www.europarl.europa.eu/news/expert/infopress_page/042-77910-186-07-28-907-20100706IPR77909-05-07-2010-2010-false/default_en.htm.

[114] Eijfiger, Directorate General For Internal Policies Policy Department A: Economic and Scientific Policies: Economic and Monetary Affairs Adjustments to the Accountability and Transparency of the European Central Bank, 2009, http://www.europarl.europa.eu/document/activities/cont/200909/20090923ATT61086/20090923ATT61086EN.pdf.

[115] The ECB published its opinion on three proposals for regulations of the European Parliament and of the Council establishing a European Banking Authority, a European Insurance and Occupational Pensions Authority and a European Securities and Markets Authority, 8 January 2010, (CON/2010/5), (2010/C 13/01), http://www.ecb.de/ecb/legal/pdf/c_01320100120en00010009.pdf.

[116] FSA, The Turner Report: A response to the Global Financial Crisis, March 2009, http://www.fsa.gov.uk/pubs/other/turner_review.pdf.

[117] The Tripartite Review: A review of the UK's tripartite system of financial regulation in relation to financial stability, March 2009; see also: Osborne welcomes Sassoon report into tripartite financial regulation, 9 March 2009, http://www.conservatives.com/News/News_stories/2009/03/Osborne_welcomes_Sassoon_report_into_tripartite_financial_regulation.aspx; The Future of Banking Commission, 13 June 2010, http://commission.bnbb.org/banking/sites/all/themes/whichfobtheme/pdf/commission_report.pdf, Elliott, George Osborne unveils sweeping City reforms, The Guardian, 16 June 2010, http://www.guardian.co.uk/business/2010/jun/16/george-osborne-city-fsa-banking.

need to be clarified and strengthened so that in a future crisis the relevant authorities are able to respond with some rapidly.[118] Under the Commission proposals similar clarity will be required with regard to the powers conferred on the ESRB and the ESAs.

(v) At the micro-prudential level the ESAs will have the power to issue binding interpretations of EU legislation and cross-border activity will be regulated at this level. However, the definition of banks to be regulated at this level becomes crucial, the level of information provided by national regulators needs to be agreed and the relationship between national regulators clarified with the split in the responsibilities clearly defined. The proposal to establish 'colleges of supervisors' provides only a partial solution to the supervision of firms operating across national boundaries, because it endorses the prominent role of the home-country regulator and fails to address the conflicts of interest between the home-country and host-country regulators. While host countries could seek to protect their interests by imposing capital controls this would clearly damage the levels of financial integration achieved within the EU Member States and would be contrary to EU law.

(vi) The level of EU supervisory powers granted to any central EU bodies will remain a problem while national governments remain the fiscal authorities[119] and the responsibility for bailing out failing financial institutions remains a national level concern. Professor Goodhart,[120] appearing before the House of Lords, European Union Committee, expressed the view that if crisis management were to be transferred to a European agency then a 'federal source of money' would be required. Lord Turner[121] also expressed the view that national governments would be unwilling to cede national micro-prudential supervisory powers to a EU body while having the responsibility for bailing out financial banks. The pan-European regulatory structure provides that the work and objectives of the new committees will not impinge on the fiscal responsibilities of the Member States.[122]

Those countries likely to oppose the pan-European model must recognise that the alternative is likely to require a rebalance in the regulatory powers between the host and home regulator control, particularly with countries like China and India who only recently allowed foreign direct investment and whose economies were relatively unscathed by the financial collapse. Yet, giving more powers to the host countries has its own limitations and host regulators are unlikely to have the resources or the knowledge to dissect complex group structures and monitor and challenge the activities of such groups. What, therefore, is needed is an effective pan-European regulator, or even a global regulator, that can monitor home-country and host-country relations, with enforcement powers.

---

[118] This view is supported by the House of Lords, European Union Committee, 14th Report of Session 2008–09, The future of EU financial regulation and supervision, 2009.

[119] Whelan, Directorate General for Internal Policies Policy Department A: Economic and Scientific Policies Economic and Monetary Affairs, The ECB Role in Financial Supervision, 2009, http://www.europarl.europa.eu/document/activities/cont/200909/20090922ATT61027/20090922ATT61027EN.pdf.

[120] House of Lords, European Union Committee, 14th Report of Session 2008–09, The future of EU financial regulation and supervision, 2009.

[121] FSA, The Turner Report: A response to the Global Financial Crisis, March 2009, http://www.fsa.gov.uk/pubs/other/turner_review.pdf.

[122] Article 6.2.11, Proposal for a Regulation of the European Parliament and of the Council establishing a European Banking Authority, Brussels, 23.9.2009 COM (2009) 501 final, 2009/0142 (COD). This in itself has been seen as a limitation of the proposals; House of Lords, European Union Committee, 14th Report of Session 2008–09, The future of EU financial regulation and supervision, 2009.

Some national barriers to the establishment of a global regulator

While national firms need an effective national regulator the regulation of global firms offering global products and services needs an equally effective global regulator who understands the complexity of the global market, its customer base, stresses and risks. Domestic regulators are generally accountable to a minister, government department or parliament. This is a means of ensuring that the regulator serves the public interest and its decisions are subject to scrutiny. Within the UK, the FSMA 2000 imposes on the Financial Conduct Authority (FCA) a framework, in the form of statutory objectives[123] through which the FCA is required to discharge its public duties.[124] An international regulator, at present, cannot be appointed through or integrated into a political structure or be made accountable to an elected parliament, although the pan-European regulator will be accountable to both the national supervisors forming the European Supervisory Authority and ESRB. These regulatory bodies also report to the European Commission so that failings can, if necessary, be rectified by EU legislation, and be scrutinised by the domestic and European courts and ministers.[125]

A difficult issue to be resolved before the development of a global regulator is whether national governments, and their citizens, will subscribe to the idea and reality of surrendering legislative sovereignty[126] and enforcement powers in the financial services sector to, what might be perceived as, a remote global group.[127] The answer must lie in the extent of the benefits gained, the economies of scale, the effectiveness in containing financial instability and maintaining customer confidence, and the level of accountability of the group. A right of participation and representation will enable ownership of policy but for many countries any such development is likely to be incremental and over a period of time. Within the global markets, a crisis like that recently experienced may in fact hasten the markets and governments towards a global regulator. Any form of a regional or global regulator will involve, to some extent, a transfer of sovereignty. EU Member States have long been accustomed to the idea that membership of the EU entails a transfer of and limitation to sovereignty in certain fields.[128] In particular the provisions on EMU imply a significant constraint on national competences, particularly in the field of monetary policy, for those countries that have adopted the euro.[129] While the concept, therefore, of a regional regulator remains remote elsewhere,

---

[123] Section 2(2) FSMA 2000.

[124] Indeed, Sir Howard Davies of the FSA characterised these objectives as a 'very effective discipline on our internal processes', which makes some effort to identify, unlike previous legislation, the ends to which the FSA ought to apply its powers. Additionally, the FSA was part of a tripartite system of regulation with the Treasury and the Bank of England exercising distinct functions, which require coordination, cooperation and oversight by the other parties to the arrangement, including the Treasury (2006 Memorandum of Understanding).

[125] For example, warnings and recommendations issued by the ESRB must be transmitted to the Council, while those related to supervisory issues should also be transmitted to the relevant ESA.

[126] Giovanoli (2000) *International Monetary Law Issues for the New Millennium*, Oxford: OUP, Chapter 1.

[127] The current prudential system of prudential regulation is based on the principles of home-country control and thus while there are common rules within the Member States these rules do not infringe national sovereignty; Member States and financial institutions are governed by the respective national legal framework.

[128] Case 26/62 *Van Gen en Loos* [1963] ECR 1; and *Costa v ENEL* [1964] ECR 585.

[129] Eijffinger and De Haan (2000) *European Monetary and Fiscal Policy*, Oxford: Oxford University Press.

citizens of the EU Member States are more familiar with the concept of ceding sovereignty. However, whether the creation of a pan-European regulator is popular with its citizens remains to be seen. The loss of sovereignty, where this occurs, is not absolute as members of the supranational body individually have an influencing and developmental role, and collectively an ownership stake. The key issue is whether the loss of sovereignty is redressed by the ensuing benefits and stability of the financial markets. Traditionally, countries such as the USA have been reluctant to surrender any sovereignty to international institutions partially because of perceived costs but also because, until recently, of their supremacy in business and finance. Significantly, whether the strong emerging economies, like China and India, would be willing to surrender their sovereignty in an area of the economy so integral to their success is questionable.

Challenges for a global regulator

The international regulatory framework in place in 2008 failed to stem the global financial crisis. Growing risks were not properly identified or monitored and international standard-setting agencies were not effective in dealing with the systemic global financial problems. A system of global regulation needs to address a number of existing gaps in the regulation of the global financial sector, some of which are now explored.

Prudential supervision

Most domestic regulators undertake some form of prudential supervision that involves initial authorisation, the grant of a licence and permission to undertake a 'regulated activity' including the acceptance of deposits. Such authorised institutions are then regulated and supervised on a continuing basis. Within the UK, the FSMA 2000[130] sets out a number of principles of good regulation, which are intended to underpin the manner in which the FCA is expected to discharge its statutory obligations. The FCA should have regard to: efficiency and economy; the role of governance and management; that the regulation must be proportionate to the benefits; innovation; the international character of the financial services markets; the desirability of maintaining the competitiveness of the UK financial services sector; and minimising the possible adverse impact on competition of the FCA's regulation.[131] The FCA has a formal obligation to ensure that sound management of the financial services sector remains the key priority but the FCA must have regard to this in the context of the wider environment, including the internationalisation of the services markets and products available. A well-regulated banking sector will result in local confidence and also enjoy the confidence of foreign investors and lenders. Regulation based on international standards should result in added confidence and attract foreign business and inward investment and therefore the concept of a global regulator has several advantages, for example, such a regulator will also be able to monitor international

---

[130] As amended by the Financial Services Act 2010.

[131] FSA, Principles of good regulation, 1 October 2007, http://www.fsa.gov.uk/Pages/about/aims/principles/index.shtml; see also: FSA, A new Regulator for the new Millennium, January 2000, para. 19. Following the announcement by George Osborne to reform UK banking regulation in the UK the responsibilities for banking regulation will be redefined with the Bank of England again assuming a regulatory and supervisory role: see The Future of Banking Commission, 13 June 2010, http://commission.bnbb.org/banking/sites/all/themes/whichfobtheme/pdf/commission_report.pdf; and Elliott, George Osborne unveils sweeping City reforms, *The Guardian*, 16 June 2010, http://www.guardian.co.uk/business/2010/jun/16/george-osborne-city-fsa-banking.

capital flows and the imbalances that may result. Thus, global risks can be identified and removed[132] with the global regulator having power to take appropriate action.[133]

Since prudential regulation is seen as independent of daily government and carried on by an independent regulator the work of the global regulator could be undertaken by organisations such as the Basel Committee, the Bank for International Settlements, the International Monetary Fund or groupings of central banks and other financial regulators who have been responsible for developing voluntary international regulations, which to date domestic governments and regulators have not been compelled to implement. While there would be some loss of sovereignty in delegating financial regulation to an international regulator the benefits of increased stability and added robustness of the global financial sector would probably outweigh any concerns. Insofar as consumers are concerned the assurance that their investments and savings are placed with well-regulated institutions and giving them a reasonable return is paramount; the nature of the regulator, or where it is based, is unlikely to cause much dissatisfaction. The loss of sovereignty is possibly a greater worry for the politician rather than the consumer. In order to ensure its independence the prudential regulator would need a budget either by a levy on governments or the financial services industry itself via a tax on profits of individual institutions,[134] or based on the size of the domestic sector.

Bankruptcy regime

An effective bankruptcy regime may itself bring benefits to an economy since it helps to allocate repayment of loans and other debts to lenders. Financers will therefore have greater certainty and assurances of an equitable allocation of assets for the purposes of repayment of debts. The principal benefits of a personal insolvency regime, therefore, is to ensure a fair division of the insolvent debtor's assets to his creditors allowing the insolvent debtor, in due course, to make a new start free from the burden of continuously accumulating debt. By contrast the corporate insolvency regime allows the corporate entity an opportunity to restore the company to health and, possibly, trade its way to profitability, giving the company a long-term future and thereby safeguarding the interests of creditors who may in the long-term recover the full amounts of any debts owed to them. In the absence of the company being restored to health, the insolvency regime will again provide for the equitable repayment of company debts with creditors being ranked in order of priority depending on the nature, type, time and date of registration of security.

An equitable bankruptcy regime will, therefore, encourage investment, as creditors are more likely to risk their investment and extend credit where the law provides for clear rules which will apply in the event of insolvency and where management are likely to be held accountable for wrongdoing, leading to, or in connection with, the insolvency. In dealing with distressed multinational banks, consistency of approach is possible either through the adoption of an international regime on cross-border insolvency based on the work of the United Nations Commission on International Trade Law (UNCITRAL) or on the basis of work undertaken at the European level on the winding up of banking groups or cross-border

---

[132] The ESRC will be tasked with identifying systemic risks in the European financial sector, The High-Level Group on Financial Supervision in the EU, chaired by Jacques de Larosière, para. 174.

[133] The High-Level Group on Financial Supervision in the EU, chaired by Jacques de Larosière, paras 181–182.

[134] Peston, IMF proposes two big new bank taxes to fund bail-outs, BBC News, 21 April 2010, http://news.bbc.co.uk/1/hi/8633455.stm.

banks. UNCITRAL adopted the Model Law on Cross-border Insolvency in May 1997[135] which deals with the recognition of foreign insolvency proceedings, cooperation between judicial authorities and administrators and issues relating to the coordination of concurrent insolvency proceedings. It purpose includes cooperation between states to ensure fair and efficient administration of cross-border insolvency and to protect debtors' assets. In 1999, UNCITRAL commenced work on the Legislative Guide on Insolvency Law, which was adopted by the UN General Assembly on 2 December 2004.[136] The World Bank has coordinated the effort of the UNCITRAL Guide with its own Global Bank Insolvency Initiative to establish a set of standards on insolvency and creditor rights.[137] The UNCITRAL Working Group V on insolvency has also started working on the treatment of corporate groups in insolvency, examining cross-border and domestic issues but the UNCITRAL model recognises that specialist institutions, like banks and insurance companies, may require specialist treatment in a separate insolvency regime. A more recent development is the new Basel Working Group[138] to study the regulation of cross-border banks.

In 2009, the de Larosière Group recommended that while, crisis management should be left with national supervisors in the case of domestic banks an EU-wide response is advocated in the case of cross-border institutions.[139] The 2001 Directive on the Reorganisation and Winding up of Credit Institutions[140] is not intended to harmonise national legislation but is aimed at ensuring the mutual recognition of Member States' reorganisation measures and winding-up proceedings. There are inconsistencies between national legislation, which prevents the efficient handling of distressed cross-border banks: for example creditor claims may be ranked differently under domestic law in Members States, in some countries greater protection is given to the institution rather than creditors, the application of the rules relating to set-off in bank insolvency,[141] the role of supervision and the treatment of financial contracts and the protection of the payment system. The lack of consistent crisis management tools places the wider global economy at a major disadvantage and the work of these international organisations could be used as a platform for establishing a global bankruptcy regime.

Sovereign bankruptcy

While a personal bankrupt or corporate insolvency may support the repayment of personal or corporate debt to creditors the insolvency of a sovereign state presents different issues for consideration. There have been several famous sovereign debt crises[142] with the Organisation

---

[135] http://www.uncitral.org/pdf/english/texts/insolven/insolvency-e.pdf.

[136] UNCITRAL Legislative Guide on Insolvency Law, New York 2005, http://www.uncitral.org/pdf/english/texts/insolven/05-80722_Ebook.pdf.

[137] See: The World Bank Principles for Effective Insolvency and Creditor Rights Systems (Revised) 2005, http://siteresources.worldbank.org/GILD/Resources/FINAL-ICRPrinciples-March2009.pdf.

[138] Established in December 2007.

[139] At present the EU insolvency regime consists of the Council Regulation on Insolvency Proceedings (EC) No. 1346/2000 of 29 May 2000; the Directive on the reorganisation and winding up of credit institutions, Directive 2001/24/EC of 4 April 2001; and the Directive concerning the reorganisation and winding up of insurance undertakings, Directive 2001/17/EC of 19 March 2001; see also Lastra (2009) Northern Rock, UK bank insolvency and cross-border bank insolvency, 9(3), *Journal of Banking Regulation*, 165–186.

[140] Directive on the reorganisation and winding up of credit institutions, Directive 2001/24/EC of 4 April 2001.

[141] International Financial Conglomerates: Implications for Bank Insolvency Regime, Richard Herring, Wharton School University of Pennsylvania, July 2002.

[142] See discussion on the role of the IMF in Sovereign debt crisis by Gianviti (2000) The prevention and resolution of international financial crises: A perspective from the International Monetary Fund, ch. 4, in *International Monetary Law Issues for the New Millennium*, ed. Giovanoli, Oxford: OUP.

for Economic Cooperation and Development looking at the crises in Mexico (1994–95), Asia (1997), Russia (1998) and Argentina (2001). It found that investment banks charge higher underwriting fees on sovereign debt well before such crises actually occur and before investors in sovereign bonds detect default risks. More recently, when Dubai World asked for a moratorium on its debt in December 2009, the losses stretched from Asia to Wall Street. Bank shares plunged on fears of exposure, and investors fled to the dollar and away from assets that were perceived as riskier, such as commodities in this case. While Abu Dhabi came to the rescue of Dubai, the questions and rumours as to who might default next will continue for some time.[143] Investors rushed to sell Greek bonds when the newly elected government of George Papandreou revealed that the national deficit would soar to over 12 per cent of gross domestic product this year, well above previous official projections.[144] The terms of a bail-out from the EU and IMF has led to social unrest and violence.[145] Greece's predicament has escalated concerns about contagion in other European countries whose finances are in poor shape and credit ratings agencies warned Spain, Portugal and the UK of possible down-gradings in their national ratings.[146] The UK was downgraded in April 2013.[147] In March 2013, Cyprus, the smallest country in the EU, received a bail-out from the IMF on terms which included savers deposits being taxed to support the bail-out.[148]

Within the UK, although house prices and the economy are beginning to recover and unemployment is close to peaking, sovereign credit will come under renewed stress if the economic recovery falters and if the new government withdraws its fiscal stimulus measures early. The issue therefore is whether there should be some kind of sovereign bankruptcy regime and who should exercise such powers. The absence of an international bankruptcy regime for sovereign states or a sovereign entity adds uncertainty. One such uncertainty that needs to be resolved is to establish a sovereign bankruptcy court applying a uniform set of rules and procedures. There are a number of proposals that may be used as the foundation of an international framework. The Jubilee framework envisages a bankruptcy based on Chapter 9 of the US Bankruptcy Code, which deals with municipal bankruptcy and is enforced by an independent panel of experts convened for specific proceedings.[149] Additionally, the IMF proposed the Sovereign Debt Restructuring Mechanism (SDRM) as a uniform and systemic

---

[143] *Wall Street Journal*, Playing the sovereign debt crisis, tricky for professional traders; a minefield for retail investors, 17 December 2009.

[144] Debt disaster fears rumble from Athens to London: Game of chicken for bond spreads: Will the EU honor 'no bailout'? 16 December 2009?

[145] *The Daily Telegraph*, IMF launches Greek rescue plan, 16 April 2010, http://www.telegraph.co.uk/finance/financetopics/financialcrisis/7594805/IMF-launches-Greek-rescue-plan.html; Reuters, EU, IMF agree $147 billion bailout for Greece, http://www.reuters.com/article/idUSTRE6400PJ20100502.

[146] This would run the risk of Greece not having access to the global credit markets, Elliott, Three unpleasant choices: devaluation, default or deflation: next stop the IMF, *The Guardian*, 12 February 2010, http://www.guardian.co.uk/commentisfree/2010/feb/11/germany-greece-debt-crisis-euro.

[147] http://www.bbc.co.uk/news/business-22219382.

[148] Das, Effects of bailout will be felt far beyond Cyprus, *The Independent*, http://www.independent.co.uk/news/business/comment/satyajit-das-effects-of-bailout-will-be-felt-far-beyond-cyprus-8539842.html; see also: McDonald-Gibson and Savaricas, Cyprus government considers capital restrictions if banks reopen in wake of no vote on bailout plan, 20 March 2013, http://www.independent.co.uk/news/world/europe/cyprus-government-considers-capital-restrictions-if-banks-reopen-in-wake-of-no-vote-on-bailout-plan-8541257.html.

[149] Resolving international debt crisis – the Jubilee Framework for international insolvency, Pettifor, January 2002, www.jubileeplus.org/analysis/reports/jubilee_framework.html.

approach to dealing with sovereign debt although this development was shelved in 2003. The IMF's proposal was based on four main principles:

1 Majority restructuring – this would enable the affirmative vote of a qualified majority of creditors (75 per cent majority) to bind a dissenting minority to the terms of a restructuring agreement. From the perspective of creditors this would provide confidence that any forbearance exercised by the majority when agreeing to a restructuring would not be abused by free riders who could otherwise press for full payment after an agreement was reached. From the perspective of the sovereign, the resolution of these collective action issues will make it more likely that it will be able to reach early agreement with creditors on the debt restructuring. Moreover, it eliminates the threat of disruptive litigation by dissenting creditors after the restructuring takes place.

2 Stay on creditor enforcement – in the event that an agreement had not been reached prior to a default, a temporary stay on creditor litigation after a suspension of payments but before a restructuring agreement is reached would support the effective operation of the majority restructuring provision.

3 Protecting creditor interests – the SDRM would need to provide safeguards that give creditors adequate assurances that their interests are being protected during the period of the stay. The sovereign debtor would be required not to make payments to non-priority creditors; this would avoid the dissipation of resources. There would also have to be assurances that the debtor would conduct policies in a fashion that preserves asset values. Working with the IMF to implement policies would be evidence of good faith.

4 Priority financing – the SDRM could also be used to facilitate the provision of new money from private creditors during the period of the stay. It is in the collective interests of private creditors and the sovereign debtor that new money is provided in appropriate amounts. Such financing, when used in the context of good policies,[150] can help limit the degree of economic damage and help preserve the member's capacity to generate the resources to service its debts. The SDRM proposal gave the IMF an active role in the implementation of the SDRM. A Sovereign Debt Dispute Resolution Forum would be established to determine disputes between creditors and debtors with the IMF having a nomination and endorsement role. The IMF proposal stalled because of the role proposed for itself by the IMF, including a determination whether or not a nation was qualified for debt restructuring, the determination of a nation's debt sustainability from which the necessary amount of debt reduction would be made not by the Sovereign Debt Dispute Resolution Forum but by the IMF, the proposal for the SDRM applied only to commercial bank debt and not the Paris Club,[151] the IMF and the World Bank debt which were left out of the equation and the fact that the laws that were to be applied had not yet been drafted. The IMF was therefore seeking support and ratification for something that had not yet been developed or designed. The recent credit crisis may be the catalyst needed to review this proposal and implement it in some form, with appropriate revisions.

---

[150] Kreguer, A new approach to debt restructuring, IMF 2002, http://www.imf.org/external/pubs/ft/exrp/sdrm/eng/sdrm.pdf; see also Dodd (2002) Sovereign Debt Restructuring, Derivative Study Centre, 9(1.4), *The Financier*, http://www.financialpolicy.org/dscsovdebt.pdf.

[151] Calleghy, Innovation in the Sovereign Debt Regime: From the Paris Club to Enhanced HIPC and Beyond, p. 14, Department of Political Science, University of Pennsylvania, 2002, http://lnweb90.worldbank.org/OED/oeddoclib.nsf/DocUNIDViewForJavaSearch/4BC77E9BEC2CAAFC85256E4A00536A04/$file/hipc_wp_sovereign_debt.pdf.

Lender of last resort

The instability of the banking systems has been demonstrated yet again by the recent financial crisis that led to bail-outs of banks on a global basis. All nations have a lender of last resort (LoLR) who is intended to provide stability and confidence within the national banking systems. The LoLR role, while normally fulfilled by central banks, may also be undertaken by some other organisation, for example the Treasury in the USA, but is associated with the prevention and mitigation of financial crises that arise with the loss of confidence in a financial institution or assets. There is no accepted definition of LoLR but Meltzer[152] described the role as having the capacity and the ability to lend to prevent failures of solvent banks in periods when no other lender is capable or willing to lend in sufficient volume to prevent or end financial panic.

The overall objective of the LoLR role is to prevent panic induced declines in the stock market so that the position of the wider economy does not deteriorate leading to an economic recession. The role of LoLR has two integrated aspects: namely, the lender of last resort in a crisis, and the role of crisis manager with a view to developing policy to reinforce confidence. The LoLR, however, will provide such facilities in return for security being given and at a punitive interest rate. Thus, while the LoLR is able to provide large amounts of money to maintain consumer confidence at short notice that will be done at a penal interest rate so that management does not become reliant on the LoLR and moral hazard is avoided. The role of the Bank of England, acting in its capacity as LoLR, is demonstrated throughout the Bank's history but the disclosure, in September 2009, that the Bank of England had poured £20 billion into Royal Bank of Scotland over the weekend of the 11 and 12 October 2008, after other banks had refused to lend RBS crisis funding and that RBS was depositing assets with the Bank of England in return for the funding,[153] shows its continuing strategic significance.

There is currently no LoLR in the international financial system but the need for an international LoLR arises because international capital flows are not only extremely volatile but also contagious and an international lender of last resort will help mitigate the effects of instability and loss of confidence in the international markets. The flows of capital in the international markets also help support and develop the international economies, maintain employment and grow wealth in both the developing and advanced nations. It is therefore submitted that the need and case for an international LoLR is stronger than ever.[154] The IMF already discharges some of the functions associated with a LoLR, including the promotion of international monetary cooperation, surveillance and the associated provision of information; and technical assistance including policy advice and monitoring. Although the IMF is not a central bank its structure is close to that of a credit union and it has access to resources, which it can re-lend to member countries. As crisis manager, it has been assigned the lead in negotiating with member countries in a crisis, and it cooperates in arranging financing

---

[152] Meltzer (1986) Financial Failures and Financial Policies published in *Deregulating financial services: Public Policy in Flux*, eds Kaufman and Kormandi, Cambridge, Massachusetts; Bullinger, cited in On the need for an international lender of last resort, Stanley Fisher, 1999, Paper presented to the American Economic Association and the American Finance Association, New York, http://www.petersoninstitute.org/fischer/pdf/Fischer122.pdf.

[153] Elliott and Treanor, UK was hours from bank shutdown, FSA ready to close cash machines during crisis, *The Observer*, 6 September 2009.

[154] Saxton, An International Lender of Last Resort, The IMF, and the Federal Reserve, http://www.house.gov/jec/imf/lolr.htm.

packages. The question is whether it has sufficient resources to support and lend in a crisis situation. A quota, which has not kept pace with the growth of the global economy, increases the funds available to the IMF, but the Fund could still assemble a sizeable package in response to a financial crisis. The IMF, however, does not have the capacity to issue currency.

Indeed, the IMF has some experience of the LoLR role. In 1997, the IMF introduced the Supplemental Reserve Facility (SRF),[155] which can make short-term loans in large amounts at penalty rates to countries in crisis. SRF loans have been made to Korea, Russia and Brazil. There would need to be some reform to the IMF funding policies, for example the IMF normally lends and organises a bail-out of crisis-hit countries subject to economic reform and usually makes funding available over a period of time so the recipient country can show compliance with IMF required reforms. A LoLR will impose conditions on the emergency funding but the nature of these may have to be reviewed if the IMF is to be the LoLR and funds can clearly not be withheld in a crisis situation pending proof of compliance with the conditions imposed.

Deposit Guarantee Schemes

The recent financial crisis has demonstrated that Deposit Guarantee Schemes were insufficient[156] to maintain confidence in the banking markets and significantly were not, in some cases, fully implemented. Consequently, the EFTA Surveillance Authorities have brought Iceland before the EFTA court for failure to implement the Financial Conglomerates Directive.[157] The Directive enhances financial stability between sectors and is a significant improvement in the protection of depositors, insurance policy-holders and investors.

Such guarantee schemes serve both a social and economic purpose and are intended to help preserve the stability of the financial system.[158] The rapid growth of international banking leaves the issue of who is responsible for compensating the customer where an overseas bank, or a bank from another EU Member State, offers banking facilities across national boundaries. This was a particularly prominent question when the Icelandic government seized the Icelandic banks, including Icesave, in an attempt to shore up the Icelandic banks at the height of the financial crisis.[159] On Tuesday, 7 October 2008, UK savers were unable to access their Landsbanki-run Icesave accounts and were faced with a message telling them the bank was unable to process requests for deposits or withdrawals. Icesave offered competitive rates and had therefore attracted more than 200,000 accounts of UK residents.[160]

The passport arrangements for EU financial institutions grant an institution authorised in one Member State an automatic right to establish branches, as opposed to subsidiaries, in other Member States. The host supervisor in the country in which the branch is established has little oversight of the activities of the group. Under the current DGSs the customer will be compensated under the home DGS up to the level of guarantee given in the home state. Thus,

---

[155] IMF Approves Supplemental Reserve Facility, http://www.imf.org/external/np/sec/pr/1997/PR9759.HTM.

[156] PR (10) 23, Financial Services: Iceland brought to Court for failure fully to implement Directive, 24 April 2010, http://www.eftasurv.int/press--publications/press-releases/internal-market/nr/1219.

[157] The Directive was intended to be implemented into national laws by 1 August 2005, 2002/87/EC.

[158] Arrigunaga (2000) Deposit Insurance Schemes: Reconciling Market Discipline with financial stability, Chapter 17 in *International Monetary Law Issues for the New Millennium*, ed. Giovanoli, Oxford: OUP.

[159] In 2008 the internet deposit business operated by the UK branch of Landsbanki Islands hf grew to £4.5 billion.

[160] Iceland government seizes control of Landsbanki, David Teather, guardian.co.uk, 7 October 2008, Iceland%20government%20seizes%20control%20of%20Landsbank.

the Icelandic DGS underwrites the first €22,000 (roughly £17,000) held and balances in excess up to £50,000 are guaranteed by the British government.[161] The seize anti-terrorism legislation was used to the assets of Icelandic banks held in the UK in an effort to pressurise the Icelandic government to meet its obligations. Generally domestic governments and regulators are, therefore, left to implement a DGS but the recent crisis saw some countries break ranks and guarantee the full amount held by customers with their banks. Thus, Ireland acted to guarantee deposits held by its banks for a two-year period to restore confidence after shares plunged 26 per cent in Dublin.[162] Beyond the EU the extent of the DGS is based on local domestic regulations for accounts held overseas and the laws of that country will bind a subsidiary established in an overseas country. Whether the parent company will stand behind the obligations and debts of an overseas subsidiary remains a controversy[163] but perhaps parent companies that attempt to abuse the separate entity rule should be forced to recognise there is no hiding place for them.

The de Larosière Group has explored the idea of a EU fund composed of national deposit guarantee funds but this has found no support because of the perceived political and practical problems this would create. However, in principle there is no reason why a EU-wide or, indeed, a global DGS cannot be established, again through the IMF or BIS.

Summary

The systemic failure of the global financial markets has led to calls for extensive reforms and overhaul of the global financial structures that have been found to be woefully defective or sometimes absent. The global markets cannot be allowed to operate on an almost unchecked basis when the financial sector, financial products and financial business operate on a global scale. The commitment for reform must not be allowed to wane as the financial markets begin the process of recovery. The impetus for reform within the existing international regulatory agencies has never been greater and the 'loopholes that were at the heart of the crisis'[164] must be plugged and certain sectors of the financial markets clearly need particular oversight, for example derivatives and cross-border financial firms. This chapter has attempted to explore the work already undertaken by the current international regulatory agencies and to highlight some of the weaknesses in the current international financial regulatory structure. The global regulation must be complete, robust and transparent with sanctions for non-compliance. It may be an objective that can be achieved only in incremental stages and that requires long-term coordinated action. Governments must also act in the short term, perhaps with some restrictions on the movement of capital or a tax on capital movements to maintain financial stability. Rather than restrict enterprise and business innovation it is time governments and regulators got their houses in order and coordinated an international regulatory regime.

---

[161] The UK government responded by guaranteeing the savings of customer accounts with Icelandic banks (UK Freezes Icelandic Bank Assets; Threatens Lawsuit (Update2)), http://www.bloomberg.com/apps/news?pid=20601102&sid=aarH9BaUZJZY&refer=uk.

[162] Ireland Guarantees Bank Deposits, Debt for Two Years (Update2), Dara Doyle and Ian Guider, 20 September 2008, http://www.bloomberg.com/apps/news?pid=newsarchive&sid=aGywJhwA3qf.

[163] Within the UK the separate entity rule was first examined in *Salomon v Salomon Co Ltd* [1897] AC 22.

[164] The White House, Office of the Press Secretary, Remarks of the President on Financial Rescue and Reform, Federal Hall, New York, 14 September 2009, http://whitehouse.gov/thepressoffice/Remarks-by-the-President-on-Financial-Rescue-anxsxsd-Reform-at-Federal-Hall.

The attempts by the EU to establish a pan-European financial sector may be a first step. The institutional reform proposed by the European Commission is intended to integrate the European financial markets further but while that will allow regional coordination, global integration and coordination will be ineffective unless the US and emerging Asian financial regulators are willing to cooperate. The EU Member States have already agreed to cede sovereignty in certain areas of policy; whether the US and other regulators can be persuaded to pool financial supervision and regulation to strengthen the global financial markets remains to be seen: it may prove to be a step too far.

Conclusion

This chapter is intended to give the reader an overview of the role of the City of London as an international financial centre and the nature of services provided by it. The chapter then explores the efforts of inter-governmental agencies to establish common banking standards of business and regulation. The chapter concludes with a discussion of the new Pan-European regulatory authorities, their functions, roles and relationships with national authorities, and the challenges that a creation of an global regulator would present.

Further reading

➤ King, M. (2007) Through the looking glass: reform of the international institutions, *Australian Business Review*, 123.
This paper is based upon a speech delivered by Mervyn King which identifies the importance of globalisation and the dependence which stems from it. In turn, this paper concludes that countries should not rely upon the commitments made 60 years ago. King concludes that failure to reform the international institutions risks condemning these institutions to irrelevance and obscurity.

➤ Hanson, S., Kashyap, A. and Stein, J. (2011) A Macroprudential Approach to Financial Regulation, *Journal of Economic Perspectives*, 25(1), 3–28.
This paper identifies that many critics argued that the regulatory framework in place prior to the global financial crisis was deficient due to its micro-prudential character. Accordingly this paper proposes a detailed vision of how a macro-prudential regime might be designed.

➤ The EU High-level Group on Financial Supervision in the EU Report, Chaired by Jacques de Larosière, Brussels, 25 February 2009, http://ec.europa.eu/internal_market/finances/docs/de_larosiere_report_en.pdf.
The report of the de Larosière high-level group on financial supervision was established to examine the future of European financial regulation and supervision. The report noted that the European Union's framework of regulation remains seriously fragmented, and action is required at national, European and global levels to achieve an effective regulatory framework.

➤ Communication for the Spring European Council: Driving European Recovery, Brussels, 4 March 2009, COM (2009) 114 final, http://eur-lex.europa.eu/LexUriServ/LexUriServ.do?uri=COM:2009:0114:FIN:EN:PDF.

The corporate governance failings in financial institutions and directors' legal liability

The aim of this chapter is to:

➤ Explore some of the failings in corporate governance that individually contributed to the financial crisis and which collectively resulted in the collapse of the global financial markets.

➤ Examine some of the governance responsibilities imposed by the companies legislation, the Combined Code on Corporate Governance and the Financial Services and Markets Act 2000 on the management of banks and other financial institutions.

➤ Examine why good governance of banks is important and the position of bank depositors, as stakeholders.

Introduction

Alistair Darling, Chancellor of the Exchequer in June 2009, summed up the failings in good management and governance of banks and other financial firms when he said:

> Last summer, just as the crisis began to bite, a senior banker told me that 'from now on we will only lend when we understand the risks involved'. I did wonder what they had been doing up until then. Months later we were the majority shareholder of that bank.[1]

A number of failings in corporate governance have been blamed for exacerbating the 2007–09 global financial crisis, including reckless board practices, insufficient risk management, excessive executive remuneration and reckless bonus policies that encouraged short-termism and rewarded high levels of risk-taking, sometimes to the detriment of the firm.[2] Although poor governance was one of the contributing factors to the recent financial crisis, it is widely

---

[1] Speech by the Chancellor of the Exchequer, the Rt Hon Alistair Darling MP, at Mansion House, London, 17 June 2009, http://www.hm-treasury.gov.uk/press_57_09.htm.

[2] The High-Level Group on Financial Supervision in the EU Report, chaired by Jacques de Larosière, Brussels, 25 February 2009 for a summary of the causes of the crisis; see also: A regulatory response to the global banking crisis, FSA, March 2009; and A review of corporate governance in UK banks and other financial industry entities, Final Recommendations, 26 November 2009.

acknowledged to have been an important factor leading to, and during the financial crisis.[3] Failures in corporate governance, however, are not new and it is not the first time that these failures have been recognised as significant contributory causes to institutional failure and yet regulators, supervisors and boards of companies appear to have learnt few lessons from previous experiences to safeguard the long-term fortunes of the companies under their management and supervision. Even when warned of the developing difficult market conditions the board of Northern Rock failed to sufficiently safeguard the bank or to take steps to reinforce its position; not even as a precaution.[4] They did not anticipate that a tightening in the credit markets would extend to good quality credit.[5]

Corporate governance failure has been at the root of both regional crises[6] and failure in individual banks.[7] It has been suggested that ineffectual corporate governance was responsible for the Japanese banking crisis[8] and that the continued weaknesses in the corporate governance culture impeded recovery. The Asian financial crisis too was blamed on a failure of corporate governance, lack of transparency and poor quality information flows that resulted in markets not having a true and accurate picture of the banking sector and corporations.[9] When that information became available the markets reacted adversely and there was a collapse of confidence in the banking sector. Failures in corporate governance played a major role in the 2007–09 global financial crisis.

In the case of banks and other financial institutions (BOFI), the statutory corporate governance responsibilities under the Companies Act 2006 are supplemented by the 'comply or explain' principles of the Combined Code on Corporate Governance[10] and by the Financial

[3] HM Treasury, A review of corporate governance in UK banks and other financial entities, Final Recommendations, 26 November 2009, http://www.hm-treasury.gov.uk/walker_review_information.htm; see also FSA, Effective Corporate Governance (Significant influence controlled functions and the Walker review), January 2010, Consultation 10/3, http://www.fsa.gov.uk/pubs/cp/cp10_03.pdf.

[4] House of Commons Treasury Committee, The run on the Rock, Fifth Report of Session 2007–08, Volume 1, Ordered by The House of Commons, printed 24 January 2008, HC 56–I, http://www.parliament.the-stationery-office.com/pa/cm200708/cmselect/cmtreasy/56/56i.pdf.

[5] House of Commons Treasury Committee, The run on the Rock, Fifth Report of Session 2007–08, Volume 1, Ordered by The House of Commons, printed 24 January 2008, HC 56–I, pp. 15–16, http://www.parliament. the-stationery-office.com/pa/cm200708/cmselect/cmtreasy/56/56i.pdf.

[6] The recent global crisis has strong parallels with the collapse of the Japanese banking sector in the 1990s when Japanese innovation, economic development and growth outstripped the advanced western economies. This was matched by dramatic rises in property prices, which outstripped prices both in the US and the UK. Japanese banks operating in an environment of inadequate prudential regulations lent heavily to customers with less than a perfect credit; indeed some banks transferred the responsibility of undertaking credit checks to non-bank entities. The collapse of the Japanese property market, when it came, saw the Japanese economy go into a recession from which it has even yet not fully recovered although an extensive government stimulus package during 1992–95 supported some vigorous growth in 1996, see: Japan's Economic Crisis and Policy Options, 1998, http://www.imf.org/external/pubs/ft/weo/weo1098/pdf/1098ch4.pdf; see also IMF Working Paper: Monetary and Exchange Affairs Department, The Japanese Banking Crisis of the 1990s, WP/00/07, Kanaya and Woo, http://www.imf.org/external/pubs/ft/wp/2000/wp0007.pdf.

[7] In 1995 Barings Bank collapsed following the mismanagement of derivative trading by Leeson, a Barings trader in Singapore, which passed unchecked as a result poor internal controls and lack of monitoring.

[8] IMF Working Paper: Monetary and Exchange Affairs Department, The Japanese Banking Crisis of the 1990s, WP/00/07, Kanaya and Woo, http://www.imf.org/external/pubs/ft/wp/2000/wp0007.pdf.

[9] IMF Working Paper: Monetary and Exchange Affairs Department, The Japanese Banking Crisis of the 1990s, WP/00/07, Kanaya and Woo, http://www.imf.org/external/pubs/ft/wp/2000/wp0007.pdf.

[10] Financial Reporting Council, The Combined Code on Corporate Governance, June 2008, http://www.frc.org.uk/ documents/pagemanager/frc/Combined_Code_June_2008/Combined%20Code%20Web%20Optimized% 20June%202008(2).pdf. The revised version came into force from 29 June 2010.

Services and Markets Act 2000 as amended. Financial institution regulation is also extends to capital, liquidity, risk management and other internal aspects that prevent, or deal with, the consequences of failure, such as depositor protection and the position of counterparties. The result is that arrangements for corporate governance for banks reflect a combination of prescriptive legislation, codes of best practice, custom and market incentives.

This chapter will therefore explore (i) the failings in corporate governance in the 2007–09 financial crisis; (ii) why good corporate governance of banks is important; (iii) the position of depositors as stakeholders; and (iv) the failings in bank governance and the duties owed by directors under the Companies Act 2006. Aspects of corporate governance that are regulated under the Financial Services and Markets Act 2000, particularly the statutory objects which govern the parameters of regulation, the conduct of business rules, the fit and proper person requirements, and the role of auditors will be discussed in outline to highlight issues relating to governance.

What were the failings in corporate governance?

The role of and failures in corporate governance in BOFIs, during and before the financial crisis, has now been recognised at various levels[11] including by Lord Turner[12] who was asked by the then Chancellor of the Exchequer, Alistair Darling, to review the causes of the financial crisis and make recommendations on changes in regulation and supervision needed to establish a more robust banking system. While Lord Turner was happy to await the outcome of the report then under preparation by Sir David Walker,[13] who had been asked, in February 2009, by the Prime Minister, Gordon Brown, to review corporate governance in the UK banking industry, Lord Turner[14] indicated a number of areas of concern in respect of corporate governance. These included the need to improve professionalism and independence of risk management; to embed risk management considerations into remuneration so as to avoid incentives for undue risk-taking; to raise the levels of skill and time commitment of non-executive directors; and to enhance the ability of the shareholders to constrain the firm's risk-taking. The Walker report,[15] when published, made recommendations in five main areas: board size,

---

[11] International standards setting agencies, for example, the OECD, concluded the crisis can 'to an important extent be attributed to failures and weaknesses in corporate governance arrangements which did not serve their purpose to safeguard against excessive risk taking in number of financial service companies' Kirkpatrick, The Corporate Governance Lessons from the Financial Crisis, OECD, February 2009, http://www.oecd.org/dataoecd/32/1/42229620.pdf. The EU high-level Group on financial supervision in the EU Report, chaired by Jacques de Larosière, Brussels, 25 February 2009, also suggested there were strong links between poor risk management and corporate failings, http://ec.europa.eu/internal_market/finances/docs/de_larosiere_report_en.pdf.

[12] FSA, The Turner Review, A regulatory response to the global banking crisis, March 2009, http://www.fsa.gov.uk/pubs/other/turner_review.pdf.

[13] The remit of this review was later extended to examine corporate governance in the whole finance industry, HM Treasury, A review of corporate governance in UK Banks and other financial entities, Final Recommendations, 26 November 2009, http://webarchive.nationalarchives.gov.uk/+/http:/www.hm-treasury.gov.uk/d/walker_review_261109.pdf.

[14] FSA, The Turner Review, A regulatory response to the global banking crisis, March 2009, http://www.fsa.gov.uk/pubs/other/turner_review.pdf.

[15] HM Treasury, A review of corporate governance in UK Banks and other financial entities, Final Recommendations, 26 November 2009, http://webarchive.nationalarchives.gov.uk/+/http:/www.hm-treasury.gov.uk/d/walker_review_261109.pdf.

composition and qualifications of the board; functioning of the board and evaluation of performance; the role of institutional shareholders: communication and engagement; governance of risk; and remuneration.[16]

What is obvious, as a result of the financial crisis, is that there were severe shortfalls in the arrangements of prudential supervision and board due diligence in respect of key areas of oversight and management; shortfalls that became the target of serious scrutiny and heavy criticism only when the markets stalled and management failures could no longer be swept aside under the asset bubble of rising house prices, increases in share prices and high dividend yields. The fact that some financial institutions were able to weather the credit crisis significantly better than others is a reflection of the different qualities, and capabilities of governance and management experience.[17] Failings in the good governance of BOFIs may be summarised under the following headings.

Failures of directors

The board of directors[18] is responsible for forging, reviewing and overseeing the implementation of corporate strategy and risk policy. The latter clearly needs to be central to broad strategy and requires the involvement of senior management with an appropriate balance of skills and experience to meet the needs of the business. The Combined Code, with which all public companies are expected to comply, or to explain non-compliance, requires directors not only to have the appropriate skills and knowledge but also to regularly update their skills and knowledge.[19] This requirement is reinforced by duties imposed under the Companies Act 2006 and their application by the courts.[20] Channels of communication must be maintained so that risk information may be effectively transmitted. The global financial crisis revealed catastrophic failure in management practices, defective due diligence and imprudent business judgement, including acquisitions.[21] In his report Kirkpatrick[22] noted that in a number of cases boards were not aware of strategic decisions and had not put in place controls to oversee and manage risk. The report examining the failure of HBOS recognised that senior management

---

[16] The five key themes of the review received much support in the consultation process, and perhaps with improved focus, remained: see: A review of corporate governance in UK banks and other financial industry entities, Final recommendations, 26 November 2009, pp. 11–12, http://webarchive.nationalarchives.gov.uk/+/http:/www.hm-treasury.gov.uk/d/walker_review_261109.pdf.

[17] Kirkpatrick, The Corporate Governance Lessons from the Financial Crisis, OECD, February 2009, http://www.oecd.org/dataoecd/32/1/42229620.pdf.

[18] It is outside the scope of this work to deal with the roles, functions and regulations of boards of directors and for further discussion you are referred to texts in Company Law generally. Reference may be made to Hannigan's *Modern Company*, 3rd edn, Oxford University Press.

[19] FRC, The Combined Code on Corporate Governance, 2008, Principles A.3, A.5; *Re Barings (No 5)* [1999] 1 B.C.L.C 433; *Commonwealth Bank of Australia v Friedrich* (1991) 9 ACLC 946.

[20] See p. 108.

[21] For example, HSBC purchased consumer credit group, Household Finance, in the USA, resulting in unexpected losses in 2005–06 attributable to the failure to integrate the new firm into the HSBC risk management system, HSBC pays £9 billion for credit card group, BBC News, 14 November, 2002, http://news.bbc.co.uk/1/hi/business/2471827.stm; see also: Worthington: HSBC to Writedown $17.2 billion; Pressured to Sell U.S. Business Unit, *HSBC Finance*, 3 March 2008, http://www.glgroup.com/News/HSBC-to-Writedown-$17.2-Billion-Pressured-to-Sell-U.S.-Business-Unit---HSBC-Finance-22313.html.

[22] OECD, The Corporate Governance Lessons from the Financial Crisis, Financial Market Trends, 2008, ISSN 1995-2864, http://ftalphaville.ft.com/blog/2009/02/11/52320/hbos-the-moore-memo/.

drawn largely from the retail and insurance sides of the group paid insufficient attention to its corporate lending business[23] and NEDs failed to understand the core risks the group was running.

The complexities in establishing a risk strategy and controlling risk in financial institutions means that the need for relevant industry experience on the boards of BOFIs is greater than that in non-financial institutions where the failure of the institution will be more likely to be limited to shareholders and creditors, rather than the wider economy. Specific risks faced by banking institutions include maturity transformation (i.e. borrow short and lend long), which means that liquidity risks become a serious concern. Closely associated with liquidity risk is reputational risk, which was only managed during the financial crisis, in some cases, by governmental guarantees. Stress testing is therefore part of the risk management[24] tools used by boards in their oversight of management and review and guiding strategy to determine how the BOFI would react to different financial situations. Certain boards only had a limited technical understanding of products (such as mortgage-backed securities) and a lack of control over balance sheet growth and liquidity needs.[25] Risk control therefore is central to broad strategy and requires the involvement of senior management with appropriate channels of communication so that risk information may be effectively transmitted, with clear reporting lines to the risk committee. The report of the Senior Supervisors Group[26] found that senior management who felt more comfortable with the risks they faced and who managed to avoid significant unexpected losses, had experience in the capital markets. Consequently, the prolonged market instability played to their strengths and experience.[27]

One of the serious flaws in bank corporate governance has been in the role of Non Executive Directors (NEDs) who are expected to act as a counter-weight to executive directors to ensure transparency and accountability in the board's decisions, while at the same time contributing to the leadership of the company.[28] Both executive and NEDs owe the same extent of duties to the company and serious failures on the part of NEDs to challenge the

---

[23] Parliamentary Commission on Banking Standards, An accident waiting to happen: The Failure of HBOS, Fourth Report of Session 2012–13, House of Commons and House of Lords, HL Paper 144; HC 705, http://www.publications.parliament.uk/pa/jt201213/jtselect/jtpcbs/144/144.pdf.

[24] Hector Sants, former Chief Executive of the FSA, stressed the importance of firms having an effective risk management function with clear reporting lines to the risk committee with the risk officer being recognised as unit head to emphasise the importance of the function. The FSA also expected to see an executive director on the board of each high-risk firm solely responsible for risk, The regulator's role in judging competence, Speech at the Securities and Investment Institute Conference, 7 May 2009; http://www.fsa.gov.uk/pages/Library/Communication/Speeches/2009/0514_hs.shtml; see also: The International Finance Report (IIF) which stressed that a solid risk culture throughout the firm is essential and there appears to be need to re-emphasise the respective roles of CEO and the board in the risk management process in many firms. The report then suggests that board oversight needs to be strengthened in risk issues; boards need to be educated on risk issues and be given the means to understand the firm's risk appetite and performance against it.

[25] The OECD highlighted that the less effective boards of directors were unaware of strategic decisions being made by management and had failed to implement effective systems to enable the board to oversee the banks' risk appetite.

[26] Observations on risk management practices during the recent market turbulence, 6 March 2008.

[27] Kirkpatrick, The Corporate Governance Lessons from the Financial Crisis, OECD, February 2009, http://www.oecd.org/dataoecd/32/1/42229620.pdf.

[28] The Cadbury Report stated the committee believes that the calibre of the NEDs is of special importance to setting and maintaining standards of corporate governance, para. 4.10. The Combined Code now recognises the important role of NEDs (June 2008 edn, and currently under review).

executive board have been raised as corporate governance failings. The Commons Treasury Committee[29] was critical of the failures of Northern Rock NEDs to restrain the CEO. Failures by NEDs in urging prudence within the management of other 'high impact' firms were also noted. The Treasury Committee looking into the failure of Northern Rock[30] noted:

> The non-executive members of the Board, and in particular the Chairman of the Board, the Chairman of the Risk Committee and the Senior non-executive director, failed in the case of Northern Rock to ensure that it remained liquid as well as solvent, to provide against the risks that it was taking and to act as an effective restraining force on the strategy of the executive members.

The Observer reported:

> the independent directors, who are supposed to act as a check on the executive folly, did not restrain . . . the chief executive, from his turbo-charged business model, which was a bit like putting a Ferrari engine into a Micra.[31]

Failures in business management – liquidity

A feature of the financial crisis has been the failure of boards to manage liquidity needs and balance sheet growth. Some boards had not put in place mechanisms to monitor the implementation of strategic decisions and they failed to price properly the risk that exposures could have and that certain off-balance-sheet liabilities might have to be funded by on-balance-sheet transactions precisely when it became difficult or expensive to fund externally. Both Bear Stearns and Northern Rock argued that the risk of liquidity drying up could not have been foreseen and in any event they were adequately capitalised. The directors of Northern Rock acknowledged that they had read the Bank of England's Financial Stability Report and an FSA report, both of which drew explicit attention to liquidity risks[32] and at that stage (2007) no emergency lending lines were arranged. The management of Northern Rock was also adamant that it was not reasonable to expect them to foresee that all its funding markets might close simultaneously, as happened on 9 August 2008, or that the crisis would be so prolonged. It is questionable whether these would be viable defences and stress-testing scenarios might have anticipated liquidity drying up and a prolonged financial downturn, particularly keeping in mind that previous regional crises, for example, the Japanese and Asian crisis, have both had long-term repercussions and markets are less predictable.

---

[29] House of Commons Treasury Committee, The run on the Rock, Fifth Report of Session 2007–08, Volume 1, Ordered by The House of Commons, printed 24 January 2008, HC 56–I, http://www.parliament.the-stationery-office.com/pa/cm200708/cmselect/cmtreasy/56/56i.pdf.

[30] House of Commons Treasury Committee, The run on the Rock, Fifth Report of Session 2007–08, Volume 1, Ordered by The House of Commons, printed 24 January 2008, HC 56–I, http://www.parliament.the-stationery-office.com/pa/cm200708/cmselect/cmtreasy/56/56i.pdf.

[31] Sunderland, King not only culprit in a right royal mess, *The Observer*, 23 September 2007, http://www.guardian.co.uk/business/2007/sep/23/8.

[32] House of Commons Treasury Committee, The run on the Rock, Fifth Report of Session 2007–08, Volume 1, Ordered by The House of Commons, printed 24 January 2008, HC 56–I, http://www.parliament.the-stationery-office.com/pa/cm200708/cmselect/cmtreasy/56/56i.pdf.

Failures in remuneration policies

There is general consensus that badly designed remuneration policies[33] and compensation schemes in the financial services sector contributed to 'short-termism' and excessive risk-taking without regard to the long-term performance of financial institutions.[34] The Senior Supervisors Group[35] noted that 'an issue for a number of firms is whether compensation and other incentives have been sufficiently well designed to achieve an appropriate balance between risk appetite and risk controls . . .'. Thus, the legitimacy of excessive remuneration and pensions packages, which not only damage shareholder wealth but also warp and jeopardise the executive function, are questionable and leave room to challenge the reasonableness of such awards. One of the weaknesses of the system of voting remuneration packages to senior management is that remuneration committees, while intended to be independent of the executive, are made up of NEDs nominated and appointed by executive directors and there is a serious risk of conflict of interests or lack of independence.[36]

Institutional shareholders

The significance of institutional investors, mainly pension funds and insurance companies, has increased significantly over the past 40 years. The Cadbury Committee expressed the view that institutional investors should use their influence in companies in which they hold shares to persuade compliance with the Code.[37] The Combined Code[38] states that institutional shareholders should enter into dialogue with companies based on a 'mutual understanding of objectives'. The Walker Report[39] recognised the significance of communication and engagement between companies and their shareholders and the report identified potential for long-term shareholders, as owners, to influence the quality of governance in the financial services sector. The report recommended that firms should disclose their shareholder engagement strategies and activities.

---

[33] Failures in remuneration, and government response following the credit crisis, is dealt with separately in Ch. 5.

[34] HM Treasury, A review of corporate governance in UK Banks and other financial entities, Final Recommendations, 26 November 2009, http://webarchive.nationalarchives.gov.uk/+/http:/www.hm-treasury.gov.uk/d/walker_review_261109.pdf.

[35] The Report of the Financial Stability Forum, Enhancing market and institutional resilience (2008) shared similar concerns, p. 7, http://www.financialstabilityboard.org/publications/r_0804.pdf.

[36] In early 2008, the FSA conducted a review of remuneration policies and concluded that remuneration structures in financial firms had encouraged employees to pursue risky business policies which effectively undermined the firm's own systems of risk control. The FSA therefore issued a 'Dear CEO' letter to all high-impact banks and building societies warning of the need to ensure that remuneration practices were consistent with sound risk management. The letter outlined examples of good and poor practice and asked firms to review their remuneration policies against this guidance, ahead of decisions about their end-of-year remuneration reviews. This was followed by a policy statement on Reforming remuneration practices in financial services, PS 09/15, http://www.fsa.gov.uk/pubs/policy/ps09_15.pdf.

[37] Report of the Committee on the Financial Aspects of Corporate Governance, (1992). Similar views were expressed in the Greenbury Report (1995) and the Hampel Report (1998).

[38] Financial Reporting Council, The Combined Code on Corporate Governance, June 2008, http://www.frc.org.uk/documents/pagemanager/frc/Combined_Code_June_2008/Combined%20Code%20Web%20Optimized%20June%202008(2).pdf. The revised version came into force from 29 June 2010.

[39] HM Treasury, A review of corporate governance in UK Banks and other financial entities, Final Recommendations, 26 November 2009, http://webarchive.nationalarchives.gov.uk/+/http:/www.hm-treasury.gov.uk/d/walker_review_261109.pdf.

Oversight of controller shareholders

The Banking Act 1979 introduced the policy of monitoring controlling shareholding interests in licensed deposit-taking institutions.[40] The collapse of a number of banks, including Johnson Matthey Bankers, in the early 1980s resulted in these requirements being extended to all deposit-taking institutions with s.49 of the FSMA 2000 imposing the current 'fit and proper' person requirement in respect of shareholders. The section requires shareholder 'controllers' of deposit-taking institutions to be 'fit and proper' persons before they are authorised to acquire the controlling interest, with subsequent changes in controlling shareholders also being notified to the regulator prior to changes in control.[41] The FSMA provides that a person acquires control if, *inter alia*, he acquires or holds 10 per cent or more of the shares in an authorised institution and is able to exercise significant influence over its management through his shareholding or voting rights. A person who proposes to acquire a significant holding in a deposit-taking institution must notify the FCA of his intention.[42] The FCA will require the shareholder, or potential shareholder, to be judged on whether such a person is 'fit and proper' to have such a holding[43] and whether he is financially sufficiently secure to ensure that the holding does not weaken the bank. Certain types of persons are likely to be disapproved by the FCA as 'fit and proper' persons, for example a person convicted of serious fraud or financial deception, as are certain types of foreign nationals, or governments. Such requirements are imposed on shareholders of banks for a number of reasons, including ensuring banking stability and customer confidence.

To enhance the transparency of corporate governance, in July 2013, the Secretary of State for Business, Innovation and Skills, Vince Cable, launched the *Transparency & Trust Discussion Paper*.[44] This paper affirms the UK's commitment to implement a central registry of company beneficial ownership information, to ensure that the ownership and influence of companies remains transparent.

The audit function

The Report of the Parliamentary Committee on Banking Standards recognised that a more robust internal audit function could play a significant role in supporting the executive and non-executive directors of BOFIs. The report blamed 'conflicts of interest' and suggested too close a relationship between top accountants and senior bank management which meant 'auditors failed to act decisively and fully to expose risks being added to balance sheets throughout the period of highly leveraged banking expansion'. The Commission also found 'evidence' that indicated that 'auditors did not act as the last line of defence against banks' questionable reporting on their own businesses and, at worst, they were cheerleaders for it'. The Chartered

---

[40] However, recognised banks were left free from much of the rigours of the legislation. See: White Paper on Banking Supervision (Cmnd 9695).

[41] The Financial Services and Markets Act 2000 (Controllers) Regulations 2009 (SI 2009/53).

[42] Sections 178–192 FSMA 2000; see also SUP 11: Controllers and Close Links.

[43] SUP 11.7.5 G(1)–(2).

[44] Department for Business Innovation & Skills, Transparency & Trust: Enhancing the Transparency of UK Company Ownership and Increasing Trust in UK Business, Discussion Paper, July 2013, https://www.gov.uk/government/uploads/system/uploads/attachment_data/file/212079/bis-13-959-transparency-and-trust-enhancing-the-transparency-of-uk-company-ownership-and-increaing-trust-in-uk-business.pdf.

Institute of Internal Auditors[45] consequently issued new guidance intended to enhance the effectiveness of the internal audit functions and the impact and influence they have within the organisations. In exercising their supervisory judgement, the FCA will consider the nature and extent of compliance with the guidance in any assessment of internal audit effectiveness within regulated firms. The FCA has incorporated the internal audit into its SYSC[46] and also in the approved functions regime.[47] The most recent definition of internal audit is provided in the Code of Ethics and International Standards for the Internal Auditing Profession,[48] which provides that:

> Internal auditing is an independent, objective assurance and consulting activity designed to add value and improve an organisation's operations. It helps an organisation accomplish its objectives by bringing a systematic, disciplined approach to evaluate and improve the effectiveness of risk management, control and governance processes.

The definition highlights the independence and objectivity of the internal auditor and that the principles established within the code are intended to develop integrity, objectivity, confidentiality and competency. These principles are further developed in the rules of conduct, which bind internal auditors in respect of the integrity of their work so that internal auditors perform their work with honesty, diligence and responsibility, or not to participate in any activity that impairs their independence. However, internal auditors will communicate their findings to those who can act on their findings and recommendations. They, therefore, have access to directors and the board of management to whom they may disclose their findings. However, internal audit will only be successful if the senior management is willing to act to remedy issues and defects once identified, and to implement recommendations. The internal audit of Barings raised a number of concerns, which were never acted on by the management. The internal auditor must establish an efficient and effective system to maintain and enhance quality assurance within an organisation to improve internal operation but he does not have a direct channel of communication to the FCA or other regulatory bodies. The internal auditor is not in the formal role of a 'whistleblower' and a survey by the Basel Committee on Banking Supervision found reluctance to move the role in that direction.[49] Nevertheless, banking auditors do have a duty of care towards the FCA's functions to ensure that 'information in the regulatory returns is consistent' with the information audited but the bank auditors for Northern Rock expressed the view that the auditor 'was not under a duty of care to point out certain aspects of the structure of Northern Rock's liabilities' to the FSA[50] (the then financial services regulator).

[45] Chartered Institute of Internal Auditors, Effective Internal Audit in the Financial Services Sector, http://www.iia.org.uk/media/354788/0758_effective_internal_audit_financial_webfinal.pdf.

[46] FSA Handbook, Handbook, Senior Management Arrangements, Systems and Controls, Release 062, December 2007, SYSC 6.2, http://www.fshandbook.info/FS/html/FCA/SYSC/6/2.

[47] FSA Handbook, Senior Management Arrangements, Systems and Controls, Release 062, February 2007, SYSC 6.2.1.

[48] Institute of Internal Auditing – UK and Ireland (1 January 2004) Code of Ethics and International Standards for the Professional Practice of Internal Auditing, at: http://www.theiia.org/?doc_id=1499, copyright © by The Institute of Internal Auditors, Inc. All Rights Reserved.

[49] Basel Committee on Banking Supervision (August 2002), Internal audit in banks and the supervisor's relationship auditors: A survey.

[50] House of Commons Treasury Committee, The run on the Rock, Fifth Report of Session 2007–08, Volume 1, Ordered by The House of Commons, printed 24 January 2008, HC 56–I, http://www.parliament.the-stationery-office.com/pa/cm200708/cmselect/cmtreasy/56/56i.pdf.

The audit committee

The audit committee is required, *inter alia*, to monitor the integrity of financial statements;[51] review internal financial controls and management systems; monitor and review the internal audit function; assist in the appointment of external auditors and their remuneration package; monitor and review the independence, objectivity and effectiveness of external auditors; and devise and implement a policy to govern non-audit work provided by the external auditor.[52] The audit committee has a significant role in overseeing the affairs of the company and is required to meet at least three times a year, with the expectation that it will meet more frequently[53] and it is anticipated that the chair of the committee will liaise continuously with key office-holders within the company. The report emphasises that the company will be required to provide resources to enable the audit committee to discharge its functions appropriately[54] and the remuneration package of the audit committee needs to be commensurate with the time needed to discharge its duties[55] with the membership having the appropriate skills and expertise.[56] The company is required to provide the appropriate training and induction to enable members of the audit committee to discharge their duties.[57] The audit committee also needs to oversee the appointment of the external auditors and oversee their work.[58] The audit committee must consist of individuals who are familiar with regulation and supervisory requirements of the business within which they function.

So while there is clear evidence that corporate governance failings contributed heavily to the financial crisis it is necessary to explore why good governance of banks is critical.

Why is good governance of banks important?

It is necessary that the regulation of banks integrate strong governance standards in order to protect stakeholders who have an economic and social interest in a robust banking system. For most stakeholders, for example customers, suppliers, employees etc., their economic welfare depends on a sound and stable banking system and because of the dangers of systemic risk[59] that bank failure poses on the economy and society generally a robust governance system that balances the various, sometimes competing, interests is essential. The essential external framework of prudential regulation and supervision must be supplemented by high standards of internal self-regulation to ensure good management and the drive for profits must not be allowed to create instability in the system or, adversely, affect depositor interests and market confidence. A balance has to be maintained between the parameters in which

---

[51] Smith (2003) Audit Committees Combined Code Guidance Report and Proposed Guidance (Smith Report), report by the FRC-appointed group chaired by Sir Robert Smith; available at www.frc.org.uk/images/uploaded/documents/ACReport.pdf.

[52] Para. 2.1.

[53] Paras 3.5 and 3.9.

[54] Paras 3.11–3.14.

[55] Para. 3.15.

[56] Para. 3.19.

[57] Para. 3.19.

[58] Paras 5.14–5.18.

[59] De Bandt and Hartmann, *Systemic Risk: A Survey*, ECB Working Paper No 35, November 2000, examine the nature and effect of systemic risk in the banking sector, http://www.ecb.int/pub/pdf/scpwps/ecbwp035.pdf.

regulation will allow business to be undertaken and innovate, and the ability of the board to develop and execute its business strategy. The Walker report concluded that:

> The massive dislocation and costs borne by society justify tough regulatory action . . .

The good corporate governance of BOFIs is therefore fundamental because instability within the banking and financial sector can have a major ripple effect which may affect individual bank depositors and the wider economy. The statement of the Basel Committee on Banking Supervision on Corporate Governance for Banking Organisations recognises the special role of banks:[60]

> Banks are a critical component of any economy. They provide financing for commercial enterprises, basic financial services to a broad segment of the population and access to payments systems. In addition, some banks are expected to make credit and liquidity available in difficult market conditions. The importance of banks to national economies is underscored by the fact that banking is virtually a universally regulated industry and that banks have access to government safety nets. It is of crucial importance therefore that banks have strong corporate governance.

Strong banks and strong bank corporate governance is necessary because of the social costs of bank failure. The loss of confidence and resulting instability may have long-term consequences beyond the individual institution or even the banking sector, and adversely impact the wider economy from which it may take considerable time to recover. Further, the effect of a banking crisis does not contain itself within national boundaries and, as we have seen recently, a subprime mortgage that started in the USA rapidly developed into a global banking crisis.[61]

While the fear of an old fashioned run on the bank should be sufficient to curb reckless management decisions, that threat has proven to have insufficient force to ensure good management. The leverage the depositor has in reality to curb management excess is limited partly because of the limited information customers, particularly small retail customers, have available to them and in a systemic collapse there may be limited alternatives or opportunity for depositors to transfer funds to more stable institutions. In many instances, the customer is unable to ascertain whether his bank is at risk and if it has a management that is fully engaged with a robust business strategy, until it is too late.

We will now examine the position of the bank customers as stakeholders in a bank.

The position of depositors as stakeholders

The legal position of the depositor, customer, was examined in *Foley* v *Hill*[62] where the House of Lords held that a banker and customer relationship is essentially that of creditor and debtor and in *Space Investments Ltd* v *Canadian Imperial Bank of Commerce Trust Co (Bahamas)*[63] Lord Templeman expressed the view that:

---

[60] Basel Committee on Banking Supervision, Enhancing Corporate Governance for Banking Organizations, Bank of International Settlements, 1999, http://www.ecgi.org/codes/documents/basel_committee.pdf.

[61] Calomiris, The Subprime Turmoil: What's Old, What's New, and What's Next, Paper presented at the 9th Jacques Polak Annual Research Conference, hosted by the International Monetary Fund Washington, DC, 13–14 November 2008, http://www.imf.org/external/np/res/seminars/2008/arc/pdf/CWC.pdf.

[62] (1848) 9 ER 1002.

[63] [1986] 1 WLR 1072.

If the bank becomes insolvent the customer can only prove in the liquidation of the bank as an unsecured creditor for the amount which was, or ought to have been, credited to the account at the date when the bank went into liquidation.

The line of cases from *Foley* v *Hill*[64] set to rest the debate around the view that the banker and customer relationship was one of agent and principal which bound the bank in a continuous duty to account to the customer in respect of the deposit balance. Therefore, while the bank is a going concern, it is only contractually accountable to repay the amount deposited as and when the customer demands repayment.[65]

While, this has the effect of enabling the bank to treat the deposits placed with it as its own and thereby largely free to utilise that money in the course of its business, the common law offers the customer little redress in the event of his bank going into liquidation. It is for this reason that most countries with advanced banking systems have implemented some form of a compulsory insurance scheme. In the UK, the Financial Services Compensation Scheme (FSCS) is effectively the compensation scheme of last resort and will provide limited redress to a depositor who finds himself as an unsecured creditor and therefore liable to bear the worst of the excesses of mismanagement. The FSCS is also a tool for maintaining confidence and stability within the banking sector, although such guarantees proved inadequate in the recent crisis.

The practical reasons for opening a bank account, as opposed to investing, will vary and therefore depositors are less likely to follow trends in the banking markets[66] and even likely less to monitor risk, which gives banks a customer base having only a limited interest in their accounts. This gives banks almost complete freedom to use the deposits to support their daily business; particularly as fairly small amounts of the balances deposited will be required to be repaid at any one time. It is because the bank is only legally obliged to return an amount equivalent to the monies deposited, and not the amount *in species*, together with the fact that the customer has only limited knowledge and understanding of the risks bank management might engage in during the course of the business that moral hazard between the bank and depositors is limited. *In species* refers to an asset in its present form without selling it for cash, for example fractional share distributions. Bank managers, therefore, have strong incentives to increase risk because they can transfer the risk of loss to their depositors, customers, while receiving profits made using the monies deposited by those customers. The bank is only accountable to the depositors for any profits through the payment of agreed interest, if any.[67] However, the recent financial crisis has taken the loss of risk a step further with the decisions to bail out failing banks, when to prevent systemic collapse, the then government decided to nationalise, or part nationalise, several banks.[68] In such circumstances, government intervention in the form of nationalisation or a guarantee that depositors would not bear the burden of failing banks transferred the risks of bank failure to the taxpayer.

---

[64] (1848) 9 ER 1002.

[65] See Ch. 1 for a more detailed discussion.

[66] Garten, Banking on the market: Relying on Depositors to Control Bank Risk, 4 *Yale J of Regulation*, 129 at 134.

[67] *Re Head, Head* v *Head (No) 2* [1894] 2 Ch 236 at 238 where the court distinguished between current accounts, which at that time carried no interest, and savings accounts that bore interest but against which it was not possible to draw cheques. Banking practice now is that current accounts that are in credit will result in interest payable to the customer calculated on a daily basis.

[68] See Ch. 5.

It is now intended to explore the nature of obligations company directors owe under the Companies Act 2006 and the impact of that legislation specifically on BOFIs.

Failings in bank governance and the duties owed by directors under the Companies Act 2006

The framework of corporate governance places the interests of the company and its shareholders centre stage. The role of the executive board is to protect and advance the interests of the company by setting the strategic direction of the company and appointing management that is capable and experienced. Embedded within this overarching responsibility is the need to ensure that management makes an informed and considered decision about which businesses to pursue and to what extent; the kinds and levels of risks the firm should engage in, which need to be carefully assessed against the overall, long-term objectives of the company. Directors, including NEDs, other than those of an insolvent or near-insolvent company, owe a number of duties to their company.[69]

These duties, although initially developed by the rules of the common law and equity, are now enshrined and codified by ss.172–177 of the Companies Act 2006. The codification of directors' duties was in itself a major leap forward; this was the first time under UK law that directors' duties have been committed to writing and, significantly, in a single place. The new statutory statement is intended to capture a cultural change in the way in which companies conduct their business.[70] However, it must be remembered that the duties merely impose minimum standards of good behaviour against which the conduct of directors of BOFIs will be judged; the duties are not intended to tell the directors what to do but establish minimum standards with which they are required to conform. However, directors of BOFIs must be familiar with the duties they owe the company and they should be able to identify any training or expert advice they may need to ensure continued compliance with such duties. This is key to a working environment where both business products and practices have changed significantly and within which the pace of future development is not likely to slow. Some of the duties[71] owed by directors of BOFIs under which they may be held liable, in the context of the recent financial crisis, are described under the following headings.

Promoting the success of the company?

The new duty to promote the success of the company is set out in s.172 of the Companies Act 2006. This duty is developed from one of the overriding principles of the fiduciary duties, i.e. the duty to act in good faith in the interests of the company. The Act imposes a duty on the director to act in the way that would, in good faith, be most likely to promote the success of the company (the first limb).[72] The section appears to be a codification of the equitable

---

[69] Sections 170–177 Companies Act 2006.

[70] Hodge, Companies Act 2006, Duties of company directors, Ministerial statements, June 2007, http://www. berr.gov.uk/files/file40139.pdf.

[71] It is outside the scope of this work to deal with duties owed by company directors in detail and for further discussion you are referred to texts in Company Law generally. Reference may be made to Hannigan's *Company Law*, 3rd edn, Oxford: Oxford University Press.

[72] Section 172(1) Companies Act 2006.

principles and in *Re Southern Counties Fresh Foods Ltd*[73] the court compared the new form of wording with the wording under the equitable principles and concluded that they implemented the same principles and came to the same thing, with the modern formulation giving a more readily understood definition of the scope of the duty. The court also confirmed that the test under s.172(1) remains subjective in nature and that it will therefore need to determine whether the director honestly believed that he was acting in a way most likely to promote the success of the company. Therefore, in *Extrasure Travel Insurance Ltd v Scattergood*, the court held that the test is whether the director honestly believes that he was acting in the best interests of the company although that belief appears unreasonable to the court.[74] This mirrors the pre-2006 position established in *Re Smith & Fawcett Ltd.*[75] While the 2006 Act does not define how success is to be judged for a commercial company, it will be determined by the long-term increase in the value of shares,[76] by board strategy and by the members of the company. A firm's business and significantly risk balance, therefore, reflects the view of its senior management and what risks they, in good faith, believe are commensurate with the firm's strategy, having regard to the interests of the shareholders. Keay[77] points out that the section does not require directors to guarantee success and there is therefore no reasonable care requirement within the scope of the section, although there may be multiple sections under which liability may be imposed.

However, s.172 does enshrine a radical change in the law and culture within which companies must conduct their business. Section 172(1)(a)–(f) (the second limb) purports to capture the corporate governance objective that requires directors to have regard to shareholder considerations and imposes on directors the duty to have regard to the long-term interests of the company, its members as a whole and non-shareholder interests.[78] For the first time, UK company law expressly recognises the significance of paying attention to the interests of a wider group of stakeholders but in the context of the overriding obligation that requires directors to 'promote the success of the company for the benefit of its members as a whole'.

The approach in s.172 is a legal response to modern business practices and articulates the connection between business practices under which the company has regard to a wider range of issues in pursuing success and 'what is good for society at large'.[79] Pursuing the interests of shareholders and embracing these wider responsibilities are objectives that are intended to be complementary and not necessarily in conflict. Thus, when exercising this duty under s.172 directors are required to have regard to the non-exhaustive factors listed, including the long-term consequence of the decisions; the interests of the employees; the relationships with suppliers and customers; the impact of the decision on the community and environment; the desirability of maintaining a reputation for high standards of business conduct; and the need

---

[73] [2008] EWHC 2810.

[74] [2003] 1 B.C.L.C. 598 at 619.

[75] [1942] Ch 304.

[76] Lord Goldsmith, Lords Grand Committee, 6 February 2006, column 255, Companies Act 2006, Duties of company directors, Ministerial statements, June 2007, http://www.berr.gov.uk/files/file40139.pdf.

[77] Legislative Comment: Section 72 (1) of the Companies Act 2006: an interpretation and assessment, (2007) Company Lawyer 106 at 108.

[78] This is supplemented by the enhanced business review requirement under s.417 which compels corporate disclosure of information on stakeholder issues.

[79] Hodge, Companies Act 2006, Duties of company directors, Ministerial statements, June 2007, http://www.berr.gov.uk/files/file40139.pdf.

to act fairly as between members of the company. The duty to promote the success of the company is, therefore, a duty to act for the collective good of the members as a whole, not merely the majority shareholder.[80] It remains to be seen how in practice directors will balance these, sometimes conflicting, considerations: for example, environmental considerations might not always be consistent with shareholders' interests, or the interests of depositors' to have their account balances safeguarded may not be compatible with shareholder motives to enhance profits, and in cases of conflict, the Act cannot always intend that shareholder interests take precedence.

Further, whether s.172 is intended to extend the scope of liability to stakeholders, such as bank depositors, who are in law unsecured creditors, remains to be seen. The question remains whether banks are expected to have regard to the social costs of bank failure and the scope of that liability, if any.

The interests of creditors become paramount only in the insolvency of the company and depositors are classed merely as unsecured creditors of the company with no rights to have their interests taken into consideration while the company is a going concern, unless s.172(b)–(f) can come to their aid. Section 172(1)(d) requires directors to have regard to the 'desirability of maintaining a reputation for high standards of business conduct'. The majority of bank depositors are dependent on the services, advice and information provided to them by their banks regarding the nature of accounts and, sometimes investment opportunities, and therefore expect high standards of business and integrity from their banks. Section 172(1)(f) provides directors must act fairly as between the members of the company. So could depositors, as unsecured creditors, sue for breach of s.172(1)(f); does the section give an unidentified class of depositors a right to bring an action? It should be noted that the courts refused to allow an action against the then UK bank regulator, the Bank of England, for negligence in respect of its handling of BCCI and its eventual closure on the basis that depositors were too remote a class to whom a duty of care was owed (an unidentified class who could not establish proximity).[81] Moreover, the Bank of England, as the banking regulator, is granted statutory immunity from prosecution unless deliberate wrongdoing can be established.[82] This protection is now extended to the PRA and FCA (and previously the FSA) but there is no similar immunity extended to directors; indeed they now owe duties to various stakeholders under s.172(1)(b)–(f), but lack of proximity may well defeat any action by depositors (unsecured creditors).

Duty to exercise reasonable skill and diligence

The legal duties placed on directors against which their conduct will be judged are critical, as board competence is difficult, particularly for an outsider, to judge.[83] A company director is required under s.174 of the CA 2006 to exercise reasonable skill and care in the discharge of his functions and responsibilities. The duty of skill and care at common law was based on

---

[80] Lord Goldsmith, Lords Grand Committee, 6 February 2006, column 255, Companies Act 2006, Duties of company directors, Ministerial statements, June 2007, http://www.berr.gov.uk/files/file40139.pdf.

[81] *Three Rivers DC v Bank of England* [2001] UKHL 16.

[82] Banking Act 1987, s.1(4).

[83] The interim report of the Institute of International Finance Committee on Market Best Practices concluded that: 'events have raised questions about the ability of certain boards properly to oversee senior managements and to understand and monitor the business itself', 2008, Washington, DC.

competence and the fiduciary concepts of honesty and loyalty.[84] The initial expressions of the duty to exercise reasonable skill and care have stood the test of time and even the more modern formulation of the duty of care is based on the statement by Romer J in *Re City Equitable Fire Insurance Co Ltd*[85] where it was held that 'a director need not exhibit in the performance of his duties a greater degree of skill than may reasonably be expected from a person of his knowledge and experience'. The modern view of the duty to exercise skill and care is, however, a reflection of the fact that directors are expected to be more professional and experienced in the discharge of their responsibilities to stakeholders and the public, and the courts demand a more objective standard of care. Holding a directorship is no longer a hobby for the gentleman seeking a not too demanding distraction. In *Commonwealth Bank of Australia v Friedrich*,[86] Tadgell J expressed the view that:

> In particular, the stage has been reached when a director is expected to be capable of under-standing his company's affairs to the extent of actually reaching a reasonably informed opinion of its financial capacity . . . I think it follows that he is required by law to be capable of keeping abreast of the company's affairs, and sufficiently abreast of them to act appropriately if there are reasonable grounds to expect that the company will not be able to pay all its debts in due course and he has reasonable cause to expect it.

Similar views have been expressed by the UK courts in *Norman v Theodore Goddard*[87] and in *Re D'Jan of London Ltd*,[88] in the context of an examination of s.214 of the Insolvency Act 1986, which introduced a more objective standard of care through consideration of the general knowledge that may be reasonably attributed to a director in the same position. More recently, examining the duty to exercise reasonable skill and care in *Lexi Holdings (in administration) v Luqman and Other*[89] the court described s.214 of the Insolvency Act 1986 as the model from which s.174 of the Companies Act 2006 is derived. All directors must, therefore, attend to their duties including taking reasonable steps to supervise and control the conduct of their company's business.

An action for misfeasance under s.212 of the Companies Act 2006 may be available, as an alternative, against the directors. Such action provides a remedy where the directors have misapplied or retained, or become accountable, for money or assets of the company, or where they commit a breach of fiduciary duty owed to the company. Following *Re D'Jan of London Ltd*, misfeasance can include a breach of duty of care, as the court held signing a form without reading it amounted to negligence, thus giving rise to misfeasance.[90]

A number of failings in corporate governance could amount to a breach of duty of care. The FSA, the previous financial services regulator, raised concerns, in 2004, that key parts of the Halifax Bank of Scotland (HBOS) group were posing 'medium or high' risks to maintaining market confidence and protecting customers and yet the board continued to expand the business base and was vulnerable when HBOS, in 2009, became the victim of short-selling.

---

[84] Hasio, A sprouting duty of honesty and loyalty? Companies Act 2006 (2009) 20 *International Company and Commercial Law Review* 201 at 306.

[85] [1925] Ch 407 and which itself was based on *Overend & Gurney Co v Gibb* (1871–72) L.R. 5 H.L. 480 at 486–487.

[86] (1991) 9 ACLC 946 at 965.

[87] [1992] B.C.C. 14.

[88] [1993] B.C.C. 646.

[89] [2008] EWHC 1639.

[90] [1993] B.C.C. 646.

By early 2007, a number of governmental standard-settings agencies had started to issue warnings about the level of defaults and liquidity.[91] The directors of Northern Rock acknowledged to the parliamentary inquiry that they had read the FSA's warnings about liquidity risk, but considered their systems of raising short-term finance sound.[92] Despite these warnings Northern Rock did not have in place sufficient liquidity insurance to protect itself from the worsening market situations. The House of Commons Treasury Committee laid the blame for this failure to respond to changing circumstances in the market clearly on the bank's management.[93] Inadequate financial industry experience of NEDs has also been identified as one of the elements of failure at board level[94] and NED failures to mount a robust challenge to executive decisions may amount to a failure of due diligence.[95] Executive directors responsible for appointing NEDs may also be liable, among others, for failure to ensure that NEDs had appropriate experience, training and skills. However, banking experience is clearly not enough; Northern Rock had two board members with banking experience while Bears Stearns had 7 out of 13 directors who had banking experience, although at Lehman Brothers 4 of the 10 members of the board were over 75 years of age and only one had a current banking background.[96]

The law recognises the power of the directors to delegate their duties in appropriate circumstances,[97] for example delegating power to company accountants and auditors to prepare proper financial records of the business, but where delegation is permitted the board and individual directors retain an obligation to supervise and control the conduct of persons to whom powers are delegated.[98] Where delegation takes place the law does not distinguish

---

[91] The lack of an active risk committee was cited by the OECD report as a possible reason for ineffective risk management. The Lehman Brothers' risk committee was noted as having convened only twice, in 2006 and 2007, and Bear Stearns' committee was formed just prior to its collapse. The US Securities and Exchange Commission (SEC) also highlighted that a feature of the Bear Stearns' failure was that staff involved in risk assessment worked in close proximity to traders, which led the SEC to conclude that risk managers were hampered by a lack of independence in discharging their duties.

[92] House of Commons Treasury Committee, The run on the Rock, Fifth Report of Session 2007–08, Volume 1, Ordered by The House of Commons, printed 24 January 2008, HC 56–I, http://www.parliament.the-stationery-office.com/pa/cm200708/cmselect/cmtreasy/56/56i.pdf.

[93] The Committee condemned the 'high-risk, reckless business strategy of Northern Rock, with reliance on short- and-medium-term wholesale funding and an absence of sufficient insurance and a failure to arrange standby facility or cover that risk, meant that it was unable to cope with the liquidity pressures placed upon it by the freezing of international capital markets in August 2007. Given that the formulation of that strategy was a fundamental role of the Board of Northern Rock, overseen by some directors who had been there since its demutualization, the failure of that strategy must be attributed to the Board.'

[94] HM Treasury, A review of corporate governance in UK Banks and other financial entities, Final Recommendations, 26 November 2009, http://webarchive.nationalarchives.gov.uk/+/http:/www.hm-treasury.gov.uk/d/walker_review_261109.pdf; also House of Commons Treasury Committee, The run on the Rock, Fifth Report of Session 2007–08, Volume 1, Ordered by The House of Commons, printed 24 January 2008, HC 56–I, http://www.parliament.the-stationery-office.com/pa/cm200708/cmselect/cmtreasy/56/56i.pdf.

[95] Watson and Bauer, Don't bank on strong governance: Observations on corporate governance in US banks, Special Comment, New York, August 2005, concluded that: 'too few banks have adopted the approach in other financial service sectors of appointing retired industry executives or advisors with industry experience such as accountants or consultants'. http://v3.moodys.com/sites/products/AboutMoodysRatingsAttachments/2003700000425158.pdf.

[96] Kirkpatrick, The Corporate Governance Lessons from the Financial Crisis, OECD, February 2009, http://www.oecd.org/dataoecd/32/1/42229620.pdf.

[97] Originally recognised in *Re City Equitable Fire Insurance Co Ltd* [1925] Ch 407.

[98] *Re Barings Plc (No 5)* [1999] 1 B.C.L.C. 433.

between the duty to supervise management functions delegated to employees and the duty to supervise management functions delegated to a fellow director,[99] and following *Re Barings Plc (No 5)* it was clear that directors can be disqualified for failing to have adequate internal controls in place to prevent reckless (there was no evidence of dishonesty or fraud) trading which produced losses and which eventually led to the collapse of the entire bank. In that case Nick Leeson, a futures trader in Singapore working for the former Barings Bank entered into a number of contracts in breach of the bank's internal audit recommendation. He subsequently fraudulently doctored the bank's accounts, and reported large profits, while in fact trading at losses. Following an earthquake in Kobe, Japan, the stock market went into a downward spiral, and his losses were uncovered. The Secretary of State sought director disqualification orders under the Company Directors Disqualification Act 1986 against three directors of Barings for their failure to supervise his activities. They were alleged to be incompetent, and therefore 'unfit to be concerned in the management of a company'.

Duty to exercise independent judgement

While directors of a company, acting with due diligence, may delegate functions in appropriate circumstances the law, under s.173 Companies Act 2006 still requires them to exercise independent judgement. The duty does not prevent a director, acting diligently and to promote the success of the company, from relying on the advice or work of others, but the final decision must be his responsibility. In certain circumstances a director may be in breach of his duties if he fails to take appropriate advice, for example legal advice, but as with all advice it does not absolve a director from his responsibilities to make a considered decision on the basis of the information and his overall knowledge of the business. It would, therefore, not excuse the failures of the Northern Rock management to suggest they took legal or FSA advice without actually looking at its relevance to the Northern Rock scenario and then making a properly considered decision. Neither the legal advisers, nor indeed the FSA, were there to actually manage Northern Rock's business and the failures must be imputed to the management alone.[100]

Actions in the insolvency of the company

Claims against directors for fraudulent trading[101] are less common simply because of the difficulty of establishing fraud. The liquidator must establish that directors carried on business with the intent to defraud creditors or for some other fraudulent purpose. The section requires 'actual dishonesty, involving real moral blame',[102] and although the wrongdoing must be proven 'on the balance of probabilities' the more improbable the alleged dishonest conduct, the more compelling the evidence of the act must be.[103] However, a liquidator is less

---

[99] *Lexi Holdings (in administration)* v *Luqman and Others* [2008] EWHC 1639.

[100] Unless of course misfeasance, or deliberate wrongdoing, can be ascribed to the FSA since it has immunity from prosecution for acts done in its regulatory capacity or unless negligence can be imputed to those giving legal advice, s.19 FSMA 2000.

[101] Section 213 Insolvency Act 1986.

[102] *Re Patrick and Lyon Ltd* [1933] Ch 786.

[103] *Aktieselskbet Dansk Skibfinansiering* v *Brothers* [2001] 2 BCLC 324.

likely to rely on having to prove fraudulent trading, when an action on wrongful trading requires a lower standard of proof and yet is wide enough to extend and include all actions for wrongful trading.[104]

Corporate governance under the Financial and Services and Markets Act 2000 (FSMA 2000)

Until the new 'twin peaks' regulatory system was implemented[105] the Financial Services Authority (FSA), together with the Bank of England and the Treasury, have overall regulatory responsibility for deposit-taking, insurance and investment business.[106] The division of responsibility was based on the principles of clear accountability, transparency, avoidance of duplication and regular information exchange so that each authority could efficiently and effectively discharge its functions in support of the tripartite arrangements. The FSMA 2000, as amended, amalgamates the components of the regulatory regime designating the regulatory authority with powers to undertake authorisation and supervision of the banking sector, with enforcement sanctions and powers. The Act recognises that the regulation of banks must be flexible and differentiates between individual firms on the basis of a risk-based approach and the new regulatory authorities, the FCA and PRA have delegated statutory authority to implement rules and practices to support its statutory functions.

The FCA is required to execute its regulatory and supervisory functions in a proactive manner that prevents instability within the banking sector, rather than as a reactive body. However, market conditions can develop and alter so rapidly that, to some extent, the discharge of its regulatory role will inevitably be reactive. Since neither the FCA nor its representatives are involved on a daily basis in the management of banks its perception and knowledge of the firm is bound to be once removed, and therefore subject to informational gaps. The FCA needs, therefore, to ensure that despite, sometimes, turbulent market conditions its regulatory and oversight strategy is sufficiently robust that banks are able to weather any turbulence, foreseen or otherwise, with minimal repercussions to their customer base.

UK banking regulation is therefore intended to be adaptable and sufficiently robust to accommodate the uniqueness of each individual firm. However, the FCA's functions must be carried out in a manner that complies with its statutory objectives and within the parameters in which the FCA is authorised to act. The Financial Services and Markets Tribunal and, if necessary, the courts can therefore determine the lawfulness of the FCA's conduct.[107] The statutory objectives are a means of ensuring internal and external accountability of the FCA.[108] They are intended to maintain the integrity of the financial services sector and thus maintain consumer confidence and protection while, at the same time, ensuring the reputation of the financial services sector by regulating institutions and personnel. The FSMA 2000

---

[104] Section 214 Insolvency Act 1986.
[105] See Ch. 4.
[106] Memorandum of Understanding between HM Treasury, the Bank of England and the Financial Services Authority, http://www.bankofengland.co.uk/financialstability/mou.pd.
[107] Draft Financial Services and markets Bill, Delegated Powers and Deregulation Committee, para. 11
[108] Section 2(1) provides that the FSA must act in a manner 'reasonably' compatible with its regulatory objectives.

tasks the FCA with the statutory objectives to: maintain market confidence; enhance understanding; protect consumers; and reduce financial crime.[109]

The FCA's corporate governance regime

Authorisation under the FSMA 2000 as amended will allow deposit-taking institutions to operate within the perimeters of the Act so that regulated activity can be undertaken without the threat of criminal sanctions.[110] The prudential regulation of banks is undertaken through the FCA's established principles and practices because banks normally operate on a small asset reserve and generally hold a large proportion of illiquid assets, thereby making them susceptible to failure. The fragile nature of banking is reinforced by the fact that the inter-bank markets are made up of a network of large creditor and debtor relationships and the lack of liquidity, as evidenced in the recent crisis, can damage the markets and lead to systemic collapse.[111] It should be noted that Northern Rock's problems stemmed not from the bank being insolvent but from loss of liquidity and confidence in the inter-bank markets.[112]

The FSMA 2000 has a direct impact on corporate governance standards within the banking and financial services sector with the Act requiring, and imposing, high standards of conduct and integrity on senior managers and key persons, including controller shareholders. The basis of the regulation is that transparency of information and conduct will result in greater accountability. The Act, therefore, establishes a number of principles of good regulation intended to underpin the discharge of the regulated firm's statutory obligations. Section 2(3)(a)–(f) FSMA 2000 provides a series of principles to ensure the FCA achieves the sound management of financial services within the context of the wider economic environment. Moreover, the FCA's Principles for Businesses provide 'fundamental obligations' which a regulated firm is required to observe. These principles require regulation of the regulated institutions and their global networks while considering the interests of consumers, regulators and financial intermediaries.

Nevertheless, as a result of the collapse of Northern Rock, the Financial Services Act 2012 amended the regulatory framework established under FSMA 2000 to disband the Financial Services Authority (FSA). In turn, the Financial Conduct Authority (FCA) has been created with the operational objectives to: secure an appropriate degree of protection for consumers; protect and enhance the integrity of the UK financial system; and promote effective competition in the interests of consumers. The Prudential Regulation Authority (PRA) has been created to promote the safety and soundness of financial firms with the broader goal of maintaining the stability of the UK financial system.

---

[109] See Ch. 2.

[110] Sections 19 and 23 of the FSMA 2000.

[111] It was the failure of Northern Rock to borrow on the inter-bank markets or find a private injection of capital through a private merger that resulted in it turning to the Bank of England, as lender of last resort, and that led to its eventual nationalisation, House of Commons Treasury Committee, The run on the Rock, Fifth Report of Session 2007–08, Volume 1, Ordered by The House of Commons, printed 24 January 2008, HC 56–I, http://www.parliament.the-stationery-office.com/pa/cm200708/cmselect/cmtreasy/56/56i.pdf.

[112] House of Commons Treasury Committee, The run on the Rock, Fifth Report of Session 2007–08, Volume 1, Ordered by The House of Commons, printed 24 January 2008, HC 56–I, http://www.parliament.the-stationery-office.com/pa/cm200708/cmselect/cmtreasy/56/56i.pdf.

The FCAs principles for businesses

These principles provide 'fundamental obligations' which a regulated firm is required to observe and that reinforce the FCA's regulatory objectives.[113] They apply not merely to regulated institutions but across the group and its global activities,[114] and provide the context within which the regulated business is undertaken. Failure to comply with these principles may result in intensive supervision, enforcement actions, withdrawal or restrictions on permission to undertake regulated activities.[115] The interests of consumers, regulators and financial intermediaries feature heavily in these principles although they do not give the consumer a cause of action for breach; the remedy lies with the FCA. A breach of the principles will be judged on the basis of the objective 'reasonable care' test although a subjective test will be applied in respect of honesty.[116] The FCA will, therefore, take into consideration whether the act or omission deviates from standards of general practice[117] within the banking sector and against the standards expected of a skilled person.[118] The FCA also has to consider the likelihood of the risk reoccurring and any precautionary measures that a reasonable and prudent person would take[119] having regard to that person's skill and expertise.

Principles 1 and 2 require that deposit-taking institutions must conduct their business with integrity and with due skill, care and diligence.[120] Thus, Abbey National Asset Managers was fined £320,000 for, *inter alia*, its breach of Principle 2 in not exercising the appropriate level of 'skill and care' in dealing effectively with concerns expressed by its compliance officers.[121] Principle 3[122] requires regulated businesses to take reasonable care to organise and control their affairs responsibly and effectively, with adequate risk management systems. In 2005, the FSA fined Citigroup Global Markets[123] £4 million for its failure to comply with Principles 2 and 3 as a result of the implementation of a trading strategy that manipulated the trading system in the bond market. Citigroup Global Markets was fined approximately £9 million when the FSA concluded that Citigroup had failed to exercise due care. In 2007, the FSA fined the Nationwide Building Society £980,000, for a failure to maintain satisfactory security systems and to take reasonable care of confidential customer data when a laptop was stolen from an employee's home.[124] Principle 4 requires that regulated businesses must maintain adequate

---

[113] The FCA Handbook of Rules and Guidance issued under ss.138 and 157 of the FSMA 2000 established under delegated authority establish rules supplementary to the Act. The Act is made up of six main blocks that consist of High Level Standards etc., which authorised institutions and persons must comply with. Block 1 – High Level Standards consist of a number of core Principles for Businesses (PRIN) with which all firms must comply. See Ch. 1 and Ch. 2.

[114] FCA, Principles for Businesses, PRIN 3.3, http://www.fshandbook.info/FS/html/FCA/PRIN/3/3#D23.

[115] FCA, Principles for Businesses, DEPP.1.1, http://www.fshandbook.info/FS/html/FCA/DEPP/1/1.

[116] *Royal Brunei Airlines* v *Tan* [1995] AC 378 at 389.

[117] *Kraji* v *McGarth* [1986] 1 All ER 54 at 61.

[118] *Bolam* v *Friern Management Committee* [1957] 2 All ER 118 at 122.

[119] *Bolton* v *Stone and Others* [1951] 1 All ER 1078 at 1081.

[120] Previously the FSA's Principles for Businesses, now FCA's PRIN 1 and 2 for Businesses, http://www.fshandbook.info/FS/html/FCA/PRIN/2/1.

[121] FSA (2003) 9 December, Final Notice: Abbey National Asset Managers Ltd, http://www.fca.org.uk/static/pubs/final/abbey-asset_9dec03.pdf.

[122] Previously the FSA's Principles for Businesses, now FCA's PRIN 1 and 2 for Businesses, http://www.fshandbook.info/FS/html/FCA/PRIN/2/1.

[123] FSA, 2005, 28 June, Final Notice, Citigroup Global Markets Ltd.

[124] FSA (2007) 14 February, Final Notice: Nationwide Building Society, http://www.fsa.gov.uk/pubs/final/nbs.pdf.

financial resources.[125] Principles 6–10 affect the relationship between the regulated firm and its customers with Principle 6 requiring the regulated business to pay due regard to the interests of its customers and treat them fairly. Professor Buiter in his written evidence to the Treasury Committee concluded that Northern Rock's 'funding policies were reckless'[126] and evidence to the Treasury Committee[127] on Northern Rock also found failures on the part of management that could amount to breaches of these principles.

Senior management: systems and controls

The FSA during its time as the financial services regulatory authority expanded on Principle 3 of the Principles for Businesses in its senior management arrangements, systems and controls (SYSC).[128] These require regulated businesses to exercise 'reasonable care' over their business and to ensure they have 'adequate risk management' systems in place.[129] The need for proper accountability and transparency is emphasised so that the business does not become inured in fraud. The FSA was mindful of fulfilling its statutory objectives and safeguarding confidence in the financial services sector and protecting consumer interests.[130]

SYSC require a regulated business to apportion management responsibility so that the firm is able to monitor and control its business affairs with reasonable care.[131] The senior management guidance indicates that responsibilities in a regulated firm need to be apportioned to the chief executive, a director or a senior manager[132] with the board of directors having the ultimate responsibility of apportioning functions. The apportionment of responsibilities must comply with good corporate governance. SYSC requires that a firm must take 'reasonable care to establish and maintain such systems and controls as are appropriate to its business', and a firm must take 'reasonable care to establish and maintain effective systems and controls for compliance with applicable requirements and standards . . .'.[133] The latter require that

---

[125] Previously the FSA's Principles for Businesses, now FCA's PRIN 4 for Businesses, http://www.fshandbook.info/FS/html/FCA/PRIN/2/1.

[126] House of Commons Treasury Committee, The run on the Rock, Fifth Report of Session 2007–08, Volume 1, ordered by The House of Commons, printed 24 January 2008, HC 56–I, http://www.parliament.the-stationery-office.com/pa/cm200708/cmselect/cmtreasy/56/56i.pdf.

[127] House of Commons Treasury Committee, The run on the Rock, Fifth Report of Session 2007–08, Volume 1, Ordered by The House of Commons, printed 24 January 2008, HC 56–I, http://www.parliament.the-stationery-office.com/pa/cm200708/cmselect/cmtreasy/56/56i.pdf.

[128] FSA Handbook, Senior Management Arrangements, Systems and Controls, Release 026, December 2003, SYSC 2, now FCA handbook, Senior Management Arrangements, Systems and Controls, http://www.fshandbook.info/FS/html/FCA/SYSC/2/1; http://www.fsa.gov.uk/pubs/hb-releases/rel26/rel26sysc.pdf.

[129] FSA Handbook, Senior Management Arrangements, Systems and Controls, Release 072, December 2007, SYSC 4.1.6, now FCA Handbook, Senior Management Arrangements, Systems and Controls, SYSC 4.1.1.R, http://www.fshandbook.info/FS/html/FCA/SYSC/4/1.

[130] FSA Handbook, Senior Management Arrangements, Systems and Controls, Release 026, December 2003, SYSC 3.2.6.

[131] FSA Handbook, Senior Management Arrangements, Systems and Controls, Release 061, January 2007, SYSC 1.1.4, FCA Handbook, Senior Management Arrangements, Systems and Controls, SYSC 5.1, http://www.fshandbook.info/FS/html/FCA/SYSC/5/1.

[132] FSA Handbook, Senior Management Arrangements, Systems and Controls, Release 061, January 2007, Release 80, 2008, SYSC 2.1; SYSC 2.1.1R; 2.1.3R and 2.1.5G, now FCA Handbook, Senior Management Arrangements, Systems and Controls, SYSC 2.1, http://www.fshandbook.info/FS/html/FCA/SYSC/2/1.

[133] FSA Handbook, Handbook, Senior Management Arrangements, Systems and Controls, Release 061, December 2007, SYSC 1.1.4, now FCA Handbook, Handbook, Senior Management Arrangements, Systems and Controls, SYSC 3.1, http://www.fshandbook.info/FS/html/FCA/SYSC/3/1.

appropriate management committees be established within the firm to ensure that a reasonable standard of care is exercised in discharging management duties and functions. Where responsibilities for systems and controls are delegated any such delegation must be appropriately supervised and controlled.

◼ Significant persons and controlled functions

Regulated firms are required to 'take reasonable care to establish and maintain such systems and controls as are appropriate to the business and the FCA requires senior management to play a leading role in ensuring that effective governance structures are in place, with clear lines of responsibility among directors and senior managers'.[134] The FSMA regulates the activities of individuals who exert 'significant influence' on the conduct of a bank's affairs in relation to regulated activities. The FCA divides these individuals into two groups: (i) members of governing bodies of firms, e.g. directors, members of managing groups of partners, and management committees who have responsibility for setting the business strategy and ethical standards of the firm; and (ii) senior management to whom the firm's governing body has delegated significant aspects of their controlled functions, for example those who deal with customers.[135]

Bank management and controller shareholders are required by the FSMA 2000 to comply with the 'fit and proper' person requirements, both initially and on a continuous basis. The rules and principles are deemed to be fundamental to depositor protection. The FCA has a formal obligation to ensure that sound management of the financial services remains the key priority but the FCA must have regard to the wider environment, including the internationalisation of the financial services markets and products available. Within that, the FCA will demand 'fit and proper' management responsible for the protection of depositors and consumer interests. The objectives placed on the FCA are not intended to impose an extra layer of management on 'authorised institutions' or to encroach into commercial decisions[136] but they are intended to ensure stable and responsible management. The objective is to ensure that the 'right people are in place for all key roles and they take the necessary actions to deliver the right outcomes'.[137] Firms are responsible for nominating candidates for controlled functions and for undertaking sufficient due diligence on the candidate while the FCA will judge the applicant against the 'fit and proper'[138] person criteria of honesty, integrity and reputation; competence and capability; and financial soundness. The FCA will look at financial industry experience and it will in future also examine the relevant qualifications of the

---

[134] FSA, Senior Management Arrangements, Systems and Controls, SYSC 2.1; now FCA, Senior Management Arrangements, Systems and Controls, SYSC 2.1, http://www.fshandbook.info/FS/html/FCA/SYSC/2/1.

[135] FSA, Effective Corporate Governance, Significant influence controlled functions and the Walker review, January 2010, Consultation Paper 10/3, http://www.fsa.gov.uk/pubs/cp/cp10_03.pd.

[136] FSA, A New Regulator for the New Millennium, January 2000, para. 19, http://www.fsa.gov.uk/pubs/policy/P29.pdf.

[137] FSA, Effective Corporate Governance, Significant influence controlled functions and the Walker review, January 2010, Consultation Paper 10/3, http://www.fsa.gov.uk/pubs/cp/cp10_03.pd.

[138] Section 61 of the FSMA 2000 requires an application may only be approved if a person is fit and proper to perform a controlled function.

applicant.[139] The FCA has made it clear that its future focus will be on attitudes and competencies and probity of those tasked with governance[140] and while management must avoid the 'heard mentality' the FCA, for its part, must appoint committed and experienced management capable of robust decision-making.[141] The 'fit and proper person' test has been used to judge the context of fraud and bankruptcy but, in view of excessive risk-taking, there appears to be strong justification for extending the criteria to professional skills and risk management. The test could also be extended to include the case of objectivity and independence.[142]

The significant persons regime applies to NEDs through their being recognised as carrying out controlled functions. Hector Sants, Former Chief Executive of the FSA,[143] called for a 'different calibre of NED, with a different mindset', as a significant component to the FSA's armoury against management accountability and oversight.[144]

---

[139] Although the Chairman and Chief Executive of Northern Rock were 'extremely experienced', the Commons Treasury Committee found it of some concern that neither of them, and particularly the Chief Executive, was a qualified banker. The Committee concluded that the FSA should not have allowed two appointments of a Chairman and Chief Executive to a 'high impact' financial institution where both lacked relevant financial qualifications. The qualifications of the former Chairman of Northern Rock also came under scrutiny and were subject to comment, House of Commons Treasury Committee, The run on the Rock, Fifth Report of Session 2007–08, Volume 1, Ordered by The House of Commons, printed 24 January 2008, HC 56–I, http://www.parliament.the-stationery-office.com/pa/cm200708/cmselect/cmtreasy/56/56i.pdf.

[140] See: The regulator's role in judging competence, 7 May 2009; and The challenges facing bank regulation, FSA Association of Corporate Treasurers,14 May 2009, Hector Sants, Former Chief Executive, http://www.fsa.gov.uk/pages/Library/Communication/Speeches/2009/0514_hs.shtml.

[141] As from 2010 the FSA will place particular focus on those with significant influence functions and interview candidates for a number of the key appointments in high-impact firms, for example, those applying for the positions of chair, CEO, finance director or risk director, FSA, Effective Corporate Governance, Significant influence controlled functions and the Walker review, January 2010, Consultation Paper 10/3, para. 4.20, http://www.fsa.gov.uk/pubs/cp/cp10_03.pdf.

[142] Supervisors will look more critically at the performance of SIFs especially in high-impact firms and this will include reviewing the competence of SIFs as part of the ongoing assessment of a firm's management, governance and culture. In the first six months of the enhanced approval process, 51 SIF interviews were undertaken and a number of applications were withdrawn following interviews, FSA, Effective Corporate Governance, Significant influence controlled functions and the Walker review, January 2010, Consultation Paper 10/3, para. 4.20, http://www.fsa.gov.uk/pubs/cp/cp10_03.pdf; see also: Speech by Hector Sants, Former Chief Executive, The challenges facing bank regulation, FSA Association of Corporate Treasurers, 14 May 2009, http://www.fsa.gov.uk/pages/Library/Communication/Speeches/2009/0514_hs.shtml.

[143] Sants suggested the creation of 'provisional NEDs' who will become full NEDs on acquiring certain technical skills in order to exercise rigorous oversight and an ability to demonstrate competence with regard to risk management, regulation and an understanding of the business model of the firm, The regulator's role in judging competence, Speech to the Securities and Investment Institute Conference, 7 May 2009, http://www.fsa.gov.uk/pages/Library/Communication/Speeches/2009/0514_hs.shtml. NEDs, in the future, will need to have relevant and diverse expertise with a willingness to challenge the executive and independence of thought. The FSA Consultation paper on Effective Corporate Governance recognises that there needs to be flexibility in making such appointments and an individual lacking such knowledge may nevertheless be an excellent candidate. In such circumstances the board will need to assess the impact his appointment would have on the board and whether there is sufficient industry wide experience across the other NEDs for the board to meet its collective responsibilities; and that there is a structured development plan to properly induct the candidate and bring him 'up to speed'. The practical effect of the increased demands on them is that NEDs are likely to become full-time and will need to be appropriately remunerated. This in itself could cause problems in the future as NEDs' remuneration and livelihood becomes more closely tied into the company.

[144] Some banks have reported difficulties in recruiting non-executive directors with high-level financial expertise and some European banks report that many potential candidates are already working for rival banks, Ladipo, A Comparative Corporate Governance Study Board Profile, Structure and Practice in Large European Banks, 2008, http://www.nestoradvisors.co.uk/fileadmin/user_upload/articles/ExecSum.pdf.

BANKING LAW IN PRACTICE

UK companies make up over 60 per cent of private enterprises and create over 80 per cent of private employment and 95 per cent of the economic turnover. Businesses, investors, employees and consumers must all have confidence that companies are acting fairly. To enhance the transparency of corporate governance, in July 2013, the Secretary of State for Business, Innovation and Skills, Vince Cable, launched the Transparency & Trust[145] Discussion Paper. This paper affirms the UK's commitment to implement a central registry of company beneficial ownership information, to ensure ownership and influence on companies remains transparent. Currently, there is no registry of those who can influence the company or its management, i.e. beneficial owners,[146] and that raises possibilities that companies can be used for illegal activity. The UK Action Plan provides that the companies will be required to obtain and hold information about beneficial ownerships in their shares and make it available to the tax and law enforcement authorities through a central agency maintained at Companies House. Moreover, the paper identifies that stricter restrictions will be placed upon company directors who fail to follow the rules.

In particular the paper implements the recommendation of the Parliamentary Commission on Banking Standards (PCBS) that directors' duties in the banking sector should be amended to promote a more responsible approach to managing large financial institutions. The PCBS recommended that directors in large financial institutions should be placed under a legal duty to ensure that they prioritise the 'safety and stability' of their institution rather than the interests of shareholders. The primary responsibility of directors within banks is to ensure stability of the bank. The discussion paper considers whether the nature of this duty should be extended more widely. The paper also invited comments on issues relating to disqualification of company directors and specifically on whether in proceedings relating to the disqualification of directors the court should take into consideration the extent of the loss suffered by creditors and whether material breaches of sectoral regulation should be taken into consideration. Further the paper pursues the possibility of allowing actions available to the liquidator for wrongful and fraudulent trading to be assigned or sold to a third party, thereby allowing action to be pursued where the liquidator no longer has funds to support the action. The time limit for disqualification will be extended from two to five years. The consultation period ended in September 2013.

---

[145] Department for Business Innovation & Skills, Transparency & Trust: Enhancing the Transparency of UK Company Ownership and Increasing Trust in UK Business, Discussion Paper, July 2013, https://www.gov.uk/government/uploads/system/uploads/attachment_data/file/212079/bis-13-959-transparency-and-trust-enhancing-the-transparency-of-uk-company-ownership-and-increaing-trust-in-uk-business.pdf.

[146] Money Laundering Regulations 2007 define beneficial owners as anyone who holds more than 25 per cent of the shares or voting rights in the company or anyone who can exercise influence over the management.

Conclusion

Outside the sphere of insolvency there are relatively few cases in UK corporate jurisprudence of company litigation against directors. Offending directors are more likely to be persuaded to resign rather than companies pursue acrimonious litigation through the courts to the possible professional detriment of both the directors and the commercial reputation of the company. Moreover, in an action for the breach of statutory duties it must be remembered that the courts will not second-guess the wisdom of decisions of company directors. However, where a company's performance has been badly affected, for example by the credit crisis, it may be that there is likely to be changes in management to return stability to the company. The new management may make former directors the target of a claim. In limited circumstances, a shareholder may also bring proceedings to enforce obligations owed by a director to his company and thereby enforce rights vested in the company. On behalf of the company and in the case of company insolvency the liquidator may seek to hold directors accountable for the benefit of the creditors. These provisions are reinforced by s.235 of the Insolvency Act which require directors, and former directors, of a company to cooperate with office-holders (administrator, administrative receiver, liquidator or provisional liquidator) and provide such office-holders with information about the company, formation, business, dealings and affairs as required by the office-holders. If cooperation under s.235 is not achieved then office-holders may make a formal application to the court[147] to submit an affidavit to the court of their dealings with the company, or to produce any books or other records in relation to the company.

The aftershocks of recent credit crises are still being felt globally and governments have implemented measures to restore stability and confidence.[148] Financial firms, customers, the wider economy and governments, with the threat of sovereign debt default still rumbling, have felt the ripples of the crises.[149] This chapter has attempted to explore the interplay between company law, bank regulation and self-governance. All have failed miserably to prevent a banking crisis resulting from a reckless disregard of the standards of corporate governance. The interests of the customer and other stakeholders have been eroded in an environment of greed and personal gain.

---

[147] Section 236 Insolvency Act 1986.

[148] The response of the UK government to the financial crisis is explored in Ch. 5.

[149] Damor, Greece Sovereign Debt Crisis, The Way Forward, if Any!, 11 February 2010, The Market Oracle, http://www.marketoracle.co.uk/Article17169.html; see also: Iceland celebrates after rejecting Icesave payback plan, http://www.marketoracle.co.uk/Article17169.html.

Further reading

➤ The EU high-level Group on financial supervision in the EU Report, chaired by Jacques de Larosière, Brussels, 25 February 2009, also suggested there were strong links between poor risk management and corporate failings, http://ec.europa.eu/internal_market/finances/docs/de_larosiere_report_en.pdf. The report of the de Larosière high-level Group on financial supervision was established to examine the future of European financial regulation and supervision. The report noted that the European Union's framework of regulation remains seriously fragmented, and action is required at national, European and global levels to achieve an effective regulatory framework.

➤ FSA, The Turner Review, A regulatory response to the global banking crisis, March 2009, http://www.fsa.gov.uk/pubs/other/turner_review.pdf. The Turner Review was commissioned by the Chancellor of the Exchequer Alistair Darling in October 2008 to review the causes of the financial crisis. The Turner Review makes a series of recommendations on the changes in regulation and supervision to create a more robust banking system for the future. The Review recognises the difficult task of enhancing stability in the macro-economic climate of the financial crisis.

➤ HM Treasury, A review of corporate governance in UK banks and other financial entities, Final Recommendations, 26 November 2009, http://webarchive.nationalarchives.gov.uk/20130129110402/http://www.hm-treasury.gov.uk/d/walker_review_261109.pdf. The Walker Review was commissioned by the Prime Minister Gordon Brown to review corporate governance in the UK banking sector in light of the experience of critical loss and failure throughout the banking system. The overall recommendations covered a broad scope of issues, including the need to ensure that non-executive directors (NEDs) have the knowledge and understanding of the business to enable an effective contribution through continuous training.

➤ House of Commons Treasury Committee, *The Run on the Rock, Fifth Report of Session 2007–08*, Volume 1, Ordered by The House of Commons, printed 24 January 2008, HC 56–I, http://www.parliament.the-stationery-office.com/pa/cm200708/cmselect/cmtreasy/56/56i.pdf. In this report, the Treasury Select Committee analyses the causes and consequences of the run on Northern Rock. The Committee emphasises the advantages of legislative change on a cross-party basis and makes proposals for such changes, and for reforms of the tripartite arrangements on that basis. The Committee states that the Financial Services Authority (FSA) systematically failed in its regulatory duty to ensure that Northern Rock would not pose a systemic risk.

➤ Garten, H. (1986) Banking on the Market: Relying on Depositors to Control Bank Risk, 4, *Yale J of Regulation*, 129. Helen Garten considers the idea of market discipline in relation to the banking sector. The article considers the difficulty in achieving a balance between market discipline and maintaining public confidence in the banking industry.

➤ Hsiao, M. (2009) A Sprouting duty of honesty and loyalty? Companies Act 2006, 20, *International Company and Commercial Law Review*, 201. Mark Hsiao's article examines the scope of the directors' duties enshrined in ss.170–177 of the Companies Act 2006. Hsiao notes the development of directors' duties from a common law to a statutory basis. In relation to boards of directors who exercise day-to-day management, Hsiao examines the extent to which directors act in a fiduciary capacity.

4   The UK response to the credit crisis

Chapter overview

The aim of this chapter is to:

➤ Examine the government reviews during and following the 2007–09 crisis and the key recommendations it made to the actual and perceived shortcomings in the regulation of the banking sector.

➤ Examine the government's response to the financial crisis, including the effect of:

- the Banking (Special Provisions) Act 2008,
- the Banking Act 2009,
- the new structure of bank regulation and proposals to ring-fence the retail banking sector, and
- the remuneration code and control of the bonus culture.

Introduction

By mid-2007 it was apparent that a large number of the US and non-US banks had participated, either directly or indirectly, in the US housing market either by lending in the subprime market or participating in the securitisations markets. Many banks were left with exposure to 'toxic' asset-backed securities or with debt obligations that could not be financed out of their own capital. Accounting practices required the value of securities be adjusted to reflect the price at which they were then being traded and this led to banks holding huge debts with the urgent need to raise further capital or to reduce lending. In this environment panic among the banking community led to a refusal, and a freeze, in inter-bank lending.[1] Banks that relied on short-term finance (e.g. deposits from customers) to fund long-term lending commitments found they lacked liquidity and in that environment the UK Banking

---

[1] Concerns about insolvency resulted in inter-bank lending drying up with LIBOR (the rate at which banks lend to each other), on 9 September 2007, soaring to a nine-year high. By Autumn 2008, LIBOR was approximately 2 per cent above the Bank of England base rate (about ten times higher than banks normally lent to each other), Northern Rock to be Nationalized, 17 February 2008, http://news.bbc.co.uk/1/hi/business/7249575.stm.

sector saw the collapse of Northern Rock,[2] with failed attempts to find a private sector solution.[3]

Weaknesses in the markets were being exploited by aggressive short-selling of stock which drove down the price of bank shares, particularly the Halifax Banking Group,[4] which combined with lack of depositor confidence resulted in a hastily arranged merger to try to stabilise the markets.[5] Investment banks were even more exposed to the financial crisis than commercial banks since they took greater risks and with a smaller capital cushion; without a depositor base investment banks relied wholly on the capital and money markets for fund raising and short-term liquidity.

Panic in this sector led to banks refusing to lend to each other. Northern Rock was therefore forced to ask the Bank of England, as lender of last resort, for emergency support. This chapter will examine some of the immediate and continuing government responses to stabilise the banking sector and ensure that a longer-term capability to deal with future crises is in place.

The Banking (Special Provisions) Act 2008

Emergency legislation, namely the Banking (Special Provisions) Act 2008, was passed to legitimise the nationalisation of Northern Rock, and later to take into public ownership the Bradford and Bingley Building Society.[6] The Treasury was given specific powers to nationalise failing banks, or to compel a takeover by a designated 'body corporate'. While, the 2008 Act was merely an interim measure to enable a governmental response to the banking crisis it was nevertheless a significant measure, being the first piece of UK legislation passed specifically to deal with failing banks. The Act applied to any FSA (the then financial services regulator) regulated deposit-taking institution[7] and the Treasury could, where it deemed it 'desirable',[8] exercise powers for the following purposes:

- Maintaining stability of the UK financial system.[9]

- Protecting public interest where the Treasury had provided 'financial assistance' to the deposit taker.[10]

'Financial assistance', under the Act, referred to a situation where the Bank of England had provided financial assistance to a deposit taker, and the Treasury had assumed liability in

---

[2] See: Listra, Northern Rock, UK Insolvency and cross-border bank insolvency, *Journal of Banking Regulation*, 9(3), pp. 165–186 for an analysis of the Northern Rock collapse.

[3] Vina and Loveday, Northern Rock Nationalized as U.K. Rejects Virgin Bid (Update2), 17 February 2008, http://www.bloomberg.com/apps/news?pid=20601087&sid=aR399_tyWImw; *Northern Rock to be Nationalized*, 17 February 2008, http://news.bbc.co.uk/1/hi/business/7249575.stm.

[4] Fletcher, FSA clamps down on short selling investors, *The Telegraph*, 14 June 2008, http://www.telegraph.co.uk/finance/newsbysector/banksandfinance/2791623/FSA-clamps-down-on-short-selling-investors.html.

[5] Kennedy, Webster and Seib, Lloyds TSB agrees to merger with HBOS, 17 September 2008, Timesonline, http://business.timesonline.co.uk/tol/business/industry_sectors/banking_and_finance/article4776447.ece.

[6] Bradford & Bingley: A history of how and when it when it all went wrong, 28 September 2008, http://www.telegraph.co.uk/finance/financialcrisis/3097348/Bradford-and-Bingley-A-history-of-how-and-when-it-all-went-wrong.html.

[7] Banking (Special Provisions) Act 2008, s.1.

[8] Banking (Special Provisions) Act 2008, s.2(1).

[9] Banking (Special Provisions) Act 2008, s.2(2)(a).

[10] Banking (Special Provisions) Act 2008, s.2(2)(b).

respect of that assistance, or the Treasury, either with or without the support of the Bank of England, had put in place a guarantee liability in respect of the deposit taker.[11]

The transfer of ownership of a bank

Under s.3 of the Banking (Special Provisions) Act 2008 the Treasury, effectively the Chancellor of the Exchequer, was given the power to order the transfer of securities, for example shares, of a deposit-taking institution to the Bank of England, or an entity controlled by the Treasury, or to some other body corporate,[12] for example another bank. When a transfer was affected under s.3 any subscription rights of third parties were extinguished[13] and once the transfer was effected, a scheme to compensate those shareholders who had lost their shares was to be established.[14] The Treasury, using its powers under the Banking (Special Provisions) Act 2008, announced on 22 February 2008 that it had acquired all the shares in Northern Rock, including all the preference shares, and that all share options and other entitlements to shares issued by Northern Rock had been extinguished by a Transfer Order made under the 2008 Act.[15]

The Banking Act 2009

The Banking (Special Provisions) Act 2008 lapsed on 21 February 2009. At the same time the Banking Act 2009[16] came into force. A discussion paper issued by the tripartite authorities and four consultation papers preceded the Act. Most G-10 countries have adopted a special insolvency scheme to deal with distressed banks. Although the schemes vary from country to country they nevertheless apply special rules to deal with failing banks rather than the rules that apply in the insolvency of non-banking institutions. That option was not available in the UK because of the lack of special legislation.

Under the Banking Act 2009, the corporate insolvency regime developed in the UK is designed to support the restructuring of a distressed company and the orderly liquidation of a company if there is no prospect of restoring the company to health in the long term and treating shareholders and creditors fairly. The insolvency of a bank is very different and such insolvency can affect the stability of the financial system and the wider economy. The application of the general rules of insolvency law to a distressed bank could aggravate the situation rather than minimise sector wide distress. Even solvent banks can be faced with solvency problems if there is loss of public confidence and a resultant run on the bank. In bank insolvency situations the solution needs to be found quickly with, if necessary, the authorities being able to override the wishes of the shareholders and creditors. The disadvantages of a lack of special insolvency regime were demonstrated with the events that befell Northern Rock in mid-2007.

Without a Special Resolution Regime (SRR) for banks the authorities had no powers to take control of Northern Rock away from the shareholders and management and put in place a private sector solution, so government had no option but to nationalise Northern Rock. The

---

[11] Banking (Special Provisions) Act 2008, s.2(3)(b).
[12] Banking (Special Provisions) Act 2008, s.3(1).
[13] Banking (Special Provisions) Act 2008, s.4.
[14] Banking (Special Provisions) Act 2008, s.3.
[15] Northern Rock now in public hands, 22 February 2008, http://news.bbc.co.uk/1/hi/uk_politics/7258492.stm.
[16] Banking Act 2009, Parts 1 to 4, and some of Part 7.

consultation for a SRR showed support for a special regime for failing banks particularly, for example, from international regulatory institutions like the IMF and BIS. Almost all respondents accepted the need for change and a framework that facilitated orderly bank resolution. The main features of an SRR regime are to give the authorities the power to implement resolution measures and the rights of shareholders of the bank are subordinated to the powers of the authorities. These features are replicated in the UK SRR scheme introduced by the Banking Act 2009.

The most significant aspect of the 2009 Act is the SRR, which gave the government, the then banking regulator, the FSA (now the FCA)[17] and the Bank of England special powers to deal with banks in financial difficulty.[18] The Act also provides new bank insolvency[19] and administration procedures,[20] makes changes to the financial services compensation scheme,[21] and the regulation of inter-bank payment systems.[22] The most controversial aspect of the 2009 Act is the SRR, which creates three stabilisation options – a private sector transfer, a bridge bank transfer and temporary public ownership – and is used when a bank or part of a bank's business has, or is likely to encounter, financial difficulties. The authorities are given wide powers, which sometimes override contractual arrangements and property rights. To some extent the Banking Act 2009 erodes the right of bank stakeholders and creditors. The Bank of England and the Treasury can also effectively remove and appoint directors to the bank's board.[23] The Banking Act 2009 applies to banks, which are defined as UK incorporated entities that have permission, from the regulatory bodies, to accept deposits thereby excluding branches of foreign banks.[24] The Act does not extend to building societies or credit unions, but provides how the special resolution regime may be applied to them.[25]

The Act was aimed at putting in place a regime for deposit-taking institutions and the protection, *inter alia*, of depositors' interests. It was not originally intended to include investment banks within its regime, but after the collapse of Lehman Brothers it became apparent that some method of dealing with investment banks and managing the complexities of such a collapse was necessary. The term 'bank' may extend to insurance companies with permission to accept deposits. The SRR, therefore, extends to a range of financial institutions[26] and it sets out the legal framework within which the authorities may exercise their intervention powers, if a bank is in difficulty. Although the government did not have explicit intervention powers at the time of the Northern Rock problems such powers were conferred by the Banking (Special Provisions) Act 2008 which enabled the nationalisation of the building society. The Banking Act 2009 and the two statutory instruments which came into force at the same time,[27] protect specified arrangements with a UK bank from interference if the bank is brought within the regime and deal with compensation payable to third parties in the event of a failing bank. The Act provides a permanent statutory regime to allow intervention in the private banking sector.

---

[17] Section 1A of the Financial Services and Markets Act 2000, inserted by Financial Services Act 2012, Part 1A, Chapter 1.

[18] Part 1 Banking Act 2009.

[19] Part 2 Banking Act 2009.

[20] Part 3 Banking Act 2009, as amended by the Financial Services Act 2012.

[21] Part 4 Banking Act 2009, as amended by the Financial Services Act 2012, schedule 10.

[22] Part 5 Banking Act 2009.

[23] Banking Act 2009, s.20.

[24] Banking Act 2009, s.2.

[25] Banking Act 2009, s.2.

[26] Banking Act 2009, ss.232–233 and s.236.

[27] The Banking Act 2009 (Restriction of Partial Property Transfers Order) 2009, S.I. 2009/332 and The Banking Act 2009 (Third Party Compensation Arrangements for Partial Property Transfers) Regulations 2009, S.I. 2009/319.

Statutory objectives

In exercising their powers under the Banking Act 2009, the authorities must have equal regard to the statutory objectives[28] intended to govern the use of their powers under the Act. The Financial Conduct Authority (FCA), Bank of England and the Treasury are to have regard to the following objectives when exercising their powers:[29]

- Protect and enhance the stability of the UK financial system.[30]
- Protect and enhance confidence in the UK banking system[31] so that public confidence is not undermined by a bank failure.
- Protect depositors,[32] including safeguarding the interests of depositors while dealing with a failing bank by ensuring fast payments to depositors and the continuity of banking services.
- Protect public funds[33] by safeguarding taxpayers' interests, if the Treasury provides financial assistance to a bank.
- Avoid interfering with property rights[34] within the context of the Human Rights Act 1998.

Section 96 of the Financial Services Act 2012 introduces two new statutory objectives as follows:

- To protect client assets.
- To minimise adverse effects on institutions that support the operation of financial markets, such as investment exchanges.

Although the SRR specifies a set of objectives in the legislation, the Act does not define terms such as 'financial stability', which is defined in the context of the overarching need to ensure financial stability. These objectives are not listed in order of priority; rather they are to be balanced in the circumstances of any given case.[35] While the objectives may prove contradictory in practice certainly one or more of them are likely to be met in the case of a failing bank. Thus, for example, the need to protect in full UK depositors with Icelandic banks[36] placed strains on the public purse and will have put the third and fourth objectives at loggerheads.[37] The difficult balance between these objectives is further illustrated by the 2013 banking crisis in Cyprus.[38] The objectives, while intended to protect the banking industry, are capable also of fulfilling political goals. The objectives are further clarified in the Code of Practice

---

[28] As amended by s.96 of the Financial Services Act 2012.

[29] Banking Act 2009, s.4.

[30] Banking Act 2009, s.4(4).

[31] Banking Act 2009, s.4(5).

[32] Banking Act 2009, s.4(6).

[33] Banking Act 2009, s.4(7).

[34] Banking Act 2009, s.4 (8).

[35] Banking Act 2009, s.4(10).

[36] New services and products, for example Internet banking, have created a new type of customer willing to transfer accounts when rivals offer a high rate of interest. Thus, overseas banks, for example Landsbanki of Iceland, were able to win substantial deposits from UK bank customers by offering higher rates of interest than the UK banking sector, but were unable to meet customer demand when the financial crisis paralysed the Icelandic banking sector.

[37] UK seeks return of Iceland cash, 10 October 2008, http://news.bbc.co.uk/1/hi/uk_politics/7662599.stm.

[38] Cyprus bank crisis: the legacy, 26 March 2013, http://www.bbc.co.uk/news/world-europe-21937077.

published along with the Act.[39] The Act makes it explicit that the continuity of banking services is included as a priority of the special resolution objective.[40]

The SRR regime

The FCA, the Bank of England and the Treasury collectively have powers to exercise the stabilisation regime. This will enable the authorities to intervene in respect of the failing bank while it has some net worth, thereby increasing the likelihood of an orderly resolution in support of public policy objectives.[41] The FCA determines whether the bank falls within the general conditions that bring the stabilisation regime into effect.[42] These conditions demarcate the boundary that must be crossed before the stabilisation powers, the bank administration or the bank insolvency procedures may be applied.[43] While the FCA determines whether or not the special regime should be applied, the Bank of England implements and runs the regime, except in cases of temporary public ownership, when the Treasury assumes responsibility.[44]

The SSR is likely to be implemented when the FCA considers[45] a bank to be 'failing, or likely to fail', taking into account two circumstances: *Condition 1*: the bank fails or is likely to fail to satisfy the threshold conditions set out in the FCA Handbook;[46] and *Condition 2* whether having regard to the timing and other relevant circumstances, it is unlikely that action will be taken to enable the bank to satisfy these conditions.[47] The terms 'failing, or likely fail', used in s.7(2) of the Banking Act 2009 are not defined and are, therefore, likely to extend to a wide range of situations a bank may find itself in, including failings relating to financial and managerial resources. The FCA threshold conditions are wide-ranging and deal with most aspects of a bank's business and so the FCA may have regard to wide ranging aspects of the institution's business. The main reason for using the threshold conditions as the trigger is that these conditions are the regulatory requirements which a UK bank undertakes to meet in order to gain authorisation from the FCA to accept deposits and carry out regulated banking activities. It is appropriate, therefore, that banks that no longer meet the conditions for authorisation, and have no prospect of doing so in future, should be placed into the SRR and may, as a result, lose their deposit-taking authority.

The FCA must consult with the Bank of England and the Treasury before determining whether, or not, the last condition is met.[48] The question for the regulatory authorities is what timeframe should be adopted before a decision to activate the stabilisation powers. At this stage the bank is not insolvent but circumstances are such that there is the likelihood of insolvency. The bank would need to convince the FCA that it could avoid insolvency but

---

[39] HM Treasury, Banking Act 2009 Special Resolution Regime Code of Practice, http://www.hm-treasury.gov.uk/d/bankingact2009_code_of_practice.pdf.

[40] Banking Act 2009, s.4(9).

[41] Financial stability and depositor protection: special resolution regime, July 2008, Cm 7459, para. 3.7, http://www.fsa.gov.uk/pubs/cp/joint_doc_stability.pdf.

[42] Banking Act 2009, s.7.

[43] Banking Act 2009, s.7.

[44] See explanation in: Financial stability and depositor protection: special resolution regime, July 2008, Cm 7459, para. 2.7, http://www.fsa.gov.uk/pubs/cp/joint_doc_stability.pdf.

[45] FCA Handbook, Threshold Conditions, http://www.fshandbook.info/FS/html/FCA/COND.

[46] Banking Act 2009, s.7(2).

[47] Banking Act 2009, s.7(3).

[48] Banking Act 2009, s.7(4).

at this stage any decisions about the viability of the bank will lie not with bank management but with the FCA, having regard to the fact that depositors' interests and the systemic effect of the collapse will be significant factors taken into consideration by the FCA. The FCA guidance on the test for determining whether a bank is placed in SSR has drawn criticism as not being onerous enough and it was suggested that the test should be that the bank was 'highly unlikely', instead of 'reasonably unlikely'[49] to meet the conditions under s.7 of the Banking Act 2009. Baroness Noakes, then Shadow Minister for the Treasury, observed that the implications of having the higher standard would mean the FSA would have to give the failing bank a longer period to work out its problems, and if unsuccessful could mean greater losses.[50] However, with regard to the standard set, the FCA needs to satisfy itself on a balance of probabilities that a bank will be unable to turn its affairs around.[51] Although this would appear to be a low threshold against which such orders might be made Lord Justice Denning in *Bater* v *Bater*[52] suggested there are degrees of probability. Thus, for example, a fraud case will require a higher degree of probability than one requiring establishing negligence, although the degree of probability required in the former case would not as high as in a criminal case.[53] However, in the case of the FCA making the decision to implement the SRR regime, with all of the consequent implications for the bank in question, and possibly the wider banking sector, any decision will require a high level of confidence regarding the action and therefore an appropriate level of evidence.

These decisions are in essence regulatory judgments and so are taken by the FCA in the UK. The UK is no different from virtually all other major countries with special regimes that assign to banking supervisors the right to trigger the SRR. This does raise the generic and frequently highlighted risk of regulatory forbearance, which means that the banking supervisors may delay too long in triggering the regime. Alternatively, the fear may be that the regulator's discretion to implement the SRR is premature and taken before a bank was genuinely in trouble. However, the FSA noted[54] that the adequacy of resources condition is likely to be the main focus of its determination and the FSA, and now the FCA, will rarely expect banks to pass directly from normal supervision straight into the SSR. The FCA is likely to heighten supervision[55] before the SRR is exercised. Since bank supervision gives rise to a set of continuing compliance obligations it will lead to opportunities to intervene to enhance supervision.[56]

---

[49] Banking Act 2009, s.7(3), *Condition 2.*

[50] Committee, HL, Banking Bill, Baroness Noakes, col. 1203, 13 January 2009.

[51] Committee, HL, Banking Bill, Lord Myners, col. 1203, 13 January 2009.

[52] [1950] 2 All ER 458 CA at 460.

[53] However, Denning LJ, was more cautious in *Hornal v Neuberger Products Ltd* [1957] 1 QB 247 CA at 254 where he expressed the view that in a civil case alleging criminal conduct, the standard should still be on a balance of probabilities. In *Heinl v Jyske Bank (Gibraltar) Ltd, The Times*, 28 September 1999, 661 at 662, Coleman J, expressed the view that when dishonesty is alleged, the standard of proof should involve a high level of probability, although not as high as the criminal standard.

[54] FSA, Financial Stability and Depositor protection: FSA Responsibilities, CP08/23, December 2008, paras 3.14–15, http://www.fsa.gov.uk/pubs/cp/cp08_23.pdf.

[55] FSA, Financial Stability and Depositor protection: FSA Responsibilities, CP08/23, December 2008, para.2.4, http://www.fsa.gov.uk/pubs/cp/cp08_23.pdf.

[56] Sants, CEO at the FSA, said that the banking industry needed to be 'frightened' about the intensity of supervision the FSA was about to adopt; in Delivering intensive supervision and credible deterrence, it says bankers should be 'very frightened' by the FSA, 12 March 2009, http://www.fsa.gov.uk/pages/Library/Communication/Speeches/2009/0312_hs.shtml#.

The failure of the regulators to act at the appropriate time may stem from the fear of possible legal challenge from shareholders, directors or creditors of the failed bank. This risk is partly addressed in the UK by a key aspect of the design of the triggers, which is that they enable a failing bank to be placed into resolution before it is balance sheet insolvent. In this respect, the UK SRR fully meets a key recommendation by the IMF and World Bank. This is intended to increase the chances of an orderly and rapid resolution in a manner that preserves as much as possible of the remaining franchise value of the bank.

A breach of Condition 1 could give rise to a number of enforcement actions, which could be used at any time, and so may be used before or with the stabilisation powers under the Banking Act 2009. For example, with the Dunfermline Building Society, before resorting to the stabilisation powers, the FSA, the then regulator, tried to use other powers to arrange a private sector takeover.[57] Further, the time provided for a bank to turn its business around will depend on a non-exhaustive list of factors, for example the extent or risk of loss and the effect on potential consumers of such loss, the seriousness of the breach, the risk to the financial system and confidence, and the likely success of any remedial action.[58] Other circumstances the FCA could take into account are divided into liquidity and capital concerns. The FCA can take into account the availability of market funding, whether the funding structure is viable and still available, whether the liquidity problem poses doubts about its capital, and the credit rating.[59] The structure of Northern Rock, with its reliance on the wholesale funding markets, would have been of concern to the regulatory authorities. In respect of capital the FCA could take into account the availability of capital, the sources and terms of capital, the success of raising capital and the interest shown by institutional investors. The FCA will also assess the potential of a takeover of all or part of the bank and the status of negotiations, the potential counterparty, shareholder approval and the suitability of a potential bidder.[60]

The regulatory toolkit and the stabilisation options

The UK SRR provides the authorities with four key tools:

1 The power to direct and accelerate a transfer of part or all of a failing bank's business to a private sector purchaser (PSP).

2 The power to take control of part or all of a failing bank's business through a bridge bank owned and controlled by the Bank of England.

3 The power to place a failing bank into temporary public ownership (TPO).

4 A modified bank insolvency procedure (BIP) to close a failing bank and facilitate fast and orderly payout of depositors' claims under the Financial Services Compensation Scheme (FSCS) or transfer of their insured deposits to a healthy private bank.[61]

---

[57] News Release – Dunfermline Building Society, 30 March 2009, http://www.bankofengland.co.uk/publications/Pages/news/2009/030.aspx.
[58] FCA Handbook, Threshold Conditions, http://www.fshandbook.info/FS/html/FCA/COND.
[59] FCA Handbook, Threshold Conditions, http://www.fshandbook.info/FS/html/FCA/COND.
[60] FCA Handbook, Threshold Conditions, http://www.fshandbook.info/FS/html/FCA/COND.
[61] Brierley, Financial Stability Paper No. 5, July 2009, The UK Special Resolution Regime for Failings Banks in the International Context, Bank of England, ISSN 1754–4362.

These tools available, in some cases, may be alternatives and in other cases complementary. In the resolution of the Dunfermline Building Society in March 2009, part of the business of the society was transferred to a PSP and another part was initially transferred to a bridge bank. Although it is not possible to be prescriptive, in many cases a transfer to a PSP, if it can be arranged quickly and at an appropriate price, is likely to be the tool best able to meet all the SRR objectives. However, in the short term a transfer to a bridge bank may be the best option particularly if a private sector solution requires more time to arrange, for example because potential PSPs need to carry out due diligence on the bank's books. It may be necessary to take a bank into TPO if there is no reasonable prospect of selling it to a PSP, either directly or through a bridge bank, in the short run and the bank's failure could represent a serious threat to financial stability.

Once the FCA has decided that a bank is unable to fulfil its threshold conditions, the next step will be for the Bank of England, in consultation with the Treasury and the FCA, to decide which of the stabilisation options to implement. The Bank of England has three stabilisation options[62] at its disposal under the Banking Act 2009 and these are intended to decide the fate of the bank and its various operations depending on the extent of the difficulties. However, once the general conditions set out in s.7 are satisfied another set of specific conditions set out in s.8 need to be satisfied and are intended to prioritise the public interest consideration when deciding which of the stabilisation options to adopt.

The three stabilisation options

Private sector transfer

The Bank of England may transfer all or part of a bank's business by way of a property or share transfer to a commercial purchaser,[63] thereby providing continuity of banking services without using public funds. The Bank may facilitate a private sector transfer in order to maintain either stability in the UK financial sector, confidence in the banking system or depositor protection.[64] The Bank will be able to decide which part of the failing bank it wants to sell off. It is not clear what incentives the Bank may negotiate to make a sale to a private purchaser but undoubtedly the acquiring bank (bank taking over the failed bank) must itself be in a sufficiently strong position to acquire and absorb the failed institution without jeopardising its existing business activities. This would be assessed as a supervisory issue. The importance of the stability of the acquiring bank, before and after the time of acquisition, is illustrated by Lloyds Banking Group's acquisition of Halifax Bank of Scotland (HBOS) in November 2008, which triggered an additional government bail-out in March 2009.[65] The risk of jeopardising existing business activities is further exemplified by the US government's bail-out of Bank of America in January 2009, which followed the acquisition of Merrill Lynch.[66]

---

[62] All three powers were used during the 2007–09 crisis: the takeover of HBOS by Lloyds TSB although the shareholders still needed to agree to the takeover whereas under the legislation the Bank of England would make the decision regarding the form and terms of the takeover; the temporary public ownership of Northern Rock and Bradford and Bingley. The second option is not familiar in the UK but nevertheless used in the case of the Dunfermline Building Society case.

[63] Banking Act 2009, s.11.

[64] Banking Act 2009, s.8(2), Condition A; see also FSA, Financial Stability and Depositor protection: FSA Responsibilities, CP08/23, December 2008, para. 2.16, http://www.fsa.gov.uk/pubs/cp/cp08_23.pdf.

[65] Government takes over Lloyds, 7 March 2009, http://www.guardian.co.uk/business/2009/mar/07/government-takes-over-lloyds.

[66] Bank of America bail-out agreed, 16 January 2009, http://news.bbc.co.uk/1/hi/7832484.stm.

Alternatively, where the Treasury has provided financial assistance then it may recommend that such a transfer is in the public interest.[67] In the case of a failing bank it is likely at least one of these conditions will be met.[68] The presumption is that if public assistance is given then the Treasury will decide which stabilisation option will best safeguard public interest and public funds. The provision does not include the FCA in the consultation, which is inconsistent with Condition A in s.8 of the Banking Act 2009.

Bridge bank transfer

The Bank of England may, after consultation with the FCA and the Treasury, transfer all or part of a failing bank to a new bank[69] established by the Bank of England, by way of one or more property transfer instruments. Under this option the Bank of England has the opportunity to stabilise the bank, preserve franchise value and ensure consumers have continued access to banking services. It will also provide the Bank of England with time to pursue a private sector solution where this could not have been immediately arranged, for example by allowing potential buyers to carry out due diligence on the business. If these measures are effective in preserving the net worth of the bank, they should encourage competitive bids from private sector purchasers.[70]

Where the Bank of England considers the bridge bank option to be appropriate it will establish a separate company, apply for FCA authorisation to carry on the relevant regulated activities and use the property transfer powers to transfer property, rights and liabilities from the failing bank to the bridge bank. A partial transfer to a bridge bank may be considered suitable where only a relatively small proportion of a bank's balance sheet poses a risk to financial stability and it may be necessary in order to stabilise the situation to transfer this portion of the bank. A partial transfer to a bridge bank may also be suitable in cases where there has been a significant deterioration in the quality of a distinct part of a bank's balance sheet (for example, if the firm has had to write down substantial losses on a particular class of asset or if there is significant uncertainty regarding the viability of an existing business line). This portion of the balance sheet could be left behind in any transfer, thereby sanitising the bridge bank from some of the difficulties faced by the failing bank. Alternatively, a private sector purchaser may be willing to buy only the 'healthy' parts of a bank and a better price may be obtained from its sale as a going concern, rather than winding up the whole of the failing bank.[71] The failing or residual bank retains the deteriorating or poorly performing assets, which can be entered into administration.

The Bank of England can facilitate a bridge bank transfer only if certain conditions, similar to those for a private sector transfer, are satisfied.[72] Lord Myners explained, 'that a crucial distinction between the "bridge bank" concept and some of the alternatives is that the failing

---

[67] Banking Act 2009, s.8(5), Condition B.

[68] While the merger of Halifax Bank of Scotland with Lloyds TSB was sufficient to lift the immediate danger of the collapse of the HBOS Group, the merger created a banking giant, with around a third of all current accounts in Britain and 28 per cent of the mortgage market. One would expect this to fall foul of normal competition authorities in Britain and the EU Competition rules.

[69] Banking Act 2009, ss.8 and 12.

[70] FSA, Financial Stability and Depositor protection: FSA Responsibilities, CP08/23, December 2008, para. 3.20, http://www.fsa.gov.uk/pubs/cp/cp08_23.pdf.

[71] FSA, Financial Stability and Depositor protection: FSA Responsibilities, CP08/23, December 2008, paras 3.37–3.39, http://www.fsa.gov.uk/pubs/cp/cp08_23.pdf.

[72] Banking Act 2009, s.8.

bank is terminated and its banking license withdrawn, and a new institution is created'.[73] Under the Banking Act 2009 other regulated activities not limited to deposit-taking activities may also be transferred to the bridge bank.[74]

Temporary public ownership

The final option is to take the bank into temporary public ownership[75] by transferring shares to a nominee of the Treasury or a company wholly owned by the Treasury. This would involve the Treasury making share transfer orders with a view to returning the failing bank, in due course, to the private sector. The power may be exercised, if necessary, in order to protect the public interest and (i) it is necessary to reduce or resolve a threat to the stability of the UK financial system,[76] or (ii) the Treasury has provided financial assistance in respect of the bank to resolve or reduce such a threat.[77] Thus, Northern Rock and parts of Bradford and Bingley were nationalised under the Banking (Special Provisions) Act 2008. In the case of Northern Rock[78] the depositors were given a 100 per cent guarantee, which protected their deposits, while Santander (via its subsidiary Abbey National Plc) bought the Bradford and Bingley savings and branch network, with the government putting the mortgage and loans business into temporary public ownership.[79] The Treasury may also take the holding company of the rescued bank into temporary public ownership if it is satisfied that:

- The general conditions are met in respect of the bank.
- The public ownership conditions are met.
- The holding company is incorporated in the UK.

The government's interests are managed by UK Financial Investments (UKFI) in Northern Rock and Bradford and Bingley, including the recapitalised RBS and Lloyds TSB and HBOS (Lloyds Banking Group), creating an arm's-length relationship between the public interest and private interests in banks.

Share and property transfer

In order to facilitate the transfer of shares or the business of a failing bank, the Bank of England, or the Treasury, in the case of a temporary public ownership, may make instruments or orders for share or property transfers. The powers under these instruments are extensive. A share transfer instrument, or order, can provide for securities to be transferred and can make provisions for or in connection with the transfer. The Bank of England makes share transfer instruments to effect the transfer of a bank to a private sector purchaser[80] or to a bridge bank.

---

[73] Myners (2009) *Financial Crisis Management and Bank Resolution*, 344–245.
[74] Banking Act 2009, s.12 (1).
[75] Banking Act 2009, s.13.
[76] Banking Act 2009, s.9(2).
[77] Banking Act 2009, s.9(3).
[78] The 'good bits' of Northern Rock were bought by the Virgin Group, in 2011, when it acquired the 75 branches with one million customers and their £14 billion of mortgages and £16 billion of savings. The sale completed in January 2012: Northern Rock sold to Virgin Money, 17 November 2011, http://www.bbc.co.uk/news/business-15769886.
[79] Banking Act 2009, s.12(1).
[80] Banking Act 2009, s.15.

The Treasury makes share transfer orders to effect the transfer of a bank[81] or its holding company to temporary public ownership.[82]

The Bank of England may, by way of a property transfer instrument, transfer all or part of the property of a bank to a private sector purchaser[83] or bridge bank.[84] Where the Treasury has made a share transfer order to bring the bank into temporary public ownership, it may make the property transfer order.[85] Property includes a bank's assets and liabilities. The property transfer instrument may not only provide for the transfer of property but also make other provisions for the purposes of, or in connection, with the transfer. The property transfer powers are broad. Thus, for example, the property transfer instrument may be made without regard to contractual or legislative restrictions on transfer.[86] In addition the Bank of England, or the Treasury, where appropriate, has the power to apportion enforceable rights and liabilities between the transferor and transferee to a specified extent and in specified ways. The property transfer instrument also enables the transferor and transferee, by agreement, to modify a provision of the instrument, provided they achieve 'a result that could have been achieved by the instrument'. It is unclear whether this provision would permit the Bank of England or the Treasury to modify or alter contractual terms pursuant to such apportionment. Where property is held under a trust the Bank of England may modify the terms of the trust to the extent necessary to effect a transfer of the legal or beneficial interest of the transferor or any rights, obligations or interest of the transferor in the property.[87]

Secondary legislation implemented by the government prevents the unfettered use of partial property transfers and provides that security interests, set-off and netting arrangements and structured arrangements are protected. The order gives wider protection to security holders to ensure that partial transfers do not interfere with security interests. Thus, liabilities and their related financial collateral must be transferred together or not at all. This protection is extended to fixed and floating charges. Netting arrangements are defined as arrangements under which a number of claims or obligations can be converted into a net claim or obligation, while a set-off is defined as an arrangement under which one debt can be offset against another to reduce the overall amount of the debt. Subject to any express exclusion, all transactions with a bank that may be offset or netted must be transferred together or not at all.

Remedies and compensation mechanisms

If a partial transfer is made in breach of the relevant restrictions, the right to exercise set-off or netting continues despite the transfer. However, in the case of a security interest or structured

---

[81] See: The Northern Rock plc Transfer Order 2008, SI 2008/432, http://www.opsi.gov.uk/si/si2008/pdf/uksi_20080432_en.pdf, which extinguished all share options and entitlements to shares issued by Northern Rock.

[82] Banking Act 2009, s.16.

[83] Under the Banking Act 2009 reverse transfer powers are not available in respect of securities or property, rights and liabilities, which have been transferred to a commercial purchaser. Section 97 of the Financial Services Act 2012 inserts a new s.26A and s.42A into the Banking Act 2009 and makes other modifications to Part 1 of that Act to permit the availability of the reverse transfer powers in relation to transfers to commercial purchasers: for example to remedy the situation in which securities or property, rights and liabilities have been transferred in error.

[84] Banking Act 2009, s.33.

[85] http://www.opsi.gov.uk/si/si2008/pdf/uksi_20080432_en.pdf.

[86] Banking Act 2009, s.34.

[87] Section 34(8) of the Banking Act 2009, inserted by s.98 of the Financial Services Act 2012.

arrangement, the party affected must notify the relevant authority of the breach and the authority must remedy it by transferring the property rights or liabilities that were not transferred in the initial partial transfer.

The Banking Act 2009 sets out a number of compensation mechanisms for creditors that are adversely affected by the partial transfer of property. The main compensation mechanism for creditors left in the residual bank is set out in the Third-Party Compensation Regulations.[88] Their premise is that a creditor of the residual bank should receive the same payout as he would have received if the transfer has not taken place and the whole bank had been instead subject to insolvency. The regulations envisage that an independent valuer[89] will calculate the dividend, if any, that creditors of the residual bank would have received from winding-up or administration of the whole bank.

Bank insolvency proceedings

In addition to the stabilisation options, the regime contains a new insolvency procedure,[90] which is essentially a modified form of administration procedure. A bank liquidator is tasked with reconciling two main objectives namely:

- To work the financial services compensation scheme to ensure that depositors' accounts are transferred to another financial institution or the depositors receive payment from or on behalf of the scheme.[91]

- To wind up the affairs of the bank so as to achieve the best result for the bank's creditors as a whole.[92]

These objectives may sometimes conflict, for example it may be in the creditors' interests for the bank liquidator to reduce costs and close certain branches, whereas the first objective may be better served by keeping the branches open and retaining staff. In such a situation the Act expressly provides that the first objective should take precedence and thus the government appears to have chosen to protect depositors' interest ahead of creditors' interests.[93]

The Bank administration procedure[94] which is largely based on the Insolvency Act 1996, as amended by the Enterprise Act 2002, also has two objectives, which are (i) to support a commercial purchaser or bridge bank in its acquisition, and (ii) to rescue the residual bank as a going concern, or to achieve a better realisation for the residual bank's creditors as a whole than would be likely in a winding-up.[95] As with bank insolvency, there may be conflicts of interest, although the Act provides that the first objective must take priority. This requires the bank administrator to provide the commercial purchaser or bridge bank with such facilities as are under the residual bank's control, which in the opinion of the Bank of England are required to operate effectively.

---

[88] Banking Act 2009, ss.59 and 60.
[89] Banking Act 2009, s.54.
[90] Banking Act 2009, s.90.
[91] Banking Act 2009, s.99, as amended by the Financial services Act 2012, s.38.
[92] Banking Act 2009, s.99(4).
[93] Banking Act 2009, s.99(4).
[94] Banking Act 2009, s.136.
[95] Banking Act 2009, s.137.

One distinctive feature of the UK toolkit is that it contains different pre-conditions for use of the different tools. This provides greater and more transparent guidance than most other regimes on the key factors influencing the choice of tools. The specific condition for exercising the PSP and bridge bank tools is specified in s.8 of the Act as requiring at least one of the 'public interest' objectives – maintaining financial stability, maintaining public confidence in the banking sector or protecting depositors – to be met. But the condition for exercising the TPO tool is set in s.9 of the Act at a higher level: this requires a serious threat to financial stability to arise from the failure of the bank. This emphasises that TPO is regarded in the UK SRR as a last resort. The regime in this respect is closer to the IMF and World Bank recommendations.

The BIP, by contrast, does not require a 'public interest' objective to be met before it may be applied. But it remains the case that the BIP is still part of the SRR toolkit: it is important from a moral hazard perspective that the SRR should not be viewed as a 'no-failure' or 'no-closure' regime. So the authorities must still be guided by the five statutory SRR objectives in deciding whether to use the BIP tool and in implementing it. The conditions for use of the tools imply that the BIP will be used if the bank's failure is not likely to trigger the public interest criteria for use of the other SRR tools.

The insolvency regime for investment banks

In light of the collapse of the investment bank Lehman Brothers International, HM Treasury commissioned a review to strengthen the administration regime for investment banks. The special administration regime for investment banks (SAR) was introduced in response to the slow return of client assets in the Lehman administration. Pursuant to ss.232 to 236 of the Banking Act 2009, HM Treasury sought to introduce further legislation to enhance the insolvency regime for investment banks. Following a consultation process, the UK government adopted the Investment Bank Special Administration Regulations 2011 to prevent bank insolvency through the creation of the Special Administration Regime (SAR). Since the regulations came into force on 8 February 2011, three firms – MF Global UK Limited, World Spreads Limited and Pritchard Stockbrokers Limited – have been placed in special administration. None of these insolvency procedures is yet complete. Section 6 (1) of the Regulations provides that the Regulations will be applicable in the following circumstances:

(a) The investment bank is, or is likely to become, unable to pay its debts.

(b) It would be fair to put the investment bank into special administration.

(c) It is expedient in the public interest to put the investment bank into special administration.

The Special Administration Regime (SAR) offers a modified insolvency procedure for investment firms, which was designed to facilitate the prompt return of client assets. The Regulations provided HM Treasury must hold an independent review of the SAR within two years of it coming into force. This requirement resulted in Peter Bloxham's Review of the Special Administration Regime for Investment Banks, published on 23 April 2013.[96]

---

[96] HM Treasury, Press Release, Review of the Special Administration Regime for Investment Banks, 23 April 2013, https://www.gov.uk/government/news/review-of-the-special-administration-regime-for-investment-banks-published.

While the Bloxham Review has been published, Peter Bloxham identified this Review should be read as an interim report, as the three cases in which the SAR has been invoked have not reached conclusion.[97] Although Bloxham recommended the SAR Review exercise should continue, several provisional conclusions were proposed.

Bloxham identifies that the Banking Act 2009 sets out a number of broad objectives for the SAR Regime, which includes 'facilitating return of client assets', 'protecting creditors' rights', alongside the general objective of 'maximising the efficiency and effectiveness of the financial services of the United Kingdom'. While the Review acknowledges the SAR has made progress towards the first two objectives, Bloxham questions whether any variant of insolvency law could be expected comprehensively to achieve all of these objectives. Nevertheless, the Review recommends the SAR regime should be retained. Additionally, the Review proposed a number of good practice recommendations for firms to improve the quality of their record keeping and to ensure clients are able readily to understand the contents of client statements. It should be noted that the development of the SAR regime will occur alongside the conclusion of the Lehman Brothers administration and the SAR for MF Global.[98]

The Financial Services Act 2012 Act will extend the SRR to certain UK investment firms, UK clearing houses and certain group companies of UK banks and UK investment firms (each a banking group company). Accordingly, this may mean that more companies within a UK bank's group may be affected by the SRR.

The failings of the FSA and bank regulation and supervision

The FSA came under heavy criticism for its failure to detect, warn against and subsequently, properly handle the 2007–09 financial crisis. These failures have been heavily documented in a series of reports and policy documents[99] and by the media.[100] In its report 'The run on the Rock', the Treasury Committee highlighted the FSA's 'systematic failure of duty' over the

---

[97] The Peter Bloxham Review, 23 April 2013, https://www.gov.uk/government/uploads/system/uploads/attachment_data/file/190983/peter_bloxham_review_of_investment_bank_sar2011_.pdf.

[98] FSA says MF Global UK in 'special administration', 31 October 2011, http://uk.reuters.com/article/2011/10/31/uk-fsa-says-mf-global-uk-in-special-admi-idUKTRE79U5NO20111031.

[99] The Turner Review: A regulatory response to the global financial crisis, March 2009, http://www.fsa.gov.uk/pubs/other/turner_review.pdf; HM Treasury, Reforming Financial Markets, White Paper, July 2009; Cm 7669; http://webarchive.nationalarchives.gov.uk/+/http://www.hm-treasury.gov.uk/d/reforming_financial_markets 080709.pdf; From Crisis to Confidence: Plan for Sound Banking, Conservative Party Policy White Paper, July 2009, http://www.conservatives.com/News/News_stories/2009/07/~/media/Files/Downloadable%20Files/PlanforSoundBanking.ashx; Sassoon, The Tripartite Review A review of the UK's Tripartite system of financial regulation in relation to financial stability, March 2009, http://www.conservatives.com/News/News_stories/2009/03/Osborne_welcomes_Sassoon_report_into_tripartite_financial_regulation.aspx; McFall Report, Banking Crisis: regulation and supervision. Fourteenth Report of Session 2008–09, July 2009, http://www.publications.parliament.uk/pa/cm200809/cmselect/cmtreasy/767/767.pdf; Georgosouli (2010) The Revision of the FSA's Approach to Regulation: An Incomplete Agenda, 7, J.B.L., 599.

[100] Treanor and Elliott, George Osborne to strip FSA of City regulation powers, The Guardian, 3 June 2010, http://www.guardian.co.uk/politics/2010/jun/03/george-osborne-fsa-city-bank; Armistead, Lords committee demands bank regulation overhaul, The Telegraph, 30 May 2009, http://www.telegraph.co.uk/finance/newsbysector/banksandfinance/5413402/Lords-committee-demands-bank-regulation-overhaul.html.

supervision of Northern Rock and its failure to spot Northern Rock's reckless 'business' plan.[101] In fact, in its own internal audit the FSA admitted its failures in supervision of Northern Rock and identified four key failings: (i) lack of sufficient supervisory engagement with Northern Rock's management regarding the firm's business model in a changing market that left Northern Rock vulnerable; (ii) lack of adequate supervision and review of the quality, intensity and rigour of the firm's supervision by FSA management; (iii) inadequate specific resource directly supervising the firm; and (iv) lack of FSA intensity in ensuring that all available risk information was taken into account to inform its supervisory action.[102] The Treasury Committee investigating the collapse of Northern Rock[103] concluded that the system of communication between the tripartite authorities was flawed and the lack of coordination between them contributed to the public's reaction, which resulted in the run on the bank. However, the Committee concluded that it would not be in the interests of the UK to dismantle the system of financial regulation and supervision but that a reformation of the system with stronger powers and clearer leadership should be implemented.

In March 2009, the Turner review[104] recognised that the FSA had traditionally focused on the supervision of individual institutions, rather than sector-wide or system-wide risks with its focus on conduct of business regulation rather than prudential regulation. The FSA had therefore failed to monitor systemic risk. Consequently, liquidity risks and the build up of trading book risks were missed. However, the Turner review[105] failed to recommend any

---

[101] House of Commons Treasury Report, The run on the Rock, Fifth Report of Session 2007– 08, Vol. 1, HC 56-1, criticised the shortfalls in the UK regulatory regime and recommended a review of the tripartite system, http://www.publications.parliament.uk/pa/cm200708/cmselect/cmtreasy/56/56i.pdf. The Turner Review: A regulatory response to the global financial crisis, March 2009, http://www.fsa.gov.uk/pubs/other/turner_review.pdf, identified the failings in UK regulatory regime. The Walker Report, A review of corporate governance in UK banks and other financial industry entities – Final Recommendations, 26 November 2009, http://webarchive.nationalarchives.gov.uk/+/http://www.hm-treasury.gov.uk/d/walker_review_261109.pdf examined the failings in corporate governance of banks and other financial institutions.

[102] FSA, FSA moves to enhance supervision in wake of Northern Rock, FSA/PN/028/2008, 26 March 2008, http://www.fsa.gov.uk/pages/Library/Communication/PR/2008/028.shtml.

[103] House of Commons Treasury Report, The run on the Rock, Fifth Report of Session 2007–08, Vol. 1, HC 56-1, criticised the shortfalls in the UK regulatory regime and recommended a review of the tripartite system, http://www.publications.parliament.uk/pa/cm200708/cmselect/cmtreasy/56/56i.pdf.

[104] The Turner review was commissioned by the then Chancellor of the Exchequer, George Osborne, to look at the causes of the financial crisis and make recommendations on the changes in regulation and supervisory approach needed to create a more robust banking system for the future, The Turner Review: FSA moves to enhance supervision in wake of Northern Rock, FSA/PN/028/2008, 26 March 2008, http://www.fsa.gov.uk/pages/Library/Communication/PR/2008/028.shtml.

[105] The Turner review, however, did remind the FSA that its approach to regulation was not merely intended as a tick box exercise. However, it failed to challenge some of the perceived shortfalls in the FSA regulatory approach, for example the problems with the FSA Handbook remained unchallenged. In fact the Turner review expressed the view that the FSA's mode of regulation was based on a clear set of prudential and conduct of business rules. The complexity and cumbersome nature of the Handbook are not commented on and the lack of general understanding of the principles-based approach established by the Principles for Business is ignored. The Turner Review: A regulatory response to the global financial crisis, March 2009, p. 86, http://www.fsa.gov.uk/pubs/other/turner_review.pdf.

radical reforms to the FSA's style of regulation but, instead, recommended working within regulatory parameters established by the FSA to make certain improvements.[106]

The authorities, including the FSA, were also criticised by Lord Sassoon in his review of the tripartite system of regulation which was commissioned by the then Shadow Chancellor, George Osborne, and intended to inform the Conservative party policy on reforming the regulation of the financial system.[107] The review concluded that the tripartite authorities were 'poorly prepared' and had, in particular, spent 'insufficient time conducting joint planning for a financial crisis'. Further there was little interaction between the tripartite authorities at the senior level prior to mid-2007.[108]

The July 2009 Government White Paper on regulatory reform concluded that the system had placed too much weight on 'ensuring that systems and processes were correctly defined rather than on challenging business models and strategies'.[109] The White Paper concluded that the financial crisis exposed the inherent weaknesses in the 'tripartite' system of regulation with perhaps the most significant failing being that no single institution had responsibility, authority or powers to oversee the financial system as a whole.[110] The Conservative Party Policy White Paper,[111] concluded that the tripartite system was 'confused and fragmented, with responsibilities, powers and capabilities split awkwardly between competing institutions'. Consequently, Keasey and Verones[112] concluded that the regulatory architecture was too cumbersome and flawed because no one organisation appeared to be in overall control.

The system was also criticised for placing responsibility for both prudential regulation and consumer protection and market conduct in the same organisation, namely the FSA. The Conservative Party Policy White Paper proposed reforms in both the architecture of financial regulation, and those associated with regulation policy. The Conservative Party proposed radical reforms of the financial services sector and plans to abolish the FSA and the tripartite system of supervision.[113]

However, on forming the Conservative/Liberal coalition government it was reported that the new Chancellor, George Osborne, had modified his plans and that the FSA would survive

---

[106] Paul Tucker, Deputy Governor of the Bank of England for Financial Stability, therefore concluded that the problem was not one of 'overlap' but 'underlap' in responsibility, The Turner Review: A regulatory response to the global financial crisis, p. 84, March 2009, http://www.fsa.gov.uk/pubs/other/turner_review.pdf. Consequently, macro-prudential risk analysis and mitigation fell within the gaps now recognised as created by the tripartite system, A new approach to financial regulation: judgement, focus and stability, July 2010, Cm 7874, Ch. 1, http://www.official-documents.gov.uk/document/cm78/7874/7874.pdf.

[107] Sassoon, The Tripartite Review: A Review of the UK's Tripartite system of financial regulation in relation to financial stability, March 2009, http://www.conservatives.com/News/News_stories/2009/03/Osborne_welcomes_Sassoon_report_into_tripartite_financial_regulation.aspx.

[108] Sassoon, The Tripartite Review: A Review of the UK's Tripartite system of financial regulation in relation to financial stability, para. 74, March 2009, http://www.conservatives.com/News/News_stories/2009/03/Osborne_welcomes_Sassoon_report_into_tripartite_financial_regulation.aspx.

[109] HM Treasury, Reforming Financial Markets, 2009, Cm 7667, at 56, http://webarchive.nationalarchives.gov.uk/+/http://www.hm-treasury.gov.uk/d/reforming_financial_markets080709.pdf.

[110] HM Treasury, A new approach to financial regulation: the blueprint for reform, June 2011, Cm 8083, http://www.hm-treasury.gov.uk/d/consult_finreg__new_approach_blueprint.pdf.

[111] From Crisis to Confidence: Plan for Sound Banking, Policy White Paper, March 2009, http://www.conservatives.com/News/News_stories/2009/07/~/media/Files/Downloadable%20Fies/PlanforSoundBanking.ashx.

[112] Keasey and Verones (2008) Lessons from the Northern Rock Affair, 16(1), Journal of Financial Regulation and Compliance, 8.

[113] Conservative Manifesto, 2010, available at http://tinyurl.com/comcys.

but with reduced powers.[114] It was not until the Chancellor's Mansion House speech[115] that his commitment to financial reform was fully revealed with the tripartite system, rather than the FSA, seen as a key weakness to financial stability although the FSA did not escaped criticism. This was reinforced by Mark Hoban, the Financial Secretary to the Treasury, who the following day in his address to the House of Commons, remarked that the tripartite system had 'failed spectacularly in its mission to ensure financial stability and that failure cost the economy billions'.[116] These remarks were followed by proposals for reform, although the document, 'A new approach to financial regulation: judgement, focus and stability', also served to move forward the consultation exercise.[117]

The proposals for reform and the new regulatory architecture

The Conservative government expressed the view that macro-prudential regulation to ensure that risks developing across the financial sector were properly identified, monitored and dealt with were key to financial stability and central banks, as lenders of last resort, had the expertise and familiarity with 'every aspect of the institutions that they may have to support'.[118] The Bank of England would, therefore, be at the centre of the new regulatory structure. George Osborne, at his Mansion House speech, explained that 'our thinking is informed by this insight: only independent central banks have the broad macroeconomic understanding, the authority and the knowledge required to make the kind of macro-prudential judgements that are required now and in the future'.[119] Adopting a variation to the twin peaks approach to supervision,[120] the government proposed to break up the FSA[121] and to place bank supervision in the hands of a number of committees, working to complement each other, with the Bank of England central to bank supervision and bank regulation. Although the new regulatory bodies, the Financial Conduct Authority (FCA) and the Prudential Regulation Authority (PRA) have been functioning since 1 April 2011, the statutory regime intended to create the new infrastructure for bank regulation was not introduced in the House of Commons, until

---

[114] Armistead, City watchdog FSA to survive in shock coalition compromise, *Daily Telegraph*, 12 May 2010, http://www.telegraph.co.uk/finance/economics/7716651/George-Osbornes-Treasury-team-the-power-behind-the-coalition-government.html; Paler, Osborne seeks to keep FSA but put it in its place under Bank, 14 June 2010, Citywire, http://citywire.co.uk/wealth-manager/osborne-seeks-to-keep-fsa-but-put-it-in-its-place-under-bank/a406642.

[115] Rt Hon George Osborne MP, Speech at the Lord Mayor's dinner for bankers and merchants of the City of London, 16 June 2010, http://www.hm-treasury.gov.uk/press_12_10.htm.

[116] Hansard, HC, cols 1056–1065, 17 June 2010, Mark Hoban MP; see also, A new approach to financial regulation: judgement, focus and stability, July 2010, Cm 7874, Ch. 1, http://www.official-documents.gov.uk/document/cm78/7874/7874.pdf.

[117] A new approach to financial regulation: judgement, focus and stability, July 2010, Cm 7874, Ch. 1, http://www.official-documents.gov.uk/document/cm78/7874/7874.pdf.

[118] Rt Hon George Osborne MP, Speech at the Lord Mayor's dinner for bankers and merchants of the City of London, 16 June 2010, http://www.hm-treasury.gov.uk/press_12_10.htm.

[119] Rt Hon George Osborne MP, Speech at the Lord Mayor's dinner for bankers and merchants of the City of London, 16 June 2010, http://www.hm-treasury.gov.uk/press_12_10.htm.

[120] See Michael Taylor, The Road from Twin Peaks – and the way back, http://insurancejournal.org/wp-content/uploads/2011/07/Abstract-21.pdf.

[121] Financial Services Act 2012, Part 2, s.6.

January 2012. Following the Financial Services Bill 2012, the Financial Services Act 2012 came into force on 1 April 2013 and provides a new framework for financial regulation in the UK which makes the Bank of England responsible for ensuring and protecting the stability of the UK financial systems.[122]

Financial Policy Committee (FPC)

One of the key criticisms of the regulatory system in force during, and before, the financial crisis was the lack of a single, focused body with responsibility for protecting the stability of the financial system, as a whole. The new FPC[123] was established to ensure that a single body, situated within the Bank of England,[124] has the expertise to monitor the financial system and identify risks to its stability.[125] Macro-prudential policy and decisions are, therefore, the responsibility of the Financial Policy Committee (FPC).

As part of the Bank of England, there will be a frequent two-way flow of information and exchange of views between the PRA and the FPC.[126] The FPC is a powerful new authority sitting at the head of the regulatory architecture, taking a system-wide view of developing risks to stability and responding accordingly. The creation of the FPC is, therefore, a keystone of the government's programme for strengthening the financial stability framework. The FPC's role is to contribute to the Bank's Financial Stability objective[127] by identifying and monitoring systemic risks and taking action to address them. Crucially, the government has decided that the FPC will be required to take economic growth into account in pursuing financial stability, recognising that stability will generally be an important enabler of growth.

Where the FPC has identified risks, it is able to offer advice and recommendations to bodies responsible for the oversight of the financial system, including the Treasury, and other relevant bodies[128] such as the Financial Reporting Council. The FPC is responsible for reducing risks to the financial system as a whole[129] and is, among other things, able to recommend changes to PRA policies and rules on a 'comply or explain' basis.[130]

The Bank of England also has other financial stability functions. Building on its responsibility for operating the Special Resolution Regime for banks, the Bank of England has responsibility

---

[122] Financial Services Act 2012; see also HM Treasury, A new approach to financial regulation: the blueprint for reform, June 2011, Cm 8083, http://www.official-documents.gov.uk/document/cm80/8083/8083.pdf.

[123] On 17 February 2011 the government and the Bank of England announced the establishment of the FPC on an interim basis, to commence work on macro-prudential issues in advance of the legislation being enacted, HM Treasury, A new approach to financial regulation: the blueprint for reform, June 2011, Cm 8083, http://www.official-documents.gov.uk/document/cm80/8083/8083.pdf.

[124] Financial Services Act 2012, schedule 1 inserts a new s.9B to the Bank of England Act 1998.

[125] Financial Services Act 2012, schedule 3 amends s.2A of the Bank of England Act 1998 and provides that the FPC is to contribute to that objective primarily by identifying, monitoring and taking action to remove or reduce systemic risks with a view to protecting and enhancing the resilience of the UK financial system.

[126] Bank of England and FSA, The Bank of England, Prudential Regulation Authority, Our approach to banking supervision, May 2011, http://www.bankofengland.co.uk/publications/other/financialstability/uk_reg_framework/pra_approach.pdf.

[127] Financial Services Act 2012, s.3 inserts a new s.9C to the Bank of England Act 1998.

[128] Financial Services Act 2012, s.3 inserts a new s.9H to the Bank of England Act 1998 and provides that the FPC may give directions to the PRA or FCA.

[129] Financial Services Act 2012, s.3 inserts a new s.9C to the Bank of England Act 1998.

[130] FSA, The Bank of England, Prudential Regulation Authority, Our approach to banking supervision, May 2011, para. 7, http://www.bankofengland.co.uk/publications/other/financialstability/uk_reg_framework/pra_approach.pdf.

for dealing with crisis situations. A new crisis management Memorandum of Understanding (MOU) sets out the responsibilities of the Bank and the Treasury with the Chancellor of the Exchequer ultimately responsible for all decisions involving public funds.[131] The Treasury may make recommendations to the FPC[132] relating to matters that the FPC should regard as relevant to the Committee's understanding of the Bank's financial stability objective, and matters to which the Treasury considers the FPC should have regard, in the exercise of its functions. For example, the Treasury could recommend that the FPC takes into account the experience of another country in using a particular macro-prudential measure.

Prudential Regulation Authority (PRA)

With the Prudential Regulation Authority (PRA)[133] established as a subsidiary of the Bank of England prudential regulation is returned to the Bank of England. The PRA[134] is responsible for prudential regulation and supervision of individual firms which manage significant balance sheet risk as a core part of their business, i.e. banks, insurers and the larger, more complex investment firms. The PRA's role, therefore, will be to contribute to the promotion of the stability of the UK financial system. It has a single objective, i.e. to promote the safety and soundness of PRA-regulated firms.[135] The PRA meets this objective primarily by seeking to minimise any adverse effects of firm failure on the UK financial system and by ensuring that firms carry on their business in a way that avoids adverse effects on the system.[136]

The main means of achieving that objective is by seeking to ensure that the way in which the business of PRA-authorised persons[137] is carried on avoids any adverse effect on the UK

---

[131] HM Treasury, A new approach to financial regulation: the blueprint for reform, para. 1.30, June 2011, Cm 8083, http://www.official-documents.gov.uk/document/cm80/8083/8083.pdf.

[132] Financial Services Act 2012, s.3 inserts a new s.9D to the Bank of England Act 1998.

[133] Financial Services Act 2012, s.6 and schedule 20 insert a new s.2A to the Financial Services and Markets Act 2000 under which the PRA will be a limited company formed under the Companies Act 2006.

[134] Financial Services Act 2012, schedule 3 inserts a schedule 1ZB of the Financial Services and Markets Act 2000, which sets out requirements for the PRA's constitution and imposes certain obligations on the Bank of England.

[135] Bank of England and FSA, The Bank of England, Prudential Regulation Authority, Our approach to banking supervision, May 2011, http://www.bankofengland.co.uk/publications/other/financialstability/uk_reg_framework/pra_approach.pdf; Financial Services Act 2012, Part 2, s.6, inserts a new s.2B(3) to the Financial Services and Markets Act 2000. This reflects the Financial Services Act 2012, s.5, which inserts a new s.2B(3) to the Financial Services and Markets Act 2000.

[136] Bank of England and FSA, The Bank of England, Prudential Regulation Authority, Our approach to banking supervision, May 2011, http://www.bankofengland.co.uk/publications/other/financialstability/uk_reg_framework/pra_approach.pdf; Financial Services Act 2012, Part 2, s.6, inserts a new s.2B(3) to the Financial Services and Markets Act 2000. This reflects the Financial Services Act 2012, s.5 which inserts a new s.2B(3) (a) to the Financial Services and Markets Act 2000.

[137] The PRA will be responsible for the prudential supervision of over 2,000 firms, of which around half will be deposit-takers. On current data, it will regulate 157 UK-incorporated banks (of which over 60 per cent form part of overseas banking groups), 48 UK building societies, 652 UK credit unions and 162 branches of overseas banks, split roughly equally between the European Economic Area (EEA) and elsewhere. Through its supervision of UK-authorised deposit-takers the PRA will be responsible for the prudential regulation of firms holding £9 trillion of assets in the UK and globally, equal to around seven times UK GDP. Within this total, UK-owned banks alone hold assets equal to five times UK GDP. Additionally, the PRA will be responsible for the prudential supervision of passported branches of EEA banks, which together hold a further £2 trillion of assets in the UK: FSA, The Bank of England, Prudential Regulation Authority, Our approach to banking supervision, May 2011, paras 20 and 22, http://www.bankofengland.co.uk/publications/other/financialstability/uk_reg_framework/pra_approach.pdf.

financial system,[138] and by seeking to ensure that, if a PRA-authorised person fails, that failure occurs in as orderly a manner as possible.[139] The PRA's approach to regulation will thus consist of policy-making to guard against a range of possible outcomes and the application of that policy through effective supervision. All firms will be subject to a baseline level of supervisory oversight designed both to reduce the probability of failure and, as it is not the PRA's role to prevent firm failure in all circumstances, to ensure that if a firm does fail, it does so in an orderly manner.[140]

Supervisory efforts and resources will be focused particularly on issues with potential systemic impact. The PRA's approach will combine regulatory policy relating to both the firm's resilience (e.g. capital, liquidity and leverage) and to the resolution of firms when they fail with the application of that policy through effective and, where necessary, intensive supervision. Addressing one of the shortfalls of the FSA's approach to supervision the PRA will seek to go beyond monitoring 'tick box' compliance with rules.[141] Firms will be expected to approach compliance in a manner that responds to the purpose and intent of the rules, and supervisors will seek to address whether firms are effectively mitigating risks.[142]

Locating the PRA within the Bank of England is a reflection of its importance in protecting financial stability and its core responsibility will be to promote the safety and soundness of the firms it regulates.[143] The PRA's approach to supervision will be judgement-led so the nature and intensity of supervision will depend on the risks posed by each firm; while every firm will be subject to a minimum baseline level of supervision to promote and support its soundness and resilience.[144]

An effective regulatory framework for financial stability needs to combine firm-specific supervision with oversight and risk management of the financial system as a whole. So the

---

[138] Financial Services Act 2012, Part 2, s.6, inserts a new s.2B(3)(a) to the Financial Services and Markets Act 2000. This reflects the Financial Services Act 2012, s.5 which inserts a new s.2B(3)(a) to the FSMA 2000.

[139] Financial Services Act 2012, Part 2, s.6, inserts a new s.2B(3)(b) to the Financial Services and Markets Act 2000. This reflects the Financial Services Action 2012, s.5 which inserts a new s.2B(3)(b) to the FSMA 2000. Section 2I(2)–(4) provides the meaning of 'failure' and includes: insolvency; being taken for the purposes of the financial services compensation scheme unable, or likely to be unable, to meet claims; and having a stabilisation option under Part 1 of the Banking Act 2009 implemented (for example transfer to a private sector purchaser (s.11 of that Act), transfer to a bridge bank (s.12 of that Act), or transfer to temporary public ownership (s.13 of that Act)). The fact that a PRA authorised person has received financial assistance from the Treasury or the Secretary of State may be relevant in determining whether that person has failed but is not a sign of failure in all cases.

[140] Bank of England and FSA, The Bank of England, Prudential Regulation Authority, Our approach to banking supervision, May 2011, para. 6, http://www.bankofengland.co.uk/publications/other/financialstability/uk_reg_framework/pra_approach.pdf.

[141] Bank of England and FSA, The Bank of England, Prudential Regulation Authority, Our approach to banking supervision, May 2011, http://www.bankofengland.co.uk/publications/other/financialstability/uk_reg_framework/pra_approach.pdf.

[142] HM Treasury, A new approach to financial regulation: the blueprint for reform, para. 1.36, June 2011, Cm 8083, http://www.official-documents.gov.uk/document/cm80/8083/8083.pdf.

[143] HM Treasury, A new approach to financial regulation: the blueprint for reform, June 2011, Cm 8083, http://www.official-documents.gov.uk/document/cm80/8083/8083.pdf.

[144] Bank of England and FSA, The Bank of England, Prudential Regulation Authority, Our approach to banking supervision, May 2011, para. 6, http://www.bankofengland.co.uk/publications/other/financialstability/uk_reg_framework/pra_approach.pdf.

PRA will work closely with the rest of the Bank, including the Financial Policy Committee (FPC).[145] The PRA supervisors will, in carrying out this function, coordinate with other authorities, including the FCA and overseas authorities in the case of multinational firms. Although, the PRA is charged with making firm-specific decisions, it is inevitable that there will be overlap between these decisions and those which the FPC is making. This will be addressed through some common membership of the PRA board and the FPC. In addition, the PRA will provide firm-specific information to feed into the FPC's assessment of the macro-prudential outlook; and the FPC's analysis of potential systemic risks will help inform the PRA's judgements on specific types of institutions, sectors and asset classes, including its approach to stress testing and its assessments of future vulnerabilities.[146] A further difference to the system of regulation under the FSA is demonstrated by the adoption of stress testing, which is utilised to analyse an institution's strength against contrasting hypothetical financial scenarios.

In the case of subsidiaries of overseas banks in the UK, the PRA's approach will mirror that for UK banks, reflecting the fact that it will have the prudential powers for such institutions. The PRA will assess both a firm's links with, and the viability of, its group as a whole. Supervision of the UK subsidiaries of the most significant global financial institutions will be an important undertaking for the PRA, as well as being an important input into the consolidated supervision.[147]

The Financial Conduct Authority (FCA)

The separation of responsibility for prudential and conduct of business regulation for systemic firms will allow the creation of the FCA[148] as an authority with the remit and capability to specialise in protecting consumers[149] and promoting confidence in financial services and markets. The FCA will fulfil this role for all consumers of financial services, from retail savers to the largest institutional investors. The FCA position paper states that:

> The FCA will need to spot things earlier; be willing to intervene early to improve standards either in specific firms or wider; take robust action to address weaknesses in competition revealed by economic analysis . . .

---

[145] Bank of England and FSA, The Bank of England, Prudential Regulation Authority, Our approach to banking supervision, May 2011, para. 6, http://www.bankofengland.co.uk/publications/other/financialstability/uk_reg_framework/pra_approach.pdf.

[146] Bank of England and FSA, The Bank of England, Prudential Regulation Authority, Our approach to banking supervision, May 2011, http://www.bankofengland.co.uk/publications/other/financialstability/uk_reg_framework/pra_approach.pdf.

[147] Bank of England and FSA, The Bank of England, Prudential Regulation Authority, Our approach to banking supervision, May 2011, http://www.bankofengland.co.uk/publications/other/financialstability/uk_reg_framework/pra_approach.pdf.

[148] The FSA is renamed the Financial Conduct Authority following amendment by part 2, s.6 of the Financial Services Act 2012. This reflects clause 5 of the Financial Services Bill 2012, which inserted a new s.1A(1) to the Financial Services and Markets Act 2000.

[149] Financial Services Act 2012, Part 2, s.6, inserts a new s.1B(2) to the Financial Services and Markets Act 2000. This reflects the Financial Services Bill 2012 clause 5 which inserts a new s.1B(2) in the Financial Services and Markets Act 2000.

The FCA's objectives do not impose on it a statutory duty to take action to secure an appropriate degree of protection for all persons who fall within the definition of 'consumer'. Instead, the objectives provide a mandate for the FCA to act where the authority identifies actual or potential consumer detriment. However, the FCA could take action, for example, under its consumer protection objective for the purposes of protecting only one category of person who falls within the definition of 'consumer,' but it need not ensure that the action taken secures an appropriate degree of protection for all persons who fall within that definition.

As an integrated conduct regulator, covering retail, wholesale and market conduct the FCA will have a broad statutory remit, which encompasses the breadth of its responsibilities. Its strategic[150] objective is, therefore, expressed in terms of promoting confidence in the UK financial system, underpinned by operational objectives[151] relating to consumer protection, promoting choice and efficiency, and market integrity. The FCA will have a statutory duty to exercise its general functions in a way, which promotes competition, insofar as compatible with its strategic and operational objectives.[152] The effect of this duty is that where the FCA decides to act in pursuance of an operational objective and has the choice between two options, one of which would have a negative impact on competition while the other would have a positive impact on competition, the FCA must choose the option that promotes competition, unless this would be incompatible with its strategic objective.

While, the FCA is able to use its general rule-making and supervisory toolkit to promote transparency in the provision of services, remove barriers to entry, or take other action in pursuit of its competition duty, it has a specific new power to require the Office of Fair Trading to consider whether structural barriers or other features of the market are creating competitive inefficiencies in specific markets.[153] In discharging its general functions the FCA must also have regard to the regulatory principles which apply to the FPC and the PRA,[154] and must have regard to the importance of taking action intended to minimise the extent to which it is possible for certain types of business to be used for a purpose connected with financial crime. This duty is placed on the FCA, rather than the PRA, as the FCA is to have responsibility for regulating the conduct of business of authorised persons and, is therefore, deemed best placed to take regulatory action to tackle financial crime.

---

[150] Financial Services Act 2012, Part 2, s.6, inserts a new s.1B(2) to the Financial Services and Markets Act 2000. This reflects the Financial Services Act 2012, s.5 which inserts a new s.1B(2) in the Financial Services and Markets Act 2000.

[151] Financial Services Act 2012, Part 2, s.6, inserts a new s.1C, 1D and 1E into the Financial Services and Markets Act 2000. This reflects the Financial Services Bill 2012, clause 5 which inserts a new s.1C, 1D and 1E in the Financial Services and Markets Act 2000.

[152] Financial Services Act 2012, Part 2, s.6, which reflects the Financial Services Bill 2012, clause 5.

[153] HM Treasury, A new approach to financial regulation: the blueprint for reform, para. 1.40, June 2011, Cm 8083, http://www.official-documents.gov.uk/document/cm80/8083/8083.pdf.

[154] Financial Services Act 2012, Part 2, s.6 inserts a new s.3B in the Financial Services and Markets Act 2000. This reflects the Financial Services Bill 2012, clause 5 which inserts a new s.3B in the Financial Services Act 2000.

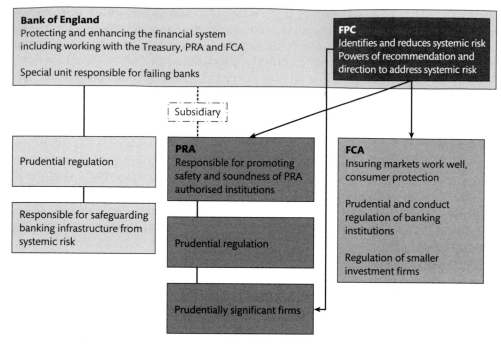

Figure 4.1 The twin peaks approach to banking regulation

The 'joined up' approach to prudential supervision

Despite previous criticisms of the Bank of England's failings in bank supervision the reforms confer on the Bank a central role in the new system of financial regulation. The main features of the new regulatory landscape are a more 'joined-up' approach to prudential regulation, with both macro- and-micro-prudential regulation brought together under the remit of the Bank of England. Additionally, the creation of a dedicated and specialist regulator to focus on consumer protection and market integrity has reinforced oversight of the financial sector. The Treasury justifies the involvement of the Bank of England on the basis that the Bank has a 'competitive advantage due to its exposure in the markets and the information it gains through its role as a supervisory authority would support it in performing other functions effectively, for example its role as provider of liquidity insurance'.

The Bank is seen to have a competitive advantage due to its exposure in the markets and yet there is debate about the Bank's ability to remain in touch with the detail of those exact markets. This lack of ability may detract from any perceived competitive edge the Bank of England may have. If the Bank of England remains overly focused on its monetary policy role then its involvement with the new system may be superficial and ineffective.[155] Cowie[156] argues that the danger is that the Bank of England has too many priorities and its resources

[155] Keasey and Verones (2008) Lessons from the Northern Rock Affair, 16(1) *Journal of Financial Regulation and Compliance*, 8.

[156] Cowie (2010) Regulation: Improving on the FSA, 41(499), *Euromoney*, 117.

will be spread too thinly. The Bank must therefore be in a position to balance its responsibilities for monetary stability with those for prudential regulation and remain in touch with the markets. Meanwhile, the Treasury has expressed the view that Bank of England involvement in supervision may assist it to carry out its other objectives.

The new structure necessitates close cooperation and coordination between the new regulatory bodies, to ensure consistency of regulation and to avoid duplication of efforts. The regulators are required to coordinate their functions for three purposes:

(i)   To ensure that a policy pursued by one regulator does not have an adverse impact on the pursuit, by the other regulator, of its objectives.

(ii) To ensure that they obtain advice or information from each other where the other regulator has a particular expertise and exercises qualifying functions.

(iii) To ensure that, where the regulators exercise qualifying functions in relation to a matter of common regulatory interest,[157] they have regard to the need to use resources efficiently and economically.

The duty to coordinate does not override the requirement that each regulator discharges its general functions in a way which advances its objectives, and it does not apply where the burden on the regulators of coordinating the exercise of their functions would outweigh the benefits.[158] One regulator may give the other directions in relation to the consolidated supervision of some or all of the members of the group for the purposes of relevant EU directives.[159] The directions may require the regulator to exercise, or not to exercise, its functions in a particular way but may not require the regulator to do something that it does not have the power to do.

Independent Commission on Banking (ICB)

On 12 September 2011[160] the Independent Commission on Banking (ICB) published its final report and recommendations on reforms to improve stability and competition in the UK.[161] The final report was followed by a government response in December 2011 in which almost all the Commission's recommendations were accepted.[162] The recommendations aim to reduce the probability and impact of a systemic financial crisis in the future; maintain the efficient flow of credit to the economy and the ability of households and businesses to manage their

---

[157] Financial Services Act 2012, s.6, inserts a new s.3D to the Financial Services and Markets Act 2000. This reflects the Financial Services Bill 2012, s.6 which inserts a new s.3D to the Financial Services and Markets Act 2000.

[158] Financial Services Act 2012, Part 2, s.6, inserts a new s.3D to the Financial Services and Markets Act 2000. This reflects the Financial Services Bill 2012, clause 5 which inserts a new s.3D to the Financial Services and Markets Act 2000.

[159] Financial Services Act 2012, Part 2, s.6, inserts new ss.3L to 3O to the Financial Services and Markets Act 2000. This reflects the Financial Services Bill 2012, clause 5 which inserts new ss.3L to 3O to the Financial Services and Markets Act 2000.

[160] Sir John Vickers, Chair, Independent Commission on Banking Final Recommendations, September 2011, http://hm-treasury.gov.uk/d/ICB-Final-Report.pdf.

[161] The report expands on the Commission's April 2011 interim report and Annex 1 contains a summary of the responses to the Commission's consultation, http://www.hm-treasury.gov.uk/d/icb_interim_report_full_document.pdf.

[162] HM Treasury, The Government response to the Independent Commission on Banking, Cm 8252, http://cdn.hm-treasury.gov.uk/govt_response_to_icb_191211.pdf; Banking reform: delivering sustainability and supporting a sustainable economy, Cm 8252.

risks and financial needs over time; preserve the functioning of the payment systems; and guarantee capital certainty and liquidity for small savers, including small and medium-sized enterprises. The recommendations on competition set out reforms for structural change in UK banking markets, for improving consumer choice and switching banking services providers, and for pro-competitive regulation of financial services. The main recommendations of the Commission were as described under the following headings.

Ring-fencing banks

The purpose of the retail ring-fence is to isolate those banking activities where the continuous provision of service is vital to the economy and to bank customers in order to ensure that this provision is not threatened, as a result of activities which are incidental to it, and that such provision can be maintained in the event of the bank's failure without government solvency support. Only ring-fenced banks will be granted permission to provide mandated services in the UK. Such services are those where even a temporary interruption to the provision of service resulting from the failure of a bank would have significant economic costs; and customers are not well equipped to plan for such an interruption. Mandated services comprise the taking of deposits from, and the provision of overdrafts to, individuals and small and medium-sized organisations.[163] The ring-fencing provisions will apply to any standalone UK bank, any UK bank that is part of a wider banking group with a head-office in the UK, and any UK bank, which is a subsidiary of a wider banking group with head-offices overseas. Mandated services could also be provided in the UK by branches of foreign banks, although any significant banks based outside the European Economic Area (EEA) wishing to carry out mandated services in the UK will generally be required to establish a UK subsidiary. No other institution may provide a mandated service in the UK. The word 'bank' in the context of ring-fenced services has a broad meaning and extends to all types of deposit-takers, in particular building societies.[164]

The Commission recommended that ring-fenced banks should be prohibited from providing certain services, including those that:

- Directly increase the exposure of the ring-fenced bank to global financial markets;

- Involve the ring-fenced bank taking risk and are not integral to the provision of payments services to customers, or the direct intermediation of funds between savers and borrowers within the non-financial sector; or

- In any other way threaten the objectives of the ring-fence. Prohibited services will include (though need not be limited to):

  (a) any service, which is not provided to customers within the EEA;
  (b) any service which results in an exposure to a non-ring-fenced bank or a non-bank financial organisation, except those associated with the provision of payments services where the regulator has deemed this appropriate;
  (c) any service, which would result in a trading book asset;
  (d) any service, which would result in a requirement to hold regulatory capital against market risk;

---

[163] Independent Commission on Banking Final Recommendations, September 2011, para. 3.13, http://hm-treasury.gov.uk/d/ICB-Final-Report.pdf.

[164] Independent Commission on Banking Final Recommendations, September 2011, para. 3.14, http://hm-treasury.gov.uk/d/ICB-Final-Report.pdf.

(e) the purchase or origination of derivatives or other contracts which would result in a requirement to hold regulatory capital against counterparty credit risk; and

(f) services relating to secondary markets activity including the purchase of loans or securities.[165]

Broadly, this will mean that the majority of the retail and commercial banking divisions of the existing UK banks could be placed in ring-fenced banks,[166] but not the wholesale and investment banking divisions.

Ring-fenced banks would be able to undertake those ancillary activities necessary for the efficient provision of mandated services. Ancillary activities would be permitted only to the extent they are required for this provision, and not as standalone lines of business. Ancillary activities would, therefore, include for example, employing staff and owning or procuring the necessary operational infrastructure. In particular, a ring-fenced bank would be permitted to conduct financial activities beyond the provision of non-prohibited services only to the extent that these are strictly required for the purposes of its treasury function, i.e. for risk management, liquidity management, or in order to raise funding for the provision of non-prohibited services.[167]

Where a ring-fenced bank is part of a wider corporate group, the authorities should have confidence that they can isolate it from the rest of the group in a matter of days and continue the provision of its services without providing solvency support. Ring-fenced banks should be separate legal entities and their balance sheets should contain only assets and liabilities arising from mandated services and activities; the wider corporate group should be required to put in place arrangements to ensure that the ring-fenced bank has continuous access to all of the operations, staff, data and services required to continue its activities, irrespective of the financial health of the rest of the group; and the ring-fenced bank should either be a direct member of all the payments systems that it uses or should use another ring-fenced bank as an agent.[168]

Loss absorbency

The 2007–09 financial crisis revealed that UK banks were severely under-capitalised and small declines in the value of their assets threatened some with insolvency. The government, fearful of the consequences of allowing systemically important banks to fail, bailed them out. In addition to direct capital injections, the taxpayer also took on enormous contingent liabilities. It became apparent that banks had not sufficiently protected themselves against the risks they were taking. So as losses started to erode their safety buffers, banks that were ill prepared had ever fewer resources to absorb further losses that might come through. In an attempt to reduce risk, banks sought to shrink their balance sheets, and so cut lending. The resulting

---

[165] Independent Commission on Banking Final Recommendations, September 2011, para. 3.39, http://hm-treasury.gov.uk/d/ICB-Final-Report.pdf.

[166] Based on the balance sheets of UK banks at the end of 2010 this construction of a retail ring-fence could lead to around £1.1–£2.3 trillion of assets being held within UK ring-fenced banks, or around 75–160 per cent of current UK GDP. This is between a sixth and a third of the total assets of the UK banking sector of over £6 trillion, Independent Commission on Banking Final Recommendations, September 2011, para. 3.40, http://hm-treasury.gov.uk/d/ICB-Final-Report.pdf.

[167] Independent Commission on Banking Final Recommendations, September 2011, para. 3.57, http://hm-treasury.gov.uk/d/ICB-Final-Report.pdf.

[168] Independent Commission on Banking Final Recommendations, September 2011, para. 3.74, http://hm-treasury.gov.uk/d/ICB-Final-Report.pdf.

contraction in the supply of credit has had a significant effect on the economy. Shareholders, in some of the largest banks, having enjoyed strong returns in the years running up to the crisis, suffered considerable losses, and some were pushed into bankruptcy or insolvency. However, bank creditors escaped largely unscathed, and many employees in wholesale and investment banking were very well paid throughout.

The Commission therefore made recommendations intended to make banks better able to absorb losses and less likely to fail, and better able to cope with losses short of failure. If they do fail, banks need to avoid the consequences of disorderly bank failure.[169] Some of these recommendations include requiring all UK-headquartered banks and all ring-fenced banks to maintain a Tier 1 leverage ratio of at least 3 per cent. Tier 1 Capital refers to a bank's core capital, and the leverage ratio is calculated by dividing the Tier 1 Capital against the bank's total adjusted assets. A bank with a 3 per cent leverage ratio may also be expressed as being 33 times leveraged which is calculated by reversing the aforementioned calculation. This is tightened to 4.06 per cent for ring-fenced banks required to have an equity ratio of at least 10 per cent, which is calculated by dividing a bank's equities against its total debts.[170] While the Commission would have been inclined to recommend higher equity requirements for ring-fenced banks than those of non ring-fenced banks, it recognised that mandating substantially higher equity requirements for ring-fenced banks (together with loss-absorbing debt) would probably invite arbitrage, i.e. the shifting of activities from the ring-fenced bank to the non-ring-fenced bank in order to exploit the difference. The Commission's recommendations on minimum equity requirements avoid creating strong incentives for such arbitrage.[171] Resolution authorities should have bail-in powers.[172] This is a process of internal recapitalisation, which is triggered once a firm becomes non-viable. Losses are imposed on certain numbers of a firm's direct stakeholders by a process of 'bailing-in', either by writing down their claims or by converting them to equity. The firm is recapitalised from within and the need for new capital resources to be provided by the public sector (i.e. a bail-out) is avoided. Bail-in will usually need to be accompanied by changes in the firm's senior management and the adoption of a new business plan that addresses the causes of the firm's failure.

A key objective of the bail-in process is to secure the continued existence of part or the entire firm on a going concern basis. If this can be done then disruption of services to customers of the firm should be minimised, while its shareholders and uninsured creditors are subject to going concern losses rather than the much larger gone concern losses that they would suffer if the firm went into insolvency or liquidation.[173]

Competition

The ICB report explored issues relating to competition in the UK banking sector in respect of structural conditions for competition, conditions for the exercise of well-informed choice

---

[169] Independent Commission on Banking Final Recommendations, September 2011, para. 4, http://hm-treasury.gov.uk/d/ICB-Final-Report.pdf.

[170] Independent Commission on Banking Final Recommendations, September 2011, para. 4.39, http://hm-treasury.gov.uk/d/ICB-Final-Report.pdf.

[171] Independent Commission on Banking Final Recommendations, September 2011, para. 4.46, http://hm-treasury.gov.uk/d/ICB-Final-Report.pdf.

[172] Independent Commission on Banking Final Recommendations, September 2011, para. 4.46, http://hm-treasury.gov.uk/d/ICB-Final-Report.pdf.

[173] FSA, Recovery and Resolution Plans, August 2011, CP11_16, para. 11.1, http://www.fsa.gov.uk/pubs/cp/cp11_16.pdf.

by consumers; and financial stability and competition. Most of the competition problems highlighted by the Cruickshank report[174] into competition in UK banking remain.[175] Market concentration of the supply side is coupled with weaknesses on the demand side. The ICB concluded that current account switching costs are perceived as being high and product comparisons are opaque. There has also been strong public dissatisfaction with aspects of bank pricing, such as unarranged overdraft charges, and widespread mis-selling in the case of PPI (Payment Protection Insurance).[176]

The Commission recommended that the PRA should work with the Office of Fair Trading (OFT) to review the application of prudential standards to ensure that prudential requirements for capital and liquidity do not unnecessarily limit the ability of new entrants to enter the banking market. To smooth the process of switching current accounts for individuals and small businesses, a current account redirection service should be established to:

- Catch all credits and debits going to the old account, including automated payments taken from debit cards as well as direct debits.
- Be seamless for the customer, ensuring that they retain full use of their banking services without being inconvenienced by debits or credits going to the wrong account.
- Ensure that annual payments are caught, by continuing for at least 13 months.
- Continue to send reminders and provide support to direct debit originators to ensure that they update their details for people who have switched accounts.
- Guarantee that customers will not suffer loss should there be mistakes during the switching process.
- Be free to the customer.

The redirection service should not impose disproportionate costs on new entrants and banks that access payments systems through agency arrangements. Small banks, building societies and small business direct debit originators should not be penalised by these changes. A maximum timescale should also be introduced for the release of security after repayment of borrowing, and banks should improve the process for transferring security. The Commission believes this should ease switching for small businesses. The OFT, and the Financial Conduct Authority (FCA) should work with the banks to improve transparency across all retail banking products, in particular for personal current accounts (PCAs) and business current accounts (BCAs).

The Commission also recommended that the government should reach agreement with Lloyds Banking Group (LBG) to ensure that the entity which results from its state aid divestiture has a funding position at least as strong as its peers, including as evidenced by its loan-to-deposit ratio (LDR) relative to its peers' LDRs at the time of the disposal; and has a share of the personal current account (PCA) market of at least 6 per cent.

---

[174] Cruickshank (2000) Competition in UK banking: The Cruickshank report, http://www.hm-treasury.gov.uk/d/2YRCshank-251104.pdf.

[175] Over the past decade the competition authorities (the Office of Fair Trading (OFT) and the Competition Commission (CC)) have been involved with banking markets on a number of occasions, for example blocking the proposed Lloyds TSB/Abbey National merger in 2001, the SME banking report of 2002, and the unauthorised overdraft case which the OFT lost before the Supreme Court in 2009.

[176] PPI – facts and figures from the 'biggest mis-selling scandal of all time', 4 March 2013, http://www.guardian.co.uk/money/2013/mar/04/ppi-facts-figures-biggest-mis-selling-scandal.

Government response to the ICB recommendations

The government response to the ICB published on 19 December 2011[177] strongly supported the objectives and recommendations to make banks better able to absorb losses, to efficiently and effectively resolve failing banks and curb incentives for excessive risk-taking. The government agreed:

(i) That vital banking services, in particular the taking of retail deposits, should only be provided by 'ring-fenced banks', and that these banks should be prohibited from undertaking certain investment banking activities.

(ii) With the ICB's recommendations on loss-absorbency and sees these non-structural reforms as an important complement to ring-fencing in making banks better able to absorb losses, easier to resolve if they fail, and in curbing excessive risk-taking.

(iii) That all banks should be subject to normal competitive market forces, which means they must be able to fail safely without relying on a government guarantee and without putting the provision of critical services at risk.

(iv) That all banks, including non-ring-fenced banks, need to be resolvable without the use of state resources. However, these powers should be complemented by the introduction of a resolution regime that covers investment firms and financial holding companies.

(v) With and supports all the recommendations on introducing competition in the banking sector and will consult with the payments council on options for enhancing the regulatory framework for the payment system.

The government White Paper,[178] giving effect to the recommendations of the ICB was considered by the Parliamentary Commission on Banking Standards (PCBS) which published its report in June 2013.[179] The PCBS also recognised the importance of effective ring-fencing, to ensure financial stability. The PCBS, however, stated the ring-fence should be 'electrified' to enforce compliance if the initial ring-fencing requirements did not reduce risk. However, the PCBS emphasised that it is important to be 'clear that it is these functions that enjoy protection and not the bank itself or its shareholders or creditors'.[180] Further, the Liikanen Group recommended that risky proprietary trading, which is conducted through the bank's own assets for the firm's own profit, should be conducted by a separate legal entity.[181]

The Banking Reform Bill, which is due to come into force in early 2014, will therefore make the following changes to the structure:

---

[177] HM Treasury, The Government response to the Independent Banking Commission, Cm 8252, http://cdn.hm-treasury.gov.uk/govt_response_to_icb_191211.pdf.

[178] HM Treasury, Banking Reform: delivering stability and supporting a sustainability economy, Cm 356, June 2012, https://www.gov.uk/government/uploads/system/uploads/attachment_data/file/32556/whitepaper_banking_reform_140512.pdf.

[179] Parliamentary Commission on Banking Standards, Changing Banking for Good, 19 June 2013, Volumes I and II, http://www.publications.parliament.uk/pa/jt201314/jtselect/jtpcbs/27/2702.htm.

[180] Parliamentary Commission on Banking Standards, Changing Banking for Good, para. 104, 19 June 2013, Volumes I and II, http://www.publications.parliament.uk/pa/jt201314/jtselect/jtpcbs/27/2702.htm.

[181] Liikanen High-level Expert Group on reforming the structure of the EU banking sector, Final Report, 2 October 2012, http://ec.europa.eu/internal_market/bank/docs/high-level_expert_group/report_en.pdf.

- Introduce a 'ring-fence' around the deposits of individuals and small businesses, to separate the high street from the dealing floor and protect taxpayers when things go wrong.
- Make sure the Prudential Regulation Authority can hold banks to account for the way they separate their retail and investment activities, giving it powers to enforce the full separation of individual banks.
- Give depositors, protected under the Financial Services Compensation Scheme, preference if a bank enters insolvency.
- Give the government power to ensure that banks are more able to absorb losses.

To make the financial system more responsive to consumers it is intended to increase competition between financial services firms, including making it easier for customers to switch their current accounts with a seven-day switching service introduced in September 2013.

The government intends that the ICB recommendations relating to ring-fenced banks will be implemented by May 2015 and banks will be expected to be complaint as soon as possible thereafter, and non-structural changes related to loss absorbency fully completed by the beginning of 2019.

Remuneration practices in banks and other financial institutions

The banking crisis exposed serious flaws in remuneration policies in the UK banking sector and propelled the issue of remuneration practices to the forefront of public[182] and political debate.[183] The Turner Review[184] concluded that there was a 'strong *prima facie* case that inappropriate incentive structures played a role in encouraging behaviour which contributed to the financial crisis', although the review went on to state that it was difficult to 'gauge precisely how important that contribution was . . .'. The Walker Report[185] concluded that Lord

---

[182] The Nobel prize-winning economist Joseph Stiglitz concluded that: 'The system of compensation almost surely contributed in an important way to the crisis. It was designed to encourage risk-taking – but it encouraged excessive risk-taking. In effect, it paid them to gamble. When things turned out well, they walked away with huge bonuses. When things turned out badly – as now – they do not share in the losses. Even if they lose their jobs, they walk away with large sums of money', You ask the questions, *Independent*, 24 March 2008, http://www.independent.co.uk/news/people/profiles/joseph-stiglitz-you-ask-the-questions-799885.html.

[183] Several reports have identified failures in remuneration policies and practices some of which include: House of Commons Treasury Committee Banking Crisis: reforming corporate governance and pay in the City: Government, UK Financial Investments Ltd and Financial Services Authority Responses to the Ninth Report from the Committee, Eighth Special Report of Session 2008–09, printed 21 July 2009, HC 462, http://www.publications. parliament.uk/pa/cm200809/cmselect/cmtreasy/462/462.pdf; House of Commons Treasury Committee Banking Crisis: reforming corporate governance and pay in the City, Ninth Report of Session 2008–09, May 2009, HC 519, http://www.iasplus.com/uk/0905treasurycommittee.pdf; FSA, The Turner Review, A regulatory response to the global banking crisis, March 2009, p. 80, http://www.fsa.gov.uk/pubs/other/turner_review.pdf; HM Treasury, A review of corporate governance in UK Banks and other financial entities, Final Recommendations, 26 November 2009, http://www.hm-treasury.gov.uk/walker_review_information.htm.

[184] FSA, The Turner Review, A regulatory response to the global banking crisis, March 2009, p. 80, http://www. fsa.gov.uk/pubs/other/turner_review.pdf.

[185] A review of corporate governance in UK banks and other financial industry entities, 16 July 2009, http:// www.audit-committee-institute.be/dbfetch/52616e646f6d4956f9ed6cb8ae5277dbec35c233bab54a5b/ walker_review_consultation_160709.pdf.

Turner had underestimated the impact inappropriate remuneration policies played on the financial crisis and it is widely accepted that failures in market discipline, including remuneration practices[186] in the banking sector were significant factors in the crisis. Executive[187] pay has become a controversial subject[188] and there was public outrage at the compensation packages awarded to some senior executives, including payments perceived as rewards for failure, in circumstances where several banking firms were saved from insolvency, only as a result of taxpayer bail-out.[189]

Bonuses have been criticised as rewarding short-term success without necessarily being objectively aligned to long-term company strategy and shareholder interests[190] and share options often used to motivate executives and give the recipient windfall gains[191] resulting from upwards movements in the market, inflationary gains and the discounted prices at which share-options were granted[192] have been criticised for not being linked to performance. While, some of the regulation on directors remuneration is subject to the companies legislation, the corporate code specific regulation of remuneration in banks and other financial institutions (BOFI) was previously under FSA, now FCA, control.

The UK remuneration landscape

Even before the credit crunch, the FSA had powers to address risks posed by inappropriate remuneration structures, although they were part of the FSA Handbook's Principles for Business and Senior Management Arrangements, Systems and Controls Sourcebook (SYSC).[193]

---

[186] HM Treasury, A review of corporate governance in UK Banks and other financial entities, Final Recommendations, 26 November 2009, http://www.hmtreasury.gov.uk/walker_review_information.htm.

[187] The group of people who might be described as 'executives' has caused some debate but Pepper described them as '. . . the very senior executives responsible for defining and executing a company's strategy, who through their actions are capable of directly affecting (positively or negatively) the company's profits, share price, reputation, market positioning and so on', Pepper (2006) *Senior Executive Reward: Key Models and Practices*, Ashgate Publishing Limited, 2006, p. 5.

[188] Lee said that 'Evidence in the US is of many companies having given away 10 per cent, and in some cases as much as 30 per cent, of their equity to executive directors and other staff in just the last five years or so. That is clearly not sustainable into the future: there wouldn't be any companies left in public hands if it were': Lee (2002) Not Badly Paid But Paid Badly, 10(2), *Corporate Governance: An International Review*, p. 69.

[189] House of Commons Treasury Committee, Banking crisis: reforming corporate governance and pay in the City, Ninth Report of session 2008–09, HC 519, published 15 May 2009, recognised two distinct areas of concern as contributing to the banking crisis: (i) the high levels of remuneration and bonuses, the excessive risk-taking and the substantial severance packages awarded to senior executives, including those of nationalised or part-nationalised banks, and (ii) the bonus culture which encouraged short-term profit and excessive and reckless risk-taking, http://www.iasplus.com/uk/0905treasurycommittee.pdf.

[190] Murphy (1999) Executive Compensation, http://windbichler.rewi.hu-berlin.de/Murphy_Executive Compensation.pdf.

[191] Behchuk, Cohen and Spamann (2010) The Wages of Failure: Executive Compensation at Bear Stearns and Lehman 2000–2008, discussion Paper 657, Harvard, Hohn M. Olin Centre for Law, Economics and Business, 27, Yale Journal on Regulation, pp. 257–282, estimate that the top-five executive teams at Bear Stearns and Lehman, during 2000–08, took out amounts totalling about $1.1 billion and $850 million respectively, exercising their share and options rights.

[192] Directors' Remuneration, Report of a Study Group, Chaired by Sir Richard Greenbury, 1995, http://www.ecgi.org/codes/documents/greenbury.pdf.

[193] FSA, Senior Management Arrangements, Systems and Controls, *FSA Handbook* H, Release 026 D, December 2003, http://www.fsa.gov.uk/pubs/hb-releases/rel26/rel26sysc.pd.

These principles continue[194] to apply to remuneration structures, for example firms must take reasonable care to organise and control their affairs responsibly and effectively, with adequate risk management systems.[195] To the extent that remuneration structures can give rise to conflicts of interest, Principal 3 (a firm must manage conflicts of interest fairly, both between itself and its customers and between a customer and another client) is also relevant, for example where remuneration structures encourage staff to act contrary to customer interests.[196] These powers are reinforced by the new UK Corporate Governance Code which exhorts remuneration committees to 'be sensitive to pay and employment conditions' within the group.[197] Additionally, the Companies Act 2006 requires oversight of directors' service contracts[198] and implements disclosure provisions of termination packages.[199] The conduct of the directors who approve such termination packages may come under scrutiny under ss.171–176 of the 2006 Act with ss.171–173 being relied on to impose liability. More recently, the FSA provided that it expects firms to avoid remuneration structures, which might encourage employees to take excessive risks in order to maximise bonuses, thereby jeopardising the prudential standing of the firm.[200]

The FSA remuneration code

In October 2008, the FSA issued a 'Dear CEO' letter to the CEOs of around 20 major banks and building societies setting out the FSAs 'initial thinking' on remuneration policies. The letter urged banks to review their remuneration policies, particularly in the light of market developments, and to take appropriate action if they were not aligned with sound risk management systems and controls. The intention was for the FSA to visit these institutions to

---

[194] Now SYSC 19A.1, http://www.fshandbook.info/FS/html/FCA/SYSC/19A/1.

[195] Principle 19.A 3.7, FSA, Senior Management Arrangements, Systems and Controls, *FCA Handbook*, http://www.fshandbook.info/FS/html/FCA/SYSC/19A/3.

[196] These controls were relied on by the FSA when it concluded that firms' remuneration structures increased the risks of advisers engaging in unsuitable sales of PPIs, http://www.fsa.gov.uk/pubs/final/alliance_leicester.pdf.

[197] On 28 May 2010, the Financial Reporting Council (FRC) published the new UK Corporate Governance Code, which applies to companies reporting on or after the 29 June 2010. FRS, *The UK Corporate Governance Code*, 2010, Section D, http://www.frc.org.uk/documents/pagemanager/Corporate_Governance/UK%20Corp%20Gov%20Code%20June%202010.pdf.

[198] Companies Act 2006, s.188.

[199] Sections 215–222 of the Companies Act 2006 establishes the rules relating to shareholder approval of director's termination packages made after October 2007. The provisions cover compensation packages for loss of directorial (or other office connected with that appointment) office or as consideration for or in connection with retirement from office, whether directly to the director or any person connected with him. The term 'payment' includes past, present and future payments made under a separation package. Such payments are unlawful unless members, who have had notice of the proposed payment, including the actual amounts, have approved them. However, members' approval is not required where payments are made in good faith in discharge of an existing legal obligation (i.e., not entered into in relation to the event giving rise to the payment for loss of office) (s.220(10(a) and (b) CA 2006) or by way of 'settlement or compromise of any claim arising in connection with termination of a person's office or employment' or by way of 'pension for past services' (s.220(1)(c) and (d) CA 2006).

[200] FSA, Revising the Remuneration Code Feedback on CP10/19 and Final Rules, SYSC 19A.2.2G, December 2010, PS 10/20, http://www.fsa.gov.uk/pubs/policy/ps10_20.pdf; FSA, Revising the Remuneration Code, Ch. 3.33, July 2010, CP 10/19, http://www.fsa.gov.uk/pubs/cp/cp10_19.pdf.

check remuneration policies and to discuss what constitutes good remuneration practice.[201] As a direct response to the credit crunch and the continuing financial crisis the FSA then published, on 26 February 2009, the draft FSA Code of Practice[202] on remuneration policies. The draft Code was expected to apply to 48 FSA-regulated banks, building societies and broker-dealers, although the possibility was raised of extending its application to all authorised firms. A revised version of the draft Code was then issued, in March 2009, as part of an FSA Consultation Paper entitled 'Reforming Remuneration Practices in Financial Services'[203] and was applied to around 26 UK financial institutions, although a number of European banks operating through UK subsidiaries and branches agreed to apply this version of the code to their UK staff.[204]

A further revised Remuneration Code[205] was published, in August 2010, as a policy statement entitled Revising the Remuneration Code.[206] The revised Code largely gave effect to the recommendations in the Walker review[207] on remuneration, and the FSF (Financial Stability Forum) Principles for Sound Compensation Practices,[208] and is generally consistent with the CRD 3 (Capital Requirements Directive 3), which requires firms to have a remuneration

---

[201] The FSA published its findings from this review in March 2009, Reforming Remuneration Practices in Financial Services, FSA Consultation Paper 09/10, http://www.fsa.gov.uk/pubs/cp/cp09_10.pdf.

[202] FSA, Draft Code on remuneration practices, http://www.fsa.gov.uk/pubs/other/remuneration.pdf.

[203] FSA, Reforming Remuneration Practices in Financial Services, CP 09/10, March 2009, http://www.fsa.gov.uk/pubs/cp/cp09_10.pdf.

[204] HM Treasury, City of London banks agree to support G20 bonus reforms, 14 October 2009, http://www.articles.scopulus.co.uk/City%20of%20London%20banks%20agree%20to%20support%20G20%20bonus%20reforms.htm; Smith (2010) Reforming the Bonus Culture, *Journal of International Banking and Financial Law*, p. 37.

[205] In June 2010, a series of amendments were agreed at EU level to the Capital Requirements Directive (2006/48/EC and 2006/49/EC) (CRD 3), leading to the FSA consulting on a revised version of its Code in July 2010, CP 10/19, http://www.fsa.gov.uk/pubs/cp/cp10_19.pdf. While the 26 or so firms subject to the Code were expected to implement the revised Code from 1 January 2011 in respect of payments made after that date, other firms were expected to implement the Code 'as soon as is reasonably possible,' but in any event by 1 July 2011. On 10 November 2010, the FSA published the CP 10/27 in which it outlined its proposals to implement the requirements of the Directive amending the Capital Requirements Directive (2006/48/EC and 2006/49/EC) (CRD), known as CRD 3, relating to the disclosure of remuneration.

[206] FSA, Revising the Remuneration Code, CP 10/19, July 2010, http://www.fsa.gov.uk/pubs/cp/cp10_19.pdf. The FSA has tried to be flexible on timing, recognising that, while the CRD 3 measures were to be implemented by 1 January 2011, it was unrealistic for firms not already subject to the Code, particularly when the formal CRD 3 text was not expected until shortly before the implementation deadline.

[207] Walker, A review of corporate governance in UK banks and other financial industry entities, Final recommendations, 26 November 2009, http://webarchive.nationalarchives.gov.uk/+/http://www.hm-treasury.gov.uk/d/walker_review_261109.pdf. The Walker review recommended, inter alia, that remuneration committees be charged with having greater oversight over firm-wide compensation systems, and that there should be one remuneration committee that established the relevant principles on a firm-wide basis. It also suggested that the remuneration committee should understand and be comfortable with the way in which these principles are incorporated into compensation structures. The review also proposed the use of both long- and short-term incentive schemes to achieve this and that BOFIs should publicly disclose the compensation of high-end directors and employees by bands of income. In addition, executive board members and high-end employees should maintain a financial interest in the relevant BOFI that is in line with their historic or expected compensation (Recommendations 28–39).

[208] See: FSB Thematic Review on Compensation, 30 March 2010, http://www.financialstabilityboard.org/publications/r_100330a.pdf?frames=0. The FSF was re-established as the Financial Stability Board in April 2009 (Ref no: 14/2009), 2 April 2009; http://www.financialstabilityboard.org/press/pr_090402b.pdf.

policy,[209] although there are some major differences in its scope. On 17 December 2010, the FSA published its policy statement on revising the remuneration code,[210] which reported on feedback received by the FSA, to its July 2010 statement.[211] The policy statement was initially due to be published in November 2010, but was deferred so the FSA could take into account the final guidelines on remuneration published by CEBS (Committee of European Banking Supervisors).[212] Consequently, over 2,500 firms are subjected to the Code with UK firms required to apply it globally to all their regulated and unregulated entities. The FSA also expressed the opinion that the CEBS high-level principles were effectively aligned to the revised Code on Remuneration.[213] The FSA statement on 'Reforming Remuneration Practices in Financial Services' therefore contains the final rules on remuneration practices, which are incorporated in the FSA Handbook (now the FCA Handbook)[214] in the form of a Code of Practice on remuneration policies. The Code is designed to achieve two objectives: (i) that boards focus more closely on ensuring that the total amount distributed by a firm is consistent with good risk management and sustainability; and (ii) that individual compensation practices provide the right incentives.[215] The main features of the FCA revised Code on remuneration policies and practices in the financial services sector are as follows.

Scope of the Code

The Remuneration Code covers all aspects of remuneration that may have a bearing on effective risk management including wages, bonus, long-term incentive plans, options, hiring bonuses, severance packages and pension arrangements,[216] and the CRD 3 provides that firms disclose 'the most important design characteristics of the remuneration system, including information on the criteria used for performance measurement and risk adjustment, deferral policy and vesting criteria'.[217] The Code recognises that if a firm's remuneration policy is not aligned with effective risk management[218] employee incentives may develop that undermine

---

[209] FSA, Revising the Remuneration Code Feedback on CP10/19 and Final Rules, SYSC 19A.1.6, December 2010, PS 10/20, http://www.fsa.gov.uk/pubs/policy/ps10_20.pdf; Directive 2010/76/EU of the European Parliament and of the Council of 24 November 2010 amending Directives 2006/48/EC and 2006/49/EC as regards Capital Requirements for the trading book and for re-securitisations, and the supervisory review of remuneration policies, L329/3, 14/12/10, http://eur-lex.europa.eu/LexUriServ/LexUriServ.do?uri=OJ:L:2010 :329:003:035:EN:PDF.

[210] FSA, Revising the Remuneration Code Feedback on CP10/19 and Final Rules, December 2010, PS 10/20, http://www.fsa.gov.uk/pubs/policy/ps10_20.pdf.

[211] FSA, Revising the Remuneration Code, July 2010, CP 10/19, http://www.fsa.gov.uk/pubs/cp/cp10_19.pdf.

[212] CEBS, Guidelines on Remuneration Policies and Practices, 10 December 2010, http://www.c-ebs.org/cebs/ media/Publications/Standards%20and%20Guidelines/2010/Remuneration/Guidelines.pdf.

[213] FSA, Reforming remuneration practices in financial services, August 2009, PS 09/15, p. 13, http://www.fsa. gov.uk/pubs/policy/ps09_15.pdf.

[214] FCA Handbook, SYSC 19.3A, http://www.fshandbook.info/FS/html/FCA/SYSC/19A/3.

[215] SYSC 19A.2.2, Remuneration Code: Remuneration principles, http://www.fshandbook.info/FS/html/FCA/ SYSC/19A/2.

[216] SYSC 19A.2.2, Remuneration Code: Remuneration principles, http://www.fshandbook.info/FS/html/FCA/ SYSC/19A/2.

[217] Directive 2010/76/EU of the European Parliament and of the Council of 24 November 2010 amending Directives 2006/48/EC and 2006/49/EC as regards Capital Requirements for the trading book and for re-securitizations, and the supervisory review of remuneration policies, L329/3, 14/12/10, http://eur-lex. europa.eu/LexUriServ/LexUriServ.do?uri=OJ:L:2010:329:003:035:EN:PDF.

[218] SYSC 19.2.2, Remuneration Code: Remuneration principles, http://www.fshandbook.info/FS/html/FCA/ SYSC/19A/2.

effective risk management; consequently the Remuneration Code is intended to ensure that firms have risk-focused remuneration policies intended to promote risk management and reduce risk exposure,[219] which the now FCA will use to assess the quality of a firm's remuneration policies. The FCA may ask remuneration committees to provide it with evidence that the firm's remuneration policies meet the Remuneration Code's principles, together with plans for improvements where there is a weakness.

Drafting the remuneration policy

CRD 3 requires each firm's board of directors 'acting in its supervisory function', to take responsibility for the firms' remuneration policy and for implementing it. It must also carry out periodic reviews[220] of the policy's general principles.[221] The CEBS remuneration guidelines state that the CEO or other executive members should not control the remuneration policy and that the management body should include non-executive members with sufficient knowledge of remuneration policies and structures.[222] In CP42, CEBS states that firms should have regard to capital and liquidity planning, as well as risk management, when devising their remuneration policies.[223] The remuneration policy should be consistent with and promote sound and effective risk management, not encourage risk-taking that exceeds the level of tolerated risk of the firm, be in line with the business strategy, objectives, values and long-term interests of the firm and incorporate measures to avoid conflicts of interest.[224]

---

[219] FSA, Revising the Remuneration Code Feedback on CP10/19 and Final Rules, SYSC 19A.1.6G, December 2010, PS 10/20, http://www.fsa.gov.uk/pubs/policy/ps10_20.pdf; CEBS guidance states that institutions should describe 'how they take into account current and future risks to which [the firm is] exposed when implementing remuneration methodologies and what these risks are. Institutions should describe the measures used to take account of these risks and the ways in which these measures affect remuneration'. This is consistent with Principle 8 of the FSA revised draft Code, which requires firms to ensure their bonus pool calculations include adjustments for all types of current and potential risks, http://www.fsa.gov.uk/pubs/cp/cp10_27.pdf.

[220] The implementation of the remuneration policies must also be subject to 'central and independent internal review', at least on an annual basis, Annex 1, Directive 2010/76/EU of the European Parliament and of the Council of 24 November 2010 amending Directives 2006/48/EC and 2006/49/EC as regards Capital Requirements for the trading book and for re-securitizations, and the supervisory review of remuneration policies, L329/3, 14/12/10, http://eur-lex.europa.eu/LexUriServ/LexUriServ.do?uri=OJ:L:2010:329:003:035:EN:PDF. CEBS remuneration guidelines state that the annual review is the responsibility of the management body, acting in its supervisory function, but that the review should be carried out in conjunction with internal control functions, e.g., internal audit, risk management and compliance, and key supervisory function committees, e.g., audit, risk and nominations committees, CEBS, Guidelines on Remuneration Policies and Practices, para. 49, http://j7.agefi.fr/documents/liens/201012/13-tgsjm4vtp31gvcg.pdf.

[221] Directive 2010/76/EU of the European Parliament and of the Council of 24 November 2010 amending Directives 2006/48/EC and 2006/49/EC as regards Capital Requirements for the trading book and for re-securitisations, and the supervisory review of remuneration policies, L329/3, 14/12/10, http://eur-lex.europa.eu/LexUriServ/LexUriServ.do?uri=OJ:L:2010:329:003:035:EN:PDF.

[222] CEBS, Guidelines on Remuneration Policies and Practices, paras 42 and 43, 10 December 2010, http://j7.agefi.fr/documents/liens/201012/13-tgsjm4vtp31gvcg.pdf.

[223] CEBS, Consultation Paper on Guidelines on Remuneration Policies and Practices (CP42), para. 66, 8 October 2010, http://www.eba.europa.eu/documents/Publications/Consultation-papers/2010/CP42/CP42.aspx; see also CEBS, Guidelines on Remuneration Policies and Practices, para. 66, 10 December 2010, http://j7.agefi.fr/documents/liens/201012/13-tgsjm4vtp31gvcg.pdf.

[224] Directive 2010/76/EU of the European Parliament and of the Council of 24 November 2010 amending Directives 2006/48/EC and 2006/49/EC as regards Capital Requirements for the trading book and for re-securitisations, and the supervisory review of remuneration policies, L329/3, 14/12/10, http://eur-lex.europa.eu/LexUriServ/LexUriServ.do?uri=OJ:L:2010:329:003:035:EN:PDF.

Proportionate in application

The FCA Code avoids a formulaic 'one size fits all' approach to the regulation of remuneration policies and for this reason the FCA Code is not overly detailed.[225] Consequently, from the firms' point of view, the implementation of the rules can be tailored to the institutions' specific characteristics and the intensity of the supervision will vary according to the risk characteristics of the firm.[226] The effect of the proportionality principle is that not all firms will have to give substance to the remuneration requirements in the same way or to the same extent. While some firms will need to apply more sophisticated policies or practices in fulfilling the requirements; other firms can meet the requirements in a simpler or less burdensome way.[227] CRD 3[228] and FSB high-level principles both reinforce the view that any response to the regulation of remuneration policy is proportionate and credit institutions comply with the requirements 'in a way that is appropriate to their size, internal organisation and the nature, scope and the complexity of their activities'.[229]

The focus of the regulation is not the levels of remuneration paid to any one individual[230] but best practice in determining remuneration policies, with improved governance and oversight of remuneration arrangements. In applying the Remuneration Code firms must have regard to applicable good practice on remuneration and corporate governance,[231] for example guidelines on executive contracts and severance issued by the Association of British Insurers (ABI) and the National Association of Pension Funds (NAPF).[232]

---

[225] This is also recognised by the FSF in its Principles for Sound Compensation Practices, 2 April 2009, http://www.financialstabilityboard.org/publications/r_0904b.pdf?frames=0.

[226] Basel Committee on Banking Supervision, Consultative Document Range of Methodologies for Risk and Performance Alignment of Remuneration, October 2010, Bank for International Settlements, http://www.bis.org/publ/bcbs178.pdf.

[227] FSA, Revising the Remuneration Code Feedback on CP10/19 and Final Rules, December 2010, PS 10/20, http://www.fsa.gov.uk/pubs/policy/ps10_20.pdf.

[228] The CRD 3 allows regulators to apply its requirements on a proportionate basis, taking account of a firm's size and complexity. The FSA has divided firms into four tiers, based mainly on their regulatory capital and types of permission. Each group will be subject to a different degree of disclosure, FSA, Revising the Remuneration Code Feedback on CP10/19 and Final Rules, December 2010, PS 10/20, http://www.fsa.gov.uk/pubs/policy/ps10_20.pdf.

[229] The proportionality principle is set out in SYSC 19A.3.3R(2) and implements para. 23, Annex V, Directive 2006/48/EC. FSA, Implementing CRD3: disclosure of remuneration, CP10/27, November 2010, http://www.fsa.gov.uk/pubs/cp/cp10_27.pdf; Consultation Paper on Guidelines on Remuneration Policies and Practices (CP42), para. 24, 8 October 2010, http://www.eba.europa.eu/documents/Publications/Consultation-papers/2010/CP42/CP42.aspx, provides guidance on the purposes of applying CRD 3 proportionately principles, CEBS, Guidelines on Remuneration Policies and Practices, para. 24, 10 December 2010, http://j7.agefi.fr/documents/liens/201012/13-tgsjm4vtp31gvcg.pdf; see also Basel Committee on Banking Supervision, Consultative Document Range of Methodologies for Risk and Performance Alignment of Remuneration, October 2010, Bank for International Settlements, http://www.bis.org/publ/bcbs178.pdf.

[230] See: FSF Principles for Sound Compensation Practices, 2 April 2009, http://www.financialstabilityboard.org/publications/r_0904b.pdf?frames=0.

[231] See: FSF Principles for Sound Compensation Practices, Principle 1, 2 April 2009, http://www.financialstabilityboard.org/publications/r_0904b.pdf?frames=0; FCA Handbook, Remuneration Code, SYSC 19A.2 Principle 4, http://www.fshandbook.info/FS/html/FCA/SYSC/19A/3.

[232] SYSC 19.3 Remuneration Code: Remuneration principles, release 97, January 2010, http://www.fsa.gov.uk/pubs/hb-releases/rel97/rel97sysc.pdf.

Personnel to whom the Code applies

Because UK registered firms are subject to the Remuneration Code globally, the Code will catch indirectly some firms, which would otherwise fall outside its scope. Staff who perform a significant influence function[233] and other senior managers[234] will be caught, as will 'all staff whose total remuneration takes them into the same bracket as senior management and risk takers[235] and whose professional activities could have a material impact on a firm's risk profile'.[236] It is not clear on what basis an employee would fall in 'the same bracket' as senior management[237] but the FCA has attempted to clarify this and stated that it would expect, for example, anyone who performs as a head of a significant business line or support and control function for all or part of the year to be subject to the Code in that year.

Independent decision-making

The Remuneration Code provides that while industry comparators may be relevant in setting remuneration they should not override the need for independent decisions[238] that are

[233] CEBS, Consultation Paper on Guidelines on Remuneration Policies and Practices (CP42), 8 October 2010, http://www.eba.europa.eu/documents/Publications/Consultation-papers/2010/CP42/CP42.aspx, suggests that these individuals will include senior staff responsible for heading the compliance, finance control, risk management, human resources, and internal audit areas; see also CEBS, Guidelines on Remuneration Policies and Practices, para. 16, 10 December 2010, http://j7.agefi.fr/documents/liens/201012/13-tgsjm4vtp31gvcg.pdf. Although human resources is not usually regarded as a control function, CEBS regards it as playing 'an essential role in the design and implementation of the remuneration policies developed by the supervisory function', CEBS, Guidelines on Remuneration Policies and Practices, para. 24, 10 December 2010, http://j7.agefi.fr/documents/liens/201012/13-tgsjm4vtp31gvcg.pdf; FCA Handbook, Remuneration Code, SYSC 19A.3.4, http://www.fshandbook.info/FS/html/FCA/SYSC/19A/3.

[234] CP42 states that the CRD3 will apply to all members of firms' management bodies (such as the board of directors), whether or not they are executive or non-executive members. CEBS has specific expectations on how such individuals should remunerated and draws a distinction in its remuneration guidelines between members of management bodies acting in a supervisory function (referred to in the remuneration guidelines as the 'supervisory function') and those members acting in a management function (referred to in the remuneration guidelines as the 'management function'), CEBS, Consultation Paper on Guidelines on Remuneration Policies and Practices (CP42), 8 October 2010, http://www.eba.europa.eu/documents/Publications/Consultation-papers/2010/CP42/CP42.aspx). The management function should not determine its own remuneration. The supervisory function should determine the remuneration of the management function. The supervisory function should usually be compensated only with fixed remuneration, CEBS, Guidelines on Remuneration Policies and Practices, para. 46, 10 December 2010, http://j7.agefi.fr/documents/liens/201012/13-tgsjm4vtp31gvcg.pdf; FCA Handbook, Remuneration Code, SYSC 19A.3.4, http://www.fshandbook.info/FS/html/FCA/SYSC/19A/3.

[235] Recital 3 of CRD 3 states that, for these purposes 'total remuneration' includes discretionary pension benefits. CEBS, Guidelines on Remuneration Policies and Practices, para. 16, 10 December 2010, http://j7.agefi.fr/documents/liens/201012/13-tgsjm4vtp31gvcg.pdf states that 'remuneration bracket' refers to the range of the total remuneration of each of the staff members in the senior manager and risk-taker categories, from the highest paid to the lowest paid in these categories, FCA Handbook, Remuneration Code, SYSC 19A.3.4, http://www.fshandbook.info/FS/html/FCA/SYSC/19A/3.

[236] CP42 states that these will be staff members who can exert influence on the institution's risk profile, including persons capable of entering into contracts or positions and taking decisions that affect the risk positions of the institution, including individual traders, specific trading desks and credit officers, CEBS, Consultation Paper on Guidelines on Remuneration Policies and Practices (CP42), 8 October 2010, http://www.eba.europa.eu/documents/Publications/Consultation-papers/2010/CP42/CP42.aspx. See also: CEBS, Guidelines on Remuneration Policies and Practices, para. 16, 10 December 2010, http://j7.agefi.fr/documents/liens/201012/13-tgsjm4vtp31gvcg.pdf.

[237] Firms should apply the principles to categories of staff whose professional activities have a material impact on their risk profiles, para. 23, Annex V, Directive 2006/48/EC.

[238] FCA Handbook, Remuneration Code, SYSC 19A.3.4, http://www.fshandbook.info/FS/html/FCA/SYSC/19A/3.

consistent with the firm's financial strategy and prospects.[239] In a reminder that remuneration committees were found to have failed their companies,[240] the Remuneration Code[241] provides that normally the remuneration committee should include one or more non-executive directors with practical skills and experience of risk management.[242] The FCA may ask the remuneration committee to prepare a statement on the firm's remuneration policy, including the implications of the policy for the firm.[243] The FCA will expect the statement to include an assessment of the impact of the firm's policies on its risk profile and employee behaviour. In drawing up the assessment, the remuneration committee should exercise its own independent judgement.[244] Although remuneration committees may need to engage professional advisers to support[245] their activities in respect of remuneration policies the FSA, the then regulator, was critical that some remuneration committees place undue reliance on such advice.[246] In an effort to ensure integrity of the system the FSF Principles for Sound Compensation Practices provide that the chief executive officer and the management team should not primarily control compensation systems.[247]

Design and structure of remuneration packages

For most firms, the most sensitive and complex issues are likely to arise in relation to Principle 12(a),[248] which requires firms to ensure that the structure of employees' remuneration

---

[239] See: FSF Principles for Sound Compensation Practices, principles 1 and 3, 2 April 2009, http://www.financial stabilityboard.org/publications/r_0904b.pdf?frames=0.

[240] The House of Commons Treasury Committee, Banking crisis: reforming corporate governance and pay in the City, Ninth Report of session 2008–09, HC 519, published 15 May 2009, http://www.publications.parliament.uk/pa/cm200809/cmselect/cmtreasy/462/462.pdf.

[241] SYSC 19A.3.12R(1) Remuneration Principle 4 (Governance) that a firm that is significant in terms of its size, internal organisation and the nature, the scope and the complexity of its activities must establish a remuneration committee, http://www.fshandbook.info/FS/html/FCA/SYSC/19A/3; FSA, Revising the Remuneration Code: Feedback on CP10/19 and Final Rules, December 2010, PS 10/20, http://www.fsa.gov.uk/pubs/policy/ps10_20.pdf.

[242] SYSC 19.3 Remuneration Code: Remuneration principles, release 97, January 2010, http://www.fsa.gov.uk/pubs/hb-releases/rel97/rel97sysc.pdf; FSF Principles for Sound Compensation Practices, Principle 1 which provides, 'that effective independence and appropriate authority of such staff are necessary to preserve the integrity of financial and risk management's influence on incentive compensation', 2 April 2009, http://www.financialstabilityboard.org/publications/r_0904b.pdf?frames=0.

[243] SYSC 19.4 Remuneration Code: Remuneration principles, release 97, January 2010, http://www.fsa.gov.uk/pubs/hb-releases/rel97/rel97sysc.pdf.

[244] CRD 3 provides that 'information concerning the decision-making process used for determining the remuneration policy, including if applicable, information about the composition and the mandate of a remuneration committee, the external consultant whose services have been used for the determination of the remuneration policy and the role of the relevant stakeholders'. Principle 4 of the revised FSA Code requires firms to establish a remuneration committee (RemCo), which must periodically review and implement the firm's remuneration policies, FSA, Implementing CRD3: disclosure of remuneration, CP10/27, November 2010, http://www.fsa.gov.uk/pubs/cp/cp10_27.pdf.

[245] This obligation is reinforced by the Companies Act 2006 s.173, which imposes a duty on directors to exercise independent judgement. While preserving the right to delegate directors must exercise independent judgement and must exercise due diligence, care and skill in the act of delegation (Companies Act 2006, s.174); see also Re Barings Plc (No 5) [2000] 1 BCLC 523.

[246] NEDs owe a duty of care in discharging their duties to their appointing company, including agreeing remuneration packages.

[247] See: FSF Principles for Sound Compensation Practices, Principle 1, 2 April 2009, http://www.financialstabilityboard.org/publications/r_0904b.pdf?frames=0.

[248] FCA Handbook Remuneration Code, SYSC 19A.3, http://www.fshandbook.info/FS/html/FCA/SYSC/19A/3.

is consistent with and promotes effective risk management. The Code requires that individual, business unit and firm-wide performance must be taken into account and when measuring individual performance[249] both financial and non-financial criteria (for example regulatory compliance), must be taken into consideration.[250] A firm must, therefore, ensure that any variable remuneration, including the deferred portion is paid, or vests, only if it is sustainable according to the financial circumstances of the firm as a whole, and justified according to the performance of the firm, the business unit and the individual concerned. The CEBS guidance recommends that firms disclose 'information relating to the design and structure of remuneration processes, such as the key features and objective of the remuneration policy'. CEBS guidance further advises that firms should disclose how they would ensure 'staff in control functions are remunerated independently of the businesses they oversee'. This is consistent with Principle 5 of the FCA Code.

Any guaranteed bonuses must be exceptional and limited to the first year of service[251] while retention awards, for example following a major restructuring,[252] may be justified, but must be notified to the FCA in advance and depending on how they are structured may need the approval of shareholders under the UK Listing Authority's Listing Rules.[253] The balance between fixed and variable pay must be appropriate, and allow for any variable component not to be paid[254] and payments on early termination must not reward failure. CEBS has suggested that firms should follow the approach taken in the EU Commission's April 2009 recommendation on the remuneration of directors of listed companies which provides that termination payments should not exceed a fixed amount or fixed number of years of annual

---

[249] FCA handbook Remuneration Code, SYSC 19A.3.3.6, http://www.fshandbook.info/FS/html/FCA/SYSC/19A/3; as part of their duty to support economic recovery the main four UK banks, namely HSBC, Barclays, Lloyds Banking Group and Royal Bank of Scotland, and Santander in the context of its lending, entered into an accord with the government which included a number of commitments relating to pay and bonuses. The banks agreed that variable compensation would be explicitly linked to performance. For all senior staff, a significant proportion of any bonuses paid will be deferred into shares and be subject to significant vesting periods. Bonuses will be subject to claw back in clearly defined circumstances. There will be no reward for failure, Project Merlin – Bank's Statement, 9 February 2011, http://www.hm-treasury.gov.uk/d/bank_agreement_090211.pdf.

[250] FCA handbook Remuneration Code, SYSC 19A.3.3.6, http://www.fshandbook.info/FS/html/FCA/SYSC/19A/3; see also: FSF Principles for Sound Compensation Practices, Principle 2, 2 April 2009, http://www.financialstability board.org/publications/r_0904b.pdf?frames=0; CRD 3 requires firms to disclose 'information on the link between pay and performance'. CEBS guidance also advises that such disclosure should include 'a description of the main performance metrics utilised for the firm, top-level business lines, and for individuals (i.e. scorecards)'. This is consistent with Principle 12 of the revised FSA Code, which sets out rules and guidance on the link between pay and performance and provides that where remuneration is performance-related, firms should ensure this is based not only on the individual's performance but also on that of the business unit and the firm as a whole (draft SYSC 19.3.34R). Non-financial performance metrics, including adherence to effective risk management and compliance with the regulatory system, should also play a significant role in the assessment process.

[251] FCA Handbook, Remuneration Code, SYSC 19.3.40, http://www.fshandbook.info/FS/html/FCA/SYSC/19A/3. Firms should not commit to guaranteed variable remuneration, which should only be paid when hiring new staff and only in then in exceptional circumstances. Its payment must be limited to the first year of their employment.

[252] FCA handbook Remuneration Code, SYSC 19A.3.43, http://www.fshandbook.info/FS/html/FCA/SYSC/19A/3.

[253] Financial Services and Markets Act 2000, s.74.

[254] FCA handbook Remuneration Code, SYSC 19A.3.44, http://www.fshandbook.info/FS/html/FCA/SYSC/19A/3.

remuneration[255] and, generally, not be more than 'two years of the non-variable component of the remuneration'.[256] Termination payments should not reward failure.

Each firm must set appropriate ratios between fixed pay and variable pay to ensure that the salary is a sufficiently high proportion of the remuneration to allow for the possibility of the bonus not being paid. The amount of the discretionary bonus pool must be based on profit and adjusted for current and future risks, and take into account the cost and quality of the business cycle, the nature of capital and liquidity required. Firms must ensure that performance related bonuses are assessed in a multi-year framework taking into account the performance of the individual, the performance of business unit and the overall results of the firm. At least 40 per cent[257] of the bonus must be deferred over a period of not less than 3–5 years taking into account the business cycle, the nature of the business, its risks and the activities of the individual.[258] Where the bonus is of a particularly high amount (the FCA suggest £500,000)[259] or where it is paid to an executive director of a tier 1 firm, at least 60 per cent[260] must be deferred. Half of the bonus is immediately payable and that part which is deferred should be paid on a net of tax basis in the form of shares and, where appropriate, capital instruments, which reflect the credit quality of the firm as a going concern, should also be used. All deferred bonuses may be subject to 'performance adjustment' and firms should be able to reduce the amount prior to vesting in the event of poor performance including employee misbehaviour or material error, firm or the business unit suffering a material downturn in its financial performance, or the firm or business unit suffering a material failure of risk management. Firms must ensure that vesting of awards granted under the long-term incentive plans are subject to appropriate performance conditions, which are adjusted for current and long-term risk factors. At least 50 per cent of a long-term incentive award must vest after three years, with the reminder vesting after not less than five years.

When the CRD 4 becomes effective on payments made from 1 January 2014, the variable pay will not be able to exceed 100 per cent of the remuneration unless at 66 per cent of the firms shareholders (or unless 75 per cent of the shareholders if there is no quorum) approve an increase to 200 per cent. Even with shareholder approval to increase the maximum bonus above 100 per cent of base salary, the new rules will require that 25 per cent of any bonus above the initial 100 per cent cap must be deferred for at least five years. For these purposes 'variable pay' is defined as remuneration that reflects 'a sustainable and risk adjusted performance as well as performance in excess of that required to fulfil the employee's job description' while 'fixed pay' is remuneration which 'primarily reflects professional level experience and organisational responsibility as set out in the employee's job description as part of the terms of employment'.

---

[255] Recommendations of the European Commission, Commission Recommendation on remuneration policies in the financial services sector, 30 April 2009, L 120.22 2009/384/EC, http://eur-lex.europa.eu/LexUriServ/LexUriServ.do?uri=OJ:L:2009:120:0022:0027:EN:PDF.

[256] CEBS, Consultation Paper on Guidelines on Remuneration Policies and Practices (CP 42), para. 71, 8 October 2010, http://www.c-ebs.org/documents/Publications/Consultation-papers/2010/CP42/CP42.aspx.

[257] FCA handbook Remuneration Code, SYSC 19A.3.49, http://www.fshandbook.info/FS/html/FCA/SYSC/19A/3.

[258] FCA handbook Remuneration Code, SYSC 19A.3.49, http://www.fshandbook.info/FS/html/FCA/SYSC/19A/3.

[259] £500,000 constitutes 'particularly high', but lesser amounts might also be regarded as 'particularly high'; for example, if the amount is significantly more than that paid to other staff in the firm subject to the code.

[260] FCA handbook Remuneration Code, SYSC 19A.3.50, http://www.fshandbook.info/FS/html/FCA/SYSC/19A/3.

Executives' Remuneration Reports Regulations 2013

UK quoted companies have been under an obligation to disclose their remuneration polices and the details of individual director's packages in the form of the directors' remuneration report (DRR) since 2002,[261] and to obtain shareholder approval of the DRR.[262] The regulations require quoted companies to provide detailed information on executive and director compensation, including details of fixed salary, share option schemes and other equity incentives, for example long-term incentive plans, and pensions of each director. On 24 June 2013, the Department of Business, Innovation and Skills (BIS) published the final version of the Large and Medium-sized Companies and Groups (Accounts and Reports) (Amendment) Regulations 2013 (Directors' Remuneration Regulations). The changes to the directors' remuneration report of a quoted company came into force for financial years beginning on or after 1 October 2013. For financial years beginning on or after 1 October 2013 the directors' remuneration report for a quoted company will include:

- A statement by the chair of the remuneration committee.
- A remuneration policy setting out the company's policy on directors' remuneration.
- An implementation policy setting out information on how the remuneration policy was implemented.

The purpose of the regulations is to enhance transparency in setting directors' pay; improve accountability to shareholders; and provide for a more effective performance linkage. The remuneration policy must set out the company's approach to every aspect of directors' remuneration, including recruitment and loss of office payments. Shareholders will have a binding vote on a resolution to approve the directors' remuneration policy and companies will have to seek shareholder approval at least every three years, or more frequently if a company wishes to change the policy.

Additionally, s.4 of the Financial Services Act 2010 gives the Treasury powers to make regulations requiring companies to prepare reports disclosing information on the remuneration paid to officers and employees who are not directors of institutions authorised under the Financial Services and Markets Act 2000, and to other employees with a specified connection to the authorised institution. In March 2010, the Treasury published draft Executives' Remuneration Reports Regulations 2010, which set out Treasury plans to use the powers under s.4 of the Financial Services Act 2010 to implement the recommendations in the Walker Review[263] for enhanced disclosure of remuneration on the part of the larger banks and building societies. The Regulations, which actually go further than the Walker Review, require disclosure of the number of relevant executives whose remuneration in the preceding financial year exceeded £500,000;[264] specify disclosure bands starting from £500,000 and

---

[261] The 'Directors' Remuneration Report Regulations applied to quoted companies from the financial year ending on or after 31 December 2002. See also the Deloittie's Report on the impact of the Directors' Remuneration Report Regulations: A Report for the Department of Trade and Industry, November 2004 which looked at the effectiveness of the regulations, http://www.bis.gov.uk/files/file13425.pdf.

[262] Large and Medium-sized Companies and Groups (Accounts and Reports) Regulations 2008, SI 2008/410, reg. 11 and schedule 8.

[263] HM Treasury, A review of corporate governance in UK Banks and other financial entities, Final Recommendations, 26 November 2009, http://www.hm-treasury.gov.uk/walker_review_information.htm.

[264] The Walker Review recommended a £1 million threshold, HM Treasury, A review of corporate governance in UK banks and other financial entities, Final Recommendations, 26 November 2009, http://www.hm-treasury.gov.uk/walker_review_information.htm.

going up in £500,000 increments to £5 million, and then up from £5 million by £1 million increments.[265]

In February 2011 the UK government announced an accord between the four major UK banks, specifically Barclays, HSBC, Lloyds Banking Group and RBS, and, in the context of lending, Santander, under the name Project Merlin. On top of the disclosure that will be required by CRD 3 a commitment was given by the Merlin banks to disclose, from and including 2010, the remuneration details of the executive directors and (on an unnamed basis) the five highest paid 'senior executive officers'.[266] For those individuals whose details are not already disclosed, the parameters of this disclosure will be based on the disclosure standard in the FCA Handbook, so that this disclosure is consistent with the aggregate Code staff disclosures the FCA will require going forward. This will go beyond international practice by disclosing the remuneration details relating to five individuals over and above executive directors. As part of these announcements the government, in December 2011,[267] indicated that it would consult on a mandatory requirement, from 2012, for all large UK banks to publish the pay of their eight highest paid senior executive officers. This follows on from this year's commitment by the four major banks to make detailed remuneration disclosures with respect to the five highest paid non-board executives within their organisations. The government's proposals would require more comprehensive disclosure of information-relating to the eight most senior executives than is required in relation to the FSA's remuneration disclosure rules, but less detailed disclosures than are required for executive directors of quoted companies in a directors' remuneration report.

A new regime on executive pay was implemented from the 1st October 2013.[268] The regulations have a significant impact on the way UK-quoted companies formulate their policy on executive remuneration and report this to shareholders.

The director's remuneration policy[269] (DRP) require companys to set out their out future policy on directors' remuneration. Shareholders will have a new binding vote (by way of ordinary resolution) on the proposed DRP at least once every three years. Once the DRP is approved, the company will only be able to make a remuneration payment, or a payment in respect of a loss of office to a director, which is in accordance with the policy, or which has been separately approved by shareholders. The regulations:

- streamline company disclosure requirements so that reports are focused on making the link between pay and performance clear;

- introduce a new requirement to report the total pay directors receive for the year as a single figure;[270]

- ensure that shareholder engagement is sustained over the long term.

---

[265] The Walker Review proposed wider bands, HM Treasury, A review of corporate governance in UK Banks and other financial entities, Final Recommendations, 26 November 2009, http://www.hm-treasury.gov.uk/walker_review_information.htm.

[266] Project Merlin – Bank's Statement, 9 February 2011, http://www.hm-treasury.gov.uk/d/bank_agreement_090211.pdf.

[267] HM Treasury, Bank Executive Remuneration Disclosure Consultation on Draft Regulations, December 2011, http://www.hm-treasury.gov.uk/d/condoc_bank_executive_remuneration_disclosure_6122011.pdf.

[268] Large and Medium-sized Companies and Groups (Accounts and Reports) (Amendment) Regulations 2013.

[269] Large and Medium-sized Companies and Groups (Accounts and Reports) (Amendment) Regulations 2013, Part 4.

[270] Large and Medium-sized Companies and Groups (Accounts and Reports) (Amendment) Regulations 2013, Part 3.

There is no leeway to make amendments to the policy or to make payments outside the scope of the DRP without first obtaining the shareholder's approval, which reinforces the importance of the policy and it will require that the DRP is carefully drafted particularly with regard to any flexibility.

There are serious consequences for directors if a payment is made outside the scope of the approved DRP. Such payments are treated as held by the recipient on trust for the company, and any directors who authorized the payment will be liable to indemnify the company for any loss resulting from it.

Any contractual provisions (e.g. in a service agreement or compromise agreement) which require payment to be made in breach of the approved DRP will be void except for remuneration or loss of office payments required to be made under an agreement concluded prior to 27 June 2012. Where such an agreement has been 'modified or renewed' on or after 27 June 2012, it will be treated as having been entered into after that date and, as such, will not benefit from the grandfathering provisions. In those circumstances, the agreement will become subject to the DRP.

The Parliamentary Commission on Banking Standards June 2013 report illustrates remuneration remains a contentious political issue.[271] The government's initial response has provoked further debate with the accusation the government's proposals do not go far enough.[272]

Conclusion

Governmental response to the 2007–09 financial crisis has been extensive with fundamental statutory changes in the regulation of the banking sector, including placing the Bank of England, once again, at the centre of bank regulation. Statutory powers to deal with distressed banks were implemented to aid Northern Rock, Bradford and Bingley and the HBOS group. Various reports placed part of the blame on poorly planned remuneration policies and while the government threatened legislation to curb a culture of excess the FCA has implemented the remuneration Code. The rate of reform has not yet slowed.

Further reading

➤ Lastra, R.M. (2008) Northern Rock, UK Insolvency and cross-border bank insolvency, 9(3), *Journal of Banking Regulation*, 165–186.
This paper deals with bank crisis management in light of the Northern Rock debacle and the ongoing credit crisis. This paper further examines the legislative and regulatory responses in the UK, including the new special solution regime (SRR) to deal with banks in distress.

---

[271] Parliamentary Commission on Banking Standards, Changing Banking for Good, 19 June 2013, Volumes I and II, http://www.publications.parliament.uk/pa/jt201314/jtselect/jtpcbs/27/2702.htm.

[272] Tyrie, Bank reform legislation 'so weak as to be virtually useless', 9 July 2013, http://www.telegraph.co.uk/finance/newsbysector/banksandfinance/10167457/Andrew-Tyrie-bank-reform-legislation-so-weak-as-to-be-virtually-useless.html.

➤ Singh, D. (2011) The UK Banking Act 2009, pre-insolvency and early intervention: policy and practice, 1, *Journal of Business Law*.
This paper analyses the Banking Act 2009, which introduced a special regime to deal with failing banks in the UK. Singh compares the UK model against the Canadian and US models of early intervention.

➤ Keasey, K. and Veronesi, G. (2008) Lessons from the Northern Rock Affair, 16(1), *Journal of Financial Regulation and Compliance*, 8.
This paper analyses the reasons behind the collapse of the Northern Rock and the broader systemic problems faced by the UK financial system. The paper proposes a return to a prudential regulatory model.

➤ The Turner Review: A regulatory response to the global financial crisis, March 2009, http://www.fsa.gov.uk/pubs/other/turner_review.pdf.
The Turner Review considers how Britain should respond to the financial crisis and proposes a series of recommendations to create a stable and effective banking system. The Review highlights the need for banks to preserve higher capital reserves, and supports closer supervision of the credit rating agency. Notably the Review's recommendations exceed the Basel Committee's requirements. The Review further calls for controlled remuneration to prevent undue risk taking.

➤ HM Treasury, Reforming Financial Markets, White Paper, July 2009; Cm 7669; http://webarchive.nationalarchives.gov.uk/+/http://www.hm-treasury.gov.uk/d/reforming_financial_markets080709.pdf.
This paper was produced as a result of the global financial crisis, and identifies a lack of understanding of the risks of interconnected markets as the root cause of the financial crisis. Moreover, the paper notes UK financial firms were exposed through inadequate capital and leverage protection, and an over-dependence on risky product schemes. This paper sets out the government's analysis of the causes of the financial crisis, and the regulatory reforms necessary to strengthen the financial system for the future.

➤ From Crisis to Confidence: Plan for Sound Banking, Conservative Party Policy White Paper, July 2009, http://www.conservatives.com/News/News_stories/2009/07/~/media/Files/Downloadable%20Files/PlanforSoundBanking.ashx.
This White Paper sets out the Conservative party's plan for sound banking to lead the British economy from crisis to confidence. The paper identifies the failure of the tripartite system of regulation and a decade of financial imprudence as the fundamental causes of the financial crisis in Britain.

➤ Sassoon, The Tripartite Review: A review of the UK's Tripartite system of financial regulation in relation to financial stability, March 2009, http://www.conservatives.com/News/News_stories/2009/03/Osborne_welcomes_Sassoon_report_into_tripartite_financial_regulation.aspx.
The Sassoon Report was commissioned by the opposition Conservative Party in October 2008 to form the Conservative Party's position on the regime of financial regulation in the UK. The Report recommended an overhaul of the tripartite regime which shared responsibilities between the Financial Services Authority (FSA), HM Treasury and the Bank of England, due to a lack of communication and awareness of who bore overall responsibility.

➤ McFall Report, Banking Crisis: regulation and supervision, Fourteenth Report of Session 2008–09, July 2009, http://www.publications.parliament.uk/pa/cm200809/cmselect/cmtreasy/767/767.pdf.
While this report states that by any measure the FSA failed in its supervision of the banking sector, it does note that the FSA attempted to rectify its mistakes to improve its regulation of banks in response to the failings exhibited in its handling of Northern Rock. The report addresses the problems that many banks are systemically significant because they are too big, conduct too many types of business, or are too complex and interconnected.

➤ Georgosouli, A. (2010) The Revision of the FSA's Approach to Regulation: An Incomplete Agenda, 7, *J.B.L.*, 599.
This article examines the FSA's approach to regulation before and after the financial crisis. The article further brings attention to certain long-standing problems that compromise its effectiveness with the view of explaining why further reform is not only essential but also already overdue.

➤ Snowdon, P., Lovegrove, S., Wicks, K. (2011) Remuneration and regulation, *Compliance Officer Bulletin*.

5 Bank regulation and supervision

Chapter overview

The aim of this chapter is to:

➤ Examine historically the approach to bank regulation and supervision with the single unitary regulator (the Financial Services Authority (FSA)) being disbanded in 2013 and the Bank of England[1] restored as the main banking regulator under a new 'twin peaks' supervisory structure.

➤ Examine the Financial Services and Markets Act 2000, as amended.

➤ Examine the scope, if any, of the legal liability of the bank supervisory authority in the event of bank insolvency.

Introduction

Bank failures are generally seen as having a greater impact on the economy and on consumer confidence than other types of business failure. This is partly due to the fear that such lack of confidence may have a domino effect not only across the banking sector but also across the wider economy, or a group of, possibly, key-players in the economy.[2] It is because banks are more closely inter-connected to each other in the way they undertake business that there is a genuine danger of systemic failure. The underlying nature of banking business necessitates that banks are interdependent; thus they regularly place deposits with each other, lend and borrow from and to each other, and their need to settle accounts with each other for third-party transfers makes them more susceptible to sometimes, unexpected influences across the sector.[3] The failure of one bank can transmit fear among a chain of banks and the failure of even an individual bank can introduce the possibility of a system-wide failure. Further, the

---

[1] It must be noted that following the 2008 financial crisis the Coalition government decided that the banking sector was best regulated by a strong Central Bank and returned the powers of bank regulation and supervision to the Bank of England.

[2] Braithwaite, Macintosh, Simonn and Reed, GM to file for Chapter 11 protection, 31 May 2009, *Financial Times*, http://www.ft.com/cms/s/0/e75423ac-4df8-11de-a0a1-00144feabdc0.html#axzz1eiNTMkfu.

[3] Kaufman, Bank Failure, Systemic Risk, and Bank Regulation, *The Cato Journal*, 16(1), http://www.cato.org/pubs/journal/cj16n1-2.html.

cumulative effect of bank failure may have a ripple effect because customer deposits form a large part of the money supply and a significant portion of bank assets.[4] Such uncertainty will affect the level of customer spending as depositors either lose savings or fear banking or economic instability. The collapse of Northern Rock and its subsequent nationalisation, together with the sale of Bradford and Bingley to the Spanish Santander Group, and the merger of HBOS Group with Lloyds Banking Group were some of the measures the Brown government was forced into, in order to prevent a banking collapse during 2007–09.[5] However, events in the UK were parallelled by events in the global markets with France, Germany, Switzerland and the USA announcing banking bad debt exposure.[6] The attempts of any single government to stabilise their domestic banking sector were hampered by events internationally[7] and the UK government was forced into announcing a massive rescue package of the banking sector.[8] Successive governments in the UK have, therefore, intervened to safeguard the banking sector through primary legislation, quasi-government bodies (e.g. the FSA, the PRA and the FCA) and soft law (Voluntary Codes of Practice).

Bank regulation refers to rules that banks are required to comply with[9] while supervision refers to the monitoring process undertaken by regulators. Apart from the initial authorisation requirements that must be complied with, prudential supervision requires continuing compliance with the statutory requirements. Accordingly[10] two types of regulation and supervision can be identified namely:

- Prudential regulation which focuses on the solvency, safety and soundness of financial institutions.
- Conduct of business regulation that focuses on the methods used by financial firms to conduct business with their customers.

---

[4] Assets held by UK banks totalled £7,616 billion at the end of 2009, down 4 per cent on the previous year. Foreign banks held 51 per cent of the total. As concerns about solvency eased, UK banks' equity prices rose by 40 per cent between March 2009 and the end of the year, recouping much of the losses of the previous nine months, International Banking Services London, Banking 2010, February 2010, http://www.thecityuk.com/media/2372/IFSL_Banking_2010.pdf.

[5] Belt-and-braces bid to banish N Rock nightmare, *The Financial Times*, 7 October 2008, http://www.ft.com/cms/s/d77c7f54-47bb-11dd-93ca-000077b07658,dwp_uuid=74d73); Bradford & Bingley's final moments, 28 September 2008, http://business.timesonline.co.uk/to1/business/industry, and Santander buys Bradford & Bingley's branches, *The Daily Telegraph*, 13 February 2009, http://www.telegraph.co.uk/finance/financetopics/financialcrisis/3100146.

[6] BBC News, Timeline: Credit Crunch to Downturn, 29 January 2009, http://news.bbc.co.uk/1/hi/business/7521250.stm.

[7] The Turner Review: A regulatory response to the global financial crisis, March 2009, http://www.fsa.gov.uk/pubs/other/turner_review.pdf concluded that what made the 2007–09 crisis was the global nature of the financial crisis.

[8] Grice, £850 bn: Official Cost of the Bank Bailout, *The Independent*, 4 December 2009, http://www.independent.co.uk/news/uk/politics/163850bn-official-cost-of-the-bank-bailout-1833830.html. A similar rescue package of the US banking sector was announced with the Obama government approving a $700 billion Troubled Asset Relief Programme: Somerville, US bank bailout estimate cut by $200 billion, Reuters, 7 December 2009, http://www.reuters.com/article/2009/12/07/us-economy-treasury-tarp-idUSTRE5B60KF20091207.

[9] The Financial Services and Markets Act 2000 not only implemented a single unified regulator for the financial services sector but also implemented minimum standards of prudential regulation across the sector.

[10] Llewellyn, The Economic Rationale for Financial Regulation, Financial Services Authority Occasional Paper, 1 April 1999, 10–11, http://www.fsa.gov.uk/pubs/occpapers/OP01.pdf.

Bank regulation and bank supervision

The case for prudential regulation and supervision of financial firms is that consumers are not well equipped to judge the safety and soundness of financial firms either because they do not have access to market information or they do not have the skills or expertise to make an informed judgement. On the other hand, conduct of business regulation helps to ensure the establishment of rules and guidelines about the proper way of dealing with customers, but fails to focus on institutional regulation. The need for banks to be regulated on the basis of prudential supervision stems from the need to prevent systemic bank failure that may result from the fact that banks work on small asset reserves which makes them susceptible to failure, and the fact that the inter-bank lending market is made up of a network of unsecured creditor and debtor relationships means that the collapse of a single bank can have a domino effect and lead to the collapse of other banks.[11]

The formal regulation of banks

Historical background

A formal system of bank regulation and supervision was introduced in the UK by the Banking Act 1979, following the collapse of the property market during 1973–76 when the Bank of England, together with a number of retail banks, launched the life-boat operation to bail out banking institutions facing crisis.[12] The Secondary Banking crisis was triggered by the collapse of London and County Securities Ltd in November 1973, as a result of it investing short-term deposits in long-term transactions and an unexpected failure in the short-term deposits not being renewed. This led to liquidity problems for the institution and because of the fears of wider public panic and the systemic effect of bank collapse on the economy, the Bank of England was forced to rescue several institutions. The aftermath of the Secondary Banking crisis led to a call for the implementation of a statutory regime of regulation in the UK banking sector.[13] The Banking Act 1979 introduced a two-tier system of authorisation under which 'recognised banks' were able, largely, to continue within an informal and flexible system of self-regulation previously operated by the Bank of England, while 'licensed institutions' were required to comply with the full rigours of the Act.[14] The Banking Act 1979 exempted from

---

[11] The 2008 credit crisis was in large due to a loss of confidence within the banking sector and the unwillingness of the banks to lend to each other, House of Commons Treasury Committee, The run on the Rock, Fifth Report of Session 2007–08, HC 56–I, http://www.publications.parliament.uk/pa/cm200708/cmselect/cmtreasy/56/56i.pdf; see also FSA Internal Audit Division, The Supervision of Northern Rock: a lessons learned review, March 2008, http://www.fsa.gov.uk/pubs/other/nr_report.pdf; see also: Freixos, Curzio, Hoggarth and Soussa, Lender of Last Resort: A Review of the Literature, http://www.bankofengland.co.uk/publications/fsr/1999/fsr07art6.pdf; Goodhart and Illing (eds), Contagion, and the Lender of Last Resort: A Reader, *Financial Crisis*, Oxford University Press, 2002.

[12] See: The Secondary Banking Crisis and the Bank of England's Support Operation, Bank of England Quarterly Bulletin, June 1978, p. 230 at 233; Reid (2003) The Secondary Banking Crisis 1973–75, London: Hindsight Books.

[13] The Banking Act 1979 also ensured compliance with the First Council Directive 77/780/EEC on the coordination of the laws, regulations and administrative provisions relating to the establishment and pursuance of business and deposit-taking institutions.

[14] Implementing the First Banking Directive, the Banking Act 1979 also introduced the Deposit Protection Scheme which initially protected customer deposits up to a maximum of £20,000.

its remit other institutions providing banking services,[15] for example building societies and the Post Office, and regulated under other statutory provisions. The system of banking supervision was embedded within the wider, and fragmented, system of financial regulation and supervision with separate regulators, resulting in a general reluctance to share information. The shortcomings of the Banking Act 1979 and the major deficiencies and complacent practices in the system of UK bank supervision were exposed following the investigation into the collapse of Johnson Matthey Bank, in October 1984.[16]

The Banking Act 1987, repealing the 1987 Act, was intended to remedy the defects highlighted by the collapse of Johnson Matthey and the 1987 Act abolished the two-tier system of bank supervision, replacing it with a single system of authorisation, which was applied to all institutions that accepted deposits, in the course of their business. While the 1987 Act strengthened and reinforced the powers of the Bank of England (banks were required to disclose exposures exceeding 10 per cent of their capital to the Bank of England and were prohibited from lending more than 25 per cent of their capital to a single borrower)[17] the Bank of England was still allowed to operate its supervisory regime within a flexible framework.[18] Thus, banking institutions subject to Bank of England regulation enjoyed a flexibility and privilege in their regulatory regime depending on how they were perceived by the regulator and more widely within the banking sector.

The Banking Act 1987, while formalising the Bank of England's approach to its supervisory functions, also placed on the Bank an express duty to supervise authorised institutions,[19] to keep under review both the operation of the Act and developments in the banking sector that might appear relevant to the exercise of its powers and functions.[20] However, despite legislative intervention there continued to be a significant emphasis on the discretionary and flexible style of prudential supervision,[21] even after the collapse of both BCCI and Barings Bank. The enforced closure of BCCI, in 1991, followed the discovery of one of the largest banking frauds and mis-management of the twentieth century and called into question the effectiveness of the Bank of England's prudential supervisory functions. The Bank's failure to intervene, in fact, highlights the dilemma faced by bank regulators: revocation of permission to continue with the business can itself lead to loss of confidence and result in a 'run' on the bank created by the actions of the bank regulator with possible long-term damage to its business,[22] while the regulator's failure to act may result in losses to customers and the wider economy. The need to protect the interests of depositors, therefore, has to be carefully balanced with the need not to damage the bank's business.

---

[15] *United Dominion Trust* v *Kirkwood* [1966] 2 QB 431.

[16] Hadjiemmanuil (1995) *Banking Regulation and the Bank of England*, London: Lloyd's of London Press, p. 43.

[17] Badell and Grau Legal Consultants, *The Formal Regulatory Approach to Banking Regulation*, http://www.badellgrau.com/legalbanking.html; p. 13.

[18] Blunden, Director of Banking Supervision, explained the Bank of England's approach to supervision as: Flexible, without rigid patterns; Personal, with each institution being judged according to its individual situation; Progressive, with institutions rising step-by-step through a status ladder; and Participative, with the opinions of each institution's peer-group taken into consideration, The Supervision of the UK Banking System, 1997, 15, *Bank of England Quarterly Bulletin*, 188.

[19] Banking Act 1987, s.1(1).

[20] Banking Act 1987, s.2(1).

[21] White Paper on Banking Supervision, Cmnd 9695, 1985, continued to place an emphasis on the flexible nature of the UK banking sector.

[22] The Right Hon. Lord Justice Bingham (1992) Inquiry into the Supervision of the Bank of Credit and Commerce International (Bingham Report), London: HMSO.

The Bank of England faced further criticism following the collapse of Barings, in 1995, which resulted in the parent company, Barings Bros & Co., in London being placed in the hands of administrators and eventually being sold to the Dutch Bank, ING, for a nominal sum of £1.[23] Although, the Barings collapse did not lead to immediate and direct change in bank regulation it did result in an extensive reassessment of banking supervision[24] which advised that clearer standards and objectives were required to clarify the Bank's approach to bank supervision, including taking a more risk-based approach.

The one stop shop to financial regulation: the Financial Services Authority (FSA)

In 1997, the Labour Party fought the general election, in part, on a promise to reform the financial services industry and in its Business Manifesto, 'Equipping Britain for the Future', it undertook to bring self-regulation to an end. In fact, the announcement on 20 May 1997, by Gordon Brown, the then Chancellor of the Exchequer,[25] amounted to a wholesale reform of the financial services sector with the establishment of what amounted to 'one stop regulation'.[26] The single system of authorisation, covering banking, insurance and investment services, was the cornerstone of the new regime. Until this reform the multiple regulators[27] within financial services had applied a range of different authorisation regimes, under a number of separate legislative regimes. Brown emphasised that reform was essential to ensure investor confidence, the overall success and stability of the economy and to reassure those employed in the financial services sector.[28] One of the most fundamental, and perhaps unexpected, intended reforms was that under the new structure the Bank of England was to lose its historic powers of bank supervision. Alan Milburn, the Chief Secretary to the Treasury, explained the rationale behind the reform:

> Nowadays, banks, securities firms and insurance companies all play in the same pond. But while the traditional sectoral boundaries are disappearing, the old regulatory structures have failed to keep pace. The result is the worst of all worlds – heavy-handed and confused regulation, with more than one supervisor, all with different rules and procedures, seeking to regulate the self-same firm. That is not just a recipe for confusion; it is costly and inefficient and, ironically, it can dilute the impact of effective regulation.[29]

The Governor of the Bank of England, while cautious in his public opposition,[30] had no option but to accept the loss of supervisory powers. Perhaps, because of the unique and

[23] Barings was brought to a situation of collapse as a result of the activities of Nick Leeson who accumulated losses totalling $827 million at Barings Futures in Singapore, Report of the Board of Banking Supervision Inquiry into the Circumstances of the Collapse of Barings, 18 July 1995, (Barings Report), London, HMSO, para. 1.2.

[24] See: Review by Arthur Anderson & Co. SC (1996) Findings and Recommendations of the Review of Supervision and Surveillance (Arthur Anderson Report), London, Arthur Anderson Consulting.

[25] HM Treasury News Release 49/97, The Chancellor's Statement To The House of Commons on the Bank of England, 20 May 1997, http://archive.treasury.gov.uk/press/1997/p49_97.html.

[26] Alan Millburn, HC Deb, 28 June 1999, c.35.

[27] Bank of England; the Building Societies Commission; the Friendly Societies Commission and the Registry of Friendly Societies; the Treasury's Insurance Directorate; the Financial Services Authority; various self-regulating organisations; and recognised professional bodies.

[28] Gordon Brown, HC Deb, 20 May 1997, c.510.

[29] Alan Milburn, HC Deb, 28 June 1999, c.37.

[30] HM Treasury News Release 49/97, The Chancellor's Statement To The House of Commons on the Bank of England, 20 May 1997, http://archive.treasury.gov.uk/press/1997/p49_97.html.

pivotal position of banks within the economy, the repeated failures of the Bank of England in supervision, changes to the methods and practices of business within the City of London and in the products available, meant that loss of supervisory power by the Bank of England was inevitable. The financial world had become too complex for a system of multiple regulators. Nevertheless, the overriding influence of the Bank of England became apparent with the appointment of Howard Hughes, the then Deputy Governor of the Bank of England, to the Chair of the Financial Services Authority (FSA) (the newly created single financial services regulatory authority); thus drawing upon the 'resident expertise' of the Bank of England.[31]

However, although the Financial Services Authority (FSA) was introduced to ensure effective regulation, events which occurred in the UK during the 2007–09 financial crisis led to the emergence of an alternative twin peaks approach to regulation. This was implemented through the Financial Services Act 2012, which came into effect on 1 April 2013, and created two new bodies: the Prudential Regulation Authority (PRA) and the Financial Conduct Authority (FCA). To ensure effective regulation and communication between these authorities, the Bank of England was given overall control of the regulatory system. However, the statutory framework within which banking regulation will be discharged remains the Financial Services and Markets Act 2000, as amended.

The Financial Services and Markets Act 2000 (FSMA)

The Financial Services and Markets Bill was subjected to unprecedented debate and scrutiny.[32] The key themes of the debate centred on a number of issues:

- Although the advantages of the single regulator were recognised, nevertheless, there was a fear that the centralisation of regulation might lead to a 'one size fits all' approach to the regulation of financial institutions that performed different functions.

- The importance of maintaining FSA accountability and scrutiny resulted in some debate.

- Critics of the FSMA were concerned that the Act would give rise to a significant compliance burden and costs would be passed to customers which might damage the competitive position of the City of London as a financial centre.

- There was also considerable debate about the role of the state in protecting consumer interest and the principle of *caveat emptor*. An issue for discussion was whether an intense legislative regime would promote 'moral hazard' and create a false sense of security leading to a failure to assess the risks.[33]

- Finally, there was much debate about the FSA's investigation and enforcement powers.

---

[31] Gordon Brown, the Chancellor of the Exchequer, HC Deb, 20 May 1997, c.511.
[32] The Bill was subjected to extensive scrutiny first by the Treasury Committee, Financial Services Regulation, Treasury Committee, HC, 73-I 1998–99 and then by the Joint Committee on Financial Services and Markets under the Chair of Lord Burns which took live and written submissions from industry practitioners, interest groups and constitutional lawyers and published two detailed reports on the Bill.
[33] Llewellyn, The Economic Rationale for Financial Regulation, Financial Services Authority Occasional Paper, 1 April 1999, 10–11, http://www.fsa.gov.uk/pubs/occpapers/OP01.pdf.

Nevertheless, the FSMA 2000 transferred the 'regulation of the financial services and markets; to provide for the transfer of certain statutory functions relating to building societies, friendly societies, industrial and provident societies and certain other mutual societies; and connected persons' to the Financial Services Authority (FSA)[34] which as the single unified regulator, was authorised to make rules relating to regulated and prohibited activities, authorisation and exemption, continuous supervision, enforcement powers and an appeals procedure. The FSA was required to discharge these functions in accordance with objectives set out in the FSMA 2000. However, following the implementation of s.6 of the Financial Services Act 2012, ss.1–18 of the Financial Services and Markets Act 2000 have been amended to substitute the Financial Services Authority (FSA) with the Financial Conduct Authority (FCA).

The twin peaks approach to bank regulation

Although the Financial Services Authority (FSA) was introduced to ensure effective regulation, the events which occurred in the UK during the financial crisis led to the emergence of an alternative twin peaks approach to regulation. This was implemented through the Financial Services Act 2012, which came into effect on 1 April 2013, and created two new bodies: the Prudential Regulation Authority (PRA),[35] and the Financial Conduct Authority (FCA).[36] The FCA has taken over the legal status of the FSA[37] and a significant portion of its previous functions. The FCA is therefore the UK regulator responsible for the business conduct of all firms previously regulated by the FSA, including also firms subject to additional prudential supervision by the Prudential Regulatory Authority (PRA). Additionally, the FCA also acts as the prudential regulator of all firms other than those subject to PRA regulation.

The PRA, a subsidiary of the Bank of England, is responsible for micro-prudential regulation of the largest firms considered 'systemically important' to the UK economy and markets. This includes insurance intermediaries, personal investment firms and mortgage intermediaries. The general objective of the PRA is to promote the safety and soundness of regulated firms.[38] The FCA also regulates firms providing market services (such as recognised investment exchanges and providers of multilateral trading facilities) and addresses conduct issues in the market more generally. The objective of the FCA is to ensure that business across the financial services industry and markets is conducted in a manner that furthers the interests of market participants[39] and consumers.[40]

The Financial Policy Committee (FPC)[41] is a committee of the Bank of England and is responsible for macro-prudential regulation of the UK financial industry. The committee

---

[34] FSA, Financial Services Authority: An Outline, Memorandum of Understanding between The Treasury, The Bank of England and the FSA, App. 2, 28 October 1997, http://www.fsa.gov.uk/pubs/policy/launch.pdf; FSA, The Financial Services Authority: Meeting our Responsibilities, 1998, http://www.fsa.gov.uk/pubs/policy/p05.pdf; FSA, A new Regulator for the New Millennium, January 2000, http://www.fsa.gov.uk/pubs/policy/p29.pdf.

[35] Financial Services Act 2012, Ch. 2 inserts a new s.2A to the Financial Services and Markets Act 2000.

[36] Financial Services Act 2012, Ch. 1 inserts a new s.1A to the Financial Services and Markets Act 2000; see also Ch. 1.

[37] Financial Services Act 2012, Ch. 1 inserts a new s.1A(1) to the Financial Services and Markets Act 2000.

[38] Financial Services Act 2012, Ch. 2 inserts a new s.2B(3) to the Financial Services and Markets Act 2000.

[39] Financial Services Act 2012, Ch. 1 inserts a new s.1D to the Financial Services and Markets Act 2000.

[40] Financial Services Act 2012, Ch. 1 inserts new ss.1C and 1E to the Financial Services and Markets Act 2000.

[41] Financial Services Act 2012, inserts a new Part 1A, s.9A to the Bank of England Act 1998.

considers prudential regulation issues across the entire UK financial system, looking at the general risks to the economy and analysing emerging trends or asset bubbles in order to prevent problems arising. Unlike both the PRA and FCA, the FPC does not have direct regulatory responsibility for any particular types of firm or specific entities.

The FPC's overall objective is to assist the Bank of England in achieving financial stability by identifying, monitoring and taking action to remove or reduce systemic risks.[42] For this purpose, 'systemic risk' is risk to the stability of the UK financial system as a whole or to a significant part of that system. The FPC implements its measures through the PRA and FCA,[43] who are responsible for applying the identified measures directly to applicable regulated firms.

The Financial Services Act 2000, as amended

Since the Treasury announced the proposed changes to the regulatory regime in June 2010, steps have been taken to ensure that there is minimal disruption during the implementation of the new regime. Firms that were already regulated by the FSA were 'grandfathered' into the new regime and did not need to reapply to the FCA or the PRA for fresh authorisations and regulatory approvals. Firms for whom the FCA is their prudential regulator will have a similar relationship with the FCA as they did with the FSA. However, PRA-authorised firms will need to adapt to supervision by two regulators and manage the impact of regulatory processes, such as the approved persons regime, being split between two regulators. Further, for these firms, the FSA ARROW risk mitigation programme is replaced by two separate programmes with two sets of mitigating actions to address. A number of transitional provisions were introduced to make the change to the new regulation system an easier process.

The FCA's objectives

The Financial Services and Markets Act 2000 (FSMA), as amended by the Financial Services Act 2012, imposes on the Financial Conduct Authority (FCA)[44] a framework, in the form of statutory objectives,[45] through which the FCA is required to discharge its public duties[46] and which help to ensure internal and external accountability of the FCA activities under the FSMA.[47]

---

[42] Financial Services Act 2012, inserts a new Part 1A, s.9C to the Bank of England Act 1998.

[43] Financial Services Act 2012, inserts a new Part 1A, ss.9H and 9I to the Bank of England Act 1998.

[44] The Financial Services Act 2012 clause 137G reflects the Financial Services Bill 2012 clause 137E, to provide that the FCA may make such rules, as appear necessary or expedient for the purposes of advancing one or more of its objectives, with respect to carrying on by them of regulated activities, or with respect to them carrying out any activities, which are not regulated activities.

[45] Financial Services and Markets Act 2000, s.2(2).

[46] Sir Howard Davies characterised these objectives as a 'very effective discipline on our internal processes', which makes some effort to identify, unlike previous legislation, the ends to which the FSA ought to apply its powers', Joint Committee on Financial Services and Markets, First Report, Minutes of Evidence, 16 March, 1999, para. 22.

[47] Financial Services and Markets Act 2000, s.2(1) provides that the FSA must act in a manner 'reasonably' compatible with its regulatory objectives.

The regulatory objectives establish the parameters within which the FCA is authorised to act and the benchmark against which the Financial Services and Markets Tribunal and, if necessary, the courts will determine the lawfulness of the FCA's conduct.[48] The FCA, itself, will determine the measures which are 'most appropriate for the purpose of meeting those objectives' and the FCA's general functions, power to make rules, to prepare and issue codes, to give general guidance, and to determine the general policy and principles which govern the performance of particular functions[49] are to be 'considered as a whole'.[50] The statutory objectives that define the scope of the FCA's purpose are:

- Maintain market confidence;[51]
- Enhance understanding;[52]
- Protect consumers;[53]
- Reduce financial crime; and
- Promoting effective competition.[54]

While these objectives are not seen as being in order of any priority, they are intended to maintain the well-being of the financial services sector and maintain consumer confidence and protection while, at the same time, ensuring the integrity of the financial services sector by regulating institutions and personnel. The Financial Conduct Authority is tasked with discharging its general functions in a way that is compatible with its strategic objective of ensuring the markets function well. Additionally, the FCA's operational objectives include: to secure an appropriate degree of consumer protection, to protect and enhance the integrity of the UK financial system, and to promote effective competition in the interests of consumers. The scope of some of these objectives will now be explored.

Market confidence

The FCA's market objective is defined as 'maintaining confidence in the financial system',[55] including financial markets and exchanges, regulated activities and connected activities. The objective, in many ways, underpins the stability of the financial services sector by requiring that those who work within it conduct business in a manner that maintains customer confidence and an environment within which investment remains an attractive proposition. The integrity of those working within the financial services sector and the orderly conduct of the markets are key to this objective. As explained by the former financial services regulator, the Financial Services Authority, in its document, 'A New Regulator for the New Millennium', stated that maintaining confidence 'involves . . . preserving actual stability in the financial system and the reasonable expectation that it will remain stable'.[56] The FCA will, therefore, be

---

[48] Draft Financial Services and Markets Bill, Delegated Powers and Deregulation Committee, para. 11.
[49] Financial Services and Markets Act 2000, s.2(4).
[50] Financial Services and Markets Act 2000, s.2(3).
[51] Financial Services and Markets Act 2000, s.3(1).
[52] The original 'public awareness' objective is superseded by the new s. 3A 'enhancing understanding' objective under the Financial Services Act 2010.
[53] Financial Services and Markets Act 2000, s.5.
[54] Financial Services Act 2012, inserts a new Part 1A, s.1E to the Financial Services and Markets Act 2000.
[55] Financial Services and Markets Act 2000, s.3(1).
[56] FSA, A new Regulator for the New Millennium, January 2000, Ch. 1 para. 2, http://www.fsa.gov.uk/pubs/policy/p29.pdf.

expected to have knowledge of both the domestic and international financial markets so it could monitor developments and risks and how they impacted on market confidence. However, the FSMA and the market confidence objective are not intended to establish a 'zero failure' regime[57] and consumers must be expected to take responsibility for their decisions.[58] Consequently, if required, the new insolvency regime put in place by the Banking Act 2009 is intended to support an orderly winding down of activities.[59]

While the market confidence objective provides a broad basis for FCA intervention, including intervention based on the conduct, or suspected conduct, of individuals, individual firms, sectoral risks and consumer interest, the objective does not expressly extend responsibility to the FCA for monitoring systemic risk. In fact systemic risk, while related to market confidence, is a separate hazard and was subjected to a separate Memorandum of Understanding between the Bank of England, The Treasury and the FSA, and it was this memorandum that imposed ultimate responsibility on the Treasury for authorising support operations in the 2007–09 banking crisis.[60]

Enhancing understanding

The FSA's[61] focus in respect of retail banking was reinforced by the Financial Services Act 2010, which replaced the public awareness objective[62] with a new objective under which the FSA, the then regulator, was expected to reinforce and enhance the understanding and knowledge of the public on financial matters (including the UK financial system) and their ability to manage their own financial affairs,[63] including promoting the advantages of financial planning, together with the risks associated with different kinds of financial dealing.[64] While, the FSA's ability to exercise its powers had been qualified by reference to protecting the interests of consumers, it was able to exercise those powers in relation to any of the statutory objectives, including financial stability. It is important that the scope of this new objective be clarified, particularly in light of the amendment to the way in which the FCA can now exercise its powers.

Consumer protection

Section 5 of the FSMA 2000 requires the FCA to secure an appropriate degree of 'consumer protection'. Both the 'enhancing understanding' and 'consumer protection' objectives are concerned with the problem of correcting the imbalances of information between the service

---

[57] For example, in 1991, the Bank of England took the decision to close BCCI and was satisfied that its closure would not result in a general loss of market confidence, or result in systemic collapse. By contrast, because of the danger of a widespread systemic collapse during the 2007–08 credit crisis and wider economic repercussions the government intervened to nationalise, or part nationalise, certain banks, e.g. Northern Rock was taken into full state ownership and the government took a 40 per cent interest Lloyds Banking Group, following its takeover of HBOS, in efforts to restore customer confidence.

[58] Financial Services Act 2012, inserts a new Part 1A, s.1C(2)(d) to the Financial Services and Markets Act 2000.

[59] See Ch. 5.

[60] Banking (Special Provision) Act 2008, s.2.

[61] The FSA was abolished on 1 April 2013 through the Financial Services Act and replaced with a twin peak approach through the Financial Conduct Authority and the Prudential Regulatory Authority: see Ch. 1.

[62] Financial Services Acts 2010 inserts s.6A to the FSMA 2000 and replaces s.4 of the FSMA 2000.

[63] Section 6A Financial Services Act 2010.

[64] The FSA must establish a consumer education body whose main functions will be to educate the public on awareness in respect of financial products and dealings and associated risks.

provider and consumer. However, it is impossible to protect the consumer against all risk and those investors willing to take high risks cannot then expect full protection against losses;[65] what the regulation has attempted to safeguard against was loss resulting to the consumer from the negligence, mis-selling or fraud of the product provider, and that imbalances which resulted in an unfair advantage to the provider were prevented. The purpose of this type of regulation is to ensure that the consumer is placed in a position to make a fully informed judgement of the costs, the potential risks and returns on the product. The former FSA therefore put in place measures intended to deal with unfairness and bad or inappropriate advice where the inherent risks are not made clear.[66] The FCA, itself, is bound by a number of objectives and duties intended to safeguard the consumer and the integrity of the markets.[67]

Promoting effective competition

Despite the Cruickshank Committee's suggestion, in its interim report, that the promotion of competition should be among the FSA's objectives, it was only one of the principles governing the operation of the then FSA in the achievement of its objectives.[68] However, the Financial Services Act 2012[69] now introduces a new competition objective which the FCA must promote. The new objective is intended to promote effective competition in the interests of consumers in the markets for regulated financial services, or services provided by a recognised investment exchange in carrying on regulated activities. The matters to which the FCA may have regard in considering the effectiveness of competition in the market for any services include: the needs of different consumers who use or may use those services, including their need for information in order to make informed choices; the ease with which consumers who may wish to use those services, including consumers in areas affected by social or economic deprivation, can access them; the ease with which consumers who obtain those services can change their service provider from whom they obtain them; the ease with which new entrants can enter the market; and how far competition is encouraging innovation.

The reduction of financial crime

This objective embraces the whole of the financial services sector and places the FCA[70] in the forefront of the fight against the reduction of financial crime, particularly as a firm's exposure to financial crime may result in loss of market confidence. Financial crime is defined as including any criminal offence involving 'fraud or dishonesty'. The responsibility for achieving this

---

[65] Section 1C of the FSMA 2000, inserted by s.2(2) Financial Services Act 2012, provides that the appropriate levels of protection for consumers will have regard to, for example, the differing degrees of risk involved in different kinds of investment; the differing degrees of experience and expertise that different consumers may have; any information which the consumer financial education body has provided to the FCA in the exercise of the consumer financial education function; the needs that consumers may have for advice and accurate information; the general principle that consumers should take responsibility for their decisions.

[66] The Unfair Contract Terms Regulatory Guide (UNFCOG1) http://fsahandbook.info/FSA/html/handbook/UNFCOG/1.

[67] Financial Services Act 2012, inserts a new Part 1A, ss.1B(3)(a) and 1C to the Financial Services and Markets Act 2000.

[68] Cruickshank, Competition in UK Banking: A Report to the Chancellor of the Exchequer, HMSO, 2000. The interim report can be found as an annex (annex F) to the final text.

[69] Financial Services Act 2012, inserts a new Part 1A, s.1E to the Financial Services and Markets Act 2000.

[70] Financial Services Act 2012, inserts a new Part 1A, s.1H(3) to the Financial Services and Markets Act 2000.

objective is placed directly on regulated persons who can monitor, and are best placed to assess, how the business can be abused, even by insiders with expert knowledge and skills, to commit fraud and criminal conduct. Regulated institutions are best placed to assess and acquire the best knowledge of their customer and business activity; for example, banks are required to comply with 'know your customer' regulations to counter anti-terrorist activity. The Royal Bank of Scotland was fined £750,000 for a breach of money-laundering rules applying to customer identification.[71]

Financial stability

The Financial Services Act 2010 introduced a financial stability objective[72] which is intended to contribute to the protection and enhancement of the stability of the UK financial sector. The FCA is required to have regard to the economic and fiscal consequences of instability in the UK, the effect on economic growth of its conduct and the impact, within the UK financial sector, and of events occurring within the international markets which may adversely impact on the UK markets. The FCA is therefore required to monitor the international financial markets and developments overseas to ensure that it responds to safeguard and protect the domestic financial markets.

Principles of regulation

The Financial Services and Markets Act 2000 (FSMA), as amended, sets out a number of regulatory principles (or principles of good regulation), which are intended to underpin the manner in which it is expected that bank regulators will discharge their statutory obligations. The principles the FCA should have regard to are: efficiency and economy;[73] the role of governance and management;[74] that regulation must be proportionate to the benefits;[75] innovation;[76] the international character of the financial services markets; the desirability of maintaining the competitiveness of the UK financial services sector;[77] and minimising the possible adverse impact on competition of the FCA's regulation.[78]

The FCA has a formal obligation to ensure that sound management of financial services remains a key priority but the FCA is required to have regard to this in the context of the wider environment, including the internationalisation of the services markets and product availability. Within that, the FCA demands fit and proper management responsible for the protection of depositor and consumer interest. Thus, the objectives placed on the FCA are not

---

[71] http://www.finextra.com/news/fullstory.aspx?newsitemid=7587.

[72] Bank of England Act 1998, s.2A, inserted by s.1 Financial Services Act 2010, is amended by the Financial Services Act 2012, s.2 which reflects the Financial Services Bill 2012, clause 2B.

[73] Financial Services and Markets Act 2000, s.2(3)(a), see also: A new Regulator for the new Millennium, FSA January 2000, para. 19, http://www.fsa.gov.uk/pubs/policy/p29.pdf.

[74] Financial Services and Markets Act 2000, s.2(3)(b), see also: A new Regulator for the new Millennium, FSA January 2000, para. 19, http://www.fsa.gov.uk/pubs/policy/p29.pdf.

[75] Financial Services and Markets Act 2000, s.2(3)(c), see also: A new Regulator for the new Millennium, FSA January 2000, para. 19, http://www.fsa.gov.uk/pubs/policy/p29.pdf.

[76] Financial Services and Markets Act 2000, s.2(3)(d), see also: A new Regulator for the new Millennium, FSA January 2000, para. 19, http://www.fsa.gov.uk/pubs/policy/p29.pdf.

[77] Financial Services and Markets Act 2000, s.2(3)(e), see also: A new Regulator for the new Millennium, FSA January 2000, para. 19, http://www.fsa.gov.uk/pubs/policy/p29.pdf.

[78] Financial Services and Markets Act 2000, s.2(3)(f), see also: A new Regulator for the new Millennium, FSA January 2000, para. 19, http://www.fsa.gov.uk/pubs/policy/p29.pdf.

intended to impose an extra layer of management on 'authorised institutions' or to be intrusive into individual commercial decisions.[79] When executing its supervisory functions and devising regulatory structures the FCA is required to maintain a level playing field between the various sectors of the financial services industry and dismantle anti-competitive measures.[80]

The prudential regulation of banks

Since the Banking Act 1979 the regulation of banks has been based on the assumption that Parliament will establish minimum acceptable standards of conduct enforced and monitored through an authorisation and permission regime. Collectively, the supervision of the banking sector is conducted on the basis of prudential supervision under the FSMA 2000, as amended, and the Codifying EU Banking Directive adds a definitional platform to ensure common terminology and implement a minimum set of banking regulatory standards. To achieve a twin peaks system of financial regulation, which encompasses financial conduct and financial stability, the Financial Services Act 2012 amended the FSMA 2000 to give responsibility for financial stability to the PRA.

Accepting deposits by way of business

The FSMA 2000 establishes the scope of the Act by prohibiting unauthorised persons from carrying on regulated activities in the UK,[81] or falsely claiming to be authorised or exempt.[82] Further, the Act prohibits authorised persons from carrying on a regulated business without permission[83] and restricts the communication of financial promotions by unauthorised persons.[84]

'Regulated activities' are at the core of the FSMA and the definition and scope of regulated activities will determine whether authorisation is required. The Treasury is entitled to specify whether an activity is 'regulated' by the Regulated Activities Order[85] and that order extends to a whole range of financial sector activities, including 'accepting deposits' by way of business,[86] retail mortgage business and electronic money. The courts and formerly the FSA have looked at what constitutes a deposit for the purposes of 'regulated activity'. In *SCF Finance Co Ltd* v *Masri*[87] Slade LJ distinguished between a deposit paid in return for the provision of services[88] and a deposit within the scope of a deposit-taking business, and

---

[79] See: A new Regulator for the new Millennium, FSA January 2000, para. 19, http://www.fsa.gov.uk/pubs/policy/p29.pdf.

[80] FSA, making Policy in the FSA: How to Take Account of Competition, A Guide to Competition Analysis in Financial Services (Guide to Competition), July 2000.

[81] Financial Services and Markets Act 2000, s.19.

[82] Financial Services and Markets Act 2000, s.24.

[83] Financial Services and Markets Act 2000, s.20.

[84] Financial Services and Markets Act 2000, s.21.

[85] Financial Services and Markets Act 2000, s.22; see also schedule 2 and for Regulated Activities Order see SI 2001/544, as amended, http://www.legislation.gov.uk/uksi/2001/544/part/II/chapter/II/made; Financial Services Act 2012, inserts a new s.22A to the Financial Services and Markets Act 2000.

[86] Financial Services and Markets Act 2000 schedule 2, para. 4, and Regulated Activities Order, see SI 2001/544, as amended, Art. 5, http://www.legislation.gov.uk/uksi/2001/544/part/II/chapter/II/made.

[87] [1987] QB 1007.

[88] Regulated Activities Order, see SI 2001/544, as amended, Art. 5 (2), http://www.legislation.gov.uk/uksi/2001/544/part/II/chapter/II/made.

concluded that the former payment would not amount to a deposit for the purposes of a regulated activity. The definition of what constitutes a 'deposit' focuses on both the extent of the business, where the bank is used as a repository for funds which the customer draws on as required by him, but also on the supply side of funds where a bank uses those deposits to lend to others, 'as money received by way of deposit is lent to others';[89]or where any other activity of the person accepting the deposit is financed, wholly or to any material extent, out of the capital of or interest on money received by way of a deposit.[90] The second limb of this definition opens up a host of commercial companies which issue debt securities in the capital markets to fund their businesses and have no intention of lending as credit institutions. However, the Regulated Activities Order excludes any sums received by a person in consideration for the issue of instruments creating or acknowledging indebtedness or government securities investments.[91] While the business of banking includes accepting deposits and lending to customers, for regulatory purposes the scope of the FSMA 2000 extends to those involved in the acceptance of deposits. A breach of s.19 of the FSMA 2000 may result in imprisonment for up to two years.[92] In 2005, the FSA took action against Alan Evitts, who was jailed for 18 months, for accepting £204,000 of unauthorised deposits.[93]

The FSMA 2000 also requires that the deposit-taking must occur 'by way of a business'[94] and while the Act does not define the term, there is considerable case law as to what amounts to a 'business'. In *Stevenson v Rogers*[95] the Court of Appeal recognised the 'varied approach of the courts in differing areas of the law' to the question of what is, or is not, done 'in the course of a trade or business'. While, there is potential for some uncertainty legal authority requires that for a business to exist there must be an element of regularity in the dealings and they must take place with a view to a profit. The FSA has previously explained that deposits must be accepted by way of a business: i.e. deposits must be accepted on a 'day-to-day' basis rather than on occasion,[96] and as part of the normal working day. The FSA has followed the view expressed by Hobhouse J in *Morgan Grenfell Co* v *Welwyn Hatfield District Council (Islington Local Council, third party)*[97] where the judge said that:

---

[89] Regulated Activities Order, see SI 2001/544, as amended, Art. 5, http://www.legislation.gov.uk/uksi/2001/544/part/II/chapter/II/made; Lord Denning in *United Dominion Trust* v *Kirkwood* [1966] 2QB 431 similarly described the term banking business as accepting money which is then lent to others, in the ordinary course of a business with an equivalent only repayable on demand.

[90] Regulated Activities Order, see SI 2001/544, as amended, Art. 5(1)(b), http://www.legislation.gov.uk/uksi/2001/544/part/II/chapter/II/made, Commissioners of the *State Savings Bank of Victoria* v *Permewan Wright & Co. Ltd* (1915) 19 CLR 457.

[91] Regulated Activities Order, see SI 2001/544, as amended, Art. 9, http://www.legislation.gov.uk/uksi/2001/544/part/II/chapter/II/made.

[92] See FSA, FSA Handbook, Release 041, April 2005, AUTH 2: *Authorization and regulated Section 2.2.1*, http://www.fsa.gov.uk/pubs/hb-releases/rel41/rel41auth.pdf.

[93] FSA (2005) Glossop accountant jailed for illegal deposit-taking, FSA/PN/070/2005, http://www.fsa.gov.uk/pages/Library/Communication/PR/2005/070.shtml.

[94] Financial Services and Markets Act 2000, s.22. Financial Services Act 2012, inserts a new s.22A to the Financial Services and Markets Act 2000 designating PRA approved activities.

[95] [1999] 2 WLR 1064, per Potter LJ.

[96] FSA, FSA Handbook, Release 041, April 2005, AUTH 2: Authorization and regulated Section 2.3.1, http://www.fsa.gov.uk/pubs/hb-releases/rel41/rel41auth.pdf. At common law in *United Dominion Trust* v *Kirkwood* [1966] 2 QB 431 Lord Denning attributed this as one of the requirements for a banking business.

[97] [1995] 1 All ER 1 at p. 13.

Regularly entering into a certain type of transaction for the purpose of profit is a good indication that the party . . . is doing so by way of business. But it is equally possible that the very first time it enters into such a contract it is doing so by way of business because it is doing so as part of its own overall business activity.

However, whether or not an activity is carried on by way of business is a question of fact and several factors may be taken into consideration, including the activity and proportion which the activity bears to other activities carried on by the same person but which are not regulated.[98] A deposit-taking activity undertaken for the first time may be undertaken 'by way of business'.

Authorisation and permission

Under the FSMA 2000, the requirements of authorisation[99] and permission are intended to work in tandem to achieve an integrated regulatory regime. Authorisation under the Act will allow such institutions to operate within the perimeters of the Act so that the regulated activity can be undertaken without the threat of criminal sanctions emanating from breach of the general prohibition,[100] or from the sanctions flowing from the provisions relating to acting contrary to the restrictions on financial promotion,[101] or falsely claiming to be authorised or exempt.[102] A person or institution seeking permission to undertake a regulated activity must satisfy the threshold conditions established under the new s.55B[103] and schedule 6 of the FSMA 2000, together with the requirements contained in the threshold condition code made by the regulators under new s.137O. The threshold conditions are the minimum conditions which a regulator must ensure that the person concerned (for example, the person making the application for authorisation) will satisfy when the regulator makes a decision relevant to that person under Part 4A of the 2000 Act. Where the person concerned is, or is seeking to become, a PRA-authorised person, each regulator will be responsible for ensuring the threshold conditions, as provided under schedule 6, are satisfied.

The requirement to ensure that the person concerned must satisfy the threshold conditions will not prevent the FCA from taking steps to advance any of its operational objectives[104] or the PRA from advancing any of its objectives.[105] For example, the PRA might delay for a short period the cancellation of the permission of a deposit taker, which does not satisfy its threshold conditions to allow preparations to be made to ensure that the failure of the deposit taker is orderly.

An application for authorisation may be made under s.55A of the FSMA 2000. Authorised persons for the purposes of the FSMA 2000 are:

- Persons who have a Part IV permission to carry on one or more regulated activities. With certain exceptions (for example, EEA firms), a person wanting to carry on any one or more

---

[98] See FSA, FSA Handbook, Release 041, April 2005, AUTH 2: Authorization and regulated Section 2.3.3, http://www.fsa.gov.uk/pubs/hb-releases/rel41/rel41auth.pdf.

[99] Financial Services Act 2012, inserts ss.55E and F to the Financial Services and Markets Act 2000.

[100] Financial Services and Markets Act 2000, ss.19 and 23.

[101] Financial Services and Markets Act 2000, ss.21 and 25.

[102] Financial Services and Markets Act 2000, s.24.

[103] Inserted by s.11 of the Financial Services Act 2012.

[104] See new s.1B(3) of the Financial Services Act 2012.

[105] See new ss.2B and 2D of the Financial Services Act 2012.

regulated activities must apply to the appropriate regulator for Part 4A permission. If the regulator gives such permission, the applicant will become an authorised person.[106]

- EEA firms or treaty firms qualifying for authorisation under schedule 3 or schedule 4A).
- Persons otherwise authorised under the Act.

The new ss.55E and 55F of the FSMA 2000, as amended, provide that the regulators may grant permission for all the activities applied for, or just some of them, or may impose limitations (for example, limitations on the class of consumer to whom the authorised person may provide services or limiting the type of insurance contracts that an authorised person could write to a particular class) or may permit activities which are wider or narrower than the activities as described in the application. A person who carries on a regulated activity without authorisation, and thereby without permission, acts in contravention of the FSMA 2000. For most UK firms the grant of permission to undertake a restricted activity will lead to recognition as an authorised person. The grant of the dual aspects of the approval process, i.e. permission and authorisation, is to facilitate the free movement of banking services across EU Member States so that European banks carrying on financial activities in the UK[107] benefit from the 'passport'[108] concept and so may carry on, in any EU Member State, the same financial activities as authorised by their home regulator.

The new s.55D of the FSMA 2000 provides that where a regulator is considering whether a person from outside the EEA satisfies or will satisfy, and will continue to satisfy, any one or more of the threshold conditions for which that regulator is responsible. For example, where a firm authorised in Singapore applies for permission to undertake a regulated activity in the UK then the regulator can have regard to a view of the Singaporean regulator which is relevant to compliance with the threshold condition, for example a view on the adequacy of a firm's resources.[109] But, if the FCA or the PRA takes the view of a non-UK regulator into account, they must, in considering how much weight to give that opinion, have regard to the nature and scope of the supervision exercised in relation to the non-EEA firm by the overseas regulator.

The authorisation requirements under the FSMA 2000 have the advantage that they act as control on the entry (and exit where the licence is revoked) of institutions to the banking business and control the market in an effort to maintain consumer confidence and market stability. However, the requirements of prudential supervision do not negate the risk of bank failure or loss resulting from fraud or mismanagement, or poor business decisions.

The threshold conditions

The permission requirement under the FSMA 2000 which needs to be satisfied prior to undertaking authorised activities requires the applicant to satisfy certain 'threshold conditions'[110]

[106] See FSA, FSA Handbook, Release 041, April 2005, AUTH 2: Authorization and regulated Section 3.2, http://www.fsa.gov.uk/pubs/hb-releases/rel41/rel41auth.pdf.
[107] Financial Services and Markets Act 2000, s.31(1)(b) or (c).
[108] Financial Services Act 2012, s.12 inserts a new s.34 and amends schedule 3 to the Financial Services and Markets Act 2000.
[109] Amendments to para. 19 of schedule 3 and to para. 20 of schedule 3 of the FSMA 2000 deal with coordination between the regulators.
[110] Financial Services Bill 2011, Part 2, clause 7 amends s.41 FSMA 2000. Reflected in s.11 of the Financial Services Act 2012, s.55B.

on a continuous basis.[111] The FCA has broad powers that are intended to have regard to its statutory objectives while ensuring that it uses its resources efficiently to mitigate the risks which ensue in the financial services sector.

The FSMA 2000[112] provides minimum criteria, which must be satisfied for the grant of permission and prior to carrying out a regulated activity. These minimum 'threshold conditions' are set out in schedule 6 to the Act and the FCA and PRA, as appropriate, must ensure that those seeking authorisation can satisfy them at both the initial authorisation stage and then continuously thereafter. The threshold conditions are broad and, while the first two conditions are absolute, the final three conditions give the FCA, and the PRA, wide discretion, although these discretionary requirements are further elaborated in the Principles for Businesses,[113] Statements of Principles for Approved Persons[114] and the Interim Prudential Sourcebook for Banks (IPSB). The five general threshold conditions[115] are as follows.

Legal status

This requires that the entity seeking authorisation to accept deposits must be either a body corporate or a partnership.[116]

Location of offices

This requirement deals with a problem that became particularly apparent following the collapse of BCCI, which avoided effective supervision because while incorporated in Luxembourg, the bank's management was based in London. The FSMA 2000[117] requires that the head-office and registered office of an authorised entity are both located in the UK, or where an entity not having a registered office, for example a partnership, has its head-office in the UK it must carry on business in the UK. Neither the Post-BCCI Directive, nor the FSMA, define what is meant by 'head-office', but the FCA has given guidance and its key focus is to determine where the 'central management and control' of the day-to-day activities is located. This requirement complies with the Post-BCCI Directive.[118]

Close links

Again this threshold deals with another Post-BCCI Directive[119] and provides that authorised persons must disclose links with other persons who may prevent the FCA from effectively supervising the applicant once authorised. The FCA can insist on the disclosure of any information about 'close links' even where that link is with an exempted person or entity.[120]

---

[111] FCA, Handbook: Threshold conditions, http://www.fshandbook.info/FS/html/FCA/COND/1/1A.

[112] Section 41(2) FSMA 2000, see also FCA, Handbook, PRIN 3, http://www.fshandbook.info/FS/html/FCA/PRIN/3/1.

[113] FCA, Principles for Businesses, http://www.fshandbook.info/FS/html/FCA/PRIN.

[114] FCA, Statements of Principles and Code of Practice for Approved Persons, http://www.fshandbook.info/FS/html/FCA/APER.

[115] http://www.fshandbook.info/FS/html/FCA/COND/1/1A.

[116] Financial Services and Markets Act 2000, schedule 6, para. 1; see FCA Handbook, Threshold Conditions, COND 2.2.1, http://www.fshandbook.info/FS/html/FCA/COND/2/2.

[117] Schedule 6, para. 2 FSMA 2000, see FCA Handbook, Threshold Conditions, COND 2.2.1, http://www.fshandbook.info/FS/html/FCA/COND/2/2.

[118] Consolidated Banking Directive 2000/12/EC.

[119] Consolidated Banking Directive 2000/12/EC.

[120] Schedule 6, para. 3 FSMA 2000, FCA, Handbook COND 2.3.1A http://www.fshandbook.info/FS/html/FCA/COND/2/3.

The term 'close links' refers to (i) links between parent and subsidiary undertaking, or (ii) an equivalent degree of control in relation to unincorporated persons, or (iii) the holding or control of 20 per cent or more of the voting rights or capital of a firm. The lead test for the requirement of disclosure is whether the 'close links' are likely to prevent effective FCA supervision, and if the person to whom the applicant is linked is an entity regulated outside the EEA, then the foreign regulation should not impede effective FCA supervision of the applicant. The close links requirement will be assessed in the context of links within the banking group[121] and the FCA will consider whether the structure and geographical spread of the group might impede the adequate and reliable flow of information to the FCA, and whether companies within the group have different accounting dates and do not share common auditors.[122] The institution applying for permission must be capable of effective supervision.[123]

Adequate resources

The fourth and fifth thresholds form the cornerstone of detailed rules in the FCA's Handbook. The FSMA 2000 provides that the resources of an authorised entity must be adequate in relation to the regulated activities it seeks to carry on[124] (or currently carries on) and the FCA may take into account, or have regard to, the provision made in respect of liabilities, the means by which it manages the incidence of risk in its business and the effect of a person's membership of a group. The authorised entity must have adequate resources on both a consolidated basis and an individual entity basis, initially on authorisation and continuously thereafter.[125] In this situation adequate resources may include provision, which the authorised entity makes in respect of both contingent and future liabilities, and the manner in which business risks, on a consolidated and solo basis, are managed, including appropriate staff training. Thus, adequate resources include not only issues relating to capital but wider resources relating to management and control of systems and staff.

The FCA may have regard, when assessing resources, as to whether the authorised entity has 'conducted sufficient enquires' into the financial services sector in which it intends to conduct business to establish that the firm has access to adequate capital to cover early losses and that client money, assets and deposits will not be placed at risk if the business fails. The FCA may also ask for a 'well constructed business plan or strategy plan for its products and service' which has been 'sufficiently tested'.[126] The level of detail required in a business plan will need to be appropriate to the complexity of the proposed regulated activities and the risks that may be posed. For firms carrying on, or seeking to carry on, a PRA-regulated activity the PRA is responsible for assessing their financial resources. Paragraphs 4D and 5D of schedule 6 to the FSMA 2000 contain the threshold conditions relating to financial resources which are relevant to the discharge by the PRA of its functions under the Act in relation to firms carrying on, or seeking to carry on, a PRA-regulated activity (in addition to additional non-financial resources threshold conditions which are also relevant to the discharge by the PRA of its functions).[127]

[121] FCA, Handbook Hout, COND. 2.3, http://www.fsahandbook.info/FSA/html/handbook/COND/2/3.
[122] FCA, Handbook Hout, COND 2.3.1B, http://www.fsahandbook.info/FSA/html/handbook/COND/2/1.
[123] FCA, Handbook Hout, COND 2.3.1B, http://www.fsahandbook.info/FSA/html/handbook/COND/2/1.
[124] FCA, Handbook Hout, COND 2.4, http://www.fshandbook.info/FS/html/FCA/COND/2/4.
[125] Financial Services and Markets Act 2000 schedule 6, para. 4, see also FCA, Handbook COND 2.4.1 (3), http://www.fshandbook.info/FS/html/FCA/COND/2/4.
[126] FCA, Handbook Hout, COND 2.4.1 (B), http://www.fshandbook.info/FS/html/FCA/COND/2/4.
[127] FCA, Handbook Hout, COND 2.4.1 (B), http://www.fshandbook.info/FS/html/FCA/COND/2/4.

Suitability of persons

The final threshold imposes the 'fit and proper'[128] purpose requirement and the FSMA 2000 provides that the FCA must be satisfied, *inter alia*, by a person's 'connection' with any other person and hence introduces an overlap with Threshold Conditions 3 and 4. However, the FCA focuses on a number of considerations under two main headings:

1 Conduct of business with integrity and in compliance with proper standards.

2 Competent and prudent management and exercise of due skill, care and diligence.

The FCA guidance provides that it will focus on key issues such as the installation of compliance procedures for a firm's 'approved persons' to be made aware of the regulatory requirements applying to them; whether a firm demonstrates readiness to comply with the FCA's regulatory requirements; whether there are arrangements for proper systems of internal control to comply with regulatory standards and requirements to be put in place; whether reasonable care has been taken to ensure that robust information and reporting systems have been developed, tested and properly installed; and whether an approved entity has made reasonable enquires to ensure that it will not pose an unreasonable risk to consumers or the financial system in the UK[129] including whether, or not, the approved entity has appointed auditors with sufficient experience in the areas of business to be undertaken.

The FCA's Principles of Business

The FCA's 'Principles for Businesses' provide 'fundamental obligations' which a regulated firm is required to observe.[130] These principles apply not merely to regulated institutions but across the group and its global activities[131] and provide the context within which the regulated business is undertaken. The principles express the main dimensions of the 'fit and proper' standard set for firms in threshold condition 5, although they do not derive their authority from that standard or exhaust its implications. Being ready, willing and organised to abide by the principles is, however, a critical factor in applications for Part 4A permission, and breaching the principles may challenge a firm's claim that it is fit and proper.[132] The interests of consumers, regulators and financial intermediaries feature heavily in these principles. A breach of the principles will be judged on the basis of an objective 'reasonable care' test,[133] although a subjective test will be applied in respect of honesty.[134]

The FCA will take into consideration whether the act or omission deviates from general practice,[135] which is interpreted to mean reasonable behaviour of a skilled person in the role assigned to him.[136] The act or omission will be judged on whether it departs from 'general

---

[128] FCA, Handbook COND 2.5, http://www.fshandbook.info/FS/html/FCA/COND/2/5.
[129] FCA, Handbook COND 2.5, http://www.fshandbook.info/FS/html/FCA/COND/2/5.
[130] FCA, Handbook, PRIN COND 1.1.2, http://www.fshandbook.info/FS/html/FCA/PRIN/1/1.
[131] FSA, Handbook for Businesses, PRIN 1.13G; 1.1.5G and 1.1.6G, http://fsahandbook.info/FSA/html/handbook/PRIN/1.
[132] FCA, Handbook, PRIN COND 1.1.4, http://www.fshandbook.info/FS/html/FCA/PRIN/1/1.
[133] FCA, Handbook, PRIN COND 1.1.5, http://www.fshandbook.info/FS/html/FCA/PRIN/1/1.
[134] *Royal Brunei Airlines* v *Tan* [1995] 2 AC 378 at 389.
[135] *Kraji* v *McGarth* [1986] 1 All ER 54 at 61.
[136] *Bolam* v *Friern Management Committee* [1957] 2 All ER 118 at 122; *Re Barings Plc (No 5)* [1999] 1 BCLC 433.

practice'.[137] In addition the FCA has to consider the likelihood of the risk occurring and any precautionary measures that a reasonable and prudent person would take[138] having regard to that person's skill and expertise.[139] A director must ensure that he continues to acquire the skills, training and knowledge required to discharge his functions.[140] The principles with which deposit-taking institutions must comply with govern the way regulated business is conducted and Principles 1[141] and 2[142] require that the firm must conduct its business with integrity and with due skill, care and diligence. Thus, Abbey National Asset Managers were fined £320,000 for, *inter alia*, its breach of Principle 2 in not exercising the appropriate level of 'skill and care' in dealing effectively with concerns expressed by its compliance officers.[143] Principle 3[144] requires regulated businesses to take reasonable care to organise and control their affairs responsibly and effectively, with adequate risk management systems. In 2007, the FSA fined the Nationwide Building Society £980,000 for a failure to maintain satisfactory security systems and to take reasonable care of confidential customer data when a laptop was stolen from an employee's home.[145] Principle 4 requires that regulated businesses must maintain adequate financial resources[146] and Principle 5[147] provides for the adherence of proper market conduct. Principle 11[148] requires regulated firms to deal with regulators in an open, transparent and cooperative manner, and firms must disclose to the FSA anything relating to the firm of which the FSA would reasonably expect notice.

Thus, Principles 6 to 10 regulate the relationship between the regulated firm and its customers. Principle 6[149] requires the regulated business to pay due regard to the interests of its customers and treat them fairly and Principle 7[150] requires regulated businesses to pay due regard to the information needs of its clients, and communicate information to them in a way that is clear, fair and not misleading. In 2005, the FSA imposed a fine of £800,000 on Abbey National plc for its failure to treat customers fairly and equitably and for its mishandling of complaints following the mis-selling of endowment mortgages. Citigroup Global Markets[151] was required to surrender profits of approximately £9 million and pay a fine of £4 million for its failure to comply with Principles 2 and 3 as a result of its trading strategy in the bond market. The FSA investigations concluded that the firm had failed to exercise due diligence. Principle 8[152] requires a firm to manage conflicts of interest fairly, both between itself and its customers and between customers *inter se*. Principle 9[153] places on

---

[137] *Bolam v Friern Management Committee* [1957] 2 All ER 118 at 122.

[138] *Bolton v Stone and Others* [1951] 1 All ER 1078 at 1081.

[139] *Re Queens, Moat Houses Plc, Secretary of State for Trade and Industry v Bairstow (No 2)* [2005] 1 BCLC 136.

[140] *Re Barings Plc (No 2)* [1999] 1 BCLC 433.

[141] FCA, Handbook, PRIN 2.1, http://www.fshandbook.info/FS/html/FCA/PRIN/2/1.

[142] FCA, Handbook, PRIN 2.1, http://www.fshandbook.info/FS/html/FCA/PRIN/2/1.

[143] FSA, Final Notice: Abbey National Asset Managers Ltd, 2003, 9 December http://www.fsa.gov.uk/pubs/final/ abbey-asset_9dec03.pdf.

[144] FCA, Handbook, PRIN 2.1, http://www.fshandbook.info/FS/html/FCA/PRIN/2/1.

[145] FSA, Final Notice: Nationwide Building Society, (2007) 14 February, http://www.fsa.gov.uk/pubs/final/nbs.pdf.

[146] FCA, Handbook, PRIN 2.1, http://www.fshandbook.info/FS/html/FCA/PRIN/2/1.

[147] FCA, Handbook, PRIN 2.1, http://www.fshandbook.info/FS/html/FCA/PRIN/2/1.

[148] FCA, Handbook, PRIN 2.1, http://www.fshandbook.info/FS/html/FCA/PRIN/2/1.

[149] FCA, Handbook, PRIN 2.1, http://www.fshandbook.info/FS/html/FCA/PRIN/2/1.

[150] FCA, Handbook, PRIN 2.1, http://www.fshandbook.info/FS/html/FCA/PRIN/2/1.

[151] FSA, Final Notice, Citigroup Global Markets Ltd, 2005, 28 June http://www.fsa.gov.uk/pubs/final/cgml_ 28jun05.pdf.

[152] FCA, Handbook, PRIN 2.1, http://www.fshandbook.info/FS/html/FCA/PRIN/2/1.

[153] FCA, Handbook, PRIN 2.1, http://www.fshandbook.info/FS/html/FCA/PRIN/2/1.

the regulated business an obligation to take reasonable care to ensure the suitability of its advice. Finally, Principle 10[154] requires regulated firms to arrange adequate protection for clients' assets when it is responsible for them.[155] In 2001, the FSA fined Credit Suisse First Boston £4 million for deliberately misleading regulatory counterparts in Japan about its derivatives business.[156]

Senior management: systems and controls

The FCA has expanded on Principle 3 of the Principles for Businesses[157] in its senior management arrangements, systems and controls (SYSC) guidance.[158] These require a regulated business to exercise 'reasonable care' over its business and to ensure that it has in place 'adequate risk management' systems.[159] The need to ensure proper accountability and transparency is emphasised so that the business does not become inured in fraud. The SYSC require a regulated business to apportion management responsibility so that the firm is able to monitor and control its business affairs with reasonable care.[160] The senior management guidance indicates that responsibilities in a regulated firm need to be apportioned to the chief executive, a director or a senior manager[161] with the Board of Directors having the ultimate responsibility of apportioning functions. SYSC 3.1.1R[162] requires that a firm must take 'reasonable care to establish and maintain such systems and controls' as are appropriate to its day-to-day management and well-being and that appropriate management committees are established within the firm to ensure that a reasonable standard of care is exercised to discharge management duties and functions. Where responsibilities for systems and controls are delegated any such delegation must be appropriately supervised and controlled.[163] A penalty of £320,000 was imposed on Abbey National Asset Managers for breach of SYSC 3.1.1 and a failure to implement satisfactory controls for its business and the failure to comply with FSA orders to implement appropriate systems within a reasonable time. A regulated firm must have in place systems and controls for handling the risks of financial crime.[164] The FSA fined the Bank of Ireland £375,000 for breach of SYSC 3.2.6 because of its failure to take reasonable care to counter the risk of its bank draft facility being used as a channel for financial crime and money laundering activities and for ensuring that staff understood their anti-money laundering responsibilities in relation to the recognition and reporting of suspicious

---

[154] FCA, Handbook, PRIN 2.1, http://www.fshandbook.info/FS/html/FCA/PRIN/2/1.

[155] FSA, Handbook Principles for Businesses, PRIN 2:21.1R, http://fsahandbook.info/FSA/html/handbook/PRIN/2.

[156] FSA, Final Notice, Credit Suisse First Boston International, 2002, 11 December, http://www.fsa.gov.uk/pubs/final/creditsuisse-fb_11dec02.pdf.

[157] FCA, Handbook, PRIN 3, http://www.fshandbook.info/FS/html/FCA/PRIN/3.

[158] FCA, Handbook, Senior Management Arrangements, Systems and Controls, http://www.fshandbook.info/FS/html/FCA/SYSC.

[159] FCA, Handbook, Senior Management Arrangements, Systems and Controls, SYSC 1.2.1, http://www.fshandbook.info/FS/html/FCA/SYSC/2/1.

[160] FCA, Handbook, SYSC 2.1.1R, http://www.fshandbook.info/FS/html/FCA/SYSC/2/1; and 3.1.1R, http://www.fshandbook.info/FS/html/FCA/SYSC/3/1.

[161] FCA, Handbook, SYSC 2.1.1–2.1.4, http://www.fshandbook.info/FS/html/FCA/SYSC/2/1.

[162] FCA, Handbook, http://www.fshandbook.info/FS/html/FCA/SYSC/3/1.

[163] FCA, Handbook, SYSC 3.2.3, http://www.fshandbook.info/FS/html/FCA/SYSC/3/2. This is reinforced by the duty to exercise reasonable skill and care in delegating responsibilities to third parties, *Secretary of State for Trade and Industry* v *Baker and others (No 5), Re Barings* [2000] 1 WLR 634.

[164] FCA, Handbook, SYSC 3.2.6R, http://www.fshandbook.info/FS/html/FCA/SYSC/3/2.

transactions. The misuse concerned 40 bank drafts issued between 1998 and 2002 worth approximately £2,000,000.[165]

BANKING LAW IN PRACTICE

In its response to the Parliamentary Commission on Banking Standards report, 'Changing Banks for Good', the government supports the Commission's proposals to strengthen individual accountability among senior employees in the banking sector. The government has therefore introduced a new criminal offence of reckless misconduct in the management of a bank, through the Financial Services Banking Reform Bill 2013. The amendment will propose that senior persons should be held accountable for contraventions of regulatory requirements in their areas of responsibility, unless they can demonstrate that they took all reasonable steps to prevent the contravention occurring or continuing. This will reverse the burden of proof, as the individual will be required to establish their lack of culpability. The Act also involves an extension to the time limit for commencing disciplinary action against senior persons. The offence is limited to senior individuals at a firm who are covered by the new Senior Persons Regime as persons with responsibility for managing the business and the key risks that the firm faces.

The introduction of the new criminal offence only serves to underline the high levels of scrutiny that senior banking personnel can expect in the future. The reversal of the burden of proof will put significant pressure on any senior individuals in the banking sector whose conduct comes under scrutiny.

◼ The approved persons regime under the FSMA 2000

The Companies Act 2006 has codified the duties developed by the courts in respect of the standard of skill and care expected from directors and senior management and this has been enhanced by the FSMA 2000. Additionally, the FCA handbook deals with specific governance features attributable to the financial services sector. Thus, while directors and senior management must display a reasonable standard of skill and care the FCA regime not only governs who can undertake regulated activities at the institutional level but also who is responsible for discharging a firm's responsibilities on its behalf.[166] Under s.59 of the FSMA 2000, a person cannot carry out a controlled function unless he is approved by the FCA and approval will only be granted if the person in question meets the FCA's 'fit and proper' person requirements before taking up appointment. The regulated firm is under a duty to exercise reasonable skill and care when appointing persons to controlled functions to ensure they are appropriate for the relevant position. Whether or not a person requires approval will depend on whether or not he performs a 'controlled function',[167] i.e. those functions that 'add value' to the regulatory process or assist the FCA in carrying out its regulatory objectives. One of the criticisms in respect of corporate governance in banks and other financial institutions following the 2007–09 crisis

---

[165] FSA, 31 August 2004, Final Notice: The Governor and Company of the Bank of Ireland, http://www.fsa.gov.uk/pubs/final/boi_31aug04.pdf.

[166] FCA, Handbook, SYSC 1.2, http://www.fshandbook.info/FS/html/FCA/SYSC/1/2.

[167] FCA, Handbook, APER 1.2G, http://www.fshandbook.info/FS/html/FCA/APER/1/2.

was that many in top management positions in the banking sector had no banking background or banking experience.[168] The FSA, the then financial services regulator, announced that, in future, its approach to senior banking appointments would be much more questioning and it would interview many more candidates for such positions.[169]

Controlled functions are not merely those functions and duties discharged by directors and senior management of a regulated firm, but extend to any activities that require a customer interface or customer contact.[170] Thus, employees who have contact with customers either in an advisory or other capacity to arrange transactions must be approved persons under the FSMA 2000. A function is controlled when it fulfils the conditions established in s.59(5)–(7) of the FSMA 2000 namely where the individual has significant influence over the conduct of approved persons and where the individual deals with the property of customer. The FCA has also listed functions that require prior approval, including: functions that relate to the governing body (directors, chief executive officer and non-executive directors); required functions (money laundering officer); systems and control functions; significant management functions (internal functions); and customer functions.

The fit and proper test for approved persons

An individual performing a controlled function is required to be approved as a fit and proper person.[171] The FCA has established a number of factors that will be taken into consideration in determining the fit and proper person requirement, such as 'honesty', 'integrity', 'reputation', 'competence', 'capability' and 'financial soundness'.[172] An assessment of the individual's character, and the nature and complexity of the regulated business will be required. The individual needs to satisfy the FCA that he is fit and proper to undertake a regulated business and the FCA has statutory authority to withdraw or restrict approval of a person, if it considers them as no longer satisfying the fit and proper person requirement. The FCA takes a cumulative approach to regulatory failure but will also take an individual incident approach.[173] PRA will apply only principles 1–4, 8 and 11 in carrying out its regulatory functions.[174]

In *Secretary of State* v *Ettinger, Re Swift*[175] the Court allowed an appeal by the Secretary of State for Trade and Industry under s.6 of the Company Directors Disqualification Act 1986 in relation to the length of the disqualification following a persistent failure by the directors to discharge their statutory obligations to file documents. The court expressed the view that the failure showed a blatant disregard for accountability and could not be condoned even if the directors lacked a dishonest intent. Taken cumulatively the administrative failures showed a persistent disregard, while the repeated failures to prepare and submit proper accounts, called into question the willingness to work with the regulators.

---

[168] See Ch. 3.

[169] See Ch. 3.

[170] FCA, Handbook, SUPP 10A 5.1, http://www./www.fshandbook.info/FS/html/FCA/SUP/10A/5.

[171] FCA, Handbook, FIT 1.1.1, http://www.fshandbook.info/FS/html/FCA/FIT/1/1.

[172] FCA, Handbook, FIT 1.3.1, http://www.fshandbook.info/FS/html/FCA/FIT/1/3; FIT 2.1–2.3, http://www.fshandbook.info/FS/html/FCA/FIT/2; also Principle 2 Statements of Principle and Code of Practice for Approved Persons, http://www.fshandbook.info/FS/html/FCA/APER/2/1A.

[173] *Secretary of State* v *Ettinger, Re Swift 736 Ltd* [1993] BCLC 896 at 900; see also: Case Comment: Failure to file accounts and keep books, Com. Law, 1993, 14(6), 120.

[174] FCA, Handbook, http://fshandbook.info/FS/html/handbook/PRIN/2/1.

[175] [1993] BCLC 896.

A person's probity is key for him to be an approved person and the FCA will have high regard for a person's honesty and integrity. The FCA will take into consideration whether the person has been convicted of any criminal offence (including spent convictions) and the FCA will pay particular regard to offences of dishonesty, fraud, financial crime or offences (whether committed in the UK or overseas) under the companies legislation or other financial services legislation.[176] The FCA takes into consideration whether a person has been convicted of illegal deposit-taking, leading to a custodial sentence, or whether the person, or any business with which he is, or has been, associated has been investigated, disciplined, censured, suspended or criticised by a regulatory body, court or tribunal[177] and whether the person has been truthful and candid in his past dealings[178] with any regulatory bodies. Thus, a person who fails to disclose convictions and a custodial sentence for illegal deposit-taking may be prohibited from undertaking a regulated business.[179] Similarly, a person who fails to disclose convictions for dishonesty will not be approved as fit and proper person by the FCA.[180]

The FCA will take into account a person's reputation and competency in determining whether he is a fit and proper person and a person's knowledge, experience and skill, and his ability to discharge his responsibilities to a standard of the reasonable man will be relevant.[181] Thus, in *Brazier v Skipton Rock Co Ltd*[182] the court said whether a person is fit and proper would depend on whether he is, on a fair assessment, able to perform a particular function in the light of the problems and the associated risk. The law will expect him to exercise reasonable skill and care in the discharge of these duties and keep abreast of the company's business.[183] The court will not expect each director to have detailed knowledge of the day-to-day conduct of the company's affairs but they must have such knowledge individually and collectively to responsibly supervise and monitor the company's affairs.[184] Following a Parliamentary Committee investigation into the 2007–09 financial crisis a criticism raised was that many of the senior banking management had no background or experience of banking itself.[185] If the director professes to have any special skills and expertise then he is expected to bring those to his office and display a higher standard of skill and care. The FCA recognises that the directors will have variable skills and bring a variable level of competence and expertise to the business and therefore a person may be fit and proper for the purposes of holding office in one firm but not fit and proper to hold office in another firm or to carry out other functions.

---

[176] FCA, Handbook, FIT 2.1.3, http://www.fshandbook.info/FS/html/FCA/FIT/2/1.

[177] FCA, Handbook, FIT 2.1.3, http://www.fshandbook.info/FS/html/FCA/FIT/2/1.

[178] FCA, Handbook, FIT 2.1.3, http://www.fshandbook.info/FS/html/FCA/FIT/2/1.

[179] FSA, Final Notice: John Edward Rourke, 18 November 2004, http://www.fsa.gov.uk/pubs/final/je-rourke_18nov04.pdf.

[180] FSA, Final Notice: Palani Jegatheeswaran, 6 December 2007, http://www.fsa.gov.uk/pubs/final/jegatheeswaran_6dec07.pdf.

[181] *Gibson v Skibs A/S Marina and Orkla Grobe A/B and Smith Coggins Ltd* [1966] 2 ALL ER 476 at 478; *Dorchester Finance Co Ltd v Stebbing* [1989] BCLC 498.

[182] [1962] 2 All ER 955 at 957.

[183] *Re Westmid Packing Services Ltd* [1998] 2 All ER 124.

[184] *Re Brian D Pierson (Contractors) Ltd* [2001] 1 BCLC 275.

[185] House of Commons Treasury Committee, Financial Crisis: Regulation and Supervision, Fourteenth Report of Session 2008–09, HC 767, http://www.parliament.the-stationery-office.co.uk/pa/cm200809/cmselect/cmtreasy/767/767.pdf.

The assessment criteria

The approved persons regime is governed by a number of principles that illustrate the standards expected of persons who undertake controlled functions. In addition to the fit and proper person principles the FCA has also developed a Code of Practice to assist with the interpretation of these principles. The Code gives examples of the kind of acts or omissions that may give rise to an approval being reviewed because of a failure to comply with the principles.[186] Principles 1 and 2 concentrate on the carrying out of approved functions with 'integrity'[187] and provide that those exercising such functions should act with due skill, care and diligence.[188] Principles 3 and 4 require the observance of proper standards of market conduct[189] and the approved persons to cooperate with the FCA. Principles 5–7 relate to those in senior management positions and recognise that such persons have additional responsibilities in respect of the business. Such persons are required to ensure that the business is organised in a manner so it can be effectively controlled with reasonable care[190] and for approved persons to exercise due skill, care and diligence in their management responsibility.[191] Principle 7 requires an approved person to ensure that their firm complies with regulatory requirements.[192] In contrast to the principles the Code highlights the kind of acts of omissions that can lead to a breach of the principles, as well as highlighting the types of conduct that may be deemed to be negligent or lead to criminal charges. Other examples of conduct, while not amounting to negligence or criminal conduct, may nevertheless, amount to a breach of the principles. Thus for example, conduct which amounts to misleading clients or producing false information may, at least, raise questions about a person's lack of integrity but could result in liability for negligence or criminal sanctions. A failure to inform a client fully about the risks associated with a financial product may lead to questions about the approved person acting with appropriate skill, care and diligence.

Withdrawal of approval as a fit and proper person

The FCA has the power to withdraw approval if it considers an individual unfit to take up a controlled function. The factors taken into account for the withdrawal of approval include the person's honesty, integrity, competence and capability. Any decision taken by the FCA in respect of a person's fitness, including the decision to withdraw approval, must be commensurate to the risks posed by the individual and a withdrawal of approval must comply with the enforcement guidelines and the decision to withdraw approval needs to comply with the

---

[186] FCA, Handbook, http://www.fshandbook.info/FS/html/FCA/FIT/2/1; also Statements of Principle and Code of Practice for Approved Persons, http://www.fshandbook.info/FS/html/FCA/APER/3.

[187] FCA, Handbook, http://www.fshandbook.info/FS/html/FCA/FIT/2/1; also Statements of Principle and Code of Practice for Approved Persons, http://www.fshandbook.info/FS/html/FCA/APER/4/1.

[188] FCA, Handbook, http://www.fshandbook.info/FS/html/FCA/FIT/2/2, also Statements of Principle and Code of Practice for Approved Persons, http://www.fshandbook.info/FS/html/FCA/APER/4/2.

[189] FCA, Handbook, Statements of Principle and Code of Practice for Approved Persons, Chapter 2, The Statements of Principle for Approved Persons, APER 2, 2.2.1.2, http://www.fshandbook.info/FS/html/FCA/APER/2/1A and APER 3, 3.1.4G (1), http://www.fshandbook.info/FS/html/FCA/APER/3/3.

[190] FCA, Handbook, Statements of Principle and Code of Practice for Approved Persons, Chapter 2, The Statements of Principle for Approved Persons, APER 4.5.1G, http://www.fshandbook.info/FS/html/FCA/APER/2/1A.

[191] FCA, Handbook, Statements of Principle and Code of Practice for Approved Persons, http://www.fshandbook.info/FS/html/FCA/APER/2/1A.

[192] FSA, Handbook, Statements of Principle and Code of Practice for Approved Persons, Chapter 2, The Statements of Principle for Approved Persons, APER 4.5.1, http://www.fshandbook.info/FS/html/FCA/APER/2/1A.

enforcement guidelines. In *Cox v The FSA (Ian Douglas Cox v Financial Services Authority)*[193] an application for approval was refused on the grounds of Cox's previous dishonest conduct that led to two insurance companies and the Inland Revenue being defrauded. The decision of the tribunal took into account that the incident, although a one-off, was not fully resolved and the Inland Revenue had not been given the opportunity to seek relief for the dishonesty. In *Hoodless and Blackwell v The FSA (Geoffrey Alan Hoodless & Sean Michael Blackwell v Financial Services Authority)*[194] the tribunal rejected the FSA's decision to withdraw approval on the basis that the individuals concerned were not fit and proper on the grounds of dishonesty in respect of incorrect statements relating to the placement of a share issue. The tribunal followed the test established in *R v Ghosh*[195] where it was said that an individual was dishonest if he must have realised, by the standards of the reasonable and honest man, that his conduct was dishonest. The tribunal concluded that failure to volunteer information to regulators was not evidence of improper motive or lack of integrity and an isolated lack of honesty did not automatically amount to dishonesty.

The appropriate regulator, FCA or PRA, may under s.33 of the FSMA 2000 cancel or withdraw the Part 4A permission and consequently there is no regulated activity the firm may undertake.[196]

FCA powers of investigations, censure and enforcement

Section 68 of the Financial Services Act 2012 enables the Treasury to appoint a person to carry out an inquiry where events have occurred which give rise to concern and which either relate to the carrying out of regulated activities, the issue of listed securities, recognised clearing houses or recognised inter-bank payment systems or collective investment schemes. Such an enquiry will be permitted where the events under investigation may not have occurred but for a serious failure in the legislative regime for regulation, or its operation. Where such a breach is investigated the Treasury may appoint a person to conduct an enquiry and issue any terms of remit. Alternatively, ss.73 and 74 of the Financial Services Act 2012 require the FCA and PRA to investigate events and to report to the Treasury on the result of the investigation. The duty applies where events have occurred which relate to those regulated by the FCA or the PRA, or within their respective regulatory remits which have, or may have caused serious harm to the values underpinning the FCAs and the PRAs operational objectives (in the case of the FCA: appropriate degree of protection for consumers, the integrity of the UK financial system, effective competition in the interests of consumers; and in the PRA where the conduct undermines financial stability), and where those events may not have occurred but for a serious failure in the legislative regime for regulation, or its operation. The powers extend to the rights to seek information and documents from regulated firms to assess the level of compliance. These powers extend to a wide range of operations and associated persons, for example, information in respect of members in order to monitor ownership or assist an overseas regulator.

The FCA may initiate an investigation if it appears that a firm or individual has contravened its permission, breached an FCA rule or is no longer a fit and proper person to

---

[193] http://www.judgmental.org.uk/judgments/UKFSM/2003/[2003]%20UKFSM%20FSM003.html.
[194] http://www.judgmental.org.uk/judgments/UKFSM/2003/[2003]%20UKFSM%20FSM007.html.
[195] *R v Ghosh* [1982] 2 WLR 110.
[196] FCA, Handbook, SUPP 6.52A and 6.5.2B, http://fshandbook.info/FS/html/handbook/SUP/6/5.

perform functions in respect of a regulated firm.[197] The investigation may require the firm or approved persons to assist the investigator by answering questions on the issue or issues.[198] The investigation process is a formal attempt to gather information and documents, to assess whether the enforcement division is required to take action. Whether the FCA makes public its investigation will take into consideration the necessity to maintain market confidence and ensure consumer protection.

In most cases fines and the threat of adverse publicity assist in maintaining market discipline without the institution's licence being restricted or revoked. Sections 63(1) and 56(2) of the FSMA 2000 provide authority for the FCA to withdraw approval or prohibit an individual from undertaking controlled functions if the FCA considers such a person is not fit and proper to perform controlled functions. The FCA may take a number of factors into consideration in deciding whether or not to exercise its power to withdraw approval, including any events outside the controlled function remit. The FCA will assess whether the approved person undertakes the controlled functions with probity, competence and integrity.[199] A breach of the regulatory objectives under the FSMA 2000 is a significant indication of whether disciplinary action should be taken. Sections 45–48 of the FSMA 2000 allows the FCA to impose, vary or remove requirements relating to acquiring control and the FCA can change the asset requirements of regulated firms. The FCA can also impose limits to control the number of customers a firm can deal with, or the types of investment undertaken or impose requirements in respect of not taking new business.

The external auditor

Following the collapse of Johnson Matthey, the Banking Act 1987 formally introduced the role of the external auditor to banking supervision and the closure of BCCI brought under scrutiny the role of external auditors who were responsible for BCCI and the group accounts. BCCI losses exceeded £9 billion and resulted in the prosecution of senior directors implicated in fraud. The external auditors, PricewaterhouseCoopers, were fined £975,000 by the Joint Disciplinary Scheme Tribunal (now the Accounting Investigation and Discipline Board) for failure to show a complete view of the way BCCI was managed in its annual audit reports and thus failed to give a 'true and fair view' of the state of the financial affairs of the bank and the group. The role of auditors again came under scrutiny with the collapse of Barings when internal failings on the part of the management, regulators and auditors were highlighted.[200]

The use of external auditors by the FSA

An audit under the Companies Act 2006 requires the auditor to verify whether the financial statements give a 'true and fair view' of the financial state of the company.[201] The audit is based on a contract between the auditor and the regulated firm, his client and the auditor

---

[197] FSMA 2000, s.168(4)–(5).

[198] FCA, Handbook, http://www.fshandbook.info/FS/html/FCA/APER/4/7.

[199] FCA, Handbook, http://www.fshandbook.info/FS/html/FCA/FIT/2/1.

[200] Bingham, Report of the Board of Banking Supervision Inquiry into the Circumstances of the Collapse of Barings, London, HMSO, 18 July 1995.

[201] The audit has a limited life and in *Berg & Sons v Adams* [1993] BCLC 1045 at 1055, Hobhouse J recognised that the utility of the audited accounts diminishes with the passage of time as more up-to-date information becomes available which provides a better idea of the financial viability of the firm.

will be required to undertake work in accordance with professional standards and ethics.[202] The auditor is required to express an opinion based on a 'true and fair view' of whether the financial statements prepared, in all material respects, are in accordance with an applicable financial reporting framework.[203]

Although the relationship between the external auditor[204] and the firm is one bound within the parameters of confidentiality which would normally prevent an auditor from disclosing information about a client (the banking firm) to a third party, the work of the auditor falls within the exceptions of confidentiality. The Banking Act 1987 originally gave the auditor the right to communicate information to the regulator and this has been revised in the new SAS 620 (Statements of Auditing Standards),[205] which require auditors to bring to the attention of the regulator any information they come across during the ordinary course of performing an audit considered to be relevant to the regulator's remit of responsibility and any matter of material significance to the regulator. SAS 620 places the auditor under a general duty to report to the regulator information obtained during an audit that warrants such disclosure or warrants being passed on in the public interest.

Methods of redress

The FSMA 2000 confers different methods of redress and accountability in favour of consumers: the single Ombudsman scheme, the Independent Complaints Commissioner and the Financial Services Compensation Scheme. Consumers therefore have recourse to these alternative remedies without having to resort to the courts for the acts or omissions of the regulated firms.

The FCA Ombudsman Scheme

The Financial Ombudsman Scheme (FOS) has allowed consumers to seek redress against financial firms once internal complaints procedures at individual firm level have been exhausted. The Financial Ombudsman scheme established under Part XVI of the FSMA 2000, places on the Ombudsman the responsibility to deal independently with disputes efficiently and with 'minimum formality'.[206] The FCA requires regulated firms to have in place an effective mechanism for handling customer complaints.[207] The internal procedure must deal with all aspects of the management of the complaint from receipt, investigation and decision[208] and if the complaint is upheld the firm will be required to pay 'fair compensation' for any acts or omissions. The final response of the firm must inform the complainant to the FOS scheme, if the customer is still unsatisfied.

The Independent Complaints Commissioner

The Independent Complaints Commissioner has been established to allow consumers and firms to seek relief for losses caused by the acts or omissions of the previously the FSA, and

[202] International Standards on Auditing 200, http://www.ifac.org/sites/default/files/downloads/a008-2010-iaasb-handbook-isa-200.pdf.

[203] International Standards on Auditing 200, para. 2, http://www.ifac.org/sites/default/files/downloads/a008-2010-iaasb-handbook-isa-200.pdf, ISA.

[204] The role of internal auditors is discussed in the context of corporate governance in Ch. 3.

[205] The auditor's right and duty to report to regulators in the financial sector, http://www.cpaireland.ie/UserFiles/File/Technical%20Resources/Auditing/SAS620%20.pdf.

[206] Section 225(1) FSMA 2000, as amended by the Financial Services Act 2012, Seced. 11.

[207] FCA, Handbook, *DISP* 2.1.1, http://www.fshandbook.info/FS/html/FCA/DISP/2/1.

[208] FCA, Handbook, *DISP* 2.1.1, http://www.fshandbook.info/FS/html/FCA/DISP/2/1.

now FCA.[209] The mandate of the Complaints Commissioner is to deal with 'allegations of misconduct' by the FCA and deal with acts or omissions relating to 'unreasonable delay', 'unprofessional behaviour' and 'bias and lack of integrity' where the complainant thinks the FCA's investigation is unsatisfactory. The remit of the Complaints Commissioner is to investigate procedural failures rather than legislative failures.[210] The guidance sets out the procedure to be followed and establishes that the FCA must first handle the complaint.

Financial services compensation scheme

The introduction of a single financial services regulator implemented a single compensation scheme and replaced the various individual schemes that existed prior to the FSMA 2000. The objective of the scheme, as highlighted by the FSA, was to secure 'the appropriate degree of protection for consumers and maintaining confidence in the financial system', although the FSMA 2000, Part XV[211] provides the framework for the compensation scheme. While, the FSA, now FCA, was responsible for establishing the scheme it is not responsible for administrating the scheme, which lies with the Financial Services Compensation Scheme Ltd (FSCS), a separate corporate body. It handles compensation claims relating to accepting deposits, designated investment and insurance business, insurance mediation, mortgage advice, arranging mortgages and all activities now regulated by the FCA. However, the FSCS is not independent of the FCA and is dependent on the FCA to confer powers, which enable it raise sufficient funds to meet the costs of discharging it duties.

The FSCS compensates those with a protected claim, which means that an individual must have an account or joint account with a regulated institution. A firm is determined to be in default when the FCA, the FSCS or the judicial authority determine that the institution is unlikely to be able to satisfy protected claims against it, i.e. the institution is unlikely to be able to repay customer deposits on demand or other agreed terms. This requires the FSCS to work with the liquidator or administrator to determine the default, to whom compensation is owed and the amount. The compensation scheme does not protect 100 per cent of the deposits held by UK authorised banks and the idea that the customer should bear some of the risk is shared in several jurisdictions. Following the 2007–09, banking crisis and to restore customer confidence following the nationalisation of Northern Rock, the loss of confidence in the Halifax Banking Group and the danger of a global systemic collapse, the Brown government raised the maximum level of protection conferred on single account holders to £50,000 (£100,000 for joint account holders) which was raised to £85,000 by the end of 2010.[212]

The time scale and speed with which claims are processed and compensation paid to depositors has also raised concerns with many BCCI depositors waiting several years for compensation. In the midst of the 2007–09 banking crisis the government passed the Banking (Special Provisions) Act 2008 which amended the powers of the Treasury and the FCA in relation to the FSCS, and the FCA proposes that compensation to depositors should be paid within a targeted seven days from the regulated firm defaulting. This includes the FSCS having an enhanced ability to settle claims without investigation where the value of the claim

---

[209] FSA, Investigation of Complaints Against the FSA, Policy Statement PS 93, August 2001, http://www.fsa.gov.uk/pubs/policy/ps93.pdf.

[210] http://www.fsa.gov.uk/Pages/Library/Communication/PR/2001/109.shtml.

[211] As amended by the Banking Act 2009, and the Financial Services Act 2012, schedule 10.

[212] Financial Services Compensation Scheme, http://www.fscs.org.uk/what-we-cover/eligibility-rules/compensation-limits/.

is likely to be less than the cost of the investigation. Section 123(1) of the Banking (Special Provisions) Act 2008 provides that compensation payments may be made or arranged by the FSCS, rather than being funded from the assets of the failed bank. Alternatively, where a transfer of accounts to another financial institution is possible so that depositors have continued access to their funds and banking services generally, the FSCS can make monies available to fund that transfer. The Act has also put in place a system to increase the liquidity of the FSCS to ensure that it can deal with all future claims expeditiously. Section 123(2) of the 2008 Act allows the Treasury to introduce a 'pre-funding' scheme that imposes levies on regulated firms in order to build up a contingency fund ahead of potential defaults.

Bank regulator liable for loss to depositors from bank insolvency?

The collapse of BCCI[213] led to extensive litigation as BCCI liquidators sought to impose liability in an attempt to recover some of the losses suffered by the depositors, creditors and employees of the bank. The litigation challenged long-established legal principles. One of the issues under consideration was whether the Bank of England, as the then bank regulator, could be made liable for misfeasance in public office. The issue of the potential liability of the banking regulator was examined and the following questions explored:

- Was there a duty of care owed by bank regulators to depositors or potential depositors?

- Was there liability for misfeasance in public office arising from the statutory duty not to act in bad faith?

Liability at common law

In terms of potential liability at common law UK bank regulators have traditionally been well protected. Cases concerning liability in negligence have been restrictive and the courts have not imposed a duty of care on regulators in respect of economic loss. This reluctance to impose a duty of care on bank regulators was confirmed in *Yuen Kun-Yeu v Attorney General of Hong Kong*[214] and then in *Davis v Radcliff*.[215]

In *Yuen Kun-Yeu v General of Hong Kong*the question before the Privy Council was whether the Commissioner of deposit-taking institutions (the banking regulator) in Hong Kong,

---

[213] In July 1991, the Bank of England presented a petition to wind up the Bank of Credit and Commerce International (BCCI) on the grounds that it was in the public interest that the bank should be wound up, or alternatively on the grounds that BCCI was insolvent. The petition was founded on allegations of dishonest and fraudulent conduct by BCCI management. The accounts and records of BCCI were maintained in a form that made it extremely difficult to reconstitute exactly what had occurred. At the time the winding-up petition was filed, the provisional liquidators estimated that there were approximately 48,400 sterling accounts with some £652 million involved. Of those, there were 36,800 depositors whose deposits were between zero and £1,000. The total owed to these depositors amounted to approximately £4.7 million. There were approximately 2,600 depositors between £1,000 and £2,000 with an estimated total owed to them of £3.6 million. There were 5,900 depositors with between £2,000 and £20,000 deposited and a total of approximately £40.5 million owed. The remaining depositors had accounts with deposits in excess of £20,000 (and of whom the largest single depositor had a credit balance of approximately £33 million) and were owed in all approximately £603.6 million. In addition non-sterling accounts held in London numbered around 17,000 with deposits totalling approximately £2.15 billion. Lord Justice Bingham, Inquiry into the Supervision of the Bank of Credit and Commerce International (Bingham Inquiry), 22 October 1992, http://www.official-documents. gov.uk/document/hc9293/hc01/0198/0198.pdf.

[214] [1988] 1 AC 175.

[215] [1990] 2 All ER 536.

owed members of the public who might place deposits with deposit-taking companies a duty to exercise reasonable care to ensure that members of the public did not suffer loss through the affairs of licensed institutions being conducted in a fraudulent or imprudent manner. The Privy Council[216] held that the matter for consideration was whether there existed between the Commissioner and potential depositors with that company such close and direct relations as to place the Commissioner under a duty of care towards would-be depositors, taking into consideration that one of the purposes of the regulatory regime was the protection of persons who deposited money. Although, the restrictions and obligations placed on deposit-taking companies safeguarded against the danger of potential loss caused by the fraudulent conduct of the management or against imprudent management, the discretion given to the Commissioner to register, or remove, such institutions was fundamental to the protection afforded to depositors, or potential depositors.

It was argued for the plaintiffs that while it may be reasonably foreseeable that if an un-creditworthy company were allowed to register, or to remain, on the register of authorised institutions, persons who may in the future place deposits with it, or existing depositors, may be lulled into leaving money with it and risk losing it by relying on the registration. The Privy Council held that the mere foresight of harm does not necessarily establish a duty of care, and future and existing depositors are not the only persons to whose interests the Commissioner should have regard. There was no direct relationship between the Commissioner and those who deposited their money with the deposit-taking institution. The Commissioner had no power to control the day-to-day activities of those who caused loss and damage although he did have the power to stop the company from continuing business: a decision, which was within his discretionary powers. The Privy Council also concluded that there was no relationship between the Commissioner and those unascertained members of the public who might, in future, become exposed to the risk of financial loss through depositing money with the company. Accordingly, the commissioner owed no duty of care because there were not the close and direct relations between him and the plaintiffs to give rise to the duty of care.

Similarly, in *Davis* v *Radcliffe*[217] a claim was brought against the Treasurer of the Isle of Man and members of the Finance Board, the regulatory authority in the Isle of Man, which alleged that the Treasurer and the members of the Finance Board owed a duty of care to the plaintiffs, a breach of which rendered them liable in damages for losses suffered as a result of having deposited money with a bank, such as SIB (South Indian Bank), which had become insolvent. Lord Goff, delivering the opinion of the Privy Council thought the *Davis* case practically indistinguishable from *Yuen Kun-Yeu* and expressed the view that a number of considerations militated against the imposition of a duty of care. He concluded that functions conferred on the Treasurer and the Finance Board were typical functions of modern government, to be exercised in the interests of the general public. These functions tended to be of the broadest kind and in establishing a system of licensing banks, regard must be had to the fact that the licensing system should provide a degree of security for those dealing with banks carrying on business in the Isle of Man, including security for those who deposit money with such banks. The legislature must have intended any licensing system should operate in the

---

[216] See: *Anns* v *Merton London Borough Council* [1978] AC 728; *Hedley Byrne & Co. Ltd* v *Heller and Partners Ltd* [1964] AC 465; *Dorset Yacht Co. Ltd* v *Home Office* [1970] AC 1004; and *Hill* v *Chief Constable of West Yorkshire* [1988] QB 60.

[217] [1990] 2 All ER 536.

interests of the public as a whole and those charged with making such decisions may have to exercise judgements with regard to the future of the banking sector on the Isle of Man, and not merely in respect of the interests of the customers and creditors of the bank. In such circumstances there may be competing considerations, which have to be carefully weighed and balanced in the public interest. Lord Goff concluded that such considerations might necessarily need to be taken into account by modern regulatory authorities. The emphasis on the broader public interest militated against the imposition of a duty of care in favour of any particular section of the public.

Lord Goff then went on to reject the submission that a duty of care could be imposed on the defendants for negligent damage caused arising from the default of a third party (SIB) and that liability might be imposed for purely financial loss flowing from the negligence of a third party. Lord Goff concluded that the circumstances in which such liability will be imposed must be rare and, in the present case, the defendants did not possess sufficient control over the management of SIB to warrant the imposition of any liability.[218] Lord Goff then went on to reject the argument that a duty of care could be imposed in favour of those who may be considering depositing their money with SIB.

Statutory immunity against liability

While, the courts may be sympathetic towards depositors who face financial hardship if their bank becomes insolvent, they have been reluctant to hold the regulator liable for the mismanagement of the boards of directors.[219] Ultimately, the courts will ensure that business decisions are made in compliance with the legal obligations imposed on directors but their role does not extend to oversight and approval of business decisions made by the management. Indeed, the FSA is given express immunity against legal action for damages under the FSMA 2000,[220] which provides that:

> Neither the Authority or any person who is, or is acting as, a member, officer or member of staff of the Authority is to be liable in damages for anything done or omitted in the discharge of the Authority's functions.

However, the immunity will not apply if the act or omission is shown to have been done in bad faith or in respect of an act or omission made unlawful as a result of s.6(1) of the Human Rights Act 1998. While, the immunity conferred by the FSMA 2000 protects both the FCA and its employees from a claim against damages the scope of this protection was examined in *Gulf Insurance Ltd v The Central Bank of Trinidad and Tobago*[221] where the Central Bank intervened to save the Trinidad Co-operative Bank Ltd by restructuring its management and providing new management. Following the recovery of the bank, the plaintiff's purchased a 0.54 per cent share in it. However, during this time two other banks experienced problems and the Central Bank entered into similar rescue plans. The asset structure of the three banks was found to be weak and because this was leaked to the press the Central Bank devised a plan to amalgamate the three banks and create a new bank with a new management. The plaintiff, as shareholder, sought to have the transfer of its assets to the new bank declared void and *ultra vires* and sought damages arguing the fact that the Governor of the Central Bank had

---

[218] cf. *Smith v Leurs* (1945) 70 CLR 256.
[219] *Johnson Matthey Plc v Arthur Young and the Governor of the Bank of England* [1989] 2 All ER 105.
[220] Section 19 (1), schedule 1.
[221] Privy Council Appeal No 78 of 2002, 9 March 2005.

made the decision was not sufficiently independent and the transfer of assets was not lawful. The Privy Council, holding in favour of the plaintiff, awarded damages in conversion on the basis that the failure of the Central Bank to obtain an independent valuation was unlawful. The Central Bank and Financial Institutions (Non-Banking) (Amendment) Act 1986 required an independent valuation of the assets before an amalgamation could be undertaken and that had not be done. Such powers should be restrictively construed and only exercised where the Central Bank acts in good faith and without negligence.

Liability for misfeasance

In *Three Rivers District Council and Others v Bank of England (No 3)*[222] approximately 6,000 former depositors of BCCI (based in the UK and abroad) with accounts in the UK brought a class action against the Bank of England accepting that while the Bank was not liable for damages for acts or omissions[223] in the discharge of its regulatory functions in the absence of bad faith, the Bank was, nevertheless, liable to them for misfeasance in public office in that it had either wrongly granted a licence to BCCI or had failed to revoke BCCI's licence when it knew, believed or suspected that it would probably collapse without being rescued. The Bank of England denied the claim arguing that the tort of misfeasance in public office was (1) an intentional tort and that the plaintiff had to prove that the defendant intended to injure the plaintiff, or that the defendant's acts or omissions were aimed at the plaintiff, or that the defendant knew that his acts or omissions of misfeasance would inevitably and/or necessarily injure the plaintiff; (2) that the plaintiffs had to establish the infringement of an enforceable legal right or interest before they could sue for misfeasance in public office; and (3) that the plaintiff's loss was caused by the fraud of those controlling BCCI and not by any act or omission of the Bank of England.

The trial judge held (and this was not disputed by either the Court of Appeal or the House of Lords) that the tort of misfeasance in public office was concerned with a deliberate and dishonest wrongful abuse of the powers given to a public officer and the purpose of the tort was to provide compensation for those who suffered loss as a result of the improper abuse of power. The tort is based on the principle that such powers must be exercised only for the public good and not for an ulterior or improper motive.[224] The imposition of this form of tort liability is to prevent the injuring of members of the public by deliberate disregard of official duty.[225] It, therefore, applies to an unlawful or unauthorised act by a person holding a public office and that includes the Bank of England, provided the wrong is committed with the requisite mental element.

The mental requirement of the tort of misfeasance

Both the judge at first instance and the Court of Appeal reiterated the principle that an invalid administrative action by itself does not give rise to a cause of action in damages by those who have suffered a loss as a consequence of that action. Something more is required in the case of misfeasance in public office and that must be related to the individual who brings the action. While the cases make it clear that the malice need not be targeted the Court

---

[222] [1996] 3 All ER 558.
[223] Banking Act 1987, s.1(4).
[224] *Three Rivers 1* [2000] 2 WLR 1230, per Lord Steyn, citing Nourse LJ in *Jones v Swansea City Council* [1990] 1 WLR 54 at 85.
[225] *Three Rivers (No 3)* CA.

of Appeal in *Three Rivers (No 3)* expressed the view that there must be a conscious disregard for the interests of those who will be affected by the making of the particular decision. Dishonesty is, therefore, an essential ingredient of the tort of misfeasance in public office. The requirement for knowledge of some sort of the illegality and knowledge (or foresight) of the consequent injury has been discussed in the authorities.[226] However, the interrelationship between dishonesty, knowledge (or foresight) and recklessness was considered in the *Three Rivers (No 3)* case. The crucial element of the tort is the mental element and its effect on the claimant. The tort can, therefore, be established in two alternative ways:

1 Where a public officer performs or omits to perform an act with the object of injuring the plaintiff (i.e. where there was targeted malice or bad faith). This requires proof that a public officer has acted with the intention of injuring the claimant, for example where the defendant, the Prime Minister and Attorney General of Quebec,[227] deprived the claimant of his restaurant licence in revenge for the claimant posting bail for members of the Jehovah's Witnesses sect, against whose activities there had been a campaign); or

2 Where he performs an act, which he knows he has no power to perform and which he knows would, in the ordinary course of events, cause damage or injury of the type, which has in fact been suffered by the claimant.[228] This form, untargeted malice, is made out when a public officer acts in the knowledge that he exceeds his powers, and that his act is likely to injure the claimant.

The most stringent form of the tort of misfeasance, therefore, requires targeted malice and requires proof that the public officer acted with the intention of injuring the claimant. The alternative form of an action for misfeasance may arise where the public officer acts in the knowledge that he exceeds his powers and that his act will probably injure the claimant. Where the tort takes this form the mental element is satisfied where the act or omission is done intentionally by the public officer (a) in the knowledge that it was beyond his powers and that it would probably cause harm to the claimant; or (b) recklessly because, although he was aware that there was serious risk that the claimant would suffer loss due to an act or omission which he knew to be unlawful, he wilfully chose to disregard that risk. It was this latter form of possible liability, which was the focus of the action (untargeted malice) before the House of Lords.

The first judgment of the House of Lords in *Three Rivers* held on the issue of knowledge of the illegality that the claimant must show either that the officer had actual knowledge that the disputed act was unlawful or that the public officer acted with a state of mind of reckless indifference to the illegality. Where the officer knows that his act will probably injure the claimant, or if the person is in a class to which the claimant belongs, it is sufficient that the officer has actual knowledge that the act was unlawful or, in circumstances in which he believes or suspects that the act is beyond his powers, that he does not ascertain whether or not that is so, or fails to take such steps as would be taken by an honest and reasonable man to ascertain the true position.

Lord Hope's judgment also clarifies the exact meaning and role of bad faith. Counsel for the Bank of England had argued that the case should be struck out because the pleadings did

---

[226] See *Bourgoin* Mann J at 740 and Oliver LJ at 777.
[227] E.g. *Roncarelli* v *Duplessis* (1959) 16 D.L.R. (2d) 698.
[228] *The Three Rivers 1* [2000] 2 WLR 1235, per Lord Steyn.

not make specific allegations of dishonesty in the subjective sense of bad faith on the part of officials of the Bank. Lord Hope rejected this argument and effectively held that proof of the elements of the tort in terms of knowledge of unlawfulness of the act or omission and its consequences was sufficient. Proof that the defendant did not care whether the consequences occurred or not is sufficient and bad faith is demonstrated by recklessness on the part of the officer in disregarding the risk. No additional element of dishonesty or bad faith is required.

This was a significant point in favour of the claimants in the *Three Rivers* case. It would have been difficult to prove bad faith outright beyond the unlawfulness and the possible consequences on the part of the officials of the Bank dealing with BCCI. This clarification of the role of bad faith is critical in the application of the tort of misfeasance in its application for remedying administrative wrongs. Reckless administrators are likely to be a more common occurrence that those who are outright dishonest.

Conclusion

The recent changes in bank regulation have followed a long line of formal and informal regulation of the banking sector, which have proven to be weak and non-responsive in the face of financial crisis. The single unitary regulator introduced by the Labour government was intended to provide a 'joined up approach' to the financial regulation. When tested, regulation through the FSA proved to be ineffective and the 2007–9 financial crisis shook confidence in financial regulation and the regulatory bodies. While the banking industry will continue to be regulated through the FSMA 2000, as amended, that regulation will be undertaken not by the FSA, now abolished, but through the Bank of England, as the Central banker. Whether the 'twin peak' approach to bank regulation through the FCA and the PRA can strengthen the banking system so it can withstand national, regional or global crises remains to be seen. History does not bode well!

Further reading

➤ HM Treasury, A new approach to financial regulation: judgement, focus and stability, CM 7874, July 2010.
The Coalition government which took office in May 2010 sought to reform the UK's financial regulatory framework. The proposals sought to provide the Bank of England with control of macro-prudential regulation and oversight of micro-prudential regulation. These proposals outlined the creation of a Financial Policy Committee within the Bank of England. Furthermore, the Financial Services Authority (FSA) would be dismantled in favour of a twin peaks approach to regulation. In place of the FSA would be the Financial Conduct Authority (FCA) and the Prudential Regulation Authority (PRA).

➤ Sassoon, The Tripartite Review: A review of the UK's Tripartite system of financial regulation in relation to financial stability, March 2009, http://www.conservatives.com/News/News_stories/2009/03/Osborne_welcomes_Sassoon_report_into_tripartite_financial_regulation.aspx.
The Sassoon Report was commissioned by the opposition Conservative Party in October 2008 to form the Conservative Party's position on the regime of financial regulation in the UK. The Report

recommended an overhaul of the tripartite regime which shared responsibilities between the Financial Services Authority (FSA), HM Treasury and the Bank of England, due to a lack of communication and awareness of who bore overall responsibility.

➤ The Turner Review: A regulatory response to the global financial crisis, March 2009, http://www.fsa.gov.uk/pubs/other/turner_review.pdf. The Review concluded that what made the 2007–09 crisis was the global nature of the financial crisis.

The Turner Review was commissioned by the Chancellor of the Exchequer Alistair Darling in October 2008 to review the causes of the financial crisis. The Turner Review makes a series of recommendations on the changes in regulation and supervision to create a more robust banking system for the future. The Review recognises the difficult task of enhancing stability in the macro-economic climate of the financial crisis.

➤ Ciro, T. (2009) The global financial crisis: causes and implications for regulation, parts 1 and 2, *Journal of International Banking Law and Financial Regulation*.

This article critically examines the global financial crisis and considers the causes of the current crisis alongside the implications for global financial regulation. In the first part of the article, the authors consider why the global financial crisis occurred, and in the second part, they assess what may be enacted to address the identified problems.

➤ Arora, A. (2006) The Statutory System of the bank supervision and the failure of BCCI, *J.B.L.*, 487.

This article reviews the legal issues considered by the House of Lords in *Three Rivers DC v Bank of England (No. 3)*. This article further details BCCI's history from before the grant of a full banking licence to its collapse in 1991, and issues of European Community law raised by the case. The article further examines the court's analysis of the requirements for the tort of misfeasance in public office and its application in relation to the grant of a banking licence in 1980, and the failure to revoke this in 1990 or before the actual closure.

➤ Dijkstra, R. (2009) Liability of financial regulators: Defensive conduct or careful supervision, 10(4), *Journal of Banking Regulation*, 269–284.

This article provides positive economic analysis to examine the impact of liability rules affecting Dutch financial regulators on these regulators' behaviour, to test the theories that subjecting financial regulators to tortious liability has a chilling effect on their performance or, alternatively, provides incentives for them to undertake careful market supervision. Outlines a basic economic model of regulator liability, and assesses its accuracy when applied to the Dutch liability regime.

The banker and customer relationship and the unfair terms in banking contracts

Chapter overview

The aim of this chapter is to:

➤ Explain the contractual nature of the banker and customer relationship with reference to the lack of a 'model contract'.

➤ Examine the question of who, in law, will be treated as a customer and some of the different types of customers the bank may deal with.

➤ The effect of standard form contracts and exclusion or limitation of liability contracts in banking law.

➤ Examine the scope and nature of the work of the Financial Services Authority and the Office of Fair Trading (before both bodies were abolished) in the area of unfair contract terms in banking contracts.

Introduction

It is trite law that the banker and customer relationship is based on the principles of contract law, but that relationship is rarely reduced to a single written contract. Where special services are provided to the customer, beyond the opening of a basic account, e.g. the provision of a loan, overdraft facility or a debit card, then the customer will sign separate agreements, which will govern the provision of these services by the bank. In almost all circumstances the customer will sign a mandate with the bank, for the provision of services, on the banker's terms. The banker and customer relationship is, therefore, governed by a variety of written terms under contract law, supplemented by implied contractual terms introduced and developed by the courts, statute and voluntary codes of banking practice.[1] In 1986, the Jack Report stated that over 90 per cent of the adult population maintained accounts with a bank[2] and by 2004 that figure had increased to 95 per cent of the adult population.[3] The 2010 Financial Inclusion

---

[1] FSA, Banking Conduct of Business Sourcebook, http://www.fsa.gov.uk/Pages/Doing/Regulated/bcobs/index.shtml.
[2] Jack, Banking Services: Law and Practice, Report by the Review Committee (Chairman: Professor R.B. Jack), Cm. 622, London 1986, para. 2 20.
[3] APACS, *Yearbook of Payment Statistics*, 2004, p. 6.

Task Force Report[4] found that 52 per cent of the UK population without access to bank accounts would like access to such facilities and the European Commission, in July 2011, adopted a Recommendation,[5] which stated that as a fundamental principle all adult consumers should have access to basic payment accounts throughout the EU.[6] This basic account should include the facility to deposit and withdraw cash into and from the account. It should also enable the consumer to make essential payment transactions such as receiving income or benefits, paying bills or taxes, and purchasing goods and services, including through direct debit, credit transfer and the use of a payment card. The basic account may also give the opportunity to the consumer to initiate payment orders via the payment service provider's online banking facilities where technically possible. However, access to credit is not an automatic component of or a right attached to a basic payment account. In the UK the banking sector responded by offering customers the basic bank account, which does not permit an overdraft, while the Post Office responded by providing universal banking.[7]

Although it is common practice for customers to sign a bank mandate when opening an account, the reality is that a customer who opens an account, with a bank will rarely read the detailed terms of the mandate, or contract, he signs and thus becomes bound by terms which he has not read, or fully understood.[8] While the mandate, or contract, will contain some[9] of the terms of the legal agreement, such terms do not attempt to exhaustively define the features of the banker and customer relationship. Even if the customer did read the terms of the mandate he is rarely in a position to negotiate such terms and will, generally, sign the contract on the basis of the standard terms imposed by the bank. The use of standard terms may, therefore, lead to a significant imbalance in the contractual relations between the parties and may undermine the interests of the contracting parties. Additionally, widespread unfair practices with regard to contractual terms may distort business practices both within the banking sector, and the wider economy.[10] Where unfair terms are found in contracts governing the banker and customer relationship the distortion will have ramifications beyond the individual customer, since such an imbalance will have a detrimental effect on the financial well-being of consumers generally, and more specifically, their ability to access the banking and credit markets. Before the nature of the work undertaken by the FAS and OFT in the area of unfair terms is discussed we will examine the question of who is a customer under the law.

---

[4] Financial Inclusion Task Force, Banking services and poorer households, December 2010, p. 6, http://www.hm-treasury.gov.uk/d/fin_inclusion_taskforce_poorerhouseholds_dec2010.pdf.

[5] Commission Recommendation 2011/442/EU, Access to a basic payment account, 18 July 2011, http://eur-lex.europa.eu/LexUriServ/LexUriServ.do?uri=OJ:L:2011:190:0087:01:EN:HTML.

[6] In 2010 it was found that 30 million adults in the EU did not have any bank account facilities: Study on the costs and benefits of policy actions in the field of ensuring access to a basic bank account, 2010, http://ec.europa.eu/internal_market/finservices-retail/inclusion_en.htm#study.

[7] See Ch. 1.

[8] *L'Estrange* v *Graucob Ltd* [1934] 2 KB 394.

[9] The Jack Committee on Banking Services rejected the concept of a 'model contract', even for business customers, on the basis that the general mandate signed by the customer, on the opening of his account, gives the bank flexibility to respond to competition and developments, Banking Services: Law and Practice, Cm 622, 1989.

[10] Commission of the European Communities, Report from the Commission on the Implementation of Council Directive 93/13/EEC of 5 April 1993 on Unfair Terms in Consumer Contracts, Brussels, 27 April 2000, COM (2000) 248 final, http://ec.europa.eu/consumers/cons_int/safe_shop/unf_cont_terms/uct03_en.pdf.

Who is a customer?

The question of who is a 'customer' within the context of the banker and customer relationship is of practical significance for the purposes of the application of certain contractual and statutory obligations, which regulate the scope of the banker and customer relationship. For example, the implied contractual terms determine the scope of duties owed by the parties to the banker and customer relationship, while statute generally determines the scope of defences available to the bank in payment transactions, as well imposing other obligations on the parties. Thus, for example, the implied contractual terms under the banker and customer relationship impose certain duties on the bank including an obligation on the bank to conform to the customer's mandate and a duty of confidentiality to its customer. Additionally, as we have seen, the nature of the standard form contract entered into between the bank and customer will subject the contract to the test of fairness under UCTA 1977 and UTCCR 1999. Other statutory provisions which regulate the banker and customer relationship, for example, are s.75(1) of the Bills of Exchange Act 1882 which deals with the right of the customer to countermand the payment of cheques, while s.75(2) deals with the termination of the banker and customer relationship on the death of the customer and s.4 of the Cheques Act 1957 deals with the liability of the collecting bank where it receives payment of a cheque for a customer who, it is discovered subsequently, does not have valid title to the instrument. Moreover, UCTA 1977 and UTCCRs 1999 provides protection under contract law to a customer, who enters into a contract with the bank, as a consumer.

While, the term 'customer' therefore remains undefined by statute, the 'customer due diligence'[11] (CDD)[12] measures implement requirements intended to assist verification of the customer's identity and support the discovery of the 'purpose and intended nature' of the business relationship. The CDD measures must be adopted when the bank establishes (a) an ongoing 'business relationship' (i.e., the normal banker and customer relationship)[13] or (b) carries out 'an occasional transaction' above 15,000 euros,[14] or (c) suspects money laundering or terrorist financing,[15] or (d) doubts the veracity of the information.[16] The measures must be adopted before acting for the 'customer' and on a 'risk sensitive' basis at other appropriate times.[17] The regulations permit for verification to be completed during the establishment of the relationship.[18]

---

[11] Previously known as 'know your customer' requirements.

[12] Money Laundering Regulations 2007, SI 2007/2157 (as amended by SI 2007/3299 and SI 2009/209).

[13] Money Laundering Regulations 2007, SI 2007/2157 (as amended by SI 2007/3299 and SI 2009/209). Regulation 7(1)(a) defines a 'business relationship' as one intended to have 'an element of duration'.

[14] Money Laundering Regulations 2007, SI 2007/2157 (as amended by SI 2007/3299 and SI 2009/209, reg. 7(1)(b)). Occasional transaction is defined under reg. 2(1) as one above the financial threshold that is not part of a 'business relationship' and 'whether the transaction is carried out in a single operation or several operations which appear linked'.

[15] Money Laundering Regulations 2007, SI 2007/2157 (as amended by SI 2007/3299 and SI 2009/209, Reg. 7(1)(c)).

[16] Money Laundering Regulations 2007, SI 2007/2157 (as amended by SI 2007/3299 and SI 2009/209, Reg. 7(1)(d)).

[17] Money Laundering Regulations 2007, SI 2007/2157 (as amended by SI 2007/3299 and SI 2009/209, Reg. 7(2)).

[18] Money Laundering Regulations 2007, SI 2007/2157 (as amended by SI 2007/3299 and SI 2009/209). Regulation 9 permits banks to open an account before verification is completed provided no transactions are carried out until completion.

The Financial Action Task Force on Money Laundering has promoted these requirements as key to acquiring a customer profile and continuing concerns with terrorist financing have given these requirements an added impetus. The Basle Committee regards these as essential to enabling banks to manage risk.[19]

So while in most circumstances the 'due diligence' requirements will assist the bank in identifying the customer and profile his banking needs there will remain situations where those requirements will not answer the question 'who is a customer?' Where a bank deals with a fund manager who does not take positions as a principal but will sell his expertise in return for a fee, then once the transaction is completed the fund manager, as the agent, simply drops out of the transaction leaving the bank to deal with the principal. In such circumstances the bank faces the problem of being unable to assess the creditworthiness of the customer. So judicial attempts to help identify 'who is a customer?' need to be explored.

Judicial attempts to identify who the customer is?

A number of judicial decisions have examined the main features of the banker and customer relationship and the courts have repeatedly expressed the view that the banker and customer relationship comes into existence only when the parties intend to enter into such a relationship,[20] so that the person intending to become a bank customer must either open the account personally with the relevant intention or instruct an agent to act for him. In *Barclays Bank Ltd v Okenarhe*,[21] Bailhache J suggested that the offer to open an account is made by the proposed customer, and its acceptance by the bank will create a binding contract on the basis of the general law of contract.

However, the bank must maintain an account, whether a current or deposit account, to instigate the banker and customer relationship and make the recipient of the banking services a customer. In *Great Western Railway Co v London and County Banking Co Ltd*[22] a rate collector had habitually cashed cheques over the counter of the defendant bank, with which the rural authority maintained an account, with the rate collector keeping part of the funds and depositing the rest to the credit of the authority's account. In one instance, the rate collector cashed a cheque over the counter obtained by fraud and the bank was sued for conversion. On the question of whether the cheque had been collected by the bank for its customer the court held that although the bank had regularly cashed cheques at the rate collector's request for a number of years, he was not a customer of the bank as he did not maintain an account with the bank personally. In respect of the fraudulent cheque the bank had, therefore, merely collected the money for itself and since it had a defective title to the instrument the bank was liable to the true owner. Where a bank, therefore, performs a casual service, even though performed with regularity, this does not make the beneficiary of that service a customer. Merely cashing cheques over the counter does not render the recipient of such services a customer.[23] In practice banks will cash cheques over the counter if accompanied by a cheque card; such a service will not render the recipient a customer unless that person maintains an account with the bank even if at a different branch of the same bank.

---

[19] Basle Committee on Banking Supervision, Due Diligence for Banks (Basle), BIS, 2001.
[20] *Robinson v Midland Bank Ltd* (1925) 41 TLR 402.
[21] [1966] 2 Lloyd's Rep 87.
[22] [1901] AC 414.
[23] *Barclays Bank Ltd v Okenarhe* [1966] 2 Lloyd's Rep 87.

The mere opening of an account is sufficient to create a banker and customer relationship even if the customer has never drawn on that account. In *Ladbroke & Co v Todd*[24] a rogue who stole a cheque opened an account with the defendant bank under the name of the payee on the instrument. On the cheque being cleared the rogue withdrew the funds and in an action for conversion by the drawer the bank sought to rely on s.82 of the Bills of Exchange Act 1882. It was argued that merely opening the account did not render the rogue a customer and the bank could not therefore rely on the defence under s.82 of the 1882 Act. Bailhache J delivering the judgment held that the rogue became a customer of the bank when the bank agreed to open the account and the fact that he had not been allowed to withdraw the proceeds of the cheque was irrelevant to the existence of the banker and customer relationship. In *Commissioners of Taxation v English, Scottish and Australian Bank Ltd*[25] a cheque payable to the Commissioners of Taxation was stolen and paid by the thief to the credit of an account opened by him with the defendant bank. An issue that needed to be resolved was whether the rogue had become a customer of the defendant bank by reason of the single transaction although related to the stolen cheque. Lord Dunedin, delivering his judgment observed that:

> the word 'customer' signifies a relationship in which duration is not of the essence. A person whose money has been accepted by a bank on the footing that they undertake to honour cheques up to the amount standing to his credit is . . . a customer of the bank . . . irrespective of whether his connection is of short or long standing. The contrast is between a casual service, such as, for instance, cashing a cheque for a person introduced by one of their customers, and a person who has an account of his own at the bank.

The view of the Privy Council in the *Commissioners of Taxation* case may be qualified to the extent that a person who merely agrees to open an account may be treated as a customer although the formalities to the opening of the account have not been completed. In *Woods v Martins Bank Ltd*,[26] the defendant's bank manager gave the plaintiff certain investment advice and consequently the plaintiff signed a letter instructing the bank to deal with funds previously held in a building society account. It was agreed that any resulting credit balances would be held for the account of the plaintiff. The court held that the banker and customer relationship came into existence from the date the bank accepted instructions contained in the letter to manage the credit balances, although the account was not formally opened until later. The fact the bank had accepted and agreed to instructions that would lead to an account being opened for the plaintiff was sufficient to impose the obligations of the banker and customer relationship. Salmon J held that the defendant bank had failed to comply with the duty of care, which it owed to the claimant under the banker and customer relationship established between them. At the time *Woods v Martins Bank* Ltd was decided the court had to recognise a breach of contractual duty, as an action in tort for negligent advice was not permissible. The law has since developed to recognise such a duty of care in tort under *Hedley Byrne & Co Ltd v Heller and Partners Ltd*.[27]

As an exception to the general principle the courts have recognised that a banking firm will be a customer of another bank where it uses that bank to regularly clear cheques although it does not maintain an account with the collecting bank. In *Importers Co Ltd v Westminster*

---

[24] (1914) 30 LTR 433.
[25] [1920] AC 683.
[26] [1959] 1 QB 55.
[27] [1964] AC 465.

Bank Ltd[28] the courts have recognised that a bank can be the customer of a collecting bank where a clearing bank, in the regular course of dealings, collects cheques remitted to it by a non-clearing bank on behalf of its customer for clearing. In such circumstances Bankes LJ said in this case the:

> business of collecting cheques was done between bank and bank, and it seems to me impossible to contend, as a matter of law, that the bank for which the [clearing bankers] were doing business were not, in reference to that business, their customer.

It may not always be easy to determine who is the bank's customer. Where a person impersonates another with a view to committing a deception he may still become a customer of the bank, if the bank intended to deal with the person physically present and not the person the rogue intended to impersonate. In *Ladbroke & Co v Todd*[29] the court held that a rogue who pretended to be the person named on a cheque tendered by him to the defendant bank was for the purposes of the banker and customer relationship, the bank's customer. Similarly, in *Marfani & Co Ltd v Midland Bank Ltd*[30] a rogue, named K, opened an account with the defendant bank in the name of a wealthy businessman, Eliazade, who was a client of K's employers. K then wrongfully paid into that account cheques drawn by the employer for the credit of Eliazade. In an action for conversion against the defendant bank, the Court of Appeal held that the bank's customer was, in fact, K, the rogue, and not Eliazade who had never intended or applied to open an account with the defendant bank. The bank had at all times intended to deal with the person before it, K, although he was impersonating someone when the account was opened. Similarly, in *Stoney Stanton Supplies (Coventry) Ltd v Midland Bank Ltd*[31] the court held that a banker and customer relationship had not been entered into with B when it was discovered that B's signature had been forged; forgery rendering the whole transaction a nullity despite the fact that the account had actually become operational.

While the law requires that there must an intention to create legal relations and a meeting of the minds for the purposes of contract law, it is possible for the rules of agency law to allow one person, an agent, to open an account on behalf of another. The rules of agency law will normally require such authority be expressly conferred on the agent, or for such authority to be tacitly given. Thus, for example a local bank, in the UK, may open an account with an overseas bank for its customer in order to facilitate certain transactions or to receive, or make, regular payments from overseas. Such consent can be given either expressly by the customer or implied from business practices of the bank. Similarly, a parent may open an account in the name of a minor child and the courts may hold that the bank owes a duty of care to the minor child. In *Rowlandson v National Westminster Bank Ltd*[32] the court held the bank owed a fiduciary duty of care to the grandchildren of a business woman who opened an account in their joint names and conferred a right on their guardians to draw on the credit balances. Although, the guardians had not expressly approved the opening of the account they did eventually learn of the account and one of them drew against the account for his personal gain.

Under the banker and customer relationship a customer is, therefore, one who maintains an account with the bank regardless of whether or not that account has become operational

---

[28] [1927] 1 KB 869.
[29] (1914) 30 LTR 433.
[30] [1968] 1 WLR 956.
[31] [1966] 2 Lloyd's Rep. 373.
[32] [1978] 1 WLR 798.

and to whom as a result of opening this account the bank owes certain duties, including the duty to conform to the customer's mandate in respect of carrying out the customer's instructions. In *Libyan Arab Foreign Bank* v *Bankers Trust*[33] Staughton J attempted to highlight those services which a bank is bound to provide its customer and are core to the relationship arising from the account facility, and those which are optional and subject to specific agreement:

> [f]or a private customer with a current account I would include in the first category the delivery of cash in legal tender over the bank's counter and the honouring of cheques drawn by the customer. Other services, such as standing orders, direct debits, banker's drafts, letters of credit, automated cash tills and foreign currency for travel abroad, may be in the second category of services which the bank is not bound to but usually will supply on demand . . . The answer may depend on the circumstances of a particular case.

Types of bank customer

The banker and customer relationship is primarily that of debtor and creditor with the credit balance standing to the credit of the customer's account being intermingled with other credit balances maintained by the bank.[34] The nature of the individual banker and customer relationship, however, will govern issues such as when the bank comes under an obligation to make payment and to whom such payment should be made.[35] While there is a debtor and creditor relationship in respect of the credit balance on the customer's account that relationship changes to agent and principal when the bank executes the customer's mandate. By complying with the payment mandate the bank satisfies two distinct functions:

(a) It discharges the debt owed by the bank to the customer to the value of the repayment.

(b) It acts as an agent in complying with the customer's mandate.[36]

The discharge of these functions does not normally cause any problems in the course of the banker and customer relationship but problems may arise if specific considerations in respect of special bank accounts are not taken into account. The bank must, therefore, safeguard its position and ensure that:

● The person giving the mandate has the authority to act in that capacity; and

● That the payment mandate is issued in favour of the person entitled to the money.

If the bank fails to act properly with regard to either of these obligations it may find itself liable to the true owner of the funds both because the mandate is defective and/or the bank has acted without authority; or because the payment is made to someone other than the true owner. The nature of the bank account and the bank's mandate are therefore important and we will now examine the main features of the different types of accounts the bank opens for customers.

---

[33] [1989] QB 728 at 749.
[34] *Foley* v *Hill* (1848) 2 HLC 28 (HL).
[35] The bank is under a duty to conform to a number of implied contractual terms, including the duty to conform to the customer's mandate: see Ch. 7.
[36] See Ch. 7 for further discussion.

Joint accounts

A joint account is one that is opened in the name of two or more persons in their personal capacity. Although any one or more of the joint account holders may be authorised to draw against the account each account holder will act either for himself or the other joint holders of the account and it is this that distinguishes joint account holders from other account holders who act in a representative or fiduciary capacity, for example directors of a company.

One of the main issues the bank will have to determine in respect of the bank account will be who has authority to draw against the account. When a joint account is opened the bank will require clear and unambiguous instructions regarding the authority to draw against the account, for example whether the signature of a single account holder will suffice to confer authority on the bank to make payment or whether the signature of both, or all, the account holders is required. A bank may find it has acted without a proper mandate either because the instruction does not bear the authorised signature (missing signature) or because one of the signatures is forged. In *Jackson* v *White and Midland Bank Ltd*[37] the plaintiff entered into negotiations with the first defendant with the intention of either becoming a partner or joint owner of the first defendant's business. The plaintiff paid £2,000 into a joint account at a branch of the defendant bank opened by him and the first defendant, with the express instructions that cheques had to be signed by both the account holders. The first defendant forged the plaintiff's signature on a number of cheques, which the bank duly paid. Business negotiations with the plaintiff broke down and the first defendant refused to repay the money misappropriated from the joint account. The plaintiff applied for an injunction against the bank ordering it to restore the amount of the debits made against cheques drawn only by the first defendant. Parke J held:[38]

> the Bank made an agreement with the plaintiff and the first defendant jointly that it would honour any cheques signed by them jointly, and also a separate agreement with the plaintiff and the first defendant severally that it would not honour any cheques unless he had signed them. It follows, therefore, as the Bank has honoured cheques not signed by the plaintiff, the plaintiff is entitled to sue for breach of that separate agreement.

The court expressed a similar view in *Catlin* v *Cyprus Finance Corporation (London) Ltd*[39] where the bank, contrary to the mandate, honoured a cheque drawn by one of the joint account holders alone. Bingham J held that although the account was a joint account and the mandate given to the bank to honour cheques jointly given by all the holders of the account, the bank owed a separate duty to conform to the mandate to each of them severally. Bingham J continued that a duty owed to the joint account holders which could only have been enforced jointly would be 'worthless' where the purpose of the account, and thereby the mandate, was to safeguard against the misconduct of one of the account holders.

Although, a joint account holder may be able to establish breach of mandate by the bank, the court will have to determine the measure of damages recovered. In normal circumstances the owner of the joint account cannot recover more than the loss incurred by him and, as a joint account holder, that means 50 per cent of the amount of the invalid cheque. However,

---

[37] [1967] 2 Lloyd's Rep. 68.
[38] Following *Welch* v *Bank of England* [1955] Ch 508; *Twibell* v *London Suburban Bank* [1869] WN 127 and the Australian case of *Arden* v *Bank of New South Wales* [1956] VLR 569.
[39] [1927] 2 KB 297.

in both the *Catlin* and *Jackson* cases the respective plaintiffs were entitled to recover the damages by reference to the value of the cheques, since they could show that the funds paid out from the respective accounts were in fact their property and never became joint property. The damages awarded were the full amounts of the cheques paid out against the unauthorised mandates. This is in contrast to an action based merely on breach of contract by the bank. Thus, in *Twibell's*[40] case where the claimant recovered an appropriate moiety of the sum for which the cheque was drawn, that is a measure of damages that compensates the claimant for his loss.

A defrauded joint account holder may not, however, be able to recover the amount of the unauthorised payment, or any part of it, if it has been used towards the payment of lawfully owing debts enforceable against the plaintiff. The equitable principle of subrogation will apply to discharge the debt owed to a third party and to that extent the bank stands in the position of the debtor. In *B. Liggett (Liverpool) Ltd v Barclays Bank Ltd*[41] the defendant bank paid a cheque payable to the claimant's trade creditors but, contrary to the mandate given to the bank, the instrument was drawn by a single director. The court held that while at common law the bank would be liable to restore the full amount of the unauthorised cheque, equitable principles may modify the harshness of the common law and the bank would, having paid off legally enforceable debts against the claimant, stand in the shoes of the trade creditors. Wright J expressed the view that in such cases the customer whose account has been debited in reality is no worse off because the bank has discharged a legally enforceable debt. This principle was followed in *Jackson v White*[42] and used to mitigate the harshness of the common law rule, which would compel the bank to restore the amount of an invalid mandate. In that case one of the cheques paid by the bank was actually drawn for the payment of goods supplied and Park J expressed the view that the bank was entitled 'to take advantage of the equitable doctrine by which a person who had in fact paid the debts of another without authority was allowed the advantage of his payments'.

The issues that arose in the *Jackson* and *Catlin* cases do not arise where either, or any, of the joint account holders can draw against the account for their own purposes. In *Re Bishop*[43] the fact that investments purchased in the joint names of the husband and wife, and sometimes in their sole names from a joint account to which they both contributed did nothing to displace the legal titles indicated by the purchase transactions. Stamp J held that where a joint account is opened then, in the absence of facts or circumstances which indicate that the account was intended, or was kept, for some specific or limited purpose, each account holder can draw upon it not only for the benefit of both account holders but also for the sole benefit of one of the account holders. Each account holder, in drawing money out of the account, is to be treated as doing so with the authority of the other.

Where one of the account holders dies the question that inevitably arises is who is entitled to the balance held to the credit of a joint account holder. In most instances the bank mandate form will contain a survivorship clause and the contract will specify the person or persons to whom the bank will pay the credit balance. However, even in the absence of a survivorship clause it is well established that legal title to the deceased's share of the credit balance vests in the survivor.[44]

---

[40] *Twibell v London Suburban Bank* [1869] WN 127.
[41] [1928] 1 KB 48.
[42] [1967] 2 Lloyd's Rep. 68.
[43] [1965] Ch 450.
[44] *Russell v Scott* (1936) 55 CLR 440 at 451.

Partnership accounts

A partnership account resembles the joint account in that it is opened in the name of more than one person. Unlike a registered company or a registered partnership, a general partnership does not enjoy separate legal status, so the account is in effect a joint account in the name of the specified partners. Under s.5 of the Partnership Act 1890 each partner acts as the agent of his co-partners and the partnership business. A partner can therefore open an account on behalf of the partnership but not in his individual name. A partner can operate the partnership account in his own right and he can also close that account. However, in *Alliance Bank Ltd* v *Kearsley*[45] Montague Smith J said that an account opened by a man in his own name is *prima facie* his private account and the other partners were, therefore, not liable to reimburse the bank for losses incurred by the partner on the account, although it was used solely for partnership purposes.

Not only must a partner act within the scope of his authority in respect of drawings made against the partnership account[46] but the bank must also conform to the strict terms of the mandate given to it with regard to the operation of the account. The nature of the partnership business will determine the scope of the partner's authority. For example, a partner of a trading or commercial firm has the authority to raise credit[47] and arrange an overdraft for the partnership.[48] The partner has the authority to grant security for any relevant loan.[49] A professional partnership, for example a solicitor's firm or medical or dental practices, will be unlikely to be authorised to borrow on the firm's behalf.[50] It is usual for the partnership agreement to expressly stipulate that a partnership may open an account and also whether it is to be operated by the joint signature of all or some of the partners.

The doctrine of survivorship, which applies to joint accounts, is inapplicable to partnership accounts. Unless the partnership agreement expressly provides, the death of a partner will dissolve the partnership.[51] However, under s.38 of the Partnership Act 1890, the surviving partners have the power to continue to act for the firm for the purposes of winding up the firm and the bank is entitled to assume that the partners act within their statutory authority. In *Backhouse* v *Charlton*[52] a father and son partnership authorised its bank that each partner was entitled to draw on the partnership account, both during and after the father's lifetime. After the father's death, the son, as the surviving partner continued to draw cheques on the partnership account and pay the proceeds into his personal account with the same bank. The court held that the bank was not liable to the father's estate and it was entitled to honour cheques drawn by the son, as the surviving partner. Similarly, in *Re Bourne*[53] the surviving partner deposited some title deeds as security for an increase in the partnership overdraft, as part of winding up its affairs. The issue before the court was whether the bank or deceased's partner's estate had priority over the deeds. Romer LJ giving judgment for the bank held that

---

[45] (1871) LR 6 CP 433.
[46] *Foster* v *Mackreth* (1867) LR 2 Ex 163; *Bank of Baroda Ltd* v *Punjab National Bank Ltd* [1944] AC 176.
[47] *Twinsectra Ltd* v *Yardley* [2002] 2 AC 164; *JJ Coughlan Ltd* v *Ruparelia* [2003] EWCA Civ 1057.
[48] *Bank of Australasia* v *Breillat* (1847) 6 Moore PC 153.
[49] *Bank of Scotland* v *Henry Butcher & Co* [2003] 1 BCLC 575.
[50] *Higgins* v *Beauchamp* [1914] 3 KB 1192.
[51] Partnership Act 1890, s.33(1).
[52] (1878) 8 Ch D 444.
[53] [1906] 2 Ch 427.

third parties dealing with the surviving partner were entitled to assume that he was acting in good faith and within his authority to liquidate the partnership.

Company contracts

A company is a separate legal entity and enjoys separate legal status from its directors and managers. Consequently, a company can enter into contractual obligations and give a valid discharge for its debts. While this feature distinguished registered companies from the partnership, the limited liability partnership, which now also enjoys a similar separate legal status,[54] blurs the distinction between them. Banks will, therefore, have similar concerns about the capacity of the business entity and the authority of the personnel for each entity since both registered companies and the limited liability partnership must act through agents. Any discussion relating to capacity must therefore distinguish between capacity of the business entity and the capacity of its agents and it is proposed to deal with both these aspects.

Capacity of the company or limited liability partnership

Section 30 of the Companies Act 2006 provides that the 'validity of an act done by a company shall not be called into question on the ground of lack of capacity by reason of anything in the company's constitution', while s.1(3) of the Limited Liability Partnership Act 2000 provides that a 'limited liability partnership has unlimited capacity'. While banks, need not concern themselves with issues of capacity in respect of either the registered company or the limited liability partnership, they are likely to follow former practice and require that the entity furnish them with copies of its constitutional documents before opening an account or making other facilities, for example an overdraft or loan, available. Furthermore, since a company's objects are now free from limitations and 'unrestricted' a company will have capacity to borrow and grant security.[55]

In any event the bank will seek to ensure that the board of directors has the power to delegate,[56] although s.40(1) of the Companies Act 2006 provides that 'the power of the directors to bind the company, or authorise others to do so, is deemed to be free of any limitation under the company's constitution', including limitations imposed by resolution at a general meeting or by a shareholders agreement. However, the protection given to a bank under s.40(1) of the Companies Act 2006 is subject to limits:

- The protection is only given to third parties and in this case the bank, which deals with the company in the context of 'any transaction or other act' to which the company is a party.[57]
- The statutory protection only applies in favour of a third party dealing with a company 'in good faith'. Since there is a statutory presumption of good faith under s.40(2)(b)(ii) of the Companies Act 2006 this requirement is unlikely to present any problems to a bank and this is supported by the requirement that a person dealing with the company is not

---

[54] Limited Liability Partnership Act 2000, s.1(2).
[55] Companies Act 2006, s.31 (1).
[56] *Southend-on-Sea Corporation v Hodgson (Hickford) Ltd* [1962] 1 QB 416.
[57] In *EIC Services Ltd v Phipps* [2005] 1 All ER 338 the Court of Appeal held this requirement was not satisfied.

bound to enquire into any limitations on the board's powers.[58] However, it may constitute bad faith not to investigate a matter further, once put on enquiry.[59] However, a person is not regarded as acting in bad faith 'by reason only' of his knowledge[60] that the act is outside the powers of the board and a bank which has had sight of the constitution without appreciating its limitations is likely to have acted in good faith. However, the bank will not be protected if it deals with an inquorate board,[61] although the bank may, depending on the circumstances, be protected by the 'indoor management rule'.[62]

● A bank will only be protected under s.40(1) if it deals directly with the board of directors. Where a bank, or third party, deals with an individual director, s.40(1) will only protect the bank from limitations on the board's power to delegate.

Capacity of directors

Whether the individual director has the power to act for his company will depend on the actual extent of the delegation to the director and the rules of agency law[63] will help determine the scope of that delegation. Where there appears to be a lack of express[64] or implied[65] authority on the part of the agent, the rules of 'apparent or ostensible' authority may cure such lack of authority. In *Freeman and Lockyer* v *Buckhurst Park Properties (Mangel) Ltd*[66] the Court of Appeal held that a person dealing with an agent without authority or defective authority might be protected if it can be shown that:

1 He relied on a representation made by the principal or purported principal as to the agent's authority;

2 The person making the representation had actual authority to make such a representation; and

3 The transaction is *intra vires*. However, changes in the law now mean that this requirement will always be satisfied by s.39(1) of the Companies Act 2006.

Thus, apparent or ostensible authority is such authority, of an agent, as may reasonably appear to others to be within the scope of that office. So while the bank will normally verify the authority of a director to draw against the company's account and to some extent the transaction may be taken at face value, the bank will nevertheless need to be alert, for example where the agent or director, draws a cheque against the company's account in his own name and deposits that cheque into his own account.

---

[58] Companies Act 2006, s.40(20)(b)(i).

[59] *Wrexham Association Football Club Ltd* v *Crucialmove Ltd* [2008] 1 BCLC 508.

[60] Companies Act 2006, s.40 (2)(b)(iii); see *Ford* v *Polymer Vision Ltd* [2009] EWHC 945.

[61] *Ford* v *Polymer Vision Ltd* [2009] EWHC 945 applying *Smith* v *Henniker-Major & Co* [2003] Ch 182.

[62] *Royal British Bank* v *Turquand* (1856) 6 E& B 327.

[63] *Freeman and Lockyer* v *Buckhurst Park Properties (Mangel) Ltd* [1964] 1 All ER 630; see also Limited Liability Partnership Act 2000, section 6.

[64] In *Freeman and Lockyer* v *Buckhurst Park Properties (Mangel) Ltd* [1964] 1 All ER 630 it was said that express authority is such when it is given by express words, for example when the board of directors passes a resolution which authorises two of their number to draw cheques.

[65] In *Freeman and Lockyer* v *Buckhurst Park Properties (Mangel) Ltd* [1964] 1 All ER 630 it was said that implied authority is that authority which is inferred from the conduct of the parties and the circumstances of the case.

[66] [1964] 1 All ER 630; see also *Hely-Hutchinson* v *Brayhead Ltd* [1968] 1 QB 549; *Armagas Ltd* v *Mundogas SA* [1986] AC 717; *British Bank of the Middle East* v *Sun Life Assurance Co of Canada* [1983] 2 Lloyd's Rep. 9.

Drawing negotiable instruments and operating a current account for the company

Any holder of a bill of exchange is entitled to know who is liable on it and so any instrument drawn in a representative capacity must make that clear. Section 26 (1) of the Bills of Exchange Act 1882 provides that a person who signs a bill as drawer, endorser or acceptor and adds his signature indicating that he signs for and on behalf of a principal, or in a representative capacity is not personally liable. However, merely adding words to his signature describing him as an agent, or as filling a representative character, does not exempt him from personal liability. Additionally, s.26(2) provides that the most favourable construction, to the validity of the instrument, will be given in determining whether a signature on a bill is that of the principal or that of the agent who draws it.

Section 52 of the Companies Act 2006 provides that a bill of exchange or promissory note is deemed to have been made, accepted or endorsed on behalf of a company, if made, accepted or endorsed in the name of, or by or on behalf or on account of, the company by a person acting under its authority. While cheques are not specifically mentioned in s.52 such instruments are defined by s.73 of the Act as a bill of exchange drawn on a banker payable on demand. Section 52, therefore, deals with a situation where an individual agent, for example director or company secretary, draws a cheque or other instrument without authority or in abuse of that authority, for example to defraud the company. However, some authorities treat the company's agent as having implied authority to draw cheques[67] and thereby protect the bank from misuse of power by the agent. Other cases, however, restrict this rule and in *Rama Corporation Ltd* v *Proved Tin and General Investment Ltd*[68] Slade J held that a person could not plead an agent's implied authority unless he could establish his reliance on it, when entering into the contract with the principal. Further, the extent of the bank's reliance on the agent's authority will depend on the agent's position in the company.[69] The bank cannot, therefore, assume the agent's authority is wider than the inference from the agent's position, or the principal's representation in respect of him, but a bank must exercise caution when it deals with a person other than a director.

In *British Bank of the Middle East* v *Sun Life Assurance Co of Canada*[70] senior officers of an insurance company were held not to have express or implied authority to give undertakings to repay amounts advanced to a property developer, by a bank. Finally, the bank may be put on enquiry in suspicious circumstances and prevent it from relying on an agent's authority if it fails to investigate further.[71] While the doctrine of constructive notice does not apply to negotiable instruments[72] the bank may in fact owe a duty of care when paying a cheque in what appears to be suspicious circumstances.

---

[67] *Biggerstaff* v *Rowatt's Wharf Ltd* [1896] 2 Ch 93; *Deys* v *Pullinger Engineering Co* [1921] 1 KB 77; *British Tomson-Houston Co Ltd* v *Federated European Bank Ltd* [1932] KB 176; *Re Land Credit Co of Ireland, ex p. Overend, Gurney & Co.* (1869) LR 4 Ch. App. 460.

[68] [1952] 2 QB147.

[69] *A.L. Underwood Ltd* v *Bank of Liverpool and Martins* [1924] 1 KB 775.

[70] [1983] 2 Lloyd's Rep. 9.

[71] *Alexander Stewart & Son of Dundee Ltd* v *Westminster Bank Ltd* [1926] WN 126; *B. Liggett (Liverpool) Ltd* v *Barclays Bank Ltd* [1928] 1 KB 48.

[72] *London Joint Stock Bank* v *Simmons* [1892] AC 201.

Unincorporated associations

Unincorporated associations are primarily non-commercial associations, for example clubs and charitable institutions, usually funded through subscriptions and donations. An unincorporated association has no separate legal existence or separate legal personality. A management, or governing, committee will operate such associations and the committee must remain within the powers conferred by its association. The management committee may delegate its powers to agents whose acts will then bind the association.[73] Such delegation is likely to include authority to undertake banking activities on behalf of the association, for example unincorporated associations will usually require a bank account in order to raise subscriptions and effect payment of services for its membership. The association may also need to borrow money to further its objectives. The association's constitution is likely to contain express powers enabling the committee to delegate powers to deal with the bank. When an association applies to open a bank account, the bank should ask for a copy of the constitution, or the resolution, to confirm the scope of the authority to open an account and the power of the named officers to draw cheques or other banking transactions. A bank will need to ensure that it acts within its authority not merely when making payments against the account but also when making loans to the association.

Since the unincorporated association is not a distinct legal entity with its own contractual capacity the association cannot be sued in its own name. Additionally, the liability of members to third parties is usually limited to the amount of their subscription or membership fee so unless they have given their express consent to a transaction they will not be liable beyond their membership fee.[74] However, assets held by the association may be targeted, by bringing a representative action against the committee members, but it may also be possible to hold the committee members personally liable. In *Coutts & Co v Irish Exhibition in London*[75] a bank granted an overdraft to an association that was in the process of being formed and on the assurance of one of the future committee members. Although the association was formed it failed before the account was transferred to the association and before the committee members were released from their liability with the result the court held the committee members personally liable.

Trust accounts

A trust account will be opened mainly by executors under a will, or by persons such as solicitors. A trust is not a separate legal entity from its trustees and the trustees will have legal title to the trust property, while the beneficiary will have equitable title. The trust deed will normally require two or more persons to be appointed trustees, so that trust property is under the control of more than one person. The trustee's role is to administer the trust assets according to the trust deed appointing him and his instructions under that deed. Additionally, the trustees have powers conferred on them by the Trustees Acts 1925 and 2000. The death of a trustee does not affect the right of survivorship and s.18 of the Trustee Act 1925 authorises the surviving trustee (or trustees or their personal representatives) to carry on the business of the trust until another person is appointed trustee, whether under

---

[73] *Bradley Egg Farm Ltd* v *Clifford* [1943] 2 All ER 378.
[74] *Howells* v *Dominion Insurance Co Ltd* [2005] EWHC 552.
[75] (1891) 7 TLR 313.

the will or by the court. They will, therefore, have the power to draw cheques on the trust account. However, trustees were not previously allowed to delegate their authority[76] and so cheques, unless the trust deed provided otherwise, had to be signed by all the trustees.[77] However, s.25 of the Trustee Act 2000 now allows trustees to delegate, even to a sole trustee, all but a few functions: for example the power to appoint trustees, the power to decide whether payment should be made out of income or capital or issues relating to whether or the way in which trust assets should be distributed.[78] Section 3(1) of the Trustee Act 1925 allows a trustee to 'make any kind of investment', which includes depositing trust money in a bank account. The right to borrow for trust purposes is restricted and s.16 of the Trustee Act 1925 provides that trustees are authorised either by law or under the trust deed to 'pay or apply capital money subject to the trust for any purpose or in any manner'. Trustees are deemed to have the power to raise any required amounts by 'sale, conversion, calling in or mortgage of all or any part of the trust property' and where the trustees have the power to mortgage they also have the power to borrow.[79] Additionally, trustees have the power to borrow for the purposes of the trust's business.[80]

Banks operating trust accounts

A bank cannot generally exercise its right to combine two or more accounts held in the name of the customer where one of the accounts so held is his personal account and the other a trust account. Thus, for example, in *Re Gross, ex p. Kingston*[81] an official maintained two accounts with the same bank, one of which was his personal account and the other account was marked 'Police Account'. The bank sought to combine the overdrawn personal account with the credit balance on the 'Police Account' when the account holder absconded. The Court of Appeal held that the bank could not combine the two accounts since the 'Police Account' was headed 'in such a way that a banker cannot fail to know it to be a trust account' and that 'the balance standing to the credit of that account will, on the bankruptcy of the person who kept it, belong to the trust'.

Even a bank account that is not specifically marked as a trust account may be treated as a trust account if circumstances should alert the bank to the fact that the trustees have, in fact, opened a trust account, for example where a bank receives funds from a company to be placed in a separate account, that fact by itself does not put the bank on inquiry concerning the rights of third parties.[82] In *Foxton* v *Manchester & Liverpool District Banking Co.*[83] the court established that once it is shown that the bank is aware that money is affected by a trust it is immaterial that the bank does not know the detailed terms of the trust. It is sufficient to make the bank liable if it knew that the fund is held in a fiduciary capacity and that a payment made by the trustees is inconsistent with their holding the fund in a fiduciary capacity.[84]

---

[76] *Re Flower and Metropolitan Board of Works* (1884) 27 Ch D 592; *Green* v *Whithead* [1930] 1 Ch 38.
[77] *Green* v *Whithead* [1930] 1 Ch 38.
[78] Trustee Act 2000, s.11.
[79] Trustee Act 2000, ss.16 and 28.
[80] *Dowse* v *Gorton* [1891] AC 190.
[81] (1871) LR 6 Ch. App. 632.
[82] See: *Union Bank of Australia* v *Murray-Aynsley* [1898] AC 693; *Barclays Bank Ltd* v *Quistclose Investments Ltd* [1970] AC 567.
[83] (1881) 44 LT 406.
[84] See: *Union Bank of Australia* v *Murray-Aynsley* [1898] AC 693.

More recently, in *Devron Potatoes Ltd v Gordon & Innes Ltd*[85] the court said that from the time 'when a bank becomes aware that the funds paid into the client's account . . . are only held by the [payer] in a fiduciary capacity, they have no right to set off funds against sums due to them by their customer under other accounts'. Any knowledge acquired by a bank officer within the scope of his employment will be imputed to the bank. In *Saudi Arabian Monetary Agency v Dresdner Bank AG*[86] the Court of Appeal held that the bank could exercise a right of combination against a trust account's credit balance when it had clear evidence that the beneficiary of that account was a customer who was overdrawn on their personal account with the bank.

A bank's liability to the beneficiaries is protected under the rules of equity. This may be done at the expense of innocent third parties who deal in good faith with the trustee who acts fraudulently or *ultra vires*. In such circumstances the bank may be held liable as a constructive trustee if it knowingly receives trust property in breach of trust, or dishonestly assists in its dissipation. A bank will only be liable if the necessary element of fault is established which in the case of knowing receipt cases requires unconscionable behaviour, and dishonesty in the case of dishonest behaviour.

The bank is unlikely to have the necessary level of fault when the proceeds of a trust, with which the bank has no specific connection, are paid into its customer's accounts without indication that the funds were trust funds. In *Thomson v Clydesdale Bank Ltd*[87] the House of Lords held that the bank did not have sufficient notice of the wrongful nature of the transaction to be imputed with knowledge of the stockbroker's breach of trust. In *Thomson* shareholders ordered their stockbroker to sell certain shares for them. The broker having sold the shares paid the cheque for the sale price into his own overdrawn personal account. The bank had knowledge that the cheque represented the proceeds of the sale of shares but was unaware whether the broker held the money represented in the cheque as agent or in his own right. The case relies on the lack of knowledge of the bank with regard to the nature of the money and whether it held the proceeds of the sale of shares held on trust. The case might have been differently decided if the broker had paid the money first into his 'clients' or other 'trust account' and then transferred the funds into his personal account, particularly where the account is designated a trust account.[88] The failure to designate an account as appropriate, for example 'trust account', does not necessarily mean that the bank may not have the requisite knowledge since a bank may actually know that the account is being used as a 'trust account'[89] and proceeds are being improperly applied.[90] Mere knowledge that the account is a trust account will not be sufficient to place the bank on notice of any misappropriation since the bank's primary focus will be on ensuring that trustees manage the account within their apparent powers, for example the bank's focus will be on the administration of the account, i.e. cheques are properly drawn with the requisite signatures against the account.

A more complex situation is where a trustee pays a cheque drawn on a trust account into his personal account where both accounts are held with the same bank, particularly where

---

[85] 2003 SCLR 103.
[86] [2005] 1 Lloyd's Rep. 12 at 23.
[87] [1893] AC 282.
[88] *Thomson v Clydesdale Bank Ltd* [1893] AC 282; *Union Bank of Australia Ltd v Murray-Aynsley* [1898] AC 693.
[89] *New South Wales v Commonwealth (No 3)* (1932) 46 CLR 246.
[90] *Re Gross, ex p. Kingston* (1871) LR 6 Ch. App. 632; *Greenwood Teale v William, Williams, Brown & Co* (1894) 11 TLR 56.

the amount involved is large. In *Foxton v Manchester and Liverpool District Banking Co*[91] the court held that the bank would be liable to the beneficiaries of a trust, where a trustee drew a cheque against a trust account in order to reduce the overdraft on his personal account, unless it could show that the payment in question was legitimate and proper. In *John v Dodwell & Co Ltd*[92] stockbrokers were held liable when cheques drawn on the employer's account were used to purchase shares in the employee's name. The approach in *Foxton* was applied in *Attorney General v De Winton*[93] where the court held that a person working as treasurer for the Council was not merely a servant and working in that capacity but owed fiduciary duties to the Council. This appears also to be the approach in *Rowlandson v National Westminster Bank Ltd*[94] where the bank was held liable to the beneficiaries when it permitted a trustee to draw cheques on the trust account for his personal purposes. However, it has been suggested that this view was too strict and a bank should only become liable for a breach of trust where it became aware of the breach of trust if, before the collection of a cheque, it became aware of the overdraft on the personal account and pressed for payment.[95] In *Grey v Johnston*[96] Lord Cairns observed that the circumstances which would most readily establish that the bank is privy to the breach of trust is where the bank stands to benefit from the trustee's breach of trust.

Solicitor's accounts

A 'client account' or 'solicitor's account' held by a solicitor is a trust account held by a solicitor to deposit client money. In *Brazill v Willoughby*[97] Peter Smith J described the main features of the solicitor's client account as:

> not a series of accounts but is one account in respect of which all clients' monies are deposited but each client's share is determined according to the amount set out in his ledger. The accounts are credited and withdrawn by reference to each individual client and there is no question (for example) of any part of the client account deposits being used for anything other than distribution as that client might nominate or decide. . . . No client obtains an interest in the client account until he has sums credited in respect of it.

Client accounts must be maintained in separate accounts by a solicitor and not co-mingled with the solicitors' personal funds.[98] The Solicitors' Accounts Rules 1998 made by the Law Society apply to all clients' accounts regardless of whether the accounts are opened in the name of a single individual or the names of several members of the practice.[99] The effect of these rules is that client money must be 'held in separate banks accounts, prescribe the records which must be kept and the circumstances in which the solicitor is permitted to draw on client money and guard against the mixing of client money and office money'.[100] This provision is

---

[91] (1881) 44 LT 406.
[92] [1918] AC 563.
[93] [1906] 2 Ch 106.
[94] [1978] 1 WLR 798.
[95] *Gray v Johnson* (1868) LR 3 HL 1; *Coleman v Bucks and Oxon Union Bank* [1897] 2 Ch 243.
[96] (1868) LR 3 HL 1.
[97] [2009] EWHC 1633.
[98] Solicitors Act 1974, s.32, amended by the Access to Justice Act 1999, schedule 15; Legal Services Act 2007, ss.177, 210 and schedule 16.
[99] Solicitors Act 1974, s.87.
[100] *Re Ahmed & Co* [2006] EWHC 480.

intended to prevent client money being used fraudulently, or otherwise misused. In respect of banks, s.85 of the Solicitors Act 1974 provides that a bank is not under a duty to enquire into, nor is it deemed to have knowledge of, any right of a person to any money paid or credited to the client's account 'which it would not incur or be under or be deemed to have in the case of an account kept by a person entitled absolutely to all money paid or credited to it'. The bank is protected against any additional liability that it may incur because the account is a solicitor's account but not against any liability it may incur regardless of the nature of the account. Thus, the bank may still be held liable as a constructive trustee on the basis of knowing receipt or dishonest assistance.[101] However, a solicitor can draw on the client account and the bank will owe no duty unless the cheque is drawn in suspicious circumstances.

However, a solicitor's creditor may, on occasion, seek a third party debt order (previously known as garnishee orders) against any credit balances on the solicitor's personal account and his client account. In *Plunkett v Barclays Bank Ltd*[102] the defendant bank froze a client account when a garnishee *order nisi* was served on it and therefore dishonoured a cheque drawn on the account and returned it to the holder marked with the words 'refer to drawer'. The solicitor brought an action against the bank for defamation and breach of contract. Du Parcq J dismissing the action rejected the submission that 'money paid into a client account kept with a bank in the name of a solicitor is a debt owing from the banker to the solicitor'.[103]

On the basis of these cases client funds may be made the subject of court orders where a third party creditor seeks to recover personal debts owed by the solicitor. There are a number of reasons why this conclusion is unlikely to be up held by the courts. Client accounts should be held incapable of attachment for personal debts owed by a solicitor because:

● The credit balance on a client account constitutes a trust fund that is not available to satisfy personal debts incurred by a solicitor.

● The Solicitors' Act 1974 prohibits a solicitor from combining credit balances on a client's account with a debit balance on the solicitor's personal account and so it is unlikely that a third party will be given the right to effectively do that, i.e., combine the credit on the client balance with a debit on the personal account.

● Combining the balance on the client account with the overdrawn solicitors' personal account wrongly assumes that the client account forms part of the personal estate of the solicitor. This also means that on the bankruptcy of a solicitor only his personal estate is subject to any bankruptcy order and not any property held as a fiduciary or as a trustee. Once a bankruptcy order is made the solicitor and the bank are required to notify the court of any accounts held by the solicitor as a trustee.

Therefore, client accounts held by a solicitor are seen as not part of the solicitor's personal estate and not subject to third party orders.

Minors' accounts

At common law a contract made by a minor, namely a person under the age of 18 years,[104] was voidable at his insistence and so a contract made by a minor could be enforced by him,

---

[101] *Lipkin Gorman v Karpnale Ltd* [1987] 1 WLR 987 at 997.
[102] [1936] 2 KB 107.
[103] *Arab Bank Ltd v Barclays Bank (DCO)*[1954] AC 495 at 532.
[104] Family Law Reform Act 1969, s.1 provides the age of majority in the UK is 18 years.

but not against him. The common law protected minors (formally known as 'infants') from adults, some of who may be unscrupulous. However, contracts for the purchase of necessary goods and services delivered or supplied to a minor will be contracts for which payment may be compelled against the minor. Insofar as goods are the subject matter of the agreement, the position at common law was affirmed by s.3(2) of the Sale of Goods Act 1979 which provides that where 'necessaries' are sold and delivered to a minor, he must pay a reasonable price for them. 'Necessaries' are those goods and services that are 'suitable to the condition in life of a minor'[105] and they must not be confused with 'necessities' of life, although regard will be had to the minor's social background and wealth. In *Chapple v Cooper*[106] the defendant minor was held liable for the funeral costs of her husband and Alderson B., said:

> Things necessary are those without which an individual cannot reasonably exist . . . it must first be made out that . . . the things furnished are essential to the existence and reasonable advantage and comfort of the infant contractor. Thus articles of mere luxury are always excluded, though luxurious items of utility are in some cases allowed.

The claimant therefore has to persuade the court that the goods or services supplied are capable of being necessaries and the next question to be decided by the court is whether in fact they are necessaries in respect of that particular minor with the latter depending on the minor's standard of living. The court will also have regard to whether the minor is already adequately supplied with the particular goods. In *Nash v Inman*[107] the defendant, while under the age of majority, which at that time was 21, purchased clothing from a Savile Row tailor and included 11 fancy waistcoats. The court heard evidence that the defendant was adequately supplied with clothing fit for his station in life and on that basis the Court of Appeal held that the goods were not necessaries and the claimant's action succeeded.

Loans made to minors for the acquisition of necessaries are recoverable, for example to pay for accommodation, food and books. Loans are also recoverable from the minor by the bank being subrogated to the supplier's rights.[108]

However, the bank should exercise caution when lending to a minor. In *R. Leslie Ltd v Sheill*[109] a lender was unable to recover his losses when a minor obtained a loan by misrepresenting his age. The court held that the amount could not be recovered by bringing an action within deceit or in quasi-contract because that would allow the lender to obtain an indirect remedy not available in contract. However, the courts of equity may grant a remedy to prevent the minor from being unjustly enriched by his own fraud. Additionally, s.3(1) of the Minors' Contracts Act 1987 provides that the courts have the power where they think it 'just and equitable' to require the minor to return the property, or 'property representing that which was acquired by him'.

Operation of a bank account by a minor

The first question, which arises is whether a bank can open an account in the name of a minor. A minor has the same capacity to enter into a contract to open a bank account as he does to

---

[105] Sale of Goods Act 1979, s.3(3).
[106] (1844) 14 M. & W. 252.
[107] [1908] 2 KB 1.
[108] *Re National Permanent Benefit Building Society* (1869) LR 5 Ch. App. 309; *Lewis v Alleyne* (1888) TLR 560.
[109] [1914] 3 KB 607.

enter into any other contract. A bank can, therefore, open an account for a minor and honour payment instructions so long as that account is in credit. As a matter of caution banks tend to open accounts either in the name of a minor's guardian or in the minor's name but on the understanding that the guardian will operate it. However, in both instances the bank's customer is the minor,[110] and because of the trust element, in such instances, the bank may become subject to fiduciary duties to the minor, especially if the withdrawals against the account, by the guardian, are out of the ordinary.[111]

With regard to the authority of the bank to pay against negotiable instruments drawn by a minor s.22(1) of the Bills of Exchange Act 1882 provides that a person's capacity to draw is the same as his capacity to enter into a simple contract. Thus, a person's capacity to incur liability on a bill is co-extensive with his capacity under the rules of contract. A minor may, therefore, sue on a bill of exchange[112] or other negotiable instrument but he cannot be made liable on a bill of exchange, cheque or other negotiable instrument. A holder in due course is not in any better position than a holder for value of the bill.[113]

A minor is not liable for a post-dated cheque although its date of payment is subsequent to his attaining his majority.[114] However, the signature of a minor does not invalidate the bill as a whole and s.22(2) of the Bills of Exchange Act 1882 provides that 'where a bill is drawn or endorsed by an infant [or minor] . . . the drawing or endorsing entitles the holder to receive payment of the bill, and to enforce it against any other party thereto'.

Problems may arise in respect of loans made to a minor although there is no legal bar to a bank permitting a minor to overdraw on his account or to extending an overdraft facility to a minor. Contracts that are not for 'necessaries' are unenforceable against a minor but the minors' immunity under such contracts may be removed by ratification of the contract once the minor has attained majority.[115] Although these contracts are unenforceable against a minor, property may pass from the minor to the other party. Where a bank does extend credit or grant a loan to a minor the bank may require a guarantee to be given by a person of full age. The question is whether a guarantor with full legal capacity will be personally liable to the bank if the minor, the principal debtor, defaults on the loan. In *Coutts & Co v Browne-Lecky*[116] an overdraft granted to a minor was guaranteed by two persons of full age and all the parties, including the bank, knew that the principal debtor was an infant (minor). The court held that the guarantors could not be made liable on the guarantee. The judge relied on *Swan v Bank of Scotland*[117] where a father who had guaranteed his infant son's overdraft could not be sued on the guarantee. Oliver J who relied on *Coutts & Co* also relied on the principle established by Pothier and quoted in de Colyar's *Law of Guarantees and Principles and Surety*,[118] where it was said:

---

[110] *Rowlandson v National Westminster Bank Ltd* [1978] 1 WLR 798.
[111] *Rowlandson v National Westminster Bank Ltd* [1978] 1 WLR 798.
[112] *Warwick v Bruce* (1813) 2 M. & S. 205.
[113] *Re Solykoff* [1891] 1 QB 413; *Levene v Brougham* (1909) 25 TLR 265.
[114] *Hutley v Peacock* (1913) 30 TLR 42; cf *Belfast Banking Co v Doherty* (1879) 4 LR Ir. 124 where the court held that a holder in due course may sue the acceptor of a debt incurred during infancy, but accepted after attaining majority.
[115] Minors' Contracts Act 1987, s.1(1).
[116] [1947] KB 104.
[117] (1836) 10 Bil NS 627.
[118] 3rd edition (1897), p. 210.

As the obligation of sureties is according to our definition an obligation accessory to that of a principal debtor, it follows that it is of the essence of the obligation that there should be a valid obligation of a principal debtor; consequently if the principal is not obliged, neither is the surety, as there can be no accessory without a principal obligation.

The law was, however, changed by the Minors' Contracts Act 1987 which repealed the Infants Relief Act 1874. Section 2 of the 1987 Act provides that where a guarantee is given in respect of an obligation to a contract made after the commencement of the Act, and the obligation is unenforceable against him because he was a minor when the contract was made, the guarantee is not to be unenforceable against the guarantor for that reason alone. The effect of the section is to ensure that a guarantee given in respect of a contract made by a minor is not invalid merely because the principal debt is unenforceable because of the minority of the debtor. Alternatively, the bank can require a person of full capacity to give an indemnity for the debts of the minor. With an indemnity the surety agrees with the lender that he will be legally liable for the existing or future indebtedness of the minor and in such circumstances the surety becomes primarily liable for the debts of the minor. His liability is not dependent on the default of the minor.[119]

Fairness in consumer contracts in the banking sector

Consumer choice and consumer access are key features of fairness in consumer contracts in the banking sector.[120] Standard form contracts, therefore, whether relating to customer accounts, payments, overdrafts or other borrowing, securities etc., in the banker and customer relationship that seek to exclude the liability of the bank, or restrict the right of the customer to seek relief, are subject to the Unfair Contract Terms Act 1977 (UCTA) and also the Unfair Terms in Consumer Contracts Regulations 1994 (UTCCR). Both highlight the struggle not only between consumer protection and freedom of contract, but also the balance between consumer protection and consumer choice,[121] and the UTCCR, specifically, attempt to redress national differences in treatment between EU Member States, by imposing minimum[122] harmonising standards in respect of consumer contracts and unfair terms. We will now examine some of the work which has been undertaken by the FSA and the OFT in the area of fair terms in banking contracts and then the effect of UCTA and UTCCR in banking contracts.[123]

---

[119] *Moschi v Lep Air Services Ltd* [1973] AC 331; *Wauthier v Wilson* (1912) 28 TLR 239.

[120] The attempt to control the nature and effect of exclusion clauses had been piecemeal before the Unfair Contract Terms Act 1977 (UCTA) with the first major attempt to control exclusion clauses being made under s.3 of the Misrepresentation Act 1967 (now replaced by an amended s.8 of UCTA), followed by the Supply of Goods (implied Terms) Act 1973 (similar provisions are now found in s.6 of UCTA). The legislative scheme introduced by UCTA is more comprehensive.

[121] See Collins (1994) *Good Faith in European Contract Law*, 14 *Oxford Journal of Legal Studies*, 229 where the author noted that the draft Directive proposed by the Commission envisaged the introduction of a general principle against substantive unfairness in consumer contracts.

[122] Although national governments may impose higher standards in order to protect their consumers: see Case C-484/08 *Caja de Ahorros y Monte de Piedad de Madrid* (3 June 2010).

[123] These areas are fundamental to the study of contract law and are dealt with in books on that subject. For a more extensive discussion see Peel (2011) *Treitel's Law of Contract*, London: Sweet & Maxwell.

The FSA regulation of the retail banking sector and fair terms in the retail banking

The FSMA 2000 required the FSA[124] to secure an appropriate degree of 'consumer protection' so that the consumer was placed in a position to make a fully informed judgement regarding the potential risks, costs and returns on the product. The Financial Conduct Authority (FCA) is now responsible for consumer protection and conduct regulation of all banks, retail and wholesale.[125] The Act also imposes a new statutory[126] objective under which the FCA is expected to reinforce and enhance the understanding and knowledge of the public on financial matters (including the UK financial system), their ability to manage their own financial affairs, and to promote the advantages of financial planning.[127] The lack of knowledge and awareness of the manner in which the financial services sector operates has been perceived by the government as a potential risk for consumers and an obstacle to sound regulation of the financial services. The knowledge and understanding imbalance will, in the majority of cases, be against the bank customer, but the new statutory objective places the onus on the FCA to ensure that it undertakes an education role. As with the, now repealed, 'public awareness' objective the new objective is intended to enhance the public's understanding of the financial system through promoting awareness of the benefits and risks associated with different kinds of investment or other financial dealing. The intention is to ensure that consumers can make reasonably informed decisions about whether, or not, to invest, including making fully informed decisions of the associated costs, with some understanding of the risks associated with the investment. The focus of these objectives is consumer empowerment. Prior to the 2012 changes in the regulatory structure the FSA had undertaken some work in the fair terms in the retail sector. It is intended to examine the nature of some of this work.

The FSA and fair terms in consumer banking contracts

The FSA was always in an anomalous position: it had to balance its ability to regulate the retail customers' core financial services relationship with its responsibility for the regulation of the payments services sector.[128] This anomaly potentially undermined the FSA's regulatory effectiveness because it was unable to look comprehensively across all risks affecting the firms' retail market activities. Voluntary Codes of Practice had been used to help customers understand and regulate obligations for a number of basic retail products, including bank accounts

---

[124] On 16 June 2010, George Osborne, the new Chancellor of the Exchequer, outlined plans to reform the regulation of the financial services sector and to abolish the tripartite system of bank regulation and to transfer the regulation of banks to the Bank of England. The FSA ceased to exist and a number of bodies established, including the Financial Conduct Authority (FCA) were established. The FCA is responsible for consumer protection and conduct regulation: see Ch. 4.

[125] Financial Services Act 2012, Ch. 1 inserts a new s.1A to the Financial Services and Markets Act 2000; see also Ch. 4.

[126] The 'public awareness' objective is superseded by the new s.3A 'enhancing understanding' objective under the Financial Services Act 2010.

[127] The FSA (now FCA) must establish a consumer education body whose main functions will be to educate the public on awareness in respect of financial products and dealings and associated risks ss.1 and 2 in the Financial Services Act 2010 insert a new s.6A: FSMA 2000.

[128] See the Payment Services Directive 2007/64/EC of the European Parliament and the Council of 13 November 2007 on payment services in the internal market amending Directives 97/7/EC, 2002/65/EC, 2005/60/EC and 2006/48/EC, 5.12.2007, OJ. L. 319/1.

and overdrafts.[129] In this atmosphere, the FSA undertook a survey into the effectiveness of the arrangements of consumer protection including a review of the effectiveness of the banking codes[130] and whether they remained appropriate in the light of its principles-based approach to regulation and the Treating Customers Fairly (TCF) initiative.[131] The review was also intended to determine whether the banking codes were the right model for the future, particularly in the light of the FSA's objective of addressing more comprehensively and efficiently the prudential and conducts risks affecting retail market activities.

The FSA identified two main types of market failure for a justification away from self-regulation, namely (i) potential failure in the retail market arising from asymmetric information held by providers and consumers, and (ii) regulatory failure arising from deficiencies in the arrangements. Furthermore, the review recognised gaps in the Voluntary Codes,[132] which included a lack of equivalence to the FSA's overarching fairness objective under Principle 6 of its Principles of Business,[133] which required firms to pay due regard to the interests of its customers and treat them fairly.[134] Following the review and consultation stages, the FSA published a policy statement on regulating the conduct of the retail banking business,[135] while at the same time as replacing the Voluntary Codes with the new Banking Conduct of Business Sourcebook (BCOBS)[136] and the implementation of the new Payment Services

---

[129] The deposit-taking products that fell within the remit, and regulation, of the codes included current, savings and deposit accounts, cash ISAs, child trust funds and payments services, including foreign exchange transactions. The codes also extended to overdrafts, personal and business loans and credit cards, http://www.bba. org.uk/bba/jsp/polopoly.jsp?d=140&a=13131.

[130] The first Banking code was implemented in March 1992 and was reviewed and revised on a number of occasions. The code was reviewed for a third time in 2007, and amendments effected from 31 March 2008, with key commitments to the fair treatment of customers and a commitment to lend responsibly being introduced, together with subscribers contacting customers they felt may be facing financial difficulties. The first Business Banking code came into effect in March 2002 with the 2008 revision giving an undertaking to give clear information about accounts and services, how they work, their terms and conditions and the interest rates which may apply, http://www.bba.org.uk/content/1/c6/01/31/27/Business_Code_2008.pdf. As at September 2008, there were 119 subscribers to one or both of the codes comprising banks, building societies, one credit union and other financial service providers (including National Savings and Investments). The codes were drawn up, and their content maintained, by the three industry 'sponsor' organisations: the British Bankers' Association (BBA), the Building Societies Association (BSA) and APACS, the UK Payments Association. Subscription to the codes was voluntary. Virtually all providers of retail deposit products (aside from credit unions) were subscribers to the Banking code. The Banking Code Standards Board (BCSB) undertook day-to-day monitoring of adherence by subscribers, and enforcement of the codes under a contractual relationship with each subscriber, http://www.fsa.gov.uk/pubs/cp/cp08_19.pdf. The codes were reviewed to reflect market developments, innovation and changes in the regulatory environment.

[131] FSA, *Regulating retail banking conduct of business*, Consultation Paper 08/19, November 2008, http://www.fsa. gov.uk/pubs/cp/cp08_19.pdf.

[132] Including in respect of enforcement which was the responsibility of the BCSB.

[133] The new framework for the regulation of retail banking applies the FSA's Principles for Businesses to regulated activities, for example accepting deposits and the FSA, Principles of Business, Principle 6 provides that 'a firm must pay due regard to the interests of its customers and treat them fairly', http://www.ecompli.co.uk/html/ FSAPrinciplesofBusiness_407.html.

[134] FSA, *Regulating retail banking conduct of business*, Consultation Paper 08/19, November 2008, http://www.fsa. gov.uk/pubs/cp/cp08_19.pdf.

[135] FSA, *Regulating retail banking conduct of business*, Policy Statement 09/6, April 2009, http://www.fsa.gov.uk/ pubs/policy/ps09_06.pdf.

[136] FSA, *Banking Conduct of Business Sourcebook*, http://www.fsa.gov.uk/Pages/Doing/Regulated/bcobs/index.shtml.

Directive Regulations.[137] The new regime was intended to deliver a framework to customers where fairness was to be the central theme to the FSA's supervision and enforcement work.[138] The BCOBS introduced new high-level outcome-focused rules that apply to retail banking services for consumers and small businesses. Those parts of the FSA's Conduct of Business Sourcebook (COBS) that were incorporated into BCOBS relate to communicating with clients, including financial promotions,[139] distance communications,[140] disclosure requirements,[141] and cancellation.[142] BCOBS was superseded by the Lending Standards Board which in 2011 issued a Lending Code which now applies to retail customers and micro-enterprises.[143]

The FSA and unfair terms in banking contracts

While assessing the effectiveness of the regulation of the retail banking services sector generally, the FSA was also looking at the impact of the unfair contract terms in the banking sector. The FSA viewed unfair contract terms as a strong indicator of failure by a financial firm to treat its customer's fairly. The FSA therefore confirmed that Treating the Customer Fairly (TCF) was now a core part of its supervisory work and a key priority within the FSA's retail strategy. In 2013 the FCA Principles for Businesses made this a key priority and PRIN 2.1 provides that firms must pay due regard to the interests of their customers and treat them fairly.[144]

However, in June 2008, the FSA had published its report, 'Fairness of terms in consumer contracts: Firms' awareness of and compliance with the Unfair Terms in Consumer Contracts Regulations',[145] that outlined the results of its review of awareness of financial firms, and compliance with, the UTCCRs 1999. The aim of this study is to ensure that firms recognise the importance that fair terms play in complying with the Treating the Customer Fairly (TCF) principle, as well as explaining good and bad practice. The report concluded that many financial firms still used unfair terms in consumer contracts and the FSA[146] warned firms to take urgent action to review and amend their terms, as necessary, and to ensure that they have in place systems and controls to ensure fairness of customer contracts. In December 2008, the FSA[147]

---

[137] SI 2009/209 which implemented the Payment Services Directive (2007/64/EC), OJ No L 319, 5.12, 2997, p. 1. The Directive replaced about 40 per cent of the Banking and Business Codes and applies to the regulated activity of accepting deposits, and replaces the non-lending aspects of the Banking Code and Business Banking Code.

[138] Annex 2 of FSA, Regulating retail banking conduct of business, Policy Statement 09/6, April 2009, http://www.fsa.gov.uk/pubs/policy/ps09_06.pdf outlines the relationship between the BCOBS and the PSRs with Appendix 1 setting out the final text of the new Handbook rules and guidance for the BPS.

[139] FSA, COBS 4.2, Fair, clear and not misleading communications, http://fsahandbook.info/FSA/html/handbook/COBS/4/2.

[140] FSA, COBS 5, The distance marketing disclosure rule, http://fsahandbook.info/FSA/html/handbook/COBS/5/1.

[141] FSA, COBS 13, The obligation to prepare product information, http://fsahandbook.info/FSA/html/handbook/COBS/13/1; FSA, COBS 14.2, Providing product information to client, http://fsahandbook.info/FSA/html/handbook/COBS/14/2.

[142] FSA, COBS 15.2, The Right to Cancel, http://fsahandbook.info/FSA/html/handbook/COBS/15/2.

[143] http://www.lendingstandardsboard.org.uk/docs/lendingcode.pdf.

[144] http://www.fshandbook.info/FS/html/FCA/PRIN/2/1.

[145] FSA, Fairness of terms in consumer contracts: Firms' awareness of and compliance with the Unfair Terms in Consumer Contracts Regulations 1999, Consumer Research 66, June 2008, prepared by GfK NOP, http://www.fsa.gov.uk/pubs/consumer-research/crpr66.pdf.

[146] FSA, Fairness of terms in consumer contracts: a visible factor in firms treating their customers fairly, June 2008, http://www.fsa.gov.uk/pubs/other/consumer_contracts_report.pdf.

[147] FSA, Update on the Treating Customers Fairly initiative and the December deadline, http://www.fsa.gov.uk/pubs/other/tcf_deadline.pdf.

issued a reminder that it expected all financial firms to ensure that they use fair terms in consumer contracts. The FSA report explained its approach to unfair contract terms in consumer contacts and stated that where the FSA identified a term as unfair it would follow procedure set out in the FSA's Unfair Contract Terms Regulatory Guide (UNFCOG).[148]

In January 2009, the FSA manager of the Unfair Contract Terms Team[149] again reiterated its approach to unfair contract terms in consumer contracts and expressed the view that firms should be proactive in reviewing the fairness of their contractual terms and, within the context of the UTCCRs, a number of factors should be taken into account when trying to determine whether a term is likely to be considered fair. Firms must ensure:

- They have in place a robust controls system to ensure that the firm's consumer contracts are fair including ensuring that senior management receive and use appropriate management information to measure the effectiveness of the systems and controls for contracts.

- That those drafting contracts are adequately skilled and there are adequate systems in place to verify that the contracts reflect legal and regulatory developments.

- That someone with appropriate expertise and experience signs off newly-drafted contracts.

- That the information in the contract and its presentation is appropriate for the target audience.

- That the content of the contract is clear, fair and not misleading.

- There are adequate systems and controls in place to ensure that terms are fairly applied.

Firms should also have in place senior management who receive and can use appropriate management information to measure the effectiveness of systems and controls for ensuring that consumer contracts are not contrary to the unfairness requirements of the regulations and that the contract is fair. In January 2012, the FSA published a statement of the types of contractual terms which are commonly seen to be of concern under the 1999 Regulations, including terms that give banks the right to unilaterally vary the contract, the right to terminate the contract, the right to transfer its obligations under the contract and terms that are not in plain and intelligible language.[150]

In April 2012, the FSA published a speech by Clive Gordon emphasising that it continued to be disappointed by the lack of attention given to unfair terms in consumer contracts and

[148] The FSA expressed the view that would form a view on whether it considered a contract term as potentially unfair, although only a court can decide whether it is actually unfair. As a risk-based and proportionate regulator, the FSA would carry out a risk assessment to assess the level of actual or potential detriment to consumers posed by an unfair contract term. When a complaint was considered to be unfair the FSA would seek the views of the firm and if unsatisfied the FSA would require the firm to amend or delete the term. If the issue is not resolved the FSA will take enforcement action through the courts. Any changes undertaken had to be notified to customers and protect them from significant financial detriment. The FSA would require the firm to give an undertaking to treat existing customers fairly by treating them as if the new, fairly drafted term formed part of the original contract. Where the FSA received a number of complaints about the same issue then that may be taken to indicate an industry wide problem regarding the particular term, for example in respect of unauthorised overdraft bank charges, FSA, Unfair Contract Terms Regulatory Guide, http://fsahandbook.info/FSA/html/handbook/UNFCOG/1/1.

[149] Webster, FSA's interpretation of the Unfair Terms in Consumer Contracts Regulations 1999, Manager of the Unfair Contract Terms Team, FSA CML's 7th annual legal issues for mortgage lenders conference, 13 January 2009, http://www.fsa.gov.uk/pages/Library/Communication/Speeches/2009/0113_kw.shtml.

[150] FSA, Unfair contract terms: improving standards in consumer contracts, January 2012, http://www.fsa.gov.uk/static/pubs/guidance/fg12_02.pdf.

the failure to review contracts routinely. The FSA remained concerned about systems and controls that firms had in place relating to contractual terms and wanted to identify the root causes of why some firms continued to have unfair terms in their contracts, and it considered that the wording of contracts should be something that firms considered at the product design stage.[151] The FSA view was that senior managers are ultimately responsible for ensuring that contractual terms are fair.[152]

The work of the Office of Fair Trading in the area of unfair contract terms

Against the background of the work undertaken by the FSA, the Office of Fair Trading (OFT) (abolished by the Enterprise and Regulatory Reform Act 2013[153] and replaced by the Competition and Markets Authority)[154] launched its market survey into Personal Current Accounts (PCAs), to assess whether the PCA market was now operating in a satisfactory manner for consumers. Two previous studies[155] had expressed concerns about the retail banking market: (i) The Cruickshank Report, in March 2000, concluded that consumers were not adequately informed about financial products, that they found it difficult to compare them and that competition was not operating effectively, and (ii) an investigation by the Competition Commission, in Northern Ireland, concluded that there was lack of information and transparency in respect of charging structures and practices for PCAs which meant that customers believed that changing banks was more difficult than in practice. The OFT survey[156] looked into the fairness of the level and application of insufficient funds charges and wider questions about competition and value for money in respect of the provision of PCAs in the UK, and specifically into the low levels of transparency and cost structures employed by UK banks for charges on unauthorised bank overdrafts; and the ease with which customers could transfer or switch accounts between banking institutions. The survey concluded that the PCA market still did not work well for consumers due to the complexity in bank charges and lack of transparency, which made it difficult for customers to assess different bank accounts.[157]

The OFT therefore concluded that complexity and lack of transparency meant that both consumers and competition focus almost exclusively on the more visible fees, and not on the

---

[151] FSA, Clive Gordon, Unfair Contract Terms – Ensuring a fair deal for consumers, 21 March 2012, http://www.fsa.gov.uk/library/communication/speeches/2012/uct-clive-gordon.shtml.

[152] FSA, Clive Gordon, Unfair Contract Terms – Ensuring a fair deal for consumers, 21 March 2012, http://www.fsa.gov.uk/library/communication/speeches/2012/uct-clive-gordon.shtml.

[153] Section 26.

[154] Section 25.

[155] See: The Cruickshank Report, Competition in UK Banking, a Report to the Chancellor of the Exchequer, 20 March 2000; and also a separate investigation by the Competition Commission in Northern Ireland, Personal Current Account Banking Services in Northern Ireland market Investigation.

[156] OFT Market Survey, Personal current accounts in the UK, July 2008, http://www.oft.gov.uk/shared_oft/reports/financial_products/OFT1005.pdf.

[157] In January 2009, the European Commission published its second annual Consumer Markets Scoreboard Report which was created by the Commission for use as a tool under its Consumer Market Watch process to help monitor markets from a consumer perspective. The aim of the Scoreboard is to develop comprehensive EU-wide comparable data on a range of issues. The Commission has, however, concluded that retail banking services is one of the most problematic areas for consumers and the report identified that there were very low rates of consumers switching accounts between providers and banks increasingly charging 'non-transparent' fees. The Commission also concluded that consumers found it hard to compare interest rates, fees and offers between Member States and explanations were not easily comprehensible. European Commission, Data collection for prices of current accounts provided to consumers, Final Report, 2009, http://ec.europa.eu/consumers/strategy/docs/prices_current_accounts_report_en.pdf.

less visible elements such as insufficient funds charges and interest forgone by customers on credit balances, despite the fact that these make up the vast bulk of banks' revenues. For insufficient funds charges, the effects were exacerbated by lack of simple mechanisms for consumers to control, or opt out of, an unarranged overdraft. Furthermore, a significant proportion of consumers still believe that it is both complex and risky to switch accounts, with the result that switching rates are very low. Paul Tucker, then Deputy Governor of the Bank of England, appearing before the Treasury Select Committee in July 2013, emphasised his support for increasing the portability of PCAs and suggested that the framework for the PCA must be adapted to facilitate enhanced portability.[158] The OFT therefore concluded that the market had become distorted in a number of ways:

1 There appeared to be a substantial cross-subsidisation from those consumers who incurred insufficient funds charges, to those who did not and to a significant extent from vulnerable low-income and low-saving consumers, to higher-income and higher-saving customers.

2 The extent of the cross-subsidisation meant there was a substantial misalignment between a bank's revenue and its cost on many of its services. This could lead to inefficiencies through under or over consumption of services by consumers.

3 The lack of consumer awareness and switching accounts provided banks with little incentive to compete and provide the best services to the customer.

Consequently, the OFT survey concluded that the market did not work well for consumers with a significant number of them not having knowledge of how much they will pay in bank charges and fees, and how individual elements of the fee structure was implemented. The OFT market survey also provided further impetus for the additional OFT investigation into Unfair Terms in Consumer Contracts Regulations (UTCCRs).[159]

In order to resolve the issues relating to unauthorised bank charges, the OFT – liaising with the FSA – entered into an agreement with seven banks and one building society[160] which constituted the largest providers of the PCAs in the UK, to launch a test case in the High Court to determine the fairness of the relevant terms and charges applied, by the institutions, to unarranged PCA overdrafts. On the same day, and in order to lend its support to the test case, the FSA announced a waiver[161] suspending the processing of customer complaints[162] in

---

[158] Treasury Select Committee, Uncorrected oral evidence, Bank of England June 2013, Financial Stability Report, 5 July 2013, http://www.parliament.uk/documents/commons-committees/treasury/TC%2002%2007%2013%20(2).pdf, p. 12.

[159] OFT, Investigation under the Unfair Terms in Consumer Contracts Regulations into the fairness of personal current account contract terms providing for unarranged overdraft charges, April 2007, http://www.oft.gov.uk/OFTwork/consumer-enforcement/consumer-enforcement-completed/UTCCRs/.

[160] The banks involved in the test case were: Abbey National Plc, Barclays Bank Plc, Clydesdale Bank Plc, HBOS Plc, Lloyds TSB Bank Plc, HSBC Plc, Royal Bank of Scotland Plc, together with the Nationwide Building Society and the Office of Fair Trading.

[161] The FSA granted the banks and the Financial Ombudsman service a waiver to enable them to stop processing customer complaints regarding unauthorised bank charges pending the outcome of the test case. The first waiver was granted in July 2007 and was followed by a further six-month waiver in July 2008, which was then extended for a further six months in January 2009. The last waiver was granted in July 2009 but withdrawn in November 2009 following the decision of the Supreme Court.

[162] The FSA revealed that almost one million complaints relating to unauthorised overdraft charges had been put on hold since July 2007. Many thousands of individual actions had been successfully brought against the banks, http://www.fsa.gov.uk/pages/Library/Communication/PR/2009/100.shtml.

respect of unauthorised overdraft charges, until the test case was settled. Further, County Court claims instituted by individual customers[163] were stayed pending the outcome of the OFT action.[164] The relevant terms on the basis of which the banks were making the charges were therefore being challenged on two fronts simultaneously:[165] (i) by the OFT investigating the fairness of the terms under which the banks imposed such charges, and (ii) by the thousands of individual claims in the County Courts disputing the charges levied by the banks not only on the basis of the UTCCR, but also on the basis that these charges amounted to penalties that were unenforceable under the rules of common law. The banks, in order to obtain a comprehensive decision, counter-claimed.

Unfair contract terms legislation and banking contracts

The Unfair Contract Terms Act 1977

The Unfair Contract Terms Act 1977 (UCTA) applies to both the provision of goods and services, including banking services, where one of the parties enters into the contract as a 'consumer'.[166] The Act is concerned with terms and clauses that seek to exclude or restrict liability,[167] rather than unfair terms generally and applies to not only contractual terms but also to non-contractual terms that purport to restrict or exclude liability in tort. Under the Act an exclusion clause is a term[168] that excludes or restricts liability in respect of a breach of contract. Such clauses are subject to the test of reasonableness[169] and the onus of proof, i.e. to the effect that the clause is reasonable, is on the bank. The Act also applies the reasonableness test to terms that purport to entitle the other party to render performance substantially different from that reasonably expected, or no performance at all in respect of the whole, or any part, of the contractual obligation.[170] Section 11(1) of UCTA provides that the term must be 'fair and reasonable' having regard to the circumstances that were, or ought reasonably to have been, known to the parties at the time the contract was concluded. Section 11 also sets out a number of non-exhaustive factors, including the resources of the parties and their

---

[163] Banks continued to deal with complaints where customers suffer hardship as a result of the processing of actions being stayed, http://www.fsa.gov.uk/pages/Library/Communication/PR/2007/090.shtml.

[164] A complaint that the UTCCR has been infringed may be pursued by an action in the County Court by an individual consumer by reference to the particular contract entered into with the service provider, or by a qualifying body (schedule 1, The Unfair Terms in Consumer Contracts Regulations 1999, SI 1999/2083), or the OFT under the s.213(1)(a) of the Enterprise Act 2002, as a 'general enforcer' of 'Community Infringements'.

[165] The learned judge, at first instance in *OFT v Abbey National Plc*, accepted the conclusion of the House of Lords in *Director General Of Fair Trading v First National Bank Plc* [2001] UKHL 52 that the then 1994 Regulations (and now the UTCCRs 1999), allow for a dual system of challenges to the validity of contractual terms but whatever the form of the challenge, the assessment of the fairness of the terms is on the basis of individual contracts entered into with the customer challenging the terms, or on the collective challenges on the basis of a notional contract with a hypothetical customer. The Regulations, therefore, make provision for a number of 'qualifying bodies' to apply to the court for injunctive relief against the use of unfair terms, schedule 1, The Unfair Terms in Consumer Contracts Regulations 1999, SI 1999/2083.

[166] Unfair Contract Terms Act 1977, s.12(1).

[167] Unfair Contract Terms Act 1977, s.13(1).

[168] Unfair Contract Terms Act 1977, s.3(2).

[169] Unfair Contract Terms Act 1977, s.11(1).

[170] Unfair Contract Terms Act 1977, s.3(2)(b).

ability to underwrite any losses, which the courts may take into consideration in determining whether the clause is reasonable. The courts have given some indication of the factors that may be relevant in determining whether a clause satisfies the requirement of reasonableness. However, in *Phillips Products Ltd v Hyland*[171] the Court of Appeal held that each decision turns on its own particular circumstances and so just because the type of clause is held as unreasonable in one case does not automatically mean it will be struck down in all other similar circumstances. The scope of discretion the courts have in interpreting s.11 of UCTA was made plain by Lord Bridge in *George Mitchell (Chesterhall) Ltd v Finney Lock Seeds Ltd*[172] where in explaining the approach of the courts as to what is 'fair and reasonable' he said:

> the court must entertain a whole range of considerations, put them in the scales on one side or the other, and decide at the end of the day on which side the balance comes down. There will sometimes be room for a legitimate difference of judicial opinion as to what the answer should be, where it will be impossible to say that one view is demonstrably wrong or the other demonstrably right . . .

The requirement of reasonableness was also explored in *Smith v Eric S Bush*[173] where Lord Griffiths said that four questions should always be considered in deciding the issue of reasonableness:

1 Were the parties of equal bargaining power?

2 In the case of advice, would it have been reasonably practical to obtain the advice from an alternative source taking into account considerations of cost and time?

3 How difficult is the task being undertaken for which liability is being excluded?

4 What are the practical consequences of the decision on the question of reasonableness?

Lord Griffiths then continued that:

> This must involve sums of money potentially at stake and the ability of the parties to bear the loss involved, which in turn raises the question of insurance . . .

The section may, therefore, apply to protect the customer when a bank seeks to limit the rights of the customer, for example to have erroneous debits against his account. The Privy Council examined the scope and effect of such limitation of liability clauses in the context of the banker and customer relationship in *Tai Hing Cotton Mill Ltd v Lui Chong Hing Bank Ltd,*[174] and held that written contracts entered into by a customer with three banks in Hong Kong, each of which contained clauses restricting the customer's right to notify banks of wrongful debits, resulting from fraudulent cheques being drawn against the customer's account and paid by the three banks with whom the customer maintained accounts, to seven days, were invalid.

The Privy Council concluded that under the general law the customer's right to have the fraudulent transactions reversed and his account re-credited could not be doubted, but the effectiveness of the express terms which sought to place the customer under an obligation to check his bank statements, and to notify the bank of any errors within a stated timeframe, had

---

[171] [1987] 2 All ER 631.
[172] [1983] AC 803.
[173] [1990] AC 831.
[174] [1986] AC 80.

to be examined by the court. The Privy Council, examining the scope and validity of these clauses, held that although the terms restricting the time of notification given to the customer were properly incorporated into the written and signed contracts, they were not expressed in language that was sufficiently robust to bring home to the customer either the intended importance of the verification of the bank statements, or the effect of the restrictions regarding the notification period. The limitation of liability clauses were, therefore, not reasonable and consequently unenforceable since they did not bring to the attention of the bank's customer the consequences of failure to notify the bank of errors on the bank statement.

The Unfair Terms in Consumer Contracts Regulations 1994

The EU Directive on Unfair Terms in Consumer Contracts[175] is clear in its objectives; namely the protection of consumers 'by adopting uniform rules of laws in the matter of unfair terms'[176] and reducing the distortions in competition between sellers of goods and suppliers of services caused by differences in national laws in consumer contracts. In *Director General of Fair Trading v First National Bank Plc*[177] Lord Steyn identified the Directive as:

> . . . Aimed at contracts of adhension, viz 'take it or leave it' contracts. It treats consumers as presumptively weaker parties and therefore fit for protection from abuses by the stronger contracting parties. This is an objective which must throughout guide the interpretation of the Directive as well as the implementing Regulations.

The Council Directive[178] was implemented in the UK, in the Unfair Contract Terms in Consumer Contract Regulations 1999,[179] which came into effect on 1 October 1999. Regulation 4(1) of the 1999 Regulations apply to 'unfair terms' in contracts concluded between a seller or a supplier and consumer and reg. 5(1) provides that a contractual term which has not been 'negotiated shall be regarded as unfair if, contrary to the requirement of good faith, it causes a significant imbalance in the parties' rights and obligations arising under the contract to the detriment of the consumer'. Regulation 6 (2) provides that the fairness of what are known as 'core terms' should not be assessed in so far are they are 'in plain intelligible language' and relate '(a) to the definition of the main subject matter of the contract, or (b) to the adequacy of the price or remuneration, as against the goods or services provided in exchange'.

Consequently, the regulations are particularly relevant to the standard form contracts which banks use as the basis of their normal banking business and consumer contracts entered into with their personal current account (PCA) customers.

It was conceded before Andrew Smith J, at first instance, in *The Office of Fair Trading v Abbey National Plc*[180] that the terms on which PCA customers will have entered into contracts for the provision of such services is not 'individually negotiated', notwithstanding that the banks received individually signed mandates in respect of their instructions regarding payments to and from their customers. Andrew Smith J was asked to assess a number

---

[175] Council Directive 93/13/EEC on Unfair Terms in Consumer Contracts, OJ L 095, 21/4/1993.
[176] Recital 10, Council Directive 93/13/EEC on Unfair Terms in Consumer Contracts, OJ L 095, 21/4/1993.
[177] [2001] UKHL 52, [2002] 1 AC 481.
[178] OJ L 095, 21/4/1993.
[179] The 1999 Regulations, SI 1999/2083, revoked and repealed the Unfair Contract Terms in Consumer Contracts Terms Regulations 1994.
[180] [2009] EWHC 36 (COMM).

of issues but the main question before the court was whether, or not, the OFT was entitled, under the UTCCRs 1999, to examine the fairness of bank charges levied on unauthorised overdrafts. It was agreed between the parties that unless such an assessment was prohibited by reg. 6(2)(b) of UTCCRs, the OFT was entitled to assess 'relevant terms' for fairness.

The learned judge held that although the terms generally used by some of the banks, in respect of PCAs, were in 'plain and intelligible language',[181] and those used by the other banks were largely in 'plain and intelligible language', except in relatively minor respects, the terms under which charges were levied were not exempt from assessment as to fairness because they were not 'core provisions' or part of the 'essential services' provided by banks. The judge examined these issues in detail.

Plain and intelligible language

Regulation 6(2) UTCCRs provides that terms in consumer contracts that have not been individually negotiated must be in 'plain and intelligible language' but Andrew Smith J examined to whom the terms must be intelligible. Regulation 6(2) requires the actual wording of individual clauses to be comprehensible to the typical consumer so that he understands how his rights and obligations are affected by the clause. The question, therefore, is whether the contractual terms proposed by the seller or supplier are sufficiently clear to enable the typical consumer to have a 'proper understanding' of them for sensible and practical purposes. Within the context of the PCA, Andrew Smith J expressed the opinion that the customer is entitled to understand the types, and circumstances, of charges the bank is entitled to levy and the amount of the fee. The customer 'does not need an education in the full complexities of banking systems' and the 1999 Regulations do not require the banks to engage in that.

Non-contractual terms given to the consumer, for example in the form of leaflets, are only relevant as an aid towards assessing whether the relevant terms are intelligible. Even if, unusually, a customer does have an understanding of how the banking systems operate, it would not necessarily mean that the customer would have knowledge, with certainty, of what funds he has in his account.[182] However, the OFT argued that for terms to be in 'plain and intelligible language', their meaning, effect and application must be apparent to the 'typical consumer' and the consumer must be able to make a fully informed choice about whether, or not, to enter into a contract.[183] The learned judge accepted that there was 'no real dispute between the parties that the question whether terms are in plain intelligible language' is to be considered from the point of view of the 'typical or average consumer'.

---

[181] As required by reg. 6(2) of the Unfair Contract Terms in Consumer Contracts Terms Regulations 1999.

[182] This will be dependent on the nature of the payment mandate given by the customer, for example, the payee of a cheque may present it for payment at any time within six months from the date in the instrument, *Byles on Bills of Exchange and Cheques* (2007) 28th edn, London: Sweet & Maxwell; the payee of a direct debit has a window of three working days during which to collect a payment in accordance with the instruction, Brindle and Cox (2004) *The Law of Bank Payments*, 3rd edn, London: Sweet & Maxwell.

[183] Andrew Smith J, *obiter*, considered the effect of an established relationship and a course of dealings with the bank and the effect on the relationship of a change in terms and concluded that 'if terms differ from previous terms or an established pattern of dealing, the modified or amended terms would need to be clearer for them to be held in "plain and intelligible language"'.

Fairness of terms

Having decided that the terms were in 'plain and intelligible language,' Andrew Smith J considered the scope of reg. 6(2)(b) and the issue of fairness; a question previously explored by the House of Lords in *Director General of Fair Trading v First National Bank Plc*[184] where the Lords had held that a default provision in a loan agreement between a bank and a consumer borrower was subject to an assessment of fairness and did not fall to be excluded from that assessment on the basis of reg. 4(2) of the 1994 regulations. The purpose of reg. 4(2) was to exclude from assessment the essential or 'core features' of the bargain and not the incidental or ancillary terms; interest payments which became payable only in the event of default were not core provisions and therefore subject to the test of fairness.

While the case left some questions unresolved, for example, how would the general guidance relating to core provisions be given effect outside the default cases, it was authoritatively relied on in the *Abbey National* case, with Andrew Smith J and the Court of Appeal concluding that the exemptions relating to core terms had to be narrowly construed and such terms as were excluded from an assessment of unfairness had to fall 'squarely within it'.[185] Andrew Smith J then went onto consider whether an assessment of fairness of the relevant terms was permitted if the terms related to the 'adequacy of the price or remuneration'.

Price or remuneration

It was argued, on behalf of the banks, that the 'relevant charges' were the price or remuneration, or part of the price or remuneration, for services supplied by them on two alternatives, although not mutually inconsistent, grounds:

- That banks supply their PCA customers with a 'bundle' or 'package' of services which enable customers to manage their day-to-day finances, and this includes services whereby customers can, without making prior arrangements, request an overdraft by issuing a payment instruction which, if granted, will increase or create a borrowing, from the bank on its standard terms. The relevant charges (together with revenue from other sources, particularly from interest paid by customers on other borrowings and the use by the bank of credit balances in the customer's account) are the price or remuneration for the package of services; or

- If the relevant charges were not regarded as part of the price or remuneration for the package of services supplied by the bank, then they were the price or remuneration for some part of those services, i.e., for the services supplied in connection with borrowing requests where no facility has been pre-arranged.

Andrew Smith J, however, rejected the argument that the consideration procedure a bank undertakes in order to determine whether, or not, to grant an overdraft facility following a 'relevant instruction' amounts to the provision of services[186] and held that the typical bank customer would not recognise such charges as the price or remuneration for those services when he opens a PCA. The Court of Appeal[187] reached the same conclusion as Andrew Smith

---

[184] [2001] UKHL 52, [2002] 1 AC 481.

[185] Lord Bingham in *Director General Of Fair Trading v First National Bank Plc* [2001] UKHL 52.

[186] This is in contrast to services supplied by an architect who prepares preliminary drawings or a doctor for medical services even if the patient is not cured.

[187] [2009] EWCA Civ 116.

J regarding the construction of reg. 6(2)(b), but it adopted a wider approach and expressed the view that under reg. 6(2)(b) the fairness of the payment obligations was exempted from assessment (in point of adequacy) only if they formed part of the core or 'essential bargain',[188] between the parties. The Court of Appeal concluded that the relevant charges levied by the banks were ancillary payment obligations and not part of the 'essential bargain' since the typical bank customer would not recognise them as the price for services supplied by the banks. The relevant terms were not the subject of bargaining between the bank (supplier of services) and the customer. The fact that the charges were contingent and not specifically negotiated were strong indicators that the charges were not the 'price or remuneration' within reg. 6(2) of the UTCCRs 1999 and therefore an assessment of the fairness of the relevant charges was not excluded.

In *The Office of Fair Trading* v *Abbey National Plc*[189] the Supreme Court held that both the judge at first instance, Andrew Smith J, and the Court of Appeal, had applied an over-complex approach to an issue, which although important to a significant number of bank customers was in fact a simple issue of construction. The Supreme Court concluded that both Art. 4(2) of the Directive and reg. 6(2) of UTCCRs were two sides of the same coin (the *quid pro quo* in consumer contracts) and the courts could not decide that some services, where the contract is one for composite services (for example an entertainer booked to perform for an hour at a children's party or a week's stay at a five star hotel offering a wide variety of services), were more essential than others. The services banks offer to their PCA customers are a comparable package and the bank charges levied on PCA customers for the grant of unauthorised overdrafts by their banks constitute part of the price to be paid for the composite package of services. It was, therefore, inappropriate to analyse the transactions as 'principal' and 'ancillary'.

Lord Walker said that consideration, in the context of the 'free-if-in-credit' PCA offered by the banks, consisted of the interest surrendered by customers, whose accounts were in credit. Interest foregone was an important part of the package for customers whose accounts were in credit, and overdraft interest and charges were an important element of the consideration for those customers who were not in credit. Just as banking services to PCA holders could be described as a package, so could the consideration that moved from the customer to the bank. The only question for the court when applying reg. 6(2)(b) was whether the relevant charges paid by PCA customers were part of the price or remuneration. The Supreme Court was content to allow a less restrictive interpretation of reg. 6 and concluded that any monetary, price or remuneration payable under the contract would naturally fall within the language of reg. 6 (2)(b), including bank charges whether contingent or not, even if incurred only by a minority of the customers, and even if the charges only constituted a part of the price. The approach of the lower courts was rejected as 'complex' and necessitating a 'value judgement'. The relevant terms and charges did fall squarely within the exclusion under reg. 6 (2)(b) and were part of the price or remuneration for banking services provided. The OFT was not therefore entitled to assess the fairness of such charges under the UTCCR 1999 in relation to their adequacy as against the services provided.

---

[188] Andrew Smith J expressed the view that the provision of an unarranged overdraft is part of the 'essential services' supplied by a bank operating current accounts. The Court of Appeal disagreed and said that the question is not 'what is an essential service?' but 'what is the core or essential bargain between the parties?'
[189] [2009] UKSC 6.

BANKING LAW IN PRACTICE

The Consumer Rights Bill 2013

The draft Consumer Rights Bill was published on 12 June 2013 and will represent a major overhaul of the UK consumer protection laws. The Bill seeks to consolidate important parts of consumer law, make it more user-friendly and robust and bring it up to date to account for the digital age. The new law, expected to come into force in June 2014, will have an impact on all business-to-consumer (B2C) businesses, including businesses that provide goods, services, digital content or any combination and whether provided online or in stores. The Bill is split into three main sections: (i) consumer contracts for goods, services and digital; (ii) control of unfair contract terms in consumer contracts; and (iii) clarification and strengthening of enforcement powers.

The Bill considerably strengthens consumer rights in relation to unfair terms. The B2C provisions in the current Unfair Terms in Consumer Contracts Regulations 1999 and Unfair Contract Terms Act 1977 will be consolidated in the new legislation.

The test for an 'unfair' term will remain the same, i.e. one which 'causes a significant imbalance' in the rights and obligations of the parties under the contract, to the detriment of the consumer. In addition to non-core terms (terms other than price or subject matter), the test is extended to apply to consumer notices (whether or not in writing). Core terms on price or subject matter will only be exempt from the fairness test if they are presented in a transparent and prominent manner. The effect of this provision is to restrict the impact of the decision of the Supreme Court in the Office of Fair Trading versus Abbey National Plc case where the court held that the relevant terms and charges fell squarely within the exclusion under reg. 6 (2)(b) and were part of the price or remuneration for the banking services provided. Such terms could not therefore not be assessed in respect of the fairness of such charges under the UTCCR 1999 in relation to their adequacy as against the services provided. As with other terms, such terms will now have to satisfy the fairness test.

The current provisions on terms having to be in plain and intelligible language will be further boosted by an obligation on the supplier to bring particularly onerous terms to the consumer's attention. The grey list of clauses that are deemed to be unfair has also been revised and expanded.

Conclusion

The banking customer often enters into a contract on the basis of standard terms imposed by banks, with no opportunity to negotiate those terms. Frequently, standard form contracts are signed without the customer having either the opportunity, or the incentive, to read the terms. While for some contracts a statutory cooling-off period may redress the balance somewhat, the customer will often enter into a contract without even a reasonable awareness of the obligations undertaken by him. Customer challenges to the nature of standard terms in banking contracts have come through in various forms, for example in charges levied for unauthorised bank overdrafts. Some of these challenges have been supported by consumer organisations. The law too has gone some way to protect the customer but further work needs to be done. The FCA is meant to champion the interests of the consumer by both educating customers and protecting their interests. This is an area of the law where further developments are likely to follow.

Further reading

➤ The Cruickshank Report, *Competition in UK Banking, a Report to the Chancellor of the Exchequer*, 20 March 2000, http://webarchive.nationalarchives.gov.uk/+/http://www.hm-treasury.gov.uk/fin_bank_reviewfinal.htm.
The scope of the review included the examination of the levels of innovation, competition and efficiency both within the industry and in comparison to international standards. This report concluded that consumers were not adequately informed about their financial products, and found it difficult to compare them, which impeded competition.

➤ Competition Commission, *Personal Current Account Banking Services in Northern Ireland Market Investigation*, http://www.oft.gov.uk/shared_oft/reports/financial_products/oft796.pdf.
Following complaints regarding the nature of competition within the personal current account market in Northern Ireland, the Competition Commission launched an investigation. This investigation concluded there was a lack of information and transparency about charging structures and practices. In turn, consumers believed switching banks was more difficult than in practice.

➤ OFT Market Survey, *Personal current accounts in the UK*, July 2008, http://www.oft.gov.uk/shared_oft/reports/financial_products/OFT1005.pdf.
The Office of Fair Trading (OFT) launched this market study into the market for personal current accounts in April 2007. Although the OFT found evidence of competition in the PCA market, the survey found the combination of complexity and lack of transparency meant the PCA market was not working well for consumers.

➤ *The Office of Fair Trading v Abbey National Plc* [2009] UKSC 6.
This case examined whether unauthorised overdrafts fell within the scope of the Unfair Terms in Consumer Contract Regulations 1999, SI 1999/2083. The House of Lords held the charges that followed from an unauthorised overdraft could not be examined under the regulations.

7 Duties arising under the banker and customer relationship

Chapter overview

The aim of this chapter is to:

➤ Explore the common law duties imposed on the bank and arising from the nature of the agency relationship which regulates the banker and customer relationship.

➤ Specifically examine the duties to conform to the customer's mandate, the duty to account, the duty of confidentiality and the duty of care arising both in contract and tort.

Introduction

As the written mandate signed by the customer when opening a current account is still largely based on implied contractual terms it lacks the detail of the legal rules the courts have developed over the years. In turn, the courts have been reluctant to impose terms that are not sufficiently well known to customers[1] and the Jack Committee[2] stressed the need for transparency and fairness in the banker and customer relationship, but recommended that this be achieved through a voluntary code of good practice.[3] In 2002, the Cruickshank Report into Competition in UK Banking[4] resulted in the banking sector publishing the Business Banking Code, which set out standards of best practice when dealing with small businesses. Both codes were last revised in 2008 and were superseded by the Banking Conduct of Business Sourcebook (BCOBS).[5] In 2009 the BCOBS was superseded by the Lending Standards Boards, which issued the Lending Code in 2011,[6] a successor to the previous two codes. The Lending

[1] See *Turner v Royal Bank of Scotland Plc* [1999] 2 All ER (Comm.) 664; and *Kitchen v HSBC Plc* [2000] (Comm.) 787 at 795, per Sedley LJ.

[2] Jack, Banking Services: Law and Practice, Report by the Review Committee Chaired by Professor R.B. Jack, CBE, 1989, London Cm. 622, paras 4.04, 6.23, 16.10–16.12.

[3] The industry response to the Jack Report came in the form of a voluntary code, which set standards of good banking practice for financial institutions when they are dealing with personal customers in the United Kingdom.

[4] Cruickshank, Competition in UK Banking – A Report to the Chancellor of the Exchequer, London, March 2000, Cm. 5319.

[5] http://www.fsahandbook.info/FSA/html/handbook/BCOBS.

[6] Revised in 2012; http://www.lendingstandardsboard.org.uk/docs/lendingcode.pdf.

Code establishes rules of good practice in respect of loans to individual and micro enterprises, credit cards and other facilities.[7] However, the customer still has to rely on a number of different sources, including the common law, statute, and the Lending Code to determine his relationship with his bank. The law therefore has become cumbersome and inaccessible.

Terms arising under the banker and customer contract

While there has been legislative and judicial intervention to protect the interests of the consumer in respect of unfair contract terms,[8] the common law has developed the fundamental obligations implied into the banker and customer relationship. The courts have therefore been, at the forefront in the development of the scope, nature and breadth of obligations owed by banks to their customers, and *vice versa*.

In examining the nature of the deposit account in *Joachimson v Swiss Bank Corporation*[9] Atkin LJ described the banker and customer relationship as a single contract made between the bank and its customer but with several obligations flowing from it. He said that the bank undertakes:

> to receive money and to collect bills for its customer's account . . . to repay any part of the amount due . . . [and not to] cease to do business with the customer except upon reasonable notice.

Additionally, in *Tournier v National Provincial and Union Bank of England*[10] the Court of Appeal established a duty of confidentiality arising out of the banker and customer contract. In *Selangor United Rubber Estates Ltd v Cradock (No 3)*[11] the court held the bank in breach of a duty of care and in *Barclays Bank Plc v Quincecare Ltd*[12] the court held that a failure to conform to this obligation might render the bank liable in both contract and tort. We will now examine the scope of the duties established by the courts.

Duty to conform to the customer's mandate

An important feature of the banker and customer relationship is that the bank must conform to the customer's mandate and act within the current account facility; that will include receiving and making payments, as directed by the customer, including acting on a countermand received in proper time. In the context of an account the mandate will specify who is entitled to draw against the credit balance, and where more than one signature is required then how many, and the identity of each signatory.[13] The mandate, therefore, embodies the agreement and the terms within which the bank must act. The positive duty to act in accordance with the customer's mandate[14] is matched by a duty on the part of the bank not to exceed the

---

[7] http://www.lendingstandardsboard.org.uk/docs/lendingcode.pdf.
[8] See Ch. 6.
[9] [1921] 3 KB 110.
[10] [1924] 1 KB 461.
[11] [1968] 1 WLR 1555.
[12] [1992] 4 ALL ER 363.
[13] See Ch. 6.
[14] See: Pollock (1901) Notes: *Fleming v Bank of New Zealand*, January, *Law Quarterly Review*, No. LXV. p. 2.

customer's mandate. In terms of the duty to act in accordance with the mandate the bank will frequently be required to act in accordance with the payment instructions given by the customer, whether that entails the traditional method of payment through a cheque or other direct debits, standing orders or automated funds transfers.

Duty to make payment

The duty to pay cheques, or other instruments, drawn by the customer on his account amounts to a duty to act as expeditiously as possible, if the instrument is properly drawn, and where it is drawn, either within the credit balance on the account,[15] or within the agreed overdraft limit.[16] Goff J explained the nature of the contractual obligations in *Barclays Bank Plc* v *W.J. Simms & Cooke (Southern) Ltd*[17] where he said:

> It is a basic obligation owed by a bank to its customer that it will honour on presentation cheques drawn by the customer on the bank, provided that there are sufficient funds in the customer's account to meet the cheque, or the bank has agreed to provide the customer with overdraft facilities sufficient to meet the cheque.

The bank will, therefore, be given a reasonable time to credit the customer's account with any amounts paid to the customer's order. In *Marzetti* v *Williams*[18] the customer made a cash payment of £40 to the credit of his account at 11.00am so the actual balance on the customer's account became £109 9s 6d. The bank dishonoured a cheque, properly drawn by the customer, for £87 7s 6d and presented at the bank's counter at 3.00pm, as the amount of £40 credited earlier that morning, had not been entered up on the ledger by then. The cheque, however, was paid the following day when it was re-presented. The court held the bank liable for breach of contract when it failed to pay the cheque presented for payment at a time when the customer's account had a sufficient credit balance. It was held that the bank was entitled to a reasonable time to credit the funds to the customer's account and the jury found the delay of four hours to be unreasonable.

If the credit balance, or the overdraft facility, falls short of the amount of the authorised payment, the bank is not obliged to make payment and may reject the payment mandate on the basis of an insufficient credit balance,[19] although the bank may find itself liable for breach of contract where the dishonour amounts to a breach of contract.[20] In *Fleming* v *Bank of New Zealand*[21] the court held that a bank was guilty of wrongful dishonour, and thereby guilty of breach of contract, when it dishonoured a cheque drawn by its customer who had overdrawn on the account with the bank's consent and who had paid into the credit of his account cash and cheques specifically agreed to be used for the purposes of paying the cheque later dishonoured by the bank. The bank was not entitled to use the amounts specifically agreed to be credited

---

[15] *Sierra Leone Telecommunications Co. Ltd* v *Barclays Bank Plc* [1998] 2 All ER 821; *Barclays BankLtd* v *W.J. Simms & Cooke (Southern) Ltd* [1980] 1 QB 682.

[16] See Ch. 6.

[17] [1980] 1 QB 677 at 699.

[18] (1830) 1 B & Ad 415.

[19] *Marzetti* v *Williams* (1830) 1B & Ad 415; *Bank of New South Wales* v *Laing* [1954] AC 135 at 154.

[20] *Marzetti* v *Williams* (1830) 1 B & Ad 415.

[21] [1900] AC 577; see also: Pollock (1901) Notes: *Fleming* v *Bank of New Zealand*, January, *Law Quarterly Review*, No. LXV. p. 2.

to the customer's account, on the understanding that they would be used to honour the cheque which the bank then later dishonoured, to set off the debit balance on the customer's overdraft. The fact that the bank received no consideration for providing the overdraft was irrelevant particularly where the bank agreed, either expressly or implicitly, to allow the customer case to overdraw, or where the bank had accepted instructions from the customer which were inconsistent with its right to use the amounts credited to the account to reduce the overdraft.

While the *Fleming* case illustrates the bank's obligation to pay a cheque, or other instrument, in accordance with a customer's mandate, it must be remembered that the bank will come under a general duty to conform to the customer's mandate,[22] regardless of the nature of the transaction, so long as the instruction is unambiguous and reasonable, and the bank has agreed to act on behalf of the customer. So, where the cheque has been properly drawn but the bank erroneously pays out an amount in excess of the figure for which the cheque is drawn, or in fact debits the same amount twice, the law provides that, in fact, the bank has paid away its own money and cannot debit the customer's account.

Duty not to exceed the customer's mandate

The positive duty to act in accordance with the customer's mandate is matched by a duty on the part of the bank not to exceed the customer's mandate; in such cases the bank is under a negative duty not to act in a manner that exceeds the customer's mandate. An example of where a bank will be deemed to exceed its mandate is where the bank pays a cheque on which the customer's signature has been forged although, on the facts, the customer may be estopped from denying that the bank acts without a mandate, if it becomes obvious that the customer has known of the forgeries, for sometime.[23] The customer's failure to act to prevent his bank account being used as a vehicle for fraud may be treated as his acquiescence and entitle the bank to debit the amount of the forged cheques. However, in normal circumstances, a forged cheque or payment is wholly inoperative[24] and the bank has no valid authority to make payment and cannot debit the customer's account where it acts on the forged instrument.[25] Forgery amounts to the material falsification of a document (e.g. placing someone else's signature on a cheque or other document without their authority) and thus amounts to bringing into existence a document, which purports to be something it is not.[26]

Another situation where a bank may discover it has exceeded its mandate is where the bank makes payment on instruments drawn by an agent, in excess of the authority conferred on him. In the same way as with forged cheques, the bank cannot debit the customer's account. Thus, in *B. Liggett (Liverpool) Ltd v Barclays Bank*[27] the court held the bank had exceeded its mandate when paying a cheque drawn on a company's account and signed by merely one director, instead of the two signatures required under the company's mandate. In that case

---

[22] *Sierra Leone Telecommunications Ltd v Barclays Bank Plc* [1998] 2 All ER 821.

[23] *Greenwood v Martin's Bank Ltd* [1933] AC 51; see also *Orr and Barber v Union Bank of Scotland* (1854) 1 Macq 512.

[24] Bills of Exchange Act 1882, s.24.

[25] *London Joint Stock Bank Ltd v Macmillan & Arthur* [1918] AC 777; *London & River Plate Bank v Bank of Liverpool* [1896] 1 QB 7.

[26] For example placing a false date on a bill of lading as in *The American Accord*; see also s.9 forgery and Counterfeiting Act 1981.

[27] [1928] 1 KB 48.

the company's two directors had authority to appoint a third but one of the director's (A) was so concerned with the management of the company's business by the other (B) that A insisted on signing all the cheques drawn in the company's name. B drew a number of cheques, which the bank honoured without reference to A. The court held the bank had exceeded its mandate when paying a cheque drawn on the company account and signed by merely one director, instead of the two signatures required in accordance with the company's mandate.

A payment instruction given by an agent of the customer will not bind the customer (principal) where the agent acts without authority. However, the courts may have difficulty in determining when the bank has notice that the agent acts without authority. In *Lloyds Bank Ltd* v *Chartered Bank of India, Australia and China*[28] cheques fraudulently drawn by an employee of the plaintiff bank who had ostensible authority were held to have been paid negligently and in excess of the mandate conferred on the defendant bank. Scrutton LJ held that a third party dealing in good faith with an agent acting within his ostensible authority is not prejudiced by the fact that, as between the customer (principal) and his agent, the agent is using his authority in such a way that the customer (principal) can complain that the agent acts for his own benefit. However, where the third party has notice of the irregularity or is put on inquiry as to whether the agent is exceeding his ostensible authority, then the paying bank will not be protected. In *Morison* v *London County and Westminster Bank Ltd*[29] the court concluded that the question of negligence, on the part of the bank, was one of fact and laid down guidelines intended to assist the courts in determining whether or not the bank is guilty of negligence:

- The question should in strictness be determined separately with regard to each cheque [or other payment mandate].
- The test of negligence is whether the transaction of paying any cheque [or other payment mandate] was so out of the ordinary that it ought to have aroused suspicion in the mind of the bank and given it cause to make inquiries.
- The negligence must be the proximate cause of the loss.

There was a suggestion in the *Selangor United Rubber Estates Ltd* v *Cradock (No 3)*[30] and *Karak Rubber Co Ltd* v *Burden (No 2)*[31] cases that the bank ought to investigate payment instructions given to it by agents to ensure they accord with the principal's intentions but it is now established that the bank will only rarely be fixed with knowledge of the impropriety of the agent's actions. In the *Selangor* case the bank provided financial assistance in connection with a takeover bid and because of the inexperience of its officer the bank failed to realise the company was financing the purchase of its own shares contrary to the Companies Act, then in force. The court held that an agent who assists in bringing about the disposal of trust property in breach of trust would be personally liable either if it knew or ought to have known about the breach. The bank was held liable in negligence with the court imposing the standard of the reasonable banker (objective test in the case). Similarly, in the *Karak* case the defendant bank paid a banker's draft against the company's account in circumstances in which it was alleged that the bank's employees should have realised that the payment was in connection with the purchase by the company of its own shares, contrary to the Companies legislation. However,

---

[28] [1929] 1 KB 40.
[29] [1914] 3 KB 356.
[30] [1968] 1 WLR 1555.
[31] [1972] 1 WLR 602.

the *Selangor* and *Karak* cases were criticised in *Lipkin Gorman v Karpnale Ltd*[32] as imposing too high a standard of care. In that case a partner in a firm of solicitors misappropriated money from his firm's client account by drawing cheques on the account (as he was authorised to do) and used the money for an unauthorised purpose (i.e. gambled it away). The Court of Appeal rejected the argument that the bank should be fixed with notice of the fact that the monies were being drawn without authority. May LJ formulated the duty on the bank as follows:

> In the simple case of a current account in credit the basic obligation on the banker is to pay his customer's cheques in accordance with his mandate. Having in mind the vast numbers of cheques which are presented every day for payment . . . whether over a bank counter or through the clearing, it is in my opinion only when the circumstances are such that any reasonable cashier would hesitate to pay a cheque at once and refer it to his or her superior, and when any reasonable superior would hesitate to authorise payment without enquiry, that a cheque should not be paid immediately upon presentation and such enquiry made. Further, it would I think be only in rare circumstances, and only when any reasonable bank manager would do the same, that a manager should instruct his staff to refer all or some of his customer's cheques to him before they are paid.

The question is one of common sense and the bank is not expected to act as an amateur detective. However, the bank acts outside the mandate if the payment is outside the scope of the instructions and that is obvious from the transaction, for example where the payment instructions involve a large sum of money from a company account to a personal account of a director, which is overdrawn. If the breach of mandate is not obvious from the facts then the bank may not be held to have notice of the lack of the agent's authority. It would be wrong to expect the bank to act in a way so as to suspect every customer to be engaged in fraudulent transactions[33] and it may be that something that appears suspicious after the event would appear normal in a busy working day.

Thus, a bank that acts in accordance with the mandate is duly authorised and entitled to debit the customer's account. However, it does not follow that a bank that acts contrary to the mandate is bound to be unauthorised. Thus, in *London Intercontinental Trust Ltd v Barclays Bank Ltd*[34] the defendant bank honoured a cheque bearing a sole signature when the given mandate required two signatures. However, the sole signatory had actual authority from the plaintiff company's board of directors to arrange the transfer of the sum in question (presumably the bank was not aware of this at the time of the payment). The plaintiff's claim was dismissed on the ground that the bank's failure to observe the discrepancy between the cheque and mandate simply had the consequence of exposing the bank to the risk that the signatory had not been instructed to arrange the transfer of funds. The fact that the signatory had been given actual authority to arrange the transfer of funds acted to give the bank authority to pay against the single signature, although the bank was unaware of the amended mandate.

Duty to obey the customer's countermand

While the bank has a duty to act in accordance with the customer's mandate to make payment, the mandate to pay may be superseded by a countermand directing the bank not to pay. The

---

[32] [1989] 1 WLR 1340.
[33] *Barclays Bank v Quincecare Ltd* [1992] 4 All ER 363.
[34] [1980] 1 Lloyd's Rep 241.

countermand order must be clear and unambiguous so that where the customer countermands payment the bank has clear information about the original mandate being countermanded. In the case of cheques, s.75(1) of the Bills of Exchange Act 1882 gives a statutory right to countermand payment. In order to be effective the countermand must provide information that allows the bank to identify the instruction being countermanded, for example, the unique identifying information on the countermanded instrument must be clear so information such as the cheque number, the amount, the name of the payee and date on cheque, must be clearly given. Where, therefore, a customer gives the wrong cheque number by mistake and the bank makes payment on the cheque ineffectively countermanded, it can debit the customer's account.

In *Westminster Bank Ltd* v *Hilton*[35] the House of Lords held that when making payment from the customer's account the bank acts as the customer's agent, and where, therefore, the customer gives erroneous or ambiguous instructions capable of several interpretations the bank is not liable if it adopts an interpretation that is reasonable, although not the one intended by the customer. In the *Westminster* case the ambiguity was caused by the customer giving the wrong serial number for the cheque intended to be countermanded. However, if the ambiguity is obvious then the bank should verify the countermanded instructions with the customer.[36] In *Reade* v *Royal Bank of Scotland*[37] the customer gave an instruction to countermand a cheque by telegram setting out the number of the cheque and the name of the payee, but failed to indicate on which of his two accounts the cheque was drawn. The bank's clerk, who processed the instruction, made a note of the stop instruction against one account only and the cheque, having been drawn against the other account was paid when presented for payment. The court held the countermand was effective and the bank not entitled to debit the customer's account. In *Remfor Industries Ltd* v *Bank of Montreal*[38] the Ontario Court of Appeal held that if the details set out in the countermand instruction are sufficient to identify the cheque, the bank comes under a duty to conform to the countermand and stop the cheque, even if the notice is defective or inaccurate in respect of one detail. Where the cheque is described with reasonable accuracy the bank must, in case of doubt, enquire whether the cheque presented is the one the customer seeks to countermand.[39]

A bank will usually need the countermand mandate to be authenticated so while a bank may accept a verbal countermand[40] over the telephone it will usually ask for written confirmation. A bank employee may refuse to accept a countermand if he cannot verify the customer's identity, and must refuse to accept the countermand instruction, or indeed any instruction, if he has doubts about the customer's identity. The court, in the *Curtice* case, accepted this view although Cozens-Hardy MR said that a telegram might 'reasonably and in the ordinary course of business, be acted upon by the bank, at least to the extent of postponing the honouring of the cheque until further enquiry can be made'.

---

[35] (1926) 43 TLR 124.

[36] *European Asian Bank AG* v *Punjab and Sind Bank (No 2)* [1983] 1 WLR 642; *Patel* v *Standard Chartered Bank* [2001] Lloyds Rep. (Bank) 229; *Cooper* v *National Westminster Bank* [2009] EWHC 3035.

[37] [1922] 2 IR 22.

[38] (1978) DLR (3rd) 316.

[39] *Giordano* v *Royal Bank of Canada* [1973] 3 OR 771 at 775–776.

[40] In *Morrell* v *Workers Savings & Loan Bank* [2007] UKPC 3 Lord Mance recognised that a bank may act on the oral instructions of the customer and be entitled to debit his account accordingly. Although not a case involving countermand of a payment instruction there is no reason why this principle should not extend to countermand instructions.

For the countermand to be effective it must come to the knowledge of the branch manager where the customer's account is maintained, prior to payment being effected.[41] In *Curtice v London City and Midland Bank Ltd*[42] a notice of countermand sent by telegram was placed in the bank's letterbox and missed when the letterbox was cleared so it did not come to the branch manager's attention until after the cheque was paid. The court held that the doctrine of constructive notice would not apply to a countermand by the customer of his mandate; only actual notice would suffice with the result that the cheque was properly paid and the notice of countermand, which came to the bank's attention after the instrument was paid, was too late. However, in these circumstances the bank could be liable to the customer for negligence in failing to ensure that the letterbox was properly and regularly cleared. In *London Provincial and South-Western Bank Ltd v Buzzard*[43] a countermand sent to another branch of the bank was held to be ineffective until it came to the attention of the branch where the account was maintained and on which the cheque was drawn.[44] In *Curtice* the court held that the constructive notice rule does not apply to countermand; the instruction must come to the attention of a bank employee with authority to act on the countermand prior to payment being effected.[45] In *Commonwealth Trading Bank v Reno Auto Sales Pty Ltd*[46] a countermand notice was held to be ineffective when given over the telephone to an employee who lacked the authority to handle such instructions from the customer and who failed to communicate the instructions to the teller in the belief that the message would be confirmed, in writing. In the *Curtice* case, although the bank's failure to ensure that its letterbox was properly and expeditiously cleared amounted to a beach of duty of care, it did not form the basis of the court's judgment since the customer's action did not plead lack of due care and the action was merely based on breach of contract.

A countermand will only be effective if it is given by the customer, drawer or his agent, and before payment is made. The countermand must be given a reasonable time before the cheque is paid in order to enable the bank to take appropriate action to act on the countermand. If the cheque is presented for payment before the bank has had time to complete its internal procedures to stop payment the bank will not be liable for paying the instrument, but if the bank takes an unnecessarily long time to stop the cheque, the customer may be able to dispute the payment on the grounds of the bank's negligence.[47] The bank will not, however, accept the countermand of a cheque where payment is guaranteed by a cheque card if the amount of the payment does not exceed the amount of the guarantee given by that card, in most cases £50 or £100, since under the terms of issue and usage allowing the use of a guarantee card amounts to a promise, by the bank, to make payment.

In 1989, the Jack Committee expressed the view that there was considerable uncertainty and confusion about the drawer's rights to countermand.[48] The Committee recommended that the customer's right to countermand the cheque must be preserved, whenever possible

---

[41] The question relating to when payment is made therefore becomes important: a question which is discussed in Ch. 1.

[42] [1908] 1 KB 293.

[43] (1918) 35 TLR 142.

[44] Cf *Burnett v Westminster Bank Ltd* [1966] 1 QB 742.

[45] *Giordano v Royal Bank of Canada* [1973] 3 OR 771 (Ont. CA).

[46] [1967] VR 790 (Vic. Sup. Ct.).

[47] *Giordano v Royal Bank of Canada* [1973] 3 OR 771 (Ont. CA).

[48] Jack, Banking Services: Law and Practice, Report by the Review Committee Chaired by Professor R.B. Jack, CBE, 1989, London Cm. 622, paras 4.04, 6.23, 16.10–16.12, para. 7.80.

and banks should make available to customers an explanation of the rights and obligations of the parties to transactions effected through the clearing systems, including rights of countermand. The Jack Committee also suggested that the customer's right to countermand payment should be preserved, whenever possible, even with the introduction of automated funds transfers systems where payment tends to occur through instantaneous or near instantaneous means.

A bank which has erroneously made payment against an instruction that has been countermanded may find itself liable for damages at common law and also in equity, where it finds it is allowed to stand in the shoes a third-party creditor who but for the bank's payment, although wrongly made, would have had a legally enforceable right against the bank's customer. The bank may therefore plead that the customer is in no worse position since the countermanded payment actually discharged a legally enforceable debt.

Damages for wrongful dishonour of a cheque

Where the bank acts in breach of its mandate and either makes payment when it should not have, or fails to make a properly authorised payment, the customer will be entitled to sue the bank for breach of contract. However, under contract law unless, the innocent customer is able to show he has sustained a loss he is only entitled to nominal damages.[49] In *Evans* v *London and Provincial Bank*[50] the customer was the wife of a naval officer and when the bank wrongfully dishonoured her cheque, she sued for breach of contract. It was held that since she had suffered no loss she was only entitled to nominal damages and she was, therefore, awarded one shilling, as damages. In *Gibbons* v *Westminster Bank Ltd*[51] the bank dishonoured a cheque drawn by a tenant in favour of a landlord and the court held that the plaintiff, customer had to plead and prove loss in order to recover substantial damages. It is unlikely that the customer will suffer any special loss under the rules of contract law and claims are, therefore, confined to nominal damages.

However, damage to a customer's reputation engaged in trade or business was recognised as early as *Marzetti* v *Williams*[52] and the rule was reaffirmed in *Rolin* v *Steward*[53] where the bank wrongfully dishonoured a cheque drawn by the bank's customer who carried on business as a merchant. The court held that:

> when . . . the [customer] is a trader . . . the jury, in estimating the damages, may take into their consideration the natural and necessary consequences which must result to the [customer] from the [bank's] breach of contract: just as in the case of an action for slander of a person in the way of his trade, or in the case of an imputation of insolvency on a trader, the action lies without proof of special damage.

In law there was, therefore, a presumption of damage in favour of a customer who was in trade and the customer did not have to plead any particular loss. Until recently, the presumption of damage applied only to business customers or tradesmen because a wrongful dishonour

---

[49] Peel (2011) *Treitel on Contract Law*, London: Sweet & Maxwell.
[50] *The Times*, 1 March 1917.
[51] [1939] 2 KB 882.
[52] (1830) 1 B & Ad 415.
[53] (1854) 14 CB 595.

of a cheque, or other payment instrument, would clearly cause loss of reputation[54] with the amount of damages awarded either by the judge, sitting alone, or with the jury.[55]

However, in *Kpohraror v Woolwich Building Society*[56] the Court of Appeal held that the distinction between the business customer and the general consumer customer should no longer be maintained. The facts of *Kpohraror* were that the customer was a 'self-employed exporter/ importer' and the bank wrongfully dishonoured a cheque to his suppliers. The customer's position was therefore analogous to a tradesman. The Court of Appeal referring to the significance of credit ratings held for members of the public concluded that, in the present social conditions, it should be presumed that the wrongful dishonour of a cheque would cause damage to any customer's reputation.[57] Further, the distinction between trade or business customers and retail customers, who are consumers, can no-longer be justified particularly as professional people, for example lawyers, accountants, dentists and physicians, are to some extent regarded akin to businessmen. The *Kpohraror* case is a reflection of social and societal changes with recognition that a wrongful refusal to honour a payment mandate can cause as much harm to members of the public generally as tradesmen.

The risk of wrongful dishonour of a cheque has not been eliminated by the introduction of the semi-automated clearing processes, or other systems of payment used for money transfers. Although, reader-sorter machines read the details encoded in magnetic ink, nevertheless there still exists the danger of human, or other, error with the recording of such details. Where a payment mandate is thus dishonoured the bank must take care in respect of any reason given for the dishonour of the payment instruction.

In cases of wrongful dishonour, a customer may also bring a claim for defamation, which requires the making of an untrue statement that would lower the plaintiff in the estimation of right-thinking members of society. Where the bank dishonours a cheque the bank will normally state the reason for the dishonour, for example 'insufficient funds', indicating the customer has an insufficient credit balance to meet the amount of the cheque drawn. Where a bank wrongfully dishonours a cheque the plaintiff's, customer's, claim is based on the fact that the defamation (i.e. the plaintiff does not have sufficient funds to meet the cheque) is published to the third party, the payee, by the bank's wrongful dishonour of the cheque and the instrument is being returned to the payee, with words which indicate that the plaintiff has insufficient funds to the credit of his account to meet the cheque. Provided that the reason given for the dishonour is capable of bearing a defamatory meaning, then the statement may be libellous.

In practice the plaintiff can sue both for breach of contract and the tort of defamation and although he will not recover two sets of damages there may be advantages in suing under both. Thus, where the bank can justify the dishonour in contract it may still be liable for defamation if the statement refusing payment is libellous. For banks the problem is that whatever reason they give for the dishonour is likely to indicate that the customer has

---

[54] *Rolin v Stewart* (1854) 14 CB 595; *Wilson v United Counties Bank Ltd* [1920] AC 102; *Gibbons v Westminster Bank Ltd* [1939] 2 KB 882; *Jayson v Midland Bank Ltd* [1968] 1 Lloyd's Rep 409; *Rae v Yorkshire Bank Plc* [1988] FLR 1.

[55] See *Wilson v United Counties Bank Ltd* [1920] AC 102 at 112 where the court said that reasonable damages are to be awarded, although a prompt apology will be taken into account as mitigation: *Davidson v Barclays Bank* [1940] 1 All ER 316 at 324. See also *Baker v ANZ Bank Ltd* [1958] NZLR 907 at 911.

[56] [1996] 4 All ER 119.

[57] An award of £5,500 was therefore upheld; the wrongfully dishonoured cheque had a face value of £4,500.

insufficient funds, or the amount of the cheque is in excess of the overdraft limit so statements such as 'present again'[58] and 'refer to drawer'[59] are capable of bearing a defamatory meaning. The innocent appearance of the words is irrelevant and if they are capable of having an innuendo that is defamatory then the bank may be liable. In *Baker v Australia and New Zealand Bank Ltd*[60] the court therefore held the words 'present again' were both legally capable of a defamatory meaning and in fact did have the effect of conveying such a meaning. In *Pyke v Hibernian Bank Ltd*[61] Black J reached a similar conclusion with regard to the words 'refer to drawer' when the bank dishonoured a cheque. In *Bumpitra-Commerce Bank Bhd v Top-A Plastic Sdn Bhd*[62] the Malaysian Court of Appeal held that placing the words 'frozen account' and 'refer to drawer' on a cheque were capable of a highly defamatory meaning and tantamount to saying that the plaintiff had gone into liquidation or been locked up.

The safest course of action is for the bank not to give any reason for the non-payment. Thus, in *Frost v London Joint Stock Bank Ltd*[63] the defendant bank returned a cheque with the words 'reason not stated' stamped on the back. In an action for defamation the court concluded that the plaintiff had failed to prove the words would naturally be understood as conveying a defamatory meaning since the words were equally capable of an innocent meaning. Where a bank dishonours a cheque, or indeed where relevant any other mandate, it may protect itself against the possibility of an action for defamation by ensuring that:

- The credit balance standing to the customer's account is insufficient to meet the cheque.
- The amount is not within any agreed overdraft limit.
- All items have been properly credited to the customer's account.
- The cheque about to be dishonoured is not backed by a cheque card.
- No post-dated cheques have been cleared prior to the date of payment specified on the instrument thereby artificially reducing the amount in the account.
- The reason for the dishonour in so far as possible does not convey a defamatory meaning.

Unauthorised payments that discharge a customer's debts

A person who has paid the debts of another without his authority, for example where the bank pays on a countermanded cheque or other payment instruction, maybe allowed to take advantage of that payment under the equitable doctrine of subrogation.[64] In such circumstances, the bank would be entitled to stand in the shoes of recipient to the extent of the benefit received by that recipient, i.e. the recipient's right to bring a legal action is extinguished. Thus, for example the payment of a countermanded cheque may discharge a valid debt owed to the payee for which the latter might have been able to bring an action to recover the debt. In such a situation the bank may take the benefit of its having discharged a debt, which would otherwise be legally enforceable. The doctrine of subrogation, therefore,

---

[58] *Baker v Australia and New Zealand bank Ltd* [1958] NZLR 907.
[59] *Jayson v Midland Bank Ltd* [1968] 1 Lloyd's Rep 409; *Pyke v Hibernian Bank Ltd* [1950] IR 195.
[60] [1958] NZLR 907.
[61] [1950] IR 195.
[62] [2008] 5 MLJ 34 [22] (Malay CA).
[63] (1906) 22 TLR 760.
[64] *Blackburn Building Society v Cunliffe, Brooks & Co* (1882) 22 Ch D 61 at 71.

applies as a defence to an action for conversion when an unauthorised payment is actually made for, and discharges a legally enforceable debt, or any part of the payment is used to reduce the account holder's indebtedness.

The application of this rule was explored in the context of cheques in *Liggett (Liverpool) Ltd v Barclays Bank Ltd*[65] where the defendant bank had paid cheques drawn on the plaintiff's account in breach of a mandate that required two signatures. In an action by the plaintiff Wright J concluded:

> the banker will be entitled to the benefit of that payment if he can show that that payment went to discharge a legal liability of the customer. The customer in such a case is really no worse off, because the legal liability which has to be discharged is discharged, though it is discharged under circumstances which at common law would not entitle the bank to debit the customer.

In *A.L. Underwood Ltd v Bank of Liverpool and Martins*[66] the defendant bank was held liable for conversion of the claimant's cheques, which had been wrongfully paid by the company director into his own account, although there was evidence to show that some of the proceeds of the cheques had been used to discharge the company's debts. The Court of Appeal did not expressly state what the position would be if legitimate company debts had been discharged with funds wrongly credited to the director's personal account but appeared to indicate, without actually deciding the point, that damages would be reduced *pro tanto*. The principle was applied by the Court of Appeal in *Lloyds Bank Ltd v Chartered Bank of India, Australia, and China,*[67] and in *Re Cleadon Trust Ltd*[68] where the court held that the equitable principle of subrogation would only apply to cases where the money was expended by an agent, or borrower, authorised to pay the legitimate debts of the plaintiff.[69] In *Cleadon* the facts were that a company had two directors and one of the directors used his personal money in discharge of debts owed by two subsidiary companies. As the company had guaranteed the debts of the subsidiaries the director who had paid off the debts of the subsidiaries expected he would be reimbursed. Although a resolution was passed purporting to authorise repayment of some of the advances this was held to be invalid under the company's articles of association. The company and the subsidiaries went into insolvent liquidation. There was no knowledge or agreement on the part of company to the payments and so it was not liable to repay the director. The court held that there was no equitable principle which imposed liability on the company because it had not authorised the transaction. The director was therefore not entitled to recover the amounts advanced by him.

The principle of subrogation does not apply to money spent by an outsider with no authority to pay the debts. In *Crantrave Ltd v Lloyds Bank Plc*[70] the bank paid out funds standing to the credit of a corporate customer on the service of an interim third party debt order. Before the interim order was made final the corporate customer was wound up. The Court of Appeal held that the bank was not entitled to rely on the equitable doctrine of subrogation and in the absence of evidence that a bank's payment had been made on the customer's

---

[65] [1928] 1 KB 48.
[66] [1924] 1 KB 775.
[67] [1929] 1 KB 40.
[68] [1939] Ch 286.
[69] Pedley (2001) Repent not that you shall lose your friend and he repents not that he pays your debt, *Journal of International Banking Law*.
[70] [2000] QB 917.

behalf and with his mandate, or subsequently ratified by him, the bank was not protected and could not stand in the creditor's shoes. However, May LJ thought there 'might conceivably be circumstances not amounting to ratification in which it would nevertheless be unconscionable to allow the customer to recover from the bank the balance of his account without deduction of a payment which the bank had made gratuitously'.

The nature of the circumstances alluded to by May LJ was not explained by him and remains unclear.[71]

Duty to collect instruments

In relation to the payment and collection of instruments the duty to conform to the customer's mandate manifests itself as a duty to act as expeditiously as possible in relation to the instruments. The bank is, therefore, under a duty to collect amounts payable to the customer by use of normal banking practice when the customer delivers the instruments for collection and to credit his account with the proceeds when received.[72] Such instruments include the payment and collection of cheques, bills of exchange, credit transfers, direct debits, and payments made through electronic funds transfers and through the post office giro system. Legally a bank is only obliged to allow a customer to draw against his account in respect of cleared cheques or against an overdraft limit.[73] Whether a bank will allow a customer to overdraw will depend on a number of factors including the customer's banking history, his status, income and the systems used by banks as part of their daily banking business to update the customer's account. In *Marzetti v Williams*[74] the court held that the bank acted in breach of contract if it failed to pay a cheque when the customer's account had a sufficient balance to meet the instrument, but that the bank was entitled to a reasonable time to credit the funds to the customer's account. A delay of four hours was held to be unreasonable. It should be noted that the delay related to the credit of £40 paid in cash over the counter at the branch where the customer's account was maintained. In the same circumstances, and accounting for modern banking techniques where customer information is accessed and amended by computer, an immediate and instant credit to the customer's account would not seem unreasonable. However, where instruments need to be presented through the clearing system to another bank there is still likely to be a delay[75] before the customer's account is credited.[76]

In *Hare v Henty*[77] the court held that a bank which receives, from a customer, an instrument for collection must present it for payment on the institution on which it is drawn or issued, as expeditiously as possible. If the instrument is to be presented for payment through the clearing system it is sufficient for the bank to present, or arrange for it to be presented, for collection on the same day or the following day. Cheques presented on another bank for

---

[71] *Gulf International Bank BSC v Albaraka Islamic Bank* [2004] EWCA Civ 416; *Tayeb v HSBC Plc* [2004] 4 All ER 1024.

[72] *Joachimson v Swiss Bank Corporation* [1921] 3 KB 110 at 127, per Atkin LJ.

[73] See Ch. 9.

[74] (1830) 1 B & Ad 415.

[75] See Ch. 1 where the system of cheque clearing is explained. The customer will start to receive interest from the second day of payment into the current account: he may not be permitted to draw against the amount until the fourth day.

[76] See Ch. 1 for discussion of the clearing systems and when payment is complete in law.

[77] (1861) 10 CB NS 66.

clearing may still take up to three or a maximum of four days to be credited to the customer's account before a customer can draw on the amount.[78] It is the bank's decision whether, or not, to allow a customer to draw against the proceeds of un-cleared instruments and in *Capital and Counties Bank Ltd v Gordon*[79] it was suggested that crediting the customer's account with the amount of an uncleared cheque gives the customer the right to draw on that amount. Although, this view was doubted in *A.L. Underwood Ltd v Bank of Liverpool* it is submitted that the view expressed in *Capital Counties Bank Ltd* is correct; to hold otherwise would require the customer to verify which amounts credited to his account have actually been cleared so he can draw on them and that surely cannot be the intention of either the banks or the law. The scope of this obligation needs to develop as banking practice develops and changes, and as the clearing system becomes fully automated; the law will need to develop to keep pace.

The bank's duty to render an account

A bank will usually provide a statement of account to the customer either on demand or periodically as agreed. Although the intervals between statements are at the discretion of the bank, statements of account will generally be sent quarterly, unless the customer requests they are sent more frequently. The computerised statement has superseded the passbook, which previously contained a record of all debit and credit transactions and which served to record all debit and credit transactions. What is, therefore, necessary is that a running total is kept of all transactions against the customer's account and the bank provides the customer with a statement of account. It is, therefore, an integral part of the contractual arrangement between the bank and its customer that the customer's account will show, at any time, either a credit or debit balance for the customer. Indeed, banks are obliged to provide paper-based[80] bank statements and they will not charge for providing the initial statements for the period in question. Where the customer asks for copies at a later stage a nominal charge may be imposed. In *Rolls Razor Ltd v Cox*[81] Winn LJ explained the nature of the current account relationship and said:

> the relationship of banker and customer upon a current account implies from its very nature an intention on the part of both parties that debits and credits arising between them shall be brought into a running account on which by reason of the customary method of keeping such account, there will at any given moment be an outstanding debit or credit balance.

Passbooks have, largely, been replaced, with the exception of some accounts maintained by the Post Office and building societies, by banks providing statements of account. As with any record-keeping exercise, whether manual or electronic and whether in the form of a passbook or otherwise, it is possible that the record may contain inaccuracies. The significant question, therefore, is whether, and to what extent the customer, or indeed the bank, will be entitled to have any error, or errors, rectified; to what extent an inaccurate statement of account binds the parties; and to what extent the law imposes an obligation on the customer to verify bank

---

[78] See Ch. 1 for discussion of the clearing systems and when payment is complete in law.
[79] [1903] AC 249.
[80] Banks now offer certain banking facilities online including checking bank balances and transactional statements.
[81] [1967] 1 QB 552 at 574.

statements, particularly where the contract seeks to impose an obligation of verification within an unreasonably short timeframe.[82]

Under the existing law a credit or debit entry in a statement of account is not conclusive evidence of the state of the account; it is merely *prima facie* evidence and can be rebutted by proof to the contrary. Consequently, in certain circumstances, either the bank or the customer may seek to have the account rendered, rectified. A bank, for example, may seek to debit the customer's account where it erroneously credits that customer's account with a payment due to another account, or credits the account with a sum larger than the amount payable to him. In such circumstances the bank will seek to debit an amount from the customer's account, and in most cases the bank will simply debit the account since it holds the account and the funds for the customer, However, the customer may object to the bank debiting his account with the erroneous entry on two possible grounds: firstly, that the bank is estopped from denying the accuracy of the credit balance as shown on either the pass-book or statement of account, or secondly that the statement constitutes an 'account settled' with the result that the bank is bound by that representation of the account.

The basis of the estoppel plea is that the customer has relied on the statement, or representation of the bank, regarding the state of the account and acted to his detriment as a result of the reliance; consequently the bank is denied its right to correct the statement of account. Thus, the customer can only plead estoppel if the erroneous statement genuinely misled him. In *Holland v Manchester and Liverpool District Banking Co*[83] the court held that where the customer acts, in good faith, on an erroneous entry made in his passbook and alters his position accordingly the bank is estopped from having the error rectified. In *Holland* a customer relying on his passbook, which showed a credit balance of £70, instead of the correct figure of £60, drew a cheque for £67, which was dishonoured, by the bank, on grounds of insufficient funds, when presented for payment. Although the court recognised the bank's right to have an error on the customer's bank statement rectified it held that the bank had no right to dishonour cheques drawn under the belief that the statement was correct. The bank would have to give reasonable notice of the error and its intention to dishonour a cheque, drawn as a result of the reliance on the statement. Until that notice is given the bank cannot reverse entries and correct the error and must honour cheques drawn in good faith, by the customer. The bank was, therefore, liable for breach of contract with the customer having acted in good faith.

The rules of estoppel may prevent the bank from reclaiming monies wrongly corrected to the customer's account where the customer is wrongfully lulled into a false belief in respect of the state of his financial affairs as a result of the bank's errors. In *Skyring v Greenwood and Cox*[84] the paymaster of a military corps credited an officer's account with money, as part of his salary, to which he was not entitled. The erroneous credits took place over five years and when the error was discovered the paymaster continued to pay the same amount to the officer's credit, as salary. It was only after the death of the officer that an action was brought to recover the amounts wrongly paid with the paymaster attempting to set off the erroneous amounts against the credit on the officer's account. The officer's estate challenged the right of set-off and the court held that the erroneous entries amounted to representations regarding the credit entries and that it would be prejudicial to the customer to allow the bank

---

[82] See Ch. 6 on UCTA 1977.
[83] (1909) 25 TLR 386.
[84] (1825) 4 B & C 281.

to recover the amounts of the mistaken payments. The paymaster's error was compounded by the fact that having discovered the amount of the salary entitlement he took no steps to rectify the error so the customer continued to be mistaken about his salary entitlement. Abbott CJ observed:

> It is of great importance to any man . . . that they should not be led to suppose that their annual income is greater than it really is. Every prudent man accommodates his mode of living to what he supposes to be his income; it therefore works a great prejudice to any man, if after having had credit given him in account for certain sums, and having been allowed to draw on his agent on the faith that these sums belonged to him, he may be called upon to pay them back.

Unless, therefore, reliance and prejudice to the detriment of the customer can be established, the bank is entitled to rectify the error within a reasonable time. The customer's belief in the accuracy of the statement is essential so that if the customer is aware of the bank's mistake, the bank is not estopped from adjusting the error. The customer can raise an estoppel against the bank only if he was misled by the bank's error. In *British and North European Bank Ltd* v *Zalzstein*[85] the customer did not discover the erroneous credit to his account until after the bank had reversed it. The court held the bank is only estopped from disputing the accuracy of the statements of account where the customer honestly believes the statements to be correct and acts accordingly. Similarly, in *United Overseas Bank* v *Jiwani*[86] the defendant customer was wrongly advised of the credit balance on his account when his account was credited twice with the amount of a single remittance. The amount involved was substantial and the defendant was not expecting any other credits to his account. The defendant used the accrued credit balance towards the completion of a transaction he was already committed to completing and which he was engaged to enter, in any event. The customer disputed the bank's right to reverse the erroneous entry when the bank realised its mistake. The court allowed the bank's action and held that the customer is not entitled to take advantage of the bank's mistake where he knows, or from the facts realises, that the amount appearing to the credit of his account is a mistake. The customer is not entitled to ignore facts staring him in the face. The court also took into consideration that the defendant customer was in a position to repay the money without any hardship or prejudice to him.

Thus, for a bank to be estopped from reclaiming the amount credited to the customer's account, three conditions have to be satisfied namely:

1 The bank must be under a duty to give accurate information about the state of the customer's account and in breach of that duty gave inaccurate information or in some other way misrepresent the state of the customer's account.

2 The customer must show that the inaccurate information misled him about the balance standing to the credit of his account.

3 The customer must show that because of his mistaken belief he changed his position in such a way as would make it inequitable to require him to repay the money wrongly credited to his account.

A statement of account is, therefore, not a final settlement of the account between the bank and its customer. It is only conclusive against the bank if the customer has relied on the statement to his detriment.

---

[85] [1927] 2 KB 92.
[86] [1976] 1 WLR 964.

There may be circumstances where the bank customer seeks to have an error on his account rectified, for example where a payment has been wrongly debited from the account twice instead of just the once, or where his account has been wrongly credited with a smaller amount than the customer is entitled, or where the account has been wrongly debited because of fraud of the third party. In most cases the bank and the customer will reach an agreed position and the bank is likely to credit the customer's account, but if substantial amounts are involved or the bank feels the customer is at fault the parties may end up before the courts, particularly if the customer is involved in the fraud or wrongdoing. However, apart from circumstances where the customer is involved in the wrongdoing in respect of his account the customer is entitled to have erroneous debit entries made against his account corrected. The principle is based on the rule that the implied duties established by the common law do not place the customer under an obligation to verify or check the statement of account.[87] The customer is allowed to dispute erroneous debits even if the customer initially returns the statement or counterfoil to his bank without referring to the error.[88] In *Tai Hing Cotton Mill Ltd* v *Liu Chong Hing Bank Ltd*[89] a clerk who had custody of his employer's chequebooks, over a number of years forged the manager's signature on a substantial number of cheques, which were paid by the three banks with which the company customer held current accounts. As the company did not maintain a regular system of audits, the clerk's forgeries were not discovered for several years and finding the company's internal systems of audit inadequate Mantell J held that the customer had contributed to the losses. This decision was affirmed by the Hong Kong Court of Appeal, which held that the company customer was in breach of a duty of care, both in contract and tort, owed to the bank. On appeal, the Privy Council reversed the Hong Kong Court of Appeal. In respect of the claim in contract Lord Scarman held that, unless there was an agreement to the contrary, the risk of wrongful payments is borne by the bank, and in this case by each of the three banks. He concluded that:

> banks offer a service, which is to honour their customer's cheques when drawn upon an account in credit or within an agreed overdraft limit. If they pay out upon cheques which are not [the customer's], they are acting outside their mandate and cannot plead his authority in justification of their debit to his account. The risk is a risk of service which it is their business to offer.

The learned judge, in *Tai Hing*, emphasised that the customer's duty to refrain from facilitating a fraud applied only in respect of the drawing of cheques, although the customer may be liable for cheques drawn negligently by him. The customer is, therefore, not obliged to adopt wider business practices aimed at preventing fraud and neither is the customer under any obligation to check his bank statements.[90] In respect of the claim in tort, Lord Scarman said that their Lordships 'do not believe that there is anything to the advantage of the law's development in searching for a liability in tort where the parties are in a contractual relationship. This is particularly so in commercial relationships.' However, the *Tai Hing* case outlines the

---

[87] *Lewes Sanitary Steam Laundry Co Ltd* v *Barclay & Co Ltd* (1906) 95 LT 444; *Kepitigalla Rubber Estates Ltd* v *National Bank of India Ltd* [1909] 2 KB 1010 at 1027–1029; *Walker* v *Manchester and Liverpool District Banking Co Ltd* (1913) 108 LT 728; *Brewer* v *Westminster Bank Ltd* [1952] 2 All ER 650 at 656; *Wealdon Woodlands (Kent) Ltd* v *National Westminster Bank Ltd* (1983) 133 NLJ 19; *Royal Bank of Scotland Plc* v *Fielding* [2003] EWHC 986.

[88] *Kepitigalla Rubber Estates Ltd* v *National Bank of India Ltd* [1909] 2 KB 1010 at 1027–1029.

[89] [1986] AC 80.

[90] *Tai Hing Cotton Mill Ltd* v *Liu Chong Hing Bank Ltd* [1986] AC 80; *Duncan* v *American Express Services Europe Ltd* [2009] SLT 112.

possibility of concurrent liability in tort and contract and this view has been supported in several cases. In *Henderson* v *Merrett Syndicates Ltd*[91] the House of Lords held that English law does not prevent a claimant from suing in contract and in tort especially where the claimant can take advantage of the practical differences that exist between contractual and tortious claims. In that case it was held that Names at Lloyd's might sue members' agents, with whom they had a contract for both negligence as well as for breach of contract. Further, in contract law only rights and obligations can be assigned whereas in tort the courts may take into account issues relating to contributory negligence. The two forms of action allow for a different measure of damages and attach different limitation periods so allowing claimants to enjoy different substantive rights. In *Tesco Stores Ltd* v *Costain Construction Ltd*[92] the court took the view that the *Tai Hing* case was out of line with current thinking and practice regarding concurrent liability. However, the courts will not impose a duty of care in tort that is inconsistent with the terms of the contract.

By rejecting these arguments the Privy Council, therefore, reaffirmed the rule that the risk of paying on forged cheques falls on the bank. An employer is therefore not responsible for the conduct of a dishonest employee who forges cheques against his employer's account although the employer (customer) is in the best position to safeguard against, and prevent, forgery. The issue of whether any vicarious liability might be raised against the employer (customer) although raised in the *Tai Hing* case, was not pursued. The Privy Council gave no consideration to the argument that both good business sense and good business practice might require the customer to verify his bank statement.[93] Otherwise the bank statement becomes an ineffective piece of paper.

The Jack Committee report, while accepting the case for reform in this area of the law, rejected the idea that bank customers should be placed under a statutory duty to examine their bank statements. However, in order to redress the balance between the bank and its customer, the Jack Committee recommended legislation which 'in an action against a bank in debt or for damages, arising from an unauthorised payment, contributory negligence may be raised as a defence, but only if the court is satisfied that the degree of negligence shown' is sufficiently serious for it to be 'inequitable that the bank should be liable for the whole amount of the debt or damages'.[94] The government response to the Jack report was to recommend an attempt to redress the imbalance between banks and their customers[95] but the government stated its intention to await the outcome of the 'Law Commission Report on Contributory Negligence as a Defence in Contract'. The report,[96] published in December 1993, recommended that damages should be apportioned, in an action in contract, on the grounds of contributory negligence where the defendant is in breach of an express or implied contractual duty to take reasonable care or exercise reasonable skill or both, but not where he is in breach of a contractual term which imposes a higher level of duty. The Law Commission accepted that this recommendation did not deal with the situation where a bank customer's

---

[91] [1995] 2 AC 145.

[92] [2003] EWHC 1487; see also *Riyad Bank* v *Ahli United Bank (UK) Plc* [2006] EWCA Civ 780; *Biffa Waste Services Ltd* v *Maschinenfabrik Ernst Hese GmbH* [2008] EWHC 6; *Galliford Try Infrastructure Ltd* v *MacDonald Ltd* [2008] EWHC 1570; *SHAH* v *HSBC Private Bank 9 (UK) Ltd* [2009] EWHC 79.

[93] See also *Arrow Transfer Co Ltd* v *Royal Bank of Canada* (1972) 27 DLR (3D) 81 at 97–103.

[94] Jack, Banking Services: Law and Practice, Report by the Review Committee Chaired by Professor R.B. Jack, CBE, 1989, London Cm. 622, paras 4.04, 6.23, 16.10–16.12, para. 6.13 and 6.14,

[95] White Paper on Banking Services: Law and Practice, Cm 1026, London 1990, at 30,

[96] Law Commission, Contributory Negligence as a Defence in Contract, No 219, London, 1993.

account is sought to be debited resulting from forged cheques and where the bank is under a strict duty to adhere to the customer's mandate.[97]

The Law Commission, like the Privy Council, adopted the view that banks were best placed to protect against the consequences of making a payment against a forged mandate. An appropriately worded clause, which is properly brought to the attention of the customer at the time the contract is entered into, requiring the customer to verify his bank statements within a reasonable time may therefore be upheld. In *Arrow Transfer Co Ltd* v *Royal Bank of Canada*[98] the customer was bound by a verification clause, which formed part of the express agreement, entered into with his bank and which formed an integral part of the contractual agreement between the bank and its customer. In *Arrow Transfer Co Ltd* the customer had agreed:

(a) To verify the correctness of each statement of account received from the bank;

(b) To notify the bank in writing of of any alleged omissions from or debits wrongly made to, or inaccurate entries in the account so stated; and

(c) That with the exception of any alleged errors notified in writing to the bank, that the bank statement was conclusive as to its correctness and the bank free from all claims.

The customer was therefore under an obligation to verify his bank statements and notify the bank of any errors within the agreed time. Thereafter, the statement constituted conclusive evidence of the transactions on the account and the balance on the account. The court relied on *B and G Construction Co Ltd* v *Bank of Montreal*[99] and *Syndicat des Camionneurs Artisans du Quebec Metropolitain* v *Banque Provinciale du Canada*[100] where the banks had effectively placed their respective customers under contractual obligations to verify bank statements and to notify them of any forged cheques. Consequently, any failure to comply with the obligation deprived the customers, respectively, of their normal remedies against the banks. While, in *B and G Construction Co Ltd* v *Bank of Montreal*[101] there was no specific reference to forgery or fraud, and in the absence of notice from the customer of any erroneous or fraudulent debits from the account, the vouchers were to be taken as 'genuine and properly chargeable' against the customer. Laskin J in *Arrow Transfer Co Ltd* while agreeing with the court concluded that the verification clause was binding on different grounds. He concluded that the verification clause had to be narrowly construed against the bank and was, therefore, ineffective. It did not exempt the bank from liability against the payment of cheques, which had been forged by the customer's employees. He held that the customer's repeated failure to verify the bank statement subsequently prevented him from disputing or denying the value of the forged cheques. Further, Martland J in *Arrow Transfer Co Ltd* held that the verification agreement was not in any way ambiguous and the customer having failed to perform his contractual obligations was bound by the agreement. The clause was held effective and imposed a duty on the customer to verify that the statements did not specifically refer to fraud but in the absence of notification from the customer of errors in respect of the transactions the statements were held to be accurate.

---

[97] Law Commission, Contributory Negligence as a Defence in Contract, No 219, London, 1993, para. 5.20.
[98] (1972) 27 DLR (3d.) 81.
[99] [1954] 2 DLR 753.
[100] (1969) 11 DLR (3d.) 610.
[101] [1954] 2 DLR 753.

The terms of business imposed by the three Hong Kong banks in the *Tai Hing Cotton Mill Ltd*[102] case were clearly not as extensive as the terms in *Arrow Transfer Co Ltd*. In *Tai Hing* the first bank provided:

> A monthly statement for each account will be sent by the bank to the depositor by post or messenger and the balance shown therein may be deemed to be correct by the bank if the depositor does not notify the bank in writing of any error therein within 10 days after sending the statement.

The terms of business of the second bank provided:

> The bank's statement of my/our account will be confirmed by me/us without delay. In case of absence of such confirmation within a fortnight, the bank may take the said statement as approved by me/us.

The terms of business imposed by the third bank were as follows:

> A statement of the customer's account will be rendered once a month. Customers are desired: (1) to examine all entries on the statement of account and to report at once to the bank any error found therein; (2) to return the confirmation slip duly signed. In the absence of any objection to the statement within seven days after its receipt by the bank, the account shall be deemed to have been confirmed.

It is submitted that the attempts to impose liability on the customer to check his bank statements and to inform the bank of any discrepancies were unsuccessful because the wording of the terms was not sufficient to place such an onus on the customer and to bring to his attention the potential consequences of failure, namely the loss of the customer's right to have his account re-credited. It will, however, be possible to impose such terms on the customer if they are sufficiently clearly worded to impose an express obligation on the customer and the terms are shown to be reasonable under the Unfair Contract Terms Act 1977 and the Unfair Terms in Consumer Contracts Regulations 1999.

The banker's duty of confidentiality

Several countries protect the rights of their bank customer's by the implementation of a statutory duty of confidentiality.[103] Within the UK, the duty of bank confidentiality is derived from the contractual terms implied into the banking contract, although there are now extensive inroads into the scope of the duty established as a result of statutory intervention and common law exceptions. The Jack Committee,[104] in its review of banking services, recommended the codification of the banker's duty of confidentiality, which it argued would allow for ease of accessibility and understanding. It recognised that the duty of confidentiality was key to the banker and customer relationship and expressed concern that any uncertainty about the scope and extent to which the duty applied to protect consumers, might undermine confidence in the banking system. The government White Paper, 'Banking Services: Law and

---

[102] [1986] AC 80.

[103] E.g. Singapore Banking Act 1999, s.47, as amended by the Banking (Amendment) Act 2001; see Ellinger (2004) 20 *BFLR* 137; and Switzerland's Federal Law on Banks and Savings 1934, Article 47.

[104] Jack, Banking Services: Law and Practice, Report by the Review Committee Chaired by Professor R.B. Jack, CBE, 1989, London Cm. 622, paras 4.04, 6.23, 16.10–16.12.

Practice',[105] however, rejected the option of codifying the duty of confidentiality as likely to introduce uncertainty and confusion. Instead, the voluntary Code of Banking Practice reaffirmed the duty of bank confidentiality and the qualifications established by Bankes LJ in the *Tournier*[106] case. The Banking Code has now been replaced by the Lending Code,[107] which specifically prohibits the exchange of customer information for marketing purposes with other entities in the same banking group without the customer's consent and further provides a commitment that personal information will be treated as private and confidential.[108]

The basis of the duty of confidentiality in the banker and customer relationship is that a customer who places confidential financial information in the hands of another should be entitled to a legal assurance that such information will not be revealed to all and sundry. The bank can, particularly over a period of time, build up a fairly comprehensive picture of the customer's financial affairs especially where the customer arranges to receive credits to his account (for example where the customer's salary is paid directly to the credit of his account and his outgoings are paid by direct debit from the account). The bank, as an agent, is in a position of trustee[109] and accordingly under an obligation to protect his customer's (principal's) interests and confidences. The bank's duty of secrecy and the general duty imposed on it, as an agent, were highlighted by Diplock LJ in *Parry Jones v Law Society*[110] where he said:

> Such a duty [of secrecy] exists not only between solicitor and client, but, for example, between banker and customer, doctor and patient and accountant and client. Such a duty of confidence is subject to, and overridden by, the duty to the party to that contract to comply with the law of the land. If it is the duty of such a party to a contract . . . to disclose in defined circumstances confidential information, then he must do so, and any express contract to the contrary would be illegal and void.

The duty of confidentiality is not unique to the banker and customer relationship and was recognised in a more general context in *Attorney-General v Guardian Newspapers Ltd (No 2)*[111] as follows:

> a duty of confidence arises when confidential information comes to the knowledge of a person (the confident) in circumstances where he has notice, or is held to have agreed, that the information is confidential with the effect that it would be just in all the circumstances that he should be precluded from disclosing the information to others . . . To this broad general principle there are three limitations . . . the first . . . is that the principle of confidentiality only applies to information to the extent that it is confidential . . . the second limiting principle is that the duty of confidence applies neither to useless information, nor to trivia . . . the third limiting principle . . . is that, although the basis of the law's protection of confidence is that there is a public interest that confidences should be preserved and protected by the law, nevertheless that public interest may be outweighed by some other countervailing public interest which favours disclosure . . .

---

[105] White Paper on Banking Services: Law and Practice, Cm 1026, London 1990.
[106] *Tournier v National Provincial and Union Bank of England* [1924] 1 KB 461.
[107] The Lending Code: Setting standards for banks, building societies and credit card providers 2011, http://www.lendingstandardsboard.org.uk/docs/lendingcode.pdf.
[108] The Lending Code: setting standards for banks, building societies and credit card providers, para. 15, 2011, http://www.lendingstandardsboard.org.uk/docs/lendingcode.pdf.
[109] Bowstead and Reynolds (2010) *Agency Law*, London: Sweet & Maxwell.
[110] [1969] 1 Ch. 1 at 9.
[111] [1990] 1 AC 109 at 281–282.

Relationships of a personal nature where one person relies on the professional expertise of another will, therefore, involve, to varying degrees, the duty of confidentiality. Thus, insurance companies, securities firms, accountants etc. will be bound by the general duty of confidentiality. Where a breach of this duty of confidentiality is threatened, but has not yet taken place, the customer may seek an injunction to restrain the disclosure but where wrongful disclosure has taken place then the only remedy available is damages for breach of contract. In *Jackson* v *Royal Bank of Scotland*[112] the customer obtained damages when the bank inadvertently disclosed its customer's mark-up, leading to the loss of a line of business. The bank was ordered to pay for the lost profit that the customer could prove had resulted.

Posner's justification for the duty of confidentiality

Prior to *Tournier* v *National Provincial and Union Bank of England*[113] the courts had expressed the view that while banks were expected to observe a duty of secrecy it was nevertheless a matter of moral, not legal obligation.[114] Banking industry opinion endorsed this approach as in harmony with common sense and banking usage, with bankers acting responsibly to honour the trust reposed in them.[115] While the imposition of a legal duty of confidentiality can be grounded in public policy the need to protect the financial information of the customer is paramount. The *Tournier* case changed the moral obligation to respect the confidential nature of the banker and customer relationship into a legal duty imposed by the common law. The court in the *Tournier* case gave little justification for the imposition of a legal duty except that '[t]he credit of a customer depends very largely upon the strict observance of that confidence'.

However, the credit of a customer does not always depend on concealing the details of his bank account and, in fact, Professor Posner[116] argues that to conceal key financial information from creditors, which if known would impair the person's reputation, is equivalent to fraud by a manufacturer in concealing defects in his goods. Posner is concerned that the duty of confidentiality is not always economically viable although there are reasons for the justification of the legal obligation to observe the duty of confidentiality, namely the protection of personal secret information particularly in respect of commercial customers whose business may be jeopardised if financial information is not respected, and the need to preserve the well-being of the banking sector and confidence in it by respecting the duty of confidentiality and ensuring client information is protected.

The duty of confidentiality in the banker and customer contract

The banker's duty of confidentiality[117] arises from the imposition of the rules of agency law on the banker and customer relationship. An agent owes a duty of loyalty and confidentiality to his principal (customer in the banking context), although the degree of the duty owed will

---

[112] [2005] UK HL 3.

[113] [1924] 1 KB 461.

[114] *Hardy* v *Veasey* (1868) LR 3 Ex.107; *Tassell* v *Cooper* (1850) 9 CB 509.

[115] Bankers and their Customers (1868) 28 Bankers' Magazine, 218–219.

[116] Posner (1978) The Right of Privacy, 12 Georgia LR, 393; Posner (1979) Privacy, Secrecy and Reputation, 28 Buff. LR, 1.

[117] For a historical examination of the duty of confidentiality see: Stokes (2011) The Genesis of Banking Confidentiality, 32(3) The Journal of Legal History, 279–294.

depend on the nature of the relationship. Thus, for example a solicitor owes an absolute duty of confidentiality to his clients,[118] whereas the banker's duty of confidentiality is qualified and subject to recognised exceptions. The scope of the legal duty of confidentiality in the banker and customer relationship was examined in *Tournier v National Provincial and Union Bank of England*[119] where the plaintiff customer's account with the defendant bank was heavily over-drawn. The plaintiff entered into a repayment plan with the bank under which he agreed to make weekly repayments to the bank. However, he failed to keep up with the repayments and the branch manager telephoned the plaintiff's employers, ostensibly to ascertain the customer's private address, but in the course of the conversation disclosed to them that the customer, their employee, was overdrawn to the bank and that he had dealings with bookmakers. As a result of this conversation the employer's failed to renew the plaintiff's contract of employment. At first instance, judgment was entered for the bank and the plaintiff appealed.

The Court of Appeal held the bank guilty of a breach of the duty of confidentiality and awarded damages against the bank. The court held that there is an implied term in the con-tract between a bank and its customer that a bank will not divulge to a third party, without the customer's consent, information either about the state of the customer's account or about any specific transactions entered into with the bank. Any unauthorised disclosure constitutes a breach of the bank's duty not to disclose information in respect of the customer and acquired in the course of the banker and customer relationship. It was crucial for the Court of Appeal to determine whether the duty of confidentiality extended to information received by the bank from the customer alone in the course of his dealings with the bank or whether it extended to any information received from other sources, for example third party transactions involving the customer.

Atkin LJ emphasised that the duty extended not merely to facts and information gleaned from the state of the customer's account but encompassed 'information obtained from other sources than the customer's actual account, if the occasion upon which the information was obtained arose out of the banking relations of the bank and its customers'.[120] In the *Tournier* case itself, the information in question received by the branch manager was based on a cheque made payable to one of the bank's customers and drawn by another customer. However, Scrutton LJ expressed a contrary view and concluded that the bank's duty of con-fidentiality did not apply to 'knowledge derived from other sources during the continuance of the relation'. May LJ in *Lipkin Gorman v Karpnale Ltd*[121] confirmed 'the correctness of the principles of law stated by the majority in *Tournier*'s case has not been doubted since the case was decided'. More recently, in *Barclays Bank v Taylor*[122] Lord Donaldson MR said that the banker and customer relationship imposes on the banker 'a duty of confidentiality in relation to information concerning its customer and his affairs which it acquires in the character of his banker'.

The question, which therefore arises, is whether information acquired prior to the opening of the account and after the termination of the relationship may fall outside the scope of the

---

[118] *Minter v Priest* [1930] AC 558; in other cases a solicitor may apply to the court for directions on how to, for example, deal with funds under his control despite the nature of the confidential relationship, *Finers v Miro* [1991] 1 WLR 35.
[119] [1924] 1 KB 461.
[120] [1924] 1 KB 461 at 485.
[121] [1989] 1 WLR 1340.
[122] [1989] 1 WLR 1066 at 1070.

duty of confidentiality.[123] In such circumstances, banks need to be careful in respect of information received about a person who subsequently becomes a customer, or information received about a customer after the relationship has terminated. Information acquired before the banker and customer relationship was established may be repeated in the course of the relationship, once established. In such a situation the information is clearly bound by the banker's duty of confidentiality and any information acquired by the bank, in reasonable anticipation of establishing the banker and customer relationship, will be subject to the duty of confidentiality. Further, information that is not subject to the banker's duty of confidentiality may be subject to the general rules of confidentiality under the principles established in *Attorney-General v Guardian Newspapers Ltd (No 2)*.[124] Additionally, the bank may expressly undertake to keep the information about the customer's affairs confidential even if the recognised parameters of the banker's duty of secrecy do not extend to the information or transactions in questions. The Lending Code provides that 'personal information will be treated as private and confidential'.[125] Further, Bankes and Atkin LJJ both expressed the view in the *Tournier* case that the duty of confidentiality does not cease merely because the customer closes his accounts with the bank but rather 'extends beyond the period when the account is closed, or ceases to be active'.[126] Similarly, Bankes LJ expressed the view that the duty of confidentiality does not cease to exist merely because the customer closes his account but that the information gained during the 'currency of the banker and customer relationship remains confidential unless released under the circumstances bringing the case within one of the classes of qualifications I have already referred to'.[127]

The qualifications to the *Tournier* rule act as a safeguard to ensure that the duty of confidentiality and the bank account, in turn, is not abused. We will now examine the qualifications to the *Tournier* case.

The qualifications to the Tournier case

The duty of confidentiality recognised in the *Tournier* case is not absolute and Bankes LJ[128] identified four qualifications:

> On principle . . . the qualifications can be classified under four heads: (a) where the disclosure is under compulsion of law; (b) where there is a duty to the public to disclose; (c) where the interests of the bank require disclosure; (d) where the disclosure is made by the express or implied consent of the customer.

The qualifications are generally regarded as exceptions to the *Tournier* principle but it is questionable whether a principle established under the common law can create exceptions to situations where disclosure is required by compulsion of law, in other words by statute. It is submitted that statute will override the common law duty of confidentiality and compel disclosure so the duty of confidentiality only prevails where statute has not intervened to

---

[123] See Scrutton LJ, and Atkin LJ, in *Tournier v National Provincial and Union Bank of England* [1924] 1 KB 461.
[124] [1990] 1 AC 109; see also *Douglas v Hello! Ltd (No 3)* [2008] 1 AC 1.
[125] The Lending Code Setting standards for banks, building societies and credit card providers, para. 15, 2011, http://www.lendingstandardsboard.org.uk/docs/lendingcode.pdf.
[126] [1924] 1 KB 461 at 485.
[127] [1924] 1 KB 461 at 475.
[128] [1924] 1 KB 461 at 473.

abrogate the duty of non-disclosure, or where one of the other common law exceptions does not justify disclosure. However, the qualifications to the *Tournier* case have been almost universally adopted and sometimes extended by codification.[129] In such cases, as with other instances, disclosure is the overriding obligation and confidentiality permitted only where statute permits. In *Parry-Jones* v *Law Society*[130] Diplock LJ said that the overriding duty to disclose is a 'duty to comply with the law of the land' and that must mean an investigation of statute first before relying on the common law.

Disclosure by compulsion of law

Recent years have seen significant inroads to the duty of confidentiality as a result of statutory and judicial intervention, which compels disclosure of what would otherwise be confidential information. Thus, it could be argued that the common law duty of confidentiality only exists to fill the vacuum that now exists once legislation and common law exceptions have compelled disclosure. It could therefore be argued that, in modern UK banking law, the duty of confidentiality has, in fact, been so eroded that the obligation now is to make disclosure and the duty of confidentiality only exists as an exception.

The statutory provisions allowing disclosure are both fairly specific and narrow in scope. The Jack Committee gave a list of 19 statutory provisions in England under which the duty of confidentiality was overridden.[131] The list, while not exhaustive at the time, has been further expanded by other significant legislation, for example the Human Rights Act 1998, the Data Protection Act 1998 and several statutes and regulations relating to money laundering.[132] A number of these statutes are of considerable importance to banks and some of the more important ones are dealt with below.

Handling data

The Data Protection Act 1998 (DPA 1998)[133] gives effect to the European Directive on the Protection of Individuals with regard to the Processing of Personal Data and the Free Movement of such Data.[134] The Directive, and the legislation implementing it, was passed because of the growth of computerisation and the development of the Internet, which meant that vast amounts of information could be stored, accessed and processed with relative ease.[135] While these developments have eased the ways information can be stored, managed, accessed

---

[129] For example, the Malaysian Banking and Financial Institutions Act 1989, ss.97–99, and the Singapore Banking Act 2003, s.2, give an exhaustive list of 'exceptions' to the duty of confidentiality, including banks being permitted to make disclosure in the insolvency of a corporate entity, in the case of a garnishee order made by the courts or in the case of probate.

[130] [1969] 1 Ch. 1 at 9.

[131] Jack, Banking Services: Law and Practice, Report by the Review Committee Chaired by Professor R.B. Jack, CBE, 1989, London Cm. 622, paras 4.04, 6.23, 16.10–16.12.

[132] See Ch. 13 relating to a discussion of money laundering legislation and the protection conferred on banks if disclosure is made if the bank has knowledge or suspicion that the account is being used for money laundering purposes.

[133] Repealed the Data Protection Act 1984.

[134] European Directive on the Protection of Individuals with regard to the Processing of Personal Data and the Free Movement of such Data, Council Directive 95/46.

[135] Spearman (2012) Disclosure of confidential information: Tournier and 'disclosure in the interests of the bank' reappraised, 27(2), B.J.I.B. & F.L., 78–82.

and communicated it has also extended the ways in which personal information stored by a bank or other financial institution can be exploited, stolen or 'hacked'.

The personal and economically valuable nature of the information held by banks meant that clarity was required in the ways banks were required to handle, store and transmit the information accessible to them. One of the problems of mass storage of information is that it may be accessed, manipulated and mishandled by unauthorised persons in ways that may have a seriously adverse affect on the person to whom it relates. Section 1 of the DPA 1998, therefore, provides that an entity processing personal data must be registered as a 'data controller'[136] and the processing must comply with the eight 'data protection principles'.[137] The latter require that personal data be used fairly and lawfully; be used for the specific purposes for which it was obtained; be adequate and relevant; not be excessive in relation to the purpose for which it was processed; be accurate and, where necessary, be kept up to date. Appropriate measures must be taken to prevent the unauthorised or unlawful use of data and its accidental loss or damage. Personal data will be processed 'fairly and lawfully' if one of a number of conditions is satisfied,[138] including that the 'data subject'[139] consents to the processing; that the processing is necessary to perform or enter into the contract, to comply with a non-contractual obligation, or to fulfil certain public purposes, e.g. the administration of justice; or that the processing is 'necessary for the purposes of legitimate interests pursued by the data controller or by a third party . . . to whom the data is disclosed'.[140] Where the relevant information includes 'sensitive personal data', for example data dealing with racial or ethnic origin, political opinions or religious beliefs, the processing will be under alternative conditions.[141] The 'data subject' is given certain rights to access personal data to prevent the accessing of personal data for marketing purposes,[142] to prevent any processing of personal data likely to cause damage or distress,[143] to receive compensation where damage results from a breach of the DPA 1998[144] and to apply to the court for correction, blocking or erasure or destruction of inaccurate information.[145]

Additionally, the Human Rights Act 1998 incorporates the Convention for the Protection of Human Rights and Fundamental Freedoms (ECHR) into English law in a number of ways: the English courts must, insofar as possible, construe all legislation in a way that is compatible with the ECHR; by making it unlawful for a 'public authority' to act in a way that is incompatible with the ECHR rights and by introducing a procedure whereby the courts can declare legislation incompatible with ECHR rights, leaving it to Parliament to amend legislation as it thinks fit. The concept of 'public authority' includes 'a court or tribunal'[146] and therefore the Act will affect judicial discretion and the development of the common law. The HRA 1998 does not give private citizens a direct 'horizontal' right of action against each other based on breaches of ECHR rights.

---

[136] Data Protection Act 1998, s.1(1).
[137] Data Protection Act 1998, s.4(4).
[138] Data Protection Act 1998, schedule 1, Part II, para. 2.
[139] Individual who is the subject of the personal data.
[140] Data Protection Act 1998, schedule 2.
[141] Data Protection Act 1998, s.2 and schedule 3.
[142] Data Protection Act 1998, s.11.
[143] Data Protection Act 1998, s.10.
[144] Data Protection Act 1998, s.13.
[145] Data Protection Act 1998, s.14.
[146] Human Rights Act 1998, s.(6)3.

Disclosure to assist regulatory authorities

Certain statutory provisions compel disclosure of confidential banking information to support, for example, regulatory and investigatory authorities to access confidential information held by a bank, about its customer. Thus, police officers may be able to access a suspect's banking records. A bank may also be compelled to disclose confidential banking information to the CFA or PRA if one of four conditions set out in the Financial Services and Markets Act 2000 are satisfied: (i) the person required to make disclosure is the person under investigation or a member of the same group as the person under investigation; (ii) the person to whom the confidence is owed is the person under investigation; (iii) the person under investigation consents to the disclosure; or (iv) authorisation has been given for disclosure to the investigating body.[147]

In *Financial Services Authority* v *Amro International*[148] the Securities Exchange Commission (SEC) requested the FSA's assistance in obtaining documents from Goodman Jones, a London-based accountancy firm, which it contended had acted for the respondents and held documents relating to transactions the SEC was investigating. The FSA, at its discretion, appointed investigators[149] and, in due course, sent a formal notice to Goodman Jones requiring the production of the documents sought by the SEC. The respondents challenged the FSA's appointment of investigators in relation to Goodman Jones as unlawful and claimed that, in any event, the SEC's request for the production of documents from Goodman Jones (and therefore the FSA's notice) was unreasonably broad. The Court of Appeal dismissing the action held that it was not for the FSA to analyse or make further enquiry of the request made by a foreign regulator. The Court could find 'no good reason why Parliament should have required the FSA to second-guess a foreign regulator as to its own laws and procedures, or as to the genuineness or validity of its requirement for information or documents'. The Court of Appeal acknowledged that the FSA is not bound to comply with the request of an overseas regulator, and observed that the FSMA sets out four factors which the FSA may take into account when deciding whether to exercise its investigative power at the request of a foreign regulator. None of these factors suggested that the FSA should also 'form a judgment as to the necessity or desirability, from the point of view of the foreign regulator, of its obtaining the information or documents it seeks'. The Court of Appeal held that, by asking 'pertinent questions' of the SEC and receiving 'sensible answers', the FSA had decided appropriately to exercise its investigative power to assist the SEC.

Under the Companies legislation a bank may be required to produce documents relevant to its customer's, company's affairs where there is an investigation in respect of an officer or manager's conduct in respect of the company's management.[150] Similarly, a disclosure order may be made against a bank believed to hold information concerning the affairs of an insolvent company customer.[151] A person associated with an insolvent company, for example a director or other officer, believed to have information concerning its affairs may under s.236 of the insolvency Act 1986, be compelled to produce documents to the court and submit an affidavit detailing his dealings with the company. The court will balance the

---

[147] Financial Services and Markets Act 2000, s.165; see also Financial Services Act 2012, s.68.
[148] [2010] EWCA Civ. 123.
[149] Financial Services and Markets Act 2000, s.169.
[150] Companies Act 2006, s.1132(2)–(4).
[151] Insolvency Act 1986, s.236.

importance of the information to the proceedings against the degree of oppression involved in granting the application.[152] Additionally, s.745 of the Income and Corporation Taxes Act 1988 gives the Inland Revenue wide investigative powers if it suspects that the provisions of the legislation preventing the transfer of assets abroad for the purposes of evading UK tax have been breached and the bank must furnish the particulars of any relevant transactions to the Inland Revenue.[153] There are also a number of offences relating to money laundering where the bank will be required to make disclosure of confidential information held by a bank where the bank knows or suspects a customer of money laundering.[154]

Other statutory provisions that allow disclosure of confidential information are broader and intended to assist the investigation of conduct where the bank account is used as a vehicle for criminal or other unlawful activity. Some of these will now be examined.

Methods of disclosure

A special procedure established for the disclosure of information, and potential evidence, is contained in the Bankers' Books Evidence Act 1879,[155] although legal developments allow the use of secondary evidence in both civil and criminal proceedings as a result of the Civil Procedure Rules[156] and the Civil Evidence Act 1995[157] which allow hearsay evidence, including in respect of bank records. The Criminal Justice Act 2003[158] also allows for hearsay documents 'created or received' by a person in the course of a trade, business, or profession to be admitted in evidence in criminal proceedings.

The purpose of the Bankers' Books Evidence Act 1879 (BBEA 1879) was primarily to relieve the bank or its officers from having to give evidence personally. The Act states that a copy of any entry in bankers' books is receivable as *prima facie* evidence not only of the entry but also of the matters, transactions and accounts recorded therein.[159] It must be established, either orally or by affidavit by an officer of the bank that the entry was made in the ordinary course of the business, and at the relevant time of making the entry, the record was made in the usual manner of recording banking business, and that the record remained in the custody and control of the bank at all times.[160] It must also be established in court proceedings that the copy has been examined against the original[161] and is a correct record.[162] Original documents are kept with the bank. The power to order inspection of the bankers' books is discretionary under the BBEA 1879 and an order will only be made where the entry is shown as relevant and likely to be admissible in legal proceedings. Any inspection order will be limited to relevant entries. While a disclosure order can be made in the course of the litigation or to

---

[152] *B & C Holdings Plc (joint Administrators) v Spicer & Oppenheim* [1993] AC 426.

[153] See *Clinch v Inland Revenue Comrs* [1974] QB 760 where the court considered the effect of a notice served under the predecessor to the 1988 Act.

[154] Anti-Terrorism Crime and Security Act 2001, Proceeds of Crime Act 2002, Money Laundering Regulations 2007, SI 2007/2157.

[155] Extended by the Banking Act 1979 and as superseded by the Banking Act 1987 and the Financial Services and Markets Act 2000.

[156] Civil Procedure Rules 1988, Part 33.

[157] Civil Evidence Act 1995, ss.8 and 9.

[158] Criminal Justice Act 2003, s.114(2).

[159] *London and Westminster Bank v Button* (1907) 51 SJ 466.

[160] *Asylum for Idiots v Handysides* (1906) 22 TLR 573.

[161] Criminal Justice Act 2003, s.133.

[162] Bankers' Books Evidence Act 1879, s.5.

support a genuine investigation (not a 'fishing expedition') it is likely to be made effective against a third party who participates in the wrongdoing or allows his account to used to hide the proceeds of a crime or wrongdoing, for example where a wife allows her account to be used to deposit funds wrongly received.[163]

Although the BBEA 1879 is no longer unique among the provisions allowing disclosure it still remains a crucial weapon in compelling disclosure of bank records. Section 7 of the BBEA 1879 allows that on an application in respect of legal proceeding, a court or judge may order a party to inspect and take copies of entries in any banker's book for the purposes of the proceedings. The rules of evidence normally require the 'best evidence' to be produced in legal proceedings, and in respect of bank records that is usually verbal testimony verified by written records. Bankers' books, in the past, would have included ledgers, daybooks, cashbooks, account books and other written records. In *Barker v Wilson*[164] Bridge LJ held that the definition of 'bankers' books' includes microfilm or any other means of maintaining a permanent record, using modern technology. This provision was reinforced by the Banking Act 1979[165] which amended the BBEA 1879, and which now provides that the definition of 'bankers' books' includes records kept on 'microfilm, magnetic tape, or any other form of mechanical or electronic data retrieval mechanism'.[166] This will extend to computer records or other means of record keeping undertaken in the ordinary course of the banking business.[167] The Act defines legal proceedings as any 'civil or criminal proceedings or any inquiry in which evidence is or may be given, and includes any arbitration'.[168] In *Wheatley v Commissioner of Police of the British Virgin Islands*[169] the Privy Council expressed the view that the purpose of the BBEA 1879, is to allow a bank to make disclosure without being liable to its customer for breach of the duty of confidentiality. In order to determine whether or not to make an inspection order under the BBEA 1879, the courts have discretion to exercise their powers, and should be guided by the principles relating to inspection and disclosure of documents in other contexts.[170] The courts will, however, exercise their powers sparingly and in *Williams v Summerfield*[171] although the court granted an order compelling disclosure of bank records to enable a police inspector to inspect and then take copies of certain bank accounts the court voiced a note of caution. Lord Widgery CJ said:

> justices should warn themselves of the importance of the step which they are taking in making an order under s.7; should always recognise the care with which the jurisdiction should be exercised; should take into account among other things whether there is other evidence in the possession of the prosecution to support the charge.

The courts will not encourage or allow their jurisdiction to be used for 'fishing expeditions' and compel disclosure where legal proceedings are commenced merely to investigate a 'suspect

---

[163] *Ironmonger & Co v Dyne* (1928) 44 TLR 579.

[164] [1980] 1 WLR 884.

[165] Superseded by the Banking Act 1998, ss.81 and 82, and now the Disclosure of Confidential Information Regulations 2001, SI 2001/2188 made under the Financial Services and Markets Act 2000.

[166] See *Williams v Williams* [1988] QB 161 but not cheques and the accompanying paying-in slips paid by a bank and stored without a proper filing system.

[167] Bankers Books Evidence Act 1879, s.9(2).

[168] Bankers Books Evidence Act 1879, s.10.

[169] [2006] Cr. App. Rep. 328.

[170] *South Staffordshire Tramways Co v Ebbsmith* [1895] 2 QB 669 at 674.

[171] [1972] 2 QB 512.

account', but an order will be made where there is *prima facie* evidence of wrongdoing which is hidden behind the curtain of bank confidentiality. In *Williams v Summerfield*[172] disclosure orders were granted to the police when a company employee was accused of misappropriating funds of his employer company. The Divisional Court of the Queen Bench Division approved the orders as there was independent evidence of the misappropriation and the disclosure would assist in determining the amount involved. However, a court is likely to refuse an application to investigate bank records where there are only unsubstantiated suspicions about the account under investigation, although the court may grant an order where there is *prima facie* evidence of unlawful activity[173] and in criminal cases the courts will only exercise powers to make a disclosure order 'with great caution'.[174]

An order will only be made against a non-party's account where there is a close nexus between the defendant and that party, for example where the account is that of a company of which the defendant is a director.[175] Although, the order may be made against the bank without notice it must be served at least three days before the bank has to comply with it, so the bank has an opportunity to object to it[176] and although it is good practice to give notice to the person whose account is likely to be subjected to a court order, it may be done without notice to him.[177] Further the bank does not owe a duty to its customer whose account may become the subject of a disclosure order to inform that such an application has been made, or is going to be made.[178] In *El Jawhary v Bank of Credit and Commerce International SA*[179] Sir Donald Nicholls concluded that a bank did not owe a duty to inform its customer that information falling within one of the qualifications had been disclosed to the BCCI liquidators, although a different view was expressed in *Robertson v Canadian Imperial Bank of Commerce*,[180] which is dealt below. In *El Jawhary* despite holding that the bank's disclosure fell within the first exception to the *Tournier* case, disclosure had in fact been sought in pursuance of the liquidators' statutory obligations.

Witness orders

Banks made the subject of a court order to disclose information, whether by way of a 'witness order' (previously known as a *subpoena duces tecum*) under the Civil Procedure Rules 1998[181] or some other disclosure order made under rule 31.17 are not under an obligation to the customer to contest an apparently lawful and proper request for access. Neither is the bank under an obligation to its customer to notify of its intention to make the disclosure, or even that such a request has been received. In *Robertson v Canadian Imperial Bank of Commerce*[182] the Privy Council held that a bank manager who had disclosed information about its customer under a court subpoena (now a witness order) had not acted in breach of the duty

---

[172] [1972] 2 QB 512.
[173] *Williams v Summerfield* [1972] 2 QB 512.
[174] *South Staffordshire Tramways Co v Ebbsmith* [1895] 2 QB 669.
[175] *South Staffordshire Tramways Co v Ebbsmith* [1895] 2 QB 669.
[176] Bankers Books Evidence Act 1879, s.7.
[177] Bankers Books Evidence Act 1879, s.7.
[178] See Lord Donaldson in *Barclays Bank Plc v Taylor* [1989] 1 WLR 1066 in respect of an 'access order' under the Police and Criminal Evidence Act 1984.
[179] [1993] BCLC 396.
[180] [1994] 1 WLR 1493.
[181] Part 34.2(1) of the CPR.
[182] [1994] 1 WLR 1493.

of confidentiality when the branch manager failed to notify the customer of the court order prior to making the disclosure. Indeed, the bank may find itself liable for the offence of 'tipping off' where it informs the customer that an order for disclosure in respect of his banking affairs had been made, or of the bank's intention to comply with it.[183] Even if the court finds that in a particular situation the bank should have notified the customer of the service of the witness order in respect his account, that duty would not extend beyond making the best endeavour possible to contact the customer. However, for such a term to be implied into the banker and customer relationship it would have to be shown that the term complied with the strict necessity requirements.[184]

Order for discovery

In respect of civil proceedings the BBEA 1879 does not grant new powers of discovery or alter the laws or practice of discovery.[185] Discovery is a pre-trial examination of the evidence and documents by parties to legal proceedings and, therefore, allows the courts to make a disclosure order prior to the start of the proceedings and to support any following proceedings. The order will normally be made under the principles established by the House of Lords in *Norwich Parmacoul Co* v *Customs & Excise Comrs*[186] where the House of Lords established that a court may order someone, including a bank, who has become 'mixed up' in the wrongful acts of another, to disclose full information and identify the wrongdoer. The person against whom the order is made must have 'participated', or been 'involved', in the civil or criminal wrongdoing[187] and the principle behind the order is that justice requires a person to cooperate in righting a wrong if that person, either wittingly or unwittingly, facilitated the wrongdoing.

A bank that maintains an account used to conceal the wrongdoing will become subject to the courts' jurisdiction under *Norwich Parmacoul*, although the bank itself is innocent of the wrongdoing. The court will not, however, grant an order under *Norwich Parmacoul* unless three conditions are satisfied: (i) it must at least be arguable that a civil or criminal wrong has been committed; (ii) the disclosure order must be required to enable an action to be brought against the wrongdoer; and (iii) the person against whom the *Norwich Parmacoul* order is sought must be 'mixed up' in the wrongdoing. However, relief under the case is discretionary and simply satisfying the three conditions will not be enough; the order must be seen as a 'necessity' and in *Koo Golden East Mongolia* v *Bank of Nova Scotia*[188] counsel for the Central Bank of Mongolia citing Lord Cross in *Norwich Parmacoul* argued that such an order should rarely be used to support a 'breach of the confidence as between the bank and its customer'. However, in *Koo Golden East Mongolia*, Sir Anthony Clarke MR described bank accounts, which are used to hold the proceeds of wrongful activity as classic examples of wrongful activity where *Norwich Parmacoul* orders may be made against a bank, although the court declined to make a disclosure order since the Bank of Mongolia, as a central bank, was a state entity and had made the contract in the exercise of its sovereign authority.

---

[183] Proceeds of Crime Act 2002, s.333; see also Wadsley (2001) Banks in a Bind: Implications of the Money laundering Legislation, 16 *JIBL*, 125; see also Ch. 13 on money laundering and the offences under the Proceeds of Crime Act 2002, Terrorism Act 2000 and the Money Laundering Regulations 2007.

[184] *Liverpool City Council* v *Irwin* [1977] AC 239.

[185] *South Staffordshire Tramways Co* v *Ebbsmith* [1895] 2 QB 669; *Waterhouse* v *Barker* [1924] 2 KB 759.

[186] [1974] AC 133.

[187] *Ashworth Hospital Authority* v *MGN Ltd* [2002] 1 WLR 2033.

[188] [2007] EWCA Civ 1443.

Such a disclosure order was made in *Bankers Trust Co* v *Shapira*[189] where the Court of Appeal ordered discovery against the defendants who held accounts for persons responsible for fraudulently depriving the plaintiffs of a considerable sum of money and who allegedly placed it in their accounts. The facts of *Shapira* were that two rogues obtained a substantial amount of money by presenting forged cheques to the claimant bank, in New York, cheques drawn on it by a bank in Saudi Arabia. On discovering that the cheques were forgeries the claimant bank in New York reimbursed the account of the Saudi Arabian bank and sought to recover its losses from the two rogues. The claimant bank sought to locate the rogues by applying for an order instructing the defendant bank to disclose, and take copies of, all correspondence between the two rogues and the defendant bank and all cheques drawn on the account. The Court of Appeal held that while the courts will not lightly use their power to compel disclosure of confidential information arising out of the banker and customer relationship an order would be granted where the claimant sought to recover funds of which he had been fraudulently deprived.

A person guilty of fraud cannot, therefore, rely on the confidential nature of the banker and customer relationship to hide the proceeds of fraud and the courts will make a disclosure order, even in interlocutory proceedings, where delay would result in the funds being dissipated or the ability to trace them diminished. However, such an order is only made in exceptional circumstances where strong evidence is available showing that misappropriated funds are held to the credit of a bank account. Lord Denning in *Shapira* expressed the view that it was 'a strong thing to order a bank to disclose the state of its customer's account and the documents and correspondence relating to it'. A plaintiff may also have to give an undertaking to compensate the bank for any award of damages and give an undertaking that the material disclosed would only be used for the purposes of the relevant action.[190] Further, in *Arab Monetary Fund* v *Hashim (No 5)*[191] Hoffman J held that a claimant relying on the *Bankers Trust* order to compel disclosure must show there is a 'real prospect' that the information sought is likely to lead to the location and preservation of the assets to which the claimant has a proprietary claim. On the facts, Hoffman J concluded that the delay was such that there was no prospect of the assets being located or preserved. The potential advantage of an order favouring disclosure of information must be weighted against the detriment to the defendant, not merely in respect of aspects for which he can be financially compensated but in respect of the invasion of his privacy and breach of confidence. In *Koo Golden East Mongolia*[192] the claimant sought an order against a bank with which the proposed defendant held an account and the disclosure of the information would help locate the identity of the third party holding the proceeds of the illegal activity.

A bank served with a *Bankers Trust* order may find itself between a rock and hard place where, for example it is served with a disclosure order under the *Bankers Trust* principles and the possibility that merely making the disclosure will alert the account holder that he is being investigated and thus risk 'tipping' him off under the money laundering legislation.[193]

---

[189] [1980] 1 WLR 1274.
[190] *Bankers Trust Co* v *Shapira* [1980] 1 WLR 1274.
[191] [1992] 2 All ER 911.
[192] [2007] EWCA Civ 1443.
[193] See Ch. 13.

Duty of confidentiality and the jurisdiction of foreign courts

By the very nature of the banking business customers may not only be able to maintain accounts in two or more jurisdictions with different banks, but also banks, or branches of the same bank in different jurisdictions, may hold confidential information about the same customer. Legal proceedings in one jurisdiction (A) may, therefore, give rise to disclosure orders in respect of the customer's banking activities in another legal jurisdiction (B). A problem may, therefore, arise where the courts in jurisdiction A order the disclosure of banking information held by a bank in jurisdiction B. The bank in jurisdiction B faces a dilemma to the effect that not only is the banking information it holds about one of its customers the subject of a disclosure order by a foreign court, but it is subject to local confidential laws in country B, so that the bank holding the information will in fact be in breach of the banker and customer relationship locally if it complies with the disclosure order of the foreign courts from jurisdiction A. However, there are two methods by which a claimant may obtain information held in another jurisdiction:

1   If the bank does not have a presence in the jurisdiction where the action takes place, or if the bank does have a branch in that jurisdiction, but the information is held abroad at the bank's head-office or relates to banking operations taking place abroad, the claimant may apply for 'letters of request' or 'letters rogatory'.

2   If the foreign bank that holds the information has a branch within the jurisdiction where the proceedings are taking place then the claimant may apply to the court hearing the proceedings for a witness summons that can be served on the officers of the bank at the branch within the jurisdiction.[194] The witness summons effectively orders bank officers to produce relevant documents, and testify, in court.

Evidence held in England to support foreign proceedings

Where the court requesting the information is located in another EU Member State (with the exception of Denmark) issues a 'letter of request' to obtain evidence held in the UK in relation to 'civil or commercial' proceedings, then Council Regulation on the Co-operation between Member States in the Taking of Evidence in Civil or Commercial Matters[195] provides that a request may be made by the court hearing the complaint for evidence intended to be used in judicial proceedings[196] to be transmitted directly to the court[197] in the prescribed form.[198] The overseas court must acknowledge receipt of the request within seven days[199] and must execute

---

[194] Civil Procedure Rules 1998, rule 34(2)(1).

[195] EC Council Regulation on the Co-operation between Member States in the Taking of Evidence in Civil or Commercial Matters, 1206/2001, 2001 OJ L 174.

[196] EC Council Regulation on the Co-operation between Member States in the Taking of Evidence in Civil or Commercial Matters, 1206/2001, 2001 OJ L 174, Article 1(2).

[197] EC Council Regulation on the Co-operation between Member States in the Taking of Evidence in Civil or Commercial Matters, 1206/2001, 2001 OJ L 174, Article 2(1).

[198] EC Council Regulation on the Co-operation between Member States in the Taking of Evidence in Civil or Commercial Matters, 1206/2001, 2001 OJ L 174, Article 4.

[199] EC Council Regulation on the Co-operation between Member States in the Taking of Evidence in Civil or Commercial Matters, 1206/2001, 2001 OJ L 174, Article 7 (1).

the request within 90 days of the receipt.[200] Therefore, a general request for all bank statements received by a person during a particular period is unlikely to be granted but a request for all bank statements received during a particular period from a named bank may be granted.[201]

Where the requesting court is located outside the Member States the letter of request is governed by the Hague Convention on the Taking of Evidence Abroad in Civil or Commercial Matters 1970, and in the UK the position is governed by the Evidence (Proceedings in Other Jurisdictions) Act 1975. The Act establishes a number of limitations on the obligation to respond to any request namely: (i) the English court will not require any action to be taken in response to the letter of request unless any compliance is required by way of obtaining evidence for the purposes of civil proceedings in the court making the request;[202] and (ii) an English court will only order the production of documents specified by the requesting court.[203] In *Land Rover North American Inc.* v *Windh*[204] Treacy J stated that, in considering the letter of request, the court should:

> ask first whether the intended witnesses can reasonably be expected to have relevant evidence to give on the topics mentioned in the amended schedule of requested testimony, and second whether the intention underlying the formulation of those topics is an intention to obtain evidence for use at the trial or some other investigatory, and therefore impermissible intention.

Even where these limitations do not apply, the English courts have discretion as to whether or not to accede to the request of the foreign court and is unlikely to comply with the request where that would involve infringement of a privilege recognised by law, for example the duty of confidentiality. The court also has discretion as to the most appropriate manner in which the information can be furnished.[205] In *Re Westinghouse Uranium Contracts*[206] the House of Lords refused to give effect to letters of request issued by the courts, in Virginia, USA, in respect of litigation instituted in Virginia against defendants, an alleged international cartel of uranium producing companies, including two English companies, who in fact were not party to the litigation, in Virginia. The House of Lords said that the production of the requested evidence would expose the English companies to fines for breaching European competition law and the companies were, therefore, entitled to claim privilege against self-incrimination. Further, since the evidence supplied could be used in any subsequent legal proceedings, in Virginia, the English companies could resist the order on the basis of the privilege against self-incrimination under the Fifth Amendment to the United States Constitution. The House of Lords, in particular Lord Wilberforce, paid regard to the intervention of the UK Attorney General who considered that the investigatory powers against foreign citizens under the US anti-trust legislation infringed UK jurisdiction and sovereignty. The court concluded that complying with the letters rogatory issued by the US court would expose British subjects to proceedings, in the USA, in respect of acts performed outside the USA, and that such an extension of extraterritorial jurisdiction was not in accordance with international law.

---

[200] EC Council Regulation on the Co-operation between Member States in the Taking of Evidence in Civil or Commercial Matters, 1206/2001, 2001 OJ L 174, Article 10.

[201] *Re Asbestos Insurance Coverage Cases* [1985] 1 WLR 331.

[202] Evidence (Proceedings in Other Jurisdictions) Act 1975, s.2(3).

[203] Evidence (Proceedings in Other Jurisdictions) Act 1975, s.2(4); *Genira Trade & Finance Inc.* v *Refco Capital Markets Ltd* [2001] EWCA Civ. 1733.

[204] [2005] EWHC 432.

[205] Dicey, Morris and Collins (2010) *The Conflict of Laws*, London: Sweet and Maxwell.

[206] [1978] AC 547.

The refusal to give effect to letters rogatory on the grounds of self-incrimination may also be used as a device for refusing to order a bank, subject to the duty of confidentiality, to comply with such requests to disclose information about a customer. In *Re State of Norway's Application*[207] the courts refused a request from the Norwegian tax authorities seeking to interview two bank officers on the basis that to comply with the request would involve the bank in breach of its duty of confidentiality, owed to the customer. However, since the duty of confidentiality under *Tournier* is qualified, complying with a request by the foreign court would not automatically be a bar to disclosure and Kerr LJ in *Re State of Norway's Application* said the court must carry 'out a balancing exercise' between the 'desirable policy of assisting a foreign court' and the 'great weight' to be given to the 'desirability of upholding the duty of confidence'. Both Glidewell and Gibson LJJ agreed with the desirability to have regard to the competing claims. However, unlike Kerr LJ who said that where disclosure is required under letters rogatory it may be justified under the first *Tournier* exception (namely compulsion of law), the former judges held that disclosure might be justified under the second *Tournier* exception, namely there is a public interest in the UK courts assisting foreign courts.

As an alternative, the US courts have often resorted to compelling bank officers based at local branches in the USA to disclose the relevant information, or face contempt of court proceedings. However, in such circumstances the courts are likely to give effect to domestic laws when faced with an order with extraterritorial effect from an overseas court. In *X AG v A Bank*[208] the US Department of Justice, in the course of an investigation into the crude oil industry, served a subpoena on the head-office of a US bank requiring the production in the USA of documents relating to bank accounts held with the bank's London branch by a group of companies, one of which had dealings in the US crude oil market. As the bank indicated its intention to comply with the request for information the corporate group obtained an interim injunction restraining the bank from disclosing the information. Leggett J in determining whether, or not, to continue with the interim injunction concluded that since the bank accounts were opened and maintained in London, English law governed the banker and customer relationship. With regard to whether the injunction should be continued the learned judge held that two factors, in particular, should be considered:

1 That compliance with the US order would potentially render the bank liable to its customer for breach of the duty of confidentiality, the scope of which was to be determined by English Law which governed the banker and customer relationship, since the accounts in question were located in London. Accordingly, implementing the order of the US courts would not only involve a 'breach of what might be termed a private interest in the sense that what is directly involved is a contract between banker and customer', but it would also involve a 'matter of public interest, because it raises issues of wider concern than those peculiar to the parties'.

2 It was unlikely that the US court would commence contempt of court proceedings if a court of competent jurisdiction at the place where the relevant records were maintained had prevented the bank, by order, from making the disclosure.

---

[207] [1987] QB 433 (CA) affd [1990] 1 AC 723; see also *Honda Giken Kogyou Kabushiki Kaisha v KJM Superbikes* [2007] EWCA Civ. 313.
[208] [1983] 2 All ER 464.

Leggett J concluded:

> I can summarise in a sentence the balance of convenience as I see it. On the one hand, there is involved in the continuation of the injunction impending the exercise by the United States Court in London of powers which, by English standards, would be regarded as excessive, without in so doing causing detriment to the bank: on the other hand, the refusal of the injunctions, or the non-continuation of them, would cause potentially very considerable commercial harm to the group, which cannot be disputed, by suffering the bank to act for its own purposes in breach of the duty of confidentiality admittedly owed to its customers.

Similarly, in *FDC Co Ltd v Chase Manhattan Bank*[209] the US revenue authorities demanded information from the defendant bank's head office in New York about the claimant's account that was held with the bank's Hong Kong branch. The Hong Kong Court of Appeal granted an injunction to prevent disclosure since complying with the order of the US courts would constitute a breach of the bank's duty of confidentiality. Huggins VP expressed the view that all 'persons opening accounts with banks in Hong Kong, whether local or foreign banks, are entitled to look to the Hong Kong courts to enforce any obligations of secrecy that is, by Hong Kong law, implied by virtue of the relationship of banker and customer'. Nor did Huggins VP consider the fact that the breach of the duty of confidentiality would occur in the USA rather than in Hong Kong would waive the breach, as 'the obligation of secrecy is not subject to territorial limits'. Nor was the disclosure of information justifiable under an order made by a foreign court under the 'compulsion of law' qualification to the *Tournier* case. Moreover, all banks carrying on business in Hong Kong owed the same extent of the duty of confidentiality irrespective of where the head office of the Hong Kong based branch is located. The Hong Kong Court of Appeal therefore gave effect to Hong Kong law rather than compel compliance with an order of a foreign court.

Although, it was argued that there was no basis for the injunction against disclosing information in Hong Kong since the transfer of information between a bank branch and its head office was merely a transfer of information between different parts of the same entity, Huggins VP held that for the purposes of holding confidential customer information 'the Hong Kong branch of the bank should for present purposes be considered as a different entity separate from its head office in New York'. Huggins VP said that although there may be circumstances (for example an internal investigation of suspected fraud) where the ordinary course of business would require an exchange of customer information between bank offices, the transfer of information in *FDC* was 'solely for the purpose of its being disclosed to the United States Government' and it would be 'closing our eyes to the reality of the situation' to allow a bank to make an internal transfer of information which it would not make in the ordinary course of business, when the 'transfer is designed for no other purpose than to bring the information within the jurisdiction of the foreign court'. Consequently, although the order appeared to be addressed to the head office of the bank in the jurisdiction it was made (the USA) Huggins VP considered that the order, in fact, had 'extraterritorial' effect and was 'aimed unashamedly' at information held in Hong Kong and subject to the laws of that country.

However, in cases involving fraud the English courts are less likely to grant an injunction to prevent disclosure of information. In *Pharaon v Bank of Credit and Commerce International SA (in liquidation)*[210] the victim of an alleged fraudulent conspiracy involving the defendant

---

[209] [1985] 2 HKC 470 (HKCA).
[210] [1988] 4 All ER 455.

bank, BCCI, started proceedings in New York, and obtained a subpoena from the US District court against BCCI's auditors for the production of documents relating to BCCI. The auditors applied to the English courts for leave to comply with the US subpoena since there was a risk that such disclosure might be against an injunction obtained by one of BCCI's customer's, in the English courts, preventing disclosure to third parties. Rattee J held that the bank's duty of confidentiality was overridden by the second qualification to the *Tournier* case, namely disclosure that is justified on the grounds of public interest since the US order was made in pursuance of revealing or uncovering fraud. The BCCI auditors were given leave to comply with the US subpoena but subject to the documents being redacted to ensure that information about customers not involved in the conspiracy were not disclosed.

Information held by branches of foreign banks carrying on business in the UK

The definition of the term 'banker' under the BBEA 1879 did not originally extend to ordering disclosure of information held by branches of foreign banks carrying on business in the UK. This was rectified by the Banking Act 1979[211] but the courts are reluctant to order disclosure of information where there would be jurisdictional issues. Thus, in *R v Grossman*[212] the Court of Appeal refused to order disclosure of information in English criminal proceedings of a bank's books held on the Isle of Man in relation to accounts maintained on the island. Similarly, in civil proceedings Hoffman J in *MacKinnon v Donaldson, Lufkin and Janrette Securities Corporation*[213] expressed the view that courts should not, except in exceptional circumstances, impose on a foreigner and in particular a foreign bank which would owe a duty of confidence to its customer regulated by the law of the country where the account is maintained, a requirement to produce documents outside the jurisdiction concerning business transacted outside the jurisdiction. He said that due regard to the sovereignty of others is especially important where banks are concerned and continued:

> If every country where a bank happened to carry on business asserted a right to require the bank to produce documents relating to accounts kept in any other such country, banks would be in the unhappy position of being forced to submit to whichever sovereign was able to apply the greatest pressure.

In the *Mackinnon* case a defunct Bahamian company allegedly committed frauds in relation to a number of international loans. The claimant obtained an order under s.7 of the BBEA 1879 which entitled him to inspect certain documents concerning the Bahamian company's account with the London branch of a New York bank. The claimant also obtained a witness order requiring an officer of the bank at the bank's London branch to attend the trial and produce certain relevant documents. Hoffmann J discharging the Master's order, held that as both the disclosure order and witness order were to take effect in New York, they infringed US sovereignty and it was important that the courts did not exercise their jurisdiction in a way that impeached another country's sovereignty.[214] The court took the view that bank

---

[211] Superseded by the Banking Act 1998, ss.81 and 82, and now the Disclosure of Confidential Information Regulations 2001, SI 2001/2188 made under the Financial Services and Markets Act 2000.

[212] (1981) 73 CR App Rep 302.

[213] [1986] Ch 482.

[214] See *Société Eram Shipping Co Ltd v Compagnie Internationale de Navigacion* [2003] 3 WLR 21 where the court refused a third party debt order over a foreign account's credit balance.

documents normally contain details not only of the bank's own business, but also those of the bank's customers, and bank confidentiality laws in different countries protect customer confidentiality to different degrees. Hoffmann J therefore expressed the view that the duty of bank confidentiality should be governed by the laws of the country where the account is kept otherwise if 'every country where a bank happened to carry on business asserted a right to require the bank to produce documents relating to accounts kept in any other such country, banks would be in the unhappy position of being forced to submit to whichever sovereign was able to apply the greatest pressure'.

In *Masri* v *Consolidated Contractors International Company SAL (No 2)*[215] Lawrence Collins LJ expressed the view that there is no absolute rule that a 'court will never have jurisdiction to make orders under the BBEA 1879 against the London branch of a foreign bank in relation to papers held by head office, nor that it will never be possible to issue witness summons against the bank's London branch officer in respect of head office transactions.' Such disclosure orders or witness summons would only be made if the circumstances of the case demonstrate 'a sufficient connection with England to justify an order'. Lawrence Collins LJ expressed the view that the *Mackinnon* case might have been differently decided if the papers held by the foreign bank's head office had related to English transactions. However, these views were doubted by Sir Anthony Clarke MR in *Masri* v *Consolidated Contractors International Company SAL (No 4)*[216] where he expressed the view that Lawrence Collins LJ may have 'somewhat understated' the relevance of presumption against extraterritoriality.

Where, however, documents are maintained, or witnesses located, in another EU Member State, the English courts may request assistance from the foreign court under Regulation EC Council Regulation on the Co-operation between Member States in the Taking of Evidence in Civil or Commercial Matters.[217]

Disclosure in the interests of the public

The second qualification to the duty of confidentiality recognised by Bankes LJ in *Tournier* relates to bank's duty to disclose relevant information where there is a duty to the public to make disclosure. Relying on the view expressed by Viscount Finlay in *Weld-Blundell* v *Stephens*[218] Bankes LJ in *Tournier* expressed the view that in certain circumstances 'State or public duty may supersede' the duty of confidentiality of the agent (bank) to his principal (customer). Thus, in times of war a bank may be required to disclose confidential information about a customer's dealings with, for example, an enemy alien. In the *Tournier* case, itself, Bankes LJ doubted that a bank was entitled to disclose to the police information because of its suspicions that the customer was involved in a crime. The circumstances in which the public interest requires a person to disclose otherwise confidential information, and the nature and scope of the information to be disclosed, may, therefore, vary according to prevailing circumstances and prevailing economic, social, cultural and political ideologies. This is an example of an area where specific statutes have intervened to impose a duty to report wrongdoing in relation to the customer's banking activities (e.g. Drug Trafficking Act 1986; Proceeds of Crime Act 2002 etc.).

---

[215] [2008] EWCA 303.
[216] [2010] AC 90.
[217] 1206/2001, 2001 OJ L 174.
[218] [1920] AC 956.

There has, therefore, been some debate about whether or not this qualification should continue to be recognised and the scope and effect of the qualification will undoubtedly reflect, at any relevant time, current social and moral standards. The private interests of the customer, in preserving the confidentiality of his financial information and dealings, will need to be balanced against the public interest in favour of disclosure. Paget[219] states that this qualification is perhaps the 'most difficult' of Bankes LJ's qualifications and given the statutory inroads to the duty of confidentiality the Jack Committee on Banking Services[220] adopted the view that the qualification no longer be recognised and had no justification in modern society. Indeed, the Jack Committee recommended the abolition of this qualification,[221] but the government White Paper,[222] in response, rejected this recommendation on the basis that the public duty qualification permits banks to make disclosure, as opposed to the various statutes, which require disclosure.

It would, therefore, appear that for the present this qualification continues to have a place in the law and a number of recent cases justify its continued recognition. The *Libyan Arab Foreign Bank* v *Bankers Trust Co*[223] case arose following the United States Presidential Order of 8 January 1986 freezing Libyan assets and interests held in the USA or in the possession or control of US persons including overseas branches of US persons and which extended, in remit, to braches of US registered banks. Following the order the Bankers Trust, in New York, was required to disclose information regarding the claimant's accounts held by it in New York and London, to the Federal Reserve, the US Central Bank. The London account being governed by English Law the claimants brought an action for breach of confidentiality relying on three of the four *Tournier* qualifications, including disclosure being justified on grounds of public interest. Staughton J rejected the first two grounds for justifying disclosure but was of the view that the public interest qualification would probably apply, although he did not have to decide the case on that ground. He expressed the view:

> But presuming (as I must) the New York law on this point is the same as English Law, it seems to me that the Federal Reserve Board, as the central bank in the United States, may have a public duty to perform in obtaining information from banks.

More recently, the continued existence of the public interest qualification was examined in *Price Waterhouse* v *BCCI Holdings (Luxembourg) SA*[224] which concerned the disclosure of confidential information by Price Waterhouse to the Bingham Inquiry, established jointly by the Chancellor of the Exchequer and the Governor of the Bank of England, following the collapse of Bank of Credit and Commerce International Group (BCCI). The Bingham inquiry was a non-statutory inquiry established to investigate the performance of the Bank of England's statutory supervisory functions in relation to BCCI. As a non-statutory investigation the inquiry had no statutory power to compel disclosure of otherwise confidential information. However, wishing to cooperate and support the inquiry, Price Waterhouse applied to the

---

[219] Hapgood (2013) *Paget's Law of Banking*, London: Butterworths LexisNexis.

[220] Jack Banking Services: Law and Practice, Report by the Review Committee, Chairman: Professor R.B. Jack, Cm. 622.

[221] Jack, Banking Services: Law and Practice, Report by the Review Committee Chaired by Professor R.B. Jack, CBE, 1989, London Cm. 622, paras 4.04, 6.23, 16.10–16.12, paras 5.30 and 5.41.

[222] White Paper on *Banking Services: Law and Practice*, Cm 1026, P.15, London 1990.

[223] [1989] QB 728.

[224] [1992] BCLC 583.

court for directions. Although the case concerned the duty of confidentiality owed by accountants to their clients the principles discussed by Millett J are of general relevance and the learned judge concluded that the public interest in maintaining confidentiality might be superseded by some countervailing interest in favour of disclosure and that the latter was not limited to the public interest in detecting or preventing wrongdoing. According to Millett J the duty of confidentiality was subject to the right, and not merely the duty, to disclose information where there was a higher public interest in the disclosure, instead of maintaining confidentiality. It was in the public interest Price Waterhouse cooperated with the judicial inquiry looking into the failures of effective supervision and regulation of authorised deposit-taking institutions and issues of depositor protection.

Millett J concluded that if it was in the public interest to disclose information to the Bank of England, then responsible for regulation of the banking sector, under s.39 of the Banking Act 1987[225] there is at least as great an interest in disclosing information to an inquiry established to review the Bank's performance in respect of BCCI provided the disclosure of the information is not broader than that authorised under the statutory powers. The case concerned the issue of disclosure of confidential information to recognised authorities concerned with a review of bank supervision. However, in *Pharaon v Bank of Credit and Commerce International SA (in liquidation)*,[226] another case following the collapse of BCCI, Rattee J held that the balance between the public interest in upholding the duty of confidentiality in the banker and customer relationship was overridden by the public interest in making confidential documents available to the parties in private foreign proceedings where there was alleged fraud involving an international bank. He added that such disclosure must be limited to what was reasonably necessary to achieve the purpose of public interest.

Disclosure in the bank's interest

Bankes LJ recognised the third qualification to the duty of confidentiality as being where disclosure is required in the interests of the bank itself. The scope of this qualification has also been the subject of some scrutiny and Cranston[227] argues that disclosure of confidential information can be justified on the basis of the public interest qualification but not on the basis of it being in the interest of the bank. Bankes LJ said that a simple illustration within this category is where 'a bank issues a writ claiming payment of an overdraft stating on the face of the writ the amount of the overdraft'. Hence litigation or some other dispute involving a customer or sometimes a third party, for example where the bank seeks to enforce a third party guarantee when the customer is in default, will be the subject of this qualification. In such circumstances the disclosure is sanctioned on the strength of the legal proceedings. In *Sunderland v Barclays Bank Ltd*[228] the bank dishonoured a cheque drawn by its customer, a married woman, because there were insufficient funds to the credit of the account, but also because the bank knew that the cheques were drawn in respect of gambling debts. The customer's husband intervened to complain on behalf of his wife and at her request, and at that stage the branch manager disclosed to the husband that the cheques were drawn in favour of bookmakers. Du Parq LJ dismissed the wife's action and held the bank was justified in disclosing confidential information to the customer's husband where the bank's

---

[225] Superseded by the Financial Services and Markets Act 2000, Part XI.
[226] [1998] 4 All ER 455.
[227] Cranston (2002) *Principles of Banking Law*, Oxford: Oxford University Press, 174–176.
[228] (1938) 5 LDB 163.

reputation was clearly under threat. He further held that the wife had given her implied consent to the disclosure of the state of her bank account by allowing her husband to intervene in the discussions, on her behalf.

While it might be argued that the wife had given her implied consent to the bank, to discuss the state of her account with her husband, it is questionable whether the wife could be said to have impliedly given her consent to the bank manager to disclose the fact that the cheques drawn by her, on her account, related to gambling debts. It is difficult to justify the decision of Du Parq LJ in the *Sunderland* case particularly if the *Tournier* case itself is followed. In the latter case the bank manager disclosed information about the customer's account to his employer and the fact that the cheques were again, in that case, drawn to settle gambling debts. While there was no justification at all in the bank manager's disclosure in the *Tournier* case where the manager took the step of calling the customer's employer, in the *Sunderland* case the manager might have acquitted himself by explaining there were insufficient funds for the bank to honour the cheque drawn by the customer, but without the need to explain that the dishonoured cheque was drawn to pay gambling debts. The qualification was reviewed in *El Jawhary* v *BCCI*[229] and *Christofi* v *Barclays Bank Plc.*[230] In the latter case the court held that the bank was under a duty to disclose information which had been made available to the recipient as a matter of statutory right; in this instance under s.22 of the Bankruptcy Act 1914.

Disclosure with the customer's authority

The final qualification recognised by Bankes LJ in the *Tournier* case, which may justify disclosure of confidential information, is where the bank acts either with the express or implied consent of the customer in making that disclosure. At the time the case was decided it was accepted that the disclosure might relate to the general state of the customer's account, or special circumstances in which the bank is only permitted to supply such information as is sanctioned by the customer. Moreover, the bank should not act in circumstances where it believes that the customer's consent was obtained under duress and not freely given. Bankes LJ himself gave the example of a customer authorising disclosure where he uses the bank to provide a credit reference. Banks have adopted the practice of making disclosure in such circumstances on the basis of the customer's implied consent.

However, in *Turner* v *Royal Bank of Scotland*[231] the Court of Appeal rejected the view that a retail customer gives implied consent to his bank to provide credit references, on his behalf, when he opens his account. In that case the plaintiff customer maintained both his personal and business accounts with the defendant bank and over a three-year period the bank responded unfavourably to a number of status enquires about his creditworthiness. On each occasion the bank made use of confidential information about the state of the plaintiff's account, prior to formally responding to the enquires. The plaintiff brought an action against the bank claiming damages for breach of the duty of confidentiality. While the bank did not dispute that it owed the plaintiff customer a duty of confidentiality it was argued, on the bank's behalf, that the duty was qualified where the disclosure was made with the customer's implied or express consent. As the plaintiff had not given his express consent to the disclosure it was argued that he had, in fact, given his implied consent to the disclosure.

[229] [1993] BCLC 396.
[230] [1999] 2 All ER (Comm) 417.
[231] [1999] 2 All ER (Comm) 664.

The bank claimed that it was normal banking practice to respond, in the ordinary course of banking business, to status enquiries about a customer's credit-worthiness from other banks and that every customer opening an account with a bank must be presumed to have agreed to this practice, whether or not they had actual knowledge. A customer would then be deemed to have given his implied consent to his bank to provide references to a third party based on otherwise confidential banking information acquired as a result of the knowledge a bank gains from the course of dealings with its customer. The Court of Appeal, upholding the decision of the trial judge and rejecting the bank's argument, that the customer had given implied consent to the disclosure of confidential information, held the bank liable for the breach of duty of confidentiality.

Sir Richard Scott VC distinguished between banking practice, which operates as 'no more than a private agreement between banks', and such practice as amounts to an established usage, which contractually binds the bank's customer, although the customer has no knowledge of it and is unaware of the practice.[232] Trade practice will only bind the customer if it is 'notorious, certain and reasonable and not contrary to the law'.[233] Scott VC concluded that he could not find evidence to suggest that the practice of providing credit references for customers without their knowledge or consent was so notorious, i.e. well known and recognised by those operating in the trade or business as to be universally accepted, as to bind *Turner*, as established usage. The learned judge also concluded that a banking practice that deprives a customer of substantive rights, for example the right to confidentiality in respect of his banking affairs, could only be relied on where the customer knew and assented to the practice.[234] The court's emphasis was on the failure to establish notoriety and not lack of reasonableness.

The *Turner* case clarifies an area of some uncertainty and previously subject to some criticism.[235] The implied consent theory was difficult to justify in the case of personal customer's who were unaware of the ramifications of the banker and customer relationship. This is still true of the vast majority of bank customer's despite attempts towards transparency and financial education.

While business customers might be expected to have a greater understanding of the terms on which they conduct banking business it would be difficult to establish notoriety in respect of the bank's right to rely on implied consent of the customer to disclose confidential information. So while the *Turner* case dealt specifically with the non-business customer it is likely the courts will extend the rule also to business customers, so a bank can only disclose confidential information with the express consent of the customer. In 1989 the Jack Committee recommended that legislation should require banks to explain clearly to customers 'how the system of bankers' opinions works, and to invite them to give, or withhold, their general consent to the bank to supply opinions on them in response to enquiries'. The industry response, in the form of the Banking Code and the Business Banking Codes, was to provide that where a bank is asked for a banker's reference it must obtain the customer's consent in writing before the reference is given. In the *Turner* case Scott VC stated that the Banking Code in respect of the giving of bankers' references merely reflected the existing common law obligations and did not establish new standards.[236] If that view is correct then the common

---

[232] [1999] 2 All ER (Comm.) 664 at 671.
[233] *Cunliffe-Owen v Teather and Greenwood* [1967] 1 WLR 385 at 391.
[234] [1999] 2 All ER (Comm.) 664 at 670 citing *Barclays Bank plc v Bank of England* [1985] 1 All ER 385 at 391.
[235] Chorley (1972) *Law of Banking*, London: Sweet & Maxwell.
[236] [1999] 2 All ER (Comm.) 664 at 671.

law requires express consent in every case of a status enquiry. This might be considered too onerous and impede banking business. It is also in contrast to the Jack Committee recommendation, which required banks to obtain general consent from their customers.

Disclosure within groups of companies

Disclosure of confidential information held by the bank is not permitted when another member of a group of companies (of which the bank is a member) is in dispute with the customer. The courts will apply the separate entity principle that exists in respect of each subsidiary company within the group to protect confidential information held by individual member companies of the group.[237] While disclosure of confidential information by a bank to a parent or subsidiary company will be in breach of the bank's duty of confidentiality the rule is not cost effective and may deny banks the opportunity to assess the customer's financial well-being, and the bank's exposure, on an overall business basis. For this reason the Jack Committee[238] recommended the law should be modified to allow the transfer, between banking companies within the same group, of confidential information, without the customer's consent, provided the disclosure is reasonably necessary for the specific purpose of protecting the bank and its subsidiaries against loss, in relation to the provision of normal banking services. The Jack Committee expressed the view that the transfer of such information, without the customer's consent, could not be justified to include disclosure to non-banking subsidiaries within the same group. The Banking Code took a somewhat different approach and prohibited disclosure to other companies in the same group for marketing purposes, unless the bank acted at the request of the customer.[239] Presumably, the use of confidential customer information is permitted for marketing and non-marketing purposes so long as the information is available to branches in the same company but carrying on a different business.

Credit reference agencies

The four qualifications to the *Tournier* case have been adapted and modified to meet current banking practice and the demands of the law. However, there is some doubt about which of the qualifications would apply to disclosure of confidential information by banks to credit reference agencies. Credit reference agencies are regulated by the Consumer Credit Act 1974[240] and are subject to the Data Protection Act 1998. The Consumer Credit Act 1974 provides that a credit reference agency is:

> a person carrying on a business comprising the furnishings of persons with information relevant to the financial standing of individuals, being information collected by the agency for that purpose.

Traditionally, banking practice had dedicated that while banks were able to use such information available to credit reference agencies to make decisions about their customer's, they were

---

[237] *Bank of Tokyo v Karoon* [1987] AC at 53.

[238] Jack, Banking Services: Law and Practice, Report by the Review Committee Chaired by Professor R.B. Jack, CBE, 1989, London Cm. 622, paras 4.04, 6.23, 16.10–16.12.

[239] Banking Code, 2005 edn, paras 8.3 and 11.1, with similar provisions contained in the Business Banking Code, 2005 edn, paras 8.3 and 11.1.

[240] Consumer Credit Act 1974, s.145(8).

unable to contribute information to credit reference agencies by passing customer information acquired in the course of the banker and customer relationship. In 1988 an agreement, effective for a 12-month period, was entered into between the banks and credit reference agencies under which banks would make available information to such agencies in respect of customers who were in default, known as 'black information'. However, there was a difference of policy between the banks about when disclosure would be made and in a lecture given by the then Governor of the Bank of England to the Chartered Institute of Bankers[241] he expressed the view that even if it has to wait a change in the law:

> the banks, and all other lenders will consider very carefully, whether they cannot provide more data, subject of course to proper safeguards about its confidentiality . . .

In its 1989 report the Jack Committee was clearly concerned about the extent of disclosure of confidential information that should be permitted and whether it should be restricted to customers who are in default (black information). Disclosure of confidential information in respect of customer's who are not in default and who have a clean credit record has proven to be more controversial and in November 1988 the then President of the Chartered Institute of Bankers expressed the view:[242]

> Market research had shown that a high proportion of customers might refuse permission for such disclosure if asked to consent to it voluntarily.

The government White Paper on Banking Services Law and Practice[243] accepted that banks could already pass information to credit reference agencies where the customer was in default (black information) but the government expressed the view that the proposed Banking Code should prohibit the disclosure of 'white information' to credit reference agencies unless with the express consent of the customer. Although the first edition of the Banking Code did not deal with this recommendation, subsequent revisions provided that while 'black' information may be disclosed to credit reference agencies, subject to 28 days' notice of such disclosure to the customer, 'white' information may only be disclosed with the express consent of the customer. This is now reinforced by the Lending Code, which came into operation in March 2011.[244]

It is difficult to justify disclosure of a customer's confidential banking information to credit reference agencies and while the government White Paper justified it on the basis of 'interests of the bank' under the *Tournier* qualifications, it is questionable whether disclosure of 'white information' under this qualification could be justified. Disclosure on the basis of the 'public interest' may be justified in the context of 'black information' but again more difficult to justify with 'white information'. Where disclosure of confidential bank information is made when the customer is not in default, and has a perfect bank record, then disclosure to a credit reference agency is probably only justified if made with the express consent of the customer.[245]

---

[241] Chartered Institute of Bankers, 29 November 1988.

[242] *Banking World*, November 1988.

[243] White Paper on Banking Services: Law and Practice, Cm 1026, P.16, London 1990.

[244] The Lending Code Setting standards for banks, building societies and credit card providers 2011, section 3, http://www.lendingstandardsboard.org.uk/docs/lendingcode.pdf.

[245] The importance of credit reference agencies in modern society was recognised in *Kpohraror v Woolwich Building Society* [1996] 4 All ER 119.

Duty to exercise care in contract and tort

The courts have examined the scope of the duty of care arising under the implied banker and customer contract. The duty may either be imposed as a result of the application of the common law rules established by the courts in the context of the banker and customer contract, or under statute by s.13 of the Supply of Goods and Services Act 1982 which implies a duty of care in contracts for the supply of services undertaken in the course of a business.

The duty of care is co-extensive and a claimant may pursue an action for breach of duty of care in contract and/or tort. The possibility of a dual cause of action might allow the plaintiff to take advantage of the potentially wider tortuous duty than the contractual counterpart, although the contractual obligations may well help define the scope of the tortuous duty. The courts will, however, be reluctant to impose obligations in tort which are inconsistent with contractual terms.[246] In *Jeremy Stone* v *National Westminster Bank Plc*[247] Sales J confirmed that a private banker who follows his bank's processes and his client's instructions, who acts honestly and who is not aware of his client's fraudulent activities is not liable (and therefore neither is his employer bank) to his client's defrauded investors. The decision confirms that a private banker's duty of care in tort is limited to the contractual duties he owes his client. The court stated, *obiter*, that this would have been the case even if the bank's back office had been in breach of its regulatory anti-money laundering duties.

Although, the duty of care recognised in contract may be concurrent with obligations in tort[248] there is no reason why the law of tort could not impose wider obligations than those arising under contract.[249] The court will not, however, impose a duty in tort that is inconsistent with the terms of the contract.[250] The scope of concurrent liability was examined in *Go Dante Yap* v *Bank Austria Creditanstalt AG*[251] where the plaintiff sued his private bank in relation to investment losses incurred during the 1997 Asian financial crisis alleging that the investments were not authorised by him and that the bank had negligently failed to provide him with investment advice on the management of his portfolio. The Singapore Court of Appeal held that the bank owed its customer a duty of skill and care in contract and tort to carry out its customer's instructions and to provide investment advice. The court held that while the bank was under an implied duty in contract to exercise reasonable skill and care in carrying out its customer's instructions it was not under an implied duty in contract with respect to providing investment advice on the management of the portfolio. On the facts, the court found that the bank had not breached its duties in contract or tort. The court went on to recognise that such duties and the standard of those duties may be excluded or substantially limited by exclusion clauses and disclaimers.

The existence of an implied contractual duty of care owed by a bank to the customer has been examined in several different circumstances, for example in the context of mandate, the

---

[246] *Tai Hing Cotton Mill Ltd* v *Liu Chong Hing Bank Ltd* [1986] AC 80.

[247] [2013] EWHC 208 (Ch).

[248] *Henderson* v *Merrett Syndicates Ltd* [1995] 2 AC 145 at 193.

[249] *Holt* v *Payne Skillington and De Groot Collis* (1995) 77 BLR 51; applied in *Sumitomo Bank Ltd* v *Banque Bruxelles Lambert SA* [1997] 1 Lloyd's Rep. 487.

[250] *Tai Hing Cotton Mill Ltd* v *Liu Chong Hing Bank Ltd* [1986] AC 80.

[251] [2011] SGCA 39.

giving of investment advice, the taking and execution of security. In *Westminster Bank Ltd v Hilton*[252] both Atkin and Bankes LJJ said:

> it is the duty of the bank, arising out of the contract, to exercise reasonable care and skill in dealing with the communications which the customer sends to [him] in relation to his banking business.

In the context of the banker and customer relationship the learned judges went onto say that:

> in essence it is a contractual relationship which involves, I think, the duty of the bank to take reasonable care in the carrying out for its customer of its customer's business.

In *Selangor United Rubber Estates Ltd v Cradock (No 3)*[253] the action arose out of a scheme to finance a take-over bid of the company. The transaction was carried out in the presence of the existing and new directors of the company and an officer of the bank, the District Bank, whose function it was to deliver a bankers' draft issued by the District Bank in exchange for a cheque drawn by the company, as payment for the bankers' draft. The effect of the transaction was that the amount standing to the credit of the current account amounted to the company paying for its own shares in the takeover situation through middlemen who in turn had agreed to lend a similar amount to those making the takeover bid to help finance the takeover bid. However, because of the complexity of the transaction and the inexperience of the bank officer the illegal nature of the transaction did not come to the attention of the bank although it was obviously aware of the takeover bid. The presence of the bank officer was intended to ensure that the bankers' draft was only delivered to the company's directors once they had handed over a properly drawn cheque as payment for the draft.

When the company went into liquidation the Official Receiver brought an action against the bank to recover the amount involved on the grounds that the bank was in breach of its duty as a constructive trustee and, alternatively, in negligence for breach of a duty of care. The action against the bank succeeded on both counts and Ungoed-Thomas J approving *Hilton v Westminster Bank Ltd*[254] in respect of the duty of care said:

> a bank has a duty under its contract with the customer to exercise 'reasonable care and skill' in carrying out its part with regard to operations within its contract with its customer. The standard of that reasonable care and skill is an objective standard applicable to bankers. Whether or not it has been attained in any particular case has to be decided in the light of all the relevant facts, which can vary almost infinitely. The relevant considerations include the prima facie assumption that men are honest, the practice of bankers, the very limited time in which banks have to decide what course to take with regard to a cheque presented for payment without risking liability for delay, and the extent to which an operation is unusual or out of the ordinary course of business . . . What intervention is appropriate in that exercise of reasonable care and skill again depends on circumstances? Where it is to inquire, then failure to make inquiry is not excused by the conviction that the inquiry would be futile, or that the answer would have been false.

Although it is difficult to understand why the presence of a bank officer whose sole purpose was to deliver the bankers' draft, an administrative function on behalf of the bank, and

---

[252] (1926) 43 TLR 124.
[253] [1968] 1 WLR 1555.
[254] (1926) 43 TLR 124.

receive a cheque for payment of the draft was sufficient to impute constructive notice of the illegality of the transaction the *Selangor* case found some support in *Karak Rubber Co Ltd* v *Burden (No 2)*.[255] The facts of *Karak* were similar to *Selangor*, and the defendant bank was party to a payment, by means of a bankers' draft, in circumstances in which it was alleged that the bank staff involved should have realised that the payment was for the purpose of, or related to, the purchase of a company's own shares. This being illegal under the Companies legislation an action was brought, against the bank, for negligence. Brightman J held the bank liable for breach of duty of care. In determining whether a duty of care is imposed the question, which must be answered, is:

> whether the banker is to exercise reasonable and skill in transacting the customer's business, including the making of such enquires as may, in given circumstances, be appropriate and practical if the banker has, or a reasonable banker would have, grounds for believing that the authorised signatories are misusing their authority for the purpose of defrauding their principal or otherwise defeating his true intentions.

Both *Selangor* and *Karak* proceeded on the basis that the duty in contract was synonymous to the duty in equity. However, it is erroneous to equate liability for breach of a duty of care in negligence to liability based on dishonesty and thus liability as constructive trustee. The complexity of the laws of contract and equity resulted in too onerous a standard of care being imposed which the banks, in those cases, failed to discharge and which subsequently caused some concerns. The law seemed to give the impression that the paying banks were expected to act as amateur detectives and that it should not be unusual to dishonour a cheque even though signed in accordance with the customer's written mandate.

The law was reviewed in *Barclays Bank plc* v *Quincecare Ltd*[256] and *Lipkin Gorman* v *Karpnale Ltd*[257] and these cases adopted a more balanced approach. In *Barclays Bank plc* v *Quincecare*[258] the plaintiff bank's claim against a corporate borrower and its guarantor was resisted on the ground that the bank, in executing a payment order given by its chairman, on behalf of the company, had been put on inquiry that the chairman was acting in an unauthorised manner and for his own benefit. Steyn J gave careful consideration to the competing factors on either side and held that in fairness to both parties the bank must refrain from executing an order if, and for as long as, it is put on inquiry in the sense that the bank has reasonable grounds, even if not proof, that the mandate is an attempt to misappropriate company funds. Having expressed the general principles regarding the duty of care in similar terms to those in the *Selangor*[259] and *Karak*[260] cases, Steyn J said a number of factors, for example the standing of the corporate customer, the bank's knowledge of the signatory, the amount involved, the need for a prompt transfer, the need to make reasonable inquires and the unusual features of the transaction may be relevant and taken into consideration. Furthermore, he expressed the view that 'in the absence of telling indications to the contrary, a banker will usually approach a suggestion that a director of a corporate customer is trying to defraud the company with an reaction of instinctive disbelief'.

[255] [1972] 1 All ER 210.
[256] [1992] 4 All ER 363.
[257] [1992] 4 All ER 409.
[258] [1992] 4 All ER 363.
[259] [1968] 1 WLR 1555.
[260] [1972] 1 All ER 210.

Thus, trust and distrust is the basis of the banker and customer relationship and places the bank under a less onerous duty of care compared to the *Selangor* and *Karak* cases where the views of the courts had left the impression that a higher standard of care was imposed; i.e. that the bank would have to act as an amateur detective. The *Quincecare*[261] case was followed by the Court of Appeal in *Lipkin Gorman v Karpnale Ltd*[262] in which Lloyds bank appealed against a finding of liability as a constructive trustee and for breach of contract.

The facts of *Lipkin Gorman* were that a partner, X, in a firm of solicitors, who had sole authority to draw against the client account drew cheques against the account to fund his gambling habit. Part of the case against the bank was that the branch manager knew of X's gambling habit. Indeed, following a meeting with X, the manager recorded that he did not believe X's assertion that the gambling was a 'controlled activity'. The manager failed to inform the firm of solicitors of X's gambling, or the large sums X had withdrawn from the firm's account. The manager made no inquiries as to the propriety of X's withdrawals. Reversing Allott J the Court of Appeal expressed the view that it had to deal with two main issues namely: (i) the relationship between liability as a constructive trustee and the law of contract; and (ii) the duty of care owed by a bank to its customer under the law of contract.

On the second issue Parker LJ approached the question of the standard of care with the warning that reported cases must be treated with caution for they are essentially cases decided on their individual facts and regard must be had to the following:

- That what may be considered to be a breach of duty at any one time may not be a breach of duty at another.[263]
- Cases relating to the collecting bank being sued for conversion for wrongful payment and those relating to the paying bank raise different considerations.
- The distinction between liability as a constructive trustee and liability for breach of contract is frequently blurred or not considered at all.

Despite the difference of approach both May and Parker LJJ concluded that the bank will not, in normal circumstances, be under a duty to enquire whether, or not, the person drawing the cheques is authorised to draw on the account and a duty will only be imposed in unusual circumstances. May and Parker LJJ held that the bank could not be held liable to its customer as constructive trustee of the monies in the customer's account unless the bank could be shown to be in breach of the contractual duty of care owed to the customer.

The bank was said to be negligent in failing to notify the solicitors of X's habit: however both evidence and the pleadings on this point were considered unsatisfactory. The Court of Appeal found that the branch manager had learnt of X's vices through X's operation of his personal account, rather than through the account of the solicitors, and the bank owed X a duty to keep such information confidential.[264] If the information came to the attention of the branch manager through X's operation of the firm's account, the branch manager would have been obliged to inform the solicitor's firm that its account was being mishandled.

---

[261] [1992] 4 All ER 363.
[262] [1992] 4 All ER 409.
[263] Citing *Marfani & Co Ltd* v *Midland Bank Ltd* [1968] 2 All ER 573.
[264] *Tournier* v *National Provincial and Union Bank of England* [1924] 1 K.B. 461.

The question was whether the bank was negligent in failing to make inquiries before honouring cheques drawn by X on the firm's account. The Court of Appeal was unanimously of the view that there was some limit on the bank's entitlement to treat a mandate as absolute. Counsel for the bank argued that the limit should be drawn when the relevant transaction was patently dishonest. The court imposed a slightly higher obligation on the bank than that argued for by counsel for the bank. May LJ said that the test established in *Selangor* imposed too onerous a test of the duty of care and a bank should not too easily be made liable for such a breach where the bank pays a cheque drawn within the scope of the agent's authority. In such cases the bank will only be liable if a reasonable banker would not pay the cheque without referring it to his superior for payment to be sanctioned and he would hesitate before approving payment:

> In the simple case of a current account in credit the basic obligation on the banker is to pay his customer's cheques in accordance with his mandate. Having in mind the vast numbers of cheques which are presented for payment every day in this country, whether over a bank counter or through the clearing, it is my opinion only when the circumstances are such that any reasonable cashier would hesitate to pay a cheque at once and refer it to his or her superior, and when any reasonable cashier would hesitate to authorise payment without enquiry, that a cheque should not be paid immediately on presentation and such enquiry made. Further, it would . . . I think be only in rare circumstances, and only when any reasonable bank manager should instruct his staff to refer all or some of his customer's cheques to him before they are paid.

Parker LJ then went on to formulate the test for the standard of care as follows:

> The question must be whether if a reasonable and honest banker knew of the relevant facts he would have considered that there was a serious or real possibility albeit not amounting to a probability that his customer might be defrauded . . . If it is established then in my view a reasonable banker would be in breach of duty if he continued to pay cheques without enquiry. He could not simply sit back and ignore the situation.

Parker LJ then went on:

> that there was a serious or real possibility that [X] was drawing on the client account and using the funds so obtained for his own and not the solicitors' or beneficiaries' purposes.

On the facts, the Court of Appeal found that there was no negligence. Parker LJ noted that not only did the manager know of X's gambling, but that the manager would not have tolerated X remaining as a customer but for X's association with the plaintiff. However, this is not enough to lead a reasonable bank manager to believe that there was any possibility that X might be stealing from the client account.

In *Go Dante Yap v Bank Austria Creditanstalt AG* the Court also held that the bank was under a duty in tort to provide investment advice because the bank had assumed such responsibility by holding itself as possessing special skill or expertise to search for, recommend and transact in emerging market securities. The standard of care was to be determined by reference to (i) the prevailing circumstances, bearing in mind the danger of hindsight in times of financial crisis; (ii) the experience and sophistication of the defendant; and (iii) the contractual framework.

We will now examine specific areas where the courts have explored the nature of the duty of care.

Tax repercussions for the customer

In *Schioler* v *Westminster Bank Ltd*[265] a Dutch national domiciled in Denmark, but resident in the UK, maintained an account with the Guernsey branch of the defendant bank. In normal circumstances dividend payments he received in respect of an investment in a Malaysian company were paid directly to the credit of his account in Guernsey, in sterling, without any liability to UK taxation on the dividends. However, on one particular occasion the payment was made by a voucher drawn in a foreign currency and the Guernsey branch, not having a facility to collect drafts in foreign currency, remitted it to the head-office in England for collection. The claimant, thereupon, became liable to UK income tax on the dividend payment, which the bank duly deducted before crediting his account with the balance of the payment.

Mocatta J dismissing the claimant's action for breach of contract held the bank had not acted negligently in failing to ask for specific instructions, particularly in respect of the tax repercussions on the claimant, when it received a payment draft in a foreign currency. The bank was not under any obligation to consult the plaintiff, or her accountant, and to impose such an obligation on the bank would be to place the bank under an impossible obligation. The bank had acted in accordance with standard banking practice and it was not in breach of a duty of care.

Thus a bank does not come under any obligation to its customer to advise on the risks or tax implications of certain types of transactions in relation to the normal banker and customer contract.[266]

'Not negotiable' and 'account payee only' crossing

It may be that the bank may be held liable for breach of contract and relevant banking practice at the time the case is decided, and the knowledge of the bank may become relevant.[267] Moreover, the court will have regard to expert testimony to determine current banking practice.[268] Similarly, in *Redmond Bank* v *Allied Irish Banks plc*[269] the court held the bank was not under a duty of care to advise or warn the customer of the inherent risks of dealing with cheques crossed 'not negotiable' and 'account payee only' and which were apparently endorsed on the back with the payee's signature.

Advise on tax implications

The bank, within the normal scope of the banker and customer relationship, does not assume any contractual obligations towards its customer to advise on a more advantageous type of account facility, or other product, it now provides. In *Sureya & Douglas* v *Midland Bank Plc*[270]

---

[265] (1970) 2 QB 719.
[266] The situation may be different if the bank undertakes to give investment advice.
[267] See *Marfani & Co Ltd* v *Midland Bank Ltd* [1968] 1 WLR 956 at 972 where Diplock LJ may not be a reliable guide in respect of current banking practice.
[268] See *Barings Plc (in liquidation)* v *Coopers & Lybrand (No 2)* [2000] 1 Lloyd's Rep. Bank. 83 where the court in Singapore allowed expert evidence on the conduct and administration of futures and derivatives trading within Barings Plc in Singapore when the issue of negligence arose in respect of the management of the bank.
[269] [1987] FLR 307.
[270] [1999] 1 All ER (Comm.) 612.

the claimants, a firm of solicitors, maintained two accounts with the defendant bank; one was a current account with a cheque book facility, which did not accrue interest, while the other paid interest but could not be used as an operating account. In 1984, the bank introduced a new interest-bearing account for its professional customers, but did not inform the claimant of this facility until some four years later. The claimant then brought an action for loss of interest for that period arguing that the bank was under an implied contractual duty to inform the customer of any new banking services relevant to him. The Court of Appeal held that the banker and customer relationship does not impose a duty on the bank to keep the customer informed of new banking products and merely adopting this as a matter of policy, did not impose a duty the customer could enforce.

Advice on the viability of a business transaction

A further question that has arisen is whether a bank, which examines a business transaction with a view to extending a loan or other facility to the customer, is under an implied contractual duty to inform the customer of the commercial viability of that project. In normal circumstances, the bank will make an assessment of the proposed transaction and the customer's creditworthiness as part of a business decision whether or not to make a loan and the issue that has arisen is whether the bank is under an obligation to advise on the commercial viability of the speculation. Unless the bank has either by express agreement or by implication undertaken any additional obligations to the customer, for example, to advise on the possible success or failure of a proposed venture, the bank is not under a duty under contract to give such advice. For example the bank will not be liable to a customer, where having extended a loan facility, it fails to inform the customer of the specific market movements. In *Lloyds Bank plc v Cobb*, unreported,[271] Scott LJ expressed the following view:

> In order to place the bank under a duty of care to the borrower the borrower must . . . make it clear to the bank that its advice is being sought. The mere request for a loan, coupled with the supply to the bank of the details of the commercial project . . . does not suffice to make clear to the bank that is advice is being sought.

More recently, Millett LJ in *National Commercial Bank (Jamaica) Ltd v Hew*[272] stated:

> The viability of a transaction may depend on the vantage point from which it is viewed; what is a viable loan may not be a viable borrowing. This is one reason why a borrower is not entitled to rely on the fact that the lender has chosen to lend him money as evidence, still less as advice, that the lender thinks that the purpose for which the borrower intends to use it is sound.

The unpredictable element in the nature of these transactions makes it difficult to impose a contractual duty of care on the bank. In *Stafford v Conti Commodity Services*[273] Mocatta J concluded that it is difficult in a volatile market to assume the bank has assumed a duty of care, particularly where the plaintiff had, in the past, failed to accept advice given by the bank. The *Stafford* case concerned the issue of liability of a stockbroker in respect of investments in the futures markets. This area of the law has been examined in a number of Australian cases where the courts, while treating the duty of care in contract and tort as being concurrent, have

---

[271] 18 December 1991 (CA).
[272] [2003] UKPC 51.
[273] [1981] 1 All ER 691.

been reluctant to impose a duty. In *Lloyd* v *Citicorp Australia Ltd*[274] the bank granted its customer a loan facility that could be drawn in a number of different currencies. The customer, who was a businessman and who had substantial experience in land development and business generally, used the facility without covering himself by a hedging agreement and having incurred losses as a result of adverse currency fluctuations brought an action against the bank because of its alleged failure to advise him generally on the management of the loan and the bank's failure to suggest a hedge. The court dismissed the action and Rogers J taking into consideration that the claimant was a man of considerable business experience and that the bank had not offered to monitor the investments stated:

> the duty [imposed on the bank] called for exercise of skill and diligence which a reasonably competent and careful foreign exchange adviser would exercise; by reason of the nature of the market to which I have already referred, I would take leave to doubt that the content of that duty would be very high. That skill and diligence is of some assistance, I do not doubt. However, the assistance to be derived from it in a market as volatile as the one for the Australian dollar has been fairly minimal.

In *McEvoy* v *ANZ Banking Group Ltd*[275] the court adopted a similar view in circumstances where a businessman of some experience took out a foreign currency loan and sustained heavy losses. The bank knew that the customer had terminated the services of his manager and that he was relying on the advice of the bank for specific transactions, although he had also been advised by other financial institutions with which he had friendly relations. The customer also knew that the bank had a policy not to advise on the type of transaction in question. The court held that the bank owed no duty of care in tort but also added that a bank cannot be expected to do something without a fee, which it had expressly refused to do, with or without a fee, in circumstances where the customer knew that others were willing to provide such a service but for a fee only.

A duty of care in contract is not usually imposed unless the bank undertakes to assume liability and views expressed are likely to be treated as expressions of opinion.[276] While such a duty may not exist under the law of contract the question has also been asked as to whether a duty of care may be imposed on the bank in negligence and the issue was examined in *Foti* v *Banque Nationale de Paris*.[277] The customers in that case were two Italian immigrants who had established a successful business, and who obtained a loan from the bank denominated in Swiss francs to finance the purchase of a shopping centre. The purpose of the borrowing in Swiss francs was to minimise interest on the loan but they were given no advice on adverse currency fluctuations. The customers sustained considerable losses from which they could not be protected by hedging contracts. In an action by the two customers the court held the bank had failed to act in a manner expected from a prudent banker and took into consideration that the bank's officers had emphasised to the customers its expertise and given them the impression that it would monitor the currency implications. The bank had therefore acted in breach of the duty of care arising from the proximity of the relationship in tort and not on the implied contractual duty of care.

---

[274] (1986) 11 NSWLR 286.
[275] [1988] ATR 80.
[276] *Westpac Banking Corporation* v *Potter* [1992] ACL Rep. 45 Qld.
[277] (1989) 54 SASR 354.

Similarly, in *Verity & Spindler v Lloyds Bank plc*[278] the claimants were a teacher and acupuncturist who were looking for a property to buy and renovate. They approached the bank because it advertised a 'tailor made' financial advisory service. They proposed to buy a property that had major structural defects but had also looked at a second property, which the bank manager encouraged them to buy as a better prospect. They purchased the property but lost money in the property slump that followed. When the bank sought to recover the money the claimants resisted on the grounds that the bank had assumed a duty of care in contract and tort, which the bank had breached because of the negligent advice. The court held the bank liable for negligence. The judge was influenced by the facts that the bank's customers were relatively inexperienced, significantly the bank manager had inspected both the properties (not usual practice) and encouraged them to purchase one of the properties, and the wording of the bank's advertisement.

The relevant expertise and experience of the customer, if any, will be important and in *Bankers Trust International plc v P.T. Dharmala Sakti Sejahtera*[279] the bank sold two-interest rate swaps to an Indonesian buyer. When the bank sued for sums due under these contracts the buyer counter-claimed for breach of duty of care and misrepresentation. Oral representations and letters from the bank emphasising the advantages of the proposed transactions had preceded each sale and the buyer alleged that by entering into these explanations the bank had assumed a duty to 'fully explain the term, meaning and effect of the transactions and the potential financial consequences'. Mance J held that the bank did not owe to the buyer any greater duty than to fairly and accurately represent the facts relating to the representations. The learned judge emphasised that the relationship under discussion was not the conventional banker and customer relationship but a commercial relationship involving the sale of complex products. However, rejecting the duty of care the court held that the relationship between the buyer and the bank was of a commercial nature in which the buyer had held himself out as both experienced and capable of understanding such transactions and their implications.

These cases raise a number of principles, a summary of which may assist in understanding the area:

- The courts are clearly reluctant to impose a duty of care in contract that is too onerous as shown in the cases following *Selangor* and *Karak Rubber*.
- It is submitted that the moderation of the test for the duty of care in *Lipkin Gorman* is now the accepted test and the bank does not owe a duty of care in implied contract in the execution of ordinary or standard services; thus the bank is not expected of have knowledge of the customer's special situation unless that has been brought to the attention of the bank and the bank has assumed a duty of care in those circumstances (*Schioler*).
- The bank does not assume a duty of care in respect of the commercial viability of a transaction (*Lloyd; McEvoy*).
- The court will have regard to (i) the nature of the transaction; (ii) the representations of both the bank, including any bank leaflets and advertisements, and the representations of the customer; and (iii) whether it was reasonable for the customer to rely on such representations (*Foti; Verity*).
- The experience of the customer in business generally and in respect of the specific transactions (*Verity; Dharmala*).

---

[278] [1995] CLC 1557 (QBD).
[279] [1995] Bank LR 381.

While the cases under discussion have focused on the circumstances in which a duty of care may be implied in contract to the bank's customer the issue of a duty of care may be extended to a third party. In *Weir v National Westminster Bank*[280] while the court held that a paying bank owes its customer's agent a duty of care to detect and report any forgeries of his signature in cheques drawn on the customer's account the bank does not owe a wider duty of care to its customer's to detect and report on forgeries of its customer's signature on cheques drawn on some other account whenever such cheques purported to bear the customer's signature came into the bank's possession. Lord Hope said to impose such a duty would be 'unreasonable' and impose a 'wholly disproportionate burden on the banker'.

Duty of care in tort

The absence of a duty of care between a bank and third party under an implied contract means any duty owed by the bank must arise in tort. Thus whether a tortuous duty of care is imposed will depend on the establishment of a 'relationship of proximity' between the parties. In *Hedley Byrne & Co Ltd v Heller and Partners Ltd*[281] the House of Lords held that a bank which provides a bankers' reference to a third party enquirer owes a duty of care on the basis of the voluntary assumption of responsibility by the bank to the third party. In *Henderson v Merrett Syndicates Ltd*[282] the *Hedley Byrne* principle was held to extend to economic loss caused by the negligent provision of services. Lord Goff said liability was imposed because of the assumption of responsibility by the defendant bank, along with the reliance by the claimant, although liability may still be imposed even if reliance is not established so long as the defendant bank's conduct caused the loss to the claimant. In *White v Jones*[283] the court held that a solicitor who accepted instructions to draft a will owed a duty of care to the intended beneficiary even if the intended beneficiary was not aware that the solicitor had been employed for this purpose. Following this line of reasoning it could be alleged that a bank in agreeing to execute a payment order owes a duty of care to the beneficiary to execute the order in accordance with those instructions. However, in *Wells v First National Commercial Bank*[284] the Court of Appeal rejected a duty of care was owed in those circumstances and *White v Jones* was distinguished as a case on its facts and a case where no other remedy was available to the claimant. In *Wells*, however, the claimant had a cause of action against the bank's customer although Evans LJ did concede that a duty of care might have arisen if there had been direct communication between the bank and the beneficiary and the bank thereupon voluntarily assumes a voluntary duty of care.

However, a duty of care may be owed to a third party even if there is no voluntary assumption of the responsibility. The issues was explored in *Customs and Excise Commissioners v Barclays Bank plc*[285] where the plaintiffs, the Customs and Excise Commissioners, notified the defendant bank of the grant of injunctions which specifically prohibited the disposal of assets held in two accounts maintained by the debtor companies. Contrary to the terms of the injunctions the defendant bank allowed the balances from the two accounts to be withdrawn

---

[280] [1995] Bank LR 249.
[281] [1964] AC 465.
[282] [1995] 2 AC 145.
[283] [1995] 2 AC 207.
[284] [1998] PNLR 552.
[285] [2004] EWHC 122.

and the plaintiff's brought an action against the bank for breach of the terms of the injunction. A preliminary issue for the court was whether the defendant bank owed a duty of care to the plaintiffs to safeguard the funds held to the credit of the accounts. The Court of Appeal, reversing the judge at first instance, held that the bank owed the Commissioners a duty of care to prevent the disposal of the credit balances held to credit of the debtor's account contrary to the terms of the injunctions. The Court of Appeal applied the threefold test established in *Caparo Industries plc* v *Dickman*[286] for ascertaining whether there was a duty of care in an economic loss case namely: (i) the test of foreseeability of damage, (ii) a relationship of proximity and (iii) whether it is fair, just and reasonable to impose the duty. The court concluded that the bank having received notice of the injunctions was required to comply with them. The bank argued that the absence of the voluntary assumption of duty was sufficient to negate the imposition of a duty of care but the court concluded that its absence was not conclusive in establishing a lack of duty of care. The court adopted the view expressed by Lord Slynn in *Phelps* v *Hillingdon LBC*[287] where he said:

> it is sometimes said that there has to be an assumption of responsibility by the person concerned. That phrase can be misleading in that it can suggest that the professional person must knowingly and deliberately accept responsibility. It is, however, clear that the test is an objective one: *Henderson v Merrett* [1995] 2 AC 145, 181. The phrase means simply that the law recognises that there is a duty of care. It is not so much that responsibility is assumed as that it is recognised or imposed by the law.

BANKING LAW IN PRACTICE

In the aftermath of the global financial crisis, the Financial Services Consumer Panel submitted that there should, in UK Law, be a statutory duty of care. The panel supported this recommendation on the grounds of rebuilding customers' trust in the financial sector, and ensuring that banks act honestly and fairly in the interests of their customers. The public perception of banks continues to be that they cannot be trusted and their level of competence continues to be questioned. A clause in the Financial Services (Banking Reform) Bill 2013 which sought to impose a duty of care which the coalition government believes will go a long way towards ensuring that consumers could have confidence that their best interests were being served and that those selling financial services products were acting in both a prudent and ethical manner was defeated in the House of Lords in November 2013. The new clause would require a ring-fenced bank not to act in a way contrary to the customer's interest while carrying out its core activities. The statutory duty of care would have imposed on a ring-fenced institution a fiduciary duty in carrying out its core services and a more general duty of care across the financial services sector. Creating a general duty of care would have removed the uncertainty whether or not a duty would be found to exist by the courts. However, such a duty would create problems relating to how the duty was to be interpreted and applied by the courts. The current law will continue to be applied to interpret owned by the institutions, and management,

➡

---

[286] [1990] 2 AC 605.
[287] [2001] 2 AC 619 at 654.

including the scope of the fiduciary duty imposed. However, establishing a statutory duty of care would have given the regulators the some basis for oversight and intervention in a contractual relationship.

The duties imposed by clause 5 will allow the courts to take all relevant considerations into account while assuring customers that the banks had the legal obligation to act fairly.

Although the need for reform in the conduct of the financial services sector is broadly accepted, Andrew Haldane, Executive Director of the Bank of England, has cautioned against the imposition of a statutory duty of care without an accurate definition of the circumstances in which the duty would be imposed. The scope of any such duty does, indeed, need to be carefully defined since imposing a fiduciary duty in respect of the core obligations undertaken by a bank, even a ring-fenced bank, could have far-reaching ramifications on the banker and customer relationship.

The duty not to terminate the banker and customer relationship

The varied nature of the services offered by a bank will mean that the specific contract will govern issues relating to termination of the contract. Some contracts for specific services will expressly provide for a maturity date and therefore the relationship will terminate at the end of a fixed period, for example fixed deposits with an ascertained maturity date. The contract, itself, may allow early termination but subject to agreed penalties and the occurrence of certain events may automatically terminate the banker and customer relationship, for example the winding up of a bank[288] or death of the account holder.[289]

In other circumstances the contractual relationship will be of an indeterminate period and the relationship terminates when the customer makes a demand for the entire credit balance, which closes the account. The right to terminate the relationship at any time without notice being expressly given is recognised by the Payment Services Regulations 2009.[290] A bank may under the Payment Services Regulations 2009, require notice to be given before the customer terminates the banker and customer relationship by closing the bank account but the notice period may not exceed one month.[291] The bank may charge the customer for closing the current account (in fact banks do not generally impose such charges) but such charges must 'reasonably correspond to the actual costs for closure of the account.[292] However, no such charges may be imposed if the account has been opened for a minimum period of 12 months.[293]

---

[288] *Re Russian Commercial and Industrial Bank* [1955] 1 Ch 148.

[289] *Re Russian Commercial and Industrial Bank* [1955] 1 Ch 148.

[290] The Payment Services Regulations 2009, SI 2009/209, http://www.legislation.gov.uk/uksi/2009/209/contents/made.

[291] The Payment Services Regulations 2009, SI 2009/209, reg. 43(1), http://www.legislation.gov.uk/uksi/2009/209/contents/made.

[292] The Payment Services Regulations 2009, SI 2009/209, reg. 43(2) http://www.legislation.gov.uk/uksi/2009/209/contents/made.

[293] The Payment Services Regulations 2009, SI 2009/209, reg. 43(3) http://www.legislation.gov.uk/uksi/2009/209/contents/made.

Any action, by the customer, to recover the amount standing to the credit of account his must be preceded by a demand[294] with the six-year limitation period running from the date of the customer's demand. In *Bank of Baroda v ASAA Mahomed*[295] the customer demanded the repayment of his credit balance and closure of his account. The bank ignoring this request continued to operate the account and the customer's solicitor, some months later, then made a further demand, in writing, for repayment of the credit balance, which too was ignored. The question which arose related to when the limitation period commenced with regard to the customer's right to bring legal proceedings. There were two options only one of which would allow the action as being within the limitation period. In the first instance the limitation period could be said to begin to run from the time of the customer's demand, which would have rendered the action statute barred; alternatively the period might be said to commence from the date of the solicitor's request for repayment, which would place the action within the limitation period. The Court of Appeal held that the limitation period commenced from the date of the solicitor's demand and the action was not statute barred. Mummery LJ said that neither the customer's first demand, nor the bank's subsequent conduct, resulted in the account being closed, or the banker and customer relationship being terminated, so there was nothing to prevent the customer from making further demands on the account, including a fresh demand for repayment and a further cause of action. The first demand was, therefore, merely treated as a demand for repayment; not a request to close the account and terminate the relationship. Mantell LJ agreed with Mummery LJ and concluded that neither the first demand of the customer nor the bank's subsequent actions and failure to comply with the demand amounted to a termination of the relationship. However, to the extent that the first demand amounted to a demand to close the account he agreed with Simon Brown LJ who held that 'if a customer, having demanded closure and repayment of his account, then changes his mind, he can notify the bank accordingly and, assuming always that the bank is content to continue holding the account, the contract will in effect start afresh. The cause of action arising from the original demand will have ended and a fresh one will arise upon the making of the demand.'

The common law position where the bank wishes to terminate the banker and customer relationship was confirmed in *National Commercial Bank of Jamaica Ltd v Olint Corporation Ltd*[296] with Hoffmann LJ holding that in the absence of a written agreement or 'statutory impediment' the bank must give reasonable notice. The Payment Services Regulations 2009 provide that where a bank wishes to terminate an account which falls within those referred to as 'framework contracts', for example a current account or individual savings account then a minimum of two months' notice must be given, provided the account contains a provision to that effect.[297] Banks are required to give a longer period of notice to terminate an account in order to enable the customer to ensure that outstanding cheques, or other payment instructions, have the opportunity to clear and the customer has the time to make alternative arrangements with regard to his banking affairs. In *Prosperity Ltd v Lloyds Bank Ltd*[298] the bank's customer, an insurance company, received insurance premiums payable by third

---

[294] *Foley v Hill* (1848) 2 HLC 28; *Joachimson v Swiss Bank Corp* [1921] 3 KB 110.
[295] [1999] Lloyd's Rep. Bank. 14.
[296] [2009] UKPC 16.
[297] The Payment Services Regulations 2009, SI 2009/209, reg. 43(4) http://www.legislation.gov.uk/uksi/2009/209/contents/made.
[298] (1923) 39 TLR 372.

parties direct into its account held with the defendant bank. The scheme run by the insurance company received adverse publicity and the bank decided to terminate the customer's account. The bank gave the customer one month's notice of its intention to close the account and the plaintiff brought an action claiming the bank could not terminate the relationship in the absence of reasonable notice being given and applied for an injunction to restrain the bank from closing its account. The court, approving *Joachimson* v *Swiss Bank Corporation Ltd*,[299] held that it is a term of the banking contract that a bank will not cease to do business with the customer without giving reasonable notice and:

> the question of reasonableness must depend on the special facts and circumstances of the account. An account might be a small account drawn upon only by cheques cashed by the customer for his own purposes. In that case a comparatively short notice might be all that was needed . . . A customer might also deal with his account by sending cheques, to the knowledge of his bank, to different parts of the continent. In that case . . . the existence of such outstanding cheques might place upon the bank a larger burden as to notice . . .

Subject to proof of loss or damage the courts will award damages for the bank's wrongful termination of the account. However, an injunction will not normally be granted and Lord Hoffmann, in *Olint*, disapproved of the practice of customers applying for an injunction against their bank, in such circumstances, to gain a tactical advantage. Lord Hoffmann approved the view expressed in *Prosperity* that damages will normally be an adequate remedy. Additionally, since the banker and customer relationship is of a personal nature the courts will not compel the parties to a contract to adhere to the contract.

Duties owed by a customer to the bank

The range of duties owed by the customer to the bank are fairly well defined and their ambit narrow. Indeed, it would be correct to say that implied contract only imposes such duties on the customer, as are necessary to ensure that his account, or other dealings with the bank, are managed without such fraud, or loss, as the customer could have prevented. Any wider duties of care imposed on the customer will only be valid if they are consistent with the terms of the implied contract and reasonable under the Unfair Contract Terms Act 1977 and the Unfair Contracts Terms Regulations. In *Tai Hing Cotton Mill Ltd* v *Liu Chong Hing Bank Ltd*[300] the Privy Council rejected a submission that a wider duty than that upheld in the *Macmillan* and *Greenwood* cases should be implied as a necessary incident of the banker and customer relationship. Lord Scarman delivering the judgment stated:

> The argument for the banks is, when analysed, no more than that the obligations of care placed on banks in the management of a customer's account which the courts have recognised have become with the development of banking business so burdensome that they should be met by a reciprocal of responsibility imposed on the customer, and they cite *Selangor United Rubber Estates Ltd* v *Cradock (No 3)* [1968] 2 All ER 1073, [1968] 1 WLR 1555 (Ungoed-Thomas) and *Karak Rubber Co Ltd* v *Burden (No 2)* [1972] 1 All ER 1210, [1971] 1 WLR 602 (Brightman J). One can fully understand the comment of Cons JA that the banks must today look for protection.

[299] [1921] 3 KB 110.
[300] [1986] AC 80.

So be it. They can increase the severity of their terms of business, and they can use their influence, as they have in the past, to seek to persuade the legislature that they should be granted by statute further protection. But it does not follow that because they may need protection as their business expands the necessary incidents of their relationship with their customer must also change.

In addition to the duty to repay on demand any sums overdrawn on the current account and the duty to repay reasonable charges for the services rendered, the customer owes a number of 'self-regarding' or 'self-interest duties' the non-conformity with which will prevent the customer from enforcing his rights against the bank. The failure to conform to these duties will normally result in the customer from being estopped from bringing an action against the bank. Thus, a payment made by a bank in excess of the customer's mandate is an unauthorised payment and the bank cannot debit the customer's account. Additionally, if the payment is a material alteration of the instrument it may be avoided under s.64 of the Bills of Exchange Act 1882 and the bank in such cases not only exceeds the mandate conferred but also pays on effectively what is a void instrument. The customer therefore has a right to object to the bank debiting the customer's account with the amount of the payment unless he, himself, has failed to comply with the duties owed by him to the bank. The customer has to comply with these duties if he wishes to preserve any rights he may have against the bank for relief.

Thus, the customer owes his bank a duty to refrain from drawing cheques or other instruments in such a manner as to facilitate fraud or forgery. This duty was upheld in *London Joint Stock Bank* v *Macmillan*[301] where a clerk, employed by the defendants, was entrusted with the duty of preparing and presenting cheques for signature to one of the partners for small amounts of petty cash. The clerk presented a cheque drawn for £2 in the space preserved for figures, with blank spaces before and after the numeral, having also left in blank the section reserved for value of the cheque to be written in words. The name of the payee was also left blank on the uncrossed instrument. The incomplete instrument was presented to the partner just as he was leaving office and who being in a hurry, failed to notice the incomplete and unusual form of the instrument. The partner was informed the instrument was for petty cash and that two pounds would be sufficient. The partner signed the instrument. The clerk subsequently completed the cheque for £120 having inserted the digit '1' before the '2' and a '0' after it, and having received the payment for £120 absconded. The House of Lords, reversing the trial judge and the Court of Appeal held in favour of the bank. Lord Finlay defined and explained the scope of the customer's duty as follows:

> if he (the customer) draws a cheque in a manner which facilitates fraud he is guilty of a breach of duty as between himself and the banker, and he will be responsible to the banker for any loss sustained by the banker as a natural and direct consequence of this breach of duty . . .
>
> As the customer and the banker are under a contractual relation in this matter, it is obvious that, in drawing a cheque, the customer is bound to take usual and reasonable precautions to prevent forgery. Crime is, indeed, a very serious matter, but everyone knows that crime is not uncommon. If the cheque is drawn in such a way as to facilitate or almost invite an increase in the amount of the forgery if the cheque should get into the hands of a dishonest person, forgery is not a remote but a very natural consequence of negligence of this description.

The House of Lords applied the principle laid down in *Young* v *Grote*[302] where it was held that a customer who draws an incomplete cheque leaving its completion to an agent cannot then

---

[301] [1918] AC 777.
[302] (1827) 4 Bing 253.

object to the bank debiting his account with the full amount fraudulently entered on the cheque even if it is done by way of alteration. The decision also imposed a wider duty of care to ensure that when the customer signs the cheque he does not leave spaces that facilitate fraud. The principle was not applied in *Scholfield v Earl of Londesborough*[303] where the Court of Appeal held that an acceptor of a bill of exchange had not acted negligently where he accepted a bill of exchange the amount of which had been fraudulently raised by the holder of the bill before the acceptance. The distinction in the decision is that the fraud had taken place before the bill was accepted and a failure to detect or notice the available blanks tendered to him for acceptance was not negligence.

It is a question of degree as to whether neglect of ordinary precaution in issuing cheques amounts to breach by the drawer of his contract with the bank. In *Société Générale v Metropolitan Bank Ltd*[304] a 'y' was inserted in a slight blank left after the word 'eight' in a bill and Bovill CJ held that 'it was the usual way of filling up blanks in a form', and no man in the City would take notice of 'eight' not being close to the next word. Similarly, in *Slingsby v District Bank Ltd*[305] the bank was held not entitled to debit the customer's account when the customer had left certain blank spaces on the cheque form which enabled a fraudulent solicitor to insert the words 'per Cumberbirch and Potts' after the name of the payee and before the words 'or order' printed on the cheque form. The court concluded that the altera-tion was such that it could not reasonably be anticipated that the cheque would be altered in the form it was. Scrutton LJ concluded that it was not a 'usual precaution' to draw lines before or after the name of the payee. Thus, it would appear that where the alteration is obvious or discernable by the exercise of reasonable care, or where the state of the cheque raises suspicion of unauthorised alteration and payment is made without inquiry, then the *Macmillan* case offers no relief to the bank.

The principle established in the *Macmillan* case relates to the drawing of individual cheques or other instruments. The courts have refused to impose a wider duty of care to take reasonable precautions in the management of its business to prevent forged cheques being presented for payment[306] or a general duty on the customer to check and verify his bank statements. In *Wealdon Woodlands (Kent) Ltd v National Westminster Bank Ltd*[307] McNeill J said that in the absence of legislative intervention no duty would be imposed on the customer to check his bank statements. Failure to do so does not amount to a breach of duty of care.

A further duty owed by the customer to his bank imposes on him an obligation to inform the bank of known forgeries. Again the scope of the duty is narrowly defined and the customer only comes under a duty to inform his bank of any forgeries in respect of his account that he has knowledge of. In *Brown v Westminster Bank Ltd*[308] the servants of an old lady forged her signature on cheques drawn on her current account over a number of years. The branch manager, on numerous occasions enquired about the authenticity of the cheques and was reassured by the lady that the cheques were genuinely drawn. Although the branch manager

---

[303] [1896] AC 514.

[304] (1873) 27 LT 849.

[305] [1932] 1 KB 544.

[306] Which is in direct contrast to the view expressed by the Hong Kong Court of Appeal in *Tai Hing Ltd v Lui Chong Hing Bank* and which the privy Council rejected on appeal [1989] 1 AC 80 and *Price Meats Ltd v Barclays Bank Plc* [2000] 2 All ER (Comm) 346.

[307] (1983) 133 NLJ 719.

[308] [1964] 2 Lloyd's Rep. 187.

had doubts about her mental state the court held that the elderly lady could not subsequently assert the fraudulent nature of the cheques and insist her account be re-credited with the amount of the forged cheques. In the *Brown* case the bank successfully raised estoppel against the customer because she had specifically represented that the cheques were properly drawn and bore her signature. Although, the *Brown* case is based on actual representations made by the bank customer, where the customer's conduct is such as to lull the bank into a false sense of security so it fails to seek relief or remedy against the fraudulent person then the customer cannot subsequently seek to have the amounts paid as a result of the fraud, restored to his account. In *Greenwood v Martins Bank Ltd*[309] the wife forged her husband's signature on a number of cheques and having cashed them applied the money for her own purposes. The husband accepted the explanation given by the wife in respect of the false cheques and agreed not to inform the bank of the forged cheques. However, when he realised that the wife had misled him about the reason for the forgeries he threatened to inform the bank and the wife committed suicide. The husband then bought an action to recover the amount of the forged cheques disputing the bank's right to debit his account. The House of Lords held that the husband was estopped from relying on the forgeries and his failure to inform the banks of the forgeries had denied the bank its right to seek a remedy against the wife. Lord Tomlin said:

> the sole question is whether in the circumstances of this case the respondents are entitled to set up estoppel.
>
> The essential factors giving rise to an estoppel are:
>
> 1 A representation or conduct amounting to a representation intended to induce a course of conduct on the part of the person to whom the representation is made.
>
> 2 An act or omission resulting from the representation, whether actual or by conduct, by the person to whom the representation is made.
>
> 3 Detriment to such person as a consequence of the act or omission.
>
> Mere silence cannot amount to a representation, but when there is a duty to disclose, deliberate silence may become significant and amount to a representation . . .
>
> The deliberate abstention from speaking in those circumstances seems to me to amount to a representation to the respondents that the forged cheques were in fact in order, and assuming that detriment to the respondents followed there were, it seems to me, present all the elements essential to estoppel.

The issue raised by this case is whether the customer owes a wider duty of care to be vigilant in respect of forgeries against his account. In *National Bank of New Zealand Ltd v Walpole and Patterson Ltd*[310] the court held that the customer is not under an obligation to keep a vigilant eye on his business with a view to detecting fraud and this view was approved in *Tai Hing Cotton Mill Ltd v Liu Chong Hing Bank Ltd*.[311]

The obligation imposed on the customer requires that he must not knowingly allow another (the bank) to be prejudiced by the use of fraudulent instruments and the courts have imposed a duty of 'fair dealing between man and man'.[312] It is immaterial that the forged signature on the bill or cheque is that of the drawer, acceptor or endorser.

[309] [1933] AC 51.
[310] [1975] 2 NZLR 7.
[311] [1986] AC 80.
[312] *Ogilvie v West Australian Mortgage and Agency Corpn Ltd* [1896] AC 269.

The courts have also looked at the issue of whether constructive knowledge of the forgery might be sufficient to found an estoppel against the customer. In *Price Meats Ltd v Barclays Bank Plc*[313] the defendant bank argued that the claimant should have been altered of the need to make enquiries by the size of the overdraft but Arden J, held that the argument went counter to the *Tai Hing* case because it was based on a duty which required the customer to take precautions in the management of the claimant's business. Consequently, it was unnecessary for Arden J to rule on the issue of whether constructive knowledge suffices to raise estoppel against the customer and she expressed the view that *McKenzie v British Linen Co*[314] and *Morison v London County and Westminster Bank Ltd*[315] both support this view. The issue was raised again in *Patel v Standard Chartered Bank*[316] where the defendant bank sought to rely on the claimant's failure to report a fraud about which the customer as a reasonable person ought to have been put on enquiry. Toulson J held that to impose a duty to enquire and report a forgery based on knowledge of circumstances that would cause a reasonable hypothetical customer to discover the existence of the fraud, and not based on the actual knowledge of the customer, would be inconsistent, as would the *Tai Hing* and *Price Meats* cases.

The silence of the customer must result in prejudice or injury to the bank, which can take the form of monetary loss but may include situations where the bank is precluded from protecting itself against subsequent forgeries or losses or the loss of opportunity to take proceedings against the forger.[317]

Conclusion

The courts, sometimes taking into consideration banking practice, have largely developed the scope and nature of the banker and customer relationship. The obligations which arise under the banking contract require not only an understanding of the rules of the debtor and creditor relationship, as modified to accommodate the special aspects of the banking business, but also the rules of agency law, contract law, trust law, tort law, property law and partnership, company and insolvency law. The complexity of the law is reflected through the complex nature of the banker and customer relationship.

Further reading

➤ *Banking Services: Law and Practice*, Report by the Review Committee, 1989, Cm. 622.
  The Report examined the nature and scope of the retail banker and customer relationship with several recommendations for reform.

[313] [2000] 2 All ER (Comm) 346.
[314] (1881) 6 App Cas 82 at 92.
[315] [1914] 3 KB 356.
[316] [2000] Lloyd's Rep Bank 229.
[317] *McKenzie v British Bank Ltd* [1914] 3 KB 356.

➤ Cruickshank Report, *Competition in UK Banking, a Report to the Chancellor of the Exchequer*, 20 March 2000, http://webarchive.nationalarchives.gov.uk/+/http://www.hm-treasury.gov.uk/fin_bank_reviewfinal.htm.
The scope of the review included the examination of the levels of innovation, competition and efficiency both within the industry and in comparison to international standards. This report concluded that consumers were not adequately informed about their financial products, and found it difficult to compare them, which impeded competition.

➤ Posner, R. (1978) The Right of Privacy 12 *Georgia LR* 393, http://digitalcommons.law.uga.edu/cgi/viewcontent.cgi?article=1021&context=lectures_pre_arch_lectures_sibley&sei-redir=1&referer=http%3A%2F%2F.
This article attempts an economic analysis of the dissemination and withholding of information primarily in personal rather than business contexts. After outlining the personal connotations of privacy, the article then examines the principles of tort law that protect a right of privacy in both personal and commercial contexts to draw a correlation between judgments in tort law and underlying economic considerations.

➤ Posner, R. (1979) Privacy, Secrecy and Reputation 28 *Buff. LR*.
This article considers several aspects of privacy, including the desire for seclusion that may lead a person to resent telephone solicitations even if the caller makes no effort to extract private information from him. The article further attempts to establish empirical foundations for the economic analysis of privacy, and extends this analysis to defamation.

➤ Stokes, R. (2011) The Genesis of Banking Confidentiality, 32(3) *The Journal of Legal History*, 279–294.
Since 1924 and the decision of the Court of Appeal in *Tournier v National Provincial and Union Bank of England*, confidentiality has been recognised as a fundamental pillar of the banker and customer relationship, existing as an implied term in the banker and customer contract. This article seeks to outline the decision in *Tournier* and analyse the development of this area of law prior to that decision while also reflecting on the dearth of reported cases on this important issue. The discussion will explain the context of the difficulties faced by the Court of Appeal in *Tournier* and offer an illustration of a time when confidentiality between banker and customer was regarded as merely a matter of professionalism based upon principles of morality.

8 The bank as the fiduciary

Chapter overview

The aim of this chapter is to:

➤ Examine the circumstances in which the banker and customer relationship based on contract law will become the subject of fiduciary duties as a result of the bank undertaking obligations which impose duties of loyalty and trust.

➤ Examine the effect of the principles of undue influence where the person acting as a surety is subject to the dominant influence of the person in whose favour the guarantee or mortgage is given.

➤ Explore the steps a solicitor must take to show he has discharged his obligation to give independent legal advice.

Introduction

The courts have stressed that on the 'face of it the relationship between a bank and its customer is not a fiduciary relationship'[1] and the core deposit-taking and lending activities undertaken by a bank are clearly not based on a fiduciary relationship.[2] However, the more complex services offered by the modern multifunctional banks may impose fiduciary duties on the bank, for example where a bank acts as a trustee of an estate or manages an investment portfolio.[3] Banks are not charitable institutions;[4] the nature of the bank's business and the fact that banks are largely private commercial enterprises which will further their business interests means that banks will place their business needs before the customer. Thus, the normal banker and customer relationship is clearly based on contract law and this is of the essence to the banker and customer relationship.

---

[1] *Governor and Company of the Bank of Scotland* v *A Ltd* [2001] Lloyd's Rep. Bank. 73; see also *Cornish* v *Midland Bank Plc* [1985] 3 All ER 513; *National Westminster Bank Plc* v *Morgan* [1985] AC 686 (HL).

[2] *Foley* v *Hill* (1848) 2 HLC 26 at 36; see also Curtis (1987) 'The Fiduciary Controversy: Injection of Fiduciary Principles into the Bank–Depositor and Bank–Borrower Relationships' 20 *Loyola LR*, 794.

[3] *Ata* v *American Express Bank Ltd, The Times*, 26 June 1998, Rix J affirmed by the CA; see also *Toronto Dominion Bank* v *Forsythe* (2000) 47 OR (3d) 321 at 327.

[4] *National Westminster Bank plc* v *Morgan* [1983] 3 ALL ER 85 at 91.

It is because the bank undertakes additional obligations, which take the relationship beyond the scope of normal banker and customer relationship and contract law, which has resulted in the fiduciary obligations being imposed. In *Bristol and West Building Society* v *Mothew*[5] the Court of Appeal, reversing Chadwick J, held there had not been a breach of fiduciary duty when a solicitor acted for both the mortgagee and purchaser; indeed the building society had expressly authorised the solicitor to act for both. While the solicitor was liable for his negligence in failing to inform the building society of the second mortgage he was not in breach of any fiduciary obligations. Millett LJ made a number of salient points in respect of the nature of the fiduciary duties:

- The distinguishing obligation of a fiduciary is the obligation of loyalty and fidelity.

- Mere incompetence is not enough either to impose fiduciary obligations or to hold a breach of the fiduciary obligations although it may give rise to an action in negligence.

- The existence of a fiduciary relationship does not mean that every duty owed by a fiduciary to the beneficiary is a fiduciary duty. For example, the trustee's duty to exercise reasonable care, though equitable, is not necessarily a fiduciary duty.

In such circumstances, the solicitor will, nevertheless, still be expected to serve each principal loyally and faithfully. However, not all fiduciaries owe the same duties and the nature of the relationship and the contract between the parties will determine the scope of the fiduciary obligations. Apart from the duty of care, those owing fiduciary obligations will owe certain core obligations and Millett LJ[6] explained:

> [T]he principal is entitled to the single-minded loyalty of the fiduciary. This core liability has several facets. A fiduciary must act in good faith; he must not make a profit out of his trust; he must not place himself in a position where his duty and his interest may conflict; he may not act for his own benefit or the benefit of a third person without the informed consent of his principal. This is not intended to be an exhaustive list, but is sufficient to indicate the nature of fiduciary obligations. They are the defining characteristics of the fiduciary.

A bank may, therefore, become liable as a trustee because it undertakes the core obligations of loyalty and fidelity recognised in the *Mothew* case. The bank will assume these obligations either by assuming the role of a fiduciary, or by knowingly dealing with a customer in circumstances where the customer is induced into believing that the bank has assumed such a role.[7] Such liability is to be distinguished from liability imposed on a bank because of the bank's proximity[8] with a trustee or agent who has committed a breach of trust or other fiduciary duty, or because of its proximity to property which was originally in the hands of a trustee. In such circumstances a bank may find itself liable as a constructive trustee because, although a stranger to the trust, it has intermeddled with trust property. In such circumstances the bank may find liability imposed on it in one of two situations: (a) where the bank has acted as an accessory by dishonestly assisting in the breach of trust;[9] or (b) where the bank has unconsciously received trust property.[10]

---

[5] [1998] Ch 1.
[6] *Bristol and West Building Society* v *Mothew* [1998] Ch 1 at 18.
[7] *Bristol and West Building Society* v *Mothew* [1998] Ch 1.
[8] *Bristol and West Building Society* v *Mothew* [1998] Ch 1.
[9] See Ch. 12.
[10] See Ch. 12.

Such duties while regulating the behaviour of the fiduciary do not tell him what to do.[11] Further, a breach of fiduciary duties will attract remedies that are intended to allow restitution rather than merely compensate.[12]

The balance between the common law and fiduciary nature of the banker and customer relationship

The courts have traditionally been reluctant to impose fiduciary obligations on banks not merely in respect of commercial customers but also in the context of individual customers who may be considered both less astute and more vulnerable than commercial customers. This reluctance was recognised in the case of commercial customers in *JP Morgan Chase Bank* v *Springwell Navigation Corporation*[13] where the judge held that what was essentially a commercial banking relationship could not give rise to the extensive fiduciary obligations contended for. The key issues were the degree to which JP Morgan Chase might be liable for losses suffered by Springwell (described as a sophisticated investor); and whether the bank had a duty to act as an investment adviser to its client, irrespective of any contractual agreement governing their relationship.

Springwell, who had a long-standing relationship with Chase, brought claims against members of the Chase group, arising from losses made on investments in 'emerging markets' instruments, which Chase had sold, or issued. By 1998, Springwell had a portfolio with a face value of approximately $700 million invested in market debt in Latin America and Russia, in particular in 'GKO-linked' notes, which were debt securities issued by the Russian Federation. However, the GKO notes defaulted, and Springwell began proceedings in New York for the losses it suffered. These proceedings were suspended because of jurisdictional issues and an action then commenced before the English courts. Springwell alleged breach of contract, breach of fiduciary duty and negligent mis-statement. Springwell also alleged there was an advisory relationship between it and Chase, but that the investments made, and the portfolio as a whole, were such that no reasonable adviser could have advised Springwell to hold the investments.

Springwell sought to support its allegation that Chase owed a duty of care on the basis that Chase knew that Springwell's representative often did not read the documents that Chase gave him. Springwell further alleged that, however the relationship might have started, it evolved over time to become an advisory one. Gloster J rejected these allegations and drew attention to Springwell's sophistication as an investor, the lack of evidence documenting any advisory obligation, the fact that although Springwell valued Chase's advice it ultimately made its own decisions, and the existence of the certain disclaimers of liability. The judge approved Lord Mustill in *Re Goldcorp*[14] where the latter said that:

> many commercial relationships involve . . . a reliance by one party on the other [honestly and conscientiously to do what it had by contract promised to do] and to introduce the whole new dimension into such relationships which would flow from giving them a fiduciary character would have adverse consequences . . . high expectations do not necessarily lead to equitable remedies.

[11] *Attorney General* v *Blake* [1998] 1 All ER 833 at 843.
[12] *Bristol and West Building Society* v *Mothew* [1998] Ch 1 at 18.
[13] [2008] EWHC 1186.
[14] *Re Goldcorp Exchange Ltd* [1995] 1 AC 74.

The purpose of the contractual documentation was to delineate the relationship between the parties and once defined the relationship was one which neither gave rise to fiduciary obligations or a duty of care. The reluctance to impose fiduciary duties on the bank when it deals with an individual customer was highlighted in *Wright* v *HSBC Plc*[15] where the bank's customer, after the death of her husband, reached a compromise with her bank and settled various claims against the bank, in return for continued banking facilities. Subsequently, the customer attempted to revive her claim against the bank on the basis that the bank had been in breach of its fiduciary duties by advising her to enter into the agreement. Despite her vulnerability Jack J held that the bank had not assumed a fiduciary role in its dealings with her. In fact, the bank had suggested that the customer, a widow, obtain independent legal advice and had not advised her to enter into the compromise arrangement but had left her to make her own decision. The court concluded that in normal circumstances there was no question of a fiduciary relationship[16] being recognised in the general banker and customer relationship[17] but the courts may impose a fiduciary relationship where a 'special relationship' or 'exceptional circumstances' are established.

A new clause 5 in the Financial Services (Banking Reform) Bill 2013 will insert into the law a duty of care. The scope of the statutory duty of care will be that the ring-fenced institution will owe a fiduciary duty in carrying out its core services and a more general duty of care across the financial services sector. The scope of this duty, if enacted, will have a fundamental impact on the banker and customer relationship.

So the question that arises is how do the courts protect those customers who do not enter into a fiduciary relationship but who are seen to have been disadvantaged as a result of unconscionable behaviour.

Protecting the vulnerable

However, there is a real lack of clarity in this area and the issue of when banks will be treated as under fiduciary obligations remains unsettled. What is clear is that the English courts will treat a person as a fiduciary where someone 'has undertaken to act for or on behalf of another in a particular matter in circumstances, which give rise to a relationship of trust and confidence'. Thus, a fiduciary is under a duty of loyalty[18] but the courts will protect the vulnerable, for example the elderly parent,[19] the spouse who gives a guarantee etc., when there is an element of dependency or influence exercised over the dependent person. In such circumstances, when the bank seeks to enforce its claim the action may be defeated because it was in a fiduciary relationship to the surety, or the bank had knowledge of the actual or constructive wrong doing. In *Lloyds Bank Plc* v *Bundy*[20] the Court of Appeal set aside a guarantee secured over the elderly customer's home to support an overdraft given by the bank to his son who had financial difficulties. The bank failed to disclose the extent of these

---

[15] [2006] EWHC 930.

[16] *Cornish* v *Midland Bank Plc* [1985] 3 All ER 522.

[17] See also *Westminster Bank Plc* v *Morgan* [1985] AC 686 where the court held that the relationship remained that of banker and customer.

[18] *Bristol and West Building Society* v *Mothew* [1998] Ch. 1.

[19] *Lloyds Bank Ltd* v *Bundy* [1975] QB 326.

[20] [1975] QB 326.

difficulties and failed to suggest that the customer obtain independent legal advice, before executing the security. The Court of Appeal set aside the guarantee on the presumption of undue influence. The vulnerability of the elderly bank customer in *Bundy*[21] placed him in a category of person who would need the protection of the courts and someone Lord Denning was concerned to protect. Sir Eric Sachs emphasised that the customer was someone of long standing and the bank manager was someone in whom the elderly customer placed 'trust and confidence', so the manager's advice was likely to be relied on by the customer. The learned judge, while not seeking to catalogue the elements in which a special relationship will be recognised to exist, said that a fiduciary relationship could arise in a number of circumstances:

> Such cases tend to arise where someone relies on the guidance or advice of another, where the other is aware of that reliance and where the person upon whom reliance is placed obtains, or may well obtain, a benefit from the transaction or has some other interest in it being concluded. In addition, there must, of course, be shown to exist some vital element . . . referred to as confidentiality.

Sir Eric Sachs went on to explain that 'confidentiality' in this context means that the banker and customer relationship has attained a level dependency and once confidence is said to exist 'influence naturally grows out of it'. A fiduciary relationship therefore arises where the customer has placed trust and confidence in the bank thereby giving influence over him.

For a number of reasons, the courts are likely to exercise caution over the application of the fiduciary principles as applied in *Bundy*.[22] Moreover, the *Bundy* case must now be interpreted in the light of *National Westminster Bank Plc v Morgan*.[23] The Court of Appeal considered *Bundy* as 'very unusual' and to involve 'special facts', and only Sir Eric Sachs decided it on the basis of breach of fiduciary duty, while Cairns LJ held the 'special relationship' between the bank and the customer gave rise to a duty to advice which, if breached, would avoid the guarantee 'on the grounds of undue influence'. Lord Denning applied the rules of undue influence to the facts in order to grant relief to the customer. Further, Sir Eric Sachs considered the conflicts of interests in the relationship between the bank, the customer and his son so significant as to impose fiduciary obligations.

Further, while agreeing with the decision in *Bundy*,[24] Lord Scarman in *National Westminster Bank Plc v Morgan*[25] cast doubt on the view expressed by Lord Denning in *Bundy*[26] that 'inequality of bargaining power' was a general ground for setting aside transactions. Lord Scarman in *Morgan*[27] expressed the view that in surety cases relief would be given on the basis of 'undue influence', rather than 'confidentiality' in the context of a relationship of trust. Lord Scarman held that the question was whether a 'meticulous examination of the facts' would show the bank 'had crossed the line' and could be held to have exercised undue influence.

---

[21] *Lloyds Bank Plc v Bundy* [1975] QB 326.
[22] *Lloyds Bank Plc v Bundy* [1975] QB 326.
[23] [1985] AC 686.
[24] *Lloyds Bank Plc v Bundy* [1975] QB 326.
[25] [1985] AC 686 (HL).
[26] *Lloyds Bank Plc v Bundy* [1975] QB 326.
[27] *National Westminster Bank Plc v Morgan* [1985] AC 686 (HL).

In *National Westminster Bank Plc v Morgan*[28] a customer who had defaulted on an earlier building society loan secured over the matrimonial home he jointly owned with his wife (who was also the bank's customer) sought to refinance the loan to prevent the building society from selling the home. The bank manager visited the matrimonial home to allow the wife to execute the necessary security documents and despite the wife's unwillingness to secure the husband's business activities over the house, the bank manager failed to explain the nature of the security and reassured her, in good faith but erroneously, that the charge only secured the amount advanced to secure the original loan. Although the bank failed to recommend that the wife obtain independent advice, the charge was held valid. Sir Eric Sachs concluded that the relationship remained that of banker and customer and that the branch manager had not exercised undue influence over the wife and therefore the bank was not obliged to recommend the wife obtain independent advice. The court concluded that the bank did not gain any hidden or undue benefit from the transaction; the wife was anxious to enter into an arrangement that would prevent the necessity of selling her house and the branch manager's explanation of the scope of the house was only technically incorrect, since the bank did not intend to enforce the charge in respect of the husband's business liabilities, although the charge was wide enough to permit that. Further, the wife understood the general nature of the charge and the fact that, without it, the building society would sell the house.

The issue was looked at again in, *Klein v First Edina National Bank*[29] where the Supreme Court of Minnesota held:

> that when a bank transacts business with a depositor or other customer, it has no special duty to counsel the customer and inform him of every material fact relating to the transaction – including the bank's motive, if material, for the transaction – unless special circumstances exist, such as where the bank knows or has reason to know that the customer is placing his trust and confidence in the bank and is relying on the bank.

Similarly, in *Woods v Martins Bank Ltd*[30] the English courts have held that a bank may find itself subject to fiduciary duties when giving investment advice to a customer. The circumstances that give rise to these duties were considered in *Woods v Martins Bank Ltd*[31] where the manager of one of the branches of the defendant bank induced the claimant to invest a substantial amount of money in the shares of a company (which was also a customer of the bank) and whose overdraft, at the relevant time, was of considerable concern to the head-office of the bank. The branch manager failed to disclose these facts to the claimant, a young man with no business experience who lost the full amount of the investment in the shares. The bank argued that the branch manager owed no duty of care to the claimant since the latter was not a customer of the bank at the time the investment advice was given and relied upon. The court, imposing liability on the bank for breach of a duty of care, held that even if a contractual relationship did not exist at the relevant time the bank had assumed fiduciary obligations towards the claimant when the branch manager undertook to act as his financial adviser. This conclusion was based on a number of factors:

[28] [1985] AC 686.
[29] 196 NW 2d 619 (1972).
[30] [1959] 1 QB 55.
[31] [1959] 1 QB 55.

- The fact that the branch manager, in his conversations with the claimant, had emphasised the expertise of the bank and had effectively agreed and undertaken to act as the claimant's financial adviser.

- The branch manager had placed considerable emphasis on a leaflet published by the bank and provided to potential customers which emphasised the expertise of the bank in the area.

- The branch manager had effectively advised the claimant to invest in the company's shares where the money from the investment would effectively be used to reduce the company's overdraft to the bank. Salmon J expressed the view that the claimant was unable to make a judgement with the full knowledge of the facts or knowledge of the bank's conflict of interest.

While Salmon J held there was no fraud on the part of the branch manager his conduct nevertheless involved a breach of fiduciary duty to exercise care arising from the fact that the claimant had clearly placed trust in the branch manager's judgement, expertise and professionalism.

The nature of the special relationship and the possibility of a conflict of interest were examined again in *Standard Investments Ltd v Canadian Imperial Bank of Commerce*[32] where the claimants planned to extend their business to other parts of Canada and for this purpose planned to acquire a controlling interest in a company which undertook business under the name Crown Trust. The claimants, who were substantial customers of the defendant bank, with the potential of directing more of their banking business to the defendant bank approached W, the then president of the defendant bank, and asked W for his advice and support in respect of the acquisition of Crown Trust. Unknown to W, the Chairman of the defendant bank had already at the request of one of the bank's directors, M, who had a personal interest in Crown Trust, agreed to purchase shares in Crown Trust for the bank itself, to help counter any takeover bid. W, acting in good faith, gave an undertaking that the defendant bank would provide the necessary support required by the claimants. When W became aware of the conflict of interest he failed to mention the bank's policy of supporting Crown Trust in its bid to remain independent but instead told the claimants that they should negotiate with M. The claimants had already met W and continued to deal with him, over a number of years, in respect of the takeover. The defendant then sold its shares in Crown Trust to another organisation, which then acquired a controlling interest in Crown Trust without the claimants having an opportunity to make a bid for its shares. The claimants suffered a substantial loss when the value of the Crown Trust shares dropped following the takeover by the other organisation.

At first instance, Griffiths J gave judgment for the bank on the grounds that the duty of confidentiality owed to Crown Trust prevented the bank from disclosing the extent of its interest in Crown Trust. The Court of Appeal reversed Griffiths J on the basis of the conflicts of interests in the bank's dealings with two customers, the claimants and Crown Trust. Further, the bank had encouraged the claimant to undertake discussions over a lengthy period with M who was not only a director of the bank but also someone who had a personal interest and close association in Crown Trust. The court held that the effect of the defendant

---

[32] (1985) 22 DLR (4th) 410.

bank's conduct was to encourage 'one of its customers to proceed with a course of action to achieve a purpose which it had already decided to thwart'.[33] The Court of Appeal[34] also rejected the view expressed by Griffiths J that the fiduciary relationship came to an end when W referred the claimants to M.

The Court of Appeal emphasised that at no time did the defendant bank or its officers indicate that the bank's offer of assistance to the claimant was withdrawn. This view is in contrast to *Arklow Investments Ltd* v *Maclean*[35] where following the claimants' rejection of the terms on which the defendant bank offered to act on their behalf, the bank withdrew its offer of assistance and in the absence of any alternative formal or informal arrangement between them the Privy Council held there were no dealings between the parties which could give rise to the imposition, or undertaking, of a fiduciary duty of loyalty on the bank. However, in *United Pan-Europe Communications NV* v *Deutsche Bank AG*[36] the Court of Appeal held that the defendant bank's undertaking of a number of activities for the claimants gave rise to fiduciary duties which could exist beyond the discharge of those activities.

Further in *Standard Investments Ltd* Goodman JA was not persuaded by the argument that the bank was unable to reveal its connection and dealings relating to Crown Trust as a result of the rules of confidentiality. He held that the defendant bank was not entitled to rely 'on the principle of confidentiality with respect to another customer, when the defendant was taking action by purchase of shares for its own account and benefit, in direct conflict with the interests of other customers who were relying on it for advice and assistance'. As the defendant bank stood to gain on its dealings in respect of the shares, Goodman JA continued:

> if the defendant felt it could not lawfully reveal the information which it possessed because of its duty of confidentiality to its customers, information which no doubt would have discouraged the [claimants], it was under an obligation to tell the [claimants] that it had a position adverse to their plans or that it had a conflict of interests.[37]

Another argument before the trial judge and the Court of Appeal was that a breach of fiduciary duty could not be established where the knowledge on which the duty, and the breach, was sought to be established was based on the dealings of two separate officers. This argument failed for a number of reasons: it was based around the fact that both officers of the bank, the branch manager, W and the bank's director, M, had full knowledge and details of the bank's policy and dealings in respect of Crown Trust at one time or another, during the course of the period in question, and the combined knowledge of both W and M (both senior officers of the bank) was attributable to the bank. The bank's breach of duty to the claimant was of a continuing nature and the bank had persistently failed to advise the claimant of the conflict of interest.

However, merely disclosing the conflict of interest will not allow the bank to avoid liability for breach of a fiduciary duty. In *Commonwealth Trading Bank of Australia* v *Smith*[38] the branch

---

[33] At p. 431.
[34] Goodman JA giving judgment.
[35] [2000] 1 WLR 594.
[36] [2000] 2 BCLC 461.
[37] (1985) 22 DLR (4th) 410 at 437.
[38] (1991) 102 Aust. L Rep. 453.

manager of the bank who was aware that two of the banks customers were interested in acquiring the same hotel introduced them to other customers wishing to sell such a hotel. The branch manager informed the purchasers that the vendors also banked with his branch and explained that he would have to keep certain information available to him, under the banking contract, as confidential. However, instead of informing the purchasers to seek independent advice he informed them that the proposed terms of the sale were favourable and that any attempt to negotiate on the price would be unsuccessful. He later failed to disclose to the purchasers that an independent valuation, obtained in respect of the mortgage, was considerably lower and the actual valuation was likely to be even lower since the valuer had mistakenly acted under the belief that the unexpired period of the lease was six rather than four years. The Federal Court of Australia held the bank to be in breach of fiduciary duty. The court held that while it was reasonable for the bank to obtain an independent valuation to protect its own interests the bank had, in respect of the purchaser, created the expectation that he would be advised on the wisdom of the proposed investment. The bank had, therefore, assumed the position of 'investment adviser' and thereby owed fiduciary obligations towards purchaser. The court took into consideration that the bank was acting on behalf of customers, neither of whom had business experience, and in respect of the purchasers the bank had failed to disclose the conflict of interest. Since the conflict bound the bank to a duty of confidentiality to the vendor, the bank should have refrained from giving any advice to the purchaser and impressed on him the necessity of obtaining independent advice. The bank was held liable although it gained no financial benefit: the liability arose from the imposition of the fiduciary obligations, with the courts holding that the bank had failed to observe those fiduciary duties.

The banks may use contractual terms to exclude or modify fiduciary duties and such a device was approved in *Kelly* v *Cooper*[39] and *Henderson* v *Merrett Syndicates Ltd.*[40] However, the Law Commission[41] recommended that professional trustees should not be able to exclude liability for breach of trust arsing from negligence. Whether the transaction can be set aside will depend on a number of factors including the Unfair Terms Act 1977, Unfair Contracts Terms Regulations and other vitiating factors, for example misrepresentation, mistake, etc.

Undue influence

Since *National Westminster Bank Plc* v *Morgan*[42] there have been significant developments in the principles of undue influence and its application to cases where the courts have to intervene to protect the interests of the wife, who agrees to act as surety, for a loan made by a bank, to secure the husband's overdraft.

---

[39] [1993] AC 205 at 214–215.
[40] [1995] 2 AC 145 at 206.
[41] Fiduciary Duties and Regulatory Rules (Report No. 236), London, 1995; The Law Commission Consultation Paper (Trustee Exemption Clauses) LCCP No. 171, London 2002.
[42] [1985] AC 686 (HL).

> ## BANKING LAW IN PRACTICE
>
> While it is necessary to ensure that the wife, or other surety, has acted of her free will to guarantee the loan or other facilities extended to the husband, there is also the need for the bank to have reasonable confidence in the strength of its security. Otherwise, it would not provide the required money. The problem lies in finding the course best designed to protect wives or other dependants, in a minority of cases, without unreasonably hampering the process of the giving and taking of security. Like every compromise, the outcome falls short of achieving in full the objectives of fully protecting either of the two competing interests. The steps required to be undertaken by the bank will not guarantee that, in future, wives or other sureties will not be subjected to undue influence or misled when standing as sureties, and short of prohibiting this type of suretyship transaction altogether, there is no way of achieving that result.

Undue influence may become significant in surety transactions because of the dominating influence exercised over the surety. In *Royal Bank of Scotland* v *Etridge (No 2)*[43] Lord Nicholls said:

> Undue influence is one of the grounds of relief developed by the courts of equity as courts of conscience. The objective is to ensure that the influence of one person over another is not abused.

Equity will set aside certain contracts or gifts on the ground that a party has behaved 'unconscionably' and obtained a benefit as a result of the exercise of undue influence. The two categories of undue influence, first established in *Allcard* v *Skinner*[44] and recognised by the Court of Appeal in *Bank of Credit and Commerce International SA* v *Aboody*[45] are:

1 *'actual undue influence'* (Class 1) where the complainant has to prove the wrongdoer exerted undue influence over him in order to enter into the disputed transaction. To establish actual undue influence it must be shown that undue pressure or intimidation was in fact applied, for example duress in the form of physical or mental pressure leading to physical or economic compulsion. However, the influence may not necessarily be physical but it must be unjustified in that it seeks to confer a benefit on the person exercising the influence; a benefit he would not otherwise have had.

2 Alternatively, the courts may be willing to recognise the existence of *'presumed undue influence'* (Class 2) in which case the complainant has to show that a confidential relationship existed which in turn raises a presumption of undue influence and the burden is then on the alleged wrongdoer to show the complainant entered into the transaction of his free will.

The *Aboody* case further divided presumed undue (class 2) into two further categories (Class 2A and Class 2B):

[43] [2002] 2 AC 773.
[44] (1887) 36 Ch D 145.
[45] [1992] 4 All ER 955.

1 The relationship between the parties is such that one party has reposed trust and confidence in the other and the courts will irrebuttably presume the existence of undue influence, for example, between a solicitor and client, or trustee and beneficiary (Class 2(A)). Moreover, the transaction in question is one that is inexplicable on any other grounds. As the banker and customer relationship does not normally fall into this category it is not proposed to discuss this in detail.

2 In the other category of presumed undue influence there is no irrebuttable presumption and undue influence will have to be proven. What is necessary is that the degree of trust and confidence reposed in the dominant party is such that he is in a position to influence the free will of the other party, either because the dominant party has day-to-day manage-ment of that person's affairs or because he undertakes to act as adviser for the dependent party (Class 2(B)). In these cases the presumption of undue influence may sometimes be refuted. The problem then is to identify those relationships that ought to put the other party on notice of undue influence; it is not enough merely to show the existence of a relation-ship where fiduciary obligations (as opposed to the existence of a fiduciary relationship) are imposed, but that the relationship is one of trust and confidence.

This distinction was recognised by the House of Lords in *Barclays Bank* v *O'Brien*[46] where the court held that a relationship between a husband and wife did not fall within the Class 2(A) category and therefore the wife had to establish that she reposed trust and confidence in the husband in relation to her financial affairs and therefore undue influence should be presumed within the Class 2(B) category. This distinction continues to be recognised and applied, not-withstanding comments by Lord Nicholls in *Royal Bank of Scotland* v *Etridge (No 2)*,[47] that the distinction is 'a little confusing' and Lord Clyde criticised it as 'illogical'. Nevertheless, it is for the person who alleges he has been wronged by undue influence to establish undue influence. In the context of the banker and customer relationship category 2(B) has produced a raft of cases.

While the reasoning in *Lloyds Bank Plc* v *Bundy*[48] may be viewed with caution the ultimate decision was undoubtedly right but in the category 2(B) cases the courts may require that undue influence be established. Thus, in *Greene King Plc* v *Stanley*[49] the Court of Appeal held that a man in his mid-forties who persuaded his elderly parents to execute a security over their house for a loan facility he was taking, to acquire an interest in a public house, had failed to rebut the presumption of undue influence. The court held as significant that the son was experienced in business while the parents were relatively naïve and elderly. More recently, Lord Hoffman in *R* v *Attorney General*[50] held that:

> Certain relationships – parent and child, trustee and beneficiary, etc. – give rise to a presump-tion that one party had influence over the other . . . if the transaction is one which cannot be reasonably explained by the relationship, that will be prima facie evidence of undue influence. Even if the relationship does not fall into one of the established categories, the evidence may show that one party did in fact have influence over the other.

---

[46] [1994] 1 AC 180.
[47] [2002] 2 AC 773.
[48] [1975] QB 326.
[49] [2002] B.P.I.R 491.
[50] Unreported 17 March 2003, Privy Council Appeal 61 of 2002.

The issue, therefore, is to be able to identify the circumstances in which the presumption of undue influence may arise. Many of the recent cases have involved partners, whether married or co-habiting, or other dependants. Thus, in *Barclays Bank Plc* v *O'Brien*[51] the husband was a shareholder in a manufacturing company with a significant unsecured overdraft. He arranged with the manager of the respondent bank for an overdraft facility, which was to be secured by means of a second charge over the matrimonial home, jointly owned by the husband and the appellant, his wife. The bank prepared the necessary documentation, including a guarantee to be provided by the husband and a charge to be signed by both the husband and his wife, who was to act as the surety. However, bank staff failed to follow the branch manager's instructions that the O'Briens should seek independent advice and be specifically asked if they did not understand any aspect of the transaction, prior to signing the documents. The wife signed the documents without reading them and her husband accompanied the appellant to the bank in order to enable her to sign the documents, as guarantor for an overdraft, to secure her husband's business. The appellant, therefore, received no direct benefit from the guarantee undertaken by her (although her action did enable her husband's business to remain solvent). Although, there was no actual undue influence imposed on her it was argued that undue influence might be presumed given that the couple were married and the relationship might be one where there is a dominant partner, who directs the other in respect of aspects of the relationship.

It was significant that Mrs O'Brien had not been separately advised in respect of her own personal liabilities under the guarantee and when the bank sought to enforce the security given by her the appellant claimed that her husband had exercised undue influence and that she had been misled by him, regarding the amount and duration of the guarantee. The House of Lords dismissed an appeal by Barclays Bank Plc and concluded that if a wife was induced by undue influence, misrepresentation or other legal wrong of her husband, to stand surety for the husband's debts the creditor would, in circumstances which should have put him on inquiry, be fixed with constructive notice of the wife's right to set aside the transaction unless the creditor has warned the wife, at a meeting not attended by the husband, of the risks involved and advised the wife to take independent advice.

In analysing Lord Browne-Wilkinson's[52] judgment in *O'Brien* the main issues that need to be examined are:

(i) *Misrepresentation*: The House of Lords accepted that Mrs O'Brien had been the victim of misrepresentation and on that basis she would be entitled to have the mortgage set aside. It was sufficient there had been a misrepresentation effected by the mortgagor and the co-surety had been induced to sign the guarantee on the basis of that misrepresentation. The mortgagee had failed to ensure that the co-surety had received independent legal advice and in the *O'Brien* case the bank staff dealing with the transaction had not followed the branch manager's instructions and ensured Mrs O'Brien was independently advised. In those circumstances the mortgagee will be fixed with constructive knowledge of that misrepresentation.

However, misrepresentation and undue influence should be carefully distinguished and although the misrepresentation in *O'Brien* was established while undue influence was unproven. Lord Nicholls in the later House of Lords decision of *Royal Bank of Scotland* v *Etridge (No 2)*[53]

---

[51] [1994] 1 AC 180.
[52] [1994] 1 AC 180.
[53] [2002] 2 AC 773.

urged caution when dealing with husband and wife cases and the possible application of the doctrine of undue influence. He said:

> Statements or conduct by a husband which do not pass beyond the bounds of what may be expected of a reasonable husband in the circumstances should not, without more, be castigated as undue influence. Similarly, when a husband is forecasting the future of his business, and expressing his hopes or fears, a degree of hyperbole may be only natural. Courts should not too readily treat such exaggerations as misstatements.

However, 'inaccurate explanations of a proposed transaction are a different matter . . .' and actionable where the statement is misleading.

(ii) *Knowledge of the bank*: there is a logical difficulty in establishing undue influence or misrepresentation in a tripartite situation where the conduct of the husband or wife (or co-habitees) is challenged on the basis of undue influence and the mortgage or guarantee sought to be set aside is in favour of a third party, the bank. The traditional view of equity in this tripartite situation seems to be that a person in the position of the wife will only be relieved of her bargain if the other party to the transaction (the bank, in the present instance) was privy to the conduct, which led to the wife's entry into the transaction. Knowledge is required.[54] The law imposes no obligation on one party to a transaction to check whether the other party's concurrence was obtained by undue influence. However, a party to a contract may lose the benefit of his contract, entered into in good faith, if he ought to have known that the other's concurrence had been procured by the undue influence of a third party.

Cases of the bank having actual knowledge of the application of undue influence or misrepresentation by the borrower are not only rare but also unlikely to cause a major difficulty since the outcome will be dependent on a straight finding of actual fact. The difficulty arises in cases where the bank does not have actual knowledge but there is the possibility of undue influence or misrepresentation, which has induced the surety to guarantee the debt. It is, therefore, necessary for the surety to establish either that the borrower was acting as the bank's agent, or that the bank ought to have known of the undue influence or misrepresentation. The bank, therefore, needs to be fixed with constructive notice of the wrongdoing and the question which Lord Browne-Wilkinson[55] said needs to be resolved is whether there was something about the transaction which ought to have put the bank on notice.

On the facts of *O'Brien* it was suggested that the bank employee's had used Mr O'Brien to co-opt his wife as a surety for the overdraft, and he had thereby become the bank's agent for these purposes. The suspicion of agency in *O'Brien* arose from the fact that the bank had proposed the surety arrangement, to support the overdraft for Mr O'Brien's company. Such an agency relationship would, *prima facie*, fix the bank with notice of those facts the agent had notice, including any misrepresentation or undue influence. Thus, Lord Browne-Wilkinson said that:

> if the wrongdoing husband is acting as agent for the creditor bank in obtaining the security from the wife, the creditor will be fixed with the wrongdoing of its agent and the surety contract can be set aside as against the creditor.

---

[54] See: *Cobbett v Brock* (1855) 20 Beav 524 at 528 and 531, per Sir John Romilly MR, *Kempson v Ashbee* (1874) LR 10 Ch App 15, 21, per James LJ, and *Bainbrigge v Browne*, 18 Ch D 188, 197, per Fry J.
[55] *Barclays Bank Plc* v *O'Brien* [1994] 1 AC 180.

In the *Etridge*[56] case Lord Hobhouse discussing the degree of notice required by the bank said that:

> notice of the risk of undue influence is not an all or nothing question. Situations will differ across a spectrum from a very small risk to a serious risk verging on the probability. There has to be a proportionality between the degree of risk and the requisite response to it.

The question to be determined is whether the bank has been 'put on inquiry' as to the exercise of undue influence or misrepresentation, so as to be required to protect itself. The court in *Etridge* also observed that the phrase 'put on inquiry' was to be preferred rather than 'to have constructive notice', as used by Lord Browne-Wilkinson in *O'Brien*.[57] In *Etridge*, Lord Nicholls recognised that even the phrase 'put on inquiry' is not completely correct usage since the bank is not required to investigate or attempt to discover that the surety's consent has been freely given with knowledge, or understanding, of the full facts. Instead, the bank should satisfy itself that the surety has had brought to her attention the practical implications of the proposed transaction and it is with regard to this that the bank is 'put on inquiry'. Thus, the two elements that combine to raise the presumption of undue influence or misrepresentation are (a) the relationship between the surety and the borrower, and (b) the nature of the transaction. It is intended to deal with these requirements:

(a) *The nature of the relationship between the surety and the borrower*: Earlier cases had established that there was not an irrebuttable presumption of undue influence between husband and wife,[58] but the courts will intervene where there is 'inequality of bargaining power' and should be watchful of any hints of undue influence over the surety.[59]

In O'Brien[60] Lord Browne-Wilkinson, however, held that in cases involving the husband and wife, the wife can, so as to raise a presumption of undue influence, demonstrate that there was a relationship of 'trust and confidence' between them. In *CIBC v Pitt*,[61] an appeal heard contemporaneously by the House of Lords to the *O'Brien*[62] case, Lord Browne-Wilkinson held that the presumption of undue influence would only arise where there is some 'manifest disadvantage' to the surety arising out of the transaction. In a narrow sense the transaction is manifestly disadvantageous to the wife since she takes a financial obligation in return for which she receives nothing. That would be a blinkered view of the transaction since the fortunes of husbands and wives are often bound together in ways in which the giving of the security may benefit the wife and family. On the facts of O'Brien, the Lords concluded that because Mrs O'Brien was acting as a surety in a transaction under which she gained no direct personal benefit, it must be presumed that she must have been subject to some undue influence. However, in *Etridge*,[63] Lord Nicholls was careful not to draw any boundaries between relationships that might put the bank on inquiry and those that might not. Following, the *Etridge* case it is likely that a bank will be 'put on inquiry', where the relationship between the surety

---

[56] *Royal Bank of Scotland* v *Etridge (No 2)* [2002] 2 AC 773.
[57] *Barclays Bank Plc* v *O'Brien* [1994] 1 AC 180.
[58] *Howes* v *Bishop* [1909] 2 KB 390; *Bank of Montreal* v *Stuart* [1911] AC 120, *MacKenzie* v *Royal Bank of Canada* [1934] AC 468.
[59] See *Yerkey* v *Jones* (1939) 63 CLR 649.
[60] *Barclays Bank Plc* v *O'Brien* [1994] 1 AC 180.
[61] [1993] 4 All ER 433.
[62] *Barclays Bank Plc* v *O'Brien* [1994] 1 AC 180.
[63] *Royal Bank of Scotland* v *Etridge (No 2)* [2002] 2 AC 773.

and the debtor is of a non-commercial nature and the transaction calls for an explanation. The latter two factors will be sufficient to put the bank on notice even though the bank has no knowledge of any circumstances suggesting undue influence or misrepresentation. The nature of the transaction and the non-commercial relationship will be sufficient to put the bank on notice.

Lord Nicholls, in *Etridge*, then went on to explain that a non-commercial relationship may be any heterosexual or homosexual relationship whether, or not, the parties are married. This approach is wider to that taken by Lord Browne-Wilkinson in *O'Brien*[64] where the analysis is confined to the husband and wife relationship. The same rule will apply to a non-sexual, non-commercial relationship, including within members of the family, such as siblings and parent and child.

On the other hand, a commercial relationship will exist in circumstances where the surety has a commercial incentive to grant security to the borrower, whether that relationship arises between corporate entities, or from the engagement of the surety by the borrower to provide the guarantee for a fee.

(b) *The nature of the transaction*: For the courts to set aside a guarantee on the grounds of undue influence it is not enough for the surety merely to establish that the bank knew of the non-commercial nature of the borrower's relationship with the surety; otherwise every transaction between a husband and wife will place the bank on inquiry. Thus, a bank would be 'put on inquiry' whenever a house was purchased in joint names and the bank or building society advancing a loan, secured by a mortgage to finance the purchase, would have to insist on meeting both the parties independently to advise them on the nature of the transaction and recommend they obtain separate independent legal advice.

Loans in the joint name of a husband and wife as opposed to loans in the sole name of the husband

In the *O'Brien*[65] case it was recognised that placing the bank under such a burden would not be in the interests of the average couple requiring a loan to purchase a home. Instead, a distinction has to be drawn between cases where the loan is made in the joint names of the husband and wife and those made in the sole name of the husband, with the wife acting as a surety to secure the loan or overdraft over, for example, the matrimonial home. In *O'Brien* the creditor was put on inquiry because the transaction was held to be 'manifestly disadvantageous' to Mrs O'Brien, the surety, since there was a substantial risk of the transaction being to the surety's disadvantage. Although, the manifest disadvantage requirement has since been doubted in the *Etridge*[66] case it was central to the House of Lords' decision in *CIBC* v *Pitt*[67] and highlights the requirement that there must be something of an unusual nature in the transaction, before the bank is fixed with notice of undue influence. The case concerned a straightforward mortgage over property, rather than a security. In that case Mr Pitt had informed the appellant, Mrs Pitt, that he wished to borrow money on the security of the house to speculate on the stock market. The appellant was unhappy with this suggestion

---

[64] *Barclays Bank Plc* v *O'Brien* [1994] 1 AC 180.
[65] *Barclays Bank Plc* v *O'Brien* [1994] 1 AC 180.
[66] *Royal Bank of Scotland* v *Etridge (No 2)* [2002] 2 AC 773.
[67] [1997] 4 ALL ER 433.

and expressed her reservations to her husband who then exerted undue influence on his wife in order to obtain her agreement to the loan being secured, by a mortgage, over the matrimonial home.

In fact, Mrs Pitt not only did not read any of the documentation relating to the loan but also only saw the first and last pages. The solicitors acting for Mr and Mrs Pitt also acted as solicitors for the bank and Mrs Pitt did not receive any independent legal advice relating to the transaction. Mrs Pitt alleged that she had entered into the transaction because of her husband's undue influence and as a result of his misrepresentation about the nature of the loan. At first instance, the court held that while there was undue influence exerted by the husband, there was no misrepresentation. However, the House of Lords held that the bank was not affected by the undue influence of the husband. Further, on the facts in *Pitt*[68] there was nothing to indicate that the transaction was anything other than a normal secured loan taken out jointly by a husband and wife. Unlike, *O'Brien*[69] where Mrs O'Brien was acting to her manifest disadvantage when acting as surety, there was nothing to raise the presumption of undue influence in the *Pitt*[70] case where the bank was found to have been extending money on an ordinary secured loan.

The *O'Brien*[71] and *Pitt*[72] cases were further clarified and developed by the House of Lords in *Royal Bank of Scotland v Etridge (No 2)*[73] where the Lords concluded that transactions where a person is required to act as a surety are examples of situations where that person may have been the victim of some undue influence or misrepresentation because they guarantee performance by another under the transaction, without acquiring any direct benefit themselves. Lord Nicholls suggested that the test of manifest disadvantage was no longer relevant but, as suggested in *O'Brien*, some notion of fixing the mortgagee with notice where a co-habitee stands to suffer some financial disadvantage continues to remain important. The approach in *CIBC v Pitt*[74] was, therefore, approved and the focus of the judgment in *Etridge (No 2)* is the position of the surety and not mortgagors generally.

In *Etridge (No 2)* Lord Hobhouse was generally supportive of the approach adopted by Lord Browne-Wilkinson but he disagreed with the application of the constructive notice test on the basis that different standards of notice would apply to set aside the transaction in each situation.[75] Thus, for example, a case involving a wife acting as a surety would require evidence of undue influence to fix the mortgagee with notice, whereas situations appearing to be a little out of the ordinary would make it more difficult to fix the mortgagee with notice of undue influence. Lord Hobhouse while not adopting the approach taken by the Australian courts did suggest that it might be better to set aside unconscionable bargains, rather than going through the gymnastics of affixing the mortgagee with notice of the undue influence. The Australian approach allows the courts to set aside transactions due to the presence of unconscionability, without having to determine whether the mortgagee had notice of that unconscionable behaviour.

---

[68] *CIBC v Pitt* [1997] 4 ALL ER 433.
[69] *Barclays Bank Plc v O'Brien* [1994] 1 AC 180.
[70] *CIBC v Pitt* [1997] 4 ALL ER 433.
[71] *Barclays Bank Plc v O'Brien* [1994] 1 AC 180.
[72] *CIBC v Pitt* [1997] 4 ALL ER 433.
[73] [2002] AC 773.
[74] [1997] 4 All ER 433.
[75] [2001] 4 All ER 449 at 449.

Lord Scott, in *Etridge (No 2)*, takes a somewhat different approach and is more focused on the co-habitee failing to give free consent to a contract where she acts under undue influence, or some misrepresentation. However, the contractual approach is complicated by the presence of a third party, i.e. the bank making the loan, and the question which needs to be resolved by the courts will be the extent of knowledge required by the bank, mortgagee, to set aside its right to repossess the property on the grounds of undue influence or misrepresentation, between the surety and their partner. The test of knowledge extends to the mortgagee being either fixed with actual knowledge itself, or having some constructive or imputed notice because of the conduct of an agent. However, what is not clear is whether the knowledge would have to be acquired either wilfully or by recklessly failing to make such inquires as a reasonable banker would have made, or but for wilfully closing its eyes to the obvious, such knowledge is sufficient to impute notice as a constructive trustee.[76] Lord Scott did however agree with Lord Nicholls that if there is some special feature in the transaction, then that will fix the mortgagee bank with knowledge of undue influence.[77]

Although their Lordships all take a slightly different approach to affixing the mortgagee bank with notice of the undue influence or misrepresentation many of the principles established in the *O'Brien* case remain relevant, except that the requirement of manifest disadvantage has been set aside in subsequent decisions.

Practical consequences of the cases on undue influence

In *O'Brien* Lord Browne-Wilkinson held that the mortgagee could take 'reasonable steps' to discharge his liability for undue influence or misrepresentation. The learned judge said that a bank can reasonably be expected simply to take steps to bring home to the surety the risk she is running by standing as surety, and to advise her to take independent legal advice. He suggested that a bank should insist that the wife attend a private meeting, in the absence of the husband, with a representative of the bank at which the extent of her liability as surety is explained, warned of the risk she is running and urged to take independent legal advice. In reality banks avoided having private meetings with the wife, or other surety, rather than risk being exposed to allegations of negligence; preferring instead that the surety take legal advice and then seeking confirmation from the solicitor that the nature and effect of the document had been explained.

In cases post-*O'Brien* and pre-*Etridge (No 2)* the courts examined the nature of steps the mortgagee was required to take to avoid liability. In *Massey v Midland Bank*,[78] Ms Massey was persuaded by her partner to charge her personal property as security, for his overdraft with the mortgagee. The bank interviewed them both together but advised Ms Massey, in her partner's presence, to obtain independent legal advice. The Court of Appeal held that the mortgagee was only required to see that the surety sought advice, not to ensure that the advice was properly given. Steyn LJ held that in these circumstances 'nothing more was required of the bank than to urge or insist that Miss Massey should take independent advice'. In *Massey* Steyn LJ urged there are two questions that require consideration namely; whether

---

[76] [2001] 4 All ER 449 at 509.
[77] [2001] 4 All ER 449 at 509.
[78] [1995] 1 All ER 929.

or not the mortgagee was put on inquiry as to the circumstances in which the co-habitee had agreed to provide the security, and secondly, if so, whether or not the mortgagee took reasonable steps to ensure that the agreement of the co-habitee to the charge was properly obtained. This test was followed in *Banco Exterior Internacional* v *Mann*[79] and in *Bank of Baroda* v *Rayarel*.[80] The bank cannot be required to ensure that the advice received was full, complete and accurate; the bank cannot be liable for the negligence of the solicitor.[81] In other words, the bank can only be required to go so far and Lord Nicholls expressly acknowledged that a bank is not required to investigate whether the surety has been the subject of undue influence.

In *Heather Padden* v *Bevan Ashford*[82] the Court confirmed that the purpose of a wife obtaining legal advice is for the solicitor to explain that the other party to the transaction will rely on the independent solicitor's involvement to counter any suggestion that the wife has been subjected to undue influence. Therefore, by giving the certificate and witnessing the confirmation, the solicitor accepts an obligation (for himself and his firm) to advise the wife and takes reasonable steps to satisfy himself that the wife had been advised to the extent that a reasonably competent solicitor would have done in the circumstances.

Lord Nicholls in *Etridge (No 2)* set out the steps the bank should take once it is put on inquiry about the possibility of undue influence of the borrower and to be able to rely on the confirmation of a solicitor that he has properly advised the surety.

1 The bank should communicate directly with the surety and ask her to nominate a solicitor who will act to advise her separately from the borrower and inform her that in order to safeguard its position the bank will require written confirmation that the solicitor has fully explained to her the nature and practical effect of documents she will be required to sign. The bank should also explain that the purpose of insisting on such confirmation is to ensure that the surety cannot later dispute that she is legally bound by the signed documents. The bank should not proceed with the transaction until the written confirmation is received.

2 It should be accepted practice that banks who intend to rely on confirmation from the surety's solicitor that appropriate advice has been given to the surety will provide relevant financial information about the borrower's affairs as necessary for the solicitor properly to advise the surety. In order to protect itself against allegations of wrongful disclosure the bank should ensure that it obtains the borrower's permission to any disclosure. While, the extent of the disclosure will depend on the facts of each individual case the information will ordinarily include, as a minimum, information regarding the purpose for which the new facility has been requested, the amount of the borrower's current indebtedness and overdraft facility, and the amount and terms of the new facility. Where the borrower has applied for the facility in writing, a copy of the application form should be sent to the surety's solicitor. If the bank, where for example the borrower refuses to consent to the disclosure, cannot provide adequate information it should not proceed with the transaction in that form.

[79] [1995] 1 All ER 939.
[80] [1995] 2 FLR 376.
[81] *Heather Padden* v *Bevan Ashford* [2011] EWCA Civ 1616.
[82] [2011] EWCA Civ 1616.

3 If the bank believes or has reason to suspect, or has any reason to believe or suspect, that the surety has in some way been misled or is not entering into the transaction of her own free will, then the bank should inform the surety's solicitor of the facts on which this belief is held.

4 The bank should, in every case, obtain from the solicitor advising the surety, written confirmation that the surety has received proper advice. It is not enough for the bank to know that the surety has been to see the solicitor because it cannot be assumed that the advice was taken.

Solicitor acting for more than one party

In *Banco Exterior Internacional* v *Mann*[83] the solicitor advised the borrower, co-habitee (surety) and the company for which the loan was sought, with the result that it was unclear whether or not the co-habitee received independent legal advice. Morritt LJ said that the position must be considered from the mortgagee's point of view and the mortgagee had been shown a certificate that the co-habitee had received legal advice and had acted reasonably in concluding that the co-habitee had agreed to the mortgage. Therefore, even if the co-habitee had not actually received independent legal advice it is enough for the mortgagee to show that the co-habitee had attested such advice had been taken. Therefore, according to *Mann* the mortgagee is not required to look behind the certificate attesting that legal advice has been received. In *Royal Bank of Scotland* v *Etridge (No 2)* Lord Hobhouse strongly expressed the view that there must be 'true independent advice' given by a solicitor, which would lead to 'real consent' to the contract.[84] However, it is submitted that it is unrealistic to expect that each party must be represented by his other own separate solicitor in such cases and a single solicitor representing all the parties to the transaction can give independent legal advice; only actual knowledge on the part of the mortgagee bank that the surety has not received independent legal advice will defeat the bank's security. If the advice received was negligent that will give a cause of action against the solicitor but not defeat the bank's right over the security.

In *Midland Bank* v *Serter*[85] the Court of Appeal held that where the solicitor had represented the mortgagee, mortgagor and the co-habitee, the mortgagee was not bound by constructive notice of any undue influence where the co-habitee had signed a certificate acknowledging receipt of legal advice even in circumstances where the mortgagee directs a solicitor to advise the co-habitee. The solicitor owes all the duties of a professional acting in that capacity and the bank can rely on the surety having obtained legal advice even if it subsequently transpires that the solicitor breaches his obligation to give independent advice and acts in a way which advantages the mortgagee or mortgagor because he fails to pass on full information to the surety about the nature of the transaction.

Similarly, in *Barclays Bank* v *Thomson*[86] the bank gave a loan to the defendant surety's husband, which was secured against a mortgage over the family home. The bank instructed a solicitor to act on its behalf in the mortgage transaction, including giving advice to the

---

[83] [1995] 1 All ER 936.
[84] [2001] 4 All ER 449.
[85] [1995] 1 FLR 367.
[86] [1997] 4 All ER 816.

defendant. The solicitors explained the effect of the mortgage to the defendant in the absence of the husband and it was held that the defendant had been properly advised on the effect of the mortgage over the family home. The bank was not therefore imputed with any notice of any undue influence or misrepresentation and the finding of constructive notice was set aside. The onus therefore on the bank is to ensure that a surety can show that legal advice has been received through the certificate rather than confirming that the surety has no rights which may set aside the security. In respect of the view expressed by Hobhouse LJ in the *Mann* case that 'true independent advice' must be given by the solicitor, the court in *Halifax BSc* v *Stepsky*[87] held that the mortgagee should be absolved from responsibility for procuring 'truly independent advice' if it is shown that the solicitor gave impartial advice to the surety. In *Stepsky* there was a suggestion that the solicitor had sought to persuade the surety to sign the agreement when it was against the surety's best interests. Obviously where there is a conflict of interest the solicitor will not be able to give impartial advice but merely because the solicitor acts for more than one party to the transaction does not impute bad faith or negligence.

Remedies for breach of common law or fiduciary duties

The remedies available for a breach of duty will be determined by the nature of the duty that is breached. A breach of a fiduciary duty will entitle the injured party to be granted restitution or other restorative relief rather than compensation in the form of damages. However, where the proprietary remedies are impossible then the courts may award compensation in lieu of rescission or restitution. However, not every breach of duty by a fiduciary will in fact be a breach of a fiduciary duty and a breach of an equitable duty will result in an award of common law damages.[88]

In cases involving a breach of duty of contract or breach of a tort the courts will award damages to compensate for the resulting loss assessed under the common law rules for the award of damages for breach of contract or breach of a duty of care.

Conclusion

While the banker and customer relationship remains entrenched in contract law and the courts are reluctant to impose fiduciary obligations on the basic relationship, nevertheless they will intervene to assist an innocent party who has been the victim of 'unconscionable behaviour'. The law in this area will continue to develop and one of the considerations is likely to be whether a doctrine of 'unconscionable behaviour' should be recognised to support the claims of the dependent wife, partner or elderly parent.

[87] [1996] 2 All ER 277.
[88] *Bristol and West Building Society* v *Mothew* [1998] Ch 1 at 18.

Further reading

➤ Rosen, A. (2001) The Myth of Independent Advice, *New Law Journal*, 296–297.
This article anticipates the House of Lords decision in *Royal Bank of Scotland plc v Etridge (No. 2)* and assesses the guidance provided on the position of solicitors when asked by banks to advise the wife when the husband plans to remortgage the family home. The article analyses previous cases alongside the Law Society's Guide to Professional Conduct.

➤ Barker, K. (2000) 'Lost in the Umbrian Hills: Seeking Direction for O'Brien', 114 *RLR*.
This article considers whether the spouse or bank had to prove the bank's constructive notice of the husband's undue influence and misrepresentation.

➤ Clayton, N. (1992) 'Banks as fiduciaries: the UK position', 315 *J.I.B.L.*
This article considers the circumstances in which a banker may be or become a fiduciary in relation to his customer. To explore this question, Clayton analyses a series of cases including *Lloyds Bank Ltd v Bundy*, and *National Westminster Bank v Morgan*.

9

The nature of the overdrawn account and the bank's self-help remedies

The aim of this chapter is to:

➤ Explore the law relating to unauthorised bank overdrafts within the context of the *Office of Fair Trading* v *Abbey National Building Society & Others* case.

➤ Examine the self-help remedies available to the bank where the customer has more than one bank account, some of which are overdrawn while others are in credit. These remedies may be especially important where the customer has become, or may become, insolvent.

Introduction

An overdraft facility is generally granted to the customer as a result of an express agreement entered into with the bank. In such a situation the bank will agree to allow the customer a contractual right to overdraw up to an agreed ceiling.[1] If a customer is offered an arranged overdraft, or an increase in his existing arranged overdraft limit, the bank should inform the customer whether the overdraft is repayable on demand,[2] or at a certain time in the future. Where the bank grants its customer an overdraft facility through the current account it effectively provides that customer with a loan facility, the amount of which may vary on a daily basis, and on which the interest payable[3] will be calculated, at a compound rate,[4]

---

[1] Lending Code: Setting standards for banks, building societies and credit card providers, July 2011 para. 76 provides: 'When providing customers with information, before a contract is entered into, about a current account offering an arranged overdraft facility, subscribers should include clear, fair and not misleading information outlining the availability of the overdraft, including whether there are qualifying criteria for accessing the overdraft.' http://www.lendingstandardsboard.org.uk/docs/lendingcode.pdf.

[2] Lending Code: Setting standards for banks, building societies and credit card providers, July 2011 para. 80 provides that the explanation to the customer could be contained in a facility letter or the terms and conditions, http://www.lendingstandardsboard.org.uk/docs/lendingcode.pdf.

[3] Lending Code: Setting standards for banks, building societies and credit card providers, July 2011 para. 77 provides: 'The customer must be provided, where relevant, with details of any charges payable, the interest rate to be applied or, if reference interest rates are to be used, the method for calculating the actual interest and the relevant date and index or base for determining such reference interest rates.' http://www.lendingstandardsboard.org.uk/docs/lendingcode.pdf.

[4] *Sempra Metals Ltd* v *IRC* [2008] 1 AC 561 (HL).

on a daily basis, although the amount may be debited from the customer's account on a periodic basis.[5]

While, the effect of the rule in *Foley* v *Hill*[6] is that the bank is a debtor to its customer for the amount of the credit balance in the customer's account, that relationship is reversed where the customer's account is overdrawn so that the bank becomes the customer's creditor for the amount of the overdraft. Once the customer becomes overdrawn any amounts paid to the credit of the customer's account will be applied to pay off the overdraft until the full amount of the overdraft is paid off. In evidence submitted to the court at first instance in *Office of Fair Trading* v *Abbey National and 7 Others*,[7] Andrew Smith J accepted that substantial numbers of customers with current accounts have a pre-arranged overdraft facility and take advantage of it.[8] However, a bank is not under any obligation to extend an overdraft facility to its customer and once the customer has availed himself of the credit balance on his account the bank's indebtedness to the customer is discharged. If the bank has agreed to grant an overdraft facility the customer is legally entitled to overdraw on that facility and the bank will be liable for wrongful dishonour of a payment if it wrongfully dishonours a payment mandate within the overdraft limit.[9]

Goff J explained the nature of the contractual obligations and rights that arise in respect of a pre-arranged overdraft facility in *Barclays Bank Plc* v *W.J. Simms & Cooke (Southern) Ltd* where he said that:[10]

> It is a basic obligation owed by a bank to its customer that it will honour on presentation cheques [or other payment instructions] drawn by the customer on the bank, provided that there are sufficient funds in the customer's account to meet the cheque [or other payment mandate], or the bank has agreed to provide the customer with overdraft facilities sufficient to meet the cheque [or other payment mandate]. Where the bank honours such a cheque [or other payment mandate], it acts within its mandate, with the result that the bank is entitled to debit the customer's account with the amount of the cheque, and further that the banks' payment is effective to discharge the obligation of the customer to the payee on the cheque, because the bank has paid the cheque with the authority of the customer.

---

[5] Lending Code: Setting standards for banks, building societies and credit card providers, July 2011 para. 90 provides: 'Subscribers should make information about overdraft interest rates available to customers via: a telephone helpline; a website; notices in branches; or information from staff.' http://www.lendingstandardsboard.org.uk/docs/lendingcode.pdf.

[6] (1848) 2 HL Cas 28; see Ch. 1 for further discussion.

[7] [2008] EWHC 875 (Comm) before Andrew Smith J, at para. 55.

[8] Approximately 50 per cent of the eligible customers of Abbey National plc had an overdraft facility and of those approximately half used the facility in any year. In the case of Barclays Bank plc, in 2006, about 56 per cent of the PCA customers had an arranged overdraft facility with about 50 per cent of Clydesdale Bank plc customers having an arranged overdraft, with about 16 per cent of the customers using the arranged overdraft facility. In 2006, approximately two-thirds of HBOS plc PCA customers had an arranged overdraft facility and approximately two-thirds of those customers used the facility, while approximately 60 per cent of HSBC plc PCA customers had an arranged overdraft, while about 96 per cent of First Direct customers had an agreed overdraft facility.

[9] See Ch. 7 for a discussion of the rules relating to payment of mandate.

[10] [1980] 1 QB 677 at 699.

BANKING LAW IN PRACTICE

In reality, however, customers may overdraw on their personal current accounts (PCAs) through an unauthorised overdraft and evidence before the court, in *Office of Fair Trading* v *Abbey National and 7 Others*,[11] showed that it was not unusual for PCA customers to overdraw without a pre-arranged overdraft facility.[12] Where there is no pre-arranged overdraft a payment mandate, which can only be paid by the extension of an overdraft facility, will be treated as an implied request for an overdraft facility. In *Cuthbert* v *Roberts Lubbock and Co*[13] the court held that the drawing of a cheque by a customer for a sum in excess of his credit balance is really a request for a loan, and if the cheque is honoured the customer has borrowed money from the bank. In law, a payment mandate, therefore, issued by a customer when there are insufficient funds to the credit of the account amounts to a request for an overdraft facility, on the bank's standard terms, e.g. the customer is deemed to agree to the payment of any bank charges in respect of the overdraft facility.[14] A customer will therefore, *prima facie*, not be in breach of his banking contract if he gives instructions to his bank to make a payment without either having the necessary funds to the credit of his account, or without a pre-arranged overdraft facility being in place at the time the payment becomes due.

In these circumstances, the customer implicitly requests the bank grant overdraft facilities to the extent of the credit required to facilitate the payment,[15] but the bank is under no obligation to honour the customer's cheques because the customer has insufficient funds to the credit of his account and does not have in place pre-arranged overdraft facilities, sufficient to meet the amount of the payment instruction. The bank has an option whether or not to comply with the payment mandate and if the bank decides not honour the mandate, it acts within its rights to refuse payment. If, however, the bank honours the cheque, it accepts the customer's mandate[16] to make payment and extend an overdraft facility; the consequences of making the payment will be the same as if the overdraft had been agreed prior to the payment which, when made in accordance with the customer's mandate,[17] discharges the customer's debt to the third party with the bank entitled to reimbursement from the customer.

---

[11] [2008] EWHC 875 (Comm) before Andrew Smith J at para. 55.

[12] Evidence from the Abbey National plc showed that 'significant' numbers of its customers overdrew without a pre-arranged overdraft thereby incurring fees,' and that a large proportion of those customers were overdrawn on a number of occasions a year. Approximately 20 per cent of Barclays Bank plc customers overdrew without prior arrangement. At the same time approximately 7 per cent of Clydesdale plc customers had an unarranged overdraft while about 17 per cent of their customers overdrew without prior arrangement at any time. About 10 per cent of HBOS plc PCA customers had unarranged overdrafts in 2006, while in September 2007, 13 per cent of HSBC plc and 7 per cent of First Direct customers had unarranged overdrafts. In 2006, about 22 per cent of Lloyds TSB plc PCA customers had unarranged overdrafts.

[13] [1909] 2 Ch 226.

[14] *Lloyds Bank Plc* v *Voller* [2000] 2 All ER (Comm) 978.

[15] Waller LJ in *Lloyds Bank Plc* v *Independent Insurance Co Ltd* [2000] 1 QB 110 at 118.

[16] This is to be distinguished from a situation where the bank pays a cheque drawn or purported to be drawn by its customer but finds itself having made payment without a mandate, for example the bank overlooks a notice of the customer's death, or if it makes payment on a forged signature of its customer. In such cases the bank cannot debit the customer's account: see *Re Beavan, Davies, Bank & Co* v *Beavan* [1913] 2 Ch 595; s.24 Bills of Exchange Act 1882; *London Joint Stock Bank* v *Macmillan* [1918] AC 777; *Liggett (Liverpool) Ltd* v *Barclays Bank Ltd* [1928]1 KB 48.

[17] *Barclays Bank Plc* v *W.J. Simms & Cooke (Southern) Ltd* [1980] 1 QB 677 at 699.

The customer's use of a cheque guarantee card,[18] provided by the bank, to guarantee payment does not alter the contractual position between banks and their customers. The use of the card merely places the bank, through the agency of its customer, under an obligation to the third party in whose favour the cheque is drawn not to dishonour the cheque on presentation for lack of funds in the customer's account; the bank will effectively extend credit and allow the customer to overdraw to facilitate payment on that cheque.[19]

Where the bank does make payment in accordance with the customer's instructions, either where there is a pre-arranged overdraft in place or in the absence of an pre-arranged overdraft facility, the bank allows the customer a credit facility and the customer is deemed to have agreed to the bank's relevant standard terms in respect of such transactions, unless the parties are deemed to have entered into to an agreement to the contrary, or unless the terms are deemed contrary to established banking practice or otherwise held unreasonable.[20]

The effect of the overdraft

Overdrafts have traditionally been thought of as relatively short-term funding but in reality many businesses fund their daily activity through this method of borrowing. However, the amount owing will continually fluctuate, resulting in balances, which vary throughout the overdraft period.

The effect of the grant of an overdraft facility, in favour of the customer, will vary depending on whether there is a pre-arranged overdraft facility resulting from a specific contractual agreement, or where the overdraft results from the bank's decision to extend an overdraft following the bank's decision to honour a payment instruction for which there are insufficient funds to the credit of the customer's account when there is no pre-arranged overdraft facility. In the former case an overdraft facility will, generally, be extended on the basis of the bank's terms of business and commits the bank to allow the customer to overdraw only for as long as the facility is in place, and the customer's payment mandate is within that limit.[21] By contrast, a request to make payment when there is an insufficient credit balance standing in favour of the customer to meet a payment mandate will be deemed, in the absence of an agreed overdraft, as a request for an overdraft facility to cover a particular payment. The overdraft facility may, therefore, take one of three forms: (i) the pre-arranged overdraft; (ii) a recurrent overdraft facility established as a result of implied practice established between the bank and individual customers; and (iii) a one off (or occasional) overdraft permitted to honour individual payment instructions which result in the grant of an overdraft.

---

[18] A cheque which was backed by a cheque guarantee card amounted to a promise by the bank to honour the cheque properly drawn by the customer. The payee of the cheque was therefore assured payment of the cheque up to the limit of the guarantee on the card, usually £50 or £100. The cheque guarantee scheme was removed in 2011.

[19] *Re Charge Card Services Ltd* [1987] Ch 150.

[20] *Emerald Meats (London) Ltd* v *AIB Group (UK) Plc* [2002] EWCA Civ 460 at para. 14.

[21] Although the facility may be granted for a specific purpose, typically it is not limited to a specific payment by the customer.

Processing a request for an overdraft facility

The processes in handling a payment request against a pre-arranged overdraft compared to a situation where the customer requests an overdraft facility by issuing a payment mandate (i.e. a request for an unauthorised overdraft) when he has an insufficient credit balance,[22] are similar and common to the vast majority of the banks,[23] even if the bank responds by considering the request and declining to make payment. However, in the case of an unauthorised overdraft facility the bank may be involved in some additional processes before it decides whether or not to make payment. For example in *The Office of Fair Trade* v *Abbey National Plc and Others*[24] it was explained that such requests are handled by the Abbey National Plc's Reject Referrals database,[25] which involve both manual and automated processes. Further, while Andrew Smith J, at first instance, recognised that banks may not be obliged to 'consider' a request for an overdraft facility, and they could automate procedures to allow any account to have a debit, or overdrawn, balance of a modest amount without the bank being in breach of its contractual obligations, nevertheless banks must show that they act in accordance both with banking practice and the banking code,[26] to which all banks, at the relevant time, subscribed and which stated:

> Before we lend you any money or increase your overdraft, or other borrowing, we will assess whether we feel you will be able to pay it.

The banks are therefore obliged, in accordance with banking practice, the banking code[27] and their express contractual terms[28] to 'consider' reasonably whether, or not, to grant a request for payment of a mandate that would result in an overdraft facility being extended. Banks, therefore, have discretion whether or not to pay in accordance with the customer's mandate an instruction that would allow the customer to overdraw (in the absence of a sufficient credit balance and in the absence of a pre-arranged overdraft),[29] but they will be in breach of contract if they act arbitrarily, capriciously or in bad faith when making their decision whether or not to make the payment. In *Abu Dhabi National Tanker Co* v *Product Star Shipping Co Ltd*[30] Leggatt LJ expressed the view that:

---

[22] What Andrew Smith J, in *The Office of Fair Trading* v *Abbey National plc and Others* [2008] EWHC 875 (Comm), called a Relevant Instruction.

[23] Bank practices and processes in handling such payments were considered by Andrew Smith J, in *The Office of Fair Trading* v *Abbey National plc and 7 Others* [2008] EWHC 875.

[24] [2008] EWHC 875 (Comm) Andrew Smith J at para. 81.

[25] The decision whether or not to pay the instruction involves an assessment by Abbey's 'risk personnel', using information from its 'risk databases'. If the banks decline to pay a Relevant Instruction they will notify the counterparty, for example BACS in the case of a direct debit or the presenting bank in the case of a cheque. Andrew Smith J accepted that other banks have comparable arrangements: *The Office of Fair Trading* v *Abbey National plc and Others* [2008] WHC 875 (Comm).

[26] The seven banks and one building society all subscribed to the banking code of practice for PCA customers. The Banking Codes have been superseded by the Lending Code, March 2011, http://www.lendingstandardsboard.org.uk/docs/lendingcode.pdf.

[27] The Lending Code, March 2011, http://www.lendingstandardsboard.org.uk/docs/lendingcode.pdf.

[28] Andrew Smith J in *The Office of Fair Trading* v *Abbey National Plc and Others* [2008] EWHC 875 (Comm) concluded that the terms of all seven banks required them to act in accordance with proper banking practice.

[29] What Andrew Smith J at first instance, in *The Office of Trade* v *Abbey National Plc and Others*, referred to as a 'Relevant Instruction' from the customer. This terminology was adopted subsequently by both the Court of Appeal and the Supreme Court.

[30] [1993] 1 Lloyd's Rep 397 at p. 404.

Where A and B contract with each other to confer a discretion on A, that does not render B subject to A's uninhibited whim. In my judgment, the authorities show that not only must the discretion be exercised honestly and in good faith, but, having regard to the provision of the contract by which it is conferred, it must not be exercised arbitrarily, capriciously or unreasonably.

Withdrawal of the overdraft facility

The common law position is that an overdraft is repayable on demand unless the bank has agreed to a different repayment arrangement. In *Rouse* v *Bradford Banking Co.*[31] Lord Herschell said:

> It may be that an overdraft does not prevent the bank who have agreed to give it from at any time giving notice that it is no longer to continue, and that they must be paid their money. This I think at least it does; if they have agreed to give an overdraft they cannot refuse to honour cheques or drafts, within the limit of that overdraft, which have been drawn and put into circulation before any notice to the person to whom they have agreed to give the overdraft that the limit is to be withdrawn.

The bank, therefore, does not owe the customer a duty to ensure that any demand for repayment is made in sufficient time to give the customer a reasonable opportunity to raise the money from other sources. However, the customer must be given reasonable time to effect the repayment. In *Cripps & Son Ltd* v *Wickendon*[32] it was held that although an overdraft may be payable on demand the customer has to be given reasonable notice before the facility is withdrawn. In *Bank of Baroda* v *Panessar*[33] Walton J was of the opinion that:

> the debtor is not in default in making the payment demanded unless and until he has had a reasonable opportunity of implementing whatever reasonable mechanics of payment he may need to discharge the debt. Of course, this is limited to the time necessary for the mechanics of payment. It does not extend to any time to raise the money if it is not there to be paid.

Any period of notice required to implement the payment is likely to be fairly short considering the almost instantaneous means of payment system available to transfer funds.

The legal position, therefore, is that where a customer who has received a demand for the repayment of an overdraft informs the bank that he does not have sufficient funds to repay the amount of the overdraft, the bank can treat the customer as being in immediate default and can take action without delay to enforce its legal rights. It may be the case that the grant of overdraft facility is accompanied by an agreement that the overdraft is for a particular period of time or purpose. The question of an express or implied agreement was considered in *Titford Property* v *Cannon Street Acceptances Ltd*[34] where the loan agreement contained the following clause: 'Clause 9: All moneys due by you, whether by way of capital or interest, shall be payable on demand and you shall have the right to repay all moneys due without notice.' However, a letter from the bank to the customer contained the following terms: 'We have pleasure in advising you of the terms and conditions upon which we are prepared to provide

---

[31] [1894] AC 586.
[32] [1973] 1 WLR 944.
[33] [1987] Ch 335.
[34] QBD, 22 May 1975.

an overdraft facility in the maximum sum of GBP 248,000 for a period of 12 months to assist you in the purchase and development of the under mentioned freehold premises.'

Goff J stated in the course of his judgment:

> It seems to me, where a bank allows an overdraft for a fixed time for a specific purpose – whether the time be such as the parties think is required for the achievement of the purpose, or only the most the bank will allow, that time is binding on the bank; otherwise the customer might well be led into a disastrous position, as has happened here. The customer, on the faith of the bank's promise to a loan, an overdraft for a fixed term, commits himself and then finds the overdraft cut off, so that he cannot meet his liabilities, and in addition he had insured indebtedness to the bank in respect of abortive expenditure.

The issue of the bank's right to withdraw an overdraft was examined in *Williams and Glyns Bank* v *Barnes*[35] where the bank granted its customer an overdraft facility to finance certain transactions intended to be undertaken by a company of which the customer was the CEO and majority shareholder. When the company's financial position deteriorated further the bank demanded immediate repayment of the overdraft. The court expressed the view that in the absence of an express agreement providing for the date of repayment, or for the duration of the overdraft facility, the court must consider whether according to the ordinary rules for the implication of terms into commercial contracts, any such terms are to be implied. If no such term is to be implied than the money lent under such a facility is repayable on demand. The mere knowledge that the customer will use the overdraft facility to underwrite a venture that will take time to come to fruition cannot give rise to an implied term requiring a period of notice to be given by the bank, with or without reference to the probable duration of the business venture for which the overdraft is used. Gibson J stated that:

> Bankers . . . regard repayability on demand as a universal or normal attribute of overdrafts, but there is nothing to suggest that they regard that attribute as overriding an agreement to the contrary. If a usage to that effect existed it would not, in my judgment, be lawful or reasonable . . . In truth, this custom or usage is no more than recognition of the rule of law which results from the nature of lending money; money lent is repayable without demand, or at the latest on demand, unless the lender expressly or impliedly agrees otherwise.

The legal position, therefore, is that banks will be able to demand immediate repayment of overdrafts provided the bank has done nothing to restrict its right to immediate repayment as in the *Titford Properties* case.

Interest on an overdraft

Interest will be calculated on the amount of the overdraft either at an agreed rate or at the bank's currently published lending rate. This is fixed by reference to the Bank of England's base rate which will be uniform for all commercial banks plus a number of percentage points over the minimum depending on the risk to the bank and the creditworthiness of the customer. The Lending Code provides[36] that 'subscribers should make information about

---

[35] [1981] Com LR 205.

[36] Lending Code: Setting standards for banks, building societies and credit card providers, July 2011, para. 90, http://www.lendingstandardsboard.org.uk/docs/lendingcode.pdf.

overdraft interest rates available to customers via: a telephone helpline; a website; notices in branches; or information from staff'.

Interest on the amount of the overdraft is charged on a daily basis although it may not be debited until the end of the current quarterly or half-yearly period. Consequently, in calculating interest on an overdraft, account is not taken of amounts credited to the customer's account until the business day following that on which the bank receives the credit item. Where an account is continuously overdrawn a substantial part of the debit may represent the interest charged, particularly as interest will be charged at a compound rate. In *Yourell* v *Hibernian Bank Ltd*[37] Lord Atkinson considered charging compound interest 'a usual and perfectly legitimate mode of dealing between banker and customer' and in *National Bank of Greece SA* v *Pinios Shipping Co (No 1)*[38] the House of Lords held that the usage under which banks are entitled to charge compound interest prevails generally as 'between bankers and customers who borrow from them and do not pay interest as it accrues'. Lord Goff of Chieveley doubted that the usage was restricted to 'accounts current for mutual transactions' and the usage therefore although developed in the context of usury laws had a general application to borrowing between customers and their banks. His Lordship also concluded that the bank could continue to charge compound interest even after the bank had demanded repayment of the overdraft and concluded:

> if it be equitable that a banker should be entitled to capitalise interest at, for example, yearly or half yearly rests because his customer has failed to pay interest on the due date, there appears to be no basis in justice or logic for terminating that right simply because the bank has demanded payment of the sum outstanding in the customer's account.

The question of whether charging compound interest is a right available to the customer was examined in *Halliday* v *HBOS Plc*[39] where the court held that no such right existed in favour of the customer where the defendant bank had made a number of wrongful deductions against the customer's account but where the bank had credited his account in full, together with any interest that might have accrued. The court further held that the bank had no obligation to repay the claimant compound interest, at a rate which it might have charged a customer for an unauthorised overdraft, on the ground that such a term could not be imposed for reasons of fairness, but could only be imposed where it was necessary to give business efficacy to a banker and customer relationship. However, as a result of *Sempra Metals Ltd* v *IRC*[40] a customer may be entitled to compound interest providing he can show that such loss was actual and foreseeable.

Appropriation of payments

One of the features of the current account is that the credit and/or debit balance standing to the credit of the customer's account will vary on a daily basis because of the nature of the relationship which is based on mutual dealings between the parties. For most purposes it will be sufficient to determine the net debit or credit balances on the customer's account,

[37] [1918] AC 372.
[38] [1990] 1 AC 637.
[39] [2007] EWHC 1789.
[40] [2007] UKHL 34.

although in some instances it may become necessary to determine which of the credit entries have discharged individual debits from the account. This may become important where, for example, a third party assumes secondary liability, for a fixed period, for an overdraft extended to the account holder. On the expiration of the agreed period of the guarantee the bank decides not to strike a balance (freezing the account or ruling off) on the account to determine the exact extent of the guarantor's liability but allows the operation of the account in the ordinary manner so that further credits and debits are made against the account. When the bank later seeks to enforce the security a dispute will probably arise about the extent of the debts covered by the guarantee. The bank's argument will undoubtedly be that the guarantee extends to the full amount of the overdraft accumulated by the customer on the account, including amounts withdrawn after the account should have been frozen or ruled off, while the guarantor will seek to minimise his liability by arguing that his liability does not extend to amounts withdrawn after the expiration of the guarantee.

Alternatively, the issue of liability may arise, for example, on the retirement of a partner but where the partnership account continues to be operated in the normal way without a balance being struck to determine the liability of the retiring partner for the amount of the overdraft extended, by the bank, to the partnership. The bank's argument will be that the retiring partner is both collectively and individually liable for the full amount of the overdraft including any amounts extended by the bank after the partner's retirement, while the retiring partner will argue his liability is limited to the amount owing on the account up to and including the day of this retirement.

This issue of appropriation of payments where there is a continuous course of transactions was examined in *Devaynes* v *Noble* (*Clayton's* case)[41] where the courts established a common law presumption in respect of the distribution of monies from a bank account. The rule is based on the presumption that payments in and out of a bank account are presumed appropriated to debit and credits in the order in which the debts are incurred. The rule is based on the notion of first-in, first-out to determine the effect of payments from an account, and will normally apply in the absence of evidence of any other intention. The facts of the case were that Clayton had an account with a partnership, which carried on a banking business under the name of Devaynes, Dawes, Noble, and Co. The amount standing to the credit of Clayton's account on the death of one of the partners, Devaynes, when by law the partnership was dissolved was £1,717. However, the surviving partners continued the banking business and eventually the partnership business became bankrupt. Clayton sought to recover the credit balance due to him or from the deceased partner's estate. However, during the period intervening the death of the partner, Devaynes, and the bankruptcy of the banking firm, Clayton had withdrawn amounts in excess of the credit balance of £1,717 but had also paid to the credit of his account substantial sums so that the credit balance on his account, at the bankruptcy of the banking partnership, was in excess of £1,717. Clayton, therefore, sued the dead partner's, Devaynes', estate for the amount of the credit balance on his account at the time of the firm's bankruptcy. Grant MR held that the deceased partner's estate was not liable for debts incurred by the partnership in respect of money deposited by Clayton after the death of the partner, Devaynes. The money paid out to Clayton, or his order, had discharged the balance of the credit balance standing to the credit of Clayton's account at the death of the partner and his estate was therefore not liable for amounts standing to the credit

[41] (1816) 1 Mer. 572.

of his account on the bankruptcy of the partnership. The learned judge explaining the presumption in respect of running accounts held:

> In such a case, there is no room for any other appropriation than that which arises from the order in which the receipts and payments take place, and are carried into the account. Presumably, it is the sum first paid in, that is first drawn out. It is the first item on the debit side of the account, that is discharged, or reduced, by the first item on the credit side. The appropriation is made by the very act of setting the two items against each other. Upon that principle, all accounts current are settled, and particularly cash accounts. When there has been a continuation of dealings, in what way can it be ascertained whether the specific balance due on a given day has, or has not, been discharged, but by examining whether payments to the amount of that balance appear by the account to have been made? You are not to take the account backwards, and strike the balance at the head, instead of the foot, of it.

The rule in *Clayton's* case is based on a probable presumption of the intention of the parties and may be displaced by a different intention. There was no such clear intention in *Clayton's* case and in *Deeley v Lloyds Bank Ltd*[42] the House of Lords held that where a bank receives notice of an advance on the second mortgage, it will lose priority in respect of subsequent advances even though monies are paid to the credit of the account and are appropriated against the current indebtedness. In the *Deeley* case the bank obtained from its customer a first mortgage to secure an overdraft. It subsequently received notice of a second mortgage executed by the customer over the same property but the bank failed to freeze or rule off the balance as it then stood and the customer continued to operate the account in the ordinary manner. In the course of operating the account the amounts paid into the account by the customer were sufficient to pay off the balance of overdraft secured by the first mortgage. The customer then became overdrawn again and while the bank sought to argue that the further debit balance on the customer's account had priority for repayment by virtue of the first mortgage which extended not only to the amount of the original overdraft but also the later debit balance, the second mortgagee claimed he had priority to repayment of his loan over the second debit balance on the customer's account. The Court of Appeal, upholding Eve J, at first instance, held that the rule in *Clayton's* case had been displaced by the intention of the parties. Fletcher Moulton LJ criticised the recognition of a legal rule which the bank could circumvent by the 'simple formality of drawing two horizontal lines in their books and making believe to commence a new account'. The House of Lords overruled both the court at first instance and the Court of Appeal, and held that the rule in *Clayton's* case had not been displaced by the conduct of the parties. The Lords expressed the view that primarily the right to appropriate a payment to the credit of an account rests with the debtor (bank) but if he did not indicate an intention then the creditor ought to do so, and in the absence of a specific appropriation the position is governed by the rule in *Clayton's* case. Lord Shaw of Dumfermline expressed the view that if either the bank or creditor had intended to appropriate the payments made to the credit of the account after notification of the second mortgage, it should always rule off the account where the bank desires to preserve a security on which further advances cannot be charged. Lord Shaw then went on:

> After notice to the bank of a second mortgage by the customer, the debit is struck at the date of notice, and in the ordinary case, that is to say, where an account is merely continued without

[42] [1912] AC 756.

alteration, or where no specific appropriation of fresh payments is made, such payments are credited to the earliest items on the debit side of the account, and continue so to be credited until the balance secured under the first mortgage is extinguished.

The question of the nature of notice of the subsequent mortgage was examined in *Deeley v Lloyds Bank Ltd*[43] and while it is clear that it is not necessary to show that at the time of the subsequent advance, the first mortgagee has knowledge, i.e., actual awareness, of the second mortgagee's interest, it is sufficient for the second mortgagee to show notice, and not knowledge. The court expressed the view that it must be shown that actual notice of an advance having been on second mortgage must be given to the person or persons who represent the mind of the first mortgagee. In respect of money advanced by a bank the court held in *Hopkinson v Rolt*[44] that where a bank receives notice of an advance on a second mortgage, it will lose its priority in respect of subsequent advances even though the money is paid to the credit of the bank account and is appropriated against the current indebtedness. The rule in *Hopkinson* was explained in *Matzner v Clyde Securities Ltd*[45] as follows:

> a mortgagee to whom the property is mortgaged for advances already made cannot, after receiving notice of a second mortgage, have priority over the second mortgagee for further advances upon the first mortgage, even if the first mortgage, to the knowledge of the second mortgagee, is expressed to be a security for further advances that may be made.

The rule in *Clayton*'s case has also been applied in cases where the partnership firm is dissolved, instead of the bankruptcy situation. In *Royal Bank of Scotland v Christie*[46] a partner in a trading firm mortgaged his own land to secure advances made to the firm by its bank. At the date of the partner's death the partnership account was overdrawn but on his death the bank continued the account unbroken. The surviving partners paid into the account amounts which exceeded the overdraft and then withdrew even larger amounts, which left the partnership account overdrawn by a larger amount. The court held that the rule in *Clayton*'s case required payments made to the credit of the partnership account by the surviving partners be credited first against the earlier debit items so the payments credited to the account went towards paying off the overdraft on the account established during the lifetime of the deceased partner and thereby to that extent discharging the mortgage. In *Re Yeovil Glove Co Ltd*[47] a company created a mortgage over the whole of its assets by way of a floating charge to secure its existing and future indebtedness to the bank. The company went into liquidation within 12 months of the creation of the charge with the result that the charge was void except as security for 'cash paid to the company at the time of or subsequently to the creation of, and in consideration for, the charge'.[48] Applying the rule in *Clayton*'s case the Court of Appeal in *Re Yeovil* held that the floating charge was valid security for advances made by the bank after it was created, but not for earlier advances. However, because the company had paid amounts into its current account since the creation of the charge, those amounts went towards satisfying its existing indebtedness under the 'first-in, first-out' rule and the advances made since the creation of the floating charge were still owing and secured by the floating charge.

---

[43] [1912] AC 756.
[44] (1861) 9 HL Cas 514.
[45] [1975] 2 NSWLR 293.
[46] (1841) 8 Cl & F 214.
[47] [1965] Ch 148.
[48] Section 322(1) Companies Act 1948, now Insolvency Act 1986, s.245.

An alternative course of action would be for the bank to strike a balance on the account and then open a fresh account in the name of the customer.[49] The rule in *Clayton*'s case can be displaced in a number of circumstances:

1 In *Siebe Gorman & Co Ltd* v *Barclays Bank Ltd*[50] Slade J expressed the view that the opening of a fresh account displaces the rule in *Clayton*'s case and the learned judge then went on to recognise two further exceptions to the rule. He said the rule does not apply in respect of secured transactions where the second mortgagee agreed to the making of fresh advances by the first mortgagee and, further, the rule does not apply where the fresh advances are made under a contractual obligation arising under the mortgage deed.

2 The rule does not apply where there are competing beneficial interests to a particular fund. In *Commerzbank Akteingesellschaft* v *IBM Morgan Plc*[51] the applicant, a German bank, held two correspondent accounts at its London branch in the name of IBM Morgan plc, a stockbroking firm based in Lagos, Nigeria. The accounts were a US dollar account and a sterling account created to receive deposits from, or make payments in respect of, financial transactions for foreign banks around the world. On 9 May 2002 the Financial Investigation Unit of the City of London Police informed Commerzbank that the accounts were being used for fraudulent purposes and Commerzbank was told that any more transactions on these accounts would constitute money laundering and the bank was forbidden to act on any further instructions from IBM Morgan. Commerzbank had to decide what to do with the amounts standing to the credit of the accounts and how to deal with the competing claims to those funds. On 19 February 2003 Commerzbank sought relief by way of interpleader proceedings in accordance with the Civil Procedure Rules.[52] The balance on these accounts at the commencement of legal proceedings was $437,973.61 and £132,579.05 respectively. The purpose of the proceedings, therefore, was to allow the parties claiming on the money to interplead among themselves and for the court to determine title to the money. All the money deposited into the two accounts had been intermingled and it was impossible to identify any individual payment as corresponding to a particular transaction or party. Commerzbank received money from IBM Morgan to be paid into the accounts without any knowledge of the identity of the beneficiaries or individual customers and insofar as Commerzbank was concerned any such individuals were customers of IBM Morgan. The court held that invariably where there are competing beneficial interests it will consider the rule in *Clayton*'s case namely that the first payment in is also the first payment out, but the rule does not apply 'where it would be both impracticable and unjust to apply . . .'. Thus, for example where money is held in a common fund and the facts suggest a common intention, which arises either expressly or by implication that the rule in *Clayton*'s case will not apply, then the courts will give effect to that intention. However, where the evidence indicates that it would be impractical or too complicated to apply the rule in *Clayton*'s case then it should not be applied and the courts should adopt the approach in *Barlow Clowes* v *Vaughan*[53] where the claims far exceeded the size of the fund available for distribution. In that case Woolf LJ described the rule in *Clayton*'s case as

---

[49] *Royal Bank of Canada* v *Bank of Montreal* (1976) 67 DLR (3d) 755.
[50] [1979] 2 Lloyd's Rep. 142.
[51] [2004] EWHC 2771.
[52] RSC Order 17, rule 3, schedule 1 of the Civil Procedure Rules.
[53] [1992] 4 All ER 22 (CA).

a rule of 'convenience', which did not have to be applied, where it might lead to injustice or where it may result in an injustice. Woolf LJ in *Barlow Clowes* said that where the evidence suggested that the investors had intended or were deemed to have intended that the money be dealt with collectively then the rule in *Clayton*'s case should not be applied. The Court also concluded that, on the particular facts in *Barlow Clowes*, the North American solution – namely that credits to a bank account made at different times and from different sources are treated as a blend or cocktail, with the result that when a withdrawal is made from the account such withdrawals are treated as a withdrawal in the same proportions as the different interests in the account (here of the investors). Lindsay J in *Russell-Cooke Trust Co v Prentis*[54] referring to the judgments in *Barlow Clowes* said that it was evident that the rule in Clayton's case could be displaced 'by even a light counterweight' where Woolf LJ had expressed the view that 'the rule need only be applied when it is convenient to do so and when its application can be said to do broad justice having regard to the nature of the competing claims'. In *Russell-Cooke* the ownership of certain funds in a solicitor's account received from a number of investors had to be determined and the court concluded that the fund should be distributed rateably instead of on the basis of the 'first-in, first-out rule'.

3   The rule in *Clayton*'s case will not apply where a trustee pays trust money into his personal account and thereby mixes trust funds with his own funds. In *Re Hallett's Estate*[55] a solicitor who misappropriated funds from a client account and had them transferred into his personal account was deemed to withdraw his personal funds first. Thus, if a trustee misappropriates money belonging to the trust, the first amounts so deemed to be withdrawn by him will not be allocated to the discharge of the funds held on trust but towards the discharge of his own personal deposits, even if his personal funds were, in fact, made later in order of time. In such cases, the fiduciary is presumed to spend his own money first before misappropriating money from the trust. The rules of equity provide that if a fiduciary has mixed his own money with sums of trust money in a private account, withdrawals are attributed to his own money as far as possible.[56]

4   The first-in, first out rule does not apply to separate bank accounts even if maintained with the same bank. In *Bradford Old Bank Ltd v Sutcliffe*[57] a customer maintained both a loan account and a current account to which payments in were made. The court held that the guarantor on the loan account could not claim that amounts credited to the current account should be applied to reduce the amounts outstanding on the loan account and thereby reduce the amount outstanding on the guarantee.

5   In *Cory Brothers & Co Ltd v Owners of Turkish Steamship, The Mecca*[58] the court held that the rule in *Clayton*'s case does not apply where the parties have merely entered into a series of transactions without the existence of a current account, nor where it is clear from the circumstances that the creditor intended the right to reserve his right to appropriate payments to the credit of the account when necessary. It therefore follows that where the bank agrees not to apply the first-in, first-out rule the rule in *Clayton*'s case will not apply.

[54] [2003] 2 All ER 478.
[55] (1880) 13 ChD 696.
[56] *Re MacDonald* [1975] Qd R 255.
[57] [1918] 2 KB 833.
[58] [1897 AC 286.

In *Westminster Bank Ltd* v *Cond*[59] the court rejected the guarantor's argument that the bank intended to apply the first-in, first-out rule when the bank continued the account unbroken after making a demand on him and the loan should be treated as having been paid off by the subsequent payments into the account. In that case the guarantee form contained an express clause preventing the operation of the rule in *Clayton*'s case and the court give effect to that clause.

Combination of accounts

It is common for customers to maintain more than one account, sometimes with the same branch and sometimes with different branches of the same bank. Sometimes, the customer may maintain more than one account for his own convenience and the better management of his finances, for example a customer may have a savings account separate from an account which he uses to pay his household expenses and bills. In other circumstances, the customer may act in a fiduciary capacity as part of his professional activity and will be required to keep any client funds he manages separate from his personal funds: for example a solicitor, accountant or trustee will be required to keep client funds in accounts separate from his own.

Despite operating separate accounts for a customer, the bank may decide to treat all the customer's accounts as one and combine the balances to produce an overall single credit or debit balance payable to, or from, the customer. The bank may decide to combine the various accounts held by the customer to produce a single balance payable to, or from, the customer where the customer is either unable or unwilling to repay the overdraft on one of his accounts while at the same time maintaining a credit balance on another account. Prior to exercising the right of set-off the bank will determine if the customer is heading towards, or is in, financial difficulties[60] and where set-off is exercised the customer must be left with sufficient funds to meet his day-to-day living expenses and any priority debts that have been identified.[61] Although there are more involved classifications of set-off – legal, equitable, transactional, self-help etc. – ultimately a right of set-off is no use if it does not afford a defence if one party decides to sue. Other forms of set-off, for example, the banker's right to combine accounts or a contractual right of set-off, will ultimately be resolved by a right to defend against a claim for the full amount owing. Set-off can, therefore, operate in one of two ways:

1 It may be a defence relied on by a debtor when called on to pay by his creditor. In other words, the debtor avoids his obligation to repay a debt in full to the creditor because the creditor in turn owes money to the debtor. This may arise where the customer is bankrupt or insolvent and the bank is an unsecured creditor in respect of an overdraft. Thus, for example, the insolvent customer has an overdraft of £5,000 on a current account (account A) and at the same time has a credit balance of £10,000 (account B). If in the insolvency of the customer the bank were to hold the £10,000 for the administrators it would clearly be disadvantaged since the bank would then have to prove as an unsecured creditor for the £5,000 of the overdraft amount, along with the other creditors, and it is very unlikely to recover the full £5,000 due to it. Instead, if the bank were to exercise its right to combine

---

[59] (1940) 46 Com Cas 60.
[60] The Lending Code, March 2011, para. 169, http://www.lendingstandardsboard.org.uk/docs/lendingcode.pdf.
[61] The Lending Code, March 2011, para. 169, http://www.lendingstandardsboard.org.uk/docs/lendingcode.pdf.

the two accounts held for the customer the bank can set off the entire amount of the £5,000 overdraft and the credit balance so it is only accountable in the insolvency for the remaining £5,000. The bank will, therefore, recover the full amount of the £5,000 overdraft in priority to other secured and unsecured creditors. Insolvency set-off is mandatory, so attempts to contract out of it will fail, but any attempt to widen the scope of it is likely to involve an expropriation of assets, which should fall into the insolvent estate and will fail. In an insolvency situation the right to set-off is more a weapon than a defence because, for example, a bank can escape loss which it would otherwise suffer, particularly if it holds no security for an overdrawn account in view of the customer's inability to repay the overdraft because the bank can set off the amount of the overdraft against other credit balances held for the same customer.

2   On the other hand, a retail customer may draw a cheque or instruct payment to be made from his account in excess of the balance standing to the credit of his account, or where the payment instruction is in excess of his overdraft. The bank would clearly be entitled to dishonour the payment mandate but combining the balances on the two accounts may enable the bank to honour the payment mandate, which would otherwise have been dishonoured. The right to combine is based on the fact that regardless of the fact that a customer may have more than one account either with the same bank or with different branches of the same bank, nevertheless the relationship is governed by a single contract under which the bank is obliged to produce a single account balance and may exercise a right of set-off in respect of mutual dealings. Debts due to the customer are due from the bank as a legal entity and not from individual branches that may hold different accounts for the customer. On that basis the bank is therefore, in certain circumstances, permitted to combine the credit and debit balances to produce a single overall balance. In *Re European Bank, Agra Bank Claims*,[62] in the insolvency of the OC bank (customer) and the A & M bank (banker with whom OC maintained three separate accounts) the Court of Appeal held it would be wrong to treat the three accounts as distinct matters. James LJ said:

> It was only for convenience that the loan account was kept separately . . . In truth, as between banker and customer, whatever number of accounts are kept in books, the whole is really but one account, and it is not open to the customer, in the absence of some special contract, to say that the securities which he deposits are only applicable to one account.

A question of terminology

Whether the right to produce an overall balance in respect of the customer's accounts in law is a right to 'combine' accounts or a 'set-off' or 'lien' has been the subject of some debate in the courts and by academic writers, particularly as the terms have been rarely consistently used.

The bank has a common law right to combine two or more of the customer's accounts without notice to him, even if those accounts are maintained at different branches of the same bank. It is a common law right, which arises from the notion that, regardless of the number of accounts a customer has with a bank, there is only one banker and customer relationship and one debt between them. In other words, after combining the debits and credits across all

---

[62] (1872) LR 8 Ch App 41.

accounts maintained for a customer there is a single debt owed to the bank or by the bank to the other party. The right to combine may also arise under contract. A set-off arises in its simplest form where a number of parties owe debts to one other so that rather than each party paying the amount it owes, the debts are netted-off so that only one debt remains outstanding. A right of set-off exists in equity, in the context of insolvency, but may also arise under contract. In the context of lenders and financially troubled borrowers, the most relevant forms of set-off are statutory insolvency set-off and contractual set-off. The overall effect of combining accounts or setting off amounts is that the bank will produce a single debit or credit balance between them allowing settlement between them by the payment of a net balance. A lien on the other hand is the right to retain and, if necessary, sell assets or property belonging to another to pay off debts owed to the creditor.

In *National Westminster Bank Ltd* v *Halesowen Presswork and Assemblies Ltd*[63] the claimants maintained a current account, 'account no. 1', with the defendant bank, which was substantially overdrawn. In April 1968 a trading account was opened, known as 'account no. 2', and the defendant bank agreed that in the absence of any material changes in circumstances 'account no. 1' would remain frozen for four months. On 20 May the claimants convened a meeting of their creditors but the bank, having received notice of the meeting, decided to leave the arrangement in place. On 12 June, the claimants passed a voluntary resolution to have the company wound-up and on 19 June the bank informed the liquidator that it had decided to set off the credit balance on 'account no. 2' against the frozen overdrawn balance on 'account no. 1'. The bank sought to exercise its statutory right to set off the balances on the two accounts under s.21 of the Bankruptcy Act 1914 (now s.323 of the Insolvency Act 1986). The liquidator objected on the grounds that the bank was bound, by the April agreement, to keep the two accounts separate. At first instance the bank's right to combine the two accounts was upheld. Roskill J, at first instance, held that the bank's agreement to keep the two accounts separate terminated with the change of material circumstances, i.e. the voluntary resolution to wind up the company. He concluded that the bank has a right to set-off which he treated as a lien. The Court of Appeal, by a majority, reversed the judge at first instance. Denning and Winn LJJs said that set-off was not available to the bank because the two amounts to be set off lacked mutuality. Further, their Lordships held that since title passed to the bank, monies deposited to the customer's account became the money of the bank and the bank could not have a lien over its own money or property, particularly when it has possession, and use, of the property as in the case of a bank holding credit balances for customers. The customer retained a right to repayment on demand of the whole or part of the money. Their Lordships were unanimous in approving the view adopted by the Court of Appeal that the bank's right to combine the customer's accounts was to be distinguished from the lien and Lord Cross concluded that to describe the right to combine several of the customer's accounts as an example of a banker's lien amounted to a 'misuse of language'. However, there may be grounds for arguing that while a bank may not exercise a lien over the credit balances held by it there is the possibility that the bank may exercise a lien over the asset represented by the bank balance which would allow it to exercise a lien over any bank account held for a particular customer, regardless of the nature of the account, i.e. whether it is a fixed account with a maturity date some time in the future or a current account. On the basis of current judicial authority the bank's right to combine the balances

---

[63] [1972] AC 785.

of a customer's accounts is in reality a right of set-off and combination is merely a specialised term for a set-off particular to banks. In *Re K (Restraint Order)*[64] Otton J sought to distinguish a bank's right to combine accounts from a right to set-off on the ground that combining accounts involves the determination of the final balance due to a customer or vice versa. In reality, a set-off also involves the same exercise with an overall balance struck to settle accounts between the bank and customer.

The bank's right to combine accounts

The bank's right to combine accounts was explained in *Garnett v McKewan*[65] where it was held that the bank was justified in dishonouring cheques drawn on an account maintained with one branch of the bank which was in credit, while the customer was counterbalanced by a debit account held with a different branch of the same bank. The facts of the case were that the bank's customer was overdrawn on an account he maintained with the 'A branch' of the bank and when he failed to clear the overdraft the bank froze account. The customer therefore opened an account with the 'B branch' of the same bank and paid into it cheques to the credit of this account. The bank, without giving notice to the customer, combined the accounts thereby reducing the balance standing to the credit of his account with the 'B branch'. The customer continued to draw cheques against the balance of the account maintained with the 'B branch' but these were dishonoured on the basis of insufficient funds. The customer sued the bank for breach of contract and defamation. The court held the bank was entitled to combine the two accounts for its own purposes, unless there was an agreement to the contrary. The court relied on the view that while the customer may open several accounts with the same bank, there is in law only a single contract between the bank and its customer. Kelly CB thought it important that there was a course of mutual dealings between the bank and its customer and as the customer had the power to order the bank to transfer amounts from one account to another, so the bank has a similar right. However, Bramwell B raised some reservations regarding the right to combine accounts held with different branches when he said:

> [t]he bank is not liable to be called on to pay at one branch just because there is a balance at another. Why, then, may the bank without notice debit the customer's account at one branch with his deficiency on another.

The learned judge, however, went on to state that it was unrealistic to allow a customer overdrawn with one branch of the bank to draw up to the credit balance he may hold in an account with a different branch and no hardship is caused to the customer if his right to draw against the account in credit is limited to the overall net balance produced after the bank has combined the debit and credit entries on the two or more accounts. The customer is bound to know he has a number of accounts with the bank, some of which may be overdrawn, and he cannot ignore that fact when drawing against credit balances he may have on other accounts. This reasoning is more likely to apply when customers are more readily able to access account balances through a variety of different sources than simply await the statement of account.

[64] [1990] 2 QB 289.
[65] (1872) LR 8 Ex 10.

The principle was re-examined in *Greenwood Teale* v *Williams, Williams, Brown & Co*[66] where the senior partner of a firm of solicitors opened three accounts namely: an office account (Account A), a deposit account (Account B) and a personal account (Account C). The bank was initially informed that client funds would be paid to the credit of the deposit account (Account B) but this was subsequently closed and both the firm's money and client funds deposited in the office account (Account A). The personal account became substantially overdrawn and the bank sought to combine the two accounts. Wright J held that the bank had a right to combine the accounts but that right was subject to three exceptions:

1 The right to combine separate accounts may be overridden by express agreement.

2 The right to combine cannot be exercised where an amount is remitted to the bank and appropriated for a given purpose.

3 A bank cannot combine a customer's private account with one that is known to the bank to be a trust account or known by the bank to be used for activities undertaken by the customer as a trustee.

The mere fact that the account is described, as an office account does not make money deposited in such an account trust funds.

In *National Westminster Bank Ltd* v *Halesowen Presswork and Assemblies Ltd*[67] the House of Lords, overruling the Court of Appeal, allowed the bank to set off the balances so the bank was only liable to restore to the liquidator the credit balance on 'account no. 2', after it had exercised its right to set off the amount overdrawn on 'account no. 1'. Lords Denning and Winn also held that, having entered into an agreement not to combine the accounts, the bank was bound by that and would have to give notice to the customer if, on the material change of circumstances, it wished to exercise that right. However, Buckley LJ in his dissenting judgment, thought that the debts were mutual and that the agreement between the company and the bank did exclude the right to set off the balances. However, the right to set off accounts is clearly recognised and recent cases have reaffirmed that right. In *Re K (Restraint Order)*[68] the court held the bank could exercise its right to set off accounts without infringing a restraining order under the Drug Trafficking Offences Act 1986 and in *Hongkong and Shanghai Banking Corporation* v *Kloeckner and Co AG*[69] Hirst J rejected the argument that the rules relating to the autonomy of a letter of credit of necessity led to the conclusion that a set-off between bank accounts held by the same customer is not permitted. Any doubts regarding the principle of set-off in relation to bank accounts raised by Swift J in *WP Greenhalgh & Sons* v *Union Bank of Manchester*,[70] which rejected the possibility of any right to combine two or more bank accounts of the same customer, have long been settled. However, while such doubts remained banks attempted to preserve their rights to combine accounts by taking letters of set-off signed by customers relying on credit balances for borrowing on other accounts although in *Midland Bank Ltd* v *Reckitt*[71] Lord Atkin cast doubt on how such a document increased the bank's rights to set-off.

---

[66] (1894) 11 TLR 56.
[67] [1975] QB654.
[68] [1990] 2 QB 298.
[69] [1990] 2 QB 514.
[70] [1924] 2 KB 153.
[71] [1933] AC 1.

Does the bank have to give notice of its intention to combine accounts?

The question of whether a bank is required to give notice to the customer of its intention to combine accounts was considered in *Garnett v M'Kewan*[72] where the court unanimously answered the question in the negative. Kelly CB said:

> In general it might be proper or considerate to give notice to that effect, but there is no legal obligation on the bankers to do, arising either from express contract or the course of dealing between the parties.

A different conclusion may however be reached where the bank enters into an agreement not to combine the accounts, or where such an agreement can be implied from the circumstances. In *Buckingham & Co v London and Midland Bank Ltd*[73] the plaintiff had current and loan accounts with the defendant bank, with the latter account secured against his house. The bank manager had the property re-surveyed and decided that the amount of the loan granted to the customer should be reduced. The bank, therefore, set off the credit balances on the current account against the loan account without giving notice to the customer. Consequently, cheques drawn by the customer against the current account were dishonoured and the customer challenged the bank's right to set-off. The jury found that there was a consistent course of dealings established between the bank and customer, which allowed the customer to draw cheques against the current account without regard to the state of the loan account.[74] However, an agreement not to combine separate accounts held by the customer may be displaced by reasonable notice or subsequent events that affect the banker and customer relationship, for example where there is a substantial change in the customer's circumstances, for example the customer becomes insolvent. In *British Guiana Bank v OR*[75] the Court recognised that an agreement to keep balances on different accounts separate will normally terminate if there is a material change in the customer's circumstances, for example where he becomes insolvent. However, in *Direct Acceptance Corporation v Bank of NSW*[76] a company account that was heavily overdrawn was frozen by the bank and a separate account opened, 'account no. 2', for current banking activities. Soon afterwards a debenture holder appointed a receiver over the company's assets and the bank sought to combine the two accounts to enable it to set off the credit balance in 'account no. 2' against the overdraft in the frozen account. The liquidator challenged the right of the bank to combine the accounts and sought to recover the full credit balance on 'account no. 2'. Macfarlan J concluded that the agreement was that the main account should be frozen by the bank and there should not be a right to set off the credit balance of 'account no. 2' against the debit balance in the main account. He expressed the view that the agreement to keep the accounts was dependent on the intention of the parties and that agreement remained in effect despite the insolvency of the customer and the appointment of a receiver. He further concluded that there was nothing to indicate 'that the agreement was to continue in operation only so long as the accounts . . . were current'. Significantly, Marfarlan J also said 'I cannot accept that when a receiver and manager is appointed, a current account necessarily ceases to be a current account . . .'.

---

[72] (1872) LR 8 Ex 10.
[73] (1895) 12 TLR 70.
[74] See also *Bradford Old Bank Ltd v Sutcliffe* [1918] 2 KB 833.
[75] (1911) 104 LT 754.
[76] (1968) 88 WN (NSW) (Pt 1) 498.

Since the appointment of a receiver does not necessarily mean that the company's business activities are terminated and the company may, in fact, continue to trade, his appointment does not necessarily affect the 'current' nature of the bank accounts. A different conclusion may be reached where, however, a winding-up petition is presented and where the company's trading activities are restricted to realising its assets specifically for the purposes of the company's liquidation, and the agreement to hold separate accounts may be affected by a material change in the customer's circumstances. In *National Westminster Bank Ltd v Halesowen Presswork and Assemblies Ltd*[77] the court concluded that the winding-up petition amounted to a material change in the customer's circumstances and thereby allowed the bank to combine the accounts in question. Furthermore, the court also recognised that the agreement restricting the bank's right to combine the accounts was, in any event, for a limited period.

Does notice have to be given before the bank exercises its right to combine accounts?

In *Garnett v M'Kewan*[78] the court expressed the view that the bank may combine separate accounts held for the same customer without giving notice of its intention to exercise its right. By contrast, in *Buckingham Co v London and Midland Bank*[79] the jury decided that the customer was entitled to reasonable notice if the bank decided to cancel the arrangement with him and the latter was entitled to draw cheques on the current account without regard to the loan account. However, even if the bank has entered into an agreement to give notice to the customer before exercising its right to combine accounts the right to receive notice may be superseded by circumstances.[80]

A period of notice could in fact defeat any advantage purportedly gained by the bank through its exercise of its right to combine credit and debit balances held for the customer. A customer who receives notice of the bank's intention to combine a debit and credit balance held under two separate accounts under his name may withdraw the credit balance on notice being given and thereby defeat the bank's purpose in combining the accounts. In *National Westminster Bank Ltd v Halesowen Presswork and Assemblies Ltd*[81] Viscount Dilhorne expressed the view that if the bank had decided to combine the accounts following the customer's decision to convene a meeting of the creditors, notice of the decision to combine the accounts would probably be required. Lord Cross of Chelsea expressed the view that:

> The choice . . . lies between a notice taking immediate effect and no notice at all. On any footing the bank would be obliged to honour cheques drawn up to the limit of the apparent credit balance before the company became aware that the bank was consolidating the accounts and so it might be said that notification to the customer was a condition precedent to the exercise by the bank of its right to consolidation but only a measure of precaution which the bank might take to end its liability to honour cheques.

It might, therefore, be argued that the notice of its intention to combine the customer's account is merely a precaution the bank may undertake so it does not end up in dispute with

[77] [1972] AC 785.
[78] (1872) LR 8 Ex 10.
[79] (1895) 12 TLR 70.
[80] *British Guiana Bank v OR* (1911) 104 LT 754.
[81] [1972] AC 785.

the customer regarding wrongful dishonour of a payment mandate but following *Garnett v M'Kewan*[82] and the *Halesowen*[83] cases the bank is not obliged to give notice of its intention to combine accounts; indeed it may decide not give notice in order to protect its interests.

The issue of whether the bank is under an obligation to honour cheques drawn by the customer but not yet presented for payment was explored by Lord Cross in *Halesowen*[84] where he expressed the view that the bank should at the very least honour those cheques drawn by the customer up to the time he was given notice of the combination of the accounts. The Lending Code provides that when a lender is 'actively considering or is likely to exercise set-off' it should inform the customer in 'clear and simple language the generic circumstances in which set-off would be used and when'.[85] Whether the courts actually interpret this clause of the Lending Code as a binding obligation and enforceable against the bank will not only depend on how the courts give effect to the rest of the Code but also the consequences of the clause. The effect of the combination of accounts is that the bank is allowed to strike a balance between credit and debit balances on different accounts maintained by the customer: the consequence of this is that the bank effectively terminates the account and banker and customer relationship without giving reasonable notice as normally required.[86]

Limitations on the bank's right to combine accounts

A number of cases have examined restrictions to the right of the bank to set off credit balances where the customer maintains more than one account with the bank. However, Macatta J examined the limitations to the bank's right of set-off in *Barclays Bank Ltd* v *Okenarhe*[87] as follows:

1   The bank does not have a right to combine accounts maintained by one person but in two different capacities, for example where the customer maintains a personal account and a trust account.[88] However, in *Union Bank of Australia Ltd* v *Murray-Aynsley*[89] the Privy Council held that where there are several accounts in the name of the same customer with a bank, but the customer does not make it clear to the bank and the bank does not know which of those accounts is a trust account, the bank is entitled to combine all the accounts.

2   The right to combine accounts is abrogated if there is an express or implied agreement not to combine the accounts. In *Re European Bank*[90] James LJ giving judgment said:

> In truth, as between banker and customer, whatever number of accounts are kept in the books, the whole is really but one account, and it is not open to the customer, in the absence of some special contract, to say that the securities which he deposits are only applicable to one account.

[82] (1872) LR 8 Ex 10.
[83] [1972] AC 785.
[84] [1972] AC 785.
[85] Lending Code, March 2011, http://www.lendingstandardsboard.org.uk/docs/lendingcode.pdf.
[86] See Chapter 7.
[87] [1966] 2 Lloyd's Rep 87.
[88] *Garnett* v *M'Kewan* (1872) LR 8 Ex. 10.
[89] [1898] AC 693.
[90] (1872) LR 8 Ch App Cas 41.

In *Bradford Old Bank Ltd* v *Sutcliffe*[91] set-off was not permissible where the bank had specifically agreed that the two accounts would be kept separate so that the credit balance on a current account could not be used to reduce liability against a loan account. Pickford and Bankes LJJ[92] mentioned that in their view it was clear on the facts that, by arrangement between the bank and the customer concerned, the two accounts in question were to be kept distinct. Lord Justice Scrutton[93] put the matter in a slightly different way and he expressed the view that:

> The first point argued appears to involve a misunderstanding of the relation of loan and current accounts. The funds paid into the current account are appropriated by the customer to that account, and cannot be used by the bank in discharge of the loan account without the consent of the customer. No customer could otherwise have any security in drawing a cheque on his current account if he had a loan account greater than his credit balance on current account. The £3,400 debit balance on loan account cannot be treated as discharged by subsequent payments into the current account.

In *Buckingham and Co* v *London and Midland Bank Ltd*[94] the bank had no right to combine a secured loan account with a current account and in *Re E.J. Morel (1934) Ltd*[95] the court recognised a limited right to combine the accounts.

If money is deposited with a bank for a special purpose the bank cannot combine the accounts. In *W.P. Greenhalgh and Sons* v *Union Bank of Manchester*[96] the court held that the bank had no right to combine the accounts because it had knowledge of the ultimate destination of the proceeds of certain bills deposited by the customer. Similarly, in *Barclays Bank Ltd* v *Quistclose Investments Ltd*[97] the House of Lords held that the bank could not claim a set-off when money was paid into an account for a specific purpose, for example the payment of a dividend, even where that purpose had failed due to the liquidation of the company. The money did not become part of the debtor's estate and set-off was therefore not permitted. In *Bieber* v *Teathers Ltd (In Liquidation)*[98] the critical issue was whether certain subscription monies remained trust monies when they were paid from an HSBC account opened to receive such funds into the partnership account. The Court of Appeal held that the claim based on a Quistclose trust in respect of the monies once paid into the partnership account could not be maintained once the partnership was in existence and the investors' subscriptions had been paid into the partnership account. The monies belonged to the partnership and vested in the general partners as joint legal owners. Each investor's beneficial ownership of his individual subscription then ceased and was replaced with a right to participate in the profits of the partnership and in its net assets on dissolution as specified in the partnership deed.

3 Combination is not possible for contingent liabilities. In *Jeffryes* v *Agra and Masterman's Bank Ltd*[99] a customer who was indebted to the bank handed to it certain bank receipts issued by another bank representing deposits lodged with that other bank.

---

[91] [1918] 2 KB 833.
[92] [1918] 2 KB 833 at pp. 839 and 843.
[93] 1918] 2 KB 833 p. 847.
[94] (1895) 12 TLR 70.
[95] [1962] Ch 21.
[96] [1924] 2 KB 153.
[97] [1970] AC 567.
[98] [2013] 1 B.C.L.C. 248 (CA (Civ Div)).
[99] (1866) LR 2 Eq 674.

4 More recently, the courts have recognised that set-off is not available where there is any doubt about the identity of the account holder. In *Bhogal* v *Punjab National Bank*[100] it was held that the right to set-off in respect of funds held in different accounts depends on the accounts belonging to the same person and in *Uttamchandani* v *Central Bank of India*[101] the Court of Appeal held that:

> Set-off has never been allowed save where the accounts are of the same customer, held in the same name, and in the same right. Even then the right of set-off may be excluded by agreement express or implied. What is unusual about the present case is that the bank is seeking to set off accounts held in different names.

The courts will not permit the bank to exercise a right to combine or set off accounts unless the accounts are held for the same customer and even then the right to combine the accounts may be excluded by express or implied agreement.

Special rules relating to insolvency

The commonest use of the right to combine accounts probably occurs where the customer becomes bankrupt or insolvent. The statutory right of set-off is mandatory once the customer has gone into liquidation and any wider rights of set-off agreed between the parties under contract will not be enforceable in the insolvency. Such contractual agreements may have the effect of widening the rights of set-off to the detriment of the general creditors and are therefore held as contrary to public policy and unenforceable.[102] Nevertheless the statutory right of set-off is fairly broad and extends to the rights of value and set-off against liabilities which are merely contingent as at the date of the insolvency,[103] for example a bank which has issued a guarantee or letter of credit at the customer's request is likely to be able to exercise set-off representing the level of any such demand.

The right to set off in such circumstances exists not merely under the common law but is reinforced by statute. Statutory set-off therefore refers to the bank's right to combine accounts under s.323 of the Insolvency Act 1986, previously s.31 of the Bankruptcy Act 1914. Section 323 of the Insolvency Act 1986 provides:

1 This section applies where before the commencement of the bankruptcy there have been mutual credits, mutual debts or other mutual dealings between the bankrupt and any creditor of the bankrupt proving or claiming to prove for a bankruptcy debt.

2 An account shall be taken of what is due from each party to the other in respect of the mutual dealings and the sums due from one party shall be set off against the sums due from the other.

3 Sums due from the bankrupt to another party shall not be included in the account taken under subsection (2) above if that other party had notice at the time they became due that a bankruptcy petition relating to the bankrupt was pending.

---

[100] [1988] 2 All ER 296.
[101] (1989) 139 NLJ.
[102] *British Eagle International Airlines Ltd* v *Cie Nationale Air France* [1975] 2 All ER 390.
[103] *Re Charge Card Services Ltd* [1987] Ch 150.

4   Only the balance (if any) of the account taken under subsection (2) above shall be provable as a bankruptcy debt or, as the case may be, be paid to the trustee as part of the bankrupt's estate.

Section 31 of the Bankruptcy Act 1914 provided as follows:

Where there have been mutual credits, mutual debts or other mutual dealings, between a debtor against whom a receiving order shall be made under this Act and any other person proving or claiming to prove a debt under the receiving order, an account shall be taken of what is due from the one party to the other in respect of such mutual dealings, and the sum due from the one party shall be set off against any sum due from the other party, and the balance of the account, and no more shall be claimed or paid on either side respectively; but a person shall not be entitled under this Section to claim the benefit of any set-off against the property of a debtor in any case where he had, at the time of giving credit to the debtor, notice of an act of bankruptcy committed by the debtor and available against him.

The statutory set-off requires 'mutual dealings' between the parties, including 'mutual credits, mutual debts or other mutual dealings'. This essentially means that the demands must be between the same parties and that each party should be debtor and creditor in the same capacity. It would not be just or equitable if cross-demands were set off in equity unless there is mutuality. In its simplest form, mutuality means that A can sue B and B can sue A. Instead, if the circumstances are such that A can sue B and B can sue C, it would not normally be equitable that the demands are allowed to be set off, because this would mean that A's asset (the claim against B) would be used to pay C's liability. This would include the situation in which A and C are related entities, for example parent and subsidiary companies. In equity, their relationship would not justify the use of A's claim to pay C's debt through a set-off. Buxton LJ said in *Muscat v Smith*[104] that the cross-claim must be against the original claimant and in *R. (on the Application of Burkett)* v *London Borough of Hammersmith and Fulham*[105] Brooke LJ, said:

It is of course the case that A, when sued by B, cannot set-off against B a debt or liability owed to A by C, however close in fact, as opposed to in law, the relationship between the three parties may be.

In *National Westminster Bank* v *Halesowen Presswork and Assemblies Ltd*,[106] dealing with the earlier provision under s.31 of the Bankruptcy Act 1914, the House of Lords examined the question of whether dealings between the defendant bank and the claimants were mutual and Lord Simon of Glaisdale agreed with earlier authorities[107] which had expressed the view that dealings between the parties would cease to be mutual if the payments were made for a special or specific purpose. He took the view that every payment of money is for a specific or special purpose in the ordinary sense of those words and something else is required to take the transaction out of the concept of mutual dealings. He then went on to define the concept of 'mutual dealings' as follows:

---

[104] [2004] HLR 6.
[105] [2004] EWCA Civ 1342.
[106] [1972] AC 785.
[107] *Re Pollitt, ex parte Minor* [1893] 1 QB 455; *Re Mid-Kent Fruit Factory* [1896] 1 Ch 567; *Re City Equitable Fire Insurance Co Ltd* [1930] 2 Ch 293.

. . . money is paid for a special (or specific) purpose so as to exclude mutuality of dealing within section 31 if money is paid in such circumstances that it would be a misappropriation to use it for any other purpose than that for which it is paid.

The House of Lords concluded that the dealings between the bank and the claimants were mutual as the agreement not to combine the accounts was effective for a limited period only and so long as the customer's circumstances remained materially unchanged.

Further, after reviewing the authorities, Viscount Dilhorne, in *Halesowen*, came to the conclusion that it was not possible to contract out of s.31 and that the word 'shall' in the section meant that set-off was mandatory. However that view is clearly *obiter*; because he went on to say that, even if he was wrong on the point, and it was possible to contract out of the section, the express agreement between the bank and the company did not allow the parties to contract out of the section and therefore did allow the set-off.[108] However, the wording of s.323 of the Insolvency Act 1986 supports this view and while it does not specifically refer to the right of set-off it provides 'an account shall be taken of what is due from each party to the other'. It therefore means that a trustee in bankruptcy will set off debts in the bankruptcy of parties regardless of any agreement between them. Lord Cross came to the opposite conclusion that the word 'shall' was intended to give the creditor (bank) a definite right of set-off as opposed to giving s.31 mandatory effect. Section 323 of the Insolvency Act 1986 supports the view that the right to set-off is mandatory and provides that an account shall be taken of what is due from each party. Where the bank is therefore a creditor of an overdrawn account but holds another account which has a credit balance in favour of the customer then allowing the bank a statutory set-off will defeat or delay the right of other creditors, many of whom might only have become creditors of the bankrupt customer because the bank allowed the customer to trade by extending overdraft facilities. This really is a case of the bank having its cake and eating it.

A question, which was not explored in *Halesowen*, was whether allowing a right of set-off amounts to a voidable preference under s.239 (insolvency of companies) or s.340 (bankruptcy of a person) of the Insolvency Act 1986. Where a preference is given to a creditor within the 'relevant time' the court has the power to set aside the transaction if the debtor was desirous of conferring a benefit on the creditor.

Conclusion

The rights of the customer to an overdraft facility is clearly at the discretion of the bank. The bank will make a business decision depending on the perceived ability of the customer to repay the overdraft, generally on demand. Where the customer is overdrawn the bank has various remedies which allow it priority of repayment even where the overdraft is unsecured; clearly an enormous benefit to the bank where the customer becomes insolvent or bankrupt and one of the special examples of the banker and customer relationship.

---

[108] See *British Eagle International Airlines Ltd* v *Cie Nationale Air France* [1975] 2 All ER 390 where the House of Lords held that once the customer goes into liquidation the set-off is mandatory.

Further reading

➤ Shea, T. (1986) 'Statutory set-off', 1(3) *Journal of International Banking Law*, 152–161.
This article considers the right to statutory set-off available under s.31 of the Bankruptcy Act 1914 which was replaced by s.332 of the Insolvency Act 1986. This article considers the development of the case law in this area and examines the differences between the old and new provisions.

➤ Collins, N. (2005) 'Tracing: Clayton's case and its exceptions', 11(9) *Trusts & Trustees* 28–29.
This article examines the Chancery Division judgment in *Commerzbank Aktiengesellschaft* v *IMB Morgan Plc* on whether the rule of first in, first out for distributing the funds of frozen bank accounts, established in *Re Clayton*'s case, applied where the accounts were set up to be managed collectively by a single stockbroking company. Outlines the tests identified by the judge for establishing a proprietary claim to the funds. Considers the implications of the decision for the future application of the *Re Clayton*'s case rule.

➤ Pawlowski, M. (2003) 'The demise of the rule in Clayton's case, Case Comment', 339 *Conveyancer and Property Lawyer*.
This article discusses the High Court ruling in *Russell-Cooke Trust Co* v *Prentis (No.1)* on the applicability of the rule in *Clayton*'s case and the method for determining ownership of funds in a secured property investment plan. This article further considers criticisms of the rule in *Clayton*'s case, with particular regard to the Court of Appeal decision in *Barlow Clowes International Ltd (In Liquidation)* v *Vaughan*, and notes the diminishing application of the rule.

➤ Bethell-Jones, R. (1994) 'Contracting out of set-off rights', 9(10) *Journal of International Banking Law*, 428–430.
This article considers the validity of the decision that it is not possible to contract out of set-off rights in insolvency in the context of the Bank of England requirements of debt subordination.

➤ McCracken, S. (1994) 'The distinction between combination and set-off: problems of terminology and substance under the banking contract', 9(2) *BJIB & FL*, 68–78.
This article examines the bank's ability to apply the credit balance on the account of a customer against the debit balance on another account of the same customer and pay him only the difference between the two accounts.

➤ Berg, A. (1996) 'Case Comment: Contracting out of set-off in a winding up', 1(Feb) *LMCLQ*, 49–57.
This article considers whether mandatory set-off in bankruptcies or winding up can be waived or excluded.

10 Bills of exchange

Chapter overview

The aim of this chapter is to:

➤ Examine the nature and scope of negotiable instruments as a vehicle for settling debts owed to third parties.

➤ Examine the requirements of the Bills of Exchange Act 1882 including the creation of a negotiable instrument, the rights and liabilities of the parties, and the unique position of the holder in due course.

Introduction

BANKING LAW IN PRACTICE

Negotiable instruments are transferable documents that embody an obligation on the part of one person to pay money to another. As such they take the place of cash. The oldest form of negotiable instrument is the bill of exchange which, in essence, is a document by which one person (the drawer) requires the drawee (often the bank) to make payment to a third party (the payee). If the drawee adds his signature to the bill he signifies his acceptance of the drawer's order and becomes known as the acceptor. The addition of the drawer's signature also places the acceptor under a primary liability to make payment on the instrument. Bills of exchange are sometimes known as 'drafts'. A bill of exchange gives rise to autonomous obligations, separate from any underlying contract under which the debt is owed, which derive from the drawing of the bill or the acceptance of the bill.[1] Bills of exchange were widely used as a payment mechanism in connection with commercial transactions, particularly the finance of international trade. Bills of exchange, other than cheques, are now rarely used in domestic trade and transactions.

➡

---

[1] *Nova (Jersey) Knit Ltd v Kammgarn Spinnerei GmbH* [1977] 1 WLR 713 at 732G; *Cardinal Financial Investments Corp. v Central Bank of Yemen* [2001] 1 Lloyds Rep. 1, para. 7.

In international commercial transactions the drawer, for example A, of a bill of exchange will be a buyer of goods, carrying on business in a country different from the seller (for example B in whose favour the instrument will be drawn), and the drawee (usually the bank) will be a person or entity who by arrangement with the buyer (A), is willing to pay the purchase price of the goods to the seller (B). However, the central characteristic of a bill of exchange is that such instruments are usually negotiable instruments, i.e., the payee (i.e. B) has the right to transfer the bill in favour of a third party by mere endorsement. This will enable the seller (B), where payment is not immediately due under the bill, to sell his rights under the bill, normally at a discount, to obtain access to immediate cash rather than wait for the date of maturity of the bill, in order to receive payment. The person, who has the right to demand payment on the bill, whether that is the original payee or a subsequent endorsee, is known as the holder. The seller's (payee's) ability to transfer the bill is enhanced by the rules which allow the transferee to take free from defects of title, including the seller's own title, and thereby acquire the rights of the holder in due course, so long he takes free from notice of the defect and has given consideration. Further, a claim by the seller (A) would succeed in his capacity as payee under the bill of exchange whereas an action for the sale price of the goods may fail. In other words, the courts will only deal with the instrument and the rights represented under that instrument, rather than become involved in disputes relating to the underlying contract of sale.

Use of bills of exchange

Bills of exchange were for centuries not only the main method of payment in international trade but also for traders in different cities. Other forms of speedier and more secure methods of payment have superseded them. However, they remain important in trade with a number of countries, for example in Africa, the Indian subcontinent and the Pacific. They are also used in Germany. They are frequently used in relation to payment under a letter of credit.

Sources of law

The law on bills of exchange developed as part of the law merchant (i.e. the system of rules recognised and adopted by traders) but it was codified by the Bills of Exchange Act 1882. Although the older pre-1882 Act cases may help to resolve difficult points, the House of Lords in *Bank of England* v *Vagliano Brothers*[2] emphasised that cases prior to the Act should not normally be necessary. While the provisions of the Bills of Exchange Act 1882 have been widely adopted in common law jurisdictions, the UK does not subscribe to any international conventions dealing with the law on negotiable instruments or bills of exchange. It has not, as yet, subscribed to the 1998 UNCITRAL Convention on International Bills of Exchange, although banks often incorporate the provisions of Uniform Rules for Collections.[3]

---

[2] [1891] AC 107.
[3] ICC No 522, 1995, published by the Commission on Banking Technique and Practice of the ICC.

The cheque as a negotiable instrument

The cheque serves a dual purpose in the payment process in that a customer who holds a current account accompanied by a chequebook can withdraw amounts from his account by means of cheques drawn in his favour.[4] In such a situation the cheque will be drawn in favour of 'self' or 'cash' and it will enable the customer to draw cash at the branch where the account is kept, or if backed by a debit card from any branch of the same or another bank. Alternatively, the cheque may be used to pay a third party to whom the customer (drawer) owes money. In such a situation the cheque will be drawn in favour of a creditor (payee) and delivered to him. The drawing of the cheque serves as a mandate or instruction to the bank to credit the payee's account with the specified amount. Payment by the bank will, therefore, discharge the drawer of the cheque to the value for which the cheque is drawn. Payment by the bank to the named payee also serves to discharge the bank's liability to the customer for the amount paid to the third party in accordance with the drawer's mandate.

Although negotiable instruments, in general, allow title in the instrument to be transferred to a third party, the Cheques Act 1957 prevents the endorsement of such instruments so that only the named payee is entitled to receive payment against it.

Definition of a bill of exchange

Section 3(1) of the Bills of Exchange Act 1882 defines a bill of exchange as follows:

> A bill of exchange is an unconditional order in writing, addressed by one person to another, signed by the person giving it, requiring the person to whom it is addressed to pay on demand or at a fixed or determinable future time a sum certain in money to or to the order of a specified person, or to bearer.

An instrument which does not comply with these conditions is not a bill of exchange. Thus, a promissory note that involves a straightforward promise from A to B to make payment without the involvement of a third party is not a bill of exchange.

The drawing of a bill of exchange

The statutory definition of a bill of exchange refers to a number of constituent elements all of which must be present for a bill of exchange to be valid. In practice the vast majority of bills, especially cheques, are drawn on standard pre-printed forms which help with the compliance requirements of the Bills of Exchange Act 1882. However, there are obviously certain aspects of the instrument which only the drawer or endorser can complete. The Bills of Exchange Act 1882 provides that for the bill to be valid it must comply with the requirements described under the following eight subheadings.

---

[4] In reality customers are more likely to use a debit card to withdraw cash from their account for personal use.

1 Must be in writing

The bill must be written and that includes typing or printing.[5] The Act envisages a document, or some physical object capable of delivery, so what is essential is that the document is in a written form, which will most commonly be paper, although that is not essential for a valid bill of exchange.[6] In *Roberts & Co v Marsh National Bank of Abu Dhabi*[7] instruments were 'scrip' cheques, that is, blank 'house' cheques kept by a gambling club, and drawn as required on an account of the customer.

The Report of the Review Committee on Banking Services[8] recommended a system whereby negotiable instruments could be created in non-paper form and where the obligations under the instrument could be recorded at a central registry in an electronic or 'dematerialised' form.[9] The government White Paper,[10] in response to the Jack Report, contained proposals to give instruments in a dematerialised form the same status as negotiable instruments but the proposal has not, to date, been implemented. The Electronic Communications Act 2000 allows a minister to modify, by statutory instrument, any enactment for the purpose of authorising the use of electronic communications or electronic storage for doing anything which is required by the enactment to be done in writing. However, no changes have been made to s.3 of the Bills of Exchange Act 1882.

2 Must be an order

The instrument must be an unequivocal mandate ordering the bank to make payment. Thus, a request on the instrument in the form 'You will oblige your humble servant . . .'[11] was held to be a mere request for payment and not a demand to make payment. However, the older authorities are, at times, difficult to reconcile and in *Ruff v Webb*[12] the court expressed the view that the mere use of polite language does not deprive words which are clearly intended to be an order of those characteristics. In *Ruff v Webb* the court, therefore, concluded that the words 'A will much oblige B by paying C 20 guineas' does not deprive the words of their instructive meaning. The modern, standard, pre-printed forms of negotiable instruments, for example cheques, normally have the word 'Pay. . . .' printed on them so the nature of the mandate is clear. It is probable that the modern courts would examine the instrument as a whole to determine whether it is intended to be a negotiable instrument and hold it as valid merely because the wording, while clearly intended to be an instruction, uses a polite form of words.

---

[5] Bills of Exchange Act 1882, s.2 and Interpretation Act 1978, schedule 1.

[6] See A.P. Herbert's fictitious case of *Board of Inland Revenue v Haddock* which related to a cheque written on a cow: Herbert (1935) 'The Negotiable Cow', *Uncommon Law*.

[7] [2008] 1 CLC 399.

[8] Jack (1989) The Report of the Review Committee on Banking Services (Chairman Professor R.B. Jack), HMSO, Cm. 622 paras 8.33–8.8.40.

[9] Jack (1989) Banking Services: Law and Practice, Report by the Review Committee Chaired by Professor R.B. Jack, CBE, London Cm. 622, commissioned Professor Shea to examine the law relating to negotiable instruments (other than cheques) and to recommend changes. His report is published as Appendix A to the Jack Report and contains a discussion of the Act as it applies to modern commercial conditions and possible changes to the law.

[10] Jack (1989) Banking Services: Law and Practice, Report by the Review Committee Chaired by Professor R.B. Jack, CBE, London Cm. 622, paras 6.9–6.10.

[11] See: *Ellison v Collingridge* (1850) 9 CB 570; *Little v Slackford* (1828) M & M 171.

[12] (1794) 1 Esp. 129.

3 Must be unconditional

A negotiable instrument, including a cheque, must be an 'unconditional order' and the Act provides that an 'instrument expressed to be payable on a contingency is not a bill, and the happening of the event does not cure the defect.'[13] Story[14] explains that the reason for this requirement is that it would greatly prejudice commercial transactions 'of mankind and diminish and narrow their credit and negotiability, if paper securities of this kind were issued into the world encumbered with conditions, and if the person to whom they were offered in negotiation were obliged to enquire when those uncertain events would be reduced to a certainty'.

Conditions or contingencies which would invalidate the bill may be of any type but if they are addressed to the drawee bank and place it under an obligation to verify a state of affairs or that the condition has been fulfilled the instrument is no-longer 'unconditional'. Thus, for example where the drawee bank is mandated to pay only if some other obligation of the drawer, or another party, has been performed then that would invalidate the bill. It was common practice for certain forms of government cheques, for example those issued by Social Security,[15] to require a receipt form printed on either the front or back of the cheque to be signed. If the order requiring the receipt to be signed placed the bank under an obligation to ensure that the receipt was signed, then the cheque was a conditional instrument, but if the direction was addressed to the payee alone then that did not render the cheque conditional. Thus, in *Bavins Junior and Sims London and South Western Bank Ltd*[16] the court concluded that an instrument drawn 'Pay to B Bavins the sum of sixty-nine pounds provided the receipt at the foot hereof is duly signed, stamped and dated' was a conditional order and therefore not a negotiable instrument. The instruction at the receipt, requiring the signature of the payee, was addressed to the drawee bank, and therefore rendered the negotiable instrument conditional but where the instruction to sign the receipt is not addressed to the payee the payment mandate remains unconditional. In both *Nathan v Ogdens Ltd*[17] and *Thairlwall v Great Northern Railway Co*[18] it was held that instructions contained at the foot of each instrument did not render them conditional. In *Nathan* a cheque was drawn in the normal format but at the foot were printed the words 'the receipt at the back hereof must be signed. . . .'. The Court held that the instrument remained unconditional despite the clause at the foot of the instrument because the request at the bottom of the signature was addressed to the payee and not the bank. The distinction between the *Bavins* and *Nathan* cases is based on to whom the instruction for the signature of the receipt is addressed.

Generally, if the direction to obtain the payee's signature appears above the space intended for the drawer's signature then the words form part of the instruction to the bank and qualify the payment mandate, but if they appear underneath the drawer's signature then the words are incidental to the payment mandate and addressed merely to the payee so the drawee bank may disregard them. In the *Thiarlwall* case the insertion at the foot of the cheque

---

[13] Bills of Exchange Act 1882, s.11.

[14] Story, Commentaries on the Bills of Exchange, 1846, available electronically: http://books.google.co.uk/boo ks?id=kJQ0AAAAIAAJ&printsec=frontcover&source=gbs_ge_summary_r&cad=0#v=onepage&q&f=false.

[15] Most social security payments are now made direct into the payee's bank account by electronic means. Consequently, such payment instruments are rarely used.

[16] [1900] 1 QB 270.

[17] (1905) 94 LT 126.

[18] [1910] 2 KB 509.

provided that the instrument will not be paid if presented to the drawee bank after six months from the date on which it was drawn. The court held that the instrument was unconditional. In some cases the instrument may bear the letter 'R' on the face of it and this is treated as an indication that the drawer requires the drawee bank to obtain the payee's signature on the receipt, regardless of whether it appears on the face or back of the instrument. Such instruments are treated as conditional since the payee's signature of the receipt is a pre-requisite of payment against the mandate. The bank is likely to dishonour such instruments. Again the use of such receipts has declined since the Cheques Act 1957 which provided that the paid cheque is *prima facie* proof of payment although banks now rarely return such cheques to the drawer.

4 Must be addressed by one person to another

A cheque is a bill of exchange drawn by one person on another, which must be a bank,[19] whereas an ordinary bill of exchange may be drawn on anyone. The standard bill of exchange identifies the addressee in the bottom left-hand corner with the drawer being identified by his signature, since the bill will be drawn as an order from A to B to make payment. However, it is possible for the drawer:

- To address himself and order himself to make payment, for example where one division of a company, or one branch of a bank, draws an instrument, on another division of the same company, or branch of the same bank or on the head-office of the same bank. Such an instrument is not a bill of exchange since the instrument is not drawn from 'one person to another'.[20] In such circumstances the Bills of Exchange Act 1882 provides that the holder may treat the instrument as a promissory note or as a bill of exchange.[21] In both instances, the holder is entitled to enforce the instrument. Thus, in *Abbey National plc v JSF Finance & Currency Exchange Co Ltd*[22] a holder for value was entitled to claim payment from Abbey National on a bankers' draft which had been issued in fraudulent circumstances.

- By accident or deliberately to address the order to a non-existent person and the courts have held that such instruments may be held payable to bearer.[23] Section 5(2) of the Bills of Exchange Act 1882 similarly provides that instruments drawn in favour of a 'fictitious person' or non-existing person may be treated as a bill of exchange or bearer instrument.

A cheque must be payable on demand,[24] while a bill of exchange may be drawn payable a number of days after date, acceptance or sight.[25] The drawer can sign the bill at any stage in its history and all that is required is that it must have been signed by the time it is enforced. The fact that the bill may be unsigned when accepted or endorsed does not affect its validity

---

[19] The term 'bank' is not defined within the Bills of Exchange Act 1882 although s.2 of the Act provides that '"Banker"' includes a body of person whether incorporated or not who carry on the business of banking.' Applying s.5(2) of the Act it has been held that a cheque drawn on a fictitious bank was to held to be a cheque for the purposes of the Gaming Act 1968 (*Aziz v Knightsbridge Gaming and Catering Services and Supplies Ltd* [1982] LS Gaz. R 1412.

[20] *Re British Trade Corp Ltd* [1932] 2 Ch 1.

[21] Bills of Exchange Act 1882, s.5(2).

[22] [2006] EWCA Civ 328.

[23] [1891] AC 107.

[24] Bills of Exchange Act 1882, s.73.

[25] Bills of Exchange Act 1882, s.10.

when the drawer subsequently adds his signature to the instrument and it is not a bill of exchange until that condition is fulfilled.[26]

The Bills of Exchange Act 1882 does not prevent the drawing of post-dated cheques and the Act provides that a bill is not invalid by reason only that is antedated or post-dated.[27] A bank is bound to pay a post-dated cheque on or after the due date of payment. In both *Whistler v Foster*[28] and *Austin v Bunyard*[29] it was held that holders of post-dated cheques could recover the amounts for which the cheques were drawn and that the instruments were to be taken to have been drawn according to the date appearing on the face of them.

A different situation arises under s.3(4) of the Bills of Exchange Act 1882, which provides that *prima facie* the instrument need not be dated. An undated instrument would presumably be payable on demand, or on presentation. In practice banks are likely to refuse to pay undated cheques without the drawer's consent and this refusal was upheld in *Griffiths v Dalton*,[30] where the plaintiff purported to fill in the date on a cheque some 18 months later. The court concluded that the delay in completing the cheque under s.20(1) of the 1882 Act was unreasonable and the bank was justified in refusing to make payment.

5 Must be signed by the drawer

Section 23 of the Bills of Exchange Act 1882 provides that 'no person shall be liable as drawer . . . of a bill who has not signed it as such'. A number of points arise for consideration, as follows.

What is a signature?

The Bills of Exchange Act 1882 does not define what constitutes an effective signature. Chalmers and Guest[31] describe a signature as 'the writing of a person's name on a bill or note in order to authenticate and give effect to some contract thereon'.

While the drawer of a cheque or bill of exchange will normally sign his name in manuscript either in his personal capacity or as an agent, for example he signs on behalf of a company, the use a permanent form of ink or print[32] will normally be required. However, a cheque written in pencil (if the other constituents are present) will be valid.[33] The courts have had to resolve the issue of whether a facsimile signature on an instrument will be sufficient. In *Goodman v J. Eban Ltd*[34] the Court of Appeal, by a majority, held that a signature affixed on a bill of costs, by means of a rubber stamp, issued by a solicitor was an adequate signature within s.65(2) of the Solicitors Act 1932. Lord Evershed MR relied on *Bennett v Brumfitt*[35] where the court had regarded to the use of a stamp as satisfying the requirement of signature under the Statute of Frauds and the Statute of Wills, although the *Bennett* case did not deal with the requirement of what would be an appropriate signature for the purposes of bills of

---

[26] A drawer of a bill may deliberately delay signature on the bill of exchange: *G & H Montage GmbH v Irvani* [1990] 1 WLR 667.

[27] *Royal Bank of Scotland v Tottenham* [1894] 2 QB 715 at 719; *Shapira v Greenstein* (1970) 10 DLR (3d) 746.

[28] (1863) 14 NS 248.

[29] (1865) 6 B & S 687.

[30] [1940] 2 KB 264.

[31] *Chalmers and Guest on Bills of Exchange and Cheques* (2009) London: Sweet & Maxwell.

[32] *Re London and Mediterranean Bank, ex parte Birmingham Banking Co* (1868) LR 3 Ch App 651.

[33] *Geary v Physic* (1826) 5 B & C 234.

[34] [1954] 1 QB 550; *Re a Debtor* [1996] 1 BCLC 538; *Re Horne, The Times*, 14 June 2000.

[35] (1867) LR 3 CP 28.

exchange. Denning LJ dissenting argued that what would constitute a signature differed depending on the statute in question and in that context questioned whether 'anyone ever supposed that a man can sign a bill of exchange or a cheque by means of a rubber stamp'.[36] He concluded that a document could not be signed by means of a rubber stamp, although a mark executed by an illiterate person would be adequate. However, the distinction between a rubber stamp or some other form of mark, and therefore presumably some form of automated signature, is not easy to understand although Lord Denning expressed the view that a rubber stamp, and therefore also some form of automated signature, is a 'thoughtless impress . . . in contrast to the reasoned attention of a sensible person'. However, the majority view in *Goodman* is supported in the Interpretation Act 1978[37] which defines 'writing' to include any 'other modes of representing or reproducing words in a visible form'. Merely printing a name will therefore not suffice and the element of facsimile is probably essential to verify authenticity.[38]

In the case of bills of exchange drawn by a company s.52 of the Companies Act 2006 provides that:

> A bill of exchange or promissory note is deemed to have been made, accepted or endorsed on behalf of a company if made, accepted or endorsed in the name of, or by or on behalf or on account of, the company by a person acting under its authority.

The agent may, therefore, either sign his name but identify that he signs on behalf of the company or the agent may either sign the name of the company (i.e. in the name of the company). Where he signs his name he must do so either in manuscript or by facsimile but where he signs in the name of the company, the only safe course is to do so by manuscript. In *Lazarus Estates Ltd* v *Beasley*,[39] Lord Denning while accepting the authority of *Goodman*, rejected that the possibility that it permitted the company to affix its name with a rubber stamp and still less by mere type.

Location of signature

The signature should appear in a place which makes it clear that it is intended to authenticate, the document. That normally means at the end of the document or beneath the text. A signature elsewhere on the face of the document would probably suffice if the intention were clear.[40] The use of initials only[41] has been held to constitute a signature but initials are normally only used to authenticate amendments so the better practice would be to place a full signature on the instrument.

Signature by an agent

Section 23 of the Bills of Exchange Act 1882 provides that no one will be liable on a bill either as drawer, endorser or acceptor of a bill unless he signs the instrument. An agent acting within the authority vested in him may place such a signature on the instrument so that the

---

[36] *Goodman* v *J. Eban Ltd* [1954] 1 QB 550 at 557.

[37] Interpretation Act 1978, schedule 1.

[38] See Lord Evershed MR in *Goodman* v *J. Eban Ltd* [1954] 1 QB 550 on *R* v *Cowper* (1890) 24 QBD 553 and *Firstpost Homes Ltd* v *Johnson* [1995] 1 WLR 1567 at 1575.

[39] [1956] 1 QB 702 at 710.

[40] *Weatherhill* v *Pearce* [1995] 1 WLR 592; *Hill* v *Hill* [1947] Ch 231.

[41] *Caton* v *Caton* (1867) LR 2 HL 127 at 143; *Hill* v *Hill* [1947] Ch 231; *Wood* v *Smith* [1993] Ch 90.

agent's principal, the bank's customer, is liable on the instrument and the bank having made payment in accordance with the cheque can debit the customer's account.

An agent may simply write his principal's name on the instrument without adding anything to indicate that he draws the instrument as an agent.[42] If an agent signs in his own name and adds words indicating that he is signing in a representative capacity then that is sufficient notice to a third party that he has limited authority from his principal and the principal will only be bound by the instrument if the agent acts within the limits of that authority.[43]

Section 25 of the Bills of Exchange Act 1882 deals with the question of a signature by procuration, and such a signature puts the person to whom the cheque is handed upon enquiry that the agent's authority to sign it is limited. It will therefore prevent the bank from becoming a *bona fide* holder without notice.[44] In *Morison v Kemp*[45] a clerk employed by the plaintiff firm was authorised to draw cheques 'per pro' (i.e. per procuration) his employers for the purposes of their business. The clerk drew a cheque in that form and made it payable to a bookmaker to settle his personal betting losses. It was held that the employers could recover the proceeds of the cheque from the bookmakers. However, in *McDonald and Co v Nash and Co*[46] Scrutton LJ expressed the view that s.25 of the Bills of Exchange Act 1882 is confined to cases where the signature on the instrument shows a special or limited authority, for example words such as 'under power of attorney or per procuration' are used and does not apply to situations where a general authority is conferred to sign 'on behalf of . . .' or 'by . . .'.

It may not be enough to place the words 'agent' or 'director' after the signature since the words merely refer to the office occupied by the signatory and not necessarily that the agent signs in that capacity.[47] In such circumstances, the signatory may be held personally liable as the principal and it makes no difference that the payee or holder has knowledge that he signed merely as an agent.[48]

The main problem which arises is with reference to the positioning of the name of the principal on the instrument in relation to the signature of the authorised agent, or the omission of words which indicate that the agent signs for or on behalf of a principal, or in a representative character. In recent cases, the courts have taken a more flexible approach that reflects business reality with regard to the imposition of personal liability on an agent. In these cases the courts have taken the view that none of the parties would have expected an individual officer or employee to undertake personal liability. In *Chapman v Smethurst*[49] the court concluded that placing the word 'director' after the signature was sufficient for the instrument to be treated as a promissory note issued by the company. The court examined the effect of s.26(2) of the 1882 Act in *Elliott v Bax-Ironside*[50] where two company directors endorsed the back of a bill of exchange 'in order to guarantee the liability of the company'. The court held that the directors would be treated as having endorsed the bill in their personal capacity since that was the only way of giving the additional guarantee required. In *Bondina Ltd v Rollaway*

---

[42] Bills of Exchange Act 1882, s.91(1).
[43] Bills of Exchange Act 1882, s.25.
[44] *Morison v London County and Westminster Bank Ltd* [1914] 3 KB 356; *Midland Bank Ltd v Reckitt* [1933] AC 1.
[45] (1912) 29 TLR 70.
[46] [1922] WN 272.
[47] *Landes v Marcus* (1909) 25 TLR 478.
[48] Leadbitter v Farrow (1816) 5 M & S 345.
[49] [1909] 1 KB 927.
[50] [1925] 2 KB 301.

Shower Blinds Ltd[51] it was held that a cheque signed by a director of a company without any indication of the capacity in which he signed the instrument was a cheque drawn by the company because in placing his signature on it the director was adopting all the wording on the cheque form, including the name of the company.

It is impossible to be certain about words which will suffice to negate personal liability since the court is entitled to look at the document as a whole, and the intention of the drawer within a commercial context, in order to discover whether he intends to sign as an agent. Where the drawer of the instrument is a company it may be possible to establish the personal liability of the signatory under s.52 of the Companies Act 2006. The section provides that where an officer of a company, or other person, acting on behalf of the company signs or authorises the signature on a negotiable instrument, or order for money or goods, which does not mention the company's name in full, he is liable to the holder for the obligations evidenced in the document. Personal liability attaches not only to the person who signs the irregular document but also to the person who expressly authorises the signature by another.[52] In *Durham Fancy Goods Ltd* v *Michael Jackson (Fancy Goods) Ltd*[53] the plaintiffs had drawn a bill on the defendants, which wrongly named them as 'M. Jackson (Fancy Goods) Ltd' and prepared a form of acceptance in the same style. A director of the company signed the acceptance without noticing the error and the bill was dishonoured on presentation. The director was held personally liable on the bill but the plaintiffs were estopped from enforcing the bill since they were responsible for the misdescription. In *Maxform SpA* v *Mariani and Goodville Ltd*[54] a director of Goodville was held personally liable on the bills drawn in its registered business name, Ital design, without any mention on the bills of the name Goodville Ltd. The court held that the word 'name' under the then s.108 of the Companies Act 1948 could only mean the company's registered corporate name. However, in *Banque de L'Indochine et de Suez SA* v *Euroseas Group Finance Co Ltd*[55] it was held that the directors of a company were not personally liable because the abbreviation 'Co' had been used, instead of the full word 'company' and that abbreviation was well understood. In *Barber and Nicholls Ltd* v *R & G Associates (London) Ltd*[56] s.108 of the Companies Act 1948 did not apply to impose personal liability on directors in respect of cheques drawn by the company because the word 'London' had been omitted from the company's name on the printed cheque forms. The omission was not that of the director but of the bank providing the pre-printed cheque forms.

It should be noted that the company cannot raise lack of contractual capacity in order to avoid liability on instruments drawn by it.[57] An agent may escape liability by adding words to indicate that he signs 'without recourse' or '*sans recours*'.

6 Must require payment on demand or at a fixed or determinable future time

This requirement recognises the distinction between those bills which are required to be paid on demand, commonly referred to as sight bills, and those which are known as term bills, i.e. payable at a date in the future. Section 10(1)(a) of the Act provides that a bill is payable

---

[51] [1986] WLR 517.
[52] *John Wilkes (Footwear) Ltd* v *Lee International Footwear Ltd* [1985] BCLC 444.
[53] [1968] 2 QB 839.
[54] [1979] 2 Lloyd's Rep 385.
[55] [1981] 3 All ER 198.
[56] (1981) 132 NLJ 1076.
[57] Companies Act 2006, s.39.

on demand if it is 'expressed to be payable on demand, or at sight, or on presentation'. A standard bill will be payable on 'sight' meaning the drawee bank is required to pay as soon as it sees the bill, on its presentation to it for payment. Further, s.11 of the Bills of Exchange Act 1882 provides that a bill is 'payable at a determinable future time', for the purposes of s.3(1), if it is expressed to be payable either 'at a fixed period after date or sight' or on or at a fixed period after the happening of a specified event which is certain to happen, though the time of the happening may be uncertain.

A bill of exchange is, therefore, payable in one of three ways: payable on demand, payable at a fixed future time, for example a specific date in the future, or payable at a 'determinable future time', such as 90 days after sight (i.e. 90 days after the instrument is presented for acceptance). The determinable date on which the bill of exchange is due to fall has to be definite and this has caused some discussion in the courts. In *Williamson* v *Rider*[58] an instrument drawn '[I] . . . agree to repay . . . the sum of £100 on or before 31 December 1956', was held not to be a promissory note within the meaning of s.83, because the words 'on or before 31 December 1956' gave the payer an option to repay on any day of his choosing before 31 December 1956, and so the court by a majority held that there was no unconditional promise to pay at a fixed time in the future, as required by s.83 of the 1882 Act. The contingency regarding the time for payment prevented the instrument being payable at 'a fixed or determinable future time'. Ormerod LJ dissenting stated that if the maker chooses to pay at an earlier date than the holder of the bill is under an obligation to accept payment; it was purely a matter for the payer to decide if he chose to pay earlier.

While the decision of the majority was reluctantly affirmed in *Claydon* v *Bradley*[59] the majority decision in *Williams* v *Rider* has been rejected by a number of Commonwealth jurisdictions in preference for the judgment of Ormerod LJ: In *John Burrows Ltd* v *Subsurface Surveys Ltd*[60] the Supreme Court of Canada in *Williams* v *Rider* and in *Creative Press Ltd* v *Harman*[61] the High Court of Ireland, both of which followed the views expressed by Ormerod LJ. In the Canadian case, Ritchie J giving the, judgment of the court, followed the reasoning of Ormerod LJ in holding that a promise to pay a sum in 9 years and 10 months from 1 April 1963 was an unconditional promise to pay the sum at a fixed and determinable future time, despite a proviso which gave the payer the option to pay the whole or any part of the sum at any earlier time upon giving 30 days' notice of intention prior to such payment. In *Byles on Bills of Exchange and Cheques*[62] the dissenting view of Ormerod LJ in *Williamson* v *Rider* is preferred.[63] It is now for the Supreme Court to clarify the position.

Section 11 refers to bills payable after a specified event and although this form of wording will rarely be used the issue may arise in respect of a bill where the wording has been altered. A bill of exchange payable on a contingency is not a bill of exchange. An instrument drawn

---

[58] [1963] 1 QB 89 at 97–98.

[59] [1989] 1 All ER 522 at 524–525.

[60] (1968) 68 D.L.R. (2d) 354.

[61] [1973] IR 313.

[62] *Byles on Bills of Exchange and Cheques* (2007) London: Sweet & Maxwell.

[63] The view of Ormerod LJ in *Williamson* v *Rider* [1963] 1 QB 89 is also preferred by Hudson, in his 1962 article 'Time and Promissory Notes' 25 MLR 593. In that article it is suggested, at p.595, by reference to the judgment of Abbott CJ in *Clayton* v *Gosling* (1826) 5 B & C 360 that a time of payment, in relation to a promissory note, is only contingent if it is a 'time which may or may not arrive'. In the present case the time for payment was bound to arrive; the money was payable on 1 July 1983 if it had not been repaid, at the option of the payer, before.

payable at 30 days after the arrival of a specific ship in a named port was not a bill of exchange but a mere waste of paper.[64] In *Novaknit Hellas SA* v *Kumar Brothers International Ltd*[65] the court held an instrument expressed to be payable 'on 60 days from the first presentation of the documents' was as certain an instrument as one payable 'at sight' since the shipment is bound to have taken place on presentation of the documents. In *Korea* v *Exchange Bank* v *Debenhams (Central Buying) Ltd*[66] a printed form had been altered so as to require payment 'at 90 days d/a of this first bill of exchange'. The Court of Appeal held that the meaning of the bill was unclear and even if it could be construed as requiring payment at 90 days after acceptance, the statutory requirement was not satisfied: the drawee might refuse acceptance. However, the courts will try and uphold the validity of bills whenever possible.

Section 10(1)(b) provides that a bill in which no time for payment is expressed is always payable on demand. While s.10 covers the situation where the bill is silent about the date for payment it does not cover the situation where a time is expressed for payment, nor does it satisfy the requirements of s.11 in respect of determination of the date of payment. In such cases the question to be decided is whether no time for payment has been expressed or that a time has been expressed but in a manner which does not satisfy the Act. Section 73 of the Act defines a cheque as a bill of exchange drawn on a banker payable on demand. However, post-dated cheques are recognised as valid instruments and payable at the earliest date on or after the date appearing on the instrument.

7 Must be for a sum certain in money

Although the Bills of Exchange Act 1882 does not define the term 'money' it will include any legal tender including foreign currency[67] and euros. The bill will rarely include a requirement to pay interest. Section 9(1)(a) provides that a requirement to pay a sum plus interest will not render the sum uncertain but the bill must specify the rate and period of interest so any interest payable can be calculated with certainty. The amount payable can be indicated in either words or figures and if both are used s.9(2) provides that words shall prevail in the event of a discrepancy. However, in *G & H Montage GmbH* v *Irvani*[68] a clerk had entered the correct amount of MN464,000 in figures but omitted the word 'thousand' in the text. German law was applied and it was accepted that there was an equivalent provision to s.9(1) in German law but Saville J accepted that, in the unusual circumstances, the figures would be allowed to prevail over words as between the original parties to the bill. It may be inferred that the learned judge would have applied the same principles under English law.

8 Must require payment to or to the order of a specified person or bearer

Section 7(1) of the Act requires that the payee 'must be named or otherwise indicated therein with reasonable certainty' so that minor inaccuracies in the spelling or designation of the payee's name will not normally give rise to any real uncertainty. A bill may be drawn in favour of joint payees or of alternative payees.[69] Normally, a bill will be payable to bearer by

[64] Guest (2009) *Chalmers and Guest on Bills of Exchange and Cheques*, London: Sweet & Maxwell, Pt IV.
[65] [1998] Lloyd's Rep 100.
[66] [1979] 1 Lloyd's Rep 548.
[67] Bills of Exchange Act 1882, s.9(1)(d).
[68] [1990] 1 WLR 667.
[69] Bills of Exchange Act 1882, s.7(2).

simply writing the word 'bearer' as the payee and a bill made payable to a fictitious person may be treated as payable to bearer.[70]

A cheque, which is made out for a specific purpose, for example 'Pay cash or order', is not a bill of exchange as it is not payable to a specific person; neither is such an instrument treated as payable to bearer under s.7(3) of the Bills of Exchange Act 1882.[71] A 'pay cash' document is no more than that, and if the amount of the instrument is paid to the person intended to receive it, the drawer cannot claim the money back from the bank.[72]

Difficulties arise where the drawer leaves the payee's name in blank. In *Daun & Vallentin* v *Sherwood*[73] it was suggested that such instruments should be treated as payable to bearer because that is their natural effect. However, the nature of the negotiable instrument and its definition militates against that interpretation and in *R* v *Randall*[74] an instrument drawn 'Pay . . . or order' was held not to be a bill, although in *Chamberlain* v *Young*[75] a similar instrument was construed as meaning it was payable to 'my order', i.e. to the order of the drawer. This case could be construed as applying the formula used in personal cheques cashed over the counter, for example where the drawer uses the words pay 'myself' or 'cash'.

Non-compliance with statutory requirements

Section 3(2) of the Bills of Exchange Act 1882, provides that a bill of exchange must not require anything to be done in addition to the payment of money. This reflects the fact that the bill is a negotiable instrument and represents a payment obligation. Section 3(4) identifies three elements that do not have to be present in a valid bill:

- It does not have to be dated.
- It does not have to specify the value given. The bill is a self-standing instrument and a party suing on it does not have to show he provided consideration.
- It does not have to specify the place where it is drawn or the place where it is payable.

Incomplete bills

A drawer may sign a bill in a form in which one or more elements required by statute are omitted, for example the identity of the payee or the date of issue. Section 20(1) of the Bills of Exchange Act 1882, provides that in such a case any person to whom the incomplete bill is delivered in order that it may be converted into a bill has '*prima facie*' authority to fill the omission 'in any way he thinks fit'. Subsection (2) provides that in order for the bill to be enforceable the completion of the bill must be within a reasonable time and in accordance with the authority of the drawer. In such circumstances, the bill will be enforceable by a

---

[70] *Bank of England* v *Vagliano Brothers* [1891] AC 107 at 153.
[71] *Orbit Mining and Trading Co Ltd* v *Westminster Bank Ltd* [1963] 1 QB 794.
[72] *Cole* v *Milsome* [1951] 1 All ER 311.
[73] (1895) 11 TLR 211.
[74] (1811) Russ & Ry 195.
[75] [1893] 2 QB 206.

holder in due course even if the original authority is exceeded. The drawer who delivers an incomplete document, therefore, does so as his own risk even though he limits the authority of the other party to fill the gaps.

Transferable and negotiable instruments

A particular feature of negotiable instruments, and what distinguishes them from other contracts, is their negotiability. Negotiation allows the transfer of title to, and rights under, the bill from one person to another.[76] Negotiability is therefore a form of assignability, but one that improves the position of the transferee of a negotiable instrument as compared to the assignee of a chose in action. The assignee of contractual rights takes 'subject to equities'[77] so if a contract is liable to be set aside on the grounds of misrepresentation or undue influence, or is illegal, or if the other party to the contract has a claim against the assignor to recover damages or a debt which can be set off against the assignor's contractual rights, the assignee obtains no greater right to the instrument than the assignor himself had. Additionally, the assignment of ordinary contractual rights has to be completed by giving notice of the assignment to the debtor. By contrast, negotiable instruments are freely transferable before they become overdue and circulate like cash. Further, a transfer or even successive transfers, of a bill can be made without knowledge of the parties liable to the bill, although it must be presented to the payer for payment. A negotiable instrument, and thereby title in it, is therefore transferable by mere delivery (an instrument payable to bearer is transferred by handing it to the transferee and an order instrument by endorsement), if accompanied by the intention to transfer title. The transferee of a negotiable instrument therefore takes free from defects of title of any prior parties[78] and free from defects available between them, if he is a holder in due course.[79]

These features of negotiable instruments make them an attractive method of payment. Thus, for example, a buyer of goods may be reluctant to pay for them until after he expects to receive the goods, or until he can arrange resale, or until he can use them in some way to make a profit. The buyer may be willing to accept a bill of exchange drawn on him by the seller or payable to the seller at a date, some time in the future. The seller, rather than wait to receive payment on maturity of the bill, can transfer the bill to a third party, for example his bank, and receive cash immediately against the bill of exchange. In such circumstances, the banker, or anyone else who buys the bill, known as discounting, will invariably pay less than the face value of the bill because he pays against the bill before it becomes due for payment and because the bank then takes the risk that it may not receive payment against the bill from the buyer who may have become bankrupt or insolvent. The bank also provides an additional service to the seller by allowing the customer to have earlier access to the money payable under the bill and for which the seller will otherwise have to await payment and seek that payment from abroad.

---

[76] Bills of Exchange Act 1882, s.31(1).
[77] Beale (2012) *Chitty on Contracts*, London: Sweet & Maxwell.
[78] Bills of Exchange Act 1882, s.38(2).
[79] Bills of Exchange Act 1882, s.29.

A number of features must therefore be satisfied if an instrument is to be treated as negotiable namely:[80]

- The terms of the instrument must not be incompatible with or such as to negate the idea of negotiability and there should be no indication that the instrument is only transferable subject to defects of title unknown to the transferee. There should be no indication that it is not transferable by delivery or endorsement and delivery.

- The obligation or rights evidenced by the instrument must be consonant with the commercial function of a negotiable instrument, namely an obligation to pay.

- The instrument belongs to a class which is treated by the mercantile community as negotiable.

The commonest forms of negotiable instruments are therefore bills of exchange, cheques and promissory notes.

Negotiation defined

Section 31 of the Bills of Exchange Act 1882 provides that negotiation takes place when a bill is transferred from one person to another in such a way that the transferee becomes the holder. The term 'transfer' is not defined in the Act but 'holder' is defined in s.2 to mean the payee or endorsee of a bill, or note, who is in possession of it, or the bearer. However, the bill or note is 'issued' to the first payee who while a holder of bill does not have the instrument negotiated to him.[81]

A bill payable to bearer is negotiated by mere delivery[82] and an endorsement is unnecessary.[83] A bill is payable to bearer which is expressed to be so payable, or one on which the only or last endorsement is in blank.[84] As between the two parties an intention to transfer the instrument on the part of the transferor is necessary if the transferee is to have an unassailable title. If the instrument is transferred to a holder in due course, the absence of an intention to transfer title between the immediate parties is a matter of personal defences and will not interfere with the title of the holder in due course. Section 21(2) of the Act provides that in the hands of a holder in due course 'a valid delivery of the bill by all parties prior to him so as to make them liable to him is conclusively presumed'. The subsection also provides that as against a transferor and transferee and some other party (other than the holder in due course) it is possible to prove that the instrument was delivered for some purpose other than with the intention to transfer title. Thus, for example, if the holder (A) of a bearer cheque hands it over to B for safekeeping for A, A is entitled to recall the cheque at any time. If B refuses to return the instrument, A can sue B for its return because B has possession only for a limited purpose. If B in turn delivers the cheque to C who knows of the circumstances in which B took possession, C can also be sued for the return of the cheque, even if he gave value to B. However, if C is a holder in due course then although A can sue B, B cannot sue C. Further, if payment on the cheque is countermanded C will still be entitled to sue the drawer, A.

[80] Jacobs (1943) *Bills of Exchange, Cheques, Promissory Notes and Negotiable Instruments Generally*, London: Sweet & Maxwell.
[81] *RE Jones Ltd* v *Waring and Gillow Ltd* [1926] AC 670.
[82] Bills of Exchange Act 1882, s.2 defines the terms 'bearer' and 'delivery'.
[83] Bills of Exchange Act 1882, s.31(2).
[84] Bills of Exchange Act 1882, s.8(3).

Fictitious or non-existent payee

Although, in *Orbit Mining and Trading Co Ltd* v *Westminster Bank Ltd*[85] the court held that s.7(3) of the Bills of Exchange Act 1882 did not apply to 'pay cash' instruments, the section may be used to hold otherwise ineffective cheques, or bills (for example instruments where there is a forged endorsement, or the payee has ceased to exist, e.g. a company that has been deregistered or never ultimately registered, or a deceased individual) as payable to bearer which means the instrument is transferable by delivery alone. In these circumstances the courts have to examine the scope of ss.7(3) and 24 of the Act.

Under s.24 of the 1882 Act a forged endorsement will render the negotiable instrument a nullity and no one can acquire a good title through an endorsement. Consequently, a person who acquires the instrument after a forged instrument has been placed on it cannot sue parties prior to the endorsement and, in particular, cannot sue the drawer or acceptor of the bill of exchange. On the other hand, s.7(3) will apply, for example, where the drawer is induced, usually mistakenly, into belief that he is indebted to a third party (payee). The person inducing the mistake will then misappropriate the instrument but in order to receive payment the dishonest person must endorse the payee's name on it. Even having forged the payee's endorsement on the instrument the dishonest person cannot pay the instrument into his account (he may not have an account) so the only way to receive payment on it is to endorse the instrument to someone who gives value for it.

However, the effect of the endorsement is that anyone who takes the instrument after the forged endorsement cannot sue a person who endorsed it prior to the endorsement: the forged endorsement breaks the chain of title. Thus, even a holder in due course cannot make the drawer who created the instrument, possibly through negligence, liable. To avoid this situation, the courts have held that s.7(3) may provide that such an instrument should be regarded payable to bearer and the forged endorsement ignored since endorsements on bearer instruments are unnecessary. The drawer, or acceptor can therefore be made liable to the holder in due course. The drawer will then bear the loss arising as a result of the instrument being paid.

In *Bank of England* v *Vagliano Brothers*[86] the House of Lords examined the effect of s.7(3) where VB employed G as a clerk for them. G forged bills purported to have been drawn on them by X, in Odessa, and on VB, in London, and payable to P. G asked VB to accept the bills, which they did so without question, adding to the form of acceptance that they were payable at the Bank of England where VB had an account. G then forged P's endorsement and obtained payment over the counter at the Bank. It was held that G was the real drawer of the bills and since the drawer never intended P to obtain payment, the bills were payable to bearer. The Bank had acted properly in making payment and could debit VB's account. In coming to this conclusion their Lordships adopted a subjective approach so the question of whether the payee was 'fictitious' or not depended on the intention of the person who actually drew the bill of exchange and although P was actually in existence when the bill was drawn G had no intention that the payee should actually receive payment on it.

Lord Herschell examining the meaning of the word 'fictitious' said that where the payee is named by way of pretence and without any intention that he should be the person to receive

---

[85] [1963] 1 QB 794.
[86] [1891] AC 107.

payment, the instrument is drawn in favour of a fictitious payee. Lord Macnaghten took the view that 'the proper meaning of the word fictitious is "feigned" or "counterfeit"' and therefore P, as the named payee, was strictly speaking a fictitious payee. The House of Lords was not united on its understanding of the meaning of the word fictitious or non-existent payee. Lords Bramwell and Field were of the opinion that the payee was not fictitious. There was a real payee called P and VB were accustomed to accepting bills drawn by P in their favour. In determining whether the payee is fictitious Lord Bramwell said it is not a question of intention but a question of fact and the bills were payable to an existing person. If there were no real payee, and the name was inserted as a mere *nominis umbra*, then and only then, would the payee be fictitious.

A different approach was adopted in *Clutton* v *Attenborough*[87] where a clerk in the accounts department of the appellants persuaded his employers to draw a cheque payable to 'John Brett' by falsely representing that it was drawn as payment for work done. The clerk obtained possession of the completed cheques, forged the payee's signature on it and negotiated the bill to the respondent who obtained payment on the cheque. Although the appellants had intended the payee 'John Brett' to receive payment for work completed for them, the House of Lords held that, as there was no such person known to the drawer, the cheque was drawn in favour of a 'non-existent' person. The payee of the cheque was treated as a fictitious person because the person committing the fraud supplied the name and the drawer had no knowledge of any person under that name. The appellants could not, therefore, have intended the payee to be a real and identifiable person. Lord Halsbury refused to give effect to the drawer's intention, as in the *Vagliano* case,[88] but determined the question objectively by simply asking whether the payee referred to on the face of the instrument actually existed or not.

The approach in the *Vagliano*[89] case would therefore appear to apply to the situation where the payee exists but the instrument is treated as fictitious because the fraudulent person supplies the name of the payee, whereas *Clutton*[90] would appear to apply to situations where the payee is unknown to the drawer and therefore 'non-existing'. The approach in the *Vagliano* case does not apply to a situation where the drawer's intention to make a cheque payable to a designated real person is in fact induced by another person's fraudulent misrepresentation. In such circumstances, although the motive for drawing the cheque is the other person's misrepresentation in respect of the drawer's liability to that person, the drawer nevertheless intends to make the cheque payable to the very person. Such a cheque would not be payable to a 'fictitious' person and therefore not payable to bearer. In *Royal Bank of Canada* v *Concrete Column Clamps (1961) Ltd*[91] a clerk in the payroll department of the defendant company induced his employers to draw a number of cheques payable to their former employers who were not, in fact, owed any salary. The majority of the Supreme Court of Canada held that the cheques were not payable to 'fictitious' payees, even though the drawer's intention, albeit fraudulently induced, was to pay those persons (i.e. the former employers to whom, in fact, no monies were owed). In an attempt to ascertain whether the payees of the cheques were

[87] [1897] AC 90.
[88] [1891] AC 107.
[89] [1891] AC 107.
[90] [1897] AC 90.
[91] [1977] 2 SCR 456.

fictitious their Lordships relied on the fourth of the four propositions set out in Falconbridge *Banking and Bills of Exchange*[92] which explains that whether a named payee is non-existing is a simple question of fact and not dependent on anyone's intention.

> The question whether the payee is fictitious depends upon the intention of the creator of the instrument, that is, the drawer of a bill or cheque or the maker of a note. In the case of a bill drawn by Adam Bede upon John Aldn payable to Martin Chuzzlewit, the payee may or may not be fictitious or non-existent according to the circumstances:
>
> 1 If Martin Chuzzlewit is not the name of any real person known to Bede, but is merely that of a creature of the imagination, the payee is non-existing and is probably also fictitious.
>
> 2 If Bede for some purpose of his own inserts as payee the name of Martin Chuzzlewit, a real person who was known to him but whom he knows to be dead, the payee is non-existing, but is not fictitious.
>
> 3 If Martin Chuzzlewit is the name of a real person known to Bede, but Bede names him as payee by way of pretence, not intending that he should receive payment, the payee is fictitious, but is not non-existing.
>
> 4 If Martin Chuzzlewit is the name of a real person, intended by Bede to receive payment, the payee is neither fictitious nor non-existing, notwithstanding that Bede has been induced to draw the bill by the fraud of some other person who has falsely represented by Bede that there is a transaction in respect of which Chuzzlewit is entitled to the sum mentioned in the bill.

In his dissenting judgment Laskins CJ agreed with the majority view that in the type of situation before them the 'discovery of the real or imaginary character of the payee is post facto: and ordinarily the drawer, induced by the fraud, would intend that the cheque take its effect in favour of the named payee'. Laskins CJ, however, thought that this general position required further analysis depending on whether the drawee bank or the drawer were at fault in any way, including whether it was possible to attribute the conduct of the fraudulent person to the drawer on the ground that the fraudulent person was acting as his agent or employee. The facts of each particular case therefore become relevant.

More recently, the Supreme Court of Canada approved the majority view in *Concrete Column Clamps (1961) Ltd* to that expressed by Laskins CJ. In *Boma Manufacturing Ltd* v *Canadian Imperial Bank of Commerce*[93] Boma Manufacturing Ltd (BML) and Panabo Sales Ltd (PSL) were two small associated family-owned companies whose sole shareholders and officers were Boris and his wife, Ursula. The companies employed a bookkeeper, Alm, who was authorised to draw cheques for both the companies with respect to bank accounts held with the Royal Bank of Canada. Cheques drawn on these accounts required the signature of only one authorised signing officer. Alm had responsibility for preparing the payroll, handling accounts receivable and payable, preparing cheques and reconciling bank statements. From 1982 to 1987 Alm defrauded the two companies of $91,289.00 by issuing and depositing to her own accounts, with the Canadian Imperial Bank of Commerce (CIBC), a total of 155 cheques drawn on the accounts of the two companies held with the Royal Bank. The cheques were made payable to a number of persons connected with the companies, including the managers, several employees, and one of the sub-contractors, Van Sang Lam. The cheques payable to Lam were,

---

[92] Falconbridge (1969) *Banking and Bills of Exchange,* Toronto: Canada Law Book Ltd, pp. 485–486.
[93] [1996] 3 SCR 277.

with one exception, made to J. Lam or J.R. Lam, the initials and the last name mimicking the name of Alm's first husband. Alm signed 146 of the cheques on behalf of the companies and fraudulently obtained the manager's signature on the other nine cheques and then deposited all of the cheques into one of her accounts at the CIBC. CIBC policy with respect to a customer wishing to deposit a third-party cheque was to require that the payee endorse the cheque. However, 107 of the cheques payable to J. Lam or J.R. Lam were accepted by the CIBC for deposit without endorsement. The bank's tellers assumed that the payee was J. Alm or J.R. Alm, Alm's first husband, and so accepted the cheques without endorsement, contrary to their policy. Those cheques that were endorsed were endorsed fraudulently by Alm. The fraudulently negotiated cheques were all paid by the Royal Bank and the cancelled cheques were sent to the companies, most of which were removed and destroyed by Alm. On discovery of the fraud the two companies brought an action in negligence, and in the alternative, conversion, against their bank and against the CIBC. The Supreme Court of Canada restored the decision of the trial judge who held that it is neither necessary nor desirable to import notions of agency or vicarious liability and it is the intention of the drawer that is of relevance. On that basis Iacobucci J reaffirmed the general principle that:

> where a drawer is fraudulently induce by another person into issuing a cheque for the benefit of a real person to whom no obligation is owed, the cheque is to be considered payable to the payee, and not to a fictitious person.

Rights and liabilities of the parties to a bill of exchange

There are normally at least two parties to a bill of exchange, the drawer and endorser, with the payee being either a third party to the bill or the drawer himself. Where the bill is negotiated the holder adds further currency to the bill by endorsing the instrument and undertaking liability on the bill by virtue of the endorsement on the bill. His position is similar to that of the drawer arising from the obligation resulting from his signature, as endorser on the bill, to pay against the instrument.

The drawer of the bill performs a dual function namely: (i) on due presentation he instructs the drawee to honour the instrument, and (ii) he undertakes that on due presentation that the bill of exchange will be accepted, where an acceptance is required, and paid.[94] The drawer, therefore, warrants that the bill of exchange will be honoured and paid by the drawee. Therefore, the requirements for incurring liability on a bill of exchange are:

- That the person concerned must have contractual capacity.
- That he has placed his signature on the document.
- That it has been delivered to a holder.
- That consideration was received for the instrument.

The Bills of Exchange Act 1882 devotes a number of sections to the question of liability on the bill of exchange. We will now examine who may be a party to such a bill and the extent of liability incurred by each party to the bill.

---

[94] Bills of Exchange Act 1882, s.55(1)(a).

Drawer

The drawer is normally the person responsible for bringing the negotiable instrument into existence. He will incur liability on the instrument if he, in addition to signing the instrument, also delivers it to the payee or his agent. The drawer of a cheque will remain primarily liable on the instrument throughout because unlike a bill of exchange, the cheque is never accepted. By contrast, if the bill of exchange is accepted then the acceptor becomes primarily liable on it and the drawer in effect becomes the guarantor.

The drawer and endorsers of a bill are jointly and severally responsible to the holder for its acceptance and payment[95] and if the bill is dishonoured the holder may enforce payment against all or any of the parties who have placed their signature on the instrument in their capacity as drawer, endorser or the acceptor, in the case of accepted bills. Section 55 of the Bills of Exchange Act 1882 deals with the liability of the drawer and provides that the drawer will compensate not only the holder but any endorser who may be compelled to make payment. The position is simpler in the case of cheques as the drawer remains primarily liable. In *Starke v Cheeseman*[96] the court held that the act of drawing a bill implies a promise from the drawer to pay for it, if the drawee does not. An endorsement by the drawer does not give him a new character as endorser, or divest him of this liability as drawer, and he remains the ultimate debtor on the bills.

The statutory estoppels available against the drawer are found in s.55(1)(b) of the Bills of Exchange Act 1882, which states that the drawer is precluded from denying to a holder in due course the existence of the payee or his capacity to endorse it. However, where the payee is fictitious or non-existent the bill may be treated as payable to bearer and consequently parties subsequent to a forged endorsement may sue the acceptor or drawer. The fact that the drawer may to attempt to deny the existence of the payee prevents the drawer making any attempt to escape liability on the grounds that the payee is non-existent.

Drawee

The drawee (the person charged with making payment on the instrument), by merely acting in that capacity, does not incur any liability on the instrument. The bill of exchange, in itself, does not amount to an assignment of funds in the hands of the drawee, and a drawee who does not accept it will not be personally liable on the instrument.[97] Hence banks, which never accept cheques, do not incur any liability on them to the payee or holder. The drawee may undertake liability on a bill of exchange under a separate agreement with the drawer or payee and will be liable under that agreement if he fails to comply.[98] For example, a bank that wrongly dishonours a bill presented for non-acceptance, drawn in accordance with the provisions of an arrangement requiring the drawee's acceptance, may be separately liable to the drawer, under contract, for the non-acceptance. A person other than the drawee of a bill of exchange cannot accept the instrument. Where the drawee does accept a bill of exchange, he becomes the acceptor of the bill, and becomes primarily liable on the bill by

---

[95] *Rouquette* v *Overmann* (1875) LR 10 QB 525.
[96] (1699) Carth 509.
[97] Bills of Exchange Act 1882, s.53(1).
[98] *Smith* v *Brown* (1815) 6 Taunt. 340; *Laing* v *Barclay* (1823) 1 B & C 398.

undertaking to make payment in accordance with the terms of the acceptance.[99] However, the defences available to him against the drawer are not normally available to subsequent holders of the bill. Acceptance is defined as the 'signification by the drawee of his assent to the order of the holder'.

The acceptance has to be written on the bill of exchange and signed by the drawee,[100] although a mere signature of the drawee will be sufficient.[101] The common practice in accepting bills of exchange is to write the word 'accepted', and sign and date the instrument. A bill of exchange may be accepted after it becomes overdue or after its dishonour, by the drawer.[102] Not all bills of exchange need to be presented for acceptance. Presentation for acceptance is required where an instrument is 'payable at a fixed time after sight' since in such cases unless the bill of exchange is presented for acceptance the date of maturity remains undetermined.[103] A bill will be required to be presented for acceptance where acceptance is expressly required by the instrument or where the bill is drawn payable other than the drawee's place of business of residence.[104]

Acceptor

The acceptance of the bill of exchange renders the acceptor primarily liable on the bill of exchange and s.54(2)(a) of the Bills of Exchange Act 1882 provides that the acceptor is precluded from denying to a holder in due course:

- The existence of the drawer.
- The genuineness of the drawer's signature (an exception to the rule in s.24 of the Act).
- The capacity and authority of the drawer to draw a bill.

Further, the acceptor is precluded from denying to a holder in due course the capacity of the drawer to endorse an order but not the genuineness or validity of his endorsement, and the existence and capacity of the payee to endorse the bill in the case of a bill payable to a named payee or his order but not the genuineness or validity of this endorsement.[105]

Payee

The original payee of the bill, cheque or note in whose possession the instrument remains cannot be a holder in due course since the instrument has to be negotiated[106] and the payee of the instrument cannot therefore claim the protection given to a holder in due course. However, as a holder the payee may sue on the instrument in his own name.[107] Professor

---

[99] Bills of Exchange Act 1882, s.54(1).
[100] Bills of Exchange Act 1882, s.17(2)(a).
[101] Bills of Exchange Act 1882, s.17(2)(a).
[102] Bills of Exchange Act 1882, s.18(2).
[103] Bills of Exchange Act 1882, s.39(1).
[104] Bills of Exchange Act 1882, s.39(2).
[105] Bills of Exchange Act 1882, s.54(2)(b).
[106] *RE Jones Ltd v Waring and Gillow Ltd* [1926] AC 670.
[107] Bills of Exchange Act 1882, s.38(1).

Shea[108] considered whether the payee should be a holder in due course and concluded that, on balance, he should not. The Act does not state what defences may be raised against the payee by the original parties to the instrument, i.e. by the drawer of the cheque or by the drawer or acceptor of the instrument. If the payee obtains the issue of an instrument by fraud, duress or other unlawful means then the title of the payee is defective and such a defence can be raised against him. As between the immediate parties and subject to the rule that negotiable instruments are to be treated as cash in the hands of the recipient, personal defences arising from the underlying contract of sale may also be raised. The position is less clear where the fraud, duress or other wrongdoing is that of the third party, e.g. where A by fraud procures B to draw a cheque in favour of C. A number of authorities have held that fraud or duress on the part of the third party cannot be raised against the original payee of the instrument who has received it as holder in due course.[109]

Endorser

The liability of the endorser is similar to that of the drawer.[110] A number of cases have explained the position of the endorser by saying that the endorser is in effect a new drawer and his endorsement gives a new mandate regarding the payment of the bill to the drawee or acceptor.[111] Consequently, the endorser's liability to an accepted bill of exchange is secondary to that of the acceptor, or if the drawer remains primarily liable throughout on the bill, the liability of the endorser is conditional and does not arise until the instrument has been dishonoured. In addition, an endorser who is compelled to pay is entitled to be indemnified by the drawer and where the bill has been accepted, by the acceptor.

An endorsement must be written on the bill itself.[112] The purpose of this is to enable a bill to operate as a negotiable instrument by 'ensuring that one piece of paper contains all the writing constituting the obligations of the bill and name of the parties to it'.[113] The assignment of an instrument by a separate document is not an endorsement.[114] However, an 'allonge' may be attached to the instrument if further space is required for endorsements.

The 'endorser' or his agent must sign the endorsement. In *Arab Bank Ltd v Ross*[115] it was recognised that the endorsement might not correspond exactly to the name of the payee or the endorsee of the instrument where Lord Denning said:

> by a misnomer, a payee may be described on the face of the bill by the wrong name, nevertheless, if it is quite plain that the drawer intended him as payee, then an endorsement on the back by the payee in his own true name is valid and sufficient to pass the property in the bill.

---

[108] Jack (1989) Banking Services: Law and Practice, Jack, R.B., Banking Services: Law and Practice, Report by the Review Committee Chaired by Professor R.B. Jack, CBE, London Cm. 622, Appendix A, paras 20.4–20.6.
[109] *Talbot v Von Boris* [1911] 1 KB 854; *Hasan v Willson* [1977] 1 Lloyd's Rep 431.
[110] Bills of Exchange Act 1882, s.55.
[111] *Penny v Innes* (1834) 1 Cr M & R 439; *Steele v M'Kinlay* (1880) 5 App Cas 754.
[112] Bills of Exchange Act 1882, s.32(1).
[113] *KHR Financings Ltd v Jackson*, 1977 SLT (Sh Ct) 6.
[114] *Harrop v Fisher* (1861) 10 CB NS 196.
[115] [1952] 2 QB 216.

Transferor by delivery

A bill is payable to bearer which states on the face of it that it is payable to bearer, or on which the 'only or last endorsement' is in blank.[116] The Act[117] provides that where the holder of a bill payable to bearer negotiates it by delivery without endorsing it, he is called a transferor by delivery and is not liable on the instrument. However, he warrants to his immediate transferee, if he is a transferee for value and not a donee, that the bill is what it purports to be (i.e. that it is not a forgery), that he has a right to transfer the bill and that at the time of the transfer he did not know of any fact which rendered the instrument valueless. These liabilities are less extensive than those of an endorser since an endorser's liability is not limited to his immediate endorser for value.

Forged or unauthorised signatures

Section 24 of the Bills of Exchange Act 1882 provides that a forged (although the term forged is not defined in the Act) or unauthorised signature is 'wholly inoperative' and no right to retain the bill, or to give a discharge, or to enforce payment against any party can be acquired through or under the signature. An example of a forged signature is where A signs B's name with the intention that it should be taken, by innocent third parties, to have been written by B himself; there is therefore an element of deception involved. It was originally thought that a signature would not be 'forged' if it were placed on a bill where B falsely purports to act with A's authority. In *Morison* v *London Country and Westminster Bank Ltd*[118] an agent had authority to sign cheques on behalf of his employers for the purposes of his employers' business. In fact, he signed cheques in his own favour and in excess of his authority. The Court of Appeal held that in accordance with the Forgery Act 1861, the cheques were not forgeries within the meaning of the Bills of Exchange Act 1882. However, the Forgery Act 1913 introduced a definition of forgery, which extended to a false claim to be authorised to sign. Consequently, in *Kreditbank Cassel GmbH* v *Schenkers Ltd*[119] the Court of Appeal (without reference to the *Morison* case) relied on the new definition to exempt a company from liability whose employee had dishonestly signed bills purportedly on its behalf. Scrutton LJ argued that 'the bills are clearly forgeries within the Forgery Act 1913, as they contain a false statement'. The inference from Scrutton LJ's judgment is that the words 'where a signature is forged' in s.24 should be interpreted in accordance with the current statutory definition of forgery in criminal law. The Forgery and Counterfeiting Act 1981, superseding the Forgery Act 1913, contains the current definition of forgery which provides that a person is guilty of forgery if he makes a false instrument, with the intention that he or another will use it to induce somebody to accept it as genuine, or by reason of so accepting it to do some act to his own or any other person's prejudice. Section 9(1) then goes on to provide the circumstances in which the instrument will be considered to be false and would appear to extend to the situation in the *Morison* case.

Whether or not a signature is unauthorised will depend on the principles of agency law. The authority to sign on behalf of the drawer, endorser or acceptor may be express, implied

---

[116] Bills of Exchange Act 1882, s.8(3).
[117] Bills of Exchange Act 1882, s.58.
[118] [1914] 3 KB 356.
[119] [1927] 1 KB 826.

or ostensible. Where the principal is a company then the Companies Act 2006 will also deal with the contractual capacity of the company and its agents.

Section 24 treats in the same way an instrument, which has been forged, and one which bears an unauthorised signature, i.e. as wholly inoperative. Thus, if the signature of the drawer on a cheque is forged and the bank makes payment against it, the bank cannot debit the customer's account and it may be compelled to re-credit the customer's account. The payee, even if he takes payment in good faith and has given value, cannot sue the drawer for payment if payment is countermanded, and if the payee has received payment he can be compelled to return it. Similarly, if the drawee's signature is forged on an acceptance on a bill of exchange, the drawee cannot be sued. The same rules apply to an endorsee whose signature is forged. However, the holder will be able to sue any endorsee on a bill who has placed his signature on the bill after the forged endorsement, but the forged signature breaks the chain of title so any signatories who have endorsed the instrument prior to the forged endorsement are discharged on the bill.

Holder in due course

The Bills of Exchange Act 1882 recognises three classes of holder:

- A holder.
- A holder for value.
- A holder in due course.

The rights and defences available to each category of holder will vary depending on the type of holder. While the Act defines the rights of the different types of holder, case law is important in understanding the relevant legislation.

Holder

Section 2 of the Bills of Exchange Act 1882 defines the 'holder' as the payee or endorsee of a bill who has possession of the bill or the bearer of the bill. The holder may, therefore, be the original holder of the bill or a transferee. Under s.38(1) of the Act the holder has a right to sue in his own name and, if he obtains payment, the person who makes payment will get a valid discharge for the bill.[120] The converse of s.38(1) is that a person who is not a holder of the bill cannot sue on the bill. While the Contracts (Rights of Third Parties) Act 1999 allows contracting parties to confer a right to enforce their contact on a third party, s.6 of the 1999 Act provides that the Act confers no rights on a third party in relation to rights conferred under a bill of exchange. The Law Commission's 'Report on Privity of Contract: Contracts for the benefit of third parties'[121] expressed the view that it would cause 'unacceptable uncertainty' to allow the possibility of third parties who are not holders being able to sue on a bill of exchange.

Holder for value

The general rules of consideration apply to bills of exchange, cheques and promissory notes and s.30(1) of the Bills of Exchange 1882 Act infers a statutory presumption that every party

---

[120] Bills of Exchange Act 1882, s.38(3)(b).
[121] Law Commission Report, No. 242, para. 12.16, Cm 3329, 1996, http://lawcommission.justice.gov.uk/docs/lc242_privity_of_contract_for_the_benefit_of_third_parties.pdf.

whose signature appears on the bill is a holder for value. The Act adopts the general principles of what constitutes adequate consideration and s.27(1) provides that valuable consideration under the Act[122] may constitute '(a) any consideration sufficient to support a simple contract of law recognises that some consideration must be given' but the section also qualifies the common law rules on consideration and provides that a bill drawn for 'an antecedent debt or liability' will be sufficient consideration.[123] In *Oliver v Davis*[124] the defendant sent her cheque to the claimant in the hope that the claimant would not sue her fiancé, who was indebted to the claimant. The defendant did not inform the claimant that she was sending the cheque and, in fact, countermanded payment on it before he received it. The Court of Appeal held that the action would not succeed, as the claimant had given no consideration for the cheque. Consequently, in *Hasan v Willson*,[125] and in line with the *Oliver* case,[126] it was said that 'antecedent debt or liability' refers to the antecedent debt or liability of the 'promissor or drawer of the bill' and not to a debt or liability of a third party (e.g. the defendant's fiancé in the *Oliver* case). If the defendant had given or agreed to give time to the defendant's fiancé to discharge the debt (in return for the defendant's cheque), that would have been valuable consideration but no such undertaking had been supplied.

Cheques and bills of exchange are frequently drawn in settlement of existing debts and liabilities so that the general principles of consideration need, to a limited extent, to be modified. However, the rule is treated as an exception to the general principle that consideration must not be past. Section 27(2) then goes on to provide that where 'value has at any time been given for a bill the holder is deemed to be a holder for value as regards the acceptor and all parties to the bill who became parties prior to such time'. A holder claiming against an acceptor, drawer or prior endorser with whom the holder has had no direct dealings is, therefore, to be treated as having given value in return for that person's obligation to pay or compensate him, provided the value has been given by someone for the bill after the acceptor, drawer or endorser became a party to the bill.[127] Thus, it is not necessary for the holder of a bill who sues on it to show that he provided consideration to the defendant. For example, A draws a bill on B, who accepts it gratuitously. C gives A value for the bill and endorses it to X as a gift. X can sue B although X gave no value for the bill and B received nothing for his acceptance. X can also sue A but X cannot sue C, as C did not become a party to the bill prior to the giving of value.

The subsection does not dispense with the requirement that, as between the holder and the person from whom he derives title, the holder should provide consideration. In *Diamond v Graham*[128] the claimant (A) sued the defendant (B) on a cheque which the defendant (B) had given to the claimant (A) in return for a loan by the claimant (A) to a friend (C) of the defendant. The claimant (A) provided consideration by making the loan, although the loan was not made to the defendant (B), but to his friend (C). Both Diplock LJ and Sachs LJ regarded it as clear that consideration had been provided within s.27(1)(a).

---

[122] Bills of Exchange Act 1882, s.27(1)(a).

[123] Bills of Exchange Act 1882, s.27(1)(b); *Elkington v Cook-Hill* (1914) 30 TLR 670, *Ayres v Moore* [1940] 1 KB 278.

[124] [1949] 2 KB 727.

[125] [1977] 1 Lloyd's Rep 431.

[126] [1949] 2 KB 727.

[127] *MK International Development Co Ltd v The Housing Bank* [1991] 1 Bank LR 74 at 80; *Clifford Chance v Silver* [1992] 2 Bank LR 11 para. 6-065.

[128] [1968] 1 WLR 1061.

However, Danckwerts LJ, who delivered the leading judgment in the *Diamond* case,[129] said that the wording of s.27(2) did not appear to require value be given by the holder. However, in *Hanson v Willson*[130] Goff J observed that it was a fundamental principle of English law that consideration must move from the promisee (the holder) and that the statement by Danckwerts LJ was not part of the actual decision in *Diamond v Graham*,[131] which, in any event, was inconsistent with the statement of law in *Oliver v Davis*.[132] The claimant's action in *Hanson* on the dishonoured cheque failed because the claimant had not provided consideration, although a third party (not an agent) had provided the defendant with a cheque in exchange. In *MK International Development Co Ltd v The Housing Bank*[133] Mustill LJ said that there was 'a clear current of authority' that the mere existence of debts owed by a third party did not furnish consideration for the cheque drawn by the defendant in that case.

Where the holder has a lien on the bill he is deemed to be a holder for value to the extent of the sum for which he has a lien.[134]

Holder in due course

For a person to qualify as a holder in due course he must have taken a bill, which is complete and regular on the face of it, under the following circumstances:

- He became a holder of the bill before it became overdue, and without notice of previous dishonour.

- He took the bill in good faith and for value, and that the time the bill was negotiated to him he had no notice of any defect in the title of the person who negotiated it.[135]

The definition contains several elements, each of which must be complied with as follows.

Bill must be complete and regular on the face

A holder of a bill may be a holder in due course only if the bill is complete and regular on the face of it, including the back of the instrument when he takes it. If the bill itself conveys a warning of possible defects because of some formal irregularity then the rule of the overt market, *caveat emptor*, applies and the holder, however honest, takes it subject to any defects of title the transferor himself has.[136] Consequently, the holder takes at his own risk a blank acceptance or a bill that has been torn and taped together. In *Ingham v Primrose*[137] the acceptor of a bill, with the intention of cancelling it, tore it into two pieces and threw them into the street. The eventual endorser picked up the pieces and joined them together and put the bill into circulation. The acceptor was held liable to a *bona fide* holder for value because although he had intended to cancel the bill he did not in fact cancel. However, the decision has been subject to criticism and would probably be decided differently now. In evidence, it was accepted by the court that there was a common practice, in the nineteenth century, that

---

[129] [1968] 1 WLR 1061 at 1064.
[130] [1977] 1 Lloyd's Rep 431 at 441–442.
[131] [1968] 1 WLR 1061.
[132] [1949] 2 KB 727.
[133] [1991] 1 Bank LR 74 at 78.
[134] Bills of Exchange Act 1882, s.27(3).
[135] Bills of Exchange Act 1882, s.29(1).
[136] *Awde v Dixon* (1851) 6 Ex 869.
[137] (1859) 7 CB NS 82.

bills sent in the post were often divided into two and the pieces sent by successive post, with the payee joining the pieces again on the receipt of the two halves. The court may therefore have concluded that there was nothing irregular on the face of the instrument.

The effect of s.29(1) was considered in *Arab Bank Ltd v Ross*[138] where the plaintiff bank sued as holder in due course of two promissory notes drawn by the defendant in favour of *'Fathi and Faysal Nabulsy Company'* and which were, in fact, endorsed on the reverse *'Fathi and Faysal Nabulsy'*. The Court of Appeal held that the endorsements were sufficient to pass title to the bank but the bank did not become a holder in due course because the endorsement was irregular, in that it did not set out the name of the payee company in full. Lord Denning stated that an irregularity in the endorsement will deprive a subsequent holder of the rights conferred on a holder in due course and an examination of the promissory note gave rise to at least a theoretical suspicion or doubt as to whether the bill had been endorsed by the named payee.

Overdue bills

A holder in due course must have taken the bill before it became overdue and without notice of any prior dishonour, if there has been a previous dishonour.[139] Where a bill is overdue it remains transferable but it cannot be negotiated so as to confer a title on a subsequent holder free from defects affecting it when it became due.[140] Where a party takes a bill, which has previously been dishonoured by non-acceptance with knowledge of that fact, he cannot be a holder in due course. However, if the bill is payable on demand and it has not been in circulation for an unreasonable time, although it has in fact been presented for payment and dishonoured, the person to whom it is negotiated can still be a holder in due course if he takes without notice of the dishonour. Once a bill is overdue, it can only be negotiated subject to any defect in title affecting its maturity and the endorser cannot give a better title than the person from whom he took the bill.[141] Professor Shea[142] felt unable to suggest a more precise statutory definition of stale bills since the appropriate time may vary with different types of bills.

Holder must take the bill in good faith for value

A holder in due course must either himself give value or derive his title through a prior holder in due course. He cannot take the benefit of the fact that he takes through a holder for value who was not a holder in due course. For example, A gives value for a bill with notice of a defect in the prior title and A then endorses the bill to B who takes it gratuitously but without knowledge of the defect. B cannot be a holder in due course since the conditions for holding in due course cannot be split among successive holders, and value and good faith must proceed from the same person to constitute a person a holder in due course. However, once a person has satisfied the requirements in order to become a holder in due course, subsequent holders of the bill enjoy the benefits and privileges of a holder in due course, and they therefore take free from defects of title, which do not affect him.

---

[138] [1952] 2 QB 216.
[139] Bills of Exchange Act 1882, s.36.
[140] Bills of Exchange Act 1882, s.36(2).
[141] Bills of Exchange Act 1882, s.36(5).
[142] Jack (1989) Banking Services: Law and Practice, Report by the Review Committee Chaired by Professor R.B. Jack, CBE, London Cm. 622, Appendix A, para. 20.9.

In order to be a holder in due course, it is essential that the holder should act in good faith. Section 90 of the Bills of Exchange Act 1882 provides that a thing is done in good faith where it is done honestly, whether or not it is done negligently. It is, therefore, a question of the state of mind of the person who takes the instrument at the time he takes it. A person who acquires a bill from an endorser whom he realises is not the true owner cannot be a holder in due course and similarly a person who shuts his eyes to the existence of an apparent defect of title cannot be a holder in due course. Once the recipient of the bill has a suspicion that something is wrong with the bill, he is put on enquiry. In *Jones v Gordon*[143] a London firm drew bills on the firm for £1,727 which the firm accepted. At the time both the drawer and acceptors were insolvent and contemplating bankruptcy, and the transaction was undertaken with a view to defraud the creditors of the acceptors. The drawer offered the bills to the plaintiff, who knew the acceptor was in financial difficulties but who thought that he might be able to pay part of the face value of the bill, and so purchased them for £200. Although the plaintiff knew someone from whom he could obtain further information he made no further enquires. The acceptor subsequently became bankrupt and the plaintiff brought an action to recover the full amount of the bills. The court held that the plaintiff had sufficient knowledge of the affairs of the acceptor to realise that he was, or he might be, a party to the fraud and he therefore could not prove the full amount of the bills. Lord Blackburn examined the meaning of good faith[144] and two important points arise from his judgment:

1 If a man suspects something is wrong with a negotiable instrument that is enough to prevent him from taking it in good faith. The suspicion need not be accurate, provided it is near the truth.

2 If a man admits that he was careless in not discovering a defect in the title to the bill, he is entitled to be treated as having acted in good faith, but when a man says he was careless, the court may conclude that he was not in fact merely careless, but did suspect something to be wrong and willfully closed his eyes to it. In that case he did not act in good faith.

The good faith requirement was discussed again in *London Joint Stock Bank v Simmons*[145] where a broker defrauded the owner of negotiable securities by pledging them to a bank as security for a personal advance.

In addition, s.29(2) of the Bills of Exchange Act 1882 provides a non-exhaustive list of defects that will affect the title of a holder in due course, including duress, fraud and any illegal means by which the transferor obtains the acceptance on the instrument. In *Osterreichische Landerbank v S'Elite Ltd*[146] the court took the view that 'want of good faith', 'dishonesty', and 'fraud' were synonyms and 'fraud' within s.29(2) of the Act means 'common law fraud'. In *Bank of Credit and Commerce International SA v Dawson and Wright*[147] the court held that a bank manager's conspiracy with a fraudulent customer might constitute lack of

---

[143] (1877) 2 App Cas 616.
[144] *Jones v Gordon* (1877) 2 App Cas 616 at 629.
[145] [1892] AC 201.
[146] [1981] QB 565.
[147] [1987] FLR 342.

good faith and knowledge of a defective title on the part of the bank. The court, therefore, held that the plaintiff bank was not a holder in due course of three cheques either by taking them for collection or by having a lien, the bank being tainted by the knowledge of the bank manager.

A party, who takes the bill in good faith whether or not he gives value, will not therefore be able to retain the bill and will obtain no better a title than the person who negotiates it.[148] Under s.38(2) of the Bills of Exchange Act 1882 a 'holder in due course' holds the bill of exchange free from defects of title of the previous parties, as well as from personal defences available to prior parties. The expression 'personal defences' refers to defences such as set-off and counterclaim. The operation of the section may be illustrated by the following: A, the holder of a bill, endorses it to B, who cannot be made liable on the bill (for example, he is a minor). The bill is stolen from B by C who then forges B's endorsement on it and disposes of the bill to D, who fulfils the conditions to be a holder in due course. D endorses the bill to E and E to F, who is also a holder in due course. F can sue D and E on the dishonour of the bill, and it makes no difference if E obtained the bill from D by fraud. However, F cannot sue A or B, who became parties to the bill before the B's endorsement was forged, which of course is a nullity.

The wording of ss.29 and 38 is in fact confusing because s.29 refers to defects in the title of a person who negotiates a bill, whereas s.38(2) speaks of a holder in due course who takes free from defect of title of prior parties while s.38(3) refers to defects in the holder's title. These modes of reference must be assumed to refer to the same things, i.e. title and the difference between the reference to the transferor's defective title and the reference to a holder in due course acquiring free from all defects of title must be considered insignificant. However, s.29(2) refers to six listed defects, but s.30(2) which imposes the onus of proving that a defect of title has occurred, lists only five defects and the reference to 'other unlawful means' is omitted from s.30(2). Illegality is included generally, whereas under s.29(2) 'illegal consideration' is specifically recognised. The intention of the Act, like the common law decisions on which the Act is based, is that a holder in due course takes a bill free from all defects of title with the exception of those to which he is made specifically subject, for example forgery.

For value

The nature of the value, which must be given, has been dealt with in the context of a holder for value. The traditional view has been that a holder must himself give value in order to qualify as a holder in due course or take from someone who himself satisfies all the requirements of a holder in due course. Professor Shea and the Jack Committee recommended amendments that would eliminate the holder for value as a class of holder of negotiable instruments. They were in favour of retaining the requirement that a holder in due course should give value as a test of good faith. In *Clifford Chance v Silver*[149] the Court of Appeal held that endorsees holding a cheque could take advantage of s.27(2) of the 1882 Act to claim as holders in due course because value had previously been given, although not by themselves.

---

[148] *Clarke v Shee* (1774) 1 Cowp 197.
[149] [1992] 2 Bank LR 11.

Conclusion

The banking industry has devised various forms of negotiable instruments in order to enable payment to be made against them. The Bills of Exchange Act 1882, codifying the common law, recognised several of these instruments as negotiable so that title and the rights to receive payment could be passed to a third party, e.g. a holder who obtained free from notice of defects and who gave consideration. The usage of paper-based bills of exchange has declined as other methods of payment have gained prominence but they continue to be heavily used in some parts of the world in support of international trade transactions. Although in English law the cheque is no longer a negotiable instrument, bills of exchange still remain negotiable so that shipping documents and the payment instrument are capable of being passed to a third party.

Further reading

The Report of the Review Committee on Banking Services (the Jack Report), HMSO, 1989, Cm. 622. The Jack Committee Report on Banking Services Law and Practice in the United Kingdom was published in February 1989. Notably the report contained 83 recommendations, including the proposals for three new laws. The report proposed: a voluntary code of practice; a statutory codification of the exceptions to the law of confidentiality; and significant changes to the law on cheques and negotiable instruments.

11 Cheques as negotiable instruments

Chapter overview

The aim of this chapter is to:

➤ Examine the nature and special rules relating to cheques including the removal of the rights of negotiation.

➤ Discuss the contractual relationships involved in the collection and payment of a cheque.

➤ Explore the protection given to the paying and collecting banks for wrongful payment.

➤ Discuss the future of cheques.

Introduction

A cheque is a bill of exchange drawn on a banker payable on demand.[1] A cheque is therefore a type of bill of exchange and unless otherwise provided the Bills of Exchange Act 1882 will apply to cheques.[2] However, cheques are used very differently to bills of exchange. A cheque, for example, unlike a bill of exchange is drawn and payable by a bank and cheques are usually crossed and collected through banks. Additionally in the UK, in practice, cheques are no longer negotiated. Although the law relating to cheques has closely followed that relating to bills of exchange it has also developed a distinct set of rules and a number of distinct statutory provisions have been enacted. In *Ramchurn Mullick* v *Luchmeechund Radakissen*[3] Parke B described cheques as 'a peculiar sort of instrument, in many respects resembling a bill of exchange, but in some entirely different'. The nature of this peculiarity led the Committee on Banking Services in its 'Law and Practice Report',[4] to conclude that it is 'something of a legal anachronism that the main body of the law relating to cheques should be contained in an Act which treats the cheque as a subset of the bill of exchange'. The Committee, therefore,

---

[1] Bills of Exchange Act 1882 s.73.
[2] Bills of Exchange Act 1882 s.73.
[3] (1854) 9 Moo PC 46 at 69.
[4] Jack (1989) *Banking Services: Law and Practice*, Report by the Review Committee Chaired by Professor R.B. Jack, CBE, London Cm. 622.

concluded that it is confusing to have the law on cheques governed by the law relating to other bills of exchange and that the law relating to cheques should be dealt with by its own legislation. The government did not adopt this suggestion[5] and although cheques as a means of payment have for now survived plans for their abandonment,[6] it is possible they may simply fall into disuse as other effective means of payment are adopted.

Terminology

Although the terminology in respect of bills of exchange was examined earlier it is proposed to deal, here, with the main terminology relevant to cheques.

The drawer of a cheque is the person who brings it into existence by signing and properly drawing it. He will issue the instrument through its first delivery, complete in form, to a holder.[7] The delivery of the cheque means the transfer of possession, actual or constructive, from the drawer to the payee who is identified on the cheque form as the intended recipient of the funds and in whose favour the cheque has been drawn; unless the cheque is drawn payable to bearer in which case the person in possession of cheque is the bearer and he is entitled to payment.

The payee may transfer his rights to payment under the cheque, by endorsement, to a third party. A cheque may be endorsed to successive holders, if it is transferable and negotiable. In the UK, the law and banking practice have combined together to remove these aspects of a cheque although other jurisdictions allow cheques to be negotiated like bills of exchange.[8]

The holder of a cheque is the payee or endorsee of it, or the bearer in possession. The holder will generally collect the amount of the cheque, by paying it into his bank account for collection. The bank presenting the cheque for collection is called the collecting or presenting bank.

The contractual nature of the relationship

The four main contractual relationships involved in the collection and payments of a cheque are:

- A contract between the drawer of the cheque and the paying bank on which the cheque is drawn.
- A contract between the payee of the cheque and the collecting bank to which the payee will deliver the cheque for collection.
- A contract between the drawer and the payee arising out of the issue of the cheque.
- A contract between the collecting bank and the paying bank in relation to the clearing of cheques.[9]

Generally, the drawer of the cheque will be in a contractual relationship with the paying bank, which will owe various obligations under contract, including the duty to honour the customer's

---

[5] HSMO, UK Government White Paper on Banking Services: Banking and Services, Cm 1026, March 1990.
[6] See Ch. 12.
[7] Bills of Exchange Act 1882 s.2.
[8] See Ch. 10 on the rules on negotiation of bills of exchange.
[9] *Barclays Bank Plc v Bank of England* [1985] 1 All ER 385 at 390.

mandate.[10] Money standing to the credit of the drawer's account, with the drawing bank, is owed in debt by the paying bank to the drawer. By paying the amount of cheques drawn by the customer, the paying bank acts as an agent to discharge the indebtedness, either in whole or in part, of the drawer to the payee, and simultaneously to reduce its indebtedness to the payee to the value of the cheque. If the paying bank deviates from the drawer's mandate it will not be able to debit the customer's account, unless it can establish a defence for breach of the mandate.[11] There is no assignment of the proceeds of a cheque to the holder of the cheque before it is actually paid and the paying bank, further, does not become liable as an acceptor of a cheque since cheques are not accepted.

The holder will generally be a customer of the collecting bank and in presenting the cheque for collection the collecting bank will act as an agent for its customer. The collecting bank may present the cheque for itself, if it has given value. The collecting bank is under a duty to take reasonable steps to obtain payment of the cheque by duly presenting it for payment and if payment is refused the bank is under an obligation to notify its customer of the dishonour.

The drawer will frequently be in a contractual relationship with the payee of the cheque, e.g. the cheque is drawn in payment for the supply of goods or services. By delivering the cheque, in payment for the goods or services, to the seller or supplier the buyer undertakes a separate obligation with regard to payment under the instrument. A buyer who has a defence to a claim under the contract of sale because defective goods have been supplied may or may not have a defence under the contract constituted by the cheque.

Finally, banks collect cheques from each other under terms and rules established not only by the courts but also by banking practice, which will determine questions such as when the payment is complete, and the time of payment.[12]

Functions of a cheque

By far the most important function of cheques is to facilitate payment between the drawer of the cheque and payment is made through the mandate issued to the paying bank. For this function, it is not necessary that the cheque enjoy the characteristics of negotiability or transferability. All that is required is that a valid payment mandate is issued by the drawer to his bank, and in this instance that mandate will take the form of a cheque drawn against the drawer's account. The other function of the cheque, in theory, is a transfer and negotiation, which would enable title to the instrument to be passed from one holder to another.

A cheque is transferable if the rights under it are capable of being transferred from one person to another by delivery of the cheque, or by endorsement and delivery. Unless restricted the cheque is transferable[13] and the transferee may, then, enforce the cheque in his own name. If, however, the cheque is restricted so that it is non-transferable then it is still a cheque[14] but it will not be possible for the payee to validly endorse the cheque to another person. The cheque is valid between the immediate parties, the payer and payee, but it is not negotiable or transferable to a third party.

[10] See Ch. 7 for a discussion of the duties arising out of the contract.
[11] See Ch. 7.
[12] See Ch. 1 for discussion on when payment is made and finality of payment.
[13] Bills of Exchange Act 1882, s.31.
[14] *Hibernian Bank Ltd* v *Gysin and Hanson* [1938] 2 KB 384; see also Cheques Act 1992, s.1.

A cheque is negotiable if title to the cheque may be transferred free from defects in the title of the transferor and this is the case where a cheque is negotiated to a holder in due course.[15] However, a 'not negotiable' crossing on a cheque will prevent the cheque being negotiable but will not prevent the transferability of the cheque. In such circumstances, the payee may validly transfer the cheque by endorsement, but the endorsee would then take title to the cheque subject to any defects in the title of the payee.[16] Consequently, although a transferee could become a holder for value, he could not be a holder in due course.

The 'account payee' crossing or 'account payee only' crossing was originally construed so as to neither restrict transferability nor negotiability of the cheque but merely acts as an instruction to the collecting bank that the proceeds of the cheque were to be applied to the credit of the named payee. The payee is the person in whose favour the cheque is drawn and not someone (the holder) who acquires the cheque by negotiation.[17] Consequently, if the collecting bank collects the proceeds of such cheques for someone other than the named payee it would risk being liable in negligence and act in breach of s.4 of the Cheques Act 1957, if that person has a defective title to the instrument.[18] The courts took the view that it was impossible for the drawee bank to know, when the cheque was passed through the clearing system, for whose account it was collected and will be credited. The drawee bank cannot therefore assume responsibility for ensuring that the proceeds are credited to the payee's account and the words 'account payee' are not treated as an instruction to the drawee bank.

The Jack Committee[19] concluded that it would impose an unreasonable burden on the paying bank to give statutory recognition to the 'account payee' crossing and instead recommended that a new non-transferable instrument should be introduced alongside the traditional cheque. However, the government rejected the idea of a new non-transferable instrument because it felt that such an instrument would result in greater confusion about the use of cheques.[20] Instead s.1 of the Cheques Act 1992[21] introduced into the Bills of Exchange Act 1882 a new s.81A, which provides:

> Where a cheque is crossed and bears across its face the words 'account payee' or 'a/c payee', either with or without the word 'only', the cheque shall not be transferable, but shall only be valid as between the parties thereto.

The new s.81A(1) of the Bills of Exchange Act 1882 means that cheques crossed 'account payee' are given effect as non-transferable and non-negotiable instruments. Such cheques are only valid as between the original drawer and the original payee. If the payee endorses the cheque in favour of a third party that person will not acquire a valid title and cannot enforce

---

[15] Bills of Exchange Act 1882, s.38(2).

[16] *Great Western v London* [1901] AC 414; *Hibernian Bank Ltd v Gysin and Hanson* [1938] 2 KB 384; Bills of Exchange Act 1882, s.81.

[17] *House Property Co of London Ltd v London County and Westminster Bank* (1915) 84 LJ KB 1846.

[18] *Akrokerri (Atlantic) Mines Ltd v Economic Bank* [1904] 2 KB 465; *House Property Co of London Ltd v London County and Westminster Bank* (1915) 84 LJ KB 1846; *Universal Guarantee Pty Ltd v National Bank of Australasia* [1965] 1 WLR 691.

[19] Jack (1989) Banking Services: Law and Practice, Report by the Review Committee Chaired by Professor R.B. Jack, CBE, London Cm 622, para. 7.18.

[20] HSMO, UK Government White Paper on Banking Services: Banking and Services, Cm 1026, March 1990, Annex 5, para. 5.6.

[21] Cheques Act 1882, s.1 came into force on 16 June 1992. The background to the Act and UK banking practice as a result of the Act is examined in *The Honourable Society of Middle Temple v Lloyds Bank and Sekerbank* [1999] Lloyd's Rep. Bank. 50.

payment on the cheque. The new s.81A(2) of the Bills of Exchange Act 1882 gives effect to another proposal in the White Paper.[22] It provides that:

> A banker is not to be treated for the purposes of section 80 . . . as having been negligent by reason only of his failure to concern himself with any purported endorsement of a cheque which . . . is not transferable.

The subsection ensures that a drawee or paying bank which pays a cheque crossed 'account payee' in favour of the original payee and ignores any purported endorsement of the cheque will still enjoy the statutory protections conferred on banks under the Bills of Exchange Act 1882 and Cheques Act 1957. Since 'account payee' cheques are neither negotiable nor transferable a collecting bank cannot become a holder for value or holder in due course of the cheque. The cheque is valid between the immediate parties, the payer and payee, but it is not negotiable or transferable to a third party.[23] It is, in theory, possible for the drawer of the cheque to delete the 'account payee' crossing so as to make the cheque negotiable but the paying bank may question this alteration on the cheque form.[24]

Since 1992 the UK banks, although not required to, have adopted the practice of issuing pre-printed cheque forms, to customers, crossed and marked 'account payee', with the word 'or order' at the end of the payee line omitted. In *The Honourable Society of Middle Temple* v *Lloyds Bank and Sekerbank*[25] Rix J, after hearing expert evidence,[26] said that 'it can now truly be said that virtually every English cheque is crossed "a/c payee", however, foreign banks may not be aware of the significance of the term'. Such cheques are non-transferable and the practice of negotiating cheques is likely to die out.

Liability of paying and collecting banks for wrongful payment

Collecting bank

In *The Honourable Society of Middle Temple* v *Lloyds Bank and Sekerbank*[27] Rix J explained the nature of liability a collecting bank might find itself under:

> it seems to me that there is an important distinction to be made between the case where the agent is in breach of some duty vis-à-vis the party which requests him to act, and the case where the agent is in breach of some duty a third party.

The collecting bank may, therefore, find itself liable to its customer if it collects a cheque in excess of the mandate,[28] or to a third party true owner if payment is collected for someone other than the true owner. In collecting cheques and dealing with the proceeds for customers,

---

[22] HSMO, UK Government White Paper on Banking Services: Banking and Services, Cm 1026, March 1990.
[23] [1999] Lloyd's Rep. Bank. 50.
[24] Letter from the British Bankers Association on 19 May 1992 advised that to cancel the pre-printed not transferable crossing, a customer could draw a line through the words 'account payee' or 'a/c payee' or write 'words deleted' over them and authenticate the changes with his signature.
[25] [1999] Lloyd's Rep. Bank. 50.
[26] Practice adopted by Lloyds Bank, Barclays Bank and Midland Bank, in 1995.
[27] [1999] Lloyd's Rep. Bank. 50.
[28] See Ch. 7.

or for itself, the collecting bank may expose itself to claims from third parties who have an interest in the cheques, or the proceeds. Although the customer who requests that the collecting bank collect a cheque will himself be at fault and liable to the claimant, the claimant may target the collecting bank which is more likely to be available and have the means to satisfy the judgment. From the collecting bank's view the most dangerous claims are likely to be personal claims which do not depend on the collecting bank retaining the proceeds of the cheque, in which the claimant has an interest. These include an action in conversion, an action for money had and received, and for knowing assistance in breach of fiduciary duty.

We will now look at conversion as a cause of action.

An action in conversion

Conversion[29] is an action for the wrongful interference with goods, including documents, by taking, using or destroying, or otherwise dealing, them in a manner inconsistent with the rights of the true owner to immediate possession.[30] It is key to this area of the law that an action in conversion could not be brought in respect of the misappropriation of money[31] so the common law developed the proprietary action for conversion of the cheque of itself, rather than the money, but allowed damages to be based on the face value of the cheque, rather than the value of paper on which the cheque is written. The acts, which may constitute conversion of the cheque, are wide in nature[32] but in the context of cheques will extend to the presentation and collection of cheques for someone other than the true owner. Liability for conversion is strict so that the absence of knowledge by the collecting bank of the wrongdoing, and the absence of negligence on the part of the collecting bank, are no defence. Diplock LJ in *Marfani & Co Ltd* v *Midland Bank Ltd*[33] expressed the view that it:

> matters not that the doer of the act of usurpation did not know, and could not by the exercise of any reasonable care have known, of his neighbour's interest in the goods. The duty is absolute; he acts at this peril . . . [A banker's] contract with his customer requires him to accept possession of cheques delivered to him by his customer, to present them for payment to the banks upon which the cheques are drawn, to receive payment of them, and to credit the amount thereof to his own customer's account . . . If the customer is not entitled to the cheque which he delivers to his banker for collection, the banker, however innocent and careful he might have been, would at common law be liable to the true owner of the cheque for the amount of which he receives payment, either as damages in conversion or under the cognate cause of action, based historically upon assumpsit, for money had and received.

It should be noted that a claim in conversion is a claim in respect of the wrongful interference with possession of 'goods' and not ownership. Thus, an owner who is not in actual

---

[29] The action is still governed mainly by the common law, although some aspects of the law have been affected by the Torts (Interference with Goods) Act 1977.

[30] *Lloyds Bank Ltd* v *Chartered Bank of India, Australia and China* [1929] 1 KB 40.

[31] In *Likpin Gorman (a firm)* v *Karpnale* [1991] 2 AC 548 where the court expressed the view that money cannot be converted, with the exception of particular exception of notes and coins: Dugdale (2012) *Clerk and Lindsell on Torts*, London: Sweet & Maxwell Ltd, para. 17–34. The debt owed by the paying bank to the drawer is a chose in action, which will be reduced *pro tanto* by the payment of the cheque. There can be no conversion of the chose in action since it does not fall within the definition of 'goods'.

[32] Dugdale (2012) *Clerk and Lindsell on Torts*, London: Sweet & Maxwell Ltd, para. 17–08.

[33] [1968] 1 WLR 956 at 971.

possession and has no immediate right to possession has no claim in conversion, but a non-owner, for example, a thief who was in possession at the time of the conversion, would be able to bring an action (subject to the defence of *jus tertii* (the right of a third party)). Although, the claim in conversion relates to the paper on which the cheque is written the damages recoverable are not the value of the piece of paper but face value of the cheque.[34]

The true owner's cause of action

Where a customer asks his bank to present a cheque for payment to the drawee bank, it assumes the role of either a collecting bank, or discounting bank, but whatever role it occupies, if the customer's title is defective, the bank may be sued by the true owner of the cheque. While the causes of action available to the true owner of the cheque are similar, the nature of defences available to the collecting bank will vary. A bank, which collects a cheque for a person who has no title to it or whose title is defective, faces the possibility of an action by the true owner of the instrument.

There are two possible causes of action available: (i) an action in conversion; and (ii) an action based on restitution for wrongdoing. In *OBG Ltd* v *Allan*[35] the court confirmed that although the availability of an action in conversion in relation to a cheque is a 'legal fiction' where a bank converts a cheque by receiving it for collection and presenting it for payment,[36] the bank is liable for the face value of the instrument. Their Lordships also confirmed that the cheque is to be treated as a chattel for the purposes of such an action. The other form of action available is based on restitution for wrongdoing and in *Morison* v *London County and Westminster Bank Ltd*,[37] where an agent drew cheques against his principal's account, in excess of his authority, and arranged for their collection to the credit of his own personal account, the true owner was held entitled to pursue an action for money had and received, instead of an action in the tort of conversion. Since the House of Lords decision in *Lipkin Gorman* v *Karpnale & Co*[38] it has also been possible, in appropriate cases, to bring an action on the grounds that the defendant has been unjustly enriched at the claimant's expense, for example where payment is made under a mistake of fact. However, the cause of action in conversion is to be preferred rather than a restitutionary action which is based on a waiver of the tort of conversion. The reason is that once an agent, acting in good faith, has paid over the money to his principal he cannot be required to return the money to the payer. In similar circumstances, a bank as an agent, acting in good faith, cannot be made accountable to the true owner, in an action for money had and received, once it has paid the money over to its principal, the customer.

If, in the course of collecting the cheque, as agent for a customer, the collecting bank incurs liability to a third party in conversion, the collecting bank may find itself liable to the true owner of the instrument. The person to whom the right of action in conversion is

---

[34] *Morison v London County and Westminster Bank Ltd* [1914] 3 KB 356; *Lloyds Bank Ltd v The Chartered Bank of India, Australia and China* [1929] 1 KB 40 at 55–56.

[35] [2008] AC 1.

[36] *Morison v London County and Westminster Bank Ltd* [1914] 3 KB 356; *AL Underwood Ltd v Bank of Liverpool* [1924] 1 QB 775; *Lloyds Bank Ltd v Savory & Co* [1933] AC 201; *Bute (Marquess of) v Barclays Bank Ltd* [1955] 1 QB 202; see also *Arrow Transfer Co Ltd v Royal Bank of Canada* [1971] 3 WWR 241 where the history of the action is examined.

[37] [1914] 3 KB 356.

[38] [1991] 2 AC 548.

available is called the 'true owner' under the Bills of Exchange Act 1882, but the Act does not define the term. It would appear to mean a holder of the instrument who can prove that he has (a) ownership and possession of the instrument, or (b) possession of it, or (c) an immediate right to possession, without either actual ownership or actual possession. The question of whether the drawer or payee of a cheque is a true owner may depend on whether the drawer was authorised to make payment in that manner, but even if the drawer retains ownership the payee may be entitled to immediate possession. In *International Factors Ltd* v *Rodriguez*[39] the plaintiffs and a company entered into an agreement under which the plaintiffs agreed to purchase all the company's book debts. It was agreed that if any payments in respect of the assigned debts were paid directly to the company it would hold the full amount on trust for the plaintiffs. The company received four cheques totalling £11,370 towards the payment of debts, which were subject to the agreement, and arranged for these to be paid into its own bank account. The court held the plaintiffs were entitled to sue in conversion because the agreement gave them an immediate right to the possession of the cheques; the company came under an immediate obligation to hand over to the plaintiffs any cheques that came into its possession.

In *Bute (Marquess of)* v *Barclays Bank Ltd*[40] three warrants, which legally constituted cheques, bearing crossings and accompanied by the words 'not negotiable' were dispatched by the drawers to M, an employee of the Marquess of Bute. M arranged for the collection and payment of these warrants, which were payable to '[M] for the Marquess of Bute', to the credit of an account opened in his own name. The Marquess of Bute brought an action for conversion of these warrants against the collecting bank. McNair J rejected the argument that for the action to succeed the Marquess had to establish that he was the owner and therefore had property in the warrants. Instead, the learned judge held that in order to bring an action in conversion all the claimant had to establish was his entitlement to the immediate possession of the instrument at the time the conversion took place. In the *Marquess of Bute* case the Marquess had never intended to pass possession to M and therefore his action in conversion was maintained. However, in *Citibank NA* v *Brown Shipley & Co Ltd*[41] dishonest persons managed to get access to a bank account held with the claimant and induced the bank to issue bankers' drafts payable to the defendant bank. The defendant bank, on obtaining assurances from the claimant bank that the drafts were regular, received the amounts under the drafts on clearing and credited the dishonest person's account with them. Waller J, dismissing the claimant bank's action in conversion, held that as a person authorised for the claimant bank had delivered the drafts to the defendant bank, and title to them and the right to possession had passed to the defendant bank.

As a general rule the true owner of the cheque is the last person to whom the instrument has been validly transferred. If the instrument has not been validly drawn or negotiated, for example the drawing of the instrument is vitiated by forgery, then the original owner remains the true owner of the cheque.[42] If the instrument has been forged, the true owner is the proprietor of the chequebook from which the form was taken without authorisation[43] but where

---

[39] [1979] QB 351.
[40] [1955] 1 QB 202.
[41] [1991] 2 Lloyd's Rep. 576.
[42] *Ladbroke & Co* v *Todd* (1914) 30 TLR 433; *Commercial Banking Co of Sydney Ltd* v *Mann* [1961] AC 1.
[43] *Morison* v *London County and Westminster Bank Ltd* [1914] 3 KB 356; *Bute (Marquess of)* v *Barclays Bank Ltd* [1955] 1 QB 202.

a cheque payable to the order of a specified person is removed from him before he has nego-tiated it, title does not pass to a third party and the purported payee remains the true owner.[44] However, where the payee endorses the instrument, if the law permits endorsement in blank, a rogue may thereafter transfer title by mere delivery.

Collecting banks defence to a claim in conversion

Section 4 of the Cheques Act 1957 provides:

> Where a banker, in good faith and without negligence (a) receives payment for a customer of an instrument to which this section applies; or (b) having credited a customer's account with the amount of such an instrument, receives payment thereof for himself; and the customer has no title, or a defective title, to the instrument, the banker does not incur any liability to the true owner of the instrument by reason only of having received payment thereof . . .

If the customer of a collecting bank deposits a cheque for the collection of his account but does not have title to the cheque, the collecting bank, at common law, is liable to the true owner in damages, regardless of how careful or however innocent the collecting bank had been. The purpose of s.4 of the Cheques Act 1957 is to mitigate the hardship of the common law and provide the collecting bank with a defence which will enable the collecting bank to avoid liability if it has acted in good faith and without negligence.

Instruments to which s.4 of the Cheques Act 1957 applies

Section 4(2) of the 1957 Act applies *inter alia* to:

- Cheques, including cheques under s.81A of the Bills of Exchange Act 1882 or those that are otherwise non-transferable.
- Any document issued by a customer of a bank, which although not a bill of exchange, is intended to enable a person to obtain payment from that bank of the sum mentioned in the document.
- Any draft payable on demand drawn by the bank upon itself, whether payable at the head-office or some other office of the bank.

The definition of a cheque has been examined[45] but a cheque which bears a forged signature is wholly inoperative and, therefore, not a cheque for the purposes of s.4 of the Cheques Act 1882. Similarly, where the cheque has been materially altered the instrument is void and therefore falls outside the scope of the Cheques Act 1957. Thus, the collecting bank is protected against an action in conversion where it collects an instrument for someone other than the true owner, on instruments which are valid payment orders but not technically cheques. In *Orbit Mining and Trading Co Ltd* v *Westminster Bank Ltd*[46] instruments in the form of cheques and made payable 'Pay Cash or order' were held to fall outside the definition of cheques, but were held to be within the scope of s.4(2)(b).

---

[44] *Lacave & Co* v *Credit Lyonnais* [1897] 1 QB 148.
[45] See Ch. 10.
[46] [1963] 1 QB 794.

Collecting bank

Section 4 of the Cheques Act 1957 applies to a 'banker' which is defined as a body of persons, whether incorporated or not, who carry on the business of banking. In order to be protected under s.4 of the Cheques Act 1957 the collecting bank must have:

- Received payment of a cheque for a holder;[47] or

- Credited a holder's account with the amount of a cheque, and then received payment of the cheque itself.[48]

While, s.4 of the Cheques Act 1957 expressly covers the receipt of the proceeds of the cheque, by a collecting bank, it also includes:

> every step taken in the ordinary course of business and intended to lead up to that result, i.e. the receipt of payment of the cheque.

Thus, where a collecting bank employs a correspondent bank to collect a cheque on behalf of a customer, each bank is protected by s.4 of the Cheques Act 1957.

Requirements of s.4 of the Cheques Act 1957

In order to claim the protection of s.4 the collecting bank must show that it received payment 'in good faith and without negligence'. Section 90 of the Bills of Exchange Act 1882, which is applied to the construction of the Cheques Act 1957 by s.6(1) of the 1957 Act, provides that 'a thing is done in good faith, within the meaning of the Cheques Act 1957, where it is in fact done honestly, whether it is done negligently or not'. It is, however, the requirement that the collecting bank acts without negligence that has resulted in considerable litigation. At common law, the collecting bank owes the true owner an absolute duty not to convert the cheque but s.4 of the Bills of Exchange Act 1882 allows the collecting bank an opportunity to escape liability so long as the bank is not negligent. The effect of the section is to impose a kind of statutory duty of care on the collecting bank, which will enable it to escape liability, which would otherwise be imposed by the common law.[49] Whether the collecting bank has been negligent is a question of fact, which should be determined separately in respect of each cheque.[50]

The courts have formulated general tests for determining whether, objectively, the collecting bank has discharged the prevailing standard of care and although the collecting bank, or its officers, cannot be expected to act as amateur detectives the collecting bank cannot assume that every person who presents a cheque for collection is honest and the true owner of the instrument.[51] In *Thackwell* v *Barclays Bank*[52] Hutchinson J examined the various tests that had been applied by the courts in a series of cases. The learned judge referred to *Taxation Commissioners* v *English Scottish and Australian Bank*[53] where the court held that the test of negligence is whether the transaction of paying the cheque, coupled with the circumstances antecedent or present, was so out of the ordinary course that it ought to have aroused doubts

---

[47] Cheques Act 1957, s.4(1)(a).
[48] Cheques Act 1957, s.4(1)(b).
[49] Hapgood (2007) *Paget's Law of Banking*, London: LexisNexis Butterworth, para. 24.10.
[50] *Morison* v *London County and Westminster Bank Ltd* [1914] 3 KB 356.
[51] *Taxation Commissioners* v *English Scottish and Australian Bank* [1920] AC 683.
[52] [1986] 1 All ER 676.
[53] [1920] AC 683.

in the bank's mind, and caused it to make enquiry. Hutchinson J then went on to examine the test established in *Lloyds Bank v EB Savory & Co*[54] where the court concluded that the standard by which the absence, or otherwise, of negligence is to be determined by reference to the practice of reasonable men carrying on the business of banks, endeavouring to act in a manner calculated to protect themselves and others against fraud. However, Hutchinson J concluded that the most suitable approach to the question of negligence of the collecting bank was that provided by Diplock LJ in *Marfani & Co Ltd v Midland Bank Ltd*[55] where the judge concluded that:

> Granted good faith in the banker . . . the usual matter with respect to which the banker should take reasonable care is to satisfy himself that his own customer's title to the cheque delivered to him for collection is not defective, i.e. that no other person is the owner of it. Where the customer is in possession of the cheque at the time of delivery for collection, and appears on the face of it to be the 'holder', i.e. the payee or indorsee or the bearer, the banker is, in my view, entitled to assume that the customer is the owner of the cheque unless there are facts which are known, or ought to be known, to the banker which would cause a reasonable banker to suspect that the customer is not the true owner.
>
> What facts ought to be known to the banker, i.e. what inquires he should make and, what facts are sufficient to cause him reasonably to suspect that the customer is not the true owner, must depend on current banking practice, and change as that practice changes. Cases decided 30 years ago, when the use by the general public of banking facilities was much less widespread, may not be a reliable guide to what the duty of a careful banker in relation to inquiries, and as to facts which ought to give rise to suspicion, is today.

The approach in the *Marfani* case was confirmed in *Architects of Wine Ltd v Barclays Bank Plc.*[56] where the Court of Appeal emphasised the importance of current banking practice to the issue of negligence. In deciding whether or not a bank has proven that it was not negligent, within s.4 of the Cheques Act 1957, the courts will look at 'all the circumstances antecedent and present'. Rix LJ explained in the *Architects of Wine Ltd* case that the enquiry is fact sensitive.

Burden of proof

It is for the collecting bank to show that it acted without negligence[57] and in accordance with the usual balance of proof in civil cases, on the balance of probabilities. This was reinforced in *Marfani & Co Ltd v Midland Bank Ltd*[58] where Diplock LJ expressed the view that 'since it [the Cheques Act 1957, s.4] takes the form of a qualified immunity from strict liability at common law, the onus of showing that he did take such reasonable care lies upon the defendant bank'.

Time for assessing the collecting bank's conduct

It might be thought that the relevant time for determining whether the collecting bank had complied with its duty of care towards the true owner of the cheque is the time it receives the

---

[54] [1933] AC 201.
[55] [1968] 1 WLR 972.
[56] [2007] 2 Lloyd's Rep 471.
[57] *Midland Bank Ltd v Reckitt* [1933] AC 1 HL 14; *Orbit Mining and Trading Co Ltd v Westminster Bank Ltd* [1963] 1 QB 794 at 813.
[58] [1968] 1 WLR 957.

payment. However, in *Marfani & Co Ltd* v *Midland Bank Ltd*[59] Diplock LJ held that the relevant time was the time when the collecting bank pays out the proceeds of the cheque to its own customer so depriving the true owner of his right to follow the money. The facts, which therefore come to the attention of the collecting bank between the time it receives the payment and the time when the holder draws against the cheque, are relevant. In *Marfani* this allowed the collecting bank to prove that it had acted without negligence when the collecting bank received favourable references for the payee who had recently opened an account. Equally, the bank might receive information, which might put the bank on enquiry, during this time.

Relevance of the collecting bank's own internal procedures

Collecting banks will have their own internal procedures for their staff intended to reduce the possibility of the bank collecting cheques to which the holder has no, or a defective, title. If these procedures are deemed to be insufficient and not stringent enough, the collecting bank may be held negligent, notwithstanding compliance with its own procedures.[60] If the collecting bank sets very stringent standards for its employees to follow, and these are breached then that in itself maybe used as evidence of negligence. However, while the courts will have regard to generally accepted banking practice, compliance with such practice would not preclude a finding of negligence.[61] If the cheque would ordinarily come to a cashier the question is whether a cashier of ordinary intelligence would have appreciated that the title of the customer was open to doubt.

Causation

Where the collecting bank has failed to prove that it received payment without negligence, it will have failed to make enquires or taken some step which, in the circumstances, it ought reasonably to have made or taken. The question is whether the collecting bank can argue that had it made those enquires or taken those steps, it would not have prevented the loss sustained by the true owner of the cheque. The decisions of the courts are in conflict on this point. In *Underwood Ltd* v *Bank of Liverpool & Martins*[62] it was said that is not open to the collecting bank to run this argument.[63] By contrast, more recent cases have taken the view that, in theory, the collecting bank could raise such an argument although the standard of proof required will be high. In *Baker* v *Barclays Bank Ltd*[64] Devlin J held that negligence on the part of the collecting bank could affirmatively show that the failure was immaterial. This was described as a heavy burden. In *Marfani & Co Ltd* v *Midland Bank Ltd*[65] Diplock LJ said that the collecting bank would not be negligent if it was 'improbable' that the enquiries would have lead to the detection of the holder's dishonest purpose. However, the weight of judicial opinion supports the view that it is no defence for the collecting bank to show that, even if it had made enquires, the true owner of the cheque would still have suffered the loss. Thus, if the collecting bank fails to show that it was not negligent and therefore falls outside the

---

[59] [1968] 1 WLR 957.
[60] *Lloyds Bank Ltd* v *E.B. Savory & Co* [1933] AC 201.
[61] *The Honourable Society of Middle Temple* v *Lloyds Bank Plc* [1999] Lloyd's Rep. Bank 50 at 66, per Rix J, citing *Lloyds Bank Ltd* v *E.B. Savory & Co* [1933] AC 201.
[62] [1924] 1 KB 775.
[63] See also *Lloyds Bank Ltd* v *E.B. Savoury & Co* [1933] AC 201.
[64] [1955] 1 WLR 822.
[65] [1968] 1 WLR 956.

scope of s.4 of the Cheques Act 1957 the bank is exposed to the full rigours of the action for conversion, or for money had and received. In such circumstances, it is not a defence to these actions to argue that had reasonable care been exercised the loss would still have occurred.

Specific examples of negligence

Below are discussed examples of negligence under specific headings.

Opening the account

Although the collecting bank's conduct at the time of opening the account may not be sufficient for it to lose the protection of s.4 of the Cheques Act 1957 the circumstances connected with the opening of the account may shed light on the question of whether or not the collecting bank has been negligent in opening the account.[66]

The procedures to verify the identity of prospective customers are largely determined by the regulations aimed at preventing money laundering[67] and the FCA's Rules[68] require banks and other financial institutions to have procedures to enable them to identify money laundering risks and that these are proportionate to the nature, scale and complexity of the activities of the business. Regulations 5 and 6 of the Money Laundering Regulations 2007[69] provide that when establishing a business relationship, for example opening a bank account, the bank must undertake 'customer due diligence'. This requires identification of the customer and, where relevant, any beneficial owners.[70] In the case of an individual customer the Guidance issued by the Joint Money Laundering Steering Group (JMLSG) provides that banks should verify the name, date of birth and residential address of the customer.[71] In the case of company customers that includes the full name, registered number, registered office in the country of incorporation and business address are required. For a private company the name of all directors and the name of individuals who own or control more than 25 per cent of the shares or voting rights are also required. The JMLSG provides that in the case of individuals the verification should be by way of a government issued document with full name and photograph and either a residential address or date of birth, for example a passport or photocard driving licence. Alternatively, a government issued document without a photograph may be used if supported by a second document issued by a government body, public sector authority or

---

[66] *Commissioners of Taxation* v *English, Scottish and Australian Bank Ltd* [1920] AC 683 at 688.

[67] See Chs 7 and 13: Money Laundering Regulations 2007, SI 2007/2157 which implement, in part, EU Directive 2005/60/EU on the prevention of the use of financial systems for the purpose of money laundering and terrorist financing. Guidance to assist in complying with the 2007 Regulations has been produced by the Joint Money Laundering Steering Group which is made up of the leading UK trade associations in the financial services sector.

[68] Under the Financial Services and Markets Act 2000; see FCA Handbook, SYSC 6.3, http://www.fshandbook. info/FS/html/FCA/SYSC/6/3.

[69] Money Laundering Regulations 2007, SI 2007/2157 (as amended by SI 2007/3299 and SI 2009/209).

[70] Money Laundering Regulations 2007, SI 2007/2157 (as amended by SI 2007/3299 and SI 2009/209), regs 5(b) and 6 define such interests as those controlling more than 25 per cent of a body corporate, partnership or trust.

[71] Joint Money Laundering Steering Group Guidance, para. 5.3.70, version 1 February 2011, http://www.jmlsg. org.uk/jmlsg-guidance.

regulated utility company with the customer's full name and either address or date of birth.[72] Depending on the circumstances, less may be required by way of verification from those on low incomes, students, asylum seekers and migrant workers.[73]

Prior to the money laundering regulations a collecting bank could be liable for negligence if it was found to have made inadequate enquires as to the customer's identity.[74] Not only will the bank be found liable for negligence but it might also be liable in negligence under s.150 of the Financial Services and Markets Act 2000 and the bank is liable in excess of the face value of the cheque.

Employer's details

The earlier cases suggest that a bank should obtain the employment details of its prospective customers before opening an account. In *Lloyd's Bank Ltd* v *E.B. Savory & Co*[75] the claimant, a stockbroker, paid its jobbers, in accordance with Stock Exchange practice, by cheques drawn in the name of a payee or bearer. Two of the claimant's employees, P and S, stole such cheques. While P paid the cheques into City branches of Lloyd's Bank for the credit of his account, at the Wallington branch, S paid the cheques into City branches of Lloyd's Bank for the credit of his wife's account at Redhill and then Weybridge branches. Lord Wright, one of three majority judges, held that in a situation where a payee is employed in a position, which involves his handling and having the opportunity to steal his employer's cheques, a collecting bank would not have taken adequate precautions if it does not enquire and ask for the name of the customer's employers.[76] Had the collecting bank known this, it would have realised, or ought to have realised, that P was paying cheques drawn on his employers.[77] In relation to opening an account for S's wife, the collecting bank obtained a reference from her landlady, but made no further enquiries. Lord Wright expressed the view that the collecting bank ought to have enquired as to her 'means and circumstance', and in relation to the husband 'something about him and his occupation or position in life'. In the circumstances, the bank was held negligent in collecting cheques for S's wife. Lords Russell and Blanesburgh, dissenting, held that an enquiry into the name of the employer was unnecessary.

In recent years there has been a move away from the rule that the collecting bank should enquire about a customer's employment. In *Orbit Mining and Trading Co Ltd* v *Westminster Bank Ltd*[78] Harman LJ held that a collecting bank is not under a duty continually to keep itself

---

[72] Joint Money Laundering Steering Group Guidance, para. 5.3.74, version 1 February 2011, http://www.jmlsg.org.uk/jmlsg-guidance.

[73] Joint Money Laundering Steering Group Guidance, para. 5.3.98, version 1 February 2011, http://www.jmlsg.org.uk/jmlsg-guidance.

[74] *Lumsden & Co* v *London Trustees Savings Bank* [1971] 1 Lloyds Rep 114.

[75] [1933] AC 201.

[76] In *Lloyd's Bank Ltd* v *E.B. Savory* [1933] AC 201 Lord Wright though it was necessary to ascertain the name of the employer where the intended customer was a stockbroker's clerk. This was in contrast with an intended customer who, for example, was a technical employee in a factory where he would not generally be expected to handle his employer's cheques.

[77] In *Lloyd's Bank Ltd* v *E.B. Savory* [1933] AC 201 Lord Warrington thought that it was usual to enquire of the name of the employer, but noted an exception, namely where there was a satisfactory reference to make such an enquiry superficial. Lord Buckmaster accepts that a satisfactory reference might have dispensed with the need to ascertain the name of the employer but, on the facts, found that this was not the case. Lord Wright however thought that both were required.

[78] [1963] QB 794 at 825.

up to date regarding the identity of the customer's employer. The collecting bank was held not negligent even though the customer presented cheques drawn on a new company, of which he was a director, for his own account. There was further reluctance, on the part of the courts, to introduce a strict rule regarding the customer's employer. In *Marfani & Co v Midland Bank*[79] Diplock LJ held that there was no absolute duty on a collecting bank to obtain details of employment from a prospective customer and viewed the *Lloyd's Bank*[80] case as a case decided on the banking practice of the 1930s. However, under the Money Laundering Regulations 2007[81] and the JMLSG Guidance, it states that employment details 'might be relevant' for personal bank account customers depending on the bank's 'risk assessment of the situation'.

Employees and agents

Cases which involve employees, and agents, usually involve such an individual either paying into his personal account cheques drawn on the employer or principal's account, or paying into his personal account cheques which name the employer or principal as the original payee of the amount.

(i) Cheques drawn on the principal or employer

In *Lloyds Bank Ltd v E.B. Savory Co*[82] a number of bearer cheques were drawn by the employer, in favour of creditors of the firm, but were stolen by an employee who paid them into his personal account. Lord Wright held that:

> The most obvious circumstances which should put a banker on his guard . . . are where a cheque is presented for collection which bears on its face a warning that the customer may have misappropriated it as for instance . . . where a servant steals cheques drawn by his employers and pays them or procures their payment into his own account.

The collecting bank was negligent in not enquiring into the payee's title to the cheque, even though the cheque was paid into a branch of the collecting bank other than where the employee maintained his account.

Further in *Lloyds Bank Ltd v The Chartered Bank of India, Australia and China*[83] the court concluded that the collecting bank could not rely on the presence of a signature on the cheque in addition to that of the employee whose account was being credited. In this case, the claimant was a bank whose fraudulent employee, L, had authority to draw cheques on other banks with which the claimant maintained accounts. L signed all the cheques, but in some cases it was necessary for him to procure the signatures of other signatories, which he did by misrepresenting the purpose of the payment. L then forwarded the cheques for collection of the defendant bank with a written instruction to credit his account. Sankey LJ relied on the fact that the collecting bank knew that L was an employee of the claimant and was transferring large sums of money from the claimant's account to his personal account. Additionally, cheques were made payable to the collecting bank with a direction to pay into his personal account; this direction should have put the bank on enquiry.

[79] [1968] 1 WLR 956.
[80] [1933] AC 201.
[81] SI 2007/2157.
[82] [1933] AC 201.
[83] [1929] 1 KB 40.

(ii) Cheques payable to employer or principal

The payment by an agent, or employee, of cheques payable to his principal, or employer, into his own account should place the collecting bank on enquiry.[84] In *Bute (Marquess) v Barclays Bank Ltd*[85] McGaw was the claimant's farm manager responsible for making applications to the Department of Agriculture for farm subsidies. After he had left the claimant's employment, McGaw received three payment warrants, which he had applied for before he left the claimant's employment. The warrants were marked 'Pay Mr D. McGaw, Kellylamont, Rothersby, Bute £133 10s in respect of Hill Sheep subsidy, 1949, for the Marquess of Bute'. McGaw opened a bank account with the defendant bank in Yorkshire and the defendant bank collected the warrants. After taking up references, the defendant bank allowed McGaw to draw against the warrants. It was held that the collecting bank had been negligent in collecting the warrants since McGaw was a complete stranger to the collecting bank and the warrants bore a clear indication that McGaw was to receive the money as an agent or in a fiduciary capacity. The proceeds of the warrants should not have been credited to his account without enquiry.

(iii) Company directors

Although similar rules to those applicable to agents and employees are likely to apply to company directors there may be greater opportunity for directors to access company bank accounts, in an unauthorised manner, and pay into their own accounts cheques drawn by the company in favour of a third party, or divert cheques payable to the company to their own accounts. Whether, it may be possible for the collecting bank to argue that the director had ostensible authority to deal with cheques has been examined. By the court this was examined in *Underwood Ltd v Bank of Liverpool & Martins*[86] where cheques payable to 'A.L. Underwood Ltd', some of which were crossed 'Account Payee' and endorsed 'A.L. Underwood Ltd – A.L. Underwood sole director', were paid into the personal account of A.L. Underwood at the defendant bank. The collecting bank argued that Underwood had apparent authority to pay the cheques into his own account as he was the sole director of the company and owned all but one of its shares. The court rejecting this argument held that the collection of the cheques for the personal account of Underwood was so unusual that it ought to have attracted the attention of the collecting bank and the judges took the view that the collecting bank ought to have asked the director whether the company had its own bank account (which it did at another bank) and why the cheques were not being paid into the company account.

The *Underwood* case can be contrasted with *Orbit Mining and Trading Co Ltd v Westminster Bank Ltd*[87] where the claimant company's cheques required the signatures of two directors, E and W. W often spent time abroad and he frequently signed cheques in blank before his departure. E fraudulently made the cheques out to 'cash', added his signature to the cheques, and presented them for collection through his bank. Despite these warning signs, the collecting bank was held not negligent since the collecting bank did not know that its payee, E, was a director of the claimant company,[88] and his signature was illegible.

---

[84] *Hannan's Lake View Central (Limited) v Armstrong* (1900) TLR 236.

[85] [1955] 1 QB 202, first instance.

[86] [1924] 1 KB 775.

[87] [1963] 1 QB 794.

[88] The bank had initially enquired as to E's employers, but at the time of the fraud E was a director or another company (*Orbit Mining and Trading Co Ltd v Westminster Bank Ltd* [1963] 1 QB 794). It was therefore not argued that the bank had been negligent in opening the account.

(iv) Public authorities

In *Ross* v *London County Westminster & Parrs Bank Ltd*[89] the court held that it was not in accordance with the ordinary course that cheques drawn payable to the officer of a public department should be endorsed for the purposes of paying sums to a private individual. In *Ross* cheques were made payable to a public department namely, 'The Officer in Charge, Estates Office, Canadian Overseas Military Forces'. The estates office did not have its own bank account, and the Officer in Charge, with a view to the cheques being sent to the paymaster general or his beneficiary, regularly endorsed them. However, a quartermaster sergeant fraudulently took the cheques to the defendant bank for the collection of his own account. The court held that the collecting bank should have been put on enquiry and was negligent in not making enquires into the fraudster's title to the cheques.

(v) Partners

In the absence of an express agreement of the other partners, cheques payable to a partnership ought to be paid into a partnership account. In *Baker* v *Barclays Bank Ltd*[90] it was argued, at first instance, that the bank could rely on the actual or ostensible authority of a partner to endorse a cheque and pay it into his personal account. Devlin J applying *A.L. Underwood Ltd* v *Bank of Liverpool*[91] held that this was no defence to an action in conversion against the collecting bank. In *Smith and Baldwin* v *Barclays Bank*[92] the collecting bank was put on enquiry as a result of a partner paying partnership cheques into his personal account. However, the bank was held to have taken sufficient steps to avoid liability for negligence since the partner had been summoned to a meeting at the collecting bank and asked for an explanation, and he had produced a certificate issued under the Registration of Business Names Act 1916, which purported to show he was the sole proprietor.

(vi) Trustees

Trustees may have authority to draw on the trust account and the collecting bank will be put on enquiry if it is aware, or ought to be aware, that cheques are being paid to the benefit of the trustees. In *Midland Bank Ltd* v *Reckitt*[93] a solicitor, Terrington, was authorised by a power of attorney to draw cheques on the client's bank account. Terrington fraudulently drew cheques on the client's bank account which were signed 'Harold G Reckitt by Terrington, his attorney', and presented to the collecting bank for the credit of his own account, which was overdrawn. The court held that the form of the cheque put the collecting bank on notice that the cheques did not belong to Terrington and the collecting bank was negligent in failing to enquire whether Terrington had authority to make such payments into his own account.

Professional people, for example solicitors, often maintain bank accounts, which contain client funds, held on trust by the solicitor. The nature of these accounts means that a wide range of cheques may be paid into the trust account without putting the bank on enquiry. In *Penmount Estates Ltd* v *National Provincial Bank Ltd*[94] cheques crossed '& Not negotiable'

---

[89] [1919] 1 KB 678.
[90] [1955] 2 All ER 571.
[91] [1924] 1 KB 775.
[92] (1944) 65 *Journal of Institute of Bankers* 5.
[93] [1933] AC 1.
[94] (1945) 173 LT 344.

received from the War Damage Commission, and payable to the claimant, were fraudulently endorsed and paid into a solicitor's client account held with the defendant collecting bank. The solicitor explained that he had an arrangement with the clients whereby he paid cheques from the War Damage Commission into his account, and sent them a cheque minus his legal fees. It was held that the collecting bank had not been negligent in collecting the cheque since there was nothing out of the ordinary in a solicitor paying into his account monies belonging to persons other than himself.

General conduct of the account

The courts have, in some cases, held that the general conduct of the payee's account should have been a factor which ought to have put the collecting bank on notice when collecting that payee's cheques. The JMLSG Guidance[95] states that information obtained about a customer at the outset of a relationship 'might include' the purpose of the bank account and the anticipated level of activity. The size of cheques paid into a payee's account, therefore, may be a factor that puts the collecting bank on notice if it is coupled with other factors that may arouse the collecting bank's suspicion. In *Nu-Stilo Footwear Ltd v Lloyds Bank Ltd*[96] a fictitious referee stated that the account holder had just started a freelance business, which would be successful in a few years. The court held that the collecting bank should have been put on enquiry and factors that should have been taken into consideration included the large numbers of the cheques being paid into the account, which were considered inconsistent with the payee starting up a new business. Other factors which should place the bank on enquiry include cheques drawn into the name of the business being endorsed to a third party without any real explanation of why the business does not have its own account. In *Baker v Barclays Bank Ltd*[97] the payee paid into his personal account cheques which were drawn 'Modern Confections' and which appeared to be properly endorsed. The collecting bank's manager accepted the payee's explanation that he was helping the owner of 'Modern Confections' with the financial side of the business with a view to entering into a partnership with the owner of the business. The court held that the bank manager ought to have refused the explanation, as there was no real reason why the business did not have its own bank account, nor any reason why the owner of 'Modern Confections' would allow the payee to handle the business's money without having any control over the account. In *The Honourable Society of the Middle Temple v Lloyds Bank Plc*[98] Rix J held that a bank acting as an agent for collection for a foreign bank ought to have been put on enquiry by a combination of factors including the fact that a cheque payable to Sun Alliance, an English insurance company, was being collected by a bank in Turkey after the cheque had been illegibly endorsed by the agent for collection. Further, the agent for collection had been asked to speed up the clearance of the cheque because the Turkish bank's customer was 'in a difficult position,' which did not seem compatible with the position of the payee, Sun Alliance, a major English insurance company.

---

[95] Joint Money Laundering Steering Group Guidance, Version 1 February 2011, http://www.jmlsg.org.uk/jmlsg-guidance.
[96] *The Times*, 19 June 1956.
[97] [1955] 2 All ER 571.
[98] [1999] Lloyd's Rep Bank 50 at 72.

Crossing and endorsements

Under s.81A[99] of the Bills of Exchange Act 1882 a cheque marked 'account payee only' is non-transferable and the original payee remains the owner of the cheque. Prior to the Cheques Act 1992 the courts had already concluded that any such endorsement placed the collecting bank on enquiry to enquire how the holder, other than the named payee, obtained possession of the cheque provided. As a result of the Cheques Act 1992, a collecting bank will have to show exceptional circumstances in order to benefit from the protection provided under the Act. A circumstance where a collecting bank may still benefit from the protection under s.4 of the Bills of Exchange Act 1882 is where the cheque is collected for a fraudster who has the same name as the payee of the cheque. Another situation where the collecting bank may benefit from the protection of s.4 of the Bills of Exchange 1882 arose in *Architects of Wine Ltd v Barclays Bank Plc*[100] where over a six-month period, in 2004, the bank credited its customer, Architects of Wine (UK) Ltd, with the proceeds of approximately 400 cheques to which the customer did not have title. The cheques in fact belonged to an associated company with a similar name, Architects of Wine Ltd. When the latter became insolvent, its liquidator sued the bank for conversion of the cheques. The Court of Appeal, reversing the summary judgment at first instance, found the bank had a defence, under s.4 of the Bills of Exchange Act 1882. The cheques were made payable either to Architects of Wine or Architects of Wine Ltd and the bank provided evidence that its staff, responsible for checking the payee's name on cheques, were trained to apply a common sense approach and look to see that the name of the payee on the cheques sufficiently (albeit not precisely) matches the account name'. The bank staff were not aware that there was an associated company with a similar name and the Court of Appeal was not prepared to pool the knowledge of others in the bank not involved in the collection of cheques. The Court of Appeal held this evidence of banking practice gave the bank an arguable defence to the claim.

In *The Honourable Society of the Middle Temple v Lloyds Bank Plc*[101] one of the main issues in the case was whether the Turkish bank and/or Lloyds Bank acted without negligence. Rix J drew a distinction between the situation where a bank acts as an agent for collection (where the bank is essentially the point of entry into the clearing system) and branch collection where the bank is acting for its own individual customer. In the latter case the bank has the opportunity to do two things, which are not open to the agent for collection. The first is to vet the bank's customer when the account is opened and subsequently. The second is to compare the customer's name on the paying in slip and the payee's name on the cheque. With this in mind, Rix J held that the agent for collection was entitled to rely on the collecting bank to carry out the necessary enquiries as to the customer's identity, unless anything came to its notice in a particular case, or if it came to its notice that the collecting bank did not carry out proper procedures to protect the true owner of the cheque.[102] In this connection there was a distinction to be drawn between the agent for collection acting for a domestic bank and where it acted on behalf of a foreign bank. The agent for collection was entitled to assume

---

[99] Inserted by s.1 of the Cheques Act 1992 which came into force on 16 June 1992.
[100] [2007] 2 Lloyd's Rep 471.
[101] [1999] Lloyds Rep Bank 50.
[102] *The Honourable Society of the Middle Temple v Lloyds Bank Plc* [1999] Lloyds Rep Bank 50.

that the domestic collecting bank was aware of its responsibilities under the Cheques Act 1992 but was not entitled to assume this in relation to a collecting banking in a foreign country. Rix J held that both Lloyds Bank and the Turkish bank had acted negligently. Lloyds Bank ought, but failed, to inform the Turkish bank of the effects of the Cheques Act 1992. The Turkish Bank failed to make sufficient enquiry as to the identity of the person presenting the cheque for collection (a new customer) and to enquire why it was in possession of an English cheque for over £180,000 payable to 'Sun Alliance'.

In *Linklaters* v *HSBC*[103] a cheque stolen from Linklaters's office and which surfaced in Spain was paid into an account with BPE, a Spanish bank. BPE used HSBC as its UK agent to collect the cheque. BPE and HSBC settled the claim with Linklaters and the matter before the court was the issue of contribution for the losses. The court held that the *Middle Temple* case[104] was correctly decided. As between the collecting bank and its agent for collection, it was the duty of the collecting bank to ensure that it was collecting the instrument for the right customer and true owner. The collecting bank could not pass that primary duty to its agent for collection. The *Middle Temple* case could not be distinguished on the ground that HSBC was both BPE's agent for collection and the paying bank. HSBC incurred liability for conversion when, on and in accordance with BPE's instructions, it credited BPE's account with the proceeds of the cheque. That it did so as BPE's agent for collection and the fact it was also the paying bank did not affect that conclusion. HSBC was therefore entitled to a complete indemnity from BPE. Any negligence committed by HSBC was practised not on BPE but the true owner of the cheque.

On the issue of banking practice, Gross J was critical of HSBC who expressed the view that the amount of the cheque and it having been specially presented for payment by a foreign bank should have put the bank on enquiry. A simple telephone call to the drawers would have revealed that Linklaters had not been paid. HSBC staff had not followed their own internal procedures and the court concluded that foreign banks would not be expected to be aware of the effect of the Cheques Act 1992, but an English bank collecting such a cheque for a foreign bank for the account of a person other than the named payee will do so at its peril.

Not negotiable

The effect of the 'not negotiable' crossing is that the holder of such a cheque will not have a better title to it than the person from whom he received it. The crossing does not affect the transferability of the cheque. In *Great Western Railway Co* v *London and County Banking Ltd*[105] Lord Brampton appears to have suggested *obiter* that a collecting bank should be put on enquiry if asked to collect a cheque marked 'not negotiable' for a customer who is not the named payee. However, in *Crumplin* v *London Joint Stock Bank Ltd*[106] Pickford J noted this view was criticised and held that it was simply a matter to be taken into consideration along with all the other circumstances surrounding the collection of the cheque. It was not *prima facie* evidence of negligence for a collecting bank to collect such a cheque for a customer who was not the named payee.

---

[103] [2003] EWHC 1113.
[104] [1999] 1 All ER 193.
[105] [1901] AC 414.
[106] (1913) TLR 99.

Cash or order

In *Orbit Mining and Trading Co Ltd* v *Westminster Bank Ltd*[107] it was argued that the collecting bank should have been put on enquiry, and made enquiries, when cheques crossed 'pay cash or order' were presented for payment. The court held that, on the basis of evidence of banking practice submitted to the court such a direction was not so unusual as to put the collecting bank on enquiry.

Collecting and discounting banks

The distinction between the collecting and discounting banks is fundamental. A collecting bank that presents a cheque for payment, on the customer's behalf, will act as an agent. The collecting bank merely incurs a commitment to credit the customer's account with an equivalent amount and not on trust.[108] The collecting bank does not acquire property in the cheque and does not become its holder. The bank's position is different if the bank discounts the cheque. This will occur where, for example, the bank permits the customer to draw against the proceeds of the cheque before it is cleared. Where the bank acts as a receiving bank it receives the amount of the cheque for itself.[109] Since cheques, in the UK, are now normally crossed 'account payee' and therefore non-transferable[110] it will be rare for a bank to collect a cheque as a discounting bank.

At one time it was thought that the bank became a discounting bank when it credited the customer's account with the amount of the cheque before clearing it.[111] However, it is now established that a cheque is discounted if, apart from crediting the customer's account before it being cleared, the bank agrees to grant the customer an overdraft against the proceeds or actually allows the customer to draw against the proceeds of the cheque. In *Re Farrow's Bank Ltd*[112] a customer's account with the F Bank was credited immediately with the amount of the cheque payable to him. The pay-in slip contained a notation under which the bank reserved to itself the right 'to defer payment of cheques against which may have been credited to the account'. As the F bank was not a member of the clearing house, it remitted the cheque to the B bank and the amount of the cheque was credited to the F bank's account, subject to recourse. The cheque was honoured when presented for payment by the B bank but the F bank suspended payment before it received advice and before the proceeds were actually credited to B bank's account with the drawee bank. There were two questions before the court namely: (i) whether the F Bank had acted as a discounting bank or as a collecting bank; and (ii) if the F Bank had acted as a collecting bank whether it had received the proceeds solely as its customer's agent, or in the context of the banker and customer relationship in which case the amount would be a debt due to the customer from his bank. In the latter situation, the customer would have had to prove in the F Bank's liquidation, as a general creditor. This would also have been the case if the F Bank had been a discounting bank but if the amount

---

[107] [1963] 1 QB 794.
[108] *Emerald Meats (London) Ltd* v *AIB Group (UK) Ltd* [2002] EWCA Civ. 460.
[109] *Capital and Counties Bank Ltd* v *Gordon* [1903] AC 240.
[110] Bills of Exchange Act 1882, s.81(A).
[111] *Capital and Counties Bank Ltd* v *Gordon* [1903] AC 240.
[112] [1923] 1 Ch 41.

had been received by the F Bank as a mere agent, the customer would have been entitled to the amount *in specie*. Astbury J held that merely crediting the customer's account did not, on the part of F bank, amount to furnishing consideration. To assume the role of a discounting bank, the F Bank would have had to permit the customer to draw against the proceeds. The case established that a cheque is discounted where the bank agrees to grant its customer an overdraft against the proceeds, or actually allows the customer to draw against them before the instrument is cleared. The bank will also assume the role of a discounting bank where the amount of the cheque reduces the customer's existing overdraft by the amount of the cheque before it is cleared so the proceeds are taken into account in calculating the balance available for drawing.[113]

However, it may not be clear whether the bank acts as a collecting or discounting bank and the distinction may not always be clear. The two roles may not be mutually exclusive. In *Barclays Bank Ltd* v *Astley Industrial Trust Ltd*[114] it was recognised that a bank might act as both the customer's collecting bank and as a discounting bank. In the *Astley Industrial Trust Ltd* case it was observed that a bank that grants its customer an overdraft of £5 against an uncleared cheque of £100 will have given value for it but it cannot be said that the bank ceases to be the customer's agent for collection.

Paying bank's statutory defences to a claim for wrongful payment

Traditionally, the cheque has performed two functions: (1) as a negotiable instrument that can be used to effect a payment of money due from the drawer to a third party and which can be transferred or negotiated freely; and (2) as a payment mandate from the customer to the bank directing the latter to make payment, in accordance with the mandate, to a named payee. The modern cheque performs the latter function with the transferability and negotiation now restricted by statute and banking practice. As the paying bank acts in accordance with the contract, it is required to make payment in accordance with the customer's mandate and the rules of agency law will determine the relationship. If the paying bank deviates from the mandate it will be in breach of the contractual mandate. In *Midland Bank Ltd* v *Seymour*[115] Lord Devlin explained the view with regard to the mandate as:

> It is a hard laws sometimes which deprives an agent of the right to reimbursement if he has exceeded his authority, even though the excess does not damage his principal's interests. The corollary . . . is that the instruction to the agent must be clear and unambiguous.

Applying this rule to an unauthorised payment of a cheque or other payment mandate means that a bank is not entitled to debit the customer's account with the amount unless it can plead one of the statutory defences. The paying bank may be able to rely on common law defences that can be raised by an agent, for example estoppel, ratification and ambiguity of mandate. The bank can also rely on equitable defences that apply where an unauthorised payment is made but the customer benefits as a valid debt owed by him to a third party is discharged.[116]

---

[113] *M'Lean* v *Clydesdale Banking Corporation* (1883) 9 App Cas 95.
[114] [1970] 2 QB 527.
[115] [1955] 2 Lloyd's Rep 147.
[116] See Ch. 7.

The paying bank will have a defence to a claim of having paid in breach of a mandate and will not be liable for having wrongly debited the account of the drawer.

The statutory defences available to the paying bank will be examined below.[117] However, neither the common law nor equitable defences give the paying bank a comprehensive defence in all instances of the cheque being wrongly paid. Thus for example, where a cheque bears a forged drawer's signature, or is signed in excess of the agent's authority, or is invalidated by a third party (for example, where the holder alters the instrument by increasing the amount for which it is drawn by the drawer) the bank has a common law defence where the customer has facilitated the fraud or allowed the bank to believe it is a valid and properly drawn instrument. On the other hand, for example, where the bank pays a countermanded cheque, the common law will protect the bank where there is ambiguity in the countermand instrument or if the countermand comes to the attention of the bank too late.

Where a bank is unable to rely on these defences the drawer may be able to bring an action for the bank's breach of mandate. Additionally, where a cheque has been paid for the credit of a person not entitled to the proceeds of the cheque, the true owner may bring an action in conversion against the paying bank. In *OBG Ltd* v *Allan*[118] the House of Lords concluded that the cheque was an item of property with a value equal to its face value and therefore provided the 'true owner' can show he is entitled to 'immediate possession' of the instrument, and if the cheque has been misappropriated or destroyed, then he may be able to bring an action for its conversion and claim face value. However, where payment is wrongfully made against the instrument by the bank it could be argued that the payment discharges the cheque and thereby amounts to destruction of the instrument as an item of property. The right of action in conversion, by the true owner, against the paying bank, derives support from *Smith* v *Union Bank of London*[119] where the payee of a cheque drawn on the defendant bank, crossed it specially to the C Bank with which he maintained an account and endorsed the instrument in blank. The cheque was stolen and transferred to an innocent third party who became a holder in due course, to the credit of his account with the L Bank. The drawee bank, the defendant, paid the cheque when presented by the L Bank despite the special crossing. The court held that since the crossing did not restrict the negotiability of the instrument the payee had ceased to be the true owner when the instrument came into the possession of the holder in due course. The payee was therefore not entitled to the immediate possession of the instrument and his action in conversion failed. Blackburn J expressed the view that if a bank had paid the cheque to a person other than the holder in due course, it would have laid itself open to an action for conversion by the true owner. However, this dictum needs to be narrowly construed since the paying bank's act of conversion is supposed to be the destruction of the negotiable character of the instrument resulting from its discharge. However, s.59 of the Bills of Exchange Act 1882[120] discharges a bill, including a cheque, when payment is made 'in due course'. This occurs when payment is made by the drawee in good faith to a holder of the instrument whose defect in title the drawee has no knowledge of. It therefore follows that payment in due course does not occur when the cheque is paid to a person who has acquired title under a forged endorsement. It therefore follows that payment to such a person

---

[117] Other defences, for example estoppel, ratification and equitable defence of payment of the customer's debt, are dealt with elsewhere.

[118] [2008] AC 1.

[119] (1875) LR 10 QB 291, affd (1875) 1 QBD 31.

[120] See Ch. 10.

does not discharge the instrument or destroy its negotiability and the paying bank is not subject to an action in conversion by the true owner. However, doubts concerning the availability of the action in conversion when a cheque has been improperly paid are found in the Court of Appeal decision in *Charles v Blackwell*[121] where the court decided that if a cheque was properly paid an action would not lie against the bank. Cockburn CJ observed:

> A cheque taken in payment remains the property of the payee only so long as it remains unpaid. When paid the banker is entitled to keep the voucher till this account with his customer is settled . . . If the cheque was duly paid, so as to deprive the payee of a right of action . . . they no longer have any property in it.

According to Cockburn CJ, the payee, or true owner, loses his property in the cheque when it is 'duly paid' but under the Bills of Exchange Act 1882 this would be when 'payment is made in due course'.

Statutory defences

The statutory defences available to the paying bank arise primarily in relation to the area of liability arising from forged endorsements on cheques. Where they apply these defences are available in addition to any common law or equitable defences. The bank's protection depends on the bank having acted either in the ordinary course of business or 'without negligence'. In other cases the bank may obtain a valid defence if it has paid a cheque 'in due course'. Payment in due course is the basic principle involved in such payments, although the payment will not necessarily confer a defence on the bank against its customer. The rationale for the defences available to the paying bank is that such a bank is not normally in a position to know whether, or not, an endorsement on a cheque is by the payee or endorsee. In the absence of statute, the paying bank would still be strictly liable if it paid a cheque, which bore a forged endorsement. The statutory defences do not apply to other instruments and do not apply to forgeries and material alterations. In such cases, the paying bank must bring itself within the common law defences of estoppel, ratification or the equitable defence of discharge of a debt owed to a third party.

Where the provisions of ss.59, 60 and 80 of the Bills of Exchange Act 1882 apply they protect the paying bank against claims by the customer, for wrongfully debiting his account, and also against an action by a third party.

Section 59 of the Bills of Exchange Act 1882

Section 59 of the Bills of Exchange Act 1882, provides that a bill is discharged by payment in due course by or on behalf of the drawee bank or acceptor. 'Payment in due course' is defined as payment made at or after the maturity of the bill to the holder in good faith and without notice that his title to the bill is defective. As cheques are payable on demand on after the date appearing on them the question of maturity does not arise. 'Holder'[122] is defined as the payee or endorsee of a bill or note who is in possession of it, or the bearer; and the term 'bearer'[123] is defined as the person in possession of a bill or note which is payable to bearer.

---

[121] (1877) 2 CPD 151.
[122] Bills of Exchange Act 1882, s.2.
[123] Bills of Exchange Act 1882, s.2.

Where, therefore, a drawee bank pays a cheque to someone other than the holder this will not constitute payment in due course.

A paying bank pays a cheque in due course if it pays the amount of the cheque to the holder in good faith and without negligence that the holder's title is defective. The cheque is thereby discharged and the drawer cannot claim, as against the paying bank, that the cheque should not have been paid. Once the cheque had been paid in due course the true owner will no longer have a proprietary interest in the cheque, since the paying bank is entitled to hold the cheque as a piece of paper until the paying bank is paid, and then the holder is entitled to it.[124] For example, the drawer of a bearer cheque who loses that cheque, or has it stolen from him, may find he has no claim against the payee bank under s.59 if a third party receives payment as the holder of the cheque. The paying bank will not be liable to the drawer for having wrongfully paid the third party since it will have complied with the mandate in making payment.

Section 60 of the Bills of Exchange Act 1882

As the use of cheques became more common banks were faced with the increased problems associated with forged cheques. A paying bank has no means of knowing or verifying the payee's signature, particularly where the cheque has been negotiated several times. Where the bank failed to discharge its obligation to make payment to the proper payee or endorsee because of a forged endorsement then, in the absence of some rule to the contrary, the bank was required to make a second payment to the true owner of the cheque and could not further debit the customer's account in respect of the first payment. The burden on the paying bank was felt to be unreasonable and s.19 of the Stamp Act 1853 was passed to protect the paying bank in respect of payments made on forged endorsements. The Stamp Act 1853 is still in effect in respect of bankers' drafts and other instruments that do not fall within the definition of a 'bill of exchange'. In so far as the Stamp Act applied to cheques it has been superseded by s.60 of the Bills of Exchange Act 1882 which provides that where a bank in good faith and in the ordinary course of business pays a cheque on which an endorsement is subsequently found to be forged or unauthorised, the payment will be treated as having been made in due course. Therefore, where s.60 applies the bank is under no obligation to make a second payment out of its funds.

For the paying bank to be protected by s.60 of the Bills of Exchange Act 1882, a payment must be made in 'good faith and in the ordinary course of business'. The good faith requirement is satisfied if the paying bank acts honestly but it does not necessarily require the bank to act with care. In *Carpenters' Co v British Mutual Banking Co Ltd*[125] Branson J held that the defendant bank had paid cheques in good faith and in the ordinary course of business and was, therefore protected by s.60, notwithstanding its negligence in collecting them on behalf of the plaintiff's clerk, who had forged the payee's endorsements on them. Whether a bank has acted in the 'ordinary course of business', for the purposes of s.60 is to be determined by reference to banking practice rather than the law.[126] In *Carpenters' Co v British Mutual Banking Co Ltd*[127] the Court of Appeal was divided on whether negligence by the paying bank was

---

[124] *Charles v Blackwell* (1877) 2 CPD 151 at 162.
[125] [1938] 1 KB 511.
[126] See: Lord Halsbury LC, in *Bank of England v Vagliano Brothers* [1891] AC 107 at 117.
[127] [1938] 1 KB 511.

intended to exclude the paying bank from protection under s.60 of the Bills of Exchange Act 1882. Greer LJ expressed the view that when a bank acts negligently it deviates from the ordinary course of business but Slesser LJ, although agreeing with Greer LJ on other grounds, expressed the view that a bank may be acting in the ordinary course of business despite its negligence. MacKinnon LJ dissenting said:

> A thing that is done not in the ordinary course of business may be done negligently; but I do not think the converse is necessarily true. A thing may be done negligently and yet be done in the ordinary course of business.

The general view is that the decision of the majority in *Carpenters* is to be preferred so that provided the paying bank acts 'in the ordinary course of business' it is protected by s.60 even though it is guilty of negligence. A similar approach has been taken in other jurisdictions in respect of statutory protection of the paying bank in respect of their equivalent to s.60. The question remains open, although in practice the issue is not likely to arise again because of the restrictions on crossing cheques. However, it must be recognised that the ordinary course of business is determined on the basis of business methods used by the reasonably careful banker and a failure to meet those standards would establish negligence.

An approach similar to that in the *Carpenters* case was adopted by the Australian Courts in *Smith* v *Commercial Banking Co of Sydney Ltd*[128] where the court expressed the opinion that a bank may be negligent and yet act in the ordinary course of business. However, a bank which pays in obviously suspicious circumstances, will lose its protection under s.60 of the Bills of Exchange Act 1882. In *Auchteroni and Co* v *Midland Bank Ltd*[129] the court held the bank was justified in paying over the counter a bill for £2876 9s, but that a different conclusion might have been reached if an office boy or a tramp had presented the bill for a larger amount. In *Questions on Banking Practice*[130] it is stated that:

> the practical guidance is that when dealing with a negotiable instrument the banker does not need to view every presentation with suspicion. Because prudence in doubtful circumstances may demand care, but the need for enquiry arises only in exceptional cases. If the appearance of the presenter or the relevant facts, including the amounts of the cheque, occasion suspicion, then the prudent course is to institute the necessary enquiries before effecting payment.

The legal authority that, therefore, exists would appear to suggest that the requirement that payment be in the ordinary course of business is less stringent than the requirement that the bank act without negligence.

The question for which s.60 of the Bills of Exchange Act 1882 does not specifically provide is whether the protection conferred on the paying bank is restricted to circumstances where the endorsement is used to negotiate the cheque or whether the defence is also available where the endorsement is merely placed to evidence receipt of payment by the bank. Banks used to insist the payee endorse all cheques before paying them to the credit of his account or cashing them. One of the purposes of this was to confer protection on the paying bank under s.60 of the Bills of Exchange Act 1882 and the collecting bank being treated as a holder of the cheque. While Byles J in *Keene* v *Beard*,[131] a case decided before the Bills of Exchange

---

[128] (1910) 11 CLR 667.
[129] [1928] 2 KB 294.
[130] Institute of Bankers (1978) *Questions on Banking Practice*, No 503 at p. 170, London.
[131] (1860) 8 CB NS 372.

Act 1882, suggested that the signature of a person receiving payment of a cheque is not an endorsement but merely a receipt, in *Brighton Empire and Eden Syndicate* v *London and County Bank*[132] the view was expressed that a signature written on the back of a cheque prior to payment in cash by the drawee bank is an endorsement under s.60 of the Act. Further, s.1 of the Cheques Act 1957 was drafted in wide terms so as to release a paying bank from any obligations to verify, or otherwise concern itself, with endorsements and from liability which might otherwise have arisen from the absence, invalidity or irregularity of an endorsement of a cheque whether the bank was actually making payment to the named payee or some other person.

Many of the problems relating to forged endorsements have been solved by the Cheques Act 1992, which provides that the effect of the account payee crossing is to render the cheque non-transferable.

Section 80 of the Bills of Exchange Act 1882

In addition to s.60 of the Bills of Exchange Act 1882, s.80 provides protection to the paying bank specifically in relation to crossed cheques. Section 80 is to be read in conjunction with s.79 of the 1882 Act, which establishes the duties of the paying bank in respect of the payment of crossed cheques. Section 80 of the Bills of Exchange Act 1882 provides that where a crossed cheque has been paid in accordance with the tenor of the crossing, in good faith and without negligence, the paying bank is placed in the same position as if the cheque had been paid to the true owner. The requirement under s.60 that payment should be made in the ordinary course of business is replaced by the requirement that payment should be made in good faith. Section 80 of the Bills of Exchange Act 1882 only applies to crossed cheques paid to a bank and is not limited to cheques payable to order. Section 80 will apply if the cheque bears a forged or unauthorised endorsement but it will not protect the paying bank if the drawer's signature has been forged or made without his authority, as the instrument is wholly inoperative. Neither, will the section protect the paying bank where the cheque has been materially altered under s.64(1) of the 1882 Act. The effect of the material alteration is to render the instrument void so it is no longer a cheque but a 'worthless piece of paper'.[133]

As the paying bank is protected, in respect of forged endorsements on crossed or uncrossed cheques, by s.60 the need for s.80 is not apparent. However, the existence of the two sections is historical. While s.60 finds its origins in the Stamp Act 1853, s.80 of the Bills of Exchange Act 1882 finds its origins in s.9 of the Crossed Cheques Act 1876, which as the title implies, was concerned exclusively with crossed cheques. The 1876 Act was repealed by the Bills of Exchange Act 1882 although its provisions were enacted in ss.76–82 of the 1882 Act. Thus, s.9 of the 1876 Act was re-enacted as s.80 of the 1882 Act. While the need to have two separate provisions was questioned by Holden,[134] recent Australian authority suggests that s.80 may have use in its own right. Thus, in *Australian Mutual Provident Society* v *Derham*[135] an assured, who had decided to surrender his policy, lodged a form requesting the

---

[132] (1904) *The Times*, 24 March 1904.

[133] *Smith* v *Lloyds TSB Bank Plc* [2001] QB 541 at 556–557.

[134] Holden (1955) *History of Negotiable Instruments in English Law*, London: Holden, p. 268; see also Guest (2009) *Chalmers and Guest on Bills of Exchange and Cheques*, London: Sweet & Maxwell, para. 14-027.

[135] (1979) 39 FLR 165 at 173.

company remit the proceeds to an agent who gave his own post office box as the assured's address. When the agent received the company's crossed cheque payable to the assured he forged the assured's endorsement and paid the cheque to the credit of his own bank account. McGregor J held that the paying bank was protected by the Australian equivalent of s.80 of the Bills of Exchange Act 1882. As the bank was not concerned with the regularity of the endorsement it had paid the cheque in question without 'negligence'. The decision in *Derham* could have been reached even if the payment were not made 'in the ordinary course of business', provided it had been made without negligence. The fact the bank was not concerned with the regularity of the endorsement followed from the Australian equivalent of s.1 of the Cheques Act 1957.

Recent English authorities, which have examined ss.60 and 80 of the 1882 Act, have held that where there are surrounding circumstances known to the bank, which places the bank on enquiry, the bank must act with due care and it must not simply rely on the customer's mandate as expressed in the cheque.[136] Consequently, a bank that insists on a duty of care from its customer when the latter issues a mandate is equally under a reciprocal duty to the customer, particularly when the bank is aware or ought to be aware that the customer's agent is acting unlawfully and dishonestly.

Section 1 of the Cheques Act 1957

Section 1 of the Cheques Act 1957 abolished the necessity for endorsements on cheques, with certain exceptions. The section provides that where a banker in good faith and in the ordinary course of business pays a cheque drawn on him which is not endorsed or is irregularly endorsed, he does not, or in doing so, incur any liability by reason only of the absence of, or irregularity in, and is deemed to have paid in due course. Sections 60 and 80 of the Bills of Exchange Act 1882 only protect the paying bank where the endorsement of an order cheque, which appears to be regular on its face, turns out to be forged. Where a payment is made for a cheque, which is irregularly endorsed, that payment is made both negligently and outside the ordinary course of business. The protection conferred by s.1 of the Cheques Act 1957 becomes important. A regular endorsement in the case of an individual is one which purports to be that of the payee or endorsee by reproducing exactly the name as shown on the cheque. In *Slingsby* v *District Bank Ltd*[137] Wright J said:

> I think the paying bank ought to require a signature indicating the position exactly as it is indicated by the mandate describing the payee.

Where the cheque is drawn 'John Smith' and is endorsed 'J. Smith', that will be treated as a regular endorsement. However, if a company endorses a cheque and omits the words 'Ltd' or 'Co' when they form part of its name, the endorsement will be irregular.[138] A person acting in a representative capacity may endorse a cheque. In such circumstances the endorsement is not regular if the representative capacity is not reasonably compatible with the authority to endorse.[139] An endorsement is irregular when it differs materially from the description of the

---

[136] See *Selangor United Rubber Estates Ltd* v *Cradock (No 3)* [1968] 1 WLR 1555; approved in *Karak Rubber Co Ltd* v *Burden (No 2)* [1972] 1 WLR 602 and *Rowlandson* v *National Westminster Bank Ltd* [1978] 1 WLR 798. See also *Ryan* v *Bank of New South Wales* [1978] VR 555.

[137] [1932] 1 KB 544.

[138] *Arab Bank Ltd* v *Ross* [1952] 2 QB 216.

[139] See *Gerald McDonald and Co* v *Nash & Co* [1924] AC 625.

person endorsing it. The discrepancy in the endorsement renders the instrument irregular, although it may not affect its negotiability.[140]

Section 1 of the Cheques Act 1957 applies to both crossed and uncrossed cheques and analogous instruments. The protection is not available where, for example, the paying bank paid a crossed cheque in cash over the counter, since that would not be in the ordinary course of business. Prior to 1957 a paying bank would dishonour any cheque that was irregularly endorsed or on which the endorsement was missing. This led to paying banks having to dishonour a large number of cheques and the Mocatta Committee on Cheque Endorsement[141] recommended that endorsements should no longer be required for cheques other than those presented for payment over the counter. This led to the enactment of s.1 of the Cheques Act 1957. However, the Committee of London Clearing Banks took the view that the use of endorsements would be retained in certain circumstances. In a circular dated 23 September 1957[142] the Committee stated that the paying bank would continue to insist on an endorsement in two circumstances: (a) where the cheques are presented over the counter; (b) in respect of combined cheques and receipt forms marked 'R'; and (c) where cheques payable to joint payees are paid into an account which is not maintained in the name of all the payees.

The Jack Committee on Banking Services[143] accepted that protection for the paying bank along the lines currently conferred is necessary. The existing statutory provisions are not, however, wholly consistent. There is considerable overlap between the sections and their scope and relationship is, at times, unclear. Section 60 of the Bills of Exchange Act 1882 and s.1 of the Cheques Act 1957 require the bank to act in 'good faith' and 'in the ordinary course of business,' while s.80 of the Bills of Exchange Act 1882 requires the paying bank to act in 'good faith' but 'without negligence'. Moreover, ss.60 and 80 apply only to cheques while s.1 applies to cheques and other analogous instruments. Sections 60 and 1 require the paying bank to act 'in the ordinary course of business,' while s.80 does not impose that requirement. Section 80, unlike s.60 applies to both order and bearer cheques.

BANKING LAW IN PRACTICE

The future of cheques

In the UK, the use of cheques peaked in 1990 with 4 billion cheque payments made: intervening years have seen the decline of the use of cheques as a means of payment as individuals and businesses have increasingly moved to automated methods of

---

[140] *Arab Bank Ltd* v *Ross* [1952] 2 QB 216.

[141] HMSO, Mocatta Committee on Cheque Endorsement, 1956, Cmnd 3, http://onlinelibrary.wiley.com/store/10.1111/j.1468-2230.1957.tb00435.x/asset/j.1468-2230.1957.tb00435.x.pdf;jsessionid=666F0C1E19752ABBB38297A1CE9CDFF5.d02t04?v=1&t=hjj1qxeb&s=54098e6baa2eec0d731ae7d9a0f79d0afbd0bc7d.

[142] http://onlinelibrary.wiley.com/store/10.1111/j.1468-2230.1957.tb00435.x/asset/j.1468-2230.1957.tb00435.x.pdf?v=1&t=hjj1viwv&s=dd36299e7b661a804b2a2c61f14b4873a80143c0.

[143] Jack (1989) Banking Services: Law and Practice, Report by the Review Committee Chaired by Professor R.B. Jack, CBE, London Cm 622.

payment.[144] In 2006 the volume of cheque transactions declined at a rate of 8 per cent to 1.8 billion and represented 1 in 25 of all payment transactions. The rate of decline was even more marked in 2008, when the volume of cheques fell by 12 per cent to 1.4 billion. A declining minority of all payments are now made by cheque but there are some major areas of business where the cheque remains heavily used, for example in the case of payments made between individuals or to small and medium-sized businesses, in particular sole traders and mail order business. Collectively these categories, in 2005, accounted for 30 per cent of all personal cheques. Cheques are also a common means of payment to schools and other small local groups who do not have the facility to accept credit card or direct debit payments.[145] In 2006, approximately 26 million consumers made a payment by cheque.[146]

Data on cheque usage in terms of age shows that those aged 65 and over are heavier users of cheques compared to the rest of the population, on average using about 50 per cent more cheques per person, but despite this over 60 per cent of those aged 65 or over wrote no more than one cheque every four weeks. By contrast cheque usage by adults under 25 is low, with only 9 per cent of this group using cheques more often than once every four weeks.[147] The total value of cheques issued by individuals is forecast to fall to £85 billion by 2015 with the most substantial falls in the personal cheque being used for payments to retailers and for regular bills; the volume of cheques used to obtain cash is projected to fall from £69 million to £15 million, between 2005 and 2015.[148] The Payment Council forecast is that cheque transactions volumes will fall further to 602 million by 2018 with consumers making 260 million such payments and businesses making 342 million such payments.[149] A number of retailers have already stopped accepting payment by cheque or are piloting alternative means of payment and by 2015 payment by cheque is expected to account for a residual volume of payments to retailers.[150] By 2016, it is expected that cheques will account for only 1 in 50 payments in the UK with the strongest decreases expected in bill payments and in payments in the retailer, travel and entertainment sectors. However, cheques are likely to remain popular for person-to-person payments and payments to and from smaller businesses.

The Payment Council, therefore, in its first national plan for future developments in payment systems in the UK concluded that the long-term decline in the use of cheques

---

[144] Payments Council, National Payments Consulting on Change in UK Payments, 2008, http://www.treasurers.org/node/2995.

[145] Office of Fair Trading, Cheques Working Group Report, November 2006, http://www.oft.gov.uk/shared_oft/reports/financial_products/oft868.pdf.

[146] Payments Council, National Payments Consulting on Change in UK Payments, 2008, p.10, http://www.treasurers.org/node/2995.

[147] Office of Fair Trading, Cheques Working Group Report, November 2006, para. 4.20, http://www.oft.gov.uk/shared_oft/reports/financial_products/oft868.pdf.

[148] Office of Fair Trading, Cheques Working Group Report, November 2006, para. 4.38, http://www.oft.gov.uk/shared_oft/reports/financial_products/oft868.pdf.

[149] Payment Council, The Future of Cheques in the UK, December 2009, http://www.paymentscouncil.org.uk/files/payments_council/the_future_of_cheques_final_version.pdf.

[150] Office of Fair Trading, Cheques Working Group Report, November 2006, para. 4.39, http://www.oft.gov.uk/shared_oft/reports/financial_products/oft868.pdf.

should be actively managed.[151] The Payments Council, on the 16 December 2008, announced that following consultation it had set a target date of 31 October 2018 as the closure date for the clearing system. The Payments Council recognised that while cheque usage had been in continuous decline since 1990, there were still a number of situations when cheques were extensively used, including person-to-person payments, payments to sole traders and other small businesses, payments to schools, clubs, societies, associations and small charities, payments from businesses to individuals, and where the individual is reluctant to share account details, and that these gaps should be filled by alternative methods of payment, by 2014.[152] Depending on progress the final decision relating to the closure of the cheque clearing system would be made in 2016 and those least equipped to change to alternative measures are not to be disadvantaged.[153] In June 2009, the Payment Council announced that the cheque guarantee scheme would close within two years, and the Cheque Guarantee Card Scheme finally closed on 30 June 2011.[154]

On 12 July 2011, following industry consultation and public concerns, the Payment Council took the decision to cancel the possible managed closure of the cheque settlement system in 2018 and announced that cheques will continue as a means of payment for as long as customers need them. A decision to proceed with the closure would only have been made in 2016, if the alternatives to cheques had proven to be acceptable to customers, specifically the needs of older people, small businesses and the charitable and voluntary sector. Additionally, following criticisms voiced by the Treasury Select Committee[155] the Payment Council concluded that cheques as a vehicle for payment should be retained for as long as customers need them. The Payment Council has therefore cancelled the targeted date for the closure of cheque clearing. The Council will, however, continue to investigate alternative methods of payment to cheques.[156]

Conclusion

While the law relating to cheques was largely settled through the Bills of Exchange Act 1882 and the Cheques Act 1957, the dangers of fraud through the wrongful negotiation of cheques persisted as a serious concern for banks. The Cheques Act 1992 restricted the negotiation of cheques and left such instruments as payable only to the named payee. Because of the

[151] Payment Council, The Future of Cheques in the UK, December 2008, http://www.paymentscouncil.org.uk/files/payments_council/the_future_of_cheques_final_version.pdf.

[152] Payment Council, The Future of Cheques in the UK, December 2008, p.8, http://www.paymentscouncil.org.uk/files/payments_council/the_future_of_cheques_final_version.pdf.

[153] Payment Council, The Future of Cheques in the UK, December 2008, p.9, http://www.paymentscouncil.org.uk/files/payments_council/the_future_of_cheques_final_version.pdf.

[154] Payment Council, Review of the UK Domestic Cheque Guarantee Card Scheme, June 2009, http://www.paymentscouncil.org.uk/files/payments_files/cheque_guarantee_report_june_2009.pdf.

[155] House of Commons, the Future of Cheques, Treasury Committee, http://www.publications.parliament.uk/pa/cm201012/cmselect/cmtreasy/1147/114707.htm.

[156] Payment Council, 2011 National Payment Plan, http://www.paymentscouncil.org.uk/files/payments_council/pc_npp_report_2011_final-pdf.pdf.

dangers of widespread fraud and the increased use of, for example, debit and credit card payments, the use of cheques, in the UK, has declined. Certain businesses no longer accept cheques in settlement of debts or a means of payment. The decline in the use of cheques has led to the closure of the cheque guarantee scheme and the payments industry has also announced plans to discontinue the use of cheques. However, that decision, for the present, has been shelved and cheques remain as a means of payment of debts. It is likely, however, that the cheque as a means of payment will disappear over the next couple of decades.

Further reading

➤ Johnson, A. (1999) Stolen cheques and the Cheques Act 1992: the decision in the Middle Temple case, 14(4) *Journal of International Banking Law*, 129–138.
This article examines the implications for clearing banks and customers of ruling on liability where an English bank acted as agent for collection on behalf of a foreign bank in respect of a stolen cheque crossed 'a/c payee only'. The article further examines the relevant of the Cheques Act 1992 and the Cheques Act 1957.

➤ Ellinger, E.P. (2004) Liabilities of bank when crossed cheque collected overseas, 120(Apr) *L.Q.R.*, 226–229.
This article considers the Commercial Court ruling in *Linklaters* v *HSBC Bank Plc* on the determination of the liability of two banks against each other when they had been involved in clearing a cheque which had been stolen, fraudulently endorsed and used to open an account. The article further examines the judge's reliance on the ruling in *Honourable Society of the Middle Temple* v *Lloyds Bank Plc*.

➤ Cook, E.S. (1997) Obligations of a collecting bank: *Boma Manufacturing Ltd* v *Canadian Imperial Bank of Commerce*, 12(4) *Journal of International Banking Law*, 165–168.
This article examines the liability of a bank which accepts fraudulently endorsed cheques or cheques deposited by third parties without endorsement.

Third party rights: wrongful dealings and liability

Chapter overview

The aim of this chapter is to:

➤ Examine the rules relating to third party rights in respect of the customer's bank account. The third party may acquire or seek to acquire rights against a credit balance when monies belonging to that third party have been misappropriated and the bank account used to facilitate that misappropriation, or hide those funds. The chapter will therefore look at:

- The circumstances in which the bank account will be held subject to a constructive trust; and
- the rules relating to tracing of money into a bank account, including the question of whether it is possible to trace into an overdrawn account.

Introduction

The last 20 years has seen a proliferation of cases in which, in particular, misapplied company assets have come into the hands of a third party, especially a bank. Much of the debate has centred on the level of knowledge required in order to find the third party liable.

BANKING LAW IN PRACTICE

The banker and customer relationship is embedded in rules of contract law, as modified to accommodate specific aspects of that relationship. The bank is, therefore, primarily liable under the contract to carry out the customer's mandate[1] and need not concern itself with third party rights. However, there may be circumstances where the bank has to take into consideration whether third party rights, to money standing to the credit of the customer's account, should be acknowledged and satisfied, or whether in accordance with the contract the customer's mandate should be given effect.[2] Banks may find themselves

➡

[1] See Ch. 7.
[2] See Ch. 7.

implicated in a breach of trust in circumstances where they simply acted to carry out the customer's mandate. The cause of action will be based on the issue of attributing liability for misdirected funds. Liability is not restricted to those involved in the original breach of trust or breach of fiduciary duty: 'his liability is strict, nor to those who assist in the original breach of trust but extends to those who consciously assist in the continuing diversion of the funds so anyone involved in covering up the trail of those funds and laundering those funds may be held liable'.[3] The potential liability of a bank to a third party was recognised in *Westpac New Zealand Ltd* v *MAP & Associates Ltd*[4] where the court concluded 'a bank may also be liable to non-customers in certain circumstances, including where it acts as a dishonest assister'.

Several areas of the law have intervened to protect third party rights and while protecting the contractual rights of its customer the bank may, in certain circumstances, be compelled by law to recognise those third party rights. Thus, for example, where a bank wrongfully collects payment on a negotiable instrument for someone other than the true owner, the collecting bank may be made liable to the true owner in conversion.[5] Additionally, the law of restitution may protect third party rights,[6] and the courts may also be willing to exercise their equitable jurisdiction to protect third party rights, for example under the rules of equitable tracing.[7] The bank may, therefore, be held liable as a trustee where it has intermeddled in trust affairs, even though it is not formally a trustee. The wrongdoer may have disappeared, or may be insolvent, and the victim of the fraud may, therefore, seek relief from the third party bank.

The type of cases where a bank may disregard its primary obligations to its customer in favour of the interests of the third party include, for example:

1 Where a dishonest employee of the company remits company funds from the employer's account to his own account, or a company director uses company funds standing to the company's account in order to make a personal gain and benefit himself. A paying bank owes to its customer a contractual duty to exercise reasonable care and skill in carrying out its obligations under the banking contract.[8] The mere fact that a paying bank has knowledge that the drawer of the cheque has been authorised by a board resolution to draw such cheques on the company's account does not exclude the bank's obligation to the company to exercise care and skill in relation to the cheque.[9] Further, if there is a duty to make inquiry then the failure is not excused because the bank is convinced that the answer given is likely to be false.[10]

---

[3] *Twinsectra Ltd* v *Yardley* [2002] 2 All ER 377 Lord Millett.
[4] [2011] 2 NZLR 90.
[5] See Ch. 11.
[6] See Ch. 16 for a discussion of the rules on money paid under a mistake.
[7] See p. 441.
[8] *Selangor United Rubber Estates Ltd* v *Cradock (No 3)* [1968] 1 WLR 1555.
[9] *Selangor United Rubber Estates Ltd* v *Cradock (No 3)* [1968] 1 WLR 1555.
[10] *Selangor United Rubber Estates Ltd* v *Cradock (No 3)* [1968] 1 WLR 1555.

2 A third party may bring an action where the bank wishes to set off a debit balance on the customer's personal account against an account maintained for a special purpose[11] or where the credit balance sought to be combined is subject to a trust.[12]

3 Where the third party claims to have an equitable title to the credit balance because the money was obtained from him by fraud or other dishonesty.

The claimant's action will attempt to invoke the courts' equitable jurisdiction and seek to make the receiving bank liable to account either as a constructive trustee, or to enforce an equitable proprietary claim to a substitute asset following an action to trace the funds. However, the reluctance of the courts to impose liability on a third party as a constructive trustee is apparent from a number of nineteenth century cases. In *Grey* v *Johnson*[13] the testator left a substantial amount of money to his widow for life and upon her death to their children. The widow, as executrix of the estate, drew a cheque for a substantial amount on an account opened for the estate, and paid it to the credit of her personal account with the same bank. The children, who sued as beneficiaries of the trust, sought to recover the money paid into the executrix's personal account, from the bank. Lord Cairns giving judgment for the bank said:

> To hold a banker justified in refusing to pay a demand of his customer, the customer being an executor, and drawing the cheque as an executor, there must, in the first place, be some misapplication, some breach of trust intended by the executor, and there must in the second place . . . be proof that the bankers are privy to the intent to make this misapplication of the trust funds.

Similarly, in *Tassell* v *Cooper*[14] the bank's customer paid into the credit of his account a cheque received for merchandise sold on behalf of his employers. Although, no fraud was involved, the employer requested the bank freeze the amount of the payment involved and furnished an indemnity in favour of the bank. The bank subsequently dishonoured a cheque drawn by the customer in reliance on the amount standing to the credit of his account, including the amount subject to the freezing order. Maule J held that the bank was not entitled to give effect to third party claims, which contrary to the banker and customer relationship would restrain the customer from exercising his rights.

The bank's liability as a constructive trustee

However, there have been cases which have sought to give recognition to third party rights by holding the bank liable as a constructive trustee. Where a third party assists the trustee in a breach of trust, or a fiduciary in a breach of fiduciary duties,[15] then the third party will be personally liable to account either to the trust or the principal to whom fiduciary duties were owed. In simplest terms, a trust is a relationship which comes into existence when one

---

[11] *National Westminster Bank Ltd* v *Halesowen Presswork and Assemblies Ltd* [1975] QB 654 where the bank's right to combine accounts was said to revive if there was a material change of circumstances, for example a winding-up resolution.

[12] See Ch. 6.

[13] (1868) LR 3 HL 1.

[14] (1850) 9 CB 509.

[15] This was said to be 'arguable' in respect of breach of fiduciary duty by directors: *Brown* v *Bennett* [1999] 1 BCLC 649.

person holds property on behalf of another. If a third party deliberately interferes in that relationship by assisting the trustee in misappropriating trust property and depriving the beneficiary of property held for him by the trustee, the beneficiary should be able to claim compensation from the third party, as well as the trustee. Allowing the beneficiary a remedy against the third party allows the beneficiary to recover his loss from the third party, should the trustee lack the means to compensate the beneficiary or be insolvent, and also acts to discourage dishonest third party behaviour.

There has been debate about the extent of knowledge of the breach of trust, or the extent of knowledge of the breach of fiduciary liability, required to establish liability. An innocent third party who has no reason to suspect a breach will not be liable. Where a third party bank is held liable, as a constructive trustee the extent of its liability will depend on the nature of the assistance rendered by it. Where the bank 'knowingly assists' in a breach of trust its liability will extend to all of the losses flowing to the fund caused by the conduct of the dishonest trustee, whether or not the misappropriated funds actually came into the hands of the bank or not,[16] whereas in the 'knowing receipt' cases the bank will be liable to account only for those funds it receives and deals with in breach of trust. A bank may, therefore, find itself subject to liability as a constructive trustee if taking into account either its actual or constructive knowledge, its conduct has resulted in the bank being involved in a breach of trust by another, or if taking into account the knowledge of the bank, it has become involved in a breach of trust by another. In *Barnes v Addy*,[17] Lord Selborne held:

> Strangers are not to be made constructive trustees merely because they act as the agents of the trustees in transactions within their legal powers, transactions perhaps of which a Court of Equity would disapprove, unless (i) those agents receive and become chargeable with some part of the trust property, or (ii) unless they assist with knowledge in a dishonest and fraudulent design on the part of the trustees.

In *Barnes v Addy*, a solicitor, who prepared a document on the instructions of a trustee, with the latter subsequently using the document for the purposes of a fraudulent conveyance, was held not liable. On the facts, it was clear that the solicitor neither had knowledge of the dishonest design on the part of the trustee, nor was the solicitor in receipt of any trust property in breach of the trust. Lord Selborne's formulation, in that case, of third party (non-trustee) liability has two elements namely:

1 Where the third party *knowingly receives* trust property in breach of trust; or

2 Where the third party *knowingly assists* in the breach of trust. In *Royal Brunei Airlines Sdn Bhd v Tan*[18] the Privy Council considered it more appropriate to refer to liability for 'knowing assistance' as liability for 'dishonest assistance'.

Lord Selborne, while describing the scope of third party liability as a constructive trustee was also concerned to protect agents, who acting honestly find themselves in the situation of having assisted in the commission of a breach of trust. He expressed the view that it is necessary that 'persons dealing honestly as agents are at liberty to rely on the legal power of the trustees, and not to have the character of trustees constructively imposed upon them'. Agents who,

---

[16] *Royal Brunei Airlines Sdn Bhd v Tan* [1995] 2 AC 378.
[17] (1874) LR 9 Ch App 244.
[18] [1995] 2 AC 378.

therefore, act in the commercial environment must be protected by the law so they can conduct their business in safety so that those who act honestly, but in a manner which results in a breach of trust, will be protected. It is those who act with a dishonest and fraudulent design who will find liability imposed on them as constructive trustees.

Under both limbs, any liability imposed on a third party is personal and not proprietary and, therefore, analogous to personal obligations undertaken by parties to a contract. As Lord Nicholls observed in *Royal Brunei Airlines Sdn Bhd* v *Tan*[19] liability under the first limb under *Barnes* v *Addy*[20] 'is concerned with the liability of a person as a recipient of trust property or its traceable proceeds' while under the second limb the liability is that of 'an accessory to a trustee's breach of trust' since it is not dependent on receipt of the trust property. The defendant is not charged with having received trust monies for his own benefit but with having acted as an accessory to a breach of trust.[21] This form of liability arises even though no trust property has reached the hands of the third party: it is a form of secondary liability in the sense that it will only arise where there has been a breach of trust. Lord Nicholls also expressed the view that while 'recipient' based liability is restitution based, accessory liability is not.[22] This point was also made in *Grupo Torras SA* v *Al-Sabah*[23] where the Court of Appeal said:

> The basis of liability in a case of knowing receipt is quite different from that in a case of dishonest assistance. One is a receipt-based liability which may on examination prove to be either a vindication of persistent property rights or a personal restitutionary claim based on unjust enrichment by subtraction; the other is a fault-based liability as an accessory to a breach of fiduciary duty.

The House of Lords will need to clarify a number of factors with regard to receipt based liability and the law of restitution, for example is liability strict if restitution based or is it still dependent, as currently, on fault and if so what is the standard of fault? By comparison the Privy Council decision in the *Tan* case has clarified aspects of accessory liability but the question remains as to what constitutes dishonesty in the context of third party liability?

Liability for dishonest assistance

Claims for dishonest assistance are allowed where the defendant has dishonestly assisted in the wrongful disposition or misapplication of property in breach of trust. Lord Selborne in *Barnes* v *Addy*[24] held that assistants or accessories in a breach of trust could not be made liable unless 'they assist with knowledge in a dishonest and fraudulent design on the part of the trustees'. In such cases the accessory is described as and is liable to account as a 'constructive trustee', although since the accessory does not have to have received trust property, it may be confusing to describe him as a trustee at all.[25] The expressions 'constructive trust' and

---

[19] [1995] 2 AC 378.
[20] (1874) LR 9 Ch App 244.
[21] Lord Millett in *Twinsectra Ltd* v *Yardley* [2002] 2 AC 164.
[22] *Royal Brunei Airlines Sdn Bhd* v *Tan* [1995] 2 AC 378.
[23] [2001] Lloyd's Rep Bank 36.
[24] (1874) LR 9 Ch App 244.
[25] *Agip (Africa) Ltd* v *Jackson* [1990] Ch 265; *Paragon Finance Plc* v *DB Thakerar & Co (a firm)* [1999] 1 All ER 400; *Governor and Company of the Bank of Scotland* v *A Ltd* [2001] 1 WLR 751.

'constructive trustee' are 'nothing more than a formula for equitable relief'[26] in circumstances intended to prevent a third party from participating in a breach of trust. However, because of the complexities in the law there is some argument for dispensing with the notion of the constructive trust and recognising dishonest participation in a breach of trust as a form of equitable wrong requiring the third party to compensate the claimant, or account in equity. This approach was adopted in *Arab Monetary Fund* v *Hashim*[27] where Chadwick J said:

> The defendant is held liable in equity not because he is, or has been, a trustee of trust property, but because his conduct in relation to trust property has been such that he ought to be liable in damages for its loss as if he were a trustee who had disposed of the trust property in breach of interest. The claim is a claim for monetary compensation based on fault.

This view was cited with approval by the Court of Appeal in *Grupo Torras SA* v *Al-Sabah*[28] which concluded that 'dishonest assistance can therefore be described as an equitable wrong-doing'. In *Twinsectra Ltd* v *Yardley*[29] Lord Millett expressed the view that a claim for 'knowing assistance' is the equitable counterpart of the economic torts and in *Yugraneft* v *Abramovich*[30] the court referred to it simply as 'an equitable wrong'.

There are four requirements for accessory liability to be imposed:[31] (a) there must have been a trust or other fiduciary relationship; (b) there must have been misfeasance involving a breach of fiduciary duty, although *Royal Brunei Airlines Sdn Bhd* v *Tan*[32] stated that such misfeasance or breach of trust need not itself be dishonest or fraudulent; (c) a person upon whom liability is to be imposed must, as a matter of fact, have been accessory to, or assisted in, the misfeasance or breach of trust; and (d) the accessory must have been dishonest. We will now look at these individual requirements.

▮ There must have been a trust or other fiduciary relationship

Claims for dishonest assistance are not restricted to situations where the primary breach results from the misappropriation of trust property by the express trustee;[33] they also lie against those who assist in the misappropriation of trust property by other fiduciaries. There must, therefore, have been a trust or other fiduciary relationship in existence. Although *Barnes* v *Addy*[34] involved a breach of trust by the appointed trustees the principles established by Lord Selborne have extended to cover breaches of fiduciary duties by other types of fiduciaries, for example partners, company directors and other agents. This form of liability has been recognised in the context of company directors who commit breaches of fiduciary duties owed by them to their company. In *Agip (Africa) Ltd* v *Jackson*[35] payment orders properly

---

[26] *Dubai Aluminium Co Ltd* v *Salaam* [2003] 2 AC 366; *Selangor United Rubber Estates Ltd* v *Cradock (No 3)* [1968] 1 WLR 1555; *Paragon Finance Plc* v *DB Thakerar & Co (a firm)* [1999] 1 All ER 400; *Ultraframe (UK) Ltd* v *Fielding* [2005] EWHC 1638 (Ch).

[27] [1989] 1 WLR 565.

[28] [2001] Lloyd's Rep. Bank. 36.

[29] [2002] 2 AC 164.

[30] [2008] EWHC 2613.

[31] *Agip (Africa) Ltd* v *Jackson* [1990] Ch. 265 as modified by the Privy Council in *Royal Brunei Airlines* v *Tan* [1995] 2 AC 378 and more recently in *Bankgesellschaft Berlin AG* v *Makris* (QBD) 22 January 1999.

[32] [1995] 2 AC 378.

[33] *Barnes* v *Addy* (1874) LR 9 Ch App 244.

[34] *Barnes* v *Addy* (1874) LR 9 Ch App 244.

[35] [1990] Ch 265.

drawn and signed on behalf of Agip, in favour of the payee, were fraudulently altered by Agip's chief accountant, who subsequently changed the payee's name so they were credited to the accounts of the defendant companies who ultimately credited the payments to third parties abroad from whom payment was irrecoverable. The defendants, a group of account-ants based in the Isle of Wight, who assisted in laundering the misappropriated funds, were held liable for knowingly assisting in a breach of fiduciary duties owed by Agip's chief accountant. Millett J noted that the misappropriation of the company's funds inevitably involved a breach of fiduciary duty on the part of Agip's employee or agent and the question of their state of mind was analysed.[36]

In more recent cases the approach has been adopted that liability to account as a construc-tive trustee should be extended to cases of dishonest assistance in all cases of breaches of fiduciary duties, and not merely limited to breaches of trust involving the misapplication or misappropriation of trust property. In *Brown* v *Bennett*[37] the claimants, shareholders of P Ltd, claimed that the directors of the company had breached their fiduciary duties deliberately or recklessly to force P Ltd into administrative receivership with the intention of the business being acquired by O Ltd: a company in which the defendants later acquired an interest. The claimants also brought proceedings against O Ltd on the grounds that by purchasing P Ltd's shares O Ltd had dishonestly assisted the directors of P Ltd in their breach of trust. The trial judge, Rattee J, examined the claim on two grounds namely: (i) that the liability for dishonest assistance 'presupposes the breach of a trust' and that it would 'represent an extension of that head of constructive trusteeship beyond the limit so far recognised' if liability also covered an act that assisted a director in breaches of fiduciary duties to his company; and (ii) since O Ltd was only acquired by the directors after the sale and purchase of P Ltd had been agreed with the receivers it could not have assisted in the alleged breach of trust. The Court of Appeal upheld the judgment of Rattee J on the second ground and therefore did not have to decide on the first of the two reasons given by the trial judge. However, Morritt LJ, giving the only reasoned judgment of the Court of Appeal, stated that he could see no reason why liability to account as a constructive trustee should be extended to a case of dishonest assistance in any breach of fiduciary duty, and should not simply be limited to breaches of trust and mis-application of trust property. The Court of Appeal further considered this question in *Satnam Investments Ltd* v *Dunlop Heywood & Co Ltd*[38] where it was contemplated, but not decided whether the action might be available in respect of breach of receipt of confidential informa-tion that had been disclosed in breach of fiduciary duty. Nourse LJ in *Satnam* concluded that 'before a case can fall in either category [knowing receipt or dishonest assistance] there must be trust property or traceable proceeds of trust property'. However, in *Goose* v *Wilson Sandiford & Co (a firm)*,[39] delivering the judgment of the Court of Appeal, Morritt LJ said:

> the issue of whether the dishonest breach of trust in which the defendant assisted must have been more than misapplication of trust property or its proceeds of sale. The formulation of the principal by Lord Nicholls of Birkenhead . . . does not embrace such a requirement. Whether or not such a requirement is an essential feature of this head of liability is not the point we have to decide and, like the Court of Appeal in that case, we should not like to shut out the possibility of such a claim in its absence.

[36] See p. 422.
[37] [1999] 1 BCLC 649.
[38] [1999] 3 All ER 652.
[39] [2001] 1 Lloyd's Rep PN 189.

Subsequent cases have also failed to address the issue and in *Gencor ACP v Dalby*,[40] Rimer J thought the point 'a difficult one' and Roger Wyand QC in *Rockbrook Ltd v Khan*[41] expressed the view that with greatest respect to Nourse LJ in *Satnam*:[42]

> I do not find this passage easy. However there is much to be said in favour of adopting a wider approach so that accessory liability is developed as a form of equitable wrongdoing: liability will therefore be imposed for any breach of equitable obligation, including the obligation any misapplication of trust property.

There must have been misfeasance involving a breach of fiduciary duty

For liability to be imposed there must be a breach of trust, or if the wider approach is adopted, a breach of fiduciary duty. In *Barnes v Addy*,[43] Lord Selborne, on the facts, expressly addressed the issue of assistance 'in a dishonest and fraudulent design on the part of the trustee' although there were cases before *Barnes*, which did not consider the law so confined.[44] Lord Selborne's dicta that the trustee's breach of trust had to be dishonest and fraudulent for the accessory to be held liable for 'knowing assistance', however, became interpreted as if statute and introduced a straitjacket in the development of the law. Attempts to sidestep the rule were steadfastly rejected and in *Belmont Finance Corporation Ltd v Williams*[45] the Court of Appeal expressed the view that to depart from the principle (that for accessory liability to be imposed on a third party, dishonest or fraudulent design had to be established) would introduce an undesirable degree of uncertainty. In examining this aspect of the law Lord Nicholls in *Royal Brunei Airways Sdn Bhd v Tan*[46] explained that the introduction of the requirement appears to have derived from the *Selangor* case[47] which highlighted the potential use of equitable remedies in connection with misapplied company funds and since then the *Barnes v Addy*[48] formulation appears to have been applied as if it were statute, particularly with the accessory limb of the *Barnes test*. The courts consequently found themselves struggling with the interpretation of the individual ingredients, particularly 'knowingly' but also 'dishonest and fraudulent design on the part of the trustees', without examining the underlying reason why a third party who had received no trust property is being made liable. It was not until the *Tan* case[49] that the need to establish dishonesty or fraud on the part of the trustee or other fiduciary was abandoned as a prerequisite to accessory liability. The facts of *Royal Brunei Airways Sdn Bhd v Tan*[50] were that Royal Brunei Airways appointed a company (BLT) to act as their travel agent. Under the terms of the agreement BLT was required to account to the airline for monies received from the sale of the tickets but was permitted a 30-day credit

---

[40] [2000] 2 BCLC 734.
[41] [2006] EWHC 101 (Ch).
[42] [1999] 3 All ER 652.
[43] (1874) LR 9 Ch App 244.
[44] *Fyler v Fyler* (1861) 30 Beav 550; *A.G. v Leicester Corpn* (1844) 7 Beav 176; *Eaves v Hickson* (1861) 30 Beav 136.
[45] [1979] 1 All ER 118.
[46] [1995] 2 AC 378.
[47] *Selangor United Rubber Estates Ltd v Cradock (No 3)* [1968] 1 WLR 1555.
[48] (1874) LR 9 Ch App 244.
[49] [1995] 2 AC 378.
[50] [1995] 2 AC 378.

period before being required to account to the airline for the sales. The agreement expressly provided that monies received from the sale of the tickets were to be held by BLT on trust for the airline. In fact, monies received from the sale of such tickets, in breach of trust, were paid into BLT's general business account and used in the course of the company's normal business. This was done with the knowledge, and assistance, of Tan, who was the managing director and principal shareholder of BLT. As BLT was insolvent, the plaintiff sought a remedy against Tan. The Court of Appeal of Brunei Darussalam held the defendant not liable on the ground that although Tan had conceded he assisted in the breach of trust with knowledge, the breach of trust had not been shown to be of a dishonest and fraudulent design, essential for accessory liability. The Court of Appeal concluded that breach of trust had been the result of poor management and not dishonesty.

The issue before the Privy Council was whether the breach of trust, a prerequisite of accessory liability, must itself be a dishonest and a fraudulent breach by the trustee. Lord Nicholls delivering the opinion of the Privy Council concluded that accessory liability for constructive trusts required a breach of trust or other fiduciary duty, but not dishonesty. With regard to the liability of a third party Lord Nicholls concluded that what matters is not the state of mind of the trustee, but the state of mind of the third party sought to be made liable. The trustee, even if innocent, will be liable for breach of trust unless excused by an exemption clause in the trust instrument. But the issue was whether the trustee's state of mind is relevant to the question of whether the third party should be made liable to the beneficiaries for breach of trust. If the liability of the third party is fault based, what is relevant is the nature of the third party fault, and not that of the trustee. Therefore dishonesty on the part of the third party is a sufficient basis for his liability, irrespective of the state of the mind of the trustee who is in breach of trust. Lord Nicholls concluded that:

> it is difficult to see why, if a third-party dishonestly assisted in breach, there should be a further prerequisite to his liability, namely, that the trustee also must have been acting dishonestly. The alternative view would mean that a dishonest third party is liable if the trustee is dishonest, but if the trustee did not act dishonestly that . . . itself would excuse a dishonest third-party from liability. That would make no sense.

The person upon whom liability is to be imposed must, as a matter of fact, have been accessory to, or assisted in, the misfeasance or breach of trust

Generally, civil law, like criminal law is 'moulded on the philosophy of autonomy'[51] so that the loss flowing from the actions of the primary wrongdoer are generally not regarded as being caused by the actions of a participant who has induced or assisted in the commission of the wrong. Civil secondary liability, however, is an exception to this rule and a defendant fixed with this sort of liability, even where there is no direct casual link between his actions and loss, will be liable for the loss. The idea of 'assistance' encompasses not only persons who assist with the original breach of trust but also those who assist with the continued diversion of trust funds or those who help to launder the proceeds. Mance LJ, in *Grupo Torras SA v Al-Sabah (No 5)*,[52] in a dishonest assistance claim, said that:

[51] Williams (1990) *Complicity, Purpose and the Draft Code*, Crim LR 4.
[52] [2001] Lloyd's Rep Bank 36.

> The starting point . . . is that the requirement of dishonest assistance relates not to any loss or damage which may have been suffered, but to the breach of trust or fiduciary duty.

This was affirmed on appeal and then reaffirmed in *Casio Computer Ltd v Sayo*[53] where Tuckey LJ stated that:

> Grupo Torras . . . establishes that in a claim for dishonest assistance it is not necessary to show a precise causal link between the assistance and the loss . . . caused by the breach of fiduciary duty.

Where a defendant's action could have made no difference to the breach of trust or fiduciary duty 'there is no causative effect and therefore no assistance . . . [so that] the requirements of conscience [do not] require any remedy'. The claimant must, at least, show that the defendant's actions have made the fiduciary's breach easier than it would otherwise have been. The causation requirement is no stronger than this and it is no excuse that the claimant's loss would have occurred anyway because the wrongdoing fiduciary would have committed the breach even if the defendant had not assisted him. The defendant can therefore be made liable for acts or omissions that occur before the commission of the breach, although he cannot be made liable if his acts or omissions occurred after the breach was fully executed. In *Brinks Ltd v Abu-Saleh (No 3)*[54] a gang was able to steal a large quantity of gold bullion because a security guard at the warehouse where the gold was stored provided them with a key and other assistance. An associate of the gang made several trips to Switzerland to launder the proceeds of the theft and his wife accompanied him on these trips. The claimant brought an action against the wife for 'dishonest assistance'. Rimer J held that although the security guard was in breach of his fiduciary obligations of honesty and loyalty to his employers, the claimant, the wife had not provided any assistance in furtherance of the breach of trust. The learned judge concluded that the wife went on these trips to Switzerland in her spousal capacity, and her presence on these trips did not constitute 'assistance' in breach of the trust. Third party conduct or acts will, therefore, not qualify as rendering 'assistance' unless they have 'some causative significance'[55] in relation to the breach of trust or fiduciary duty. Although the assistance in the breach of trust or fiduciary duty need not be direct, the acts or omissions complained of must at least have made the commission of the breach easier than it otherwise would have been, or facilitated the concealment or disposal of the funds.[56]

On this basis, banks are likely to find allegations of accessory to, or assisted in, a breach of trust difficult to avoid. Although it has been suggested that passive receipt of monies or the mere receipt of trust property does not count as assistance,[57] banks are generally more active than passive recipients of money. Banks are likely to be involved in transferring funds into and out of bank accounts and there is therefore positive conduct[58] on their part with regard to the retention or disposal of funds and that may involve them in providing services to fraudulent persons.[59] Where the breach involves a misapplication of funds, the courts are

---

[53] [2001] EWCA Civ 661.

[54] [1996] CLC 133.

[55] *Yugraneft* v *Abramovich* [2008] EWHC 2613.

[56] *Casio Computer Co Ltd v Sayo* [2001] EWCA 661; *Grupo Torra SA v Al-Sabah (No 5)* QBD (Comm. Ct) 24 June 1999; see also Baughen (2007) *Accessory Liability at Common Law and in Equity – 'The Redundancy of Knowing Assistance', Revisited*, LMCLQ 545.

[57] *Ultraframe (UK) Ltd v Fielding* [2005] EWHC 1638 (Ch).

[58] *Re-Engine Pty Ltd v Fergusson* [2007] VSC 57.

[59] *Selangor United Rubber Estates Ltd v Cradock (No 3)* [1968] 1 WLR 1555.

likely to hold that it was not fully implemented until the funds were hidden away to prevent the beneficiaries finding them with the result that those involved in money laundering activities after the funds have been wrongfully removed from the trust account can be fixed as being liable for dishonest assistance.[60]

The accessory must have been dishonest

Prior to *Royal Brunei Airlines Sdn Bhd v Tan*[61] there was considerable debate about the level of knowledge that the accessory or assister had to possess regarding the breach of trust in order to be held liable for 'knowing assistance'. The question is whether liability could be imposed only on those who have actual knowledge of the breach of trust, including those who turn a blind eye to the truth, those deemed to have constructive notice of the breach of trust or those deemed to have knowledge of circumstances that would indicate a breach to an honest and reasonable man or would put such a person on enquiry.

In other words, the question was whether negligence would be enough to impose liability on the accessory or whether dishonesty would have to be established for liability to be imposed. In *Selangor United Rubber Estates Ltd v Cradock (No 3)*,[62] the first modern case on this point, Ungoed-Thomas J concluded that liability would be imposed on a third party who had knowledge of circumstances that would indicate to 'an honest, reasonable man' that the breach in question had been committed and would put him on enquiry. In other words, liability for assisting in a breach of trust would be imposed on a third party where a third party was deemed to have constructive notice of the improper application of the customer's funds. Negligence was, therefore, enough to hold the third-party liable for assisting in a fraudulent breach of trust. Brightman J reached a similar conclusion in *Karak Rubber Co Ltd v Burden (No 2)*[63] and although doubts[64] were cast on this approach in *Belmont Finance Corporation Ltd v Williams*[65] by Buckley and Goff LJJ, it was followed in *Baden, Delvaux and Lecuit v Société Générale pour Favoriser le Developpement du Commerce et de l'Industrie en France SA (1983)*[66] where Peter Gibson J accepted a five point scale of knowledge formulated by counsel. The level of dishonest 'knowledge' required to impose liability on a third party was established as follows:

(i)   Actual knowledge.

(ii) Wilfully setting one's eyes to the truth.

(iii) Wilfully and recklessly failing to make such enquiries as a reasonable and honest man would make.

(iv) Knowledge of circumstances that would indicate the facts to an honest and reasonable man.

(v)   Knowledge of circumstances that would put a reasonable man on enquiry.

---

[60] *Heinl v Jyske Bank (Gibraltar) Ltd* [1999] Lloyd's Rep Bank 511, approving *Agip (Africa) Ltd v Jackson* [1990] Ch 265.
[61] [1995] 2 AC 378.
[62] [1968] 1 WLR 1555.
[63] [1972] 1 WLR 602.
[64] Similar doubts were expressed in Australia by Jacobs P in *DPC Estates Pty Ltd v Grey* [1974] 1 NSWLR 443.
[65] [1979] 1 All ER 118.
[66] [1993] 1 WLR 509n.

While categories (i) to (iii) represent 'dishonesty' categories (iv) and (v) represent negligent liability. Peter Gibson J concluded that 'knowledge' of any of the five types listed, including the last two, i.e. negligence, would be sufficient to impose liability on an accessory to a breach of trust or breach of fiduciary duty.

Following the *Baden* case,[67] and prior to the *Royal Brunei Airlines Sdn Bhd v Tan*[68] case, there was an influential body of case law and academic opinion[69] in favour of the test of accessory liability being one of dishonesty. Both Megarry V-C in *Montagu's Settlement Trusts*[70] and Millett J in *Agip (Africa) Ltd v Jackson*[71] expressed the view that third parties must, at least, have realised that their clients might be involved in the fraud. Thus, dishonest behaviour was key to imposing third party liability and Millett J in *Agip*[72] concluded 'the sooner that those who will provide the services of nominee companies for the purpose of enabling their clients to keep their activities secret realise it, the better'. In *Eagle Trust Plc v SBC*[73] Vinelott J stated that it could be taken as settled law that want of probity was a prerequisite accessory liability.[74] In *Royal Brunei Airlines Sdn Bhd v Tan*,[75] Lord Nicholls confirmed that the test for accessory liability is dishonesty, or lack of probity, both of which were treated as synonymous and simply meaning 'not acting as an honest person in the circumstances.' Furthermore, Lord Nicholls expressed the view that 'knowingly' was better avoided in the future and the five-point scale of knowledge set out in the *Baden* case[76] was 'best forgotten'. Dishonesty in this context is, therefore, an objective standard and not to be assessed subjectively. Lord Nicholls explaining his reasoning also said that dishonesty includes 'commercially unacceptable conduct'. The judgment has been fundamental to the development of a test for dishonesty in civil claims and central to the debate has been whether, and to what extent, the court should consider the defendant's own state of mind and view of his own honesty, as required in the criminal context. His Lordship explained:

> Whatever may be the position in some criminal or other contexts (see, for instance *R v Gosh* [1982] QB 1053, [1982] 2 All ER 689), in the context of the accessory liability principle acting dishonestly, or with a lack of probity, which is synonymous, means simply not acting as an honest person would in the circumstances. This is an objective standard. At first sight this may seem surprising. Honesty has a connotation of subjectivity, as distinct from the objectivity of negligence. Honesty, indeed, does have a strong subjective element in that it is a description of the type of conduct assessed in the light of what a person actually knew at the time, as distinct from what a reasonable person would have known or appreciated. Further, honesty and its counterpart dishonesty are mostly concerned with advertent conduct, not inadvertent conduct. Carelessness is not dishonesty. Thus for the most part dishonesty is to be equated with conscious impropriety. However, these subjective characteristics of honesty do not mean that individuals are free to set their own standards of honesty in particular circumstances. The standard of what

[67] [1993] 1 WLR 509n.

[68] [1995] 2 AC 378.

[69] See: *Re Montague's Settlement* [1987] Ch 264; *Agip (Africa) Ltd v Jackson* [1990] Ch 265; *Polly Peck International Plc v Nadir (No 2)* [1992] 4 All ER 769.

[70] [1990] Ch 265.

[71] [1990] Ch 265.

[72] [1990] Ch 265.

[73] [1992] 4 All ER 488.

[74] See also *Polly Peck International Plc v Nadir (No 2)* [1992] 4 All ER 769.

[75] [1995] 2 AC 378.

[76] [1993] 1 WLR 509n.

constitutes honest conduct is not subjective. Honesty is not an optional scale, with higher or lower values according to the moral standards of each individual. If a person knowingly appropriates another's property, he will not escape a finding of dishonesty simply because he sees nothing wrong in such behaviour . . .

With regard to what honesty required Lord Nicholls continued:

honesty is an objective standard. The individual is expected to attain the standard which would be observed by an honest person placed in those circumstances. It is impossible to be more specific. Knox J captured the flavour of this, in a commercial setting, when he referred to a person who is guilty of commercially unacceptable conduct in the particular context involved: 'see *Cowan de Groot Properties Ltd* v *Eagle Trust Plc* [1992] 4 All ER 700, 761. Acting in reckless disregard of others' rights or possible rights can be a tell-tale sign of dishonesty.

Although Lord Nicholls referred to the 'objective standard' of dishonesty, he also talked about honesty having 'a strong subjective element'. Nevertheless, his judgment was clear insomuch as it is for the court to decide objectively what was dishonest for equitable purposes. Following the *Tan*[77] case it seemed clear that dishonesty, in equity, could be established without proof that the defendant believed himself to have been dishonest. The uncertainty, which has arisen in more recent cases, arises from the interpretation of the *Tan* case by the House of Lords in *Twinsectra Ltd* v *Yardley*[78] where their Lordships examined the question of how 'dishonesty' was to be interpreted and concluded that of the three possible tests for interpreting dishonesty, the combined test of knowledge was to applied for the purposes of accessory liability. The facts of *Twinsectra* were that a solicitor (A), acting for a borrower, had given an undertaking to a lender to retain the money advanced by him pending their application for the purchase of a certain property by the borrower. Contrary to that undertaking A paid the loan money to a second solicitor acting for the borrower (B) who then paid the money to the borrower, or his order. A substantial part of the money was used for purposes other than the purchase of the agreed property. The loan was not repaid. The lender sued, among others, B, alleging dishonest assistance in the breach of trust by A. The trial judge held that although the defendant (Y) had shut his eyes to the details of the transactions, he had not acted dishonestly because the money was at the disposal of Y. The Court of Appeal overruled the judge at first instance, and substituted a finding of dishonesty. The House of Lords restored the judgment of the trial judge and Lord Hutton examined the three possible standards which might be applied to determine whether a third party has acted dishonesty:

(i) A purely subjective standard, where a person is only regarded as dishonest if he transgresses his own standard of honesty, even if that standard is contrary to that of reasonable and honest people. This has been termed the 'Robin Hood test' and has been rejected by the courts. In *Walker* v *Stones*[79] Sir Christopher Slade said a 'person may in some cases act dishonestly, according to the ordinary use of language, even though he genuinely believes that his act is morally justified. The penniless thief, for example, who picks the pocket of the mutli-millionaire is dishonest even though he genuinely considers that theft is morally justified as a fair redistribution of wealth and that he is not therefore being dishonest'.

[77] [1995] 2 AC 378.
[78] [2002] 2 AC 164.
[79] [2000] Lloyds Rep PN 864 at 877.

(ii) A purely objective standard where a person acts dishonestly if his conduct is dishonest by the ordinary standards of reasonable and honest people, even if he does not realise this.

(iii) A combined objective and subjective test requiring that before there can be a finding of dishonesty it must be established that the defendant's conduct was dishonest by the ordinary standards of reasonable and honest people and that he himself realised that by those standards his own conduct was dishonest. This is similar to the view adopted in R v Ghosh[80] where the court established the test for dishonesty in crime. That decision established a two-tier objective and subjective test so that a jury first had to decide 'whether according to the ordinary standards of reasonable and honest people what was done was dishonest'. If the jury came to the conclusion that the conduct was dishonest by those standards, it must then consider the second question namely, 'whether the defendant himself must have realised that what he was doing was [by the standards of reasonable and honest people] dishonest'.

Lord Hutton delivering the decision of the majority in *Twinsectra*,[81] therefore, concluded that dishonesty meant both that the defendant's conduct must be 'dishonest by the ordinary standards of reasonable and honest people' and that the defendant himself must have realised that 'by those standards his conduct was dishonest'. Lord Millett, however, dissenting, rejected the second element of the dishonesty requirement and stated that 'it is not necessary that [the defendant] should actually have appreciated that he was acting dishonestly; it is sufficient that he was'. Lord Millett addressed the question of whether there is a requirement of 'dishonesty in the subjective sense in which that term is used in criminal cases'. In his view, Lord Nicholls in *Tan*[82] had rejected negligence as a test for liability and replaced it with dishonesty but in 'taking dishonesty to be the condition of liability, however, Lord Nicholls used the word in an objective sense'. Lord Millett went on to refer to Lord Lane in *Ghosh*,[83] where his Lordship had drawn a distinction between dishonesty as a state of mind and dishonesty as a course of conduct, concluding that dishonesty in the criminal context required a dishonest state of mind. In Lord Millett's view, excepting cases of fraud, the requirement of a dishonest state of mind is:

> not generally an appropriate condition of civil liability, which does not ordinarily require a guilty mind. Civil liability is usually predicated on the defendant's conduct rather than his state of mind; it results from his negligent or unreasonable behaviour or, where this is not sufficient, from intentional wrongdoing.

Lord Millett also expressed the view that:

> There is no trace in Lord Nicholls' opinion that the defendant should have been aware that he was acting contrary to objective standards of dishonesty. In my opinion, in rejecting the test of dishonesty adopted in R v Ghosh [1982] QB 1053, Lord Nicholls was using the word to characterise the defendant's conduct, not his state of mind.

Lord Millett, instead, was happy to see the development of equitable remedies requiring dishonesty in this way and stated that:

[80] [1982] QB 1053.
[81] [2002] 2 AC 164.
[82] [1995] 2 AC 378.
[83] [1982] QB 1053.

Judges have frequently used the word dishonesty in civil cases in an objective sense to describe deliberate wrongdoing, particularly when handling equitable concepts such as concealed fraud . . . [since] equity looks to a man's conduct, not to his state of mind.

According to Lord Millett the key question was not whether Lord Nicholls, in *Tan*,[84] was using the word 'dishonesty' in a subjective or objective sense but whether it was necessary to show that an accessory to a breach of trust had a dishonest state of mind, therefore being subjectively dishonest as in *Ghosh*.[85] Such an analysis was not, in his view, appropriate since:

Consciousness of wrongdoing is an aspect of mens rea and an appropriate condition of criminal liability: it is not an appropriate condition of civil liability. This generally results from negligent or intentional conduct. For the purpose of civil liability, it should not be necessary that the defendant realised that his conduct was dishonest; it should be sufficient that it constituted intentional wrongdoing.

Despite Lord Millett's dissent, Lord Hutton[86] emphasised three points in favour of the 'combined test' of dishonesty. He said that a finding by the court that (i) the 'defendant had been dishonest was a grave finding, particularly grave against a professional man', for example a solicitor; (ii) notwithstanding, that the issue did not arise in a criminal context, 'it would be less than just for the law to permit a finding that the defendant had been "dishonest" in assisting a breach of trust where he knew of the trust's existence and its breach, but had not been aware that he was doing what would be regarded by honest men as being dishonest'; and (iii) requiring the defendant to know what he was doing would be regarded as dishonest by honest people 'does not involve the defendant setting his own standards of honesty because he does not regard as dishonest what he knows would offend normally accepted standards of honest conduct'.

On the facts of *Twinsectra Ltd* v *Yardley*[87] Lords Hutton, Hoffman and Millett all agreed that there were no facts L was unaware of and therefore *Twinsectra* was not a case where the defendant deliberately closed his eyes and ears, or deliberately refrained from asking questions, unlike *Barlow Clowes International Ltd* v *Eurotrust International Ltd*.[88] Here Barlow Clowes International (BC) operated a fraudulent offshore investment scheme in Gibraltar offering high returns to investors from the UK. The defendant company, ITC, based in the Isle of Man provided offshore financial services including forming and administrating offshore companies, providing offshore directors willing to act on the instructions of beneficiaries, opening accounts and, sometimes through its own client account, moving money. The Barlow Clowes scheme collapsed in 1988, but prior to its collapse ITC had made a number of payments from Barlow Clowes to a number of offshore companies, which it administered. Some of the transactions passed through ITC's client account while others had passed through companies administered by ITC. The administrator of Barlow Clowes brought proceedings against ITC and its directors alleging that they had dishonestly assisted in defrauding the investors in the Barlow Clowes scheme. The Privy Council was only concerned with the liability of one of ITC's directors, namely Mr Henwood. At first instance, the trial judge held that Mr Henwood was fully aware of the nature of the Barlow Clowes business and of the dishonest nature of those running the investment scheme. The judge also held that

---

[84] [1995] 2 AC 378.
[85] [1982] QB 1053.
[86] *Twinstectra Ltd* v *Yardley* [2002] 2 AC 164.
[87] [2002] 2 AC 164.
[88] [2006] 1 All ER 333.

Mr Henwood 'strongly suspected the funds passing through his hands were moneys Barlow Clowes had received from members of the public' but that he 'consciously decided not to make enquiries because he preferred in his own interest not to run the risk of discovering the truth'. The judge, therefore, concluded that by deliberately closing his eyes to the facts before him Mr Henwood was dishonest. On appeal Lord Hoffman, agreeing with the trial judge, concluded that Mr Henwood's deliberate failure to enquire was dishonest 'by ordinary standards'. The *Barlow Clowes*[89] case resulted in two significant points with regard to the meaning attributed to 'dishonesty' for the purposes of dishonest assistance liability. The first issue related to the debate and misgivings that followed the *Twinsectra*[90] case around the 'combined test' for dishonesty adopted in that case. The Privy Council in *Barlow Clowes*[91] attempted to clarify, what their Lordships explained as ambiguity arising as a result of the *Twinsectra*[92] case. Both the *Barlow Clowes*,[93] and subsequently *Abou Rahmah* v *Abacha*[94] case, purported to 'interpret' *Twinsectra* and *Tan*, but did so in a way that was not entirely expected.

Lord Hoffmann, delivering the leading judgment in *Barlow Clowes*,[95] set out to interpret his own judgment in *Tan*[96] and that of Lord Hutton in *Twinsectra*.[97] According to Lord Hoffmann, Lord Hutton's reference in *Twinsectra* to what the defendant 'knows would offend normally accepted standards of honest conduct' meant only 'knowledge of the pertinent facts, so that his conduct was therefore contrary to normally acceptable standards of honest conduct objectively ascertained'. In *Barlow Clowes*[98] the court said that although the dishonest state of mind 'is a subjective mental state, the standard by which the law determines whether it is dishonest is objective'. The trial judge, at first instance, in *Barlow Clowes* had concluded that Mr Henwood 'may well have lived by different standards and seen nothing wrong in what he was doing'. So applying *Twinsectra*[99] the further issue raised by this test was whether subjectively the defendant must also have been aware that his conduct was dishonest by ordinary objective standards. Their Lordships in *Barlow Clowes*[100] concluded that Lord Hutton, in *Twinsectra*,[101] by referring to 'what he [the defendant] knows would offend normally accepted standards of honest conduct' merely required that the defendant's 'knowledge of the transaction had to be such as to render his participation contrary to normally acceptable standards of honest conduct. It did not require that he should have had reflections about what those normally acceptable standards were.' Lord Hoffmann himself went on to state that a dishonest state meant 'consciousness that one is transgressing ordinary standards of honest behaviour' and was intended to require consciousness of those elements of the transaction which make 'participation transgress ordinary standards of honest behaviour. It did not also require him to have thought about what those standards were.' Their Lordships in *Barlow Clowes*[102]

---

[89] [2006] 1 All ER 333.
[90] [2002] 2 AC 164.
[91] [2006] 1 All ER 333.
[92] [2002] 2 AC 164.
[93] [2006] 1 All ER 333.
[94] [2006] 1 Lloyd's Rep 484.
[95] [2006] 1 All ER 333.
[96] [1995] 2 AC 378.
[97] [2002] 2 AC 164.
[98] [2006] 1 All ER 333.
[99] [2002] 2 AC 164.
[100] [2006] 1 All ER 333.
[101] [2002] 2 AC 164.
[102] [2006] 1 All ER 333.

therefore concluded that *Twinsectra*[103] was consistent with the approach in the *Tan*[104] case and the former did not introduce an additional subjective requirement that the defendant should have considered or thought of his behaviour as contrary to acceptable standards. Following, *Barlow Clowes* these cases have stressed that the test for dishonesty is 'predominately objective'.[105]

The second issue addressed in *Barlow Clowes*[106] was the type of knowledge that the defendant must be shown to possess before he will be liable for having transgressed the 'standards of honesty for the purposes of imposing liability for dishonest assistance'. There was some doubt as to whether for accessory liability to be found the accessory had to be aware of the breach of trust or whether awareness of some other wrongdoing (for example, breach of contract, breach of foreign exchange controls, or evasion of tax) was enough. In *Royal Brunei Airways Sdn Bhd* v *Tan*,[107] Lord Nicholls observed that in the past the law had required for the accessory to have knowledge of the breach of trust, but he did not deal with this issue following the new, wider test of dishonesty being adopted. However, dicta in subsequent cases, particularly in *Brinks Ltd* v *Abu-Saleh (No 3)*[108] suggested that it was necessary for the accessory to have knowledge of the facts giving rise to the breach of trust. Lord Millett earlier in *Agip (Africa) Ltd* v *Jackson*[109] had expressed the view that a man 'who consciously assists others by making arrangements which he knows are calculated to conceal what is happening from a third party, takes the risk that they are part of a fraud practised on that party'. And then again in *Twinsectra Ltd* v *Yardley*[110] Lord Millett stated that it was 'obviously not necessary that he [the accessory] should know the details of the trust or the identity of the beneficiary' but it is sufficient that the accessory knows 'that the money is not the free disposal of the principal', or 'that he knows that he is assisting in a dishonest scheme' or that he has 'knowledge of the arrangements which constitute the trust'. Such a person takes the risk that his conduct may assist a breach of trust.

The position has been clarified in *Barlow Clowes*[111] where Lord Hoffmann, rejecting the view expressed in the *Brinks Ltd*[112] case, held it was not necessary that the accessory knew about the existence of the trust, the facts giving rise to the trust, or even what a trust actually involves.[113] According to *Barlow Clowes* it is sufficient that the defendant 'entertained a clear suspicion' that the funds in question were held on trust or that the primary wrongdoers were not 'entitled to make free with [the funds] as they pleased'. If accessory liability is therefore to be imposed on the basis of equitable wrongdoing, rather than liability based on 'constructive trusts', the broader approach to knowledge has to be the correct.

Lord Millett was happy to develop equitable remedies requiring dishonesty in this way when he expressed the view that:

---

[103] [2002] 2 AC 164.
[104] [1995] 2 AC 378.
[105] *Abou-Rahmah v Abacha* [2006] 1 Lloyd's Rep 484.
[106] [2006] 1 All ER 333.
[107] [1995] 2 AC 378.
[108] [1996] CLC 133.
[109] [1990] Ch 265.
[110] [2002] 2 AC 164.
[111] [2006] 1 All ER 333.
[112] [1996] CLC 133.
[113] *Abou-Rahmah v Abacha* [2006] 1 Lloyd's Rep 484.

Judges have frequently used the word dishonesty in civil cases in an objective sense to describe deliberate wrongdoing, particularly when handling equitable concepts such as concealed fraud . . . [since] equity looks to a man's conduct, not to his state of mind.

While the clarification by the Privy Council in *Barlow Clowes*[114] is welcomed, the English Courts are bound by the House of Lords decision in the *Twinsectra*[115] case but the lower courts appear to be adopting what the court in *Twinsectra* 'intended' to say rather than what was actually said. Corporate defendants, including banks, are more likely to be held liable under *Twinsectra* since there is one less requirement to satisfy and the fact that it would also require the bank to show that it had acted with conscious dishonesty. The latter element is difficult to establish with regard to corporate clients[116] and in the case of banks it is unlikely that the courts will aggregate knowledge within the bank when assessing knowledge of the facts and with conscious dishonesty.[117]

However, since the test for dishonesty remains high and an objective one it is unlikely there will be a flood of successful actions against the bank. While banks are not liable for assisting merely because they entertain suspicion about the origins of the money deposited with them they will be liable if they have strong doubts or suspicions about the money and turn a blind eye.[118] In *Abou-Rahmah* v *Abacha*[119] the claimants were the victims of a complex fraud, which resulted in them paying large sums of money into an account with a Nigerian bank. The fraudsters and the money disappeared and the claimants pursued the bank for dishonest assistance in breach of trust. The Court of Appeal had to consider 'dishonesty' in the context of a bank's duties on receipt of instructions from a customer when it might have had either generalised or even specific instructions about the propriety of the customer. Rix LJ said the bank officer had 'probably suspected' in a general way that his customer's directors were involved in money-laundering transactions. The case is of limited value since it was not decided on the question of dishonest assistance but the Court of Appeal made a number of important points with regard to previous authorities. The *Twinsectra*[120] case being a House of Lords case remains the highest authority but the Court of Appeal in *Abou Rahmah*[121] asserted that the proper test in cases of dishonesty was now as explained in the *Barlow Clowes* interpretation of the *Twinsectra*[122] judgment. Rix LJ expressed the view that it was sufficient to concentrate on *Barlow Clowes*[123] with regard to the element of knowledge required to set an investigation in respect of the element of dishonesty, and the state of mind of the defendant, as it reflected in his own standards of behaviour, was not relevant. The third party's knowledge and suspicions were relevant if they were sufficient to establish that their actions were in breach of such objectively assessed standards. The judges in *Abou Rahmah*[124] took a different view of what those standards were, balancing a bank's duties to its customers and its role in

[114] [2006] 1 All ER 333.
[115] [2002] 2 AC 164.
[116] *Meridian Global Funds Management Asia Ltd* v *Securities Commission* [1995] 2 AC 500.
[117] *Galmerrow Securities Ltd* v *National Westminster Bank Plc* Ch D 20 December 1993; *A-G's Ref (No 2 of 1999)* [2000] 3 WLR 195.
[118] *Governor & Company of the Bank of Scotland* v *A Ltd (sub nom. The bank v A Ltd)* [2001] EWCA Civ 52.
[119] [2006] 1 Lloyd's Rep 484.
[120] [2002] 2 AC 164.
[121] [2006] 1 Lloyd's Rep 484.
[122] [2002] 2 AC 164.
[123] [2006] 1 All ER 333.
[124] [2006] 1 Lloyd's Rep 484.

acting against money laundering. Arden LJ agreeing with Rix LJ that the appeal should fail considered the interpretation of the dishonesty test in *Barlow Clowes*.[125] It was unnecessary to show subjective dishonesty in the sense of consciousness that the transaction is dishonest. It is sufficient if the defendant knows of the elements of the transaction which make it dishonest according to normally accepted standards of behaviour. Addressing the central issue, Arden LJ was unequivocal in making a clear distinction between dishonesty in crime and in a civil claim, stating that there was no 'overriding reason why in respect of dishonesty in the context of civil liability (as opposed to criminal responsibility) the law should take account of the defendant's views as to the morality of his actions'. The *Abou Rahmah*[126] case signalled an acceptance by the Court of Appeal that *Barlow Clowes*[127] was to be followed. However, uncertainty remained, because as Pill LJ explained, since this case did not turn on the question, the implications of *Barlow Clowes* were 'best considered in a case in which a real issue arises on its impact'. Secondly and additionally, Rix LJ in giving his judgment that the court was to follow *Barlow Clowes*, the learned judge indicated that there may still 'possibly' be an element of the test whereby the 'defendant must in some sense be dishonest himself (a subjective test of dishonesty which might, on analysis, add little or nothing to knowledge of the facts which, objectively, would make his conduct dishonest)'.

In *Jeremy Stone v National Westminster Bank Plc*[128] the claimants, Stone Consultants Limited and Jeremy Stone, alleged that the defendant bank and one of its relationship managers, X, had been guilty of dishonest assistance in breach of fiduciary duty, deceit, conspiracy, negligence and unjust enrichment. S, a school friend of the second claimant, convinced the claimants that he was a supplier of electrical goods to a number of large hotel chains. S convinced the claimants to invest in his business by way of loans. Earlier loans were repaid with later investment money in order to create the illusion that the business was thriving and to continue to attract further investments into this Ponzi scheme. S, and his co-fraudster, T held bank accounts with the defendant bank and both were clients of the same relationship manager, X, who believed the hotel business was genuine. On acquiring responsibility for the account from the previous relationship manager in late 2008, X learnt that S frequently made large cash withdrawals from his accounts. X also learnt that these transactions had been investigated by the bank's Anti-Money Laundering team, which had concluded its investigation on the basis that it had received sufficient explanations as to why their business was conducted using large cash withdrawals. Indeed, the bank's Anti-Money Laundering team looked at these transactions again in 2009 in order to check that S was not perpetrating a VAT fraud and again concluded its investigation on the basis of sufficient evidence to the contrary.

The claimants contacted X on a number of occasions to gain access to S's bank statements and to seek a loan from the bank to assist them with the running of the hotel business. The court found that on each occasion X made it clear to the claimants that he owed a duty of confidentiality to S and could not discuss any of his affairs without S's instructions. In February 2010, during the course of a discussion between the claimants and X about a loan from the bank, X learnt that the claimants believed the receipts from the hotel business were paid directly into S's account with the National Westminster bank. X knew this was not the case. Instead, he had been told that the monies were paid into S's account with Barclays Bank, and

[125] [2006] 1 All ER 333.
[126] [2006] 1 Lloyd's Rep 484.
[127] [2006] 1 All ER 333.
[128] [2013] EWHC 208 (Ch).

that the monies were then transferred to the National Westminster Bank. S's explanation for this was that Barclays had agreed to clear the hotel business' cheques on a shorter timescale than National Westminster Bank. On 28 April 2010, as a result of a computing error, and contrary to S's instructions, the claimants were able to view S's National Westminster Bank account statements. At this point it became evident to them that they had been defrauded. The claimants then took steps to have as much of the remaining money as possible transferred back to them before alerting the Serious Fraud Office of the frauds.

The court, applying *Twinsectra*, found that although X knew the claimants were mistaken about which bank was receiving the proceeds from the hotel business, he did not act dishonestly or suspect S of fraud. He believed the hotel business to be genuine and did not owe, and had not assumed, any duty to the claimants to correct their misunderstanding; and believed that the claimants had conducted their own due diligence on the hotel business and understood it better than he did.

Recent equitable developments

In recent cases of dishonest conduct the Courts of Chancery have had no reluctance in following the direction in *Abou Ramah*[129] that the *Barlow Clowes*[130] interpretation of *Twinsectra*[131] should be applied. However, the uncertainty has continued and resurfaced in *Starglade Properties Ltd* v *Nash*[132] where the Court of Appeal, overturning the first instance decision, held that a director had acted dishonestly, and in breach of trust, when making payments to some of the company's creditors in preference to others at a time when the company was technically insolvent and not able to pay its debts in full. The defendant, N, was the director of a company, Larkstore, which owed money to Starglade Properties. The debt arose as a result of an agreement under which Larkstore agreed to share the money it received as damages in litigation against a third party. Starglade had originally assigned its rights in the litigation to Larkstore, and by a side letter Larkstore agreed to hold on trust any monies it received from the third party. At the time the damages were paid to Larkstore, it was technically insolvent. N obtained advice from his solicitor in relation to payment of the money to another creditor (G) instead of Starglade but N subsequently paid the money to other creditors (not G) to deliberately frustrate Starglade's attempts to recover the money. N then applied for Larkstore to be dissolved and taken off the Companies Register. Starglade sued N, claiming that he was liable for dishonest assistance in a breach of trust by Larkstore. It was accepted that there had been a breach of trust and N had assisted in the breach. The question was whether the assistance had been dishonest. It was argued by N, among other things, that his conduct was not something that would be considered dishonest in the commercial world. Although the court considered dishonesty in the context of ss.239 to 241 of the Insolvency Act 1986 these sections were not in play, since the claim was not brought by a liquidator of Larkstore seeking to recover assets. However, in giving judgment the court considered the relationship between the statutory provisions and a claim in equity alleging preferential payments made in breach

---

[129] [2006] 1 Lloyd's Rep 484.
[130] [2006] 1 All ER 333.
[131] [2002] 2 AC 164.
[132] [2010] EWCA Civ 1117.

of trust. The claimants' action against the defendant alleged (i) a breach of trust on grounds of knowing receipt of a payment of £15,000 received by the defendant, and (ii) restitution of the entire sum due on the grounds that the defendant had dishonestly assisted in the breach of trust by paying monies away to other creditors. The breach of trust and assistance having been established the issue was what test of dishonesty the court should apply?

The trial judge and the Court of Appeal adopted very different approaches to the propriety of the defendant's actions and what constituted commercially acceptable conduct. The trial judge thought the defendant to be an honest witness and was therefore reluctant to taint his reputation with a finding of dishonesty. He found as a question of fact that the defendant did not know of the existence of a trust, or understand its significance, and consequently had no understanding that he was acting in breach of a trust. There was no appeal from that finding. The judge also found that there was a deliberate preference of other creditors by the defendant, motivated by a desire to avoid paying the claimant, 'because he felt that the claimant had taken unfair advantage of him' but held that this did not amount to dishonesty. The judge stated his interpretation of the law to be that the conduct in question must be 'at least objectively dishonest' meaning 'conduct which would be regarded as dishonest by any right-thinking person'. He continued that 'it is not always just a question of looking at the conduct and deciding whether, objectively, it was dishonest', but there may still remain a requirement that there be some subjective element, referring to the suggestion to this effect by Rix LJ in *Abou Rahmah*,[133] as authority. The judge acknowledged different standards of moral behaviour in relation to business conduct, suggesting that there may be 'cases in which different views could reasonably be held' where 'some might think the conduct dishonest, others not' in which case, a defendant would not be liable for dishonest assistance. What Lord Hoffmann in *Barlow Clowes*[134] and Lord Nicholls in *Tan*[135] had meant was that culpability rested on breach of 'normally accepted standards of conduct', which meant 'conduct which all normal people would regard as dishonest'.

The Court of Appeal overturned the trial judge, and agreeing with counsel for the claimant said that the first instance judgment reflected an analysis of the defendant's subjective view of his own honesty, instead of the objective approach adopted by the courts. Further, any suggestion that there was a 'sliding scale of honesty' was incorrect. It was irrelevant that:

> there may be a body of opinion which regards the ordinary standard of honest behaviour as being set too high. Ultimately, in civil proceedings, it is for the court to determine what that standard is and to apply it to the facts of the case.

The court continued that just because a type of standard of behaviour was common among business people that did not prevent it also being dishonest. Following his review of the authorities, the Lord Chancellor, Sir Anthony Morritt, asserted that the court should follow the interpretation of *Twinsectra*[136] by the Privy Council in *Barlow Clowes*,[137] commenting that there:

> [I]s no suggestion in any of the speeches in *Twinsectra Ltd* v *Yardley* that the standard of dishonesty is flexible or determined by any one other than by the court on an objective basis having regard to the ingredients of the combined test explained by Lord Hutton.

[133] [2006] 1 Lloyd's Rep 484.
[134] [2006] 1 All ER 333.
[135] [1995] 2 AC 378.
[136] [2002] 2 AC 164.
[137] [2006] 1 All ER 333.

Thus, Lord Hutton's combined test[138] remains but 'as explained by Lord Hutton in *Twinsectra* and Lord Hoffmann in *Barlow Clowes*'. The Lord Chancellor then added there is a 'single standard of honesty objectively determined by the court. That standard is applied to specific conduct of a specific individual possessing the knowledge and qualities he actually enjoyed'. The relevant standard was 'the ordinary standard of honest behaviour'. The 'subjective understanding of the person concerned as to whether his conduct is dishonest' was irrelevant.

The appeal succeeded on the grounds that the judge had misstated the law and asked the wrong question, in focusing on whether the defendant had acted dishonestly in preferring one creditor over another, despite the fact that this was the basis on which the claim was pleaded. There was clear evidence that the defendant was acting with the intention and desire not of preferring other creditors, but of frustrating the claimant. The role of the court was to take a view of the honesty of such behaviour, as to whether it was within the ordinary standards of honest commercial behaviour. The Court of Appeal concluded that the deliberate 'removal of the assets of an insolvent company so as entirely to defeat the just claim of a creditor is, in my view, not in accordance with the ordinary standards of honest commercial behaviour, however much it may occur'.

The court refused to accept that a person in the position of the defendant would have thought otherwise, irrespective of any advice received from his solicitor as to the legality or otherwise of his conduct. The judgment in *Starglade* affirms the movement away from a subjective requirement of dishonesty in claims for dishonest assistance in a breach of trust, but some uncertainty remains. There remains the problem of the relative precedence of the House of Lords in *Twinsectra*[139] as compared with the Privy Council in *Barlow Clowes*[140] and the Court of Appeal in *Abou Ramah*[141] and *Starglade*.[142] Further, all three judges in *Starglade* agreed with the Lord Chancellor, Sir Anthony Morritt's, judgment in that case.

Levenson LJ, in *Starglade*, made some observations indicating that he was not entirely at ease with the direction the court had taken. First, he stated that he 'would add a note of concern if the concept of dishonesty for the purposes of civil liability differed to any marked extent from the concept of dishonesty as understood in the criminal law', and went on to add that in his view the analysis

> which has governed the approach of the criminal law may fit more readily into the language of the House of Lords in *Twinsectra* prior to the explanation of the remarks on that case in *Barlow Clowes* in the Privy Council and *Abou Rahmah* in the Court of Appeal. It is all the more important, therefore, that at some stage the opportunity to revisit this issue should be taken by the Court of Appeal (Criminal Division).

More recent civil cases have examined allegations of fraud using the reasoning from the *Twinsectra*[143] line of cases in looking at dishonesty. In *Goldsmith Williams (A Firm) v Travellers Insurance Co Ltd*[144] the defendant insurance company sought to avoid liability under a clause in the insurance agreement stating that it would not be liable in respect of claims 'arising from dishonesty or a fraudulent act or omission committed or condoned by such insured'.

---

[138] *Twinsectra Ltd* v *Yardley* [2002] 2 AC 164.
[139] [2002] 2 AC 164.
[140] [2006] 1 All ER 333.
[141] [2006] 1 Lloyd's Rep 484.
[142] [2010] EWCA Civ 1117.
[143] [2002] 2 AC 164.
[144] [2010] EWHC 26 (QB).

The case required consideration of whether the claimant had acted dishonestly or fraudulently. Wyn Williams J treated the two issues together and cited *Twinsectra*[145] and *Barlow Clowes*[146] as authorities for guidance on the question of whether the claimant had acted fraudulently or dishonestly. The judge then stated that he did not find it necessary to analyse 'these decisions in detail or consider whether there is any tension between the two'. Instead he was 'content' to apply Lord Hutton's combined test, but without reference to any judicial interpretation of the later cases. Instead, the judge stated that in order to succeed the claimant must show subjective dishonesty, i.e., that the defendant himself had realised that by the ordinary standards of reasonable and honest people that his conduct was dishonest.

The later decision of *Aviva Insurance Ltd* v *Roger George Brown*,[147] however, included a more detailed analysis of the relationship between dishonesty and fraud. In this case, the claimant alleged that, in breach of the duty of 'good faith' in insurance contracts, the defendant had made fraudulent claims on an insurance policy held by him. The action was brought under the common law and under a clause in the insurance policy, which provided that the claimant would not pay any claim, which was in any respect fraudulent. The clause contained no reference to dishonesty and one of the main contentions was whether the claimant needed to establish dishonesty for the action to succeed. The defendant sought to rely on the House of Lords decision in *Manifest Shipping Co Ltd* v *Uni Polaris Insurance Co Ltd (The Star Sea)*[148] as authority that the duty owed by an insured in relation to a claim is a duty of honesty, and the statement of Roskill LJ in *Piermay Shipping Co SA* v *Chester (The Michael)*[149] that the 'relevant test must be honest belief'. Counsel for the defendant then submitted that, in order to assess the defendant's honesty, the court should adopt Lord Hutton's combined test in *Twinsectra*. Eder J however, acknowledged that counsel's suggestion was unorthodox, noting that it might not be appropriate to apply the test since '*Twinsectra* was not concerned with the definition of fraud but with "dishonesty"'. The test, however, was accepted by Eder J in *Aviva Insurance* but the learned judge applied Lord Hutton's[150] original combined test but without reference to any attempts to interpret those requirements in later cases. The judge therefore concluded that the defendant's conduct had to be shown to be objectively dishonest and the claimant also had to prove that the defendant himself was aware that he was acting dishonestly.

The judge examined how the idea of dishonesty related to the test for fraud as laid down in *Derry* v *Peek*[151] and said that fraud is established when:

> it is shown that a false representation has been made (1) knowingly, or (2) without belief in its truth, or (3) recklessly, careless whether it be true or false. Although I have treated the second and third as distinct cases, I think the third is but an instance of the second, for one who makes a statement under such circumstances can have no real belief in the truth of what he states. To prevent a false statement being fraudulent, there must, I think, always be an honest belief in its truth. And this probably covers the whole ground, for one who knowingly alleges that which is false, has obviously no such honest belief. Thirdly, if fraud be proved, the motive of the person guilty of it is immaterial. It matters not that there was no intention to cheat or injure the person to whom the statement was made.

[145] [2002] 2 AC 164.
[146] [2006] 1 All ER 333.
[147] [2011] EWHC 362 (QB).
[148] [1995] 1 Lloyd's Rep. 651.
[149] [1979] 2 Lloyd's Rep. 1.
[150] *Twinsectra Ltd* v *Yardley* [2002] 2 AC 164.
[151] (1889) 14 App Cas 337.

Eder J accepted the reservations of counsel for the defendant: (i) that motive was irrelevant regarding the assessment of fraud either under the *Derry v Peek*[152] formula or under the *Twinsectra*[153] combined test; (ii) the second limb of Lord Hutton's combined test would be satisfied in Lord Herschell's third category since 'a person who makes a false statement recklessly, careless whether it is true or false can have no honest belief in the truth of what he states'. The judge applied the combined test in *Twinsectra* and concluded that in respect of some of them, the defendant did not believe that he was acting dishonestly, and the action failed.

A finding, or allegations, of fraud in civil cases may have major ramifications and Eder J in *Aviva*, quoting the judgment of Flaux J in *Grosvenor Casinos Ltd v National Bank of Abu Dhabi*,[154] said that fraud must not be confused with incompetence, even if it amounts to gross negligence and of the importance of being satisfied 'to the necessary heightened standard of proof that was is involved is dishonesty'.

The High Court in *Aviva* has confirmed a test for dishonesty in fraud that includes a subjective element, allowing for consideration of the state of mind of the party in question. However, the judgment takes no account of judicial consideration of *Twinsectra* in later cases.

Knowing receipt

A person who receives[155] trust property, or its traceable proceeds, in breach of trust may be made personally liable if he deals with such property[156] in breach of trust. For the beneficiary to succeed in such an action it must be shown that the defendant dealt with the property in breach of trust and his conscience was affected with knowledge of the breach. Generally, for recipient liability to be imposed, the defendant will be liable for 'knowing receipt and dealing'. The first limb of *Barnes v Addy*[157] liability has traditionally been described as 'knowing receipt' and arises in circumstances where the defendant has received trust property or its identifiable proceeds, for his own benefit. The essential requirements for establishing a right to this personal remedy were stated by Hoffmann LJ in *El Ajou v Dollar Land Holdings Plc*[158] as follows:

> the plaintiff must show, first, a disposal of his assets in breach of fiduciary duty; secondly, the beneficial receipt by the defendant of assets which are traceable as representing the assets of the plaintiff; and thirdly, knowledge on the part of the defendant that the assets he received are traceable to a breach of fiduciary duty.

Although the degree of knowledge required to impose such liability has been extensively discussed by the courts there is still a lack of clarity with regard to the level of knowledge

---

[152] (1889) 14 App Cas 337.

[153] [2002] 2 AC 164.

[154] [2007] EWHC 2600 (Comm).

[155] In *Trustor v AB Smallbone (No 2)* [2001] 1 WLR 177 it was held that property will have been received by the defendant if it can be identified as in the defendant's hands in accordance with the rules of tracing in equity. Property received by a subsidiary company will not be held to have been received by the parent company unless the subsidiary was acting as an agent for the parent or the veil of incorporation is pierced.

[156] In *Satnam Investments Ltd v Dunlop Heywood Ltd* [1999] 3 All ER 652 it was contemplated, but not decided, that this action might be available in respect of confidential information which had been received in breach of a fiduciary duty.

[157] (1874) LR 9 Ch App 244.

[158] [1995] 2 All ER 213.

required to impose liability for knowing receipt. Where an agent receives property in a professional or ministerial capacity on behalf of the principal, and not for his own benefit or use, the agent will not be held liable for 'knowing receipt'. In *Twinsectra v Yardley*[159] Lord Millett accepted, *obiter*, that any knowing receipt claim in such circumstances would fail 'for want of necessary receipt'. Similarly, in *Agip (Africa) Ltd v Jackson*[160] Lord Millett, again *obiter*, expressed the view that the paying and collecting banks will not normally be brought within the category of 'knowing receipt' liability since they do not generally receive money for their own benefit, but are merely acting as the instructing customer's agent. The learned judge, however, indicated that the position may be different if the collecting bank uses the money to reduce the customer's indebtedness to the bank, for example by using the proceeds to reduce or discharge the customer's overdraft. This view has been criticised by Moore-Bick J in *Uzinterimpex JSC v Standard Bank Plc.*[161] Whether a bank receives funds that are accredited to the customer's account for its own benefit or for that of the customer may be difficult to determine where an account revolves between credit and debit balances. Lord Millett (as he now is), writing extra judicially, has emphasised that the continuation of a running account should not be sufficient to render the bank liable as a recipient and some conscious appropriation of the sum paid into the account in reduction of the overdraft should be necessary.[162] A bank would be considered to have beneficially received trust property where it debits its commission, fees or charges against trust funds credited to the customer's account,[163] or where it exercises other rights, for example set off against the funds.

Support for Lord Millett's view that using funds received into the credit of a customer's account to discharge an overdraft involves the beneficial receipt of trust property by a bank is found in the Canadian case of *Citadel General Assurance Co v Lloyd's Bank Canada*[164] where D, an insurance agent, negotiated insurance policies on behalf of Citadel, the insurer. D collected the insurance premiums from customers that were deemed to be held on trust for Citadel but were paid into D's bank account at the respondent bank. D's parent company also had an account at the same bank and having received instructions from D, the bank each day transferred the balance from D's account into the parent company's account in order to reduce the parent company's overdraft. On the insolvency of D, Citadel brought an action against the bank for knowing receipt of the funds. The Supreme Court of Canada held that although the bank had acted on valid instructions received from D's officers, the bank, in the circumstances, did not act as a mere agent. The bank, by using the insurance premiums to discharge the parent company's overdraft, had received a benefit. Further the bank was aware of the nature of the funds paid into D's account and then subsequently transferred, on a daily basis, into the parent company's account. The court concluded that a reasonable man would, with knowledge of the circumstances, be put on enquiry with regard to the possibility of a misapplication of trust funds and by failing to make the appropriate enquiries the bank had constructive knowledge of D's breach of trust and was therefore liable for knowing receipt.

[159] [2002] 2 AC 164; see also *Agip (Africa) Ltd v Jackson* [1991] Ch 547; *Polly Peck International Plc v Nadir (No 2)* [1992] 4 All ER 769.
[160] [1991] Ch 547.
[161] [2008] EWCA Civ. 819.
[162] Millet (1991) Tracing the Proceeds of Fraud, 107 *Law Quarterly Review*, 83.
[163] *Twinsectra v Yardley* [2002] 2 AC 164.
[164] (1997) 152 DLR (4th) 411 (SCC).

Following Millett J's reasoning, in *Agip*,[165] if the bank receives trust property into an account in credit, knowing it has been paid in breach of trust, the bank cannot be held liable for 'knowing receipt' although the bank may be held liable for 'knowing assistance' if the requirements of that aspect of the *Barnes* liability can be satisfied. However, it has been argued by several commentators that the bank receives all money deposited with it beneficially unless otherwise specified under the banking contract and that is even if the bank acts as an agent, irrespective of the state of the account. This follows from the general principle that legal title to money paid to the credit of an account vests in the bank, which is free to do with it as it pleases. All the bank is required to do is to return an equivalent amount to the customer on demand. In other words, following the decision in *Foley* v *Hill*,[166] it is argued that the bank receives money credited to the account beneficially even if credited into an account in credit.

The better view is that the bank may be liable for 'knowing receipt' even if it has received the amount as an agent. In *Barnes* v *Addy*,[167] Lord Selborne envisaged that liability could be incurred by 'strangers' dealing with a fraudulent trustee in respect of transactions undertaken by the stranger, for example a bank acting in the ordinary course of its business. Lord Selborne specifically referred to banks and agents in the first (knowing receipt) limb of the *Barnes* two-fold aspect of liability, even if the stranger received the funds in his capacity as an agent. Support for this view may be found in the Court of Appeal decision in *Carl-Zeiss Stiftung* v *Herbert Smith & Co.*[168] Here an East German foundation, claiming that it was entitled to the entire property of the West German foundation, alleged that funds received by the West German foundation's solicitors as fees and expenses were recoverable under the first limb of *Barnes*. Edmund Davies LJ summarised the headings under which liability could be imposed under the first limb of *Barnes* and stated that one possible situation which may give rise to liability is a case where an agent receives or deals with money, knowing that the principal has no right to pay it over or instruct him to deal with it.

Nevertheless, the distinction between beneficial and ministerial receipt offers the bank some protection when faced with an allegation of 'knowing receipt'. The speed with which bank transactions are activated and completed will leave the bank little opportunity to enquire about the validity of a mandate before receiving funds on behalf of the customer. The law will have to develop alternative protection if strict liability is to be imposed and banks treated as beneficial recipients of all payments.

Knowing receipt liability for a bank may also arise in the context of currency exchange transactions. In *Polly Peck International* v *Nadir (No 2)*[169] the Central Bank of Northern Cyprus exchanged £45 million with another bank, IBK, for an equivalent sum in Turkish lira. Nine sterling transactions were also credited to IBK's account at the Central Bank. Millett J, at first instance, held neither transaction amounted to beneficial receipt by the Central Bank. The Court of Appeal, while agreeing that the nine sterling transactions did not amount to beneficial receipts, held that the exchange of sterling for Turkish lira did amount to a beneficial receipt. Scott LJ said:

---

[165] *Agip (Africa) Ltd* v *Jackson* [1991] Ch 547.
[166] (1848) 2 HLC 28.
[167] (1874) LR 9 Ch App 244.
[168] [1969] 2 Ch 276.
[169] [1994] 4 All ER 769.

In respect of the nine sterling transfers I think that is right. The central bank received the funds transferred not in its own right but as a banker, and as banker, credited the funds to IBK in Northern Cyprus. But in respect of the bulk of the transfers the case is . . . one of 'receipt' rather than of 'assistance'. The Central Bank was exchanging Turkish lira for sterling and became entitled to the sterling not as banker for IBK but in its own right. IBK became entitled to the Turkish lira.

Knowledge required for receipt-based liability

The proliferation of cases with regard to misapplied company assets which come into the hands of third parties has also resulted in a sustained debate about the knowledge required by the recipient to found liability in 'knowing receipt'. In considering whether a constructive trust has arisen in cases of 'knowing receipt' of trust property, the basic question is whether the conscience of the recipient is sufficiently affected to justify the imposition of such a trust.[170] At a basic level, the question is whether the recipient must have actual knowledge that assets received by him result from a breach of trust or are traceable to a breach of trust. In this context 'knowledge'[171] has been assessed by reference to the five categories of knowledge identified in *Baden, Delvaux and Lecuit v Société Générale pour Favoriser le Developpement du Commerce et de l'Industrie en France SA (1983)*,[172] and therefore constructive knowledge may be sufficient to impose liability on the third party for breach of trust.

However, the authorities have not always been consistent and in a number of cases the judges have concluded that especially when the dispute relates to commercial transactions, liability may only be imposed if the first three categories of dishonesty recognised in *Baden* are established. In other words, third party-recipient liability will only arise if the recipient can be shown to have actual knowledge of dishonesty or want of probity, in cases involving commercial transactions. The English courts were reluctant to import the doctrine of constructive notice, as it had been developed in relation to land, into commercial transactions and Lindley LJ in *Manchester Trust v Furnace*[173] expressed the view that by extending the doctrine of constructive notice into commercial transactions 'we should be doing infinite mischief and paralysing the trade of the country'. Knox J and Arden J expressed similar views in *Cowan de Groot Properties Ltd v Eagle Trust Plc*[174] and in *Eagle Trust Plc v SBC Securities Ltd (No 2)*[175] respectively. In the case of non-commercial transactions, however, knowledge falling within any of the five categories (thereby including constructive notice) will be sufficient to impose liability on a third party receiving assets in breach of trust, or the traceable proceeds.[176] There is also a view that favours receipt-based liability being imposed whenever

---

[170] *Re Montagu's Settlement Trusts* [1987] Ch 264.

[171] Whether such a trust arises depends primarily on the knowledge of the recipient, and not on notice, and for clarity the word 'knowledge' should be used and the word 'notice' avoided: *Re Montagu's Settlement Trusts* [1987] Ch 264 per Sir Robert Megarry V-C.

[172] [1993] 1 WLR 509n.

[173] [1895] 2 QB 539.

[174] [1992] 4 All ER 700.

[175] *Eagle Trust Plc v SBC Securities Ltd (No 2)* [1996] 1 BCLC 121.

[176] *Eagle Trust Plc v SBC Securities Ltd* [1992] 4 All ER 488; *Eagle Trust Plc v SBC Securities Ltd (No 2)* [1996] 1 BCLC 121; *Cowan de Groot Properties Ltd v Eagle Trust Plc* [1992] 4 All ER 700.

the recipient is shown to have acted negligently.[177] By contrast, Commonwealth authorities have expressed a preference for the view that constructive knowledge, and thereby any of the five heads of liability under *Baden*,[178] will be enough to impose third party recipient liability. In *Westpac Banking Corpn v Savin*[179] and *Citadel General Assurance Co v Lloyds Bank Canada*[180] the Supreme Court of Canada held that constructive knowledge was enough to impose liability on the third party recipient of trust funds handled in breach of trust.

Recent authority, however, has recognised that the doctrine of constructive notice must be sensitive to the customs and practices of the business against which it is judged and operates, and does not require the application of a standard of notice in the form applied to land or conveyancing transactions. In other words, the courts will have regard to the demands of commercial transactions where speed and the protection of the confidential nature of the transaction are essential. Therefore, the conduct of a bank receiving a deposit of misappropriated trust funds should be measured against the standard of enquiry that may reasonably be expected of a banker. The nature and standard of the enquiry banks are expected to enter into was described by Millett J in *Macmillan Inc. v Bishopsgate Investment Trust Plc (No 3)*[181] as follows:

> Account officers are not detectives. Unless and until they are alerted to the possibility of wrong-doing, they proceed, and are entitled to proceed, on the assumption that they are dealing with honest men. In order to establish constructive notice it is necessary to prove that the facts known to the defendant made it imperative for him to seek an explanation, because in the absence of an explanation it was obvious that the transaction was probably improper.

Consequently, a bank is only under an enquiry to investigate if the suspicion of impropriety is so strong that to ignore it would amount to dishonesty and the courts will have regard to the standards of reasonable behaviour within the banking sector in order to determine whether the recipient has acted reasonably in not making enquiries. However, in *Westpac Banking Corpn v Savin*[182] Richardson J said:

> Clearly Courts would not readily import a duty to enquire in the case of commercial transactions where they must be conscious of the seriously inhibiting effects of a wide application of the doctrine. Nevertheless there must be cases where there is no justification on the known facts for allowing a commercial man who has received funds paid to him in breach of trust to plead the shelter of the exigencies of commercial life.

A similar view was recently expressed in *Bank of Credit and Commerce International (Overseas) Ltd v Akindele*[183] where the liquidators of BCCI claimed that A, a Nigerian businessman, was liable to repay the proceeds of an investment agreement that had been executed by BCCI's directors in breach of trust. The defendant, A, had entered into an agreement with a company

---

[177] *Nelson v Larholt* [1948] 1 KB 339; *Cowan de Groot Properties Ltd v Eagle Trust Plc* [1992] 4 All ER 700; *Belmont Finance Corp Ltd v Williams Furniture Ltd (No 2)* [1980] 1 All ER 393; *International Sales and Agencies Ltd v Marcus* [1982] 3 All ER 551; *Houghton v Fayers* [2000] Lloyd's Rep Bank 145; *Westpac Banking Corp v Savin* [1985] 2 NZLR 41; *Powell v Thompson* [1991] 1 NZLR 597; *Citadel General Assurance Co v Lloyds Bank Canada* (1997) 152 DLR (4th) 411 (SCC).

[178] *Baden, Delvaux and Lecuit v Société Générale pour Favoriser le Developpement du Commerce et de l'Industrie en France SA (1983)* [1993] 1 WLR 509n.

[179] [1985] 2 NZLR 41.

[180] (1997) 152 DLR (4th) 411 (SCC).

[181] [1995] 1 WLR 978.

[182] [1985] 2 NZLR 41.

[183] [2001] Ch 437.

controlled by the BCCI group, ostensibly for the purchase of shares in the group's holding company. The agreement, guaranteed A a return of 15 per cent per annum, compounded annually, on an investment of $10 million, which enabled officers of BCCI to conceal a series of fraudulent loans used by the holding company to buy its own shares, to boost artificially the amount of its capital. The trial judge found that the defendant had acted honestly. The liquidators brought an action for both 'knowing receipt' and 'dishonest assistance'. At first instance, both claims failed. Only the claim for 'knowing receipt' went before the Court of Appeal, which on dismissing the appeal examined the question of recipient knowledge, and in particular whether the recipient had to be dishonest. The Court of Appeal confirmed that in relation to knowing, receipt dishonesty is not a necessary ingredient for imposing liability on the recipient.[184] The Court rejected previous attempts to categorise the different degrees of knowledge which a recipient might have as unhelpful, and instead expressed the view that just as the courts had established a single test of dishonesty for dishonest assistance, there should be a single test of knowledge for knowledge assistance. Nourse LJ said that the relevant question was whether the recipient's state of knowledge was such that it would in all the circumstances be unconscionable for him to retain the benefit of the property received.[185]

The trial judge, in *Akindele*,[186] had found no evidence that anyone outside BCCI had reason to doubt the integrity of its management at that time and that the defendant had no knowledge of the underlying frauds within the BCCI group. He saw it simply as an arm's-length business transaction, which he had no reason to question. The high rate of interest and the artificial nature of the agreement were insufficient 'to put an honest person in the defendant's position on notice that some fraud or breach of trust was being perpetrated'. The Court of Appeal held that although the defendant acquired additional knowledge following the entry into the agreement, that knowledge did not make it unconscionable for him to retain the benefit of the receipt. The Court concluded:

> The additional knowledge went to the general reputation of the BCCI group from late 1987 onwards. It was not a sufficient reason for questioning the propriety of a particular transaction entered into more than two years earlier, at a time when no one outside BCCI had reason to doubt the integrity of its management and in a form which the defendant had no reason to question.

The Court of Appeal recognised in *Akindele*[187] that the unconscionability test might not avoid the difficulties of application previously experienced in relation to earlier tests, but the Court expressed the hope that the new test would avoid the difficulties of 'definition and allocation' that had bedevilled the previous judicial categorisations, for example the five-point scale in *Baden* relating to the requisite degree of knowledge for knowing receipt cases. Nourse LJ also said that the unconscionability test would encourage courts to give 'commonsense decisions in the commercial context in which claims in knowing receipt are now frequently made', paying equal regard to the views of Lindley LJ on the one hand, and of Richardson J on the other. The divergent previous decisions in relation to knowing receipt might be explained on the basis of the courts striving to reach 'commonsense decisions' all along, and the differing determinations in previous cases as to the state of the recipient's knowledge and the degree of knowledge required in order to trigger liability are a product of that.

---

[184] *Belmont Finance Corp* v *Williams Furniture Ltd (No 2)* [1980] 1 All ER 393.
[185] *Niru Battery Manufacturing Co* v *Milestone Trading Ltd* [2004] 1 Lloyd's Rep 344.
[186] [1999] BCC 669.
[187] [2001] Ch 437.

The rejection of the dishonesty requirement as an appropriate element for imposing fault for knowing receipt must be correct: dishonesty is more appropriate where the action is founded on culpability, for example procuring or assisting in a breach of trust rather than passive receipt. The approach in *Akindele* ideally makes the application of the requirements for 'knowing receipt' simpler but it also raises questions about how the courts will interpret the 'unconscionability' requirement and may be criticised as being open to a subjective interpretation and therefore lacking in objectivity. There is the risk that an equally complex body of case law will develop in relation to the meaning of 'unconscionability' in this context. In *Royal Brunei Airlines Sdn Bhd v Tan*,[188] the Privy Council had considered and rejected the adoption of a test of 'unconscionable conduct' for accessory liability. Lord Nicholls said:

> Unconscionable is not a word in everyday use by non-lawyers. If it is to be used in this context, and if it is to be the touchstone of liability as an accessory, it is essential to be clear on what, in this context, unconscionable means. If unconscionable means no more than dishonesty, then dishonesty is the preferable label. If unconscionable means something different, it must be said that it is not clear what that something different is. Either way, therefore, the term is better avoided in this context.

Despite criticisms, the approach adopted in *Akindele*[189] in knowing receipt cases has been applied by the Court of Appeal in *Charter Plc v City Index Ltd*[190] and in *Criterion Properties Plc v Stratford UK Properties LLC*[191] where the Court of Appeal held that assessment of unconscionability based merely on whether the recipient has actual knowledge of the circumstances giving rise to the breach of duty was a 'too narrow and one-sided view of the matter'. The court should have regard to the recipient's actions and knowledge in the context of the commercial relationships as a whole to determine whether the test of unconscionability was satisfied.

Despite recent cases it is unlikely that the law has reached a settled state with regard to knowing receipt cases.

Strict liability as a basis of knowing receipt liability

It has been suggested that 'knowing receipt' liability should be regarded as restitution based and judges and commentators have argued in favour of the standard of strict liability subject to the defence of *bona fide* purchaser without notice and change of position. Writing extra-judicially Lord Nicholls expressed the following views:

> Personal liability should be based on the combination of two separate principles of liability. First, recipient liability should cover all third-party recipients. This would be a principle of strict liability in that it will apply to every recipient with an impeachable title irrespective of fault, but it would be restitutionary in nature. It would be confined to restoring an unjust gain. Change of position would be available as a defence accordingly. Secondly, dishonest recipients should be personally liable to meet good losses as well as accounting for all benefits.

Again Lord Nicholls, *obiter* and with whom Lord Walker agreed, in *Criterion Properties Plc v Stratford UK Properties LLC*[192] suggested that the law may yet change so as to replace the

---

[188] [1995] 2 AC 378.
[189] [2001] Ch 437.
[190] [2008] 2 WLR 950.
[191] [2003] 1 WLR 2108.
[192] [2006] 1 BCLC 729.

equitable doctrine of 'knowing receipt' with a strict liability cause of action based on unjust enrichment. In such circumstances, in order to establish liability, a claimant would only have to show that the defendant had received property which had been disposed of by a third party in breach of trust or fiduciary duty. The claimant would not be required to show knowledge or fault on the part of the recipient and instead, the recipient would have the burden of establishing a restitutionary defence to the action: a *bona fide* change of position in reliance upon the receipt or a *bona fide* purchase for value.

Those in favour of strict liability for knowing receipt claims argue that it is a natural extension of the strict liability claim in *Re Diplock*[193] and available to those entitled under a will or intestacy against recipients of assets wrongly paid out of the estate, and should be developed as an equitable counterpart to the common law personal claim for money had and received, recognised as restitutionary in nature and founded on the unjust enrichment principles in *Lipkin Gorman* v *Karpnale Ltd.*[194] Others have raised concerns about the risk of speculative claims being commenced by claimants on the basis of a strict liability test.

Nourse LJ himself expressed reservations in *Akindele*[195] about the adoption of a strict liability test where he highlighted that if the strict liability test was adopted in relation to knowing receipt, a third party recipient of misapplied company assets would face the burden of defending the receipt, for example by proving a change of position. He argued that such a position would be contrary to the spirit of the indoor management rule in *Royal British Bank* v *Turquand*[196] under which a third party is protected from internal irregularities unless they are aware of or have notice to the contrary. Nourse LJ in *Akindele*[197] also expressed concern about the risks of a defendant successfully establishing a change of position defence to a claim in restitution despite the fact that it would be unconscionable for the defendant to be permitted to retain the property. Whether this concern has merit depends on the way in which the defences to a claim in unjust enrichment, such as change of position, are developed and applied. Provided the defences are robustly applied so as to do justice to the particular circumstances of the case and temper the harsh effect of the strict liability rule, this concern does not provide a satisfactory reason for the law not moving to a strict liability approach. Provided that the defences to the strict liability claim are appropriately developed and applied, the difference between Nourse LJ's in *Akindele*[198] approach and Lord Nicholls' preference for a strict liability in *Tan*[199] is largely one of who bears the evidential burden. Until there is clarity by the Supreme Court the law remains as applied in *Akindele*.

Tracing of money

The law relating to tracing is both complicated and at times inconsistent, particularly as the areas of constructive trusts, restitution and tracing begin to overlap. Where a trustee has diverted trust property in breach of trust the beneficiary may be entitled to bring a claim to

---

[193] [1948] Ch 465.
[194] [1991] 2 AC 548.
[195] [2001] Ch 437.
[196] (1856) 6 El. & Bl 327.
[197] [2001] Ch 437.
[198] [2001] Ch 437.
[199] [1995] 2 AC 378.

recover the property. Such claims are founded on the beneficiary's equitable title to the property and although such a claim is founded on the beneficiary's proprietary rights, the remedy awarded may not necessarily be a proprietary one. There are two different remedies available in respect of equitable proprietary claims:

1 A personal remedy for the value of the property which has been received by the defendant but not necessarily retained by him.

2 A proprietary remedy that allows the claimant to treat property in the hands of the defendant as belonging to the claimant. The claimant may not be able to recover the actual property that is in the hands of the defendant but instead the claimant may recover the value of the property as a proprietary remedy in priority to the defendant's other creditors.

The essential features of proprietary claims and their remedies were examined by Lord Millett in *Boscawen* v *Bajwa*[200] where his Lordship stated that equity lawyers habitually use the expression 'the tracing claim' and 'the tracing remedy' to describe the proprietary claim and the remedy which equity makes available to the beneficial owner who seeks to recover his property *'in specie'* from those whose hands it has come into. In fact tracing is neither a claim nor a remedy. Tracing is a process by which the claimant demonstrates what has happened to his property, identifies its proceeds and the persons who have handled or received it, or its proceeds. It therefore identifies the traceable proceeds of the claimant's property and allows the claimant to substitute the traceable proceeds for the original, as a subject matter of the claim. However, it does not affect or establish his claim, which will depend on a number of factors including the nature of his interest in the original asset. The claimant will normally be able to maintain the same claim to the substituted asset as he could have maintained to the original asset.

Lord Millett explained that:

> Tracing property so-called, however, is neither a claim nor a remedy but a process. Moreover, it is not confined to the case where the plaintiff seeks a proprietary remedy; it is equally necessary where he seeks a personal remedy against the knowing recipient or knowing assistant. It is the process by which the plaintiff traces what has happened to his property, identifies as the persons who has handled or received it, and justifies his claim that the money which they handled or received (and, if necessary, which they still retain) can properly be regarded as representing his property. He needs to do this because his claim is based on the retention by him of a beneficial interest in the property which the defendant handled or received.

In such cases the defendant will either challenge the plaintiff's claim that the property in question represents his property, i.e. the defendant will challenge the validity of the right to trace, or he will raise a priority claim, i.e. by claiming to be a *bona fide* purchaser for value without notice or raise the defence of change of position.

Tracing must be distinguished from 'following'. Tracing is the process of identifying a new asset, which has substituted the original,[201] either by sale, resale or modification. Following, on the other hand, is the process of following the same asset as it moves from one person to another.[202] Thus for example, the victim of fraud can 'follow' his money into the hands of the fraudster or a third party but once the money is paid into a bank account it loses

---

[200] [1996] 1 WLR 328.
[201] *Foskett v McKeown* [2001] 1 AC 102.
[202] *Foskett v McKeown* [2001] 1 AC 102.

its identity since it is intermingled with other funds. When the trustee pays the money to the credit of a bank account, legal title to the money vests in the bank. In exchange for the payment of the money to the bank the trustee acquires, as legal owner, a chose in action, which is the debt owed by the bank to the trustee in the amount of the payment.[203] The defrauded party must instead trace the money into the proceeds, i.e. in the debt due from the bank to the account holder. In such circumstances the claimant is not tracing one asset into another, but tracing the inherent value of the original asset into its substitute. In *Foskett v McKeown*,[204] Lord Millett explained the position with regard to money paid into and out of a bank account as follows:

> We speak of money at the bank, and of many passing into and out of the bank account. But of course the account holder has no money at the bank. Money paid into a bank account belongs legally and beneficially to the bank and not to the account holder. The bank gives value for it, and it is accordingly not usually possible to make the money itself the subject of an adverse claim. Instead a claimant normally sues the account holder rather than the bank and lays claim to the proceeds of the money in his hands. These consist of the debt or part of the debt due to him from the bank. We speak of tracing money into and out of the account, but there is no money in the account. There is merely a single debt of an amount equal to the final balance standing to the credit of the account holder. Normally money passes from the paying bank to receiving bank or through the clearing system (where the money flows may be in the opposite direction). There is simply a series of debit and credit which are causally and transactionally linked. We also speak of tracing one asset into another, but this to is inaccurate. The original asset still exists in the hands of the new owner, or it may have become untraceable. The claimant claims the new asset because it was acquired in whole or in part with the original asset. What he traces, therefore, is not the physical asset itself but the value inherent in it.

Tracing must also be distinguished from claiming[205] and although tracing does not affect or establish a claim, the successful completion of a tracing exercise may be preliminary to a personal or a proprietary claim involving the enforcement of either a legal or an equitable right.[206] Tracing is available both in law and in equity with different legal rules, although there is judicial and academic opinion arguing that there is no merit in having different tracing rules in law and in equity, given that tracing is merely a process by which the claimant can establish what has happened to his property.[207]

Tracing at common law

The common law has traditionally interpreted the rules of tracing restrictively so that it is not possible to trace into a mixed fund. Thus, the common law has always been able to follow a physical asset through the hands of one recipient to another.[208] The law's ability to follow an asset, although in a changed format, while remaining in the same hands was established

---

[203] *Foley v Hill* (1848) 2 HL Cas 28.

[204] [2001] 1 AC 102.

[205] *Bracken Partners Ltd v Gutteridge* [2003] 2 BCLC 84.

[206] *Boscawen v Bajwa* [1996] 1 WLR 328.

[207] *Trustees of the Property of F.C Jones & Sons (a firm) v Jones* [1997] Ch 159; there appears to be some confusion over whether *Foskett v McKeown* [2001] 1 AC 102 has unified the equitable and common law tracing rules.

[208] *Agip (Africa) Ltd v Jackson* [1991] Ch 547.

in *Taylor v Plumer*[209] where P, whose money have been misappropriated by his broker, was able to repossess bullion and American securities purchased by the broker with the misappropriated funds. In dismissing an action in conversion against P by the broker's assignee in bankruptcy, Lord Ellenborough stated that the claimant:

> is not entitled to recover if the defendant has succeeded in maintaining these propositions in point of law – viz, that the property of a principal entrusted by him to his factor for any special purpose belongs to the principal, notwithstanding any change which that property may have undergone in point of form, so long as such property is capable of being identified and distinguished from all other.

In following the plaintiff's money into an asset purchased exclusively with it there is no distinction drawn between a chose in action, such as a debt in the form of a bank account, and any other asset, but the common law will only follow a physical asset, for example a cheque or its proceeds, from one person to another.[210] Money can only be followed at common law into and out of a bank account so long as it remains identifiable and is not mixed with other funds of a subsequent transferee.[211] The owner of chattel may therefore bring an action in conversion against a person who has interfered with his rights of ownership to trace and recover the goods. Thus, the true owner of a cheque may bring an action, in conversion, against the collecting bank where the bank wrongfully collects money on a cheque to which it is subsequently discovered that the customer, on whose behalf the cheque is collected, has a defective title. The action does not depend on the continued retention of the money by the defendant.[212] The receipt of the funds is sufficient to allow a claim.

Where however the proceeds of the cheque are paid into a bank account the common law limitations relating to the identification of the 'property' present serious limitations to recovery of the funds, for example the common law does not recognise an action in conversion for money, and furthermore the action for money had and received is not available against a 'subsequent' transferee once the money has passed into a mixed fund.[213] The effect of this principle is that money is only rarely traceable at common law. When an amount is remitted by one bank to another the traditional position is that it becomes commingled or mixed with other amounts cleared on the same day and therefore loses its identity as property of the true owner.[214] This is regardless of whether the payment instructions are given by means of a cheque or giro transfer. What is significant is that settlement between the banks will be affected through the clearing system involving the Bank of England where funds paid and received will be commingled with other payments of the bank. Lord Millett, writing extra-judicially, has commented that the effect of the cheque clearing system means that only in certain limited circumstances will a common law action for tracing ever be possible where the money is paid by cheque into a bank account. The effect of collecting payment through a clearing system is that there is no physical asset that the common law tracing claim can follow.[215] Where the

---

[209] (1815) 3 M & S 562.

[210] *Re Diplock* [1948] Ch 465.

[211] *Banque Belge pour l'Etranger v Hambrouck* [1921] 1 KB 321.

[212] *Agip (Africa) Ltd v Jackson* [1991] Ch 547.

[213] *Banque Belge pour l'Etranger v Hambrouck* [1921] 1 KB 321.

[214] *Agip (Africa) Ltd v Jackson* [1991] Ch 547; *El Ajou v Dollar Land Holdings Plc* [1994] 2 All ER 685; *Bank Tejaret v Hong Kong and Shanghai Banking Corp* [1995] 1 Lloyd's Rep 239.

[215] Millett (1991) Tracing the Proceeds of Fraud, 107 *Law Quarterly Review*, 71.

payer and the payee maintain accounts with the same bank then there is simply a debit of the payer's account and a corresponding credit of the payee's account. The common law will follow a cheque or the proceeds of the cheque in these circumstances. However, if the payer and the payee maintain accounts with different banks then the common law claim will fail since the payment and corresponding book entries representing the payment are subsumed within the daily global settlement between all the banks to the clearing system. The common law can therefore only follow money so long as it does not become mixed.

The only exception to this rule might be where payment is made using a real-time gross settlement system resulting in each payment being settled individually but even in such circumstances the payment will pass through the paying bank's settlement account held with the Bank of England when it is likely to be mixed with other funds credited to the account. In *Bank of America* v *Arnell*[216] Aikens J examined how funds were mixed once transmitted through the CHAPS system. Even if it were possible to show that the fund in question remained separate and identifiable by means of respective debit and credit entries between the payer and payee's accounts, they will become part of, or mixed with, funds standing to the credit of the recipient's account. The problems relating to bank accounts have been examined in a number of cases.

In *Banque Belge pour l'Etranger* v *Hambrouck*,[217] H, a dishonest clerk, fraudulently paid crossed cheques drawn on his employer's account with the claimant's, B's, bank, to the credit of his personal account maintained with the F bank which he utilised only for the clearing of cheques so converted. H withdrew the proceeds of the cheques and gave part of the funds to his mistress, D, who spent part of the money and paid the remaining balance to the credit for her own account with the L bank. The claimant's, B's, bank, sought to recover the amount from D and further sought a declaration that the amount placed to the credit of her account was the claimant's property in equity. In her defence it was argued that D took the money without notice of H's wrongdoing and should therefore acquire a valid title. The Court of Appeal rejected this argument and found against D. However, each member of the Court of Appeal provided different reasons for their conclusions. Bankes LJ emphasised that D had paid no money to the credit of her account 'except money which was part of the proceeds of the [clerk's] frauds'. However, on that basis, Bankes LJ concluded that the money was still identifiable and could be traced at common law. Furthermore, since D had given no value for the money she was a mere volunteer and had no defence to the action. Bankes LJ did not consider it significant that at the time of paying in the misappropriated funds D had a small credit balance in the account which might strictly have resulted in the amounts being commingled and not being subject to a common law tracing action. By contrast, Scrutton LJ expressed the view that the funds had been mixed with the credit balance standing to the credit of H's account with B's bank. Consequently, while the money could not be traced at common law to D's account it could nevertheless be traced in equity. Atkin LJ agreeing with Scrutton LJ held that the funds could be traced in equity and accordingly an order should be made for the payment of the balance to B's bank. Atkin LJ also expressed the view that the funds could be recovered as monies had and received since they remained traceable in equity. His Lordship however conceded that not every amount traceable in equity necessarily remains traceable at common law. Referring to *Taylor* v *Plumer*[218] he doubted that the common law

---

[216] [1999] 1 Lloyd's Rep Bank 399.
[217] [1921] 1 KB 321.
[218] (1815) 3 M & S 562.

'ever so restricted the right to hold that the money became incapable of being traced, merely because paid into the broker's general account with his banker'. However, he took the view that in the instant case there was 'less difficulty than usual . . . in tracing the descent of the money, for substantially no other money had ever been mixed with the proceeds of the fraud'.

The problems resulting from the commingling of finds in payments made through a clearing system were examined in *Agip (Africa) Ltd* v *Jackson*[219] where an authorised signatory of the claimant (A) signed a payment order instructing A's Tunisian bankers, Banque du Sud, to transfer $518,000 to a named payee. Z, the claimant's chief accountant, over a number of years fraudulently altered the name of the payee to Baker Oil Services Ltd (BOS), a company controlled by the defendant chartered accountants who held a US dollar account with Lloyds Bank in London. On receipt of the fraudulently altered payment mandate, Banque du Sud debited A's account and telexed Lloyds Bank in London to credit BOS's account. Banque du Sud also telexed its correspondent bank, Citibank, in New York and instructed it to credit Lloyds Bank through the New York clearing system. The money was later debited from BOS's account and transferred to an account in the name of the defendants, who acting on their customer's instructions transferred all but $45,000 to unknown parties. When the fraud was discovered the claimant brought an action against the defendants for, *inter alia*, money had and received. Millett J, at first instance, held that it was not possible for the claimant to trace the funds at law through the New York clearing system where it would have been commingled with other funds handled by the clearing system. The Court of Appeal specifically approved this line of Millett J's reasoning. Millett J also expressed the view that it was not possible to trace at law money transferred using an electronic means of funds transfer. His Lordship said a distinction needs to be drawn between the situation where payment is made by means of a cheque, where there is a physical item that can be followed by the common law tracing rules, and an electronic transfer where all that passes between the parties is a 'stream of electrons'. The Court of Appeal rejected this distinction, and Fox LJ stated that it was irrelevant that some form other than a cheque initiated the payment. However, both Millett J and the Court of Appeal upheld the claimant's right to trace in equity.

Both the *Hambrouck*[220] and *Agip*[221] cases therefore limit the right to trace proceeds into a bank account in circumstances where the money is not mixed or commingled with other funds, for example where the money transferred becomes part of a general credit balance (although the court ignored the fact that in the *Agip* case the mistress (D) to whose account misappropriated funds were transferred had a small credit balance) or where it is transferred through the clearing system, even one which allows gross real-time settlement.

However, cheques are treated differently and in *Trustees of the Property of F C Jones & Sons (a firm)* v *Jones*[222] the Court of Appeal had to consider a trustee in bankruptcy's proprietary claim to funds paid into a third party's bank account by means of a cheque. The defendant, the wife of a bankrupt, paid £11,700 into an account with a firm of commodity brokers. The money was drawn from a joint bank account, held with the Midland Bank, in her husband's name and in the name of another partner of the business. The defendant used the money to deal in potato futures and having made a profit paid £50,760 into a bank account with

[219] [1991] Ch 547.
[220] [1921] 1 KB 321.
[221] [1991] Ch 547.
[222] [1997] Ch 159.

Raphaels. The Court of Appeal held that the money in the joint account belonged to the trustee in bankruptcy by the time the cheque for £11,700 was drawn. Further, the trustee in bankruptcy claimed the profit made by the defendant as result of her investing in the potato futures. The defendant conceded that the trustee in bankruptcy could at common law trace the original £11,700 but denied that he was also entitled to the profit made as a result of her investment of that original sum.

The trial judge held in favour of the trustee in bankruptcy on the grounds that the defendant had made herself a constructive trustee for him. The Court of Appeal, however, held that the defendant was not a constructive trustee and the defendant had no title to the money. The trustee in bankruptcy was entitled in law to the debt payable by Raphaels and hence to the profit made from the investment. Millett J distinguished the facts of the present case from those in *Agip*.[223] He concluded that it was not necessary to trace the passage of the money through the clearing system or the London potato futures market. The money paid by the defendant into her account could be traced back to the proceeds she received from her husband and which could be traced back to the partnership account. It was therefore possible to by-pass the cheque clearing system by following the cheques themselves from hand to hand until they reached the defendant and then trace the proceeds into the defendant's account where the amount was not mixed with any other funds. The money in the account with the commodity brokers initially and then the credit balance in the account held with Raphaels represented a chose in action to the extent of the credit balance on those accounts from time to time. Although the amount might fluctuate it represented money belonging to the trustee and therefore a debt on which the trustee in bankruptcy could sue. The defendant had neither a legal or equitable interest in any of the money, including the profit. Nourse LJ concluded:

> I recognise that our decision goes further than that of the House of Lords in *Lipkin Gorman* v *Karpnale Ltd* . . . in that it holds that the action for money had and received entitles the legal owner to trace his property into its product, not only in the sense of property for which it is exchanged, but also in the sense of property representing the original and the profit made by the defendant's use of it.

Millett LJ explained the extension in the law is justified on the particular facts of the case but more broadly, relying on the judgment of Lord Mansfield CJ in *Clarke* v *Shee and Johnson*,[224] where the learned judge said that a liberal approach may be adopted where the defendant cannot in all conscience retain the subject-matter of the action. Millett LJ concluded that the defendant could not in his view retain either the profit or the original £11,700. The defendant cannot, by making a profit through the use of money to which she had no title, acquire a better title to the profit.

It would appear that this series of cases are based on a misunderstanding of the earlier law as recognised by Millett LJ, in the *Jones* case, but his Lordship still affirmed the traditional approach that tracing at common law is not available if the property subject to the claim is mixed with other property. Further, Professor Lionel Smith[225] demonstrated that the rule preventing the common law tracing into mixed funds or substitute goods is based on a misunderstanding of *Taylor* v *Plumer*,[226] which actually turned on the tracing rules in equity and

---

[223] [1991] Ch 547.
[224] (1774) 1 Cowp 197.
[225] Smith (1995) Tracing in *Taylor* v *Plumer*: Equity in the Court of King's Bench, LMCLQ 240.
[226] (1815) 3 M & S 562.

not common law. More recently, the Supreme Court of Canada in *BMP Global Distribution Inc v Bank of Nova Scotia*[227] accepted the argument that mixing funds in a bank account does not necessarily defeat the common law claim. Even if the traditional view of the common law is accepted, the principle that there is a mixing of funds when payment is made through a clearing system misconstrues the clearing process where transactions are settled individually and funds are mixed when settlement takes place between banks. In *BMP Global Distribution Inc*, Deschamps J accepted that when tracing funds 'the clearing system should be a neutral factor' and when examining the issue of tracing the position should be examined 'after the clearing process' and we should 'not see that process as a systematic break in the chain of possession of funds'. If the English courts accept this view then payment through a clearing system will not be fatal to a common law tracing claim. Further distinctions made between situations where payment by cheque (tangible assets) and electronic fund transfer payments misconstrue that what is being traced is not the physical asset but the inherent value. Even if payment is by cheque, what must be recognised is that it is the value of that cheque the law recognises as conferring enforceable rights. The common law has not had any problems in recognising the right to claim even where the cheque has passed through the clearing system and there is no reason why payment through electronic means should be treated in any different way.

Tracing in equity

The limitations of the common law, i.e. property cannot be traced once commingled with other funds, may prevent a claimant from recovering his property.[228] However, a claimant who is unable to recover at common law may be able to trace his property in equity and seek a proprietary remedy against the recipient provided the recipient is not a *bona fide* purchaser for value.[229] Additionally, a claim may not be allowed against an innocent volunteer where it would be unfair in the circumstances to allow the action.[230] This is one situation where the law of tracing merges with the law of restitution and the third-party recipient may plead the defence of change of position in respect of his use of the property in question.[231]

The process of tracing the inherent value of the asset may become impossible if the asset in which the value resides is destroyed or dissipated, for example if the trustee, or third party recipient, uses the trust funds to buy an asset, which is uninsured and then burns down and is destroyed. In such circumstances, there is no residue in which the original trust funds can be traced and nothing in which the beneficiaries can assert a proprietary claim. The Court of Appeal in *Re Diplock*[232] explained:

> The equitable remedies [available to beneficiaries making proprietary claims] presuppose the continued existence of the [trust] money either as a separate fund or as part of a mixed fund or as latent in property acquired by means of such a fund. If such continued existence is not established equity is . . . helpless.

---

[227] [2009] 1 SCR 504.

[228] See: *Banque Belge pour l'Etranger* v *Hambrouck* [1921] 1 KB 321 and *Agip (Africa) Ltd* v *Jackson* [1991] Ch 547.

[229] *Compagnie Noga d'Importation et d'Exportation Sa* v *ANZ Banking Group Ltd* [2005] EWHC 225 (Comm).

[230] *Re Diplock* [1948] Ch 465; affirmed in *Ministry of Health* v *Simpson* [1951] AC 251.

[231] *Lipkin Gorman* v *Karpnale Ltd* [1992] 4 All ER 512; [1991] 2 AC 548; *Kleinwort Benson Ltd* v *South Tyneside Metropolitan BC* [1994] 4 All ER 972; *South Tyneside Metropolitan Borough Council* v *Svenska International plc* [1995] 1 All ER 545.

[232] [1948] Ch 465 at 521.

The equitable rules, however, require the claimant to establish that the property in which he had an equitable propriety interest was passed to the defendant in breach of fiduciary duties. The proprietary remedy granted to the claimant will normally take the form of an equitable charge or lien, or liability may be imposed as a constructive trust or the right of subrogation granted in priority to the defendants' other creditors. Thus, in *Boscawen v Bajwa*[233] the claimant was given a proprietary remedy against the proceeds of the sale of a house in priority to the claims of the vendors' other creditors.

The main benefit of seeking equitable relief is that the action is not defeated as a result of the money losing its identity because it has passed through different bank accounts or because the money has been commingled with funds belonging to innocent persons. In *Re Hallett's Estate, Knatchbull v Hallett*[234] a solicitor instructed his bank to sell certain bonds held by him on behalf of a client. The proceeds of the sale were paid to the credit of the solicitor's personal account and the solicitor then withdrew amounts from this account so that the credit balance on the account was dissipated and reduced to an amount smaller than the trust monies wrongfully credited to the account. The client claimed to be entitled to follow the amount of the proceeds realised from the sale of the bonds against the credit balance on the solicitor's personal account but this was challenged by the solicitor's trustee in bankruptcy on the grounds that the funds held by the solicitor as a fiduciary had been exhausted by the withdrawals against the account.

A strict application of the rule in *Clayton*'s case (*Devaynes v Noble, Clayton*'s case)[235] under which amounts paid out were to be appropriated against the earliest credit entries in the account, would have resulted in the conclusion that the trust monies had been withdrawn, leaving the claimant without a remedy. The Court of Appeal, however, affirming the judgment at first instance, held that the rule in *Clayton*'s case was inapplicable. The solicitor was deemed to draw on his personal funds first and he held the remaining credit balance, although dissipated, in his personal account, in a fiduciary capacity. Jessell MR expressed the view that although the solicitor was not a trustee in the strict sense of the word the client was entitled to a tracing order. The claim was not defeated by the fact that trust money was commingled with the solicitor's own funds in such a manner that it became part of the general funds standing to the credit of the solicitor's account. Jessell MR concluded 'if a bank mixes trust funds with his own, the whole will be treated as trust property'.

While the passing of the trust funds into a bank account, so it became mixed with other funds, prevents the *cestui qui trust* from claiming the money back *in specie*, the claimant 'is entitled to a charge on the property purchased for the amount of the trust-money laid out in the purchase'. On the same basis, the *cestui qui trust* would have a charge over a mixed fund of money. Jessell MR explained:

> Suppose the trust money was 1000 sovereigns, and the trustee put them into a bag, and by mistake, or accident, or otherwise, dropped a sovereign of his own into the bag. Could anybody suppose that a judge in Equity would find any difficulty in saying that the *cestui que* trust has a right to take 1000 sovereigns out of that bag? I do not like to call it a charge of 1000 sovereigns on 1001 sovereigns, but that is the effect of it.

Jessell MR concluded that it made no difference that, in the particular case, the solicitor was not a trustee in the strict sense of the word. The equitable principles in question were

[233] [1996] 1 WLR 328.
[234] (1880) 13 Ch D 696.
[235] (1816) 1 Mer. 529.

applicable whenever the funds were misappropriated and the claimant sought recovery into a mixed fund. In *Re Hallett*[236] money was traced into a fund directly under the control of the fiduciary but the courts will also allow money to be traced into the hands of a third party.[237] The right to recover from a third party may be defeated where the third party receives the money in good faith and for valuable consideration. The victim of fraud may therefore be prevented from seeking a proprietary remedy against the bank where money has been paid into an account and the bank uses that money to reduce an overdraft or discharge some other debt. The question, which has arisen, is whether a bank can argue that it gave value in the form of a promise to repay the sum at some time in the future. In *Lipkin Gorman* v *Karpnale Ltd*[238] Lords Templeman and Goff both suggested that if a thief steals money and gives it to a donee, and that donee deposits it with a bank, the bank is not a *bona fide* purchaser so value requires not only a promise or agreement to pay in the future but also actual payment. However, in *Foskett* v *McKeown*[239] Lord Millett held that where a fraudulent person pays money into a bank account, the bank usually obtains an unassailable title to the money as a *bona fide* purchaser without notice of the victim's beneficial interest. The victim is left to trace the money into its proceeds – a debt due from the bank to the account holder. The victim may still be left with a personal claim against the bank but not a proprietary claim.

There are, however, important limitations to the claimant's right to trace the proceeds of money in equity. These were summarised in *Re Diplock*[240] as follows:

- The claimant must establish that the property in which he has an equitable proprietary claim passed to the defendant as a result of a breach of duty by a fiduciary.

- The claimant's money must be identifiable. Consequently, where the claimant's money has been paid into an overdrawn account there is no property representing the claimant's property.

- The grant of the equitable remedy, i.e. the grant of tracing order, must not work an injustice.

Establishing a fiduciary relationship

The right to trace is dependent on establishing a fiduciary relationship between the claimant and the defendant, or between the claimant and a third party, for example a bank through whose hands the property has passed. This requirement has been criticised[241] but still represents current law, although recent dicta from the House of Lords indicates that given the opportunity to review the law this principle is not likely to be followed in the future. The courts have been willing to find the requirement of the fiduciary relationship more readily satisfied in some cases than others. In *Re Hallett's*[242] the requirement was satisfied because

---

[236] (1880) 13 Ch D 696.

[237] See: *Banque Belge pour l'Etranger* v *Hambrouck* [1921] 1 KB 321 where money was traced into the hands of mistress; and *Ministry of Health* v *Simpson* [1951] AC 251 where trustees of a will had, in good faith, distributed money to a donee.

[238] [1992] 4 All ER 512.

[239] [2001] 1 AC 102.

[240] [1948] Ch 465 at 521.

[241] *Agip (Africa) Ltd* v *Jackson* [1991] Ch 547.

[242] (1880) 13 Ch D 696.

the solicitor held funds credited to his client and those from his marriage settlement in a fiduciary capacity. In *Agip (Africa) Ltd*[243] the fraudulent chief accountant, as the claimant's employee, was held to owe fiduciary duties to his employer, the claimant company. Millett J expressed the view that the requirement of the fiduciary relationship is 'readily satisfied in most cases of commercial fraud, since the embezzlement of a company's funds almost inevitably involves a breach of fiduciary duty on the part of one of the company's employees or agents'.[244] The willingness of the courts to find a fiduciary relationship was illustrated in *El Ajou v Dollar Land Holdings*[245] where Millett J held that the victim of the fraud was entitled to rescind the transaction thereby reversing his equitable title at least to the extent necessary to support a tracing claim. He concluded that:

> The victims of fraud can follow their money in equity through bank accounts where it has been mixed with other moneys because equity treats the money in such accounts as charged with the repayment of their money. If the money in an account subject to such a charge is afterwards paid out of the account and into a number of different accounts, the victims can claim a similar charge over the each of the recipient accounts.

In *Bristol & West Building Society v Motthew*[246] Millett J explained that in doing so he 'was concerned to circumvent the supposed rule that there must be a fiduciary relationship or retained beneficial interest before resort may be had to the equitable tracing remedy'. In *Westdeutsche Landesbank Girozentrale v Islington London Borough Council*[247] Lord Browne-Wilkinson said that when property is obtained by fraud, whether or not in breach of fiduciary duty, equity imposes a constructive trust on the fraudulent recipient so that the property can be recovered and traced in equity. Lord Browne-Wilkinson failed to distinguish between theft and fraud so that in *Twinsectra v Yardley*[248] counsel for the claimant argued that in the case of fraud a constructive trust should be imposed on the recipient of misappropriated property at the moment of receipt.

The difficulties of finding a fiduciary relationship were examined again in *Chase Manhattan Bank NA v Israel-British Bank (London) Ltd*[249] where the court said that payment between the banks resulted not from a fiduciary relationship but as a result of a normal commercial relationship. In that case the plaintiff, on the 3 July 1974, paid to the defendant bank approximately $2 million twice instead of a single authorised payment. The defendant discovered the mistake two days later but made no attempt to reverse the amount of the mistaken payment. In August, the defendants petitioned the court for a winding-up order, which was made in December. Both the payments were made through the New York clearing system but as a result of mistake and not as a result of fraud. The question was whether the plaintiff's only right was to claim that the payment was made in error, or whether the plaintiff could also bring an action in equity to trace the amount *in specie*. The funds having been paid through the clearinghouse were mixed with other funds of the bank and therefore the common law right to trace the funds was not available. Golding J held that the defendants were liable as

---

[243] *Agip (Africa) Ltd* v *Jackson* [1991] Ch 547.
[244] *Agip (Africa) Ltd* v *Jackson* [1991] Ch 547.
[245] [1994] 2 All ER 685.
[246] [1998] Ch 1.
[247] [1996] 2 All ER 961.
[248] [2002] 2 AC 164.
[249] [1981] Ch 105.

constructive trustees of the money, which they had received in consequence of the mistake. He concluded that the fiduciary relationship necessary for an equitable tracing action did not have to arise as a result of a consensual agreement. The mere fact of the payment gave rise to a fiduciary relationship and once the initial fiduciary relationship has been established then it is irrelevant that there may be no fiduciary relationship between the trustee and subsequent recipients or as between subsequent recipients themselves.

Following the decision in *Sinclair* v *Brougham*, Golding J in *Chase Manhattan*[250] concluded that 'a person who pays money to another under a factual mistake retains an equitable property in it and the conscience of the other is subjected to a fiduciary duty to respect his proprietary right'. The fact that the defendant bank was unaware of the mistaken payment when it received the second payment was irrelevant since it was deemed to hold the mistaken payment on trust from the moment of receipt of the payment. The plaintiffs' claim in *Chase Manhattan*[251] had a number of features, which would have justified the learned judge concluding the case on the grounds of the need to achieve justice, rather than a finding of a fiduciary relationship. The defendants discovered the mistaken payment within two days of the payment but made no attempt to return it. Unlike the defendants' general creditors, the plaintiffs had not advanced credit to the defendants and did not take the risk of the defendants' insolvency. In such circumstances, allowing the defendants to retain the money would result in the defendants' general creditors receiving a windfall. However, these arguments would not apply in every case where a mistaken payment is made.

In *Westdeutsche Landesbank Girozentrale* v *Islington London Borough Council*[252] the House of Lords departed from the decision in *Sinclair* v *Brougham* and Lord Browne-Wilkinson also disapproved the reasoning in *Chase Manhattan*[253] when he said (*obiter*):

> I cannot agree with this reasoning. First, it is based on the concept of retaining an equitable property in money where, prior to the payment to the recipient bank, there was no existing equitable interest. Further, I cannot understand how the recipient's conscience can be affected at a time when he is not aware of any mistake. Finally, the judge found that the law of England and that of New York were in substance the same. I find this a surprising conclusion since the New York law of constructive trust has for a long time been influenced by the concept of a remedial constructive trust, whereas hitherto English law has for the most part only recognised and institutional constructive trust.

Although disagreeing with the reasoning in *Chase Manhattan*,[254] Lord Browne-Wilkinson considered that the case had been rightly decided. Lord Browne-Wilkinson held that the imposition of liability as a trustee 'depends upon the conscience of the holder of the legal interest being affected' so that 'he cannot be a trustee of the property if and so long as he is ignorant of the facts alleged to affect his conscience'. However, in *Chase Manhattan*, the defendant bank had become aware of the mistake two days after the payment was made. Lord Browne Wilkinson therefore concluded:

> Other than mere receipt of the money, in ignorance of the mistake, gives rise to no trust, the retention of the monies after the recipient bank learnt of the mistake may well have given rise to a constructive trust.

[250] [1981] Ch 105.
[251] [1981] Ch 105.
[252] [1996] 2 All ER 961.
[253] [1981] Ch 105.
[254] [1981] Ch 105.

Lord Millett writing extra-judicially has also criticised the reasoning in the *Chase Manhattan*[255] case:

> It is easy to agree with Lord Browne-Wilkinson that [Chase Manhattan] was wrongly decided. But it was wrongly decided not because [the transferee] had no notice of the [transferor's] claim before it mixed the money with its own, but because the [claimant] had no proprietary interest for it to have notice of. The claimant had intentionally though mistakenly parted with all beneficial interest in the money. To this extent the case is on all fours with [Westdeutsche Landesbank]. The fact that the transferor intended to part with the beneficial interest was inconsistent with the existence of a resulting trust. The fact that the money was paid by mistake affords a ground for restitution. By itself notice of the existence of the grant of restitution is obviously insufficient to found a proprietary remedy; it is merely noticeable personal right to an account and payment. It cannot constitute notice [of] an adverse proprietary interest if there is none.

However, Lord Millett concluded that the position would be different if the property transferred represented the traceable proceeds of the fraud or misappropriated trust property by an absconding express trustee. The *Chase Manhattan* case has effectively been overruled.

Tracing into an overdrawn account

The question of whether it is possible to trace into a bank account which is overdrawn has been the subject of judicial scrutiny in a number of recent cases. This question was examined in the Court of Appeal decision in *Bishopsgate Investment Management Ltd* v *Homan*[256] where the claimant, BIM, was trustee of the assets of various occupational pension schemes of companies associated with the late Robert Maxwell. The pension fund monies of BIM were, at various stages, paid into the bank accounts of Maxwell Communication Corp Plc, MCC, the holding company of a number of the Maxwell companies. At the time the payments were made the accounts were, or at some stage subsequently became, overdrawn. MCC was also insolvent and BIM sought to trace those monies into the overdrawn accounts. The claim was based on observations made by Lord Templeman in *Space Investments Ltd* v *Canadian Imperial Bank of Commerce Trust Co*[257] where he said:

> In these cases it is impossible for the beneficiaries interested in trust property misappropriated from their trust to trace their money to any particular asset belonging to the trustee bank. But equity allows the beneficiaries, or a new trustee appointed in place of an insolvent bank trustee . . . to trace the trust money to all the assets of the bank and to recover the trust money by the exercise of an equitable charge over all the assets of the bank . . . that equitable charge secures for the beneficiaries and the trust priority over the claims of the customers . . . and . . . all other unsecured creditors.

BIM's claim failed for a number of reasons. At first instance, Vinelott J held that BIM could not trace 'through' an overdrawn bank account, whether that account was overdrawn at the time of payment or whether it became overdrawn subsequent to the payment. Vinelott J, however, reserved his position in a situation where it could be shown that there was a connection between a particular misappropriation of BIM's money and the acquisition by MCC

---

[255] [1981] Ch 105.
[256] [1995] 1 All ER 347.
[257] [1986] 1 WLR 1072.

of a particular asset. The learned judge gave two examples of what he called a 'backward tracing' exercise:

- Where MCC acquired the asset with funds from an overdrawn or loan account and MCC intended that the debt obligation represented in that account should be repaid in part or in full by misappropriations of BIM's money; or

- Where BIM's money was paid into an overdrawn bank account so as to reduce the overdraft, thereby making finance available within the overdraft limit to acquire the particular asset.

The Court of Appeal, upholding Vinelott J at first instance, rejected BIMs claim to an equitable charge over all the assets of MCC. Dillon LJ dismissed Lord Templeman's observations in *Space Investments*[258] as *obiter* in that the bank trustee was authorised by the trust instrument to deposit trust money with itself as banker and so there had been no misappropriation. Secondly, following Lord Mustill in *Re Goldcorp Exchange Ltd,*[259] Lord Templeman's observations in the *Space Investments* case could be distinguished as they were not concerned with situations where trust money was paid into an overdrawn bank, or an account which has become overdrawn and thereby ceased to exist, but as a case that was concerned with a mixed fund. The Court of Appeal therefore concluded that property could not be traced in equity when it has ceased to exist, for example money paid into an overdrawn bank account, or money paid into an account which later becomes overdrawn. This rule was affirmed by Lord Neuberger in *Re BA Peters Plc*[260] where the claimants were unable to trace funds misappropriated from them and paid into a bank account that had been overdrawn at all relevant times. This is not an absolute rule and an exception is that if the cause of the overdraft is that the payment is provisional or subject to reversal then the overdrawn nature of the account will not affect the claimant's ability to trace into or through the account. In *Cooper v PRG Powerhouse Ltd*[261] the claimant was permitted to trace his payment into a company's current account that had become overdrawn on 2 August, but which the following day was credited with the payment which had caused the account to overdraw. Evans-Lombe J allowed the claimant to trace into the account, as it had never been overdrawn. The Court of Appeal also confirmed the same position lay behind the decision in *James Roscoe (Bolton) v Winder*[262] where trust money had been mixed with personal funds and the credit balance on the account reduced to £25 18s before it was replenished. The court held that the beneficiaries charge extended only to that sum unless it could be shown that by crediting further funds into the account the trustee had intended to replace the funds wrongfully mixed into the account and paid away. The beneficiary's claim would be restricted to the lowest intermediate balance on the account. Although there was a credit balance on an MCC account held with the National Westminster Bank when administrators were appointed, the Court held there was no evidence that Maxwell had 'intended to make good the misappropriation of the BIM pension moneys'.

Dillon and Leggatt LJJ delivered the two main judgments of the Court of Appeal but they took fundamentally different views of the concept of tracing through an overdrawn bank

---

[258] [1986] 1 WLR 1072.
[259] [1995] 1 AC 74.
[260] [2008] EWHC 2205 (Ch).
[261] [2008] BCC 588.
[262] [1915] 1 Ch 62.

account. Leggatt LJ was more conventional in his approach and did not think it was possible to trace into an asset that had been acquired before the misappropriation of the money had taken place. The learned judge thought that if an asset were used as security for an overdraft that was then discharged by means of the misappropriated funds, the beneficiary might obtain priority by subrogation. Dillon LJ thought backward tracing was arguable and whether it applied in the current case depended on an investigation of the facts.

Dillon LJ said that if the connection between a particular misappropriation of the owner's money and the acquisition by the trustee of a particular asset is sufficiently clearly proved 'it is at least arguable, depending on the facts, that there ought to be an equitable charge' in favour of the owner over the asset. This was not far short of a declaration that it was possible to trace through an overdrawn bank account.

The issues relating to 'backward tracing' were examined again in *Foskett* v *McKeown*[263] where the House of Lords held that the proceeds of the insurance policy could be regarded as the traceable product of the trust money and allowed the claimants to claim a proportionate share of those proceeds. Sir Richard Scott V-C was willing to accept that trust money paid into a bank account after the premium had been paid, which left the account overdrawn, with the intention throughout to use the trust money to pay the premium would not prevent the claimants from tracing their money into the premium that was paid. His Lordship said:

> The availability of equitable remedies ought . . . to depend upon the substance of the trans-action in question and not upon the strict order in which associated events happened.

However, both Hobhouse and Morritt LJJ rejected the submission that tracing could be used to follow value into a previously acquired asset. Similar doubts, although *obiter*, are expressed in *Serious Fraud Office* v *Lexi Holdings Plc*.[264] However, it must be right that where a debt is incurred to acquire an asset and then the debt discharged by use of trust property it must be possible to trace into the asset acquired.

Conclusion

This chapter has attempted to work through areas of the law which try to give redress to a third party who has been the victim of misappropriation of funds through the use of the current account. The chapter has examined the complexities of the law of constructive trusts and the rules of tracing. The discussion has focused on how the developments in these areas of the law affect the bank with regard to liability.

---

[263] [2001] 1 AC 102.
[264] [2009] 2 WLR 905.

Further reading

➤ Shine, P. (2012) Dishonesty in civil commercial claims: a state of mind or a course of conduct?, *Journal of Business Law*, 29–43.
This article reviews the case law on the test for dishonesty in civil commercial cases. The article compares the civil and criminal tests for dishonesty, and examines developments in equity, civil fraud, and disciplinary proceedings against professionals.

➤ Halliwell, M. (2006) Assistance and dishonesty: ring-a-ring o' roses, *Conveyancer and Property Lawyer*.
This article comments on the Queen's Bench Division ruling in *Abou-Rahmah* v *Abacha* on whether a bank was guilty of dishonest assistance when it released money to fraudsters, who had deceived the claimants about the creation of a family trust, without realising that the wrong name had been given on the transfer documents. The article examines the necessary components for making a claim of dishonest assistance against a third party, focusing on the meaning of dishonesty as interpreted by the courts.

➤ Millett, P. (1991) Tracing the Proceeds of Fraud, 107 *Law Quarterly Review*, 71–85.
This article argues for a restitutionary remedy based upon equitable principles for victims of fraud.

➤ Kiri, N. (2006) Recipient and accessory liability – where do we stand now?, 21(11) *Journal of International Business Law and Regulation*, 611–620.
This article discusses the case law on the mental element of recipient liability and accessory liability for breach of trust. The article considers problems with the unconscionability criteria for knowing receipt, and the case for a strict liability test based on unjust enrichment. The article further examines the criteria of dishonesty for the purposes of dishonest assistance, focusing on the objective standards to be applied.

➤ Breslin, J. (1995) Tracing into an overdrawn bank account: when does money cease to exist?, 16(10) *Company Lawyer*, 307–311.
This article examines tracing at common law and in equity, and analyses the rules on appropriation of payments and the extent to which money paid into an overdrawn bank account may be traced.

13 Money laundering

Chapter overview

The aim of this chapter is to:

➤ Examine how legislation has intervened to prevent customers from using bank accounts, and exploiting the rules of bank confidentiality, in order to use the bank account to hide the proceeds of criminal activity.

➤ Examine the specific legislative provisions which create a series of offences that make it an offence to launder the profits of criminal activity through a bank account.

➤ Examine the reporting requirements when a bank suspects an account has been, or is being, used for money laundering.

➤ Examine the offence of 'tipping off' which is intended to prevent banks from warning their customers that an investigation has been, is in process or is pending, with regard to their banking activities.

Introduction

The goal of criminal activity is to produce a profit for individuals and groups carrying out that activity[1] and money laundering is an activity that enables criminals and drug cartels to disguise the proceeds of their crimes so they can enjoy the fruits of their crimes without jeopardising their criminal activities. Money laundering is therefore a process which enables the proceeds of criminal activity to be concealed so as to prevent the discovery of illegal gains, and the illegal activity, through which the profit is produced. Although early attempts to launder money were through the use of cash intensive businesses, for example through casinos, with the development of real-time electronic transfers of funds banks may find themselves being used as the vehicles of money laundering. The veil of bank confidentiality has encouraged criminals to use bank accounts to move their ill-gotten gains and to wash their dirty money clean.

---

[1] Ryder (2011) *Financial Crime in the 21st Century Law and Policy*, Cheltenham Edward Elgar; see also FATF standards, 40 FATF Recommendations, 2003 (incorporating the October 2004 revisions), http://www.fatf-gafi. org/dataoecd/7/40/34849567.PDF.

Banks owe their customers a contractual duty of confidentiality[2] the breach of which will result in liability if the bank wrongfully discloses information about the customer's bank account, and/or other financial information acquired in the course of the banker and customer relationship. In 1989, the Jack Committee Report on Banking Services[3] recommended the codification of the duty and the common law exceptions, into a single statute, in part to make the duty more accessible but also to modernise the scope of the duty. The Committee concluded there had been a 'massive erosion' of the duty owed by banks to protect confidential information. The government rejected both the proposal to codify the duty and to update the duty, and instead preferred to set out a statement of the duty of confidentiality, and other issues raised by the Jack Committee, in a voluntary Banking Code of Practice.[4] The government also rejected the conclusion reached by the Jack Committee that there had been a 'massive erosion' of the duty. However, the number of statutory exceptions has increased considerably particularly since the 11 September 2001 attacks in New York. The burdens on banks have also increased because of the nature and extension of their statutory obligations, which require banks to volunteer information on suspicion that a bank account is being used or suspected of being used for certain offences, and failure to inform the relevant authorities may itself be a criminal offence. At the same time, banks and other businesses have come under increased obligations to protect customer information with regard to processing, storage and transfer of personal data.[5]

While the duty of confidentiality, and scope of the common law and statutory exceptions has already been examined,[6] it is intended to focus discussion here on the anti-money laundering legislation and to deal with the relevant inroads to bank confidentiality in that context.

What is money laundering?

Laundering is the method by which all proceeds of crime are integrated into the banking systems and business environments of the world . . . [T]his is the process whereby the identity of dirty money, that is the proceeds of crime and the real ownership of these assets is transformed so that the proceeds appear to originate from a legitimate source.[7]

The Financial Action Task Force (FATF) states that the goal of a large number of 'criminal actions is to generate a profit for the individual or group that carries out the act. Money laundering is the processing of these criminal proceeds to disguise their criminal origin'. International harmonisation of which criminal acts are likely to fall within the definition of criminal activity for the purpose of money laundering has happened gradually although the proceeds of the drug trade were readily recognised as being of criminal origin. The FAFT standards[8] refer to

---

[2] *Tournier v National Provincial and Union Bank of England* [1991] 1 KB 461.

[3] Jack (1989) *Banking Services: Law and Practice*, Report by the Review Committee Chaired by Professor R.B. Jack, CBE, London Cm. 622.

[4] The Code was drawn up by the British Bankers' Association (BBA), the Building Society Association (BSA) and the Association for Payment Clearing Services (APACS) and applied to personal customers in the UK. The BBA and APACS also drew up a Business Banking Code, which applied to business customers. In 2009, the Banking Code was replaced by the Banking Conduct of Business Sourcebook (BCOBS) which was superseded, in 2011, by the Lending Code and enforced by the Lending Standards Board.

[5] Data Protection Act 1998; see Ch. 7.

[6] See Ch. 7.

[7] Lilley (2000) *Dirty Dealing – The Untold Truth about Global Money Laundering*, London: Kogan Page, p.6.

[8] FATF standards, 40 FATF Recommendations, 2003 (incorporating the October 2004 revisions), http://www.fatf-gafi.org/dataoecd/7/40/34849567.PDF.

the proceeds of all serious crimes as falling within the category of crimes covered but there is a level of discretion permitted in respect of the list adopted.

In _R v Montila_[9] the House of Lords explained:

> in its typical form, money laundering occurs when criminals who profit from their criminal enterprises seek to bring their profits within the legitimate financial sector with a view to disguising their true origin. Their aim is to avoid prosecution for the offences that they committed and confiscation of the proceeds of their offences . . .

It is generally recognised that the proceeds of drug trafficking, organised crime, racketeering, human trafficking, murder, robbery, and white-collar crime such as fraud, corruption, bribery, insider dealing and market manipulation will be caught under the money laundering legislation. Some countries, like the UK, have adopted a blanket approach so that the proceeds of all crimes may be subject to the anti-money laundering regulation. It is difficult to assess how much money is actually being laundered[10] but the International Monetary Fund (IMF) estimated that it amounted to anything between 2 per cent and 5 per cent of the world's GDP[11] and this amounted to anything up to $2 trillion. In 2009 the UNODC estimated that at a global level the proceeds of criminal activity exceed $2.1 trillion or 3.6 per cent of the global GDP but other sources estimate that the actual amount may be ten times higher. For the UK it was estimated that organised crime made $15 billion of which only $125 million was recovered.[12]

There are three stages to money laundering that have generally been recognised: placement, layering and integration. In the first stage the money launderer will introduce the proceeds of the crime into, for example the financial system or the retail economy. This may be done by separating large amounts of money into smaller amounts that can be deposited into several bank accounts with the aim of avoiding any money laundering reporting requirements, or by purchasing other currencies through a foreign exchange dealer. This process is sometimes called 'smurfing' where criminals will deposit money in a financial institution in amounts that are lower than the level at which the institution is required to complete a suspicious activity report.[13] At the second stage the launderer enters into several transactions to distance the illegal money from the original supply, and the final stage is referred to as integration. It is at this stage that the illegal monies enter the economy as clean money. Money launderers frequently use a number of complex financial transactions through shell corporations to legitimise the proceeds of crime and virtually any financial transactions could involve money laundering.[14] The Treasury took the view that money laundering 'frequently involves routeing transactions through many countries to disguise the illegal origin of the money'.[15]

---

[9] [2004] UKHL 50 para. 3.

[10] Tsingou (2005) Global governance and transnational financial crime: opportunities and tensions in global anti-money laundering regime, SCGR Working Paper 161/05, May.

[11] IMF, Michael Camdessus, Address to the FAFT at the Plenary Meeting of the Financial Action Task Force on Money Laundering, 10 February 1998, http://www.imf.org/external/np/speeches/1998/021098.htm.

[12] Berghezio (2013) Special Committee on Organized Crime, Corruption and Money Laundering (CRIM 2012–2013), Thematic Paper on Money Laundering, _Money Laundering and Banks_, January, http://www.europarl.europa.eu/document/activities/cont/201302/20130204ATT60487/20130204ATT60487EN.pdf.

[13] Welling (1989) Smurfs, money laundering and the federal criminal law: the crime of structuring transactions, 41 _Florida Law Review_, pp.287–339.

[14] Financial Services Authority, Consultation Paper 46 Money Laundering The FSA's new role (FSA, London 2000) para. 3.2.

[15] HM Treasury (2004) Anti-Money Laundering Strategy, p.14.

BANKING LAW IN PRACTICE

Reasons to counter money laundering

The fight against money laundering has received new impetus since the 11 September 2001 terror attacks in New York. Governments and policy-makers see money laundering as the means by which terrorists acquire their funding. Many reasons have been given for countering money laundering and while regulation can be justified on the basis of any or all of them the reasons are inevitably linked. The reasons given for effective anti-money laundering regimes range from: (i) the need to tackle the proceeds of drug trade, human trafficking, arms trade and other criminal activity; (ii) to support the integrity and soundness of the financial systems including good governance; (iii) to control corruption and the political and economic ramifications; (iv) to promote economic development through legitimate investment so that taxes are paid to the government; and more recently (v) to prevent the financing of terrorist activity. The government's 'Anti-Money Laundering Strategy'[16] document outlines the following reasons for tackling money laundering:

- To provide a disincentive to crime by reducing its profitability and the pool of money available to finance future criminal activity.

- To aid the detection and prosecution of crime.

- To protect the integrity of the financial system and reputation of UK business.

- To avoid economic and competitive distortions.

The managing director of the IMF expressed the view that the scale of estimated money laundering can result in a dual risk, namely one prudential, the other macroeconomic.[17] Markets and even smaller economies can be corrupted and destabilised. This has been evident in countries and regions that have harboured large-scale criminal organisations. Although initially as a result of good and bad money intermingling the country or region appears to prosper there is a risk that eventually only the corrupt financiers remain so that lasting damage is done when the infrastructure that has been built up to guarantee the integrity of the markets is lost. Even in countries that have not reached such levels of penetration the impact of money laundering may be large enough so that macroeconomic policy-makers must take it into account. Potential macroeconomic consequences of money laundering include, but are not limited to: inexplicable changes in money demand, greater prudential risks to bank soundness, contamination effects on legal financial transactions, and greater volatility of international capital flows and exchange rates due to unanticipated cross-border asset transfers.[18]

Tax havens and bank secrecy laws prevent the following of the proceeds of crime and support money laundering activities, and those providing such services are placed under

---

[16] www.hm-treasury.gov.uk/media/D57/97/D579755E-BCDC-D4B3-19632628BD485787.pdf.

[17] IMF, Michael Camdessus, Address to the FAFT at the Plenary Meeting of the Financial Action Task Force on Money Laundering, 10 February 1998, http://www.imf.org/external/np/speeches/1998/021098.htm.

[18] IMF, Michael Camdessus, Address to the FAFT at the Plenary Meeting of the Financial Action Task Force on Money Laundering, 10 February 1998, http://www.imf.org/external/np/speeches/1998/021098.htm.

disclosure requirements with appropriate levels of deterrence. The anti-money laundering regimes have therefore developed on two separate fronts – prevention and enforcement – and at three different levels which are national, regional and global.[19] Prevention is mainly about regulation, supervision, reporting, customer due diligence, enforcement and sanctions. Enforcement however is about investigation, prosecution, punishment and confiscation. There are therefore significant regulatory aspects to the anti-money laundering regimes.

International initiatives

The USA led the war on drugs trafficking and the proliferation of international crime during the 1990s which, supported by the growth in the international transfer of goods, services and electronic funds transfers, has necessitated a global response to anti-money-laundering regulation. Supranational organisations, for example the Organisation of Economic Coopera- tion and Development (OECD), the Financial Action Task Force (FATF), the United Nations, the World Bank and the International Monetary Fund (IMF), have all coordinated responses to money-laundering, and this has resulted in several important initiatives. Political pressure has focused attention on governments, individuals and organisations, for example lawyers, accountants and others handling cash or money transfers, to comply with anti-money launder- ing regulations and to act in ways that counter and discourage the flight of capital. It is intended to examine, briefly, the work of some of these supranational organisations in the area of money laundering.

United Nations

The international community's efforts to counter money laundering can be identified in the United Nations (UN) policy on the control of narcotic substances. The UN Office on Drugs and Crime coordinates the efforts of the UN through its Global Program against Money Laundering and the 1939 Convention on the Suppression of the Illicit Traffic in Dangerous Drugs imposed the first obligation to confiscate the proceeds of drug related sales.[20] The UN Convention against Illicit Traffic in Narcotic Drugs and Psychotropic Substances was super- seded by the Vienna Convention which provided that signatories must, *inter alia*, criminalise the laundering of drug proceeds,[21] take measures to establish their jurisdiction[22] over the offence of money laundering, permit the confiscation[23] of the proceeds of the sale of illicit

---

[19] Tsingou (2005) Global governance and transnational financial crime: opportunities and tensions in global anti-money laundering regime, SCGR Working Paper 161/05, May.

[20] http://www.unodc.org/pdf/convention_1988_en.pdf; see also: Bosworth-Davies (2006) Money Laundering control: towards an alternative interpretation – chapter two, 9(4) *Journal of Money Laundering Control*, p.346 at 356.

[21] UN Convention against Illicit Traffic in Narcotic Drugs and Psychotropic Substances, 1988, Article 3, http://www.unodc.org/pdf/convention_1988_en.pdf.

[22] UN Convention against Illicit Traffic in Narcotic Drugs and Psychotropic Substances, 1988, Article 4, http://www.unodc.org/pdf/convention_1988_en.pdf.

[23] UN Convention against Illicit Traffic in Narcotic Drugs and Psychotropic Substances, 1988, Article 5, http://www.unodc.org/pdf/convention_1988_en.pdf.

drugs and/or materials used in their manufacturing, provide mechanisms to facilitate the extradition[24] of those involved in criminal activity and take measures to improve mutual legal assistance.[25] Article 3 criminalises property derived from the sale of narcotic or psychotropic substances and prohibits:

> (i) the conversion or transfer of property, knowing that such property is derived from any offence or offences established, . . . or from an act or participation in such offence or offences, for the purpose of concealing or disguising the illicit origin of the property or of assisting any person who is involved in the commission of such an offence or offences to evade the legal consequences of his actions; (ii) the concealment or disguise of the true nature, source, location, disposition, movement, rights with respect to, or ownership of property, knowing that such property is derived from an offence or offences established in accordance . . .

Bosworth-Davies expressed the view that, at least in theory, the Convention:

> did more to provide a sound basis upon which global money laundering efforts to combat the effects of narcotic trafficking would be achieved, than any other initiative has realised either before or since.[26]

However, the scope of the Vienna Convention was limited with its emphasis on laundering the proceeds of crimes from the sale or manufacture of drug-related activities. However, the exposure of high levels of organised crime increased international pressure to extend the scope of criminality to a wider range of offences. The scope of the Vienna Convention was therefore extended by the Palermo Convention,[27] which focused on the criminalisation of money laundering itself. Countries that ratified the latter Convention were required to commit themselves to taking measures against transnational organised crime, including the creation of domestic criminal offences which criminalised participation in an organised criminal group, money laundering, corruption and obstruction of justice; the adoption of new and sweeping frameworks for extradition, mutual legal assistance and law enforcement cooperation; and the promotion of training and technical assistance for building or upgrading the necessary capacity of national authorities.[28]

Ongoing terrorism has resulted in the UN developing other measures to combat laundering, including the International Convention for the Suppression for the Financing of Terrorism in December 1999.[29] In an effort to stop terrorist financing, Article 2 provides that the intentional or unintentional collection of funds for a terrorist act is an offence, which should be established as criminal under local law, and each signatory state is to take measures to identify, detect and seize assets associated with terrorist financing.[30] Article 12(2) provides

---

[24] UN Convention against Illicit Traffic in Narcotic Drugs and Psychotropic Substances, 1988, Article 6, http://www.unodc.org/pdf/convention_1988_en.pdf.

[25] UN Convention against Illicit Traffic in Narcotic Drugs and Psychotropic Substances, 1988, Article 7, http://www.unodc.org/pdf/convention_1988_en.pdf.

[26] http://www.unodc.org/pdf/convention_1988_en.pdf; see also: Bosworth-Davies (2006) Money Laundering control: towards an alternative interpretation – chapter two, 9(4) *Journal of Money Laundering Control*, p.346 at 356.

[27] United Nations Convention Against Transnational Organised Crime, 2000, http://www.unodc.org/documents/treaties/UNTOC/Publications/TOC%20Convention/TOCebook-e.pdf.

[28] UNODC, United Nations Convention against Transnational Organized Crime and the Protocols Thereto, http://www.unodc.org/unodc/treaties/CTOC/.

[29] http://www.un.org/law/cod/finterr.htm.

[30] International Convention for the Suppression for the Financing of Terrorism, Article 8, http://www.un.org/law/cod/finterr.htm.

that bank secrecy laws are not of themselves sufficient grounds to refuse a request for mutual assistance from another member state.

Financial Action Task Force

A further step in the development of a global anti-money laundering policy was the establishment of the Financial Action Task Force (FATF). FATF is an inter-governmental organisation whose function it is to develop and promote anti-money laundering policies. FATF was established[31] to examine measures to combat money laundering and in 1990 it issued a report containing a programme of 40 Recommendations[32] intended to provide a comprehensive blueprint, originally for action against money laundering, and covering, *inter alia*, the financial system and regulation, and international cooperation. The Recommendations have been extended to terrorist financing, which together with the nine special Recommendations on the subject provide a comprehensive framework to combat money laundering in this area. The Recommendations have been updated on a number of occasions, and the current 2003 version incorporate the 2004 revisions. The Recommendations are not a binding convention but FATF member countries[33] have made a commitment to counter money laundering and terrorist financing. A key role for the FATF task force is the need to monitor implementation of the FATF measures. The Recommendations are divided into four parts: (i) the criminalisation and confiscation of property laundered;[34] (ii) measures to be taken by financial institutions to prevent money laundering and terrorist financing;[35] (iii) institutional and other measures necessary to combat money laundering;[36] and (iv) terrorist financing and international cooperation.[37] Recommendation 4 provides that countries should ensure that 'financial secrecy laws do not inhibit the implementation of the 40 recommendations' and Recommendation 14(a) requires that local legal provisions should be enacted to ensure that bank employees who make suspicious activity reports are protected from civil or criminal liability where the report is made in good faith. The recommendation therefore provides a safe harbour for banks and their employees where a suspicious activity report is made. Further, under Recommendation 14(b) a bank and its officers and employees are prohibited from disclosing to a customer that a suspicious activity report has been made but there is nothing in the recommendation to suggest that 'tipping off' should be made a criminal offence, for example, as it is in the UK.

In addition to these global responses the World Bank and the International Monetary Fund have intensified efforts to prevent crime and terrorism through regular assessments of anti-money laundering and terrorist financing assessments. They participate in capacity building initiatives which have been developed in conjunction with FATF.

---

[31] The FATF was established by the G-7 Summit in Paris, in 1989, and has its secretariat at the OECD in Paris.

[32] FATF standards, 40 FATF Recommendations, 2003 (incorporating the October 2004 revisions), http://www.fatf-gafi.org/dataoecd/7/40/34849567.PDF.

[33] FATF currently has 33 members: 31 countries and governments, 2 international organisations and more than 20 observers, http://www.fatf-gafi.org/document/52/0,3343,en_32250379_32236869_34027188_1_1_1_1,00.html.

[34] Recommendations 1–4 define the scope of the criminal offence for money laundering and the confiscation of the proceeds of crime.

[35] Recommendations 5–25 deal with customer due diligence, record keeping, the reporting of suspicious transactions and regulation.

[36] Recommendations 26–38 deal with competent authorities and mutual legal assistance and extradition.

[37] Recommendations 30–40 deal with mutual legal assistance and extradition.

The Basel Group of Banking Supervisors

In 1981, the Basel Group of Banking Supervisors indicated that 'co-operation cannot be complete unless effective arrangements exist for the exchange of information between supervisory authorities about banking activities within their own jurisdictions on a confidential basis'.[38] The view taken by the Basel Committee was that banking secrecy impeded the flow of information from banks to regulators and although bank secrecy was not the focus of the paper, 'Banking Secrecy and International Co-operation Regarding Banking Supervision', it was recognised that it was something that must be dealt with and was subsequently addressed by FATF in Recommendation 4.

In December 1988, the Basel Committee prepared a statement of ethical principles described as the 'Prevention of Criminal Use of the Banking System for the Purpose of Money Laundering'.[39] Although the principles were not legally binding they were to be encouraged and were expected standards of behaviour. In the preamble, the Committee stated that 'all members of the Committee firmly believe that supervisors cannot be indifferent to the use of banks by criminals'. Under the fourth principle, the Basle Committee proposed that it was necessary for banks to cooperate with law enforcement authorities to the 'extent permitted by specific local regulations relating to customer confidentiality'. The banker and customer relationship is therefore not sacrosanct.

The European Union

In 1977, the Council of Europe's European Committee on Crime Problems decided to establish a select committee of experts to look into the 'serious problems raised in many countries by the illicit transfer of funds of criminal origin frequently used for the perpetration of further crime'.[40] The select committee made a formal recommendation,[41] which included a package of measures for developing a comprehensive anti-money laundering programme. Further, it stipulated that banks should ensure that identity checks are undertaken for all customers when an account is opened or money deposited. However, the recommendation was not implemented and in 1990 the Council of Europe adopted the Strasburg Convention on Laundering, Search, Seizure and Confiscation from the Proceeds of Crime which was followed by the Warsaw Convention, in 2005, which provided that each party must ensure that a prior or simultaneous conviction for a predicate crime is not a prerequisite for a conviction for money laundering. At the Council of Europe level, the Committee of Experts on the Evaluation of Anti-Money Laundering Measures and the Financing of Terrorism (MONEYVAL) was established, in 1997, in order to assess the compliance of international measures by members.

The European Commission's attempts to counter money laundering have resulted in the EU implementing three Money Laundering Directives, which have had an impact on developments in Member States as follows.

---

[38] Basel Committee: Banking secrecy and international cooperation regarding banking supervision.
[39] http://www.bis.org/publ/bcbsc137.pdf.
[40] http://www.coe.int/t/dghl/monitoring/moneyval/about/background_moneyval_EN.asp.
[41] In 1980 the Council of Europe's Committee of Ministers adopted a recommendation on measures against the transfer and safekeeping of funds of criminal origin.

First European Money Laundering Directive 91/308/EEC (the First Directive)

The UK implemented the First Money Laundering Directive[42] through the Money Laundering Regulations in 1993.[43] The Directive was primarily intended as a response to the FATF recommendations[44] and its main purpose was the intention of protecting financial institutions and markets from being abused by drug traffickers. The scope of the First Directive covered banks and other financial intermediaries and it focused on the 'placement stage' of money laundering, i.e. the entry of criminal cash into the financial system. The First Directive imposed obligations to ensure customer verification and identification, the examination and reporting of suspicious transactions, indemnities to be given for good faith reporting of suspicious transactions, identification records to be kept for five years after the customer relationship had ended, cooperation with the authorities and adequate internal procedures and training programmes in anti-money laundering matters, and the implementation of anti-money laundering compliance procedures.[45]

In respect of bank confidentiality, Arts 5 and 6 of the First Directive[46] required banks to examine suspicious transactions and inform the relevant authorities of any circumstances they discovered concerning money laundering, and Art. 9 of the First Directive provided that disclosure made in good faith did not breach any restrictions on the disclosure of information or involve liability of any kind. Reporting suspicious transactions therefore is a clear exception to the rules of bank of confidentiality.[47] In addition 'tipping off' or disclosing to any person or third party that a suspicious transaction report had been made to the authorities was prohibited.[48]

However, by the end of the 1990s there was a consensus that the Directive had failed in its objectives.

Second European Money Laundering Directive 2001/97/EC (The Second Directive)

The Second Directive was an amending Directive intended to address two main themes. The fact that the First Directive focused on the proceeds of drug-related laundering was accepted as a major weakness. Money laundering is not only related to the proceeds of drug trafficking, but also other criminality such as human trafficking, fraud, corruption, gunrunning, theft, robbery and other serious criminal offences. Therefore, the range of predicate offences for which suspicious transaction reports became compulsory was expanded from drug trafficking offences to include all serious crime.

[42] European Council, Directive on the Prevention of the Use of the Financial System to Launder Money, 91/308, 1993 OJ (L 166).
[43] SI 1993/1933.
[44] FATF standards, 40 FATF Recommendations, 2003 (incorporating the October 2004 revisions), http://www. fatf-gafi.org/dataoecd/7/40/34849567.PDF.
[45] FATF standards, 40 FATF Recommendations, 2003 (incorporating the October 2004 revisions), http://www. fatf-gafi.org/dataoecd/7/40/34849567.PDF.
[46] 91/308/EEC.
[47] See Recital 15 of the First Money Laundering Directive 91/308/EEC.
[48] 91/308/EEC, Art. 8.

Another compelling reason for the amendment of the First Directive was the perceived ability of the various non-financial sectors to be abused by money laundering. The sectors regulated by the anti-money laundering legislation were therefore widened to include a range of professions known as gatekeepers and those handling money, for example lawyers, notaries, tax advisers, accountants, real estate agents, casinos and dealers in high-value assets, including the sellers of cars, jewellers and art dealers.

These changes were also driven by the FATF recommendations[49] and the UK implemented the Second Directive through the Money Laundering Regulations 2003.[50] However, within the EU, the implementation of the Second Directive was fragmented and the difference in approach to the measures, supervision requirements and implementation resulted in 'regulatory arbitrage' where jurisdictions with less stringent anti-money laundering regulations, supervision and due diligence requirements 'benefited' from the illicit profits of serious crime. The national differences were seen as unnecessarily bureaucratic, costly and inhibiting business with the failure to provide an effective and complete mutual recognition system within Member States burdensome.

Moreover, since the amendments to the First Directive resulting from the Second Directive were made prior to the 11 September 2001 New York terrorist attacks the additional nine FATF special recommendations on terrorist financing were not implemented in the amendments and this necessitated the implementation of the Third Directive.

Third European Money Laundering Directive 2005/60/EU (The Third Directive)

The Third Directive is substantially different from the two preceding directives and although it was regarded as a revision of the earlier directives, the changes were substantial enough to mean that the Third Directive supplanted the preceding directives. The Third Directive[51] was necessitated by the need to incorporate the amendments to the FATF 40 recommendations[52] and to include measures required by the additional nine special recommendations concerning terrorist financing.[53] The Third Directive is now the single piece of legislation throughout the EU dealing with money laundering and consists of the FATF recommendations, and requires suspicious reporting as an exception to bank confidentiality. It imposes a range of other obligations on banks, financial institutions and gatekeepers. An agreement was reached on the Third Directive in June 2005 and Member States were given until 15 December 2007 to fully implement the Directive. The Third Directive has been implemented in all Member States except France. Within the UK, the Third Money Laundering Directive was implemented through the Money Laundering Regulations 2007.[54]

---

[49] FATF standards, 40 FATF Recommendations, 2003 (incorporating the October 2004 revisions), http://www.fatf-gafi.org/dataoecd/7/40/34849567.PDF.

[50] SI 2003/3075.

[51] Directive 2005/60/EEC.

[52] FATF standards, 40 FATF Recommendations, 2003 (incorporating the October 2004 revisions), http://www.fatf-gafi.org/dataoecd/7/40/34849567.PDF.

[53] FATF standards, 40 FATF Recommendations, 2003 (incorporating the October 2004 revisions), http://www.fatf-gafi.org/dataoecd/7/40/34849567.PDF.

[54] SI 2007/2157.

Fourth European Money Laundering Directive (The Fourth Directive)

In February 2013, the European Commission published a proposal for the fourth Money Laundering Directive.[55] The European Commission has stated the main objectives of the proposed measures are to strengthen the internal market and to safeguard the interests of society from criminality and terrorism. Notably the scope of the proposed Fourth Directive encompasses providers of gambling services, and broadens the definition of Politically Exposed Persons (PEPs) to include domestic and foreign individuals entrusted with prominent public functions. While the European Banking Federation (EBF), which represents the interests of around 4,500 financial institutions, has welcomed the proposals for the Fourth Directive, the EBF has requested further clarification regarding the risk-based approach.[56] The Law Society in England and Wales summarised the key changes to the Anti-money Laundering Directive as follows: enhanced risk assessments, enhanced due diligence, simplified due diligence, record-keeping requirements and minimum sanctions.[57] Furthermore, the Law Society highlighted the proposal regarding beneficial ownership, which provides companies must ensure they hold accurate up-to-date information on their beneficial owners. In summary, the Fourth Directive will amend the Money Laundering Regulations 2007 and be implemented into UK law in late 2014 or 2015.

The UK anti-money laundering legislation

HM Treasury has led the UK's money laundering policy and in its 2004 policy document[58] the Treasury stated that its strategy was based on three objectives:[59]

(i) Effectiveness: HM Treasury expressed the view that the UK continues to ensure that it preserves an effective anti-money laundering regime in order to meet its international implementation and compliance obligations. This has been achieved through a series of domestic measures including the Proceeds of Crime Act 2002, the Money Laundering Regulations 2007,[60] the National Guidance issued by the Joint Money Laundering Steering Group and specific anti-money laundering rules. These measures also seek to comply with the International Standards set by FATF,[61] and those contained in the Vienna[62] and Palermo[63] Conventions.

(ii) Proportionality: this means that the government will continue to adopt a risk-based approach to money laundering. The approach seeks to ensure that anti-money laundering

---

[55] European Commission, Proposal for a Directive on the prevention of the use of the financial system for the purpose of money laundering and terrorist financing, 2013/0025 (COD), 5 February 2013, http://eur-lex.europa.eu/LexUriServ/LexUriServ.do?uri=COM:2013:0045:FIN:EN:PDF.

[56] European Banking Federation, EBF Position on the European Commission Proposal for a 4th EU Anti-Money Laundering Directive, EBF_001279, 22 April 2013, http://www.ebf-fbe.eu/uploads/EBF_001279-2013%20%20EBF%20Position%20on%20the%20EC%20Proposal%20for%20a%204th%20EU%20AML%20Directive.pdf.

[57] The Law Society, Fourth European Money Laundering Directive proposals released today, 5 February 2013, http://www.lawsociety.org.uk/advice/articles/new-money-laundering-directive/.

[58] HM Treasury, *Anti-money laundering Strategy*, HM Treasury: London, 2004 at p.12.

[59] HM Treasury, *Anti-money laundering Strategy*, HM Treasury: London, 2004 at p.12.

[60] SI 2006/308.

[61] FATF standards, 40 FATF Recommendations, 2003 (incorporating the October 2004 revisions), http://www.fatf-gafi.org/dataoecd/7/40/34849567.PDF.

[62] United Nations Convention against Illicit Traffic in Narcotic Drugs and Psychotropic Substances, 1988.

[63] United Nations Convention against Transactional Organized Crime, 2000.

measures are cost-effective so that firms can adopt a flexible approach to meeting their obligations. This principle was primarily a reaction to the criticism by the regulated sector about the inflexibility of the anti-money laundering regime under the Second Directive[64] and consequently the Third Directive[65] takes a more focused approach with greater risk methodology and management mechanisms.

(iii) Engagement: the final objective provides that the authorities will continue to work with firms to ensure that the consultation process is fully utilised so that feedback regarding the performance of the regulated sector is communicated back to them.

HM Treasury has indicated that it aims to achieve these objectives through a range of measures including the use of criminal law 'to punish money-launderers and to deprive them of their proceeds' and by obligations 'on the financial services sector and certain other sectors and professions to identify their customers and to report suspicious activities when necessary'.

Criminalising money laundering

The international commitment to anti-money laundering initiatives extended the requirement to combat money laundering to cover the proceeds of all serious crimes. The regime applied not only to the financial sector, but also to other non-financial activities and professions, for example lawyers, who may be vulnerable to misuse by money launderers. The primary money laundering legislation is contained in Part 7 of the Proceeds of Crime Act 2002,[66] and was amended by the Serious Organised Crime and Police Act 2005. The 2002 Act replaced and expanded the earlier anti-money laundering legislation (the Criminal Justice Act 1933 and the Drug Trafficking Act 1994) with the exception of the Terrorism Act 2000. The Proceeds of Crime Act 2002 applies 'where money-laundering activities took place on or after 23rd of February 2003'. The main objectives of the Act are to criminalise the receipt of any benefit from 'criminal property', which includes money laundering; to criminalise 'tipping off'; and to require disclosure of specified types of dealings to the authorities. Money laundering is therefore not limited to dealings with money but includes assets of any type. At the same time the Act creates a defence for those who have reported their suspicions in an appropriate manner, and a further defence for those who intended to report but have a reasonable defence for not having done so, and for those who believe that the relevant monies emanated from abroad but which did not constitute an offence there.

 Under the Proceeds of Crime Act 2002 it is a criminal offence to:

1 Conceal, disguise, convert, transfer or remove criminal property from the UK (s.327).[67]

2 Become concerned in an arrangement which a person knows or suspects facilitates the use or control of criminal property (s.328).[68]

3 Acquire, use or have possession of criminal property (s.329).[69]

We will now examine the scope of these sections separately.

[64] Directive 2001/97/EEC.
[65] Directive 2005/60/EEC.
[66] The Proceeds of Crime Act 2002 came into effect on 24 February 2003.
[67] Proceeds of Crime Act 2002, s.327.
[68] Proceeds of Crime Act 2002, s.328.
[69] Proceeds of Crime Act 2002, s.329.

◾ Conceal, disguise, convert, transfer or remove criminal property from the UK (s.327)

An offence is committed under s.327 if a person seeks to conceal criminal property, disguise criminal property, convert criminal property, transfer criminal property or remove criminal property from England and Wales, Scotland or Northern Ireland. Criminal conduct is such conduct, which is a criminal offence in any part of the UK, or would be an offence in the UK if it occurred there,[70] for example property is the result of criminal conduct if it is the result of theft, extortion, blackmail etc. Lord Nicholls in *R v Saik*[71] said 'the property in question must emanate from a crime'. His Lordship continued that the 'criminal provenance of the property is a fact necessary for the commission of the offence'.

The offences relate to conduct or dealings in relation to 'criminal property' as defined in s.340(3) of the Proceeds of Crime Act 2002, which provides:

(a) It constitutes a person's benefit from criminal conduct or it represents such a benefit (in whole or part and whether directly or indirectly), and

(b) The alleged offender knows or suspects that it constitutes or represents such a benefit.

Property, therefore, is criminal property, regardless of where it is situated, or which represents a 'person's benefit (in whole or in part and whether emanating directly or indirectly) from criminal conduct' and the 'alleged offender knows or suspects that it constitutes or represents a benefit' from such criminal activity.[72] However, no offence is committed by a deposit-taking body, e.g. a bank, if, through the operation of an account the institution converts or transfers criminal property with a value of less than £250.[73] The UK has therefore taken a sweeping view by criminalising dealings with the proceeds of all crime. There are two requirements for the offence to be satisfied: (i) property is criminal property if the 'benefit' flows from the 'criminal conduct' and therefore (ii) any 'gain' that is attributable directly to the criminal activity falls within the parameters of the definition. The 'gain' is not necessarily restricted to the cash received once the property is sold and so a benefit or any benefit in kind, which flows from the criminal activity, will be criminal property. Further, while the gain must flow from the criminal activity the offence is not restricted to a financial gain and it may therefore extend to improvements in a person's standard of living or other profits derived from the criminal activity.[74] Any person who benefits from the crime will commit the offence but it is unclear when the chain of causation may be broken. Thus, the criminal's family will benefit if they move to a bigger house purchased with criminal property but it may be difficult to identify some benefits as 'property', for example the hire of a gardener or housekeeper. If the gardener or housekeeper is paid, for example with illicit cash, then the cash would be the property and the gardener or housekeeper, if the *mens rea* was satisfied, e.g. if they suspected, would be guilty of an offence (as would the employer subject to *mens rea*). The issue relates to when the courts are likely to hold that the benefit or gain is no longer reasonably attributable to the proceeds of the crime.

---

[70] Proceeds of Crime Act 2002, s.340(2).
[71] [2006] UKHL 18 relying on *R v Montila* [2004] 1 WLR 3141.
[72] Proceeds of Crime Act 2002, s.340(3).
[73] Proceeds of Crime Act 2002, s.327(2C).
[74] Hudson (2013) *The Law of Finance*, London: Sweet & Maxwell.

The second limb in the definition of 'criminal property' under s.340(3) is that the 'alleged offender knows . . . that it constitutes or represents such a benefit'. This obviously would be the case if the defendant had actual knowledge of the criminal activity. However, what is less clear is whether constructive knowledge, i.e. that the defendant ought to have known, or that a reasonable person would have known, would be sufficient to impose liability. In *R v Saik*,[75] in dealing with a prosecution relating to conspiracy to launder criminal property, Lord Nicholls considered the question whether a person can 'know' that property is the proceed of crime unless that person participated in the crime itself: otherwise the person can merely suspect that that is in fact the case. For the purpose of conspiracy under s.1(2) of the Criminal Law Act 1977, Lord Nicholls concluded that the test of knowledge was limited strictly to actual knowledge. In coming to his decision Lord Nicholls in the *Saik*[76] case recognised the difference in approach to the earlier cases of *R v Ali*[77] where it was suggested that to 'know' meant merely to 'believe', whereas in *R v Montila*[78] the meaning of the word to 'know' was taken to require that the defendant had actual knowledge. However, in relation to money laundering a person can be found guilty where suspicion can be established and therefore constructive knowledge will be sufficient to impose liability under s.340(3) of the Proceeds of Crime Act 2002.

We will now look at the nature of 'suspicion' for the purposes of the Proceeds of Crime Act 2002.

Suspicion that there is a benefit from criminal activity

Section 340(3)(b) of the Proceeds of Crime Act 2002 provides that the defendant will be taken to have sufficient knowledge of the source of the property in circumstances in which 'the alleged offender . . . suspects that it constitutes or represents such a benefit'. Both the House of Lords and the Court of Appeal have considered the concept of 'suspicion' in relation to offences under s.327(1) of the Proceeds of Crime Act 2002, but not in relation to s.340(1): offences which although similar are not the same. The cases under s.327 have usually been in relation to whether the defendant must have suspected the property was the subject of the criminal conduct and whether the criminal conduct must actually have taken place before the conspiracy was formed so that there is some criminal property in existence, and whether it must have been reasonable for the defendant to have suspected that there had been a criminal activity committed in the circumstances. In *R v Da Silva*[79] the court of first instance had to consider whether A may 'suspect' B of being involved in criminal conduct for the purposes of s.93A of the Criminal Justice Act 1988 if A has 'the imagining of something without evidence or on slender evidence, inkling, mistrust'. The trial judge in *Da Silva*[80] adopted the dictionary definition of the word 'suspecting' and suggested that a slight suspicion might suffice for a person to be taken to have suspected another's criminal conduct. Longmore LJ adopted a different approach in the Court of Appeal when his Lordship held:

---

[75] [2006] UKHL 18.
[76] [2006] UKHL 18.
[77] [2006] 2 WLR 316.
[78] [2004] 1 WLR 3141.
[79] [2006] EWCA Crim 1654.
[80] 2006] EWCA Crim 1654.

It seems to us that the essential element in the word 'suspect' and its affiliates, in this context, is that the defendant must think that there is a possibility, which is more than fanciful, that the relevant facts exist. A vague feeling of unease would not suffice. But the statute does not require the suspicion to be 'clear' or 'firmly' grounded and targeted on 'specific facts', or based upon 'reasonable grounds'. To require the prosecution to satisfy such criteria as to the strength of the suspicion would, in our view, be putting a gloss on the section.

The approach taken by Lord Hope in *R v Saik*[81] in respect of the offence of conspiracy to launder was different to the approach taken by Longmore LJ in *R v Da Silva* and Lord Hope instead favoured a test of reasonableness in the suspicion. The defendant in *Saik* had operated a currency exchange office in London. It was alleged that in the course of that business he had converted a substantial amount of pounds sterling provided by others in the form of cash into foreign currency, and that the cash was, or represented, the proceeds of drug trafficking or other criminal activity. At trial the defendant pleaded guilty to the offence subject to the qualification that he had not known that the money had been the proceeds of crime and he had merely suspected that that was the case. Although reasonable grounds for suspicion were sufficient for the substantive offence of money laundering under s.93C(2), the issue for consideration was whether the suspicion was enough for a conspiracy to commit that offence. On appeal the Court of Appeal held that a defendant would not be guilty of conspiracy to commit the substantive offence of money laundering where he did not know, and therefore did not intend, that the money he had agreed to convert would be the proceeds of crime, when at a date in the future he performed his part of the agreement with his co-conspirators. Reasonable grounds for suspicion were sufficient for the substantive offence but not for conspiracy. The mental element in conspiracy was distinct from and superseded the mental element in the substantive offence. Lord Hope explained as follows:

> The assumption is that the person has a suspicion, otherwise he would not be thinking of doing what the statute contemplates. The objective test is introduced in the interest of fairness, to ensure that the suspicion has a reasonable basis for it. The subjective test – actual suspicion – is not enough. The objective test – that there were reasonable grounds for it – must be satisfied to.

Lord Hope suggests that the defendant must have actual suspicion (the subjective element) and also a reasonable basis (the objective element) for having that suspicion, as well as the property being used for criminal purposes. The issue, which has therefore raised debate, is the extent of knowledge required by the defendant to impose liability on the basis of suspicion. While criminal liability usually requires that the defendant appreciate his own mental state civil liability generally would impose liability on the defendant if it can be established that a reasonable person would not have acted in the manner of the defendant. However, *K v National Westminster Bank, HMRC, SOCA*[82] suggests that the interpretation of 'suspicion' is the same in civil and in criminal law. Section 340(3)(b) requires simply that there was suspicion and that:

> in most cases, the statement by those making a SAR that they have a suspicion will be enough. It will be exceptional for the courts to require those that report the suspicion to provide justification for having a suspicion. In reality, it will be for those challenging the making of a SAR to prove that no suspicion existed.

[81] [2006] UKHL 18.
[82] [2006] EWCA Civ 1039.

the court need only satisfy itself that the bank's discloser was in fact suspicious (the reasonableness of that suspicion being irrelevant, subject to bad faith). Following *Shah*, banks seem to take a belt and braces approach and show reasonableness of the disclosure by reference to factors that tend to be objective rather than subjective, which led to the suspicion: for a money laundering reporting officer (MLRO), in a court, to say merely 'I was suspicious, so there' would not be the most helpful approach. This view was adopted by Scott LJ in *Polly Peck v Nadir (No 2)*[83] who expressed the view that it would be sufficient to demonstrate knowledge (for the purpose of civil liability for knowing receipt) if a reasonable bank acting in the circumstances ought to have been suspicious that payments passing through its accounts were derived from breaches of fiduciary duties. In *Shah v HSBC Private Bank*[84] the customer had dealings in Zimbabwe, which the bank regarded as suspicious. The bank therefore blocked his accounts and reported the matter to the Serious Organised Crime Agency (SOCA). The block lasted only a few days because SOCA provided the necessary consent to operate the accounts. However, in the interim compliance with payment instructions had been delayed and the customer claimed to have suffered losses as a result. The court held that the customer's claim did not succeed on the basis that once the bank became suspicious it was under an obligation to notify SOCA. Whether or not the bank had a 'suspicion' was essentially a subjective test and the customer could not challenge the bank's view on the basis that there were no reasonable grounds for it, unless it could be established that the bank had acted in bad faith. Further the bank could not be liable for breach of contract solely as a result of complying with its obligations under the Proceeds of Crime Act 2002. Given the statutory framework and the subjective nature of any suspicion it would not be appropriate to impose any objective requirement of reasonableness on the bank in relation to its conduct under the Proceeds of Crime Act 2002. A bank will not therefore be made liable to customers in damages as a result of complying with its obligations under the Proceeds of Crime Act 2002.

In *Jeremy Stone v National Westminster Bank Plc*[85] the court found that National Westminster was not in breach of its anti-money laundering obligations and that any breaches which would have been 'relatively technical in nature', would not have been sufficient to satisfy the relevant test of bad faith. The bank's relationship manager, X, 'did not suspect money laundering', and was entitled not to suspect such activity based on the information he had received. X was also entitled to believe that National Westminster Bank's anti-money laundering team had 'fully investigated matters and made such reports as might be necessary to the authorities'. Accordingly, it appears the Court was mindful of the very low level of suspicion that is required in order to engage a money laundering reporting obligation.

Become concerned in an arrangement which a person knows or suspects facilitates the use or control of criminal property (s.328)

The second criminal offence created by the Proceeds of Crime Act 2002 provides that a person commits an offence if they enter or become concerned in an arrangement which they know or suspect facilitates 'the acquisition retention, use or control of criminal property by

---

[83] [1992] 4 All ER 769.
[84] [2009] All ER (D) 204.
[85] [2013] EWHC 208 (Ch); see Ch. 12 for facts and fuller discussion of the case.

or on behalf of another person'. The prosecution must prove that A became concerned in an arrangement which he knew or suspected would facilitate B to acquire, retain, use or control criminal property and, furthermore, that A also knew or suspected that the property constituted or represented benefit from criminal conduct or criminal involvement. For a person to be guilty under this section the definition of criminal property becomes important. The *actus reus* of the offence relates to entering into an arrangement either through a contract or any other consensual behaviour which enables another person to acquire, retain, control or use criminal property. The *mens rea* of the offence is to either 'know' or 'suspect' that any component of the act is being affected. In *Squirrell Ltd v National Westminster Bank Plc*[86] it was said that:

> The purpose of s.328(1) is not to turn innocent third parties like [banks] into criminals. It is to put them under pressure to provide information to the relevant authorities to enable the latter to obtain information about possible criminal activity and to increase the prospect of being able to freeze the proceeds of crime. To this end, a party caught by s.328(1) can avoid liability if he brings himself within the statutory defence created by s.328(2) [of making an authorised disclosure, for example where the bank is operating an account].

The interpretation of phrases such as 'becomes concerned in', 'arrangement', and 'facilitates' under s.328 has caused uncertainty among professionals. The High Court attempted to interpret s.328 in *P v P* and concluded that where a solicitor suspects his client will become involved in an arrangement, an authorised disclosure must be made and consent from the National Criminal Intelligence Service (NCIS)[87] is required, for example, for the solicitor to continue with the transaction. In that case the solicitor was concerned with the potential conflict of interest between his duty of confidentiality to his client and the duty to disclose suspicions. The court concluded that the amount or value of the criminal property was immaterial and disclosure must be made. However, in *Bowman v Fels*[88] the Court of Appeal held that just because a lawyer discovers or suspects involvement with criminal property in the course of advising his client in legal proceedings does not mean that the lawyer commits an offence under s.328(1) because the provision is not intended to cover or affect the ordinary conduct of litigation by legal professionals.

There are a number of defences available against an action for breach of ss.327 and 328, i.e. where authorised disclosure is made under s.338: (i) if the defendant makes an authorised disclosure under that relevant section; (ii) if the person believed that the offence took place outside the UK; and (iii) a deposit-taking institution does not commit the offence if disclosure is made with consent, i.e. consent of the person to whom disclosure is made.

Acquire, use or have possession of criminal property (s.329)

Section 329 of the Proceeds of Crime Act 2002 provides that a person commits an offence if he acquires, uses or has in his possession criminal property. The section does not require an element of dishonesty and mere suspicion is enough.

---

[86] [2006] 1 WLR 637.

[87] The Serious Organised Crime Agency, which assumed the functions of the National Criminal Intelligence Service on 1 April 2006.

[88] [2005] 1 WLR 3083.

The defences available under ss.327 and 328 are also available under s.329(2)(a) and (b). However, additionally a person does not commit an offence under s.329 if he acquired, used or obtained possession of the property for an 'adequate consideration'. The defence replicates that available under the offences in s.93B of the Criminal Justice Act 1988. It is available where funds or property have been acquired for a proper market price or similar exchange and attempt to cover situations where an injustice might otherwise arise: for example, an innocent trader or supplier of goods or services is paid for consumable goods and services in money that comes from crime. The defence will also be available where professional advisers, for example solicitors or accountants, receive money for or on account of costs, whether from the client or from another person on the client's behalf. The defence would not be available to a professional where the value of the work carried out or intended to be carried out on behalf of the client is not equivalent to market value or is significantly less than the money received for or on account of costs.

If a person pays proper consideration but it can be shown that he knows or suspects that such payment may help another to carry out criminal conduct then he is not treated as having paid proper consideration.[89]

Failure to make disclosure (s.330)

The Proceeds of Crime Act 2002 creates three criminal offences relating to failure to disclose information in respect of money laundering, or where the defendant knows or suspects or has reasonable grounds to believe that offences in respect of the money laundering provisions are, or have been, committed. It is also an offence for a recipient to fail to disclose information or other material of which he has knowledge or suspicion, or of which he has reasonable grounds for such knowledge or suspicion, which has been acquired by him in the course of a business in the regulated sector. It is sufficient that the information, or suspicion of certain facts, is acquired without knowledge of whether money laundering has actually taken place. The specific offences created under s.330 are detailed as follows.

Persons in the regulated sector (including bank employees) who obtain information in the course of business which gives reasonable grounds for suspecting money laundering commit an offence if they fail to make a report (s.330)

In addition to the substantive money laundering offences two further offences created under the Proceeds of Crimes Act 2002 are of relevance to bankers: (i) reporting offences under ss.330–332, and (ii) tipping off under s.333A.

The greatest challenges to bankers under the anti-money laundering provisions are caused through the Suspicious Activity Report (SAR) regime, and in particular s.330 of the 2002 Act. Section 330 creates a universal 'all-crime' duty to disclose knowledge or suspicion of money laundering; something previously limited to the laundering of drug trafficking or terrorist funds. This development was led by European initiatives, although the Working Group on Confiscation[90] also considered that the absence of an all-crime money laundering reporting

---

[89] Proceeds of Crime Act 2002, s.328(3)(c). There is a definition of inadequate consideration in sub-section (3).
[90] Home Office Organised and International Crime Directorate, Third Report, *Criminal Assets*, November 1998, http://www.nationalarchives.gov.uk/ERORecords/HO/421/2/P2/OICD/JCU/WGCONF2.HTM.

duty left a gap in the UK's anti-money laundering defences. This is unlikely since the severe nature of the penalty for failing to disclose knowledge or suspicion of trafficking or terrorist money laundering would have led to 'defensive' reporting. Under s.330 of the 2002 Act a person commits an offence if the following four conditions are satisfied: (i) if a person knows or suspects, or has reasonable grounds of knowing or suspecting that another person is engaged in money laundering; (ii) if the information giving rise to his knowledge or suspicion, or which provided reasonable grounds for the knowledge or suspicion, was received in the ordinary course of the business in the regulated sector;[91] (iii) if the recipient of the information can identify the person who is involved in the money laundering or can identify the whereabouts of any of the laundered property, or believes, or it is reasonable to expect the recipient to believe, that the information or other material will assist in identifying that other person or the whereabouts of any of the laundered property;[92] and (iv) the recipient must make disclosure of these matters as soon as is practicable after obtaining the information or other material. Disclosure must be made to a nominated officer, or an authorised person for the purposes of SOCA.

An offence is not committed under s.330: if the recipient has a reasonable excuse for not making the required disclosure; or if he is a professional legal adviser or an accountant, auditor or tax adviser, and the information came to him in privileged circumstances; or if he did not suspect money laundering had taken place or had not been given the requisite training; or if he knew or believed that the offence was being committed in another jurisdiction. In deciding whether an offence is committed under s.330 the court must consider whether the recipient has followed any relevant guidance issued by a supervisory authority or any other appropriate body, and whether it has been monitored and approved by the Treasury and then published in an approved manner as appropriate. The incorporation of negligence-based liability for non-disclosure through s.330(2)(b) is somewhat controversial. This is clearly a major departure from the previous statutory framework, which omitted to punish merely negligent non-disclosures. The negligence test prevents professional persons operating within the regulated sector from claiming ignorance of any suspicion (or of course *knowledge*) regarding a money laundering transaction as a defence in circumstances where the reasonably competent professional would have been put on alert by the transaction in question and made the necessary disclosure. While penal sanctions, and indeed *severe* penal sanctions for negligent non-disclosures, may perhaps operate in something of a draconian manner, rightly or otherwise they serve as a clear statement of intent by the government in its fight against money laundering.

In addition to s.330 there are two further disclosure requirements under ss.331 and 332 namely: (i) a money laundering reporting officer (MLRO) in the regulated sector commits an offence if an employee makes a report to the MLRO that gives reasonable grounds for suspicion, but the MLRO does not make an onward suspicious transaction report (STR) to the Serious Organised Crime Agency (whose functions were taken over by the National Crime Agency in October 2013); and (ii) MLROs not in the regulated sector will also commit an offence if they do not make an STR when they know or suspect as a result of a disclosure to them that a person is engaged in money laundering (s.332).

---

[91] The term 'regulated sector' is defined in schedule 9 of the Proceeds of Crime Act 2002 so the section extends to 'credit institutions' (banks) and most activities regulated by the financial regulatory authorities.
[92] This condition was inserted by the Serious Organised Crime and Police Act 2005, s.104.

The offence of 'tipping off'

The offence of 'tipping off' was inserted in the Proceeds of Crime Act 2002 in the form of a new s.333A, which replaced the old offence in s.333 under that Act. Under the new s.333A(1), it is an offence for any person to disclose any information, relating to money laundering, which came to him in the course of employment in the regulated financial sector. Section 333A(1) therefore provides that a person commits an offence if:

(i) He knows or suspects that a disclosure has been made to the MLRO or SOCA under the Proceeds of Crime Act 2002.

(ii) He reveals to a third party that such disclosure has been made and that disclosure is likely to prejudice any resulting investigation.

(iii) The information came to him in the course of his employment in the regulated sector.

If a bank blocks an account on the basis of suspicion of money laundering it must therefore avoid alerting the customer of the fact that a report has been made or an investigation is being, or may be, undertaken. As the bank must expedite the customer's mandate, not complying with the mandate may place the bank in a difficult position. In such circumstances the bank may apply to the court for directions about the nature of information that can be disclosed to the customer. In *Governor and Company of the Bank of Scotland v A Ltd*[93] the bank was concerned that money standing to the credit of the account may represent the proceeds of a fraud on third parties and that if sued by its customer it would not be able to use the evidence in its possession to defend the claim because it might alert the customer of the investigation. The Court of Appeal held that in the absence of an agreement with SOCA, the bank could apply to the court to determine the nature and scope of the information and evidence which could be disclosed as part of the defence.

There is a further offence under s.342 of making a disclosure that is likely to prejudice an investigation when the bank knows or suspects that a money laundering investigation is being or is about to be conducted under s.341. In *C v S*[94] the plaintiff alleged that its funds had been misappropriated by various defendants, not including B, the bank, who was made party to the proceedings for disclosure purposes and to assist C in tracing its missing funds. C successfully obtained a freezing order against the other defendants, and a disclosure order against B. Unknown to C, B had already made reports to the Economic Crimes Unit of the National Criminal Intelligence Service (NCIS) under the money laundering regulations in respect of one of the defendants. B was therefore placed in a difficult position since it was bound to obey the disclosure order but its disclosure of information to C would place it in a position where it might face prosecution under the then s.93D of the Criminal Justice Act 1988.[95] The section made it an offence for someone, when knowing or suspecting that the police are or are about to conduct an investigation into money laundering activities relating to the proceeds of crime, to disclose to another person information likely to prejudice the investigation. The NCIS would not give any assurances to B that if it made the disclosure in compliance with the court order it would not face prosecution. There was,

[93] [2001] 3 All ER 58.
[94] [1999] Lloyd's Rep. Bank. 26.
[95] Now s.342 of the Proceeds of Crime Act 2002.

therefore, a real possibility that the bank (B) would end up in court either in contempt of court for disobeying the court order if it failed to make a disclosure or for tipping off. On the facts the Court of Appeal decided that a disclosure would not prejudice the action but the court took the opportunity to give some guidelines in case a bank found itself in a similar situation:

- Immediately when a bank becomes aware that an order is being sought which may involve disclosure of information that may prejudice an investigation, the bank should alert the NCIS about the situation and the information which may be sought to be disclosed.

- The NCIS is then required to identify any material it does not wish to have disclosed and indicate how it would prefer the order to be dealt with. The NCIS may give guidance relating to which information may be disclosed and in some cases partial disclosure may be acceptable

- Where limited disclosure is not acceptable then guidance from the court must be sought. The burden is on the NCIS to persuade the court to curtail the scope of the order by showing that full disclosure would prejudice the investigation.

- The court would seek to protect the claimant's interests and the court must have material facts if it is to deprive the applicant of his normal rights.

Terrorism Act 2000

The Terrorism Act 2000, as amended by the Anti-Terrorism, Crime and Security Act 2001, deals with money laundering and terrorist property. Terrorism is defined in s.1 of the 2000 Act as involving 'violence against the person', or 'serious damage to property' or 'endangering a person's life', or 'creating a serious link to the health or safety of the public' or 'is seriously is designed to interfere with' or 'disrupt any electronic system'. In addition, the intention must be to influence the government or intimidate the public, and advance a political, religious or ideological cause.

It is an offence under s.18 of the Terrorism Act 2000 to enter into an arrangement or to become concerned in an arrangement, which facilitates the retention or control by or on behalf of another person of terrorist property. It is a defence to show that one did not know, and had no reasonable cause to suspect, that the arrangement related to terrorist property. Section 19 of the Terrorism Act 2000 provides that there is a duty on a person to disclose information to a constable as soon as reasonably practicable of their belief or suspicion that money laundering under s.18 has taken place. The defendant must have received the information in the course of a trade or profession, except for example in the regulated financial sector. The duty to disclose such information in the context of the financial sector is set out in s.21A of the Terrorism Act 2000. The duty under this section resembles that under s.330 of the Proceeds of Crime Act 2002 and provides that if the defendant knows or suspects, or has reasonable grounds for knowing or suspecting, that another person has committed an offence under s.18 of the 2000 Act, and if the information came to his in the course of a regulated sector business, then failure to disclose the information to a constable as soon as is practicable is an offence. It is also an offence under s.21D of the 2000 Act to disclose that an investigation is being or might be conducted.

Money Laundering Regulations 2007

The Money Laundering Regulations 2007 (MLR) came into force on 15 December 2007 and implemented the Third Money Laundering Directive 2005. The Regulations are intended to deny money launderers access to the financial system so necessary for their activities. The Regulations are concerned with the general regulatory objectives of promoting market confidence, of protecting consumers and reducing financial crime. The purpose of the MLR is to impose standards of behaviour in respect of 'know your customer' requirements. The requirements include:

- A duty to carry out customer due diligence (CDD) measures.[96]
- An obligation to maintain relevant obligations.[97]
- An obligation to introduce and maintain appropriate policies and procedures to counteract money laundering and terrorist financing.[98]
- An obligation to train staff to identify suspect transactions.[99]

Failure to comply with the requirements is a criminal offence. The institutions governed by these regulations are those through which amounts of cash or securities could be passed and therefore money laundered. While the term 'customer' therefore remains undefined by statute, the 'customer due diligence'[100] (CDD)[101] measures implement requirements intended to assist verification of the customer's identity and support the discovery of the 'purpose and intended nature' of the business relationship. The CDD measures must be adopted when the bank establishes a relationship with a customer.[102]

The CDD measures must be complied with when the bank establishes (a) an ongoing 'business relationship' (i.e. the normal banker and customer relationship)[103] or (b) carries out 'an occasional transaction' above €15,000,[104] or (c) suspects money laundering or terrorist financing,[105] or (d) doubts the veracity of the information.[106] The measures must be adopted before acting for the 'customer' and on a 'risk sensitive' basis at other appropriate times.[107] Since the regulations require customer due diligence, a bank is only required to

---

[96] Regulations 5–18 of the 2007 Regulations.
[97] Regulation 19 of the 2007 Regulations.
[98] Regulation 20 of the 2007 Regulations.
[99] Regulation 21 of the 2007 Regulations.
[100] Previously known as 'know your customer' requirements.
[101] Money Laundering Regulations 2007, SI 2007/2157 (as amended by SI 2007/3299 and SI 2009/209).
[102] See Ch. 6.
[103] Money Laundering Regulations 2007, SI 2007/2157 (as amended by SI 2007/3299 and SI 2009/209, reg. 7(1)(a)) defines a 'business relationship' as one intended to have 'an element of duration'.
[104] Money Laundering Regulations 2007, SI 2007/2157 (as amended by SI 2007/3299 and SI 2009/209, reg. 7(1)(b)). Occasional transaction is defined under reg. 2 (1) as one above the financial threshold that is not part of a 'business relationship' and 'whether the transaction is carried out in a single operation or several operations which appear linked'.
[105] Money Laundering Regulations 2007, SI 2007/2157 (as amended by SI 2007/3299 and SI 2009/209, reg. 7(1)(c)).
[106] Money Laundering Regulations 2007, SI 2007/2157 (as amended by SI 2007/3299 and SI 2009/209, reg. 7(1)(d)).
[107] Money Laundering Regulations 2007, SI 2007/2157 (as amended by SI 2007/3299 and SI 2009/209, reg. 7(2)).

undertake identification and verification processes in relation to its own account holders and not the identity of other persons involved in a particular transaction. The regulations permit for verification to be completed during the establishment of the relationship[108] but it may become necessary to carry out further CDD measures if the bank later suspects the account is being used for money laundering. If the customer fails to provide any required CDD material the bank must not carry out any transactions for that customer and a failure to provide the information may require consideration whether a report should be made under the Proceeds of Crime Act 2002 or the Terrorism Act 2000. Regulation 8 of the MLR provides for 'ongoing monitoring' of the relationship with the customer.

The MLR require institutions to maintain the identification evidence, together with a record of all transactions carried out for the customer, for a minimum of five years. A financial institution must establish internal policies and procedures to ensure compliance with CDD, and have in place ongoing monitoring and record-keeping requirements under which employees can report any knowledge or suspicion of money laundering to a MLRO. Banks must have in place appropriate training procedures so that employees are made aware of the requirements of the 2007 Regulations and the applicable provisions of the Proceeds of Crime Act 2002 or the Terrorism Act 2000, and employees are able to recognise and deal with transactions which may involve money laundering.

The Financial Action Task Force on Money Laundering has promoted these requirements as key to acquiring a customer profile and continuing concerns with terrorist financing have given these requirements an added impetus. The Basle Committee regards these as essential to enabling banks to manage risk.[109]

Conclusion

In order to comply with its money laundering obligations a bank may decide to block a customer's account because either it has knowledge or it suspects that an account is being used for money laundering purposes, and it must notify the appropriate authorities. However, at the same time, it is under an obligation to make sure it does not alert the customer that his account is under suspicion or possible investigation. The bank will therefore find itself in a difficult situation because it is under a legal obligation to make a suspicious activity report in certain circumstances and yet is under a contractual obligation to comply with the customer's mandate. The duty of confidentiality is also set aside where the bank suspects the account is being used for criminal or fraudulent activity. There are, however, provisions which seek to protect a bank against an action for wrongful disclosure or breach of contract where the bank acts to comply with its obligations under the anti-money laundering legislation. However, banks may find themselves walking a fine line.

---

[108] Money Laundering Regulations 2007, SI 2007/2157 (as amended by SI 2007/3299 and SI 2009/209, reg. 9) permits banks to open an account before verification is completed provided no transactions are carried out until completion.

[109] Basle Committee on Banking Supervision, Due Diligence for Banks (Basle), BIS, 2001.

Further reading

➤ Stokes, R. and Arora, A. (2004) The duty to report under the money laundering legislation within the United Kingdom, *Journal of Business Law*, May, 332–356.
  This article discusses the law relating to the duty to disclose financial information in relation to suspected money laundering imposed on lawyers and others in the banking and finance sector. The article focuses on the Criminal Justice Act 1993, the Money Laundering Regulations 1993 and the key provisions of the Proceeds of Crime Act 2002, including those on: (1) concealing criminal property; (2) entering into, or becoming concerned with, an arrangement which facilitates the acquisition, retention, use or control of criminal property; (3) acquisition, use and control of criminal property; (4) failure to disclose in the regulated sector; (5) failure to disclose nominated officers; (6) disclosure of information prejudicial to an investigation; and (7) suspicion as the basis for the UK reporting regime.

➤ Marshall, P. (2010) *Does Shah v HSBC Private Bank Ltd* make the anti-money laundering consent regime unworkable? *Journal of International Banking and Financial Law*, 287.
  This article examines the Court of Appeal ruling in *Shah v HSBC Private Bank (UK) Ltd* on whether a bank customer in respect of whom a suspicious activity report (SAR) had been made was entitled to require the bank to disclose the basis for, and investigate the nature of, the suspicion. This article reviews the background to, and practical effect of, the anti-money laundering regime introduced by the Proceeds of Crime Act 2002, in particular the 'consent regime'. The article further comments upon the extent to which the ruling represents a change of approach to the consent regime.

➤ Demetis, D. and Angell, I. (2007) The risk based approach to AML: representation, paradox, and the 3rd Directive, 10(4) *Journal of Money Laundering and Control*, 412–428.
  This article analyses the risk-based approach to anti-money laundering (AML) control, particularly the assumption that it reduces hazard, and applies the insights to Directive 2005/60 (the Third Money Laundering Directive). The article further examines, with reference to Niklas Luhmann's theories of risk, how the act of drawing distinctions between suspicious and non-suspicious activities in AML work is itself a location of risk. The article also discusses the problems involved in risk representation.

➤ Wadsley, J. (2001) Banks in a Bind: The Implications of the Money Laundering Legislation, 16(5) *JIBL*, 125.
  This article examines the extent to which money laundering offences and police advice to banks conflict with banker – customer relationships. This is exemplified in *C v S* and *Bank of Scotland v A Ltd*, alongside examples from the FSA's money laundering guidance notes.

➤ Norman, M. (2013) An appraisal of United Nations and other money laundering and financing of terrorism counter-measures,16(3) *Journal of Money Laundering Control*, 249–265.
  This article highlights impediments to the adoption by individual states of United Nations resolutions on terrorist financing and other anti-money laundering counter-measures, noting the ease of implementation of soft law instruments.

14 Nature and type of electronic fund transfer systems

Chapter overview

The aim of the chapter is to:

➤ Examine the systems of fund transfers, including credit and debit transfers, BACS, CHAPS and SWIFT transfers.

➤ Examine and discuss the legal implications of funds and the issues relating to completion and countermand of payment.

Introduction

Giro[1] systems have operated as an alternative means of money transfers to cheques in the UK since the 1960s, when the post office offered an alternative means of paying bills to the cheque account facility offered by banks. The essential feature of the giro system was to allow for the rapid transmission and circulation of money to and from a single centre with the overriding purpose of creating a safe, quick and economical means of payment. In the UK, the first attempt to introduce a giro system was made in 1926 when the Trades Union Congress adopted a resolution in favour of a post office cheque system. In 1928, a member of the General Council of the TUC gave evidence in favour of the establishment of a postal cheque system, to the Committee of the Post Office Advisory Council, set up to consider the possible introduction of such a system. The Committee, while opposed to a giro system similar to that in existence in many Continental countries, recommended that consideration should be given to the Post Office offering cheque facilities to its savings bank customers.

The Radcliffe Committee on the Working of the Monetary System[2] recommended that in the absence of the existing banking institutions moving forward to offer such services, there would be a case for investigating the possibility of the Post Office operating a giro system. In August 1965, this recommendation became a reality when the Labour government issued a White Paper, 'A Post Office Giro',[3] which proposed that a Post Office Giro, offering similar

---

[1] The word 'giro' comes from the Greek word 'guros' meaning a ring, circle, revolution or circuit.
[2] Radcliffe Committee on the Working of the Monetary System, 1959; see also: The National Giro, 1871–1969, The National Archives, http://www.nationalarchives.gov.uk/a2a/records.aspx?cat=2060-giro&cid=-1#-1.
[3] The National Archives, http://www.nationalarchives.gov.uk/a2a/records.aspx?cat=2060-giro&cid=0#0.

facilities to those offered by the European countries, would be a valuable addition to the existing methods of money transmission and settling bills. The White Paper outlined a system, which would use the Post Office and Sub-Post Office counters as its business outlets and have a fully automated central system for processing all transactions. The White Paper laid down the criteria one needed to be eligible to open an account and the basic services the Post Office Giro would offer including transfers between accounts, deposits into the account, and payments in the form of withdrawals and by post 'cheque' to a third party. Hence, in 1968 the National Giro system was established when the Postmaster General was empowered to operate 'a service of the kind commonly known as a giro system'.[4] Wider powers were subsequently granted to offer 'banking services' under the Post Office (Banking Services) Act 1976. In 1978, the system was renamed the National Girobank. In 1985, it was incorporated as Girobank Plc and became a member of the clearing house. However, in 1989, the government announced that it wished to sell Girobank, and in 1990 the Alliance & Leicester Building Society completed its purchase. At present, Santander UK Plc, which currently owns the business originally operated by National Girobank, is a member of the clearing companies operating under the umbrella of the UK Payments Administration (UKPA).[5] The National Giro is amalgamated with the bank giro, the name adopted by the clearing banks to cover their money transfer services, namely credit transfers and direct debits.

BANKING LAW IN PRACTICE

The nature of fund transfers

A transfer of funds involves the movement of a credit balance from one bank account to another, which is brought about by adjusting the balances between the payer's and payee's accounts. The process does not result in the transfer of any property but merely in the adjustment of the separate property rights (i.e. choses in action) between the payer and payee against their bank accounts.[6] There is no actual transfer of notes and coins from the payer and payee and no assignment of the debt owed by the payer to his own bank. In *Libyan Arab Foreign Bank* v *Bankers Trust Co*[7] Staughton J observed:

> Transfer may be a misleading word, since the original obligation is not assigned (notwithstanding dicta in one American case which spoke of assignment) a new obligation by a new debtor is created.

The debt owed to the payer by his bank is extinguished or reduced by the amount of the transfer to the payee, while the amount owed to the payee by his bank is increased by the amount of the credit. The instruction to make the transfer will be given by the payer or his agent in the case of cheque payments or credit transfers, although in the case of debit transfers the payee may set up the instructions. Fund transfers can be divided into credit and debit transfers according to whether the payer or payee gives the transfer instruction.

The transfer instruction will be given to the payer's bank either directly by the payer himself, in credit transfers, or by the payee acting under the payer's authority to make a

---

[4] Post Office (Borrowing Powers) Act 1967, s.2.
[5] See Ch. 1.
[6] *R v Preddy* [1996] AC 815.
[7] [1989] QB 728 at 750.

debit transfer. The transfer is effected either through a paper-based or electronic fund transfer system. The bank giro system is a paper-based fund transfer system where the payer's money transfer order is transferred manually from his bank to the payee's bank. By contrast, BACS and CHAPS are the main electronic fund transfer systems operating in the UK. The distinguishing feature of an electronic fund transfer system is that the inter-bank communication of the payment instruction is by electronic means, for example, by magnetic tape, disc or a telecommunication link.[8] The original payment instruction, whether given by the payer or the payee, may be embodied in paper and include the payer or payee's signature. In a paper-based fund transfer system the paper embodying the payment instruction is physically transferred from one bank to another, for example by courier or by a centralised clearinghouse. The Cheque and Credit Clearing Company is a paper-based fund transfer system. However, so long as the inter-bank communication is by an electronic means the fund system will be classified as electronic.

Credit and debit transfers

A credit transfer is a 'push' of funds by the payer to the payee. The payer instructs his bank to debit his account and credit the payee's account. The payer's instructions may be for an individual credit transfer, for example by CHAPS, or for recurring periodic transfers of fixed amounts under a standing order, for example the payment of monthly rental, instalments due under a hire agreement or annual subscriptions.[9] When the payer's instruction has been received, the payer's bank will debit his account and forward the payment to the payee's bank, which will credit the payee's account. The bank is not obliged to make a payment under the standing order if on the date a payment falls due the payer's account has insufficient funds. However, the bank may decide to extend an overdraft facility in order to allow the standing order to be honoured. Standing orders are instructions given by the customer to his bank to make regular payments for a fixed amount to a named payee. The clearing banks have their own *pro forma* standing order forms with the payer supplying information about the frequency and dates of the relevant payments and the details of the payee and his bank account details, as well as details of the payer's account to be debited. Only those customers who maintain an account with the transferring bank can use the credit transfer system to facilitate standing order payments. The standing order is a self-contained payment instruction that need not be accompanied by cash or cheque from the payer to meet the payments under the standing order. The *pro forma* used by the bank contains a clause that authorises the bank to debit the payer's account with the amount of each payment when made. Payment of standing orders is effected through the CHAPS 'Faster Payments Service'.

Direct debit transfers

A direct debit transfer is a 'pull' of funds from the payee to the payer's account. The payee will convey the payment instruction to his own bank to collect money from the payer's bank. The

---

[8] Geva (1992) *The Law of Electronic Funds Transfers*, New York: LexisNexis, p.103.
[9] Bank For International Settlements, Payment Systems in the UK, para. 2.2.1 http://www.bis.org/cpss/paysys/UnitedKingdomComp.pdf.

direct debit system facilitates the punctual payment of amounts due under commercial or consumer contracts by allowing the supplier, dealer or other creditor to obtain payment of amounts due to him by issuing a direct demand for payment of his debtor's bank. On receipt of the payment instruction from the payee, the payee's bank will provisionally credit the payee's account with the amount to be collected and forward the payment instruction to the payer's bank, which will debit the payer's account provided there are sufficient funds to honour the instruction, or the bank is willing to extend an overdraft facility. The credit to the payee's account will become final when the debit to the payer's account becomes irreversible. The payment instruction may sometimes be initiated by the payer himself and passed to the payee for collection, for example as with the collection of cheques. The advantage of the direct debit payment is that it enables the payee to obtain regular payments, the amount of which may vary, for example household bills which may vary with each payment.

A direct debit mandate signed by the payer will authorise the payee to make demand for payment from the payer's bank. The mandate is then either forwarded by the payee to the payer's bank, or where the Automated Direct Debt Instruction Service (AUDDIS) is used, the mandate is kept by the payee's bank and the details of the mandate transmitted electronically to the payer's bank. The mandate acts as the authorisation to the bank to honour the demands of the payee.[10] Direct debits are made through the BACS system and as part of the BACS' Direct Debit Guarantee Scheme the payee must give the payer at least ten working days' notice of the amount and date of the first direct debit and of any subsequent changes to the amount and date of the direct debit. The payee must then collect the direct debit payment on or within three working days of the specified payment. Although direct debiting can be used for the settlement of any types of payments the system is largely used for payment of varying amounts falling due for payment at regular or irregular intervals, for example the payment of electricity or gas bills.[11] While the direct debit system is open to abuse there are inbuilt safeguards, for example a firm wishing to collect payments by direct debit must be sponsored by a bank or building society that operates the scheme. Sponsorship is dependent on the sponsor being satisfied about a number of factors, for example the financial status and administrative capacity of the firm wishing to participate in the scheme. Furthermore, the firm must provide all banks and building societies operating the scheme with an indemnity against any direct or indirect losses caused by the actions of the firm, unless the bank or building society is itself responsible for the wrongdoing. Under the Direct Debit Guarantee Scheme,[12] the payer is guaranteed a full and immediate refund from his bank where a payment is made due to an error either on the part of the payer or payee, for example where the payer's bank makes a payment after the direct debit mandate has been cancelled. Where the payment is made due to an error on the part of the payee bank, the payer's bank can claim a refund under the terms of the indemnity. Figures 14.1 and 14.2 show the movement of payment instructions and funds in credit and debit transfers.

Where payment is to be by direct debit, a subsequent cancellation of the direct debit mandate by the payer gives the payee a claim for breach of contract. In *Esso Petroleum Co Ltd*

---

[10] *Esso Petroleum Ltd* v *Milton* [1997] 1 WLR 938.

[11] Bank For International Settlements, Payment Systems in the UK, para. 2.2.3 http://www.bis.org/cpss/paysys/ UnitedKingdomComp.pdf.

[12] Bank For International Settlements, Payment Systems in the UK, para. 2.2.3 http://www.bis.org/cpss/paysys/ UnitedKingdomComp.pdf.

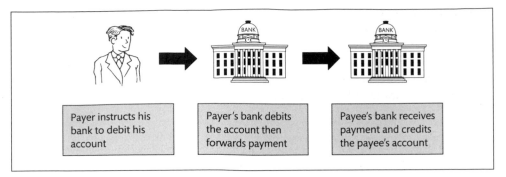

Figure 14.1 Credit transfer – a push of funds

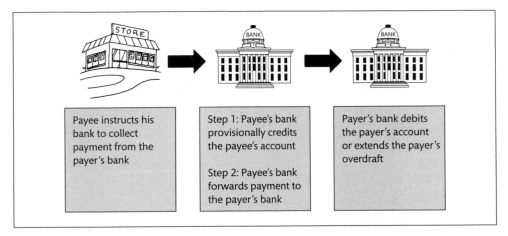

Figure 14.2 Debit transfer – a pull of funds

v *Milton*[13] the claimants owned two garages operated and managed by the defendant under licence. The two licence agreements obliged the defendant to purchase all his petrol supplies from the claimants and pay for them by direct debit. The defendant was forbidden to sell petrol at prices greater than those notified to him by the claimants. Towards the end of 1955, and in the face of competition, the claimants instructed the defendant to cut the price of petrol and also increased his rent. The defendant complained that this made his operations unprofitable and cancelled his direct debit mandate when approximately £170,000 was owing to the claimants. The claimants applied for summary judgment and the defendant argued that the stringent terms of business imposed by the claimant amounted to repudiation of the contract and he counterclaimed both damages and a set-off, in equity.

The judge, at first instance, dismissed the claimants' application for summary judgment but the claimants appealed on two grounds (i) the defendant's counterclaim, even if valid, would not give rise to an equitable set-off, and (ii) that no counterclaim or set-off was available where payment was made, or agreed to be made, by direct debit. On the latter issue the Court of Appeal applied the rule established in the case of cheques and bills of exchange, that there can be no set-off or counterclaim arising from the underlying contract, unless there

[13] [1997] 1 WLR 938.

is fraud or a failure of consideration. According to Thorpe LJ this was a 'natural evolution' of the rule that applies to bills of exchange and cheques and reflected the modern practice of treating a direct debit in the same way as payment by cheque. Simon Brown LJ, dissenting, held that there were insufficient similarities between cheques and direct debits to treat the two in the same way. However, the majority of the court ignored the fact that the cheque, if dishonoured, creates a right, in favour of the payee, to sue the drawer for breach of the obligation to make payment embodied in the cheque itself.[14] The direct debit contains no such obligation or promise and revocation of the mandate does not itself create a separate cause of action arising from the agreement to pay by direct debit. Where the direct debit mandate is revoked, the payee's cause of action arises under the underlying contract and no set-off is available for amounts due between the payer and payee. The no set-off rule applies to bills of exchange and cheques (until recently cheques were freely negotiable) and if made subject to personal disputes between the parties would hamper the negotiability of such instruments. However, direct debits are not transferable and do not require the same protection as bills of exchange. The Court of Appeal expressed the view that if payment is to be by direct debit, the payer loses any right of set-off arising from the underlying contract. It is questionable, however, whether any such terms may be applied into the underlying contract of sale and any attempt to exclude the right of set-off should be expressly set out, in the contract. In *Milton*[15] the claimant attempted to rely on an express term of the licence agreement that purported to exclude any right of set-off but the Court of Appeal held such a term unreasonable under the Unfair Contract Terms Act 1977.

Comparison between giro and cheque payments

There are three main differences between a bank giro system and cheques:

1 In theory cheques, in the UK, can facilitate the transfer of the right to payment from the payee to a third party holder who has acquired title to the cheque by transfer or negotiation, from the true owner. However, since most cheques are now pre-printed 'account payee only',[16] only the named payee may now receive payment against the cheque. Nevertheless, it might be possible for the payee to open the 'account payee only' crossing to make the cheque transferable to a third party.[17] The bank giro, on the other hand, is only payable to the specified payee.

2 The cheque system allows the payee (or holder) of the instrument to collect payment from the drawer's account at any bank (unless the cheque is 'specially crossed')[18] whereas a giro transfer can be made only to the payee's account at the bank specified in the payment instruction.

3 The cheque system allows the payee of a cheque to collect payment in cash over the counter of the drawee bank (if the cheque is uncrossed), whereas the payee of the giro transfer must receive payment through a bank account.

[14] Bills of Exchange Act 1882, s.55(1)(a).
[15] *Esso Petroleum Co Ltd* v *Milton* [1997] 1 WLR 938.
[16] See Ch. 11.
[17] See Ch. 11.
[18] See Ch. 11.

In addition to the differences in the two systems, there are a number of advantages to the giro system, which help to reduce the element of fraud involved with cheque payments. One of the main avenues for fraud is where the payee, in possession of a cheque, alters the amount of the cheque and increases the amount payable on the instrument.[19] There is also the potential for fraud where an agent of the drawer, an employee, fraudulently completes cheque forms left blank by the principal customer.[20] The potential for fraud is increased if the number of people who have access to the cheque increases, particularly where the cheque is not crossed 'account payee only'. The bank giro system reduces the potential for fraud because the giro forms are generally posted or delivered to the transferring bank, and not the payee, so the fraud, if it exists, is likely to be perpetrated by the payer's employee.

Further, the payment process reduces the possibility of dishonoured payment instructions. Under the cheque clearing system, the payee's account is credited before the cheque is transmitted for payment to the payee bank.[21] If the cheque is dishonoured by the drawee bank, either because the drawer's accounts has insufficient funds or there is an irregularity on the face of the instrument, the cheque has to be returned to the collecting bank which will reverse the credit entry in the payee's account and return the cheque to him. In giro operations (excluding direct debits) the money transfer form is initially processed by the payer's bank: it is only when the payer's bank is satisfied that the mandate is in order, that the payee bank will be involved. The payer's account is debited before the payee's account is credited, which completes the payment cycle and finalises the payment. The bank giro clearing thereby reduces the extent of dishonoured payments, although payment reversals may become necessary if there is an error in the amount of the payment, or there is an error in the decoding of the instructions. However, the extent of errors made by the payer wrongly filling in the giro form have been reduced since January 1998 when the banks introduced pre-printed forms for inter-bank transfers.[22] However, bank giro forms may be used for intra-bank transfers so the payer has to insert the details of the payee's bank account, his name and the amount (the latter two being similar to the cheque form).

The clearing of giro transfers

Currently there are four main clearing methods for giro payments with one of these being a paper based method involving the manual transmission of giro forms, and is similar to the clearing of cheques. The other methods namely BACS, CHAPS Sterling and CHAPS 'Faster Payment Service' involve electronic clearing. The clearing method employed is a matter of banking practice and this helps to define the legal roles assumed by the parties. Regardless of the method used they result in the transfer of bank payments to a third party to help pay debts owed with the collecting and paying banks acting as an agent for their respective customers.

---

[19] Bills of Exchange Act 1882, s.64. See also: *London Joint Stock Bank* v *Macmillan* [1918] AC 777; *Young* v *Grote* (1827) 4 Bing 253.

[20] *Midland Bank Ltd* v *Reckitt* [1933] AC 1; *Bute (Marquess)* v *Barclays Bank Ltd* [1955] 1 QB 202.

[21] See Ch. 1.

[22] In January 2003, APACS (now UKPA) implemented the Bank Giro Credit Certification Scheme to rationalise the design of giro credits and their code lines, thereby reducing misreads and rejections during the clearing process (see APACS, Best Practice Guidelines for the Design and Use of Bank Giro Vouchers), August 2003, http://www.ukpayments.org.uk/files/publications/exisiting_publications/cheques/chequesgiro-credits-bgc-6.pdf.

The manual clearing of bank giro credits

The procedure for the clearing of bank giro credits is fundamentally the same as that used for cheques.[23] The payer will deliver to his bank a bank giro credit accompanied by either a cheque or a withdrawal mandate. The branch at which the payer's account is maintained will enter the relevant data on the bank giro credit forms, in magnetic ink. Where the payee supplies the payer with pre-printed credit forms, the payee's account details are already encoded on the credit from so the payer's bank need only magnetically encode the amount of the transfer on the credit. The encoding usually takes place at the branch although some banks have centralised this process so encoding takes place at regional centres. The printed information, similar to cheques, sets out the clearing codes for the payer's bank and the relevant branch, the sort codes for the payee's bank and his branch, the account numbers of the payer and payee, and the amount to be transferred. The payer's account is debited with the amount of the instruction by means of a message keyed into the computer terminal at his branch. The bank giro credit is then transferred to the clearing office of the payer's bank and the next day the clearing office delivers the form through the clearinghouse to the clearing office of the payee bank, although some banks and building societies exchange paper-based credits directly between themselves under bilateral arrangements. The procedure may vary if the bank giro credit is delivered at a bank other than the one where the payer maintains his account.

Where the payer delivers a bank giro credit and accompanying cheque to a bank with which he does not maintain an account, the credit and cheque will be transmitted through the respective clearing systems, so the credit reaches the payee's banks and the cheque the drawer's branch. The manual clearing system of credit transfers is both cumbersome and slow. The payment cycle normally takes three days and may sometimes take an additional day. Where the payer and payee hold accounts with the same branch of the same bank, the bank giro credit does not pass through the clearing system. The credit and debit adjustments to the payer and payee's account are made at the branch where the accounts are maintained. Where the payer and payee hold accounts at different branches of the same bank, the bank giro credit will not pass through the clearing system and either the payer's branch will send the credit to the bank's central clearing department for transmission to the payer's branch, or the payer's branch will itself send the credit directly to the payee's branch. Despite this the manual clearing system of money transfer orders continues to be used for individual bank giro credits, although the volume of such transfers has declined.[24]

BACS clearing

In 1971 the London and Scottish clearing banks combined together to form a company (BACS) to provide a cost-effective automated clearing house service for inter-bank clearing of payments and collection transactions originating either from customers sponsored by BACS

---

[23] See Ch. 1.

[24] UK Payment Council and APACS, Annual Summary of Payment Clearing Statistics 2008, London 2009, reported that during 2008 the volume of paper-based giro credits cleared in England and Wales dropped by 10.3 per cent and the volume of such transfers declined by 9.8 per cent, http://www.ukpayments.org.uk/files/publications/exisiting_publications/general/apacsannualsummary2008060209.pdf. UK Payments Council & APACS, Clearing Statistics May 2009, London 2009, continue to reported a decline in volume and value of credit transfers from 2002 to 2009, http://www.theukcardsassociation.org.uk/wm_documents/Quarterly%20statistical%20release%20Q4%202008.pdf.

or from the sponsoring banks themselves. HM Treasury recognises BACS for the purposes of oversight by the Bank of England under s.185 of the Banking Act 2009.

In 1986, following the recommendations of the Child Committee, the company changed its name to BACS Ltd and in 2004 BACS Ltd separated into two companies: (i) a company responsible for the provision and development of services which adopted the name BACS Payments Schemes Ltd, and (ii) a company to operate the infrastructure, which retained the name BACS. This company later became Voca Ltd and is now called VocaLink Ltd: a company, currently, owned by 16 banks and building societies,[25] with 747 BACS-approved bureaux and 40 affiliates.[26] Users can submit payment instruction data from 2 to 71 days in advance of the payment being initiated.[27]

VocaLink also provides the infrastructure for other payment systems including debit cards, VocaLink ATMs and Faster Payments.[28] Typically BACS deals with high-volume, but low-value, transfers of funds, although there is an upper limit of £20 million on each individual payment submitted via BACS.[29] The two main services provided by BACS are direct credits,[30] and direct debits. BACS direct credits are payments, which are initiated by the payer, in contrast to direct debits,[31] which are initiated by the payee. The types of payments commonly initiated by the payer include the payment of salaries and wages,[32] state benefits, dividends and pensions, and the collection of regular payments, for example utility bills, credit card payments, mortgage repayments and insurance premiums. The main difference between this system and the manual clearing of cheques and bank giro credits is one of method. There is no distinction between the manual and automated system in respect of the time taken for processing payments and BACS, therefore, operates as a deferred multilateral net settlement (DNS) system, with a three-day cycle.[33]

Each BACS member has direct access to the BACS system and will supply BACS with credit and debit instructions as computer, or input, data for processing. Members may also sponsor non-member banks and building societies, and corporate customers, to enable them to submit their own input data to BACS, either directly or through a computer bureau. However, sponsored customers remain the responsibility of their sponsoring bank and any transfer they submit must still be processed by the sponsoring bank.[34] BACS is the UK's largest payment system by

[25] http://www.vocalink.com/payments-services/bacs.aspx.

[26] Bank of International Settlements, Payment, Clearing and Settlement Services in the CPSS Countries, Vol. 12, p.462, November 2012, http://www.bis.org/publ/cpss105.pdf; for earlier figures see: Bank of England, Payments Systems Oversight Report, 2011, p.11, para. 2.1.3, http://www.bankofengland.co.uk/publications/Documents/psor/psor2011.pdf.

[27] Bank of International Settlements, Payment, Clearing and Settlement Services in the CPSS Countries, Vol. 12, p.463, November 2012, http://www.bis.org/publ/cpss105.pdf.

[28] http://www.vocalink.com/payments-services/faster-payments.aspx.

[29] Bank of International Settlements, Payment, Clearing and Settlement Services in the CPSS Countries, Vol. 12, p.454, November 2012, http://www.bis.org/publ/cpss105.pdf.

[30] BACS Direct Credit is used for paying five million wages every week and 23 million salaries a month, 10 December 2012, http://www.bacs.co.uk/Bacs/Corporate/BacsServices/Pages/BacsServices.aspx.

[31] VocaLink, Bacs, Three-quarters of UK adults have at least one direct debit commitment; the average person has at least six, http://www.vocalink.com/payments-services/bacs.aspx.

[32] VocaLink, Bacs, There are over two billion of these every year, including over 90% of all UK salaries and 98% of state benefits, http://www.vocalink.com/payments-services/bacs.aspx.

[33] Bank of England, Payments Systems Oversight Report, 2011 p.11, para. 2.1, http://www.bankofengland.co.uk/publications/Documents/psor/psor2011.pdf.

[34] The rules and procedures governing the operation of BACS are set out in the BACS Users Manual and in agreements reached between the BACS members themselves.

volume,[35] although with the growth of CHAPS 'Faster Payments' there has been a decline in both the volume and value of BACS payments. There were 1,403 million BACS payments in the second quarter of 2012 with a total value of £1,038 billion. Compared to 2011 these figures show a decline of 29 million payments and a decline of £37 billion in value. On average the value of a BACS payment was £740.[36] This decline is largely due to the availability of CHAPS 'Pay Faster'.

Users can submit electronic files of payment instructions to BACS either via their own bank, or by using a telecommunications service, known as BACSTEL-IP, a service that offers direct communication to the BACS processing centre. BACSTEL-IP is a secure online channel for the submission of input data to BACS by members and enables members to track and view payment files, and to receive and store reports electronically. Direct submitters can access the service through the Internet, dial-up Extranet, Broadband Direct, DSL Connect and fixed Extranet Connect. 'Direct submitters' can access BACSTEL-IP by either using the BACS Approved Software Service (BASS) or by using a secure website called 'BACS Payment Services'.

Input data must be received by 10.30pm on day 1 of the clearing cycle so it can be processed overnight. Input data is validated and recorded by BACS and an input report is sent to the user. BACS will then sort the data and produce a series of credit and debit instructions (output data) for each member bank and building society. To that extent BACS is a self-balancing system in that every instruction to credit an account is accompanied by a corresponding debit item against the payer's account. Individual output reports recording output data relevant to the accounts of that member's customers are produced by BACS for each member bank and building society. Thus, where an employer, who is a direct submitter, wishes to pay salaries it will prepare a file of payments setting out details of the amount of each salary payment, the name of the payee and details of the payee's bank, branch and account number. This data, together with instructions to credit the bank accounts of the named employees and to debit the employer's account, is transmitted to BACS. BACS computers, at their processing centre, sort the items and group them by recipient bank. BACS will complete the processing by 6.00am on day 2 of the clearing cycle, by which time all the output data will have been dispatched to member banks and building societies. On day 2 of the clearing cycle, member banks and building societies process the output data received from BACS and ensure credits and debits are made to customer accounts by the opening of business at 9.30am on day 3. The inter-bank obligations that arise through BACS are settled at the Bank of England on a multilateral basis on day 3 of the payment cycle through the CHAPS real-time gross settlement processor.[37] However, BACS has a data storage facility so that members and their sponsored customers can dispatch credit and debit instructions to BACS between 2 and 71 days in advance of the payment date.

Payments through BACS direct credit are initiated by instructions issued by the payer. In the case of direct debits, the trading firm (the payee) is authorised by the customer (the payer) to demand payment from the latter's bank. The payee acts as the payer's agent. If

---

[35] Bank of England, Payments Systems Oversight Report, 2011, p.11, para. 2.1. http://www.bankofengland.co.uk/publications/Documents/psor/psor2011.pdf.

[36] Payments Council, Quarterly Statistical Report, 7 September 2012, http://www.paymentscouncil.org.uk/files/payments_council/card_expenditure_statistics/payments_council_statistical_release_2012_q2_final.pdf.

[37] Bank for International Settlements – Committee on Payments and Settlement Services, Payment, Clearing and Settlement Services in CPSS Countries, Vol. 2, November 2012, 463, http://www.bis.org/publ/cpss105.pdf.

the demand is made through BACS, the payee's bank will issue a demand for payment and not an order to transfer or pay funds. If the payee is a 'direct submitter' it can issue the instructions direct to BACS. The procedure involved, however, is the same as for payment instructions with the only difference being that the 'recipient bank' is required to pay rather than receive payments. Since January 2012, the Payment Services Regulations 2009 require that any refusal to execute a payment order must be refused before the end of day 1 of the clearing cycle.[38] Similarly, the payer may not revoke the direct debit payment after the end of the business day preceding the day agreed for the debiting of the funds.[39]

BACS is an immediate payment system in that the debiting of the payer's account and crediting of the payee's account take place simultaneously at the start of day 3 of the payment cycle. However, BACS is not a true immediate electronic fund transfer system because the order to pay or collect must be made at least two days before the payment date. In 2005, in order to deal with the possibility of a member bank defaulting, BACS introduced a legally binding loss-sharing agreement (Liquidity Funding and Collateralisation Agreement (LFCA)) to ensure settlement in the eventuality of a member defaulting on its obligations. All direct members collectively are required to provide liquidity to fund any shortfall created by the default up to a limit determined by reference to the average net debit position of direct members over the previous 12 months.[40] Each member is also required to pledge collateral with the amount depending on the highest net debt position of the direct members over the previous 12 months. In the event of default the collateral pledged is used to reimburse the surviving members, either in full or in part.[41]

Clearing through CHAPS

The Clearing House Automated Payment system, also known as CHAPS, became operational in 1984, as an inter-bank system for the making of guaranteed sterling payments from one bank to another. The original CHAPS system operated solely with sterling-denominated transfers and became known as CHAPS Sterling. This distinguished it from CHAPS Euro, which started processing on 4 January 1999, as a same day value electronic credit transfer system for euro-denominated payments. CHAPS Euro was connected to the various real-time gross settlement systems of Member States by TARGET, which facilitated high-value payments in euros to be made in real-time within Member States. In August 2001, CHAPS Sterling and CHAPS Euro were consolidated into a dual-currency RTGS system called NewCHAPS so the two systems could operate under the same generic SWIFT technical infrastructure and were governed by the same set of CHAPS rules.[42] All payments made under CHAPS were denominated either in sterling or euros and settled on an individual basis in real time. In May 2008, TARGET was replaced by TARGET2 which provided for a higher level of integration but as the Bank of England decided not to participate in TARGET2, CHAPS Euro was decommissioned on 16 May 2008 and NewCHAPS once again became CHAPS Sterling. In July 2011 the International

---

[38] Payment Services Regulations, 2009, regs 66(2) and 70(1).

[39] Payment Services Regulations, 2009, reg. 67(3).

[40] Bank for International Settlements – Committee on Payments and Settlement Services, Payment, Clearing and Settlement Services in CPSS Countries, Vol. 2, November 2012, 463, http://www.bis.org/publ/cpss105.pdf.

[41] Bank for International Settlements – Committee on Payments and Settlement Services, Payment, Clearing and Settlement Services in CPSS Countries, Vol. 2, November 2012, 463, http://www.bis.org/publ/cpss105.pdf.

[42] The current rules were established in June 2012. CHAPS Clearing Company Ltd, CHAPS Scheme Rules, Version 7 – June 2012, http://www.chapsco.co.uk/files/chaps/membership_rules.pdf.

Monetary Fund report described the UK CHAPS system of payments as benefiting from 'a robust legal environment that ensures settlement finality can occur in real time'.[43]

CHAPS Sterling

The Working Group on EC Payment Systems in its report on the 'Minimum Common Features for Domestic Payment Systems' recommended that as far as possible, and in order to reduce systemic risks associated with payment systems, EC central banks should consider a more extensive use of real-time gross-settlement (RTGS) systems.[44] Within the UK, at present there are 20 banks that are the over 4,500 settlement members of CHAPS Sterling. Direct members of CHAPS act as correspondent banks for financial institutions non-member, processing payments on their behalf.[45] The payments are highly concentrated with the five most active members accounting for approximately 80 per cent of payment value, and the two most active accounting for half of the total value.[46] In 2009, the average size of payments transferred by CHAPS was £1.76 million although the average was skewed by a small number of very large payments: approximately 94 per cent of payment value was attributable to 5 per cent of payment volume.[47] During the period January–September 2010, approximately £243 billion was settled in payments through CHAPS and in 2013 over £70 trillion was processed through the system.[48]

The members[49] are bound by the CHAPS rules and they use their SWIFT interface[50] to communicate directly with other settlement members over the SWIFT network. Typical payments are large financial transactions, either between banks or between banks and corporations. Some retail transactions such as housing market purchases also go through CHAPS. Each member agrees that it accepts responsibilities and liabilities under these CHAPS Rules as principal and not as agent for any other party.[51] A Memorandum of Understanding between the Bank of England and CHAPS Co sets out services the RTGS will provide with the service level expected.[52]

The settlement members send, and receive, credit transfer messages to and from member banks via the SWIFT interface. The CHAPS Sterling[53] system currently operates between

---

[43] International Monetary Fund, Washington DC, Financial Sector Assessment Program Update, July 2011, IMF Country Report No. 11/237.

[44] Working Group on EC Payment Systems, Report to Committee of Governors of the Central Banks of the Member States of the European Economic Community on Minimum Common Features for Domestic Payment Systems, 1992, http://www.ecb.europa.eu/pub/pdf/othemi/commonfeaturesen.pdf.

[45] Bank for International Settlements – Committee on Payments and Settlement Services, Payment, Clearing and Settlement Services in CPSS Countries, Vol. 2, November 2012, 460, http://www.bis.org/publ/cpss105.pdf.

[46] International Monetary Fund, Washington DC, Financial Sector Assessment Program Update, July 2011, IMF Country Report No. 11/237.

[47] International Monetary Fund, Washington DC, Financial Sector Assessment Program Update, July 2011, IMF Country Report No. 11/237.

[48] Bank for International Settlements – Committee on Payments and Settlement Services, Payment, Clearing and Settlement Services in CPSS Countries, Vol. 2, November 2012, 460, http://www.bis.org/publ/cpss105.pdf. See also CHAPS Co, about CHAPS, www.chapsco.co.uk/about_chaps/.

[49] CHAPS Scheme Rules, Version 7 – June 2012, para. 1.4.2, http://www.chapsco.co.uk/files/chaps/membership_rules.pdf.

[50] CHAPS Scheme Rules, Version 7 – June 2012, para. 1.3.1, http://www.chapsco.co.uk/files/chaps/membership_rules.pdf.

[51] CHAPS Scheme Rules, Version 7 – June 2012, para. 2.1, http://www.chapsco.co.uk/files/chaps/membership_rules.pdf.

[52] Bank for International Settlements – Committee on Payments and Settlement Services, Payment, Clearing and Settlement Services in CPSS Countries, Vol. 2, November 2012, 460, http://www.bis.org/publ/cpss105.pdf.

[53] CHAPS Clearing Company Ltd, CHAPS Scheme Rules, Version 7 – June 2012, para. 1.3.2 and 4.1.1, http://www.chapsco.co.uk/files/chaps/membership_rules.pdf.

6.00am and 4.20pm with the deadline of 4.00pm for submitting customer payments, and a further 20 minutes for inter-bank payments.[54] CHAPS Sterling members may enter into contractual arrangements with their corporate, or institutional, customers (for example a bank which is not a settlement member) allowing them to participate in the CHAPS system. These 'indirect participants'[55] are usually treated like branches of the settlement members and may be linked to the settlement member's payment processing system. The participant cannot access the CHAPS Sterling system directly but must go through the settlement member. As with all CHAPS payment messages transmitted through its SWIFT interface, the settlement members are responsible for the authenticity of any payment messages transmitted by the participant and payment must be guaranteed by the sending settlement members. The operation of CHAPS is shown in Figure 14.3.[56]

Customers may use a variety of means to instruct their branch to issue a CHAPS Sterling payment message, for example by telephone, telex or in writing. The customer must provide the bank with the names of the payer and payee, details of the banks and branches against which the payment is to be debited, the relevant account numbers and the amounts to be transferred.

Each CHAPS Sterling message is settled across members' accounts at the Bank of England before full payment data are sent to the 'receiving bank'. Consequently, all CHAPS members

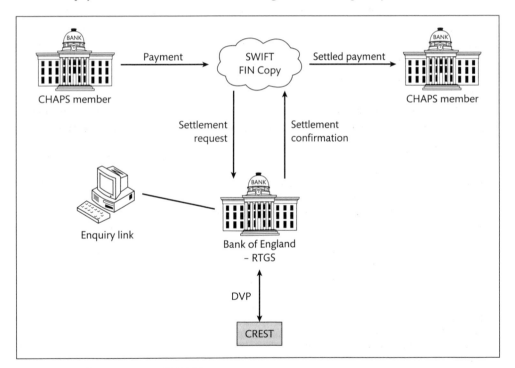

Figure 14.3 The operation of CHAPS

[54] Bank for International Settlements – Committee on Payments and Settlement Services, Payment, Clearing and Settlement Services in CPSS Countries, Vol. 2, November 2012, 461, http://www.bis.org/publ/cpss105.pdf.

[55] CHAPS Scheme Rules, Version 7 – June 2012, para. 1.4.3, http://www.chapsco.co.uk/files/chaps/membership_rules.pdf.

[56] CHAPS Co., CHAPS Technical Requirements, http://www.chapsco.co.uk/files/chaps/technical_requirement_document.pdf.

must hold a Sterling Settlement Account at the Bank of England, which the Bank of England has agreed may be used for the purpose of settling CHAPS payment obligations.[57] The SWIFT 'Y-Copy service'[58] will ensure that the settlement request, derived from each payment message received by the CHAPS Sterling Closed User Group,[59] is sent initially to the Bank of England. If there are sufficient funds in the account of the 'sending bank', the Bank of England settles the transaction by debiting the account of the sending bank and then crediting the account of the 'receiving bank'. A confirmation form is added to the full message stored by the SWIFT 'Y-Copy Service' and the full payment message and confirmation are then automatically released to the 'receiving bank'. The receiving bank will authenticate the message and it immediately transmits a positive user acknowledgement (or UAK) back to the 'sending bank'. The UAK confirms the safe receipt and acceptance of the output message and the 'receiving bank', on receipt of the full payment message, plus the confirmation, has the assurance that the amount has been credited to its settlement account.

The Bank of England[60] concluded that the main form of financial risk associated with RTGS is liquidity risk. For each payment message, settlement takes place in real time against funds in the sending bank's account. CHAPS payments cannot be made unless the paying bank has sufficient funds (or liquidity) available on its settlement account with the Bank. If there was insufficient liquidity in the system as a whole (or it was not distributed sufficiently well) to permit a regular flow of payments, the result could be gridlock. However, to avoid gridlock (i.e. the risk that in a gross settlement or payment system one or more participants defer the performance of their settlements until such time as they have received sufficient credits from other participants and thereby preventing the system from operating in real-time) the Bank of England provides CHAPS Sterling banks with intra-day liquidity so an even flow of funds can be maintained. More recently, a 'circles processing facility' has been developed which provides a central scheduling[61] and queue management for CHAPS members at the Bank of England. This is a simultaneous management facility for CHAPS members at the Bank of England and allows simultaneous settlement of payments queued on behalf of different banks. Under this facility a CHAPS Sterling settlement request is received by the central scheduler from CHAPS Sterling members, which will enable members to prioritise payments, hold individual payments or prioritise individual payments by value or by counterparty so long as that counterparty is also a CHAPS member. The central scheduler releases payments to the RTGS settlement process. At this point payment requests are either queued awaiting funds, or settled immediately if funds are available. Members are able to allocate a priority to the payment, which determines the queuing order once payments are forwarded to the RTGS processor. However, a member may amend that order or cancel the payment at any time up

---

[57] CHAPS Scheme Rules, Version 7 – June 2012, para. 1.4.1, http://www.chapsco.co.uk/files/chaps/membership_rules.pdf.

[58] See also SWIFT, FIN Secure Reliable and Cost-effective Messaging, http://www.swift.com/products/fin; SWIFT, FINCopy, The simple solution to your message duplication needs, http://www.swift.com/dsp/resources/documents/factsheet_fin_copy.pdf.

[59] CHAPS Scheme Rules, Version 7 – June 2012, para. 3.1.3, http://www.chapsco.co.uk/files/chaps/membership_rules.pdf.

[60] Bank of England, Annexes to Payment Systems Oversight Report, 2008, Detailed assessments of payment systems, Annex A, April 2009, Issue No. 5, http://www.bankofengland.co.uk/publications/Documents/psor/psorannex2008.pdf.

[61] Bank For International Settlements, Payment Systems in the UK, para. 3.2.4 http://www.bis.org/cpss/paysys/UnitedKingdomComp.pdf.

to settlement. Members are able to reserve part of their liquidity to enable urgent payments to be settled without awaiting the arrival of funds from other CHAPS members.

CHAPS subjects its members to various rules including that payment made through CHAPS Sterling must not be conditional.[62] This is in accordance with the 2009 Payment Services Regulations, which provide that as a general rule a payer cannot revoke his payment introduction once his bank has received it.[63] The CHAPS rules also provide that a payment message cannot be revoked by the sending settlement member, or any other party once the relevant member's settlement account is debited[64] and the receiving settlement member 'must for the purposes of making payments through CHAPS . . . accept and give same day . . .' value. It might, therefore, be argued that a payee who is due to receive a same day payment through CHAPS may have an action for breach of contract if his bank fails to give him same day access to the funds, as provided by the CHAPS rules.[65]

In *Hare* v *Henty*[66] the court held that the customer is entitled to the collection of funds as expeditiously as possible and applying the CHAPS rules, same day sterling payment is a reasonable usage of banking practice in respect of CHAPS payments. Further, the payee may have an action for breach of statutory duty under the Payments Services Regulations 2009 if the payee's bank fails to give the payee same day value in respect of CHAPS sterling transfers received.[67] In *Tayeb* v *HSBC Plc*[68] the 'receiving bank', being suspicious of the origin of money that had been transferred into its customer's account using CHAPS and, without its customer's consent, returned the funds to the 'sending bank' on the grounds that the transaction was an attempt to launder funds. Coleman J held that where a bank that opens an account for its customer, which is available for receiving incoming CHAPS transfers, undertakes that it will accept for the customer's account all CHAPS payments that comply with the CHAPS rules and that are in accordance with the terms of the account. The 'receiving bank' is therefore indebted to its customer for the amounts transferred once receipt of the payment is acknowledged and the customer's account is credited with the amount of the payment. Coleman J held that the CHAPS payment was normally irreversible once the 'receiving bank' had authenticated the transfer and had sent an acknowledgement informing the 'sending bank' that the transfer had been received and had credited the funds to the customer's account. This had taken place in the *Tayeb* case.

Coleman J observed that the payment in question had taken place prior to 2000 when changes to the CHAPS system had taken place but emphasised that the 'questions raised by these proceedings are pertinent also to the present CHAPS system'.[69] Given that the CHAPS rules contain specific provisions for the return of unapplied or erroneous transfers, and there are no other provisions for the reversal of credit entries following authentication, there was a 'strong implication that following application to the customer's account, in the absence of error, the banking practice relating to CHAPS transfers is that they are made ordinarily

---

[62] CHAPS Clearing Company Ltd, CHAPS Scheme Rules, Version 7 – June 2012, para. 4.1.1 http://www.chapsco.co.uk/files/chaps/membership_rules.pdf.

[63] Payment Services Regulations, 2009, regs 65(1) and 67(1).

[64] CHAPS Scheme Rules, Version 7 – June 2012, para. 3.2.1. http://www.chapsco.co.uk/files/chaps/membership_rules.pdf.

[65] CHAPS Scheme Rules, Version 7 – June 2012, http://www.chapsco.co.uk/files/chaps/membership_rules.pdf.

[66] (1861) 10 CBNS 65.

[67] Payment Services Regulations 2009, regs 73(1)–(2) and 120(1)(c).

[68] [2004] 4 All ER 1024.

[69] [2004] 4 All ER 1024 at 10.

irreversible'[70] Such transactions proceed on the basis that once a transfer has been accepted the payee can treat the funds as irrevocably his own. The real-time element is therefore crucial. However, Coleman J, drew an analogy with documentary letters of credit where, at the time of the presentation of documents, a bank with evidence of fraud can decline to make payment.[71] He also added that the same exception is likely to apply in the case of illegal transactions. However, most CHAPS payments are likely to fall within Part 6 of the Payments Services Regulations 2009, which provide that generally a payer cannot revoke his payment instruction once his bank has received it.[72] While the 2009 Regulations govern the revocability of CHAPS sterling transfers falling within their scope, the *Tayeb* case is still relevant to the issue of irrevocability and completeness of CHAPS payments, as between the payee and his bank.

CHAPS 'Faster Payments Service'

Following the Cruickshank Report[73] responsibility for regulating and reforming the UK payments systems was transferred to the Office of Fair Trading,[74] which, in 2004, set up the Payment Services Task Force. The latter suggested the development of a system for streamlining low-value electronic payments: an important innovation for the banking industry and consumer.[75] The work of the Task Force was based largely, but not exclusively, on the recommendations of the Cruickshank Report[76] and further developed, following its establishment in 2007, by its successor, the UK Payments Council.

In May 2008, CHAPS launched the 'Faster Payments Service' intended to provide a same-day clearing service for high-volume, low-value, sterling-denominated credit transfers. The 'Faster Payments Service' is an automated clearing service for standing orders and electronic retail transactions.[77] It benefits customers by speeding up one-off payments made over the Internet or by phone, reducing the BACS three-day clearing cycle to enable these payments to be cleared within hours, rather than days. However, the system is a net settlement service, rather than RTGS. The 'Faster Payments Service' enables single immediate credit transfer payments to be made all day and every day. Individual one-off payments may be diarised so that a credit transfer can be made at some specified time in the future. Standing order payments can be made when the payer wishes to make a series of payments to the named payee

---

[70] [2004] 4 All ER 1024 at 60.

[71] *United City Merchants (Investments) Ltd* v *Royal Bank of Canada* [1983] 1 AC 16.

[72] Payment Services Regulations 2009, regs 65(1) and 67(1).

[73] Cruickshank (2000) Competition in UK Banking – A Report to the Chancellor of the Exchequer, London, March.

[74] HM Treasury, Regulator to ensure a better deal for bank customers, 148/00, 21 December 2000, 148/00, http://archive.treasury.gov.uk/press/2000/p148_00.html.

[75] UK Payments Council, Annual Review 2008 – Driving Change in UK Payments, London 2008, http://www.paymentscouncil.org.uk/files/payments_files/annual_review_2008.pdf.

[76] Office of Fair Trading, Final Report of the Payment Systems Task Force, OFT 901, February 2007, https://docs.google.com/viewer?a=v&q=cache:ubE2ieTu5-4J:www.oft.gov.uk/shared_oft/reports/financial_products/oft901.pdf+Payment+Services+Task+Force,+final+Report+of+the+payments+system+2007&hl=en&gl=uk&pid=bl&srcid=ADGEEShEO09p4EacRBZSk3NNa3ukHQVgvdEEs8X-ZrmljvyqhfVPttaPvA2-IuoYK6rzjrJXr_XuDONVHumglVWKTBc6EKLIfZ2GHUIWBTPr3YCAjC1bO371Yz0F0DCYlpL7H8bwAExQ&sig=AHIEtbQY_n5JmYXPKCx0cey8ilMvTm3Emw.

[77] Bank of England, Payments Systems Oversight Report, 2011, p.11, para. 2.1.3, http://www.bankofengland.co.uk/publications/Documents/psor/psor2011.pdf.

on a regular fixed or indefinite period. The initial limit on the payments through the 'Faster Payments Service' for Internet and phone payments was £10,000 and the individual payment limit for standing orders is £100,000. From 6 September 2010, the maximum limit for all types of 'Faster Payments Service' is raised to £100,000. Each member being subject to a cap, which is determined by a formula, further mitigates risk of default and once the cap is reached the member cannot make further payments using the system until the cap recedes by payment being received or settlement.[78] The Faster Payments Service (FPS) processing services are outsourced to VocaLink Ltd. HM Treasury recognises 'Faster Payments Service' for the purposes of oversight by the Bank of England under s.185 of the Banking Act 2009.

The system supports transfer of value between retail customers' accounts in near real time, 24 hours a day, seven days a week. Membership is open to credit institutions with a settlement account at the Bank of England. Settlement between member banks takes place across accounts at the Bank of England three times per working day. There are ten direct members of the 'Faster Payments Services' scheme and 234 agency users.[79] The system works so that the paying member sends a message to the Faster Payments network service (called a Faster Payments switch) run by IPL. Once this is done the payment instruction cannot be cancelled. After ensuring that the payment message is properly formatted and has all the required details, the Faster Payments switch sends a message confirming the payment instruction to the receiving member bank and the paying member bank. The receiving member bank will verify the details of the payee's account and send a message to the Faster Payments switch confirming whether or not it accepts the payment. If the payment is accepted the switch will arrange for the amount of the payment to be incorporated into the relevant net settlement amount. The Faster Payments switch will also send a message to the paying bank to confirm that payment has been made. Individual payment messages are sent using a secure Internet service approved by BACS.

Files of payment instructions may also be used to make multiple payments. For example, where a corporate user or agency bureau has direct access to the 'Faster Payments Service', the user will submit payment requests in files to the Faster Payments switch. The Faster Payments switch will send a message to the sponsor for authorisation before the payments process can continue.

International payments

Society for Worldwide Interbank Financial Tele-Communication (SWIFT)

SWIFT is the international secure messaging system between banks, which underpins many international payment systems. Apart from the euro clearing and settlement systems almost all cross-border transfers involve inter-bank transfer of funds. In the past, such transfers were made using bankers' drafts, mail transfers and telegraphic transfers (telegrams or telex),

---

[78] Bank for International Settlements – Committee on Payments and Settlement Services, Payment, Clearing and Settlement Services in CPSS Countries, Vol. 2 November 2012, 464, http://www.bis.org/publ/cpss105.pdf.

[79] Bank of England, Payments Systems Oversight Report, 2011, p.11, para. 2.1.4, http://www.bankofengland.co.uk/publications/Documents/psor/psor2011.pdf.

which could lead to delays, errors, mistakes and loss of instructions. Today SWIFT will usually be used to transmit cross-border inter-bank payments through the telecommunications network. In *Dovey* v *Bank of New Zealand*[80] the New Zealand Court of Appeal, approving the trial judge's finding, concluded that SWIFT constituted 'the almost universal system for transferring funds across international boundaries'. Although, SWIFT is not a transfer system, it facilitates the transfer of funds through the use of a secure and reliable international communications network which has several advantages:

- SWIFT is owned by the members who use standardised message formats to increase efficiency and certainty in the payment instruction.

- SWIFT uses a common language, English, which reduces ambiguity.

- SWIFT is owned by the member banks and specialises in their needs and service provision.

- SWIFT operates a message acknowledgement and storage system, which provides greater certainty that the message has been processed; the storage service allows users to access message trails if necessary.

SWIFT is a non-profit cooperative company organised under Belgian law and wholly owned by its member banks, eligible securities broker-dealers and regulated third-party investment management institutions, whose shareholding will vary annually according to their usage of SWIFT. The shareholders elect a board of directors, which has power to implement changes in provisions governing SWIFT's allocation of liability, admit new members and expel members. SWIFT was established in 1973, by 239 banks in 15 different countries, and commenced operations in 1977. In 2012, SWIFT served over 10,240 members, sub-members and participants in 212 countries, known as users.[81] On 1 December 2011, SWIFT recorded a new peak in terms of traffic volumes with 19,992,265 messages resulting from a combination of high payments and securities volumes.[82]

By 2005, SWIFT had moved to an internet-based infrastructure, known as SWIFTNet and a new protocol known as SWIFT phase 2. The SWIFTNet messaging service (FIN)[83] includes authentication of messages, restrictions on the nature and types of messages users can send (closed user groups and relationship management application) and confirmation of receipt of messages. Messages are stored by SWIFT and forwarded to the recipient when online.[84] The store-and-forward facility removes the uncertainty and inconvenience of not knowing whether the correspondent is online at the time the sending institution wants to send the message. The message is delivered when the recipient is ready to receive it.[85]

[80] [2000] NZLR 641 at 645.

[81] SWIFT, SWIFT in Figures, October 2012, http://www.swift.com/about_swift/company_information/swift_in_figures/archive/2012/SIF_2012_10.pdf.

[82] SWIFT, The New Normal Annual Review, 2011, http://www.swift.com/resources/documents/Annual_Review_2011.pdfSWIFT.

[83] SWIFT, FIN Secure Reliable and Cost-effective Messaging, http://www.swift.com/products/fin; SWIFT, FINCopy, The simple solution to your message duplication needs, http://www.swift.com/dsp/resources/documents/factsheet_fin_copy.pdf.

[84] SWIFT, Messaging Secure Reliable and cost-effective messaging service, http://www.swift.com/dsp/resources/documents/factsheet_messaging_services.pdf.

[85] SWIFT, Messaging Secure Reliable and cost-effective messaging service, http://www.swift.com/dsp/resources/documents/factsheet_messaging_services.pdf.

Individual banks have access to the SWIFT system through the regional SWIFT access points (SAPs) with each country assigned to SAPs. The UK's SAPs is located at BACS's headquarters. The SAPs are linked together by slice processors located in the Netherlands and the USA. When a customer instructs the bank to carry out a money transfer transaction or other similar financial transaction, his instruction is conveyed by the bank's terminal to the regional SAP by the special SWIFT link. The SAP will encode the message and dispatch it to the slice processor. As with other forms of money transfer messages, the SWIFT message will set out all the relevant details of the transfer, including the name of a correspondent bank overseas, which the transmitting bank wishes to use to complete the payment. The slice processor transmits the message, after verifying the encoded security numbers contained in it, to the appropriate SAP in the country of destination. The message is decoded and transmitted to the recipient direct, or through the agency of a correspondent bank using the domestic fund transfer system. SWIFT undertakes to transmit transaction instructions on the day they are received from the paying customer, although time zones may mean that payment instructions have to be stored until the receiving bank comes online. Messages arriving at their destination after the close of business are stored at the SAP and processed on the next business day in the order in which they are received, except priority payments which involve extra cost, and are processed ahead of non-priority payments.

The rules governing the operation of SWIFT are set out in the FIN Policy module of the SWIFT User Handbook and explain SWIFT's own obligations and those of the sending and receiving banks. Messages are normally delivered, or non-delivery notified, within 30–60 minutes depending on the nature of the message and the system is available 24 hours, seven days a week. SWIFT also accepts responsibility for maintaining the security of that part of the system it controls. It is responsible for the complete network, namely SAPs, slice processor and system control centres, communication facilities and transmission lines between SAPs and the system control. However, each member institution is responsible for controlling the use of their terminals once they have gained SWIFT access; the authentication and maintaining the confidentiality and integrity of payment messages;[86] security of telecommunication links between their terminals and the regional SAP; and ensuring that SWIFT acknowledges their messages and delivery to the receiving bank. SWIFT's general policy accepts liability for breach of its duties subject to restrictions. Clause 9 of SWIFT's General Terms and Conditions[87] provides that:

> SWIFT accepts liability to the customer (whether in contract, tort, or otherwise), only for negligence, wilful default, or fraud . . .

Liability for claims relating to physical damage or loss of tangible property is limited to €5 million and claims relating to the provision or use of SWIFT services and products is limited to €50 million but excludes liability for unforeseeable loss or damage, loss of profit and indirect loss.[88] SWIFT specifically accepts limited liability for certain breach of duties including loss of interest arising out of a late payment due to its fault. SWIFT's overall annual liability for

---

[86] SWIFT, General Terms and Conditions, para. 5, https://www2.swift.com/uhbonline/books/public/en_uk/sgtc_20121207/index.htm.

[87] SWIFT, General Terms and Conditions, para. 9, https://www2.swift.com/uhbonline/books/public/en_uk/sgtc_20121207/index.htm.

[88] SWIFT, General Terms and Conditions, para. 9.1.3, https://www2.swift.com/uhbonline/books/public/en_uk/sgtc_20121207/index.htm.

loss of interest arising out of late payment may not exceed €1,235,000. SWIFT is not liable for any loss or damage arising out of unauthorised messages, negligence or a user, lack of cooperation between users, and a user's failure to follow required procedures where the failure is an 'essential element' in the event leading to the loss or damages incurred.

Legal implications of payment fund transfers

Although the law relating to the payment of fund transfers is entrenched in the rules of contract and agency laws, the Payment Services Regulations 2009[89] implement a new authorisation regime, and confer rights on customers in relation to issues of irrevocability of payment instructions, charges and execution time. At the same time, the Financial Markets and Insolvency (Settlement Finality) Regulations 1999[90] attempt to safeguard the integrity of the settlement procedures established by payment and securities settlement systems in the event of insolvency of a participant by providing that these settlement procedures will apply over the general rules of insolvency law. In addition the Financial Collateral Arrangements (No 2) Regulations 2003[91] gave effect to the EC Directive on Financial Collateral Arrangements and are aimed at promoting the effectiveness and robustness of these systems.

The application of the rules of agency law

Although, there is considerable divergence between the methods of fund transfers, nevertheless the systems available ultimately allow funds to be transferred between parties, with the banks acting as an intermediary. Banks, and other financial institutions, have, therefore, played a key role in the development and innovation of effective fund transfer systems. Thus, for example, a credit transfer is not a single process and, in fact, represents a number of distinct contractual relationships between (i) the paying customer and paying bank; (ii) the paying bank and the receiving (payee) bank; (iii) the receiving bank and the recipient (payee); and (iv) payer and payee. In addition, there may be other relationships that arise out of the transaction. Thus, if the payer's bank is not a settlement bank, it will have to clear the payment through a bank, which is a settlement bank. The position may be the same with a payee bank. If the payment has a cross-border dimension other relationships may be added, for example correspondent bank and foreign settlement systems may be used to make or receive payment.

The paying or transferring bank (the payer's bank)

Position of the paying or transferring bank at common law

At a basic level the paying, or transferring, bank will act as an agent, or the payer when making credit transfers. The bank is under a duty not merely to conform to the customer's mandate but also to carry out the customer's mandate with reasonable skill and care in accordance

---

[89] The Payment Services Regulations 2009 implement the Payment Services Directive 2007/64/EC.
[90] Implementing the EC Directive 98/26 on Settlement Finality Directive [1998] OJ L166.
[91] SI 2003/3226.

with current banking practice.[92] In the context of the agency relationship the paying bank's obligation is to make a payment in conformity with the customer's mandate[93] and a bank which fails to comply with this obligation will not be entitled, as agent, to reimbursement. The duty to act in accordance with the customer's mandate also extends to acting in accordance with a countermand.[94] In *Royal Products Ltd v Midland Bank Ltd*[95] the plaintiffs, Royal Products, a Maltese company, instructed the defendant bank, Midland, to transfer £13,000 by cable from its current account with Midland, in the UK, to its account with the Bank of Industry, Commerce and Agriculture Ltd (BICAL), in Malta. Midland regularly employed the Bank of Valletta (Valletta) in Malta as its correspondent and telexed Valletta, instructing it to transfer £13,000 to BICAL. Although Valletta was aware that BICAL was facing liquidity problems, Valletta made the transfer to BICAL and notified BICAL that the amount was to be credited to the account of Royal Products. The following day BICAL collapsed and Royal Products failed to receive the funds. Royal Products brought an action against Midland alleging that (i) National, as agents of Midland, were in breach of certain duties and obligations of a fiduciary nature; and (ii) even if National were not their agents, Midland owed Royal a duty of care in carrying out the transaction, which National's breach made Midland liable. Webster J, rejecting the arguments advanced for Royal Products, gave judgment for Midland. On the question of the relationship between Royal Products (the payer) and Midland (paying bank) the learned judge considered the legal implications of the payment instruction given by Royal Products to Midland. Webster J observed:

> . . . they are to be regarded simply as an authority and instruction, from a customer to its bank, to transfer an amount standing to the credit of that customer with that bank to the credit of its account with another bank, that other bank being impliedly authorised by the customer to accept that credit by virtue of the fact that the customer has a current account with it, no consent to the receipt of the credit being expected from or required . . . It is, in other words, a banking operation, of a kind which is often carried out internally, that is to say, within the same bank or between two branches of the same bank and which, at least from the point of view of the customer, is no different in nature or quality when, as in the present case, it is carried out between different banks.

Webster J held that there was an agency relationship between Royal Products (the payer) and Midland (the paying bank), and also an agency relationship between Midland and National (the correspondent). He concluded that there was no agency relationship between Royal Products and National (i.e. between the payer and the correspondent). Although, Midland (the agent) had the implied authority of Royal Products (the principal) to employ National (sub-agents) to facilitate the transfer, Midland did not have authority to create a contract between Royal Products and National (i.e. between the principal and the sub-agent). It followed that National did not owe any duties, including fiduciary duties, to Royal Products.

However, in *Royal Products Ltd v Midland Bank Ltd*[96] Webster J held that although Midland had not specifically entered into a contract to transfer funds to Royal Products, nevertheless

---

[92] *Selangor United Rubber Estates Ltd v Craddock (No 3)* [1968] 1 WLR 1555; *Karak Rubber Co Ltd v Burden No 2* [1972] 1 WLR 602; *Barclays Bank Plc v Quinceacre Ltd* [1992] 4 All ER 363.

[93] The instructions given by the customer must be clear and unambiguous (*Midland Bank Ltd v Seymour* [1955] 2 Lloyd's Rep 147).

[94] *Mellon Bank v Securities Settlement Corp* 710 F Supp. 991 (D.NJ, 1989).

[95] [1981] 2 Lloyd's Rep 194.

[96] [1981] 2 Lloyd's Rep 194.

the two parties were in a contractual relationship because of the underlying banker and customer relationship. However, in many cases, the paying bank will enter into a specific contract for the transfer of funds with the payer and charge him a fee for the service. The specific contract will then determine the nature of the terms and obligations and any limitations of liability.

At common law, the payer's bank generally owes a duty to exercise reasonable skill and care to a payer or transferor, who is also its customer.[97] The duty will be implied as part of the banker and customer relationship and owed concurrently in tort. While the payer will in most cases be a customer of the bank there may be circumstances where the bank may carry out an operation for someone who is not a customer, for example a Giro operation. If the amount the payer wishes to transfer is paid to the credit of a customer of the bank he approaches, the sum is received on behalf of the payee. While the bank owes a contractual duty to the payee to exercise care in executing the payment instruction, it is not so obvious whether a tortious duty is also owed to the payer. In *Abou-Rahmah* v *Abacha*[98] the claimants, who were the victims of an international fraud, instructed Gulf Bank to transfer funds to the payee (Trust International) by crediting the account of the defendant (City Express Bank of Lagos) held with the HSBC in London. Following the defendant's release of funds to 'Trusty International', rather than 'Trust International' as indicated in the SWIFT message, the payer argued that the defendant had breached the common law duty of care. Treacy J rejected the existence of a duty of care since the claimants were not the defendant's customers; there was no contract between the parties prior to the defendant bank's receipt of funds; and the bank had not undertaken any 'special responsibility' to the claimant.

Position of the paying (or transferring bank) (the payer's bank) under the Payment Services Regulations 2009

Part 5 of the Payment Services Regulations 2009 introduces certain minimum requirements in respect of the information that the payer's bank must provide its customer.[99] Where the payer is a consumer, a micro-enterprise or a charity the information is mandatory but may be disapplied by contrary agreement.[100] The nature of the information required would depend on whether the payer makes a one-off request for the transfer of funds from a bank with which there is not necessarily a continuing commercial relationship (a single payment service contract),[101] or whether the payment request is made within the context of an ongoing contractual or account relationship (a framework contract).[102] It is likely that 'single payment service contracts' will involve business-to-business transfers whereas most consumer contracts, usually from a current or flexible savings account, are likely to constitute 'framework contracts'.

---

[97] Where the Payment Services Regulations 2009 apply the paying bank's potential liability to the payer will be the same regardless of whether the payer is a customer of the paying bank or not.

[98] [2005] EWHC 2662, affd. on a different point [2007] 1 Lloyd's Rep 115.

[99] The requirements relating to the information that must be supplied during the course of a 'framework contract' (Payment Services Regulations 2009, reg. 41) or when there is a change to such a contract (Payment Services Regulations 2009, reg. 42) are disapplied in relation to regulated contracts falling under the Consumer Credit Act 1974.

[100] Payment Services Regulations 2009, reg. 33(4).

[101] Payment Services Regulations 2009, reg. 2(1).

[102] Payment Services Regulations 2009, reg. 39.

Under the 'single payment service contract', the payer's bank has to make certain information available to the payer either before the contract is concluded or 'immediately' after if the payer's request is by distance communication, for example telephone or Internet.[103] This includes information, for example, information that the payer needs to provide his bank to ensure the instruction is properly executed, the maximum time it will take for the transfer to be effected, the charges for the services provided by the payer's bank and a breakdown of the charges and any exchange rate that will be applied by the payer's bank.[104] Additional information required to be provided by the payer's bank is set out in schedule 4 of the Payment Services Regulations 2009. Following receipt of the payment order from the payer, the payer's bank must immediately provide information to the payer,[105] including a reference to enable the payer to identify the payment and the payee's details, the amount and currency of the payment transaction, details of the amount and currency of the payment transaction, the amount and breakdown of the charges payable by the payer, details of the rate and amount of the conversion, and the date when the payer's bank received the payment instruction.[106] In addition to the information to be disclosed, there are certain minimum standards regarding the manner of the disclosure including that the information must be in an easily accessible manner, in easily understood language that is clear and comprehensible, and in English or any agreed language.[107] The payer has the right to request a hard copy of any information that his bank is required to disclose[108] and to receive the information free of charge.[109]

Part 6 of the Payment Services Regulations 2009 governs the authorisation and execution of a payment instruction and establishes a regime governing the right and obligations of the parties to a payment transaction. Although Part 6 of the 2009 Regulations does not expressly distinguish between 'framework contracts' and 'single payment service contracts' the distinction may still be important. Where a payer has an account with his bank which he may use to give instructions for a payment transaction (a framework contract) the payer's bank may provide the payer with a device[110] that must be used to initiate a payment transaction on the account, or with a special password, or additional procedures that must be followed in order to initiate a payment transaction online. These security features are likely to occur in the context of an ongoing account relationship (framework contract) and are less likely to be required in the context of a one-off request for payment (single payment service contract). The use of a payment instrument in order to initiate a payment transaction may lead to the payer and his bank incurring additional legal responsibilities.[111]

The payer's bank will execute those payment transactions to which the payer has given his consent,[112] which is normally required before the execution of the payment transfer but may

---

[103] Payment Services Regulations 2009, reg. 36(1).
[104] Payment Services Regulations 2009, reg. 36(2).
[105] Payment Services Regulations 2009, reg. 37(1).
[106] Payment Services Regulations 2009, reg. 37(2).
[107] Payment Services Regulations 2009, reg. 47(1).
[108] Payment Services Regulations 2009, reg. 47(1).
[109] Payment Services Regulations 2009, reg. 48(1).
[110] For example, a device that generates a random security number which is entered into the bank's website.
[111] Obligations imposed on the payer bank regarding the payment instruments are intended to ensure that the personalised security features are not accessible to persons other than the payer; to refrain from sending the payer unsolicited payment instruments unless they are replacements for instruments previously issued etc., Payment Services Regulations 2009, reg. 59(1),
[112] Payment Services Regulations 2009, reg. 55(1).

be given afterwards, if so agreed between the parties,[113] and in accordance with the procedure agreed by the payer and his bank.[114] Where a payment instrument is used, in order to initiate the payment transaction, the payer must use the payment instrument in accordance with the terms and conditions of use[115] and must comply with any monetary limits that the payer and his bank have agreed should apply to any transactions initiated with the payment instrument,[116] for example where payment is made by card. The payment bank will not refuse payment that complies with any relevant 'framework contract,' unless it would be unlawful for the bank to comply with the transaction.[117] Where the payer's bank refuses to carry out the payment instruction it must generally notify the payer of the refusal, the reasons for the refusal and the steps required to be followed to rectify any factual errors.[118] The notification must be given in the agreed manner and at the 'earliest opportunity,'[119] but generally no later than the end of the working day following the bank's receipt of the of the payer's instructions.[120] The bank may under the 'framework contract' reserve the right to charge the payer for notifying him about the refusal to comply with the payment instruction, provided the bank's refusal is reasonably justified.[121] Where the payment transaction is initiated using a 'payment instruction', the payer's bank can reserve the right to refuse payment where it has reasonable concerns about the security of the 'payment instrument', about the suspected unauthorised or fraudulent use of the 'payment instrument' or about the payer's ability to repay when the use of the 'payment instrument' caused him to exceed his credit limit.[122] The payer's bank must inform the payer, before the dishonour, of its intention to stop payment of the 'payment instrument' and give reasons for its dishonour.[123] If it is not possible to give notification that payment has been stopped beforehand, then the payer's bank must inform the payer 'immediately' afterwards.[124] However, the payer bank need not comply with any of the notification requirements, when it would be unlawful.[125]

The payer's bank may impose charges against the payer's account, for making payment, according to the payer's instructions, provided the charges have been agreed with the payer and reflect actual costs incurred.[126] The payer's bank is not entitled to deduct these charges from the amount transferred, and must impose such charges separately, so the full amount is transferred to the payee's bank.[127] The payment instruction must be executed in the currency agreed between the payer's bank and payer[128] and the payer's bank must disclose, before initiating the payment, all charges together with the exchange rate to be applied in relation

[113] Payment Services Regulations 2009, reg. 48(2)(a).
[114] Payment Services Regulations 2009, reg. 48(2)(b).
[115] Payment Services Regulations 2009, reg. 57(1)(a).
[116] Payment Services Regulations 2009, reg. 56(1).
[117] Payment Services Regulations 2009, reg. 66(5).
[118] Payment Services Regulations 2009, reg. 66(1).
[119] Payment Services Regulations 2009, reg. 66(2).
[120] Payment Services Regulations 2009, reg. 70(1).
[121] Payment Services Regulations 2009, reg. 66(3).
[122] Payment Services Regulations 2009, reg. 66(3).
[123] Payment Services Regulations 2009, reg. 56(3).
[124] Payment Services Regulations 2009, reg. 56(4).
[125] Payment Services Regulations 2009, reg. 56(5).
[126] Payment Services Regulations 2009, reg. 52(1)(b)–(c).
[127] Payment Services Regulations 2009, reg. 68(1).
[128] Payment Services Regulations 2009, reg. 49(1).

to the payment.[129] Where the payer has supplied the paying bank with a 'unique identifier' for the payee, for example an account number, and sort code or SWIFT code for the payee's bank, a payment in accordance with such information supplied is deemed to be properly executed[130] and the paying bank is not liable for the non-execution, or defective execution, of the transaction. However, the paying bank must make reasonable efforts to recoup the funds involved and may charge the payer for such services, if permitted under the contract.[131]

The Payment Services Regulations 2009 also impose certain time limits within which the payer's bank must comply with the payer's instructions. The time limits are generally calculated to run from the 'time of receipt' of the payer's instruction which is defined as the time at which the payer's bank receives the instruction to make the payment transfer, either directly from the payer in the case of a credit transfer, or indirectly by or through the payee, in the case of a direct debit.[132] If a standing order payment is to be made on a certain date then the 'time of receipt' will be treated as the agreed date,[133] or if the payment is received on a non-business date then the 'time of receipt' for payment instruction will be treated as the next working day.[134] The 2009 Regulations make it mandatory for the payer's bank to comply with the time limits where the payment instructions are in euro or sterling, or the payment transaction involves a single conversion between the euro and sterling, and in the case of cross-border payments take place in euros.[135]

The payer can withdraw (revoke) his consent to the transaction[136] but generally cannot revoke the payment instruction once it has been received by the payer's bank.[137] The payer's bank may set a time limit by which it must receive the payment instruction if it is to be treated as received on that day. In the case of the revocation of direct debit instructions the payer may not revoke his payment instruction after the end of the preceding day agreed for the debiting of funds.[138] Where the payer and his bank have agreed that the payment transaction is to be executed on a certain date (for example in the case of a standing order) the payer may not revoke the payment after the end of the business day preceding the agreed day of payment.[139] In the case of a direct debit, the payer must also obtain the payee's consent before the payment instruction can be revoked out of time.[140]

Where the payer's bank has executed a payment that has not been authorised[141] by the payer or is revoked before payment becomes irrevocable,[142] the bank must refund the amount of the unauthorised transaction to the payer. If the amount of the unauthorised transaction is debited from the payer's account then the bank must, as part of the refund process, restore

---

[129] Payment Services Regulations 2009, reg. 49(2).
[130] Payment Services Regulations 2009, reg. 74(1).
[131] Payment Services Regulations 2009, reg. 78(2).
[132] Payment Services Regulations 2009, reg. 65(1).
[133] Payment Services Regulations 2009, reg. 65(4).
[134] Payment Services Regulations 2009, reg. 65(3).
[135] Payment Services Regulations 2009, reg. 69(1).
[136] Payment Services Regulations 2009, reg. 65(2).
[137] Payment Services Regulations 2009, regs 65(1) and 67(1).
[138] Payment Services Regulations 2009, reg. 67(3).
[139] Payment Services Regulations 2009, reg. 67(5)(a).
[140] Payment Services Regulations 2009, reg. 67(5)(b).
[141] Payment Services Regulations 2009, reg. 55(1) and (2).
[142] Payment Services Regulations 2009, reg. 67.

the payer's account to its pre-transaction position.[143] The payer must, however, notify the bank 'without delay' on becoming aware of the unauthorised transaction; this cannot exceed 13 months from the date when the payer's account was debited.[144] The payer is not obliged to notify the bank of the unauthorised payment if it can be shown that the bank failed to comply with the information requirements contained in Part 5 of the Payment Services Regulations 2009.[145] The bank will bear the burden of proving that the payment was, in fact, so authorised but the mere fact that the payer's bank can produce records to show that the 'relevant instrument' was used to initiate the payment transaction is not in itself necessarily sufficient to prove that the payer himself authorised it.[146]

There are limited grounds on which the payer's bank can pass some of the losses resulting from an unauthorised credit transfer or direct debit to the payer. Generally, the payer will only bear the loss for such a transaction when it can be shown that he acted fraudulently.[147] Where the payer is required to use a 'payment instrument' in order to initiate the payment transaction, the payer will be liable in cases of fraud, as well as losses resulting from an unauthorised payment transaction, if he either intentionally or with 'gross negligence' failed to comply with his statutory obligations regarding the instrument,[148] for example using the instrument according to the terms and conditions governing usage,[149] to notify the bank 'without undue delay' on becoming aware of the loss, theft, misappropriation or unauthorised use of the payment instrument[150] and to take reasonable steps to keep the personalised use of the payment instrument.[151] In the absence of fraudulent, intentional or grossly negligent conduct on the part of the payer, he will only be liable up to a maximum of £50 for any losses resulting from an unauthorised transaction, caused by the theft or loss of the payment instrument. Apart from cases of fraud, however, the payer will not be liable for any losses incurred after the payer has informed the bank of the loss, theft, misappropriation or unauthorised use of the payment instrument. Neither, will the payer be liable where the bank has failed to provide the payer with an appropriate means of notifying it.[152]

A payer may also be entitled to a refund from his bank in respect of a payment transaction initiated by or through the payee (for example a direct debit) even when such a transaction is authorised.[153] Such a refund is usually available when the payer did not specify the exact amount of the payments when the direct debit was initially authorised and the amount of a particular payment is in excess of the amount the payer could reasonably have expected, taking into account the payer's previous spending pattern, the conditions of the framework agreement and the circumstances of the case.[154] This provision is intended to protect the payer from a situation where the payee might abuse his position by increasing the amount of the payment.

---

[143] Payment Services Regulations 2009, reg. 61(b).
[144] Payment Services Regulations 2009, reg. 59(1).
[145] Payment Services Regulations 2009, reg. 59(2).
[146] Payment Services Regulations 2009, reg. 60(3)(a).
[147] Payment Services Regulations 2009, reg. 62(2)(a).
[148] Payment Services Regulations 2009, reg. 62(2)(b).
[149] Payment Services Regulations 2009, reg. 57(1)(a).
[150] Payment Services Regulations 2009, reg. 57(1)(b).
[151] Payment Services Regulations 2009, reg. 57(2).
[152] Payment Services Regulations 2009, reg. 62(3).
[153] Payment Services Regulations 2009, reg. 63(1).
[154] Payment Services Regulations 2009, reg. 63(2).

The role of the correspondent (or intermediary) bank

Relationship between the payer and the correspondent bank at common law

There may be circumstances, for example where the paying bank is unable to transfer funds according to the customer's instructions directly to the payee, where the paying bank uses a correspondent bank to effect the payment. The correspondent bank will act as an agent of the paying bank; there is no direct relationship between the paying customer and correspondent bank. In such circumstances the agent, the transferring bank, has appointed a sub-agent, the correspondent bank, to carry out the customer's instructions, although the payer's bank may find itself vicariously liable for the negligence or default of the correspondent.[155] In *Calico Printers' Association v Barclays Bank Ltd*[156] Wright J observed that, as a general rule, there is no privity of contract between a principal and his agent's sub-agent. This rule was affirmed, by Webster J, in *Royal Products*[157] where he said there was no privity of contract between the customer, the payer, and the correspondent bank. Thus, in that case as between Royal Products (the principal, customer) and National (the sub-agent) there was no contract. This is also true in cases involving commercial letters of credit, where the issuing bank employs a correspondent bank in the beneficiaries' country to inform the beneficiary of the opening of the credit.[158] In exceptional cases, however, the courts will recognise a contractual relationship between the original customer and the correspondent. Where banks participate in a settlement system the contractual relationships between banks are particularly important Banks may enter into bilateral arrangements, for example, where a member of a clearing system agrees to act as an agent for a non-member bank in the clearing. However, other arrangements, for example SWIFT or CHAPS, depend on multilateral contracts under which each member bank is bound by the rules of the system. In such cases, each member will enter into a contract with the system provider to conform to the rules of the provider. The payer and payee are not privy to the contract with the service provider unless the terms under which the service provider operates are expressly incorporated into the contract between the customer and its bank. The customer will, therefore, have a contractual relationship with his own bank, the basis of which may imply certain obligations with regard to the use of fund transfer systems, for example to act as expeditiously as possible[159] and in accordance with the terms of the system. A bank will therefore be deemed to have undertaken to act in accordance with the reasonable usage of bankers.[160] Any terms limiting or excluding liability will be subject to the Unfair Contract Terms Act 1977.

Thus, in *Silverstein v Chartered Bank*[161] the American court held the transferor did have a contract with his bank's correspondent as the customer had expressly selected the correspondent. Similarly, in *Evra Corporation v Swiss Bank Corporation*[162] the United States District

---

[155] *Equitable Trust Co of New York v Dawson Partners Ltd* (1927) 27 Ll. L Rep. 49.
[156] (1931) 36 Com Cas 71.
[157] *Royal Products Ltd v Midland Bank Ltd* [1981] 2 Lloyd's Rep 194.
[158] *Bank Melli Iran v Barclays Bank (Dominion, Colonial and Overseas)* [1951] 2 Lloyd's Rep 367.
[159] *Hare v Henty* (1861) 10 CBNS 65.
[160] *Hare v Henty* (1861) 10 CBNS 65.
[161] (1977) 392 NYS 2d 296.
[162] (1981) 522 F Supp 820.

Court held that the correspondent was liable in damages for breach of contract and negligence. Although the decision was reached on other grounds, the appellate court did not question the existence of a contract between the charterers and the correspondent bank.

Relationship between the paying and correspondent banks under the Payment Services Regulations 2009

A paying bank may appoint a correspondent, or intermediary, bank to complete a payment transaction on its behalf. In such circumstances the correspondent, or intermediary, bank will act as an agent for the purposes of carrying out the instructions of the payer's bank. It will normally be entitled to an indemnity for any expenses incurred from the paying bank which instructs it.[163] At common law the correspondent, or intermediary, will owe a contractual duty of skill and care[164] and may also have a concurrent duty in tort.

The liability of the correspondent, or intermediary, bank to its instructing party differs where the fund transfer falls within the scope of the Payment Services Regulations 2009. Where a failure to carry out the payment order, whether at all or in a timely manner,[165] is attributable[166] to the correspondent, or intermediary, bank that bank must compensate the payer's bank (or in the case of a debit transfer, the payee's bank) for losses incurred as a result of the non-execution or defective payment mandate.[167] The correspondent, or intermediary, bank may escape liability where it is unable to execute the payment due to the provision of an incorrect unique identifier or *force majeure*.[168] The statutory position differs in two ways: (i) a correspondent, or intermediary, bank may be liable under the 2009 Regulations, if the losses in question are 'attributable' to it although the regulations do not appear to require fault on the part of the correspondent, or intermediary, bank; and (ii) where there is a chain of correspondents, the common law rules of compensation are based on privity of contract and the paying bank will normally be limited to seeking relief against the bank it instructed. The 2009 Regulations, however, appear to enable the payer's bank to bring a claim directly against the correspondent, or intermediary, bank that is responsible (attributable) even if the bank responsible for the loss is a remote party with whom the paying bank has no direct contractual relationship.

The role of the receiving or recipient bank (the payee's bank)

The role of the receiving (or recipient) bank at common law

The position of the payee bank, at common law, is less certain than under the Payment Services Regulations 2009. The difficulty is created by having to determine for whom the payee bank is acting at any particular time in the payment transaction. However, in some

---

[163] *Honourable Society of the Middle Temple* v *Lloyds Bank Plc* [1999] 1 All ER (Comm) 193; *Linklaters (a firm)* v *HSBC Plc* [2003] 1 Lloyd's Rep 545.

[164] Where the correspondent, or intermediary, bank is appointed by the payee bank similar duties will be owed.

[165] Payment Services Regulations 2009, regs 75–76.

[166] Payment Services Regulations 2009, reg. 78.

[167] Payment Services Regulations 2009, reg. 78.

[168] Payment Services Regulations 2009, reg. 79.

types of fund transfer systems the contracts between the banks will provide a solution, for example in SWIFT transfers the master agreement between the participating banks will deal with the allocation of liability for defective payments or a failure to make payments. Where the service provider contract fails to resolve issues of liability then the rules of common law will apply. However, the legal position of the payee bank will depend on the nature of the fund transfer system being used, for example in the case of a direct debit system, the payee's bank acts as the payee's agent. When the payee initiates the direct debit, he will act as the payer's agent in giving the payment mandate, but when he selects the bank, and account, into which payment is to be made he accepts the payment in his own right.

The position is less certain in the case of credit transfers. The receiving bank will act on the instructions received from the transferring, or its correspondent, bank and must credit the payee's account according to the instructions received, including crediting the payee's account with the specified amount, either immediately or within a reasonable time. To that extent it was accepted in *Shawmut Worcester County* v *First American Bank and Trust Co*[169] that the receiving bank acts as the agent of the transferring bank for the purposes of receiving the amount transferred. However, it must follow that once the amount received by the receiving bank is credited to the account of the payee the receiving bank acts not as an agent of the transferring bank, but as an agent of the payee to whose account the funds have been credited. The courts have looked at the question whether in a credit transfer transaction the recipient bank is an agent of the payee. In *Mardorf Peach and Co Ltd* v *Attica Sea Carriers Corp of Liberia*[170] Lords Denning MR and Lawton LJ held that payment of hire for a ship by the charterers had taken place when the payment order was handed to the receiving bank, as agent for the owners and accepted by it without objection. The court concluded that payment orders are treated as equivalent to cash and that after the payment order was handed over to the receiving bank, as agent, for the owners, the charterers were to be treated as having no control over the payment. Although the House of Lords[171] allowed the appeal on other grounds the assumption that the receiving bank was the agent of the owners was not questioned. Nevertheless, the House of Lords accepted that the receiving bank, although an agent of the owners, had limited authority to accept payment and that authority extended only to acceptance of a payment made punctually. On the basis of the limited authority conferred on the receiving bank the question that arises is whether the relationship between the payee and his bank is that of debtor and creditor, or agent and principal. The better view is that the agency relationship is only temporary and is converted into a debtor and creditor relationship once the funds are unconditionally credited to the account. In *Balmoral Supermarkets Ltd* v *Bank of New Zealand*[172] McMullen J suggests that funds become the subject of the traditional debtor and creditor relationship between the bank and customer at the moment that they are deposited into an account with the bank. Similarly, in *Midland Bank Ltd* v *Conway Corp*[173] the court held that the bank was acting solely under its duty as a banker to receive any money paid into the account. It was, therefore, not possible to draw an inference that there was a special relationship between the bank and its customer that converted the bank into an agent for the purposes of receiving rental payments. The court did not consider whether the bank

[169] 731 F Supp 57.
[170] [1976] QB 835.
[171] *Mardorf Peach and Co Ltd* v *Attica Sea Carriers Corp of Liberia* [1977] AC 850.
[172] [1974] 2 NZLR 155.
[173] [1965] 1 WLR 1165.

might be an agent in the limited sense of *Mardorf Peachand Co*. Support for this view was implicit in *Royal Products Ltd v Midland Bank Ltd* where Webster J expressed the view that it is implied in the banker and customer relationship that the bank should receive sums to the credit of the customer's account. There was no question of a 'special relationship' to take the parties outside the principle of *Foley v Hill*.

Article 10 of the UNCITRAL Model Law states that the receiving bank is the agent of the transferring or correspondent bank until the receiving bank accepts the funds for the credit of the payee's account. The answer, however, is not so simple, especially where electronic fund transfer systems are used. In such circumstances, the contract governing the payment system may resolve the situation. Where the payee bank is acting as the payee's agent the payer may, nevertheless, try to hold the payee's bank liable. Although there is no privity of contract, the payer may argue the existence of a common law duty of care. In *Abou-Rahmah v Abacha*[174] the claimants, who were the victims of an international fraud instructed Gulf Bank to transfer funds to the payee (Trust International) by crediting the account of the defendant (City Express Bank of Lagos) that was held with HSBC in London. Following the release of funds to 'Trusty International' rather than 'Trust International' as indicated in the SWIFT message, the payer argued that the defendant had breached its common law duty of care. Treacy J rejecting this argument held that there was 'no special relationship' between the defendant and the claimants. The conclusion that there was no voluntary assumption of responsibility was based largely on the fact that the payer was not a customer of the payee bank and there was no contract between the parties before the payee's bank received the funds.[175] The learned judge also rejected the existence of a duty of care on the basis of the 'threefold test' and held that it was not 'fair, just and reasonable' to impose a duty on the payee's bank because it received the funds as the payee's agent, to whom it already owed a duty of care under contract. Treacy J, relying on a number of Canadian authorities,[176] concluded that banks have 'a huge number of potential [payers] who can remit money without significant control by the bank' and the fact that, in the absence of special circumstances, the imposition of a duty of care would 'impose a very heavy burden on banks and significantly hamper their efficiency'. Some support for this view is found in *So v HSBC Bank Plc*.[177] As an alternative to the argument that the payee's bank had breached its common law duty of care to the payer by crediting the wrong account, the payer in *Abou-Rahmah* also sought to recover the funds transferred from the payee's bank on the ground that it dishonestly assisted in a breach of trust, and that the funds were held under a *Quistclose* trust by the payee's bank for the claimants, and the payee's bank was liable for money had and received. Treacy J rejected the first two propositions but held that as payment had been made under an operative mistake the claimants were entitled to recover the sums credited by the payee's bank to the wrong account.[178]

---

[174] [2007] 1 Lloyd's Rep 115.

[175] In *Wells v First National Commercial Bank* [1998] PNLR 552 Evans LJ denied the existence of a duty of care owed by the payer's bank to the payee, but felt that such a duty might be owed on the basis of the principles in *Hedley Byrne & Co v Heller & Partners* if there was a direct contract between the parties.

[176] *Grooves-Raffin Construction Ltd v Bank of Nova Scotia* (1975) 64 DLR (3d) 78; *Toor v Bank of Montreal* (1922) 2 Bank LR 8; *Dennisson v Cronin* (1994) 45 ACWS (3d) 1279; *Kyserv Bank of Montreal* (1999) 88 ACWS (3d) 1156.

[177] [2009] EWCA Civ 296.

[178] See Ch. 17 for a discussion on money paid under mistake.

The role of the receiving (or recipient bank) (the payee's bank) under the Payment Services Regulations 2009

The majority of domestic fund transfers fall within the scope of the Payment Services Regulations 2009, which place the payee's bank under certain disclosure requirements. Where the payee's bank operates an account for the customer that may be used to receive and make fund transfers, the bank will have to satisfy the information requirements for a 'framework contract' and most direct debit and standing order payments are likely to be covered by these information requirements. Where the payment transaction is initiated by the payee who approaches the bank to act and receive funds on his behalf (i.e. debit transfer) the payee bank is required to make certain information available before the contract is concluded, or immediately after, for example where the payee's approach is made by 'means of distance communication' or by Internet or phone. This includes information the payee needs to provide for the proper execution of the order; the maximum time it will take for the transfer to be effected; the charges for the service provided by the payee's bank and any exchange rate to be applied. Additionally, the payee's bank must provide any such information from Schedule 4 of the 2009 Regulations, as relevant to a 'single payment service contract'. Once the information has been provided to the payee (regardless of whether the payment is made pursuant to a 'framework contract' or 'single payment service contract') the payee's bank must transmit the payment order to the payer's bank unless it notifies the payee of its reasons for refusing.[179] In the case of direct debit instructions, the payee's bank must transmit the payment order within the time limits agreed with the payee.[180] Once the payment has been received from the payer's bank, the payee's bank must immediately[181] credit the payee's account with the amount of the payment,[182] or otherwise make available the funds, if the payee has no account with the payee bank. The transferred amounts must start to earn interest by the end of the business day on which the payee's bank received the funds.[183] The full amount of the payment must be transferred to the payee's account and the payee bank must not deduct any charges unless this is previously agreed and the bank gives details of the amounts deducted.[184] The payer's bank will be responsible for reimbursing the payee in respect of unauthorised deductions where the payer initiates the payment.[185]

Regardless of whether the payer or payee initiated the transaction and following its execution, the payee bank is required to provide the payee with certain additional information: for example a reference number that will allow the payee to identify the payment transaction and, where appropriate, the payer and any information transferred as part of the transaction; the amount of the transaction stated in the currency in which the funds are placed in the payee's account; the amount and breakdown of any charges payable by the payee; the exchange rate applied by the payee's bank and the amount of the payment before the currency conversion; and the date on which the funds will be credited to the payee's account for the purposes of earning interest.[186]

---

[179] Payment Services Regulations 2009, reg. 66(1).
[180] Payment Services Regulations 2009, reg. 70.
[181] Payment Services Regulations 2009, reg. 73(1).
[182] Payment Services Regulations 2009, reg. 70(5).
[183] Payment Services Regulations 2009, reg. 73(1).
[184] Payment Services Regulations 2009, reg. 68(2).
[185] Payment Services Regulations 2009, reg, 68(3).
[186] Payment Services Regulations 2009, reg, 38(2); see also: Payments Council, Payment Services Regulations Industry Best Practice Guidance on Selected Issues, October 2009, http://www.paymentscouncil.org.uk/files/payments_council_psrs_guidance_oct_09.pdf.

The allocation of responsibility for a defective payment, or non-execution of a payment instruction, will depend on whether the payer or payee instituted the payment instruction. Where the payer initiates the payment, for example in the case of CHAPS or standing order payments, the payer's bank will bear the primary responsibility for executing the payment instruction and is generally liable for failure to execute, or a defective execution of, the mandate unless the paying bank can establish that the funds were in fact received by the payee bank.[187] Where the payer's bank can show it executed the payment in a timely manner then the responsibility for the defective execution or non-execution transfers to the payee bank, which must make the funds available to the payee immediately.[188] Where the payment transaction is initiated by the payee, for example direct debits, the payee's bank bears the prime responsibility for effecting the transfer and is liable to the payee 'for the correct transmission of the payment order'.[189] Where the payee's bank fails to transmit, or defectively transmits, a payee initiated payment instruction it must immediately re-transmit the payment order in question to the payer's bank[190] and the payee's bank must, if requested, make immediate efforts to trace the payment and notify the payee of the outcome.[191] Where the payee bank can demonstrate that it correctly transmitted the payment instruction to the payer's bank then responsibility for the defective execution, or non-execution, of the payment shifts to the payer bank who must refund the payer and restore the debited account to the state it would have been in had the defective payment transaction not taken place.[192]

Although generally the payee bank is liable for payment instructions not properly transmitted, the bank may escape liability if it can show that the payee delayed unreasonably in notifying the bank of the defective payment. Notice must in any event be given, no later than 13 months after the debit date and on becoming aware of the unauthorised or incorrectly executed payment transaction.[193] However, this limitation of liability is not valid where the payee bank has failed to comply with the provisions of Part 5 of the 2009 Regulations.[194]

Are money transfer orders negotiable instruments?

Since many of the instruments originally recognised by the common law as negotiable had their origins in mercantile usage, strictly speaking the categories of negotiable instruments are not closed.[195] While a test based on mercantile usage as a means of recognising negotiable instruments may lead to an element of unpredictability a key feature which the instrument must comply with, is that the instrument mandates the transfer of funds. The fund transfer

---

[187] Payment Services Regulations 2009, regs 70(1), 75(2) and 75(4).
[188] Payment Services Regulations 2009, reg. 75(5).
[189] Payment Services Regulations 2009, reg. 76(2).
[190] Payment Services Regulations 2009, reg. 76(3).
[191] Payment Services Regulations 2009, reg. 76(4).
[192] Payment Services Regulations 2009, reg. 76(5).
[193] Payment Services Regulations 2009, reg. 59.
[194] Payment Services Regulations 2009, reg. 59(2).
[195] In *Goodwin* v *Robarts* (1875) LR Exch. 337 at 352, Cockburn CJ, after referring to bills of exchange, promissory notes and cheques said: 'It thus appears that all these instruments which are said to have derived their negotiability from the law merchant had their origin, and that at no very remote period, in mercantile usage, and were adopted into the law by our Courts as being in conformity with usages of the trade.'

order will, generally, be an instruction by the payer to his bank to transfer funds from his bank account to the credit of the payee. The mandate may, typically, be given on standard forms issued by the bank, for example cheques, standing orders or bank giro credits but an instruction to transfer funds may also be given by letter, facsimile or telex. In *The Brimnes*[196] the Court of Appeal considered the legal status of a fund transfer mandate, which had been given by telex. The court concluded that the telexed instruction was not a negotiable instrument and further the telex could not be equated to negotiable instruments such as cheques. Cairns LJ held:

> . . . property in money passes on delivery; so does the property in a cheque. Partly by operation of the law merchant and the Bills of Exchange Act 1882, partly by the customs of business, cheques have become regarded as the equivalent of money (subject always to being afterwards defeated by dishonour). I do not think that the telex message in this case can be regarded in the same way. It was not a negotiable instrument. It could have been revoked by [the payer's bank] at any time before being acted upon by the [payee's bank], and if it had been so revoked, no action could have been brought on it as it could on a stopped cheque.

It is likely that the courts would reach the same conclusion in respect of fund transfer mandates regardless of the manner in which the instruction is given. Further, there is no mercantile custom that establishes that fund transfer orders are capable of being transferred or negotiated from one person to another by delivery (or endorsement and delivery) and they give the *bona fide* holder for value a title which is free from defects of title of the prior parties.[197] In practice the fund transfer order is sent directly by the payer to his bank to execute payment and the payee does not have the opportunity to transfer, to a third party, the fund transfer order. The fund transfer order is, therefore, not a negotiable instrument.

A fund transfer order, therefore, falls outside the definition of negotiable instruments for the purposes of the Bills of Exchange Act 1882. Section 3 of the 1882 Act defines that a bill of exchange as:

> an unconditional order in writing, addressed by one person to another, signed by the person giving it, requiring the person to whom it is addressed to pay on demand or at a fixed or determinable future time a sum certain in money to, or to the order of, a specified person, or to bearer.

Arguably, a payment instruction conveyed to the paying bank in electronic form, for example a communication network such as CHAPS, may fall outside the definition of s.3 of the Bills of Exchange Act 1882 that requires the payment instruction be 'in writing' and although the Electronic Communications Act 2000[198] gives the Secretary of State the power to amend legislation 'in such manner as he may think fit for the purpose of authorising or facilitating the use of electronic communication or electronic storage' no such order has yet been made in respect of the Bills of Exchange Act 1882. However, even if the fund transfer instruction is embodied in a written form it is unlikely to constitute a bill of exchange since the instruction mandate will not:

---

[196] *Tenax Steamship Co Ltd* v *Reinate Transoceania Mavegacion SA, The Brimnes* [1975] 1 QB 929.
[197] See Ch. 10 for a discussion on negotiable instruments.
[198] Electronic Communications Act 2000, s.8.

(a) *Be payable at a determinable future time or on demand*. The Bills of Exchange Act 1882 requires payment on sight or on presentation, which means that payment should be effected when demanded by the payee or holder. However, the bank giro form is delivered to the drawee bank, and not the payee, so payment is made when the drawee bank (payer's bank) is in a position to make payment. Where a bill of exchange does not bear a date on it, it may be treated as payable on demand. This is also the case with bank giro payments although the payee will not get the opportunity to claim payment since the payment instruction is communicated directly to the drawee bank.

(b) *Be payable to a specified person or to bearer*. The bank giro falls outside the definition of bills of exchange since the payment order is not payable to the order of a specified person or to bearer. The form will nominate a specific payee to whom, or to whose account, the money will be credited. The bank giro form cannot be transferred to a third party and the payee is not given the opportunity of deciding whether the payment should be made to a third party.

(c) *Words must contain an instruction*. Usually, bills of exchange contain words that can be construed as a formal instruction given by the payer to the paying bank. The nature of the bank giro form, used in the UK, does not include words that can be construed as an instruction or 'order' to the drawee bank.

Giro forms, therefore, do not constitute negotiable instruments and the remedies available to the parties will, therefore, depend on the rules of agency law and law of contract, rather than the Bills of Exchange Act 1882. Further, the EC Directive on Payment Services,[199] which applies to 'payment orders', including instructions to a bank to execute a fund transfer are distinguished from cheques, bills of exchange and promissory notes, which are outside the scope of the Directive.

Despite the fact that the fund transfer orders are not treated as a negotiable instrument, payment by a direct debit mandate is treated like a payment by cheque and equivalent to cash with the payer unable to rely on any rights of set-off or counterclaim arising under the underlying contract of sale (except in cases of fraud or failure of consideration). In *Esso Petroleum Co Ltd v Milton*[200] the plaintiff, an occupier of a petrol station, was required to pay for delivery by direct debit, shortly after delivery. He cancelled the direct debit mandate at a time when approximately £170,000 was outstanding for the petrol previously supplied. The Court of Appeal held the payment arrangement between the parties, to pay by direct debit, was to be treated as equivalent to payment by cheque. Consequently, the defendant was denied the right to set off the amounts, which he claimed were due to him in respect of various breaches of contract committed by the plaintiffs, under the underlying contract of sale. Thorpe LJ expressed the view that this was a 'natural evolution' of the rule which applies to bills of exchange and cheques and, according to Sir John Balcombe, reflected the modern commercial practice of treating a direct debit in the same way as payment by cheques. However, it is debatable whether this view is correct[201] although the reasoning could be applied to other forms of credit and direct debit transfers.

---

[199] Directive 2007/64/EC, [2007] OJ L319/1 implemented in English Law from 1 November 2009, by the Payment Services Regulations 2009 (SI 2009/209).
[200] [1997] 2 All ER 593.
[201] See: Hooley (1997) Direct Debits and Set-off – the Tiger Roars! *CLJ*, 500; and Tettenborn (1997) Pay now, Sue Later: Direct Debits, Set-Off and Commercial Practice 113 *LQR*, 374.

Is a money transfer an assignment?

The question whether an instruction to effect an EFT payment amounts to an assignment of funds has considerable significance in respect of the revocability of the payment and the rights of the payee against the payer's bank. In terms of an assignment, the payer would be the 'assignor', the payee would be the 'assignee' and the payer's bank would be the 'debtor'.[202] If the payer's account was in credit, that credit balance would constitute a chose in action to be assigned, either in whole or in part, as instructed by the assignor (payer-customer). Under s.136 of the Law of Property Act 1925, notification to the payer's bank as debtor would complete the assignment,[203] while in the case of an equitable assignment an intention to assign the chose in action and 'some outward expression by the assignor of his intention to make an immediate disposition of the subject of the assignment'[204] would complete the assignment, without the need for any writing or consideration. Thus, payment would be complete once the bank puts in motion the steps necessary to transfer the funds even if the debtor (assignee) is not notified of the transfer.[205] In *Delbrueck* v *Manufacturers Hanover Trust Co*[206] it was argued that money credited by a customer in an account with the transferring bank was a chose in action and therefore capable of being assigned. The Court of Appeal for the Second Circuit concluded that amounts deposited to the payer with his bank constituted a chose in action and were thus capable of assignment. Moore J stated that under the law of the United States:

> In order for there to be a valid assignment of a chose in action there must be a specific direction to transfer by the assignor and notice of the assignee.

The order to transfer funds having been given to the transferring bank, the court concluded that delivery of the credit slip to the receiving bank was sufficient notice of the transfer where the receiving bank acted as an agent of the payee.

Although the American authority is persuasive in favour of the EFT transaction arguably being an assignment, the English courts will not treat the giro payment as an assignment for a number of reasons. Firstly, a money transfer order usually involves the part payment of a credit balance (debt) due from the bank to the customer. Section 136 of the Law of Property Act 1925 does not permit the assignment of part payment of a debt. Secondly, a money transfer order does not always relate to funds standing to the credit of the customer, payer's account, at the time the instruction is issued. Although, the payer assumes that the funds required to make the payment will be available at the time the payment is to be effected, at some time in the future, this is, nevertheless, a mere expectancy. As such, it is not possible to assign a future payment of funds under s.136 of the Law of Property Act 1925.[207] Further, it may be argued that regardless of the method of payment used since the object of the payment instruction is to perform a service on behalf of the payer (the bank's customer and principal) the final result is to effect the transfer of funds to the payee and consequently

[202] See Chorley (1974) *Law of Banking*, London: Sweet & Maxwell, pp.268–269.
[203] *Hockley* v *Goldstein* (1920) 90 LJ KB 111.
[204] *Allied Carpets Group Plc* v *Macfarlane* [2002] EWHC 1155; *Daleri v Ltd* v *Woolworths Plc* [2008] EWHC 2891.
[205] *William Brandt's Sons & Co* v *Dunlop Rubber Co Ltd* [1905] AC 454.
[206] (1979) 609 F 2d 1047.
[207] *Durham Bros.* v *Robertson* [1898] 1 QB 756.

the answer in law with regard to the mandate must be the same, regardless of the method of payment.

In most money transfer orders it is assumed that the payer may revoke the instruction, at least until the payment reaches the payee's bank. This is reinforced by the fact that there appears to be no evidence of any intention to assign amounts to the credit of the payer's bank account to pay off debts as and when they arise. Further, money transfer orders involve a string of operations carried out by different banks acting in a representative capacity. In *Royal Products Ltd* v *Midland Bank Ltd*[208] Webster J expressed the view that money transfers are to be regarded:

> simply as an authority and instruction, from a customer to its bank, to transfer an amount standing to the credit of that customer with that bank to the credit of its account with another bank, that the other bank being impliedly authorised by the customer to accept that credit by virtue of the fact that the customer has a current account with it, no consent to the receipt of the credit being expected from or required of that other bank, by virtue of the same fact. It is, in other words, a banking operation, of a kind which is often carried out internally, that is to say, within the same bank or between two branches of the same bank and which, at least from the point of view of the customer, is no different in nature or quality when, as in the present case, it is carried out between different banks.

The House of Lords in *R* v *Preddy*[209] confirmed the fact that such operations do not amount to an assignment of a debt. The defendants, in that case, were charged with obtaining, or attempting to obtain, mortgage advances from lending institutions by deception contrary to s.15(1) of the Theft Act 1968. In making their applications the defendants had deliberately given false information to the lending institutions. Where the applications were approved, the advances were paid, not in cash, but by CHAPS electronic fund transfers from the bank account of the lending institution to the account of the defendant, or his solicitor.[210] The significant question before the House of Lords was whether under this process the defendant had obtained 'property belonging to another' under s.15(1) of the Theft Act 1968 and the Lords, reversing the Court of Appeal, held that it did not amount to obtaining 'property belonging to another'. Lord Goff distinguished the situation where the account of the lending institution was in credit and the situation where the lender's account was overdrawn. Where the lending institution's account was in credit, the credit balance standing in the account represented property, i.e. a chose in action, of the lender.[211] Where funds were 'transferred' to the account of the defendant, or his solicitor, that chose in action was reduced, or extinguished, and the defendant's, or his solicitor's, chose in action against his own bank was increased. However, Lord Goff emphasised that the defendant's, or his solicitor's, chose in action against his own bank had never belonged to the lender: it was a newly created proprietary right distinct from the lender's chose in action against its own bank. Where the

---

[208] [1981] 2 Lloyd's Rep 194.

[209] [1996] AC 815.

[210] Although some transfers were made by telegraphic transfer the House of Lords held, for the purposes of the case, that no distinction need be drawn between the CHAPS system and telegraphic transfers ([1996] AC 815 at 833D). In some cases the payments were made by cheque and although the Lords were not required to consider such payments Lord Goff did make some statements, *obiter*, regarding payments by cheque (at 835–837).

[211] Applying the general principles of banking law that the relationship between the bank and its customer is that of debtor and creditor: *Foley* v *Hill* (1848) 2 HL Cas. 28.

lender's account was overdrawn, Lord Goff recognised that it might have been argued that it was the bank's property, and not the lender's property, which had been 'obtained' by the defendant, but he concluded that as a result of the transfer the defendant, or his solicitor, would be given a new chose of action against his own bank; a chose in action, which had never belonged to the lender's bank. However, where the account of the defendant, or his solicitor, is overdrawn, he would not acquire a chose in action against his own bank; rather the bank's chose in action against him is reduced.

The significance of *R v Preddy* goes beyond the field of criminal law and confirms that it is a contradiction of terms to talk about 'transfer' of funds in a fund transfer operation. Thus, for example, cash (note and coins) is not transferred from one account to another and the debt owed to the payer by his bank, assuming his account is in credit, is not assigned to the payee.[212] The case highlights the distinction between the transfer of property rights and the extinction and creation of property rights. Lord Jauncey in *Preddy* said:

> . . . in applying these words [belonging to another] to circumstances such as the present there falls to be drawn a crucial distinction between the creation and extinction of rights on the one hand and the transfer of rights on the other. It is only in the latter situation that the words apply.

Is a money transfer a trust?

Where the payer sends a fund transfer instruction to the paying bank, it may be important, and necessary, to determine whether the fund transfer order gives the payee any rights over the funds in the payee's account before the funds are actually effected. For example, if the payer becomes insolvent before the funds are transferred, the payee will be in a better position if the fund transfer gives him rights over the funds in the payer's account in advance of the unsecured creditors. Legal title remains in the bank until the funds are transferred. Although it is not necessary to use the word 'trust'[213] to create a trust of the funds to be transferred, there must be an intention to create a trust. The placing of money in a separate account by a bank, or the setting aside of money for a specific purpose in a bank account, does not constitute a trust in favour of the intended payee.[214] In *Abou-Rahmah v Abacha*[215] the argument that a fund transfer instruction effected by SWIFT created a purpose trust when there were discrepancies between the name of the payee in the transfer and the account to which the funds were credited was rejected. These cases are distinct from *Barclays Bank Ltd v Quistclose Investments Ltd*[216] and *Re Kayford Ltd*[217] where the courts held that if money is placed in a separate account by the bank for the specific purpose of being returned to the creditor, if the purpose for which it is lent is not satisfied, then the money is held on trust for the creditor.[218] Thus, in *Re Kayford Ltd*[219] the instruction given by the account holder (customer),

---

[212] *Libyan Arab Foreign Bank v Bankers Trust Co* [1988] 1 Lloyd's Rep 259.
[213] *Re Kayford Ltd (In Liquidation)* [1975] 1 All ER 604 at 607.
[214] *Lister and Co v Stubbs* (1890) 45 ChD 1; *Moseley v Cressey's Co* (1865) LR 1 Eq 405.
[215] [2007] 1 Lloyd's Rep 115.
[216] [1970] AC 567.
[217] [1975] 1 WLR 279.
[218] See also: *Re Nanwa Gold Mines Ltd* [1955] 1 WLR 1080.
[219] [1975] 1 All ER 604.

to the bank was to create a 'Customer's Trust Deposit Account' and to protect the customers, whose money was paid into the account, in the event of the insolvency of the account holder. That is not normally the type of intention evinced in an ordinary fund transfer instruction.

Countermand of payment and time of payment

The problem

An examination of the legal contractual relationships between the parties to a money transfer does not always provide an answer to the question of when payment is complete. At one level it may be argued that payment is complete when it is no longer capable of revocation, or countermand, but it could equally be argued that the payment is no longer capable of revocation, or countermand, when it is executed (complete) and payment received by the payee or his agent; thereby producing a circuitous debate which fails to answer the question. The question therefore has to be answered by establishing a single test for determining the moment when the payee or his agent receives funds, although the answer will be different depending on the nature and system of money transfer involved. Thus, the moment when a SWIFT transfer is executed and complete will differ from when a BACS payment is executed and complete. The solution, therefore, will depend on the question of when a payment becomes irreversible between the payer and payee's respective agents even if the payee does not, at that stage, have the funds made available to him. In some cases the master agreement between the banks may provide a solution to the question by providing when the payment becomes irreversible. The importance of the role played by the rules of the payment transfer system has been reinforced by the Directive on Settlement Finality in Payment and Securities Settlement Systems[220] which provides that a transfer order may not be revoked by a participant in a system covered by the Directive, or by a third party, from the moment defined by the rules of that system.[221] The payment could therefore be regarded as complete and payment made when the payment becomes irreversible under the master agreement. In situations where the master agreement does not provide a solution, the principles of common law may provide one.

Further, the time of payment may depend on the number of parties involved in the transaction and payment process, and the role assumed by each party. At the simplest level the payment may involve an inhouse transfer where the payer and payee maintain accounts with the same branch of the bank. On the other hand the transaction may be a payment overseas involving the payer, the payer's bank, the correspondent or intermediary bank, the payee's bank and the payee. Other parties may also be involved, for example a transmission network such as SWIFT. It is possible that as the payment instruction proceeds through the chain of

---

[220] [1998] OJ L166/45 (as amended by Directive 2009/44/ EC and Directive 2010/78/EU). The Directive has been implemented in the UK by the Financial Markets and Insolvency (Settlement Finality) Regulations 1999, SI 1999/2979 (amended by the Financial Markets and Insolvency (Settlement Finality) (Amendment) Regulations 2006, SI 2006/50; Financial Markets and Insolvency (Settlement Finality) (Amendment) Regulations 2007, SI 2007/832; and Financial Markets and Insolvency (Settlement Finality) (Amendment) Regulations 2009, SI 2009/1972.

[221] Directive on Settlement Finality in Payment and Securities Settlement Services, Art. 5, [1998] OJ L166/45 (as amended by Directive 2009/44/EC and Directive 2010/78/EU).

parties that payment has been executed by some parties and therefore becomes irreversible in their hands but yet remains executory as far as other parties are concerned.[222] Whether the payment is irreversible as far as the payee is concerned will depend on the nature of the payment system used and the question remains whether the payer can countermand the instruction even though the payee has not received access to the funds or had them credited to his account, and yet some of the banks have executed and completed their obligation.

The answer to these issues may also depend on practical considerations, for example the question of the payee bank's right to receive payment. Thus, for example, where the payer's bank purports to reverse a payment, or stop payment, the payee may argue that payment is complete immediately on his bank (payee bank) receiving payment even though his account is not yet credited with the payment with the result that payment becomes irreversible even though the payee has not received express notification of the credit. The question here is the issue of the payee bank's authority to receive payment, including the argument that the payee implicitly gives his bank authority to receive payment when he opens an account.[223] Potentially, and depending on the system of transfer of funds used, there are a number of different points when a money transfer may arguably be complete namely:

- When the payment instruction is transmitted to the payer's bank; or
- When the payment reaches the payee's bank or his agent; or
- When the payee's bank sets in motion the machinery for crediting the payee's account; or
- The time when the payee's account is credited; or
- The time when the payee is notified of the receipt of the funds; or
- When the payment is credited to the payee's account, or otherwise made available to him under an express or implied agreement.

The common law cases in this area can be divided into two groups: (i) cases dealing with countermand or reversal of payment; and (ii) cases concerning completion of payment. Although the PSR 2009 may have an impact in both these areas the regulations are not always applicable and as the regulations have already been discussed the common law rules will be examined.

Countermand of payment

Under the rules of agency law, the paying bank acts on the customer's mandate when carrying out any payment instruction on behalf of the customer. The general principle is that the customer, as principal, may revoke the payment instruction at any time prior to the payment being executed, by the paying bank, the agent.[224] However, a principal may not revoke his agent's authority after the agent has commenced performance of the mandate and incurred liabilities for which the principal must indemnify the bank, the agent.[225] Professor Cranston summarised the principles applicable, in the absence of an express agreement, to the countermand of payment instructions in a fund transfer as follows:

[222] *Libyan Arab Foreign Bank* v *Bankers Trust Co* [1988] 1 Lloyd's Rep 259.
[223] See Webster J, in *Royal Products Ltd* v *Midland Bank Ltd* [1981] 2 Lloyd's Rep 194.
[224] *Campanari* v *Woodburn* (1854) 15 CB 400.
[225] *Warlow* v *Harrison* (1859) 1 E & E 309.

a customer who instructs its bank to hold funds to the disposal of a third party can countermand at least until the time when the funds have been transferred or credit given to the transferee . . .[226] a customer who instructs its bank to transfer funds to a third party cannot revoke from the moment the bank incurs a commitment to the third party . . .[227] A customer who instructs its bank to pay another bank to the order of a third party cannot revoke once the payee bank has acted on the instructions. This may be a point prior to crediting the payee's account.[228]

In all cases, it is irrelevant, from the point of view of revocation, whether the third party has been informed.

However, attempts to countermand money transfer instructions may arise in different circumstances. In *Rekstin v Severo Sibirsko Gosundarstvennoe Akcionernoe Obschestvo Komseverputj*[229] a customer instructed his bank to transfer the credit balance on his account to another customer who maintained an account with the same bank. After the bank had made the necessary ledger entries recording the transfer, but before the payee was notified the credit, a judgment creditor served a garnishee order nisi (now known as an interim third party debt order) attaching the payer's account. The Court of Appeal held that at the time the order nisi was served the payer did not owe any debt to the payee and there was nothing to indicate that the payee had anticipated the payment. Consequently, there was nothing to indicate an assent by the payee, express or implied to the transfer of the payment, and the payee bank could not be regarded as having the authority to hold the amount as a debt accrued to the payee. The garnishee order nisi therefore attached to the amount of the credit balance.

This *Rekstin* case, however, should be narrowly construed and in modern bank transfers the payee's bank is likely to be treated as having the implied authority to credit the payee's account from the circumstances preceding the execution of the money transfer. In *Singer v Yokohama Specie Bank Ltd*[230] the claimant was owed approximately $557,561, by the Tokyo office of the YS Bank, and they instructed the amount be remitted to him in the USA. The Tokyo office instructed its agent bank in New York to make the amount available to the claimant. The agent bank notified the claimant and requested he obtain the necessary Treasury authorisation for payment of the funds. Before this was obtained the agent bank was put into liquidation by the Alien Property Custodian and the question before the Supreme Court of New York was whether the amount involved had accrued to the claimant at the time the agent bank was placed in liquidation. Consequently, the question was whether the payee's bank was liable to the payee and whether and when, if at all, payment had been completed. The court concluded that a mere representation that funds were held at the payee's disposal was inconclusive, even if it was supported by permission to draw against the funds. The Appellate Division confirmed this decision although it was overruled, on this point, by the New York Court of Appeals, which held that notification of the transfer to the claimant 'served to create an foreseeable legal obligation by the New York agency to make such payment'. This decision was followed by the New York Supreme Court in *Guaranty Trust Co of New York v Lyon*[231] where, on similar facts (except that the funds were remitted to the payee at the order of a third party) the court held that the New York agency of the Japanese bank,

---

[226] *Gibson v Minet* (1824) 130 ER 206.
[227] *Warlow v Harrison* (1859) 1 E & E 309.
[228] *Astro amo Compania Naviera SA v Elf Union SA, The Zopraphia M* [1976] 2 Lloyd's Rep 382.
[229] [1933] 1 KB 47.
[230] 47 NYS 2d 881 (NY Sup. Ct., 1944).
[231] 124 NYS 2d 680 (NY Sup. Ct., 1953).

acting as the recipient of funds transferred from Tokyo, obtained the amount on behalf of the payee and when the payee was informed of the amount standing to his credit, the funds were available to him and payment regarded as irreversible.

As a result of these decisions it would appear that the transfer of the amount involved to the payee's bank, acting as the payee's agent, would equate to the receipt of the funds by the payee himself. This is supported by the decision in *Manufacturas International Ltd* v *Manufacturers Hanover Trust Co*[232] where the court concluded that a fund transfer is complete at the moment the receiving bank receives the credit message and not when the payee acquires the funds. This basic principle is supported by the rules of agency law under which the principal will be deemed to have received funds when they are placed in the hands of an authorised agent. However, the difficulty that arises is that it is not always clear at which point in time the payee's bank will make the decision to accept the amount on the payee's behalf. The significance of determining the moment at which payment accrues to the payee was demonstrated in *Momm* v *Barclays Bank International Limited*[233] where the court concluded that:

> The issue is whether or not a completed payment had been made by the defendants to the [claimants] on June 26. If the answer is 'Yes', it is not contested that the [claimants] have a good cause of action. If there were no authorities on this point, I think that the reaction, both of a lawyer and a banker, would be to answer this question in the affirmative. I think both would say two things. First, that in such circumstances a payment has been made if the payee's account is credited with the payment at the close of business on the value date, at any rate if it was credited intentionally and in good faith and not by error or fraud. Secondly, I think they would say that if the claimant requires to be made on a certain day by debiting a [payer] customer's account and crediting a payee customer's account, then the position at the end of that day in fact and in law must be that this has either happened or not happened, that position cannot be left in the air. In my view both these propositions are correct in law.

Kerr J in giving judgment distinguished the *Rekstin* case as having been decided on special facts. Kerr J stressed that it was significant in *Rekstin* that the payee knew nothing of the proposed transfer, that there was no underlying transaction between the payer and payee and that the payee had therefore never assented to his account being credited with the funds that were purportedly transferred to him. In contrast, in *Momm*, the claimant had specifically designated that payment of sums due under the contract should be made to the credit of his account held with the defendant bank. The bank, therefore, in *Momm*, clearly had the claimant's authority to accept the transfer of funds for him. Kerr J emphasised that the question of whether payment had been completed on a particular date should be assessed at the end of the 'value date', which is the date on which the funds are made available to the payee. Although the end of the 'value date' reflects banking practice in respect of inhouse transfers, nevertheless the bank may be allowed to reverse erroneous entries made during the course of the banking day. In *Tayeb* v *HSBC Bank Plc*,[234] Coleman J stressed that *Momm* is not authority for the proposition that once the account has been credited on the value date with the incoming transfer, the entry can be reversed at any time up to the end of that business day.

Further litigation, in the USA, following the collapse of the Herstatt Bank resulted in a discussion of the question of the claimant's completion in respect of the CHIPS payment.

---

[232] 79 F Supp. 180 (EDNY, 1992).
[233] [1977] QB 790.
[234] [2004] EWHC 1529.

In *Delbrueck & Co v Manufacturers Hanover Trust Co*[235] the claimant, a German bank, which maintained an account with the defendant bank in the USA, entered into exchange contracts with the Herstatt Bank under which approximately $12.5 million was payable by the claimant to Herstatt Bank on 26 June. On 25 June, the claimant sent a telex message to the defendant bank requesting it to credit Herstatt Bank's account with the Chase Manhattan Bank. At 10.30am on 26 June (at Eastern standard time prevailing in New York), Herstatt Bank was closed down by the German Reserve Bank. At 11.40am approximately the defendant bank transferred to Chase Manhattan the amount of $12.5 million, using the US CHIPS system. Within the next 30 minutes the claimant telephoned the defendant bank in order to stop this payment and immediately confirmed the countermand by telex. At 9.00pm the same day, Herstatt Bank's account with Chase Manhattan was formally credited with the amount. The claimant, in an action for negligence, claimed that the defendant bank committed a breach of its duty of care when it failed to act on the countermand, given to it at 11.40am, during business hours on 26 June. Moore J examined the technology involved in the CHIPS's transfer and concluded that a transfer executed through this network invariably reaches the payee's bank almost immediately (assuming there are no correspondent banks) the payment mandate is released or executed by the computer terminal of the payer's bank. It was the understanding of all the banks participating in the CHIPS system that the payee may draw on funds transferred by CHIPS, as soon as the payee bank received the electronic message. The learned judge concluded that the transfer of funds to the credit of the Herstatt Bank's account was complete immediately the defendant bank effected payment. The fact that the credit entry was not made to the credit of Herstatt Bank's account until 9.00pm on 26 June was merely an internal administrative matter and therefore irrelevant. Moore J observed:

> Based on the nature of the CHIPS system, and the fact that the member banks viewed the transactions as irrevocable . . . we hold that the CHIPS transfers were irrevocable when made.

The defendant bank had, therefore, not acted negligently when it failed to revoke the transfer of the funds to Chase Manhattan. Moore J also held that a money transfer executed by means of CHIPS could not be revoked, stopped or countermand once transmission, by an electronic message executed on the 'value date', was set in motion.

Although the decisions in *Momm* and *Delbrueck* appear to be inconsistent the variance can be explained as arising from the different methods of payment. In *Momm*, Kerr J based his decision on the finding that the method of payment employed to execute an inhouse transfer of funds made provision for a reversal of entries on the day of the execution.[236] In contrast, Moore J had regard to banking practice in respect of CHIPS transfers, which precludes revocation once the transfer is 'released' by the computer terminal of the payer's bank. Banking practice and the rules of the system through which payment is facilitated will govern the question of countermand and completion of payment. This view received further support in *Tayeb v HSBC Plc*[237] where Coleman J concluded that the *Momm* case had no application to payments made by CHAPS Sterling transfers, which involve same-day value and also a real-time transfer of funds. This view is consistent with payments made through the CHIPS network in *Delbrueck*.

---

[235] 609 F 2D. 1047 (2nd Cir., 1979).

[236] This part of the judgment was highlighted by Lord Penrose in *Sutherland v Royal Bank of Scotland Plc* [1997] 6 Bank LR 132.

[237] [2004] EWHC 1529.

In *Royal Products Ltd* v *Midland Bank Ltd*[238] Webster J confirmed the importance of banking practice in fund transfer cases when he concluded that three events had to take place before payment was complete, namely:

1 The recipient bank had to be placed in a position where it was entitled to draw on the funds made available for transmission to the claimant's account.
2 The recipient bank had to be informed that the funds were to be made available to the claimants.
3 The transfer was complete before the claimants, as payees, were notified that the funds had been credited to their account.

As the payer and payee in *Royal Products* was one and the same person it can clearly be implied that the bank had its customer's implied authority to receive the credit on behalf of its customer. However, it will not always be assumed that the bank has its customer's implied authority to receive funds from a third party on the customer's behalf, and for the credit of his account, merely because the bank holds an account for the customer. In *Customs and Excise Commissioners* v *National Westminster Bank Plc*[239] the claimants, the Customs and Excise authorities, were instructed by the taxpayer, Car Disposals Ltd (CDL), to pay a refund of tax duty due to them to their solicitors' account because of difficulties the taxpayer was experiencing with its bank. The Customs and Excise authorities, by error, paid the amount of the overpaid tax into the taxpayer's bank account with the National Westminster Bank. On discovering the error CDL complained to Customs and Excise who immediately paid a second amount to the taxpayer's solicitor and sought to recover the amount erroneously paid into the taxpayer's account, from the National Westminster, who refused. Customs and Excise commenced proceedings. National Westminster Bank claimed the payment had been made for good consideration, which was a defence to an action for recovery of amounts paid by mistake. The bank argued that it was authorised to accept payment on behalf of CDL and that the payment duly discharged the debt owed by Customs and Excise to CDL but Customs and Excise argued that a payment made in a manner contrary to CDL's instructions could not discharge the debt due from the revenue. Judge Rich QC held that mistaken payment to CDL's bank, for the credit of CDL's account, did not discharge the debt owed to CDL. An unsolicited payment to a creditor's bank account did not constitute payment of a debt unless it was accepted as such, and there was no indication of the payment being accepted by CDL. The judge then examined the decision in *Royal Products*[240] and accepted that a bank was impliedly authorised by its customer to accept a credit 'by virtue of the fact that the customer had a current account with it'.

Judge Rich QC observed that this was in the context of an instruction to a bank of which the claimant was a customer, to transfer funds to another bank, of which he is also the customer. This rule did not apply when the credit came from a third party who was not a customer of that bank. He, therefore, concluded that there was no general rule to the effect that National Westminster was, merely by virtue of holding an account for CDL, authorised to receive payment from Customs and Excise (a third party creditor) on CDL's behalf so as to discharge its debt to CDL. This view was confirmed in *PT Berlian Laju Tanker TBK* v *Nuse Shipping Ltd*[241] where Clarke J observed:

[238] [1981] 2 Lloyd's Rep 194.
[239] [2003] 1 All ER (Comm) 327.
[240] [1981] 2 Lloyd's Rep 194.
[241] [2008] EWHC 1330.

Payment under a contract cannot be made without the consent of the creditor. Even if payment is to be in cash, i.e. legal tender, the creditor may not necessarily accept it. If payment is made through the banking system, a bank may have authority to receive payment; but it will not be able to accept payment in discharge of the debt without the authority of the creditor.

Following the *Momm*, *Delbrueck* and *Royal Products* cases it is established that a money transfer is complete when the funds are made available to the payee's bank and intentionally accepted by it, on the payee's behalf. This view is supported by *Libyan Arab Foreign Bank* v *Manufacturers Hanover Trust Co (No 2)*[242] in respect of a transfer instructed by the customer, between two accounts maintained with two different branches of the same bank. The court, therefore, concluded that the transfer was complete when the transferring branch credited the recipient branch's account with it and the receiving branch effected a matching 'intentional and *bona fide*' credit entry to the payee's account. Hence the fund transfer was complete, and irreversible, when the funds were credited to the payee's account, although his bank may not have notified him of the credit.

Payment out of time

The question of whether payment is made out of time generally arises in contracts where payment is of the essence to the contract and payment out of time may allow the creditor to exercise his rights under a forfeiture clause. This type of situation may arise in respect of hire payments due, for example under a charter agreement, whereby ship owners may be allowed to withdraw a vessel on the grounds that rental due from the charterer was made out of time. Although the basic question is one of the underlying contract between the hirer (payer) and ship owner (payee), in banking terms the question is when is payment made, and therefore complete, where payment is made through the intermediary of a bank and amounts transferred between bank accounts. The basic rule was established in *The Brimnes*[243] where the Court of Appeal held that in order to determine whether an amount due under a charter party was paid on time, an analogy had to be drawn with cases concerning the question of when payment was complete if made in cash. Edmund-Davies LJ concluded:

> The owners' contention, however, that the tendering of the commercial equivalent of cash would suffice found favour with Brandon J [the trial judge]. In particular, he concluded that any transfer of funds [to the payee's bank] for the credit of the owners' account so as to give them the unconditional right to the immediate use of funds transferred was good payment. In my judgment, that was clearly right.

Megaw LJ was in support of this view when he said that payment by means of a credit entry was complete when the creditor was bound to treat it as equivalent of cash, in the sense that he was able to draw on the balance accrued.

Where the underlying contract between the payer and payee contains some express or implied condition that must be satisfied before the payee can access the funds, then that condition must be satisfied. For example, where the underlying contract requires not only for the payee's account to be credited with cleared funds, but also to be notified of that fact, then that condition must be satisfied.[244] In other cases the position may not always be so clear cut.

---

[242] [1989] 1 Lloyd's Rep 608 at 631–632.
[243] *Tenax Steamship Co Ltd* v *Brimnes (Owners of)*, *The Brimnes*, [1975] 1 QB 929.
[244] *Rick Dees Ltd* v *Larsen* [2007] 3 NZLR 577.

Thus, in *Mardorf Peach & Co Ltd v Attica Sea Carriers Corporation of Liberia, The Laconia*[245] the payee's bank received a telex message requiring it to credit the ship owners' account with the amount due under a charterparty. The telex was received late and after the date agreed under the charterparty, but shortly before the instruction was given by the ship owner to refuse the late payment. The tender was accepted by the owners' bank without objection and the bank began steps to credit the ship owners' account, but on receiving the instruction to reject the payment, it refunded the amount to the payer's bank before the actual entry was complete. The charterers argued that the late payment had been waived by the acceptance of the late tender of payment by the owners' agents, the payee's (beneficiary's) bank. The House of Lords, giving judgment for the ship owners, held that the transfer had not been completed before the amount was refunded since the payee's bank had not manifested a conscious decision to accept payment. The internal steps taken by the payee bank to process the payment were purely provisional and procedural, and therefore the bank was entitled to reject the payment. The case is authority for the point that payment as between the payer and payee will only be complete where the payee's bank has the payee's actual or apparent authority both to receive and accept the transfer of funds on the payee's behalf.

Their Lordships held that the ship owners' bank had only limited authority to receive payment and that did not extend to the acceptance of late payments on behalf of the ship owners.

Whether it could be argued by the payer that the payee bank has apparent authority to accept, what is effectively a late payment, will depend on the circumstances and the appearance given by the payee bank. To succeed with this argument the payer would have to establish that he relied on the bank's appearance of authority which he will be unable to do if knows, or ought reasonably to have known, of the bank's limited authority to received funds transfers.

In *Mardorf Peach*, Lord Salmon observed that the ship owners could have been deemed to accept payment if their bank had kept it for an unreasonable time and in *TSB Bank of Scotland Plc v Welwyn Hatfield District Council and Council of the London Borough of Brent*[246] Hobhouse J held that a payee would be deemed to have accepted an unauthorised payment made into this account where he dealt with the transferred funds as his own. In that case the learned judge held that, despite initial protests, the retention and use of the money for three weeks and its eventual return without interest amounted to acceptance of the tender by the payee local authority, and therefore payment. By contrast, in *HMV Fields Properties Ltd v Bracken Self Selection Fabrics Ltd*[247] a tenant continued to pay rent through the bank giro system for several weeks after being served with a notice of forfeiture for breach of a covenant in the lease. When the payments came to the landlord's attention they were returned to the tenant using the giro system. The court held that the landlord was entitled to exercise the forfeiture clause and that 'acceptance' of money was a question of fact. Despite the landlord's initial delay of several weeks before returning the rent money, there had been no acceptance. The payee had no knowledge of the payment being made into the account, whereas in the *Welwyn Hatfield* case the payee was aware of the payment.

A giro transfer is considered conditional, and therefore not an effective payment, where it fails to provide the payee with the same availability as cash. In *A/S Awilco of Oslo v Fulvia SpA*

---

[245] [1976] QB 835.
[246] [1993] Bank LR 267.
[247] 1991 SLT 31.

di Navigazione of Cagliari, The Chikuma[248] Lord Bridge held that payment in the context of money transfers encompassed settlement not only by legal tender but also by means of final credit entries. Therefore, payment is effected when the payee has the unconditional use of the amount settled by means of the ledger entry. Although payment by means of legal tender is not expected in cases such as these, the payee is, however, entitled to expect the full equivalent, and transferred funds that could not yet be used for investment purposes, for example, by earning interest on the funds, were not the equivalent of cash. Lord Bridge continued:

> The book entry made by the owners' bank on January 27 in the owners' account was clearly not the equivalent of cash, nor was there any reason why the owners should have been prepared to treat it as the equivalent of cash. It could not be used to earn interest, e.g., by the immediate transfer of a deposit account. It could only be drawn subject to a (probable) liability to pay interest. In substance it was the equivalent of an overdraft facility which the bank was bound to make available.

On this basis, the amount remitted could not be regarded as the equivalent to cash as the ship owners, as payees, did not have the unconditional use of it on the due date.

Lord Bridge's judgment has been criticised on the ground that the case should have been regarded as governed by English Law under which the funds would have accrued to the ship owners unconditionally when credited to their account, regardless of the stipulated 'value date'. However, the criticism appears to be unfounded because even if the case had been decided on the basis of English Law, the payment would not have been considered as equivalent to cash. The reason is that English banks would regard the stipulation of a 'value date', in money transfer orders, as an indication that the payee's account ought not to be credited before that date, i.e. 26 January, which would have rendered the payment out of time.

The cases emphasise the need to make funds available to the payee by the stipulated date, but funds are only so available if the payee can utilise them without any restrictions as if they constituted amounts in cash.

Distinction between countermand of payment and completion of payment

The cases concerning countermand of payment and completion of payment emphasise distinct stages of the payment process. In the countermand situation the courts have established that that there is no room for countermand of payment, or reversal of the payment mandate, once the funds are made available to the payee's bank and the bank has agreed, either expressly or impliedly, to receive payment for the payee. Banking practice and the payment system, or network, rules are determining factors in this situation. The question of completion of payment will be governed by the underlying contract of sale and the agreement between the parties. The issue is when is payment equivalent to legal tender, or cash, between the payer and payee. The question therefore is when does the payment become unconditional to the credit of the payee. The Supreme Court needs an opportunity to pronounce on this issue.

Bank confidentiality and electronic fund transfers

The data or computer department of the customer's bank has access to a wide range of information recorded about each customer. Additionally, computer centres, for example BACS and SWIFT, acquire a great deal of information about the customers of participating banks.

---

[248] [1980] 2 Lloyd's Rep 409.

This will be through information directly obtained from customers themselves, for example, in the case of certain BACS transactions, or from data transmitted by the banks. While the bank owes a duty of confidentiality to the customer under the banking contract, information or data acquired about an individual is also protected under the Data Protection Act 1998 (DPA 1998) which was passed to implement EC Directive 95/46 on the Protection of Individuals with regard to the Processing of Personal Data and on the Free Movement of Such Data.[249] The DPA 1998 repeals and replaces the Data Protection Act 1984, although the two enactments have a number of similar features, for example the Data Protection Commissioner under the DPA 1998 replaces the Data Protection Registrar. The DPA 1998 itself has been amended by the Freedom of Information Act 2000, so that the Data Protection Commissioner is now known as the Information Commissioner.[250] The Act is intended to protect the storage and handling of 'personal data' which is defined under s.1(1) of the DPA 1998 as data relating to a living individual who can be identified from that data, or from that data and other information in the possession of the data controller. The definition of 'personal data' was examined in *Durant* v *Financial Services Authority*[251] where the Court of Appeal established the following principles:

- The concept of 'personal data' in the DPA 1998 should be given a narrow meaning and therefore does not include all information retrieved from a search against an individual's name or unique identifier.
- The mere mention of an individual in a document held by a data controller does not mean that the document contains personal data in relation to that individual.
- Whether the information is capable of constituting personal data will depend on where it falls in a continuum of relevance or proximity to the data subject.
- In answering that question it is necessary to consider whether the information is biographical in a significant sense, and whether it has the putative data subject as its focus.
- That personal data is information that affects the privacy of the data subject.

More recently, in *Common Services Agency* v *Scottish Information Commissioner*[252] the House of Lords held that information derived from 'personal data' may not qualify as such if steps have been taken to anonymise it fully.

The definition of 'data' goes beyond information held in computerised databases and includes information 'recorded as part of a relevant filing system or with the intention that it should form part of a relevant filing system'.[253] A relevant filing system is defined as:

> any set of information relating to individuals to the extent that, although the information is not processed by means of equipment operating automatically in response to instructions given for that purpose, the set is structured, either by reference to individuals or by reference to criteria relating to individuals, in such a way that specific relating to a particular individual is readily accessible.[254]

---

[249] [1995] OJ L281/31.

[250] DPA 1998, s.6(1) as substituted by the Freedom of Information Act 2000, s.18(4), schedule 2, Part 1 para. 13(1),(2).

[251] [2004] FSR 28.

[252] [2008] 4 All ER 851.

[253] Data Protection Act 1998, s.1(1)(c).

[254] Data Protection Act 1998, s.1(1).

Documents kept in a box, for example, without any form of filing or structure are not within the scope of a 'relevant filing system' and do not constitute 'data' even if they can be easily scanned and turned into digital information.[255] The question whether information is data within the meaning of the DPA 1998 is to be determined at the time when the data subject makes his request to the data controller as to whether, and what, information is held on him.[256]

A 'data controller' is defined as someone who, either alone or with others, determines the purposes for which, and the manner in which, any personal data are, or are to be processed, and hence the bank and its computer centre is a 'data controller'.[257] By contrast, a 'data processor' is someone (other than an employee of the data controller) who processes the data on behalf of the data controller.[258] It would appear that BACS, which merely processes data and does not determine the purpose for which it is processed, would appear to fall within this definition. Liability for failing to register with the Information Commissioner, and for failing to comply with the Data Protection Principles, rests on the data controller and the data processor.[259]

The DPA 1998 reinforces the bank's duty of confidentiality in a number of ways and complements the common law rules. The conditions for the fair and lawful processing of personal data, as set out in schedule 2 to the DPA 1998, are similar to the qualifications to bank confidentiality, for example the disclosure may be sanctioned under the DPA 1998 by a court order or legislation, or be may justified in the public interest or in the interest of the data controller or may be allowed where it has been consented to by the data subject.[260] The duty of confidentiality is, therefore, reinforced in a number ways:

1 Personal data may be treated as processed fairly,[261] and in accordance with the first Data Protection Principle, only where disclosure of the personal data does not infringe the disclosure requirements contained in schedules 2 and 3 to the DPA 1998.

2 Any disclosure of personal data must be in conformity with the fifth Data Protection Principle, namely that the information must be obtained for specific purposes and is used only in a way compatible with those purposes, personal data must be adequate, relevant and not excessive in relation to the purpose for which the is processed, the personal data must be accurate and, where necessary, kept up to date; and personal data must not be kept longer than is necessary for the specified purpose or purposes for which it is required.

3 Any disclosure of personal data must take account of the rights of the data subject to object to processing likely to cause damage or distress and the right of the data subject to have inaccurate personal data relating to him rectified, blocked, erased or destroyed and have third parties to whom the inaccurate data has been communicated notified of the rectification, blocking, erasure or destruction.

---

[255] *Smith v Lloyds TSB Bank Plc* [2005] EWHC 246 (Ch).
[256] *Smith v Lloyds TSB Bank Plc* [2005] EWHC 246 (Ch).
[257] Data Protection Act 1998, s.1(1).
[258] Data Protection Act 1998, s.4(1).
[259] Data Protection Act 1998, ss.1(1), 17(1) and 21(1).
[260] Data Protection Act 1998, schedule 2, paras 1, 3, 5 and 6(1). See also s.55(2)(a) which provides that s.55(1) does not apply to a person who shows that the obtaining, disclosing or procuring was (i) necessary for the purpose of preventing or detecting crime, or (ii) was required by or under any enactment, by any rule of law, or by the order of a court.
[261] Data Protection Act 1998, s.4(4).

4 Appropriate security measures must be taken, in accordance with the sixth Data Protection Principle, to prevent unauthorised or unlawful processing and against accidental loss, destruction or damage to personal data and the data controller is required to ensure that any data processor employed by him has similar effective security measure in place.

5 The data processor, or third party, commits an offence if he knowingly or recklessly obtains, procures or discloses personal data without the consent of the data controller.[262] It is also an offence to sell personal data obtained or data obtained contrary to s.55(1).

Conclusion

The development of automated fund transfer systems has been a natural consequence of advances in telecommunication and the pace of development in the business world. The systems have supported efficiency in the banking sector, and led to innovation and faster means of payment, but they have also posed challenges for the banking industry and the law. This chapter has examined the development of automated fund transfer systems and the ensuing developments in the law. However, the ease and speed with which payments can be made across international boundaries has raised its own problems and encouraged international crime, for example the global nature of the money laundering industry.

Further reading

➤ Hooley, R. (1997) Direct Debits and Set-off – the Tiger Roars!, 56(3) *Cambridge Law Journal*, 500–503.
This article examines whether unliquidated counterclaims for damages could be set off in equity against liquidated claims in debt resulting from cancelled direct debits.

➤ Tettenborn, A. (1997) Pay now, Sue Later – Direct Debits, Set-Off and Commercial Practice, 113 *Law Quarterly Review*, 374.
This article examines whether a set-off of counterclaim for repudiatory breach of contract can be pleaded in an action brought on a cancelled direct debit.

➤ Ellinger, E.P. (2005) Irrevocability of CHAPS Money Transfer, 121 *Law Quarterly Review*, 48.
This article examines the Commercial Court ruling in *Tayeb* v *HSBC Bank Plc* on whether a bank which had received money through CHAPS and had credited the amount received to its customer's account was entitled to transfer the funds back to the remitting bank when suspicions were raised about the background and object of the payment. The article discusses the issue of finality of payment and the effect of payment through CHAPS on a real-time basis. The article further considers the effect of the Criminal Justice Act 1988 ss.93A and 93D and the need to avoid the risk of a constructive trust action.

➤ Vroegop, J. (1990) The time of payment in paper-based and electronic funds transfer systems, *LMCLQ*, 64.

---

[262] Data Protection Act 1998, s.55(1).

15 Plastic money

Introduction

The use of plastic cards, in the UK, has revolutionised the payments industry. The first charge cards were used in the USA and designed to allow businesspeople to charge their expense accounts, for example the Diners Club Card[1] and American Express Card[2] were used by business executives for the payment of expenses relating to business travel and entertainment. The Diners Club Card is still used as an important method of payment by business executives but its use has been overshadowed by the development of the credit card. Other charge cards may be limited, in use, to the payment of a particular commodity or service, for example 'fuel cards' which could only be used for petrol at participating garages, were an issue in *Re Charge Card Services Ltd.*[3] Other cards may only be used in particular stores. The modern charge cards, unlike the original charge cards, are not limited to their usage and may be used at a wide range of authorised dealers. Credit cards, however, have come to overshadow the charge cards.

---

[1] BMO Financial Group acquired the Diners Club North American franchise on 31 December 2009. The agreement gives BMO Financial Group exclusive rights to issue Diners Club Cards to corporate and personal clients in the USA and Canada, https://www.dinersclubcanada.com/home/about/dinersclub/story.

[2] https://www.americanexpress.com/ca/en/content/all-cards/.

[3] [1987] 1 Ch 150.

BANKING LAW IN PRACTICE

Barclaycard, launched in 1966, was the first credit card in the UK. The use of plastic money has increased dramatically and in 2009 there were 162.6 million plastic cards, in issue, in the UK alone and 85 per cent of the adult population held at least one or more plastic cards. Spending on plastic cards, in the UK, in 2009,[4] amounted to approximately £389 billion, and accounted for 66 per cent of all retail spending.[5] Approximately, 97 per cent of all cash withdrawals were made using debit or ATM cards, totalling £171 billion. For 2013, total plastic card spending amounted to £532 billion with 10.9 billion transactions, compared to £501 billion and 10.3 billion, respectively, in 2012.[6]

More recently, the use of plastic cards has been encouraged by the introduction of other benefits, for example, free travel insurance, free membership of a road breakdown service, a points accumulation system which can then be exchanged towards the purchase of holidays, and other products etc. Other types of cards have also become popular, for example, store cards and prepayment cards. The expansion in the usage of cards has considerably reduced the need to carry large amounts of cash.

Plastic cards have developed considerably in their nature and function since they were originally launched and they have moved away from being simple cards only capable of carrying out a single function to intelligent multifunctional cards that are used routinely in banking transactions. Probably the most decisive factor in the development of the card industry was the development of the magnetic strip, which allowed banks to decypher and store customer information. The information held by the magnetic strip could then be read by electronic bank terminals and the customer's identity verified. The front of such cards are normally embossed with the name of the cardholder, his account number and details of his bank and branch. The magnetic strip on the back of the card contains the same information as that embossed on the front, including personal identification numbers and security devices such as a three-digit security number unique to the card. The ability to emboss the necessary details of the cardholder (debtor) and his bank allowed account details to be transferred onto the sales slips under the original manual system of credit cards payments, leaving only the amount of the transaction to be entered manually. The signature of the purchasing customer then authenticated the transaction. The modern plastic card transactions enable the bank's terminal to produce a receipt that is given to the customer to verify the transaction including the date of the transaction, the name of the service provider, and the amount. The transaction is verified not by signature, but by a unique personal identification number (PIN). The smart-card used in modern plastic card transactions has a microprocessor embedded in the card which can process information, for example it can assess whether the PIN entered by the cardholder

---

[4] European Monetary Institution, Payment Services in the European Union, April 1996. In contrast, at the end of 1994, over 19,000 ATMs were in service in the UK. Almost all belonged to three reciprocal agreements (LINK, MINT and FOUR BANKS) which allowed customers of participating banks and building societies access to their accounts through the ATMs of any member institution. During 1994, there were over 1.1 billion ATM withdrawals, totalling about £54 billion; http://www.ecb.int/pub/pdf/othemi/bluebook1996en.pdf.

[5] £263.5 billion on debit cards, and £125.4 billion on credit and charge cards, UK Cards Association.

[6] The UK Cards Association, Card Expediture statistics, December 2013: http://www.ukcardassociation.org.uk/wm_documents/December 2013.

at the terminal matches with the PIN carried on the card. The smartcard can, therefore, both identify the cardholder and authorise the transaction in offline transactions.

Essentially there are five different types of plastic card functions, some of which may be combined in varying ways: credit cards, debit cards, credit and charge cards, ATM cards, pre-paid cards, and all other forms of digital cash. The use of cheque cards has declined as the use of cheques has reduced and although cheques, along with the cheque guarantee card scheme, were due to close in 2011 as a means of payment. However, the Payments Council decided to retain cheques although the UK Cheque Guarantee Card Scheme was discontinued in 2011.[7] However, debit cards are now set to overtake cash in consumer transactions[8] and credit cards remain popular especially as they are a convenient means of paying for Internet purchases or for company expenses. Pre-paid or e-money cards offer an alternative for low-value transactions and where cash is still required it is frequently obtained from an ATM, using an ATM card. A single plastic card will commonly serve several functions, for example many cards operate as cheque cards, ATM cards and debit cards. As the legal consequences associated with the use of the cards will vary depending on the nature of the contract which subsists between the cardholder and card-issuer, and in the case of debit and credit cards, on the provisions of the contract between the supplier of goods and services and his bank, it is intended here to examine the nature of the cards separately.

Payment card fraud continues to be a major issue, particularly where the cardholder is not present, for example where goods and services are purchased by mail order, by telephone or on the Internet. In 2008, card fraud on UK issued credit and debit cards amounted to a total of £609.9 million[9] and losses resulting from fraudulent transactions where the cardholder was not present amounted to around £320.4 million. The terms and conditions of issue and use of plastic cards, therefore, become paramount with regard to who will bear the risk of losses arising from the fraud. However, total losses due to fraud have continued to decline from a high in 2008 and between 2010–2011 such losses amounted to £341 million; the lowest annual total since 2000[10] due to increased security measures by card-issuers and greater precautions by users. The introduction of security numbers printed on the signature strip, on the back of the card, is intended to improve security. These, although not encoded on the magnetic strip are designed to reduce fraud, particularly where the cardholder is not present, by ensuring that the user has the card physically in his possession. The other major development has been the use of a smart chip, which has allowed signatures to be replaced as a means of authentication by the customer and instead uses a secret PIN, which the card reader or bank terminal can verify as matching the data included on the chip.

As the use of plastic cards has increased the terms relating to the use of such cards have become subject to a number of different and, sometimes, overlapping regulation. The main

---

[7] Payments *Council Cheque Guarantee Scheme*, www.paymentscouncil.org.uk/current_projects/cheque_guarantee_card_scheme/.

[8] Personal debit card spending was predicted to overtake the use of cash in value terms in 2010 and in terms of volume of transactions by 2015, Payments Council Annual Review, 2009. In fact, the running of debit card spending (£272 billion) overtook the cumulative amount of cash spent (£269 billion) over the August 2010 Bank holiday; Payments Council, *Britain moves away from cash as debit cards overtake notes and coins for the first time ever*, http://www.paymentscouncil.org.uk/media_centre/press_releases/-/page/1219/. Consumer spending on credit and debit cards combined first took over cash in 2004, APACS.

[9] Financial Fraud Action UK, Fraud: The Facts 2012. The definitive overview of payment industry fraud and measures to prevent it, http://www.theukcardsassociation.org.uk/wm_documents/Fraud_The_Facts_2012.pdf.

[10] Financial Fraud Action UK, Fraud: The Facts 2012. The definitive overview of payment industry fraud and measures to prevent it, http://www.theukcardsassociation.org.uk/wm_documents/Fraud_The_Facts_2012.pdf.

source of statutory regulation is the Consumer Credit Act 1974, as amended by the Consumer Credit Act 2006. In addition card-issuers need to comply with the Unfair Contract Terms Act 1977 and the Unfair Terms in Consumer Contracts Regulations 1999. The Financial Services Act 2012 tasks the Financial Conduct Authority with protecting consumers' interests and the Act inserts a new consumer protection objective which imposes various requirements in respect of consumer education. The banks must also comply with the FCA's conduct of business rules and when acting as a payment service provider, banks must also comply with the requirements of the Payment Services Regulations 2009. The Lending Code outlines the responsibilities of the subscriber banks and building societies in respect of loans and certain types of plastic cards.[11] When acting as an issuer of electronic money banks must comply with the FCA's regulations on electronic money.[12]

We will now examine the main features of the different types of plastic cards.

Debit cards

By contrast to cheque cards,[13] which merely enhanced the acceptability of cheques, debit cards may be used by the cardholder to actually pay for goods or services. Although there are similarities between the use of debit and credit cards, the debit card is used to electronically transfer funds from the customer (purchaser's account) to the merchant or supplier's account, without the need for cash or cheques changing hands. The cardholder pays for the goods or services by presenting the card, in the case of over-the-counter transactions or, in the case of mail-order or telephone transactions, by citing his card number and other security details which are then used to process payment. Debit cards are a more flexible and speedier means of payment then the cheque. In many instances the debit card transaction is processed by a system known as 'Electronic Funds Transfers Point of Sale' (EFT–POS). The concept of the EFT–POS[14] system was described in the Jack report:[15]

> EFT–POS is a payment system designed to allow retail payments to be made by transferring funds electronically from customers' to suppliers' accounts without any need for cash or cheques. With a typical EFT–POS system, a customer passes his card through a reader terminal installed at the supplier's point of sale, and information encoded in the card, and that relating to the transaction, is sent to a central processing point where the validity of the card is authenticated. The customer then authorises the transaction, either by signing a receipt slip produced by the terminal or by inserting his PIN at a special keyboard. Full details of the transaction are then sent back up the line to the central processor, and from there the supplier's account is credited and the customer's account debited automatically.

[11] http://www.lendingstandardsboard.org.uk/thecode.html.

[12] FCA Handbook, Reporting under Electronic Money Regulations, Sup.16.15, http://www.fshandbook.info/FS/html/FCA/SUP/16/15.

[13] The cheque guarantee card scheme was closed in 2011.

[14] Initial discussions on setting up a national EFT–POS system in the UK began in 1974 and a company named EftPos UK Ltd was incorporated in October 1985. EftPos is a clearing company originally set up through APACS. The aim of setting up a national EFT–POS system was never realised and participating institutions found it difficult to agree on the types of system that should be developed. Notwithstanding the failure of the national scheme, EFT–POS flourishes in the UK and in 1987 Barclays Bank launched its 'Connect' card scheme and Lloyds Bank its 'Card-point'. In 1988, Midland Bank, National Westminster Bank and Royal Bank of Scotland launched their scheme, called 'Switch'.

[15] Jack (1989) Banking Services: Law and Practice, Report by the Review Committee Chaired by Professor R.B. Jack, CBE, London Cm. 622, at para. 9.09.

The EFT–POS system described in the Jack Report is an online system where the supplier's computer terminal enabled near instantaneous communication with the bank's central computer, so that details of the transaction taking place between the cardholder and the supplier, as well as details of the cardholder's account with his bank, could be transmitted back and forth from one computer to another while the transaction between the cardholder and the supplier is taking place. With the online system, a cardholder's account is instantly debited the moment the transaction is completed with the merchant or service provider, although even with the online electronic fund transfer systems, the debit from the customer's account may still, sometimes, take up to three days. However, not all EFT–POS systems are online. It is possible for an online electronic fund transfer system to work offline, in which case there is no immediate communication between the supplier's computer and the bank's computer. In such cases, the supplier's terminal simply reads various details from the magnetic strip on the card as it is swiped through the machine. To a lesser extent, some debit card transactions are processed not by EFT–POS but by way of mechanical ink printers, which transfer the details embossed on the card onto paper vouchers.

Contractual relations

Debit card transactions involve either three or four discreet contractual relationships as follows. If the supplier and the cardholder hold accounts with the same bank, then effecting a transfer of monies from the cardholder's account to the supplier is straightforward and only the first three contractual relations described below are relevant. These are described as three-party transactions.[16] The card-issuing bank, under its agreement with the cardholder customer, has the right to debit the customer's account with the amount of his purchases, and the bank will simply credit the amount to the supplier's account, deducting any agreed service charge. In *Re Charge Card Services Ltd*[17] Millett J examined the nature of the three contractual relations as follows:

> on the use of the card, three separate contracts come into operation. First, there is the contract of supply between the supplier and the cardholder (either in his own right or as agent for the account holder); secondly, there is the contract between the supplier and the card-issuing company, which undertakes to honour the card by paying the supplier on presentation of the sales voucher; and, thirdly, there is the contract between the card-issuing company and the account holder by which the account holder undertakes to reimburse the card-issuing company for payments made or liabilities incurred by the card-issuing company to the supplier as a result of the cardholder's use of the card. There are thus three separate contracts and three separate parties, each being privy to two of the three contracts but neither party nor privy to the third.

In a three-party transaction the first three contractual scenarios are relevant:

1. *Cardholders and supplier*: this is the underlying contract of the sale of goods/or services between the cardholder and supplier. As with other such contracts, the implied terms under the Sale of Goods Act 1979, or Supply of Goods and Services Act 1982 where applicable, will be of considerable importance in supplementing any express terms. In *Re Charge Card Services Ltd*[18] Millett J refused to draw a distinction between those cases where the customer pays for the goods, or services, by way of card (whether a debit, or credit or charge card) and those where

---

[16] *OFT v Lloyds TSB* [2004] EWHC 2600 (Comm).
[17] [1986] 3 All ER 289.
[18] [1986] 3 All ER 289.

the customer pays by cash. Millett J rejected any argument that the consideration for the supply of goods, or services, to the cardholder was anything other than the price, where he explained:

> Three possibilities have been canvassed. The first is that the consideration for the supply is not the price (which is to be paid by the card-issuing company, a stranger to the contract of supply) but production of the card and signature of a voucher. I reject this analysis, which is quite unrealistic. Production of the card and signature of the voucher are not the consideration itself but the means of obtaining it. Moreover, a sale of goods requires a monetary consideration: see s.2(1) of the Sale of Goods Act 1979. This analysis would thus lead to the conclusion that, where payment is to be made by credit or charge card, the contract of supply is not a sale of goods, with the result that the statutory conditions and warranties are not implied.

In the context of modern banking practice and contract law it is submitted that Millett J was correct in not drawing a distinction between payment by way of card, whether debit, credit or charge card, and those transactions where the customer pays by cash or cheque.

2. Card-issuing bank and cardholder: under this contract the cardholder is authorised by the card-issuing bank to use the card for the payment of goods and/or services from the supplier. Additionally, the cardholder authorises the bank to debit his account with the amount of any card transaction entered into. The terms and conditions of use of debit cards are usually included with those for the use of the bank generally. They will require the bank to make any debit card payments where the card is used in accordance with its terms provided the customer has funds available or an agreed overdraft. The terms and conditions under which the card is issued will normally specify how liability for unauthorised use of the debit card is to be allocated between the bank and cardholder, and circumstances in which the bank would reimburse the payment. Where debit cards are used to make payment for a 'distance contract' the Consumer Protection (Distance Marketing) Regulations 2004 will apply.[19] In other sales transactions there is some debate as to whether the Consumer Credit 1974 or the Payment Services Directive will apply. Since 2009, when the relevant sections of the Payment Services Directive came into effect, those payment cards not regulated by the Consumer Credit Act 1974 are subject to limits on liability for misuse provided in the Payment Services Regulations 2009 and any contract is required to set these out. The Payment Services Regulations 2009 apply to debit and credit card payments, generally, but those parts of the regulations limiting liability, only apply where the Consumer Credit Act 1974 does not apply[20] with the result that there continues to be debate about the regime as it applies to debit cards. Under both sets of rules, the cardholder is liable if he is shown to have acted fraudulently in denying a transaction, which in fact was authorised by him,[21] and the card-issuer is liable if the card goes missing in transit and never reaches the cardholder.[22] The differences in cardholder's liability for misuse under the different regimes are as follows:

- The Consumer Credit Act 1974 allows the cardholder to be made liable without limit for use of the card by someone who acquires possession of it with the consent of the cardholder, up to the point when notice is given that it may be misused, when liability ceases.[23]

---

[19] SI 2004/2095.

[20] Payment Services Regulations 2009, reg. 52.

[21] Consumer Credit Act 1974, s.171(4)(b)(i); Payment Services Regulations 2009, reg. 60(1)(a); Consumer Protection (Distance Selling) Regulations 2000, reg. 21(2).

[22] Consumer Credit Act 1974, ss.66 and 171(4)(a); Payment Services Regulations 2009, reg. 58(2).

[23] Consumer Credit Act 1974, ss.83(1), 84(2) and (3).

Apart from that case, liability for the unauthorised use of the card resulting from loss, theft or other misuse of the card up until notice is given, is limited to £50,[24] even where losses to the cardholder exceed that amount.

- The Payment Services Regulations 2009 make the cardholder liable for losses in excess of £50 when the cardholder 'with intent or gross negligence' fails to comply with reg. 57,[25] which requires the cardholder to use the card in accordance with its terms and conditions, to notify of loss, theft, misappropriation or unauthorised misuse in the agreed manner and without undue delay, and take all reasonable steps to keep the security features safe.[26] The Consumer Credit Act 1974 does not recognise the concept of 'gross negligence'. Perhaps, unreasonably failing to report the theft or loss of the card might amount to 'gross negligence', and if the Payment Services Regulations 2009 apply, rather than the Consumer Credit Act 1974 (which applies to debit cards used for transactions other than distance contracts) the cardholder's liability may exceed £50. However, under the 2009 Regulations, the cardholder must challenge the transaction within 13 months.[27]

- Where a payment card, including a debit or credit card, is used fraudulently in connection with a distance contract by another person, or one not acting as the cardholder's agent, the cardholder is entitled to be re-credited, or to have the sum returned by the card-issuer.[28] The cardholder is not even liable for the first £50[29] (even if the Consumer Credit Act 1974 otherwise applies) and nor is the cardholder liable where the loss is due to gross negligence.[30]

The terms and conditions of different agreements will normally provide that the cardholder is obliged to notify the card-issuing bank if it is lost, or the PIN otherwise compromised. The Payment Services Regulations 2009 and the Consumer Credit Act 1974 both make it obligatory for banks to provide information on how notification should be given[31] and the card-issuing bank is liable for loss resulting from such failure.[32]

The Payment Services Regulations 2009 impose certain minimum obligations on the cardholder,[33] including an obligation to take reasonable steps to keep personalised security features, for example the PIN, safe but the regulations do not prevent additional terms being imposed,[34] so long as the cardholder is informed of the steps required of him, for example the requirement that the card should be signed immediately on receipt, or that the cardholder is prohibited from allowing anyone else to use the card etc.

The Payment Services Regulations 2009 provide that the cardholder cannot prevent payment or revoke[35] a debit card payment once it has been received by the cardholder's bank

---

[24] Consumer Credit Act 1974, s.84(1).

[25] Payment Services Regulations 2009, reg. 62(2)(b).

[26] Payment Services Regulations 2009, reg. 57.

[27] Payment Services Regulations 2009, reg. 59(1).

[28] Consumer Protection (Distance Selling) Regulations 2000, reg. 21(1).

[29] Consumer Credit Act 1974, s.84(3A), (3B) and (3C).

[30] Payment Services Regulations 2009, reg. 62(3)(c).

[31] Payment Services Regulations 2009, reg. 40 and schedule 4 para. 5 (d); Consumer Credit Act 1974, s.84(4).

[32] Payment Services Regulations 2009, reg. 62 (3)(b); Consumer Credit Act 1974, s.84(3).

[33] Payment Services Regulations 2009, reg. 57. This provision applies whether or not debit cards are otherwise subject to the Consumer Credit Act 1974 (reg. 52).

[34] Payment Services Regulations 2009, schedule 4 para. (5)(a).

[35] Payment Services Regulations 2009, reg. 67. This provision applies whether or not debit cards are otherwise subject to the Consumer Credit Act 1974 (reg. 52).

(unless the bank agrees to stop payment after that point). The card-issuer is given discretion to vary, on notice, the terms and conditions on which the card is held under the Payment Services Regulations 2009, which require, at least two months' notice, unless the change relates to changing interest or exchange rates in favour of the cardholder.[36] The Payment Services Regulations 2009 also restrict the charges that can be levied on cancellation of the agreement and impose certain obligations on the payment service provider in relation to security and the execution of payment transactions made with the card.

3. *Supplier and card-issuing bank*: under this contract, the supplier is authorised and obliged to accept certain cards in payment for goods or services, and the bank agrees to pay the supplier the value of such goods and services. It is normal for banks to have a single 'Merchant Agreement' containing standard terms governing, between themselves and suppliers, not only payment by debit cards but also bank-issued credit cards. Generally, the contract between the card-issuing bank and the supplier will consist of a form specifying the cards that the supplier is allowed to accept, the various floor limits or transaction limits, and the scale of charges which the bank will levy. Authorisation to accept telephone or Internet transactions will also be given in selected cases.

The main obligation assumed by the supplier is to honour all valid and current cards, accepted by the scheme, and presented by cardholders in consideration of the full range of goods and services offered by the supplier, and to complete and issue such documentation as suppliers may require in respect of each transaction, for example in the case of debit cards the supplier generally undertakes to offer for the goods or services sold at his normal cash price.[37] Where the terms and conditions of payment are observed, the bank for its part promises to pay the supplier the amount of such card transactions as evidenced by the documentation.

The sales procedure will differ depending on whether the transaction is an over-the-counter sale or one effected without the customer being present (CNP sales). In the case of over-the-counter sales the supplier is presented with the card and he will be responsible for checking that the card contains the necessary identifying features, and that it is valid and signed by the customer. The sale may be effected by the supplier completing a paper sales voucher or using a mechanical imprint which the customer signs (both of which are now rare in the UK), or more commonly by swiping the card through an electronic terminal and asking the customer to enter his PIN to authorise the transaction. The terminal will produce a printed slip giving details of the transaction, a copy of which is given to the customer, as a record. Authorisation may be required for the transaction if the amount is in excess of the floor limit, or if there is some suspicion about the card, or because the transaction is unusual in some other respects. Once the transaction is confirmed the supplier is normally given a code to write on the sales voucher or terminal printout. Mail, telephone, Internet or other remote sales may be effected without the customer being present (CNP sales) and the supplier having no sight of the card, the cardholder or his signature. Since the risk of fraud is greater, banks are more reluctant to grant suppliers such facilities. The basic safeguard against fraud results from the information that the supplier is required to obtain from the cardholder which typically includes the card number, the card expiry date, the issue number,

---

[36] Payment Services Regulations 2009, reg. 42.

[37] The Monopolies and Mergers Commission held such terms, in the case of credit cards, to be contrary to the public interest and for that the obligations does not extend to credit cards: see The Report of the Monopoly and Mergers Commission, Credit Card Services: A Report on the Supply of Credit Card Services in the UK, HMSO, 1989, Cm. 718.

the cardholder's name and initials as shown on the card, the security numbers shown on the signature strip and the cardholder's address for the purposes of billing and statements.

When using a debit card to purchase goods or services, the cardholder may also use the debit card to obtain a cash advance from the supplier. This is termed 'cashback'. Cash advances may also be obtained against a credit card but must only be completed in sterling.

4. *Participating banks*: with the absence of the single national EFT–POS system, most card schemes will involve the participation of more than one bank and will therefore most likely be four- (or more) party transactions.[38] The involvement of several banks necessitates a fourth contract between the participating banks and the card scheme regulating those relationships, including the acceptance procedure for cards and the manner of transferring money from the cardholder's account to that of the supplier. Although the 'master agreements', to some extent, are confidential between the members of the scheme, the courts have considered some aspects of these arrangements. In *OFT* v *Lloyds TSB*[39] it was common ground that there was some sort of contractual link between the card-issuers and 'merchant acquirers' resulting from their common agreement under the scheme rules. Gloster J drew an analogy with cases of clubs, which would support contractual relationship between suppliers authorised to accept the scheme's cards and other members of the scheme.[40]

Legal consequences of debit card use

In *Re Charge Card Services Ltd*[41] Millett J said that the supplier's acceptance of a charge card was merely an agreement by which the consideration under the contract for the sale of goods or services might be satisfied. The true consideration remains the price of the goods or services, to be paid by the customer. The supplier is obliged, by virtue of his agreement with the bank, to accept all valid and current cards in return for the payment of goods or services while the cardholder has the choice, whether to pay in cash or by card. Where a cardholder offers payment by debit card the question that remains is whether the customer discharges his obligation by merely producing the card and authenticating payment, or whether payment by debit card merely amounts to conditional payment so that if the card-issuing bank refuses payment, or goes insolvent, the question that arises is whether the purchasing customer become primarily liable to fulfil the payment obligation directly to the supplier of goods or services. The UK courts have considered the issue in the context of credit and charge cards, and it is submitted the same answer will apply by analogy.

Thus, in *Re Charge Card Services Ltd*,[42] Millett J held that the question of whether a payment by card constituted an absolute or conditional payment depends on the terms of the contract between the cardholder and the supplier. The contract of sale will not normally expressly deal

---

[38] In *OFT* v *Lloyds TSB* [2004] EWHC 2600 (Comm) Gloster J described the differences between the three and four (or more) party transactions which was upheld by the Court of Appeal and is not affected by the reversal of her judgment on the application of the Consumer Credit Act 1974, s.75 to overseas transactions.

[39] [2004] EWHC 2600.

[40] Mastercard has made its rules available online except for those relating to security and authorisation procedures: Mastercard Worldwide, Mastercard Rules, 14 June 2013, http://www.mastercard.com/us/merchant/pdf/BM-Entire_Manual_public.pdf.

[41] [1986] 3 All ER 289.

[42] [1986] 3 All ER 289.

with this question and therefore the meaning of the contract will have to be inferred. It will be necessary to consider the provisions of the contract between the cardholder and the card-issuing bank, and the supplier and his bank. Millett J concluded that where payment was made by means of a credit or charge card, the circumstances of the payment might be sufficient to displace any presumption that payment by card is conditional only. Indeed, the terms of the contract may support the presumption in favour of the payment by card being absolute. He went on to explain:

> ... The essence of the transaction, which in my view has no close analogy, is that the supplier and customer have for their mutual convenience each previously arranged to open an account with the same company, and agree that any account between themselves may if the customer wishes, be settled by crediting the supplier's and debiting the customer's account with that company.

It is submitted that where payment is by debit card, the same presumption regarding absolute payment applies. Comparison can be drawn between debit cards and credit cards, whereas a comparison between a payment by cheque and debit card with regard to whether the payment would amount to an absolute discharge, is more difficult to justify. Bearing in mind Millett J's judgment it is reasonable to conclude that payment by debit card amounts to an absolute discharge of the customer's obligation to make payment. The use of the card, therefore, as payment of the purchase price is not conditional on the bank honouring its agreement with the supplier, and therefore the supplier will have no recourse against the cardholder for payment if the bank fails, for whatever reason, to make payment to the merchant or service provider.

Credit cards and charge cards

The distinction between credit and charge cards is that in the case of charge card agreements the whole of the outstanding balance is required to be paid in full within a certain period after the date of the monthly statement sent by the card-issuer to the cardholder, whereas credit card agreements provide the cardholder with the option of extended credit, subject to the obligation to make a minimum monthly payment. Credit cards are regulated by the Consumer Credit Act 1974, whereas charge cards are exempt under s.16(5A) of the Act and Art. 3(1)(a)(ii) of the Consumer Credit (Exempt Agreements) (No 2) Order 1985.[43] In all other respects charge cards and credit cards are similar and are, therefore, discussed together.

The method of processing credit or charge card transactions is identical to debit card transactions. Like debit card transactions the credit card transaction may be 'three-party' or 'four-party'.[44] In *OFT v Lloyds TSB*[45] Gloster J explained the credit card transaction and the parties to it as follows:

[43] SI 1985/757.
[44] See *OFT v Lloyds TSB* [2004] EWHC 2600 where Gloster J concluded that there are approximately 100 Visa card-issuers and probably a similar number of MasterCard issuers in the UK, most of which do not acquire merchants.
[45] [2004] EWHC 2600.

Credit card-issuers operate under the Visa, MasterCard and American Express international network schemes, of which they are members. This membership permits them to print the respective trademarks 'Visa', 'MasterCard' and 'American Express' on their cards issued to card-holders under their credit agreements. The networks have comprehensive rules governing the operation of the respective schemes. In particular the rules provide that suppliers are recruited only by a limited number of members of the networks, who are given the status of 'Merchant Acquirers'. A supplier enters into a contract with a Merchant Acquirer, which contract obliges the supplier to accept all cards bearing a trademark of the relevant network as payment for goods or services supplied by them to such cardholders. In return, the Merchant Acquirer agrees to pay the supplier for any such transaction, less a discount. The Merchant Acquirer recoups his payment to the supplier from the card-issuer through a settlement system organised by the network, together with a fee representing a proportion of the discount. The card-issuer in turn is paid the supply price in full by the cardholder pursuant to the credit card agreement. A credit card transaction of this nature is referred to in the industry as a 'four-party transaction', with debtor, creditor, Merchant Acquirer and supplier involved. It is contrasted to the 'three-party transaction' where the card-issuer also 'acquires' the merchant.

Contractual relations

Typically, between participating members and suppliers the relationship will be governed by a 'master agreement', which sets out the terms of use. This agreement is likely to cover both debit and credit cards in the same agreement. However, as between the cardholder and card-issuers, credit cards are normally subject to a separate agreement from other banking services because of the need to ensure compliance with the requirements of the Consumer Credit Act 1974.

1. *Cardholder and supplier*: payment by a credit or charge card will be an absolute discharge of liability on the part of the cardholder. Thus, where the supplier accepts payment by credit or charge card, the supplier cannot subsequently demand payment from the cardholder, even if the card-issuer becomes insolvent. Millett J, therefore, concluded that once accepted the card-issuing company becomes primarily liable for the payment of amounts due from the cardholder and his liability is extinguished. In *Re Charge Card Services Ltd*[46] Millett J explained the relationship as follows:

> Credit and charge cards are used mainly to facilitate payment of small consumer debts arising out of transactions between parties who may well not be known to each other, and the terms of which are usually not subject of negotiation. The identity of the card-issuing company is necessarily a matter for agreement, since the card must be one which the customer is authorised to use and the supplier has the necessary equipment to accept . . . The availability of the card as a method of payment is advantageous to both parties: the customer obtains free credit for a period longer than that which the supplier is prepared to give even to the card-issuing company, or than he himself would obtain from the use of a cheque, with or without a bank card; while the supplier obtains not only better security . . . but the convenience of having a single debtor in place of many, and the prospect of extra trade by reason of the credit facilities he is able to extend (without providing them himself) to the customer. Finally, the terms on which the supplier is entitled to payment from the card-issuing company are quite different from those on which the card-issuing company is entitled to payment from the customer; and both differ

---

[46] [1987] 1 Ch 150.

from those on which the supplier would be entitled to payment from the customer if he were subject to any residual liability not discharged by the use of the card. The card-issuing company is liable to pay the supplier very shortly after the receipt of the sales vouchers and claim form, but is entitled to deduct its commission; while the customer is liable to pay the full face value of the voucher, but is entitled to much longer credit. If the customer is liable to pay the supplier on the failure or default of the card-issuing company, it is on terms more onerous than either, for he must be liable to make immediate payment of the full face value of the voucher. It is difficult to find any justification for imputing to the customer an intention to undertake any such liability.

2. *Cardholder and card-issuing bank*: where the cardholder uses the credit or charge card to make payment, the card-issuing bank undertakes to make immediate payment to the supplier for such purchases, minus the facility fee. In return the cardholder agrees to make payments (on receipt of a transaction statement from the card-issuing bank) in the prescribed manner and also agrees to pay any credit charges (if in the case of credit cards the cardholder does not pay the full amount of the statement balance) and, where applicable, any annual fee. The contract between the cardholder and card-issuing bank is concluded on the standard terms of the card-issuer but such contracts are now subject to the unfair consumer contracts legislation[47] and regulations.[48] Agreements between the cardholder and the card-issuing bank, in respect of credit cards, also frequently constitute a 'regulated credit agreement' within the Consumer Credit Act 1974 under which the card itself is treated as a 'credit token' and the agreement, if regulated, is known as a 'credit-token agreement'. Although, charge cards are not subject to the Consumer Credit Act 1974, the terms and conditions for their use tend to be similar in practice, except there is no option for extended credit. In addition, the Payment Services Regulations 2009 will also apply to most payment card agreements, but the regulations are disapplied where the agreement is a 'regulated agreement'. Where the credit or charge card agreement is a distance contract, the provisions of the Financial Services (Distance Marketing) Regulations 2004, will apply.[49]

3. *Supplier and card-issuing bank or merchant acquirer*: under the master agreement between the issuer, or merchant acquirer, and supplier of goods and services the issuer or merchant acquirer agrees to pay the dealer such amounts as are due to him, provided the goods or services are supplied on the agreed terms. The dealer must confirm the transaction with the card-issuer or merchant acquirer if it exceeds the 'floor limit'. If the signature is still used as a means of authentication then the supplier must verify the cardholder's signature against the card. The merchant agreement will specify the procedures the merchant must follow in authenticating transactions and will define the circumstances in which the merchant acquirer will have the right to chargeback, i.e. debit sums previously granted to the supplier. Generally, the merchant agreement will give the merchant acquirer the right to make a chargeback whenever a card-issuing bank makes chargeback in respect of the transaction involving a supplier. Chargeback rights will typically arise when the cardholder challenges a transaction is authorised, or makes a claim under s.75 of the Consumer Credit Act 1974.

---

[47] Unfair Contract Terms Act 1977.

[48] Unfair Terms in Consumer Contracts Regulations 1999, http://www.legislation.gov.uk/uksi/1999/2083/contents/made.

[49] SI 2004/2095. These regulations impose requirements about pre-contract information and provide cancellation rights. Where the debtor also has cancellation rights under the Consumer Credit Act 1974, the longer period will be implemented.

The result of these terms is largely to transfer risk to the supplier, particularly with regard to CNP transactions.

The card-issuer will obtain an agreed percentage of the amount of each transaction as consideration for the facility rendered to the supplier. This agreement is not subject to the Consumer Credit Act 1974 and the bank is free to contract out of the protection given under Parts 5 and 6 of the Payment Services Regulations 2009.

Cash cards

A cashpoint or automated teller machine (ATM) is an electronic funds transfer terminal capable of performing many of the roles traditionally undertaken by a bank cashier. The ATM terminal can handle deposits, transfers between accounts, balance enquiries, cash withdrawals and the payment of bills. Some ATM systems also deal with simple loan facilities. The two main types of cash cards are: online and offline. The offline card operates by means of an identification of the PIN, which is encoded on the card itself, by the automatic teller machine (ATM). An online ATM will verify the customer inserted PIN by comparing it with the customer's PIN retained by the central computer to which the computer is linked. The PIN is a numerical code which identifies the cardholder as the authorised account holder and when the customer keys the PIN into the terminal, and requests a service, the computer will verify the correctness of the customer's PIN and his credit balance. Although online cards have enhanced the security features of the cash point, and other cards, the disadvantage is that the system may be subject to mechanical breakdown and disturbance. Most banks have moved to the system of online cards, and most banks and building societies have entered 'master agreements' and become members of networks which have enabled their customers to get easy access to cash and other ATM facilities, including withdrawing cash overseas. The use of the cashpoint card at another bank's[50] ATM gives rise to a unilateral contract between the cardholder and that bank, although the other bank may merely be an agent of the cardholder's bank. The general view is that the Consumer Credit Act 1974 does not apply to ATM cards although the Payment Services Regulations 2009 do apply to the use of ATM cards, as between the cardholder and his own bank,[51] but not as between the cardholder and another bank which owns the ATM machine in which the card is used.[52] The terms and conditions for the use of the ATM card must therefore conform to the 2009 Regulations, unless the card-issuer is permitted and has contracted out.[53]

The growth in the use of PIN numbers and plastic cards has exacerbated problems relating to the misuse and abuse of ATM cards. Customers tend to forget their PIN or become

[50] On 31 August 2012, the House of Commons Treasury Committee published a report on access to cash machines for basic bank account holders. The report recommends that the Royal Bank of Scotland (RBS) and the Lloyds Banking Group (Lloyds) remove restrictions on customers with basic bank accounts using cash machines run by other banks and independent third parties, Treasury Committee, Access to cash machines for basic bank account holders, Third Report of Session 2012–13, HC 544, 31 August 2012, www.publications. parliament.uk.
[51] Payment Services Regulations 2009, schedule 1, Part 1 para. 1(b).
[52] Payment Services Regulations 2009, schedule 1, Part 1 para. 2(o).
[53] Contracting out of Parts 5 and 6 is permitted only where the cardholder is not a consumer, micro-enterprise or charity: see Payment Services Regulations 2009, regs 33 and 51.

confused especially where they hold a number of cards each with a separate PIN. Some may seek to solve this problem by carrying written records of their PIN numbers and misuse may arise if the card and the written record are wrongly accessed. Liability for misuse of ATM cards has to be considered in the light of the Consumer Credit Act 1974 under which cash cards are treated as 'regulated agreements', and the Payment Services Regulations 2009 for other cash cards. As certain non-consumer cardholders may contract out of the provisions of the 2009 Regulations, the common law still remains relevant.

The US courts have examined the question of misuse of ATM cards in a series of cases and these serve as persuasive authority in the UK. In *Judd* v *Citibank*[54] the cardholder disputed the debiting of her account with the amount of an $800 withdrawal, which was shown as having been made by the use of her checkpoint card. The ATM was programmed to permit withdrawals only if the card was verified and the PIN numbers encoded in the magnetic strip matched the PIN keyed in by the user. However, the cardholder was able to establish that at the time of the disputed withdrawal transaction she was at work, and that she had neither given her card nor her PIN to anyone. The Civil Court of the City of New York concluded that the cardholder had discharged the burden of proof and the bank could not debit her account. The court took into consideration that the ATM terminals were subject to breakdowns and malfunction. A similar conclusion was reached in *Porter* v *Citibank*[55] where the cardholder had on a number of occasions unsuccessfully attempted to withdraw money from her account on two separate days. The cardholder notified the bank immediately, but the bank had debited her account with the amounts of the unsuccessful withdrawals attempted. At the trial, the bank admitted that the ATM terminal in question was on average out of balance once or twice a week and conceded that, due to a defect in the machine, the money could have been dispensed to the next customer. Taking these factors into consideration the court gave judgment for the cardholder. There have, however, been cases where the cardholder's action has not succeeded. In *Feldman* v *Citibank*[56] the court dealt with two separate cases. In one instance the court decided in favour of the cardholder whose testimony was accepted while in the other case the court rejected the cardholder's testimony. In the latter instance, the court concluded that the cardholder had been fraudulently induced to make an extra withdrawal by the person standing next to him at the ATM. The court gave judgment in favour of the bank, although the cardholder testified that nobody had stood next to him at the time of the withdrawal.

The US courts were therefore careful to take into consideration their assessment of the cardholder's integrity and credibility. The English courts will need to do the same where the Payment Services Regulations 2009 do not apply, although where cash cards are covered by the regulations the burden of proof falls on the card-issuer to establish that its terminals and system were operating properly.

A further issue for the English courts to determine, in the case of cash cards not covered by the 2009 Regulations, is the effectiveness of the standard clause in the master agreement between the bank and the cardholder under which the bank's record is deemed conclusive proof of transactions undertaken through the use of the ATM. It is submitted that in this situation the existing rules that apply to the banker and customer relationship will provide

---

[54] 435 NYS 2d 210 (1980).
[55] (1984) 472 NYS 2d 582.
[56] 443 NYS 2d 845 (1981).

an answer for the courts. It has already been established that bank statements showing credit or debit transactions, and the balance, are merely *prima facie* evidence of the state of the account[57] and both the bank and the customer are entitled to have any errors rectified, unless the rules of estoppel apply. There is no reason why withdrawals made by the use of ATM cards from a computer terminal should be treated any differently, especially where the bank statement will evidence all transactions against the account, whether through the use of cheques or other payment instruments including where a plastic card is used to make the withdrawal.

The US courts have also dealt with the risks associated with misuse of cards. In *Ognibene v Citibank NA*[58] the cardholder's PIN was memorised by a rogue standing near an ATM terminal being used by the genuine cardholder. The rogue, who pretended to be engaged in servicing the terminals, used an adjacent telephone to conduct a fictitious conversation, after which he asked the cardholder for the use of his card to ensure that the terminal was working properly. The rogue withdrew money from the cardholder's account and returned the card to the cardholder indicating that the terminal was indeed working properly. The cardholder challenged the bank's right to debit the account with the amount of the withdrawal. The Civil Court of the City of New York concluded that the bank had been negligent in not alerting customers to the nature of the deception undertaken by the rogue, of which the bank was aware. It is difficult to predict how the English courts would respond to similar facts except that it should be noted that the customer allowed an unknown person to use his card, although the customer did not disclose his PIN to the rogue. It is highly likely that a genuine person servicing ATM terminals would have their own equipment, including if required a plastic card, to check whether the terminal is working properly after servicing it. Additionally, the Payment Services Regulations 2009 impose mandatory obligations on cardholders and issuers.

Digital money

It is expected that the existing forms of plastic card will continue to develop with more use of online systems, so that a cardholder's account balance, overdraft limit or unused credit limit can be electronically confirmed while the sales transaction is being carried out. The implementation of faster payment systems for transactions made by telephone, online or direct debit has reduced the delay in payments being debited from the cardholder's account and credited to the supplier's account.

Smartcards have allowed the development of payment cards that serve not only as a replacement for debit, credit or ATM cards but as a replacement for cash itself by way of 'digital cash' or electronic purse. These cards resemble physical cash in that a monetary value can be stored on them in the form of digital information, which may instantaneously be transferred from the cardholder to the retailer in order to settle payment obligations. The customer is using his own money, albeit in electronic form. The electronic value credited to the card will be denominated in the currency of the country in which the scheme is operating and there are

---

[57] See Ch. 7.
[58] 446 NYS 2d 845 (1981).

various options for loading value depending on the scheme through the Post Office or 'Pay Point', 'Pay Zone' or similar outlet, or by way of a transfer from a bank account or ATM.

Although, these cards resemble other forms of plastic cards they are treated as equivalent to cash[59] and may be used to immediately transfer funds from the cardholder to the supplier, up to the value stored on the card, in satisfaction of the payment obligation. Digital cash, like currency, is a medium of exchange where the movement of electronic value from one person to another involves the transfer of intangible property rights.[60] By contrast, a credit card transaction will result in the customer being indebted to the card-issuing company each time the card is used. Digital cards are, therefore, sometimes known as 'stored value cards' or 'prepaid cards'. However, digital cash systems are privately run and have no endorsement from the government; in other words they are not legal tender. An originator, therefore, issues digital money to participating banks, which pay for it, and the banks then re-issue it to customers in the form of electronic purses. However, the ability to accept digital cash in the form of prepaid cards depends on participation in the relevant scheme and only merchants who have an agreement with an originator can accept payment by way of prepaid cards. The holder of digital money has a right of redemption, as against the issuer, unless the holder is a supplier who has accepted the digital cash in payment for goods or services. The potential problems stemming from the creation of digital cash by private companies is exemplified through reference to Bitcoin, a virtual currency launched in 2009. Notably Bitcoin has experienced security challenges alongside extreme fluctuations in terms of value.[61]

The Consumer Credit Act 1974

The issue of whether the Consumer Credit Act 1974 applies to any given type of plastic card is not straightforward. The questions, which need to be considered, are:

(i) Whether the card constitutes a 'credit token' within the meaning of s.14(1) of the Consumer Credit Act.

(ii) Whether the agreement between the card-issuer and cardholder falls within the definition of a 'credit-token agreement' under s.14(2) of the Act.

Section 14(1) defines the term 'credit token' as a cheque,[62] card, voucher or some other 'thing' issued to an individual, i.e. not to a company or partnership of more than three members.[63]

---

[59] Directive 2000/46/EC specifically states in its preamble that electronic money can be considered as electronic surrogate for coins and banknotes.

[60] The European Monetary Institute recommended that only authorised credit institutions are allowed to issue smart cards or electronic money. That recommendation was implemented by Directive 2000/28/EC which expands the definition of credit institutions to cover electronic money issuers and Directive 2000/46/EC which established a new regulatory regime for electronic money institutions, although less stringent than the one which applies to banks. These Directives were implemented in the UK by the Electronic Money (Miscellaneous Amendments) Regulations 2002 (SI 2002/765) and the Financial Services Act 2000 (Regulated Activities Amendment) Order 2002 (SI 2002/682).

[61] SEC warns of Bitcoin scams, accuses Texas man of Ponzi scheme, 23 July 2013, http://www.reuters.com/article/2013/07/23/us-sec-bitcoin-idUSBRE96M0SI20130723.

[62] 'Cheques' are documents which entitle the holder to acquire goods at designated shops and that are issued on terms that the holder will pay the issuer their face value, plus interest, by instalments.

[63] Consumer Credit Act 1974, s.189(1).

The issuer must be someone who carries on 'a consumer credit business', i.e. someone who is in the business of making regulated credit agreements[64] and undertakes either (i) on the production of the token, that he will supply cash, goods or services 'on credit',[65] or (ii) where a third-party supplies cash, or goods or services against the production of the token, the issuer will pay the third party for them.[66] Section 14(2) then defines a credit token agreement as 'a regulated' agreement for the provision of credit in connection with the use of a 'credit token'. Section 8 defines a regulated consumer agreement as an agreement between a creditor and an individual for the provision of credit, which is not exempt under ss.16, 16A or 16B of the 1974 Act.[67]

The first alternative under s.14(1) extends to bipartite credit tokens and only falls within the definition of s.14 if the issuer himself undertakes to supply cash, goods or services 'on credit'. There is no express requirement within the second alternative that credit should be extended and s.14(3) states that the issuer is taken to provide credit when cash, goods, or services are supplied by the third party. There are different views on whether a credit require-ment is implied with s.14(3) merely identifying when, and by whom, the credit is supplied. If a credit requirement is not implicit, a tripartite credit token arises in the second alternative even if there is no express undertaking to provide credit, with s.14(3) 'deeming' credit to arise.[68] The academic view is that the undertaking to provide credit is implicit in the second situation.[69] It is irrelevant whether or not the issuer deducts commission from the amount paid to the supplier. It is also irrelevant whether the cash, goods or services are supplied against the mere production of the token or whether 'some other action is also required'.[70] These words are intended to cover the fact that a signature or PIN is frequently required when the token is used. In *Elliott* v *Director General of Fair Trading*[71] a token was held to fall within s.14 although only a provisional card had at that stage been supplied which was later to be exchanged for the final card when the cardholder supplied some financial details about himself and entered into a written credit agreement. These requirements will help to con-stitute 'some other action' which did not take the provisional card outside the scope of s.14. The court held it immaterial that the undertaking given in the provisional card was not contractually binding.

The definition of a credit-token is fairly wide[72] and may take any tangible form. It is not restricted to the traditional plastic card and includes a book of vouchers, which the debtor may use, by agreement, in order to draw on the account, provided the issuer undertakes to pay against these vouchers. Whether or not the issuer has extended credit will depend on the nature and terms under which the voucher is issued and the use made. Cheque forms, therefore, issued

---

[64] Consumer Credit Act 1974, s.189(1).

[65] Consumer Credit Act 1974, s.14(1)(a).

[66] Consumer Credit Act 1974, s.14(1)(b).

[67] Consumer Credit Act 2004 s.8, as amended by the Consumer Credit Act 2006, which removed the financial threshold, except in respect of credit agreements entered into for business purposes.

[68] See Jones (1988) Credit Cards, Card Users and Account Holders, *JBL*, 457.

[69] It should be noted that at the time the Consumer Credit Act was passed, in 1974, the only form of tripartite card was the credit card, which resulted in the deferment of payment and hence credit being provided. Thus those types of tripartite cards that were subsequently introduced (e.g. cashcards, debit cards that cannot cause a bank account to be overdrawn) are probably not credit tokens.

[70] Consumer Credit Act 1974, ss.14(1)(a) and (b).

[71] [1980] 1 WLR 977.

[72] Consumer Credit Act 1974, s.14.

by banks are outside the definition of credit tokens because the bank undertakes to its customer to pay against the instrument, and not for the supply of goods, services or cash.[73] Credit cards, however, do fall within the scope of s.14 of the Consumer Credit Act 1974. They involve a tripartite arrangement for the supply of cash, goods or services to the cardholder by dealers at the issuer's expense who will eventually be reimbursed by the cardholder. Charge cards now fall within the scope of s.14[74] and give rise to credit-token agreements, although these cards are exempted from s.75 of the Consumer Credit Act 1974.

Cashpoint cards normally constitute credit tokens,[75] unless the bank account against which the card may be used and from which money is withdrawn, does not have an overdraft facility and the account cannot go into debit. Under s.14 the distinction may need to be drawn between cards that are used to withdraw money from the issuing bank's own ATMs, and those 'shared' terminals resulting from mutual agreements between various card-issuers. In the case of the two-party situation, there must be an undertaking to supply cash 'on credit'[76] and therefore such cards will only constitute credit tokens if there is an agreement that the ATM will supply cash to the customer even if the withdrawal results in an overdraft arising against the account. Therefore, if the terminal is online and programmed so that an overdraft cannot arise, then the card is not a credit token. However, some terminals function on the basis of the balance at the close of the preceding day the transaction takes place and so the customer may become overdrawn, without agreement. In such circumstances the system will give rise to an implied undertaking to supply cash on credit unless the cardholder is expressly prohibited from incurring an overdraft and the card will then not be a credit token.[77] In respect of charge cards used at shared ATM terminals, unless the cash-dispensing bank is regarded as the agent of the issuer the situation falls within the second alternative of the definition under s.14 as being a 'credit token', i.e. the token is produced to a third party. As discussed above there is some debate about whether this alternative requires the issuer to provide 'credit'.

Debit cards also raise similar questions arising mainly from the fact that they were devised after the Consumer Credit Act 1974 was passed and how the Act applies to them is uncertain. Debit cards are credit tokens to the extent that the third-party supplies goods or services against the card and the card-issuer will then debit the cardholder's account. They will, therefore, be credit tokens if they fall within the second alternative of the definition under s.14. Again it would appear that if the account cannot go into overdraft than the debit card is not a credit token.

But not every agreement involving the use of a credit token falls within the scope of the Consumer Credit Act 1974. Under s.14(2) a 'credit-token agreement' is a regulated agreement for the provision of credit in connection with the use of a credit token. Even if the card is a credit token under the Act, there is no credit-token agreement unless the card is issued under

---

[73] Guest and Lloyd (1975) *Encyclopedia of Consumer Credit Law*, London: Sweet & Maxwell.

[74] Prior to the implementation of the Consumer Credit Directive 2008/48/EC charge cards were generally 'exempt agreements' and therefore the cards were not treated as credit tokens and credit-token agreements did not arise. Such an exemption is now incompatible with the Directive.

[75] Consumer Credit Act 1974, s.14(4) under which the use of an object, for example a plastic card, to operate a bank terminal provided by the issuer or a third party is deemed production of the object to that person.

[76] Consumer Credit Act 1974, s.14(1)(a).

[77] Guest and Lloyd (1975) *Encyclopedia of Consumer Credit Law*, London: Sweet & Maxwell; see also Dobson (1977) The Cheque Card as a Consumer Credit Agreement, *JBL*, 126.

a regulated agreement for the provision of credit with the use of the credit token. If the credit-token agreement merely permits the cardholder to overdraw on his current account then some of the formalities under Part V of the Act need not be complied with. However, not all cash cards are restricted to such arrangements and if the card provides other forms of credit to the cardholder, for example loans, then the agreement is not likely to be exempted and will fall within the scope of the 1974 Act. In respect of tripartite agreements, the issuer of such a token is deemed to provide the cardholder with credit whenever a third party supplies him with cash, goods or services and such an agreement is therefore a credit-token agreement unless it is exempt under s.16 of the 1974 Act.[78]

An agreement which results in the issue of the token may be within the scope of the 1974 Act even if the card itself is not a credit token, for example a current account with which the customer is issued a cheque card. The 1974 Act suggests that the contract under which a bank supplies a cheque card to the customer is a credit agreement because the cardholder can draw cheques, which the bank is bound to honour even if the cardholder continues to be overdrawn. Such an agreement is an unrestricted-use debtor–creditor agreement under s.13(C) of the 1974 Act.

Misuse of the card by a third party

Payment cards are vulnerable to fraudulent use by persons other than the cardholder debtor.[79] The policy behind the Consumer Credit Act 1974 is to transfer risk of loss principally upon the creditor where the card has been taken without the debtor's consent. The general rule applicable to regulated agreements is set out in s.83(1) of the Consumer Credit Act 1974, which provides that a debtor under a consumer credit agreement is not liable to the creditor for any loss arising from the use of the credit facility by an unauthorised person. However, s.84 establishes a number of exceptions to the general rule set out in s.83:

(i) In the case of credit-token agreements the Act allows the card-issuer to insert a clause in the agreement making the cardholder liable to the extent of £50 for loss arising from the use of the card when the card was not in his possession.[80]

(ii) The cardholder may be made liable for any loss caused by the misuse of the card by a person who acquires possession of card with the consent of the cardholder.[81]

(iii) The cardholder cannot be rendered liable unless the credit-token agreement sets out the details of the person or body to whom the theft or loss of the card must be notified.[82]

(iv) The cardholder's liability terminates (even with regard to the first £50) when he gives notice of the loss to the card-issuer.[83] The notice may be given orally or in writing and will take effect when received. The oral notice may have to be confirmed in writing and in such cases the cardholder must give written notification within seven days of the oral communication.[84]

---

[78] Guest and Lloyd (1975) *Encyclopedia of Consumer Credit Law*, London: Sweet & Maxwell.
[79] Payments Council, Annual Security and Fraud Review 2010, gives an indication of the losses resulting from plastic card fraud during 2005–09, http://www.paymentscouncil.org.uk/files/payments_council/new_website/annual_fraud_review.pdf.
[80] Consumer Credit Act 1974, s.84(1).
[81] Consumer Credit Act 1974, s.84(2).
[82] Consumer Credit Act 1974, s.84(3)–(4).
[83] Consumer Credit Act 1974, s.84(3).
[84] Consumer Credit Act 1974, s.84(5).

(v) Any sum paid by the cardholder for the issue of the card is to be treated as paid towards his liability for loss, unless it has previously been set off against amounts due for the use of the token.[85] Where more than one token is issued under one agreement, the provisions of s.84 apply to each token separately.[86]

The cardholder's liability under s.84 will only apply where the agreement between the parties contains appropriate clauses and if the agreement is silent the cardholder's position is governed by s.83, which frees the cardholder from liability for loss in cases of misuse. However, s.83 only applies to the unauthorised use of the credit facility. The term 'credit facility' is not defined but any account that maybe overdrawn by the use of the credit token can constitute a credit facility, even where, at a given moment, the account is in credit. A facility may therefore be subject to the terms of the Consumer Credit Act 1974 in some instances but outside its operation in others.

The Distance Marketing Directive excludes the scope of s.84 of the Consumer Credit Act 1974 in respect of contracts concluded over the Internet, email, or telephone. Such contracts made through the fraudulent use of the payment card are cancellable, with the cardholder entitled to have his account re-credited. The general rule under s.83 of the Consumer Credit Act 1974 will therefore apply with reference to such contracts.

Unsolicited credit tokens and credit card cheques

The Consumer Credit Act 1974 prohibits card-issuers from 'giving'[87] unsolicited credit tokens[88] and the unsolicited dispatch or delivery of such a token constitutes a criminal offence. The object of the prohibition is to prevent consumers being tempted into debt beyond their means by the provision of easy credit. The prohibition does not apply where the issuer sends an unsolicited credit token under a credit-token agreement already made and the provision is inapplicable in respect of replacement tokens (cards) even if the agreement under which they are sent is varied.[89] In all other circumstances, creditors must ensure that they have received a request for the card before it is issued. The cardholder's request for a credit token is usually in writing and signed by him.[90] Where a cardholder uses an unsolicited credit token he will be under a duty to reimburse the creditor card-issuer.

As a result of concerns about credit cardholders over-committing themselves by using 'cheques' to draw on their credit card accounts the Financial Services Act 2010 adds a new prohibition in respect of the provision of unsolicited credit card cheques[91] which result in the provision of credit under a credit-token agreement.

The credit-token agreement

The credit-token agreement, made between the card-issuer and the cardholder, is a regulated consumer agreement and the creditor must comply with his obligations relating to

---

[85] Consumer Credit Act 1974, s.84(6).
[86] Consumer Credit Act 1974, s.84(8).
[87] Defined under s.189(1) as 'deliver or send by post to . . .'.
[88] Consumer Credit Act 1974, s.51(1).
[89] Consumer Credit Act 1974, s.51(1).
[90] Consumer Credit Act 1974, s.51(2).
[91] Financial Services Act 2010, ss.51A–B, added by s.15 of the 2010 Act.

pre-contractual information, the form of agreement requirements and the copy requirements. Ordinarily, the card-issuer must send a copy of the agreement to the cardholder within seven days following the agreement being executed.[92] The Act lays down detailed requirements relating to the form and content of the agreement and provides that the credit-token agreement must be in writing and signed by both the prospective cardholder and card-issuer.[93] On the payment of a nominal fee, the cardholder is entitled to a copy of the executed agreement and certain other information. The agreement must give information in relation to, for example, the credit limit, the rate of interest, the timing of the repayments and other charges payable. If the card-issuer fails to comply with these requirements, the agreement is not properly executed and cannot, during the period of default, be forced. The Act requires that a minimum of seven days' notice must be given before any effective variation of the contract. Where the rate of interest is varied, notice can be given by publishing the variation in at least three national newspapers and, where reasonably practicable, through publicity in the card-issuer's branches

Connected lender liability

A cardholder may have the benefit of a claim against the card-issuer for any breach of contract committed by the retailer in respect of credit card agreements and where payment is made by credit card.[94] In credit arrangement transactions, there is a connection between the card-issuer and the cardholder and the acquisition of the goods or services from the supplier. This connection stems from the fact that the cardholder is able to use his credit card only where the card-issuer has entered into contracts with the appointed dealers or suppliers (in the case of 'three-party' transactions) or by a 'merchant acquirer' (in the case of 'four-party' transactions). The credit card transaction is a 'debtor–creditor–supplier' agreement[95] and s.75 of the Consumer Credit Act 1974 provides that the cardholder (debtor) has a claim based either on misrepresentation[96] or for breach of contract against the dealer (supplier) and against the card-issuer (creditor).[97] The cardholder has this claim even if, when entering into the agreement with the supplier, he has exceeded the credit limit set by the card-issuer.[98] In *Office of Trading* v *Lloyds TSP Bank Plc*[99] the House of Lords held that this liability extends in relation to domestically issued credit cards that are used to finance transactions with a foreign supplier. Section 75 applies only to 'regulated agreements' and to 'debtor–creditor–supplier' agreements, i.e. agreements where there are arrangements between the card-issuer and the dealer.

Charge-card agreements are generally not regulated and therefore offer the protection of s.75 of the Consumer Credit Act 1974 to charge-card holders. Moreover, transactions involving cheque cards are not debtor–creditor–supplier agreements, as the bank's guarantee under

---

[92] Consumer Credit Act 1974, s.61(2).
[93] Consumer Credit Act 1974, s.61(1).
[94] Consumer Credit Act 1974, s.75.
[95] Consumer Credit Act 1974, s.12(b)–(c).
[96] Consumer Credit Act 1974, s.75.
[97] Agreements for the purchase of items for less than £100 or for more than £30,000 are excluded, as well as 'non-commercial' agreements: s.75(3) Consumer Credit Act 1974.
[98] Consumer Credit Act 1974, s.75(4).
[99] [2008] 1 AC 316.

the card is made to the world at large. The cardholder is therefore not bound to seek out a designated supplier.

Default and termination of agreements

Where the cardholder is in breach of his agreement the card-issuer may terminate the agreement and demand repayment of the outstanding balance on the card.[100] Section 87 provides that prior to taking enforcement action the card-issuer must first serve the cardholder with a default notice, informing the cardholder of the breach. The cardholder must be given at least seven days' notice from service to make up the breach or to pay compensation.[101] If the cardholder does so then the breach is treated as not having occurred.[102]

The Payment Services Regulations 2009

Most of the cards considered in this chapter fall within the definition of a 'payment instrument' issued under a 'payment services' contract within the meaning of the Payment Services Regulations 2009 (PSR). Such cards are therefore subject to the contractual provisions relating to consumer protection, and the rights and liabilities of the parties.[103] The PSR 2009 permits the contracting out of most of these provisions unless the 'payment services user' is a 'consumer', a 'micro-enterprise' or a 'charity'; terms which are defined in the regulations. The 2009 Regulations define a 'payment instrument', broadly speaking, as any personalised device or set of procedures used to initiate a payment transaction by a payment service provider.[104] This extends to all payment cards examined in this chapter except cheque guarantee cards,[105] store cards issued by the retailer for use in that specific store and for electronic purses that may only be used in a number of outlets.[106] The cardholder also falls within the definition of 'payment service user' while the card-issuer is the 'payment services provider'. For payment cards issued under 'regulated agreements' under the Consumer Credit Act 1974, the PSR 2009 consumer protection provisions are generally excluded in so far there would be duplication of the provisions, but where the PSR impose obligations over and above the Consumer Credit Act 1974, then these obligations are also imposed in relation to 'regulated agreements' under the Consumer Credit Act 1974. Additionally, the PSR contain provisions

---

[100] Consumer Credit Act 1974, s.87.

[101] Consumer Credit Act 1974, s.88.

[102] Consumer Credit Act 1974, s.89.

[103] Subscribers to the lending code have agreed to show compliance with these rules by agreeing to observe them in the lending code where the general principles are set out in user friendly terms: http://www.lending standardsboard.org.uk/docs/lendingcode.pdf.

[104] The definition of 'payment instrument' refers to initiating a 'payment order', which is then defined as an instruction to a 'payment service provider' requesting the execution of a 'payment instruction' which is defined as placing, transferring or withdrawing funds.

[105] Paper-based cheques are not 'payment services' by PSR 2009, reg. 2(1), schedule 1.

[106] Payment Services Regulations 2009, schedule 2 para. 2(k) excludes service-based instruments that can only be used to acquire goods or services (i) in or on the issuer's premises, or (ii) under a commercial agreement with the issuer, either within a limited network of service providers or a limited range of goods or services: the word limited is narrowly construed so as to exclude credit, charge, debit, cashcards and electronic purses.

in relation to 'low-value payment instruments'[107] modified so that only minimal[108] informa-tion need be provided and contracting out of some of these provisions is permitted.[109]

Of special relevance to payment cards covered by the PSR 2009, provisions concerning 'payment instruments', for example the right of the card-issuer to place cards on a 'stop' list, is regulated with the cardholder being entitled to be given reasons for the stop and to have the stop lifted if the reasons have ceased to exist. Further, there are detailed provisions relating to the unsolicited sending of cards and misuse of cards. These are now considered.

Misuse of cards

The 2009 Regulations provide a framework in respect of liability in relation to that misuse of payment cards within the regulations. Express obligations are imposed on the cardholder to 'take all reasonable steps' to keep his unique security features, for example PIN, safe[110] and to notify the card-issuer once he becomes aware of the loss, theft, misappropriation, or other unauthorised use of the card 'in the agreed manner and without delay'.[111] These obligations apply even in relation to credit tokens covered by the Consumer Credit Act 1974. Except in the case of agreements regulated by the Consumer Credit Act failure to comply with these obligations 'with intent or gross negligence' renders the cardholder liable for all losses incurred in respect of an authorised transaction.[112] Corresponding obligations are imposed on the card-issuer to ensure that 'appropriate means are available at all times' to the cardholder so he can give notification of possible misuse of the card[113] and to prevent its use once notification is given.[114] The card-issuer is also under an obligation to ensure that the cardholder's unique security features 'are not accessible' to third parties[115] and the card-issuer bears the risk of sending the card and any unique security features.[116] Where the cardholder disputes a transaction, the onus is on the card-issuer to prove that the transaction was 'authenticated',[117] accurately recorded, and 'not affected by a technical breakdown or some other deficiency'.[118] The mere use of the card as requested by the card-issuer 'is not in itself necessarily sufficient' to prove either that the transaction was authorised by the cardholder or that the cardholder acted fraudulently, or failed 'with intent or gross negligence' to comply with his notification obligations[119] so as to make him liable to an unlimited extent.[120] These

---

[107] Where individual payment transactions of €60 or less (if the payment transaction is executed in the UK, otherwise the limit is €30), or having a spending limit of €300 or less (if the payment transaction is executed in the UK, otherwise the limit is €150) or in the case of electronic purses that store funds do not exceeds €500 (PSR 2009, regs 35 and 53).
[108] Payment Services Regulations 2009, reg. 35(2)(a).
[109] Payment Services Regulations 2009, reg. 35(2)(b).
[110] Payment Services Regulations 2009, reg. 57(2).
[111] Payment Services Regulations 2009, reg. 57(1).
[112] Payment Services Regulations 2009, reg. 62(2).
[113] Payment Services Regulations 2009, reg. 58(1)(c).
[114] Payment Services Regulations 2009, reg. 58(1)(e).
[115] Payment Services Regulations 2009, reg. 58(1)(a).
[116] Payment Services Regulations 2009, reg. 58(2).
[117] Payment Services Regulations 2009, reg. 60(2).
[118] Payment Services Regulations 2009, reg. 60(1).
[119] Payment Services Regulations 2009, reg. 57(1)(b).
[120] Payment Services Regulations 2009, reg. 62(2).

card-issuer obligations also apply in relation to regulated agreements covered by the Consumer Credit Act 1974.[121]

Liability, under the PSR, for misuse of the card is similar, but not identical, to that applicable to credit tokens issued under the credit-token agreements under the Consumer Credit Act 1974. The Act applies, instead of the PSR 2009, where cards are issued under an agreement regulated by the 1974 Act but there are some important differences between the two regimes:

1 There is a general provision in the PSR 2009,[122] which requires the card-issuer immediately to refund any transactions that are 'not authorised' in accordance with the PSR 2009 relating to the giving of consent to payment transactions by the cardholder.[123] There is a corresponding provision in s.83 of the 1974 Act but the section only applies to the use of a credit facility and says nothing about immediate refunds.

2 Both the PSR 2009 and the 1974 Act provide derogations from the general principle so as to impose some liability on the cardholder. However, the PSR 2009 derogations apply in law and therefore, unlike the position under the 1974 Act, do not have to be contractually imposed. Although, the 2009 derogations are similar to those under the 1974 Act there are some differences, for example the cardholder is generally liable up to a maximum of £50 for loss arising from the use of a lost, stolen or misappropriated[124] card.[125] However, the cardholder is liable for all loss where he has acted fraudulently or where the cardholder has 'with intent or gross negligence' failed to comply with his obligations to 'take all reasonable steps' to keep his unique security features safe and to notify the card-issuer 'in the agreed manner and without undue delay' once it becomes aware of the possible misuse of the card.[126] Where the card-issuer has not complied with his obligation to ensure that appropriate means are available to the cardholder at all times to notify of the possible misuse or loss of the card, then unless the cardholder has acted fraudulently, he is not liable for any loss, even for the first £50. And unless the cardholder has acted fraudulently, his liability terminates (even for the first £50) when he gives the card-issuer notice 'in the agreed manner' of possible misuse.[127] These rules are reinforced by the voluntary code of practice that subscribers agree to be bound by under the Lending Code.[128]

There is no provision in the PSR 2009 that corresponds to s.66 of the Consumer Credit Act 1974 which only imposes liability on a cardholder once he has 'accepted' the card. The PSR 2009 states that the provisions relating to the misuse of cards apply instead of s.66 to payment cards not issued under agreements regulated by the 1974 Act. Further, the

---

[121] Contracting out is not permitted in relation to the obligations under the Payment Services Regulations 2009, reg. 58.

[122] For example the cardholder's obligation to notify the card issuer on becoming aware of the possible misuse of the card (reg. 57(1)(b)).

[123] Payment Services Regulations 2009, reg. 55.

[124] Where the cardholder has failed to keep his unique security features safe.

[125] Payment Services Regulations 2009, reg. 62(1).

[126] Payment Services Regulations 2009, reg. 62(2).

[127] Payment Services Regulations 2009, reg. 62(3)(b).

[128] http://www.lendingstandardsboard.org.uk/docs/lendingcode.pdf.

PSR 2009 also state that the card-issuer is to bear the risk of sending the card or the unique security features[129] and that the burden is on the card-issuer to prove that the transaction was authenticated,[130] i.e. using any procedure to verify the use of the card, including the unique security features.

Unsolicited payment cards

The PSR 2009 contain a similar prohibition to that found in s.51 of the Consumer Credit Act 1974, under which they forbid the sending of an unsolicited 'payment instrument', except one that is a replacement for one already issued.[131] The Lending Code provides that subscribers to the code will not provide credit cards unless requested or unless intended to replace an existing card.[132] This prohibition, however, is not applied in the case of agreements regulated by the 1974 Act, which continue to be the subject of that Act. The PSR 2009 is not disapplied in relation to unsolicited credit tokens that are sent before any regulated agreement is made with the cardholder and, therefore, the prohibitions in both the 1974 Act and the PSR 2009 will apply.

The card agreement

Card agreements are 'framework contracts' for the purposes of the PSR 2009 and the relevant 'information' provisions in Part 5 of the regulations will apply. However, the PSR provisions are generally excluded in relation to agreements that are 'regulated agreements' under the 1974 Act.[133] The exclusion, however, is not complete and additional information is required under the regulations, which must also be given in the case of regulated agreements.[134] Under the PSR 2009 the information requirements are as follows: pre-contracting information must usually be provided 'in good time' to the cardholder before he is bound by the contract;[135] the cardholder is given the right, during the contract and free of charge,[136] to obtain certain information and terms relating to the contract;[137] there are provisions concerning the notification of variations in the contractual information and terms;[138] and there are provisions concerning information to be provided in relation to each payment transaction[139] and provisions governing the termination of the contract by either party.[140] These requirements are reinforced in the Lending Code so that all subscribers agree to observe them.[141]

---

[129] Payment Services Regulations 2009, reg. 58(2).
[130] Payment Services Regulations 2009, reg. 60(1).
[131] Payment Services Regulations 2009, reg. 58(1)(b).
[132] http://www.lendingstandardsboard.org.uk/docs/lendingcode.pdf.
[133] Payment Services Regulations 2009, reg. 34.
[134] Payment Services Regulations 2009, reg. 34(b) and (c).
[135] Payment Services Regulations 2009, reg. 40.
[136] Payment Services Regulations 2009, reg. 40.
[137] Payment Services Regulations 2009, reg. 41.
[138] Payment Services Regulations 2009, reg. 42.
[139] Payment Services Regulations 2009, regs 44–46.
[140] Payment Services Regulations 2009, reg. 43.
[141] http://www.lendingstandardsboard.org.uk/docs/lendingcode.pdf.

Distance marketing

The 'distance marketing' of goods and services is subject to two EU Directives which were implemented by the Consumer Protection (Distance Selling) Regulations 2001[142] and the Financial Services (Distance Marketing) Regulations 2004.[143] Originally, both Directives gave protection to consumers where their 'payment cards' were used 'fraudulently', by a third party, to make payment in connection with a distance contract. The protection in relation to Financial Services has been repealed and replaced the Payment Services Directive.[144] In relation to distance contracts, other than those for financial services, the consumer is entitled to cancel the payment and have all sums paid, by the card-issuer. This protection only applies in relation to a 'distance contract', i.e. a contract made in the context of an 'organised distance sales or service-provision scheme' operated by the supplier where there has been no face-to-face contact between the supplier and consumer up to and including the time of the conclusion of the contract,[145] so contracts by email, the Internet or the telephone which result from an organised marketing campaign are covered. Further, only consumers are protected so that persons acting in the course of their trade, business or profession are excluded.[146] The protection applies to the use of a 'payment card', which includes 'a credit card, a charge card, a debit card and a store card'.[147] The Lending Code provides that where details of a customer's account have been misused while the card has been in the customer's possession and the customer has not acted with gross negligence or fraudulently then the customer will not be liable for any resulting loss.[148]

Criminal liability for the misuse of cards

In the case of misuse of cards either by the cardholder himself or a third party, the card-issuer is entitled to its return and will usually take steps to try and prevent further misuse of the card by placing it on a 'stop list', although this will not prevent a complete misuse of the card.

The misuse of cards can give rise to criminal liability and prior to the Fraud Act 2006 the 'deception' offences under the Theft Act 1968 (as amended) and 1978 were largely relied on. However, one of the difficulties under these Acts was the problem of establishing 'deception' when an automated terminal was used to receive funds or pay for services in that a machine cannot be deceived. The Fraud Act 2006 replaces the deception offences with a more general 'fraud' offence that applies to any person who 'dishonestly makes a false representation' and thereby intends to make a gain or cause a loss.[149] The *actus reus* is therefore the making of the false representation, without the need to prove deception. In *Metropolitan Police Commissioner v Charles*,[150] a case of obtaining a pecuniary advantage by deception under the Theft Act 1968, the House of Lords held that a cardholder who used his cheque card in order to exceed his

---

[141] Directive 97/7/EC implemented by the Consumer Protection (Distance Selling) Regulations 2001, SI 2001/2334.

[142] Directive 2002/65/EC (amended by the Payment Services Directive, Directive 2007/64/EC) implemented by the Financial Services (Distance Marketing) Regulations 2004, SI 2004/2095.

[144] Directive 2007/64/EC.

[145] SI 2001/2334, reg 2(1).

[146] SI 2001/2334, reg 2(1).

[147] SI 2001/2334, reg 21(6).

[148] http://www.lendingstandardsboard.org.uk/docs/lendingcode.pdf.

[149] Fraud Act 2006, ss.1 and 2.

[150] [1977] AC 177.

overdraft limit represented to the payee that (i) he had the required funds with the bank to meet the cheques; and (ii) not just that the cheques would be paid by the bank. Under the new fraud offence a conviction would be secured under (i) because any such representation is false but not under (ii) because the bank guarantees to make payment when drawing a cheque backed by a cheque guarantee card, if certain conditions are satisfied. In another case, *R v Lambie*,[151] the credit-card holder exceeded her credit limit on a number of occasions so the bank demanded the card's return. The House of Lords concluded that a merchant would not accept a credit card if he knew that the cardholder was using it in breach of the contract with the card-issuer and therefore held that the cardholder had obtained credit by falsely representing that she was using the card in compliance with the contract. The use of the card, whether a charge or credit card, which the holder is no longer entitled to use would therefore involve a false representation and would fall within the new 'fraud' offence, and obtaining the card itself by false representations will also be covered.

Since the introduction of the new s.24A[152] of the Theft Act 1968 it is an offence to retain a 'wrongful credit' made to a bank account with the knowledge and belief that it is wrongful. Using payment cards to transfer funds to which the cardholder is not entitled into his bank account may be caught under this provision although it is aimed at persons who retain (i.e. who fail to take such steps as are reasonable to secure the cancellation of) an amount erroneously credited to their account.

Conclusion

While bank cards have changed the face of the payments system industry globally their legal regulation has not always kept apace. The Consumer Credit Act 1974 and the Payment Services Regulations 2009 have responded to the challenges posed by the plastic card sector, especially where the card is used as a means of extending credit. Both the 1974 Act and the 2009 Regulations attempt to regulate contractual relations and protect the consumer. The courts, where the opportunity has arisen, have not only attempted to develop the law but also explain and clarify the contractual relations that arise between the parties.

Further reading

➤ Jones, S.A. (1988) Credit Cards, Card Users and Account Holders, *JBL*, 457.
  This article explores the relationship between the account holder and the card user, and the card user and the other parties to the agreement. The contractual analysis of the relationship of the card user with other parties to the credit card agreement is of importance whether or not the agreement falls within the scope of the Consumer Credit Act 1974.

[151] [1982] AC 449.
[152] As amended by the Fraud Act 2006, s.14(1) and schedule 1, para. 7.

16 Overdrafts and bank loans

Chapter overview

The aim of this chapter is to:

➤ Examine some of the more common forms of bank loans available to the customer, these include:

  ● the bank overdraft;
  ● fixed term loans; and
  ● commonly for the corporate customer, the syndicated loan.

➤ Examine the legal and practical requirements and, where appropriate, analyse the distinctions between them.

Introduction

Lending has always been considered to be one of the two core activities undertaken by a bank or deposit-taking institution. Banking business is defined as 'an undertaking whose business is to receive deposits or other repayable funds from the public and to grant credits for its own account'.[1] As retail customers, most individuals are aware of the overdraft facility although the nature, extent and charges may not be fully transparent.[2] Commercial lending by banks can take various forms and banks often use the generic term 'bank facility'[3] to describe them. A term loan may have a fixed repayment schedule and the bank may allow the customer a revolving facility during which the customer can not only repay amounts but also re-borrow on the loan, so long as the overall limit of the facility is not exceeded. To that extent the revolving credit is similar to an overdraft on a bank account although the latter is generally repayable on demand.[4]

Although lending agreements may vary in detail, for example the simple overdraft facility letter may be short, for other loans the lending agreement may be considerably longer and complex. However, there are common features in most such agreements, which are intended to

---

[1] Cranston (2002) *Principles of Banking Law*, Oxford: Oxford University Press.
[2] See Ch. 9.
[3] Cranston (2002) *Principles of Banking Law*, Oxford: Oxford University Press.
[4] See Ch. 9.

identify and mitigate the credit risk the bank will face in respect of the loan facility. The more elaborate, and international, loan facilities carry specific risks, for example currency fluctuations, market disruptions and governmental action, which may affect not only the performance of the customer's obligations but sometimes also the legality of the contract. Bank loans may be granted for consumer or business purposes and a distinction must be made for the purposes of protection under the Consumer Credit Act 1974. Banking industry guidelines setting out best practice also differs depending on whether the loan is to a consumer, small business or large corporation.[5]

Before making a loan the bank will need to satisfy itself that the loan is a viable sound business decision for it, as lender, and be satisfied as to the soundness of the borrower, the purpose of the borrowing, i.e. that it is legal, and that the intended use is reasonably likely to produce a profitable outcome for it. While banks will avoid speculative projects it is not unreasonable for a bank to undertake a 'fair trade risk'.

Facility letters and loan agreements

Although a consumer customer may have little opportunity to negotiate the terms of the overdraft, or other loan agreement, there may be protracted negotiations between a bank and a corporate customer which eventually result in a document being drawn up setting out the nature of the contemplative loan and some or all of the terms to which the loan agreement is subject.

There are various terms that may be used to describe these documents, for example, offer documents, heads of agreement or commitment letters. The extent to which these documents may be legally enforceable may become important when the customer refuses to repay the fee referred to in the document, or when one of the parties refuses to complete the more formal documentation intended. In exceptional cases the loan, or part of the loan, may actually be paid over to the customer before the written agreement is finalised. In these circumstances a contract may be inferred from the conduct of the parties and the courts' willingness to apply the rules of agency law, where necessary. In other circumstances, there may be a common understanding that the loan is contingent on the agreement being concluded, so that if, for whatever reason, negotiations break down, any advances of the loan will become immediately repayable. Another possibility that may arise is one where an agreement is signed but further details have yet to be agreed. Although the latter may not necessarily make the agreement void, the courts may conclude that those terms, which have been agreed, are not sufficient to result in an enforceable contract.

English law does not countenance agreements to agree[6] and works on the assumption, especially in commercial transactions, that negotiations are adversarial. The law therefore overlooks the fact that negotiations may be completed in stages and even businesspeople are comfortable with agreements to agree. The manner in which the document is described may be some indication as to whether it is provisional until a legal agreement is drawn up and a

---

[5] See the Lending Code (March 2011), http://www.lendingstandardsboard.org.uk/docs/lendingcode.pdf; see also British Bankers' Association (BBA), A Statement of Principles: Banks and Micro-enterprises-Working Together (November 2009).

[6] *Walford* v *Miles* [1992] 2 AC 128.

commitment[7] letter, which contains a reasonably complete statement of the proposed terms, is a strong indication as to whether or not it is intended to be binding. There are various types of commitment letters and their legal character depends on their individual nature. A commitment letter 'subject to contract' will not automatically be regarded as not binding and in some cases the parties may agree to convert such a letter into a contract. Thus, there may be representations that give rise to a collateral contract, or estoppel may arise to prevent the parties from denying the terms and effect of the transactions envisaged by it. The test is whether the commitment letter was intended to be binding, or whether the binding letter is consistent with the reasonable expectations of the parties. The courts may have regard to the following:

- How the document is described is some indication whether it is intended to be legally enforceable. If the document is expressed as an 'agreement' and contains a sentence that 'this is a provisional agreement until a fully legalised agreement is drawn up' then this may indicate an intention to be bound. In some circumstances the term 'commitment' itself may not connote a binding commitment, but only a 'definite interest'.[8]

- Whether the commitment letter contains a reasonably complete statement of the proposed terms is a good indication, but is not definitive. A commitment letter may contain so few of the terms which would be expected in the formal document that it cannot be said that the parties intended to be bound, and omission of the interest rate, the currency (in the case of an international loan) and the terms of repayment would be serious flaws to the agreement being legally enforceable.

- Reference to the steps preceding and subsequent to the completion of the commitment letter may indicate whether it is intended to be legally binding.

Merely because a commitment letter is not binding does not mean that the expenses and fees mentioned in it are not payable.

The overdraft facility and the term loan

An overdraft facility is generally granted to the customer as a result of an express agreement entered into with the bank, although there may be circumstances in which the bank may decide to grant an overdraft facility when it is presented with a mandate which, if honoured, will result in the customer overdrawing without prior agreement. Where an overdraft is agreed with the bank it will allow the customer a contractual right to overdraw up to an agreed ceiling.[9] If a customer is offered an arranged overdraft, or an increase in their existing arranged overdraft limit, the bank should inform the customer whether the overdraft is repayable on

---

[7] The use of the term 'commitment' itself may not indicate a binding commitment but only a definite interest: *Governor of the Bank of England v 3i Plc* [1993] BCLC 968.

[8] *Governor of the Bank of England v 3i Plc* [1993] BCLC 968.

[9] Lending Code: Setting standards for banks, building societies and credit card providers, July 2011, para. 76 provides: 'When providing customers with information, before a contract is entered into, about a current account offering an arranged overdraft facility, subscribers should include clear, fair and not misleading information outlining the availability of the overdraft, including whether there are qualifying criteria for accessing the overdraft', http://www.lendingstandardsboard.org.uk/docs/lendingcode.pdf.

demand,[10] or at a certain time in the future. Where the bank grants its customer an overdraft facility through the current account it effectively provides that customer with a loan facility, the amount of which may vary on a daily basis, and on which the interest payable[11] will be calculated, at a compound rate,[12] on a daily basis, although the amount may be debited from the customer's account on a periodic basis.[13] As the nature of the overdraft has already been discussed[14] it is intended here only to highlight those features of the overdraft relevant in comparison with the term loan.

The overdraft facility predominates among the nature and types of loans made by banks, particularly loans made to consumer customers. The Lending Code[15] sets out the basic principles governing the overdraft and loan transactions in respect of individual customers and micro enterprises. Technically an overdraft is a fact, not a transaction. It arises where the customer of the bank draws on his current account so extensively that he eliminates any credit balance and produces a negative balance. This may be said to be particularly true of unauthorised overdrafts where the customer overdraws without a prearranged overdraft facility.[16] The interesting point to note is that the overdraft may be permitted without the express consent of the bank,[17] and consequently the reversal of roles, which occurs (so that the customer becomes the bank's debtor) arises without the express consent of the bank; although where the bank does extend an overdraft the courts are generally willing to hold the existence of an implied agreement.[18] In the absence of an express agreement, the bank may, however, refuse to pay any further amounts to the customer, or to honour any payment mandate, or obligation either to the customer or a third party.[19] However, if the bank agrees to allow the customer to overdraw in return for a consideration provided by him, the customer is legally entitled to overdraw on his account up to the agreed limit, and the bank will be liable to him in damages if it wrongfully refuses, or dishonours, the payment mandate up to the amount of the agreed limit of the overdraft.[20] Any amounts subsequently paid to the credit of the bank account will be used to eliminate the customer's indebtedness to the bank.[21]

---

[10] Lending Code: Setting standards for banks, building societies and credit card providers, July 2011, para. 80: where the lending code provides that the explanation to the customer could be contained in a facility letter or the terms and conditions, http://www.lendingstandardsboard.org.uk/docs/lendingcode.pdf.

[11] Lending Code: Setting standards for banks, building societies and credit card providers, July 2011, para. 77 provides: 'The customer must be provided, where relevant, with details of any charges payable, the interest rate to be applied or, if reference interest rates are to be used, the method for calculating the actual interest and the relevant date and index or base for determining such reference interest rates', http://www.lendingstandardsboard. org.uk/docs/lendingcode.pdf.

[12] *Sempra Metals Ltd* v *IRC* [2008] 1 AC 561 (HL).

[13] Lending Code: Setting standards for banks, building societies and credit card providers, July 2011, para. 90 provides: 'Subscribers should make information about overdraft interest rates available to customers via: a telephone helpline; a website; notices in branches; or information from staff', http://www.lendingstandardsboard.org.uk/ docs/lendingcode.pdf.

[14] See Ch. 9.

[15] The Lending Standards Board, The Lending Code, 2011, http://www.lendingstandardsboard.org.uk/docs/ lendingcode.pdf.

[16] *Office of Fair Trading* v *Abbey National and 7 Others* [2008] EWHC 875 (Comm) before Andrew Smith J at para. 55.

[17] Waller LJ in *Lloyds Bank Plc* v *Independent Insurance Co Ltd* [2000] 1 QB 110 at 118; see also Ch. 9.

[18] See Ch. 9.

[19] *Office of Fair Trading* v *Abbey National and 7 Others* [2008] EWHC 875 (Comm) before Andrew Smith J.

[20] *Barclays Bank Plc* v *W.J. Simms & Cooke (Southern) Ltd* [1980] 1 QB 677 at 699; see Chs 7 and 9.

[21] See Ch. 9.

The purposes for which a customer borrows from a bank, whether by way of an overdraft or by a fixed-term loan, are generally not the concern of the law provided the contract is legal and the amount is used for lawful purposes. In the case of company customers the abolition of the *ultra varies* rule has removed the problems in respect of the company's capacity.[22] Although the purpose for which a company may borrow money by way of an overdraft may not be material when considering the range of the company's borrowing it will remain of importance in planning the financing of the company's activities and the potential liability of its directors.[23] Although, originally, banks only financed a company's trading transactions by way of an overdraft, increasingly they have permitted overdrafts for the acquisition of capital assets.

An overdraft is repayable by the customer immediately on demand being made by the bank,[24] unless the bank agrees otherwise. In other words, a bank may demand immediate repayment of an overdraft at any time it thinks fit, and it does not owe the customer any duty to ensure that the demand is made in sufficient time before it becomes effective, so as to enable the customer a reasonable opportunity to raise the money elsewhere, if necessary.[25] However, the bank cannot treat the customer as being in default until it has given him sufficient time to obtain the money to repay the overdraft from a bank, in the locality of his residence or business address. The customer is therefore not in default until he has had time after the demand for repayment to fetch the money from another bank; it is no excuse on his part that there is no bank locally at which he has the money.[26] However, with instantaneous methods of money transfers accommodating the movement of funds relatively quickly there is now no reason why, within a reasonably short time, a customer will not be able to arrange a transfer of funds to an overdrawn account, and therefore these decisions must take into consideration developments in money transfer systems and banking practices. However the bank has an immediate right to set off an amount credited to another account and maintained by the same customer where the customer has both an overdrawn account and an account in credit.[27] Where the customer either becomes bankrupt or goes into insolvency the statutory insolvency rules take precedence to the banker's right of set off.[28] In respect of overdrafts repayable on demand the limitation period within which the bank may sue its customer to recover the amount overdrawn commences only from the date of the demand.

A major disadvantage of the overdraft, particularly where it is used to finance business operations, is that repayment may be called for without the bank giving any length of notice, and payment may therefore be demanded by the bank at a time when the company's liquid resources are low, even though its trading prospects are good. In a number of cases, where banks have attempted to enforce securities given to them, either for an overdraft or a term loan, the courts have implied a duty on the part of the bank not to enforce the security when it would be unreasonable to do so, i.e. when the company has committed a technical

---

[22] Companies Act 2006, s.39.

[23] Companies Act 2006, s.40.

[24] See Ch. 9; also see: *Rouse v Bradford Banking Co* [1894] AC 586; *Bank of Baroda v Panessar* [1987] Ch. 335.

[25] *Bank of Baroda v Panessar* [1987] Ch 335.

[26] *Toms v Wilson* (1863) 4 B 7 S 442; *Moore v Shelley* (1883) 8 App Cas 285; *Cripps (Pharmaceuticals) Ltd v Wickenden* [1973] 1 WLR 944; *Bank of Baroda v Panessar* [1986] 3 All ER 751.

[27] *Garnett v McKewan* (1872) LR 8 Ex 10.

[28] Insolvency Act 1986, ss.23(1)(2) and (4); Insolvency Rules 1986, rule 4.90(1), (2) and (4).

default[29] in respect of the facility but the company debtor is financially sound. However, the courts have held that the bank, as creditor, does not owe the customer, the debtor, a duty to act reasonably when deciding whether or not to take proceedings to enforce the security to recover a debt owed; the bank may consult only its own interests and not those of the customer when determining whether or not to enforce the security. A creditor bank's duty of care arises only when it takes steps to enforce the security for the debt; it must then act reasonably to obtain the best available price, but the choice whether and when to enforce the security is entirely that of the bank's.[30] It, therefore, follows that a bank may call in and enforce the security even in respect of an overdraft at any time and need not have regard to the effect of doing so on its customer. The customer may, of course, attempt to obtain a grace period from the bank which if conceded by the bank, even gratuitously, will then deny the bank its immediate right for payment of the overdraft without giving the customer a reasonable opportunity to borrow from elsewhere, or at least without giving the customer reasonable notice of the bank's intention to withdraw from the grace period permitted.[31]

Consumer credit aspects of the overdraft

The Consumer Credit Act 1974 applies in respect of regulated credit agreements and the relevant provisions apply if credit[32] is extended to an 'individual'.[33] The bank overdraft falls within the definition of the regulated consumer credit agreement for unrestricted-use[34] running account credit, even if the bank extends it without prior arrangement with the customer.[35] The 1974 Act applies where the bank has agreed to grant the customer an overdraft but has not finalised details of the arrangement, for example where the bank informs the customer that no bank charges will be levied while the account is in credit, but that charges will apply, if the account becomes overdrawn.[36] Often, at this stage, a maximum limit for an available overdraft will be fixed. Such agreements have been set to encompass a multiple agreement within the meaning of s.18(1)(a) of the Consumer Credit Act 1974 and under s.18(2) each transaction is treated as a separate agreement for the purpose of the Act.[37] Originally, most overdrafts were excluded from the documentation and cancellation provisions in Part V of the Consumer Credit Act 1974 but the implementation of the Consumer Credit Directive[38] has resulted in the imposition of certain requirements. Thus for example, the Directive

---

[29] *Shamji* v *Johnson Matthey Bank Ltd* [1986] BCLC 278.

[30] *Standard Chartered Bank Ltd* v *Walker* [1982] 1 WLR 1410.

[31] *Williams and Glyn's Bank Ltd* v *Barnes* [1981] Com LR 205.

[32] Consumer Credit Act 1974, s.9 under which credit includes a 'loan and any other form of financial accommodation'.

[33] Consumer Credit Act 1974, s.8.

[34] Consumer Credit Act 1974, s.10(1).

[35] Consumer Credit Act 1974, schedule 2.

[36] The Lending Code provides that where relevant the customer must be provided with details of any charges payable, the interest rate to be applied or if reference interest rates are to be used then the method of actually calculating the interest, para. 77, http://www.lendingstandardsboard.org.uk/docs/lendingcode.pdf.

[37] Guest and Lloyd (1975) *Encyclopedia of Consumer Credit Law*, London: Sweet & Maxwell.

[38] European Commission Directive 2011/90/EU was adopted by the EC in May 2008 and legislation implementing its provisions came fully into force on 1 February 2011.

provides that in the case of 'overrunning'[39] the bank must give detailed information about the rates of interest and any other charges in the current account agreement, which must be re-issued annually. If there is actual significant[40] overrunning, then details about the rates of interest and other charges are required to be given 'without delay'.[41]

The Act draws a distinction between 'authorised business overdrafts' and 'authorised non-business overdrafts' and maintains the concessions in relation to business overdrafts,[42] since business credit is outside the scope of the Directive. However, the duty to assess the credit-worthiness of the debtor[43] and the new special duty to supply a document containing the terms of the overdraft agreement[44] have been extended to all such overdrafts. The duty to notify changes of interest rate is modified in the case of all overdrafts so that it only applies to increases in the rate.[45] The 'authorised non-business overdrafts' are generally subject to pre-contract disclosure requirements and the form and content of the agreement requirements. Most overdrafts are not subject to the right of withdrawal or cancellation.

Current accounts opened at a distance, for example Internet accounts, are subject to the Distance Marketing Directive[46] under which the customer must receive 'pre-contract' information and has a right of cancellation exercisable for 14 days after the account is opened. However, these protections do not apply if the customer has visited the branch with proof of identification in compliance with the bank's money-laundering procedures,[47] since the contract will no longer be regarded as a 'distance contract'. Advertisements in respect of overdrafts need not state the 'representative APR' nor disclose any compulsory contract for 'ancillary services'. Further, only advertisements that allow overdraft drawing on a current account may use the term overdraft. The Consumer Credit Act 1974 also prohibits the canvassing of overdrafts off trade premises. Both the Act and the Directive preserve the bank's right to demand repayment of an overdraft without notice, although if the loan is for a specific period the creditor is required to give at least seven days' notice before he can enforce the agreement.[48] Although, the Directive introduced new provisions for the termination of agreements of no fixed duration, whether by the debtor or the creditor,[49] these provisions do not apply to overdrafts[50] where repayment is demanded because of default and default notice under s.87 is required.

---

[39] The term is used in the Directive to cover situations where an overdraft is permitted but has not been arranged or exceeding an arranged overdraft limit.

[40] I.e., for a 'significant' amount (see Consumer Credit Act 1974, s.74B(3) if an extra charge is payable or if the overrunning will have an adverse effect on the customer's ability to access more credit for a period of one month (or three months if the overdraft is secured on land).

[41] Unless notice has already been given during that period (Consumer Credit Act 1974, s.74B added by SI 2010/1010, reg. 22) as amended by SI 2010/1969 from 1 February 2011.

[42] Consumer Credit Act 1974, s.74(1)(b).

[43] Consumer Credit Act 1974, s.55B, inserted by SI 2010/1010, reg. 5 from 1 February 2011.

[44] Consumer Credit Act 1974, s.61B, inserted by SI 2010/1010, reg. 9 from 1 February 2011.

[45] Consumer Credit Act 1974, s.78A, inserted by SI 2010/1010, reg. 27 from 1 February 2011; see also the Lending Code, 2011, paras 77, 78, 81 and 82; http://www.lendingstandardsboard.org.uk/docs/lendingcode.pdf.

[46] Directive 2002/65/EC.

[47] See Ch. 13.

[48] Consumer Credit Act 1974, s.76 (enforcement without termination of agreement) and s.98 (termination of agreement).

[49] Consumer Credit Act 1974, s.98A, inserted by SI 2010/1010, reg. 39 from 1 February 2011.

[50] Consumer Credit Act 1974, s.98A(8).

Term loans

Term loans, as their name suggests, are made for a fixed-term period of time. They may be made to an individual or a corporate company. Where a term loan is made to an individual the loan will normally, for example, be secured by a mortgage. Where the loan is made to a company the security is likely to take the form of a guarantee, or debenture over the company assets, which may take longer to realise or mature.

The bank, therefore, will take a number of factors into account when safeguarding its interests. The bank needs, among other things, to consider the cash flow of the borrower, the source of the repayments and the nature of the repayments, for example whether the loan will be repaid by way of fixed equal instalments (amortised repayments), whether the repayments will increase over the loan period (balloon repayments) or whether the repayments will come in one shot at the end (bullet repayment).[51] Generally, the bank will attempt to identify the source of the repayments, although that need not be the exclusive source.

Banks may make term loans to smaller businesses and companies for periods up to five years (depending on the financial condition of the company and the use to which the loan will be made) and larger companies for longer periods of up to ten or more years. Term loans are generally made at rates of interest which will vary with market rate during the lifetime of the loan, and the agreement will tend to contain provisions for the acceleration of the repayment date, on the happening of certain contingencies. Some of these contingencies may relate to breaches of contract, or default of the terms of the borrowing. Very large term loans made to multinational companies may be made by a syndicate of banks who share between themselves the agreed proportion of the advance, the cost of borrowing and the associated risks.

Term loan agreements usually provide that the borrowing customer will be given the facility by the bank, or banks, to borrow up to a stated maximum amount and that the borrowing customer may draw that amount down on stated dates during an initial period after the loan agreement has been signed. The 'draw down' facility may be either through a single drawing of the whole amount or by successive instalments. Amounts of the facility, which have not been drawn by the end of the agreed period, may not be drawn thereafter, and the facility is cancelled in respect of any amounts not drawn down. In the case of very large loans, the borrowing customer may be required to give a specific number of days' notice to the lending bank that it intends to 'draw down' a stated amount of the loan on the next drawing date so the bank can ensure funds are readily available. This is particularly important when the borrowing customer can 'draw down' the amount of the loan in a number of different agreed currencies. Banks will normally charge a small percentage fee (commitment fee) on the undrawn balance, which they have agreed to lend to the borrowing customer. This fee is charged periodically at the time when interest payments fall due and it terminates when the whole amount of the loan has been drawn down. Term loans will specify the date or dates, and the manner by which the amount of the loan is to be repaid. In contrast to overdrafts, term loans, made by the bank when no date for repayment of the term loan is agreed, are treated in law as implying a term that the loan advance will become repayable only when the bank

---

[51] Loan Market Association, Guide to Syndicated Loans, http://www.lma.eu.com/uploads/files/Introductory_Guides/Guide_to_Par_Syndicated_Loans.pdf.

has given the customer reasonable length of notice demanding repayment.[52] The customer, on the other hand, would be entitled to repay such a loan at any time without giving notice in advance. A term loan by agreement will usually be repayable either in a single sum on one specified date, or more usually by quarterly, bi-annually or yearly instalments, commencing on a date specified in the agreement. The commencement and duration of the repayment or the repayment period is subject to negotiation between the borrowing company and the lead bank. The agreed repayment terms are reciprocally binding on the borrowing company and the lending bank or banks. Consequently the banks cannot require the borrowing customer to repay the loan earlier than the agreed date or dates (although there may be provision for repayment to be accelerated under a default clause) and the borrowing customer cannot save interest by repaying the loan before the agreed date or dates. It is usual, however, for the term loan agreement to permit the borrowing company to repay the whole or part of the outstanding loan on any of the dates the interest is charged under the loan agreement, but it is usual to specify the earliest date on which this may be permitted and the multiples of payment permitted. Once the borrower has repaid a term loan, it cannot be re-drawn.[53]

Non-recourse loans

Term loans made to large companies to finance projects which will become income produc-ing on or shortly after completion (e.g. loans to finance the exploration for, and exploitation of, oil bearing localities) may contain an option for the borrowing company to convert the outstanding balance of the loan, on any date for repayment of the instalment during the repay-ment period, into a non-recourse loan if certain specified financial conditions are satisfied. The non-recourse loan always carries a higher rate of interest than the initial loan, but it is repayable, with interest, during a longer period and only out of earnings or profits arising out of the financed project. The importance of a non-recourse loan is that the borrowing company will only make repayment of capital, and interest, out of profits generated from the financed project. Consequently, any liability on the part of the borrowing company arising in an insolvency situation will be avoided. The other assets of the company are therefore avail-able to sell, lease or otherwise dispose of, free from any charge or security created to finance the specific project, and are also available to be used as security for further borrowing by the company customer. The lending bank does not take an equity participation in the project and is still a creditor of the borrowing company. If the project does not produce sufficient earnings in order to repay the bank, the lending bank will normally have the power under the loan agreement to appoint a receiver to take over the management of the project and also to sell the company's assets comprised in it.

The loan facility

Commercial loan agreements usually contain: (i) conditions precedent in respect of the avail-ability of the loan; (ii) representations, warranties and covenants given by the borrower, and (iii) extensive default clauses. We will now examine the purpose of each, in turn:

---

[52] *Bradford Old Bank Ltd* v *Sutcliffe* [1918] 2 KB 833; *Buckingham & Co* v *London Midland Bank Ltd* (1895) 12 TLR 70.
[53] Loan Market Association, Guide to Syndicated Loans, http://www.lma.eu.com/uploads/files/Introductory_ Guides/Guide_to_Par_Syndicated_Loans.pdf.

(i) *Conditions precedent*: such terms must be complied with before the borrowing customer can 'draw down' the funds. Normally the borrowing customer will be required to supply the lender with specific documentation, for example although not significant for the purposes of determining the company's capacity,[54] the bank is still likely to ask for a copy of the company's constitutional documents, a copy of the board resolution approving the facility and, in the case of cross-border loans, legal opinion of the relevant foreign lawyers on its validity.[55] The bank will have wide discretion as to which documents must be produced as conditions precedent. The issue, in respect of such clauses, is whether the conditions precedent are conditions to the agreement coming into effect, or whether they are conditions precedent to the bank's performance under the loan facility. The approach appears to be that there is a binding contract once the parties have agreed to the terms, but that until the conditions precedent are satisfied the bank need not make the funds available or allow the customer to 'draw down'. Common conditions precedent may require the borrowing customer to confirm that there have been no events of default and that the representations and warranties remain accurate,[56] or may be those relating to commercial aspects of the loan including the credit standing of the borrowing customer and his financial condition.[57] Whether the bank needs to cooperate in respect of the conditions precedent will depend on the nature of the clause, for example there may be conditions precedent that require the bank to initiate action and unless the bank acts, the borrowing company will be unable to fulfil its obligations. In such circumstances, the bank will need to act with due care so that its conduct is not deemed by the borrowing customer as waiving compliance with the conditions precedent. Where a condition precedent can be construed as imposing on the bank a duty to act, the bank's failure may not only render it liable in damages but may also prevent it from claiming that the condition has not been satisfied. However, some conditions precedent may depend on the actions of a third party, for example where a regulated body needs to approve the facility and the borrower needs to obtain that approval.

(ii) *Representations and warranties*: these clauses usually have several purposes. They endeavour to provide remedies for misrepresentation in the event of inaccuracy; they operate as an estoppel against the borrower;[58] and they may enable the lender to cancel the loan commitment and accelerate repayment if they are linked to an event of default.[59] Representations and warranties usually fall into two basic categories: (a) those relating to legal aspects, for example the legal status, powers and authority of the borrowing customer and the validity of any documents; and (b) those relating to the credit standing and financial status of the borrowing customer. Additionally, the borrower will be required to make representations on certain other matters, for example that its accounts are accurate and have suffered no material adverse change since they were drawn up and that there are no legal proceedings pending that may have an adverse affect on the customer. Where there is a syndicate of banks involved in the loan, there will be representations

---

[54] As a result of the Companies Act 2006, s.39 provides the company has full contractual capacity.

[55] Loan Market Association, *Multicurrency Term and Revolving Facility Agreement*, May 2004, cl. 4.1 and schedule 2, Part 1.

[56] Loan Market Association, *Multicurrency Term and Revolving Facility Agreement*, cl. 4.2.

[57] Loan Market Association, *Multicurrency Term and Revolving Facility Agreement*, cl. 4.2.

[58] *Balkis Consolidated Co v Tomkinson* [1893] AC 396.

[59] *MacKenzie v Royal Bank of Canada* [1934] AC 468.

relating to the accuracy of the information memorandum sent to potential members. Representations and warranties, therefore, perform an investigative[60] function and will normally be undertaken in conjunction with a due diligence exercise relating to the borrower and the project being financed. Representations and warranties are usually drafted on an 'evergreen' basis, which means that they are deemed to be repeated on each 'draw down' of the funds by the borrowing customer and/or other specified intervals, and their accuracy verified.[61] The loan agreement will usually specify that it is an event of default by the borrowing customer to make a representation or warranty that is inaccurate in any material respect. Representations and warranties may relate not only to the borrowing customer but also to its parent company or any subsidiaries within the group, and borrowers will therefore need to consider whether they can accurately make representations about other companies in the group, particularly those based overseas.

(iii) *Covenants*: these are undertakings given by the borrowing customer to the lending bank which restrict the customer's conduct in respect of his business and thereby give the bank control over the borrower's business so as to ensure that the borrowing customer's business structures and financial position are preserved. As with other undertakings, the nature of the covenants will depend on a number of factors including the size and duration of the loan, the position of the borrower and his negotiating strength, and competition from other banks.[62] The main covenants usually demanded from a corporate borrower relate to: (a) the provision of financial information, for example financial statements;[63] (b) maintenance of certain financial ratios, for example maintaining minimum tangible net worth and gearing ratios;[64] (c) restrictions on the disposal of assets; (d) restrictions on the grant of security to other creditors[65] (a negative pledge clause); and (e) undertaking that such obligations under the loan agreement will rank at least equally (a *pari passu* clause) with other unsecured creditors.[66]

Protecting the bank's interest: events of default

All lending agreements will usually specify certain 'events of default' that confer on the lender the option of terminating the commitment to make any further advances and accelerating repayment of the capital sum and interest. The events of default must be expressly specified in the loan agreement and will not be implied by the courts. Any rights of default specifically set out in the loan agreement are in addition to the rights conferred by the common law in respect of the borrowing customer's default of the loan contract. Whether there has been a breach of the covenants under the loan agreement will depend on their interpretation. Specific performance of the default clauses will generally be inadvisable since it is unlikely the customer would have defaulted had he been able to comply with the terms of the loan

---

[60] Wood (1995) *International Loans, Bonds and Securities Regulations*, London: Sweet & Maxwell, p.29.

[61] Loan Market Association, *Multicurrency Term and Revolving Facility Agreement*, cl. 19.14.

[62] Day and Taylor (1995) Evidence on the Practice of UK Bankers in Contracting for Medium-Term Debt, 9 *JIBL*, 394; Day and Taylor (1996) Bankers' Perspectives on the Role of Covenants in Debt Contracts, 5 *JIBL*, 201.

[63] Loan Market Association, Multicurrency Term and Revolving Facility Agreement, cl. 20.

[64] Loan Market Association, Multicurrency Term and Revolving Facility Agreement, cl. 21.

[65] Loan Market Association, Multicurrency Term and Revolving Facility Agreement, cl. 22.5.

[66] Loan Market Association, Multicurrency Term and Revolving Facility Agreement, cl. 19.12.

agreement and continuation of the agreement, if possible, could further jeopardise the bank's commitment. Similarly, an injunction is likely to be inappropriate on the basis that the borrowing customer is unlikely to be able to perform his obligations even if the bank could undertake preventative action. Typical events of default in a loan agreement might include the failure to repay any capital or interest when due, the bankruptcy of the customer, the appointment of the official receiver or the company being wound up. Any 'material adverse change' in the borrowing customer's financial position or business operations may also be a specified default event.

Material adverse change clause

Most facility agreements will contain a material adverse change (MAC) clause. These clauses are intended to provide the lender with protection against unforeseen events, which have, or may have, a significant detrimental effect on the borrower. The purpose of the MAC clauses is to give the lender the right to accelerate the loan if the MAC event occurs. Until recently there had been few reported English cases on the use of such clauses in facility agreements. Before 2013, one of the few reported cases where an English court has upheld a lender's use of a MAC clause was *BNP Paribas* v *Yukos Oil* where the court probably had little alternative but to uphold that a MAC event had occurred. It would be hard to avoid that a $3.3 billion tax bill, frozen assets and a press release referencing a threat of insolvency did not constitute a MAC. However, two recent decisions have resulted in a review of such clauses namely *Cukurova* v *Alfa Telecom*[67] and *GrupoHoteleroUrvasco SA* v *Carey Value Added SL and another*.[68]

In the *Cukurova* case[69] Alfa Telecom argued that there had been a material adverse change as a result of an arbitration award made against Cukurova for breaching an agreement with another party. The award had ordered specific performance of Cukurova's breached obligation but the Privy Council accepted that the award 'clearly implied a potential, indeed a virtual certainty, of a very substantial order for damages against [Cukurova]' on the basis that Cukurova would not be able to satisfy the requirement for specific performance. In the Privy Council's opinion, this substantial contingent liability was unquestionably 'reasonably likely to have a material adverse effect on [Cukurova's] financial condition'. The clause under consideration stated that default would result from '[an] event or circumstance, which in the opinion of [Alfa] has had or is reasonably likely to have a material adverse effect on the financial condition, assets or business of [Cukurova]'. While the MAC is a subjective clause the Privy Council concluded that even, on an objective basis, 'the court has to be convinced by admissible evidence that [the lender] did in fact form the requisite opinion'. The lender's notification that it considered the default event an MAC would not itself be sufficient to satisfy the requirement. While lenders will usually want MAC clauses to be subjective rather than objective, and as wide as possible, there may be doubt about whether the clause covers a particular event. Lenders are, therefore, usually reluctant to rely on this clause alone to accelerate a facility.

---

[67] [2013] UKPC 25.
[68] [2013] EWHC 1039 (Comm).
[69] [2013] UKPC 25.

In *GrupoHoteleroUrvasco SA* v *Carey Value Added SL*[70] the High Court looked at the interpretation of a representation, which stated that 'there has been no material adverse change in [the] financial condition [of the obligors] (consolidated if applicable) since the date of this Loan Agreement'. The lender's argument was that the borrower was in default under the loan agreement for breaching the representation that there had been no material adverse change in the obligors' financial condition. The dispute focused on the general deterioration in the obligors' financial position over a period of time, rather than on any particular event or events. The court found there was no breach of the representation on the facts. However, the court gave guidance on some principles for interpreting MAC clauses namely:

- If a lender is trying to show there has been a MAC in a company's 'financial condition', this will be determined chiefly by reference to its financial information covering the relevant period. 'Financial condition' would not usually cover a company's prospects or more general economic or market changes.

- A change in financial condition is only materially adverse if it significantly affects the company's ability to perform its obligations under the relevant agreement, and in particular its ability to repay a loan.

- A lender cannot enforce a MAC clause based on circumstances of which it was aware when it entered the agreement.

- A change must not be merely temporary.

- The burden of proof is on the lender to show that the event or circumstance described in the clause has occurred.

However, the enquiry was not necessarily limited to the financial information if there was other compelling evidence. The adverse change would be material if it significantly affected the borrower's ability to repay the loan in question.

A breach of any of the events of default will not automatically activate default proceedings and grace periods may be implemented under the loan agreement. However, the lending banks exercise of its discretion to invoke its remedies under the 'events of default' clauses is not subject to statutory review. While a consumer customer may be able to rely on the Unfair Terms in Consumer Contracts Regulations 1999, which invalidates certain terms as 'unfair', no such scrutiny is available in respect of corporate borrowers. In *Director General of Fair Trading* v *First National Bank Plc*[71] the loan contained a term that should the borrowing customer default on the repayments, interest would continue to be payable at the contract rate until any judgment obtained by the bank was discharged. The House of Lords held that the term was subject to the UTCCR 1999 and it did not fall within the terms that related to (a) the definition of the main subject matter of the contract, or (b) the adequacy of the price or remuneration for the goods or services provided, which terms are not subject to scrutiny before the courts. On that basis it was open to the Lords to consider whether the term was 'unfair'. Their Lordships then went on to hold that the term was not 'unfair' as it did not cause a significant imbalance in the parties' rights and obligations under the contract to the detriment of the consumer. Its purpose was to ensure the borrowing customer did not enjoy

[70] [2013] EWHC 1039 (Comm).
[71] [2002] 1 AC 481.

the benefit of the outstanding amount after judgment, without satisfying the obligation to pay interest as provided for in the contract.

In addition to the UTCCR 1999, an individual or an unincorporated firm will be able to rely on the Consumer Credit Act 1974 and both the consumer and the commercial borrower can rely on the common law remedies. In respect of the bank declining to grant a loan to a consumer customer or micro enterprise, the Lending Code provides that the bank should give reasons for declining the loan.[72]

Consumer Credit Act 1974

Part V of the Consumer Credit Act 1974 introduces measures for the protection of consumers, including rights of cancellation and withdrawal, and cancellation rights in respect of 'distance' contracts. The provisions of the Act dealing with bank loans under s.60 empower the Secretary of State to make regulations prescribing, *inter alia*, the form of regulated consumer credit agreements. The Consumer Credit (Agreements) Regulations[73] made under this provision must be strictly complied with if the loan is to be enforceable by the bank, without a court order. Further, the Consumer Credit (Disclosure of Information) Regulations[74] require 'pre-contract' information to be given in the prescribed form before the loan is concluded. Again the agreement will be unenforceable without a court order, if the pre-contract information is not given.

The Consumer Credit (Agreements) Regulations require certain 'information' to be contained in the agreement and prescribe that the agreement bears a heading specifying that it is an agreement regulated by the Consumer Credit Act 1974, and that it contains statutory notices advising the debtor of his rights under the Act and that the signature is executed in the prescribed form.[75] The terms of the agreement (other than implied terms) must be set out in the document.[76] The Agreement Regulations provide for the extensive 'information' required in the document and the manner of the disclosure. The disclosure must relate to the amount of the credit or credit limit, the contract duration, the total amount payable, the timing and amount of repayments, information about the APR, detailed information about the total charge for credit (with a list of its constant constituents), the annual rate of interest, how interest is calculated and, if the APR is variable, the circumstances in which the variation will occur. Additionally, any security must be described, default charges must be listed, and information about rebates on early settlement must be given.

---

[72] The Lending Standards Board, The Lending Code, 2011, paras 166 and 167, http://www.lendingstandardsboard.org.uk/docs/lendingcode.pdf.

[73] There are two separate regimes: (i) Consumer Credit (Agreements) Regulations 1983, SI 1983/1553, as amended by SI 2004/1482 are applicable to agreements secured on land unless the creditor has 'opted into' the newer regime; and (ii) the Consumer Credit (Agreements) Regulations 2010, SI 2010/1014.

[74] The Consumer Credit (Disclosure of Information) Regulations 2004, SI 2004/1481 (The Financial Services (Distance Marketing) Regulations 2010, SI 2010/1013 as amended by SI 2010/1969, will apply to distance contracts).

[75] Consumer Credit (Agreements) Regulations 1983, reg. 6 (amended by the Consumer Credit Act 1974 (Electronic Communications) Order 2004, SI 2004/3236, reg. 4 in order to facilitate electronic contracting) and the Consumer Credit (Agreements) Regulations 2010, reg. 4.

[76] Consumer Credit Act 1974, s.61(1)(b).

Any modifications to the agreement, for example where a further advance is made under an existing agreement, or where the security for the loan is varied, modification of the agreement will need to comply with the regulations.[77] Whether modification has occurred may be debatable, for example where the bank grants an indulgence to the customer by allowing him to defer payment of the instalment or the bank reduces the amount of an instalment or extends the customer's time to make payment, compared to a situation where the customer is required to furnish consideration, for example by paying a higher rate of interest on an overdue amount.

Where the loan agreement is secured on land[78] the Consumer Credit Act 1974 contains special provisions, which require the bank to send the customer an advance copy of the agreement and legal charge. The bank must allow the customer at least a seven-day period during which the customer may cancel the agreement. At the end of this period, and if the customer has not cancelled, the bank must send him the agreement and legal charge for signature. This must then be followed by a further seven-day 'consideration period', during which the bank must not approach the customer in any way, except at the customer's request. The object of these provisions is to enable the customer to make up his mind without pressure from the bank, and also to ensure that the customer does not rush into the transaction. The bank must also take care to comply with the requirements relating to the provision of copies of the agreement. Unless the Consumer Credit Directive applies, two copies of the agreement must be given to the customer: the first unexecuted copy must be supplied when the agreement is delivered, or sent to the customer for signature, and the second copy of the executed agreement must be given within seven days following the making of the agreement.[79] If there are joint borrowers, each of them must receive these copies.[80]

The creditor's duties of disclosure under the Act do not end on the execution of the agreement and the bank is obliged to give periodic statements of account and must provide the debtor, at his request, with a copy of the agreement and details of the financial state of the transaction, when required. The creditor must also give notice of unilateral variations to the agreement and written notice of variations in interest rates must be given. Where the borrowing customer defaults in payment, the bank must give at least 14 days' notice before it calls in the loan or enforces any security (including any guarantee). The notice must be given in the statutory form, which advises the customer that, if he pays off the arrears, no further action will be taken against him or the surety. The notice must also inform him that if he has difficulties in making the payments he can apply to the court, which may make an order giving him time to pay off the amount. The bank may also serve notice in the case of non-default, for example where it wishes to call in the loan, or terminate the agreement on bankruptcy of the customer. Where the agreement is not of fixed duration both the debtor and creditor may terminate the agreement by giving notice: the debtor by giving a minimum of one month's notice to terminate, and the creditor by giving at least two months' notice.

---

[77] SI 1983/1553, reg. 7 and schedule 8 and SI 2010/1014, reg. 5 amended by SI 2010/1969.
[78] Other than s.58(2) cases.
[79] Consumer Credit Act 1974, s.62–63.
[80] Consumer Credit Act 1974, s.185.

Syndicated loans

Although the detailed provisions of different loan agreements may vary, each such agreement will contain certain similar provisions. Some attempt has been made to standardise the documentation and, in October 1998, the Loan Market, working with the British Bankers' Association, the Association of Corporate Treasurers, and the major City law firms introduced recommended forms of facility agreements for use in the syndicated lending market. Evidence indicates that by 2000 the forms were being widely used.[81] However, the purpose of the loan will shape the agreement concluded between the lending bank and the borrowing customer.

A syndicated loan will involve two or more banks with each bank in the syndicate contributing a proportion of the loan to the corporate borrower on common terms. Large commercial loans will be syndicated where a single bank is unable or unwilling to either advance the full amount of the loan, or to take the full extent of the risk associated with the loan. The amount and size of the loan is likely to determine the size of the syndicate.[82] A syndicated loan must be distinguished from a loan participation where only a single bank will enter into a loan agreement with the borrowing customer and then sell part of its interest in the loan to other banks (the participant banks). A bank may decide to sell part of its interest in a loan subsequently either because it wants to reduce its exposure or because it wants to diversify its portfolio. The *Guide to Syndicated Loans*[83] provides two types of loan facility that are usually syndicated namely: (i) the term loan, which has been discussed above; (ii) and the revolving loan facility. The guide provides that the second type of loan that may be syndicated is the revolving credit,[84] which provides the borrower with a maximum aggregate amount of capital available at any time over a specified period of time. Unlike a term credit the revolving credit allows the borrower to draw down, repay and re-draw funds advanced to him during the period of the facility. Each loan is borrowed for a set period after which it technically becomes repayable. Repayment of the revolving credit is achieved through repayment of the whole amount at a set date or by instalments.

Mechanisms of syndication

The syndicate process will begin when the borrowing customer grants a mandate to a single bank to arrange the syndicated loan. The commitment of the lead bank may vary depending on the terms of the agreement with the borrowing customer but the main function of the lead bank is to put together the loan facility, although the lead bank may agree to underwrite the loan if it is unable to form the syndicate. In most cases the customer will merely require the lead bank to use its 'best efforts' to arrange a suitable syndicate, although the term has not been legally defined. Once the basic terms and conditions of the loan have been agreed with the borrowing customer, the lead bank may solicit interest from potential participants and send out 'term sheets' to selected banks. These 'term sheets' include brief information of

---

[81] Campbell (2000) The LMA Recommended Form of Primary Documents, *JIBFL*, 53.
[82] Financing for the construction of the Eurotunnel involved more than 200 lending banks.
[83] Loan Market Association, *Guide to Syndicated Loans*, http://www.lma.eu.com/uploads/files/Introductory_Guides/Guide_to_Par_Syndicated_Loans.pdf.
[84] Loan Market Association, *Guide to Syndicated Loans*, http://www.lma.eu.com/uploads/files/Introductory_Guides/Guide_to_Par_Syndicated_Loans.pdf.

the borrower, the actual proposal and that the structure applicable at different levels of the syndicate.

At the same time the lead bank will work with the borrowing customer to prepare a detailed information memorandum about the borrowing customer and the loan which will then be used to market the loan to the potential banks in the syndicate. The information memorandum is a document used in order to sell the loan. Its legal status and the obligations to which it gives rise will depend on the nature of the information it contains, and the circumstances surrounding its distribution. In the majority of cases, the borrowing customer will have supplied the information contained in the memorandum and only in rare cases will the lead bank attempt to verify the information. The information memorandum commonly contains extensive clauses intended to limit the potential liability of a participant bank in respect of information contained in the memorandum, in the event of inaccuracy. In *Re Colocotronics Tanker Securities Litigation*[85] an action was brought against the lead bank (the European–American Banking Corporation (EABC)) alleging that EABC held itself out to be skilled in international finance and an expert in investigating, analysing and recommending potential participations in syndicated loans, such as those granted in favour of the Colocotronics shipping group. It was also alleged that EABC had a duty to the plaintiffs to advise them of all material facts relevant to the loans and that EABC was guilty of making untrue statements of material facts and of the omission of other material facts, which had induced the plaintiffs to participate in the syndicated loans. Although the litigation was settled by the lead bank, EABC, agreeing to underwrite the entire transaction, nevertheless the banking sector started to look at the question of potential liability for incorrect information contained in the information memorandum.

In this respect potential liability may include fraudulent[86] and negligent misrepresentation.[87] Since there may be substantial potential liability imposed on the lead bank, appropriate measures may be required in order to safeguard the position of that bank, by providing that the information memorandum is merely intended to provide the basis of information which each potential bank should supplement by making its own independent economic and financial investigations of the borrowing customer.

Terms of a syndicated loan

Attempts to standardise documentation in syndicated loans have generally been successful and, in October 1999, the Loan Market Association, the Association of Corporate Treasurers, and major City law firms introduced recommended forms of primary loan documentation. Syndicated loan agreements provide that:

- Each participating bank will make loans up to its specific commitment during an agreed period.
- Each bank's obligations are several and independent.
- Each bank's rights are divided.[88]

---

[85] 420 F. Supp 998 (SDNY 1976).
[86] *Derry* v *Peek* (1889) 14 App Cas 337.
[87] *Hedley Byrne & Co Ltd* v *Heller & Partners Ltd* [1964] AC 465.
[88] LMA.MTR.03, cl. 2.

These provisions recognise the severability of each participating bank's rights and obligations against the borrowing customer, since each bank effectively agrees to make a separate loan to the customer. The execution of the loan will create direct contractual relations between the borrowing customer and the syndicate banks, and each bank enters into a debtor and creditor relationship with the borrowing customer. Therefore, the failure of one participating bank to perform its loan obligations does not absolve the other member banks of their obligations. Participating banks in a syndicate will not normally underwrite the obligations of the other banks.[89] The divided nature of each bank's rights and obligations reinforces the fundamental basis of the syndicated loan, i.e. that each separate loan is made by each participating bank individually. Consequently, each bank may enforce its own rights separately, unless the bank has agreed to refrain from so doing under the loan agreement. While the rights of each participating bank are legally separate, the syndicate banks will usually undertake to abide by the decision of the majority[90] of the syndicate members in respect of the administration of the loan, particularly with regard to such matters as, for example, the enforcement of a breach of covenant, or the giving of consent to the relaxation of covenants, or in respect of a decision to accelerate the loan in the event of default.[91] The majority lender must act in good faith, but need not exercise its powers for the benefit of the participating banks as a whole.[92]

A syndicated loan agreement will contain a *pro rata* sharing clause,[93] in accordance with which each bank agrees to share with the other banks any amounts recovered from the borrowing customer (whether by way of a banker's right of set-off, litigation or repayment by the borrower) in excess of what the other banks have recovered, taking into consideration the proportion that each bank has contributed overall. Such clauses are intended to share sums received by one bank among the other participating members of the syndicate. However, the principles of the sharing clause appear to be honoured more in the breach than the compliance.[94]

While forming a syndicate of banks willing to make the loan the lead bank itself may also be one of the banks advancing funds to the borrowing customer and in such circumstances it will assess not only the extent of its own risk, but also negotiate the terms of the loan facility and security with the borrowing customer. At this stage the lead bank's responsibilities will be completed, although the loan agreement will normally provide for the appointment of a bank to act as an agent for the syndicate (agent bank) in respect of dealings with the borrowing customer and the administration of the loan facility.

The role of the agent bank

The agent bank's functions commence on appointment and although the lead bank may often assume such a function it is not uncommon for a different bank to perform the role of agent bank. The distinction between the lead bank and the agent bank may be blurred in some loan agreements because the same bank often performs both functions. However, most

---

[89] LMA.MTR.03, cl. 2.2(a).
[90] Majority requires either more than half or two-thirds of the relevant votes which are measured in accordance to the amounts of the bank's participation; see LMA. MTR. 03, cl. 1.1.
[91] LMA.MTR.03, cl. 26.7.
[92] *Redwood Master Fund Ltd* v *TD Bank Europe Ltd* [2002] EWHC 2703.
[93] LMA.MTR.03, cl. 28.
[94] Hughes (2000) Loans agreements – Single Banks and Syndicated, *JIBFL*, 115.

loan agreements make a clear distinction between the two roles particularly as the responsibilities of the agent bank only come into operation after those of the lead bank have seized, namely, on the execution of the agreement. The agent bank acts as agent of the syndicate banks and most syndicated loan agreements will include a clause which states that they have appointed the agent. The functions of the agent bank are basically administrative, for example the receiving and forwarding of documents required to satisfy the conditions precedent; calculating the interest rate in the case of floating rate loans; acting as a conduit for payment and repayment; and forwarding financial and other information received from the borrowing customer. The syndicated loan agreement may also confer discretionary powers on the agent bank, for example the power to call for a compliance certificate and financial information from the borrowing customer, or the power to accelerate the loan on default, without confirming the views of the other participating banks, in certain urgent situations. The agent bank is usually paid a fee for carrying out such obligations.

While it might be possible that the granting of discretionary powers to the agent bank might subject it to fiduciary duties it is usually provided that the loan agreement does not constitute the agent bank as a trustee or fiduciary of the participating banks.[95] The agent bank, however, will be expected to act with care, skill and diligence in respect of the other participating banks' interests.

Unauthorised acts by the agent bank

An agent bank may be liable to a borrowing customer for breach of warranty of authority, for example if the agent bank incorrectly confirms that the participating banks have consented to a waiver of the terms of the loan facility. In English law the rule is that a person, or institution, who wrongly either expressly or impliedly warrants that it has the authority of another is liable for breach of warranty of authority, to any person to whom the warranty is given and who in reliance suffers damage by acting on the faith of the warranty.[96] However, for such liability to arise the borrowing customer must have relied on the agent's representation as to the warranty of authority. Therefore, if the borrowing customer has knowledge that the agent bank has no such authority his action will not succeed. Where the agent bank acts in excess of his authority, it is possible for the remaining banks in the syndicate to ratify the agent bank's conduct.[97] Conversely, the syndicate of banks may find itself bound by the acts of its agent if they have expressly or impliedly represented that the agent bank has apparent or ostensible authority, even if the agent is not actually authorised to undertake the act, for example where the bank's have privately placed limits on the agent's authority.

Where the agent bank is given discretion by the participating banks, the agent bank must exercise reasonable skill, care and diligence in the performance of its duties. If the agent bank complies with the standard of reasonable care, it will not be liable for negligence even though

---

[95] Clarke and Farrar (1982) Rights and Duties of managing and Agent Banks in Syndicated Loans to Government Borrowers, *U.Ill. L. Rev*, 229.
[96] *Collen v Wright* (1857) 8 E & B 647.
[97] *Firth v Staines* [1897] 2 QB 70.

it has made a mistake or error of judgement. In *Chown v Parrott*[98] an attorney exercising reasonable skill and care was found not liable for having compromised his client's action without his consent and in *Re Kingston Cotton Mill Co*[99] the court held that the standard of skill and care required to discharge the duty will depend on the circumstances of each case. A sophisticated agent bank will, therefore, be expected to exercise a higher standard of care in the performance of its duties. However an agent bank will not be liable for failure to go beyond its reasonable duty of care and skill, even though the loss occasioned could have been avoided by exercising an extra level of care, skill and diligence.[100]

Whether an agent bank is under a positive duty to monitor the financial condition of the borrowing customer to ensure that the interests of the syndicate members are protected will depend on the express or implied terms of the agency contract and relationship. Where the agent bank has express power, for example to call for financial information and compliance certificates from the borrowing customer, the frequency with which and the circumstances in which such powers are exercised will be determined in the light of the contractual terms, or in the absence of express provisions, in accordance with the agent's duty to exercise reasonable skill and care in the interests of the syndicate member banks. Normally the agent bank will call for compliance certificates at fixed intervals depending on the complexity of the loan, and may do so additionally if it appears that an un-notified default has occurred. The loan agreement may provide that the agent bank is to act as a representative of the other syndicate banks for the purpose of receiving formal notification from the borrowing customer. Any such formal notification so provided is effective if the agent bank receives it within the scope of his actual or apparent authority, whether or not it is subsequently communicated to the member banks. This will not, however, be the case if the borrowing customer knew that the agent bank intended to conceal the notification from the other syndicate banks.[101] Accounts and other formal notices received from the borrowing customer should be passed to the syndicate members without delay. Whether an agent bank is under a duty to pass on information to the syndicate bank depends on the express and implied terms of the agency contract. In the absence of a specific clause, the agent bank is under a duty to keep the member banks advised on matters material to the agency, i.e. the loan.[102]

Legal nature of a loan syndicate

Although there has been some legal uncertainty about the nature of the relationship between the banks participating in a syndicated loan, it is generally accepted that banks do not enter into a partnership arrangement since they do not enter into a relationship in which the net profits are shared between them.[103] Further, to impose a partnership relationship between the participating syndicate banks would result not only in the imposition of fiduciary obligations between the member banks, but also result in them having joint liability for each other's actions and with each bank, as agent for the other, being able to bind the other banks to

---

[98] (1863) 14 CBNS 74.
[99] [1896] 2 Ch 279.
[100] *Morten v Hilton Gibbes & Smith* (1908) [1937] 2 KB 176.
[101] *Blackley v National Mutual Life Association of Australasia* [1971] NZLR 1038.
[102] *Keppel v Wheeler and Atkins* [1927] 1 KB 577.
[103] Partnership Act 1890, s.2.

legal obligations. However, in exceptional circumstances members of the syndicate many find themselves subject to fiduciary duties, in particular between the lead bank and other member banks. In *UBAF Ltd* v *European American Banking Corporation*[104] the defendants, the lead bank, invited UBAF to participate in two loans that the defendants intended to make to two companies which were part of a shipping group. UBAF claimed that the defendants had represented to them that the loans were 'attractive financing to companies in a sound and profitable group' and that in reliance on these representations, UBAF had participated in the loan. When the borrowing customer later defaulted on the loans, UBAF alleged that the defendant was liable, *inter alia*, for deceit, misrepresentation under s.2(1) of the Misrepresentation Act 1967 and negligence. As the issue before the Court of Appeal concerned whether to set aside service of a writ out of jurisdiction, it was not necessary to consider the specific question of the lead bank's relationship with the syndicate members. However, Ackner LJ *obiter* stated that:

> the transaction into which [UBAF] was invited to enter, and did enter, was that of contributing to a syndicate loan where, as seems to us, quite clearly [the defendant] were acting in a fiduciary capacity for all the other participants. It was [the defendant] who received [UBAF's] money and it was [the defendant] who arranged for and held, on behalf of all the participants, the collateral security for the loan. If, therefore, it was within [the defendant bank's] knowledge at any time while they were carrying out their fiduciary duties that the security was as [UBAF] allege, inadequate, it must we think, clearly have been their duty to inform the participants of that fact and their continued failure to do so would constitute a continuing breach off their fiduciary duty.

This view, however, must be read with caution[105] since it was merely *obiter* in an interlocutory appeal on a jurisdictional point where the court did not have the opportunity to hear full arguments on issues of fiduciary liability. The reluctance to impose fiduciary duties on the lead bank has been supported by the US courts where they will look for 'unequivocal contracting language' to that effect in the loan agreement.[106] The US courts accept that the relationship between the lead bank and the other participating banks in the loan syndicate is an arm's-length contractual agreement between experienced commercial parties and the relationship should be governed by the terms of contract entered into by them.[107] Most loan agreements now provide terms which state 'nothing in this agreement constitutes the agent or the arranger as a trustee or fiduciary of any other person'.[108] This is a legitimate and effective technique for controlling the intervention of fiduciary obligations into a contractual relationship.[109]

The argument in favour of imposing a fiduciary relationship between the lead bank and the syndicate members derives often from the desire to impose a duty of disclosure on the lead bank. The participating banks may argue that the lead bank fails to disclose information that may materially have affected their decision to join the syndicate, or the amount and terms of the loan. In the absence of a fiduciary relationship, nondisclosure by the lead bank

---

[104] [1984] 1 QB 713.

[105] Cranston (2002) *Principles of Banking Law*, Oxford: Oxford University Press.

[106] *Banque Arabe et Internationale d'Investissement* v *Maryland National Bank*, 819 F. Supp. 1282 (SDNY 1993).

[107] Brooks (1995) Participation and Syndicated Loans: Intercreditor Fiduciary Duties for Lead and Agent Banks under US Law, *JIBFL*, 275.

[108] LMA. MTR.03, cl. 26.4.

[109] *Kelly* v *Cooper* [1993] AC 205; *Henderson* v *Merrett Syndicates Ltd* [1995] AC 145.

will not generally constitute a misrepresentation or breach of a duty of care and in *IFE Fund SA v Goldman Sachs*[110] the Court of Appeal held that the implication of a duty of care was inconsistent with the terms on which the lead bank provided the information memorandum and that there was no implied representation on its part that the information contained in the memorandum was, or continued to be, accurate. In *Goldman Sachs* it was alleged that, between the date of the information memorandum and the claimant's investment, the lead bank had received further negative reports from the accountants who had previously prepared the report attached to the information memorandum, but the lead bank had failed to disclose the further information received. Gage LJ expressed the view that the only representation made by the lead bank when sending the information memorandum to potential participating syndicate members was the representation of good faith and the lead bank would only be liable if it 'actually knew that it has in its possession information which made the information in the [memorandum] misleading . . . this would amount to an allegation of dishonesty'. This view was supported in *RaiffeisenZentralbankOsterreich AG v Royal Bank of Scotland Plc*,[111] which again involved a syndicate member bank seeking to imply a representation against the lead bank. Clarke J examined a number of features that indicated such implied representations would not generally be imposed, including the fact that the lead and syndicate banks were:

> sophisticated participants in the syndicated loans market [and that] whilst the bank could reasonably expect that the principal credit issues were addressed, it could not reasonably assume that the [information memorandum] contained everything that anyone might think relevant (even on credit issues).

These two facts would appear to negate the possibility that the lead bank might be liable to the participating banks, unless the failure to disclose particular information in the information memorandum amounted to a deliberate failure or deliberate concealment, or some positive misrepresentation, or an assumption of responsibility to the particular bank to disclose certain terms can be established. Whether the lead bank assumes fiduciary obligations or a duty of care was examined again in *Natwest Australia Bank Ltd v Trans Continental Corporation Ltd*[112] where the Supreme Court of Victoria was willing to impose a duty of care, the breach of which resulted in the lead bank being held liable to the participant banks for negligence. In that case the lead bank prepared and distributed an information memorandum to prospective participants but failed to disclose that the borrowing customer had given third-party guarantees supporting company obligations, including a guarantee in favour of the lead bank itself. The borrowing customer's most recent accounts failed to disclose these liabilities and when the customer subsequently went into receivership, a participant bank brought a claim that the lead bank had been negligent in failing to disclose the existence of the borrowing customer's liabilities. The participant who had, indeed, enquired specifically about contingent liabilities before agreeing to participate in the syndicate claimed it would not have participated in the loan had the guarantees been disclosed. The Supreme Court of Victoria held the lead bank was liable for the breach of its common law duty of care and under the Trade Practices Act 1974, and that the specific enquiries made by the participant had placed the lead bank under a duty to disclose the existence of the guarantees.

---

[110] [2007] 1 Lloyd's Rep 264.
[111] [2010] EWHC 1392.
[112] [1993] ATPR (Digest) 46–109.

Compared to the *IFE Fund* and *Raiffeisen* cases, which held the lead bank was not liable in the absence of 'something more', the *Transcontinental* case deals with the situation where the lead bank has specifically assumed responsibility to a particular syndicate member for the accuracy of information. While the commercial nature of the contracts and the sophistication of the participating banks will make the imposition of duties on the lead bank difficult, nevertheless the possibility of imposing liability on the basis of a voluntary assumption of responsibility was recognised in *Sumitomo Bank Ltd* v *Banque Bruxelles Lambert SA*[113] where the court held that the lead bank's duties, rights and obligations under the loan agreement did not prevent a general duty of care arising in tort. The fact that the lead bank owed a limited nature of duties under the terms of the loan agreement did not mean that other and wider duties could not arise given the nature of the relationship between the parties. Langley J, therefore, held that the lead bank owed a duty of care to the members of the syndicate when disclosing information.

Loan participation

In loan participation, the lead bank may enter into a loan agreement with the borrowing customer and then sell part of his interest in the loan to other banks (the participants). The main methods for granting participation in such circumstances are:

- Assignment.
- Novation.
- Sub-participation.
- Risk participation.

Assignment

An assignment will involve the outright transfer of the lead bank's rights to all, or part, of its interest in the loan to the participants. The participant acquires a proprietary interest in the chose in action representing the loan. An assignment may either be statutory under s.136 of the Law of Property Act 1925, or equitable, but as loan participations usually only involve the transfer of part of the loan to any one participant, the assignment will take effect in equity. A limitation of the equitable assignment of a legal chose in action, for example a debt or contractual rights under a loan agreement, is that the equitable assignee must join the assignor to any action he may bring to enforce the assigned chose against the debtor. However, a term in the loan agreement may prohibit the assignment of a loan by the lead bank, or make the assignment subject to certain pre-conditions. In such circumstances, any purported assignment may be void against the borrowing customer.[114] Further, an assignment will only transfer the rights of the lead bank, and not the obligations, to the participant.[115]

---

[113] [1977] 1 Lloyd's Rep 487.
[114] *Linden Gardens Trust Ltd* v *Lenesta Sludge Disposals Ltd* [1994] 1 AC 85.
[115] *Tolhurst* v *Associated Portland Cement Manufacturers Ltd* [1902] 2 KB 660; *Linden Gardens Trust Ltd* v *Lenesta Sludge Disposals Ltd* [1994] 1 AC 85.

Novation

A novation involves the substitution of a new contract for the existing contract. In a loan participation, novation of the contract involves an agreement between the borrowing customer and the lead bank which releases the lead bank of its obligations and that the participant bank will take the lead bank's place as the substituted party to the loan agreement for all purposes. The participant's agreement to provide further finance to the borrowing customer constitutes the consideration required to support the new contract. Unlike an assignment, which does not require the borrowing customer's consent, novation requires the consent of all the parties. It is possible for the parties to provide for novation in advance by establishing in the contract for novation to occur on the happening of certain events[116] and is a technique used to transfer the lead bank's obligations and rights in the loan participation. In such circumstances the loan agreement constitutes a standing offer to novate made by the parties to the loan agreement and must be accepted in accordance with its terms.[117] The loan agreement may require the parties to follow particular procedures before a novation becomes effective.[118] The agreement usually provides for a prescribed form of 'transfer certificate' signed by the lead bank and the participants, to be served on the agent bank. Once the agent bank executes the form the novation becomes effective at that point.

Sub-participation and risk participation

These can be distinguished from assignments and novation in that they have no impact whatsoever on the underlying loan agreement between the lead bank and the participant bank. Sub-participations and risk-participations are separate contracts made between the lead bank and the participant. In the case of a sub-participation, the participant places a deposit with the lead bank for the amount of its participation and the lead bank agrees to pay the participant amounts equal to the participant's share of the proceeds. The participant has no claim against the borrowing customer but is exposed to the risk of default by the borrowing customer and by the lead bank. In the case of a risk participant, that bank does not provide any funding to the lead bank, but simply assumes part of the risk in the event of the borrowing customer's default.[119]

Regardless of the loan participation employed there are a number of key issues which will need to be addressed by the parties, for example the lead bank is under a duty of confidentiality to the borrowing customer that might limit the transfer of information about the loan to potential participants. This issue may be addressed through a provision in the loan agreement under which the borrowing customer gives his consent to the disclosure of information about the loan, which would otherwise be in breach of the duty of confidentiality.[120] Furthermore, the lead bank may disclaim liability to the participant in respect of the accuracy of information relating to the borrowing customer and thereby leave the participant to satisfy itself about such matters.[121] Moreover, it may be necessary to transfer to the participant the

---

[116] McKendrick (2010) *Goode on Commercial Law*, London: Penguin, p.117.

[117] Hughes (2000) Contracts, Consideration and Third Parties, *JIBFL*, 79.

[118] LMA.MTR.03, cl. 24.5.

[119] *Lloyds TSB Bank plc v Clarke* [2002] 2 All ER (Comm.) 992.

[120] LMA.MTR.3, cl. 24.7.

[121] In the UK such a disclaimer will be subject to UCTA 1977 and the test of reasonableness: *National Westminster Bank v Utrecht-America Finance Company* [2001] 3 All ER 733; *Raiffeisen Zentralbank Ostrreich AG v Royal Bank of Scotland Plc* [2010] EWHC 1392.

benefit of any security given by the borrowing customer, especially in the case of an assignment and novation where the participant is given direct rights against the borrowing customer. The protection of security rights is especially important with regard to novation, which involves the cancellation of the borrowing customer's original debt to the lead bank, thereby threatening the priority of the security rights. Novation of the security should therefore be avoided[122] since the new security will probably require registration and may not have the same priority as the earlier security. The solution would be for the lead bank to hold the security on trust for the participants but if the security is not held on trust, it should be assigned rather than novated.

Lender liability

The term lender liability is a flexible term, which can be used to cover a range of liabilities based on a number of legal doctrines.[123] It brings together separate claims that may be made against the lender by the borrowing customer or a third party, but it does not represent a single concept of liability. Lender liability may arise in a variety of circumstances where, for example, the bank is guilty of misrepresentation, gives negligent advice to the borrowing customer, fails to exercise reasonable skill and care, or knowingly receives trust property in breach of trust and is liable as a constructive trustee etc. These forms of action have already been dealt with elsewhere and this section will therefore explore liability against commercial lenders in a number of distinct areas as detailed under the succeeding headings.

Pre-contractual negotiations

Where a bank gives investment advice it assumes a contractual duty of care to its customer, and potentially, on an assumption of responsibility under *Hedley Byrne & Co v Heller Partners Ltd*,[124] a duty of care to third parties. Once the bank has assumed the role of financial adviser, the bank owes a duty to exercise reasonable skill and care in the performance of that duty, and the execution of its functions. Generally, a bank does not owe a duty of care to advise its customer on the soundness of the transaction for which the borrowing customer requires a loan or overdraft. In *Williams & Glyn's Bank Ltd v Barnes*[125] the defendant was an experienced businessman and a customer of the defendant bank, as was his company. He personally borrowed in excess of £1 million to invest in his company, which was heavily indebted to the bank. When the company collapsed and the bank called in the personal loan, the defendant argued that the bank was under a duty of care and should have warned him that the transaction he proposed to enter into was an unsound investment. The court, rejecting this argument, held that the bank was under no duty in law to consider the prudence of the loan from the customer's point of view or to advise on its commercial soundness. Ralph Gibson J said:

> no duty in law arises upon the bank either to consider the prudence of the lending from the customer's point of view, or to advise with reference to it. Such a duty could only arise by

---

[122] Cranston (2002) *Principles of Banking Law*, Oxford: Oxford University Press.
[123] Cranston (2002) *Principles of Banking Law*, Oxford: Oxford University Press.
[124] [1964] AC 465.
[125] [1981] Com. LR 205.

contract, express or implied, or upon the principle of the assumption of responsibility and reliance stated in *Hedley Byrne* or in cases of fiduciary duty. The same answer is to be given to the question even if the bank knows that the borrowing and application of the loan, as intended by the customer, are imprudent.

The mere grant of a loan will, therefore, not involve the bank in an assumption of a duty of care under the *Hedley Byrne* case, nor does it involve an imposition of a fiduciary[126] relationship between the borrowing customer and the lending bank. This reasoning was followed in *Lloyds Bank Plc v Cobb*[127] where the court held that the mere request for a loan coupled with the supply of information to the bank in respect of the project for which the finance is being sought is not sufficient to make clear to the bank that it is being asked to give advice on the prudence of the transaction, for which the loan will be used. Scott LJ expressed the view that:

> In order to place the bank under a duty of care to the borrower the borrower must, in my opinion, make clear to the bank that its advice is being sought. The mere request for a loan, coupled with the supply to the bank of the details of the commercial project . . . does not suffice to make clear to the bank that its advice is being sought.

More recently, in *National Commercial Bank (Jamaica) v Hew*[128] Lord Millett observed:

> The viability of a transaction may depend on the vantage point from which it is viewed; what is a viable loan may not be a viable borrowing. This is one reason why a borrower is not entitled to rely on the fact that the lender has chosen to lend him money as evidence, still less as advice, that the lender thinks that the purpose for which the borrower intends to use it is sound.

When the bank, therefore, examines a proposal submitted by the borrowing customer for a loan, the bank does this for its own purposes as lender and not with a view to signalling the viability, or soundness, of the purpose for which the loan will be used. The policy adopted by the courts reflects sound business policy. While the bank will lend against proposals, which from its point of view may be reasonably certain of achieving a return on its investment (i.e. the return of the capital sum lent plus commission and interests), there may be a myriad of events that could occur on a day-to-day basis over which the bank has no control and which may affect the viability of the project. Similarly, the bank is under no duty to assess the borrowing customer's capacity to repay the loan,[129] or where the lending bank requires the following customer to act in a certain way, for example under a condition precedent, the bank does not owe the borrowing customer a duty to consider whether it is in fact a prudent course for the customer to fulfil that particular condition.

Although the broad effect of the *Barnes* case is to prevent the imposition of liability on lending banks against claims that they did not take sufficient steps to advise the borrowing customer on the prudence of a particular investment or course of conduct, nevertheless

---

[126] *Governor and Company of the Bank of Scotland v A Ltd* [2001] Lloyd's Rep Bank 73; *Murphy v HSBC Bank Plc* [2004] EWHC 467; *Wright v HSBC Plc* [2006] EWHC 930; *Kotonou v National Westminster Bank Plc* [2010] EWHC 1659.

[127] CA, 18 December 1991.

[128] [2003] UKPC 51.

[129] This principle remains unaffected although banks have been held contributorily negligent because they did not make adequate enquires of borrowers, or they lent on too high a proportion of the value of the property: *Platform Loans Ltd v Oyston Shipways Ltd* [2002] 2 AC 190.

lending banks may be assumed to have voluntarily undertaken such responsibility. However, any such liability, if imposed, is likely to result from express, rather than implied, contractual obligations. Thus, for example, in *Verity and Spindler* v *Lloyd's Bank Plc*[130] the claimants approached the bank because it advertised a 'tailor made' financial advisory service and the bank manager, having inspected certain properties in respect of a loan the claimants would require, encouraged them to buy a particular property. The bank eventually sought to recover the loan and the claimants resisted on the grounds that the bank had assumed a duty of care in contract and tort, which the bank had breached because of the negligent advice. The court held the bank liable for negligence. The judge was influenced by the fact that the bank customers were relatively inexperienced, and significantly the bank manager had inspected both the properties (not usual practice) and encouraged them to purchase one of them, and the wording of the bank's advertisement. The borrowing customer's financial experience and business acumenship have become considerations the courts will take into account when deciding whether or not to impose a duty of care in respect of the advice given by the bank.[131] In the *Barnes* case[132] itself the judge laid stress on the fact that the borrowing customer was a businessman of full age and competence and rejected arguments in favour of imposing a duty of care, which would require the bank to consider the prudence of the transaction from the borrowing customer's point of view. In comparison, in *Woods* v *Martin's Bank Ltd*[133] Salmon J when imposing a fiduciary duty of care on the bank in respect of the investment advice given by it, was influenced by the fact that the claimant was a young man with no business experience. Banks should, therefore, exercise care when dealing with financially inexperienced customers and should advise borrowing customers to obtain independent financial advice in respect of the prudence of a loan from the customer's point of view.

Management and termination of the loan facility

Under English law, the terms of the loan facility are generally considered to be paramount and the courts will only construe these terms to give effect to the intention of the parties. However, in exceptional circumstances the court may be willing to imply additional duties into loan contracts, for example a duty to increase the facility, or a duty to give adequate notice of refusal to do so.[134] However, the lending bank must act consistently with the terms of the loan agreement; otherwise the borrowing customer may be able to raise an estoppel or waiver against the bank. Thus, for example, in *Emery* v *UCB Bank Plc*[135] the bank was estopped from enforcing its security without further notice to the borrowing customer following an interim agreement to reschedule payments due from the borrowing customer. However, there was no general power given to the English courts to view the fairness of terms imposed on corporate borrowers, although relief may be available for harsh bargains, for example penalty clauses. Nevertheless, there is no general doctrine of 'unconscionability' under English Law.

---

[130] [1995] CLC 1557.
[131] *Foti* v *Banque Nationale de Paris* [1990] Aust. Torts Rep. 81 (SASC).
[132] *Williams & Glyn's Bank Ltd* v *Barnes* [1981] Com. LR 205.
[133] [1959] 1 QB 55.
[134] *Williams & Glyn's Bank Ltd* v *Barnes* [1981] Com. LR 205.
[135] CA, 15 May 1997.

The Unfair Terms in Consumer Contracts Regulations 1999 allow the courts to set aside a term in consumer contracts if it has not been individually negotiated and 'if, contrary to the requirement of good faith, it causes a significant imbalance in the parties' rights and obligations arising under the contract, to the detriment of the consumer'.[136] In *Director General of Fair Trading v First National Bank plc*[137] a standard term in the bank's loan agreement provided that, in the event of default by the borrowing customer, interest would continue to be payable at the contractual rate until any judgment obtained by the bank had been discharged. The House of Lords held that the term was not unfair and did not cause a significant imbalance to the detriment of the customer. On the contrary, the term was intended to ensure that the 'borrower does not enjoy the benefit of the outstanding balance of the judgment without fulfilling the corresponding obligation which he has undertaken to pay interest on it as provided for in the contract'.

Although, the court takes a strict approach to the lender's right to terminate a loan facility, where the facility agreement gives the lending bank the right to terminate the agreement, the court will not readily interfere with the exercise of that right. However, in exceptional circumstances, the lending bank may have acted in such a way as to prevent the withdrawal of the loan facility, under the rules of estoppel, without giving reasonable notice, or may be deemed to have waived its right to terminate the agreement, or where the wording of the facility agreement is unclear the court may impose an obligation to give reasonable notice.[138]

In respect of an overdraft or on demand facility, the courts are reluctant to imply an obligation on the bank to give reasonable notice before it refuses further lending.[139] There may be justifiable commercial reasons for the lending bank taking this approach and Ralph Gibson J in *Williams & Glyn's Bank v Barnes*[140] expressed the view:

> A bank which lent on overdraft might find urgent need for funds so lent because of commercial misfortunes or other demands and had to be free to call for repayments as and when the terms of the loan permitted it to do so.

Further, an express term, for example in respect of the repayment of an overdraft loan on demand, will be upheld by the courts unless the facility agreement, when construed as a whole, shows the term to be contrary to the main provisions of that agreement. In *Bank of Baroda v Panessar*[141] the court expressed the view that money payable 'on demand' is repayable immediately and the bank was entitled to appoint a receiver within one hour of demanding repayment. Walton J expresses the view that:

> Money payable 'on demand' is repayable immediately on demand being made . . . Nevertheless it is physically impossible in most cases for a person to keep some money required to discharge the debt about his person. He may in a simple case keep it in a box under his bed; it may be at the bank or with a bailee. The debtor is therefore not in default in making the payment demanded unless and until he has had a reasonable opportunity of implementing whatever reasonable mechanisms of payment he may need to employ to discharge the debt. Of course, this is limited to the time necessary for the mechanics of payment. It does not extend to any time to raise the money if it is not there to be paid.

---

[136] UTCCR 1999, reg. 5(1).
[137] [2002] 1 AC 481.
[138] *Crimfil Ltd v Barclays Bank plc* [1995] CLC 385.
[139] *Socomex Ltd v Banque Bruxelles Lampert SA* [1966] 1 Lloyd's Rep 156.
[140] [1981] Com LR 205.
[141] [1987] Ch 335.

Following the view expressed in the *Bank of Baroda* case, in *Sheppard & Cooper Ltd v TSB Bank Plc*[142] the court concluded that the bank had been entitled to send in the receivers within 30 minutes after demanding repayment of over £600,000 from the debtor. In providing further guidance on the 'mechanics of payment' test Blackburne J held:

- The time available to the debtor to implement the mechanics of payment depends on the circumstances of the case.

- If the sum demanded is an amount that the debtor will likely have in a bank account, the debtor must be given whatever time is reasonable in all the circumstances for the debtor to contact his bank and make the necessary arrangements for the relevant sum to be transferred from his bank to the creditor.

- If the demand is made outside banking hours the period is likely to be longer than if the demand is made during banking hours and is likely to involve waiting until banks reopen.

- Where proper demand has been made, and the debtor makes it clear to the creditor that the necessary monies are unavailable, the creditor need not give the debtor any further time before treating him as in default.

More recently, in *Lloyds Bank Plc v Lampert*[143] it was argued that the 'mechanics of payment' test should give way to a more liberal approach similar to that adopted in Canada and Australia where the borrower is given reasonable time[144] to raise money from other sources. Kennedy LJ, however, expressed the view that this approach should not be overstated and his Lordship referred to *Whonnock Industries Ltd v National Bank of Canada*[145] where the British Columbia Court of Appeal reviewed the authorities and concluded that where the amount is very large Canadian law requires that lenders should be given 'at least a few days' in which to meet the demand, but that reasonable notice might range from a few days to no time at all. However, it was unnecessary for Kennedy LJ in *Lampert* to decide the issue as evidence suggested that the borrowing customer would not have been able to raise the necessary amount to repay the overdraft. The suggestion that the customer be given a reasonable time to repay the amount of an 'on demand' overdraft would add uncertainty and delay with the bank having to decide what is a reasonable time[146] before enforcing the security in circumstances

---

[142] [1996] 2 All ER 654.

[143] [1991] 1 All ER (Comm) 161.

[144] For the Canadian approach see: *Ronald Elwyn Lister Ltd v Dunlop Canada Ltd* (1982) 135 DLR (3d) 1; *Whonnock Industries Ltd v National bank of Canada* (1987) 42 DLR (4th) 1; *Royal Bank of Canada v W. Got & Associates Electric Ltd* (2000) 178 DLR (4th) 74; *Leby Properties Ltd v Manufacturers Life Insurance Co* [2006] NBCA 14; *Royal Bank of Canada v Profor Kedgwick Ltd* [2008] NBQB 78; see also Ogilve (2001) Canadian Bank Lender Liability: Semper Caveat Lender, in Blair, *Banks, Liability and Risk*. For Australian authorities see: *Bunbury Foods Pty Ltd v National Bank of Australasia Ltd* (1984) 153 CLR 49; *Pioneer Park Pty Ltd v ANZ Banking Group Ltd* [2002] NSWSC 883. Later cases in Australia have adopted a more narrow approach to the 'mechanics of payment' test: *Bond v Hong Kong Bank of Australia* (1991) 25 NSWLR 286; *Parras Holdings Pty Ltd v Commonwealth Bank of Australia* [1998] FCA 682, affd. [1999] FCA 391; *Commonwealth Bank of Australia v Renstel Nominees Pty Ltd* (VSC, 8 June 2001).

[145] (1987) 42 DLR (4th) 1.

[146] In *Whonnock Industries Ltd v National Bank of Canada* (1987) 42 DLR (4th) 1 the court, at first instance, held seven days' notice was not reasonable. However, on appeal the Court of Appeal said (42 DLR (4th) 1 at 11): 'The Canadian law demonstrated in the decisions does not contemplate more than a few days and cannot encompass anything approaching 30 days. In the decisions noted nothing approaching the 7 days permitted here has been classed as unreasonable. Cases in which the requirement for reasonable notice evolved deal with notice of an hour or less. None of them holds that a notice of more than one day was inadequate and none refers to the need for a notice of more than a few days.'

where delay would impair the bank's security and giving reasonable notice may lead to arguments about what is reasonable.

Insolvency of the borrowing customer

Where the borrowing customer faces financial difficulties it may be in the interests of the bank to provide the customer with some assistance by entering into some arrangement which allows the customer to trade out of his difficulties, rather than enforcing its formal rights under the loan agreement and enforcing the security. Since banks are encouraged to explore the possibility of saving the business rather than withdrawing their financial support, they are discouraged from taking premature action. However, a bank must take care to ensure that its actions do not operate to the detriment of the borrowing customer's other creditors and that it does not take advantage of the customer's financial position to improve its position over the borrower's other creditors. The Insolvency Act 1986, will allow the liquidator to challenge transactions entered into at undervalue,[147] voidable preferences,[148] and certain floating charges.[149] These provisions apply also in relation to 'connected persons', which includes the company's shadow directors and raises the question whether a bank could be treated as a shadow director of a corporate customer. This is important not merely in respect of the avoidance provisions, but it may also be important for determining the bank's potential liability for wrongful trading.[150] The term 'shadow director' is defined in ss.251(1) and (2) of the Companies Act 2006, and s.22(5) of the Company Directors Disqualification Act 1986, although the definition for the purpose of 'wrongful trading' liability is found in s.251 of the Insolvency Act 1986. In *Re a Company (No. 005009 of 1987)*[151] Knox J, although refusing to give reasons for the decision, held that there was a triable issue as to whether the bank had become a 'shadow director' for the purpose of imposing liability for wrongful trading. However at trial this argument was 'rightly abandoned'.[152] As a result of these cases, some concern has been raised about banks withdrawing their financial support from their corporate customers, rather than supporting them through their difficulties, but Millett J, writing in the *Insolvency Practitioner*,[153] eased concerns when he stated that a bank would have to step outside the ordinary bank-customer relationship before being treated as a 'shadow director'. Subsequently, in *Re Hydrodan (Corby) Ltd*[154] the court held that for a defendant bank to become a 'shadow director' it was necessary to allege and prove:

(i) Who the company's directors are, whether *de facto* or *de jure*;

(ii) That the defendant directed those directors how to act in relation to the company or that he was one of the persons who did so;

(iii) That those directors acted in accordance with such directions; and

(iv) They were accustomed to so act.

---

[147] Insolvency Act 1986, s.238; see also *Phillips v Brewin Dolphin Bell Lawrie Ltd* [2001] 1 WLR 143.
[148] Insolvency Act 1986, s.239.
[149] Insolvency Act 1986, s.245.
[150] Insolvency Act 1986, s.214.
[151] [1981] BCLC 324.
[152] *Re M.C. Bacon* [1990] BCLC 324; see also *Ultraframe (UK) Ltd v Fielding* [2005] EWHC 1638(Ch).
[153] Millett (1991) Shadow Directorships – A Real or Imagined Threat to the Banks, *Insolvency Practitioner*, 14.
[154] [1994] 2 BCLC 181.

In *Re Unisoft Group Ltd (No 2)* Harman J emphasised that the shadow director is someone who controls the whole, or at least a majority, of the board and the directors must act on that person's instructions as a matter of regular practice and not just on isolated occasions. Subservience or surrender of discretion by the board is not, however required but what is needed is that the board is accustomed to act on the directions or instructions of the shadow director, although such directions do not have to extend over all or most of the corporate activities of the company; nor is it necessary to demonstrate 'compulsion in excess of that implicit in the fact that the board is accustomed to act in accordance with them'.[155]

Applying these principles and the views expressed by Millett J it is unlikely that the typical lending relationship with the bank will constitute the lender as a 'shadow director'. The negotiations which result in the loan agreement, including the lending bank requiring the borrowing customer to comply with warranties, condition precedents and covenants, do not give directions or instructions to the borrowing company on how to act, but are merely terms which the bank is willing to provide or continue, regarding financial support for the borrowing customer which the company is free to accept or reject. However, the bank may face a greater risk of being held liable as a shadow director in the event of a potential default by the borrowing customer. A bank renegotiating the loan facility will want to support the borrowing customer, but will certainly also want to safeguard its interests. In *Re PTZFM Ltd*[156] Judge Baker QC rejected the allegation that the lenders had become 'shadow directors' of their borrowing customer simply by 'trying to rescue what they could out of the company using their undoubted rights as secured creditors'. The court, therefore, concluded that 'where the creditor made terms for the continuation of credit in the light of threatened default', the borrowing customer was not bound to act in accordance with the lending bank's instructions as the directors 'of the company were quite free to take the offer or leave it'. In *Ultraframe (UK) Ltd v Fielding*[157] the court accepted the view that 'a lender is entitled to keep a close eye on what is done with his money, and to impose conditions on his support for the company' and more recently the view has been expressed that where there is 'doubt whether the act of a person were referable to an assumed directorship or to some other capacity . . . The person in question must be entitled to the benefit of the doubt'.[158]

However, there may be circumstances where it is difficult to distinguish simply between 'advising' the borrowing customer how to act, and giving 'directions' or 'instructions' to the borrowing customer that might make the lender a 'shadow director'. The courts will assess objectively whether a 'direction' or 'instruction' constitutes the lending bank a 'shadow director'. Thus, where the lending bank commissions a report on the borrowing customer's affairs that the customer implements it may be argued that the bank becomes a 'shadow director'. In such circumstances the lending bank may implement the proposals in the report as conditions for the bank's continued financial support and although the borrowing customer may have no option but to accept the lending bank's conditions, in law the borrowing customer has a choice between accepting the terms of the refinancing or having its liabilities accelerated;

---

[155] *Secretary of State for Trade and Industry v Deverell* [2001] Ch 340.
[156] [1995] 2 BCLC 354.
[157] *Re Ultraframe (UK) Ltd v Fielding* [2005] EWHC 1638.
[158] *Re Mea Corporation Ltd* [2007] 1 BCLC 618.

the existence of such a choice will generally negate a suggestion that the lender is a 'shadow director'.[159] The other situation in which the question of liability as shadow director for the lending bank may arise is where the lender seeks to appoint a representative to the borrowing customer's board. Generally, this will not cause a problem since the lending bank,[160] which may nominate one or more board representatives, will not acquire control of the board as is required for a shadow directorship.[161]

Conclusion

The chapter has examined the legal effect of borrowing whether by overdraft or in the case of corporate borrowing by means of a syndicated loan. The legal liability of the parties to the loan is examined, as is the rights conferred on the parties. This is an area where the law has tried to accommodate commercial banking developments and provide solutions to, at times, specialist forms of bank finance.

Further reading

➤ Brooks, J.N. (1995) Participation and Syndicated Loans: Intercreditor Fiduciary Duties for Lead and Agent Banks under US Law, *JIBFL*, 275.
This article addresses litigation which occurs between lenders in the context of multi-creditor loans. This article discusses whether the lead bank owes a fiduciary duty to its co-lenders in a multi-creditor loan facility.

➤ Hughes, M. (2000) Loans agreements – Single Banks and Syndicated, *JIBFL*, 115. Should be on Lexis Library from 1995.
This article focuses upon loan agreements and examines a range of issues, including the contractual framework, interest rates and dispute resolution.

➤ Clarke, L. and Farrar, S.F. (1982) Rights and Duties of managing and Agent Banks in Syndicated Loans to Government Borrowers, *U.Ill. L. Rev*, 229.
As governments often have to borrow large amounts of funds exceeding those offered by a single lender, a syndicate of lenders may be formed to finance an appropriate loan. This article outlines the duties of managing and agent banks. Further, the article discusses a range of theories to consider when the managing and agent banks might be held liable for losses stemming from a syndicated loan to a government borrower.

➤ Hughes, M. (2000) Loans agreements – Single Banks and Syndicated, *JIBFL*, 115.

---

[159] *Re Ultraframe (UK) Ltd* v *Fielding* [2005] EWHC 1638.
[160] *Lord* v *Sinai Securities Ltd* [2005] 1 BCLC 295.
[161] *Kuwait Asia Bank EC* v *National Mutual Life Nominees Ltd* [1991] 1 AC 187.

17 Recovery of money paid by mistake

Chapter overview

The aim of this chapter is to:

➤ Examine the circumstances in which money paid by a bank under mistake of fact can be recovered by the parties involved.

➤ Explore the nature and circumstances under which money may be paid by mistake and the problems which arise in practice.

➤ Explore the rules relating to recovery of money paid under a mistake and the defences available in such circumstances.

➤ Provide an outline of the rules of tracing applicable in cases of recovery of payments made under a mistake.

Introduction

The law of restitution deals with whether a claimant can claim a benefit from the defendant, rather than compensation for the loss suffered by him. Thus, for example, A commits a wrong against B who sues in respect of that wrong or injury. A will, normally, be liable to compensate B for the wrong and the courts will usually award damages by reference to the loss resulting from the wrongful act. However, in some circumstances it may be open to B to seek restitution, instead of damages. It will be in B's interest to do this if the profit that A has made by his wrongful act is greater than the loss suffered by B. Restitution is, therefore, a distinct remedy compared to those normally available for an action for tort or contract. Lord Wright[1] recognised this when he said:

> any civilised system of law is bound to provide remedies for cases of what has been called unjust enrichment or unjust benefit, that is, to prevent a man retaining the money of, or some benefit derived from, another which it is against conscience that he should keep. Such remedies in English law are generally different from remedies in contract or in tort, and are now recognised to fall within a third category of the common law which has been called quasi-contract or restitution.

---

[1] *Fibrosa Spolka Akcyjna* v *Fairbairn Lawson Combe Barbour Ltd* [1943] AC 32 at 61.

While the House of Lords has recognised that restitution is available where the defendant has been unjustly enriched at the expense of the claimant[2] the remedy will also be available where the defendant obtains a benefit by the commission of a wrong, or where the claimant can bring a claim to recover property held by the defendant in which the claimant has a proprietary interest.[3]

BANKING LAW IN PRACTICE

The obligation to make restitution can arise in a variety of circumstances but, at common law, such circumstances usually involve a special relationship between two people where the law imposes a duty on one person to pay a sum of money, or sometimes to deliver specific property, to another. The relationship is, therefore, based either on the involuntary nature of the payment or transfer, its qualified nature, or the conduct of the transferee. A claim in restitution resembles a contractual claim in that liability is imposed on one person to pay money, or transfer property to another, but its difference lies in the fact that the law, regardless of the agreement between the parties, imposes restitutionary liability. More recently, in *Sempra Metals Ltd* v *Inland Revenue Commissioner*[4] the House of Lords held that a mistaken payer should be entitled to recover compound interest as a matter of right from the payee for the period between the payee's receipt of the payment and the payer's recovery of the funds with the interest representing the 'time value' of the mistaken payment and the full benefit the payee derived from the funds.[5]

Additionally, equity has separately developed principles aimed at giving the obtained benefits to the claimant. In equity, restitutionary remedies may involve restoring value to the claimant or the return of property obtained or tracing into the proceeds, or substitute. In equity the principles of restitution have influenced a number of areas, for example: (i) in the case of constructive trusts, a defendant is deemed to be a trustee of the property for the claimant by operation of law so the claimant is able to recover what is due to him; (ii) the claimant is allowed to recover property, or its substitute, from the defendant despite its being mixed with other property; and (iii) the equitable concept of uncon-scionability has proved important in the development of certain grounds of unjust enrichment, especially those relating to the exploitation of the claimant by the defendant. In respect of the law of restitution for unjust enrichment it is accepted that there is no need to treat the action for money had and received and an action for an equitable remedy 'as any longer depending upon the different concepts of justice'.[6]

---

[2] *Lipkin Gorman* v *Karpnale & Co.* [1991] 2 AC 548.
[3] *Foskett* v *McKeown* [2001] 1 AC 102.
[4] [2008] 1 AC 561.
[5] Hayton (2008) Developing the Company Law where statute has spoken, 29 *Co. Lawyer*, 2.
[6] *Westdeutsche Landesbank Girozentrale* v *Islington LBC* [1994] 4 All ER 890.

Mistaken payments: some general principles

In *Kleinwort Benson Ltd* v *Lincoln City Council*[7] Lord Hope said that subject to any defence that may arise from the circumstances a claim for restitution for money paid under a mistake of fact raises three questions:

- Was there a mistake?
- Did the mistake cause the payment?
- Did the payee have a right to receive the sum, which was so paid to him?

Strictly speaking a bank can only debit the customer's account if it makes payment against a valid mandate.[8] However, mistaken payments may occur for a variety of reasons, for example a clerical or technological error within the paying bank may lead to a mistaken payment, or a customer may effectively have countermanded payment on a cheque but the bank erroneously overlooks the countermand and makes payment,[9] or the bank may due to an error make payment twice when the mandate relates to a single payment.[10] Alternatively, there may be fraud involved in the transaction, either by an officer of the bank or some third party. While the majority of cases deal with the situation where the mistaken payment is made under a negotiable instrument, other examples of mistaken payments can result from errors arising in respect of payment mandates which do not originate through the issue of a negotiable instrument, for example mistakes relating to a CHAPS, SWIFT or Giro payment. While the courts have scrutinised the law relating to mistaken payments in respect of negotiable instruments they have not yet had the opportunity to fully explore the latter area.

Who can bring the action?

In order to succeed with its personal action for restitution the bank must show that it mistakenly paid away money to the payee who is unjustly enriched. Although the ownership of the money mistakenly paid passes to the payee that does not affect the bank's claim for restitution and as there is a direct relationship between the payee and the paying bank, to the extent that the latter makes payment and the former receives it, an action for tracing, or following, is not required. By contrast, where the bank seeks to recover money the recipient has received through a third party it must be able to assert a legal title to the money, or its substitute.

---

[7] [1999] 2 AC 349.

[8] In *Barclays Bank Ltd* v *WJ Simms Son & Cooke (Southern) Cooke Ltd* [1980] QB 677 Robert Goff J (as he then was) said: 'It is a basic obligation owed by a bank to its customer that it will honour on presentation cheques drawn by the customer on the bank, provided that there are sufficient funds in the customer's account to meet the cheque, or the bank has agreed to provide the customer with overdraft facilities sufficient to meet the cheque. Where the bank honours such a cheque, it acts within its mandate, with the result that the bank is entitled to debit the customer's account with the amount of the cheque, and further that the bank's payment is effective to discharge the obligation of the customer to the payee on the cheque, because the bank has paid the cheque with the authority of the customer.'

[9] *Barclays Bank Ltd* v *WJ Simms, Sons & Cooke (Southern) Ltd* [1980] QB 677.

[10] *Chase Manhattan Bank NA* v *Israel British Bank (London) Ltd* [1981] Ch 105.

Until recently, the prevailing view was that an action in quasi-contract or for money had and received could only be brought by the paying bank and not by the customer whose account had been mistakenly debited. This view was based on the rule in *Foley* v *Hill*,[11] which held that once money was credited to the customer's account, title in that money passed to the bank, with a resulting debtor and creditor relationship between the bank and the account holder. Consequently, funds paid to the credit of the customer's account became the bank's money. On that basis the account-holding customer who no longer had any title to the funds in question, could not bring an action for recovery of money paid under mistake of fact. However, this reasoning was been challenged in *Agip (Africa) Ltd* v *Jackson*[12] and *Lipkin Gorman* v *Karpnale Ltd*[13] both of which concluded that an action for recovery of money paid by a bank under a mistake may be brought either by the bank itself or by the customer whose money has been wrongfully paid out. In *Agip (Africa) Ltd* v *Jackson* the claimant company, Agip, sought to recover large amounts of money that had fraudulently been transferred by its chief accountant, to the credit of accounts maintained by the defendant. It was argued for the defendants that as the money transferred conceptually, under *Foley* v *Hill*, belonged to the paying bank the claimant company had no right to the money and therefore no cause of action could be maintained by Agip. At first instance, Millett J rejecting this argument, held that:

> by honouring the customer's cheque in favour of a third party and debiting his account, the bank acts as principal in repaying part of the debt to its customer and as agent of the customer in paying his money to the third party.

On appeal, the Court of Appeal, while affirming the rule in *Foley* v *Hill*, under which money once credited to the account becomes the bank's money, expressed the view that the application of that principle 'only tells half the story'. Fox LJ said:

> The banker's instruction is to pay from the customer's account. He does so by a payment from his own funds and a corresponding debit. The reality is a payment by the customer, at any rate in a case where the customer has no right to require a recrediting of his account. Nothing passes in specie. The whole matter is dealt with by accounting transactions partly in the paying bank and partly in the clearing process.

Fox LJ also agreed with the conclusion reached by Millett J that the position was not altered by the fact that the paying bank was deceived into paying on the basis of the forged instruction and, therefore, acted without a mandate. His Lordship observed that if the paying bank 'paid away Agip's money, Agip must be entitled to pursue such remedies as there may be for its recovery'.

In *Lipkin Gorman (a firm)* v *Karpnale Ltd*,[14] C, a partner in a firm of solicitors, fraudulently obtained £323,222.14 from the client account in order to gamble at the defendant's casino and lost a total of £154,695. The House of Lords, reversing the Court of Appeal, held that the solicitors were entitled to recover from the defendants the net amount lost at their tables by C. Their Lordships held that the solicitors had title to the money that could be traced, at common law, into the funds retained by the club. Consequently, both the *Agip* and *Gorman*

---

[11] (1848) 2 HL Cas 28.
[12] [1990] Ch 265.
[13] [1991] 2 AC 548.
[14] [1991] 2 AC 548.

cases recognised that a bank customer is entitled to bring a restitutionary claim for money wrongfully paid out of the account. In *Lipkin Gorman* Lord Goff said:

> Before [C] drew upon the solicitors' client account at the bank, there was of course no question of the solicitors having any legal property in any cash lying at the bank. The relationship of the bank with the solicitors was essentially that of debtor and creditor; and since the client account was at all material times in credit, the bank was the debtor and the solicitors the creditors. Such a debt constitutes a chose in action, which is a species of property; and since the debt was enforceable at common law, the chose in action was legal property belonging to the solicitors at common law . . . There is in my opinion no reason why the solicitors should not be able to trace their property at common law in that chose in action, or any part of it, into its product, i.e. cash drawn by [C] from their client account at the bank. Such a claim is consistent with their assertion that the money so obtained by [C] was their property at common law.

Lord Goff's view in *Lipkin Gorman* is consistent with the approach in the *Agip* case although his view is based on the solicitor's right to trace their property in the debt, while the *Agip* case focused on the right a bank's customer has in the funds paid out at his request. Their Lordships, although applying different rules, reached the same conclusions. Both decisions, however, recognise that where money is paid by mistake to a third party, an action to recover money so misapplied may be brought either by the bank or the account-holding customer. However, a customer is unlikely to bring an action where he can compel the bank to restore the amount wrongfully debited from his account and so the bank will be left to pursue an action against the recipient who receives the money as a result of the mistake. From a practical point, the Court of Appeal's decision in the *Agip* case probably makes more commercial sense. If the bank is obliged to reverse the debit entry, for example where the bank pays against a cheque or mandate that has been properly countermanded the bank acts without a mandate and cannot debit the customer's account. In such cases, the payee is not enriched at the customer's expense since the customer will look towards his bank to recover the amount of the wrongful payment. Most cases for restitution will generally be brought by banks unable to debit their customer's account The legal rules applicable to claims by banks are largely equally applicable to claims by customers although, where relevant, differences will be discussed in the chapter.

Recovery in cases of payments not involving negotiable instruments

The requirements for an action

(i) Payer's liability and payee's entitlement

The vast majority of payments that are held to be recoverable are those where the payer is erroneously led to believe that he is under a liability to pay money to the payee. In *Kelly* v *Solari*[15] an insurance company paid out a sum due under a life insurance policy overlooking the fact that the policy had been cancelled before the assureds' death. The Court of Exchequer held that unless the directors had paid out on the policy without caring whether the policy

---

[15] (1841) 9 M & W 54.

was valid or not, the company was entitled to recover the money in an action for money had and received.[16] Parke B, expressed the view that:

> where money is paid to another under the influence of a mistake, that is, upon the supposition that a specific fact is true, which would entitle the other to the money, but which fact is untrue, and the money would not have been paid if it had been known to the payer that the fact was untrue, an action will lie to recover it back, and it is against conscience to retain it; though a demand may be necessary in those cases in which the receiving party may have been ignorant of the mistake.

The view expressed by Parke B is deemed to define the nature of an action for recovery of money paid under a mistake of fact, although similar rules will apply where the action is based to recover money paid under a mistake of law.[17]

There is a view that the rule expressed by Parke B narrows the scope of the remedy because, according to the learned judge, the mistake must induce the payer to believe that he is under a present liability to make payment and satisfy the payee's demand. However, banks are under a contractual obligation to conform to their customer (payer's) mandate, and the duty is not owed to the payee. Luntz, however, points out that the relevant words are not included in the report in the *Law Journal* and the better view is that they are unduly restrictive.[18]

There are other cases where recovery has been allowed where the payer could not be said to have thought that he was presently liable to make payment. In *Kerrison v Glyn, Mills, Currie & Co*[19] a Mexican mining company drew bills of exchange on a New York bank. In order to facilitate payment, the claimants, who had an interest in the company, remitted £500 to the defendant bank, the London agents of the New York bank. The defendant bank credited the New York bank's overdrawn account with the amount involved. Neither the claimants nor the defendant bank were aware that, at the time, the New York bank had just become insolvent and was unable to pay against the bills of exchange. The claimants demanded repayment of the money on the basis of money paid under a mistake of fact. The House of Lords, restoring the first instance decision of Hamilton J, held that the claimants were entitled to recover the amount paid, although they were under no obligation to remit it even if the New York bank had remained solvent. The mistake was operative, as the claimants had made the payment in anticipation of the proper conclusion of a transaction (which would have resulted in future liability) in which they had a commercial interest. It was clear that the mistake did not lead the claimants to believe that they were under any existing liability at the time of payment. Similarly, in *R.E. Jones Ltd v Waring and Gillow Ltd*[20] a rogue named Bodenham obtained from the respondents furniture to the value of over £13,000 on hire purchase. Bodenham defaulted on the agreement and the respondents repossessed the goods.

---

[16] See also *Norwich Union Fire Insurance Society Ltd v Wm. H. Price Ltd* [1934] AC 455.

[17] *Kleinwort Benson Ltd v Lincoln City Council* [1999] 2 AC 349. See the issue of mistaken payments under law was examined by the Law Commission and in its report the Commission concluded that the issue of whether mistaken payments under a mistake of law were likely to be the subject of judicial developments which curtail the principle that such payments were irrecoverable. The Law Commission recommended reform of the rule that payments made under a mistake of law could not be recovered: *Restitution: Mistakes of Law and Ultra Vires Public Authority Receipts and Payments*. Report under s.3(1)(e) of the Law Commission Act 1965, Cm 2731.

[18] Goff and Jones (2011) *The Law of Unjust Enrichment* (formerly *The Law of Restitution*), London: Sweet & Maxwell.

[19] (1911) 17 Com Cas 41.

[20] [1926] AC 670.

Bodenham then approached the claimants informing them that he represented a firm of motor manufacturers called International Motors and acting on the latter's behalf he agreed to the claimants being appointed as franchise holders, provided the claimants agreed to pay a deposit of £5,000 for the purchase of 500 cars. Bodenham asked that the cheque be made payable to the defendants who, he claimed, were financing the manufacturers. These facts were untrue and Bodenham delivered the cheque to the defendants in order to obtain the release of the furniture they had seized when Bodenham defaulted under the hire purchase agreement. The House of Lords, affirming the decision of the trial court, held that the £5,000 was recoverable as money paid under a mistake of fact. However, it should be noted that when the claimants drew the cheque, they were not under the mistaken belief that they had a contractual relationship with the defendants, who were the payees. Their mistake related to their supposed contractual relationship with the car manufacturers or with the fraudster, Bodenham.

Where a transaction involves two parties, the payer's liability is a reflection of the payee's right to payment and Luntz[21] points out that so long as there are only two parties to a transaction then 'if the recipient is entitled to the money, then the payor is liable to pay him'. In such cases a mistake as to the payer's liability is matched by a mistake as to the recipient's entitlement to receive payment.

However, where more than two parties are involved then it may be possible for the recipient to be entitled to the money without the payer being liable to him: in such circumstances the recipient (payee) may be entitled to claim against a third party. Thus, liability and entitlement are not necessarily concurrent and that will inevitably be the situation where a bank is involved.[22] In this 'triangular situation' the other two parties involved are the bank customer (A), who has ostensibly given the payment instruction, the paying, or drawee, bank (B) and the third party recipient (or payee) (C) of the mistaken payment and, in such circumstances, the bank will have made payment when it has no mandate from the account-holding customer (A).[23] Enrichment of this nature is sometimes referred to as 'indirect enrichment'. Even where the paying bank is entitled to debit[24] its customer (A)'s account with the wrongful payment, it may take the decision to pursue the recipient,[25] rather than its own customer with whom

---

[21] Luntz (1968) The Bank's Right to Recover Cheques paid by Mistake, 6 *Melb ULR*, 308.

[22] Luntz (1968) The Bank's Right to Recover Cheques paid by Mistake, 6 *Melb ULR*, 308.

[23] In *Barclays Bank Ltd* v *WJ Simms Son & Cooke (Southern) Cooke Ltd* [1980] QB 677 Robert Goff J (as he then was) dealing with the point of mistaken payment said: 'a bank which pays a cheque drawn or purported to be drawn by its customer pays without a mandate. A bank does so if, for example, it overlooks or ignores notice of its customer's death, or if it pays a cheque bearing the forged signature of its customer as drawer; but, more important for present purposes, a bank will pay without mandate if it overlooks or ignores notice of countermand of the customer who has drawn the cheque. In such cases the bank, if it pays the cheque, pays without mandate from its customer; and unless, the customer is able to and does ratify the payment, the bank cannot debit the customer's account, nor will its payment be effective to discharge the obligation (if any) of the customer on the cheque, because the bank had no authority to discharge such obligation'.

[24] In some such instances, the customer may be a estopped from challenging the bank's right to debit his account. Alternatively, for example, the Bills of Exchange Act 1882 confers statutory protection on the paying and collecting banks in certain circumstances where the bank in fact acts without a valid mandate: see Ch. 11.

[25] In this chapter the term used to describe the fraudulent or unauthorised person receiving the money is 'recipient' rather than 'payee', although the terms are used interchangeably at times. This term is also used by Luntz (1968) The Bank's Rights to Recover on Cheques Paid by Mistake, 6 *Melb ULR*, 308, at 309 where he explains that the term 'payee' may cause confusion between the designated payee on a cheque or bill of exchange and the person who actually receives payment.

it may wish to maintain good relations, or it may alternatively seek to recover the money from the recipient's agent bank (collecting bank) who has deeper pockets. However, in some circumstances the mistaken payment may give rise to an action by A against C.[26] Further, once the mistake is realised the recipient bank will often simply reverse the payment. However, that may be resisted in certain circumstances, especially where fraud is involved and the fraudulent recipient has absconded or spent the money, or the money has been passed on to a third party. In order to recover the money paid under a mistake of fact the bank must be able to assert a legal title to the money, or its substitute, that is now held by the recipient.

In *Kelly* v *Solari*[27] the court held that the payee has a right to retain the money when he has an entitlement to it, be it against the payer or the third party, for example the payer's principal. However, where the payee has no entitlement to the funds received then according to Parke B, 'it is against conscience to retain it'. However, most cases take a contrary view. In *Imperial Bank of Canada* v *Bank of Hamilton*[28] the amount of a certificated cheque was fraudulently raised from $5 to $500. The bank was allowed to recover from the holder, in due course, the excess amount paid as a result of the fraud. The certification of the cheque did not bind the bank. The bank's mistake as to the validity of the cheque formed the basis of the action for restitution and the mistake was operative even though the bank was only mistaken about the extent of its liability. This was despite the fact that the holder, in due course, might have been able to recover the full amount of the altered cheque from the drawer. Similarly, in *Colonial Bank* v *Exchange Bank of Yarmouth, Nova Scotia*[29] the claimant bank which had been instructed by its customer to make payment to the X Bank, in fact paid it by mistake to the defendant bank. As the customer was heavily overdrawn against its account with the defendant bank, it purported to retain the amount and reduce the amount of the customer's overdraft. The claimant bank was entitled to recover the amount paid. Luntz concluded that the case shows 'that mistake as to the recipient's 'entitlement' . . . is not a necessary condition for the recovery of money paid in such circumstances'. Similarly, in *R.E. Jones Ltd* v *Waring & Gillow Ltd*[30] the claimants, who had made a mistake concerning their liability to pay Bodenham or the car manufacturers, did not make a mistake about the payee's entitlement to receive the money.

The conclusion, therefore, is that a payer's mistake, which forms the basis of his action in restitution, need concern neither his own liability to pay the amount nor the payee's entitlement to the money. His right to recover the amount is unaffected by a claim that the payee may have against a third party. It is sufficient that the payer is under an operative mistake concerning his own reasons for the payment or his own motive. A mistake made by the paying bank is operative whenever it causes the relevant payment. In *Barclays Bank Ltd* v *WJ Simms Son & Cooke (Southern) Ltd*[31] Goff J held that the bank's mistake about the existence of a valid mandate for the payer's extra payment was sufficient to justify the grant of an order for restitution.

---

[26] See: Van Zyl (1998) Unauthorised Payment and Unjust Enrichment in Banking Law, Ch. 1 in *Restitution and Banking Law*, F. Rose (ed.), Toronto: Mansfield Press.

[27] (1841) 9 M & W 54.

[28] [1903] AC 49.

[29] (1885) 11 App Cas 84.

[30] [1926] AC 670.

[31] [1980] QB 677.

(ii) Nature of the operative mistake

Not every mistake made by the payer operates to grant relief under the principles of restitution. Some decisions have held that money cannot be recovered unless the mistake is one 'as between' the plaintiff and defendant, or is one 'with which the defendant has nothing to do'. On the basis of these, first instance, cases it has been held that money so paid is irrecoverable.[32]

In *Kleinwort, Sons & Co v Dunlop Rubber Co*[33] the sellers of rubber assigned the purchase price due to him to M1. However, due to an error, the buyers paid the amount to M2 who had been the assignee in other transactions and who received the amount in the belief that they were entitled to it. After the purchasers were ordered to pay the amount again to M1, who was entitled as an equitable assignee to the amount, they brought an action to recover the amount paid by them to M2. The House of Lords held that the purchasers were entitled to succeed as the mistake, which concerned the relationship between the payer and payee, was the sole cause of the payment. However, in *Porter v Latec Finance (Qld.) Pty. Ltd*[34] Barwick CJ raised doubts about the views expressed in *Kleinwort* case and concluded that if an operative mistake had to be between the payer and payee, and concerned the relationship between them, recovery would be ruled out unless the mistake was common to both the parties. The latter principle would effectively mean that, for example, where the bank paid against a counter-manded cheque it would not be able to recover the amount of the countermanded cheque since the bank's mistake relates to the oversight of the customer's instructions not to make payment: a mistake between the bank and its customer and not a mistake between the bank and payee. To invoke 'privity' to defeat the payer's claim and insist the mistaken payment 'as between' the payer and payee is to insist on an 'implied contract'.[35] The modern authoritative view, however, is that it is the payer's mistake alone which should be relevant to allow recovery. Only if it is accepted that the mistake has to relate to mutual rights and duties between the payer and payee would it follow that the mistake has to be 'between them'.

The decisions of the House of Lords in *Kleinwort Sons & Co v Dunlop Rubber Co,*[36] *Kerrison v Glyn, Mills, Currie & Co*[37] and *Colonial Bank v Exchange Bank of Yarmouth, Nova Scotia*[38] authoritatively rejected the proposition that a payer could only recover the payment if his mistake was 'as between the payer and payee' in the sense of a mistake shared by both the parties: the payer was liable to the defendant to make the payment. In *Colonial Bank v Exchange Bank of Yarmouth, Nova Scotia*[39] a firm, B. Rogers & Son, instructed the plaintiff bank to transfer money to a bank in Halifax, Nova Scotia. Owing to a mistake on the part of the plaintiff bank, the money was paid to the defendants who refused to return the money because the firm of Rogers was indebted to them. The Privy Council, reversing the Supreme Court of Nova Scotia, held:

---

[32] *Barclay & Co v Malcolm & Co* (1925) 133 LT 512; *Weld-Blundell v Synott* [194] 2 KB 107; *Commonwealth Trading Bank v Reno Auto Sales Ltd* [1967] VR 790; *Royal Bank of Canada v Boyce* (1966) 57 DLR (2d) 683.

[33] (1907) 97 LT 263.

[34] (1964) 111 CLR 177.

[35] Goff and Jones (2011) *The Law of Unjust Enrichment* (formerly *The Law of Restitution*), London: Sweet & Maxwell.

[36] (1907) 97 LT 263.

[37] (1912) 81 LJKB 465.

[38] (1885) 11 App Cas 84.

[39] (1885) 11 App Cas 84.

it is said that the plaintiff's have no interest to recover the fund because they were originally set in motion by Rogers who paid them. But if it were only to relieve themselves from all questions about the mistake that their agents made in New York, and to relieve themselves from liability to be sued for the whole consequences proceeding from the mistake, the plaintiffs would have an interest to recover the money. They were told to convey the money to a certain quarter. They, through their agents, were the authors of the mistake by which it went to another quarter. It seems a perfectly untenable position to say that an agent in that position has not got an interest to recall the money, so that it may be put into the right channel.

In *Kleinwort Sons & Co v Dunlop Rubber Co*,[40] a customer directed the respondents to make a payment to a third party but they mistakenly made payment to the appellants who received the money in good faith. The House of Lords held that the respondents could recover the money although they never held the belief that they were liable to pay the appellants. Similarly, in *R.E. Jones Ltd v Waring & Gillow Ltd*[41] where the plaintiffs were mistakenly led to believe by a fraudulent third party's misrepresentation to make payments to the defendants whom they mistakenly thought to be the nominee of a company whose representative was the third party. The House of Lords allowed the plaintiffs to recover the mistaken payment; there was no suggestion that recovery had been allowed on the grounds that the plaintiffs mistakenly believed they were liable to make the payment. Lord Sumner's statement of the facts indicates that the payer mistakenly thought that he was discharging an obligation to the company and not to the defendants.

This 'formidable line of authority' led Goff J to conclude in *Barclays Bank Ltd v WJ Simms, Sons & Cooke (Southern) Ltd*[42] that a bank could recover money paid against a cheque which had been countermanded, and which it paid due to clerical oversight. The learned judge concluded that if the mistake had caused the payment to be made, the mistake did not have to be 'between' the bank, as payer, and the payee in the sense of a mistake shared by both the parties: the payer was liable to the defendant to make the payment.[43] The payer mistakenly thought that he owed a duty to another to make the payment and it was this mistake which led him to pay: this was sufficient to ground recovery. The principle under-lying these decisions is also consistent with the Privy Council in *Imperial Bank of Canada v Bank of Hamilton* where it was held that if a bank pays the holder of a certificated cheque, the amount which has been fraudulently raised, the bank may recover the excess from the holder even though it would not have been liable to the holder if the facts had been as it supposed. The learned judge analysed the earlier cases, which were used to support the argument that no action would lie to recover money paid under a mistake of fact, unless the mistake was 'as between' the payer and payee. He said the opinion of Erle CJ in *Chambers v Miller*[44] had been misinterpreted and taken out of context. The learned judge also rejected the views expressed in *Aiken v Short*[45] and *Kelly v Salori*[46] and concluded that the supposed rule that payment must be 'between' the parties was inconsistent with the decision in *R.E. Jones*

---

[40] (1907) 97 LT 263.
[41] [1926] AC 670.
[42] [1980] QB 677.
[43] Cf *Commercial Bank of Australia v Younis* [1979] 1NSWLR 444.
[44] (1862) 12 CB NS 125.
[45] (1856) 1 Hurl & N 210.
[46] (1841) 9 M & W 54.

Ltd v *Waring and Gillow*.[47] The view that money cannot be recovered because the mistake is not one 'as between' the plaintiff and defendant is therefore not likely to be followed. Since Goff J's judgment the English courts have consistently followed the *Simms* case and a causation test when determining whether a payer's mistake renders the defendant's enrichment unjust.

(iii) The mistake must have caused the plaintiff to make the payment

The burden is on the plaintiff to show he would not have made the payment but for the mistake of fact. The question the courts have tended to ask is whether the payer would have made the payment had he known the true facts. If he would have made the payment, then he cannot recover, but if the plaintiff can show he would not have made the payment and such action was induced by the mistake then he can recover.[48] Although the burden of proof should not cause the plaintiff any difficulty it may, at times, do so, but in any event it should not be necessary to demonstrate that the mistake was 'fundamental'. The burden is on the payer to demonstrate that 'but for' the mistake he would not have made the payment[49] but the mere fact that the payer had some doubt as to his liability to pay does not necessarily make him a 'risk taker' who is precluded from recovering his payment.[50]

(iv) Who may be made liable?

The paying bank may decide to sue both the collecting bank and the ultimate recipient, jointly. However, there are distinctions in pursuing an action against the collecting bank, which result from the fact that it receives the payment in a representative capacity, while the payee will receive the payment for himself, as principal. In essence the question in such situations is which of the two parties will bear the loss resulting from the wrongdoing of another. Where a bank pays money as a result of a mistake of fact or law[51] it may bring a common law action for money had and received against the payee. The action is frequently referred to as 'a personal claim in restitution at common law'.[52] The term payee is understood in a wide context for these purposes and the claim is founded on the basis of the unjust enrichment of the recipient at the bank's expense, and the bank's mistake renders the enrichment of the recipient unjust because it vitiates the bank's intention to transfer the benefit to him. The return of the mistaken payment and the reversal of the transaction and thereby the reversal of the unjust enrichment is the foundation of the action[53] and a claim will crystallise on the recipient having received the money and not its continued retention.[54]

---

[47] [1926] AC 670.

[48] *Barclays Bank Ltd* v *WJ Simms, Sons & Cooke (Southern) Ltd* [1980] 1 QB 677.

[49] *Deutsche Morgan Grenfell Group Inc.* v *Inland Revenue Commissioners*.

[50] *Marine Trade SA* v *Pioneer Freight Futures Co Ltd BVI* [2009] EWHC 2656.

[51] Until recently, English law allowed a common law action to recover money paid by mistake only where the mistake was one of fact and not of law: this limitation was criticised in *Woolwich Equitable Building Society* v *IRC* [1993] AC 70 at 164 and 199. See also Law Commission Report No. 227, *Restitution, Mistakes of Law and Ultra Vires Public Authority Receipts and Payments*, 1994.

[52] *Westdeutsche Landesbank Girozentrale* v *Islington* [1996] AC 669 at 683.

[53] *Lipkin Gorman (a firm)* v *Karpnale Ltd* [1991] 2 AC 548; *Westdeutsche Landesbank Girozentrale* v *Islington* [1986] AC 669; *Kleinwort Benson Ltd* v *Glasgow CC* [1997] 3 WLR 923 at 237; see also Van Zyl (1998) Unauthorised Payment and Unjust Enrichment in Banking Law, Ch. 1 in *Restitution and Banking Law*, F. Rose (ed.), Toronto: Mansfield Press.

[54] *Agip (Africa) Ltd* v *Jackson* [1991] Ch 547 at 563.

Defences

A claim for recovery of money paid under mistake is subject to general defences, which apply to all restitutionary claims: (a) change of position; (b) estoppel; and (c) the agent's defence of payment over. Developments in the last two defences will, in the future, be affected by the continued developments in the defence of change of position. In *Kleinwort Benson* v *Lincoln City Council*[55] Lord Goff recognised that:

> the law must evolve appropriate defences which can, together with the defence of change of position, provide protection where appropriate for recipients of money paid under a mistake of law in those cases in which justice or policy does not require them to refund the money.

However, the House of Lords was reluctant to recognise any special defences to claims founded on mistake of law. The defences are fundamentally different and are now considered.

(a) Change of position

The defence of change of position is like estoppel but the element of a representation is not required. The enriched payee will succeed if he can show that he acted to his detriment on the faith of the receipt. All the payee has to show is that on the faith of his position having improved he spent more than he would have done and so altered his position, or spent more than he would otherwise have done. The defence is based on the payee's change of position and on the consideration that it would be inequitable to insist that the money be repaid when the payee has relied on it to his detriment. It is, therefore, inequitable that the payee repays the money where he has, in reliance on the receipt, incurred a liability or given up an advantage. The defence is limited to detriment suffered as a result of the direct reliance on the payment and although the English courts were reluctant to recognise it,[56] Goff J in *Barclays Bank Ltd* v *WJ Simms, Sons & Cooke (Southern) Ltd*[57] expressed the view that, in certain circumstances, the recipient of funds, paid to him under a mistake of fact, was entitled to retain them provided that he has 'changed his position in good faith or is deemed in law to have done so'. In *Lipkin Gorman (a firm)* v *Karpnale Ltd*[58] their Lordships gave careful consideration and full recognition to the defence. In that case a partner in a firm of solicitors misappropriated money from the firm's client account and purchased gaming chips at the defendant's casino. Although, he occasionally won and paid back some of the misappropriated funds he lost £154,695 out of the total £323,222.14 stolen from the partnership firm. The firm brought an action to recover the money from the casino. The House of Lords held that the supply of gambling chips paid for with the money acquired fraudulently did not constitute the furnishing of a separate lawful consideration by the club. The dishonest partner's transactions with the gambling club involved contracts that were void and the club had not furnished value for the funds. The partnership firm therefore, subject to defences, was entitled to recover its money.

However, the House of Lords then went on to consider the amount which the firm was entitled to recover, i.e. the total amount misappropriated and placed on the gambling tables, or only the net amount lost gambling by the dishonest partner. Their Lordships concluded

---

[55] *R.E. Jones Ltd* v *Waring and Gillow Ltd* [1926] AC 670.
[56] [1926] AC 670.
[57] [1980] QB 677.
[58] [1991] 2 AC 548.

that the casino having changed its position to the extent of the amounts paid out to the dishonest partner, was only liable for the net amount lost by him. In reaching this conclusion their Lordships gave effect to the doctrine that an action in restitution could not be brought against a person who had in good faith changed his position in reliance on the money received. While their Lordships accepted change of position as a general defence to all restitutionary claims they agreed that 'it would be unwise to attempt to define its scope in abstract terms, but better to allow the law on the subject to develop on a case-by-case basis'. Lord Goff,[59] however, analysed the defence and observed that:

> Where an innocent defendant's position is so changed that he will suffer an injustice if called upon to repay in full, the injustice of requiring him so to repay outweighs the injustice of denying the [claimant] restitution. If the [claimant] pays money to the defendant under a mistake fact, and the defendant then, acting in good faith, pays the money or part of it to charity, it is unjustified to require the defendant to make restitution to the extent that he has so changed his position.

The House of Lords thereby introduced a general defence of change of position to restitutionary claims but whether this defence is available in all restitutionary claims remains to be determined. In *Foskett* v *McKeown*[60] Lord Millett distinguished between a restitutionary claim based on the reversal of unjust enrichment and one that seeks to vindicate property rights. In *Lipkin Gorman*[61] the plaintiff firm's claim, although personal, was based on its title to the property. However, Lord Goff does not suggest that change of position is not a defence to a proprietary restitutionary claim. In *Re Diplock*[62] the Court of Appeal held that the next-of-kins' equitable proprietary claim failed if it would be 'inequitable' to allow them to trace their money into the hands of innocent volunteers. The *Allcard* v *Skinner*[63] case suggests a similar limitation of the equitable proprietary claim. In that case the novice nun's claim to set aside her gifts was defeated by her own *laches* (delay) and affirmation of the transaction. Even if the action, based on the undue influence of her Lady Superior, had succeeded she would have recovered only that part of the funds gifted that 'had not been spent in accordance with the wishes of the plaintiff but remained in the hands of the defendant'.

In *Lipkin Gorman*,[64] Lord Goff emphasised that not every change of position by the payee would allow him to plead the change of position defence. The learned judge said:

> It is, of course, plain that the defence is not open to one who has changed his position in bad faith, as where the defendant has paid away money with knowledge of the facts entitling the [claimant] to restitution; and it is commonly accepted that the defence should not be open to the wrongdoer.

The defence therefore balances the claims of the plaintiff seeking restitution of another's unjust enrichment against the defendant's good faith belief that the asset received was his to keep.[65] Lord Goff emphasised that the mere fact that the payee had spent the money did not, in itself, involve a change of his position that would bring the defence into play. The

---

[59] *Lipkin Gorman (a firm)* v *Karpnale Ltd* [1991] 2 AC 548.
[60] [2001] 1 AC 102.
[61] *Lipkin Gorman (a firm)* v *Karpnale Ltd* [1991] 2 AC 548.
[62] [1948] Ch 465.
[63] (1887) 36 Ch D 145.
[64] *Lipkin Gorman (a firm)* v *Karpnale Ltd* [1991] 2 AC 548.
[65] *Dextra Bank and Trust Co* v *Bank of Jamaica* [2002] 1 All ER (Comm) 193.

'expenditure might in any event have been incurred by him in the ordinary course of things'.[66] If the payee were to succeed in this defence he must show that he has changed his position, and incurred expenditure, in a way he would not otherwise have done so as to render it unjust that he should be compelled to return the money. The defendant's change of position may, and often does, involve a deliberate act, although the courts have recognised that the defence also 'adds further possibilities which do not depend on deliberate choices by the recipient'. Thus, receipt of payment may lead the defendant to give up a job when he is of an age where the possibility of finding an alternative position is not readily available. Robert Walker LJ, in *Scottish Equitable Plc* v *Derby*, however, accepted that a defendant may rely on the defence if it can be demonstrated that he has foregone an income generating opportunity, or that it may induce him to take up a flat on, for example, a ten-year lease which would not be easy to dispose of.[67] It is, therefore, a question of fact in each case as to whether there is a casual link between the change of position and the unjust enrichment. In *National Westminster Bank Plc* v *Somer International UK Ltd*[68] the trial judge concluded, which the Court of Appeal later accepted, that it could not be said that the defendant had lost an opportunity to pursue its debtor for overpayment of the debt. There was no causal link between the receipt of the mistaken payment and the lost chance. Valuation of that change of position was nil. However, where the payee spends the money on goods or services, the benefit of which he still retains may result in him being unjustly enriched equal to their value.

In *Scottish Equitable Plc* v *Derby*[69] the defendant invested some of his money in an individual pension policy with the claimant life assurance company. He subsequently exercised an option to take an early retirement benefit, but due to an error the company failed to record the exercise of that option. When the defendant reached the age of 65 the claimant sent him a statement showing a total fund of £201,000, resulting from the failure to take into consideration the defendant's exercise of the early retirement benefit, and the fact that the fund actually stood at approximately £29,500. After receiving confirmation from the claimant that the statement was correct, the defendant took £51,300 as a lump payment and reinvested £150,600 with another pension company, NU. The defendant was, therefore, overpaid approximately £172,500, including an overpayment of £121,100 reinvested with NU. Because of the overpayment the defendant received an annual pension approximately £11,000 higher than he would otherwise have done. With the lump sum payment (£51,300), the defendant spent approximately £41,700 reducing his mortgage and the balance was spent on making modest improvements to his lifestyle. On discovering the error the claimant sought to recover the overpayment from the defendant on the ground that he had been unjustly enriched by the amount of the overpayment. The defendant, partially because he was in the middle of a divorce, was facing severe financial difficulties and sought, at first instance, to rely on the defence of change of position, arguing that because of the claimant's error and his receipt of the overpaid amount he had not sought alternative sources of income or made savings which he might otherwise have done. The trial judge rejected the change of position defence on the basis that 'there must be some causal link between the receipt of the payment and the change of position such that it would be inequitable to require the recipient to return

---

[66] *United Overseas Bank* v *Jiwani* [1976] 1 WLR 964.
[67] Robert Walker LJ in *Scottish Equitable Plc* v *Derby* [2000] 3 All ER 793.
[68] [2002] QB 1286.
[69] [2001] 3 All ER 818.

the money to its owner'. The judge held that the defendant's general financial difficulties resulting from his separation from his wife were not causally linked to the mistaken payment. Moreover, the defendant had been in no position to make any savings and there was no realistic prospect of the defendant obtaining further employment, given his age and health. The extra income had not caused a change of position to the extent that he had not foregone an opportunity he would otherwise have taken advantage of or any additional income, which he had lost as result of relying on the overpayments. Nor had the defendant incurred a change of position in respect of the overpayment to him of the extra £121,000 invested with the NU, since the NU had agreed to unwind the policy and put him in the same position he would have been in had the overpayment not been made. Finally, the learned judge held that the defendant had not changed his position in respect of the £41,700 used to reduce his mortgage for two reasons namely: (i) that the money was used to pay an existing debt that would have been paid in any event;[70] and (ii) he had the benefit of the increased equity of that amount in the house and he could realise the asset to repay the claimant. The Court of Appeal, affirming Harrison J, at first instance, stressed that for the change of position defence to be available:

(a) There must be a causal link between the recipient's change of position and the mistaken payment which makes it inequitable for the recipient to be required to make restitution; and

(b) A court should not apply too demanding a standard of proof when an honest recipient can show that he has spent the overpayment by improving his lifestyle cannot produce detailed accounts.

The Court of Appeal accepted that the change of position defence was to be available not only to those who to their detriment had relied on the mistaken payment (the 'narrow view') but also to those who had suffered some other misfortune, for example the innocent recipient of a payment which is then stolen from him, so long as the misfortune can be causally linked to the mistaken receipt (the 'wide view'). Both Robert Walker LJ in *Scottish Equitable Plc* v *Derby*[71] and Peter Gibson LJ in *National Westminster Bank plc* v *Somer International UK Ltd*[72] accepted that the defence 'is not limited to specific identifiable items of expenditure' and that 'it may be right for the court not to apply too demanding a standard of proof when an honest defendant says that he has spent an overpayment by improving his lifestyle, but cannot produce any detail accounting'. Jonathan Parker J continued in *Philip Collins Ltd* v *Davis*[73] that 'it may well be unrealistic to expect the defendant to produce conclusive evidence of change of position, given that when he changed his position he can have had no expectation that he might thereafter have to prove that he did so, and the reason why he did so in a court of law'.

In the *Davis* case,[74] royalties were mistakenly paid over during a six-year period and the claimant, in due course, sought only to recover the overpayments from any future payment of royalties. Jonathan Parker J allowed the claim to succeed in respect of part of the overpayment, but held a claim subject to the defence of change of position in respect of the other

---

[70] *United Overseas Bank* v *Jawani* [1976] 1 WLR 964.
[71] [2000] 3 All ER 793.
[72] [2002] 1 All ER 198.
[73] [2000] 3 All ER 808.
[74] [2000] 3 All ER 793.

half. He expressed the view that the overpayments had caused a general change of position by the defendants in that they increased their level of outgoings by reference to the sums so paid. It was significant that the overpayments took the form of periodic payments over a considerable period of time. While the defendants' financial affairs did not lend themselves to detailed analysis the judge was prepared to take a broad approach and concluded that on a conservative assessment the defence of change of position extended to approximately half of the payments. He stressed that the defence should be applied in accordance with the legal principles and not as a matter of fairness. The learned judge then went on to identify four principles that would be regarded as relevant to the application of the defence namely that:

1 The evidential burden is on the defendant to make good the defence of change of position. However, in applying this principle the judge expressed the view that the court should be aware of applying too strict a standard and, depending on the circumstances, it may be unrealistic to expect a defendant to produce conclusive evidence of change of position, given that when he changed his position he would not have anticipated having to prove that he had done so in a court of law, and the reason why.

2 In accordance with the view expressed in *Lipkin Gorman*,[75] for the change of position defence to withstand scrutiny there must be something more than the mere spending of the money sought to be recovered, because the expenditure might in any event have been incurred in the ordinary course of things.

3 There must be a causal link between the change of position and the overpayment. In other words the change of position must be referable in some way to the payment of that money.

4 In contrast to the defence of estoppel the change of position defence is not an 'all or nothing' defence: it is available only to the extent that the change of position renders recovery unjust.

In *South Tyneside Metropolitan Borough Council* v *Svenska International Plc*[76] Clarke J held that the defence of change of position was only available where the defendant had changed his position after receipt of the enrichment. Consequently, an anticipatory change of position was not sufficient to raise the defence. In *South Tyneside* the bank had entered into *ultra vires* swap transactions with the local authority, which the bank protected by hedging contracts. In the event, the local authority was the net payer under the swaps, and the bank was liable to make restitution. The bank, however, sought to set off losses incurred in consequence of having entered into the hedging transactions against the net payments received. Clarke J held that the bank had changed its position before the receipt of any payments and therefore could not rely on the defence of change of position, 'otherwise the bank would in effect be relying upon the supposed ability of avoided transaction'. This limitation has been heavily criticised in *Dextra Bank & Trust Co Ltd* v *Bank of Jamaica*[77] where Lords Bingham and Goff expressed the view that anticipatory expenditure resulting in a change of position was sufficient to raise the defence. The Privy Council was not convinced that a distinction should be drawn between the situation where the defendant 'expends on some extra ordinary expenditure

---

[75] *Lipkin Gorman (a firm)* v *Karpnale Ltd* [1991] 2 AC 548.
[76] [1995] 1 All ER 545.
[77] [2002] 1 All ER (Comm) 193.

all or part of the money received from the plaintiff' and one 'in which the defendant incurs such expenditure in the expectation that he will receive the sum of money from the plaintiff which he does in fact receive'. Lords Bingham and Goff continued:

> since ex hypothesi the defendant will in fact have received the expected money, there is no question of the defendant using the defence of change of position to enforce, directly or indirectly, a claim to that money. It is surely no abuse of language to say, in the second case as in the first, that the defendant has incurred expenditure in reliance on the plaintiff's payment or, as it is sometimes said, on the face of the payment. It is true that, in the second case, the defendant relied on the payment being made to him in the future (as well as relying on such payment, when made, being a valid payment); but, provided that his change of position was in good faith, it should provide, *pro tanto* at least, a good defence because it would be inequitable to require the defendant to make restitution, or to make restitution in full . . . The defence should be regarded as founded on the principle of justice designed to protect the defendant from a claim to restitution in respect of the benefit received by him in circumstances in which it would be inequitable to pursue that claim, or to pursue it in full.

In *Commerzbank AG v Gareth Price-Jones*[78] the Court of Appeal followed the *Dextra* case and held that a change of position in anticipation was to be treated in the same way as one where the change of position came afterwards.

For the change of position defence to apply not only must there be a causal link between the receipt of payment by the defendant and his change of position but the events must be referable to each other. Additionally, the defendant's position must also have changed in circumstances, which make it inequitable for him to make restitution to the claimant. Lord Goff in *Lipkin Gorman*[79] emphasised that the defence of change of position was not available to someone who acts in bad faith and a defendant who is a wrongdoer cannot rely on the defence. Since, *Twinsectra v Yardley*[80] bad faith (including dishonesty) is defined subjectively so that the defendant must realise that his conduct would be regarded as dishonest by the standards of reasonable and honest people. However, bad faith goes further than the subjective test of dishonesty and in *Niru Battery Manufacturing Co v Milestone Trading Ltd*[81] the court held that the lack of good faith was a concept 'capable of embracing a failure to act in a commercially acceptable way and sharp practice of a kind that falls short of outright dishonesty as well as dishonesty itself'. On appeal the Court of Appeal, stressed that the key question was whether it would be equitable or unconscionable to deny restitution. Bad faith does not include negligence.[82] Further, the defendant cannot rely on the change of position defence where he knows that the claimant has paid under a mistake and will be entitled to restitution,[83] or where he knew that there was a possibility he was not entitled to the money,[84] or where he took a risk that no claim would be brought for recovery.[85] The view has also been expressed that the change of position defence is not available to the careless recipient[86]

---

[78] [2003] EWCA Civ. 1663.
[79] *Lipkin Gorman (a firm) v Karpnale Ltd* [1991] 2 AC 548.
[80] [2002] 2 AC 164.
[81] [2002] 2 All ER (Comm.) 705.
[82] *Dextra Bank & Trust Co Ltd v Bank of Jamaica* [2002] 1 All ER (Comm.) 193.
[83] *RBC Dominion Securities Inc. v Dawson.*
[84] *South Tyneside Metropolitan Borough Council v Svenska International Plc* [1995] 1 All ER 545.
[85] *Re Tain Construction Ltd, Rose v AIB Group (UK) Plc* [2003] BPIR 1188.
[86] *South Tyneside Metropolitan Borough Council v Svenska International Plc* [1995] 1 All ER 545.

although the better view[87] is that since the careless payer can claim restitution for a mistaken payment, the careless payee should be treated no differently. This issue was examined in *Dextra Bank & Trust Co Ltd v Bank of Jamaica*[88] where Lords Bingham and Goff stated that a judge should not 'balance the equities' and apportion loss according to the parties' relative merits. Their Lordships also expressed the view that any attempt to apply the defence of change of position to reflect a level of fault would render it 'hopelessly unstable'. *Dextra* is also authority for the rule that good faith on the part of the recipient is a sufficient requirement for the defence of change of position. Thus, negligence on the part of the recipients is not sufficient to deprive him of the change of position defence.[89]

(b) Good consideration

The claimant's action to recover money paid under a mistake will fail if the defendant has provided 'good consideration' for the payment[90] which excludes such consideration as is illegal or contrary to public policy, for example valuable consideration was not provided in *Lipkin Gorman*[91] where money was paid to the defendant under a void gaming contract. The 'good consideration' defence must be distinguished from the *bona fide* purchaser defence and that of change of position. However, there has been some debate among the judges in relation to the consideration defence and application of these defences. In *Lloyds Bank Plc v Independent Insurance Co Ltd*[92] Waller LJ assumed that the defence of good consideration was a form of change of position and Peter Gibson LJ, although separating good consideration from change of position, characterised good consideration as a form of defence of *bona fide* purchaser for value. The view has also been taken that 'good consideration' is not a defence at all, but operates to bar the claimant's action since the defendant's enrichment will not be unjust where he has given good consideration.[93] On that basis it would be for the claimant to show that the defendant's enrichment was unjust, i.e. he had not given good consideration.[94] The provision of good consideration must also be distinguished from the defence of change of position,[95] which requires the defendant to change his position by incurring expenditure, which he would not otherwise have done, as a result of relying on the payment received from the claimant. Furthermore, the defence of 'good consideration' can only be raised where the claimant expected the consideration provided.

The defence of 'good consideration' applies where the claimant, under a mistake, pays the defendant and this has the effect of discharging a debt owed to the defendant.[96] Goff J in *Barclays Bank Plc v WJ Simms Son & Cooke (Southern) Ltd*[97] explained that 'good consideration' is given for the mistaken payment where:

---

[87] *Banque Finaanciere de la Cite v Parc (Battersea) Ltd* [1999] 1 AC 221; *Scottish Equitable Plc v Derby* [2000] 3 All ER 793.

[88] [2002] 1 All ER (Comm.) 193.

[89] *Dextra Bank & Trust Co Ltd v Bank of Jamaica* [2002] 1 All ER (Comm.) 193.

[90] *Barclays Bank Ltd v WJ Simms Son & Cooke (Southern) Cooke Ltd* [1980] QB 677.

[91] *Lipkin Gorman (a firm) v Karpnale Ltd* [1991] 2 AC 548.

[92] [2000] QB 110.

[93] *South Tyneside Metropolitan Borough Council v Svenska International Plc* [1995] 1 All ER 545.

[94] Virgo (1999) Restitution Developments in Restitution of Mistaken Payments, *CLJ*, 478.

[95] Goff J dealt with them separately in *Barclays Bank Ltd v WJ Simms Son & Cooke (Southern) Cooke Ltd* [1980] QB 677.

[96] *Jones v Churcher* [2009] 2 Lloyd's Rep 94.

[97] [1980] QB 677.

the money is paid to discharge, and does discharge, a debt owed to the payee (or a principal on whose behalf he is authorised to receive payment) by the payer or by a third party by whom he is authorised to discharge the debt.

In *Simms* the payee resisted the return of the mistaken payment on the grounds that it had gone towards discharging a legally enforceable debt due, by the customer, to the payee. Goff J resisted this argument on the ground that the payment was made outside the bank's mandate and without the authority of the customer account holder, who had countermande payment. A payment, which has been countermanded and, therefore, made without the authority of the customer, cannot discharge the customer's underlying debt to the payee.

Goff J also distinguished between payments made within the bank's mandate and those made without a mandate. He held that where a bank makes a payment within the mandate given by the customer it is entitled to debit the customer's account with the amount of the authorised payment. Furthermore, the payment will effectively discharge the obligations of the customer to the payee, because the bank has made payment with the customer's authority, for example where the bank makes payment in accordance with a validly drawn cheque which has not been countermanded. In contrast, where the bank makes payment without a mandate, for example where the bank makes payment against a cheque which has been countermanded, or where the bank overlooks notice of the customer's death, or pays a cheque bearing a forged drawer's signature, the bank cannot debit the customer's account, and the payment will not absolve the customer's obligation to the payee, unless the customer is able and does ratify the payment. Goff J went on to examine the type of mistaken payment which would fall within the category of being made within the bank's mandate. Such a payment occurs where the bank honours the customer's payment instruction in the mistaken belief that there are sufficient funds to the credit of the customer's account to meet the payment, or the bank mistakenly believes that the payment is within an agreed overdraft facility. In such cases, the effect of the bank's payment is to accept the customer's request for an overdraft facility, or to increase the amount of an agreed overdraft. The payment would, therefore, be within the bank's mandate and not only is the bank entitled to recover the amount of the payment from the customer but the customer's obligation to the payee is also discharged. This is despite the fact that payment has been made as a result of the bank's mistake and the money is recoverable from the payee unless the payment transaction itself is set aside. Thus for example, in *Lloyds Bank Plc v Independent Insurance Co Ltd*[98] the customer paid a cheque into his account with the claimant bank and instructed the bank to transfer the amount to the defendant as soon as possible to discharge a debt. The bank agreed to act in accordance with this instruction but only once the cheque had been cleared, as there were insufficient funds in the account to meet the payment. However, before the cheque was cleared CHAPS transferred the money into the defendant's bank account. When the error was discovered, the bank tried to recover the payment from the defendant as money paid under a mistake of fact. Applying the *Simms* case, the Court of Appeal held that the bank was not entitled to restitution of a payment, which had been made with the customer's actual authority and since it discharged a debt owed by the customer to the defendant the payment had been made for good consideration. It was the bank, not the customer, which had imposed the qualification that the transfer was not to be made before the cheque cleared. In contrast, in *Simms*,[99]

[98] [2000] QB 110.
[99] [1980] QB 677.

Goff J held that payment of a countermanded cheque fell outside the bank's mandate, and did not discharge the drawer's debt to the payee thereby allowing the drawee bank to recover the payment from the payee, as money had and received. Professor Goode[100] has been critical of Goff J and argues:

1 That while the countermand terminates the bank's actual authority to pay the cheque, the payee was entitled to rely on the bank's continued apparent authority to make payment, so that this was effective to discharge the drawer's liability to the payee on the cheque. This argument was rejected by the Court of Appeal in *Lloyds Bank Plc v Independent Insurance Co Ltd*[101] on the grounds that there was no holding out that the bank had authority to make a payment, and further there was no reliance by the payee on the bank having authority to pay.

2 Goode further raises the criticism that a payee who gives up a cheque in which he has a valid claim in exchange for payment suffers a change of position, since he no longer has the instrument in his hands, and any claim he wishes to pursue against the drawer will have to be on the basis of the original consideration, and not on the cheque, so that he loses valuable rights. However, under s.63(3) of the Bills of Exchange Act 1882, cancellation of a negotiable instrument under a mistake is inoperative and in such a case it may be possible for the bank to restore the cheque to the payee to enable him to take proceedings against the drawer. Further, any detriment under the mistaken payment must out outweigh the injustice of denying the bank the right to recover the money. In *B & H Engineering v First National Bank of SA Ltd*[102] the South African courts have held that payment of a countermanded cheque by the drawee bank discharges the underlying debt between the drawer and payee, so the drawee bank has no claim against the payee for mistaken payment but has a restitutionary claim against the drawer based on his unjust enrichment at the bank's expense. This view is based on the premise that the unauthorised payment discharges the drawer's indebtedness to the payee. The English courts took a similar view in *B. Liggett (Liverpool) Ltd v Barclays Bank Ltd*[103] where Barclays Bank paid a cheque to a trade creditor of its customer but in circumstances where it has been drawn by only one signatory, instead of the required two. Wright J, held the bank had a good defence to the claim on the grounds that the bank was entitled to take over the former creditor's remedies against the claimant under the rules of subrogation.

3 The paying bank may be estopped by representation from recovering money paid under a mistake of fact but a number of requirements must be satisfied:

- There must be representation by the paying bank leading the recipient to believe that he is entitled to treat the money as his own, for example where the crediting of funds to the customer's account and its entry in the statement of account results in the customer honestly believing he is entitled to the money.
- The recipient must have relied on the representation.
- The recipient must have suffered a detriment and he must not be at fault.

[100] Goode (1981) The Bank's Right to Recover Money Paid on a Stopped Cheque, LQR, 254.
[101] [2000] QB 110.
[102] 1995 (2) SA 279.
[103] [1928] 1 KB 48.

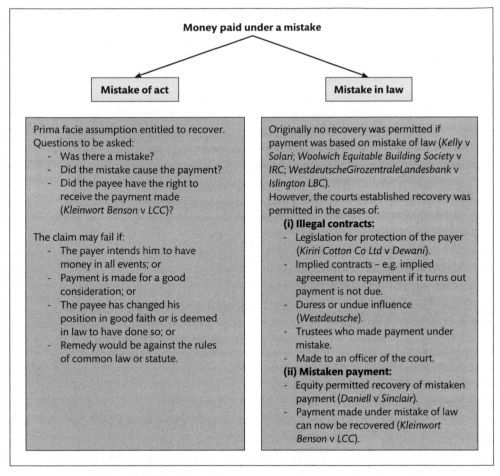

Figure 17.1 Money paid under a mistake

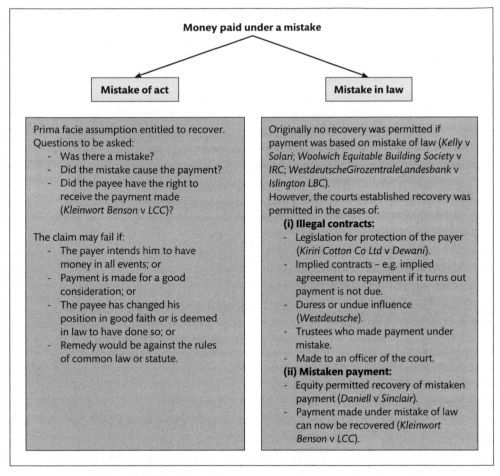

Figure 17.2 Defences to restitutionary claims

The estoppel defence differs from change of position in two ways: (i) it depends on a representation by the person making the payment whereas the change of position defence does not; and (ii) because estoppel gives a total defence to the claim whereas change of position provides only a *pro tanto* defence. In *Scottish Equitable* v *Derby*[104] the court held that it was unconscionable or inequitable to allow the recipient to keep the whole of the mistaken

[104] [2000] 3 All ER 793.

payment of £172,451 when his resultant irrecoverable expenditure was limited to £9,662. The Court of Appeal adopted a similar approach in *National Westminster Bank Plc v Somer International (UK) Ltd*[105] and concluded that it was unconscionable for the defendant to retain the balance of a mistaken payment of $76,700 when the defendant's detrimental reliance was $21,600. The limitations of the defence of estoppel as an 'all or nothing defence' leaves the future of the defence uncertain in recovery of mistaken payment cases. In *Philip Collins Ltd v Davis*[106] Parker J suggested that the law has now developed to the point where a defence of estoppel by representation is 'no longer apt in restitutionary claims where the more flexible defence of change of position is in principle available'.

Action against the collecting bank

In the majority of cases payments to the recipient's account are received to his account with the bank acting merely as the collecting agent. The agent bank acts as a conduit for the money, which is treated as paid over to the principal, not to the agent, so that the principal is the proper party to be sued. In *Jones v Churcher*[107] the court said:

> Ministerial receipt is a different defence to change of position. It is available only when a collecting bank has received funds as agent for the customer and has paid away the funds to the customer. Once the collecting bank has dealt with the funds in such a way that the credit to the customer is irreversible, the bank is entitled to plead a defence of ministerial receipt to any restitutionary claim by the payer to get the funds back. The defence complements the defence of change of position which may additionally be available to the collecting bank depending on the circumstances.

The rules governing the position of a bank, which receives funds as the payee customer's agent, can be traced back to *Buller v Harrison*.[108] This principle, however, was reiterated in *Gowers v Lloyds and National Provincial Foreign Bank Ltd*[109] where Greene MR said that money paid to an agent under a mistake of fact could be recovered from him so long as he had it in his possession, but once the agent has paid away the money it can no longer be recovered from the agent (bank) and the only remedy, in common law, is to pursue an action against the principal (recipient customer). In that case a retired army officer's widow fraudulently continued to receive his pension by representing that he was still alive. The payments were obtained by means of certificates, presented through the defendant bank, which included an attestation by an alleged medical practitioner to the effect that the army officer was alive and well. The sums were remitted to the bank, which paid them out to the widow. The Court of Appeal, affirming the court at first instance, held the amounts were not recoverable from the bank.

The principle has resulted in an inconsistency in situations where the collecting bank finds itself acting for a fraudulent customer. Where a bank collects such instruments for the customer it will be liable to the true owner in conversion, or alternatively in a restitutionary

---

[105] [2002] QB 1286.
[106] [2000] 3 All ER 808.
[107] [2009] 2 Lloyd's Rep 94; see also: Stevens (2005) Why Do Agents Drop Out?, *LMCLQ*, 101; Bant (2007) Payment Over and Change of Position: Lessons from Agency Law, *LMCLQ*, 225.
[108] (1777) 2 Cowp 565.
[109] [1938] 1 All ER 766.

action for damages equal to the amount of the instrument. The bank's only defence is that provided by s.4 of the Cheques Act 1957, under which the bank must show that it acts without negligence. The fact that the bank has paid the proceeds to the customer is no defence. However, where the bank receives the payment, for example under a money transfer or giro credit, which does not involve a negotiable instrument it escapes liability for restitution when it pays the amount to the fraudulent customer. The bank's negligence is immaterial in such cases. The practical differences in the principles governing negotiable instruments and money transfers are not that wide. The defence of ministerial receipt does not apply where the bank receives the money as principal, or in its own right. In *Continental Caoutchouc and Gutta Percha Co v Kleinwort Sons & Co*[110] two banks, the defendants and B & Co., regularly financed a firm of rubber merchants, K. The purchasers of some of K's rubber were ordered to remit part of the price to the defendants and the balance to B & Co., but mistakenly remitted the full amount to the defendants, who received the money in good faith and credited K's account with the amount. The Court of Appeal, affirming Bingham J's judgment held that the amount mistakenly paid was recoverable by the purchasers. Collins MR distinguished between two types of action:

- Where a bank received payment as a mere agent, then any amount erroneously paid could not be recovered from the bank once it was paid to the principal; and

- Where the bank received payment for itself then it is in the same position as any other ultimate payee to whom payment is made under a mistake of fact.

Support for this view in the *Continental Caoutchouc* case is found in *Thomas v Houston Corbett & Co*[111] where the court expressed the view that whether the payee's bank receives the amount as an agent or as a principal depends on his understanding of the transaction and the capacity in which he purports to act. Moreover, the court held that the defendant bank will not escape making repayment by establishing he was acting as an agent if:

(i) He had notice of the plaintiff's claim before paying the money to the principal or otherwise disposing of it on his behalf;

(ii) In the course of the transaction he acted as the principal; and

(iii) He received the money in consequence of some wrongdoing to which he was a party or of which he had knowledge.

It may not be easy to determine whether the bank receives money as an agent or as principal. If the bank allows a customer to draw against an uncleared cheque the bank will, subsequently, receive the money for itself, as principal, when the cheque is cleared. In such circumstances the payer, like any other payee, may sue the bank in restitution[112] although following *Lipkin Gorman* the bank may be able to plead change of position. Where a bank sanctions a small overdraft against an uncleared cheque for a larger amount, it will be deemed to act as both a collecting bank and as a discounting bank. It may therefore be difficult to decide in which capacity the bank receives the funds.

---

[110] (1904) 90 LT 474.
[111] [1969] NZLR 151.
[112] *Dominion Bank v Union Bank of Canada* (1908) 40 SCR 366.

In *Continental Caoutchouc* the court also considered the situation where the collecting bank receives the money as an agent but it is then applied in reduction of an existing overdraft. In such a case the money is effectively used to discharge a debt due from the principal to the agent (collecting bank). Collins LJ observed:

> [Such agent] has no doubt benefited by getting his debt paid, but he has done so in discharging his primary duty of passing the money on to his principal. He has constructively sent it on and received it back, and has done nothing incompatible with his position as a conduit-pipe or intermediary. He was entitled to be paid, and had been paid by his debtor, who was no doubt put in funds to do by the receipt of the money, and who therefore, and not the intermediary, has had the benefit of the windfall. Hence the care with which the courts have considered whether the sum has in fact been effectively passed out of the hands of the agent into those of the principal, no entry by the agent in his books sufficing until the assent of the principal has completed the transaction.

In reality the express 'assent' of the principal to the effect that any amounts paid to the credit of an overdrawn account will be used towards of the reduction of the overdraft is given at the outset, on opening the account. In *Kleinwort Sons & Co v Dunlop Rubber Co*,[113] where there was a similar type of mistake, Loreburn LJ said that an amount received by the bank in reduction of the customer's overdraft had not been paid over. It was also held that it was immaterial that the payment involved induced the bank to extend the customer's overdraft.

However, where the bank collects amounts to the credit of a current account, where a running total is usually maintained, a situation may arise where the amount mistakenly paid to the credit of the account is later paid out, subject to the payee's mandate, before the error is discovered. It may also happen that further amounts are credited to the payee's account and the question which then arises, is whether the money mistakenly credited to the customer's account has been actually paid over to the customer's account. A strict application of the first-in, first-out rule under Clayton's case (*Devaynes v Noble*)[114] would mean that the mistaken payments may be exhausted as having been paid out. However, the courts may decide that a strict application of this rule will not be allowed to work an injustice. The courts may, therefore, hold that where the total credit balance does not fall below the amount of the mistaken credit the payee customer who is unjustly enriched is deemed to use that part of the credit balance to which he is properly entitled and the bank is required to restore the amount of the mistaken payment to the payer. In *Australia and New Zealand Banking Group Ltd v Westpac Banking Corporation*[115] the plaintiff, ANZ, by mistake sent a telegraphic instruction to transfer approximately $114,000 instead of the intended amount of approximately $14,000 to Westpac for the credit of J Pty Ltd, whose account was overdrawn by about $68,000. By the time ANZ notified Westpac of the mistaken payment mandate a series of transactions had taken place on the account, which resulted in all but about $17,000 of the mistaken payment having been used by J Pty Ltd. The court held that Westpac's liability to repay the amount of the mistaken payment was limited to the unspent $17,000. It was argued, unsuccessfully, that payments out should be regarded as utilising and exhausting the whole of the available overdraft facility before being treated as applying any funds representing the overpayment

[113] (1907) 97 LT 263.
[114] (1816) 1 Mer 529.
[115] (1988) 164 CLR 662.

and that, to the extent that the available overdraft would not suffice, the funds representing the overpayment should be treated as replenished by subsequent payments into the account. Support for this argument is found in *Holland* v *Russell*[116] where Cockburn CJ suggested that the amount was to be regarded as paid over when it had been made the subject of a 'settled account' or an account stated. However, a bank statement does not constitute a settled account and the bank is only estopped from reversing a payment credited to the account if the customer has changed his position relying on the statement.[117] Hence, so long as the credit entry remains capable of reversal, any money paid by mistake should be recoverable. It should, therefore, be possible to join the bank as a party to an action in restitution brought against the payee, by the payer. In *Jones* v *Churcher*[118] it was emphasised that for the purposes of the ministerial receipt defence 'the crucial point is the point at which the crediting of funds to the customer's account can no longer be reversed'. The issue in that case was to identify the point at which a CHAPS payment represented cleared funds in the customer's account and could not therefore be recalled. It was argued, on behalf of the collecting bank, that the CHAPS payment represented cleared funds the moment the money was credited to the customer's account and the bank had a defence from the moment when the funds were credited to the customer's account.[119] The learned judge rejected this argument. The main reason for rejecting the argument was that to accept such a contention would effectively give collecting banks immunity against an action in relation to CHAPS payments. Accordingly, even in respect of CHAPS payments, a collecting bank will only have the ministerial receipt defence to the extent that the bank has drawn on the relevant funds before it has notice that the funds are being reclaimed.

Mistaken payments involving negotiable instruments

There are specific problems which arise where money is paid by a bank in respect of the discharge of negotiable instruments. In the case of current account, the bank's mandate will usually require that payment be made against a valid instruction and subject to the customer having a sufficient credit balance, or overdraft facilities.[120] The bank must, therefore, act within the mandate conferred upon it and furthermore the payment must be authorised. Thus, the bank cannot debit the customer's account if it makes payment against an instrument that bears a forged drawer's signature or where the payment has been countermanded. The underlying contract between the drawer and payee is irrelevant in respect of the rights and obligations arising between the bank and its customer. A bank, which makes payment in accordance with the customer's mandate and in accordance with its authority, has no interest in the underlying contract and merely acts as a conduit for payment and the discharge of the debt between its customer and the third party payee. In respect of negotiable instruments the question

---

[116] (1861) 30 LJ QB 308.

[117] A customer who therefore realises or should realise that the payment credited to his account is erroneous cannot rely on the mistaken entry and cannot raise estoppel against the bank: *United Overseas Bank Ltd* v *Jawani* [1976] 1 WLR 964.

[118] [2009] 2 Lloyd's Rep 94.

[119] Relying on the argument put forward by Ellinger and Lomnicka (2005) *Modern Banking Law*, Oxford: Oxford University Press, pp.498–499.

[120] *Barclays Bank Ltd* v *WJ Simms Son & Cooke (Southern) Ltd* [1980] QB 677.

arises whether where the paying bank makes payment without a mandate, for example where the cheque bears a material forgery (the drawer's signature is forged), or where the instrument has been countermanded, the payment is sufficient to discharge the customer's obligations or debt under the underlying contract and whether the bank can recover the unauthorised payment. The mistake may, therefore, be in relation to (i) the existence of a mandate, or (ii) its liability to pay.

The existence of the mandate

There may be different circumstances under which a bank makes a mistaken payment, for example, where a cheque against which the bank makes payment bears a forged drawer's signature,[121] or where the cheque bears a material alteration, for example the amount for which the cheque is drawn is fraudulently raised,[122] or the bank pays the cheque to someone who holds it under a forged endorsement,[123] or the bank makes payment against a cheque which has been countermanded. In these circumstances the bank will make payment in the belief that it makes payment against a valid mandate when that mandate was either void or has been revoked. The bank consequently acts without a mandate and cannot debit the customer's account.[124] The mistake, therefore, is fundamental and operates to induce the bank to make payment.

However, the question arises whether the bank can recover money paid under a mistake resulting from its own negligence. The earlier cases supported the view that payment on a negotiable instrument caused by the negligence of the bank cannot be recovered. In *Price v Neal*[125] the plaintiff sued to recover two sums of £40 each, paid to the defendant on two bills of exchange of which the defendant was the drawee. The defendant, an endorsee for valuable consideration of the first bill, presented it for payment on maturity and the plaintiff made payment. The plaintiff also accepted the second bill and endorsed it to the defendant for valuable consideration. Subsequently, payment was also made on the bill. In fact both bills had been forged by a third party and when this was discovered the plaintiff sought to recover the $80 he had paid to the defendant who had acted in good faith and without notice of the forgeries. Lord Mansfield held that in neither case could the plaintiff recover his money and that an acceptor would know the handwriting of the drawer, and it is rather by his fault or negligence than by mistake if he pays on a forged signature. In *Smith v Mercer*[126] it was held that payments made under a mistake of fact could not be recovered when, having discovered the mistake, there was a delay in informing the defendant. In *Cocks v Masterman* the court explained the lack of the right to recover the proceeds paid under a mistake of fact on the ground that the holder is entitled to give notice of dishonour on the very day on which the bill is dishonoured and the parties who pay the bill ought not to be able, by their negligence, to deprive the holder of any right or privilege. In *London and River Plate Bank Ltd v Bank of*

---

[121] *Price v Neal* (1762) 3 Burr 1354; *Smith v Mercer* (1815) 6 Taunt 76; *Cocks v Masterman* (1829) 9 B & C 902; *Imperial Bank of India v Abeyesinghe* (1927) 29 NLR (Ceylon) 257; *National Westminster Bank Ltd v Barclays Bank International Ltd* [1975] QB 654.

[122] *Imperial Bank of Canada v Bank of Hamilton* [1903] AC 49.

[123] *London and Riverplate Bank Ltd v Bank of Liverpool Ltd* [1896] 1 QB 7.

[124] *Barclays Bank Ltd v WJ Simms Son & Cooke (Southern) Ltd* [1980] QB 677.

[125] (1762) 3 Burr 1354.

[126] (1815) 6 Taunt 76.

Liverpool Ltd[127] Matthew J considered that the principle applying to these cases was that if the plaintiff 'so conducted himself as to lead the holder of the bill to believe that he considered the signature genuine, he could not afterwards withdraw from his position'.

However, in *Kelly v Solari*[128] the Court of Exchequer held that money paid by directors under an insurance policy, which had lapsed by reason of non-payment of premiums, could be recovered even though the means of knowing that the policy had so lapsed was available to the plaintiffs. Parke B, said that if money:

> is paid under the impression of the truth of a fact which is untrue, it may, generally speaking, be recovered back, however careless the party paying may have been, in omitting to use due diligence to inquire into the fact.

This is now the general rule although there is said to be one exception and in *Byles on Bills of Exchange*[129] it was said:

> If the drawee discovers, after payment, that the bill or cheque is a forgery he may in general, by giving notice on the same day, or within a reasonable time, recover back the money. So, too, if a forged note is discounted, the transferee, on discovery of the forgery within a reasonable time, may recover back the money paid, the imagined consideration totally failing. But any fault or negligence on the part of him who pays the money on the note will disable him from recovering.

This rule has been applied to negotiable instruments. In *Imperial Bank of Canada v Hamilton*[130] where payment was made on a fraudulently altered cheque, the Privy Council held that money was recoverable on the basis of *Kelly v Solari*.[131] In *National Westminster Bank Ltd v Barclays Bank International Ltd*[132] the plaintiff bank paid a cheque on which the signature of the drawer, its customer, was subsequently discovered to be forged. The plaintiff bank claimed that the payment on the cheque had been made under a mistaken fact on the basis of its honestly held belief that the drawer's (their customer) signature was genuine, when in fact it was forged and rendered the instrument a nullity. An action was brought against both the collecting bank and the payee for recovery of the amount paid. In allowing the action Kerr J observed:

> the main issues raised in this action, which is of some general importance to bankers and apparently arises for the first time for decision in an English court, is whether if bank which has honoured an apparently genuine cheque in which the signature of its customer was in fact skilfully forged can recover the money from the payee of the cheque after he has acted to his detriment in reliance on the cheque having been honoured . . .

Kerr J, while being prepared to assume that the defendant had acted innocently, nevertheless held the plaintiffs were able to recover the proceeds of the mistaken payment. The learned judge held that a bank does not by paying a cheque make any representations to the recipient of the genuineness of its customer's signature and the bank is not under any duty to 'recognise

---

[127] [1896] 1 QB 7.
[128] (1841) 9 M & W 54.
[129] Elliott, Odgers and Phillips (2007) *Byles on Bills of Exchange and Cheques*, London: Sweet & Maxwell, p.146.
[130] [1903] AC 49.
[131] (1841) 9 M & W 54.
[132] [1975] QB 654.

its customer's signature'. Kerr J therefore rejected the plea of negligence holding that 'in deciding whether or not to honour a customer's cheque, at any rate when it is in proper form and the customer's signature appears genuine, the bank owes no duty of care to a payee'.

The issue of the bank's mandate with regard to the countermand of cheques has been looked at recently. In *Commonwealth Trading Bank v Reno Auto Sales Ltd*[133] the court held that an action would fail where the mistake was between the bank and the drawer and not, as required, between the bank (payer) and the payee, although more recent authorities have held that since the bank's mistake is operative as it relates to the motive for the payment, i.e. the bank's belief in the existence of the customer's mandate, such a mistake will entitle the bank to recover the amount paid in an action for restitution. In *Barclay's Bank Ltd v WJ Simms & Cooke (Southern) Ltd*[134] the plaintiff, due to an error, overlooked the countermand and mistakenly made payment on the cheque. The action to recover the amount of the mistaken payment was successful. Goff J held that the issue under consideration was as follows:

> This case raises for decision the question whether a bank, which overlooks its customer's instructions to stop payment of a cheque and in consequence pays the cheque presentation, can recover the money from the payee as having been paid under a mistake of fact. The point is one on which there is no decision in this country . . .

The learned judge reviewed the leading authorities and established a number of principles:

1 If a person pays money to another under a mistake of fact which causes him to make the payment, he is prima facie entitled to recover it as money paid under a mistake of fact.

2 His claim may however fail if: (a) the payer intends that the payee shall have the money at all events, whether the fact be true or false, or is deemed in law so to intend; (b) the payment is made for good consideration, in particular if the money is paid to the discharge, and does discharge, a debt owed to the payee (or a principal on whose behalf he is authorised to receive the payment) by the payer or by a third party . . . ; or (c) the payee has changed his position in good faith, or is deemed in law to have done so.

The next question addressed by the judge was in what circumstances a bank, which has paid a cheque drawn on it by one of its customers, may recover the amount of the cheque, from the payee. The learned judge made the following observations:

> It is a basic obligation owed by a bank to its customer that it will honour on presentation cheques drawn by the customer on the bank, provided that there are sufficient funds in the customer's account to meet the cheque, or where the bank has agreed to provide the customer with overdraft facilities sufficient to meet the cheque. Where the bank honours such a cheque, it acts within its mandate, with the result that the bank is entitled to debit the customer's account with the amount of the cheque, and further that the bank's payment is effective to discharge the obligation of the customer to the pay on the cheque, because the bank has paid the cheque with the authority of the customer . . .
>
> In other cases, however, a bank which pays a cheque drawn or purported to be drawn by its customer pays without mandate. A bank does so if, for example, it overlooks or ignores notice of its customer's death, or if it pays a cheque bearing the forged signature of its customer as drawer; but, more important for present purposes, a bank will pay without mandate if it overlooks or ignores notices of countermand of the customer who has drawn the cheque. In such

---

[133] [1967] VR 790.
[134] [1980] QB 677.

cases the bank, if it pays the cheque, pays without mandate from its customer; and unless the customer is able to and does ratify the payment, the bank cannot debit the customer's account, nor will its payment be effective to discharge the obligation (if any) of the customer on the cheque, because the bank had no authority to discharge such obligation.

The learned judge stressed the legal nature of the relationship between the bank and customer as being one of mandate and if the bank therefore makes payment on a forged cheque or contrary to the demand, it acts in breach of its obligation to make payment in accordance with the mandate. Such a payment will deprive the bank of its right to debit the customer's account with the amount paid out. The purported payment does not serve to discharge the customer's obligation to the payee in terms of the underlying agreement between them under which the obligation to payment arises. In such circumstances the customer (drawer) remains obligated to make payment under the underlying contract while the bank, having acted contrary to the mandate, cannot debit the customer's account with the result that the bank remains out-of-pocket. The question, which then arises, is whether the bank can recover the mistaken payment from the payee. Goff J had no doubts about the bank's right, *prima facie*, to recover the money from the payee, except where the payee has in good faith changed his position, or is deemed in law to have done so.

Bank's right to trace the proceeds

A bank which seeks to recover money paid under a mistake of fact may not only recover the money from the collecting bank or the person to whose account the money is credited (as a direct recipient of the mistaken payment), on the basis that he had legal title to the money before payment was made so that he can claim that the person receiving from him has been unjustly enriched, but it may also recover the money from a third party who holds the money by derivation. In such circumstances the payer must assert a proprietary title based on the fact that he has retained legal title to the money paid under a mistake of fact. If the payer is able to follow or trace his money at law into the hands of the indirect recipient he will be able to hold the recipient personally liable for money had and received. The recipient is personally liable at the time he receives the money: it does not matter that he did not retain the money.[135] In *Lipkin Gorman (a firm) v Karpnale Ltd*[136] money was stolen from the claimant solicitors' client account by one of its partners who had gambled it at the defendant's casino. The House of Lords held that the defendant casino was liable to make restitution to the claimants. The defendant was the innocent indirect recipient of the claimant's money, it having reached the casino via the dishonest partner, so it was necessary for the claimant to establish a basis on which he is entitled to the money. This he does by showing he has legal title to the money.

What is tracing?

The owner of property will have a right to trace his interest in the property, including, ownership in money, so that where his interests in the property have been jeopardised by

---

[135] *Agip (Africa) Ltd v Jackson* [1990] Ch 265.
[136] [1991] 2 AC 548.

another, the true owner may either claim that property back, or alternatively claim rights over other property which has been acquired with his property. The person against whom the action is brought has generally acted in breach of some trust or fiduciary duties owed to the owner of the property. However, the right to trace may also be exercised against subsequent recipients of the property and where the property has been commingled with property belonging to others. The tracing claim, in such circumstances, is subject to equitable doctrines, which protect a *bona fide* purchaser for the value of the property. Further, the claim may not be allowed against an innocent volunteer[137] where it would be unfair in the circumstances to allow the claim.

Tracing is only available at common law if the property, which is the subject of the tracing claim, has not become mixed with property belonging to others. The payer must show that he still has legal title to the money paid by mistake. In other words, he must show either that he has retained a continuing proprietary interest in the property because the mistake is so fundamental that title to the money did not pass to the recipient, or that the mistake was induced by the fraudulent representation which enables the payer to elect whether or not to rescind the transaction and re-vest the title in him. However, the fact the claimant is mistaken does not prevent legal title to money passing to the recipient. In *Banque Belge pour I'Etranger v Hambrouck*,[138] H fraudulently obtained a number of cheques from his employer which he then paid into his own account; payments on which were collected by his bank and credited to his own account. H then withdrew these sums by cheques drawn in favour of his mistress, D, who paid the cheques into her own account. The employer's bank sought to recover the amounts of the misappropriated cheques received by D and further sought a declaration that the amounts placed to her credit were the bank's property, in equity. It was argued that D obtained the money without notice of H's wrongdoing and she acquired a valid title. The court rejected this argument on the grounds that D was a volunteer and concluded that the only person immune, in such circumstances, from the paying bank's claim is one who has given value. Atkin LJ concluded that the proceeds of the fraud, at common law, could be traced into a mixed fund but this conclusion is at variance with the judgments of Scrutton and Bankes LJJ. Atkin LJ is also at variance with the judgment in *Sinclair v Brougham*.[139] Nevertheless, it is accepted at common law that once money is mixed with other funds, i.e. where it becomes part of the general balance in the current account or is transferred to the account of a subsequent holder, it cannot be traced at common law. In *Chase Manhattan Bank NA v Israel-British (London) Bank Ltd*[140] Goulding J assumed that the payee acquired legal title to the second payment of $2 million made under a mistake to the defendant and dealt with the action to recover the money in equity. Legal title to the money was deemed to have passed because the mistaken payment became mixed with other money in the defendant's bank account so it was no longer possible to identify the claimant's property. Goulding J rejected the argument that equitable tracing was only available where a fiduciary relationship existed between the payer and payee at the time of the payment. Payment itself, made into the wrong hands, was enough to give rise to a fiduciary relationship resulting from the mistaken payment and the payer retained equitable title in

---

[137] *Re Diplock* [1948] Ch 465.
[138] [1921] 1 KB 321.
[139] [1914] AC 398.
[140] [1981] Ch 105.

the funds. Further, the payee's conscience would be subject to a fiduciary duty in respect of the money.

Even where the payer can establish that he retained legal title to the mistaken payment his right to recover the payment may be challenged on the basis of the defence of a *bona fide* purchaser.

Action against the collecting bank

Money paid to an agent under mistake of fact can be recovered from him but once has he paid it away it cannot be recovered from him. The agent merely acts as conduit for the payment. Therefore the money must be recovered from the third party (*Gowers v Lloyds National Provincial Foreign Bank Ltd*).

An alternative remedy is through tracing either at common law or in equity.

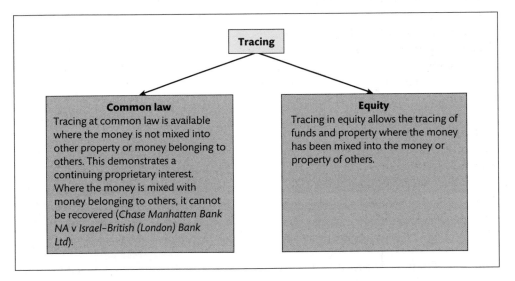

Figure 17.3 Tracing

Conclusion

A bank may make payment under a mistake of fact or law where it will not be entitled to debit the customer's account. The bank will seek to recover the amount of the wrongful payment from the ultimate recipient, whether that is the payee or a third party who receives the amount of the mistaken payment. There are a number of mechanisms whereby such payments may be recovered either as a result of the application of the rules of the common law or the rules of equity. The law in this area is complex and attempts to allow the mistaken payer to recover the mistaken payment, but the law has to be aware of the need to protect the innocent recipient or third party. A number of defences are therefore available which may defeat the right of recovery.

Further reading

➤ Watts, P. (1991) Case Comment: Unjust enrichment and misdirected funds, 107 (Oct) *Law Quarterly Review*, 521.

This article examines the House of Lords' decision in *Lipkin Gorman v Karpnale Ltd* [1991] 3 WLR 10. It focuses upon the leading judgments of Lord Templeman and Lord Goff, and analyses the connections to consideration, gambling, restitution and unjust enrichment.

➤ Birks, P. (1989) Misdirected funds, 105 *LQR*, 352–356.

This article examines whether personal restitutionary liability of the recipient of misdirected funds is strict or fault based.

➤ Burrows, A. (1990) Misdirected funds – a reply, 106 *LQR*, 20.

This article responds to Professor Birks' argument ((1989) 105 LQR 352 and 528) that the personal restitutionary liability of the recipient of misdirected funds is and should be strict and not fault-based. It shows that this argument stems from previous decisions rather than preferred policy. In turn, Burrows argues that personal restitutionary liability is and should be fault based.

18 Securities for bank borrowing

Chapter overview

The aim of this chapter is to:

➤ Examine the form of security frequently given by the borrowing customer and obligations that may arise under that security.

➤ Examine the following types of security and the assets that may be given as security:

  ➤ propriety securities;
  ➤ possessory securities;
  ➤ personal securities.

All businesses will need to raise finance at some stage during the course of the business. In return, the lender will frequently ask for some form of security. The nature, type and terms of the security form important considerations in the business decision taken by the lender in which the protection of the investment will be paramount.

Introduction

Credit is the lifeblood of the modern industrialised economy.[1] Some borrowers have access to credit on an unsecured basis but small and medium-sized companies particularly, and even public companies, may be required to give security in order to access finance. The creation of a security is essentially the creation of a contractual arrangement which although the subject of statutory regulation, for example in respect of the rules protecting the rights and interests of creditors, is subject to contractual rules, for example relating to the intention of the parties and the provision of a valid consideration. The nature of the security and the assets over which it applies will need to be examined as these determine whether the security interest has to be registered. The main object of the security is to protect the creditor in the event that the debtor is unable or unwilling to repay the loan. Where a debtor becomes insolvent the secured creditor will have priority for repayment over the unsecured creditor and will be able to recover the debt against the secured assets. Where the creditor has propriety rights he will be able to assert his rights in priority to other claimants, for example judgment creditors. However, the precise extent of the security, for example the extent of the indebtedness over

---

[1] Report of the Review Committee on Insolvency Law and Practice (1982) Cmnd 8558 (The Cork Committee).

which the security applies, will also need to be determined. Generally, this question will not pose a challenge, for example a debenture will generally secure all monies from time to time owed by the customer. However, a security may be limited to a certain type of facility, for example where a security is given for a syndicated loan and not intended to be available for other separate loans.

While the courts are willing to recognise oral contracts that have an effect on the immediate parties to the agreement they may require more formal evidence of an agreement where third party rights are likely to be affected. Therefore Lord Millett in *Agnew* v *Commissioners of Inland Revenue*[2] suggested that a two-stage analysis was necessary in order to determine the nature of the transaction: (i) determine (as a matter of fact) what obligations the parties agreed to undertake, and (ii) determine (as a matter of law) the legal effect of those obligations. In *Welsh Development Agency* v *Export Finance Co Ltd*[3] the Court of Appeal had to determine whether the transaction in question was a sale or a registrable charge and concluded that the transaction was indeed a sale. The Court, however, made it clear that it will look at the 'substance' of the transaction and is not bound by 'labels'. Since, the purpose of a security is to establish a proprietary interest in the subject matter, its creation will have an effect on the rights of creditors in the insolvency of the debtor, and it is natural that the law should demand a greater degree of formality. Thus, the law will require that the security agreement be reduced to writing and that the security be registered. The Companies Act 2006 (Amendment of Part 25) Regulations 2013[4] introduced a new framework for the registration of company charges. When the bank takes security it does not become the absolute owner of the property but will instead acquire certain rights over the property until the debt is repaid: for example these rights may include whether and to what extent the assets can be sued to create subsequent rights.

Classification of securities

Securities are classified as possessory or proprietary depending on the nature of the security given and the subject matter of the security.

Proprietary securities are those where the creditor has the right to seize the goods in case of default or insolvency of the debtor. During the loan arrangement the property will be left in the possession of the borrowing (debtor) customer. Mortgages of chattels and land are illustrations of a proprietary security, as are fixed and floating charges over the assets of a company. In such circumstances the mortgagee may enter into possession of the property but in reality, particularly in the case of banks, other remedies are likely to be exercised, for example the appointment of a receiver or liquidator or sale of property. The types of securities subject to a mortgage are likely to be title deeds of property, life policies, stocks and shares and other choses in action.

Possessory securities are based on the creditor acquiring possession of the chattel that serves as the security. Such assets therefore are those that may be the subject of a pledge or banker's lien so that the bank acquires possession of them, in the ordinary course of its business, e.g. cheques, bills of exchange or other instruments deposited with the bank for collection. In the

---

[2] [2001] 2 AC 710.
[3] [1992] BCLC 148.
[4] Replacing ss.860–894 of the Companies Act 2006, which replaced ss.395–409 of the Companies Act 1985.

case of a pledge, the pledgee is entitled to the exclusive possession of the property until the debt is discharged, and in certain circumstances the pledgee may have the power of sale although the ownership remains with the pledgor. Unlike a lien, it is not essential that the pledgor has actual ownership of the goods pledged, but the pledge must be created with the consent of the owner. Securities that are subject to the pledge are usually goods, chattels and fully negotiable securities.

The distinction between possessory and propriety securities is not appropriate where a security is created over money or choses in action, for example contractual rights. A security over such rights may be acquired by way of an assignment, for example an assignment of a credit balance of a bank account, book debts or an insurance policy.

A further classification of securities divides them into consensual (i.e. those created by agreement between the parties) and those created by operation of law. The securities created by agreement are: the pledge, the contractual lien, the mortgage and the charge. Various types of liens are created by operation of law, for example the banker's lien, or the unpaid vendor's lien etc. Another classification of securities is open-ended and closed securities. An open-ended security is one that covers all or some of the property of the debtor for the time being, for example floating charges which allow the debtor to use the assets in the course of his business including the ability to dispose of them. Any subsequently acquired assets become subject to the charge. A banker's lien is similar in nature and attaches to, for example shares acquired while the share certificate is in the possession of the bank. By contrast, the closed-ended security attaches to a specific item of property.

Guarantees are sometimes called 'personal securities' and are personal obligations under-taken by a third party to a transaction under which the guarantor undertakes a secondary liability for the repayment of the loan.

The effect of security in insolvency

When an individual or a partnership becomes bankrupt, the position is governed by the Insolvency Act 1986.[5] The bankrupt's estate vests in the trustee in bankruptcy whose function it is to realise the assets of the bankrupt and distribute them to the creditors who are divided into three groups: preferential claims, general creditors and deferred claims. Preferential claims include, for example, payments of wages to employees for up to four months prior to the bankruptcy. Any amounts left, or realised, after the preferential claims have been met will be used to pay general creditors on a *pro rata* basis. Only after that will certain deferred claims be met. Where a company goes into liquidation, again the Insolvency Act 1986 will provide the legal framework within which the insolvency will take place and the order of the payment of creditors. Subject to certain modifications, the rights of creditors in a bankruptcy apply also to the liquidation of a company. Regardless of whether it is the rules of bankruptcy that apply or winding up in the case of a liquidation, trade creditors will be general creditors who will be repaid *pro rata* amounts due to them. Similarly, if it is a bank which goes into liquidation bank depositors will, in law, be general unsecured creditors who will receive a pro rata repayment of their deposit.[6]

[5] Previously, the Bankruptcy Act 1914 and then the Insolvency Act 1985. The Insolvency Act 1985 was repealed and the Insolvency Act 1986 enacted.

[6] However, the Financial Services Compensation Scheme guarantees up to £85,000 of the deposit held by each customer with each bank and bank customers therefore have a cushion against the event of a bank's insolvency.

A trade creditor who therefore holds a security will be in a position of advantage and will be able to recover his debt in priority to the general creditors. The asset will therefore be realised to repay the secured creditor and any additional amount realised will be made available to the trustee in bankruptcy or liquidator.

The effect of the Consumer Credit Act 1974 on securities

Part VIII of the Consumer Credit Act 1974, although not enacted with a focus on the banker and customer relationship, has a considerable impact on securities taken by banks with respect to regulated credit agreements. The main object is to protect the person giving the security. Section 189(1) of the 1974 Act describes 'security' as a mortgage, a charge, a pledge, a bond, a debenture, an indemnity and guarantee, a bill or note and 'any other right provided by the debtor, or at his express or implied request by another person, to secure the performance of the agreement involved'. The Act therefore applies to securities provided by the debtor or by a third party on his behalf. So applies to securities over land, insurance policies, bank balances etc. but also to guarantees given by third parties. The Act applies to securities given in respect of concluded agreements but also in relation to prospective agreements.[7] The security becomes subject to the Act once the agreement is concluded and until then the security is unenforceable. If the main agreement, for example a loan agreement, is not executed the bank will not require the security to be executed, and if the surety gives notice of his intention to withdraw from the proposed undertaking then the bank may decide not to proceed with the loan transaction.

The Consumer Credit Act 1974 defines the term 'surety' so as to include the debtor if he furnishes security, any third party who provides security, and any 'person to whom his rights and duties in relation to the security have passed by operation of law'.[8] This may arise where a third party has subrogated the rights of the surety. The Act distinguishes between a security granted by the debtor and a security effected by a third party, in which case the security must be in writing and must comply with s.105 of the Act. The Act implements measures aimed at regulating the taking of securities in respect of regulated agreements: (i) the form and contents of securities is by s.105 and a security that is not executed properly is only enforceable by an order of the court. If the court refuses such an order the security is avoided[9] and the surety will be entitled to any amount realised, (ii) that certain specified information is provided and is furnished to the surety;[10] (iii) regulations may be made in respect of the realisation of the security; and (iv) the security device may not be used in order to evade provisions in respect of regulated agreements under the Act.

---

[7] Consumer Credit Act 1974, s.189(1).
[8] Consumer Credit Act 1974, s.189(1).
[9] Consumer Credit Act 1974, s.106.
[10] Consumer Credit Act 1974, ss.107–108 and 111, as amended by the Consumer Credit Act 2006, in respect of third party surety, and Consumer Credit Act 1974, ss.77–78, as amended by the Consumer Credit Act 2006 in respect of the debtor providing a security.

Form of security

Section 105(4) of the Consumer Credit Act 1974 establishes certain requirements in respect of the proper execution of the 'security instrument'. The surety must sign the document, which needs to embody all the express terms of the security. The document must be legible when presented for signature and he must be provided with a copy when the document is either sent or presented to him for signature. Informal arrangements with banks will therefore be contrary to the requirements of the Consumer Credit Act 1974. If these requirements are not complied with the security is enforceable only by order of the court.[11]

Information provided by the creditor

A creditor is required to provide information to a surety on request. The Consumer Credit Act 1974 draws a distinction between different types of agreements namely (i) agreements for fixed term credit;[12] and (ii) agreements for running-account credit. The creditor is required to supply the surety with a copy of the regulated agreement and the security instrument, a financial statement, which states the amount payable under the regulated agreement.[13] The information required by the surety must be supplied within 12 working days.

The creditor is also under an obligation to serve on the third party surety a copy of any default notice served on the debtor. If the creditor fails to comply with this the security is enforceable only by order of the court.

Proprietary securities

As with any asset offered as security, the bank will need to verify that the borrower debtor (or mortgagor) owns the asset and the bank lender (mortgagee) is entitled to take security over it for the value of the loan. Different interests in the same piece of real estate may be recognised:

- A 'freehold' interest is a permanent and indefensible interest in land, but its value may be diminished by the existence of other interests, for example leases or other third party rights.

- A 'leasehold' interest implies the right to occupy the property for a set period of time from the date of the lease. Possession or occupation of the property reverts to the freeholder on the expiry of the lease term. Leases of 99 years or 999 years are commonly given and freely transferable by the leaseholder and so the real value resides in the leasehold interest, rather than the freehold.

Rights in a freehold or in leasehold may exist in law or equity. The distinction between legal estates and equitable interests is based on the Law of Property Act 1925. A freehold or leasehold interest is registered at the Land Registry and the intending mortgagor is shown as the owner of the interest. The lender (bank) must take a number of factors into consideration when deciding the value of the security offered on it:

---

[11] Consumer Credit Act 1974, s.105(7) in respect of security instruments and s.65 in respect of security provided by the debtor.

[12] Consumer Credit Act 1974, s.107 (third party surety) and 77, 77A and 110 (debtor surety).

[13] Consumer Credit Act 1974, ss.107(1)(c), 108(1)(c) (third party surety) and 77(i)(c), 78(i)(c) and 110 (debtor surety).

(i) Whether the propriety interest will be subject to any adverse rights or interests which appear on the register itself, for example leases or sub-lease.

(ii) The value of the property which may be affected by extrinsic factors, for example the grant of any planning permission or development of other projects in the vicinity. These are not issues which will be found on the land register so extra enquiries may need to be made.

(iii) Certain interests remain valid and binding as against a mortgagee even though not recorded on the register. So, for example, the interests of someone in actual possession[14] may override interests of the lender. For banks this has caused problems when, for example, a bank has taken a mortgage from the husband and it subsequently transpires that the wife has contributed to the cost of maintenance and has therefore acquired an 'overriding interest' in the property.[15] Banks must therefore ensure that the spouse or partner of the registered landowner consents to postponement of their beneficial interest.

In the case of unregistered land, the bank first has to arrange for a search of the deeds, which are usually held by the freeholder or leaseholder except where the property is already subject to a mortgage and the deeds may already be in the hands of the mortgagee. In addition to the deeds, the bank may also search the register kept under the Land Charges Act 1972, which will bring to light details of rights and interests not disclosed on the deeds.

Mortgages and equitable charges

There are three types of security that can be given over land:

1 The legal mortgage confers a legal interest on the mortagagee and may only be granted by the mortgagor who has legal title in the land: i.e. a fee simple or a lease. Since the Law of Property Act 1925, a legal mortgage must be created either (a) by granting the mortgagee a lease in the legal estate (mortgage by demise), or (b) by conferring a charge by deed expressed to be by way of a legal mortgage over the legal estate (mortgage by charge). A legal mortgage must vest a term of years in the mortgage and any attempt to by the mortgagor to convey the whole of his legal estate in the land to the mortgagee operates automatically as a grant of a term of years leaving the reversionary legal estate vested in the mortgagor.[16] The term of years granted is subject to a termination on the redemption of the mortgage. The mortgagor retains the legal estate but subject to the term of years, and this will enable him to create further legal mortgages which take effect as legal charges or as demise for a term of years longer by at least a day than the preceding mortgage. The second method of creating a legal mortgage in land is by way of a legal charge.[17] Where a charge is created the lender is in the same position as if he had been granted a mortgage by demise and the legal chargee has the same rights and remedies as a legal mortgagor. The difference between a legal mortgage and legal charge is that the legal charge does not contain a conveyance of a legal estate to the mortgagee so that the mortgagor remains vested with his original estate

[14] Formerly s.70(1)(g) of the Land Registration Act 1925, now ss.11 and 12 of the Land Registration Act 2002.
[15] See: *Williams & Glyn's Bank Ltd v Boland* [1981] AC 487.
[16] Law of Property Act 1925, s.85(2).
[17] Law of Property Act 1925, s.87(1).

instead of holding a reversionary interest. Instead of granting the chargee a legal estate the mortgagor or chargor charges the land by way of legal mortgage with the payment of the principal amount, the interest and any other monies secured by the charge. Further there is no provision for redemption of a legal charge, which simply determines on repayment of the amount secured on it. In practice the mortgage by the creation of a charge is the most common. In the case of registered land the legal mortgage can only be created by way of a charge (and not by demise).

2 The equitable mortgage will confer an equitable interest on the mortgagee. A mortgagor who has a legal estate may grant an equitable mortgage. Where the mortgagor has only an equitable interest in the land (e.g., as a beneficiary under a trust) he may only create an equitable mortgage by assigning his interest to the mortgagee as security, with a proviso for reassignment on redemption. The equitable mortgage is used where less formality is preferred. The mortgagee will normally require that the deeds or the land certificate are deposited with him. Following the Law of Property (Miscellaneous Provisions) Act 1989, s.2 provides that such an agreement must be in writing. The effect of s.2 was examined by the courts in *United Bank of Kuwait Plc* v *Sahib*[18] where the Court of Appeal held that the former rule that a deposit of title deeds creates a valid equitable charge on the basis it amounted to an act of part performance to create a mortgage was inconsistent with the requirements of the 1989 Act, which requires that dispositions of interests in land must be evidenced in writing. Therefore, equitable mortgages by deposit of deeds must be accompanied by a written contract. In practice banks will use a standard form contract to secure an equitable mortgage. Such security is used mainly for short-term loans.

3 The equitable charge confers an equitable interest on the chargee but with more limited rights than the equitable mortgage. The equitable charge may be created by agreement between the borrowing customer and the bank, and is appropriated towards the discharge of some debt or obligation. The remedies of the equitable chargee in equity are the same as those of the equitable mortgagee, except that he is not allowed to foreclose and acquire the mortgagor's estate in the land or to take possession of it. Like an equitable mortgage an equitable charge must be evidenced in writing, but that may be dispensed with if the agreement to create the charge has been partly performed.

Extent of the security

A lender would be advised to take care when determining the extent of his security, especially when second or subsequent mortgagees are involved. An important issue is how much of the facility extended by the first mortgagee will enjoy priority if the lender (first mortgagee) advances further funds after he acquires notice of the second mortgage. Mortgages take priority in the order in which they are created unless there is something to disturb that order. Mortgages that are prior in time may be postponed by reason of (a) statutory provisions relating to registration which render mortgages ineffective against certain persons if not protected by proper registration,[19] or which rank in order of registration rather than creation,[20]

---

[18] [1996] 3 WLR 272.
[19] Land Charges Act 1972, s.4(5) and Land Registration Act 2002, s.48.
[20] Land Registration Act 2002, s.3, and Law of Property Act 1925, s.97.

and (b) legal principles which render equitable interests ineffective against *bona fide* purchasers of the legal interest without notice of those equitable interests or that which postpones a mortgagee that has not acted appropriately, for example the doctrine of 'tacking' may disturb the usual priority of mortgages.

Unless the first mortgagee is able to gain priority for both the original advance and any subsequent advances after the second mortgage the first mortgagee's security will only extend to those advances made prior to notice of the second mortgage. Payments made into the account by the borrowing customer will therefore reduce the amounts entitled to priority under the first mortgage and further drawings from the account, while still secured by the mortgage, will rank after the subsequent security.[21] Where a bank receives notice of a second mortgage it should 'rule off' the account so that the earlier advances are preserved and a new account opened for further advances, which may be subordinate to the second charge. The first mortgagee however may be able to 'tack' the subsequent payments to the first mortgage, thereby ousting the application of the rule in *Clayton*'s case,[22] i.e. that payments credited to the account will be used to write down the earliest debts first (the first-in, first-out rule). Such a process will give priority in respect of advances made after the second mortgage.

In relation to unregistered land s.94 of the Law of Property Act 1925 enables further advances to be tacked onto the first mortgage if the second mortgagee consents; or the bank had no notice of the second mortgage; or if the first mortgage obliged the bank to make further mortgages. Merely registering the second mortgage does not constitute notice where the first mortgage is created to secure an overdraft given by a bank. In the case of registered land s.94 of the Law of Property Act 1925 is excluded in respect of registered charges. Instead s.49 of the Land Registration Act 2002 applies and the bank may tack later advances if the second mortgagee consents, or the first mortgagee had no notice of the second or subsequent mortgage, or the original mortgage actually obliged the bank to make further advances and this obligation is entered on the register, or the first mortgage contained a maximum amount to be secured and this was entered on the register. This allows for the loan to be drawn on in tranches up to the maximum specified. This is likely to be especially useful to banks, which will allow customers to overdraw on an account over a period of time, or where a revolving credit facility is made available.

The right of redemption

The mortgagor (debtor) is entitled to redeem his mortgage by repaying any amount outstanding on the mortgage.[23] The right of repayment is available even where the date of repayment has passed and even if steps have been taken to sell the mortgaged property.[24] The right of redemption cannot be excluded by agreement and any provision that seeks to restrict such a right (known as a clog) is void. However, the parties may agree to postpone

---

[21] See *Deeley* v *Lloyds Bank Ltd* [1012] AC 756.
[22] (1816) 1 Mer. 572.
[23] *Fairclough* v *Swan Brewery Co Ltd* [1912] AC 565; *Krelinger* v *New Patagonia Meat and Cold Storage Co Ltd* [1914] AC 25.
[24] *Duke* v *Robson* [1973] 1 WLR 267.

the exercise of the right of redemption for a certain period.[25] However, the right of redemption is only lost when the mortgagor, in accordance with his rights, has sold the property. The person primarily entitled to exercise the right of redemption is the mortgagor (debtor) but can be any other person who has an interest in the mortgaged property, for example a tenant who wishes to remain in occupation. Any person who exercises the right of redemption must redeem it in full.[26]

Remedies of the mortgagee

The purpose of the mortgage, as with other forms of security, is to protect the interests of the mortgagee. Where the borrower defaults there may be a number of remedies available to the mortgagee including a statutory power of sale,[27] the power to appoint a receiver,[28] and the power to take possession.[29] The bank has a right to take possession of the land although it is rarely likely to exercise this power except where the bank wishes to ensure vacant possession or to preserve the property. The bank is more likely to obtain a court order: for example if the mortgaged property is a dwelling house then the court has a discretion to adjourn the action if it appears likely that the mortgagor is able within a reasonable time to pay the sums due.[30] If the mortgagee secures a loan regulated by the Consumer Credit Act 1974, a similar protection is accorded to the mortgagor, or if the possession is not sought *bona fide* for the purposes of enforcing the security the court may refuse possession.[31] The bank is more likely to appoint a receiver in order to collect any income the land is producing. This may be attractive where the bank wishes to continue with the mortgage. The Act provides how the receiver must deal with the income received by him. The receiver is designated an agent of the mortgagor and therefore must act in a way to preserve the property. In the sale of the property the receiver must obtain the best price reasonably obtainable. Once it becomes clear that the mortgagor is likely to remain in default of his obligations then the bank is likely to seek its right to sell the property. The proceeds of sale are held in trust by the mortgagee and any surplus after satisfying the outstanding amounts are due to the mortgagor.[32] Finally, the bank will have the right to foreclose the mortgage. This requires an order of the court and the order extinguishes the right of the mortgagor to redeem the land. Such an order is rarely requested where the value of the land is equal to, or less than, the value of the interest in the land. The court will otherwise order a sale of the land.

An equitable mortgagee is likely to reserve the power of sale. If the mortgage is under seal he will have a statutory right to appoint a receiver. An equitable mortgagee has neither a right to possession nor to foreclose.

---

[25] *Williams v Morgan* [1906] 1 Ch 804 where an agreement to postpone the exercise for 14 months was held valid.
[26] *Hall v Heward* (1886) 32 Ch D 430.
[27] Law of Property Act 1925, s.101(1).
[28] Law of Property Act 1925, s.101(1)(iii).
[29] *Four-Maids Ltd v Dudley Marshall Properties Ltd* [1957] Ch 317.
[30] Administration of Justice Act 1970, s.36; Administration of Justice Act 1973, s.8; Mortgage repossessions (Protection of tenants) Act 2012.
[31] *Quennell v Maltby* [1979] 1 WLR 318.
[32] Law of Property Act 1925, s.105.

The Consumer Credit Act 1974

A number of agreements secured by land are 'exempt agreements' and therefore outside the scope of the Consumer Credit Act 1974 if the creditor falls within a defined class of lender, including authorised institutions. The Act contains two provisions in respect of regulated agreements secured by land namely: (i) s.67 of the Consumer Credit Act 1974, which confers on the debtor a right of cancellation in certain cases, does not apply to a regulated agreement secured on land, or to a restricted-use credit agreement to finance the purchase of land. The Financial Services (Distance Marketing) Regulations 2004 also exclude 'restricted use' land mortgages and bridging loans from the right of cancellation. Instead s.58 provides a different withdrawal procedure for regulated agreements secured by land. (ii) The other special provision applicable to land mortgages securing a regulated agreement is s.126 under which such a mortgage is enforceable by an order of the court only.

Securities granted by companies

For trading companies, trading stock and book debts often constitute their most valuable assets. A company will usually raise finance by means of a debenture secured by a fixed or floating charge over such assets or part of such assets. However, at common law it was not possible to create a security over future or contingent property, nor was it possible to create a mortgage over shifting assets or stock in trade since it would need the consent of the mortgagee each time the mortgagor wanted to sell or dispose of his stock in trade. Equity came to provide solutions to both these situations. First, in *Holroyd v Marshall*[33] the court held that a charge over future property would automatically attach to the property on acquisition. The case involved an equitable mortgage over existing plants and new machinery acquired as replacement. The court upheld the validity of the mortgage which was held to extend to any property acquired after the date of the charge being executed (after acquired property). The second device recognised by equity was the floating charge and in *Re Panama, New Zealand and Australian Royal Mail Co*[34] the court held that the debenture holders had a charge over all of the company's property, including future property, and they stood in a position superior to the general creditors who could exercise no rights over the property until the debenture holders had been paid.

A debenture is defined in s.738 of the Companies Act 2006 as 'including debenture stock, bonds and any other securities of a company, whether or not constituting a charge on assets of the company'. The debenture therefore is the contract or document, which evidences the indebtedness and the form of security given by the company. The most widely used form of security used to secure advances made to a company is the charge. However, the charge is not commonly used to finance individual traders or unincorporated business firms. Charges created by incorporated companies fall outside the Bills of Sale Act 1878 and are instead registrable under the Companies Act 2006, which imposes less onerous requirements relating to form and after-acquired property.

---

[33] (1862) 10 HL Cas 191.
[34] (1870) LR 5 Ch App 318.

In comparison to the mortgage, which transfers property to the creditor, and a pledge, which gives the creditor actual or constructive possession, the charge gives the creditor a right to apply to the court[35] to realise the property, subject to the charge, in the event of default. A valid fixed charge over the assets of the company attaches to the property, which is subject to the charge and assures the chargee the benefit of the proceeds of the sale, subject only to the costs of marketing and sale. It creates a greater degree of certainty than a floating charge which is subject to the rights of certain preferential creditors.

Fixed or floating charges

The flexibility of the floating charge makes it attractive to banks that finance ongoing commercial transactions of their customers. The floating charge is unique to English Law and other jurisdictions[36] have either refused to recognise it or it has been recognised only when statute has intervened.[37] The advantage of the charge attaching to after acquired property has facilitated two types of company charges. A floating charge must either be fixed or floating. The floating charge is the antithesis of a specific charge and will cover both existing and future assets of the company. A fixed charge is created over specific property and gives the chargee an immediate proprietary interest in existing property, or when the company acquires an interest in future property that too is subject to the charge. The consent of the creditor is therefore required before the company can deal with the charged property. The distinguishing feature of a floating charge is that the company is free to deal with the charged assets in the ordinary course of its business:[38] the floating charge therefore 'hovers' over the assets subject to the charge and the company is free to deal with the assets without the consent of the holder of the floating charge.[39] The concept of the fixed and floating charges has resulted in considerable debate and categorising whether the charge is fixed or floating is not always straightforward. Lord Millett in *Agnew* v *Inland Review Commissioners*[40] explained:

> In deciding whether a charge is fixed or a floating charge, the Court is engaged in a in a two-stage process. At the first stage it must construe the instrument of charge and seek to gather the intentions of the parties from the language they have used. But the object at this stage of the process is not to discover whether the parties intended to create a fixed or a floating charge. It is to ascertain the nature of the rights and obligations which the parties intended to grant each other in respect of the charged assets. Once these have been ascertained, the Court can then embark on the second stage of the process, which is one of the categorisation. This is a matter of law. It does not depend on the intention of the parties. If their intention, properly gathered from the language of the instrument, is to grant the company rights in respect of the charged assets which are inconsistent with the nature of the fixed charge, then the charge cannot be a fixed charge however they may have chosen to describe it.

---

[35] The power to realise the property without recourse to the courts may be conferred by contract or by statute, Law of Property Act 1925, s.101.

[36] In the USA it has not been recognised on the basis that it fails to give the chargee adequate control over the charged assets.

[37] In Scotland the floating charge was recognised by the Companies (Floating Charges) (Scotland) Act 1962.

[38] *Ashborder BV v Green Gas Power Ltd* [2004] EWHC 1517.

[39] *Re Panama, New Zealand and Australian Royal Mail Co* (1870) LR 5 Ch App 318.

[40] [2001] 2 AC 710.

The distinction between fixed and floating charges came to prominence again in relation to a case concerning charges over book debts. This reasoning was approved by the House of Lords in *Re Spectrum Plus Ltd*[41] in which case their Lordships placed emphasis on the freedom of the company to deal with the assets in the ordinary course of the business rather than the nature of the assets. Thus, if the chargee, for example a bank, does not have complete control over how the chargor uses the proceeds of its book debts, the charge will be classified as a floating charge. In *Re Keenan Bros Ltd*[42] the company was required to pay the proceeds of its book debts into a special account over which the chargee (bank) had an absolute discretion in deciding whether to allow the company to transfer monies into a working account. The Supreme Court of Ireland concluded that the chargee's control over the account was such as to deprive the company of its freedom to use the proceeds and therefore a fixed charge had been created. However, in *Siebe Gorman & Co Ltd v Barclays Bank Ltd*[43] while the debenture given to Barclays Bank, described as a 'first fixed charge' over the present and future book debts of the company, required the company to pay the proceeds of its book debts into a designated account and from charging or assigning its book debts without the consent of the bank, nevertheless the company was free to use the funds in that account. Slade J held that the charge was fixed because the restrictions on the company's power to deal with the proceeds of the debts gave the bank a degree of control which was inconsistent with a floating charge. In *Re New Bullas Trading Ltd*[44] the Court of Appeal held that it was possible to combine a fixed and floating charge. In that case the debenture provided for a fixed charge over the company's uncollected book debts but once the proceeds were collected they were placed in a designated account and a floating charge took effect over them. The House of Lords in *Re Spectrum Plus* overruled both *Siebe Gorman* and *Re New Bullas*. Lord Scott explained that where the chargor is free to deal with the charged assets or their proceeds without first obtaining the chargee's permission, the charge must be a floating charge. He continued:

> the Bank's debenture place no restriction on the use that Spectrum could make of the balance on the account available to be drawn by Spectrum. Slade J in [*Siebe Gorman*] thought that it might make a difference whether the account were in credit or in debit. I must respectfully disagree. The critical question, in my opinion, is whether the chargor can draw on the account. If the chargor's bank account were in debit and the chargor had no right to draw on it, the account would have become, and would remain until the drawing rights were restored, a blocked account. The situation would be as it was in *Re Keenan Bros Ltd*. But so long as the chargor can draw on the account, and whether the account is in credit or debit, the money paid in is not being appropriated to the repayment of the debt owing to the debenture holder but is being made available for drawings on the account by the chargor.

Following *Re Spectrum Plus*, for a charge to be fixed the chargee must restrict totally the chargor's freedom to deal with the assets so charged, so they are maintained for the benefit of the chargee.

[41] [2005] 2 AC 680.
[42] [1986] BCLC 242.
[43] [1979] 2 Lloyd's Rep 142.
[44] [1994] 1 BCLC 465.

Registration of company charges

It is accepted that there should be a public record of charges created by companies over their property. Diamond concluded that there is almost universal support for a system of company charges and there is no demand for the abolition of the system of company charges.[45] The Law Commission,[46] citing Diamond, noted:

> Apart from the objective of providing information for persons proposing to deal with the company so they, or credit reference agencies on their behalf, can assess its creditworthiness, persons considering whether to provide secured credit can find out whether the proposed security is already the subject of a charge; by the same token, a registration system benefits the company itself if it is enabled to give some sort of assurance to a prospective secured creditor that the property it is offering as security is unencumbered.
>
> Registration can also ease the task of a receiver or liquidator in knowing whether to acknowledge the validity of an alleged mortgage or charge . . .
>
> One can also recognise that, in addition to the use of information by financial analysts and persons considering whether to invest in a company, there is today a general climate of opinion in favour of public disclosure of companies' financial activities.
>
> It is also important the law should set clear rules to resolve disputes when two or more parties lay claim to the same property. This may occur, for example, when the same asset has been charged to two separate lenders, and where charged property has been sold to an innocent buyer. Priority disputes may arise rarely but the rules have a significant impact on the steps that potential secured lenders and buyers of company property have to take to safeguard their interests.[47]

Despite there being support for a system of registering company charges, the pre-2013 scheme for registration had been criticised for many years. The Law Commission[48] explained the problems in following terms:

> The Scheme for registering company charges dates back to 1900 and is now inappropriate to modern needs. It is particularly inefficient in two ways.
>
> First, it requires charge documents to be submitted in paper form, although the register of company charges maintained at the Companies House is electronic.
>
> Secondly registry staff must check the particulars submitted against lengthy legal documents before the register issues a conclusive certificate of registration. This requires a significant number of staff and is, in our view, unnecessary and impossible to justify. A system of electronic online registration, with the party filing being responsible for ensuring that the information registered is accurate, would be far more efficient.

The Companies Act 2006 (Amendment of Part 25) Regulations 2013[49] came into force on 6 April 2013 and repealed and replaced the previous Part 25 of the Companies Act 2006 in relation to registration of security interests created by UK companies over their assets. The primary purpose of the regulations is to provide a single scheme applicable for the registration, alteration and satisfaction of all charges created by UK companies, and to clarify

---

[45] Diamond (1989) A Review of Security Interests in Property (The Diamond Report), para. 11.1.7.

[46] Law Com (No 296, 2002) drawing on the review conducted by Diamond (1989) A Review of Security Interests in Property (The Diamond Report), para. 11.1.5.

[47] Law Com (No 296, 2002), para. 1.5.

[48] Law Com (No 296, 2002).

[49] http://www.legislation.gov.uk/ukdsi/2013/9780111533208/contents.

perceived uncertainties under the previous regime. The new regime represents a change in emphasis but in practice retains many of the features of the previous regime. A company that has created a charge, or any person interested in the charge, may register the charge unless the charge is exempted. However, registration may also be affected by electronic filing of the statement of particulars and the charge instrument so the responsibility for accuracy of the registration is with the chargee. There is now a single UK-wide scheme covering all UK registered companies. Instead of a list of registrable charges, as previously set out in the Companies Act 2006, all charges created by UK companies can be registered unless falling within an exception. The three exceptions are rent security deposits, Lloyd's trust deeds and charges excluded from registration requirements by other legislation, such as financial collateral, by virtue of the Financial Collateral Arrangements (No. 2) Regulations 2003.[50] However, given that the consequence of non-registration is retained by the regulations, namely that the charge will be void against a liquidator, administrator or creditor of the company, the incentive to ensure registration of all registrable charges remains. UK companies will no longer be required to maintain their own registers of security with their books, but will need to have copies of relevant instruments available for inspection.

What survives from the previous regime?

While major changes are made to the scheme for registration of company charges a number of aspects of the pre-2013 regime will continue to apply:

- The time period for registration remains 21 days,[51] beginning with the day after the date of creation of the charge. However, the new rules clarify what the 'date of creation'[52] of a charge means.

- If a registrable charge is not registered within the 21-day period, it becomes void against an administrator, liquidator or creditor[53] of the company, and any debt secured by the charge becomes immediately repayable. If registration does not occur within the 21-day time limit for registration, it remains necessary to apply to court to extend the time period.[54]

- All security granted by an overseas company remains non-registrable.

However, registration is no longer compulsory (i.e. it is not a criminal offence not to register the charge and therefore there is no sanction for failure to register). From the chargee's perspective, registration of a registrable security is no more 'voluntary' than it was before, since an unregistered security will be void against the liquidator, administrator or receiver. However,

---

[50] Section 859A(6) of the Companies Act 2006, inserted by schedule 2 of The Companies Act 2006 (Amendment of Part 25) Regulations 2013.

[51] Section 859A(4) of the Companies Act 2006, inserted by schedule 2 of The Companies Act 2006 (Amendment of Part 25) Regulations 2013.

[52] Section 859B(6) of the Companies Act 2006, inserted by schedule 2 of The Companies Act 2006 (Amendment of Part 25) Regulations 2013.

[53] Section 859H(3) of the Companies Act 2006, inserted by schedule 2 of The Companies Act 2006 (Amendment of Part 25) Regulations 2013.

[54] Section 859F(3) of the Companies Act 2006, inserted by schedule 2 of The Companies Act 2006 (Amendment of Part 25) Regulations 2013.

the new registration system is hardly voluntary, given that on a failure to register the secured debt becomes immediately repayable. The statement of particulars must include information on whether the charge contains: a floating charge and, if so, whether it is expressed to cover all the property and undertaking of the company; and/or provisions which prohibit or restrict the company from creating further security that will rank equally with or ahead of the charge. As well as the statement of particulars, a certified copy of the charge instrument will be on the public register.[55]

Unlike under the old rules, the registration form must now state whether the security document contains a negative pledge. On this basis it might be argued that a later security provider has constructive notice of any negative pledge to the same extent as it has constructive notice of the charge itself. This may make a registered floating charge less vulnerable to subsequent security interests.

The security document rather than the registration form is now the key registered document for providing information about the security to third parties. The parties should therefore ensure that the security documents contain full details of the scope of the security; in particular, definitions of any assets subject to the security should be included in the security document itself. This will ensure a third party has the best possible notice of the scope of the security.

Where a previously registered charge is amended by the addition of provisions prohibiting or restricting the company from creating further security that will rank equally with or ahead of the charge, or a variation in the ranking of the charge in relation to any fixed security or any other charge, the chargor may notify Companies House of the changes.

Registration as notice to third parties

Although the reasons for the registration of company charges were clearly set out in the Diamond Report[56] it must be remembered that the security will be registered for several reasons. It is important to preserve the rights of the chargee and the rights of third party creditors, and the priority gained by registering the charge can affect those rights. The extent to which a third party can acquire a right in assets free from the existing security may depend on whether that third party has: (i) notice of the existing security; or (ii) where the security is a floating charge, with a negative pledge in favour of the floating charge holder, has notice of the charge. Under the 2013 Regulations it is not necessary to register the negative pledge separately at the time the third party acquires its interest. The information on the register is clearly notice of the charge, but under the pre-2013 law the registration of the charge was not deemed registration of the negative pledge which had to be registered separately. Under the 2013 Regulations registering any information that must be registered also gives constructive (or deemed) notice to those who might reasonably be expected to look for the constructive charge: the negative pledge does not therefore have to be registered separately. An incidental benefit of registering securities at Companies House can therefore be that it helps to protect the priority of the security holder.

---

[55] Section 859D(6) of the Companies Act 2006, inserted by schedule 2 of The Companies Act 2006 (Amendment of Part 25) Regulations 2013.

[56] Diamond (1989) A Review of Security Interests in Property (The Diamond Report).

Possessory securities

The very nature of this type of security may present a number of problems. Goods may be perishable, the price of commodities may fluctuate, storage charges may be expensive and goods manufactured for one purpose may be inappropriate for resale. It may therefore be difficult for a bank to dispose of goods, where it has taken a security over certain types of commodities, and in the event of default the assistance of the customer may be required. We will now examine the rights acquired by a bank over goods or documents that are in its possession as a result of default by the customer.

Pledge

One of the forms of security available to the bank is a legal pledge of the goods in question and this will be created by delivery of the subject matter to the bank as creditor, thereby giving it a legal right of possession until the debt is paid, for example under a letter of credit. The essence of the pledge is that the security vested in the pledgee consists exclusively of the possession of the goods in question and not any derivative proprietary interest in them. If the pledgee returns the goods to the pledgor otherwise than as an agent for the pledgee the pledge comes to an end.[57] Although the pledgee has no proprietary interest in the goods, a pledge confers an implied right for the pledgee to realise the security by selling the goods. Shipping documents held by the pledgee may be used for this purpose. A pledge will arise only as a result of an express agreement of the parties and the incidents of the pledge are also determined by agreement. The pledge by its very nature is a contract of bailment, with the pledgee acquiring both possession of the items subject to the bailment and certain specific rights in them, for example a power of sale.[58] In *The Odessa*[59] the Privy Council, however, explained that the pledgee's only power was to sell the goods upon the pledgor's default and concluded that this was not a right of property but a 'special interest'. This qualification to the pledgee's rights reflects that property in the items remains vested in the pledgor.[60]

It has been said that the pledge ranks between a mortgage, which confers a property right, and a lien which is purely possessory in nature.[61] On the basis of the decision in *The Odessa* the pledge is likely to be considered closer to the lien than the mortgage. One of the limitations of the pledge from a bank's view is that the bank is not in the business of handling goods or machinery: it will not have the expertise to go into the market to sell them and it is unlikely to have facilities for storage. However, the bank may acquire possession of documents used in the ordinary course of the banking business, namely shipping documents, negotiable instruments and market securities. Otherwise the bank is likely to have constructive possession of the goods subject to the pledge.[62] Negotiable instruments and marketable securities transferable by delivery can be the subject of a pledge because they are choses in action and confer a right to the proceeds on the holder and are also choses in possession. A

---

[57] *North Western Bank Ltd v John Poynter, Son and MacDonalds* [1895] AC 56.
[58] *Re Hardwick, ex p. Hubbard* (1886) 17 QBD 690.
[59] [1916] 1 AC 145.
[60] *Attenborough v Solomon* [1913] AC 76.
[61] *Halliday v Holgate* (18680 LR 3 EX 299.
[62] *Young v Lambert* (1870) LR 3 PC 142; *Hilton v Tucker* (1888) 39 Ch D 669; *Wrightson v McArthur and Hutchinsons* (1919) Ltd [1921] 2 KB 807.

pledge is not possible over other documents, for example share certificates, which are not negotiable in character. In *Harrold v Plenty*[63] Cozens-Hardy MR held that the deposit of share certificates involved the creation of an equitable charge on the shares or an arrangement to execute a transfer of the shares by way of mortgage and not a pledge of the shares. At common law the pledge of a bill of lading constitutes a pledge of the goods.[64]

The pledge can be created by delivery to the pledgee of the actual or constructive possession of the goods pledged. If the goods are in the hands of the pledgor, he can effect the pledge by actual delivery of the goods. In other cases he can give possession by some other sufficient act, e.g. handing over keys to the warehouse where the goods are stored so as to vest control over them in the pledgee. If the goods are in the hands of a third party who holds them on behalf of the pledgor, a pledge may be effected by the pledgor instructing the third party to hold the goods on behalf of the pledgee (i.e. acknowledging that he holds the goods on behalf of the pledgee so the latter has constructive possession of them). Where the goods are represented by documents, the mere delivery of the documents to the pledgee does not generally vest possession of the goods themselves in the pledgee unless the person who has custody of the goods is notified of the agreements and agrees to hold the goods on behalf of the pledgee. In the absence of such an agreement the pledge of the goods is incomplete and ineffective. However, an exception was recognised in *Barber v Meyestein*[65] where the court held that the pledge of the goods by means of a deposit of documents relating to them is possible either if the document is a negotiable instrument or if it is a current bill of lading. Thus, the endorsement and delivery of the bill of lading while the ship carrying the goods represented by the bill is at sea operates in exactly the same way as the delivery of the goods to the consignee or his endoresee after the arrival of the ship. Similarly, in *Sewell v Burdick*[66] the House of Lords stated that endorsement and delivery of the bill of lading by way of a pledge was equivalent, and no more than equivalent, to delivery of the goods themselves. The rule has been applied in subsequent cases although its application has been somewhat restricted. In *Official Assignee of Madras v Mercantile Bank of India Ltd*[67] it was held that the rule relating to bills of lading cannot be extended to railway consignment notes, warehouse warrants or documents used in connection with the transport and storage of goods. In *William M'Ewan and Sons v Smith*[68] it was held that the issue or transfer of a delivery order calling on a warehouse keeper to deliver goods to the person who presents the order is not, without an attornment by the keeper, sufficient to bring about a transfer or pledge of documents of title to the goods and does not amount to a transfer or pledge of the goods themselves; a pledge of such documents is merely a pledge of the documents regarded as physical objects, except in the case of a bill of lading. A delivery order does not transfer the ownership or possession of the goods and even if it is endorsed the transfer of a delivery order is not sufficient to estop the owner from asserting his rights in the goods.[69] Since the pledge involves the transfer of possession it does not have to be registered under the Bills of Sales Act 1878–1891, or in the case of a corporate pledgor under s.860 of the Companies Act 2006.

---

[63] [1901] 2 Ch 314.
[64] *Official Assignee of Madras v Mercantile Bank of India Ltd* [1935] AC 53.
[65] (1870) LR 4 HL 317.
[66] (1884) 10 App Cas 74.
[67] [1935] AC 53.
[68] (1849) 2 HL Cas 309.
[69] See *Official Assignee of Madras v Mercantile Bank of India Ltd* [1935] AC 53; *Inglis v Robertson* [1898] AC 616.

The common law has been supplemented by legislation, which was been enacted to protect banks that made advances to mercantile agents. Under s.2(1) of the Factors Act 1889 a pledge of any documents of title to goods, whether a bill of lading, rail or road consignment note, air waybill, dock or warehouse warrant or a delivery order may create a valid pledge, but only if the pledgor is a factor. The section is supplemented by s.3 of the Act which provides that a pledge of the documents of title to the goods is to be deemed a pledge of the goods and, for the purposes of the Act, the expression 'pledge' is to include 'any contract, pledging, or giving a lien or security on the goods'. In *Lloyds Bank Ltd v Bank of America National Trust and Savings Association*[70] the court held that the statutory exception in respect of a pledge by a factor applies whether the factor acts as a mercantile agent for a third person or on his own account.

A further statutory exception was created by s.25(2) of the Sale of Goods Act 1893 (now s.25(1) of the Sale of Goods Act 1979) which provides that a bank which makes an advance has a valid pledge if the buyer of goods has received the documents of title to them before the seller's lien or right of stoppage in transit for the price payable under the contract of sale. However, the statutory exceptions raise uncertainties and are therefore rarely relied on in practice. Further, the unpaid seller's lien is suspended if he takes a bill of exchange for the purchase price.

Where the bank is owed money advanced by it to pay for the price of the goods it will probably release the shipping documents to the buyer so that he can sell the goods and reimburse the bank. The question for the bank is whether having released the documents to the buyer, its charge or security over the goods is in any way affected. In *North Western Bank Ltd v John Poynter, Son and MacDonalds*[71] the House of Lords held that delivery of the goods, either actual or constructive, to the debtor destroyed the possibility of the pledge continuing or subsequently arising. However, on the facts of the case the court concluded that the bank took a pledge of the goods by delivery of the bill of lading relating to them and gave the applicant only a limited authority to sell the goods as its agent. Consequently, the bank did not give up possession of the goods and its pledge continued so that it was entitled to the proceeds of the sale in priority to any general creditors of the pledgor. The limited authority given to the buyer of the goods whose purchase is financed by a letter of credit to deal with the goods if the bank releases them to him so that he may sell them as the bank's agent does not in any way prevent the pledge in favour of the bank from continuing, even though the buyer has physical control of the goods for the purposes of the sale.

The logical consequences of this rule were explored by the court in *Re David Allester Ltd*[72] where the court held that the bank was entitled to have the value of the goods realised by experts, in this case the pledgor. Therefore, handing over the bills of lading for the purpose of selling the goods did not deny the continuing rights of the pledgee, the bank. Both *North Western Bank Ltd*[73] and *Re David Allester Ltd*[74] were approved by the Privy Council in *Official Assignee of Madras*[75] where it was held that the respondents had merely parted with possession

---

[70] [1938] 2 KB 147.
[71] [1895] AC 56.
[72] [1922] 2 Ch 211.
[73] [1895] AC 56.
[74] [1922] 2 Ch 211.
[75] [1935] AC 53.

of the railway receipts to the insolvent merchants for a limited purpose, i.e. as agents for the respondents for the purpose of dealing with the goods. A different situation may arise where the bank releases the documents of title, other than the bill of lading, to its customer, who undertakes to deal with the goods on behalf of the bank but who fraudulently pledges the documents of title to a third party who takes them in good faith. It has been held that in such a case the bank is not estopped as against the third party from setting up its title to the goods, even though the third party acted in good faith.[76]

The pledgor has a right to redeem the pledge, notwithstanding his default and regardless of the terms of the contract, at any time preceding the sale of the property pledged.[77]

Sections 114–122 of the Consumer Credit Act 1974 govern the giving of pledges under a regulated agreement although pledges of documents of title and of bearer bonds are excluded from most of the statutory requirements.

The banker's lien

A lien confers the right to retain property belonging to another, in this case the principal debtor, until the debt has been discharged. A bank, by mercantile usage, has a lien over commercial paper over which it acquires possession in the ordinary course of business. There is, therefore, no need for an express agreement between the parties to bring the lien into existence.[78] A lien may arise as a result of a particular transaction connected with the property that is subject to the lien but a 'general lien' will arise not only out of the particular transaction but also as a result of the general dealings between the parties. For example, an issuing or confirming bank under a letter of credit is entitled to hold the shipping documents it receives from the beneficiary as security for the amount paid, or committed, to the beneficiary of the credit in exchange for the shipping documents, including the bill of exchange. The general lien will secure the customer's total indebtedness to the bank at any particular time but the extent of the lien can be limited to by express or implied agreement. In *Re Bowes*[79] an insurance policy was deposited with the bank, accompanied with a memorandum, which stated that it would constitute a security for sums up to £4,000. The court held that the lien did not secure any borrowings in excess of the agreed amount. The lien may also be avoided by the circumstances surrounding the transaction, for example where a lien given for specific purposes is left with the bank after the loan is paid off and is subsequently used for general advances to the customer.[80]

The banker's lien arises by operation of law as a result of the instructions given, for example, to the issuing bank to open the credit. The lien is independent of any other security the bank may take under the express agreement and can be created over all negotiable and semi-negotiable instruments, for example cheques, bills of exchange, promissory notes, bonds and share warrants. The banker's lien is therefore in addition to any other security expressly created and is not superseded by any express security.

The ordinary right of the bank under the lien is merely a right to retain possession of the shipping documents, but in the case of shipping documents which represent title to the

---

[76] *Mercantile Bank of India Ltd* v *Central Bank of India Ltd* [1938] AC 287.
[77] *Re Morritt, ex p. Official Receiver* (1886) 18 QBD 222.
[78] *Brandao* v *Barnett* (1846) 12 Cl & F 787.
[79] (1886) 33 Ch D 586.
[80] *Re London and Globe Finance Corporation* [1902] 2 Ch 416.

goods, the lien also carries with it the right to sell the goods represented by those documents. As such it approximates more closely to a pledge than to a common law lien. In the case of other documents over which a bank has a lien there is no implied power of sale or realisation. In *Brandao* v *Barnett*[81] the court expressed the view that banks have a general lien on all securities deposited with them, as bankers, by a customer unless there is an express contract, or a contract can be implied from the circumstances, which is inconsistent with the grant of a lien. This view was reinforced in *Halesowen Presswork and Assemblies Ltd* v *Westminster Bank Ltd*[82] where the court accepted the view that bankers generally have a lien against all documents deposited with them by their customers.

The lien extends to all documents under which money will be paid to the customer, or by which money may be obtained by the customer, whether or not the documents are negotiable. Where documents relate to goods themselves, if the customer fails to reimburse the bank it can sell the goods and realise the amount of the advance made to the customer. The essential factor in deciding whether or not the documents are subject to a lien depends on whether, or not, they came into the hands of the bank in the ordinary course of its business. The bank therefore has a general lien, or a right of retention, over documents belonging to a customer over which it has possession and it can hold these documents until loans and advances have been paid back to the bank. The bank may therefore exercise a lien over cheques payable to the customer,[83] bills of exchange, share certificates and investment securities generally. In *Sewell* v *Burdick*[84] securities were held to include bills of lading and other documents representing goods in transit. An issuing bank will therefore have a lien over shipping documents taken up under a letter of credit as security for reimbursement for payment. The House of Lords then went onto hold that the deposit of a bill of lading by way of security does not divest the shipper of his proprietary rights in the goods. A lien therefore gives the bank security over the shipping documents but it does not transfer the ownership of the goods to the bank since no man can have a lien over his own property.[85] In *Aschkenasy* v *Midland Bank Ltd*[86] it was held that a bank, which instructs another bank to make a payment to a third party, is itself a customer of the paying bank. It therefore follows that a confirming bank may claim a lien over shipping documents taken up by it for its immediate customer, the issuing bank. The fact that the applicant of the credit, on whose instruction the letter of credit was issued, had placed the issuing bank in funds does not affect the right of the confirming bank to retain the documents until it is reimbursed the funds. However, it does not attach to documents that evidence mere choses in action so in *Wylde* v *Radford*[87] it was held that a deed in respect of a conveyance of land was not covered by a banker's lien although in *Re Bowes* a lien was recognised over an insurance policy. Hapgood[88] suggests that where title deeds in respect of land are deposited with a bank a special type of charge akin to a lien is created although this is not to be confused with a banker's lien.

[81] (1846) 12 Cl & Fin 787.
[82] [1972] AC 785.
[83] *Barclays Bank Ltd* v *Astley Industrial Trust Ltd* [1970] 2 QB 527; *BCCI* v *Dawson* [1987] FLR 342.
[84] (1884) 10 App Cas 74.
[85] *Halesowen Presswork and Assemblies Ltd* v *Westminster Bank Ltd* [1972] AC 785.
[86] (1935) 51 TLR 34.
[87] (1863) 33 LJ Ch 51.
[88] Hapgood (2007) *Paget's Law of Banking*, London: LexisNexis.

The lien does not however attach to securities or documents deposited with the bank for safekeeping. In such circumstances the bank holds the documents as bailee unless there is evidence to the contrary, and not in the ordinary course of the banking business.[89] Neither does the lien attach to a balance standing to the credit of the customer's bank account since the credit balance represents a debt due to the customer. The bank instead has a right of set off against the credit balance. Where an account is held in a foreign currency, however, the position is more complex and will depend on whether the account is held with a foreign correspondent or bank, or with the customer's own bank, but the debt is expressed in foreign currency. In *Choice Investments Ltd* v *Jeromnimon (Midland Bank, Garnishee)*[90] the court attached the credit balance by way of a garnishee order and concluded that such a credit balance could be the subject of a valid set off, but not a banker's lien.

A banker's lien, like a pledge, is not registrable under the Bills of Sale Act 1878 in respect of individual customers, or under the Companies Act 2006 in respect of registered companies.

Letters of hypothecation, letters of trust or trust receipts

In order to overcome the difficulties of the pledge as a form of security, banks may resort to two other forms of security in order to support the purchase of goods, namely the letter of hypothecation and the letter of trust (or trust receipt). A letter of hypothecation creates an equitable charge over the goods which ensures that if the goods are sold by the applicant the proceeds of sale are subject to a first charge in favour of the bank. If the applicant becomes bankrupt, or if a company is wound-up, the bank will rank as a secured creditor and is entitled to be paid in priority out of the proceeds of the sale. The letter of hypothecation has largely been superseded by the letter of trust or trust receipt, which evidences an agreement between the bank and the customer that the bank will hand the documents of title to the customer so as to enable him to obtain delivery of the goods. In turn the customer will hold the documents of title, the goods when they are received and eventually the proceeds of sale of the goods on behalf of the bank.

The letter of trust or trust receipt is either embodied in the application for the issue of the letter of credit by the bank, or is given separately by the applicant, buyer, when the shipping documents have been taken up by the issuing or confirming on arrival. Under the letter of trust, the buyer undertakes to hold the proceeds of sale as a trustee for the bank absolutely and to pay the whole of the proceeds of sale to the bank, which will retain what is owed to it and return the balance to the applicant of the credit. If the applicant departs from the authority given to him to deal with the goods he is guilty of a breach of trust and it is this trust relationship, which is treated by the courts as creating a valid security interest of the bank.[91]

The courts have in fact given the banks greater protection under letters of trust and trust receipts by holding that not only is the customer guilty of a breach of trust by wrongfully disposing of the goods, but that the bank may sue him and the disponee for conversion of the shipping documents. In *Midland Bank Ltd* v *Eastcheap Dried Fruit Co*[92] the court held that

---

[89] *Leese* v *Martin* (1873) LR 17 Eq 235.
[90] [1981] 1 All ER 225.
[91] *Re David Allester Ltd* [1922] 2 Ch 211.
[92] [1962] 1 Lloyd's Rep 359.

the defendants were in breach of the contract constituted by the delivery of the documents to them with the collection note attached, and also that the defendants were guilty of conversion of the documents since they had interfered with the plaintiff's possessory title to the documents. In this situation a person to whom the purchaser of the goods wrongfully disposes of shipping documents, which he has received under a trust receipt, is guilty of conversion of the documents despite the fact that he gives value for them and acts in good faith so that in equity he has a good title to the goods themselves.

The equitable proprietary interest of the bank over the goods, and subsequently over the proceeds of sale, subsists only so long as the bank is in a position to fulfil its obligations to the customer. If the bank repudiates these obligations expressly or impliedly, e.g. where the bank becomes bankrupt, it will lose its proprietary interest. In *Sale Continuation Ltd* v *Austin Taylor and Co* it was said that in such circumstances the bank's proprietary interest in the goods ceases automatically and the applicant may retain the shipping documents, the goods or the proceeds of sale for his own benefit.

Choses in action as security

Choses in action, for example money standing to the credit of a bank account, constitutes a debt due either on maturity or as agreed under the terms of the contract. They are assets in the creditor's balance sheet and so can be used in the creditor's business by converting them into cash. Alternatively, a supplier may sell all the amounts (receivable) due from his customer at a discount. In such transactions the purchaser of the 'receivables' acquires the right to be paid by the traders. Choses in action may therefore be used as collateral and, unlike other forms of security whose value may fluctuate, such assets are of fixed value and easily realisable. A security interest over choses in action has to be effected in a form recognised either in law or equity. A pledge over choses in action is ineffective since it is not possible to take possession of mere rights, although legally enforceable, but it may be possible to have a pledge over negotiable instruments or marketable securities, since such instruments represent both choses in action and choses in possession. Transactions over choses in action are effected by means of a statutory or equitable assignment. Section 136 of the Law of Property Act 1925 involves an outright transfer of the debt to the assignee, with notice of the assignment being given to the debtor in writing. The equitable assignment may be effected merely by means of an intention to assign.

Securities over book debts and other securities

A lender may wish to take security over debts due and owing, to the borrower. Book debts are amounts owing to a company or unincorporated business in the course of its business.[93] Book debts have been described as debts that would ordinarily be entered in a trader's books, regardless of whether or not they are so entered in a given case.[94] Generally, credit balances on a bank account are not 'book debts'. Although the credit balance is a debt due from the bank to the customer it is not, however, due to the customer in the ordinary course of his trading operations or ordinary course of his business. Hence, goods sold on credit, rentals

---

[93] *Shipley* v *Marshall* (1863) 14 CB (NS) 571.
[94] *Independent Automatic Sales Ltd* v *Knowles & Foster* [1962] 1 WLR 974.

due under a hire-purchase agreement or equipment leases, and amounts due from clients to traders or professionals, for example accountants and lawyers are within the definition of book debts. Credit balances are deposits made for investment purposes or for enabling regular drawings against the account.

Whether a chose in action is a 'book debt' is important for the purposes of determining whether a charge is registrable under the Bills of Sales Act 1878 or under the Companies Act 2006. Otherwise the term 'receivables' is now used to describe debts owed to (and receivable) by a business. The term is wider than book debts and includes all monetary obligations owed to a business underpinning its cash flow. The value of receivables as collateral is based on the debtor's obligation to make payment. Banks will take such security where they finance either the entire business operations of their customer or some specific aspect of it. Frequently, this form of security is in addition to a charge over goods. The bank may demand a charge over goods purchased by means of a credit facility and also over the sale of the goods. A fixed charge is preferable to a floating charge in order to protect the interests of the bank.

The question of whether a charge over book debts is fixed or floating has posed problems in the past. However, a number of issues have now been clarified:

1 There is now no doubt that a lender may take a floating charge over book debts and a charge will be characterised as such if it is intended that the borrower should be able to use the proceeds of those receivables in the ordinary course of the business.[95] A purported fixed charge over book debts may be valid as between the chargor and chargee even though notice of the charge is not given (or immediately given) to the underlying debtor.[96] However, once notice of the assignment is given to the debtor, the debtor cannot acquire further rights of set off as against the creditor in respect of that debt by entering into future debts through transactions with him, since he deals with the creditor with the knowledge of the assignee's interest. In *Business Computers Ltd v Anglo-African Leasing Ltd*[97] it was recognised that a debtor who receives a notice of assignment can continue to exercise a right of set off against that debt, in priority to any rights the assignee might have acquired, in three circumstances: (i) in relation to debts which have accrued (i.e. the debt must have become unconditionally payable although the debt is not due for payment at that stage[98]) before the notice is given; (ii) in relation to a debt which arises out of the same contract; (iii) in relation to a debt which does not arise out of the contract relating to the assigned debt but is nevertheless closely connected with it (e.g. the contracts while formally separate were entered into in the same context or venture).

2 In *Siebe Gorman & Co Ltd v Barclays Bank Ltd*,[99] Slade J concluded that there was no valid reason why a fixed charge could not be created over receivables (book debts) if supported by (i) an undertaking to credit all proceeds to a designated account of the chargor with the lender bank; and (ii) an undertaking not to charge or assign those debts in favour of any third party. Consequently, the terms of the debenture were sufficient to negate the inference that the chargor could deal with the receivables in the ordinary course of

---

[95] *Illingworth v Houldsworth* [1904] AC 355.

[96] *Holt v Heatherfield Trust Ltd* [1942] 2 KB 1; such a charge takes effect as an equitable charge since notice to the debtor is one of the necessary ingredients of a legal charge over debts.

[97] [1977] 2 All ER 741.

[98] *Christie v Taunton, Delmard, Lane & Co* [1893] 2 Ch 175.

[99] [1979] 2 Lloyd's Rep 142.

the business so the charge could not be characterised as a floating charge.[100] However, if the debenture merely created a charge without restricting the borrower's dealings with its book debts and their proceeds, then that would amount to a floating charge only.[101] By contrast in *Re Spectrum Plus Ltd*,[102] a case identical on the facts, the House of Lords held that the charge over the book debts was a floating and not a fixed charge and the debenture did not sufficiently restrict the use by the chargor of the book debts as part of the ordinary course of the business. Their Lordships held that it was not sufficient that the bank could intervene in the future to preclude further drawings. Such an act would crystallise the floating charge.

3   A further confusion was introduced into the law as a result of the decision in *Re Bullas Trading Ltd*[103] where a creditor was given (i) a floating charge over the company's assets and (ii) a charge stated to be a 'fixed charge' over its uncollected book debts. The proceeds of the book debts were to be paid into the company's bank account and consequently they were then released from the fixed charge, but caught by the floating charge. The agreement gave the chargee a power, never exercised, to direct the proceeds to be paid into a separate account to be nominated by him. The Court of Appeal held it was conceptually possible for the parties to distinguish between a book debt and its proceeds, with the result that a charge over the receivables could be classed as a fixed charge but the proceeds could be regarded as a floating charge so available to the chargor in the ordinary course of its business. While the outcome of the decision was highly convenient for lenders and borrowers, the distinction was highly artificial and commercially unrealistic. The distinction in *Re Bullas* was rejected in *Agnew v Commissioners of Inland Revenue*,[104] where the Privy Council concluded that the charge over the company's uncollected book debts was a floating charge because the company's freedom to deal with the proceeds was inconsistent with the fixed charge. This reasoning was followed in *Re Spectrum Plus*[105] and *Re Bullas* and *Siebe Gorman* are now overruled. The Privy Council in *Agnew* and the House of Lords in *Re Spectrum Plus* emphasised the need for a sufficient degree of control over both the charged receivables and their proceeds. As a result of these decisions it is accepted that the chargor must pay the proceeds of any receivables into a separate account which should be blocked by the lender to ensure exclusive control by the lender.

Credit balances as security

A balance standing to the credit of a customer's account is repayable on the agreed terms or on demand. While the account is in credit the balance constitutes a debt owed by the bank to its customer.[106] As such, the debt is an asset and the customer may utilise it as a security in respect of a transaction financed by a bank or other financial institution. However, using a credit balance as a security may cause difficulties, e.g. the customer making withdrawals may

---

[100] See the third criterion in *Re Yorkshire Woolcombers Ltd* [1903] 2 Ch 284.
[101] *Re Brightlife Ltd* [1987] Ch 200.
[102] [2005] 2 AC 680.
[103] [1994] BCC 36.
[104] [2001] 2 AC 680.
[105] [2005] 2 AC 680.
[106] *Foley v Hill* (1848) 2 HL Cas. 28.

reduce the credit balance, or the credit balance may be made the subject of a garnishee order. Problems can arise if the customer becomes bankrupt or insolvent. Although, these problems can be overcome, using a credit balance as security is likely to result in restrictions on the account holder's right to utilise the account. The method of granting security over the credit balance will depend on whether the security is given to the bank with whom the account is maintained, or with a third party bank.

Security in favour of bank which maintains the account

Where a security is created in favour of a bank which maintains the account, the bank has a right to set off of any amounts owed to it by the creditor (customer). The right to set-off is a procedural right and does not confer on the party entitled to exercise it a propriety right. Although the equitable right to set-off is invaluable for bankers (for example, where a bank is required to make payment under a guarantee it can reimburse itself by exercising a set-off against the customer's credit balance), it is subject to several limitations. Thus, until such time as the bank acquires a right of set-off the customer can make withdrawals against the credit balance thereby reducing the amount available for set-off. Further, the right of set-off is subordinate to the right of a judgment creditor who has served a garnishee order before the set-off is exercised.

When the customer is adjudicated bankrupt or becomes insolvent the bank's right to set-off is governed by s.323 of the Insolvency Act 1986. It is not possible to contract out of the statutory right of set-off, in the sense that the parties cannot by agreement limit the statutory right of set-off.[107] However, the statutory right of set-off is considerably wider than the general law. In particular, the bank is entitled to set off liabilities payable at a future date and unliquidated liabilities against the deposit. However, what was uncertain was whether a purely contingent liability could be set off, e.g. under a counter-indemnity taken in connection with the issue of a performance bond that has not yet been called. Some support can be found for the view that a contingent liability could not be set off against a present debt.[108] However, following *Re Charge Card Services Ltd*[109] the better view appears to be that contingent debts are capable of being set off provided that they satisfy certain requirements laid down. A significant requirement is that of mutuality, i.e. the debts must be between the same parties in the same right, with the result that only a liability owed to the bank by the depositor in the same capacity may be set off against the credit.

However, because of the limitation attached to the equitable and statutory rights of set-off, it has become the practice of banks to take a contractual right of set-off. This right may be subject to special agreement (letter of set-off) or may be created by means of specific clauses incorporated in the underlying financial agreement between the bank and its customer. The object of the clause is to enable the bank to set off against the credit balance any claims the bank has, whether such claims are existing, contingent, unconditional, liquidated or unliquidated. The purpose of the clause is to restrict the right of the customer to make withdrawals so long as the liability is contingent. However, the bank must ensure that the customer's need for liquidity in respect of his account is not hampered.

---

[107] *National Westminster Bank Ltd* v *Halesowen Presswork and Assemblies Ltd* [1972] AC 785.
[108] See *Re Fenton* [1931] 1 Ch 85.
[109] [1987] Ch 150.

A variation to the set-off agreement is the 'flawed asset' arrangement. The arrangement imposes a 'flaw' on the customer's asset, i.e. the arrangement restricts the customer's right to utilise the credit balance. In its simplest form, the arrangement consists of the deposit of money under an agreement by which the depositor agrees that the deposit is not to become repayable until certain liabilities have been satisfied, or if the liabilities are contingent, are no longer capable of arising. Thus, the bank is entitled to freeze the bank balance until such time as the customer's liability is discharged. A number of problems may arise in respect of the set-off agreement namely:

- A credit balance may be assigned in equity or under s.136 of the Law of Property Act 1925. Regardless of the form of assignment, the assignee's rights are subject to equities available to the bank against the assignor. However, an equity could be set up only if it accrued before the debtor was given notice of the assignment.

- A credit balance with a bank will not normally be treated as a book debt and therefore the issue of registration should not normally arise.[110] In the case of an unincorporated customer, the answer would be the same even if the balance constituted a book debt, since registration is not required where the debtor is specified in the instrument creating an assignment.[111] The position differs where the customer is incorporated, since any charge on book debts will need to be registered under the Companies Act 2006.

- The final problem arises in respect of an incorporated customer, which enters into a set-off arrangement with the bank, and is being wound up. The Insolvency Act 1986 provides that all claims which are not given a special status (i.e. preferential creditors) rank *pari passu*. In *British Eagle International Airlines Ltd* v *Compagnie Nationale Air France*[112] the House of Lords held that a clearing arrangement that purported to oust the statutory rules on set-off was against public policy. The case is based on the rule that in the insolvency of a debtor under a multi-party set-off or a clearing agreement, the agreement cannot prejudice the rights of other parties in the insolvency. It has been argued that on the same reasoning the courts would invalidate a contractual set-off and a flawed asset arrangement.[113]

Charges over bank balances

A credit balance in a bank account is a chose in action and may be the subject of a mortgage or charge affected by means of an assignment. Where a charge is created over cash deposited with a bank, the bank seeks to rank in priority as a secured creditor in the customer's insolvency. A charge over a bank deposit will often be created by way of security for the customer's obligation to indemnify the bank against a call under a guarantee, bond, documentary credit or other instrument issued by the bank of the customer. In ordinary circumstances, a security interest in a debt is created either by means of a mortgage or charge. The method by which a debt may be mortgaged is by way of an absolute assignment under s.136 of the Law of Property Act 1925. The assignment will be coupled with an express or implied equity of

---

[110] Goode (2003) *Legal Problems of Credit and Security*, London: Sweet & Maxwell.
[111] Insolvency Act 1986 s.344(3)(b).
[112] [1975] 1 WLR 758.
[113] Cresswell et al. (1996) *Encyclopaedia of Banking Law*, Vol. 1, London: Sweet & LexisNexis, para. E2478.

redemption in favour of the assignor.[114] It was at one time suggested that a charge over a bank balance required a tripartite transaction and that the bank that maintained the account, since on assignment back to the debtor the debt would cease to exist, could not hold a mortgage.[115] Millett J in *Re Charge Card Services Ltd*[116] considered this issue and the learned judge held that a charge in favour of a debtor of his own indebtedness to the chargor is conceptually impossible. The facts of the case were that Charge Card Ltd, which carried on the business of issuing credit cards used by holders for purchases made at petrol stations, assigned its receivables to Commercial Credit. The factoring agreement provided that the debts involved would be collected by Commercial Credit and paid to the credit of an account maintained by it in Charge Card Ltd's name. Under the credit, Commercial Credit was granted the absolute discretion to retain money standing to the credit of the account as security for any amount required to meet Charge Card Ltd's liabilities. As issue that arose on Charge Card Ltd's insolvency was whether the clause was void against the liquidator as an unregistered charge over book debts. Millett J giving judgment for Commercial Credit held that the right of retention did not amount to a charge since the money deposited with the bank became the bank's own money. The real effect of the clause in question was to grant Commercial Credit a contractual set off which was effective to the extent that it complied with s.31 of the Bankruptcy Act 1914 (now s.323 of the Insolvency Act 1986). The view that a bank cannot have a charge over its customer's bank balance (charge back) but must rely on contractual arrangements is supported by Goode who argues that a bank balance is a mere chose in action due from the bank to the customer and the essence of an assignment is to enable the assignee to recover the debt. The bank, which would be both a debtor and assignee, cannot sue itself to recover the debt. The *Re Charge Card Ltd* case had a hostile reception within the banking community where charge-backs are common practice. The problem could be resolved by a 'triple cocktail' of agreements to obtain security, including a contractual right of set-off, a flawed asset arrangement.[117]

The issue was resolved by the House of Lords in *Re Bank of Credit and Commerce International SA (No 8)*[118] where a bank went into liquidation after making several loans to a number of companies. The loans had been secured by charges executed by third parties over their bank accounts maintained with the same bank. The liquidator applied for directions to determine whether in trying to recover the loans from the principal debtors (companies) he could set off amounts standing to the credit of the third party deposit accounts. Lord Hoffman disagreed with the view in *Re Charge Card* that it was 'conceptually impossible' for a bank to take a charge over an amount it held to the credit of its customer. The solution he advocated was that instead of the chargee having to claim payment from the debtor, realisation would take the form of a 'book entry'.

In *Goodbody Stockbrokers* v *Allied Irish Banks and Patterson*[119] the account holder, P, held a share portfolio account with the plaintiff stockbrokers. Mrs Patterson argued it was agreed before the marriage that both she and her husband would share the portfolio account. She therefore argued that the purported pledge to the bank was ineffective either in whole, or

---

[114] *Durham Brothers* v *Robertson* [1898] 1 QB 765.
[115] Goode (2003) *Legal Problems of Credit and Security*, London: Sweet & Maxwell.
[116] [1987] Ch 150.
[117] Blair (1983) Charges over cash deposits, November *International Law Review*, 14.
[118] [1998] AC 214.
[119] [2013] IEHC 155, 16 April 2013.

in part, and at least half of the value of the account belonged to her, or was held on trust for her. The bank argued that the wife had never contributed to the account and so had no beneficial interest in it. Furthermore the bank took the charge over the account from P in good faith and without notice of the wife's claim. The bank further argued that the wife had also waived her right to complain about the charge because an excessive amount of time (five years) had passed since its execution. Birmingham J held in favour of the bank on the basis that the wife did not hold an interest in the account that prevented her husband from validly pledging it to bank. The judge found that the bank accepted the security in good faith without notice of the wife's interest; she had not protested or asserted any right over the account at the time the security was created, nor when it was later renewed or subsequently extended and so 'the fact that no steps were taken to regularise the situation, as seen from her perspective, militates against the cause that she is advancing'. The fact that she did not contribute to the account was 'highly relevant'. The best practice for lenders is of course to procure spousal consent coupled with declarations of beneficial ownership from the party giving security.

Personal securities

Guarantees are widely used by a bank where it seeks additional recourse in the event that the primary borrower, for example an individual, trader, partnership or limited company, is unable to repay the loan. Partners or directors of a company may give personal guarantees in respect of loans extended to the business and, it may be, that a parent company may be asked to give a guarantee in respect of the loan made to a subsidiary company. This in turn may mean that the cost of the borrowing is reduced.

Under a guarantee, the person or company guaranteeing the debts of another undertakes to 'answer for the debt, default or miscarriage' of another person known as the 'principal debtor'. The transaction has been described as 'an accessory contract by which the promisor undertakes to be answerable to the promisee for the debt, default or miscarriage of another person, whose primary liability to the promisee must exist or be contemplated'.[120] The borrowing customer will remain primarily liable on the debt and the guarantor's liability will only arise if the primary debtor defaults on the loan.[121] By the very nature of the guarantee contract an overall arrangement between three parties will be required under which a bank agrees to extend a loan to the principal debtor in return for the primary obligation to make payment. In addition, the bank will also require, either under the same contract or by means of a separate contract, an undertaking by a third-party guarantor under which that person undertakes a secondary obligation to make payment in the event of default by the principal debtor. Consequently the principal debtor cannot stand surety for his own obligations,[122] nor can the creditor stand as the guarantor of monies owing to him.[123] A number of obligations flow from the creation of a guarantee and since the guarantor may find himself liable for both the principal debt and any interest flowing from the debtor's breach both the law and the

---

[120] *Halsbury's Laws of England*, Guarantees and Indemnity, para. 101.
[121] *Moschi v LEP Air Services Ltd* [1973] AC 331.
[122] *Lakeman v Mountstephen* (1874) LR 7 HL 17.
[123] *Re Hoyle* [1893] 1 Ch 84.

Lending Code[124] provide that private individuals proposing to give a guarantee must be advised with regard to a number of factors, for example:

- That by giving the guarantee or a third-party security, liability may be imposed on them instead of, or as well as, the principal debtor.[125]

- That the guarantor should seek independent legal advice[126] before entering into the guarantee or third-party security.

Additionally certain formal requirements must be complied with if the guarantee is to be enforceable. Thus, the guarantee is unenforceable unless it is executed in writing and signed by the guarantor or his agent. A guarantee that is not reduced to writing is not void but is merely unenforceable.[127] The guarantor's signature is usually witnessed although that is not strictly necessary. A contract of guarantee must be supported by consideration, unless it is under seal or unless the agreement takes effect as a deed. The consideration need not be stated in the document but it must be proven. In most cases this requirement will be satisfied because, in return for the guarantee, the bank will agree to advance a loan to the borrower. Where the consideration is that 'further advances' will be permitted against an existing overdrawn account, it must be shown that such further advances have been made.[128] A guarantee may also be given in consideration of the bank deferring the demand for repayment against the borrower (principal debtor) who has run into financial difficulties. If a guarantee is given at the request of the bank in such circumstances, then it may be inferred that the guarantee is given in order to avert an immediate demand for payment and valid consideration has been given.[129] The guarantee is only legally binding if it is entered into with the intention to create legal relations. In such circumstances it may be necessary to examine the terms of the document and the circumstances surrounding the conclusion of the agreement. Sometimes, instead of a guarantee a letter of comfort may be encountered. Such letters are not guarantees and if given in lieu of a guarantee the courts may conclude there was no intention to create legal relations.[130]

Further a person who enters into a guarantee agreement must have contractual capacity. Since the abolition of the *ultra vires* rule the capacity of a registered company to give a guarantee has not been doubted and a director of the company may bind his company to such a contract unless the bank has knowledge of such limitations on the powers of the company director. So any limitations placed on the contractual capacity of directors to enter into a guarantee on behalf of their company is largely of concern to the directors and its shareholders

---

[124] http://www.lendingstandardsboard.org.uk/docs/lendingcode.pdf.

[125] Lending Code para. 68: http://www.lendingstandardsboard.org.uk/docs/lendingcode.pdf.

[126] Lending Code para. 68: http://www.lendingstandardsboard.org.uk/docs/lendingcode.pdf.

[127] Statute of Frauds 1677, s.4.

[128] *Provincial Bank of Ireland* v *Donnell* [1934] 36 DLR (3d) 130.

[129] *Greenham Ready Mixed Concrete Ltd* v *CAS (Industrial Development) Ltd* (1965) 109 Sol Jo 209.

[130] In *Kleinwort Benson Ltd* v *Malaysia Mining Corporation Berhad* [1989] 1 WLR 379 the letter of comfort stated that it was the policy of the Malaysian parent company 'to ensure that the business of MMC Metals Ltd is at all times in a position to meet its liabilities to you under the above arrangement . . .'. It was held that this did not create a legally binding obligation, although in part because a full guarantee would have required the approval of the central bank under the Malaysian Exchange Control Act. However, in *Chemo Leasing SpA* v *Rediffusion Plc* [1987] 1 FTLR 201 the court appeared more willing to enforce the terms of the letter of comfort. In the event, however, the court declined enforcement on the basis that the lender had not complied with some of the conditions of the comfort letter.

and outsiders, including banks, dealing with a company are largely insulated from the effects of such limitations.[131] Under s.39 of the Companies Act 2006, the validity of a guarantee cannot be called into question on the ground that the constitution of the company did not confer the necessary capacity to undertake such an obligation. It is therefore no longer incumbent on the banker or other lender to examine the constitutional documents to determine whether the proposed guarantee contract falls within the scope of the company's capacity.[132] Additionally, in favour of the bank dealing with a guarantor company in good faith, the power of the board of directors to bind the company, or to authorise others to do so, is deemed to be free of any limitation under the company's constitution.[133] The bank is, again, relieved of any obligation to examine the articles of association of the guarantor because it 'is not bound to enquire as to any limitations on the powers of the directors to bind the company'.[134] Consequently the bank is not concerned with borrowing limits and other internal restrictions on the powers of the board, nor is the bank under any obligation to ensure that any quorum requirements have been satisfied.[135] There is however a good faith requirement on the bank and that presumption is not rebutted merely because the bank has actual knowledge of the relevant limitation on the director's powers under the constitution.[136] The presumption however may be rebutted and the bank will need to exercise particular caution in the case of a corporate guarantee. The directors of a company must act in good faith for the benefit of the company itself: a guarantee therefore given for the benefit of someone other than the company may be set aside if directors give a guarantee in breach of their fiduciary duties. Under these circumstances, a bank, which accepts a corporate guarantee, is placed on notice of a possible irregularity and it may be unable to satisfy the good faith requirement[137] unless it has taken steps to satisfy itself that the guarantor company does derive a benefit from the transaction, or that it is consistent with the directors' fiduciary duties.[138]

Liabilities and rights under a guarantee

The courts have generally been protective of the guarantor so that any ambiguity in the contract of guarantee or any onerous or unfair terms will be construed against the bank. However, a bank is not under any duty to offer advice to a perspective guarantor about the merit of giving the requested guarantee.[139] Apart from other considerations this would result in direct conflicts of interest since it is the bank that will be the beneficiary of the guarantee arrangement. Thus, while the bank will make its own decisions about whether or not to enter into a guarantee arrangement any investigations and enquiries will be for its own benefit. Credit approval for a particular facility will not therefore imply any positive advice or recommendation to the prospective guarantor.[140]

---

[131] Companies Act 2006, ss.39, 40 and 41.
[132] See Companies Act 2006, s.31.
[133] Companies Act 2006, s.40(1).
[134] Companies Act 2006, s.40(2)(b)(i).
[135] *Smith* v *Henniker-Major* [2002] BCC 544.
[136] Companies Act 2006, s.40(2)(b)(ii) and (iii).
[137] Directors' Duties were codified under the Companies Act 2006.
[138] *Criterion Properties Plc* v *Stratford Properties LLC* [2004] UKHL 28.
[139] *Barclays Bank Plc* v *Khaira* [1992] 1 WLR 623; *Union Bank of Finland* v *Lelakis* [1995] CLC 27.
[140] *National Commercial Bank (Jamaica) Ltd* v *Hew* [2003] UKPC 51.

It will therefore be necessary to ascertain the nature and extent of the guarantee undertaking. Where two or more persons give a guarantee their liability may be joint or several, or joint/several. In a joint guarantee, each co-guarantor is liable for the whole of the sum guaranteed and they should be sued together. If proceedings are only taken against one or some of the co-guarantors, the remaining co-guarantors not included in the action are not discharged from liability, and may subsequently be sued.[141] On the death or bankruptcy of a joint co-guarantor the deceased's estate is freed from liability under the guarantee and the bank will have to enforce the guarantee against the remaining co-guarantors. In a several guarantee, each of the co-guarantors may be made separately liable for the whole of the guaranteed debt and judgment against one of the several guarantors will not prevent an action against those remaining. Where there are co-guarantors, the bank should ensure that all the proposed co-guarantors execute the contract and no advance should be made to the principal debtor until all the co-guarantors sign the guarantee. If one or more of the co-guarantors fails, or refuses, to sign the guarantee, then the co-guarantors who signed the document on the understanding of it being signed by all of them, and who can show that it was understood it would be signed by all of them, will be discharged from liability.[142]

Most guarantees given to a bank are intended to cover a series of transactions, for example a fluctuating overdraft, over a period of time. The bank will normally seek a guarantee over the 'whole debt' and any amendments that limit the extent of the security should be avoided if the bank is likely to make further advances. An advance, which takes the total amount lent up to the agreed limit, will exhaust a single or specific guarantee, i.e. the guarantor will be liable for up to a specified amount that might thereafter be reduced by the application of the rule in *Clayton*'s case on the current account. By contrast a continuing guarantee will cover all debts on the same account and will not be affected by any payments into the principal debtor's account, since it does not secure any particular advance but rather the final combined balance on all the principal debtor's accounts.[143]

The principal debtor may give an express right of indemnity, in which case the guarantor's rights will be governed by the indemnity. A guarantor has an implied right to be indemnified by the principal debtor if he gives a guarantee at the request of the principal debtor. Under the implied right of indemnity, the guarantor has, unless the guarantee provides, an immediate right against the principal debtor on each occasion he pays the guarantee, although he has no right to accelerate that right by paying a guaranteed debt before it falls due.[144]

A co-guarantor has a 'right of contribution' against the other co-guarantors of the same debt with each guarantor being liable proportionately to the amount of his guarantee. If one of the guarantors becomes insolvent, any deficiency must be borne by the other guarantors ratably. The right of contribution against the other co-guarantors exists whether they are bound severally, or jointly/severally.[145] However, there is no right of contribution if the co-guarantors are liable under separate contracts for equal portions of the same principal debt, e.g. where each guarantor has entered into a separate transaction with the bank.[146]

---

[141] Civil Liability (Contribution) Act 1978, s.3.
[142] *National Provincial Bank of England* v *Brackenbury* (1906) 22 TLR 797.
[143] *Re Sherry London and County Banking Co* v *Terry* (1884) 25 Ch D 692.
[144] *Coppin* v *Gray* (1842) 1 Y & C Ch Cas 205.
[145] *Scholefield Goodman and Sons Ltd* v *Syngier* [1985] 3 All ER 105.
[146] *Coope* v *Twynham* (1823) Turn & R 426.

Before making payment to the bank any co-guarantor can compel the other co-guarantors to contribute towards satisfying the common liability and apply to the court for a declaration of his right to the contribution.[147] If a co-guarantor is sued by the bank for payment under the guarantee, he can assert his right of contribution by joining the other co-guarantors as defendants in the action, or by obtaining an order directing that when he has paid his own share of the common liability, the co-guarantor should indemnify him from further liability. A guarantee given by a company in respect of the liabilities of an unconnected company necessarily places the duty of enquiry on the bank, and the good-faith requirement will not be satisfied unless that duty is discharged.[148] Similarly if the bank knows that the guarantee is given for an improper corporate purpose, it will not be able to enforce the company to the guarantee.[149]

Termination of the guarantee

Termination of the guarantee means only that the guarantor is excused from all further liability incurred by the debtor. The guarantor will not be excused liabilities that have already been accrued.[150] Where the guarantor guarantees the debit balance of a bank customer's current account the ruling in *Clayton*'s case will have the effect of gradually discharging the guarantor's liability if payments are made to the credit of the account, since the debts for which the guarantor became liable were 'fixed' at the time the guarantee was terminated. However, this may be prevented if the guarantee contains a term, for example the 'guarantor's liability for the amount due from the debtor at the time when the guarantee is determined shall remain notwithstanding any subsequent payment into or out of the account by or on behalf of the debtor'.[151] Alternatively the bank may stop the principal customer's current account, and open another account for him. In practice banks will include terms of the contract of guarantee, such as the one used in the *Westminster Bank Ltd* v *Cond* case, and also stop the account.

Corporate guarantees

The company as a separate legal entity enjoys separate legal status regardless of whether its shareholders consist of individuals or other corporate entities.[152] Companies within a group each enjoy the benefits of separate corporate status and each company within the group is responsible for its own debts and liabilities.[153] Inter-corporate guarantees however are a routine commercial transaction and such guarantees effectively negate the limited liability of shareholders for corporate debt. The guarantees enable a corporate group to secure borrowing as a single unit although under company law each company enjoys separate corporate status. These guarantees facilitate the availability of finance in situations where a particular corporate

---

[147] *Womershausen* v *Gullick* [1893] 2 Ch 514.
[148] *Rolled Steel Products (Holdings) Ltd* v *British Corporate Steel Corporation* [1986] Ch 246.
[149] *Re Introductions Ltd* [1970] Ch 199.
[150] *Westminster Bank Ltd* v *Sassoon* (1926) Times, 27 November.
[151] *Westminster Bank Ltd* v *Cond* (1940) 46 Com Cas 60.
[152] [1897] AC 22.
[153] See Hannigan (2012) *Modern Company Law*, Oxford: OUP.

entity's assets alone would not support the grant of the credit facility. In some instances, the lender may not be willing to lend to an individual company unless an affiliate agrees to guarantee the loan. Consequently, the terms of the guarantee provide the lender with additional assets against which to secure the ultimate repayment of the loan. Further, the collective borrowing base may result in an upgrade in the group's credit, allowing the group collectively to obtain borrowing at a lower cost.

When a company gives a guarantee or grants some other form of security to secure an affiliate's debt two questions will need to be examined: (i) whether the guarantor company was insolvent at the time the guarantee was given; and (ii) whether the guarantor received less than adequate consideration. If the answer to both of these questions is positive, then the grant of the security may be voidable as a fraudulent transfer. A surety, or guarantor, who guarantees the obligation of the principal debtor, will acquire a blend of liabilities and assets in exchange. The guarantor incurs a contingent liability since it may become obligated to pay the principal debt at some stage in the future, if the principal debtor defaults. The guarantor, however, receives a blend of benefits, which may be classified as follows:

- Business benefits.
- Equitable right of exoneration, reimbursement, segregation and contribution.

The distinction between business benefits and equitable rights is important because the benefits the guarantor receives will depend on the relationship of the guarantor and the principal debtor (i.e. whether the guarantor is the parent or subsidiary), while the equitable rights that the guarantor receives are independent of the relationship between the guarantor and the principal debtor.

Business benefits

The business benefit is a benefit received by a guarantor as a result of giving the guarantee regardless of whether or not the principal debtor defaults. Such benefits may or may not be tangible and need not be assets in the traditional sense. An important benefit that may accrue is that within an affiliated group the collective borrowing may result in upgrading the credit rating of the group and also lower the cost of the borrowing in comparison to individual loans. Frequently, a guarantee given by one very strong member within the group will lift the credit rating of the group as a whole. However, although the weaker members of the group may benefit from a group loan there may be circumstances where the strong affiliate's credit rating may be weakened because of links with the weaker affiliate. Another business benefit that may result from the joint guarantee is the 'convenient factor'. When a corporate group borrows as a unit, the potential lender will analyse the consolidated group's financial statement, rather than each affiliate's financial statement. This will lower the borrowing costs since the group only needs to give the bank one set of audited consolidated statements rather than audited financial statements from each member of the group.

Guarantor's equitable rights

On executing a guarantee, a guarantor becomes entitled to certain equitable rights and remedies against the principal debtor and co-guarantors. If the principal debtor defaults and the guarantor's liability is fixed, these rights enable the guarantor to bring an action for equitable relief. When the guarantor company pays under the guarantee, it becomes entitled to certain monetary relief. The rights and remedies available to the guarantor are as follows:

- *Exoneration*: this is a right to compel the principal debtor and the co-guarantors to pay.
- *Reimbursement*: this is the guarantor's right to be repaid by the principal debtor, any amounts it is required to pay on the principal debtor's behalf in its capacity as guarantor.
- *Subrogation*:[154] once the guarantor has paid the whole of the outstanding amount of the principal debt, subrogation will entitle the guarantor to be substituted to the position of the credit or who has been fully paid and to enjoy the rights and benefits of the creditor, including rights over the security interests and liens etc.
- *Contribution*: if there are multiple guarantors of the same debt, the right of contribution entitles paying guarantor to have the co-guarantors pay a proportionate share of the principal debt. The right of contribution exists because the co-guarantors and the creditor may still collect the whole amount of the debt from any of the co-guarantors.

The extent of the contribution in each case will be determined by the terms of the contract. Although these rights are only effective after the demand for repayment has been made against the borrower, the bank cannot entirely ignore these rights. The lender bank must ensure that, in such cases, the security is not released, but is instead made available to the guarantor. The lending bank will not wish to find itself in competition with the guarantor to recover the loan and so the standard form guarantee will defer the exercise of the right of subrogation until the lender has been repaid in full. A lender should therefore cover the entirety of the debt even if there is a financial limit on the guarantor's total liability. If the lender merely takes a guarantee of part of the debt, then the guarantor's right of subrogation will apply when he had paid that amount even if the balance of the debt remains outstanding.[155]

⬤ Downstream, cross-stream and upstream guarantees

Guarantees by affiliate companies may be classified as follows:

- A downstream guarantee is where the parent company guarantees its subsidiary's obligations.
- A cross-stream is where one subsidiary guarantees the obligations of another subsidiary company. In such cases, a lender will often require that the non-borrowing affiliate guarantees the obligation of the borrowing company.
- An upstream guarantee is where a subsidiary guarantees the obligations of its parent company.

A downstream guarantee given by a parent company to support a loan to a subsidiary company will not generally cause concerns about fraudulent transfers because the parent company, through its stock ownership of the subsidiary company, will receive the benefits of the loan proceeds reflected in the increased value of the stock. However, upstream and cross-stream guarantees may be the subject of litigation on liquidation as fraudulent transfers, either on the basis of lack of consideration or that the consideration provided is considerably less than

---

[154] See *Owen v Tate* [1976] QB 402.
[155] *Re Sass* [1896] 2 QB 12.

its value (i.e. the transaction is at an undervalue and therefore contrary to s.238 of the Insolvency act 1986). In *Phillips v Brewin Dolphin Bell Lawrie*[156] the House of Lords held that in deciding the value of the consideration received by the company in a transaction alleged to be at undervalue, regard must be had to the events occurring at the time of the transaction and to those occurring after the transaction (*ex post facto* events).

Conclusion

This chapter is intended as a brief outline of the types, nature and the law relating to securities a bank may take in return for providing a loan facility to a customer. The law in this area is complex. While facilitating banking practice the law has developed to ensure that individual customers in particular are protected through consumer legislation. In the case of corporate clients protection is given to creditors, shareholders and investors through registration of charges.

Further reading

➤ Blair, W. (1983) Charges over cash deposits, November *International Law Review*, 14.

[156] [2001] 1 WLR 143.

Index